2018

广西统计年鉴

GUANGXI STATISTICAL YEARBOOK

广西壮族自治区统计局 编

Compiled By Guangxi Statistical Bureau

图书在版编目(CIP)数据

广西统计年鉴. 2018:汉英对照/广西壮族自治区统计局编. —北京:中国统计出版社,2018.8
ISBN 978-7-5037-8520-7

Ⅰ. ①广… Ⅱ. ①广… Ⅲ. ①统计资料-广西-2018-年鉴-汉、英 Ⅳ. ①C832.67-54

中国版本图书馆 CIP 数据核字(2018)第 160935 号

广西统计年鉴—2018

作　　者/ 广西壮族自治区统计局
责任编辑/ 钟　钰
装帧设计/ 韦含锡
出版发行/ 中国统计出版社
地　　址/ 北京市丰台区西三环南路甲 6 号
邮政编码/ 100073
电　　话/ 邮购(010)63376909　书店(010)68783171
网　　址/ http://www.zgtjcbs.com
印　　刷/ 广西民族印刷包装集团有限公司
经　　销/ 新华书店
开　　本/ 890mm×1240mm　1/16
字　　数/ 1600 千字
印　　张/ 44.25
版　　别/ 2018 年 8 月第 1 版
版　　次/ 2018 年 8 月第 1 次印刷
定　　价/ 360.00 元

本书附同版本 CD-ROM 一张,光盘内容以书面文字为准。
如有印装差错,由本社发行部调换。

编者说明

一、《广西统计年鉴—2018》是一部全面反映广西壮族自治区国民经济和社会发展情况的大型资料性年刊。本书收录了全自治区2017年和1978年以来重要年份的主要统计数据，各市县（区）2017年的主要统计数据。

二、全书内容分为23个篇章，即：1.综合； 2.人口；3.国民经济核算；4.从业人员和职工工资；5.物价；6.人民生活；7.财政、金融和保险；8.资源与环境；9.能源生产与消费；10.固定资产投资；11.城市概况；12.对外经济贸易； 13.农业；14.工业；15.建筑业；16.批发和零售业；17.住宿餐饮业和旅游；18.交通、运输和邮电通信； 19.教育、科技和文化；20.体育、卫生、社会福利及服务业；21.区域经济；22.各市基本情况；23.县（市、区）基本情况。为便于读者更直观地了解全书内容和正确使用资料，篇章的后面附有主要统计指标解释。附录内容有：2017年广西国民经济和社会发展统计公报。

三、资料中所使用的度量衡单位均采用国际统一标准计量单位。

四、本年鉴部分数据合计数或相对数由于单位取舍不同产生的计算误差均未作机械调整。

五、本年鉴对以前发表的统计资料重新进行审核，凡与本年鉴资料有出入的，均以本年鉴为准。

六、本年鉴的资料来源：大部分来自统计年报，部分来自抽样调查。

七、本年鉴表中的符号使用说明：

“…”表示数据不足本表最小计量单位数；

“空格”表示该项统计数据不详或无该项统计数据；

“#”表示其中的主要项。

八、鉴于统计制度的改革，对统计年鉴中某些统计指标数据相应作了调整，对这些指标我们作了脚注，请读者在使用数据时要加以注意。

九、年鉴中涉及到经济普查的有关专业数据已按照第三次全国经济普查数据进行了调整，对此在各篇中我们也相应做了说明。

十、根据全国第二次农业普查，对2006年和2007年的农林牧渔业总产值以及粮食经济作物和主要畜禽水产等指标数据进行衔接，但2005年以前的数据均未修正。

2016年实施了研发支出核算改革，并根据国家统计局的布置对2007−2015年的GDP数据进行了衔接，相关GDP计算所得数随之调整。在《广西统计年鉴2018》中，2017年度的所有涉及GDP的数据均为快报数。

十一、在本年鉴的编辑过程中，得到了许多单位和同志的大力支持，在此我们深表谢意。限于我们的水平，年鉴中的错误和不足之处在所难免，恳请广大读者给予批评指正。

PREFACE

Ⅰ. Guangxi Statistical Yearbook is an annual statistics publication, which covers very comprehensive data in 2017 and some selected data series in historically important years since 1978 of the whole autonomous region, the main statistical data of city, county (district) in 2017 and therefore, reflects various aspects of Guangxi' s social and economic development.

Ⅱ. This book contains the following twenty-three parts, 1.General Survey; 2.Population; 3.National Economic Accounting; 4.Employment & Wages; 5. Price; 6. People' s Livelihood; 7. Finance, Banking & Insurance; 8.Natural Resources & Environment; 9. Energy Production & Consumption; 10.Investment in Fixed Assets; 11. General Survey of Cities; 12.Foreign Economy & Trades; 13. Agriculture; 14. Industry; 15. Construction; 16. Wholesale & Retail Trades; 17. Hotels Catering Services & Tourism; 18. Transportation, Postal & Telecommunication Services; 19. Education, Science & Culture; 20. Sport, Public Health, Social Welfare & Service Industry; 21. Economic Zones; 22. Basic Statistics of Cities; 23.Basic Statistics of Counties (Cities, Districts). In Order to make readers understand the whole content of this book and use the materials correctly, most of the chapters are equipped with explanatory notes on main statistical indicators at the end. Moreover, addenda (Statistical Communique on National Economic & Social Development of Guangxi in 2017) is attached at the end of the book.

Ⅲ. The international standard unit of measurement is applied in this book.

Ⅳ. Statistical discrepancies in this book due to rounding are not adjusted.

Ⅴ. In this yearbook, the statistical materials published before have been verified again, and the data that tally with this book should take the data of this book as standard.

Ⅵ. The major data sources of this publication are obtained from annual statistical reports and some from sample surveys.

Ⅶ. Notations used in this yearbook:

"…" indicates that the figure is not large enough to be measured with the smallest unit in the table;

"(blank)" indicates that the data are not available;

"#" indicates the major items of the table.

Ⅷ. Because of innovation in statistical system, some statistical data in this yearbook have been adjusted accordingly, and we have made footnote to these indicators. The users should notice that when using these data.

Ⅸ. Since the comprehensive survey of economy has not been publicized, data that related to national economy account are from preliminary reports, and it is explanted in the chapters.

Ⅹ. According to the 2rd Agriculture Census, the data of gross output value of farming, forestry animal husbandry and fishery, and the output of grains crops, economic crops and major animals in 2006 and 2007 has been adjusted, while the data in 2005 and before hasn' t.

Due to the reform of R&D expenditure accounting by National Statistics Bureau, the data of GDP from 2007 to 2015 has been recalculated, so as the related data. All the data of GDP in 2017' s are from quick statistics data, so as the related data.

XI. During the editions of this yearbook, we have won wide support from many departments and comrades, and we deeply thanks for these all. Based on our limited level, perhaps there are some mistakes in the book, we welcome all candid comments and criticism from our readers.

《广西统计年鉴—2018》编辑委员会及编辑人员

Editorial Board & Staff of Guangxi Statistical Yearbook–2018

Editorial Board

Editorial Staff

广西主要经济指标占全国的比重（2017年，%）

Proportion of Guangxi to Nation on Major Indicators (2017, %)

广西生产总值及增速

Guangxi Gross Domestic Product & Its Growth Rate

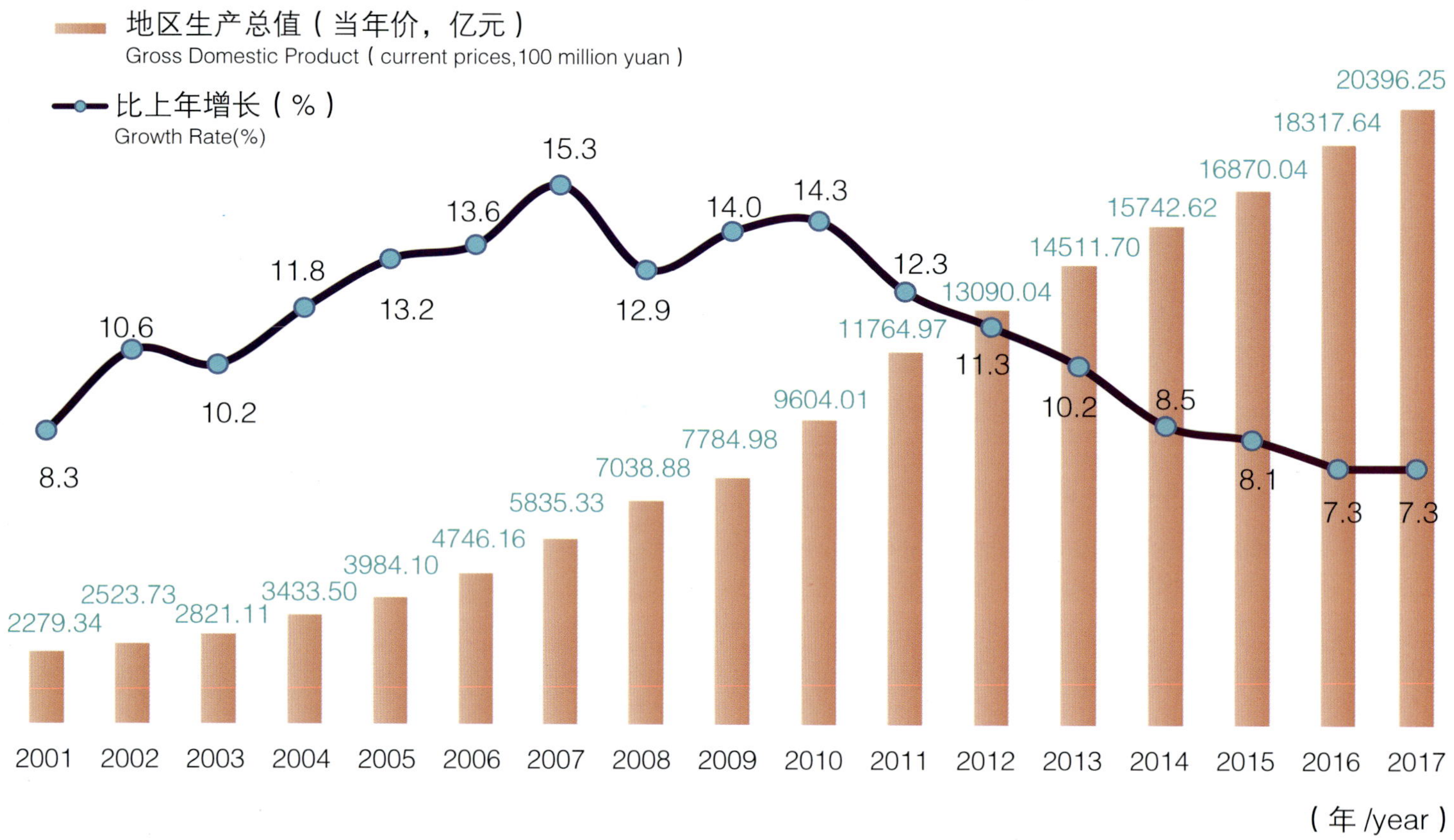

地区生产总值（当年价，亿元）
Gross Domestic Product（current prices,100 million yuan）
比上年增长（%）
Growth Rate(%)
2279.34
2523.73
2821.11
3433.50
3984.10
4746.16
5835.33
7038.88
7784.98
9604.01
11764.97
13090.04
14511.70
15742.62
16870.04
18317.64
20396.25
8.3
10.6
10.2
11.8
13.2
13.6
15.3
12.9
14.0
14.3
12.3
11.3
10.2
8.5
8.1
7.3
7.3
2001
2002
2003
2004
2005
2006
2007
2008
2009
2010
2011
2012
2013
2014
2015
2016
2017
（年/year）

地区生产总值构成（%）

Composition of Guangxi Gross Domestic Product （%）

第一产业
Primary Industry
17.4
35.3
47.2
第三产业
Tertiary Industry
第二产业
Secondary Industry
2010年

第一产业
Primary Industry
第三产业
Tertiary Industry
14.2
40.2
45.6
第二产业
Secondary Industry
2017年

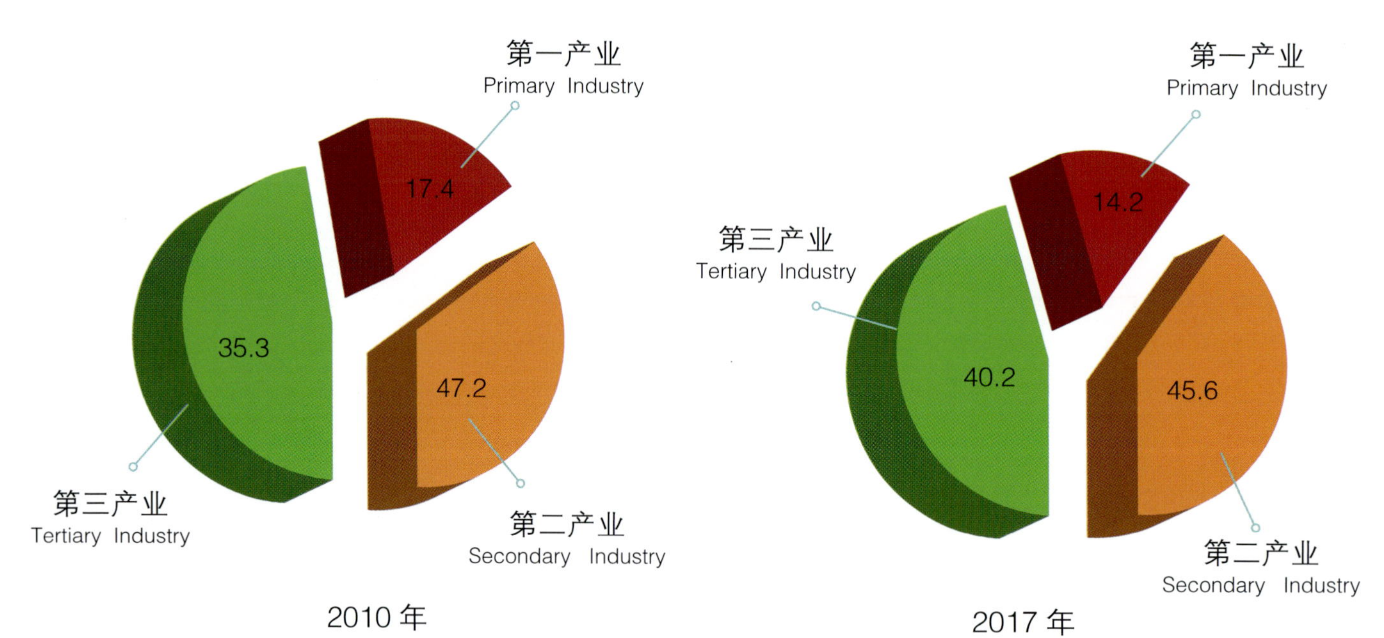

人均地区生产总值（元）

Per Capita Gross Domestic Product （yuan）

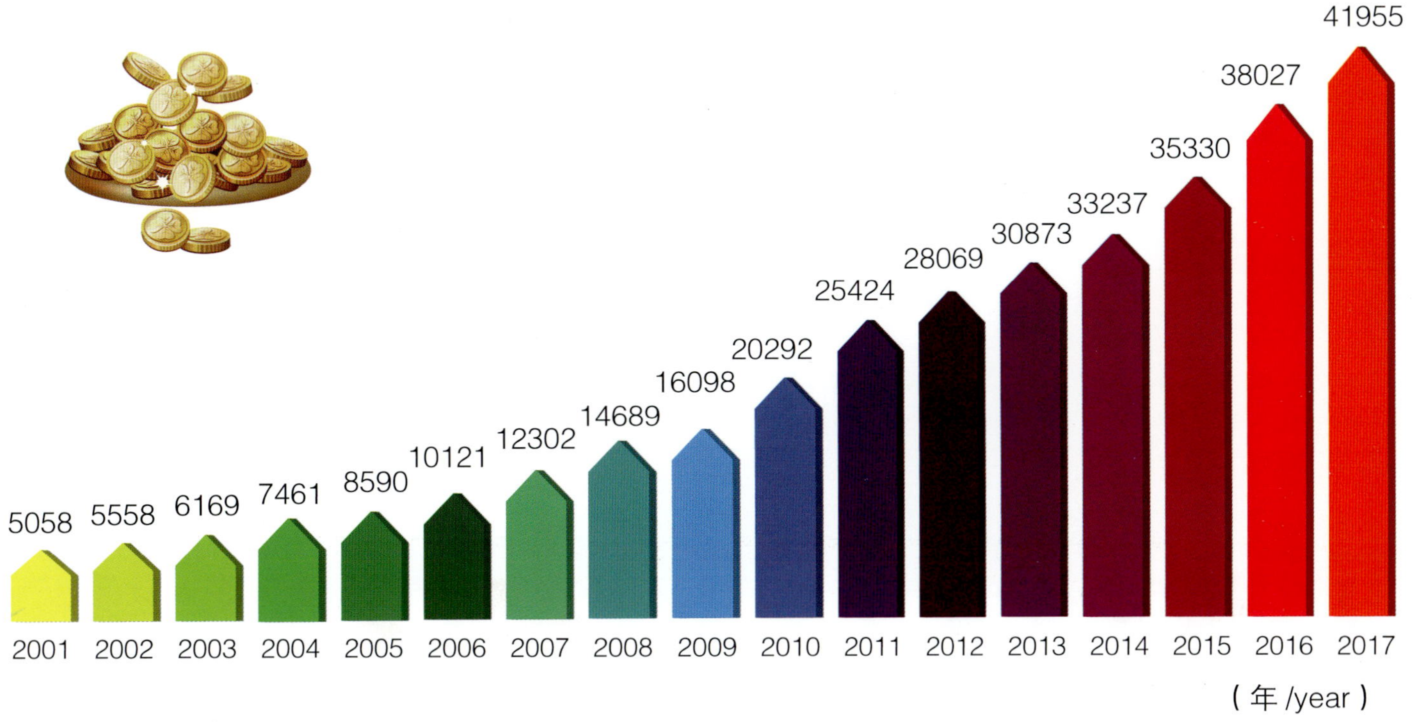

年末总人口（万人）

Total Population （10 000 persons）

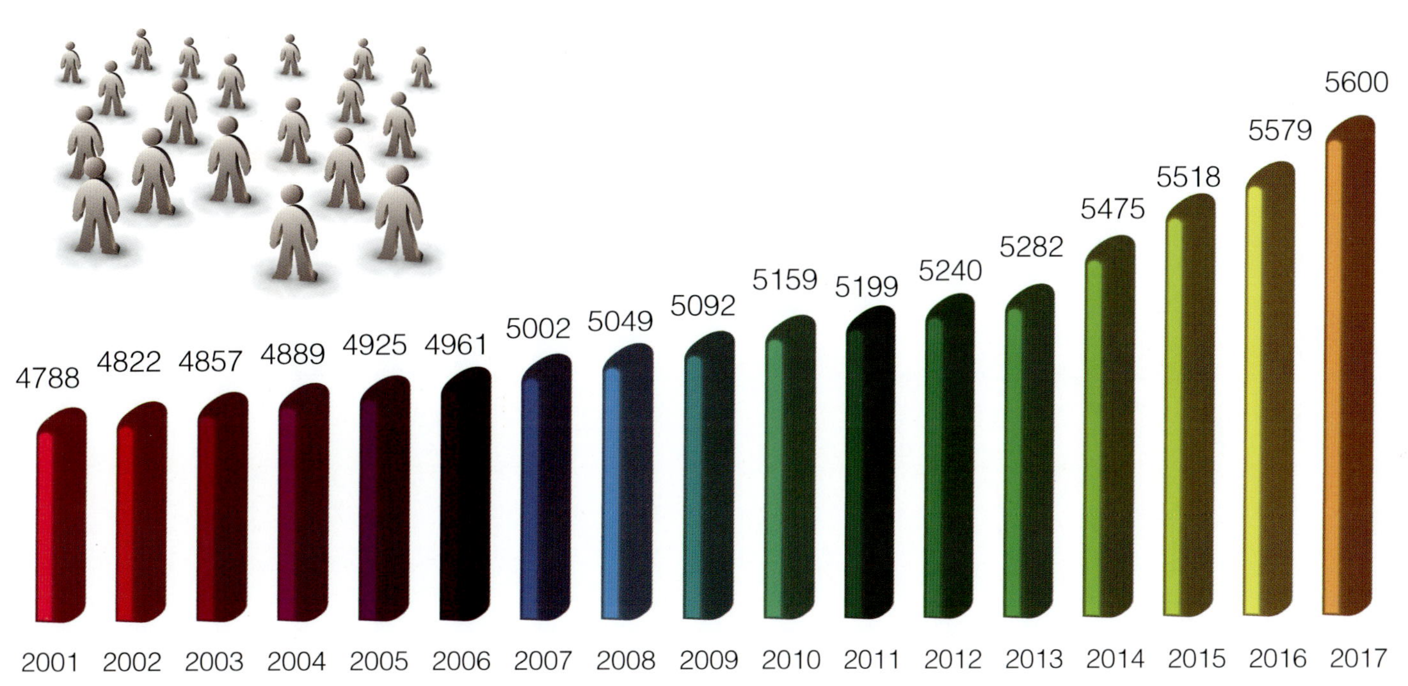

性别比（以女性为 100）

Sex Ratio （Female=100）

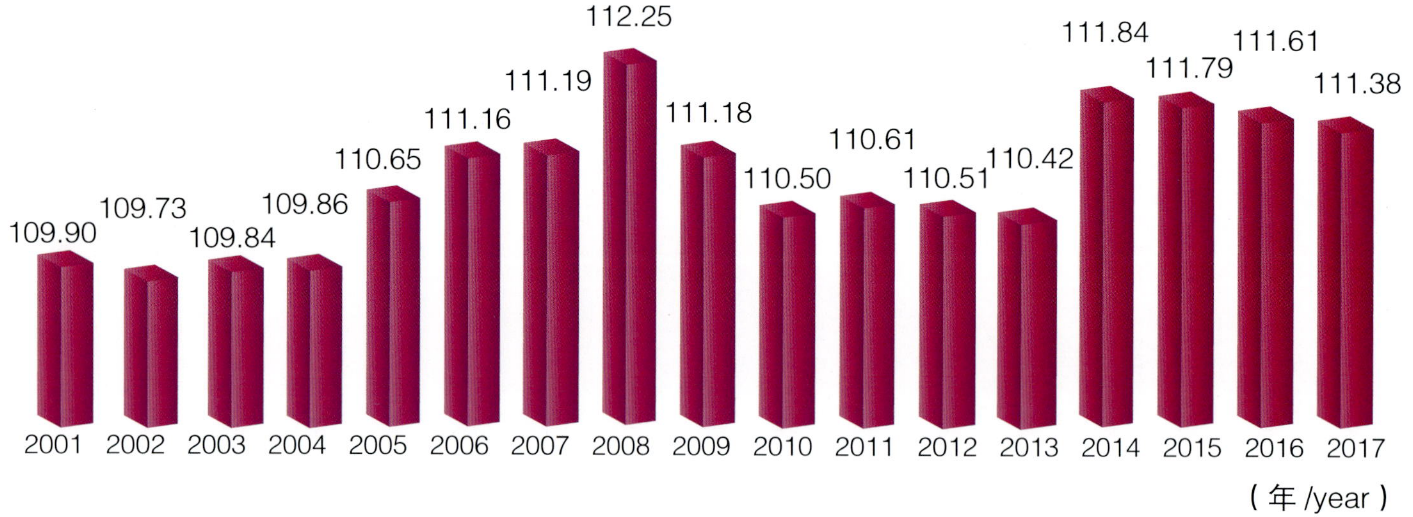

人口增长（‰）

Growth of Population （‰）

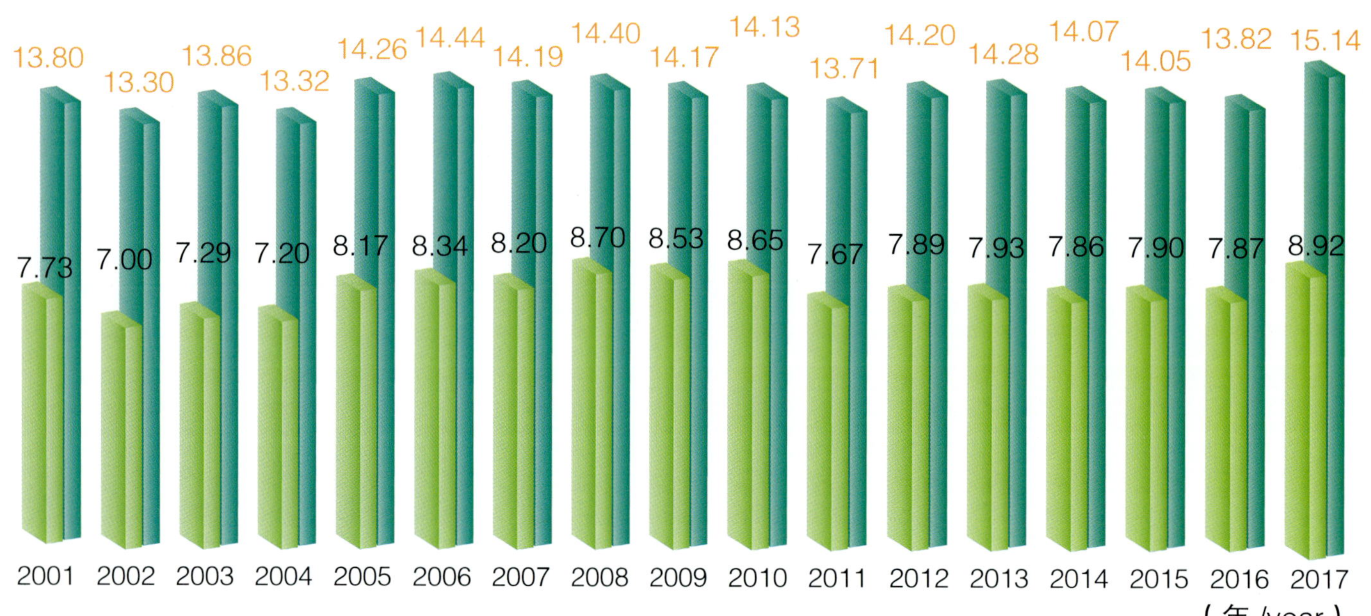

全社会从业人员（万人）

Total Employed Persons (10 000 persons)

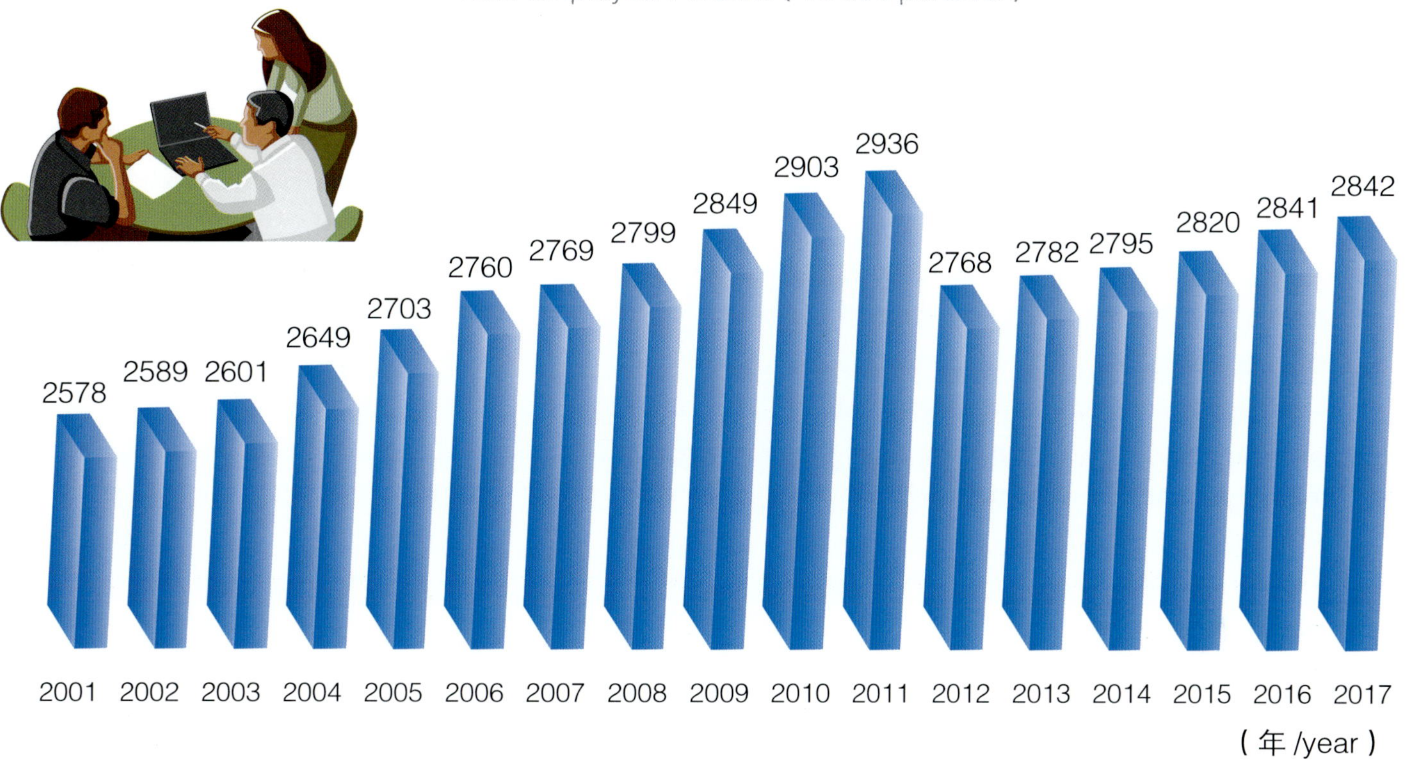

全社会从业人员构成（%）

Composition of Employment (%)

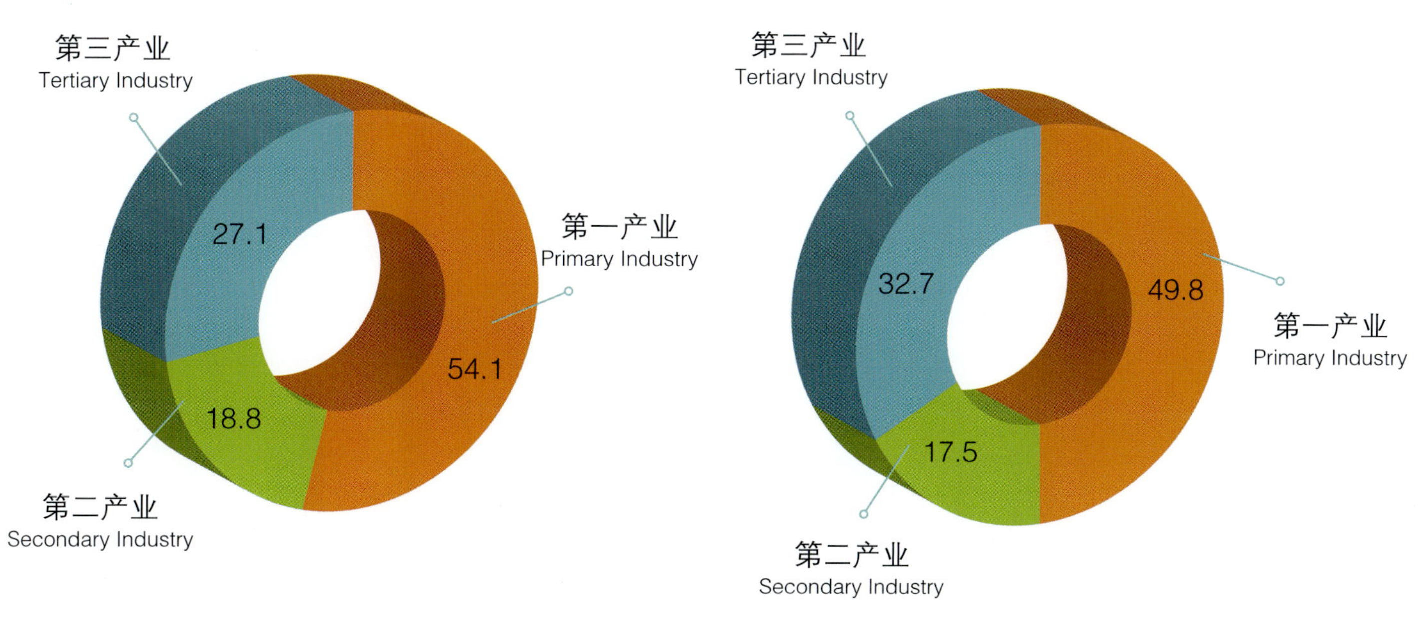

城镇单位在岗职工平均工资（元）

Average Wages of Staff & Workers at Post in Urban Units （yuan）

（年 /year）	
2017	66456
2016	60239
2015	54983
2014	46846
2013	42637
2012	37614
2011	34150
2010	31842
2009	28302
2008	25660
2007	21898
2006	18064
2005	15461
2004	13579
2003	11953
2002	10774
2001	9075

全社会固定资产投资（亿元）

Total Investment in Fixed Assets（100 million yuan）

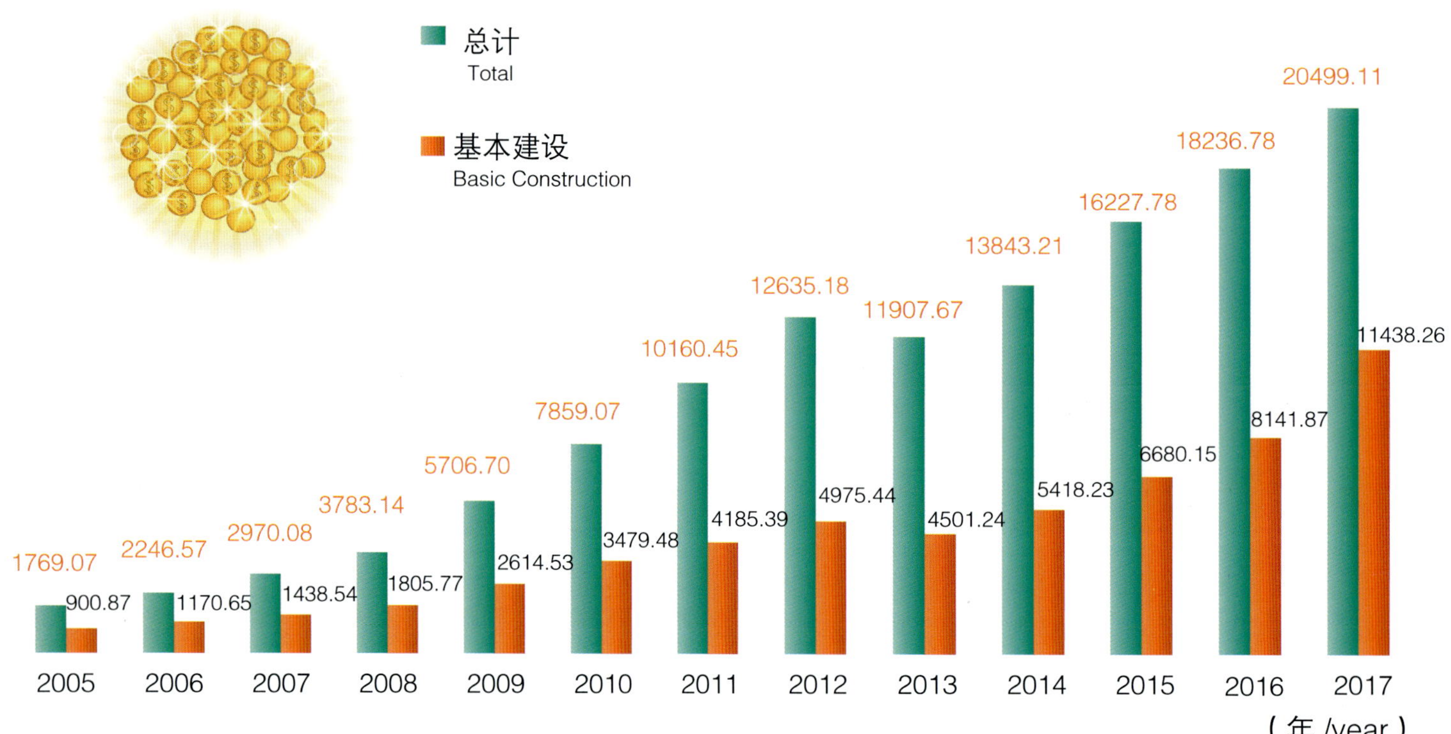

房地产投资完成额（亿元）

Real Estate Development（100 million yuan）

286.79
369.98
536.28
627.34
813.68
1206.22
1517.47
1554.94
1614.63
1838.49
1909.09
2397.99
2683.48
2005
2006
2007
2008
2009
2010
2011
2012
2013
2014
2015
2016
2017
（年 /year）

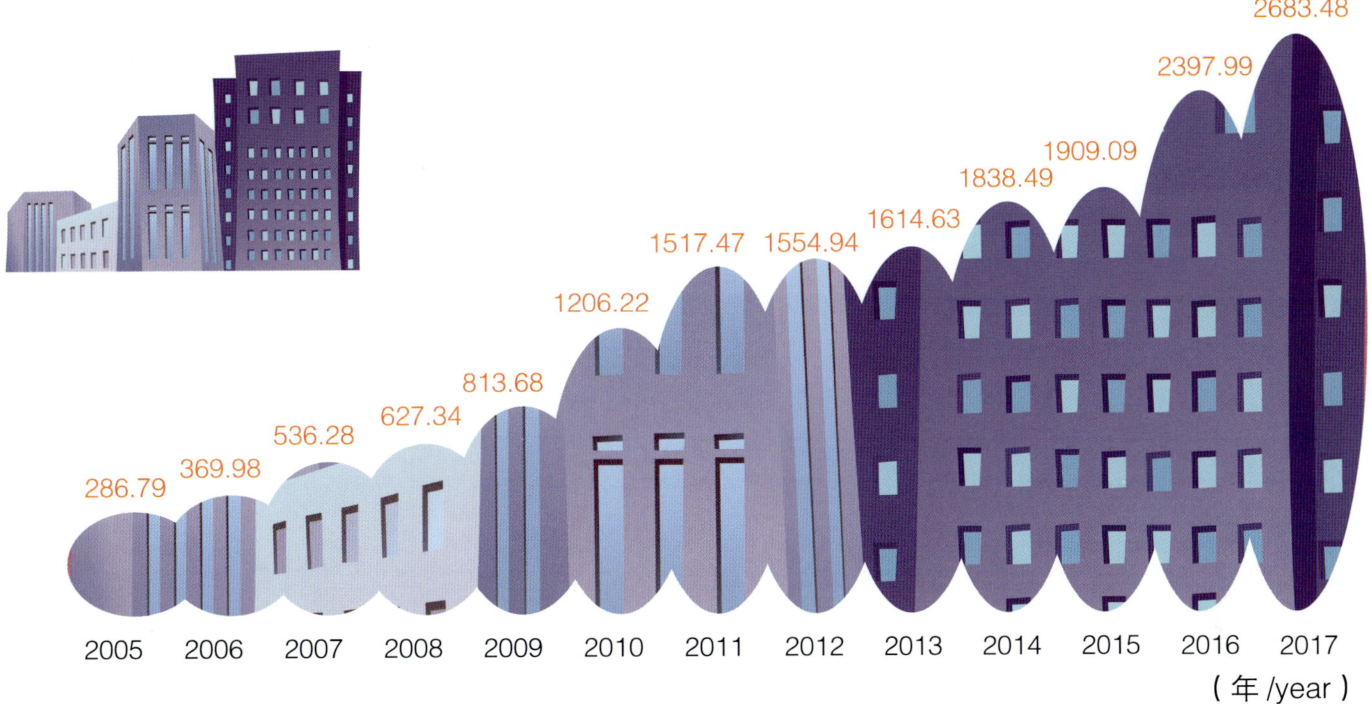

社会消费品零售总额（亿元）

Total Retail Sales of Consumer Goods （100 million yuan）

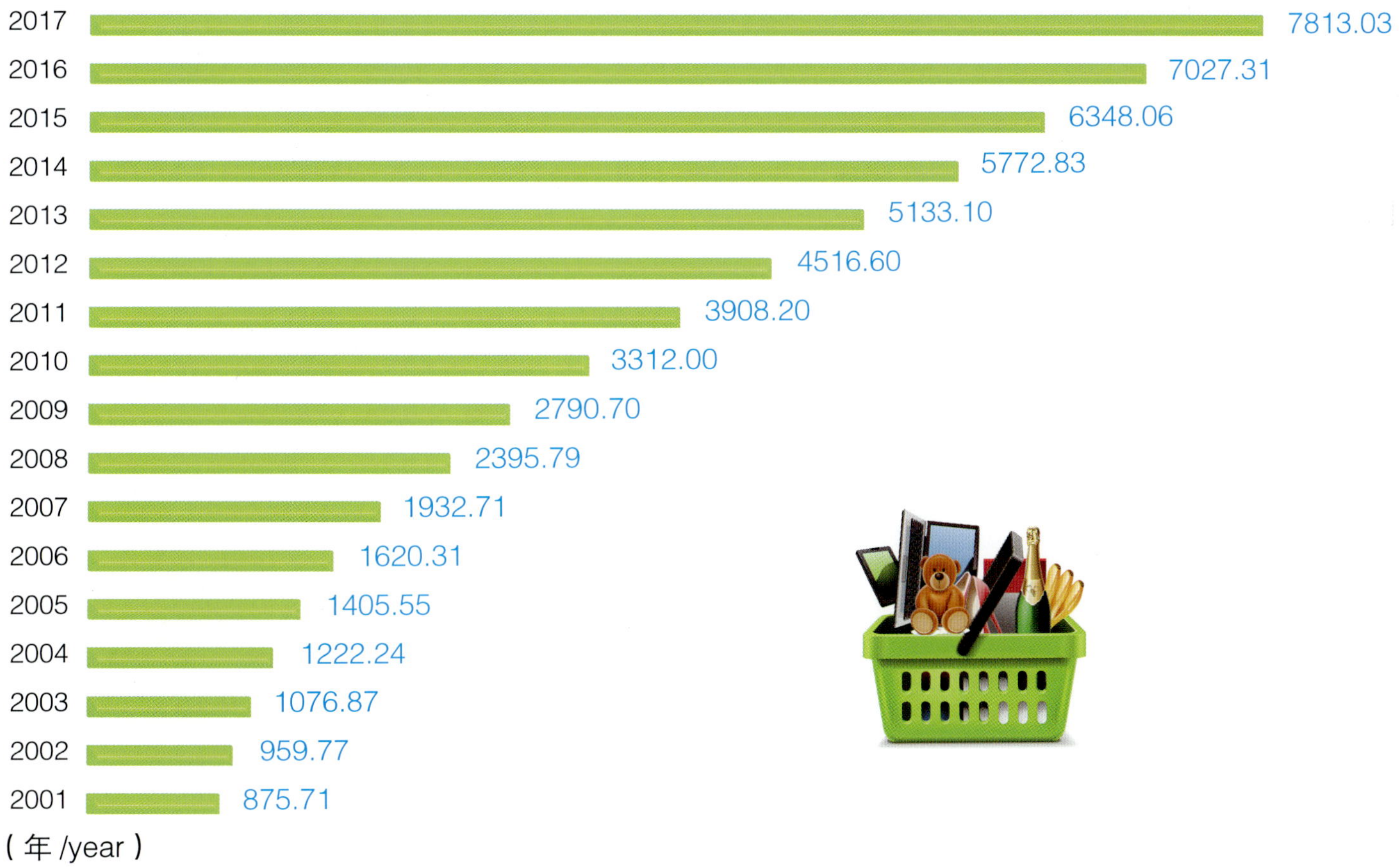

2017 7813.03
2016 7027.31
2015 6348.06
2014 5772.83
2013 5133.10
2012 4516.60
2011 3908.20
2010 3312.00
2009 2790.70
2008 2395.79
2007 1932.71
2006 1620.31
2005 1405.55
2004 1222.24
2003 1076.87
2002 959.77
2001 875.71
（年 /year）

进出口总额（亿美元）

Total Import & Export Value （USD 100 million）

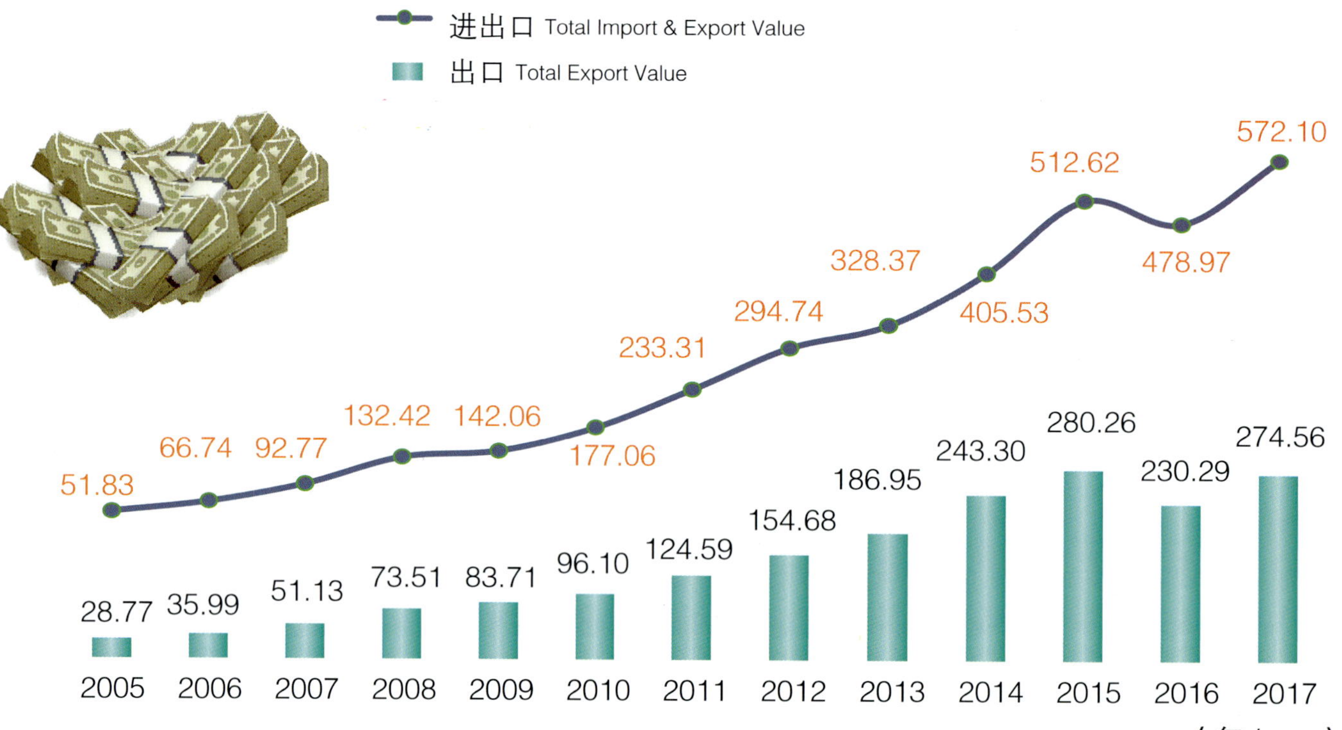

外商直接投资（亿美元）

Foreign Direct Investment （USD 100 million）

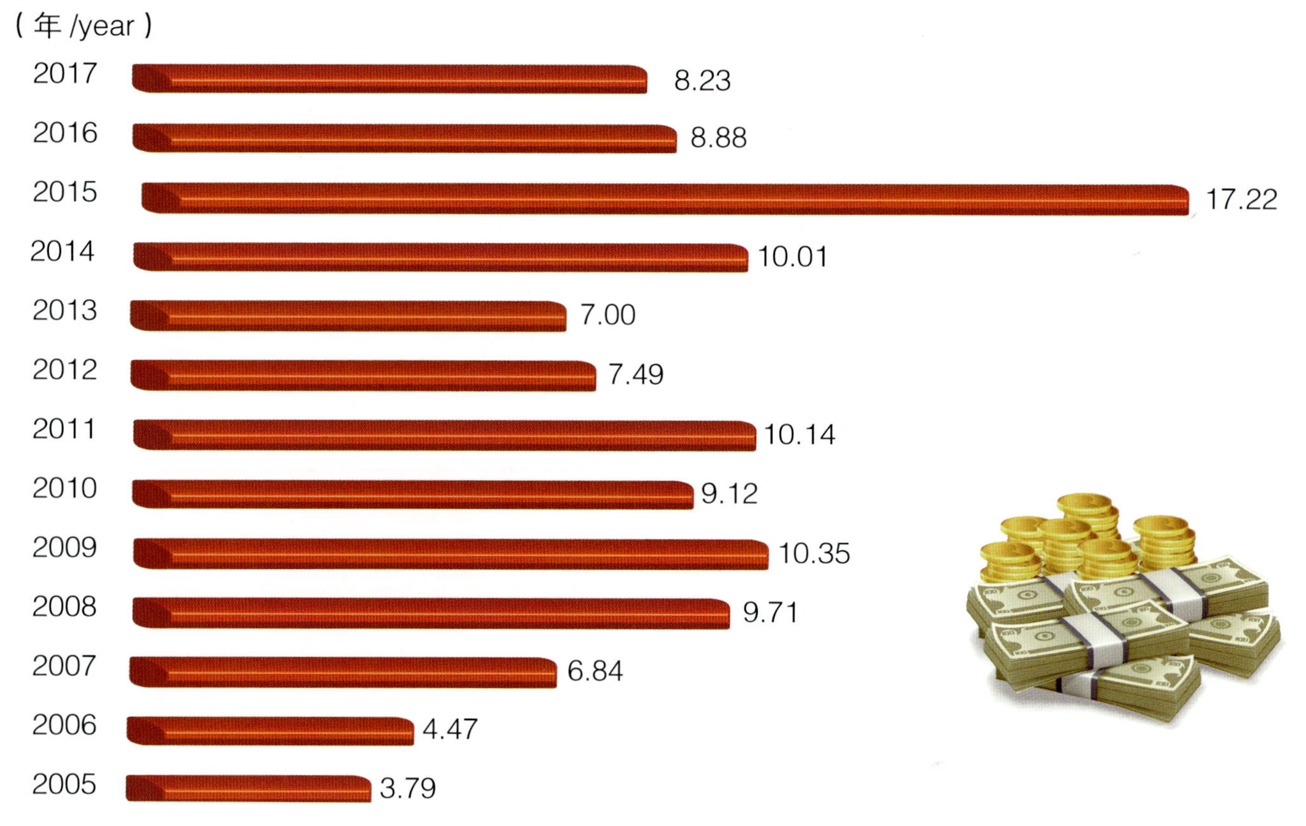

国际旅游人数（万人次）

Number of International Tourism （10 000 person-times）

国际旅游外汇收入（亿美元）

Income of International Tourism （USD 100 million）

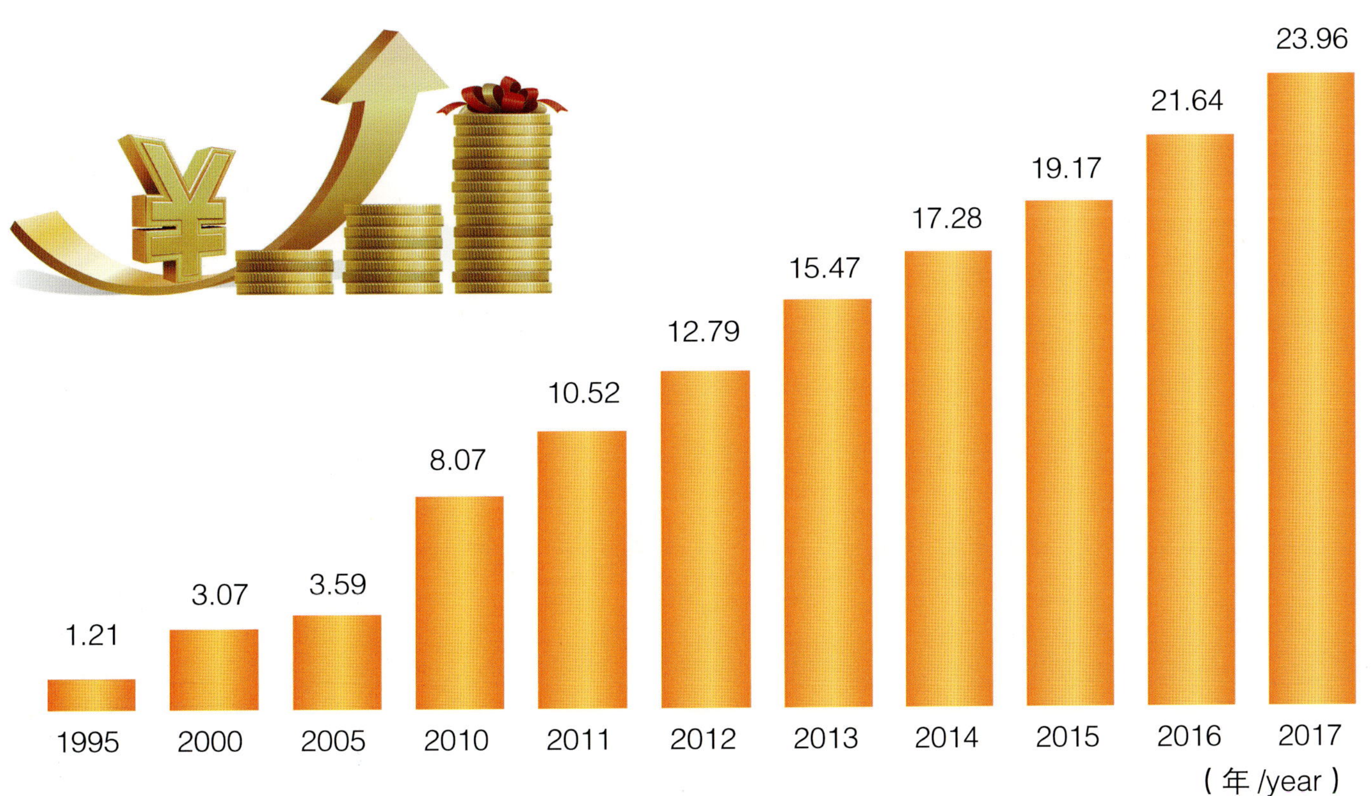

每万元 GDP 消费能源（吨标准煤）

Per 10 000 Yuan GDP Energy Consumption （ton of SCE）

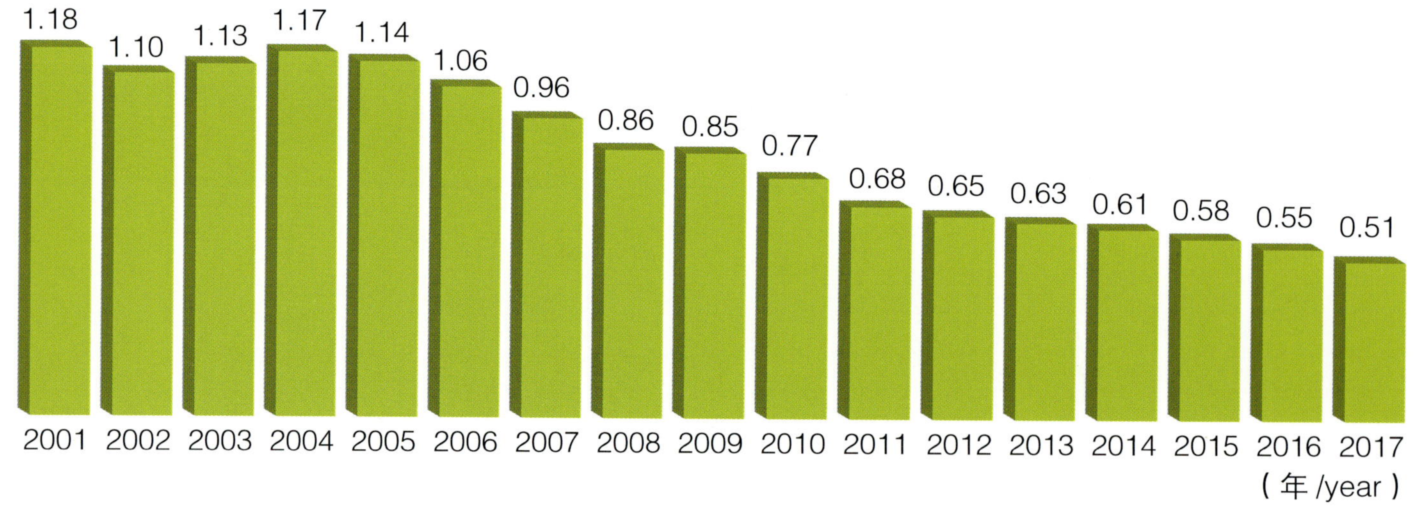

每万元工业总产值消费能源（吨标准煤）

Per 10 000 Yuan Gross Output Value of Industry Energy Consumption （ton of SCE）

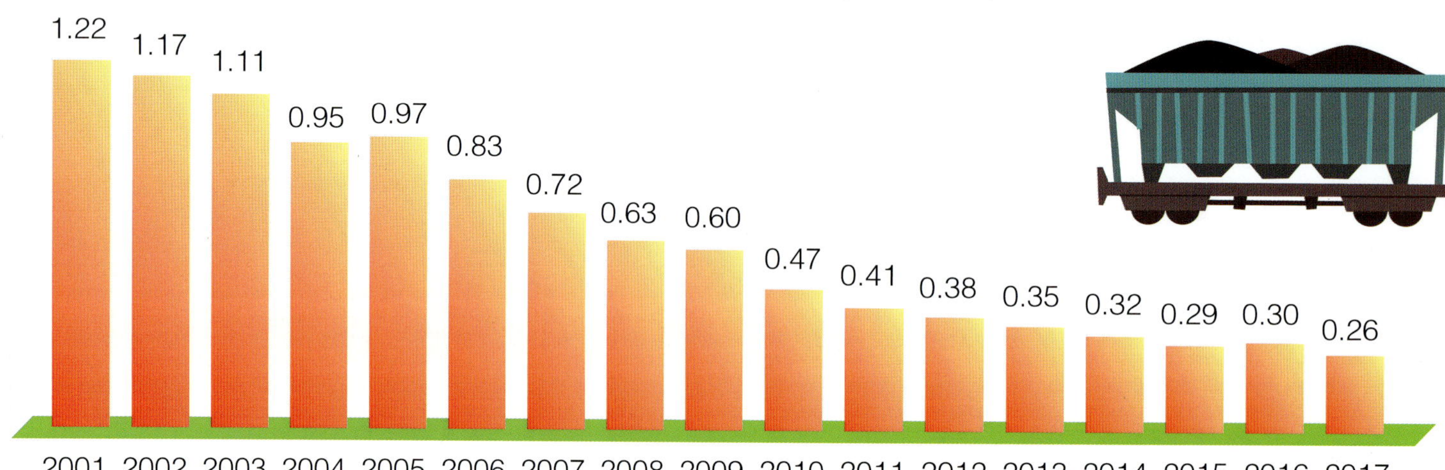

消费弹性系数

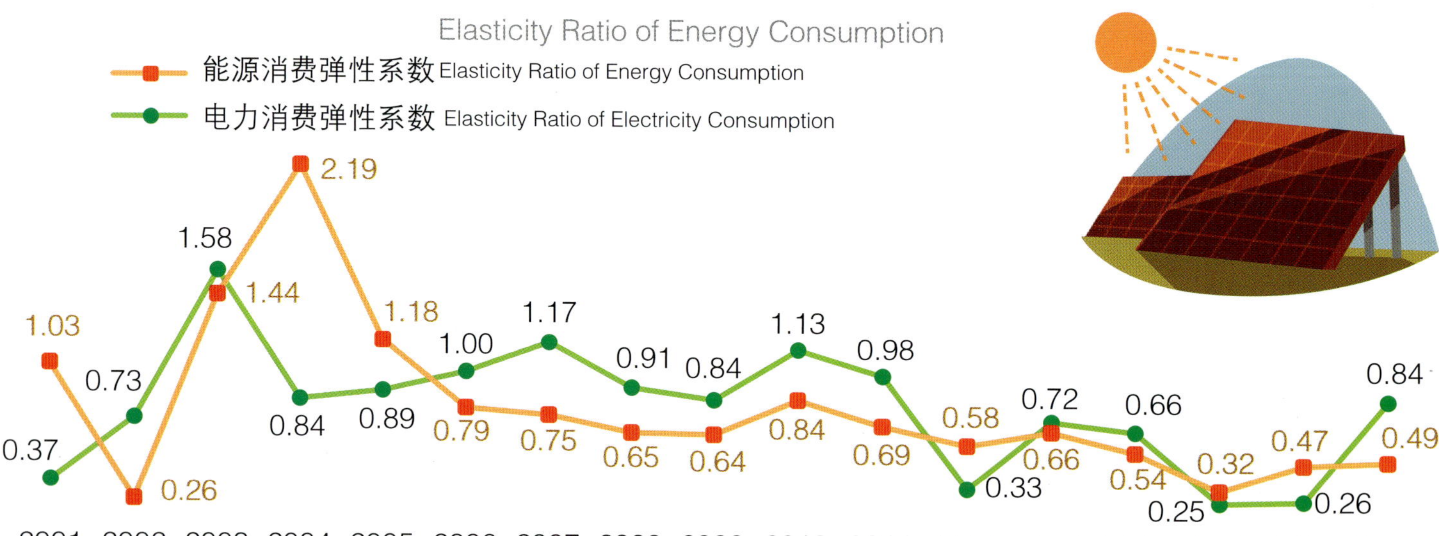

财政收入（亿元）

Financial Revenue （100 million yuan）

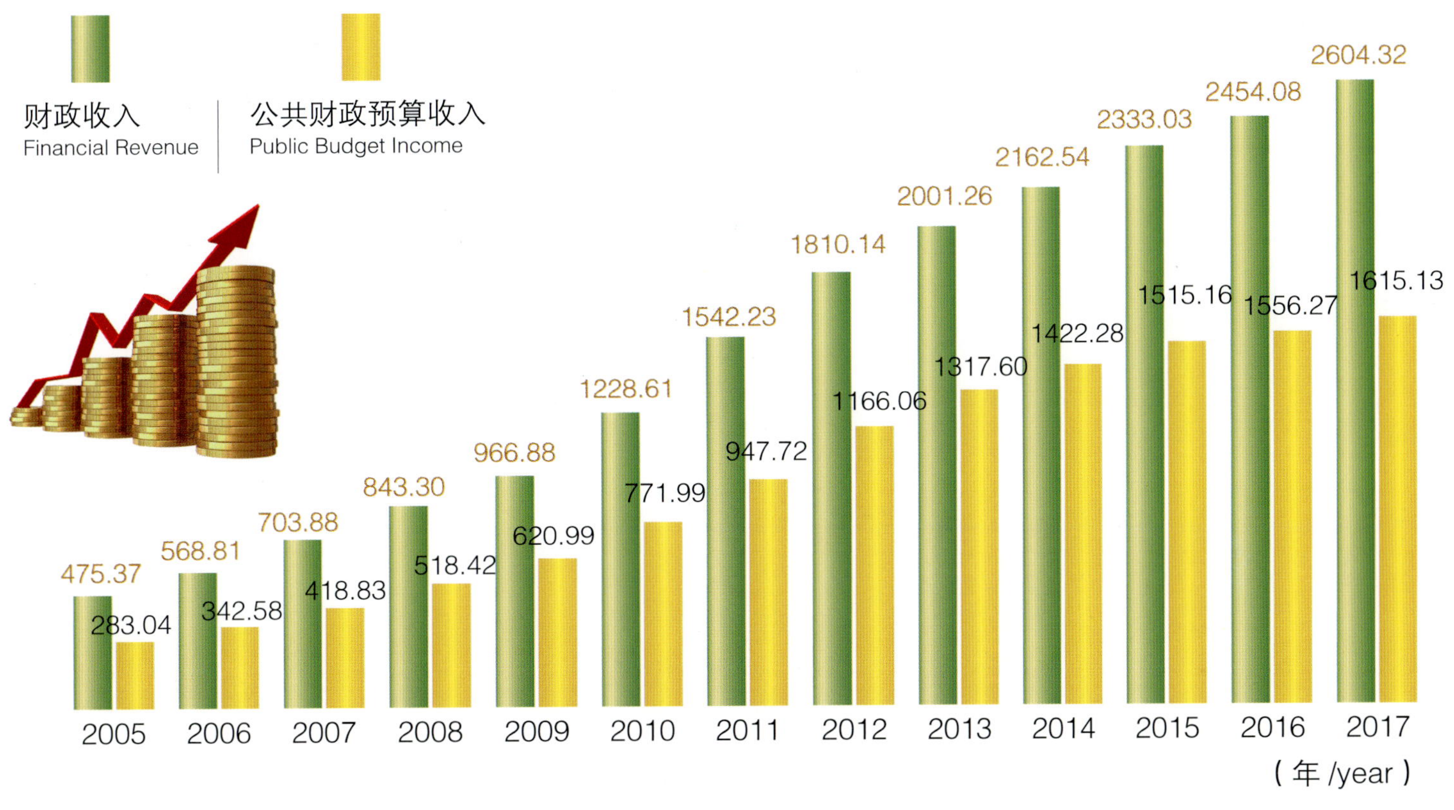

公共财政预算支出构成（%）

Composition of Public Budget Expenditure（%）

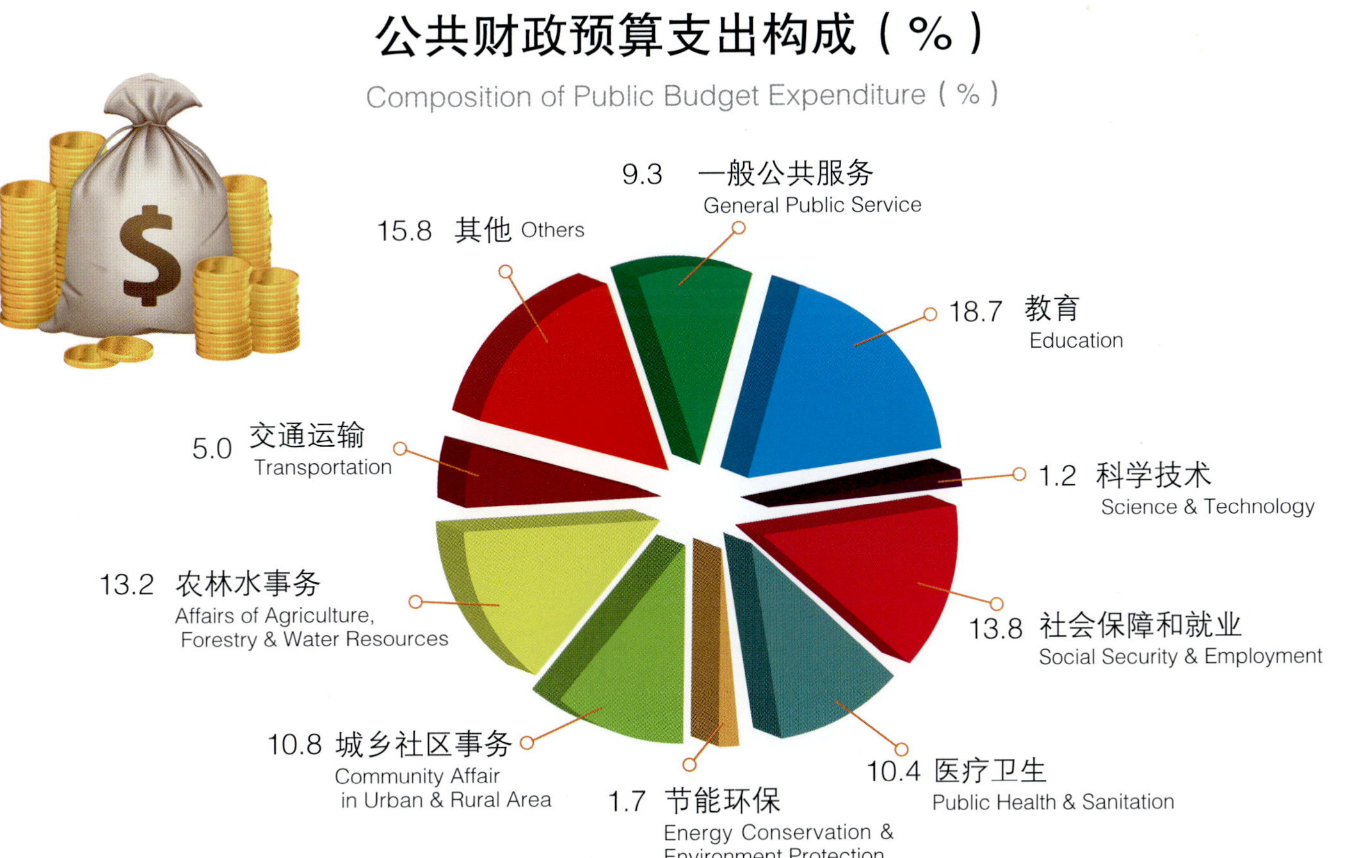

个人存款（亿元）

Personal Deposits （100 million yuan）

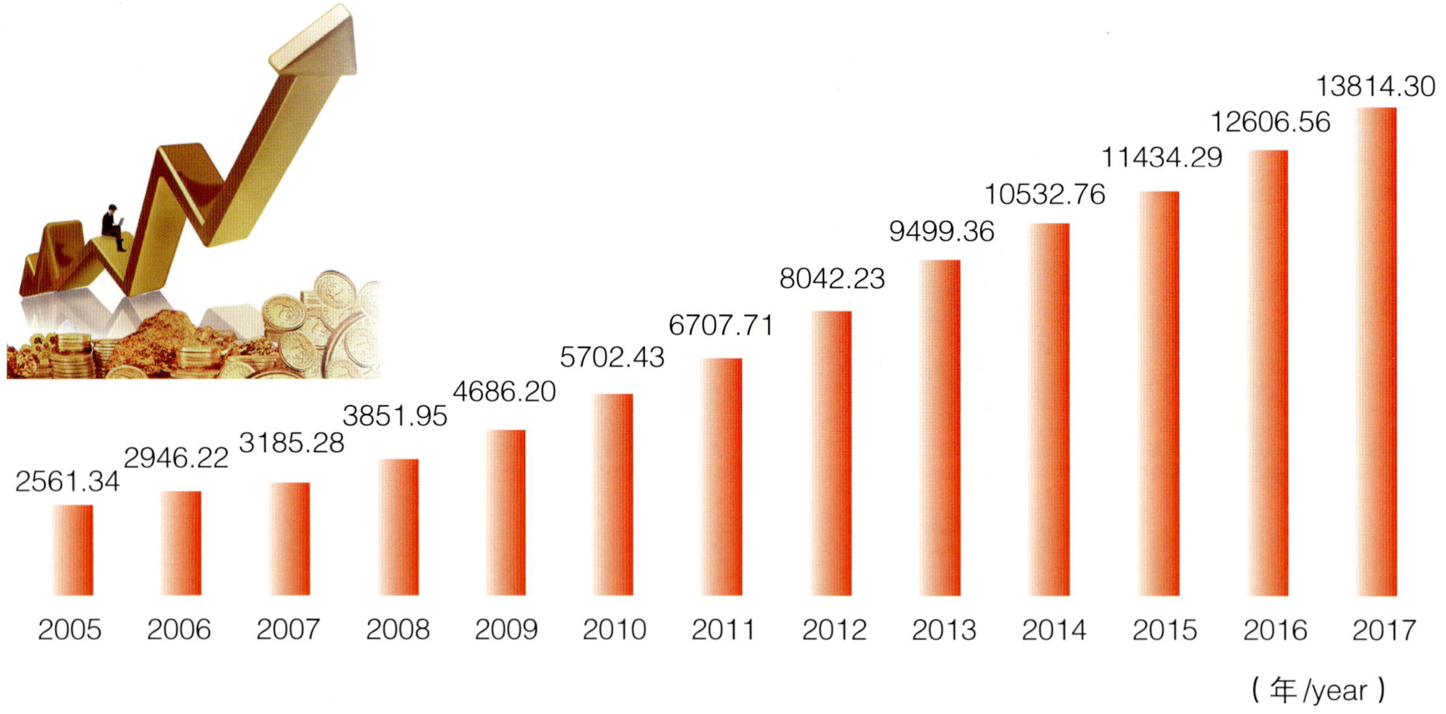

说明：根据中国人民银行南宁中心支行报表的调整，自 2011 年起，本图表中原指标“城乡居民储蓄存款”改为“个人存款”。

Note: Accroding to the reports adjustment of the Central Branch in Nanning of the People's Bank of China, the indicator "Urban & Rural Saving Deposits" has changde into "Personal Deposits" since 2011.

物价指数（上年 =100）

Price Indices （preceding year = 100）

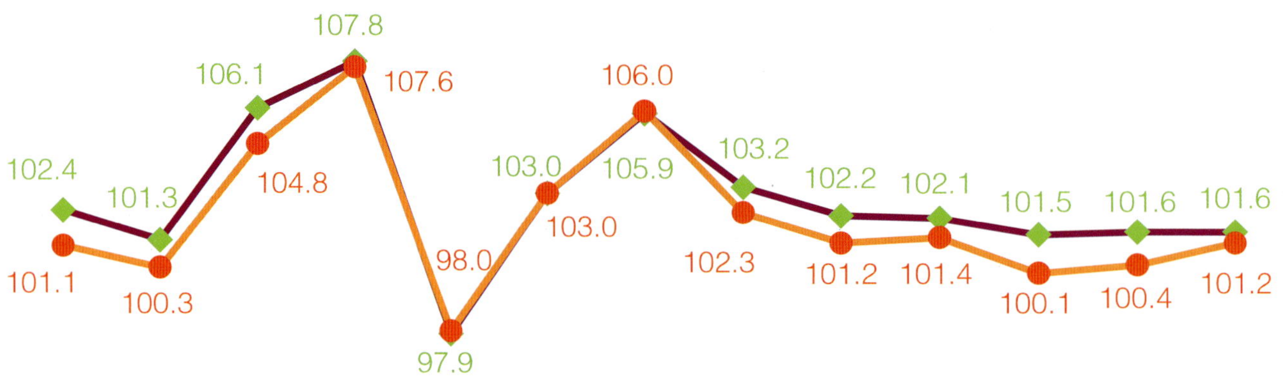

居民消费价格指数（上年=100）

Consumer Price Index （preceding year = 100）

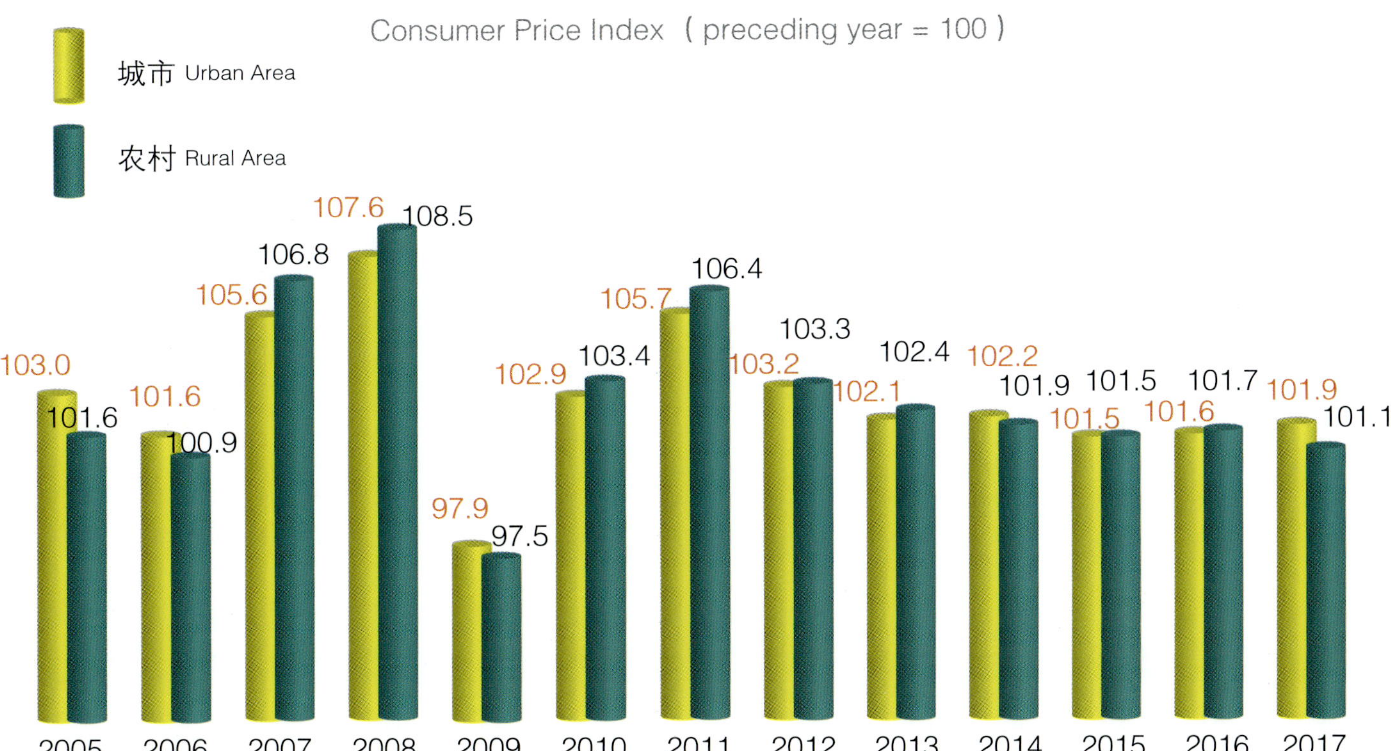

工业生产者出厂价格指数、工业生产者购进价格指数（上年=100）

Producer Price Indices for Industrial Products, Purchasing Price Indices for Industrial Producers（preceding year = 100）

工业生产者出厂价格指数
Producer Price Indices for Industrial Products

工业生产者购进价格指数
Purchasing Price Indices for Industrial Producers

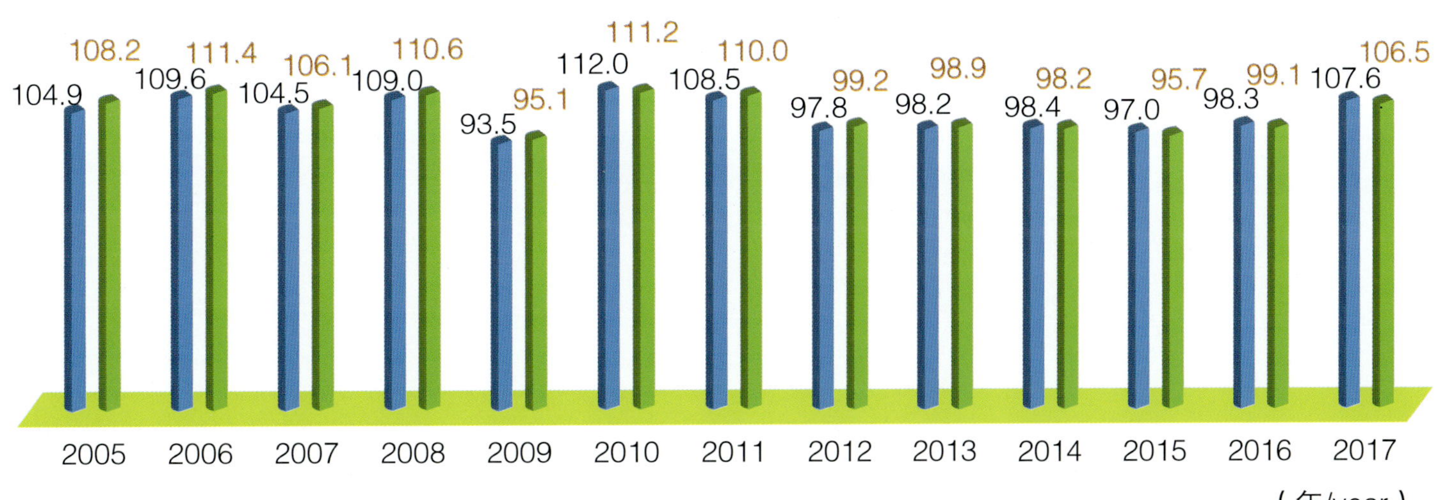

城镇居民人均可支配收入（元）

Per Capita Disposable Income of Urban Households （yuan）

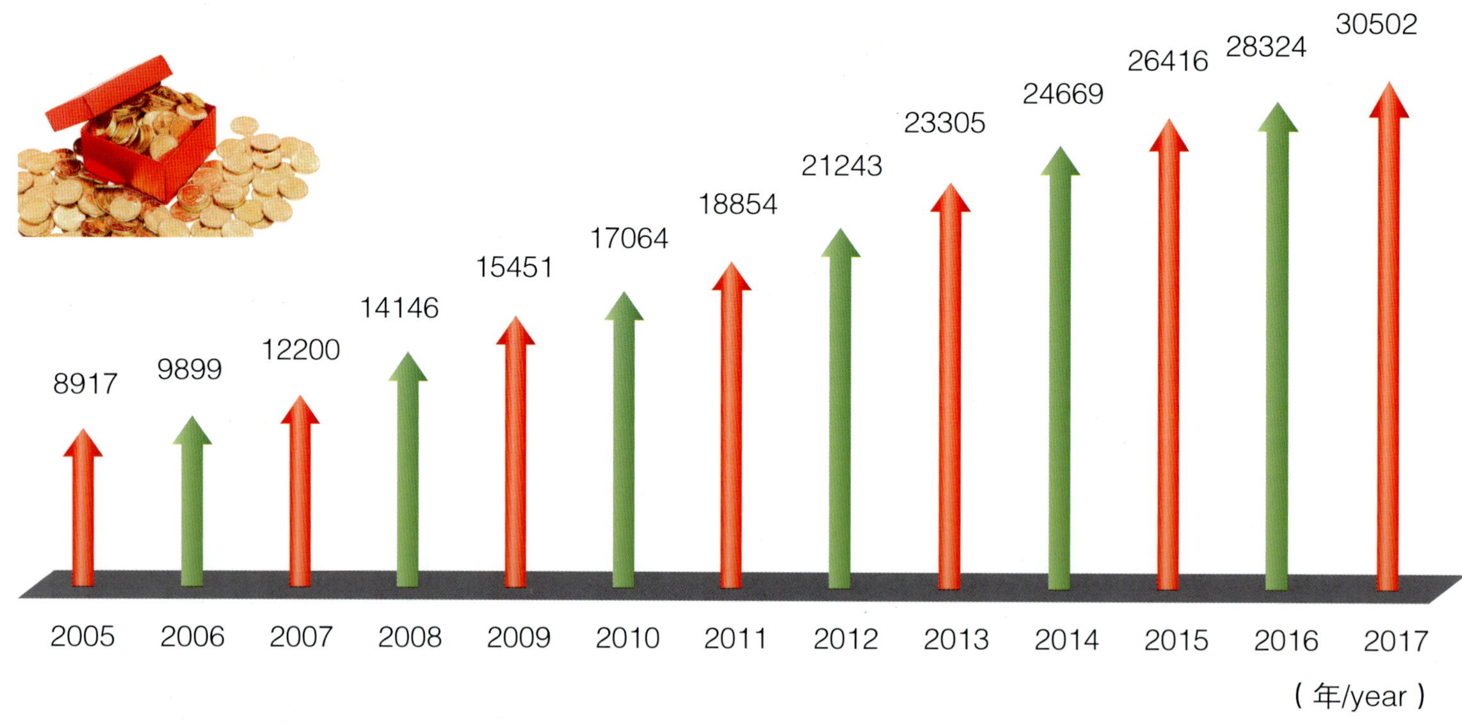

2017年城乡居民人均消费构成（%）

Composition of Per Capita Consumption Expenditure of Urban & Rural Households in 2017（%）

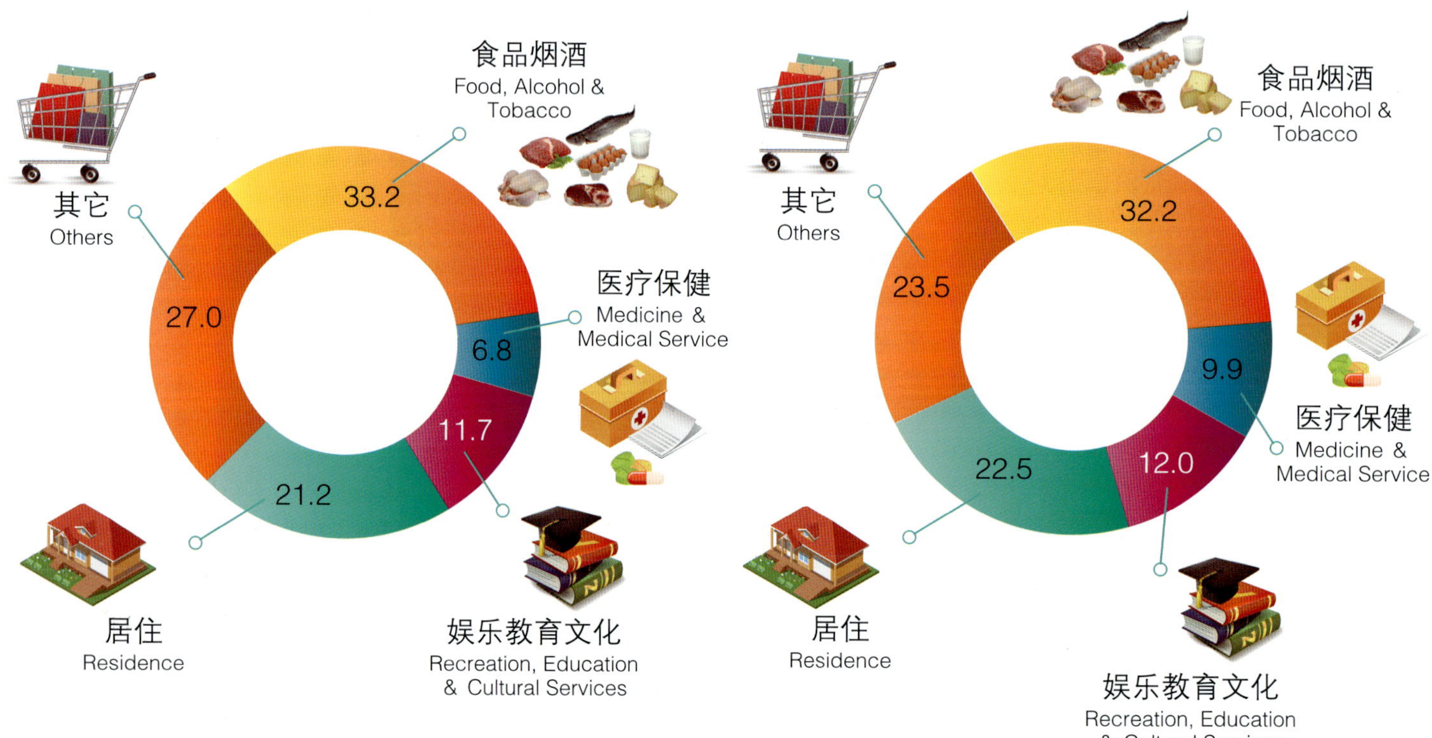

城镇居民人均消费构成
Composition of Per Capita Annual Consumption Expenditure of Urban Households

农民人均消费构成
Composition of Per Capita Annual Consumption Expenditure of Rural Households

农民人均纯收入（元）

Per Capita Net Income of Rural Households （yuan）

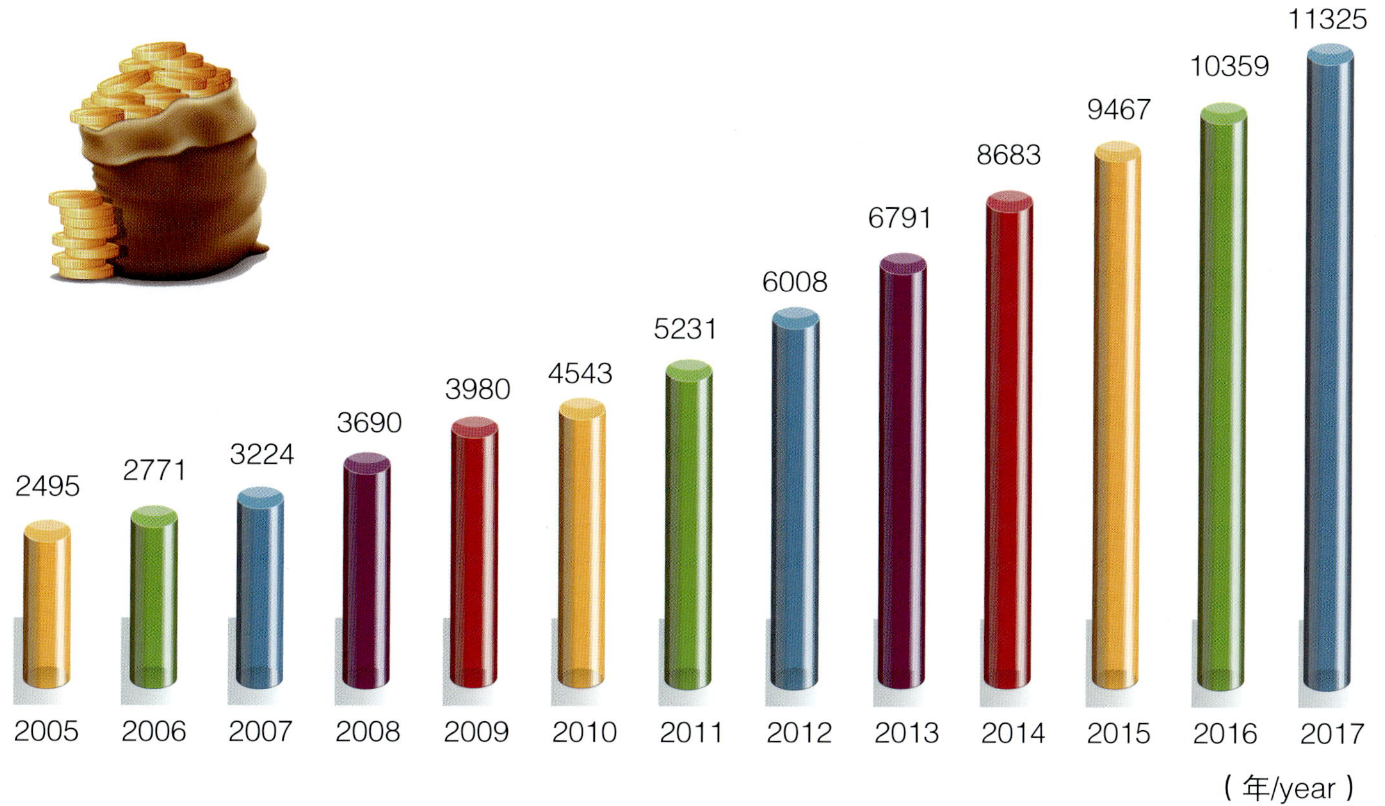

说明：2015年起为农民人均可支配收入。

Note: The data is "per capita disposable income of rural households" since 2015.

污染治理投资完成额（亿元）

Completed Investment in Pollution Treatment Projects（100 million yuan）

年/year	2005	2006	2007	2008	2009	2010	2011	2012	2013	2014	2015	2016	2017
亿元	10.37	6.94	18.19	14.98	11.71	9.28	12.97	12.73	18.32	17.89	24.72	13.04	8.65

公园绿地面积（公顷）

Park Green Area （ hectare ）

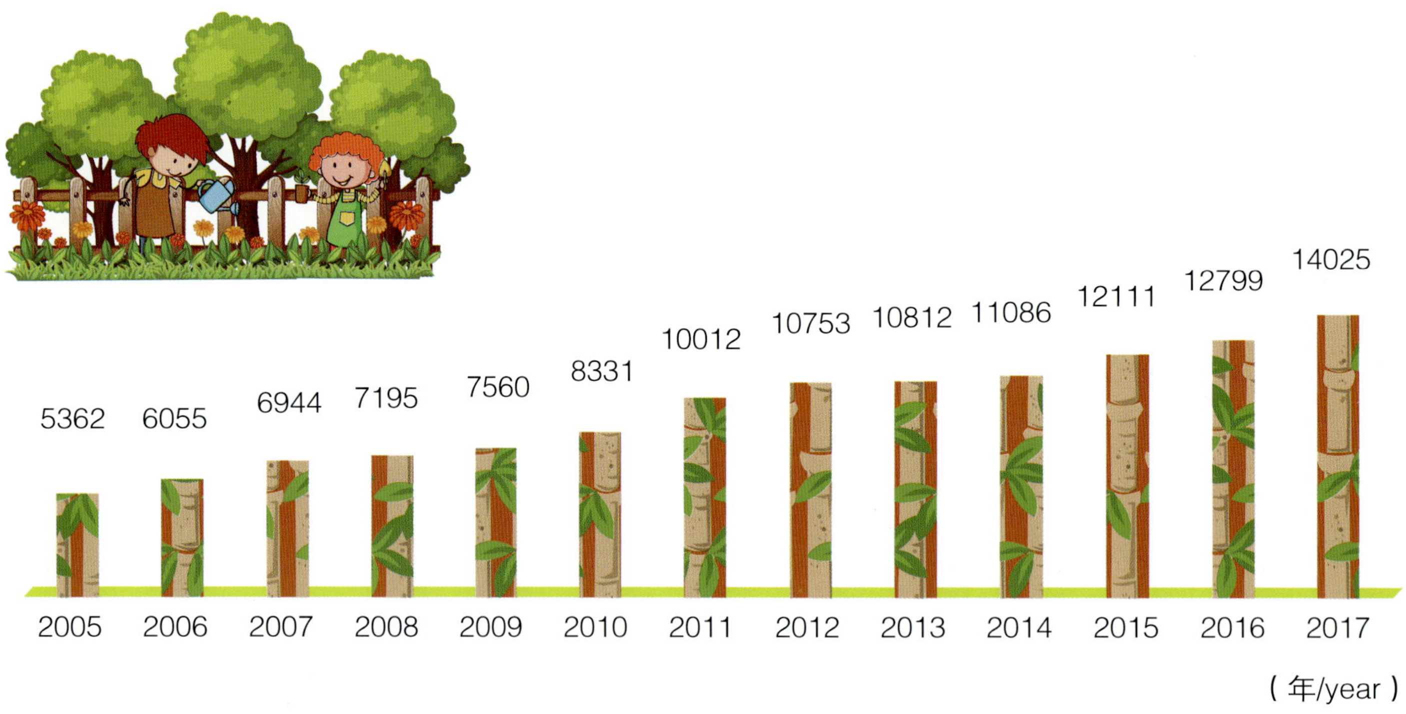

污水处理能力（万立方米/日）

Treatment Capacity of Pol luted Water （10 000 cu.m/day）

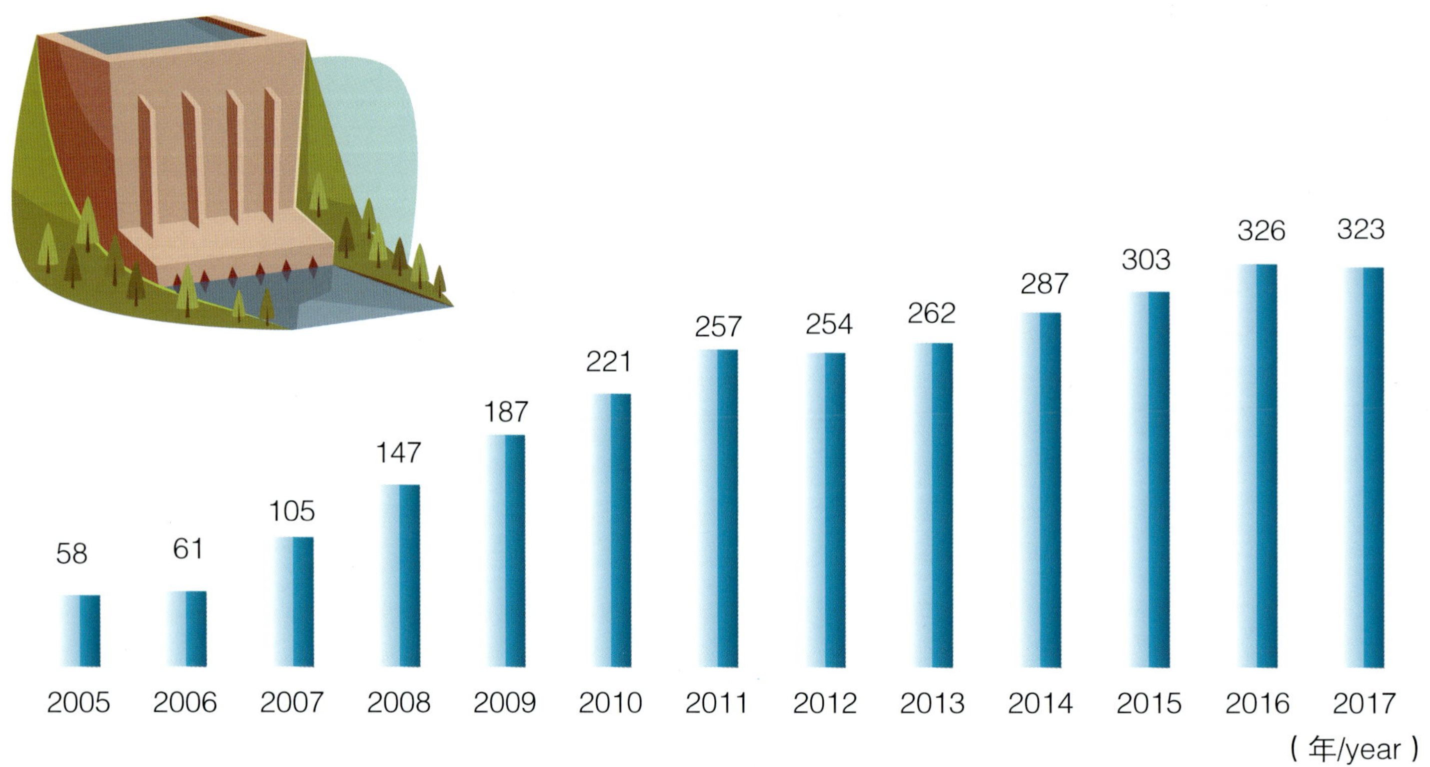

农林牧渔业总产值（当年价，亿元）

Gross Output Value of Farming,Forestry,Animal Husbandry & Fishery
(at current prices,100 million yuan)

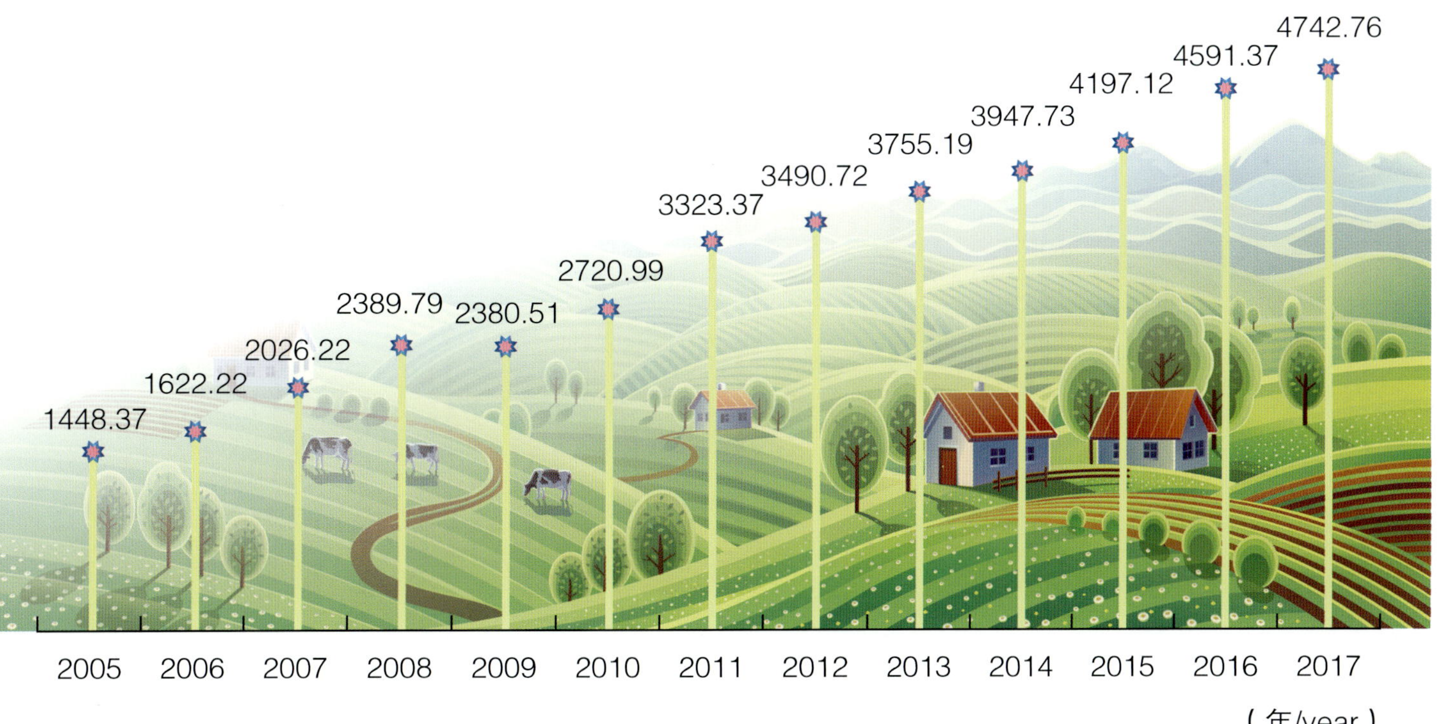

农林牧渔业总产值构成（%）

Composition of Gross Output Value of Farming,Forestry,Animal Husbandry & Fishery (%)

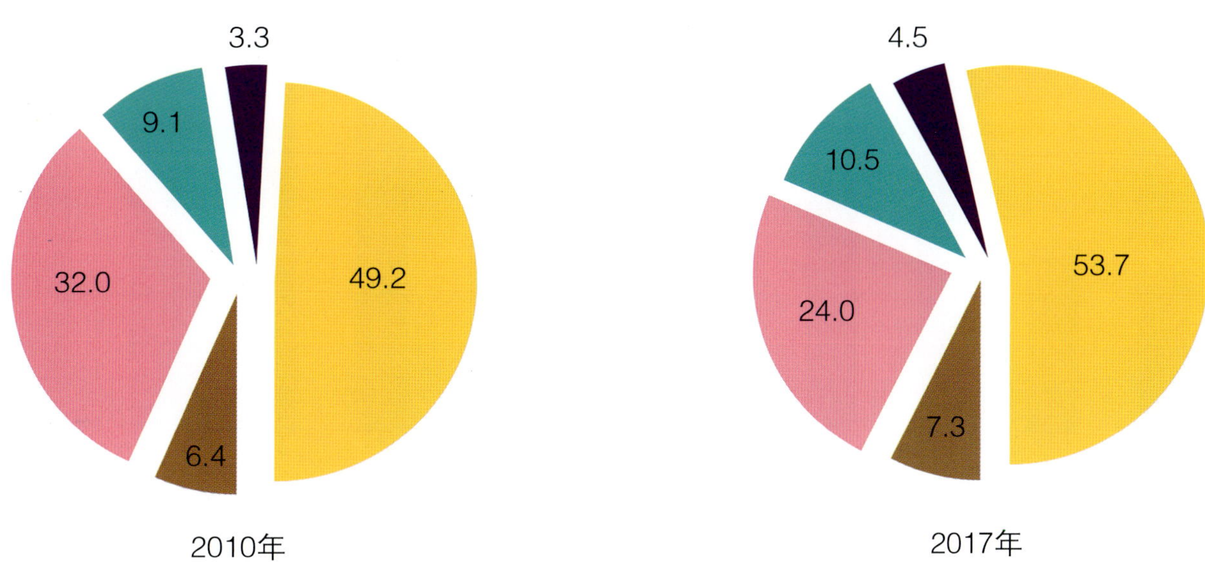

人均农产品产量（公斤）

Per Capita Major Agricultural Products （ kg ）

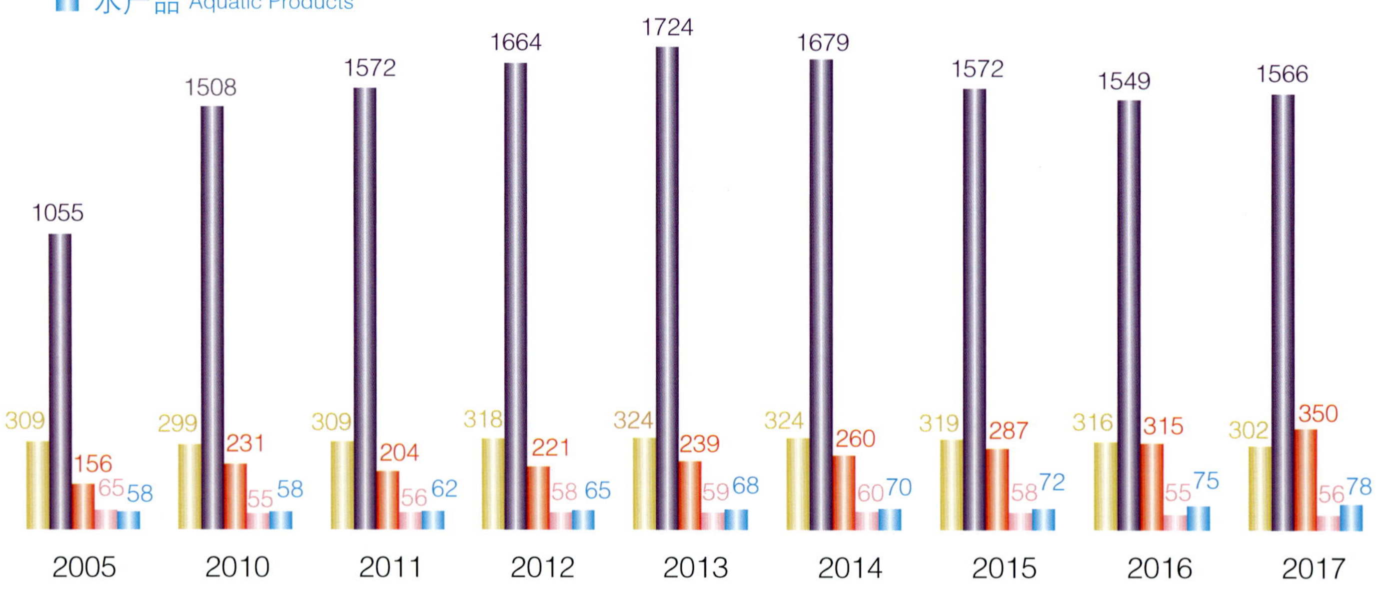

注：本表按年平均常住人口计算。

Note: The data is calculated by the annual everage permanent population.

全部工业总产值（当年价，亿元）

All Included Gross Industrial Output Value

（At Current Prices,100 million yuan）

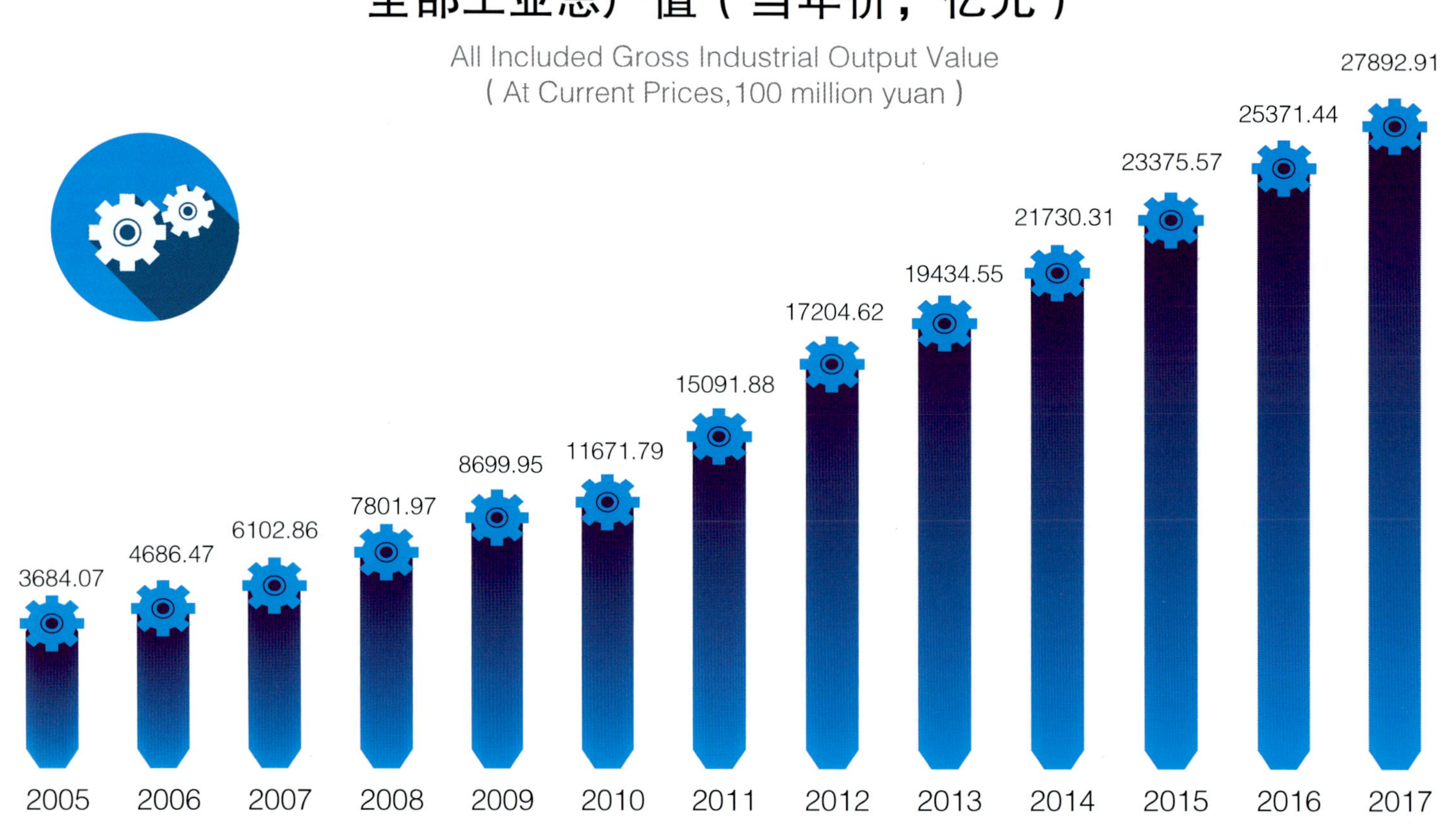

规模以上工业利润总额（亿元）

Total Profits of Industrial Enterprises above Designated Size
(100 million yuan)

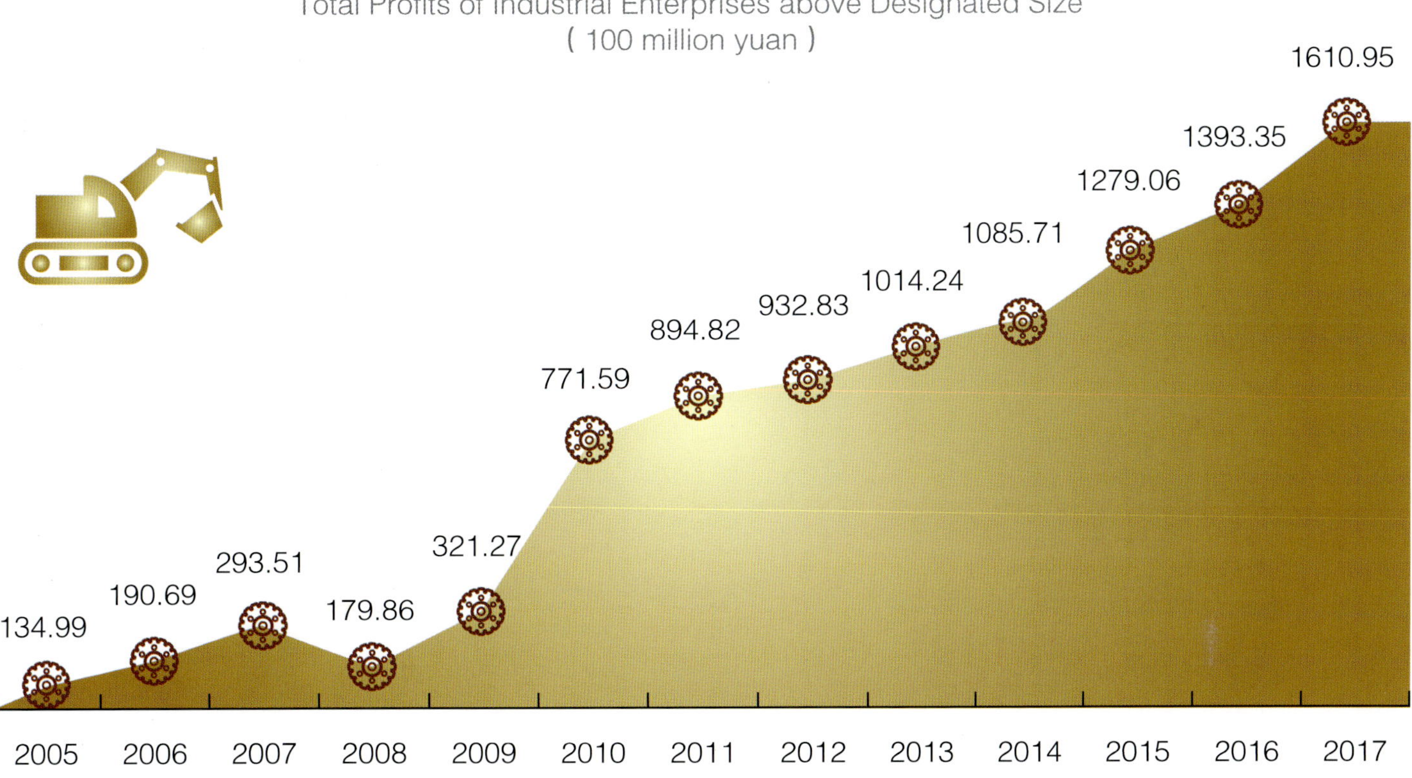

建筑业总产值（三级及三级以上，亿元）

Gross Output Value of Construction Enterprises
(Third & Higher Grade,100 million yuan)

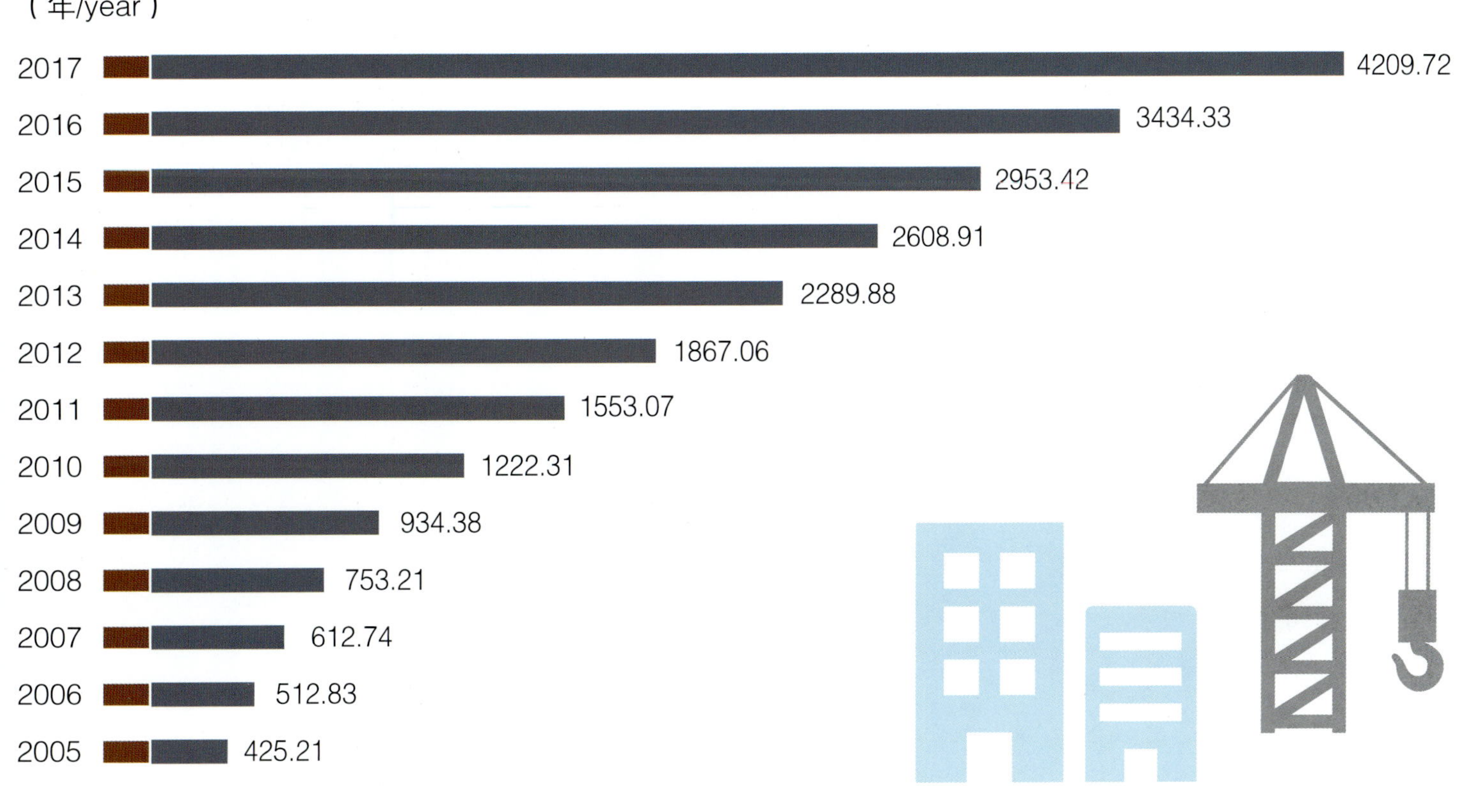

建筑业从业人员（三级及三级以上企业，万人）

Number of Employed Persons in Construction Enterprises
(Third & Higher Grade,10 000 persons)

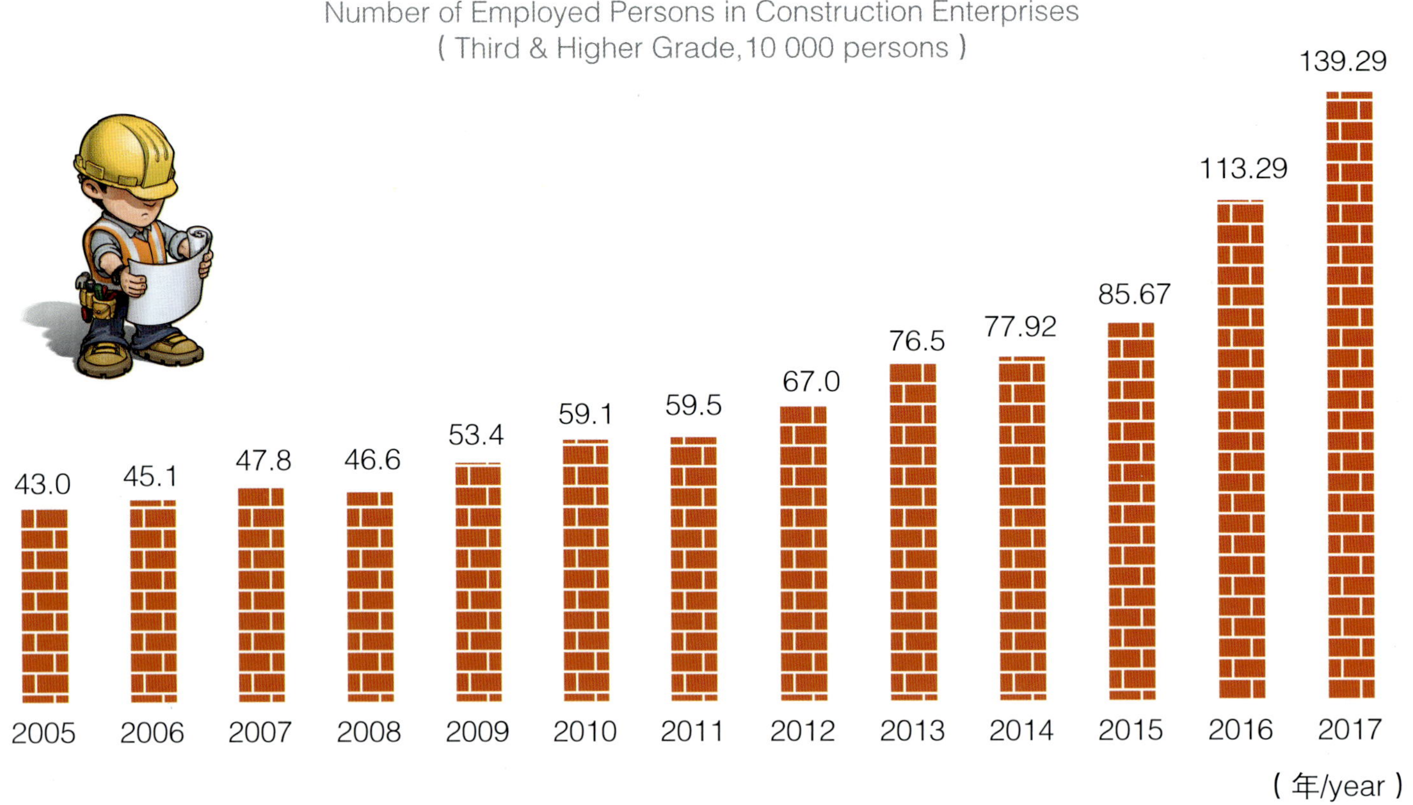

（年/year）

客货运输量

Total Passenger & Freight Traffic

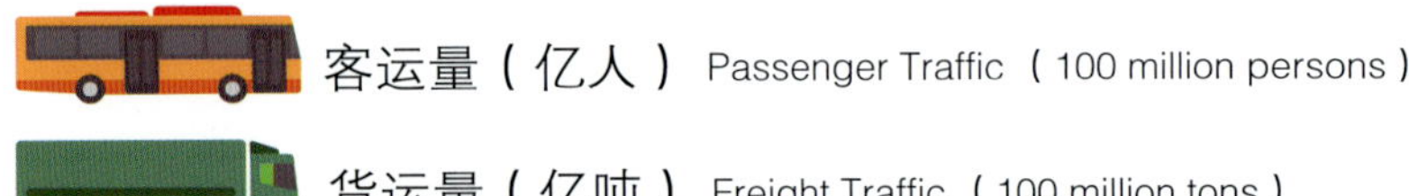

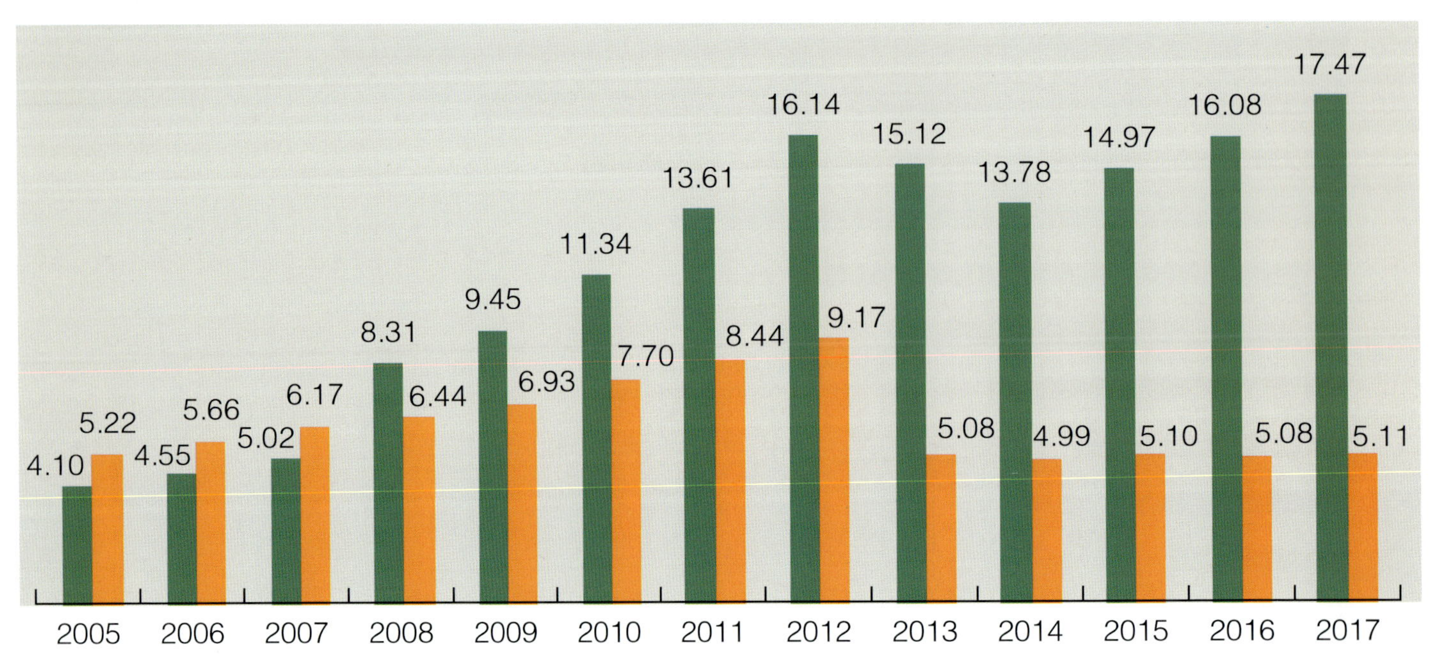

（年/year）

高速公路里程（公里）

Lenth of Expressway（km）

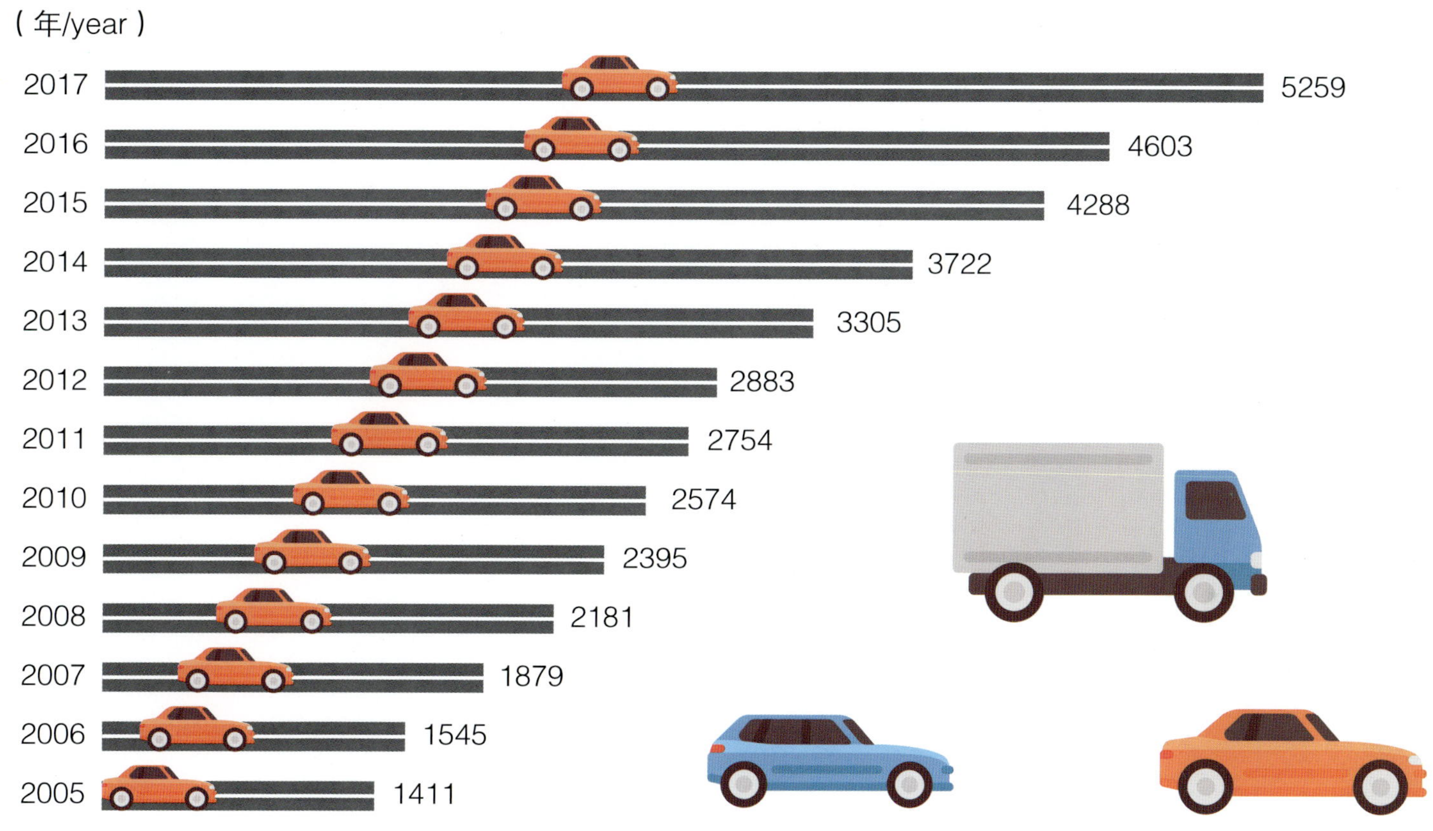

平均每万人拥有电话机（部）

Average Number of Telephone Subscribers per 10 000 Persons Owned （set）

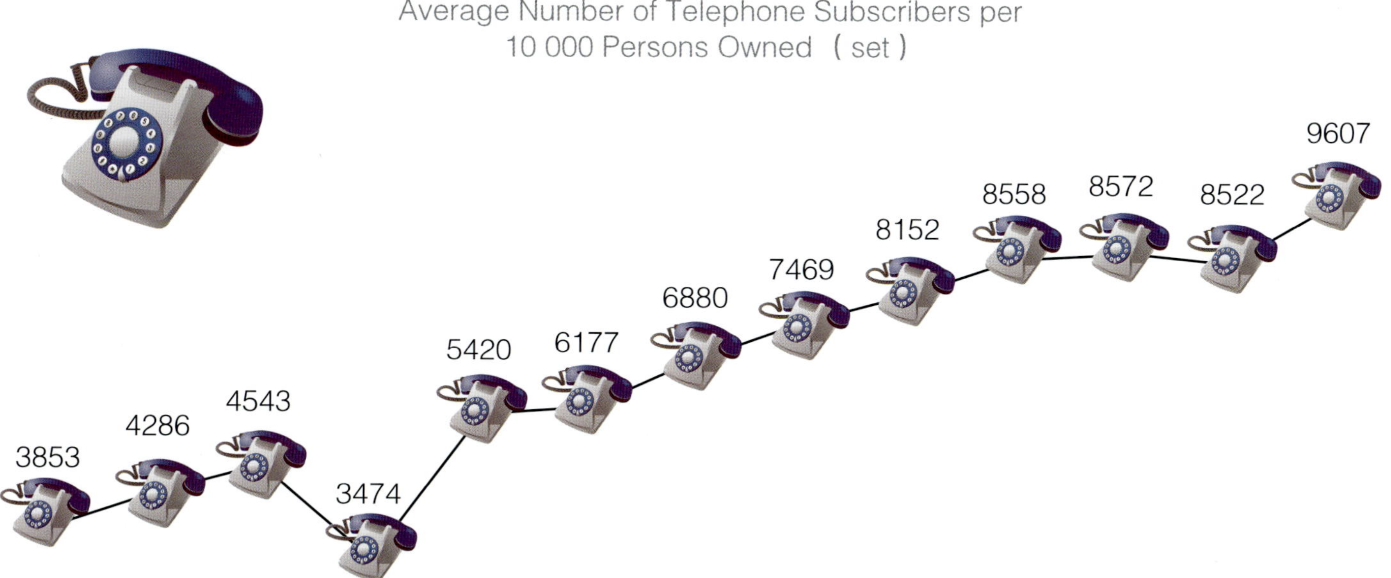

每万人在校大学生（人）

Number of University & College Students
per 10 000 Persons（person）

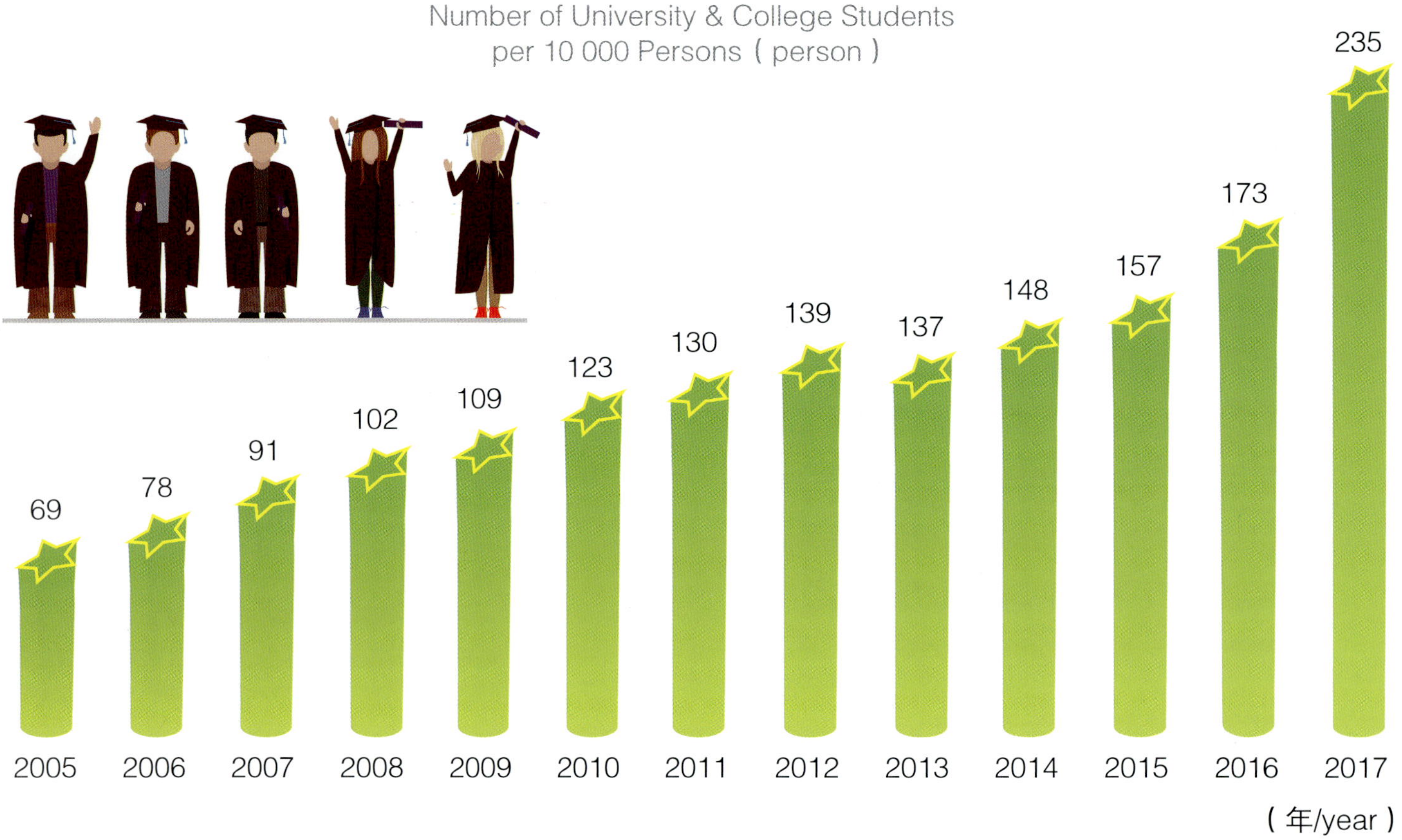

69
78
91
102
109
123
130
139
137
148
157
173
235
2005
2006
2007
2008
2009
2010
2011
2012
2013
2014
2015
2016
2017
（年/year）

科技活动人员（万人）

Number of Persons Engaged in Scientific &
Technological Activities（10 000 persons）

5.60
6.04
6.87
7.07
8.71
8.91
10.29
10.77
10.87
10.72
11.37
12.08
2005
2006
2007
2008
2009
2010
2011
2012
2013
2014
2015
2016
2017
（年/year）

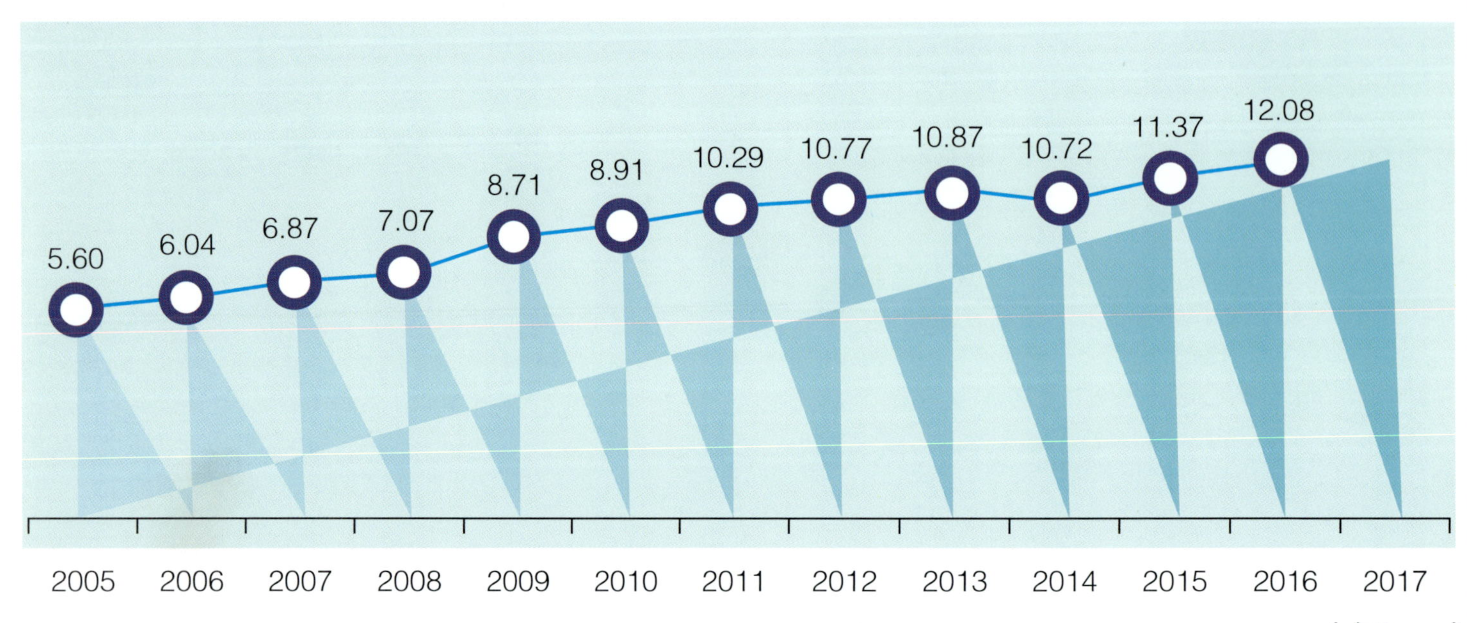

报纸、图书出版数量

Number of Publications of Newspaper & Books

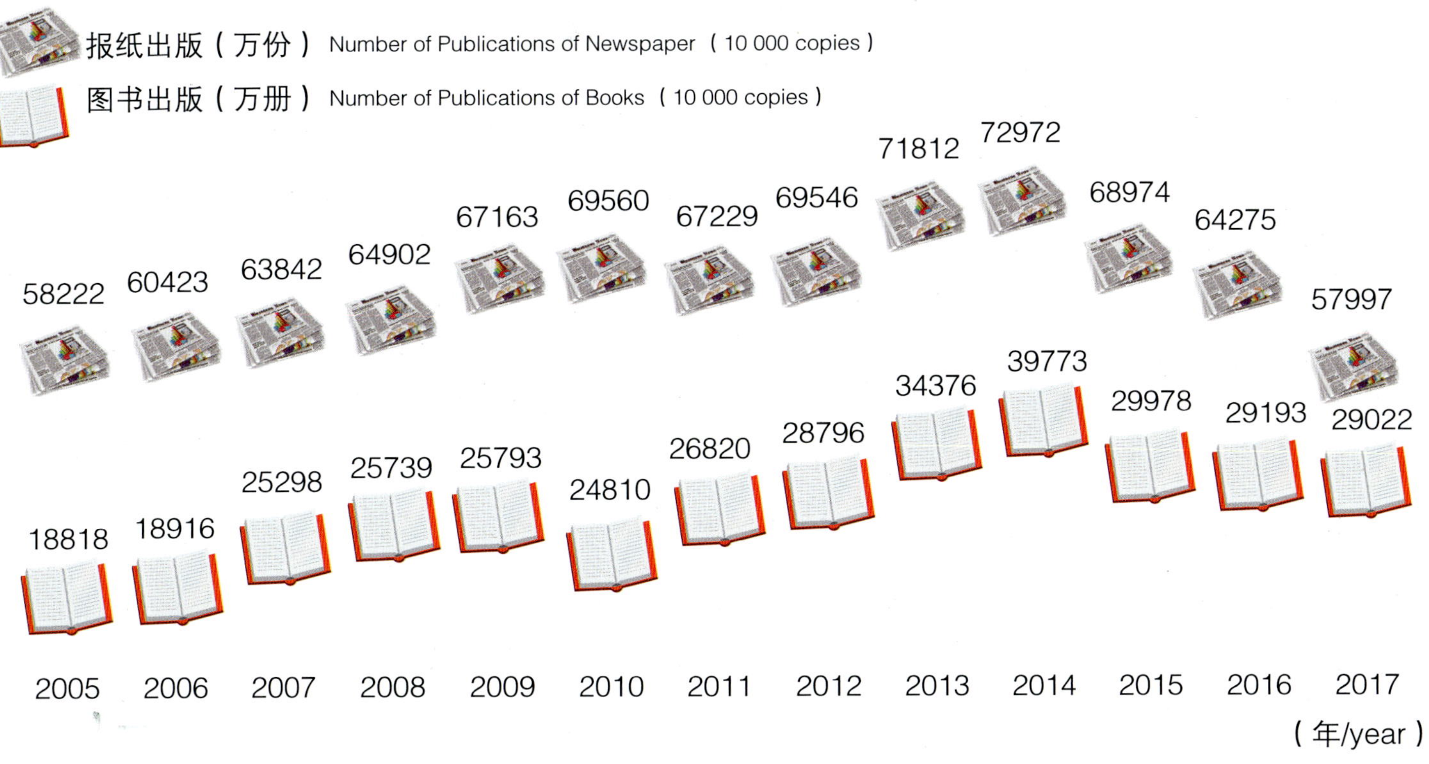

每万人医院、卫生院病床（张）

Number of Hospital Beds per 10 000 Persons （bed）

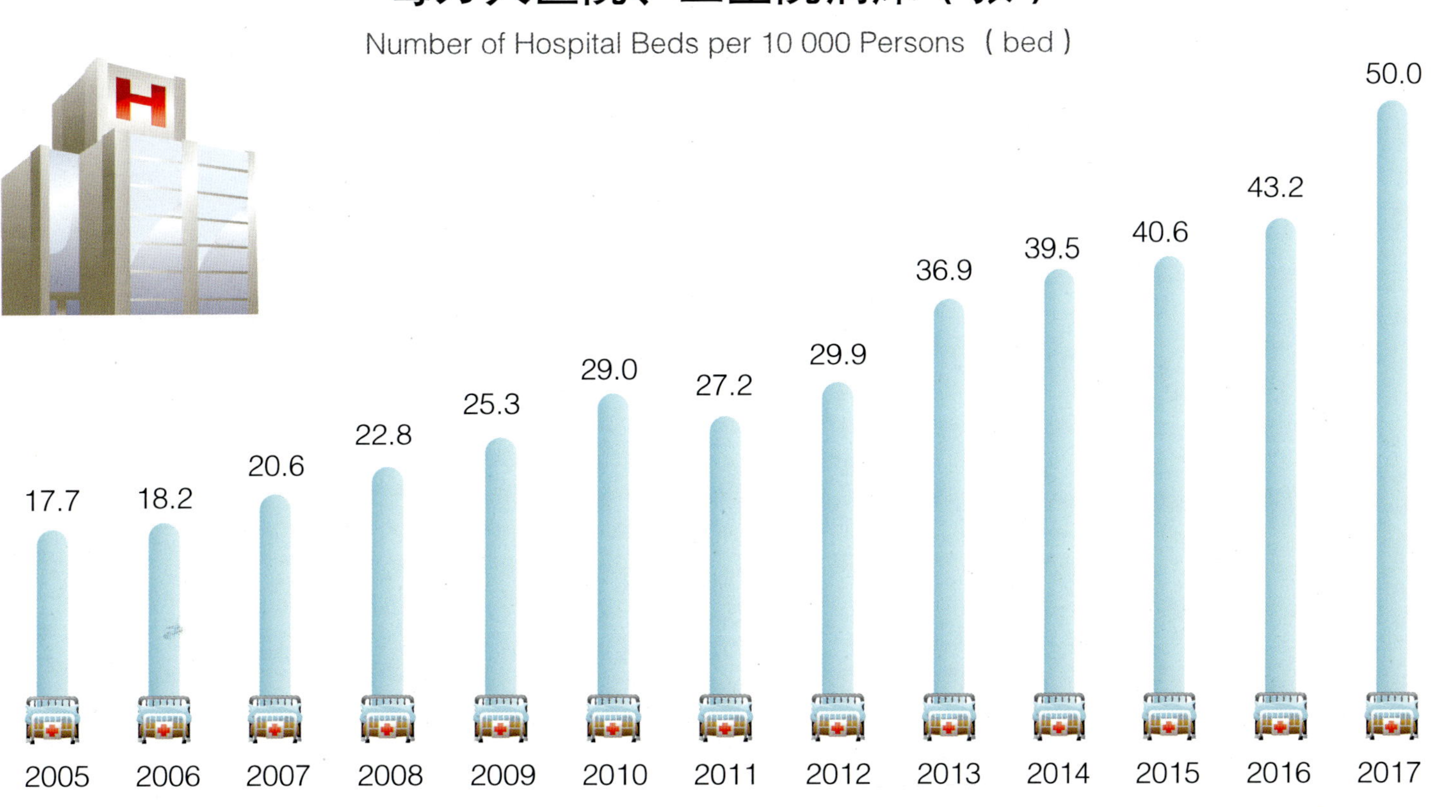

每万人卫生技术人员（人）

Number of Medical Technical Personnnel per 10 000 Persons （person）

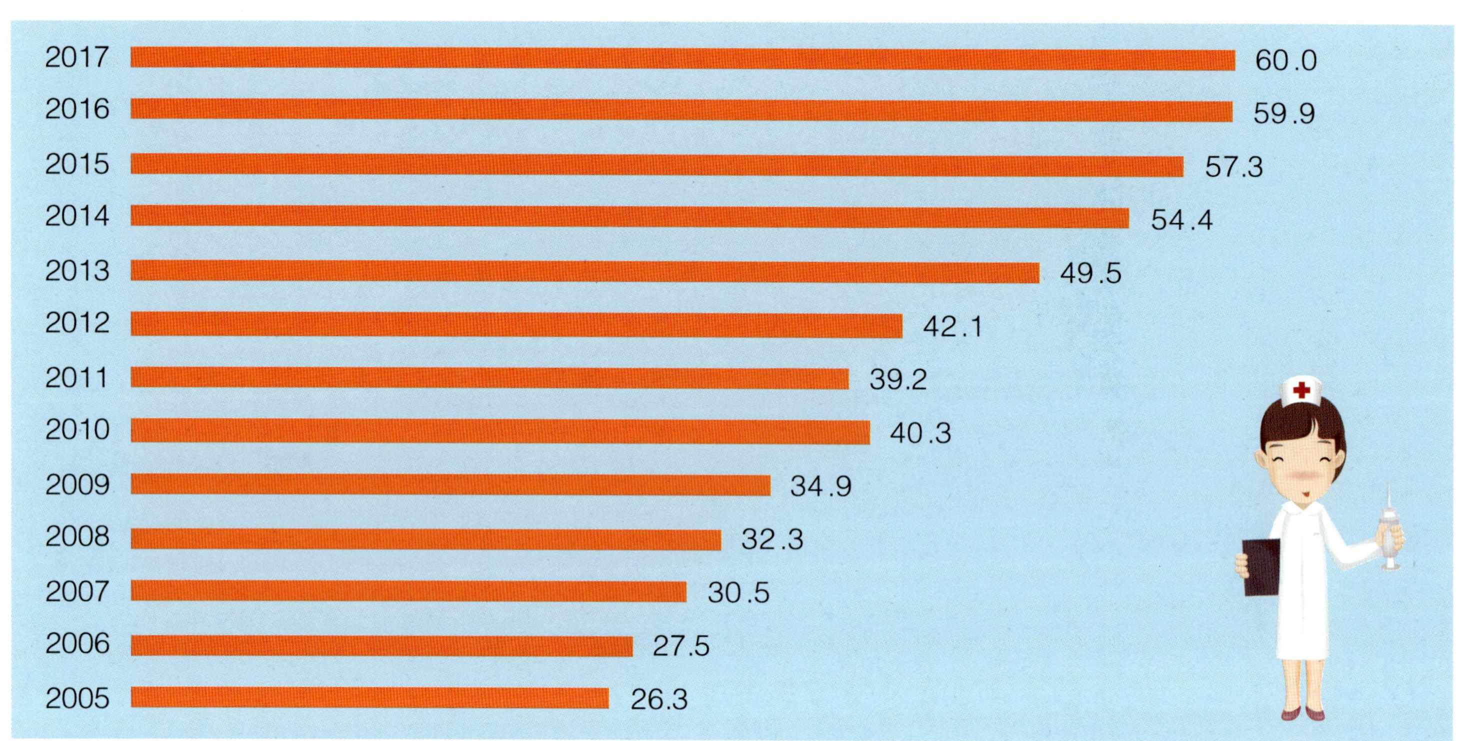

城乡居民生活最低保障人数（万人）

Population Receiving Lowest Cost-of-Living in Urban & Rural Area （10 000 persons）

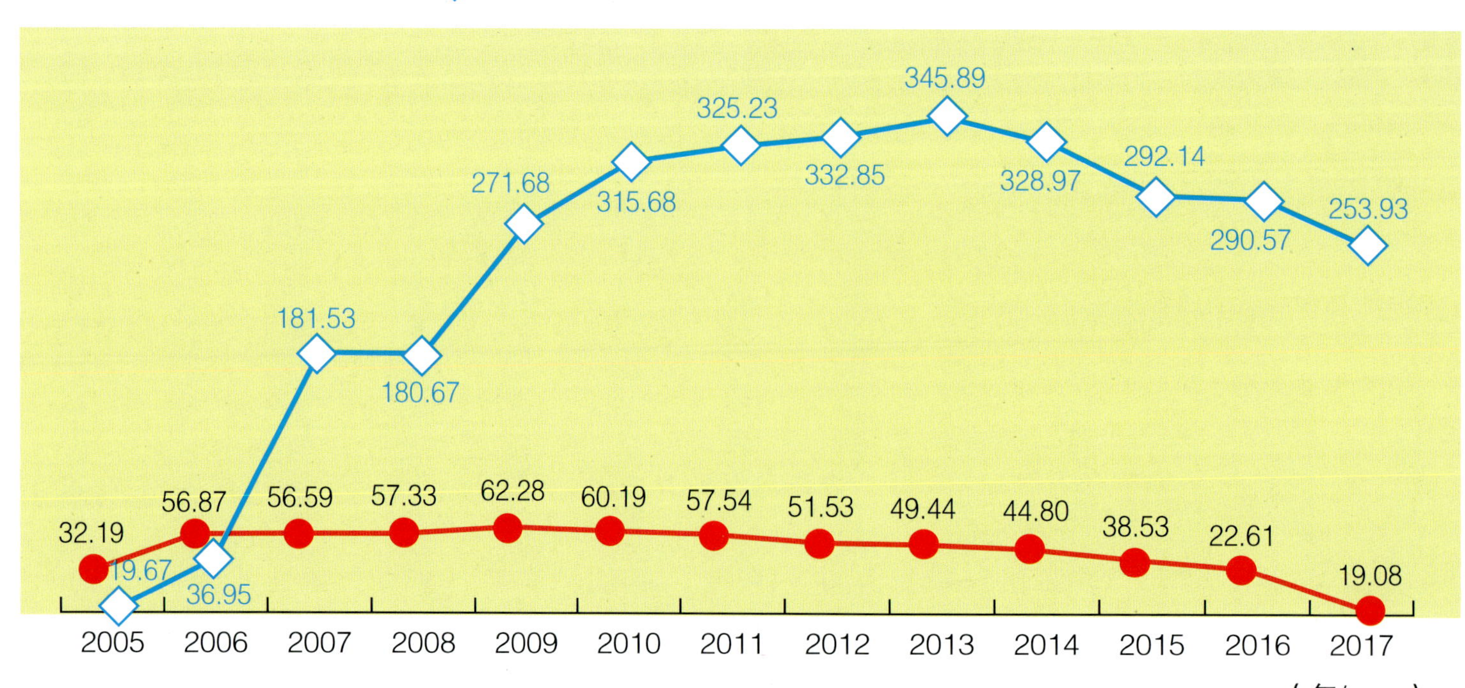

目　　录

CONTENTS

第一篇　综　合

CHAPTER 1　GENERAL SURVEY

1－1　行政区划（2017年末）……(3)
Divisions of Administrative Areas（End of 2017）

1－2　县级以上行政区划（2017年末）……(7)
Division of Administrative Areas at & above County Level（End of 2017）

1－3　主要年份国民经济和社会发展主要指标……(8)
Major Indicators on National Economic & Social Development in Main Years

1－4　主要年份国民经济和社会发展速度指标……(13)
Growth Rates of Major Indicators on National Economic & Social Development in Main Years

1－5　主要年份国民经济和社会发展结构指标……(18)
Composition Indicators on National Economic & Social Development in Main Years

1－6　主要年份国民经济和社会发展比例和效益指标……(22)
Indicators on Proportions & Efficiency in National Economic & Social Development in Main Years

1－7　主要年份人均主要工农业产品产量……(25)
Per Capita Output of Major Industrial & Agricultural Products in Main Years

1－8　各个时期主要经济指标……(26)
Main Economic Indicators of Each Period

1－9　各个时期主要经济指标平均增长率……(28)
Average Growth Rate of Main Economic Indicators of Each Period

1－10　主要年份平均每天主要社会经济活动……(30)
Selected Indicators on Average Daily Social & Economic Activities in Main Years

1－11　按行业分组的法人单位数……(32)
Number of Legal Entities Grouped by Sector

1－12　各市按机构类型分组的法人单位数（2017年）……(34)
Number of Legal Entities Grouped by Region & Type of Institutions（2017）

1－13　各市按主要行业分组的法人单位数（2017年）……(36)
Number of Legal Entities Grouped by Region & Major Sector（2017）

1－14　按行业、营业状态分组的企业法人单位数（2017年）……(38)
Number of Legal Entities Grouped by Sector & Operating State（2017）

1－15　按行业、登记注册类型分组的企业法人单位数（2017年）……(40)
Number of Legal Entities Grouped by Sector & Registration Status（2017）

1－16　各市按三次产业分组的法人单位数（2017年）……(44)
Number of Legal Entities Grouped by Three Strata of Industry（2017）

主要统计指标解释……(45)
Explanatory Notes on Main Statistical Indicators

第二篇　人　口

CHAPTER 2　POPULATION

2－1　总人口及其构成 .... (51)

Population & Its Composition

2－2　人口自然变动情况 .... (52)

Status of Population Natural Changes

2－3　主要年份按居住地分的城乡人口 .... (53)

Population by Urban & Rural by Living Areas in Main Years

2－4　主要年份各市按居住地分的城乡人口 .... (54)

Population by Urban & Rural By Living Areas by City in Main Years

2－5　各市县人口数（2017年） .... (55)

Population by City & County（2017）

2－6　主要年份婚姻情况 .... (59)

Marital Status in Main Years

2－7　主要年份各种规模家庭户构成 .... (60)

Composition of Various Size of Family Household in Main Years

2－8　主要年份人口年龄构成 .... (61)

Population Composition by Age in Main Years

2－9　6岁及以上人口受教育程度构成 .... (62)

Composition of Educational Status of Ages in 6 & above

主要统计指标解释 .... (63)

Explanatory Notes on Main Statistical Indicators

第三篇　国民经济核算

CHAPTER 3　NATIONAL ECONOMIC ACCOUNTING

3－1　广西生产总值（1978－2017年） .... (69)

Gross Domestic Product（1978－2017）

3－2　广西生产总值构成（1978－2017年） .... (70)

Composition of Gross Domestic Product（1978－2017）

3－3　广西生产总值指数（1978－2017年） .... (71)

Indices of Gross Domestic Product（1978－2017）

3－4　广西生产总值指数（1978－2017年） .... (72)

Indices of Gross Domestic Product（1978－2017）

3－5　三次产业贡献率（1990－2017年） .... (73)

Contribution Rate of Three Industries（1990－2017）

3－6　各市生产总值、人均地区生产总值（2017年） .... (74)

GDP & Per Capita GDP by City（2017）

3－7　各市生产总值、人均地区生产总值指数（2017年） .... (75)

Indices of GDP & Per Capita GDP by City（2017）

3－8　支出法广西生产总值（1978－2016年） .... (76)

Gross Domestic Product by Expenditure Approach（1978－2016）

3－9　支出法广西生产总值构成（1978－2016年） .... (77)

Composition of Gross Domestic Product by Expenditure Approach （1978－2016）

3－10　支出法广西生产总值指数（1978－2016年） .... (78)

Indices of Gross Domestic Product by Expenditure Approach（1978－2016）
3－11 支出法广西生产总值指数（1978－2016年）…… (79)
Indices of Gross Domestic Product by Expenditure Approach（1978－2016）
3－12 主要年份按支出法计算的广西生产总值…… (80)
Gross Domestic Product by Expenditure Approach in Main Years
主要统计指标解释…… (81)
Explanatory Notes on Main Statistical Indicators

第四篇 从业人员和职工工资

CHAPTER 4 EMPLOYMENT & WAGES

4－1 主要年份就业和劳动报酬基本情况…… (88)
Resource of Labor Force & Number of Employed Persons in Main Years
4－2 城乡从业人员及城镇单位在岗职工平均工资（1978－2017年）…… (90)
Urban & Rural Employed Persons, Average Wages of Staff & Workers at Post in Urban Units（1978－2017）
4－3 按产业、经济类型分组的从业人员（2017年）…… (91)
Number of Employed Persons Grouped by Industry & the Categories of Registration（2017）
4－4 城镇单位从业人员（2017年）…… (92)
Number of Employed Persons in Urban Units（2017）
4－5 按行业、经济类型分组的城镇单位女性从业人数（2017年）…… (93)
Number of Female Employed in Urban Units Grouped by Industry & the Categories of Registration（2017）
4－6 城镇单位从业人员工资总额（2017年）…… (94)
Earning of Employed Persons in Urban Units（2017）
4－7 城镇单位从业人员平均工资（2017年）…… (95)
Average Earning of Staff & Workers in Urban Units（2017）
4－8 城镇单位在岗职工平均工资（2017年）…… (96)
Average Earning of Staff & Workers in Urban Units（2017）
4－9 分市城镇单位在岗职工人数（2017年）…… (97)
Number of Employed Persons in Urban Units by City（2017）
4－10 分市城镇单位在岗职工平均工资（2017年）…… (98)
Average Wages of Staff & Workers at Post in Urban Units by City（2017）
4－11 分市城镇单位从业人员工资总额（2017年）…… (99)
Earning of Employed Persons in Urban Units by City（2017）
4－12 分市城镇单位从业人员平均工资（2017年）…… (100)
Number of Employed Persons in Urban Units by City & Sector（2017）
4－13 城镇单位分市分行业从业人员（2017年）…… (101)
Number of Employed Persons in Urban Units by City & Sector（2017）
4－14 城镇单位分市分行业女性从业人数（2017年）…… (103)
Number of Female Employed Persons in Urban Units by City & Sector（2017）
4－15 城镇单位分市分行业从业人员平均工资（2017年）…… (105)
Average Earning of Staff & Workers at Work in Urban Units by City & Sector（2017）
4－16 主要年份离休、退休、退职人员和保险福利费用情况…… (107)
Statistics of VCSR, Retired & Resigned, Insurance & Welfare Funds in Main Years
4－17 参加社会保险人员…… (108)
Number of Persons Joined Social Security in Main Years

4－18 分市社会保险参保人数（2017年）……（109）
Number of Persons Joined Social Security by City（2017）
4－19 城镇私营单位从业人员平均工资（2017年）……（110）
Average Wages of Employed Persons in Urban Private Units（2017）
主要统计指标解释……（111）
Explanatory Notes on Main Statistical Indicators

第五篇 物 价
CHAPTER 5 PRICES
5－1 居民消费及商品零售价格总指数（1978－2017年）……（117）
Consumer & Retail General Price Indices（1978－2017）
5－2 各地区商品零售和农业生产资料价格指数（2017年）……（118）
Retail & Agricultural Means of Production Price Indices by Region（2017）
5－3 各地区居民消费价格指数（2017年）……（124）
Consumer Price Indices by Region（2017）
5－4 主要年份工业品出厂价格（工业生产者出厂价格）分类指数……（130）
Ex-Factory Price Indices of Industrial Products in Main Years
5－5 主要年份工业生产者购进价格指数……（132）
Purchasing Price Indices for Industrial Producers in Main Years
5－6 主要年份固定资产投资价格指数……（132）
Price Indices of Investment in Fixed Assets in Main Years
主要统计指标解释……（133）
Explanatory Notes on Main Statistical Indicators

第六篇 人民生活
CHAPTER 6 PEOPLE' S LIVING CONDITIONS
6－1 城乡居民家庭人均收入及恩格尔系数（1978－2017年）……（137）
Per Capita Income & Engle Coefficient of Urban & Rural Households（1978－2017）
6－2 主要年份城镇居民家庭基本情况……（138）
Basic Conditions of Urban Households in Main Years
6－3 主要年份城镇居民人均可支配收入及构成……（139）
Per Capita Disposable Income of Urban Households & Its Composition in Main Years
6－4 主要年份城镇居民人均现金可支配收入及构成……（139）
Per Capita Cash disposable Income of Urban Households & Its Composition in Main Years
6－5 主要年份城镇居民人均消费支出……（140）
Per Capita Consumption Expenditure of Urban Households in Main Years
6－6 主要年份城镇居民人均现金消费支出……（140）
Per Capita Cash Consumption Expenditure of Urban Households in Main Years
6－7 主要年份城镇居民人均消费支出细项……（141）
Breakdown of Per Capita Consumption Expenditure of Urban Households in Main Years
6－8 主要年份城镇居民人均现金消费支出细项……（142）
Breakdown of Per Capita Cash Consumption Expenditure of Urban Households in Main Years
6－9 主要年份城镇居民人均消费主要食品数量……（143）
Per Capita Consumption of Major Foods of Urban Households in Main Years

6－10 主要年份城镇居民每百户主要耐用消费品拥有量 …… (144)
Ownership of Major Durable Consumer Goods Per 100 Urban Households in Main Years
6－11 主要年份城镇居民人均第二、三产业生产经营收支情况 …… (145)
Production & Management Expenditure Conditions of per Capita Secondary & Tertiary Industry of Urban Households in Main Years
6－12 主要年份城镇居民人均可支配收入分五等份收入组 …… (145)
Per Capita Disposable Income of Urban Households by Income Quintile in Main Years
6－13 主要年份农村居民家庭基本情况 …… (146)
Basic Conditions of Rural Households in Main Years
6－14 主要年份农村居民人均可支配收入及构成 …… (147)
Per Capita Disposable Income of Rural Households & Its Composition in Main Years
6－15 主要年份农村居民人均现金可支配收入及构成 …… (148)
Per Capita Cash disposable Income of Rural Households & Its Composition in Main Years
6－16 主要年份农村居民人均消费支出 …… (149)
Per Capita Consumption Expenditure of Rural Households in Main Years
6－17 主要年份农村居民人均现金消费支出 …… (149)
Per Capita Cash Consumption Expenditure of Rural Households in Main Years
6－18 主要年份农村居民人均消费支出明细 …… (150)
Breakdown of Per Capita Consumption Expenditure of Rural Households in Main Years
6－19 主要年份农村居民人均现金消费支出明细 …… (151)
Breakdown of Per Capita Cash Consumption Expenditure of Rural Households in Main Years
6－20 主要年份农村居民人均消费主要食品数量 …… (152)
Per Capita Consumption of Major Foods by Rural Households in Main Years
6－21 主要年份农村居民每百户主要耐用消费品拥有量 …… (153)
Ownership of Major Durable Consumer Goods Per 100 Rural Households in Main Years
6－22 主要年份农村居民人均第一产业生产经营收支情况 …… (154)
Production and Management Expenditure Conditions of Per Capita Primary Industry of Rural Households in Main Years
6－23 主要年份农村居民人均可支配收入五等份收入分组 …… (154)
Per Capita Disposable Income of Rural Households by Income Quintile in Main Years
6－24 各市城镇居民人均可支配收入和农村居民可支配收入 …… (155)
Per Capita Disposable Income of Urban & Rural Households by City
主要统计指标解释 …… (156)
Explanatory Notes on Main Statistical Indicators

第七篇 财政、金融和保险

CHAPTER 7 FINANCE, BANKING & INSURANCE

7－1 公共财政预算收支总额及指数（1978－2017年） …… (161)
Total Volume & Index of Public Budget Income & Expenditure（1978－2017）
7－2 主要年份财政分项目收入 …… (162)
Local Government Revenue by Items in Main Years
7－3 主要年份财政分项目支出 …… (164)
Local Government Expenditure by Accounting Items in Main Years
7－4 金融机构存贷款情况（期末余额，2005－2017年） …… (166)
Deposits & Loans of Financial Institutions（Year-end，2005－2017）

7－5 2017年全社会金融机构本外币信贷收支平衡表（期末余额）……（167）
Balance Sheet of Credit Funds in RMB & Foreign Currencies of Total Financial Institutions in Main Years （2017，Year-end）
7－6 2017年全社会金融机构人民币信贷收支平衡表（期末余额）……（169）
Balance Sheet of Credit Funds in Renminbi of Total Financial Institutions in Main Years（2017,Year-end）
7－7 主要年份保险业务……（171）
Major Indictors of Insurance Business in Main Years
主要统计指标解释……（173）
Explanatory Notes on Main Statistical Indicators

第八篇 资源与环境

CHAPTER 8 NATURAL RESOURCES & ENVIRONMENT

8－1 自然资源（2017年）……（179）
Natural Resources（2017）
8－2 主要河流基本情况（2017年）……（181）
Major Rivers（2017）
8－3 水资源基本情况……（182）
Water Resources of Guangxi
8－4 供水用水情况（2017年）……（183）
Statistics of Water Supply & Consumption（2017）
8－5 主要城市气象站点平均气温（2017年）……（184）
Monthly Average Temperature at Meteorological Stations of Major Cities（2017）
8－6 主要城市气象站点降水量（2017年）……（186）
Monthly Average Precipitation at Meteorological Stations of Major Cities（2017）
8－7 主要年份城市公用事业基本情况……（188）
Basic Statistics on Urban Public Utilities in Main Years
8－8 城市市政公用设施水平（2017年）……（189）
Level of Urban Public Utilities in Cities（2017）
8－9 城市人口和建设用地（2017年）……（191）
Population & Developed Areas in Cities（2017）
8－10 城市供水情况（2017年）……（192）
Statistics of Water Supply in Cities（2017）
8－11 城市园林绿化情况（2017年）……（193）
Basic Statistics on Parks, Gardens & Green Areas in Cities（2017）
8－12 城市市政设施情况（2017年）……（194）
Basic Statistics on Municipal Utilities in Cities（2017）
8－13 城市公共交通、清洁卫生和供气情况（2017年）……（195）
Basic Statistics on Public Traffic, Urban Sanitation & Gas Supply in Cities（2017）
8－14 主要年份工业污染治理项目建设情况……（197）
Construction of Industrial Pollution Treatment Projects in Main Years
8－15 主要年份工业污染排放及处理利用情况……（198）
Discharge, Treatment & Utilization of Industrial Pollution in Main Years
8－16 环境污染治理投资情况……（199）
Investment in Environment Pollution Treatment

8－17 重点调查工业废水排放及治理情况（2017年） (200)
Discharge & Treatment of Waste Water by Branch of Industry（2017）
8－18 重点调查工业废气排放及治理情况（2017年） (202)
Discharge & Treatment of Waste Gas by Branch of Industry（2017）
8－19 重点调查工业固体废物排放及治理情况（2017年） (206)
Discharge & Treatment of Industrial Solid Wastes（2017）
主要统计指标解释 (210)
Explanatory Notes on Main Statistical Indicators

第九篇 能源生产与消费

CHAPTER 9 ENERGY PRODUCTION & CONSUMPTION

9－1 能源生产、消费总量（1978－2017年） (216)
Production & Consumption of Energy（1978－2017）
9－2 能源生产、消费构成（1978－2017年） (217)
Composition of Energy Production & Consumption（1978－2017）
9－3 能源利用效益主要指标 (218)
Economic Results Indicators for the Utilization of Energy
9－4 能源消费弹性系数 (219)
Elasticity Ratio of Energy Consumption
9－5 主要年份分行业能源消费量和构成 (220)
Consumption & Composition of Energy by Sector in Main Years
9－5－1 主要年份规模以上工业分行业综合能源消费量 (224)
Consumption of Comprehensive Energy by Sector above Designated Size in Main Years
9－5－2 主要年份各市规模以上工业综合能源消费量 (226)
Industrial Comprehensive Enevgy Consumption above Designated Size by City in Main Years
9－6 主要年份电力消费量 (228)
Consumption of Electricity in Main Years
9－7 主要年份万元工业总产值电力消费量 (230)
Electricity Consumption of Gross Output Value of Industry per 10,000 Yuan in Main Years
9－8 能源消费水平 (232)
Annual Average per Capita Energy Consumption
9－9 能源主要产品生活消费量 (233)
Household Energy Consumption of Main Energy Products
9－10 主要年份石油及燃料消费量 (234)
Consumption of Petroleum & Fuel in Main Years
9－11 能源可供量（2017年） (234)
Energy Available for Consumption（2017）
主要统计指标解释 (235)
Explanatory Notes on Main Statistical Indicators

第十篇 固定资产投资

CHAPTER 10 INVESTMENT IN FIXED ASSETS

10－1 全社会固定资产投资及增长速度（1978－2017年） (238)
Investment in Fixed Assets & Its Growth Rate（1978－2017）

10－2 国有单位固定资产投资及增长速度（1978－2017年）……（240）
Investment in Fixed Assets of State-owned Units & Its Growth Rate（1978－2017）
10－3 主要年份全社会固定资产投资总额……（242）
Total Investment in Fixed Assets in Main Years
10－4 主要年份固定资产投资资金来源……（244）
Investment in Fixed Assets by Source of Funds in Main Years
10－5 按登记注册类型分的固定资产投资（2017年）……（246）
Investment in Fixed Assets Grouped by Registration Status（2017）
10－6 按登记注册类型分的投资资金来源（2017年）……（248）
Sources of Funds for Investment in Fixed Assets Grouped by Registration Status（2017）
10－7 按登记注册类型分的新增固定资产（2017年）……（250）
Newly Increased Fixed Assets Grouped by Registration Status（2017）
10－8 分行业固定资产投资（2017年）……（252）
Investment in Fixed Assets by Sector（2017）
10－9 工业分行业固定资产投资（2017年）……（254）
Investment in Urban Fixed Assets by Industrial Sector（2017）
10－10 基本建设分行业固定资产投资（2017年）……（256）
Investment in Fixed Assets in Basic Construction by Sector（2017）
10－11 工业行业基本建设投资（2017年）……（258）
Investment in Basic Construction by Industrial Sector（2017）
10－12 基本建设分行业投资项目和新增固定资产（2017年）……（260）
Basic Construction Projects & Newly Increased Fixed Assets by Sector（2017）
10－13 分行业更新改造投资（2017年）……（262）
Investment in Innovation by Sector（2017）
10－14 工业分行业更新改造投资（2017年）……（264）
Investment in Innovation by Industrial Sector（2017）
10－15 分行业更新改造投资项目和新增固定资产（2017年）……（266）
Investment in Innovation Projects & Newly Increased Fixed Assets by Sector（2017）
10－16 国有单位分行业投资项目和新增固定资产（2017年）……（268）
Investment Projects & Newly Increased Fixed Assets of States-owned Units（2017）
10－17 集体分行业投资项目和新增固定资产（2017年）……（270）
Investment Projects by Sector & Newly Increased Fixed Assets of Urban Collective Owned Units（2017）
10－18 私营个体固定资产投资和新增固定资产（2017年）……（272）
Investment in Fixed Assets & Newly Increased Fixed Assets of Urban Private & Individual Units（2017）
10－19 主要年份房地产开发主要指标……（274）
Major Indicators of Real Estate Development in Main Years
主要统计指标解释……（276）
Explanatory Notes on Main Statistical Indicators

第十一篇 城市概况

CHAPTER 11 GENERAL SURVEY OF CITIES

11－1 广西各市市辖区社会经济主要指标（2017年）……（284）
Main Social & Economic Indicators of Municipal Districts of Cities（2017）
主要统计指标解释……（296）
Explanatory Notes on Main Statistical Indicators

第十二篇　对外经济贸易

CHAPTER 12　FOREIGN ECONOMY & TRADES

12－1　外贸进出口总额（1978－2017年）……………………………………（300）
Total Import & Export Value of Foreign Trade（1978－2017）

12－2　主要年份外贸进出口总额（按贸易方式分）……………………………（301）
Total Import & Export Value of Foreign Trade in Main Years（by Type of Trade）

12－3　主要年份外贸出口总额（按贸易方式分）………………………………（302）
Total Export Value of Foreign Trade in Main Years（by Type of Trade）

12－4　主要年份外贸进口总额（按贸易方式分）………………………………（303）
Total Import Value of Foreign Trade in Main Years（by Type of Trade）

12－5　主要年份外贸进出口总额（按企业性质分）……………………………（304）
Total Import & Export Value in Main Years（by Nature of Enterprises）

12－6　广西同主要国家（地区）进出口商品总值（2017年）…………………（306）
Total Import & Export Value by Country & Region（2017）

12－7　广西与东盟进出口商品总值（2017年）…………………………………（307）
Total Import & Export Value from Guangxi to ASEAN（2017）

12－8　各市进出口商品总值……………………………………………………（308）
Total Import & Export Value by City

12－9　主要出口商品数量及金额（2017年）……………………………………（309）
Volume & Value of Major Export Commodities（2017）

12－10　主要进口商品数量及金额（2017年）…………………………………（311）
Volume & Value of Major Import Commodities（2017）

12－11　外商直接投资额（1979－2017年）……………………………………（312）
Foreign Direct Investment（1979－2017）

12－12　主要年份实际利用外资及对外承包工程情况…………………………（312）
Basic Statistics of Foreign Capital Actually Utilized & Overseas Contracted Projects in Main Years

12－13　主要年份分市新签外商直接投资项目和金额…………………………（313）
Items & Value of Utilization of Foreign Direct Investment Through Newly Signed Agreement by City in Main Years

主要统计指标解释…………………………………………………………（314）
Explanatory Notes on Main Statistical Indicators

第十三篇　农　业

CHAPTER 13　AGRICULTURE

13－1　主要年份农村基本情况……………………………………………………（318）
Basic Statistics of Rural Area in Main Years

13－2　农林牧渔业总产值（1978－2017年）……………………………………（320）
Gross Output Value of Farming, Forestry, Animal Husbandry &Fishery（1978－2017）

13－3　农林牧渔业总产值指数（1978－2017年）………………………………（322）
Indices of Gross Output Value of Farming, Forestry, Animal Husbandry & Fishery（1978－2017）

13－4　主要年份主要农作物播种面积……………………………………………（323）
Sown Area of Major Farm Crops in Main Years

13－5　主要年份主要农作物产品产量……………………………………………（324）
Output of Major Farm Crops in Main Years

13－6　主要年份主要农作物单位面积产量……(326)
Output of Major Farm Crops Per Hectare in Main Years
13－7　主要年份农业生产条件基本情况……(326)
Basic Statistics on Agricultural Production Conditions in Main Years
13－8　主要年份农作物播种面积构成……(327)
Sowing Areas Structure of Farm Crops in Main Years
13－9　主要年份林业生产情况……(328)
Basic Statistics on Forestry in Main Years
13－10　主要年份畜牧水产主要产品生产情况……(330)
Basic Statistics on Main Products of Animal Husbandry & Fishery in Main Years
13－11　各市农林牧渔业总产值及构成（2017年）……(332)
Gross Output Value & Its Composition of Farming, Forestry, Animal Husbandry & Fishery by City（2017）
13－12　各市农作物播种面积构成（2017年）……(333)
Sowing Areas Structure of Farm Crops by City（2017）
13－13　各市主要农作物播种面积（2017年）……(334)
Sown Area of Major Farm Crops by City（2017）
13－14　各市主要农作物产量（2017年）……(335)
Output of Major Farm Crops by City（2017）
13－15　各市主要农产品人均占有量（2017年）……(336)
Ownership of Per Capital Major Agricultural Products by City（2017）
主要统计指标解释……(337)
Explanatory Notes on Main Statistical Indicators

第十四篇　工　业

CHAPTER 14　INDUSTRY

14－1　全部工业总产值及指数……(342)
All Included Gross Industrial Output Value & Its Related Index
14－2　主要年份工业企业主要指标……(344)
Major Indicators of Industrial Enterprises in Main Years
14－3　工业企业分行业主要指标（2017年）……(350)
Major Indicators of Industrial Enterprises by Industrial Sector（2017）
14－4　国有控股工业企业主要指标（2017年）……(354)
Major Indicators of State-owned & State-holding Industrial Enterprises（2017）
14－5　国有工业企业主要指标（2017年）……(358)
Major Indicators of State-owned Industrial Enterprises（2017）
14－6　非公经济工业企业主要指标（2017年）……(362)
Major Indicators of Non-public Industrial Enterprises（2017）
14－7　私营工业企业主要指标（2017年）……(366)
Major Indicators of Private Owned Industrial Enterprises（2017）
14－8　大中型工业企业分行业主要指标（2017年）……(370)
Major Indicators of Large-scale & Medium-scale Industrial Enterprises by Industrial Sector（2017）
14－9　工业企业主要经济效益指标（2017年）……(374)
Major Economic Efficiency Indicators of Industrial Enterprises（2017）
14－10　国有控股工业企业主要经济效益指标（2017年）……(376)
Major Economic Efficiency Indicators of State-owned & State Holding Industrial Enterprises（2017）

14－11　大中型工业企业主要经济效益指标（2017年）……（378）
Major Economic Efficiency Indicators of Large & Medium Industrial Enterprises（2017）
14－12　主要年份主要工业产品产量……（380）
Output of Major Industrial Products in Main Years
14－13　广西分市规模以上工业企业主要经济指标（2017年）……（384）
Major Indicators Economic of Industrial Enterprises above Designated Size by City（2017）
主要统计指标解释……（386）
Explanatory Notes on Main Statistical Indicators

第十五篇　建筑业

CHAPTER 15　CONSTRUCTION

15－1　主要年份三级及三级以上建筑业企业主要指标……（393）
Major Indicators of the Third & Higher Grade Construction Enterprises in Main Years
15－2　主要年份国有及国有控股建筑企业主要指标……（394）
Major Indicators of State-owned & State-holding Construction Enterprises in Main Years
15－3　主要年份地方国有建筑企业主要指标……（395）
Major Indicators of Local State-owned Construction Enterprises in Main Years
15－4　建筑企业生产情况（2017年）……（396）
Major Production Indicators of Construction Enterprises（2017）
15－5　按主要行业分组的建筑企业生产情况（2017年）……（397）
Major Production Indicators of Construction Enterprises by Sector（2017）
15－6　建筑企业主要财务状况（2017年）……（398）
Major Financial Indicators of Construction Enterprises（2017）
15－7　按主要行业分组的建筑企业财务状况（2017年）……（399）
Major Financial Indicators of Construction Enterprises by Sector（2017）
15－8　各种分组的建筑企业主要经济效益指标（2017年）……（400）
Major Economic Efficiency Indicators of Construction Enterprises by Various Groups（2017）
主要统计指标解释……（402）
Explanatory Notes on Main Statistical Indicators

第十六篇　批发和零售业

CHAPTER 16　WHOLESALE & RETAIL TRADES

16－1　限额以上批发和零售业企业基本情况（2017年）……（406）
Basic Conditions of Enterprises above Designated Size in Wholesale & Retail（2017）
16－2　主要年份限额以上批发和零售业企业商品购进、销售和库存总额……（409）
Total Purchases, Sales & Stock of Enterprises above Designated in Wholesale & Retail Sale Trade in Main Years
16－3　限额以上批发和零售业企业商品购进、销售、库存总额（2017年）……（410）
Total Purchases, Sales & Stock of Enterprises above Designated in Wholesale & Retail Sale Trade by Sector（2017）
16－4　限额以上批发和零售业企业主要财务指标（2017年）……（416）
Main Financial Indicators of Enterprises above Designated in Wholesale & Retail Sale Trade（2017）
16－5　按登记注册类型分连锁批发和零售企业基本情况（2017年）……（424）
Basic Condictions of Chain-retail Enterprises by Categories of Registration（2017）

16－6 亿元以上商品交易市场基本情况（2017年）………………………………（425）
Basic Conditions of Commodity Exchange Markets of Transaction Value over 100 Million Yuan（2017）
16—7 社会消费品零售总额及指数………………………………（426）
Total Retail Sales of Consumer Goods & Relate Indices
16－8 各市社会消费品零售总额………………………………（427）
Total Retail Sales of Consumer Goods by City
16－9 主要年份个体工商业发展情况………………………………（428）
Development of Individual Industrial &Commercial Enterprises in Main Years
主要统计指标解释………………………………（430）
Explanatory Notes on Main Statistical Indicators

第十七篇 住宿餐饮业和旅游

CHAPTER 17 HOTELS,CATERING SERVICES & TOURISM

17－1 限额以上住宿和餐饮业企业基本情况（2017年）………………………………（434）
Basic Conditions of Accommodation above Star-rated & Catering Service above Designated Size（2017）
17－2 限额以上住宿和餐饮业企业经营情况（2017年）………………………………（436）
Business of Enterprises above Designated Size of Hotels & Catering Services（2017）
17－3 限额以上住宿和餐饮业企业主要财务指标（2017年）………………………………（438）
Main Financial Indicators of Enterprises above Designated in Wholesale & Retail Sale Trade（2017）
17－4 主要年份限额以上住宿和餐饮业企业经营情况………………………………（442）
Business Circumstance of Enterprises above Designated Size in Hotel & Catering in Major Years
17－5 旅游机构数（2017年）………………………………（442）
Number of Tourism Institutions（2017）
17－6 主要年份旅游人数及消费………………………………（443）
Number of Oversea Visitor Arrivals & Tourism Consumption in Main Years
17－7 主要年份各市接待入境旅游者人数………………………………（444）
Number of Oversea Visitor Arrivals & International Tourism Receipts by City in Main Years
17－8 主要年份各市国际旅游消费………………………………（446）
International Tourism Expenditure by City in Main Years
17－9 主要年份各市接待入境旅游者平均每人消费额………………………………（447）
Per Capita Expenditure of Oversea Visitor Arrivals by City in Main Years
17－10 各市接待国内游客人数………………………………（448）
Number of Domestic Visitors by City
17－11 各市国内旅游消费………………………………（449）
Tourist Consumption of Domestic Visitors by City
17－12 各市旅游总消费………………………………（450）
Total Tourist Consumption by City
17－13 广西国家A级旅游景区一览表（2017年）………………………………（451）
Schedule of National A-Grade Scenic Spots in Guangxi（2017）
主要统计指标解释（旅游）………………………………（462）
Explanatory Notes on Main Statistical Indicators

第十八篇　交通、运输和邮电通信业

CHAPTER 18　TRANSPORTATION,POSTAL & TELECOMMUNICATION SERVICES

18－1　主要年份民用车辆保有量……（467）

Possession of Civil Vehicles in Main Years

18－2　主要年份民用运输船舶拥有量……（468）

Possession of Civil Transport Vessels in Main Years

18－3　主要年份内河、沿海规模以上港口基本情况……（468）

Basic Statistics of Major Ports of Inland & Coast in Main Years

18－4　主要年份运输线路里程……（469）

Length of Transportation Routes in Main Years

18－5　主要年份规模以上港口货物吞吐量……（469）

Cargo Handled at Major Ports in Main Years

18－6　全社会客运量及旅客周转量（1978－2017年）……（470）

Total Passenger Traffic & Turnover of Passenger Traffic（1978－2017）

18－7　全社会货运量及货物周转量（1978－2017年）……（472）

Total Freight Traffic & Turnover of Freight Traffic（1978－2017）

18－8　公路线路长度（按等级分类，1978－2017年）……（474）

Total Length of Highways（Grouped by Class,1978－2017）

18－9　主要年份邮电通信水平……（475）

Level of Postal & Telecommunications Services in Main Years

18－10　主要年份邮政和电信主要指标……（476）

Major Indicators of Postal & Telecommunications Services in Main Years

主要统计指标解释……（477）

Explanatory Notes on Main Statistical Indicators

第十九篇　教育、科技和文化

CHAPTER 19　EDUCATION,SCIENCE,TECHNOLOGY & CULTURE

19－1　主要年份各类学校基本情况……（482）

Basic Statistics of Schools by Type in Main Years

19－2　普通高等学校本科学生数（2017年）……（483）

Student Statistics in Institutions of Higher Education by Field of Study（2017）

19－3　普通高等学校专科学生数（2017年）……（483）

Student Statistics in Institutions of Higher Education by Field of Study（2017）

19－4　中等职业专业学校分科学生数（2017年）……（484）

Number of Students by Field of Study in Secondary Vocational Schools（2017）

19－5　主要年份教师负担学生数……（485）

Student-teacher Ratio of School by Field in Main Years

19－6　主要年份各级各类教育平均每万人在校学生数……（485）

Number of Students Enrollment by Level & Type per 10 000 Persons in Main Years

19－7　主要年份各级成人教育在校学生数……（486）

Student Enrollment in Various Adult Education in Main Years

19－8　主要年份义务教育普及程度……（486）

Level of Compulsory Education Popularization in Main Years

19－9　主要年份科技活动基本情况……（487）

Basic Statistics for Scientific & Technical Activities in Main Years
19－10 大中型工业企业科技活动基本情况（2017年） .... （488）
Basic Statistics for Scientific & Technical Activities Organized by Large &Medium Industrial Enterprises（2017）
19－11 主要年份工业企业科技活动情况 .... （492）
Statistics for Technical Activities of Large & Medium Industrial Enterprises in Main Years
19－12 主要年份县及县以上政府部门所属研究与开发机构基本情况 .... （493）
Basic Statistics on Governmental Department Research & Development Institutions at & above County Level in Main Years
19－13 县及县以上政府部门所属研究与开发机构情况（2017年） .... （494）
Basic Statistics on Governmental Department Research & Development Institutions at & above County Level（2017）
19－14 县及县以上政府部门所属研究与开发机构课题情况（2017年） .... （495）
Projects of Governmental Department Research & Development Institutions at & above County Level（2017）
19－15 县及县以上政府部门所属研究与开发机构成果情况（1990－2017年） .... （496）
Achievement of Governmental Department Research & Development Institutions at & above County Level（1990－2017）
19－16 文化及相关产业机构和从业人员（2017年） .... （497）
Institutions, Staff & Workers of Cultural & Relevant Industries（2017）
19－17 文化及相关产业增加值（2017年） .... （498）
Added Value of Culture & Relevant Industries（2017）
19－18 文化部门主要文化产业单位基本情况 .... （498）
Basic Situation of Major Units of Culture Industries in Culture Department
19－19 主要年份广播事业发展情况 .... （501）
Basic Statistics on Broadcasting in Main Years
19－20 各市公共图书馆基本情况（2017年） .... （502）
Basic Situation of Public Libraries by City（2017）
19－21 主要年份电视事业发展情况 .... （504）
Basic Statistics on Television Stations in Main Years
19－22 主要年份图书、报纸及杂志出版情况 .... （504）
Basic Statistics of Books, Newspaper & Magazines in Main Years
主要统计指标解释 .... （505）
Explanatory Notes on Main Statistical Indicators

第二十篇 体育、卫生与社会福利

CHAPTER 20 SPORT, PUBLIC HEALTH & SOCIAL WELFARE

20－1 主要年份体育事业发展情况 .... （511）
Statistics on Sports in Main Years
20－2 运动队体育比赛成绩（2017年） .... （511）
Scores of Sports Groups in Sport Matches（2017）
20－3 主要年份卫生事业基本情况 .... （512）
Basic Situation of Public Health in Main Years
20－4 医疗机构诊疗人次和入院人数（2017年） .... （513）
Number of Hospital Patients & Admissions（2017）
20－5 收养性社会福利单位基本情况（2017年） .... （513）
Basic Statistics of Adopting Social Welfare Units（2017）

20－6　主要年份优抚和社会福利单位机构和人员 (514)
Institutions & Persons Engaged for Martyrs & Social Welfare in Main Years
20－7　主要年份社会救济对象享受救济情况 (515)
Basic Statistics of Persons Receiving Subsidies or Relief Funds in Main Years
20－8　主要年份殡葬管理情况 (515)
Condition of Burial Administration in Main Years
20－9　广西残疾人工作主要情况 (516)
The Major Situation of the Disabled Work in Guangxi Autonomous Region
主要统计指标解释 (517)
Explanatory Notes on Main Statistical Indicators

第二十一篇　区域经济

CHAPTER 21　ECONOMIC ZONES

21－1　各个经济区域主要经济指标 (522)
Main Economic Indicators of Each Economic Zone
21－2　各个经济区域主要经济指标占全区比重 (524)
Percentage of Main Regional Economic Indicators to Guangxi
21－3　北部湾经济区主要经济指标（4市，2006－2017年） (526)
Main Economic Indicators of the Beibu Gulf Economic Zone（4 cities, 2006－2017）
21－4　北部湾经济区主要经济指标（6市，2006－2017年） (528)
Main Economic Indicators of the Beibu Gulf Economic Zone（6 cities, 2006－2017）
21－5　桂西资源富集区主要经济指标（2006－2017年） (530)
Main Economic Indicators of the Resource-rich Area of Western Guangxi（2006－2017）
21－6　珠江—西江经济带广西七市主要经济指标（2006－2017年） (532)
Main Economic Indicators of the Zhujiang River-Xijiang River Economic Belt（7 cities, 2006－2017）

第二十二篇　各市基本情况

HAPTER 22　BASIC STATISTICS OF CITIES

22—1　各市社会经济主要指标（2017年） (536)
Main Social & Economic Indicators by City（2017）
22－2　南宁市主要经济指标情况（1978—2017年） (546)
Main Economic Indicators of Nanning（1978－2017）
22－3　柳州市主要经济指标情况（1978—2017年） (548)
Main Economic Indicators of Liuzhou（1978－2017）
22－4　桂林市主要经济指标情况（1978—2017年） (550)
Main Economic Indicators of Guilin（1978－2017）
22－5　梧州市主要经济指标情况（1978—2017年） (552)
Main Economic Indicators of Wuzhou（1978－2017）
22－6　北海市主要经济指标情况（1978—2017年） (554)
Main Economic Indicators of Beihai（1978－2017）
22－7　防城港市主要经济指标情况（1978—2017年） (556)
Main Economic Indicators of Fangchenggang（1978－2017）
22－8　钦州市主要经济指标情况（1978—2017年） (558)
Main Economic Indicators of Qinzhou（1978－2017）

22－9　贵港市主要经济指标情况（1996—2017年） ……………………………………………………………………………（560）
Main Economic Indicators of Guigang（1996－2017）
22－10　玉林市主要经济指标情况（1978—2017年） ……………………………………………………………………………（562）
Main Economic Indicators of Yulin（1978－2017）
22－11　百色市主要经济指标情况（1978—2017年） ……………………………………………………………………………（564）
Main Economic Indicators of Baise（1978－2017）
22－12　贺州市主要经济指标情况（2002—2017年） ……………………………………………………………………………（566）
Main Economic Indicators of Hezhou（2002－2017）
22－13　河池市主要经济指标情况（1978—2017年） ……………………………………………………………………………（568）
Main Economic Indicators of Hechi（1978－2017）
22－14　来宾市主要经济指标情况（1978—2017年） ……………………………………………………………………………（570）
Main Economic Indicators of Laibin（1978－2017）
22－15　崇左市主要经济指标情况（2003—2017年） ……………………………………………………………………………（572）
Main Economic Indicators of Chongzuo（2003－2017）
22－16　广西农垦管区社会经济主要指标……………………………………………………………………………………………（574）
Main Social & Economic Indicators by Guangxi State Farms

第二十三篇　县（市、区）基本情况

HAPTER 23　BASIC STATISTICS OF COUNTIES（CITIES, DISTRICTS）

23－1　110个县域社会经济主要指标（2017年） ……………………………………………………………………………（578）
Main Social & Economic Indicators by County（2017）

附　录

GENERAL SURVEY

2017年广西壮族自治区国民经济和社会发展统计公报…………………………………………………………………………（647）
Statistical Communique on National Economic & Social Development of Guangxi Zhuang Autonomous Region in（2017）

第一篇

综合

GENERAL SURVEY

（校对编辑：黄浩洲　焦　夕）

1—1 行政区划（2017年末）

Divisions of Administrative Areas (End of 2017)

单位：个　(unit)

年 份 Year	地级单位合计 Number of Regions at Prefecture Level	县级单位合计 Number of Regions at County Level	市辖区 Districts under the Jurisdiction of Cities	县级市 Cities at County Level	县 Counties	自治县 Autonomous Counties
1978	14	84	2	2	73	7
1980	14	99	17	2	73	7
1985	14	110	22	6	73	9
1990	14	111	21	7	71	12
1995	14	117	28	9	68	12
2000	14	120	29	10	69	12
2001	14	119	28	10	69	12
2002	14	115	32	7	64	12
2003	14	109	33	7	57	12
2004	14	109	33	7	57	12
2005	14	109	34	7	56	12
2006	14	109	34	7	56	12
2007	14	109	34	7	56	12
2008	14	109	34	7	56	12
2009	14	109	34	7	56	12
2010	14	109	34	7	56	12
2011	14	109	34	7	56	12
2012	14	109	34	7	56	12
2013	14	110	36	7	55	12
2014	14	110	36	7	55	12
2015	14	110	37	8	53	12
2016	14	111	40	7	52	12
2017	14	111	40	7	52	12

注：本表资料由自治区民政厅提供。

Note: The data in this table is provided by Guangxi Civil Bureau.

1—1 续表 1 continued

单位：个 (unit)

年 份 Year	乡镇级单位合计 Number of Regions at Townships Level	镇 Towns	乡 Townships	民族乡 Nationality Townships	街道办事处 Street Communities	居民委员会 Neighborhood Committees	村民委员会 Village Committees
1978		66					
1980							
1985	1248	265	962	60	21	937	13873
1990	1412	359	1012	58	41	1154	76073
1995	1442	627	738	60	77	1233	28243
2000	1422	745	616	63	61	1250	14750
2001	1410	749	598	61	63	1261	14743
2002	1388	750	576	61	62	1555	14443
2003	1395	748	576	61	71	1621	14398
2004	1396	748	576	61	72	1611	14333
2005	1232	700	426	61	106	1644	14359
2006	1230	700	426	58	104	1649	14363
2007	1230	702	424	58	104	1648	14361
2008	1230	702	424	58	104	1701	14353
2009	1232	702	424	58	106	1701	14345
2010	1234	702	424	58	108	1714	14355
2011	1235	702	424	58	109	1725	14336
2012	1243	715	411	58	117	1791	14345
2013	1247	722	405	59	120	1835	14313
2014	1243	773	350	59	120	1891	14323
2015	1251	773	350	59	128	1924	14273
2016	1246	788	330	59	128	1931	14276
2017	1251	799	319	59	133	1969	14258

1－1 续表2 continued

单位：个 (unit)

地 区	Region	地级单位合计 Number of Regions at Prefecture Level	县级单位合计 Number of Regions at County	市辖区 Districts under the Jurisdiction of Cities	县级市 Cities at County Level	县 Counties	自治县 Autonomous Counties
全区合计	**Total**	**14**	**111**	**40**	**7**	**52**	**12**
南宁市	Nanning	1	12	7		5	
柳州市	Liuzhou	1	10	5		3	2
桂林市	Guilin	1	17	6		9	2
梧州市	Wuzhou	1	7	3	1	3	
北海市	Beihai	1	4	3		1	
防城港市	Fangchenggang	1	4	2	1	1	
钦州市	Qinzhou	1	4	2		2	
贵港市	Guigang	1	5	3	1	1	
玉林市	Yulin	1	7	2	1	4	
百色市	Baise	1	12	1	1	9	1
贺州市	Hezhou	1	5	2		2	1
河池市	Hechi	1	11	2		4	5
来宾市	Laibin	1	6	1	1	3	1
崇左市	Chongzuo	1	7	1	1	5	

注：本表资料由自治区民政厅提供。
Note: The data in this table is provided by Guangxi Civil Bureau.

1－1 续表3 continued

单位：个 (unit)

地 区	Region	乡镇级单位合计 Number of Regions at Townships Level	镇 Towns	乡 Townships		街道办事处 Street Communities	居民委员会 Neighbourhood Committees	村民委员会 Village Committees
					民族乡 Nationlity Townships			
全区合计	**Total**	**1251**	**799**	**319**	**59**	**133**	**1969**	**14258**
南宁市	Nanning	127	86	16	3	25	386	1383
柳州市	Liuzhou	117	53	33	6	31	277	935
桂林市	Guilin	147	86	48	15	13	237	1654
梧州市	Wuzhou	67	53	5	2	9	140	861
北海市	Beihai	30	22	1		7	85	342
防城港市	Fangchenggang	30	17	6	2	7	51	280
钦州市	Qinzhou	66	54			12	98	932
贵港市	Guigang	74	55	12	2	7	88	1069
玉林市	Yulin	110	102			8	162	1332
百色市	Baise	135	75	58	13	2	77	1796
贺州市	Hezhou	61	47	10	5	4	48	707
河池市	Hechi	139	65	73	11	1	148	1497
来宾市	Laibin	70	43	23		4	80	716
崇左市	Chongzuo	78	41	34		3	92	754

1—2 县级以上行政区划（2017年末）
Division of Administrative Areas at & above County Level（End of 2017）

市	City	县（市、区）名称	Name of County (City,District) Level
南宁市	Nanning	兴宁区 青秀区 江南区 西乡塘区 良庆区 邕宁区 武鸣区 隆安县 马山县 上林县 宾阳县 横县	Xingning, Qingxiu, Jiangnan, Xixiangtang, Liangqing, Yongning, Wuming, Long'an, Mashan, Shanglin, Binyang, Hengxian
柳州市	Liuzhou	城中区 鱼峰区 柳南区 柳北区 柳城区 柳江区 鹿寨县 融安县 融水苗族自治县 三江侗族自治县	Chengzhong, Yufeng, Liunan, Liubei, Liucheng, Liujiang, Luzhai, Rong'an, Rongshui Miao Autonomous County, Sanjiang Dong Autonomous County
桂林市	Guilin	秀峰区 叠彩区 象山区 七星区 雁山区 临桂区 阳朔县 灵川县 全州县 兴安县 永福县 灌阳县 龙胜各族自治县 资源县 平乐县 荔浦县 恭城瑶族自治县	Xiufeng, Diecai, Xiangshan, Qixing, Yanshan, Lingui, Yangshuo, Lingchuan, Quanzhou, Xing'an, Yongfu, Guanyang, Longsheng all of Nationality Autonomous County, Ziyuan, Pingle, Lipu, Gongcheng Yao Autonomous County
梧州市	Wuzhou	万秀区 长洲区 龙圩区 苍梧县 藤县 蒙山县 岑溪市	Wanxiu, Changzhou, Longxu, Cangwu, Tengxian, Mengshan, Cenqi
北海市	Beihai	海城区 银海区 铁山港区 合浦县	Haicheng, Yinhai, Tieshangang, Hepu
防城港市	Fangchenggang	港口区 防城区 上思县 东兴市	Gangkou, Fangcheng, Shangsi, Dongxing
钦州市	Qinzhou	钦南区 钦北区 灵山县 浦北县	Qinnan, Qinbei, Lingshan, Pubei
贵港市	Guigang	港北区 港南区 覃塘区 平南县 桂平市	Gangbei, Gangnan, Qintang, Pingnan, Guiping
玉林市	Yulin	玉州区 福绵区 容　县 陆川县 博白县 兴业县 北流市	Yuzhou, Fumian, Rongxian, Luchuan, Bobai, Xingye, Beiliu
百色市	Baise	右江区 田阳县 田东县 平果县 德保县 那坡县 凌云县 乐业县 田林县 西林县 隆林各族自治县 靖西市	Youjiang, Tianyang, Tiandong, Pingguo, Debao, Napo, Lingyun, Leye, Tianlin, Xilin, Longlin all of Nationality Autonomous County, Jingxi
贺州市	Hezhou	八步区 平桂区 昭平县 钟山县 富川瑶族自治县	Babu, Pinggui, Zhaoping, Zhongshan, Fuchuan Yao Autonomous County
河池市	Hechi	金城江区 宜州区 南丹县 天峨县 凤山县 东兰县 罗城仫佬族自治县 环江毛南族自治县 巴马瑶族自治县 都安瑶族自治县 大化瑶族自治县	Jinchengjiang, Yizhou, Nandan, Tian'e, Fengshan, Donglan, Luocheng Mulao Autonomous County, Huanjiang Maonan Autonomous County, Bama Yao Autonomous County, Du'an Yao Autonomous County, Dahua Yao Autonomous County
来宾市	Laibin	兴宾区 忻城县 象州县 武宣县 金秀瑶族自治县 合山市	Xingbin, Xincheng, Xiangzhou, Wuxuan, Jinxiu Yao Autonomous County, Heshan
崇左市	Chongzuo	江州区 扶绥县 大新县 天等县 宁明县 龙州县 凭祥市	Jiangzhou, Fusui, Daxin, Tiandeng, Ningming, Longzhou, Pingxiang

注：本表资料由自治区民政厅提供。

Note: The data in this table is provided by Guangxi Civil Bureau.

1—3 主要年份国民经济和社会发展主要指标
Major Indicators on National Economic & Social Development in Main Years

指 标	Indicators	2000	2005	2010	2013	2014	2015	2016	2017
人口与就业	**Population & Employment**								
人 口（万人）	**Population (10 000 persons)**								
年末总人口	Year-end Population	4751	4925	5159	5282	5475	5518	5579	5600
男性	Male	2484	2587	2708	2772	2891	2913	2943	2951
女性	Female	2267	2338	2451	2510	2584	2605	2636	2649
常住人口	Permanent Population	4489	4660	4610	4719	4754	4796	4838	4885
市镇人口	Urban Population	1337	1567	1849	2115	2187	2257	2326	2404
乡村人口	Rural Population	3414	3093	2761	2604	2567	2539	2512	2481
就 业（万人）	**Employment (10 000 persons)**								
从业人员	Employment	2566	2703	2903	2782	2795	2820	2841	2842
城镇登记失业人数	Number of Registered Unemployed Persons in Urban Area	11.30	18.51	19.07	18.09	18.66	18.13	18.13	14.72
宏观经济	**Macroeconomic Indicators**								
国民核算（亿元）	**National Accounting (100 million yuan)**								
地区生产总值	Gross Domestic Product	2080.04	3984.10	9604.01	14511.70	15742.62	16870.04	18317.64	20396.25
第一产业	Primary Industry	557.38	912.50	1675.06	2290.64	2413.44	2565.45	2796.80	2906.87
第二产业	Secondary Industry	732.76	1510.68	4536.66	6778.48	7378.14	7766.34	8273.66	9297.84
#工业	Industry	612.33	1264.84	3885.20	5647.39	6118.23	6408.64	6816.64	7663.71
第三产业	Tertiary Industry	789.90	1560.92	3392.29	5442.58	5951.04	6538.25	7247.18	8191.54
人均地区生产总值（元/人）	Per Capita GDP (yuan/person)	4652	8590	20292	30873	33237	35330	38027	41955
支出法地区生产总值	Gross Demestic Product by Expenditure Approach	2080.04	3984.10	9604.01	14511.70	15742.62	16870.04	18317.64	
#最终消费	Final Consumption Expenditure	1448.30	2463.52	4936.44	7501.50	8182.66	8873.15	9834.45	
居民消费	Resident Consumption	1091.00	1808.47	3745.84	5604.51	6131.54	6645.66	7231.78	
政府消费	Government Consumption	357.30	655.05	1190.60	1896.99	2051.12	2227.49	2602.67	
资本形成总额	Total Capital Formation	676.10	1798.25	7974.75	10197.57	10864.54	11524.47	12363.85	
固定资本	Fixed Assets Formation	670.70	1749.87	7825.45	9793.74	10537.80	11336.95	12114.06	
存货增加	Inventory Increasement	5.50	48.38	149.30	403.83	326.74	187.52	249.79	
固定资产投资（亿元）	**Investment in Fixed Assets (100 million yuan)**								
全社会固定资产投资	Total Investment in Fixed Assets	660.01	1769.07	7859.07	11907.67	13843.21	16227.78	18236.78	20499.11
#基本建设	Capital Counstruction	281.54	900.87	3479.48	4501.24	5418.23	6680.15	8141.87	11438.26
更新改造	Innovation	80.16	274.73	2215.90	4319.06	5038.93	5897.85	6523.26	5322.28
房地产开发	Real Estate Development	38.67	286.79	1206.22	1614.63	1838.49	1909.09	2397.99	2683.48
其他	Others	59.26	59.97	260.24	319.75	311.14	360.46	589.83	464.25

注：1. 总人口中，2000年、2010年为人口普查数，其他年份为人口变动抽样调查推算数。2012年从业人员按常住人口口径统计。
2. 根据国家统计制度要求，2013年我区固定资产投资统计起点由项目计划总投资50万元提高到500万元；2013年各增长数据根据2012年度国家口径数据作为基数计算；2013年度全区固定资产投资与国家公布的各省数据口径完全一致（不包括跨省项目投资），各市投资包含跨省项目投资，因此各市投资合计与全区固定资产投资不一致。其他投资2015年起包含农村投资。
3. 2016年实施了研发支出核算改革，根据国家统计局的布置对2007—2015年GDP数据进行衔接，相关GDP计算所得数随之调整。

Note: 1. The data on the total population in 2000 and 2010 is taken from the National Population Survey, and the data on the total population in other years is estimated by the sample survey of population variation. The employment in 2012 is calculated by the permanent population.
2. According to the National Statistical System, the statistical floor level of total planned projects investment in fixed assets of Guangxi has been raised from 500 000 Yuan to 5 000 000 Yuan. The data on growth rates in 2013 is calculated on the data of national statistical range in 2012. The statistical range of data on investment in fixed assets of Guangxi in 2013 is completely the same as the data of other provinces published by National Bureau of Statistic (excluding investment in inter-provincial projects). Due to the investment in inter-provincial projects is included in the investment of cities separately, there are differences between the summary of investment of cities and investment of Guangxi. Investment of "Others" include one from rural areas.
3. Due to the reform of R&D expenditure accounting by National Statistics Bureau, the data of GDP from 2007 to 2015 has been recalculated, so as the related data.

1—3 续表1 continued

指　标	Indicators	2000	2005	2010	2013	2014	2015	2016	2017
财　政（亿元）	**Public Finance (100 million yuan)**								
财政收入	Financial Revenue	220.01	475.37	1228.61	2001.26	2162.54	2333.03	2454.08	2604.32
#公共财政预算收入	Public Budget Income	147.05	283.04	771.99	1317.60	1422.28	1515.16	1556.27	1615.13
公共财政预算支出	Public Budget Expenditure	258.49	611.48	2007.59	3208.67	3479.79	4065.51	4441.70	4908.55
物价总指数（上年=100）	**Price Indices (preceding year=100)**								
居民消费价格总指数	General Consumer Price Index	99.7	102.4	103.0	102.2	102.1	101.5	101.6	101.6
城　市	Urban Area	100.0	103.0	102.9	102.1	102.2	101.5	101.6	101.9
农　村	Rural Area	99.5	101.6	103.4	102.4	101.9	101.5	101.7	101.1
商品零售价格总指数	General Retail Price Index	98.6	101.1	103.0	101.2	101.4	100.1	100.4	101.2
利用外资（亿美元）	**Utilization of Foreign Capital (100 million USD)**								
外商直接投资	Foreign Direct Investment	5.25	3.79	9.12	7.00	10.01	17.22	8.88	8.23
能源生产与消费（万吨标准煤）	**Production & Consumption of Energy (10 000 tons of SCE)**								
能源生产总量	Total Energy Production	833.28	1220.99	1951.85	2129.80	2372.52	3274.39	3147.49	3255.17
能源消费总量	Total energy Consumption	2487.40	4536.74	7379.23	8530.56	9515.34	9760.65	10092.36	10458.46
产　业	**Industry**								
农　业	**Agriculture**								
农林牧渔业劳动力（万人）	Labor Force of Farming, Forestry, Animal Husbandry & Fishery (10 000 persons)	1557	1503	1571	1481	1450	1427	1423	1415
农林牧渔业总产值（亿元）	Gross Output Value of Farming, Forestry, Animal Husbandry & Fishery (100 million yuan)	828.97	1448.37	2720.99	3490.72	3947.73	4197.12	4591.37	4742.76
主要农产品产量（万吨）	Output of Major Farm Products (10 000 tons)								
粮　食	Grain	1667.24	1516.29	1412.32	1484.90	1534.41	1524.75	1521.30	1467.70
油　料	Oil-bearing Crops	58.61	63.18	45.81	53.94	61.30	64.68	68.95	71.62
甘　蔗	Sugar Cane	2937.89	5154.69	7119.62	7829.71	7952.57	7504.92	7461.32	7611.69
园林水果	Fruits (grove)	360.14	571.58	841.77	1030.95	1233.30	1369.76	1525.20	1701.30
肉　类	Meat	287.26	418.60	387.77	410.99	420.03	417.27	407.94	412.35
水产品	Aquatic Products	239.86	284.19	275.09	303.47	332.12	345.62	361.37	378.79
工　业	**Industry**								
全部工业总产值（亿元）	All Included Gross Industrial Output Value(100 million yuan)	1800.24	3684.07	11671.79	17204.62	21730.31	23375.57	25371.44	27892.91
轻工业	Light Industry	862.00	1461.05	3857.83	5395.91	6343.78	6711.34	7273.34	7817.23
重工业	Heavy Industry	938.24	2223.02	7813.96	11808.71	15386.52	16664.23	18098.10	20075.68

1－3 续表2 continued

指 标	Indicators	2000	2005	2010	2013	2014	2015	2016	2017
主要工业产品产量	Output of Major Industrial Products								
成品糖（万吨）	Machine-made Sugar (10 000 tons)	325.76	504.34	705.46	1010.89	1077.16	925.74	914.69	936.20
机制纸及纸板（万吨）	Machine-made Paper (10 000 tons)	82.55	125.37	225.11	413.90	338.67	284.05	289.03	301.21
粗钢（万吨）	Steel (10 000 tons)	104.73	496.29	1204.57	2223.65	2085.62	2146.05	2109.57	2265.26
钢材（万吨）	Steel Products (10 000 tons)	102.63	519.88	1506.34	2791.68	3263.68	3545.75	3645.08	3271.11
十种有色金属（万吨）	Nonferrous Metal (10 000 tons)	60.59	66.63	140.55	123.86	137.54	157.67	180.45	230.21
发电量（亿千瓦时）	Electricity (100 million kwh)	289.09	446.04	1032.15	1249.53	1310.03	1299.90	1346.50	1401.11
原 煤（万吨）	Coal (10 000 tons)	706.67	700.34	757.57	640.34	615.43	425.50	432.50	442.68
农用化肥（折纯100%，万吨）	Chemical Fertilizer (10 000 tons)	53.30	84.02	86.90	105.71	111.49	116.91	95.56	84.90
水 泥（万吨）	Cement (10 000 tons)	2198.35	3306.13	7516.51	11202.83	10744.58	11144.43	12056.42	12218.75
汽 车（万辆）	Motor Vehicles (10 000 sets)	13.12	37.72	136.61	186.91	209.23	229.40	245.45	248.61
建筑业（三级及三级以上企业）	**Construction**								
建筑企业年末从业人数（万人）	Number of Employed Persons (10 000 persons)	33.30	43.00	59.06	76.50	77.92	85.67	113.29	139.29
建筑业总产值（亿元）	Gross Output Value (100 million yuan)	150.92	425.21	1222.31	2289.88	2608.91	2953.42	3434.33	4209.72
交通运输业	**Transportation**								
货运量（万吨）	Freight Traffic (10 000 tons)	31270	41025	113445	151155	163043	149727	160774	174656
#铁路	Railways	5843	8517	7052	6916	6687	5779	5898	6634
客运量（万人）	Passenger Traffic (10 000 persons)	42952	52197	76967	50846	53881	50986	50765	51056
#铁路	Railways	2508	2037	3163	3275	4770	7046	8388	9838
公路里程（公里）	Length of Highways (km)	52910	62003	101782	111384	114900	117993	120547	123259
规模以上港口货物吞吐量（万吨）	Volume of Freight Handled at Major Ports (10 000 tons)	2879	6877	18575	29276	31025	31421	32041	34449
邮电通信业	**Post & Telecommunication Services**								
年末电话用户数（万户）	Number of Subscribers of Telephone (10 000 subscribers)	485.96	1890.4	2923.4	3831.9	4053.63	4034.63	4123.09	4692.79
固定电话年末用户（万户）	Number of Subscribers of Fixed-line Telephone (10 000 subscribers)	319.12	869.40	708.9	546.3	499.85	439.67	348.94	307.71
城 市	Urban	233.48	557.70	430.3	354.7	336.91	312.01	244.36	221.31
农 村	Rural	85.64	311.70	278.6	191.6	162.94	127.65	104.58	86.40
移动电话用户数	Motor Telephone (10 000 sets)	167	1021	2215	3285.6	3553.78	3594.96	3774.15	4385.08
邮电业务总量（亿元）	Business Volume of Post & Telecommunication Services (100 million yuan)	96.36	322.87	807.81	392.82	503.24	651.74	452.66	799.92
国内商业	**Domestic Trade**								
社会消费品零售总额（亿元）	Total Retail Sales of Consumer Goods (100 million yuan)	804.14	1405.55	3312	5133.10	5772.83	6348.06	7027.31	7813.03
对外经济贸易和国际旅游	**Foreign Trade & International Tourism**								
进出口总额（亿美元）	Total Exports & Imports (100 million USD)	20.38	51.83	177.06	328.37	405.53	512.62	478.97	572.10
出口总额	Exports	14.93	28.77	96.1	186.95	243.30	280.26	230.29	274.56
进口总额	Imports	5.45	23.05	80.96	141.42	162.23	232.36	248.68	297.54
接待入境旅游者人数（万人次）	**Number of International Tourists (10 000 persons)**	**124.03**	**146.16**	**250.24**	**391.54**	**421.18**	**450.06**	**482.52**	**512.44**
国际旅游收入（亿元）	Earnings from International Tourism (100 million yuan)	21.78	25.93	54.85	95.80	106.15	117.79	143.71	161.75

注：2016年起，外贸进出口数据以人民币计价。

1—3 续表3 continued

指 标	Indicators	2000	2005	2010	2013	2014	2015	2016	2017
金融、保险（亿元）	**Finance & Insurance (100 million yuan)**								
金融机构本外币存款余额	Total Saving Deposit in RMB & Foreign Currency of Financial Institutions	2269.07	4262.30	11813.90	18400.48	20298.54	22793.54	25477.80	27899.64
金融机构本外币贷款余额	Total Loan Balances in RMB & Foreign Currency of Financial Institutions	1613.25	3104.60	8979.87	14081.01	16070.95	18119.30	20640.54	23226.14
财产险保费收入	Premium Income from Property Insurance	12.16	23.88	69.19	118.88	140.67	160.68	179.86	213.21
人身险保费收入	Premium Income from Life Insurance	18.82	49.24	109.86	156.60	172.56	225.07	289.31	351.89
教育、科技、文化	**Education, Science & Technology, Culture**								
教 育	**Education**								
专任教师数（万人）	Full-time Teachers (10 000 persons)								
普通高等学校	Institutions of Higher Education	0.93	1.96	3.17	3.74	3.77	3.86	4.15	4.32
普通中等专业学校	Special Secondary Schools	0.88	0.70	2.05	2.05	2.04	2.02	2.07	2.09
普通中学	Secondary Schools	12.67	15.24	16.08	16.98	16.62	16.97	17.68	18.57
小 学	Primary Schools	19.90	20.48	22.02	20.95	21.07	22.20	22.43	23.78
在校学生数（万人）	Student Enrollment (10 000 persons)								
普通高等学校	Institutions of Higher Education	11.79	33.83	56.75	64.42	70.19	75.12	81.03	86.67
普通中等专业学校	Special Secondary Schools	15.87	17.04	80.95	82.22	78.27	73.64	69.86	68.68
普通中学	Secondary Schools	285.63	303.87	275.79	276.96	278.90	282.88	290.64	300.94
小 学	Primary Schools	536.79	452.79	430.06	426.26	431.81	440.10	451.37	463.75
科 技	**Science & Technology**								
科技活动人员数（万人）	Personnel in Scientific & Technological Activities (10 000 persons)	4.86	5.67	8.91	10.87	10.72	11.37	12.08	
研究与发展经费内部支出（亿元）	Inner Expenditure of Funds for Research & Development (100 million yuan)	8.36	14.67	62.52	107.68	111.90	105.91	117.75	142.18
文 化	**Culture**								
图书出版数量（万册）	Number of Books Published (10 000 copies)	23691	18818	24810	34376	39773	29978	29193	29022
期刊出版数量（万册）	Number of Magazines Issued (10 000 copies)	5242	5571	4268	4870	4808	4754	4236	4090
报纸出版数量（万份）	Number of Newspapers Issued (10 000 copies)	56008	58222	69560	71812	72972	68974	64275	57997
家庭 生活 环境									
家 庭	**Family**								
家庭总户数（万户）	Total Number of Households (10 000 households)	1140	1329	1347	1383	1567	1575	1586	1586
城镇居民平均每户家庭人口（人）	Average Persons Per Household in Urban Areas (person)	3.19	3.09	3.15	3.25	3.22	3.46	3.35	3.38
农村居民平均每户家庭人口（人）	Average Persons Per Household in Rural Areas (person)	4.82	4.75	3.47	3.38	3.37	3.62	3.56	3.51

注：2006以后中等专业学校在校学生包括中等职业学校学生。

Note: The "Student Enrollment of Special Secondary Schools" after 2006 includes the students of vocational schools for secondary education.

1—3 续表4 continued

指 标	Indicators	2000	2005	2010	2013	2014	2015	2016	2017
居 住	**Housing**								
城镇居民人均居住面积（平方米）	Per Capita Net Floor Space of Urban Residents (sq.m)	18.91	25.20	28.88	29.90	37.72	38.63	39.24	39.54
农村居民人均生活用房面积（平方米）	Per Capita Net Floor Space of Rural Residents (sq.m)	23.40	28.67	33.94	36.81	43.25	45.22	46.28	47.23
生 活	**Livelihood**								
城镇居民人均可支配收入（元）	Per Capita Disposable Income of Urban Households (yuan)	5834	8917	17064	23305	24669	26416	28324	30502
农村居民人均纯收入（元）	Per Capita Net Income of Rural Residents (yuan)	1865	2495	4543	6791	8683	9467	10359	11325
工资和福利	**Wages & Welfare**								
在岗职工平均工资（元）	Average Annual Wages of Staff & Workers (yuan)	6772	15461	31842	42637	46846	54983	60239	66456
离退休退职职工保险福利费用（亿元）	Insurance & Welfare Funds of VCSR, Retired & Resigned (100 million yuan)	52.89	127.22	324.40	544.10	613.34	710.44	599.56	829.63
卫 生	**Health Care**								
卫生机构数（个）	Health Institution (unit)	13707	9432	10341	11195	11469	11770	11991	12288
＃医院、卫生院	Hospital	1868	1753	1728	1755	1756	1794	1810	1853
医院、卫生院病床数（万张）	Hospital Beds (10 000 beds)	8.30	8.71	13.39	17.40	18.77	19.97	20.90	22.41
卫生技术人员（万人）	Medical Technical Personnel (10 000 persons)	12.70	12.92	18.57	23.38	25.86	27.47	28.99	30.53
市政建设	**City Construction**								
全年供水总量（亿吨）	Volume of Tap Water Supply (100 million tons)	13.58	13.29	14.73	16.17	16.22	17.33	17.67	18.36
排水管道长度（公里）	Length of Sewer Pipelines (km)	2885	4116	6417	8309	8771	10588	11480	12305
园林绿地面积（公顷）	Area of Gardens & Green Land (hectare)	44149	29689	60225	69870	72414	82382	84484	88789
环 境	**Environment**								
工业污染治理本年完成投资额（亿元）	Actual Investment for Industrial Pollution Treatment in the Year (100 million yuan)	7.37	10.37	9.28	18.32	17.89	24.72	13.04	8.65
工业污染治理本年施工项目（个）	Implementation Project of Industrial Pollution Treatment in the Year (unit)	1270	389	175	143	109	137	119	102
工业废水排放量（万吨）	Volume of Industrial Waste Water Discharged (10 000 tons)	81571	145609	165211	89508	72936	63253	32554	35950
工业废气排放总量（亿标立方米）	Volume of Industrial Waste Gas Discharged (100 million cu.m)	4607	8339	14520	29051	18631	16773	13485	14158

注：1. 因城乡住户一体化改革造成指标变动，2014—2015年居住类指标名称为期内城镇居民人均自有现住房面积和农村居民人均自有现住房面积，2014—2015年生活类指标名称为城镇常住居民人均可支配收入和农村常住居民人均可支配收入，与上年数据不可比。

2. 2003年以后职工工资及平均工资为在岗职工。

3. 市政建设指标为全区21个设市城市合计数。

Note: 1. According to the change of indicators caused by the integrate reforming on the survey of urban & rural residents, The indicators of housing in 2014 and 2015 are "Per Capita Self-owned Floor Space of Urban Residents" and "Per Capita Self-owned Floor Space of Rural Residents", and the indicators of livelihood in 2014 and 2015 are " Per Capita Annual Disposable Income of Urban Households" and "Per Capita Annual Disposable Income of Rural Households" uses the new statistical range of integration, and the data of them is not comparable with the data in preceding years.

2. Since 2003, the total wages and average annual wages of staff and workers refers to the ones at work.

3. The data on city construction refers to the summary of 21 cities in Guangxi.

1—4 主要年份国民经济和社会发展速度指标

Growth Rates of Major Indicators on National Economic & Social Development in Main Years

单位：% (%)

指 标	Indicators	指数（2017年为下列各年）Index (2017 as Percentage of the Following Years)				平均增长速度 Average Annual Growth Rate			
		2000	2005	2010	2015	2001-2005	2006-2010	2011-2015	2016-2017
人口与就业	**Population & Employment**								
人 口	**Population**								
年末总人口	Year-end Population	117.9	113.7	108.5	101.5	0.7	0.9	1.4	0.7
男性	Male	118.8	114.1	109.0	101.3	0.8	0.9	1.5	0.7
女性	Female	116.9	113.3	108.1	101.7	0.6	0.9	1.2	0.8
常住人口	Permanent Population	108.8	104.8	106.0	101.9	-0.4	-0.2	0.8	0.9
市镇人口	Urban Population	179.8	153.4	130.0	106.5	3.2	3.4	4.1	3.2
乡村人口	Rural Population	72.7	80.2	89.9	97.7	-2.0	-2.2	-1.7	-1.1
就 业	**Employment**								
从业人数	Employment	110.8	105.1	97.9	100.8	1.0	1.4	-0.6	0.4
城镇登记失业人数	Number of Registered Unemployed Persons	130.3	79.5	77.2	81.2	10.4	0.6	-1.0	-9.9
宏观经济	**Macroeconomic Indicators**								
国民核算	**National Accounting**								
地区生产总值	Gross Domestic Product	980.6	511.9	212.4	120.9	10.8	14.0	10.1	7.3
第一产业	Primary Industry	521.5	318.6	173.5	113.3	5.4	5.3	4.5	3.7
第二产业	Secondary Industry	1268.9	615.5	204.9	119.7	13.8	19.3	12.1	7.0
#工业	Industry	1251.6	605.9	197.3	119.6	13.8	19.5	11.8	7.0
第三产业	Tertiary Industry	1037.0	524.8	241.5	125.3	11.2	12.7	9.8	8.9
人均地区生产总值	Per Capita GDP	18.7	10.1	4.3	2.5	10.0	13.0	9.3	6.3
支出法地区生产总值	Gross Domestic Expenditures					10.8	14.0	10.1	
#最终消费	Total Consumption					9.5	11.3	9.4	
居民消费	Resident Consumption					8.9	12.0	9.2	
政府消费	Public Consumption					11.4	9.3	10.2	
资本形成总额	Total Investment					19.1	31.5	6.4	
固定资本	Fixed Assets					18.7	31.8	6.3	
存货增加	Inventory Increasement					47.0	20.2	13.0	
固定资产投资	**Investment in Fixed Assets**								
全社会固定资产投资	Total Investment in Fixed Assets	3105.9	1158.8	260.8	126.3	21.8	34.7	21.6	12.4
#基本建设	Capital Construction	4062.7	1269.7	328.7	171.2	26.2	31.0	20.1	30.9
更新改造	Innovation	6639.6	1937.3	240.2	90.2	27.9	51.8	27.8	-5.0
房地产开发	Real Estate Development	6939.4	935.7	222.5	140.6	49.3	33.3	9.6	18.6
其他	Others	783.4	774.1	178.4	125.1	0.2	34.1	46.2	11.8

1—4 续表1 continued

单位：% (%)

指 标	Indicators	指数（2017年为下列各年）Index (2017 as Percentage of the Following Years)				平均增长速度 Average Annual Growth Rate			
		2000	2005	2010	2015	2001-2005	2006-2010	2011-2015	2016-2017
财 政	**Public Finance**								
财政收入	Financial Revenue	1183.7	547.9	212.0	111.6	16.7	20.9	13.7	5.7
#公共财政预算收入	Public Budget Income	1098.4	570.6	209.2	106.6	14.0	22.2	14.4	3.2
公共财政预算支出	Public Budget Expenditure	1898.9	802.7	244.5	120.7	18.8	26.8	15.2	9.9
利用外资	**Utilization of Foreign Capital**								
#外商直接投资	Foreign Direct Investment	156.8	217.2	90.2	47.8	-6.3	19.2	13.6	-30.9
能源生产与消费	**Production & Consumption of Energy**								
能源生产总量	Total Energy Production	390.6	266.6	166.8	99.4	7.9	9.8	10.9	-0.3
能源消费总量	Total energy Consumption	420.5	230.5	141.7	107.1	12.8	10.2	5.8	3.5
产 业	**Industry**								
农 业	**Agriculture**								
农林牧渔业总产值	Gross Output Value of Farming, Forestry, Animal, Husbandry & Fishery	572.1	327.5	174.3	113.0	6.1	5.7	4.5	3.8
主要农产品产量	Output of Major Farm Products								
粮 食	Grain	88.0	96.8	103.9	96.3	-1.9	-1.4	1.5	-1.9
油 料	Oil-bearing Crops	122.2	113.4	156.3	110.7	1.5	-6.2	7.1	5.2
甘 蔗	Sugar Cane	259.1	147.7	106.9	101.4	11.9	6.7	1.1	0.7
园林水果	Fruits	472.4	297.6	202.1	124.2	9.7	8.0	10.2	11.4
肉 类	Meat	143.5	98.5	106.3	98.8	7.8	-1.5	1.5	-0.6
水产品	Aquatic Products	157.9	133.3	137.7	109.6	3.4	-0.6	4.7	4.7
工 业	**Industry**								
全部工业总产值	All Included Gross Industrial Output Value	1549.4	757.1	239.0	119.3	14.0	25.9	14.6	9.2
轻工业	Light Industry	906.9	535.0	202.6	116.5	10.4	21.4	12.2	7.9
重工业	Heavy Industry	2139.7	903.1	256.9	120.5	17.1	28.6	15.8	9.8
主要工业产品产量	Output of Major Industrial Products								
成品糖	Machine-made Sugar	287.4	185.6	132.7	101.1	9.1	6.9	5.6	0.6
机制纸及纸板	Machine-made Paper	364.9	240.3	133.8	106.0	8.7	12.4	4.8	3.0
粗 钢	Steel	2163.0	456.4	188.1	105.6	36.5	19.4	12.2	2.7
钢 材	Steel Products	3187.3	629.2	217.2	92.3	38.3	23.7	18.7	-4.0
十种有色金属	Nonferrous Metal	379.9	345.5	163.8	146.0	1.9	16.1	2.3	20.8
发电量	Electricity	484.7	314.1	135.7	107.8	9.1	18.3	4.7	3.8
原 煤	Coal	62.6	63.2	58.4	104.0	-0.2	1.6	-10.9	2.0
农用化肥	Chemical Fertilizer	159.3	101.0	97.7	72.6	9.5	0.7	6.1	-14.8
水 泥	Cement	555.8	369.6	162.6	109.6	8.5	17.9	8.2	4.7
汽 车	Motor Vehicles	1894.9	659.1	182.0	108.4	23.5	29.4	10.9	4.1

1—4 续表2 continued

单位：% (%)

指 标	Indicators	指数（2017年为下列各年）Index (2017 as Percentage of the Following Years) 2000	2005	2010	2015	平均增长速度 Average Annual Growth Rate 2001-2005	2006-2010	2011-2015	2016-2017
建筑业	**Construction**								
建筑企业年末从业人数	Number of Employed Persons	417.5	323.3	235.4	162.3	5.2	6.6	7.7	27.5
交通运输业	**Transportation**								
货运量	Freight Traffic	558.5	425.7	154.0	116.6	5.6	22.6	5.7	8.0
＃铁路	Railways	113.5	77.9	94.1	114.8	7.8	-3.7	-3.9	7.1
客运量	Passenger Traffic	118.9	97.8	66.3	100.1	4.0	8.1	-7.9	0.1
＃铁路	Railways	392.3	483.0	311.0	139.6	-4.1	9.2	17.4	18.2
公路里程	Length of Highways	233.0	198.8	121.1	104.5	3.2	10.4	3.0	2.2
规模以上港口货物吞吐量	Volume of Freight Handled at Major Ports	1196.6	500.9	185.5	109.6	19.0	22.0	11.1	4.7
邮电通信业	**Post & Telecommunication Services**								
年末电话用户数	Number of Subscribers of Telephone	965.7	248.2	160.5	116.3	31.2	9.1	6.7	7.8
固定电话年末用户	Number of Subscribers of Fixed-line Telephone	96.4	35.4	43.4	70.0	22.2	-4.0	-9.1	-16.3
城 市	Urban	94.8	39.7	51.4	70.9	19.0	-5.1	-6.2	-15.8
农 村	Rural	100.9	27.7	31.0	67.7	29.5	-2.2	-14.5	-17.7
移动电话用户数	Motor Telephone	2628.0	429.5	198.0	122.0	43.7	16.7	10.2	10.4
国内商业	**Domestic Trade**								
社会消费品零售总额	Total Retail Sales of Consumer Goods	971.6	555.9	235.9	123.1	11.7	18.7	13.9	10.9
对外经济贸易	**Foreign Trade**								
进出口总额	Total Exports & Imports	2807.2	1103.8	323.1	111.6	20.5	27.9	23.7	5.6
出口总额	Exports	1839.0	954.3	285.7	98.0	14.0	27.3	23.9	-1.0
进口总额	Imports	5463.3	1291.8	367.8	128.1	33.4	28.6	23.5	13.2
国际旅游	**International Tourism**								
接待入境旅游者人数	Number of International Tourists	413.2	350.6	204.8	113.9	3.3	11.4	12.5	6.7
国际旅游收入	Earnings from International Tourism	742.6	623.8	294.9	135.5	3.5	16.2	16.8	16.4

1—4 续表3 continued

单位：% (%)

指 标	Indicators	指数（2017年为下列各年）Index (2017 as Percentage of the Following Years)				平均增长速度 Average Annual Growth Rate			
		2000	2005	2010	2015	2001-2005	2006-2010	2011-2015	2016-2017
金融、保险	**Finance & Insurance**								
金融机构存款余额	Total Saving Deposit in RMB & Foreign Currency of Financial Institutions	1229.6	654.6	236.2	122.4		22.6	14.0	10.6
金融机构贷款余额	Total Loan Balances in RMB & Foreign Currency of Financial Institutions	1439.7	748.1	258.6	128.2		23.7	15.1	13.2
财产险保费收入	Premium Income from Property Insurance	1753.4	892.8	308.2	132.7	14.5	23.7	18.4	15.2
人身险保费收入	Premium Income from Life Insurance	1869.8	714.6	320.3	156.3	21.2	17.4	15.4	25.0
教育、科技、文化	**Education, Science & Technology, Culture**								
教 育	**Education**								
专任教师数	Full-time Teachers								
普通高等学校	Institutions of Higher Education	464.5	220.4	136.3	111.8	16.1	10.1	4.0	5.8
普通中等专业学校	Special Secondary Schools	237.5	298.6	102.0	103.7	-4.5	24.0	-0.3	1.8
普通中学	Secondary Schools	146.6	121.9	115.5	109.4	3.8	1.1	1.1	4.6
小 学	Primary Schools	119.5	116.1	108.0	107.1	0.6	1.5	0.2	3.5
在校学生数	Student Enrollment								
普通高等学校	Institutions of Higher Education	735.1	256.2	152.7	115.4	23.5	10.9	5.8	7.4
普通中等专业学校	Special Secondary Schools	432.8	403.1	84.8	93.3	1.4	36.6	-1.9	-3.4
普通中学	Secondary Schools	105.4	99.0	109.1	106.4	1.2	-1.9	0.5	3.1
小 学	Primary Schools	86.4	102.4	107.8	105.4	-3.3	-1.0	0.5	2.7
科 技	**Science & Technology**								
科技活动人员数	Personnel in Scientific & Technological Activities	0.0	0.0	0.0	0.0	3.1	9.5	5.0	
研究与发展经费内部支出	Inner Expenditure of Funds for Research & Development	1700.7	969.2	227.4	134.2	18.8	33.6	11.1	15.9
文 化	**Culture**								
图书出版数量	Number of Books Published	80.3	101.1	76.7	63.5	-4.5	5.7	3.9	-20.3
期刊出版数量	Number of Magazines Issued	78.0	73.4	95.8	86.0	1.2	-5.2	2.2	-7.2
报纸出版数量	Number of Newspapers Issued	123.2	118.5	99.2	100.0	0.8	3.6	-0.2	-8.3
家庭 生活 环境	**Family, Livelihood & Environment**								
家 庭	**Family**								
家庭总户数	Total Number of Households	139.1	119.3	117.7	100.7	2.9	0.3	3.2	0.3
城镇居民平均每户家庭人口	Average Persons Per Household in Urban Areas	106.0	109.4	107.3	97.7			1.9	-1.2
农村居民平均每户家庭人口	Average Persons Per Household in Rural Areas	72.8	73.9	101.2	97.0			0.8	-1.5

1—4 续表4 continued

单位：%　　(%)

指　标	Indicators	指数（2017年为下列各年）Index (2017 as Percentage of the Following Years)				平均增长速度 Average Annual Growth Rate			
		2000	2005	2010	2015	2001-2005	2006-2010	2011-2015	2016-2017
居　住	**Housing**								
城镇居民人均居住面积	Per Capita Net Floor Space of Urban Residents	209.1	156.9	136.9	102.4	5.9	2.8	6.0	1.2
农村居民人均生活用房面积	Per Capita Net Floor Space of Rural Residents	201.8	164.7	139.2	104.4	4.1	3.4	5.9	2.2
生　活	**Livelihood**								
城镇居民人均可支配收入	Per Capita Annual Disposable Income of Urban Households	522.8	342.1	178.8	115.5	8.9	13.9	9.1	7.5
农村居民人均纯收入	Per Capita Net Income of Rural Residents	607.2	453.9	249.3	119.6	6.0	12.7		9.4
工资和福利	**Wages & Welfare**								
在岗职工平均工资	Average Annual Wages of Staff & Workers	981.3	429.8	208.7	120.9	18.0	15.5	11.5	9.9
离退休退职职工保险福利费用	Insurance & Welfare Funds of VCSR, Retired & Resigned	1568.6	652.1	255.7	116.8	19.2	20.6	17.0	8.1
卫　生	**Health Care**								
卫生机构数	Health Institution	89.6	130.3	118.8	104.4	-7.2	1.9	2.6	2.2
#医院、卫生院	Hospital	99.2	105.7	107.2	103.3	-1.3	-0.3	0.8	1.6
医院、卫生院病床数	Hospital Beds	270.1	257.3	167.4	112.2	1.0	9.0	8.3	5.9
卫生技术人员	Medical Technical Personnel	240.3	236.3	164.4	111.2	0.3	7.5	8.1	5.4
市政建设	**City Construction**								
全年供水总量	Volume of Tap Water Supply	135.6	138.5	125.0	106.3	5.2	2.1	3.3	2.9
排水管道长度	Length of Sewer Pipelines	426.5	299.0	191.8	116.2	17.7	9.3	10.5	7.8
园林绿地面积	Area of Gardens & Green Land	201.1	299.1	147.4	107.8	-2.0	15.2	6.5	3.8
环　境	**Environment**								
工业污染治理本年完成投资额	Actual Investment for Industrial Pollution Treatment in the Year	117.4	83.4	93.2	35.0	7.1	-2.2	21.6	-40.8
工业污染治理本年施工项目	Implementation Project of Industrial Pollution Treatment in the Year	8.0	26.2	58.3	74.5	-21.1	-14.8	-4.8	-13.7
工业废水排放达标量	Volume of Meeting Standard for Industrial Sewage Discharged	44.1	24.7	21.8	56.8				-24.6

说明：因2015年起农村居民人均纯收入改为农村居民人均可支配收入，相关年份数据不可比。

Note: Since the indicator "Per Capita Net Income of Rural Residents" is changed into "Per Capita Disposable Income of Rural Households" in 2015, the data in relevant year is incomparable.

1－5 主要年份国民经济和社会发展结构指标

Composition Indicators on National Economic & Social Development in Main Years

单位：% (%)

指 标	Indicators	2000	2005	2010	2013	2014	2015	2016	2017
人口与就业	**Population & Employment**								
人 口	**Population**								
城乡结构（常住人口口径）	Structure of Urban & Rural (Permanent Population)								
市镇人口	Urban	28.1	33.6	40.1	44.8	46.0	47.1	48.1	49.2
乡村人口	Rural	71.9	66.4	59.9	55.2	54.0	52.9	51.9	50.8
性别结构	Sexual Structure								
男	Male	52.6	52.5	52.5	52.7	52.8	52.8	52.8	52.7
女	Female	47.7	47.5	47.5	47.3	47.2	47.2	47.2	47.3
就 业	**Employment**								
从业人员结构	Employment Structure of Industry								
第一产业	Primary Industry	61.2	56.2	54.1	53.1	51.9	50.6	50.1	49.8
第二产业	Secondary Industry	10.8	11.9	18.7	19.0	19.3	18.2	17.6	17.5
第三产业	Tertiary Industry	28.0	31.9	27.1	27.9	28.8	31.2	32.3	32.7
宏观经济	**Macroeconomic Indicators**								
国民核算	**National Accounting**								
地区生产总值产业结构	Industrial Structure of GDP								
第一产业	Primary Industry	26.8	22.9	17.4	15.8	15.3	15.2	15.3	14.2
第二产业	Secondary Industry	35.2	37.9	47.2	46.7	46.9	46.0	45.1	45.6
第三产业	Tertiary Industry	38.0	39.2	35.3	37.5	37.8	38.8	39.6	40.2
地区生产总值支出结构	Expenditure Structure of GDP								
最终消费	Final Consumption	69.6	61.8	51.4	51.7	52.0	52.6	53.7	
居民消费	Personal Consumption	52.5	45.4	39.0	38.6	38.9	39.4	39.5	
农村居民	Urban Households	24.4	18.3	11.3	10.7	10.9	11.2	11.3	
城镇居民	Rural Households	28.1	26.5	27.7	27.9	28.0	28.2	28.2	
政府消费	Government Consumption	17.2	16.4	12.4	13.1	13.0	13.2	14.2	
资本形成总额	Gross Capital Formation	32.5	45.1	83.0	70.3	69.0	68.3	67.5	
固定资本	Fixed Assets Formation	32.2	43.9	81.5	67.5	66.9	67.2	66.1	
存货增加	Inventory Increasement	0.3	1.2	1.6	2.8	2.1	1.1	1.4	
固定资产投资	**Investment in Fixed Assets**								
全社会投资管理渠道结构	Administrative Channels of Total Investment								
基本建设	Capital Construction	42.7	50.9	44.3	37.8	39.1	41.2	44.6	55.8
更新改造	Innovation	12.2	15.5	28.2	36.3	36.4	36.3	35.8	26.0
房地产开发	Real Estate Development	5.9	16.2	15.3	13.6	13.3	11.8	13.1	13.1
其他投资	Other Investment	9.0	3.4	3.3	2.7	2.2	10.7	6.4	5.1

1—5 续表1 continued

单位：% (%)

指标	Indicators	2000	2005	2010	2013	2014	2015	2016	2017
资金来源结构	**Structure of Funded Sources**								
国家预算内资金	State Budgetary Appropriation	9.0	8.7	5.0	6.0	5.9	6.8	9.3	9.2
国内贷款	Domestic Loans	24.5	18.9	15.4	15.6	13.5	14.1	12.2	12.5
利用外资	Foreign Investment	3.7	3.9	0.9	0.1	0.1	0.2	0.1	0.1
自筹和其他投资	Fundraising & Others Investment	45.3	68.5	78.7	78.3	80.5	78.9	78.4	78.2
财　政	**Government Finance**								
财政收入结构	Structure of Government Revenue								
中央	Central Government	33.2	40.5	37.2	34.2	34.2	35.1	36.6	38.0
地方	Local Government	66.8	59.5	62.8	65.8	65.8	64.9	63.4	62.0
财政支出结构	Structure of Government Expenditures								
#社会保障和就业	Social Security & Employment			10.8	10.8	11.1	11.3	12.1	13.8
农林水事务	Affairs of Agriculture, Forestry & Water Resources			13.0	11.6	11.2	12.2	12.9	13.2
教育	Education			18.3	19.0	19.0	19.4	19.2	18.7
能源生产和消费	**Production & Consumption of Energy**								
能源生产总量结构	Structure of Energy Production								
原　煤	Coal	36.0	29.4	22.0	14.7	11.9	6.9	7.2	6.3
原　油	Petroleum Crude Oil	0.6	0.4	0.2	2.5	2.9	2.4	2.2	1.9
水电及其他	Hydropower	63.4	70.2	77.9	82.8	85.2	90.7	90.6	91.8
能源消费总量结构	Structure of Energy Consumption								
煤　炭	Coal	49.3	56.0	53.9	57.5	52.8	46.0	47.0	45.4
石　油	Petroleum Crude Oil	15.2	17.6	16.6	15.9	16.7	18.0	18.4	18.4
水电及其他	Hydropower	20.5	17.6	19.2	26.7	30.4	35.9	34.6	36.2
产　业	**Industry**								
农　业	**Agriculture**								
农林牧渔业产值结构	Structure of Gross Output Value of Agriculture								
农　业	Farming	50.5	49.1	49.2	49.8	50.5	51.1	51.1	53.7
林　业	Forestry	4.7	4.3	6.4	7.7	7.7	7.5	7.0	7.3
牧　业	Animal Husbandry	33.2	35.3	32.0	29.3	27.5	27.2	27.6	24.0
渔　业	Fishery	11.6	9.9	9.1	9.8	10.5	10.2	10.1	10.5
农林牧渔服务业	Service Industry for Farming, Forestry, Animal Husbandry & Fishery		1.4	3.3	3.4	3.8	4.0	4.1	4.5
工　业	**Industry**								
全部工业总产值结构	Structure of Gross Output Value of Industry								
轻工业	Light Industry	47.9	39.7	33.1	30.0	29.2	28.7	28.7	28.0
重工业	Heavy Industry	52.1	60.3	66.9	70.0	70.8	71.3	71.3	72.0

1—5 续表2 continued

单位：% (%)

指 标	Indicators	2000	2005	2010	2013	2014	2015	2016	2017
建筑业(三级及三级以上企业)	**Construction**								
建筑业总产值结构	Structure of Gross Output Value of Construction Industry								
#国有及国有控股企业	State-owned Enterprises	58.9	58.4	52.8	48.5	46.6	45.2	44.2	40.6
城镇集体企业	Urban Collective-owned Enterprises	30.9	15.0	9.6	6.7	6.6	6.5	5.9	5.6
交通运输业	**Transportation**								
货运量结构	Structure of Freight Traffic								
#铁路	Railways	18.7	20.8	6.2	4.6	4.9	3.9	3.7	3.8
公路	Highways	75.2	67.9	82.5	82.5	78.6	79.6	79.8	79.9
水运	Waterways	6.1	11.3	11.3	12.9	16.6	16.5	16.6	16.3
客运量结构	Structure of Passenger Traffic								
# 铁路	Railways	5.8	3.9	4.1	6.4	9.6	13.8	16.5	19.3
公路	Highways	91.6	93.4	93.8	89.7	85.8	81.4	78.3	74.6
水运	Waterways	1.8	1.7	0.5	0.8	1.0	1.0	1.1	1.3
对外经济贸易	**Foreign Trade**								
进出口结构	Structure of Imports & Exports								
出口	Structure of Exports	73.3	55.5	54.3	56.9	60.0	54.7	48.1	48.0
进口	Structure of Imports	26.7	44.5	45.7	43.1	40.0	45.3	51.9	52.0
国际旅游	**International Tourism**								
来华旅游人数结构	Structure of Tourists								
外国人	Foreigners	40.8	59.7	56.5	54.2	52.6	53.2	52.2	49.8
港澳台同胞	Compatriots from Hongkong, Macao & Taiwan	58.9	40.1	43.5	45.8	47.4	46.8	47.8	50.2
教育、科技、文化	**Education, Science & Technology & Culture**								
教 育	**Education**								
在校学生结构	Structure of Students Enrollment								
大学生	College & University Students	1.4	4.2	6.7	7.8	8.1	8.5	9.0	9.3
中学生	Secondary School Students	35.5	40.3	42.3	42.8	42.3	41.6	41.1	41.0
小学生	Primary School Students	63.1	55.5	51.0	49.4	49.6	49.9	49.9	49.7
专任教师结构	Structure of Full-time Teachers								
大学	College & Universities	2.7	5.1	7.3	8.4	8.6	8.5	8.9	8.8
中学	Secondary School	39.4	42.1	41.9	44.3	43.5	42.7	43.2	42.9
小学	Primary School	57.9	52.8	50.8	47.3	47.9	48.8	47.9	48.3
科 技	**Science & Technology**								
政府部门从事科技活动人员结构	Structure of Personnel in Scientific & Technological Activities in Government Department								
自然科学	Natural Sciences		8.5	9.8	10.4	10.5	10.9	10.4	10.4

注：本表在校生和专任教师结构自2013年起，大学生包括研究生和普通高等学校在在校生，专任教师仅指普通高校专任教师，中学包括普通中等专业学校、技工学校和普通中学（高中、初中）。科技活动人员结构范围为县及县以上政府部门。

Note: Since 2013, the "College & University Students" includes postgraduate students and internal students of regular higher education institutions, the "Full-time Teachers" only includes full-time teachers in regular institutions of higher education,the "Secondary School" includes specialized secondary schools, skilled workers schools and regular secondary schools (senior, junior). The range of data in "Structure of Personnel in Scientific & Technological Activities" is in governmental departments at and above county level.

1－5 续表3 continued

单位：% (%)

指 标	Indicators	2000	2005	2010	2013	2014	2015	2016	2017
农业科学	Agricultural Sciences		39.6	36.3	33.7	33.3	33.2	39.4	40.9
医药科学	Medical Sciences		13.1	15.9	16.7	17.6	17.4	23.9	24.2
工程与技术科学	Engineering & Technology Sciences		28.6	28.7	30.2	29.9	29.9	14.6	13.9
人文与社会科学	Humanities & Social Sciences		10.2	9.3	9.0	8.7	8.6	11.7	10.5
生活 环境	**Livelihood & Environment**								
生 活	**Livelihood**								
城镇居民消费结构	Consumption Structure of Urban Residents								
#食品类	Food	39.9	42.5	38.1	37.9	35.2	34.4	34.4	33.2
衣着类	Clothing	6.5	7.3	8.1	6.6	5.3	5.2	5.1	4.9
家庭设备用品及服务	Household Facilities, Articles & Services	9.0	5.9	7.4	7.0	6.0	5.8	6.0	6.0
居住	Residence	15.5	11.5	10.2	10.8	22.5	22.2	21.9	21.2
农村居民消费结构	Consumption Structure of Rural Residents								
#食品类	Food	55.4	50.5	48.5	40.0	36.9	35.4	34.5	32.2
衣着类	Clothing	3.5	3.4	3.2	3.3	3.1	3.1	3.0	3.0
家庭设备用品及服务	Household Facilities, Articles & Services	4.2	4.1	5.6	5.4	5.9	6.0	5.5	5.2
居住	Residence	13.5	16.2	20.0	26.1	23.2	22.8	22.8	22.5
卫 生	**Health Care**								
卫生技术人员结构	Structure of Medical Technical Personnel								
#执业（助理执业）医师	Practitioner Doctors & Practitioner Assistant Doctors	36.2	42.3	36.2	33.3	33.5	33.3	33.4	33.1
注册护士	Registered Nurses	31.8	34.5	37.6	40.2	40.2	41.2	42.3	43.1
环 境	**Environment**								
工业污染治理投资结构	Used of Funds in Industrial Pollution Treatment								
治理废水	Waste Water Treatment	54.3	32.5	51.0	35.8	18.4	6.4	8.4	10.7
治理废气	Waste Gas Treatment	36.5	54.8	29.3	60.2	59.3	75.9	80.2	53.6
治理固体废物	Solid Waste Treatment	3.7	1.8	18.3	0.3	9.6	10.8	10.8	0.3
治理噪声	Noise Treatment	0.1	0.5	0.1	0.1	0	0	0	0
其他	Others	5.3	10.4	1.2	3.6	12.7	6.9	0.6	35.4

注：因城乡住户一体化改革造成指标变动，城乡居民家庭设备用品及服务指标从2015开始改为生活用品及服务。

Note: According to the change of indicators caused by the integrate reforming on the survey of urban & rural residents,the data on "Household Facilities, Articles & Services" of urban and rural livelihood is changed into "Daily Necessities & Services" since 2015.

1—6 主要年份国民经济和社会发展比例和效益指标
Indicators on Proportions & Efficiency in National Economic & Social Development in Main Years

指 标	Indicators	2000	2005	2010	2013	2014	2015	2016	2017
人口与就业	**Population & Employment**								
人 口	**Population**								
人口出生率（‰）	Birth Rate (‰)	13.6	14.3	14.1	14.3	14.07	14.05	13.82	15.14
人口死亡率（‰）	Death Rate (‰)	5.7	6.1	5.5	6.4	6.21	6.15	5.95	6.22
人口自然增长率（‰）	Natural Growth Rate (‰)	7.9	8.2	8.7	7.9	7.86	7.90	7.87	8.92
就 业	**Employment**								
三次产业就业者比例（以第一产业为100）	Employment Ratio by Types of Industry (Employment in primary industry=100)								
第一产业	Primary Industry	100.0	100.0	100.0	100.0	100.0	100.0	100.0	100.0
第二产业	Secondary Industry	17.7	21.2	34.6	35.8	37.2	35.9	35.1	35.2
第三产业	Tertiary Industry	45.6	56.7	50.1	52.4	55.5	61.7	64.5	65.7
城镇登记失业率（%）	Unemployment Rate in Urban Area (%)	3.2	4.2	3.7	3.3	3.2	2.9	2.9	2.2
宏观经济	**Macroeconomic Indicators**								
国民核算	**National Accounting**								
三次产业增加值比例（以第一产业为100）	Ratio of Value-added by Tape of Industry (Value-added in primary industry=100)								
第一产业	Primary Industry	100.0	100.0	100.0	100.0	100.0	100.0	100.0	100.0
第二产业	Secondary Industry	131.5	165.6	270.8	295.9	305.7	302.7	295.8	319.9
第三产业	Tertiary Industry	141.7	171.1	202.5	237.6	246.6	254.9	259.1	281.8
全社会劳动生产率（元/人）	Overall Labor Productivity (yuan / person)	8106	14740	33083	52158	56324.2	59823	64476	71767
第一产业	Primary Industry	3548	6007	10662	15494	16644.4	17978	19654	20543
第二产业	Secondary Industry	26358	46915	83394	128142	136632.2	151391	165468	186704
第三产业	Tertiary Industry	11017	18108	43049	70240	73926	74298	78976	88176
固定资产投资	**Investment in Fixed Assets**								
全社会固定资产投资相当于地区生产总值比例（%）	Proportion of Investment in Fixed Assets to GDP (%)	31.7	44.4	81.8	82.1	87.9	96.2	99.6	100.5

1－6 续表1 continued

指　标	Indicators	2000	2005	2010	2013	2014	2015	2016	2017
财　政	**Government Finance**								
财政收入相当于地区生产总值比例（%）	Proportion of Financial Revenue to GDP (%)	10.6	11.9	12.8	13.8	13.7	13.8	13.4	12.8
公共财政预算收入相当于地区生产总值比例（%）	Proportion of Public Budget Income to GDP (%)	7.1	7.1	8.0	9.1	9.0	9.0	8.5	7.9
公共财政预算支出相当于地区生产总值比例（%）	Proportion of Public Budget Expenditure to GDP (%)	12.4	15.3	20.9	22.1	22.1	24.1	24.2	24.1
能源生产与消费	**Production & Consumption of Energy**								
能源消费弹性系数	Elasticity Ratio of Energy Consumption	1.01	1.18	0.84	0.66	0.54	0.32	0.47	0.49
每万元地区生产总值消耗的能源（吨标准煤）	Energy Consumption per 10 000 yuan GDP (ton of SCE)	1.28	1.22	0.83	0.68	0.61	0.58	0.55	0.51
产　业	**Industry**								
农　业	**Agriculture**								
每公顷播种面积农产品产量（公斤）	Output of Farm Crops Per Hectare of Sown Area (kg)								
粮食	Grain	4563	4525	4614	4947	5002	4984	5031	4931
甘蔗	Sugarcane	57756	68950	66583	72032	73530	77073	78455	81409
工　业	**Industry**								
产值利税率（%）	Ratio of Per-tax Profits to Gross Output Value (%)	11.67	11.51	13.7	10.5	10.4	10.3	9.9	
成本费用利润率（%）	After-Tax Profits/Cost (%)	3.86	5.82	8.8	6.3	6.2	6.7	6.8	7.3
建筑业	**Construction**								
技术装备率（元/人）	Value of Machinery per Laborer (yuan/person)	7784	8843	6960	5280	-	5292	3726	3139
产值利税率（%）	Ratio of Per-tax Profits to Gross Output Value(%)	3.4	3.8	3.9	3.5	3.7	3.8	2.4	2.1
全员劳动生产率（元/人，按总产值计算）	Overall Labor Productivity (yuan/person, in terms of gross output value)	56937	125917	257132	385924	343180	344720	373289	368255
运输邮电业	**Transportation, Post & Telecommunication Services**								
铁路网密度（公里/万平方公里）	Railway Density (km/10 000 sq.km)	115	115	133	168	198	214	216	216

1－6 续表2 continued

指 标	Indicators	2000	2005	2010	2013	2014	2015	2016	2017
公路网密度（公里/万平方公里）	Highway Density (km/10 000 sq.km)	2235	2619	4284	4688	4836	4966	5074	5188
电话普及率（部/万人，含移动电话）	Access to Telephones (set/10 000 persons, including mobilephone)	1102	3853	6177	8152	8558	8572	8522	9607
对外贸易	**Foreign Trade**								
进出口总额相当于地区生产总值比例（%）	Proportion of Total Exports & Imports to GDP (%)	8.1	10.5	12.3	13.8	15.8	18.9	17.3	19.0
金 融	**Finance**								
金融机构存款相当于地区生产总值比例（%）	Bank Deposits as Percentage of GDP (%)	109.1	105.5	123.0	126.8	128.9	135.1	139.1	136.8
金融机构贷款相当于地区生产总值比例（%）	Bank Loans as Percentage of GDP (%)	77.6	77.9	93.5	97.0	102.1	107.4	112.7	113.9
教育、科技、文化	**Education, Science & Technology & Culture**								
教 育	**Education**								
学龄儿童入学率（%）	Rate of School-age Children Enrollment (%)	98.7	99.1	99.4	99.6	99.6	99.4	99.6	99.8
每万人在校小学生（人）	Number of Primary School Students per 10 000 Persons (person)	1139	926	934	903	908	918	933	949
每万人在校中学生（人）	Number of Secondary School Students per 10 000 Persons (person)	693	711	799	783	775	768	768	757
每万人在校大学生（人）	Number of University & College Students per 10 000 Persons (person)	25	69	123	137	148	157	173	235
科 技	**Science & Technology**								
研究与发展经费内部支出相当于地区生产总值比例（%）	R&D Expenditures at & above County Level as Percentage of GDP (%)	0.4	0.4	0.7	0.7	0.7	0.6	0.6	0.7
文 化	**Culture**								
广播人口覆盖率（%）	Listener Rating (%)	85.0	88.7	95.0	96.2	96.6	96.7	96.9	97.2
电视人口覆盖率（%）	Viewer Rating (%)	90.0	93.5	97.0	98.0	98.2	98.3	98.4	98.6
卫 生	**Health Care**								
每万人卫生技术人员（人）	Number of Medical Technical Personnel per 10 000 Persons (person)	26.7	26.3	36.0	49.5	54.4	57.3	59.9	60.0
每万人医院、卫生院病床数（张）	Number of Hospital Beds per 10 000 Persons (unit)	17.4	17.7	26.0	36.9	39.5	40.6	43.2	50.0

1—7 主要年份人均主要工农业产品产量
Per Capita Output of Major Industrial & Agricultural Products in Main Years

指 标	Indicators	2000	2005	2010	2013	2014	2015	2016	2017
粮食产量（公斤）	Grain (kg)	352	309	298	324	324	319	316	302
油料产量（公斤）	Oil-bearing Crops (kg)	12	13	10	12	13	14	14	15
甘蔗产量（公斤）	Sugarcane Crops (kg)	621	1050	1504	1724	1679	1572	1549	1566
水果产量（公斤）	Fruits (kg)	76	156	178	305	329	360	391	425
猪牛羊肉（公斤）	Pork, Beef & Mutton (kg)	49	65	55	59	60	58	55	56
水产品（公斤）	Aquatic Products (kg)	51	58	58	68	70	72	75	78
原煤（吨）	Coal (ton)	0.15	0.14	0.16	0.14	0.13	0.09	0.09	0.09
发电量（千瓦时）	Electricity (kwh)	611	909	2181	2658	2766	2722	2795	2882
水泥（公斤）	Cement (kg)	465	674	1588	2383	2268	2334	2503	2513
糖产量（公斤）	Sugar (kg)	69	103	149	215	227	194	190	193
机制纸及纸板（公斤）	Machine-made Paper & Paperboard (kg)	17	26	48	88	72	59	60	62

注：本表2007年起按年平均常住人口计算。自2013年起水果包括果用瓜。
Note: The data from 2007 in this table is calculated with the average permanent population in this year, and the fruits include the melons since 2013.

1－8 各个时期主要经济指标
Main Economic Indicators of Each Period

单位：亿元 (100 million yuan)

时 期	Period	地区生产总值 Gross Domestic Product	第一产业 Primary Industry	第二产业 Secondary Industry	#工业 Industry	第三产业 Tertiary Industry	固定资产投资 Investment in Fixed Assets
“一五”时期	“First Five-Year Plan” Period	88.96	50.35	22.59	19.89	16.02	6.19
“二五”时期	“Second Five-Year Plan” Period	125.03	57.92	37.65	31.64	29.46	19.58
	1963—1965	83.12	43.66	22.42	19.26	17.04	7.21
“三五”时期	“Third Five-Year Plan” Period	165.90	89.17	41.41	36.68	35.32	19.42
“四五”时期	“Fourth Five-Year Plan” Period	287.04	133.80	91.39	82.80	61.85	32.87
“五五”时期	“Fifth Five-Year Plan” Period	393.84	172.14	132.55	119.91	89.15	48.79
“六五”时期	“Sixth Five-Year Plan” Period	708.45	321.87	202.77	175.97	183.81	120.68
“七五”时期	“Seventh Five-Year Plan” Period	1592.80	627.12	479.93	417.65	485.75	337.65
“八五”时期	“Eighth Five-Year Plan” Period	4732.74	1465.25	1655.27	1423.97	1612.19	1314.72
“九五”时期	“Ninth Five-Year Plan” Period	9477.90	2829.42	3283.83	2772.24	3364.65	2808.14
“十五”时期	“Tenth Five-Year Plan” Period	15041.78	3567.49	5366.53	4462.13	6107.76	5586.27
“十一五”时期	“Eleventh Five-Year Plan” Period	35009.36	6861.12	15300.46	13099.14	12847.77	22565.56
“十二五”时期	“Twelfth Five-Year Plan” Period	71979.37	11489.12	33917.72	28376.54	26572.53	64774.33
“十三五”时期	“Thirteenth Five-Year Plan” Period	38713.89	5703.67	17571.50	14480.35	15438.72	38735.89

1—8 续表 continued

单位：亿元 (100 million yuan)

时 期	Period	公共财政预算收入（亿元）Public Budget Income (100 million yuan)	公共财政预算支出（亿元）Public Budget Expenditure (100 million yuan)	外贸进出口总额（亿美元）Total Exports & Imports (100 million USD)	#出口总额 Exports	社会消费品零售总额（亿元）Total Retail Sales of Consumer Goods (100 million yuan)	货运量（万吨）Freight Traffic (10 000 tons)
"一五"时期	"First Five-Year Plan" Period	15.33	12.61	1.74	1.74	41.80	4344
"二五"时期	"Second Five-Year Plan" Period	23.66	34.70	1.48	1.48	59.36	12595
	1963—1965	12.64	15.92	1.24	1.21	42.88	5191
"三五"时期	"Third Five-Year Plan" Period	25.24	34.25	2.37	2.19	84.47	11523
"四五"时期	"Fourth Five-Year Plan" Period	48.32	61.57	7.77	7.21	114.48	21750
"五五"时期	"Fifth Five-Year Plan" Period	61.72	87.53	13.66	12.82	177.10	26379
"六五"时期	"Sixth Five-Year Plan" Period	72.99	105.13	21.12	17.46	321.52	30448
"七五"时期	"Seventh Five-Year Plan" Period	177.90	265.93	37.97	28.32	720.45	94604
"八五"时期	"Eighth Five-Year Plan" Period	354.75	923.09	104.11	71.14	1656.07	138187
"九五"时期	"Ninth Five-Year Plan" Period	589.95	1009.68	126.74	91.87	3433.48	155717
"十五"时期	"Tenth Five-Year Plan" Period	1089.87	2334.06	168.91	99.86	5540.13	178259
"十一五"时期	"Eleventh Five-Year Plan" Period	2672.81	6641.98	611.05	340.44	12051.51	389077
"十二五"时期	"Twelfth Five-Year Plan" Period	6368.82	16284.48	1774.57	989.78	25678.80	736188
"十三五"时期	"Thirteenth Five-Year Plan" Period	3171.40	9350.25	504.85	546.43	14840.34	335430

注："十三五"起，外贸进出口数据以人民币计价。

1—9 各个时期主要经济指标平均增长率
Average Growth Rate of Main Economic Indicators of Each Period

单位：% (%)

时 期	Period	地区生产总值 Gross Domestic Product	第一产业 Primary Industry	第二产业 Secondary Industry	#工业 Industry	第三产业 Tertiary Industry	固定资产投资 Investment in Fixed Assets
"一五"时期	"First Five-Year Plan" Period	10.8	6.5	11.2	12.1	27.5	41.7
"二五"时期	"Second Five-Year Plan" Period	1.2	-4.5	3.9	4.7	8.4	-0.9
	1963—1965	7.5	11.5	9.5	8.4	0.0	27.8
"三五"时期	"Third Five-Year Plan" Period	5.1	2.6	5.3	5.1	8.7	15.6
"四五"时期	"Fourth Five-Year Plan" Period	9.6	6.2	15.0	16.5	9.9	5.3
"五五"时期	"Fifth Five-Year Plan" Period	6.2	3.9	4.8	5.5	12.2	10.5
"六五"时期	"Sixth Five-Year Plan" Period	8.3	4.4	9.9	9.2	13.3	27.4
"七五"时期	"Seventh Five-Year Plan" Period	6.1	5.0	8.7	9.7	4.4	10.2
"八五"时期	"Eighth Five-Year Plan" Period	15.1	8.4	24.3	24.2	13.6	43.9
"九五"时期	"Ninth Five-Year Plan" Period	8.5	6.5	8.6	8.5	9.7	9.3
"十五"时期	"Tenth Five-Year Plan" Period	10.8	5.4	13.8	13.8	11.2	21.8
"十一五"时期	"Eleventh Five-Year Plan" Period	14.0	5.3	19.3	19.5	12.7	34.7
"十二五"时期	"Twelfth Five-Year Plan" Period	10.1	4.5	12.1	11.8	9.8	21.6
"十三五"时期	"Thirteenth Five-Year Plan" Period	7.3	3.7	7.0	7.0	8.9	12.4

注：本表增长率按可比价格计算。
Note: The average growth rates in this table are calculated at comparable prices.

1—9 续表 continued

单位：% (%)

时　期	Period	公共财政预算收入 Public Budget Income	公共财政预算支出 Public Budget Expenditure	外贸进出口总　额 Total Exports & Imports	#出口总额 Exports	社会消费品零售总　额 Total Retail Sales of Consumer Goods	货运量 Freight Traffic
"一五"时期	"First Five-Year Plan" Period	6.4	14.7	47.1	47.1	13.2	39.8
"二五"时期	"Second Five-Year Plan" Period	2.7	2.0	-20.3	-20.3	6.1	1.7
	1963—1965	12.9	18.7	37.1	33.5	7.1	19.9
"三五"时期	"Third Five-Year Plan" Period	8.5	8.3	0.3	0.4	2.9	5.9
"四五"时期	"Fourth Five-Year Plan" Period	8.6	7.5	33.5	33.2	8.1	11.5
"五五"时期	"Fifth Five-Year Plan" Period	2.1	5.8	11.4	12.7	11.9	-2.4
"六五"时期	"Sixth Five-Year Plan" Period	10.4	11.3	6.7	0.3	14.1	23.5
"七五"时期	"Seventh Five-Year Plan" Period	18.3	16.9	11.4	14.4	14.6	9.0
"八五"时期	"Eighth Five-Year Plan" Period	11.1	16.7	29.0	25.2	23.2	7.5
"九五"时期	"Ninth Five-Year Plan" Period	13.1	13.0	-8.7	-7.8	10.1	1.8
"十五"时期	"Tenth Five-Year Plan" Period	14.0	18.8	20.5	14.0	11.7	5.6
"十一五"时期	"Eleventh Five-Year Plan" Period	22.2	26.8	27.9	27.3	18.7	22.6
"十二五"时期	"Eleventh Five-Year Plan" Period	14.4	15.2	23.7	23.9	13.9	5.7
"十三五"时期	"Thirteenth Five-Year Plan" Period	3.2	9.9	5.6	-1.0	10.9	8.0

1—10 主要年份平均每天主要社会经济活动
Selected Indicators on Average Daily Social & Economic Activities in Main Years

指 标	Indicators	2000	2005	2010	2013	2014	2015	2016	2017
每天创造的财富	**Daily Production**								
地区生产总值（亿元）	Gross Domestic Product (100 million yuan)	5.70	10.92	26.31	39.76	43.13	46.22	50.05	55.88
第一产业	Primary Industry	1.53	2.50	4.59	6.28	6.61	7.03	7.64	7.96
第二产业	Secondary Industry	2.01	4.14	12.43	18.57	20.21	21.28	22.61	25.47
#工业	Industry	1.68	3.47	10.64	15.47	16.76	17.56	18.62	21.00
第三产业	Tertiary Industry	2.16	4.28	9.29	14.91	16.30	17.91	19.80	22.44
#运输、仓储及邮政业	Transport, Storage & Post	0.44	0.59	1.32	1.86	2.01	2.20	2.34	2.56
批发零售、餐饮业	Wholesale, Retail & Catering Businesses	0.76	1.25	2.46	3.95	4.05	4.13	4.41	4.78
公共财政预算收入（亿元）	Public Budget Income (100 million yuan)	0.40	0.78	2.12	3.61	3.90	4.15	4.25	4.43
公共财政预算支出（亿元）	Public Budget Expenditure (100 million yuan)	0.71	1.68	5.50	8.79	9.52	11.14	12.14	13.45
粮 食（万吨）	Grain (10 000 tons)	4.57	4.15	3.87	4.17	4.20	4.18	4.16	4.02
油 料（万吨）	Oil-bearing Grops (10 000 tons)	0.16	0.17	0.13	0.16	0.17	0.18	0.19	0.20
甘 蔗（万吨）	Sugar Cane (10 000 tons)	8.03	14.12	19.51	22.20	21.79	20.56	20.39	20.85
猪牛羊肉（万吨）	Meat (10 000 tons)	0.63	0.88	0.71	0.72	0.74	0.76	0.72	0.74
水产品（万吨）	Aquatic Products (10 000 tons)	0.66	0.78	0.75	0.87	0.91	0.95	0.99	1.04
成品糖（万吨）	Machine-made Sugar (10 000 tons)	0.89	1.38	1.93	2.77	2.95	2.54	2.50	2.56
原 煤（万吨）	Coal (10 000 tons)	1.94	1.92	2.08	1.75	1.69	1.17	1.18	1.21
发电量（亿千瓦时）	Electricity (100 million kwh)	0.79	1.22	2.83	3.39	3.59	3.56	3.68	3.84
粗 钢（万吨）	Stee (10 000 tons)	0.29	1.36	3.30	6.09	5.71	5.88	5.76	6.21
钢 材（万吨）	Steel Products (10 000 tons)	0.28	1.42	4.13	7.65	8.94	9.71	9.96	8.96
水 泥（万吨）	Cement (10 000 tons)	6.02	9.06	20.59	30.69	29.44	30.53	32.94	33.48

1—10 续表 continued

指 标	Indicators	2000	2005	2010	2013	2014	2015	2016	2017
每天消费量	**Daily Consumption**								
最终消费（亿元）	Final Consumption Expenditure (100 million yuan)	3.97	6.75	13.52	20.55	22.42	24.31	26.87	
居民消费	Resident Consumption	2.99	4.95	10.26	15.35	16.80	18.21	19.76	
农村居民	Rural Resident	1.39	1.99	2.98	4.24	4.71	5.17	5367.00	
城镇居民	Urban Resident	1.60	2.96	7.28	11.11	12.09	13.03	14.08	
政府消费	Government Consumption	0.98	1.79	3.26	5.20	5.62	6.10	7.11	
能源消费量（万吨标准煤）	Energy Consumption (10 000 tons of SCE)	7.31	13.34	21.70	24.93	26.07	26.74	27.57	28.65
社会消费品零售总额（亿元）	Total Retail Sales of Consumer Goods (100 million yuan)	2.20	3.85	9.07	14.06	15.82	17.39	19.20	21.41
每天其他经济活动	**Other Daily Economic Activities**								
资本形成总额（亿元）	Gross Capital Formation (100 million yuan)	2.04	4.89	21.85	27.94	29.77	31.57	34.21	
固定资产形成	Fixed Assets Formation	2.03	4.80	21.44	26.83	28.87	31.06	33.53	
存货增加	Inventory Increasement	0.88	6.05	0.41	1.11	0.90	0.51	0.68	
货运量（万吨）	Freight Traffic (10 000 tons)	85.67	112.40	310.81	492.59	446.69	410.21	439.27	478.51
客运量（万人）	Passenger Traffic (10 000 persons)	117.68	143.01	210.87	267.89	147.62	139.69	138.70	139.88
规模以上港口货物吞吐量（万吨）	Volume of Freight Handled at Major Ports (10 000 tons)	7.89	18.84	50.89	80.21	85.00	86.08	87.57	94.38
邮电业务总量（万元）	Revenue from Postal & Telecommunication Services (10 000 yuan)	2640	8846	22131.88	10762.19	13787.40	17855.89	12401.64	21915.62
进出口总额（万美元）	Total Exports & Imports (10 000 USD)	558	1420	4850.98	8996.41	11110.42	14044.42	13122.45	15673.97
出口总额	Exports	409	788	2632.84	5121.92	6665.76	7678.27	6309.41	7522.19
进口总额	Imports	149	632	2218.14	3874.50	4444.66	6366.15	6813.04	8157.53
外商直接投资（万美元）	Foreign Direct Investments (10 000 USD)	143.74	103.74	249.86	191.80	274.25	471.80	243.41	225.40
来华旅游人数（人次）	Number of International Tourists (10 000 persons-time)	3398	4004	6856	10727	11539	12330	13184	14039
每天人口变动和婚姻	**Daily Population Changes & Marriages**								
出生（人）	Births (person)	1753	1918	1973	2055	1973	1973	2110	2247
死亡（人）	Deaths (person)	712	822	685	904	822	822	795	877
结婚（对）	Marriages (couple)	873	862	1439	1288	1294	1150	1073	1032
离婚（对）	Divorces (couple)	80	133	200	255	221	228	254	272

1－11 按行业分组的法人单位数

单位：个

行业门类	Sector	1996	2001	2004	2005	2006
总计	**Total**	**96356**	**123298**	**120706**	**130209**	**139566**
农、林、牧、渔业	Farming, Forestry, Animal Husbandry & Fishery	4487	8081	193	3536	4034
采矿业	Mining	2157	1165	1503	1639	1935
制造业	Manufacturing	17703	15105	16068	17110	18752
电力、热力、燃气及水生产和供应业	Production & Supply of Electricity, Heat, Gas & Water	970	1069	1578	1723	1865
建筑业	Construction	1841	1905	1586	1821	2131
批发和零售业	Wholesale & Retail Trades	14306	14921	14365	16291	18775
交通运输、仓储和邮政业	Transport, Storage & Post	1412	2430	1925	2068	2282
住宿和餐饮业	Hotels & Catering Services	1798	1891	1918	2056	2258
信息传输、软件和信息技术服务业	Information Transmission, Software & Information Technology	614	2052	2300	2721	3044
金融业	Financial Intermediation	1904	2085	1151	1191	1241
房地产业	Real Estate	1218	2417	3189	3644	4402
租赁和商务服务业	Leasing & Business Services	2433	5389	4781	5406	6140
科学研究和技术服务业	Scientific Research & Technical Services	1112	1811	4901	5083	5310
水利、环境和公共设施管理业	Management of Water Conservancy, Environment & Public Facilities	1074	3026	1481	1582	1626
居民服务、修理和其他服务业	Service to Household, Repair & Other Services	630	1230	972	1124	1339
教育	Education	8309	18650	17326	17477	17643
卫生和社会工作	Health & Social Service	3178	6227	6264	6204	6405
文化、体育和娱乐业	Culture, Sports & Entertainment	1255	2290	2574	2559	2667
公共管理、社会保障和社会组织	Public Management, Social Security & Social Organization	29955	31554	36631	36974	37717

注：1. 2004年和2008年及2013年农、林、牧、渔业法人单位数为兼营第二、三产业的农、林、牧、渔业法人单位。
2. 本表1996年、2001年、2004年、2008年及2013年均为普查数据，其余为年报数据。
3. 本表数据2011年以前按GB/T4754-2002标准分类，2012年以后按GB/T4754-2011标准分类。

Note: 1. The indicator of "Farming, Forestry, Animal Husbandry & Fishery" in 2004, 2008 & 2013 refers to the juridical entities operating primary industry also operating secondary industry or tertiary industry on the side.
2. The data of this table in 1996, 2001, 2004, 2008 & 2013 is based on the Economic Census, data in other years is based on the annual reports.
3. The data in and before 2011 in this table is sorted out by the standard of GB/T4754-2002, and by the standard of GB/T4754-2011 since 2012.

Number of Legal Entities Grouped by Sector

(unit)

2007	2008	2009	2010	2011	2012	2013	2014	2015	2016	2017
149472	**154748**	**180744**	**204970**	**238483**	**274666**	**238440**	**334564**	**402586**	**474480**	**539342**
4306	210	2630	4486	10310	23041	3420	49601	61109	76497	85439
2225	2258	2716	3079	3396	3656	2988	3386	3443	3686	3854
20307	19683	22156	24381	27106	27725	24215	28087	31491	34750	38027
1999	2271	2508	2628	2700	2771	2587	2750	2885	3055	3328
2455	2329	3130	3951	5035	5713	4730	7516	10728	15299	20038
22034	21560	33174	42384	54820	67375	64262	84623	106962	131838	153421
2586	3178	3929	4634	5459	6107	5092	6647	8512	10650	12514
2445	2152	2378	2764	3177	3466	3472	4103	5172	6264	7266
3479	5040	5610	5997	6508	6952	2546	3851	6486	9612	13404
1280	636	938	1249	1649	1643	1610	2321	2972	2509	2703
5218	5628	7084	9013	10224	11034	8447	11513	13475	16006	18677
7238	10535	12964	15394	18798	22108	18610	25498	35285	46247	56993
5573	7141	7627	8397	9020	9959	10361	12613	15433	18547	21935
1698	2081	2227	2376	2571	2748	2762	3129	3496	3887	4344
1552	1607	2152	2666	3417	4093	3541	4709	6487	7572	8590
17786	16435	16776	17126	17497	17788	18301	20043	21541	22010	23151
6480	6207	6363	6446	6573	6644	5387	5745	6059	5021	5059
2760	2600	2795	3005	3180	3489	6665	7302	7962	8818	9168
38051	43197	43587	44994	47043	48354	49444	51127	53089	52212	51431

1—12 各市按机构类型分组的法人单位数（2017年）

单位：个

地 区	Region	法人单位数 Number of Legal Entities	企业 Enterprise	事业单位 Institution
广 西	**Guangxi**	**539342**	**409009**	**41509**
南宁市	Nanning	99475	85745	4907
柳州市	Liuzhou	57136	46930	2810
桂林市	Guilin	63284	48264	4265
梧州市	Wuzhou	29966	22463	2684
北海市	Beihai	28391	24512	1437
防城港市	Fangchenggang	16243	12808	1059
钦州市	Qinzhou	28515	21144	2171
贵港市	Guigang	32852	23247	3070
玉林市	Yulin	51347	39068	4595
百色市	Baise	38837	26800	3534
贺州市	Hezhou	20188	13343	2481
河池市	Hechi	31827	19544	3648
来宾市	Laibin	20710	12964	2077
崇左市	Chongzuo	20571	12177	2771

Number of Legal Entities Grouped by Region & Type of Institutions (2017)

(unit)

机关 Agency	社会团体 Social Organization	农民专业合作社 Farmer Specialized Cooperation	其他法人 Others
8568	**12562**	**39985**	**27709**
844	1120	2959	3900
674	1104	3117	2501
1006	1676	4988	3085
498	1056	1769	1496
268	428	801	945
289	609	852	626
469	717	2505	1509
392	498	3496	2149
611	1027	3318	2728
1021	1207	3485	2790
493	841	1749	1281
917	1034	4501	2183
535	735	3051	1348
551	510	3394	1168

1—13 各市按主要行业分组的法人单位数（2017年）

单位：个

地 区	Region	合计 Total	农、林、牧、渔业 Farming, Forestry, Animal Husbandry & Fishery	采矿业 Mining	制造业 Manufac-turing	电力、热力、燃气及水生产和供应业 Production & Supply of Electricity, Heat, Gas & Water	建筑业 Construction	批发和零售业 Wholesale & Retail Trades	交通运输、仓储和邮政业 Transport, Storage & Post	住宿和餐饮业 Hotel & Catering Services
广 西	**Guangxi**	**539342**	**85439**	**3854**	**38027**	**3328**	**20038**	**153421**	**12514**	**7266**
南宁市	Nanning	99475	6800	197	5806	224	4462	35251	2343	1583
柳州市	Liuzhou	57136	5996	262	4887	236	1542	19920	1353	735
桂林市	Guilin	63284	9168	500	5133	970	2910	15920	1002	1317
梧州市	Wuzhou	29966	5341	255	1989	205	1049	8424	558	325
北海市	Beihai	28391	1594	70	1376	48	1685	8947	780	603
防城港市	Fangchenggang	16243	1810	95	739	70	804	4728	965	209
钦州市	Qinzhou	28515	4735	222	2213	124	1301	7473	1199	306
贵港市	Guigang	32852	5548	182	3572	130	1139	8553	821	286
玉林市	Yulin	51347	11576	287	4901	348	1385	13937	1011	566
百色市	Baise	38837	8823	455	2189	269	1250	9355	700	561
贺州市	Hezhou	20188	4917	198	1158	265	653	4434	325	156
河池市	Hechi	31827	8724	598	1730	194	674	7035	451	306
来宾市	Laibin	20710	5270	332	1237	125	709	4620	371	154
崇左市	Chongzuo	20571	5137	201	1097	120	475	4824	635	159

Number of Legal Entities Grouped by Region & Major Sector (2017)

(unit)

信息传输、软件和信息技术服务业 Information Transmission, Software & Information Technology	金融业 Financial Intermediation	房地产业 Real Estate	租赁和商务服务业 Leasing & Business Services	科学研究和技术服务业 Scientific Research & Technical Services	水利、环境和公共设施管理业 Management of Water Conservancy, Environment & Public Facilities	居民服务、修理和其他服务业 Service to Household, Repair & Other Services	教育 Education	卫生和社会工作 Health & Social Service	文化、体育和娱乐业 Culture, Sports & Entertainment	公共管理、社会保障和社会组织 Public Management, Social Security & Social Organizations
13404	**2703**	**18677**	**56993**	**21935**	**4344**	**8590**	**23151**	**5059**	**9168**	**51431**
4160	339	3684	15760	5337	512	2054	3848	606	1396	5113
1931	322	1865	6925	2593	380	1064	1546	506	977	4096
2000	460	2132	7306	2583	729	1296	2065	567	1069	6157
582	173	927	2789	1173	214	345	1639	238	473	3267
984	172	2825	4204	1228	151	465	1023	157	509	1570
311	131	989	1896	536	143	256	410	119	243	1789
533	151	965	2454	1264	191	458	1211	221	555	2939
464	211	890	2846	1137	214	531	2430	307	721	2870
806	168	1421	3666	1647	455	625	3240	453	714	4141
426	196	838	3193	1267	315	513	1408	623	768	5688
351	87	442	1344	619	212	172	1292	176	392	2995
311	118	672	1832	1166	376	384	1068	485	660	5043
326	82	529	1405	689	218	215	914	251	360	2903
219	93	498	1373	696	234	212	1057	350	331	2860

1—14 按行业、营业状态分组的企业法人单位数（2017年）

单位：个

行 业	Sector	单位数 Number of Legal Entities	营业 Operating	停业（歇业） Shutout (closed)
总计	**Total**	**409009**	**373299**	**8372**
农、林、牧、渔业	Farming, Forestry, Animal Husbandry & Fishery	47251	42851	743
采矿业	Mining	3854	3052	388
制造业	Manufacturing	37894	33612	1288
电力、热力、燃气及水生产和供应业	Production & Supply of Electricity, Heat, Gas & Water	3276	2955	77
建筑业	Construction	20035	18263	238
批发和零售业	Wholesale & Retail Trades	152188	140445	3104
交通运输、仓储和邮政业	Transport, Storage & Post	12094	11124	216
住宿和餐饮业	Hotels & Catering Services	7228	6631	121
信息传输、软件和信息技术服务业	Information Transmission, Software & Information Technology	12980	11970	112
金融业	Financial Intermediation	2652	2458	40
房地产业	Real Estate	18567	16615	525
租赁和商务服务业	Leasing & Business Services	55054	50516	884
科学研究和技术服务业	Scientific Research & Technical Services	15240	13887	256
水利、环境和公共设施管理业	Management of Water Conservancy, Environment & Public Facilities	2252	1963	62
居民服务、修理和其他服务业	Service to Household, Repair & Other Services	8332	7731	128
教育	Education	2254	2028	26
卫生和社会工作	Health & Social Service	818	727	8
文化、体育和娱乐业	Culture, Sports & Entertainment	7034	6466	156
公共管理、社会保障和社会组织	Public Management, Social Security & Social Organization	6	5	

Number of Legal Entities Grouped by Sector & Operating State（2017）

（unit）

筹建 Preparing to Construct	当年关闭 Closedown in the Present Year	当年破产 Bankrupted in the Present Year	当年注销 Write-off in the Present Year	当年吊销 Revoked in the Present Year	注册未经营 Registered but not Operating	其他 Others
18188	**3431**	**145**	**50**	**27**	**1054**	**4443**
2272	287	12	5		66	1015
231	106	13	3	1	6	54
1880	580	51	11	5	62	405
170	24				9	41
1166	92	2	3	1	80	190
5644	1294	33	19	13	435	1201
508	120	4			27	95
304	98	3			22	49
726	40	3		1	45	83
107	14				4	29
751	149	6	3		55	463
2617	382	10	4	3	142	496
867	61	1	1		46	121
163	17	1			11	35
327	55	1	1	2	12	75
142	16	1			15	26
63	4				5	11
250	92	4		1	12	53
						1

1—15 按行业、登记注册类型分组的企业法人单位数（2017年）

单位：个

行 业	Sector	合计 Total	内资 Domestic Funded	国有 State-owned	集体 Collective-owned	股份合作 Cooperative Share Holding
总计	**Total**	**409009**	**406872**	**4012**	**4729**	**513**
农、林、牧、渔业	Farming, Forestry, Animal Husbandry & Fishery	47251	47165	281	744	11
采矿业	Mining	3854	3827	38	37	10
制造业	Manufacturing	37894	37066	468	847	138
电力、热力、燃气及水生产和供应业	Production & Supply of Electricity, Heat, Gas & Water	3276	3205	266	172	35
建筑业	Construction	20035	20006	115	216	17
批发和零售业	Wholesale & Retail Trades	152188	151921	1044	1588	86
交通运输、仓储和邮政业	Transport, Storage & Post	12094	12037	313	186	16
住宿和餐饮业	Hotels & Catering Services	7228	7163	170	97	16
信息传输、软件和信息技术服务业	Information Transmission, Software & Information Technology	12980	12919	21	5	3
金融业	Financial Intermediation	2652	2528	47	11	79
房地产业	Real Estate	18567	18345	303	248	25
租赁和商务服务业	Leasing & Business Services	55054	54898	369	270	29
科学研究和技术服务业	Scientific Research & Technical Services	15240	15174	320	179	16
水利、环境和公共设施管理业	Management of Water Conservancy, Environment & Public Facilities	2252	2221	69	20	1
居民服务、修理和其他服务业	Service to Household, Repair & Other Services	8332	8316	44	63	18
教育	Education	2254	2249	27	30	4
卫生和社会工作	Health & Social Service	818	811	17	6	3
文化、体育和娱乐业	Culture, Sports & Entertainment	7034	7015	99	9	6
公共管理、社会保障和社会组织	Public Management, Social Security & Social Organization	6	6	1	1	

Number of Legal Entities Grouped by Sector & Registration Status（2017）

(unit)

联营 Joint-owned	国有联营 State Joint-owned	集体联营 Collective Joint-owned	国有与集体联营 State & Collective Joint-owned	其他联营 Other Joint-owned	有限责任公司 Limited Liability Company	国有独资公司 State Sole Invest-ment	其他有限责任公司 Other Limited Companies
175	**15**	**71**	**8**	**81**	**26597**	**1455**	**25142**
43		18	1	24	1066	25	1041
1	1				247	19	228
26	1	11	3	11	2923	110	2813
11	3	5		3	575	85	490
3				3	1368	58	1310
45	3	22	1	19	7877	223	7654
4		3		1	1124	84	1040
6	2	2		2	616	10	606
3		2	1		876	21	855
1		1			340	25	315
4	1	1		2	2554	136	2418
8	1	1		6	4552	488	4064
6	1	1		4	1183	51	1132
					327	72	255
5		2		3	468	12	456
3			1	2	127	1	126
					63	2	61
6	2	2	1	1	310	32	278
					1	1	

1—15 续表

行 业	Sector	股份有限公司 Share Holding Limited	私营 Individual	私营独资 Individual Sole Investment	私营合伙 Private Partnership	私营有限责任公司 Private Limited Liability Company	私营股份有限公司 Private Share Holding Limited	其他内资 Other Domestic Funded
总计	**Total**	**2618**	**368061**	**77936**	**5684**	**280489**	**3952**	**167**
农、林、牧、渔业	Farming, Forestry, Animal Husbandry & Fishery	139	44816	29181	683	14712	240	65
采矿业	Mining	41	3451	1238	312	1834	67	2
制造业	Manufacturing	345	32304	9141	1106	21606	451	15
电力、热力、燃气及水生产和供应业	Production & Supply of Electricity, Heat, Gas & Water	56	2088	431	742	883	32	2
建筑业	Construction	115	18171	808	97	17056	210	1
批发和零售业	Wholesale & Retail Trades	641	140588	25040	962	113304	1282	52
交通运输、仓储和邮政业	Transport, Storage & Post	110	10284	576	92	9482	134	
住宿和餐饮业	Hotels & Catering Services	58	6192	1411	166	4531	84	8
信息传输、软件和信息技术服务业	Information Transmission, Software & Information Technology	78	11933	502	75	11210	146	
金融业	Financial Intermediation	306	1744	49	60	1518	117	
房地产业	Real Estate	183	15024	350	75	14377	222	4
租赁和商务服务业	Leasing & Business Services	349	49316	2287	737	45671	621	5
科学研究和技术服务业	Scientific Research & Technical Services	84	13385	683	106	12410	186	1
水利、环境和公共设施管理业	Management of Water Conservancy, Environment & Public Facilities	28	1775	132	30	1587	26	1
居民服务、修理和其他服务业	Service to Household, Repair & Other Services	32	7685	1583	147	5885	70	1
教育	Education	22	2035	489	88	1438	20	1
卫生和社会工作	Health & Social Service	7	714	296	62	346	10	1
文化、体育和娱乐业	Culture, Sports & Entertainment	24	6554	3739	144	2638	33	7
公共管理、社会保障和社会组织	Public Management, Social Security & Social Organization		2			1	1	1

continued

港澳台商投资 Funded by Enterprises from Hong Kong, Macao & Taiwan	与港澳台商合资经营 Joint Venture	与港澳台商合作经营 Coopera-tive Operation	港澳台商独资 Sole Invest-ment	港澳台商投资股份有限公司 Share Holding Limited	其他港澳台商投资 Others Funded by Enterprises from Hong Kong, Macao & Taiwan	外商投资 Foreign-funded	中外合资经营 Joint Venture	中外合作经营 Coopera-tive Operation	外资企业 Sole Invest-ment	外商投资股份有限公司 Share Holding Limited	其他外商投资 Other Foreign-funded
1100	**368**	**56**	**630**	**20**	**26**	**1037**	**295**	**43**	**470**	**199**	**30**
43	15	3	22	2	1	43	15		21	7	
15	8	2	5			12	4	1	5		2
472	139	16	299	8	10	356	148	9	169	21	9
43	15	3	23	1	1	28	10	3	12	3	
7	2		4		1	22	5	10	4	3	
138	40	3	89	1	5	129	21	3	83	17	5
35	11	10	13	1		22	10	5	4	1	2
43	16	2	25			22	6	1	13	2	
26	7	1	13	2	3	35	7		12	15	1
4			3	1		120	2		25	92	1
131	65	8	57	1		91	30	5	47	5	4
66	13	5	43	2	3	90	19	2	44	21	4
34	19	2	12		1	32	10	1	15	5	1
20	7		12	1		11	2	1	5	3	
6			5		1	10	3	2	5		
2	2					3			2	1	
5	3		2			2			1	1	
10	6	1	3			9	3		3	2	1

1－16 各市按三次产业分组的法人单位数（2017年）

Number of Legal Entities Grouped by Three Strata of Industry（2017）

单位：个 (unit)

地 区	Region	法人单位数 Number of Legal Entities	第一产业 Primary Industry	第二产业 Secondary Industry	第三产业 Tertiary Industry
广 西	**Guangxi**	**539342**	**77842**	**64913**	**396587**
南宁市	Nanning	99475	6087	10639	82749
柳州市	Liuzhou	57136	5540	6868	44728
桂林市	Guilin	63284	7544	9460	46280
梧州市	Wuzhou	29966	5116	3473	21377
北海市	Beihai	28391	1413	3145	23833
防城港市	Fangchenggang	16243	1641	1701	12901
钦州市	Qinzhou	28515	4239	3833	20443
贵港市	Guigang	32852	4813	5011	23028
玉林市	Yulin	51347	11074	6902	33371
百色市	Baise	38837	8351	4146	26340
贺州市	Hezhou	20188	4628	2268	13292
河池市	Hechi	31827	8027	3182	20618
来宾市	Laibin	20710	4769	2395	13546
崇左市	Chongzuo	20571	4600	1890	14081

主要统计指标解释

发展速度 是表示某一时期内某一指标发展程度的相对数，它是报告期与基期水平之比，一般用百分数表示，即把基期水平定为1（或100%），以报告期的指标数值除以基期指标数值的商乘100%，即得发展速度。由于比较的标准时期不同，发展速度可分为定期发展速度和环比发展速度两种。发展速度的计算公式为：

发展速度=（指标当期数值/指标基期数值）×100%

增长速度 是反映社会经济增长程度的指标，它是报告期增长量与基期水平之比，又称增长率。其计算公式为：

增长速度=（指标当期数值/指标基期数值-1）×100%

或=发展速度-1（或100%）。

平均每年增长速度 我国计算平均增长速度有两种方法,一种是习惯上经常使用的“水平法”，又称几何平均法，是以间隔最后一年的水平同基期水平对比来计算平均每年增长（或下降）的速度；另一种是“累计法”又称代数平均法或方程法，是以间隔年内各年水平的总和同基期水平对比来计算平均每年增长（或下降）的速度。

在一般正常情况下，两种方法计算的平均每年增长速度比较接近，但在经济发展不平衡出现大起大落时，两种方法计算的结果差别较大。

本年鉴内所列的平均每年增长速度都是用水平法计算的。从某年到某年平均增长速度的年份，均不包基期年在内。如1981—2004年平均每年增长速度，是以1980年为基期，2004年为报告期，年份从1981年算起，共24年。

当年价格 是报告期当年的实际价格，也称现价或现行价格。使用当年价格计算的以货币表现的物量指标，反映当年的实际情况，可用于考核社会经济效益，便于对生产、流通、分配、消费之间进行经济核算和综合平衡。

可比价格 亦称固定价格。指在不同时期的价值指标对比时，扣除了价格变动因素，以确切反映物量的变化。按可比价格计算有两种方法：一种是直接用于产品产量乘其不变价格；一种是指数法换算。

不变价格 用某一时期的同类产品的平均价格作为固定价格，来计算各个时期的产品价值。目的是为了消除各个时期价格变动的影响，保证各时期间、地区间的可比性。

指数 指数是一种表明社会经济现象动态的相对数，一般用百分数表示。运用指数可以测定不能直接相加和直接对比的社会经济现象的总动态；可以分析社会经济现象总变动中各因素变动的影响程度；可以研究总平均指标变动中各组标志水平和总体结构变动的作用。它是在把各个年份的产值换算成可比价格的基础上，根据定基数等于相应各个环比指数的连乘积这个换算关系计算出来的。

本《年鉴》所列“国内生产总值指数”等都是按可比价格计算的，如计算有关年份产值增长情况，可用定期指数（即简称年度为100的定基指数）直接进行对比。例如，求2000年国内生产总值为1980年的百分比，按表上2000年指数，1980年指数，两者相除即得，其余以此类推。

各个计划时期 本年鉴表内所用各个“时期”代表的年份如下：第一个五年计划时期（简称“一五”时期）为1953到1957年；第二个五年计划时期（简称“二五”时期）为1958到1962年；第三个五年计划时期（简称“三五”时期）为1966到1970年；第四个五年计划时期（简称“四五”时期）为1971到1975年；第五个五年计划时期（简称“五五”时期）为1976到1980年；第六个五年计划时期（简称“六五”时期）为1981到1985年；第七个五年计划时期（简称“七五”时期）为1986到1990年；第八个五年计划时期（简称“八五”时期）为1991到1995年；第九个五年计划的时期（简称“九五”时期）为1996到2000年；第十个五年计划时期（简称“十五”时期）为2001到2005年；第十一个五年计划时期（简称“十一五”时期）为2006到2010年;第十二个五年计划时期（简称“十二五”时期）为2011年到2015年；第十三个五年计划时期（简称“十三五”时期）为2016年到2020年。

Explanatory Notes on Main Statistical Indicators

Development Rate is a relative indicator that reflects the development extends of a certain indicator in a certain period. It is calculated by comparing the level of report period to the level of base period, and is expressed with percentage. Namely to set the value of base period for 1 (or 100%), the development rate equals to multiply the quotient that the indicator valve in report period comparing to base period by 100%. Development rate can be classified into fixed-base development rate and chain-base development rate. The formula is:

Development Rate = (Value of Indicator in Report Period / Value of Indicator in Base Period) × 100%

Growth Rate is a indicator that reflects the growth extend of social economy, and is calculated by growth level of report period to base period. The formula is:

Growth Rate = (Value of Indicator in Report Period/ Value of Indicator in Base Period−1) × 100%

or :

=Development Rate−1 (or 100%)

Average Annual Growth Rate Two methods for calculating average annual growth rate are applied in China, one is often called level approach or the method of calculating geometric average, which is derived by comparing the level of the last year of the interval with that of the beginning year; the other is called "accumulative approach" or algebraic average or equation method, which is derived by the summation of the actual figure of each year in the interval divided by the figure in the base year.

Usually the results calculated by the two methods are fairly close, but they differed sharply when uneven economic development occurred with striking fluctuation in growth.

The average annual growth rates listed in this statistical yearbook are calculated by "level approach". The base year are not listed when the year are listed for average annual growth rates. For instance, the average annual growth rate of 24 years since 1981 is listed as average annual growth rate of 1981—2004, among which 1980 is the base year and 2004 is the reference year.

Current Price refers to the actual price in the reference period. The quantum indicators calculated in accordance with actual prices in current year can reflect the actual situation in the reference year. It can be used to check the social economic effect, and to carry though economic accounting and comprehensive balance during production, circulation, distribution and consumption.

Comparable Price also called fixed price. It is applied when comparing indicators of value over time to reflect accurately the changes in real them. Two methods are used for calculating comparable prices: (1) multiplying the output of products by their constant prices of certain year; (2) conversion of the data in current prices by relevant price index.

Constant Price refers to the average price of a given product in certain year, which is used for comparison of output value over time. As the output value at constant prices removes the factor of price changes, it reflects the trend of production development over time.

Index Index is a kind of relative indicator that reflects the trends of social economic phenomena, and is usually expressed with percentage. Using indexes can determine the whole trend of social economic phenomena that cannot be added up or compared directly; can analysis the degree of various factors impacting during the whole variation of social economic phenomena; and also can research the actions of levels and general construction movements of groups of indicators during the variation of total average indicator. It is calculated on the converting relation that fixed cardinal number equal to the continues product of corresponding chain index, when the output value in various years has been converted into comparable prices.

All of the indexes of GDP listed in this yearbook are calculated at comparable prices. The situation of output value growth in certain years can be calculated by comparing term indexes (fixed base indexes that set annual data =100) directly. For instance, the GDP in 2000 as the percentage of in 1980 can be calculated by multiplying index of 2000 to index of 1980 listed in table, and this method by analogy apply to others.

Various Plan Periods The years represented by the various "periods" in tables of this yearbook are as follows: First Five-year Plan Period refers to 1953—1957; Second Five-year Plan Period refers to 1958—1962; Third Five-year Plan Period refers to 1966—1970; Fourth Five-year Plan Period refers to 1971—1975; Fifth Five-year Plan Period refers to 1976—1980; Sixth Five-year Plan Period refers to 1981—1985; Seventh Five-year Plan Period refers to 1986—1990; Eighth Five-year Plan Period refers to 1991—1995; Ninth Five-year Plan Period refers to 1996—2000; Tenth Five-year Plan Period refers to 2001—2005; Eleventh Five-year plan period refers to 2006—2010; and Twelfth Five-year Plan Period refers to 2011—2015; Thirteenth Five-year Plan Period refers to 2016—2020.

2018广西统计年鉴

第二篇

人口

POPULATION

（校对编辑：周慧妮）

2—1 总人口及其构成
Population & Its Composition

年 份 Year	总户数 (万户) Total Households (10 000 households)	总人口 (万人) Total Population (10 000 persons)	男 性 Male	女 性 Female	性别比 (以女性为100) Sex Ratio (Female=100)	常住人口 (万人) Permanent Population (10 000 persons)	人口密度 (人/平方公里) Population Density (person/sq.km)
1978	661	3402	1753	1649	106.31		144
1980	676	3538	1822	1716	106.18		149
1985	757	3873	2005	1868	107.33		164
1990	896	4242	2205	2037	108.25		179
1991	918	4324	2250	2074	108.49		183
1992	950	4380	2285	2095	109.07		185
1993	973	4438	2317	2121	109.24		187
1994	997	4493	2346	2147	109.27		190
1995	1020	4543	2377	2166	109.74		192
1996	1040	4589	2398	2191	109.45		194
1997	1069	4633	2421	2212	109.45		196
1998	1092	4675	2442	2233	109.37		198
1999	1110	4713	2463	2250	109.51		199
2000	1140	4751	2484	2267	109.56		201
2001	1178	4788	2506	2282	109.90		202
2002	1197	4822	2521	2301	109.73		204
2003	1235	4857	2542	2315	109.84		205
2004	1285	4889	2559	2330	109.86		206
2005	1329	4925	2587	2338	110.65	4660	208
2006	1374	4961	2612	2349	111.16	4719	209
2007	1416	5002	2634	2368	111.19	4768	201
2008	1459	5049	2659	2390	111.25	4816	203
2009	1499	5092	2681	2411	111.18	4856	205
2010	1347	5159	2708	2451	110.50	4610	195
2011	1359	5199	2730	2469	110.54	4645	196
2012	1361	5240	2759	2481	110.51	4682	197
2013	1383	5282	2772	2510	110.42	4719	199
2014	1567	5475	2891	2584	111.84	4754	201
2015	1575	5518	2913	2605	111.79	4796	202
2016	1586	5579	2943	2636	111.61	4838	204
2017	1586	5600	2951	2649	111.38	4885	206

注：本表数字按当年行政区划计算，2000年总人口为根据第五次人口普查资料推算，2010年为人口普查数，2011－2013年为人口抽样调查推算数。其余年份为户籍统计年报数，人口密度从2007年起按常住人口计算。

Note: The data in this table is calculated on the administrative division of the year, the total population in 2000 is estimated by the 5th Population Census, the data in 2010 is estimated by the population census, the data from 2011 to 2013 is estimated by population Sample Survery,and total population in other years is based on the annual reports of the household registration.Population density has been calculated by permanent population since 2007.

2—2 人口自然变动情况
Status of Population Natural Changes

年 份 Year	总人口比上年增减 Total Population Changes in Comparison with Last Year		出生人口 (万人) Birth Population (10 000 persons)	出生率 (‰) Birth Rate (‰)	死亡人口 (万人) Mortality Population (10 000 persons)	死亡率 (‰) Mortality Rate (‰)	自然增长率 (‰) Natural Growth Rate (‰)
	绝对数 (万人) Population (10 000 persons)	增长速度 (%) Growth Rate (%)					
1978	73	2.19	83	24.69	19	5.79	18.90
1980	68	1.96	88	25.17	20	5.80	19.37
1985	67	1.76	98	25.51	22	5.60	19.91
1990	92	2.22	85	20.20	28	6.60	13.60
1991	63	1.48	93	21.89	31	7.24	14.65
1992	56	1.30	87	20.19	32	7.28	12.91
1993	58	1.32	86	19.58	28	6.35	13.23
1994	55	1.24	84	18.84	29	6.60	12.24
1995	50	1.11	79	17.54	29	6.53	11.01
1996	46	1.01	77	16.83	31	6.82	10.01
1997	44	0.96	74	15.93	30	6.40	9.53
1998	42	0.91	74	15.87	32	6.86	9.01
1999	38	0.81	70	14.96	32	6.93	8.03
2000	38	0.81	64	13.60	26	5.70	7.90
2001	37	0.78	66	13.80	29	6.07	7.73
2002	34	0.71	64	13.30	30	6.30	7.00
2003	35	0.73	67	13.86	32	6.57	7.29
2004	32	0.66	65	13.32	30	6.12	7.20
2005	36	0.74	70	14.26	30	6.09	8.17
2006	36	0.73	71	14.44	30	6.10	8.34
2007	41	0.83	71	14.19	30	5.99	8.20
2008	47	0.94	72	14.40	29	5.70	8.70
2009	43	0.85	72	14.17	29	5.64	8.53
2010	67	1.32	72	14.13	25	5.48	8.65
2011	40	0.78	71	13.71	31	6.04	7.67
2012	41	0.79	74	14.20	33	6.31	7.89
2013	42	0.80	75	14.28	33	6.35	7.93
2014	53	0.98	72	14.07	30	6.21	7.86
2015	43	0.79	72	14.05	30	6.15	7.90
2016	61	1.11	77	13.82	29	5.95	7.87
2017	21	0.37	82	15.14	32	6.22	8.92

注：1. 1978、1980年的“三率”数字，根据第三次人口普查资料进行了调整。2000年、2010年为人口普查数，其余年份为人口抽样调查数。
2. 1990年以前和2014—2017年的总人口增减绝对数、增长速度为户籍统计年报数，其余年份为人口抽样调查数。

Note: 1. The Third Population Census adjusted the data of birth rate, mortality rate and natural growth rate in 1978 and 1980, and the data in 2000 and 2010 is from the population census, data in other years is based on population sample survey.
2. The absolute figures of the total population variation,the growth rate are based on the annual reports of the household registration before 1990 and from 2014 to 2017, and in the other years are based on the population sample survey.

2—3 主要年份按居住地分的城乡人口

Population by Urban & Rural by Living Areas in Main Years

单位：万人 (10 000 persons)

年 份 Year	按城乡分 Population by Urban & Rural		占总人口比例（%） As Percentage of Total Population(%)	
	市镇人口 Urban	乡村人口 Rural	市镇人口 Urban	乡村人口 Rural
1990	641	3601	15.10	84.90
1995	838	3705	18.45	81.55
2000	1337	3414	28.15	71.85
2001	1350	3438	28.20	71.80
2002	1365	3457	28.30	71.70
2003	1411	3446	29.06	70.94
2004	1550	3339	31.70	68.30
2005	1567	3093	33.62	66.38
2006	1635	3084	34.64	65.36
2007	1728	3040	36.24	63.76
2008	1838	2978	38.16	61.84
2009	1904	2952	39.20	60.80
2010	1849	2761	40.11	59.89
2011	1942	2703	41.80	58.20
2012	2038	2644	43.53	56.47
2013	2115	2604	44.81	55.19
2014	2187	2567	46.01	53.99
2015	2257	2539	47.06	52.94
2016	2326	2512	48.08	51.92
2017	2404	2481	49.21	50.79

注：本表1990、2000、2010年为根据人口普查推算，其余年份为人口抽样调查推算数。2005年起为常住人口数。

Note: The data in 1990, 2000 and 2010 is estimated by the population census, and the data since 2005 is based on permanent population, while the data in the other years is estimated by the population sample survey.

2—4 主要年份各市按居住地分的城乡人口

Population by Urban & Rural By Living Areas by City in Main Years

单位：万人 (10 000 persons)

地 区 Region	按城乡分 Population by Urban & Rural	2005	2010	2012	2013	2014	2015	2016	2017
南宁市	市镇人口 Urban	286.58	350.52	382.21	395.24	403.70	414.32	425.34	438.83
Nanning	乡村人口 Rural	359.74	315.64	296.87	290.13	287.68	284.29	280.88	276.50
柳州市	市镇人口 Urban	166.89	206.91	222.77	229.53	237.32	243.64	249.44	256.03
Liuzhou	乡村人口 Rural	200.30	168.96	159.68	156.07	151.33	148.63	146.43	143.97
桂林市	市镇人口 Urban	165.36	184.02	207.05	215.46	224.12	231.29	238.48	247.34
Guilin	乡村人口 Rural	314.78	290.78	276.89	272.59	267.79	264.87	262.46	258.41
梧州市	市镇人口 Urban	109.43	123.87	137.21	142.00	145.57	149.18	152.71	156.88
Wuzhou	乡村人口 Rural	187.84	164.35	155.73	153.44	151.98	150.76	149.13	146.86
北海市	市镇人口 Urban	71.16	74.82	81.76	84.49	87.33	89.96	92.52	96.01
Beihai	乡村人口 Rural	79.02	79.11	75.44	74.53	73.04	72.61	71.85	70.32
防城港市	市镇人口 Urban	31.82	41.85	46.05	47.66	49.09	50.63	52.36	53.94
Fangchenggang	乡村人口 Rural	46.52	44.84	42.64	42.24	41.71	41.21	40.54	40.08
钦州市	市镇人口 Urban	79.73	94.57	106.97	111.66	114.88	118.84	122.59	127.77
Qinzhou	乡村人口 Rural	233.43	213.40	206.36	204.26	203.18	202.09	201.71	200.23
贵港市	市镇人口 Urban	113.51	165.65	183.08	189.22	194.18	199.75	207.78	214.46
Guigang	乡村人口 Rural	302.29	246.23	235.60	232.83	231.38	229.62	225.42	223.08
玉林市	市镇人口 Urban	177.95	217.32	241.03	249.66	258.10	265.45	272.07	280.02
Yulin	乡村人口 Rural	372.48	331.42	317.09	312.59	307.91	305.27	303.53	301.06
百色市	市镇人口 Urban	88.33	92.23	104.89	110.26	116.85	122.66	127.40	132.35
Baise	乡村人口 Rural	264.14	254.45	246.92	244.26	240.03	237.01	234.62	232.30
贺州市	市镇人口 Urban	60.31	68.95	77.39	80.51	83.72	86.36	89.66	92.95
Hezhou	乡村人口 Rural	144.13	126.46	121.34	119.47	117.62	116.23	114.21	112.72
河池市	市镇人口 Urban	104.13	92.14	103.70	109.80	115.12	121.97	126.16	130.60
Hechi	乡村人口 Rural	265.79	244.79	237.85	233.39	230.02	225.71	223.74	221.75
来宾市	市镇人口 Urban	57.80	69.65	77.71	80.52	85.47	88.76	92.83	97.08
Laibin	乡村人口 Rural	164.85	140.32	135.80	134.38	130.90	129.44	127.22	124.78
崇左市	市镇人口 Urban	54.15	59.36	66.53	68.96	72.10	74.54	77.00	79.88
Chongzuo	乡村人口 Rural	157.55	140.07	135.44	133.85	131.88	130.91	129.92	128.80

注：本表按常住人口口径统计。2010年为人口普查数，其余年份为人口抽样调查推算数。

Note: The data in this table is based on permanent population, the data in 2010 is from the population census , while the data in the other years is estimatel by the population sample survey.

2－5 各市县人口数（2017年）
Population by City & County（2017）

单位：万人 (10 000 persons)

市、县	City & County	户籍户数（万户）Total Households (10 000 households)	户籍人口 Total Household Registered Population	男性 Male	女性 Female	#城镇户籍人口 Urban Household Registered Population	常住人口 Permanent Population
南宁市	**Nanning**	**225.78**	**756.87**	**394.48**	**362.38**	**332.49**	**715.33**
市辖区	District	117.66	375.38	191.86	183.52	232.92	433.49
兴宁区	Xingning District	10.35	33.41	16.94	16.47	23.08	43.54
青秀区	Qingxiu District	23.60	73.34	36.32	37.02	61.42	79.17
江南区	Jiangnan District	16.46	52.43	26.87	25.56	36.33	64.03
西乡塘区	Xixiangtang District	25.19	79.60	39.97	39.63	61.94	123.38
良庆区	Liangqing District	8.57	28.85	15.18	13.67	13.88	37.61
邕宁区	Yongning District	10.20	36.18	19.27	16.91	14.94	28.58
武鸣区	Wuming District	23.29	71.57	37.32	34.25	21.33	57.18
隆安县	Long'an	11.57	42.24	22.43	19.81	8.95	31.54
马山县	Mashan	15.86	57.12	30.11	27.02	10.55	41.11
上林县	Shanglin	14.74	49.97	26.30	23.68	10.24	36.32
宾阳县	Binyang	30.49	105.59	56.45	49.14	33.29	82.03
横　县	Hengxian	35.45	126.56	67.34	59.22	36.54	90.84
柳州市	**Liuzhou**	**113.65**	**386.60**	**199.70**	**186.90**	**191.47**	**400.00**
市辖区	District	55.31	179.68	90.86	88.82	132.82	224.55
城中区	Chengzhong District	5.42	16.28	7.92	8.36	15.86	17.39
鱼峰区	Yufeng District	11.14	35.09	17.46	17.63	32.04	48.94
柳南区	Liunan District	12.14	36.07	18.11	17.96	35.45	52.27
柳北区	Liubei District	11.37	35.12	17.58	17.54	31.78	45.05
柳江区	Liujiang District	15.25	57.12	29.79	27.33	17.69	60.90
柳城县	Liucheng	12.42	40.97	21.15	19.82	16.21	37.11
鹿寨县	Luzhai	11.62	40.97	21.58	19.39	16.66	35.20
融安县	Rong'an	10.48	32.76	17.44	15.31	9.96	30.01
融水苗族自治县	Rongshui	13.07	51.97	27.41	24.55	10.50	42.01
三江侗族自治县	Sanjiang	10.75	40.26	21.26	19.00	5.32	31.12
桂林市	**Guilin**	**163.26**	**534.08**	**276.55**	**257.53**	**178.21**	**505.75**
市辖区	District	40.62	130.40	65.15	65.25	81.56	157.23
秀峰区	Xiufeng District	3.71	11.13	5.35	5.78	11.13	16.51
叠彩区	Diecai District	4.92	15.06	7.28	7.78	13.14	18.82
象山区	Xiangshan District	8.58	24.24	11.78	12.46	22.85	29.44
七星区	Qixing District	7.46	21.69	10.52	11.18	20.90	30.72
雁山区	Yanshan District	1.82	6.93	3.45	3.48	1.02	13.83
临桂区	Lingui District	14.14	51.34	26.76	24.58	12.52	47.91
阳朔县	Yangshuo	9.38	32.86	16.98	15.88	6.92	28.82

2－5　续表1　continued

单位：万人　　(10 000 persons)

市、县	City & County	户籍户数（万户）Total Households (10 000 households)	户籍人口 Total Household Registered Population	男　性 Male	女　性 Female	#城镇户籍人口 Urban Household Registered Population	常住人口 Permanent Population
灵川县	Lingchuan	11.81	39.09	19.75	19.34	9.63	37.23
全州县	Quanzhou	24.70	84.15	45.36	38.79	10.83	66.57
兴安县	Xing'an	12.47	39.09	20.12	18.97	9.04	34.50
永福县	Yongfu	8.10	28.87	15.26	13.62	6.20	24.67
灌阳县	Guanyang	10.58	29.57	15.81	13.76	7.98	24.32
龙胜各族自治县	Longsheng	4.78	17.25	8.79	8.45	2.79	16.11
资源县	Ziyuan	5.70	18.03	9.42	8.61	3.15	15.50
平乐县	Pingle	14.91	46.19	24.44	21.75	16.30	38.71
荔浦县	Lipu	11.15	38.24	19.68	18.57	16.62	36.15
恭城瑶族自治县	Gongcheng	9.07	30.36	15.81	14.55	7.19	25.94
梧州市	**Wuzhou**	**99.48**	**349.06**	**185.57**	**163.49**	**163.68**	**303.74**
市辖区	District	24.64	79.46	40.78	38.68	59.60	81.77
万秀区	Wanxiu District	10.21	29.90	15.06	14.84	23.87	32.31
长洲区	Changzhou District	5.81	18.43	9.19	9.24	14.60	20.80
龙圩区	Longxu District	8.62	31.14	16.54	14.60	21.13	28.66
苍梧县	Cangwu	10.40	40.72	21.82	18.90	12.01	33.01
藤　县	Tengxian	30.24	110.40	59.75	50.65	43.15	87.70
蒙山县	Mengshan	7.42	22.39	11.80	10.58	5.98	20.23
岑溪市	Cenxi	26.77	96.09	51.42	44.68	42.93	81.03
北海市	**Beihai**	**44.54**	**175.42**	**91.95**	**83.47**	**57.14**	**166.33**
市辖区	District	18.93	67.04	33.84	33.20	37.64	72.76
海城区	Haicheng District	9.86	31.39	15.56	15.84	28.27	37.39
银海区	Yinhai District	4.69	17.18	8.78	8.41	7.17	19.94
铁山港区	Tieshangang District	4.37	18.47	9.51	8.96	2.21	15.43
合浦县	Hepu	25.61	108.37	58.11	50.26	19.49	93.57
防城港市	**Fangchenggang**	**25.34**	**97.79**	**52.84**	**44.95**	**36.19**	**94.02**
市辖区	District	14.59	57.97	31.14	26.83	23.27	56.65
港口区	Gangkou District	4.18	13.97	7.24	6.73	8.55	17.49
防城区	Fangcheng District	10.41	44.00	23.90	20.09	14.72	39.16
上思县	Shangsi	6.83	24.85	13.88	10.98	5.08	21.45
东兴市	Dongxing	3.92	14.96	7.82	7.14	7.84	15.92
钦州市	**Qinzhou**	**98.48**	**410.92**	**224.02**	**186.91**	**65.16**	**328.00**
市辖区	District	33.88	150.82	82.88	67.94	36.87	128.58
钦南区	Qinnan District	15.23	64.58	34.56	30.02	22.27	57.26

2－5 续表 2 continued

单位：万人 (10 000 persons)

市、县	City & County	户籍户数（万户）Total Households (10 000 households)	户籍人口 Total Household Registered Population	男 性 Male	女 性 Female	#城镇户籍人口 Urban Household Registered Population	常住人口 Permanent Population
钦北区	Qinbei District	18.65	86.23	48.32	37.91	14.60	71.32
灵山县	Lingshan	40.91	166.17	90.24	75.93	15.68	121.96
浦北县	Pubei	23.69	93.93	50.90	43.04	12.61	77.46
贵港市	**Guigang**	**156.75**	**555.71**	**294.97**	**260.74**	**122.40**	**437.54**
市辖区	District	60.40	201.49	105.35	96.14	54.08	160.01
港北区	Gangbei District	21.77	70.88	36.71	34.17	32.83	62.04
港南区	Gangnan District	21.18	70.00	37.01	33.00	13.05	54.52
覃塘区	Qintang District	17.45	60.61	31.64	28.97	8.20	43.45
平南县	Pingnan	42.86	152.47	82.06	70.41	33.41	119.16
桂平市	Guiping	53.49	201.74	107.55	94.19	34.91	158.37
玉林市	**Yulin**	**207.71**	**724.19**	**388.20**	**335.99**	**243.77**	**581.08**
市辖区	District	30.82	111.81	59.05	52.76	57.32	113.35
玉州区	Yuzhou District	19.05	68.09	35.23	32.86	43.07	73.33
福绵区	Fumian District	11.78	43.72	23.82	19.90	14.25	40.02
容 县	Rongxian	28.79	86.63	45.98	40.66	23.42	66.99
陆川县	Luchuan	33.32	110.11	58.56	51.54	31.39	80.28
博白县	Bobai	51.98	188.11	102.87	85.24	63.06	141.30
兴业县	Xingye	21.52	76.02	41.12	34.90	18.64	58.87
北流市	Beiliu	41.27	151.50	80.62	70.88	49.94	120.29
百色市	**Baise**	**111.58**	**417.57**	**217.28**	**200.28**	**106.26**	**364.65**
右江区	Youjiang District	9.88	36.31	18.31	18.00	13.70	40.01
田阳县	Tianyang	10.58	35.61	17.97	17.64	10.98	32.80
田东县	Tiandong	11.30	43.66	22.79	20.87	10.28	37.60
平果县	Pingguo	14.26	51.60	26.97	24.63	16.80	46.07
德保县	Debao	10.14	36.87	19.66	17.21	8.58	30.83
那坡县	Napo	6.06	21.74	11.44	10.29	4.33	16.14
凌云县	Lingyun	5.97	22.36	11.66	10.70	4.96	19.53
乐业县	Leye	4.97	17.81	9.40	8.42	3.35	15.59
田林县	Tianlin	6.87	26.55	13.66	12.89	5.93	23.37
西林县	Xilin	4.16	16.15	8.40	7.75	1.95	14.64
隆林各族自治县	Longlin	10.75	43.00	22.18	20.82	9.13	35.83
靖西市	Jingxi	16.63	65.91	34.85	31.06	16.28	52.24
贺州市	**Hezhou**	**64.69**	**243.53**	**128.39**	**115.14**	**34.19**	**205.67**
市辖区	District	32.06	120.12	62.53	57.59	17.12	106.18

2—5 续表3 continued

单位：万人 (10 000 persons)

市、县	City & County	户籍户数(万户) Total Households (10 000 households)	户籍人口 Total Household Registered Population	男性 Male	女性 Female	#城镇户籍人口 Urban Household Registered Population	常住人口 Permanent Population
八步区	Babu District	19.96	74.02	38.42	35.60	13.33	64.95
平桂区	Pinggui District	12.10	46.10	24.12	21.98	3.79	41.23
昭平县	Zhaoping	12.70	44.81	24.11	20.69	5.32	35.66
钟山县	Zhongshan	11.00	44.85	23.97	20.88	6.55	36.74
富川瑶族自治县	Fuchuan	8.93	33.75	17.78	15.97	5.20	27.09
河池市	**Hechi**	**125.22**	**429.87**	**223.83**	**206.04**	**97.40**	**352.35**
市辖区	District	31.34	100.88	52.16	48.72	31.36	93.24
金城江区	Jinchengjiang District	10.99	34.36	17.74	16.62	17.17	34.81
宜州区	Yizhou District	20.34	66.52	34.42	32.10	14.18	58.43
南丹县	Nandan	9.74	32.43	17.01	15.42	7.81	29.23
天峨县	Tian'e	5.06	17.55	9.21	8.34	3.46	16.28
凤山县	Fengshan	5.99	22.05	11.57	10.48	3.54	16.97
东兰县	Donglan	8.50	31.19	16.47	14.72	3.91	22.35
罗城仫佬族自治县	Luocheng	12.10	38.70	20.01	18.69	10.73	31.13
环江毛南族自治县	Huanjiang	11.81	37.69	19.98	17.71	5.04	28.21
巴马瑶族自治县	Bama	7.82	29.42	15.33	14.09	4.07	23.42
都安瑶族自治县	Du'an	19.48	72.06	37.34	34.72	19.90	53.88
大化瑶族自治县	Dahua	13.38	47.90	24.74	23.16	7.58	37.64
来宾市	**Laibin**	**78.26**	**268.11**	**140.82**	**127.29**	**65.42**	**221.86**
兴宾区	Xingbin District	31.15	113.36	59.79	53.57	28.51	96.97
忻城县	Xincheng	12.87	43.09	22.41	20.69	8.05	32.89
象州县	Xiangzhou	11.32	36.92	19.42	17.49	8.34	29.88
武宣县	Wuxuan	13.15	45.49	24.15	21.33	11.43	37.13
金秀瑶族自治县	Jinxiu	5.10	15.69	8.07	7.62	4.15	13.13
合山市	Heshan	4.68	13.56	6.97	6.59	4.95	11.86
崇左市	**Chongzuo**	**70.78**	**249.94**	**131.90**	**118.04**	**55.08**	**208.68**
江州区	Jiangzhou District	10.99	37.34	20.00	17.33	11.04	34.30
扶绥县	Fusui	14.95	46.00	24.53	21.48	11.91	40.18
宁明县	Ningming	11.34	44.13	23.53	20.60	7.92	35.39
龙州县	Longzhou	8.01	27.23	13.95	13.28	5.12	22.72
大新县	Daxin	10.22	38.26	19.79	18.47	7.90	30.73
天等县	Tiandeng	11.89	45.55	24.17	21.37	7.17	33.42
凭祥市	Pingxiang	3.38	11.44	5.94	5.50	4.03	11.94

注：本表为公安统计年报数，常住人口为人口抽样调查推算数。

Note: The data in this table is based on the annual report from Public Security Bureau of Guangxi ,and the permanent population is estimated by the population sample survey.

2—6 主要年份婚姻情况
Marital Status in Main Years

项　目	Item	2000	2005	2010	2012	2013	2014	2015	2016	2017
内地居民登记结婚（万对）	Registered Marriages of Inland Residents (10 000 couples)	31.86	31.47	52.51	48.98	47.01	47.22	41.97	39.18	37.66
涉外婚姻（对）	Registered Foreign Marriage (couple)	3700	3411	2018	1881	1747	1653	1613	2366	3064
#国内公民（人）	Domestic Individuals(person)	3700	3411	2017	1872	1747	1653	1611	2366	2808
#男　性	Male	504	196	231	429	554	503	612	981	777
女　性	Female	2196	3215	1786	1443	1193	1150	999	1385	2031
初婚（万人）	First Marriage(10 000 persons)	61.43	59.70	98.59	90.45	86.38	84.54	73.90	71.53	63.97
再婚（万人）	Remarriage(10 000 persons)	2.28	3.92	6.84	7.89	8.01	9.91	10.26	6.82	12.02
#女　性	Female	1.12	1.51	3.33	4.25	4.37	5.43	5.77	3.41	6.94
离婚人数（万对）	Divorces (10 000 couples)	2.90	4.85	7.31	8.59	9.30	8.08	8.33	9.27	9.93
#民政部门批准	Divorces Approved	2.60	7.32	11.25	13.42	14.68	6.10	8.35	9.27	9.93
法院调判	Mediated by the Court	3.20	2.37	3.36	3.76	3.92	2.01			

注：本表为民政部门统计数。

Note: The data in this table is provided by civil affairs department.

2—7 主要年份各种规模家庭户构成

Composition of Various Size of Family Household in Main Years

单位：% (%)

年份 Year	合计 Total	1人户 Family of 1 Person	2人户 Family of 2 Persons	3人户 Family of 3 Persons	4人户 Family of 4 Persons	5人户 Family of 5 Persons	6人户 Family of 6 Persons	7人户 Family of 7 Persons	8人及以上户 Family of 8 & More Persons	家庭户平均每户人数（人） Average Population of One Family (person)	城镇家庭户平均每户人数 Average Population of One Urban Family	乡村家庭户平均每户人数 Average Population of One Rural Family
1995	100	6.50	9.58	16.84	23.75	19.30	12.50	6.40	5.12	4.31		
2000	100	10.05	13.86	21.67	23.43	17.54	7.63	3.34	2.48	3.81		
2005	100	11.18	20.45	24.71	21.82	13.02	5.25	1.98	1.59	3.37		
2007	100	6.75	18.06	26.33	26.67	13.29	5.67	1.89	1.34	3.56		
2008	100	6.87	19.17	26.56	26.69	12.62	5.31	1.66	1.12	3.48		
2009	100	4.79	9.97	20.81	28.04	20.11	9.28	3.92	3.09	3.53		
2010	100	11.30	12.98	20.23	23.41	16.35	7.97	4.00	3.76	3.34	3.15	3.47
2011	100	13.82	22.09	24.87	19.70	10.99	5.29	1.64	1.61	3.24	3.19	3.29
2012	100	13.27	21.01	23.86	20.68	11.75	5.86	1.87	1.70	3.32	3.03	3.47
2013	100	14.43	20.73	23.32	21.09	10.99	5.61	2.03	1.80	3.29	3.25	3.38
2014	100	13.73	21.13	24.41	19.78	11.29	5.77	2.08	1.81	3.30	3.22	3.37
2015	100	12.57	18.72	22.70	20.96	12.74	6.55	2.81	2.95	3.51	3.46	3.62
2016	100	12.90	19.34	22.91	21.01	12.32	6.36	2.62	2.55	3.46	3.35	3.56
2017	100	13.30	19.96	22.16	20.85	12.17	6.40	2.63	2.53	3.44	3.38	3.51

注：本表为按常住人口口径统计。2000、2010年为人口普查数,其余年份为人口抽样调查推算数。

Note: The data in this table is based on permanent population. The data in 2000 and 2010 is based on the population census, while the data in other years is estimated by the population sample survey.

2—8 主要年份人口年龄构成
Population Composition by Age in Main Years

单位：% (%)

年 份 Year	0～14岁占总人口的比重 Ages Ranging from 0 to 14 as Percentage of Total Population	15～64岁占总人口的比重 Ages Ranging from 15 to 64 as Percentage of Total Population	65岁及以上占总人口的比重 Ages in & above 65 as Percentage of Total Population
1990	33.38	61.20	5.42
2000	26.20	66.49	7.31
2005	23.76	66.67	9.57
2007	22.28	68.45	9.27
2008	22.07	68.48	9.45
2009	22.10	68.50	9.40
2010	21.71	69.05	9.24
2011	21.80	68.37	9.83
2012	21.96	68.30	9.74
2013	21.57	68.77	9.66
2014	21.58	68.75	9.67
2015	22.09	67.94	9.97
2016	22.08	67.97	9.95
2017	22.11	67.94	9.95

注：本表为按常住人口口径统计。1990、2000、2010年为人口普查数，其余年份为人口抽样调查数。

Note: The data in this table is based on permanent population. The data in 1990, 2000 and 2010 is based on the population census, while the data in other years is based on the population sample survey.

2—9　6岁及以上人口受教育程度构成
Composition of Educational Status of Ages in 6 & above

单位：%　　(%)

年份 Year	小　学 Primary Schools	初　中 Junior Secondary Schools	高中（含中职） Senior Secondary Schools (including specialized secondary schools)	大专及以上 Junior Colleges & above
2000	45.60	35.20	10.40	2.60
2005	39.84	38.19	9.89	3.96
2007	34.64	42.50	12.37	4.64
2008	34.70	43.63	11.39	4.51
2009	33.30	44.42	11.38	5.06
2010	34.85	42.64	12.14	6.58
2011	34.80	42.60	12.20	6.60
2012	33.28	43.97	12.40	6.63
2013	32.57	44.17	12.72	6.92
2014	32.32	44.17	12.79	7.10
2015	31.20	41.10	13.65	9.21
2016	31.12	41.08	13.98	9.21
2017	30.75	41.07	14.50	9.22

注：本表为按常住人口口径统计。2000、2010年为人口普查数,其余年份为人口抽样调查数。

Note: The data in this table is based on permanent population. The data in 2000 and 2010 is based on the population census, while the data in other years is based on the population sample survey.

主要统计指标解释

户数 包括家庭户（含单身独居）和集体户。

人口数 指一定时点、一定地区范围内有生命的个人的总和。

人口出生率 指在一定时期内（通常为一年）一定地区的出生人数与同期平均人数（或期中人数）之比，一般用千分率表示。计算公式：

$$人口出生率=\frac{年出生人口}{年平均人口}\times 1000‰$$

式中：出生人数指活产婴儿，即胎儿脱离母体时（不管怀孕月数），有过呼吸或其他生命现象。年平均人数指年初、年底人口数的平均数，也可用年中人口数代替。

出生人数 指活产婴儿，即胎儿脱离母体时（不管怀孕月数），有过呼吸或其他生命现象。

人口死亡率（又称粗死亡率） 指在一定时期内（通常为一年）一定地区的死亡人数与同期平均人数（或期中人数）之比，一般用千分率表示。计算公式：

$$人口死亡率=\frac{年死亡人数}{年平均人数}\times 1000‰$$

人口自然增长率 指在一定时期内（通常为一年）人口自然增加数（出生人数减死亡人数）与该时期内平均人数（或期中人数）之比，一般用千分率表示。计算公式：

$$人口自然增长率=\frac{本年出生人数-本年死亡人数}{年平均人数}\times 1000‰$$

或人口自然增长率=人口出生率－人口死亡率

性别比 反映两性人口间比例的指标，指在总人口中或各年龄组人口中，男性人数与女性人数之比。通常以每100个女性人口相对应的男性人口数来表示。计算公式：

$$性别比=\frac{男性人口}{女性人口}\times 100$$

常住人口 包括：

（一）居住本乡、镇、街道，并已在本乡、镇、街道办理常住户口登记的人；

（二）已在本乡、镇、街道居住半年以上，常住户口在本乡、镇、街道以外的人；

（三）在本乡、镇、街道居住不满半年，但已离开常住户口登记地半年以上的人；

（四）居住本乡、镇、街道，户口待定的人；

（五）原住本乡、镇、街道，在国外工作或者学习，暂无常住户口的人。

市人口 指居住在城区区域上的人口。城区是指在市辖区和不设区的市，区、市政府驻地的实际建设连接到的居民委员会和其他区域。

镇人口 指居住在镇区区域上的人口。镇区是指在城区以外的县人民政府驻地和其他镇，政府驻地的实际建设连接到的居民委员会和其他区域。

户籍人口 是指公民依照《中华人民共和国户口登记条例》，已在其经常居住地的公安户籍管理机关登记了常住户口的人。这类人口不管其是否外出，也不管外出时间长短，只要在某地注册有常住户口，则为该地区的户籍人口。

城镇户籍人口 指城镇区域范围内的户籍人口。

家庭户规模 家庭的大小，亦即家庭成员的多少。

Explanatory Notes on Main Statistical Indicators

Households include family household (including single household) and collective households.

Total Population refers to the total number of people alive at a certain point of time within a given area.

Birth Rate refers to the ratio of the number of births to the average population during a certain period of time (usually a year) in a certain region, which is often expressed in ‰.The following formula is used:

$$\text{Birth Rate} = \frac{\text{Number of Births}}{\text{Annual Average Number of Population}} \times 1000‰$$

In this formula, number of births refers to live births, i.e. the births babies had showed any vital phenomena regardless of the length of pregnancy, and annual average number of population refers to the average number of the beginning and end of the year (also can be replaced by midyear population).

Number of Births refers to live births, i.e. the births babies had showed any vital phenomena regardless of the length of pregnancy.

Death Rate refers to the ratio of the number of deaths to the average population (or mid-period population) during a certain period of time (usually a year) which is often expressed in ‰. The following formula is used:

$$\text{Death Rate} = \frac{\text{Annual Average Number of Population}}{\text{Number of Deaths}} \times 1000‰$$

Natural Growth Rate of Population refers to the ratio of natural increase in population (number of births minus number of deaths) in a certain period of time (usually a year) to the average population (or mid-period population) to the same period which is often expressed in ‰. The following formula are applied:

$$\text{Natural Growth Rate of Population} = \frac{\text{Number of Births} - \text{Number of Deaths}}{\text{Average Number of Population}} \times 1000‰$$

or: Natural Growth Rate of Population = Birth Rate – Death Rate

Sex Ratio is the indicator reflects the ratio of the population of male to female in total population or various age groups. Generally, it is often expressed in the ratio of male population to 100 female. The calculating formula:

$$\text{Sex Ratio} = \frac{\text{Male Population}}{\text{Female Population}} \times 100$$

Permanent Population includes:

1. the population living in the local countries, towns or streets, and registered as permanent residences in the local countries, towns or streets.

2. the population having been living in the local countries, towns or streets for more than half a year, with the permanent residences outside the local countries, towns or streets.

3. the population having been living in the local countries, towns or streets for less than half a year, but having been apart from the countries, towns or streets where registered their permanent residences for more than half a year.

4. the population living in the local countries, towns or streets, with undetermined residences.

5. the population once living in the local countries, towns or streets, working or studying in foreign countries now, and without permanent residences temporarily.

City Population refers to the population living in the urban area. Urban area refers to the municipal districts, the cities without district being set up, the neighborhood committees connected with the actual construction of governments of districts and cities and other areas.

Town Population refers to the population living in the town areas. The town area refers to the seat of town governments and other town beside the urban areas, the neighborhood committees connected with the seat of governments and other areas.

Total Household Registered Population refers to the population of citizens registered permanent residence in the public security household registration authorities of their permanent living places in accordance with the Regulations of the People's Republic of China on Residence Registration. Those who registered permanent residence are counted as household registered population, whether and how long they go out.

Urban Household Registered Population refers to the household registered population in the urban areas.

Household Size refers to the size of a family, or the number of family members.

第三篇

国民经济核算

NATIONAL ECONOMIC ACCOUNTING

（校对编辑：陈家芹　梁　源）

3-1 广西生产总值（1978-2017年）
Gross Domestic Product （1978-2017）

（按当年价格计算） （calculated at current prices） 单位: 亿元（100 million yuan）

年 份 Year	广 西 生产总值 Gross Domestic Product	第一产业 Primary Industry	第二产业 Secondary Industry	第三产业 Tertiary Industry	#工 业 Industry	#建筑业 Construction	#交通运输、仓储及邮政业 Transport, Storage & Post	#批发、零售和住宿餐饮业 Wholesale, Retail Trade, Hotel & Catering Services	人均地区生产总值（元/人） Per Capita GDP (yuan/person)
1978	75.85	31.01	25.81	19.03	23.29	2.52	2.91	4.43	225
1979	84.59	37.57	27.98	19.04	25.12	2.86	2.94	3.98	246
1980	97.33	44.07	30.79	22.47	27.78	3.01	3.80	5.00	278
1981	113.46	52.58	33.01	27.87	29.71	3.30	4.01	10.40	317
1982	129.15	63.15	34.72	31.28	30.98	3.74	4.25	11.36	354
1983	134.60	63.59	37.09	33.92	32.39	4.70	4.70	11.17	363
1984	150.27	66.26	43.26	40.75	36.97	6.29	5.46	12.31	399
1985	180.97	77.49	54.69	48.79	45.92	8.77	6.11	14.56	471
1986	205.46	85.62	69.03	50.81	58.41	10.62	7.17	12.30	525
1987	241.56	99.94	81.79	59.83	70.96	10.83	9.14	13.55	607
1988	313.28	118.25	100.69	94.34	86.38	14.31	12.46	28.23	770
1989	383.44	149.98	109.97	123.49	97.11	12.86	16.21	44.41	927
1990	449.06	176.77	118.45	153.84	104.79	13.66	20.45	57.53	1066
1991	518.59	195.17	141.02	182.40	123.66	17.36	30.65	62.03	1211
1992	646.60	233.03	187.48	226.09	161.44	26.04	38.96	74.92	1490
1993	871.70	250.11	321.10	300.49	273.03	48.07	48.49	101.66	1982
1994	1198.29	333.79	469.81	394.69	404.59	65.22	55.12	130.96	2675
1995	1497.56	453.15	535.86	508.55	461.25	74.61	73.76	168.97	3304
1996	1697.90	534.88	587.37	575.65	503.32	84.05	88.77	200.72	3706
1997	1817.25	582.74	614.07	620.44	524.49	89.58	95.20	223.52	3928
1998	1911.30	586.70	667.29	657.31	561.34	105.95	98.65	247.04	4346
1999	1971.41	567.72	682.34	721.35	570.76	111.58	114.07	267.96	4444
2000	2080.04	557.38	732.76	789.90	612.33	120.43	125.36	290.02	4652
2001	2279.34	576.34	771.18	931.82	639.55	131.64	145.86	312.68	5058
2002	2523.73	601.99	846.89	1074.85	699.15	147.74	174.63	342.28	5558
2003	2821.11	658.78	984.08	1178.25	813.79	170.29	184.12	375.96	6169
2004	3433.50	817.88	1253.70	1361.92	1044.80	208.90	211.15	416.50	7461
2005	3984.10	912.50	1510.68	1560.92	1264.84	245.84	213.99	455.80	8590
2006	4746.16	1032.47	1878.56	1835.12	1592.33	286.23	235.72	515.23	10121
2007	5835.33	1241.35	2434.00	2159.98	2098.73	335.27	266.90	583.37	12302
2008	7038.88	1453.75	3050.82	2534.31	2640.34	410.48	337.30	664.77	14689
2009	7784.98	1458.49	3400.42	2926.07	2882.54	517.88	378.75	759.14	16098
2010	9604.01	1675.06	4536.66	3392.29	3885.20	651.46	480.17	898.17	20292
2011	11764.97	2047.22	5707.57	4010.18	4883.31	824.26	588.20	1111.36	25424
2012	13090.04	2172.37	6287.19	4630.48	5318.97	968.22	625.57	1346.64	28069
2013	14511.70	2290.64	6778.48	5442.58	5647.39	1134.51	677.77	1442.63	30873
2014	15742.62	2413.44	7378.14	5951.04	6118.23	1264.16	733.63	1477.11	33237
2015	16870.04	2565.45	7766.34	6538.25	6408.64	1358.56	803.10	1508.12	35330
2016	18317.64	2796.80	8273.66	7247.18	6816.64	1458.41	855.67	1613.23	38027
2017	20396.25	2906.87	9297.84	8191.54	7663.71	1635.71	932.61	1745.09	41955

注：1. 表中数据按国民经济新行业划分进行了调整。
2. 2016年实施了研发支出核算改革，根据国家统计局的布置对2007－2015年GDP数据进行衔接，相关GDP计算所得数随之调整。
3. 本篇中2017年GDP及其相关数据均为快报数。

Note: 1. The data in this table has been adjusted by new divisions of trades in national economy.
2. Due to the reform of R&D expenditure accounting by National Statistics Bureau, the data of GDP from 2007 to 2015 has been recalculated, so as the related data.
3. The GDP data of 2017 in this chapter are from quick statistics data.

3－2　广西生产总值构成（1978－2017年）
Composition of Gross Domestic Product（1978－2017）

（按当年价格计算）（calculated at current prices）　　单位：%（%）

年　份 Year	广　西 生产总值 Gross Domestic Product	第一产业 Primary Industry	第二产业 Secondary Industry	第三产业 Tertiary Industry	#工　业 Industry	#建筑业 Construction	#交通运输、仓储及邮政业 Transport, Storage & Post	#批发、零售和住宿餐饮业 Wholesale, Retail Trade, Hotel & Catering Services
1978	100.0	40.9	34.0	25.1	30.7	3.3	3.8	5.8
1979	100.0	44.4	33.1	22.5	29.7	3.4	3.5	4.7
1980	100.0	45.3	31.6	23.1	28.5	3.1	3.9	5.1
1981	100.0	46.3	29.1	24.6	26.2	2.9	3.5	9.2
1982	100.0	48.9	26.9	24.2	24.0	2.9	3.3	8.8
1983	100.0	47.2	27.6	25.2	24.1	3.5	3.5	8.3
1984	100.0	44.1	28.8	27.1	24.6	4.2	3.6	8.2
1985	100.0	42.8	30.2	27.0	25.4	4.8	3.4	8.0
1986	100.0	41.7	33.6	24.7	28.4	5.2	3.5	6.0
1987	100.0	41.4	33.9	24.8	29.4	4.5	3.8	5.6
1988	100.0	37.7	32.1	30.1	27.6	4.6	4.0	9.0
1989	100.0	39.1	28.7	32.2	25.3	3.4	4.2	11.6
1990	100.0	39.4	26.4	34.3	23.3	3.0	4.6	12.8
1991	100.0	37.6	27.2	35.2	23.8	3.3	5.9	12.0
1992	100.0	36.0	29.0	35.0	25.0	4.0	6.0	11.6
1993	100.0	28.7	36.8	34.5	31.3	5.5	5.6	11.7
1994	100.0	27.9	39.2	32.9	33.8	5.4	4.6	10.9
1995	100.0	30.3	35.8	34.0	30.8	5.0	4.9	11.3
1996	100.0	31.5	34.6	33.9	29.6	5.0	5.2	11.8
1997	100.0	32.1	33.8	34.1	28.9	4.9	5.2	12.3
1998	100.0	30.7	34.9	34.4	29.4	5.5	5.2	12.9
1999	100.0	28.8	34.6	36.6	29.0	5.7	5.8	13.6
2000	100.0	26.8	35.2	38.0	29.4	5.8	6.0	13.9
2001	100.0	25.3	33.8	40.9	28.1	5.8	6.4	13.7
2002	100.0	23.9	33.6	42.6	27.7	5.9	6.9	13.6
2003	100.0	23.4	34.9	41.8	28.8	6.0	6.5	13.3
2004	100.0	23.8	36.5	39.7	30.4	6.1	6.1	12.1
2005	100.0	22.9	37.9	39.2	31.7	6.2	5.4	11.4
2006	100.0	21.8	39.6	38.7	33.5	6.0	5.0	10.9
2007	100.0	21.3	41.7	37.0	36.0	5.7	4.6	10.0
2008	100.0	20.7	43.3	36.0	37.5	5.8	4.8	9.4
2009	100.0	18.7	43.7	37.6	37.0	6.7	4.9	9.8
2010	100.0	17.4	47.2	35.3	40.5	6.8	5.0	9.4
2011	100.0	17.4	48.5	34.1	41.5	7.0	5.0	9.4
2012	100.0	16.6	48.0	35.4	40.6	7.4	4.8	10.3
2013	100.0	15.8	46.7	37.5	38.9	7.8	4.7	9.9
2014	100.0	15.3	46.9	37.8	38.9	8.0	4.7	9.4
2015	100.0	15.2	46.0	38.8	38.0	8.1	4.8	8.9
2016	100.0	15.3	45.1	39.6	37.2	8.0	4.7	8.8
2017	100.0	14.2	45.6	40.2	37.6	8.0	4.6	8.6

3－3 广西生产总值指数（1978－2017年）
Indices of Gross Domestic Product（1978－2017）

（按可比价格计算，以上年为100） (calculated at comparable prices, preceding year = 100)

年 份 Year	广西生产总值 Gross Domestic Product	第一产业 Primary Industry	第二产业 Secondary Industry	第三产业 Tertiary Industry	#工 业 Industry	#建筑业 Construction	#交通运输、仓储及邮政业 Transport, Storage & Post	#批发、零售和住宿餐饮业 Wholesale, Retail Trade, Hotel & Catering Services	人均地区生产总值 Per Capita GDP
1978	111.7	102.3	100.2	148.2	100.0	103.6	119.5	123.6	109.1
1979	103.4	105.5	105.4	98.3	105.2	109.1	100.7	91.8	101.3
1980	110.2	112.6	107.5	110.2	108.5	92.1	129.2	114.9	108.2
1981	108.0	102.5	105.5	123.0	106.9	92.7	106.2	205.2	105.9
1982	112.5	118.5	105.0	110.6	104.1	114.7	106.9	106.8	110.5
1983	103.3	99.3	106.9	107.0	105.0	125.6	104.0	100.6	101.5
1984	106.9	97.8	113.6	115.5	112.6	122.0	117.8	108.0	105.2
1985	111.0	105.0	119.0	111.1	117.8	128.2	107.7	109.2	108.9
1986	106.4	105.7	118.1	93.7	119.4	109.2	106.5	79.8	104.6
1987	109.2	105.7	112.0	110.8	114.5	92.6	119.7	103.3	107.3
1988	104.5	93.8	108.8	114.2	108.1	115.0	117.6	137.3	102.3
1989	103.6	112.4	99.2	99.0	100.7	86.1	102.4	82.9	101.8
1990	107.0	108.5	106.4	105.8	106.6	104.3	93.3	96.8	105.2
1991	112.7	108.8	115.9	114.8	114.8	125.0	131.7	106.2	110.9
1992	118.3	112.9	128.0	116.6	127.9	128.5	119.7	112.8	116.8
1993	118.3	99.6	144.9	115.1	145.1	143.8	108.4	116.9	116.7
1994	115.2	106.0	127.3	110.7	128.3	120.0	111.7	104.2	113.2
1995	111.4	115.6	108.6	111.1	108.2	111.4	116.0	111.2	110.0
1996	108.3	107.2	109.3	108.2	109.4	108.8	113.5	113.3	107.2
1997	108.0	111.2	106.4	107.3	106.4	106.1	106.6	111.3	107.0
1998	110.0	106.8	112.8	109.8	112.7	113.7	101.9	117.8	109.0
1999	108.0	107.6	106.6	109.8	106.1	109.5	113.9	109.6	107.1
2000	107.9	100.2	108.3	113.4	108.2	108.9	112.1	108.6	107.0
2001	108.3	103.4	108.0	111.8	108.0	108.2	107.2	109.7	107.4
2002	110.6	107.3	111.3	112.0	110.9	113.1	110.6	110.1	109.8
2003	110.2	104.0	114.6	110.0	114.6	114.6	112.5	109.0	109.4
2004	111.8	105.4	117.1	110.7	117.0	117.4	116.8	105.6	111.1
2005	113.2	107.1	118.4	111.3	118.9	116.2	107.3	109.4	112.3
2006	113.6	106.5	119.3	112.1	120.1	115.1	109.8	109.7	112.3
2007	115.3	105.5	121.2	114.7	122.6	113.7	104.5	109.6	114.0
2008	112.9	104.9	117.5	111.9	118.7	110.6	121.5	106.1	111.7
2009	114.0	105.2	117.9	113.8	115.9	130.3	107.5	114.6	113.0
2010	114.3	104.6	120.5	111.1	120.4	121.2	117.0	110.9	113.9
2011	112.3	104.8	116.5	110.5	116.5	116.4	109.8	115.9	112.0
2012	111.3	105.6	114.2	109.9	113.8	116.5	102.0	114.7	110.4
2013	110.2	104.1	111.6	110.9	110.7	117.3	105.2	105.6	109.3
2014	108.5	103.9	110.1	108.1	110.3	109.0	105.0	104.4	107.7
2015	108.1	103.9	108.1	109.6	107.8	109.6	111.3	102.0	107.2
2016	107.3	103.4	107.4	108.6	107.3	108.0	104.7	106.1	106.3
2017	107.3	104.1	106.6	109.2	106.8	105.6	106.5	106.5	106.3

3-4 广西生产总值指数（1978-2017年）

Indices of Gross Domestic Product（1978-2017）

（按可比价格计算，以1978年为100） (calculated at comparable prices, 1978 = 100)

年份 Year	广西生产总值 Gross Domestic Product	第一产业 Primary Industry	第二产业 Secondary Industry	第三产业 Tertiary Industry	#工业 Industry	#建筑业 Construction	#交通运输、仓储及邮政业 Transport, Storage & Post	#批发、零售和住宿餐饮业 Wholesale, Retail Trade, Hotel & Catering Services	人均地区生产总值 Per Capita GDP
1978	100.0	100.0	100.0	100.0	100.0	100.0	100.0	100.0	100.0
1979	103.4	105.5	105.4	98.3	105.2	109.1	100.7	91.8	101.3
1980	113.9	118.8	113.3	108.3	114.2	100.5	130.2	105.4	109.4
1981	123.1	121.8	119.6	133.3	122.1	93.2	138.2	216.4	115.8
1982	138.4	144.3	125.6	147.3	127.2	106.9	147.7	231.1	127.7
1983	143.0	143.2	134.3	157.7	133.5	134.2	153.6	232.5	129.8
1984	152.9	140.1	152.6	182.1	150.2	163.8	181.0	251.1	136.5
1985	169.7	147.2	181.6	202.2	177.0	210.0	194.8	274.3	148.8
1986	180.6	155.6	214.6	189.5	211.4	229.4	207.5	218.8	155.5
1987	197.2	164.4	240.2	209.8	242.1	212.6	248.3	226.0	166.8
1988	206.0	154.2	261.3	239.6	261.8	244.3	292.1	310.3	170.5
1989	213.5	173.3	259.2	237.2	263.5	210.4	299.0	257.3	173.8
1990	228.4	188.0	275.7	251.1	280.9	219.4	279.1	249.1	182.6
1991	257.5	204.5	319.6	288.2	322.3	274.3	367.5	264.4	202.4
1992	304.7	230.9	409.1	336.1	412.3	352.5	440.0	298.4	236.3
1993	360.4	230.0	592.8	386.9	598.2	506.8	476.9	348.8	275.7
1994	415.2	243.8	754.5	428.2	767.4	608.2	532.6	363.5	312.0
1995	462.4	281.7	819.3	475.8	830.5	677.7	618.0	404.1	343.3
1996	500.9	301.9	895.4	515.1	908.2	737.1	701.4	457.8	368.1
1997	541.2	335.6	952.4	552.8	966.3	782.4	747.8	509.6	393.8
1998	595.4	358.4	1074.3	607.0	1089.0	889.5	762.0	600.4	429.3
1999	643.0	385.6	1145.2	666.5	1155.4	974.0	867.9	658.0	459.8
2000	693.8	386.4	1240.3	755.8	1250.2	1060.7	972.9	714.6	492.0
2001	751.4	399.5	1339.5	844.9	1350.2	1147.7	1043.0	783.9	528.4
2002	831.0	428.7	1490.9	946.3	1497.4	1298.1	1153.5	863.1	580.2
2003	915.8	445.8	1708.5	1041.0	1716.0	1487.6	1297.7	940.8	634.7
2004	1023.8	469.9	2000.7	1152.3	2007.7	1746.4	1515.7	993.4	705.1
2005	1159.5	503.2	2369.6	1282.3	2387.0	2029.3	1626.2	1087.3	791.9
2006	1317.2	535.9	2826.9	1437.5	2866.8	2335.7	1785.6	1192.8	889.3
2007	1518.7	565.4	3426.2	1648.8	3514.7	2655.7	1866.0	1307.3	1013.8
2008	1714.6	593.1	4025.8	1845.0	4171.9	2937.2	2267.2	1387.0	1132.4
2009	1954.6	623.9	4746.4	2099.6	4835.2	3827.2	2437.2	1589.5	1279.6
2010	2234.1	652.6	5719.4	2332.7	5821.6	4638.6	2851.5	1762.8	1457.5
2011	2508.9	683.9	6663.1	2577.6	6782.2	5399.3	3130.9	2043.1	1632.4
2012	2792.4	722.2	7609.3	2832.8	7718.1	6290.2	3193.5	2343.4	1802.2
2013	3077.2	751.8	8492.0	3141.6	8543.9	7378.4	3359.6	2474.6	1969.8
2014	3338.8	781.1	9349.7	3396.1	9423.9	8042.5	3527.6	2583.5	2121.5
2015	3609.2	811.6	10107.0	3722.1	10159.0	8814.6	3926.2	2635.2	2274.2
2016	3872.7	839.2	10854.9	4042.2	10900.6	9519.8	4110.7	2795.9	2417.5
2017	4155.4	873.6	11571.3	4414.1	11641.8	10052.9	4377.9	2977.6	2569.8

3—5 三次产业贡献率（1990—2017年）
Contribution Rate of Three Industries（1990—2017）

（按可比价格计算）（calculated at comparable prices） 单位：%

年 份 Year	地区生产总值 Gross Domestic Product	第一产业 Primary Industry	第二产业 Secondary Industry	第三产业 Tertiary Industry	#工 业 Industry
1990	100.0	48.3	31.1	20.7	28.1
1991	100.0	27.2	33.0	39.8	27.1
1992	100.0	26.8	41.5	31.7	36.3
1993	100.0	-0.8	72.3	28.5	63.6
1994	100.0	12.0	64.5	23.5	58.6
1995	100.0	38.6	30.1	31.4	25.3
1996	100.0	26.3	40.1	33.6	34.9
1997	100.0	41.2	28.4	30.4	24.5
1998	100.0	21.1	45.7	33.2	39.1
1999	100.0	28.5	30.2	41.3	24.0
2000	100.0	0.8	39.2	60.1	33.1
2001	100.0	11.1	34.3	54.6	28.7
2002	100.0	17.7	37.7	44.6	30.4
2003	100.0	9.8	51.0	39.2	42.4
2004	100.0	10.7	53.3	36.0	44.1
2005	100.0	12.0	54.1	33.9	46.3
2006	100.0	11.0	54.0	35.0	47.1
2007	100.0	7.7	55.1	37.2	49.5
2008	100.0	7.6	57.0	35.5	51.9
2009	100.0	6.8	55.5	37.6	42.4
2010	100.0	5.5	64.8	29.7	54.6
2011	100.0	6.8	63.1	30.1	54.1
2012	100.0	8.0	61.7	30.3	51.4
2013	100.0	6.1	57.0	36.9	44.9
2014	100.0	6.5	60.3	33.2	52.1
2015	100.0	6.7	52.0	41.3	42.3
2016	100.0	7.2	47.1	45.7	38.3
2017	100.0	8.3	41.9	49.8	35.7

3—6 各市生产总值、人均地区生产总值（2017年）
GDP & Per Capita GDP by City（2017）

（按当年价格计算）（calculated at current prices） 单位：亿元（100 million yuan）

城市	City	地区生产总值 Gross Domestic Product	第一产业 Primary Industry	第二产业 Secondary Industry	第三产业 Tertiary Industry	#工业 Industry	人均地区生产总值（元/人） Per Capita GDP (yuan/person)
南宁市	Nanning	4118.83	404.18	1599.50	2115.15	1189.89	57948
柳州市	Liuzhou	2755.64	189.49	1487.08	1079.07	1345.13	69249
桂林市	Guilin	2045.18	381.83	791.94	871.41	609.71	40632
梧州市	Wuzhou	1338.10	136.41	785.71	415.98	729.57	44193
北海市	Beihai	1229.84	190.54	668.66	370.64	612.00	74378
防城港市	Fangchenggang	741.62	89.27	421.23	231.12	369.45	79351
钦州市	Qinzhou	1309.82	234.95	625.01	449.86	487.18	40160
贵港市	Guigang	1082.18	193.65	465.86	422.68	378.53	24857
玉林市	Yulin	1699.54	276.91	734.14	688.49	564.86	29387
百色市	Baise	1361.76	189.24	789.33	383.20	690.07	37479
贺州市	Hezhou	548.83	115.76	210.91	222.16	132.15	26802
河池市	Hechi	734.60	158.96	231.49	344.15	168.58	20921
来宾市	Laibin	663.69	159.96	250.08	253.65	183.98	30037
崇左市	Chongzuo	907.62	181.25	398.20	328.17	334.52	43678

3－7 各市生产总值、人均地区生产总值指数（2017年）
Indices of GDP & Per Capita GDP by City（2017）

（按可比价格计算，以上年为100） (calculated at comparable prices, preceding year = 100)

城 市	City	地区生产总值 Gross Domestic Product	第一产业 Primary Industry	第二产业 Secondary Industry	第三产业 Tertiary Industry	#工业 Industry	人均地区生产总值 Per Capita GDP
南宁市	Nanning	108.0	104.1	108.6	108.4	109.5	106.7
柳州市	Liuzhou	107.1	103.7	104.4	111.6	104.5	106.1
桂林市	Guilin	103.9	104.3	99.5	108.5	98.7	102.9
梧州市	Wuzhou	106.7	104.4	105.2	110.4	105.5	106.0
北海市	Beihai	110.2	103.7	110.5	113.3	111.3	108.9
防城港市	Fangchenggang	106.7	103.9	106.4	108.3	106.3	105.5
钦州市	Qinzhou	108.8	103.9	111.2	108.9	111.9	107.6
贵港市	Guigang	109.0	104.2	111.3	108.8	111.3	108.0
玉林市	Yulin	107.6	103.2	108.1	109.1	107.4	106.6
百色市	Baise	108.8	104.5	109.5	109.8	109.6	108.1
贺州市	Hezhou	105.3	104.3	101.6	109.9	97.1	104.5
河池市	Hechi	107.8	103.8	109.4	108.7	108.4	107.1
来宾市	Laibin	107.4	104.6	105.3	111.5	105.4	106.5
崇左市	Chongzuo	109.3	104.4	110.8	110.6	110.5	108.5

3－8 支出法广西生产总值（1978－2016年）

Gross Domestic Product by Expenditure Approach（1978－2016）

（按当年价格计算）（calculated at current prices） 单位：亿元（100 million yuan）

年 份 Year	支出法广西生产总值 Gross Domestic Product by Expenditure Approach	最终消费 Final Consumption Expenditure	居民消费 Resident Consumption	农村居民 Rural Households	城镇居民 Urban Households	政府消费 Government Consumption	资本形成总额 Total Capital Formation	固定资本 Fixed Assets Formation	存货增加 Inventory Increasement
1978	75.85	58.50	49.40	35.90	13.50	9.10	26.80	20.90	5.90
1979	84.59	64.60	54.50	38.80	15.70	10.10	26.20	20.60	5.60
1980	97.33	76.90	64.90	45.70	19.20	12.00	29.10	26.80	2.30
1981	113.46	86.00	73.10	52.00	21.10	12.90	32.70	27.00	5.80
1982	129.15	102.90	87.50	65.60	21.90	15.40	30.60	19.10	11.50
1983	134.60	108.70	91.80	67.90	23.90	16.90	32.40	23.30	9.10
1984	150.27	123.50	100.70	73.60	27.10	22.80	36.50	34.40	2.10
1985	180.97	142.80	115.50	87.80	27.70	27.30	61.80	42.20	19.60
1986	205.46	166.00	136.40	93.00	43.40	29.60	72.00	55.20	16.80
1987	241.56	186.50	153.50	102.40	51.10	33.00	79.70	62.70	17.00
1988	313.28	251.00	199.60	121.40	78.20	51.40	104.30	75.60	28.70
1989	383.44	293.10	231.10	142.20	88.90	62.00	111.50	70.80	40.70
1990	449.06	342.90	268.90	162.20	106.70	74.00	107.40	72.60	34.80
1991	518.59	391.30	303.60	175.30	128.30	87.70	137.10	99.40	37.80
1992	646.60	441.50	336.70	190.90	145.80	104.80	227.40	150.10	77.30
1993	871.70	566.00	439.60	230.40	209.20	126.40	350.50	278.10	72.50
1994	1198.29	790.20	622.10	300.20	321.90	168.10	472.30	382.60	89.70
1995	1497.56	1009.30	799.10	382.60	416.50	210.20	618.80	423.40	195.40
1996	1697.90	1214.10	968.20	482.90	485.30	245.90	597.00	483.60	113.40
1997	1817.25	1265.10	989.70	485.30	504.40	275.40	578.60	487.30	91.30
1998	1911.30	1312.00	1007.10	494.70	512.40	304.90	650.60	573.10	77.50
1999	1971.41	1350.40	1041.00	498.10	542.90	309.40	654.60	629.10	15.60
2000	2080.04	1448.30	1091.00	507.00	584.00	357.30	676.10	670.70	5.50
2001	2279.34	1595.40	1159.40	523.00	636.40	436.00	769.00	735.60	33.50
2002	2523.73	1699.70	1250.90	560.20	690.70	448.80	877.90	842.70	35.20
2003	2821.11	1859.50	1360.20	576.70	783.50	499.30	1030.40	990.70	39.70
2004	3433.50	2097.20	1538.00	625.10	912.90	559.20	1356.35	1296.55	59.80
2005	3984.10	2463.52	1808.47	727.32	1081.15	655.05	1798.25	1749.87	48.38
2006	4746.16	2779.59	2006.99	754.49	1252.50	772.60	2200.39	2141.72	58.67
2007	5835.33	3341.39	2425.83	833.08	1592.75	915.56	3008.82	2805.91	202.91
2008	7038.88	3877.14	2947.82	945.78	2002.04	929.32	4114.10	3783.61	330.49
2009	7784.98	4371.51	3369.86	1015.40	2354.46	1001.65	5825.96	5563.43	262.53
2010	9604.01	4936.44	3745.84	1088.89	2656.95	1190.60	7974.75	7825.45	149.30
2011	11764.97	5594.12	4248.30	1276.15	2972.15	1345.82	10087.62	9797.29	290.33
2012	13090.04	6527.43	4923.64	1442.13	3481.51	1603.79	9484.95	8963.83	521.12
2013	14511.70	7501.50	5604.51	1548.73	4055.78	1896.99	10197.57	9793.74	403.83
2014	15742.62	8182.66	6131.54	1718.09	4413.45	2051.12	10864.54	10537.80	326.74
2015	16870.04	8873.15	6645.66	1888.82	4756.84	2227.49	11524.47	11336.95	187.52
2016	18317.64	9834.45	7231.78	2076.80	5154.98	2602.67	12363.85	12114.06	249.79

注：根据国家统计局的布置，2005－2008年数据进行了调整。

Note: The data in from 2005 to 2008 has been adjusted by arrangement of National Statistic Bureau.

3-9 支出法广西生产总值构成（1978-2016年）
Composition of Gross Domestic Product by Expenditure Approach （1978-2016）

（按当年价格计算） (calculated at current prices) 单位：%（%）

年份 Year	支出法广西生产总值 Gross Domestic Product by Expenditure Approach	最终消费 Final Consumption Expenditure	居民消费 Resident Consumption	农村居民 Rural Households	城镇居民 Urban Households	政府消费 Government Consumption	资本形成总额 Total Capital Formation	固定资本 Fixed Assets Formation	存货增加 Inventory Increasement
1978	100.0	77.1	65.1	47.3	17.8	12.0	35.3	27.6	7.8
1979	100.0	76.4	64.4	45.9	18.6	11.9	31.0	24.4	6.6
1980	100.0	79.0	66.7	47.0	19.7	12.3	29.9	27.5	2.4
1981	100.0	75.8	64.4	45.8	18.6	11.4	28.8	23.8	5.1
1982	100.0	79.7	67.8	50.8	17.0	11.9	23.7	14.8	8.9
1983	100.0	80.8	68.2	50.4	17.8	12.6	24.1	17.3	6.8
1984	100.0	82.2	67.0	49.0	18.0	15.2	24.3	22.9	1.4
1985	100.0	78.9	63.8	48.5	15.3	15.1	34.1	23.3	10.8
1986	100.0	80.8	66.4	45.3	21.1	14.4	35.0	26.9	8.2
1987	100.0	77.2	63.5	42.4	21.2	13.7	33.0	26.0	7.0
1988	100.0	80.1	63.7	38.8	25.0	16.4	33.3	24.1	9.2
1989	100.0	76.4	60.3	37.1	23.2	16.2	29.1	18.5	10.6
1990	100.0	76.4	59.9	36.1	23.8	16.5	23.9	16.2	7.7
1991	100.0	75.5	58.5	33.8	24.7	16.9	26.4	19.2	7.3
1992	100.0	68.3	52.1	29.5	22.5	16.2	35.2	23.2	12.0
1993	100.0	64.9	50.4	26.4	24.0	14.5	40.2	31.9	8.3
1994	100.0	65.9	51.9	25.1	26.9	14.0	39.4	31.9	7.5
1995	100.0	67.4	53.4	25.5	27.8	14.0	41.3	28.3	13.0
1996	100.0	71.5	57.0	28.4	28.6	14.5	35.2	28.5	6.7
1997	100.0	69.6	54.5	26.7	27.8	15.2	31.8	26.8	5.0
1998	100.0	68.6	52.7	25.9	26.8	16.0	34.0	30.0	4.1
1999	100.0	68.5	52.8	25.3	27.5	15.7	33.2	31.9	0.8
2000	100.0	69.6	52.5	24.4	28.1	17.2	32.5	32.2	0.3
2001	100.0	70.0	50.9	22.9	27.9	19.1	33.7	32.3	1.5
2002	100.0	67.3	49.6	22.2	27.4	17.8	34.8	33.4	1.4
2003	100.0	65.9	48.2	20.4	27.8	17.7	36.5	35.1	1.4
2004	100.0	61.1	44.8	18.2	26.6	16.3	39.5	37.8	1.7
2005	100.0	61.8	45.4	18.3	27.1	16.4	45.1	43.9	1.2
2006	100.0	58.6	42.3	15.9	26.4	16.3	46.4	45.1	1.2
2007	100.0	57.3	41.6	14.3	27.3	15.7	51.6	48.1	3.5
2008	100.0	55.1	41.9	13.4	28.4	13.2	58.4	53.8	4.7
2009	100.0	56.2	43.3	13.0	30.2	12.9	74.8	71.5	3.4
2010	100.0	51.4	39.0	11.3	27.7	12.4	83.0	81.5	1.6
2011	100.0	47.5	36.1	10.8	25.3	11.4	85.7	83.3	2.5
2012	100.0	49.9	37.6	11.0	26.6	12.3	72.5	68.5	4.0
2013	100.0	51.7	38.6	10.7	27.9	13.1	70.3	67.5	2.8
2014	100.0	52.0	38.9	10.9	28.0	13.0	69.0	66.9	2.1
2015	100.0	52.6	39.4	11.2	28.2	13.2	68.3	67.2	1.1
2016	100.0	53.7	39.5	11.3	28.2	14.2	67.5	66.1	1.4

3－10　支出法广西生产总值指数（1978－2016年）

Indices of Gross Domestic Product by Expenditure Approach（1978－2016）

（按可比价格计算，以上年为100）　　(calculated at comparable prices, preceding year = 100)

年份 Year	支出法广西生产总值 Gross Domestic Product by Expenditure Approach	最终消费 Final Consumption Expenditure	居民消费 Resident Consumption	农村居民 Rural Households	城镇居民 Urban Households	政府消费 Government Consumption	资本形成总额 Total Capital Formation	固定资本 Fixed Assets Formation	存货增加 Inventory Increasement
1978	111.7	110.1	106.5	108.4	101.5	132.2	109.3	109.3	109.3
1979	103.4	101.8	100.6	97.2	110.4	108.5	91.5	92.1	90.2
1980	110.2	117.4	117.1	117.8	115.4	118.1	95.1	121.2	41.9
1981	108.0	111.2	111.8	114.0	106.5	107.9	100.0	89.6	221.7
1982	112.5	116.6	116.8	123.9	98.8	115.7	95.2	67.5	225.5
1983	103.3	104.4	103.6	102.9	105.9	108.7	106.5	130.2	73.0
1984	106.9	110.6	105.6	103.5	112.1	137.8	103.1	135.1	22.6
1985	111.0	111.0	111.5	110.4	114.6	108.8	159.9	115.1	831.6
1986	106.4	103.5	103.3	102.1	106.8	104.4	110.1	122.3	84.8
1987	109.2	104.9	104.9	102.9	110.2	104.8	102.6	105.2	94.8
1988	104.5	107.4	105.3	100.2	117.8	116.2	90.2	78.2	129.9
1989	103.6	95.3	98.4	100.7	93.6	83.5	110.5	97.0	137.6
1990	107.0	108.4	107.6	104.2	115.1	112.2	102.2	89.1	120.7
1991	112.7	113.3	111.9	108.6	116.8	118.5	112.6	115.7	106.0
1992	118.3	110.3	106.0	104.6	108.1	124.9	153.7	135.8	194.3
1993	118.3	107.8	110.8	102.0	122.8	99.3	151.8	196.0	81.5
1994	115.2	113.0	115.0	106.8	124.3	106.6	118.8	122.5	104.5
1995	111.4	112.1	113.3	115.9	110.7	108.2	122.6	107.0	192.8
1996	108.3	111.0	110.8	114.6	107.0	111.7	94.7	110.3	55.9
1997	108.0	107.7	105.0	103.6	106.5	117.8	97.2	100.5	81.3
1998	110.0	108.5	106.0	107.0	105.0	116.5	112.1	116.1	87.5
1999	108.0	107.4	107.7	108.9	106.4	106.4	106.9	114.4	46.5
2000	107.9	108.8	106.6	106.2	107.0	115.6	105.5	105.1	114.3
2001	108.3	108.5	105.1	102.5	107.3	118.9	112.0	107.5	658.9
2002	110.6	107.2	108.4	108.9	108.0	103.9	113.9	114.2	108.3
2003	110.2	107.1	106.1	100.4	110.8	110.0	115.2	115.5	110.1
2004	111.8	109.3	109.3	101.7	115.1	110.4	125.2	125.1	126.1
2005	113.2	115.4	115.7	115.4	116.0	114.5	130.3	133.1	69.4
2006	113.6	111.5	109.7	102.8	114.4	116.4	120.8	121.0	112.3
2007	115.3	112.8	113.1	101.4	120.3	111.9	133.0	128.1	322.1
2008	112.9	109.5	112.0	102.0	117.1	103.1	127.3	125.6	153.4
2009	114.0	112.6	116.8	110.0	119.9	100.5	144.3	149.2	82.3
2010	114.3	110.1	108.5	103.8	110.5	115.5	133.3	136.7	54.9
2011	112.3	106.3	106.1	108.4	105.2	106.7	119.5	118.3	181.1
2012	111.3	112.6	111.6	107.9	113.1	115.6	93.5	91.0	180.6
2013	110.2	112.6	111.5	104.8	114.3	115.8	107.3	109.0	78.3
2014	108.5	107.8	108.4	110.8	107.5	105.9	106.6	107.6	81.4
2015	108.1	108.1	108.3	109.7	107.7	107.5	106.7	107.3	88.3
2016	107.3	106.8	107.3	107.9	107.0	105.5	107.7	107.2	134.8

3－11 支出法广西生产总值指数（1978－2016年）

Indices of Gross Domestic Product by Expenditure Approach（1978－2016）

（按可比价格计算，以1978年为100） (calculated at comparable prices, 1978＝100)

年份 Year	支出法广西生产总值 Gross Domestic Product by Expenditure Approach	最终消费 Final Consumption Expenditure	居民消费 Resident Consumption	农村居民 Rural Households	城镇居民 Urban Households	政府消费 Government Consumption	资本形成总额 Total Capital Formation	固定资本 Fixed Assets Formation	存货增加 Inventory Increasement
1978	100.0	100.0	100.0	100.0	100.0	100.0	100.0	100.0	100.0
1979	103.4	101.8	100.6	97.2	110.4	108.5	91.5	92.1	90.2
1980	113.9	119.5	117.8	114.5	127.4	128.1	87.0	111.6	37.8
1981	123.1	132.9	131.7	130.5	135.7	138.3	87.0	100.0	83.8
1982	138.4	155.0	153.8	161.7	134.1	160.0	82.8	67.5	188.9
1983	143.0	161.8	159.4	166.4	142.0	173.9	88.2	87.9	137.9
1984	152.9	178.9	168.3	172.2	159.1	239.6	91.0	118.8	31.2
1985	169.7	198.6	187.6	190.2	182.4	260.7	145.4	136.7	259.2
1986	180.6	205.6	193.8	194.2	194.8	272.2	160.1	167.2	219.8
1987	197.2	215.6	203.3	199.8	214.6	285.2	164.3	175.9	208.4
1988	206.0	231.6	214.1	200.2	252.9	331.4	148.2	137.5	270.7
1989	213.5	220.7	210.7	201.6	236.7	276.8	163.8	133.4	372.5
1990	228.4	239.2	226.7	210.0	272.4	310.5	167.4	118.9	449.6
1991	257.5	271.1	253.7	228.1	318.2	368.0	188.4	137.5	476.6
1992	304.7	299.0	268.9	238.6	343.9	459.6	289.6	186.7	926.0
1993	360.4	322.3	297.9	243.4	422.4	456.4	439.7	366.0	754.7
1994	415.2	364.2	342.6	259.9	525.0	486.5	522.3	448.4	788.6
1995	462.4	408.3	388.2	301.3	581.2	526.4	640.4	479.8	1520.5
1996	500.9	453.2	430.1	345.2	621.9	588.0	606.4	529.2	849.9
1997	541.2	488.1	451.6	357.7	662.3	692.6	589.5	531.8	691.0
1998	595.4	529.6	478.7	382.7	695.4	806.9	660.8	617.4	604.6
1999	643.0	568.7	515.6	416.8	739.9	858.6	706.4	706.4	281.2
2000	693.8	618.8	549.6	442.6	791.7	992.5	745.2	742.4	321.4
2001	751.4	671.4	577.6	453.7	849.5	1180.1	834.7	798.1	2117.4
2002	831.0	719.7	626.2	494.0	917.4	1226.1	950.7	911.4	2293.2
2003	915.8	770.8	664.4	496.0	1016.5	1348.7	1095.2	1052.6	2524.8
2004	1023.8	842.5	726.2	504.5	1170.0	1489.0	1371.2	1316.9	3183.7
2005	1159.5	972.3	840.2	582.1	1357.2	1704.9	1786.6	1752.7	2209.5
2006	1317.2	1084.1	921.7	598.4	1552.6	1984.5	2158.3	2120.8	2481.3
2007	1518.7	1222.9	1042.4	606.8	1867.8	2220.7	2870.5	2716.7	7992.3
2008	1714.6	1339.1	1167.5	618.9	2187.2	2289.5	3654.1	3412.2	12260.2
2009	1954.6	1507.8	1363.6	680.8	2622.5	2300.9	5272.9	5091.0	10090.1
2010	2234.1	1660.1	1479.5	706.7	2897.9	2657.5	7028.8	6959.4	5539.5
2011	2508.9	1764.7	1569.7	766.1	3048.6	2835.6	8399.4	8233.0	10032.0
2012	2792.4	1987.1	1751.8	826.6	3448.0	3278.0	7853.4	7492.0	18117.8
2013	3077.2	2237.5	1953.3	866.3	3941.1	3795.9	8426.7	8166.3	14186.2
2014	3338.8	2412.0	2117.4	959.9	4236.7	4019.9	8982.9	8786.9	11547.6
2015	3609.2	2607.4	2293.1	1053.0	4562.9	4321.4	9584.8	9428.3	10196.5
2016	3872.7	2784.7	2460.5	1136.2	4882.3	4559.1	10322.8	10107.1	13744.9

3－12　主要年份按支出法计算的广西生产总值
Gross Domestic Product by Expenditure Approach in Main Years

（按当年价格计算）（calculated at current prices）　　单位：亿元（100 million yuan）

指　标	Item	2005	2010	2013	2014	2015	2016
支出法广西生产总值	**Gross Domestic Product by Expenditure Approach**	**3984.10**	**9604.01**	**14511.70**	**15742.62**	**16870.04**	**18317.64**
最终消费	Final Consumption Expenditure	2463.52	4936.44	7501.50	8182.66	8873.15	9834.45
居民消费	Resident Consumption	1808.47	3745.84	5604.51	6131.54	6645.66	7231.78
农村居民	Rural Households	727.32	1088.89	1548.73	1718.09	1888.82	2076.80
食品类支出	Expenditure for Food	370.61	474.81	547.02	599.32	676.36	727.29
衣着类支出	Expenditure for Clothes	24.82	31.30	44.85	47.31	51.71	63.64
居住类支出	Expenditure for Housing	50.61	68.35	139.11	150.77	355.85	363.43
家庭设备、用品及服务类支出	Expenditure for Household Equipment, Facilities & Services	29.82	61.44	73.76	82.34	92.16	116.24
医疗保健类支出	Expenditure for Medical Appliances & Articles	38.53	110.70	224.67	249.02	286.59	247.18
交通和通信类支出	Expenditure for Transportation & Communication	66.85	98.19	135.47	147.77	146.65	250.62
文教娱乐用品及服务类支出	Expenditure for Facilities & Services for Culture, Education & Entertainment	70.70	51.73	72.48	78.06	88.95	112.70
金融中介服务虚拟支出	Virtual Expenditure for Financial Agency Services	7.36	71.81	102.85	136.44	146.85	126.81
金融机构实际消费支出	Actual Expenditure for Financial Institutions	0.66	6.09	102.85			126.81
保险服务消费支出	Expenditure for Insurance Services	1.94	3.47	10.18	10.81	12.40	17.26
自有住房服务虚拟支出	Virtual Expenditure for Services for Private-owned Houses	51.32	93.34	171.44	183.97		
其它商品和服务类支出	Expenditure for Other Goods & Services	13.88	17.66	26.90	32.28	31.30	51.63
城镇居民	Urban Households	1081.15	2656.95	4055.78	4413.45	4756.84	5154.98
食品类支出	Expenditure for Food	413.73	828.85	1212.92	1349.11	1466.03	1360.80
衣着类支出	Expenditure for Clothes	71.17	175.60	210.95	226.94	249.27	303.13
居住类支出	Expenditure for Housing	99.81	221.18	345.22	386.11	704.60	784.85
家庭设备、用品及服务类支出	Expenditure for Household Equipment, Facilities & Services	57.48	161.80	225.60	247.12	272.66	305.67
医疗保健类支出	Expenditure for Medical Appliances & Articles	57.83	185.63	378.03	391.69	411.67	433.03
交通和通信类支出	Expenditure for Transportation & Communication	98.13	373.99	532.61	533.16	584.37	756.54
文教娱乐用品及服务类支出	Expenditure for Facilities & Services for Culture, Education & Entertainment	131.22	235.75	432.74	453.34	509.67	523.22
金融中介服务虚拟支出	Virtual Expenditure for Financial Agency Services	29.44	152.19	239.99	318.37	347.86	380.44
金融机构实际消费支出	Actual Expenditure for Financial Institutions	2.65	12.91	239.99			380.44
保险服务消费支出	Expenditure for Insurance Services	7.75	31.23	91.66	97.33	114.43	155.33
自有住房服务虚拟支出	Virtual Expenditure for Services for Private-owned Houses	46.16	165.70	257.17	275.96		
实物消费支出	Expenditure for In-kind Consumption	9.85	49.90	48.64	48.02		
其它商品和服务类支出	Expenditure for Other Goods & Services	32.44	62.22	80.25	86.30	96.28	151.97
政府消费	Government Consumption	655.05	1190.60	1896.99	2051.12	2227.49	2602.67

注：公共医疗消费支出数据从2009年开始合并到医疗保健支出中，2014年金融中介服务虚拟支出和金融机构实际消费支出合并为银行中介服务支出，2015年自有住房服务虚拟支出合并到居住支出中。

Note: The data on "Expenditure for Public Medical Care" has been combined into "Expenditure for Medical Appliances & Articles" since 2009. The indicator "Virtual Expenditure for Financial Agency Services" and "Actual Expenditure for Financial Institutions" have been combined as "Expenditure for Intermediary Services of Banks", and the indicator "Virtual Expenditure for Services for Private-owned Houses" is merged into "Expenditure for Housing" since 2015.

主要统计指标解释

地区生产总值（原国内生产总值） 是指一个地区所有常住单位在一定时期内生产活动的最终成果。地区生产总值有三种表现形态,即价值形态、收入形态和产品形态。从价值形态看，它是所有常住单位在一定时期内所生产的全部货物和服务价值超过同期投入的全部非固定资产货物和服务价值的差额，即所有常住单位的增加值之和；从收入形态看，它是所有常住单位在一定时期内所创造并分配给常住单位和非常住单位的初次分配收入之和；从产品形态看，它是最终使用的货物和服务减去进口货物和服务。在核算中， 地区生产总值的三种表现形态表现为三种计算方法，即生产法、收入法和支出法。三种方法分别从不同的方面反映地区生产总值及其构成。根据国家统计局有关我国GDP核算和数据发布制度的规定，广西国内生产总值自2004年起更名为“广西生产总值”，简称“广西GDP”。

地区生产净值 是市场价格计算的地区生产净值的简称，它等于地区生产总值减去所有常住单位的固定资产折旧。

地区收入总值 是按市场价格计算的地区收入总值的简称。它是一个国家或地区所有常住单位在一定时期内收入初次分配的最终成果。一地区常住单位从事生产活动所创造的增加值在初次分配过程中主要分配给该地区的常住单位，但也有一部分以生产税及进口税（扣除生产和进口补贴）、劳动者报酬和财产收入等形式分配给非常住单位，同时，地区外生产所创造的增加值也有一部分以生产税及进口税（扣除生产和进口补贴）、劳动者报酬和财产收入的形式分配给该地区的常住单位，从而产生了地区收入总值概念。它等于地区生产总值加上来自地区外的净要素收入。地区生产总值是一个生产概念，而地区收入总值总值是个收入概念。

地区收入净值 是按市场价格计算的地区收入净值简称，它等于地区收入总值减所有常住单位的固定资产折旧。

三次产业 是根据社会生产活动历史发展的顺序对产业结构的划分，产品直接取自然界的部门称为第一产业，对初级产品进行再加工的部门称为第二产业，为生产和消费提供各种服务的部门称为第三产业。

我国的三次产业划分是:

第一产业：农业（包括种植业、林业、牧业和渔业）。

第二产业：工业（包括采掘业，制造业，电力、煤气及水的生产和供应业）和建筑业。

第三产业：除第一、第二产业以外的其他各业。由于第三产业包括的行业多，范围广，根据我国的实际情况，第三产业又分为两大部分：一是流通部门，二是服务部门。

增加值 是指常住单位生产过程中创造的新增价值和固定资产的转移价值。它可以按生产法计算，也可以按收入法计算。按生产法计算，它等于总产出减去中间投入；按收入法计算，它等于劳动者报酬、生产税净额、固定资产折旧和营业盈余之和。

劳动者报酬 是指劳动者因从事生产活动所获得的全部报酬。它包括劳动者获得的各种形式工资、奖金和津贴，既包括货币形式的，也包括实物形式的，还包括劳动者所享受的公费医疗和医药卫生费、上下班交通补贴和单位支付的社会保险费等。单位支付的社会保险费，就是单位直接支付给负责社会保险的政府单位（一般指劳动部门）的社会保险金或为本单位职工离退休、发生死亡、伤残、医疗保险等而支付的保险费。对于个体经济来说，其所有者所获得的劳动报酬和经营利润不易区分，这两部分统一作为劳动者报酬处理。

生产税净额 是指生产税减生产补贴后的差额。生产税指政府对生产单位生产、销售和从事经营活动以及因从事生产活动使用某些生产要素，如固定资产、土地、劳动力所征收的各种税、附加费和规费。具体包括销售税金及附加、增值税、管理费中开支的各种税、应交纳的养路费、排污费和水电费附加、烟酒专卖上缴政府的专项收入等。生产补贴与生产税相反，是政府对生产单位的单方面收入转移，因此视为负生产税处理，包括政策亏损补贴、粮食系统价格补贴、外贸企业出口退税收入等。

固定资产折旧 是指一定时期内为弥补固定资产损耗按照核定的固定资产折旧率提取的固定资产折旧，或按国民经济核算统一规定的折旧率虚拟计算的固定资产折旧。它反映了固定资产在当期生产中的转移价值。

营业盈余 是指常住单位创造的增加值扣除劳动者报酬、生产税净额和固定资产折旧后的余额。它相当于企业的营业利润加上生产补贴，但要扣除从利润中开支的工资和福利等。

支出法地区生产总值 指一个地区所有常住单位在一定时期内用于最终消费、资本形成总额、以及货物和服务的净流出总额，它反映本期生产的地区生产总值的使用及结构。

最终消费 是指常住单位在一定时期内对于货物和服务的全部最终消费支出，也就是常住单位为满足物质、文化和精神生活的需要，从本地区经济领土和国外购买的货物和服务的支出。它不包括非常住单位在本地区经济领土内的消费支出。最终消费分为居民消费和政府消费。

居民消费 指常住住户在一定时期内对于货物和服务的全部最终消费支出。居民关于货物的最终消费支出在货物的所有权发生变化时记录，关于服务的最终消费支出在服务提供的时候记录。居民消费按市场价格计算，即按居民支付的购买者价格计算，货物的购买者价格是购买者取得交货所支付的价格，它包括购买者支付的运输和商业费用。

政府消费 指政府部门为全社会提供的公共服务的消费支出和免费或以较低的价格向居民住户提供的货物和服务的净支出，前者等于政府服务的产出价值减去政府单位所获得的经营收入的价值，政府服务的产出价值等于它的经常性业务支出加上固定资产折旧；后者等于政府部门免费或以较低价格向居民住户提供的货物和服务的市场价值减去向住户收取的价值。

资本形成总额 指常住单位在一定时期内对固定资产和存货的投资支出合计，包括固定资本形成总额和存货增加。

固定资本形成总额 指常住单位在一定时期内购置、转入和自产自用的固定资产，扣除固定资产的销售和转出后的价值。可分为有形固定资本形成总额和无形固定资本形成总额。

存货增加 指常住单位在一定时期内存货实物量变动的市场价值，即期末价值减期初价值的差额，存货增加可以是正值，也可以是负值，正值表示存货上升，负值表示存货下降。它包括生产单位购进的原材料、燃料和储备物资等存货，以及生产单位生产的产成品、在制品和半成品等存货等。

货物和服务净流出 指货物和服务流出减货物和服务流进的差额。流出包括常住单位向非常住单位出售或无偿转让的各种货物和服务的价值；流进包括常住单位从非常住单位购买或无偿得到的各种货物和服务的价值。

来自国（地区）外的净要素收入 指一个国家（地区）来自国外（地区外）的生产税及进口税（扣除生产及进口补贴）、劳动者报酬和财产收入，减去支付给国外（地区外）的生产税及进口税（扣除生产及进口补贴）、劳动者报酬和财产收入的差额。国内（地区）生产总值加上来自国外的净要素收入等于国民生产总值（或地区收入总值）。

Explanatory Notes on Main Statistical Indicators

Gross Domestic Product (GDP) refers to the final products of all resident units in a region during a certain period of time. Gross domestic product is expressed in three different forms, i.e. value added, income, and products respectively. The form of value added refers to the total value of all products and services produced by all resident units during a certain period of time minus total value of input of materials and services of the nature of non-fixed assets of the summation of the value added of all resident units; the form of income includes all the income created by all resident units and distributed primarily to all resident and non-resident units; the form of products refers to all final goods and services minus imports of goods and services. In the practice of national accounting, gross domestic product is calculated with three approaches, i.e. product approach, income approach, and expenditure approach respectively to reflect gross domestic product and its composition from different aspects.

Net Value of Domestic Product is the abbreviation for net value of domestic product calculated in market prices. It equals to gross domestic product minus the depreciation of fixed assets of total resident units.

Gross National Product is the abbreviation for net value of domestic national product calculated by market prices. It is the final income that after first distribution of all resident units in a country (or region) in a certain period of time. The added value created during productive activities in resident units in a country is mainly distributed to the resident units in this country, while a part of it to non-resident units in form of taxes on production and import (deducted subsidies for production and importation), laborers' remuneration and income from property, then come out the concept of gross domestic product. It equals to gross domestic product adds income of net elements from foreign countries. GDP is a concept of production, while GNP is a concept of income.

Net Value of Gross National Product is the abbreviation for net value of national product calculated in market prices. It equals to gross national product minus the depreciation of fixed assets of total resident units.

Three Industries Industry structure has been classified according to the historical sequence of development. Primary industry refers to extraction of natural resources; secondary industry involves processing of primary products; and tertiary industry provides services of various kinds for production and consumption. Industry in China comprises:

Primary industry: agriculture (including farming, forestry, animal husbandry and fishery).

Secondary industry: industry (including mining and quarrying, manufacturing, and electricity, gas and water production and supply).

Tertiary industry: all other industries not included in primary or secondary industry. Since tertiary industry includes various trades and is with extensive coverage, it is divided into 2 parts according to our country's actual situation: circulation department and service department.

Value Added refers to the newly increased value and the transfer value of fixed assets created by all resident units in a country (or a region) during a certain period of time. It can be calculated by production approach and income approach. In terms of product approach, it is the total output minus intimidates input. In terms of income approach, it is the summation of laborers' remuneration, net taxes on production, depreciation of fixes assets and operating surplus.

Laborers' Remuneration refers to the whole payment of various forms earned by the laborers from the productive activities they are engaged in. It includes wages, bonuses and allowance the laborers earned in monetary form and in kind. It also includes the free medical services provided to the laborers and the medicine expenses, traffic subsidies and social insurance free paid by the laborers'working units for them. Social insurance free paid by the laborers' working units refers to the social insurance directly paid by units to government institutions in charge of social insurance, or premiums paid by units for retired employees, death, invalidity and medical treatment of workers and staff in this unit. As the individual economy is concerned, since the laborers' remuneration is not easily distinguished from the operating profit, both are treated as laborers remuneration.

Net Taxes on Production refers to the residual of the taxes on production minus the subsidies on production. The taxes on production refer to the various taxes, extra charges and fees levied on the production units on their production, sail and business activities as well as on some factors of production, such as fixed assets land and labor force, used in the production activities they are engaged in. Concretely, they include taxes on sales, additional tax, value added tax, various taxes from expense for administration, way maintenance fee, waste discharging fee and electricity and water bills should be paid, and specific income from monopoly tobacco and liquor turned in government. In contrast to the taxes on production, the subsidies on production refer to the unilateral transfer of part of the government's revenue to the production units and are therefore regarded as negative taxes on production. They include subsidies on the loss due to implementation of government policies, price subsidies to the grain institutions, foreign trade corporations' receipts from drawback, etc.

Depreciation of Fixes Assets refers to the depreciation of fixed assets of a given period, drawn in accordance with the stipulated depreciation rate for purpose of compensating the wear loss of the fixed assets or the depreciation of fixed assets calculated in a fictitious way in accordance with the stipulated unified depreciation rate in the national economic accounting system. It reflects the value of transfer of the fixed assets in the production of the current period.

Operating Surplus refers to the balance of the value added created by the resident units deducting the laborers' remuneration, net taxes on production and the depreciation of fixed assets. It is equivalent to the business profit of the enterprises plus subsidies on production, but the wages and welfare expenses paid from the profits should be deducted.

GDP Calculated by Expenditure Approach refers to total expenditure on final consumption, total capital formation and net export of goods and services by resident units of a region in a certain period of time. It reflects the composition of GDP by its use.

Final Consumption refers to the total expenditure of resident units on final consumption of goods and services in a certain period, namely the expenditure of the resident units for purchase the goods and services from domestic economic territory and abroad to meet the requirements of material, cultural and spiritual life. It excludes the expenditure of non-resident units on consumption in the economic territory of the country. The final consumption is classified into household consumption and government consumption.

Household Consumption refers to the total expenditure of resident households on the final consumption of goods and services in a certain period. The expenditure of resident households on the final consumption of goods is recorded when the proprietary rights of goods changed, and the expenditure of resident households on the final consumption of services is recorded when the services are providing. The households' consumption is calculated at market prices, namely the purchaser's prices that the households pay; the purchaser's prices of goods are the prices the households pay when they obtain the goods including the transport and commercial expenses paid by the households.

Government Consumption refers to the expenditure on the consumption of the public services provided by the government to the whole society and the net expenditure on the goods and services provided by the government to the households at free charge or lower prices. The former equals to the output value of the government services minus the value of operating income obtained by the government departments, and the output value of the government services equals to its current operating expenditure plus depreciation of fixed assets. The latter equals to the market value of goods and services provided by the government free of charge or at low prices to the households minus the value received by the government from the households.

Total Capital Formation refers to the fixed assets acquired minus those disposed and the change in inventory including the total fixed assets formation and the increase in inventory.

Total Fixed Capital Formation refers to the value of fixed assets purchased, transferred in by the resident units and those produced and used by themselves deducting the value of fixed assets sold and transferred out. It can be classified into total tangible assets formation and total intangible formation.

Increase in Inventory refers to the market value of the change in inventory, i.e. the difference of value between the beginning and the end of the period. The increase in inventory can be positive or negative. A positive value indicates the increase in inventory while a negative value indicates the decrease in stock. The inventory includes the raw materials, fuels, and reserve materials purchased by the production units as well as the inventory of finished products, products work-in-progress and semi finished products ect.

Net Export of Goods and Services refers to the difference of the exports of goods and services minus the imports of goods and services. The imports include the value of various goods and services sold or gratuitously transferred by the resident units to the non-resident units. The imports included the value of various goods and services purchased or gratuitously acquired by the resident units from the non-resident units.

Income of Net Elements from Foreign Countries (Regions) refers to the balance, which taxes on production and import (deducted subsidies for production and importation), laborers' remuneration and income from property from foreign countries (regions) minus the ones paid to foreign countries (regions). GDP adds income of net elements from foreign countries (regions) equals GNP.

第四篇

从业人员和职工工资

EMPLOYMENT & WAGES

（校对编辑：韦　昆）

4—1　主要年份就业和劳动报酬基本情况

指　标	Items	1995	2000	2005	2010
劳动力资源总数（万人）	**Total Resource of Labor Force(10 000 persons)**	**2907**	**3203**	**3536**	**3732**
占人口总数比重（%）	Proportion in Total Population (%)	64.0	67.4	71.8	72.3
劳动力资源利用率（%）	Utilization Ratio of Resource of Labor Force (%)	82.0	80.1	76.4	77.8
从业人员合计（万人）	**Employed Persons (10 000 persons)**	**2383**	**2566**	**2703**	**2903**
第一产业	Primary Industry	1583	1571	1519	1571
第二产业	Secondary Industry	282	278	322	544
第三产业	Tertiary Industry	518	717	862	788
从业人员构成（%）	**Composition of Employment Persons(%)**				
第一产业	Primary Industry	66.4	61.2	56.2	54.1
第二产业	Secondary Industry	11.8	10.8	11.9	18.7
第三产业	Tertiary Industry	21.8	28.0	31.9	27.1
按城乡分从业人员	**Employed Persons by Urban & Rural**				
城镇从业人员（万人）	Urban Employed Persons (10 000 persons)	405	421	785	1003
国有单位	State Owned Units	293.45	234.52	199.00	203.32
城镇集体单位	Urban Collective Owned Units	48.72	28.36	20.00	17.27
股份合作单位	Cooperative Share Holding Units		1.39	2.00	2.96
联营单位	Joint-owned Units	0.42	0.34	1.00	0.75
有限责任公司	Limited-liability Companies		15.09	34.00	49.82
股份有限公司	Share Holding Limited Companies	6.00	8.79	11.00	15.15
港澳台商投资单位	Enterprises Funded by Hong Kong, Macao & Taiwan	1.62	2.97	5.50	8.23
外商投资单位	Foreign-funded Enterprises	5.66	3.83	6.20	8.99
私营企业	Private Enterprises	9.01	22.14	54.00	100.00
个体	Individual	52.99	67.86	90.00	141.00
在岗职工人数（万人）	Number of Staff & Workers at Post (10 000 persons)	343.00	283.00	269.00	291.98
国有单位	State-owned Units	283.00	225.00	189.00	187.53
城镇集体单位	Urban Collective Owned Units	47.00	26.00	18.00	13.57
其他类型单位	Others	13.00	32.00	62.00	90.87
乡村从业人员（万人）	Rural (10 000 persons)	1965	2145	2275	2387
城镇单位从业人员劳动报酬	**Remuneration of Staff & Workers in Urban Units**				
非私营单位从业人员平均劳动报酬（元）	Average Remuneration of Staff & Workers in Non-private Enterprise (Yuan)	5105	6772	15079	30673
国有单位	State-owned Units	5226	7081	15668	32587
城镇集体单位	Urban Collective owned Units	4064	4471	10392	21533
城镇私营单位从业人员平均劳动报酬（元）	**Average Remuneration of Staff & Workers in Private Enterprise (Yuan)**				
城镇登记失业人数（万人）	**Registered Unemployment in Urban Areas (10 000 persons)**	**10.10**	**11.30**	**18.51**	**19.07**
城镇登记失业率（%）	**Registered Unemployment Rate in Urban Areas (%)**	**2.4**	**3.2**	**4.2**	**3.7**

注：1. 2002年以后城镇从业人员数含农村进城从业人员。2012年按常住人口口径统计，劳动力资源总数、从业人员人数不包括外出自治区以外半年以上的人员。
2. 根据国家劳动统计报表制的统一规定，从2013年年报起，将原属于乡镇企业的“四上”企业（即规模以上工业企业，有资质的建筑业及全部房地产开发经营企业，限额以上批发和零售业、限额以上住宿餐饮业企业，部分规模以上服务业企业）纳入城镇单位从业人员与工资统计范围。
3. 本篇“城镇单位”均指“城镇非私营单位”。（下同）

Note:1. Employed population in urban areas since 2002 include employed persons entering urban areas from rural areas.sinve 2012, the statistical range of excludes the persons leaving Guangxi for more than half a year.
2. Accoding to the standard of National Statistical System of Labour Report,the onterprises of “4 Aboves” (industrial enterprises above designated size, qualified construction enterprises and all of the enterprises of real estate development & management, whloe sale & retail trade hotels & catering above designated size, and some service enterprises above designated size) which belonged to rural enterprises have been included to the statistical range of employment & wages of urban units since 2013.
3. In this chapter,urban corporate units refers to urban corporate unit excluding private units.

Resource of Labor Force & Number of Employed Persons in Main Years

2011	2012	2013	2014	2015	2016	2017
3777	**3349**	**3373**	**3399**	**3438**	**3465**	**3498**
72.7	71.5	71.5	71.5	71.7	71.6	71.6
77.7	82.7	82.5	82.3	82.0	82.0	81.3
2936	**2768**	**2782**	**2795**	**2820**	**2841**	**2842**
1565	1481	1478	1450	1427	1423	1415
562	520	529	540	513	500	498
809	767	775	805	880	918	929
53.3	53.5	53.1	51.9	50.6	50.1	49.8
19.1	18.8	19.0	19.3	18.2	17.6	17.5
27.6	27.7	27.9	28.8	31.2	32.3	32.7
1035	1113	1120	1145	1198	1236	1247
209.49	214.03	210.93	206.48	202.37	201.82	201.61
18.76	16.25	14.39	15.09	13.27	13.21	12.44
2.78	3.29	2.18	2.04	2.06	1.88	1.67
0.79	0.99	0.21	0.15	0.14	0.11	0.07
58.11	68.55	108.38	113.59	125.21	123.25	125.95
19.69	19.81	27.73	27.66	27.55	27.41	24.62
9.53	11.18	17.41	17.20	16.36	16.17	16.38
11.06	10.53	14.42	13.43	12.92	12.98	11.39
123.00	137.34	130.00	152.00	168.00	247.00	248.67
157.00	139.15	168.00	190.00	212.00	252.00	270.30
293.60	303.45	330.23	326.50	329.60	325.50	316.73
187.90	190.45	186.35	184.15	178.80	178.36	175.28
15.41	12.12	11.15	10.82	10.08	9.62	8.78
90.27	100.88	132.73	131.54	140.72	137.50	132.67
2407	1655	1662	1650	1622	1605	1595
33032	36386	41391	45424	52982	57878	63821
34886	37706	42552	46065	57247	63751	70407
22123	28819	32197	36874	40510	43064	46457
					36089	38227
18.81	**18.94**	**18.09**	**18.66**	**18.13**	**18.13**	**14.72**
3.5	**3.4**	**3.3**	**3.2**	**2.9**	**2.9**	**2.2**

4－2　城乡从业人员及城镇单位在岗职工平均工资（1978－2017年）
Urban & Rural Employed Persons, Average Wages of Staff & Workers at Post in Urban Units（1978－2017）

年　份 Year	从业人员（万人） Employed Persons(10 000 persons)			城镇单位在岗职工平均工资 Average Wages of Staff & Workers at Post in Urban Units	
	第一产业 Primary Industry	第二产业 Secondary Industry	第三产业 Tertiary Industry	绝对数（元） Absolute Number (yuan)	指数（上年=100） Indices (Preceding year=100)
1978	1171	153	132	462	104.5
1980	1283	125	142	609	108.5
1985	1463	160	207	1077	99.9
1986	1501	177	218	1282	128.6
1987	1529	193	239	1438	108.1
1988	1548	205	259	1720	106.9
1989	1575	203	269	1819	108.9
1990	1614	207	288	2049	137.2
1991	1643	215	313	2262	105.7
1992	1628	235	355	2634	111.8
1993	1594	253	428	3368	111.0
1994	1589	268	479	4468	130.4
1995	1583	282	518	5105	121.4
1996	1600	283	534	5397	118.2
1997	1606	283	565	5540	107.5
1998	1620	283	596	5779	108.2
1999	1619	276	619	6254	108.1
2000	1571	278	717	7650	118.9
2001	1570	275	733	9075	117.1
2002	1571	270	748	10774	121.6
2003	1556	279	766	11953	108.7
2004	1532	283	817	13579	110.1
2005	1519	322	862	15461	115.1
2006	1521	334	905	18064	118.8
2007	1521	419	829	21898	116.3
2008	1528	424	847	25660	115.0
2009	1561	516	771	28302	121.0
2010	1571	544	788	31842	107.0
2011	1565	562	809	34150	104.0
2012	1481	520	767	37614	113.0
2013	1478	529	775	42637	114.5
2014	1451	540	805	46846	110.0
2015	1427	513	880	54983	118.0
2016	1423	500	918	60239	109.5
2017	1415	498	929	66456	108.6

4—3 按产业、经济类型分组的从业人员（2017年）

Number of Employed Persons Grouped by Industry & the Categories of Registration（2017）

单位：万人 (10 000 persons)

行业	Sector	从业人员 Employed Persons	国有单位 State-owned Units	城镇集体单位 Urban Collective Owned Units	其他类型单位 Others
总计	**Total**	**2842**	**201.61**	**12.44**	**183.97**
第一产业	**Primary Industry**	**1415**	**6.59**	**0.02**	**0.65**
农、林、牧、渔业	Farming, Forestry, Animal Husbandry & Fishery		6.59	0.02	0.65
第二产业	**Secondary Industry**	**498**	**11.20**	**8.50**	**127.53**
工业	Industry		4.79	1.46	75.83
采矿业	Mining		0.12	0.03	3.27
制造业	Manufacturing		2.86	1.38	62.62
电力、煤气及水的生产和供应业	Electricity, Gas & Water Production & Supply		1.81	0.05	9.94
建筑业	Construction		6.41	7.03	51.70
第三产业	**Tertiary Industry**	**929**	**183.82**	**3.93**	**55.80**
交通运输、仓储和邮政业	Transportation, Storage & Postal Services		2.17	0.63	9.93
信息传输、计算机服务和软件业	Information Transmission, Computer Service & Software Industries		9.47	0.42	9.12
批发和零售业	Wholesale & Retail Trade		0.76	0.07	3.61
住宿和餐饮业	Hotel & Catering Trade		0.25	0.00	3.77
金融业	Finance		4.84	1.37	8.45
房地产业	Real Estate		0.61	0.14	7.13
租赁和商务服务业	Leasing & Business Service		2.99	0.76	7.01
科学研究、技术服务和地质勘查业	Scientific Research, Technology Service & Geological Prospecting		6.65	0.08	1.59
水利、环境和公共设施管理业	Water Conservancy, Environment & Public Facility Management		7.31	0.09	0.51
居民服务和其他服务业	Residents & Other Services		0.23	0.12	0.36
教育	Education		60.05	0.18	2.21
卫生、社会保障和社会福利业	Public Health, Social Security & Social Welfare		32.24	0.04	1.04
文化、体育和娱乐业	Culture, Sports & Entertainment		2.34	0.00	0.97
公共管理和社会组织	Public Administration & Social Organizations		53.90	0.02	0.10
国际组织	International Organizations				

4—4 城镇单位从业人员（2017年）
Number of Employed Persons in Urban Units (2017)

单位：人 (person)

项 目	Item	从业人员年末人数 Total Employed Persons at Year End	在岗职工 Staff & Workers at Post	劳务派遣工 Labor-dispatched Workers	其他从业人员 Others
总　计	**Total**	**3980260**	**3167341**	**495862**	**317057**
按登记注册类型分	**By Registered Style**				
国有单位	State-owned Units	2016121	1752789	94356	168976
城镇集体单位	Urban Collective Owned Units	124406	87795	8148	28463
其他类型单位	Others	1839733	1326757	393358	119618
内资	Domestic Capital	1562055	1073390	377757	110908
外商投资	Foreign Investment	113850	104383	6375	3092
港、澳、台投资	Enterprise Funded by Hong Kong, Macao & Taiwan	163828	148984	9226	5618
按企业、事业、机关分	**By Enterprise,Institution & Agency**				
企业	Enterprise	2285990	1641808	453223	190959
事业	Institution	1198183	1096387	17203	84593
机关	Agency	464634	405814	23121	35699
民间非营利组织	Nongovernmental Nonprofit Organizations & Others	11203	10796	115	292
其他	others	20250	12536	2200	5514
按国民经济行业分	**By Sector**				
农、林、牧、渔业	Farming,Forestry,Animal Husbandry & Fishery	72575	45316	174	27085
采矿业	Mining	34253	31180	1862	1211
制造业	Manufacturing	668708	605815	37865	25028
电力、煤气及水的生产和供应业	Electricity, Gas & Water Production & Supply	117905	110170	3918	3817
建筑业	Construction	651386	242230	345632	63524
批发和零售业	Wholesale & Retail Trade	127344	115888	4267	7189
交通运输、仓储和邮政业	Transportation, Storage & Postal Services	190175	156737	22570	10868
住宿和餐饮业	Hotel & Catering Trade	44410	42272	605	1533
信息传输、计算机服务和软件业	Information Transmission, Com- puter Service & Software Industries	40165	35597	3123	1445
金融业	Finance	146658	100968	5656	40034
房地产业	Real Estate	78815	69367	4222	5226
租赁和商务服务业	Leasing & Business Service	107708	77776	23554	6378
科学研究、技术服务和地质勘查业	Scientific Research, Technology Service & Geological Prospecting	83177	74230	2030	6917
水利、环境和公共设施管理业	Water Conservancy, Environment & Public Facility Management	79014	60726	4797	13491
居民服务和其他服务业	Residents & Other Services	7067	5382	745	940
教育	Education	624407	577533	4908	41966
卫生、社会保障和社会福利业	Public Health,Social Security & Social Welfare	333140	316107	2782	14251
文化、体育和娱乐业	Culture, Sports & Entertainment	33127	30204	565	2358
公共管理和社会组织	Public Administration & Social Organizations	540226	469843	26587	43796
国际组织	International Organizations				

4—5 按行业、经济类型分组的城镇单位女性从业人数（2017年）
Number of Female Employed in Urban Units Grouped by Industry & the Categories of Registration（2017）

单位：人 (person)

行 业	Sector	合 计 Total	国有单位 State-owned Units	城镇集体单位 Urban Collective owned Units	其他类型单位 Others
总 计	**Total**	**1559238**	**941381**	**31127**	**586730**
按企业、事业、机关分	**By Enterprise, Institution & Agency**				
企业	Enterprise	706259	109934	27988	568337
事业	Institution	679889	672908	1657	5324
机关	Agency	157114	156657	34	423
民间非营利组织	Nongovernmental Nonprofit Organizations	8256	296	366	7594
其他	Others	7720	1586	1082	5052
按国民经济行业分	**By Sector**				
第一产业	**Primary Industry**	**25909**	**23735**	**43**	**2131**
农、林、牧、渔业	Farming, Forestry, Animal Husbandry & Fishery	25909	23735	43	2131
第二产业	**Secondary Industry**	**364458**	**19593**	**16331**	**328534**
工业	Industry	303992	14429	6169	283394
采矿业	Mining	7453	172	89	7192
制造业	Manufacturing	263048	8186	5958	248904
电力、煤气及水的生产和供应业	Electricity, Gas & Water Production & Supply	33491	6071	122	27298
建筑业	Construction	60466	5164	10162	45140
第三产业	**Tertiary Industry**	**1168871**	**898053**	**14753**	**256065**
批发和零售业	Wholesale & Retail Trade	63250	7544	2435	53271
交通运输、仓储和邮政业	Transportation, Storage & Postal Services	49526	23008	1651	24867
住宿和餐饮业	Hotel & Catering Trade	27146	4389	476	22281
信息传输、计算机服务和软件业	Information Transmission, Computer Service & Software Industries	17397	831	1	16565
金融业	Finance	80946	26339	5317	49290
房地产业	Real Estate	31945	2563	566	28816
租赁和商务服务业	Leasing & Business Service	36080	10265	1639	24176
科学研究、技术服务和地质勘查业	Scientific Research, Technology Service & Geological Prospecting	28417	23150	259	5008
水利、环境和公共设施管理业	Water Conservancy, Environment & Public Facility Management	41026	38236	471	2319
居民服务和其他服务业	Residents & Other Services	3213	817	606	1790
教育	Education	362100	345627	1034	15439
卫生、社会保障和社会福利业	Public Health, Social Security & Social Welfare	229341	221943	245	7153
文化、体育和娱乐业	Culture, Sports & Entertainment	15500	10738		4762
公共管理和社会组织	Public Administration & Social Organizations	182984	182603	53	328
国际组织	International Organizations				

4—6　城镇单位从业人员工资总额（2017年）

Earning of Employed Persons in Urban Units （2017）

单位：万元　　　　(10 000 yuan)

指　标	Item	从业人员全年工资总额 Total Remunerationl	在岗职工工资总额 Wages of Staff & Workers at Post	劳务派遣工工资总额 Total Wages of Labor-dispatched Workers	其他从业人员工资总额 Remuneration Payment to Other Employed Persons
总　计	**Total**	**24874547**	**21535962**	**2342096**	**996490**
按登记注册类型分	**By Registered Style**				
国有单位	State Owned Units	14053504	13221281	366070	466153
城镇集体单位	Urban Collective Owned Units	551413	422472	31071	97870
其他类型单位	Others	10269630	7892209	1944955	432466
内资	Domestic Funds	8766096	6491130	1881147	393819
外商投资	Foreign Investment	751792	706966	30807	14018
港、澳、台投资	Enterprises Funded by Hong Kong, Macao & Taiwan	751743	694113	33001	24629
按企业、事业、机关分	**By Enterprise,Institution & Agency**				
企业	Enterprise	13127698	10263899	2205463	658336
事业	Institution	8294553	8013346	51222	229985
机关	Agency	3311940	3149562	73524	88854
民间非营利组织及其他	Nongovernmental Nonprofit Organizations & Others	140357	109154	11888	19314
按国民经济行业分	**By Sector**				
农、林、牧、渔业	Farming, Forestry, Animal Husbandry & Fishery	264009	191677	559	71772
采矿业	Mining	183186	169361	8990	4835
制造业	Manufacturing	3564052	3313819	164132	86101
电力、煤气及水的生产和供应业	Electricity, Gas & Water Production & Supply	925712	901089	16620	8003
建筑业	Construction	3118001	1160369	1746518	211113
批发和零售业	Wholesale & Retail Trade	686295	645543	18426	22325
交通运输、仓储和邮政业	Transportation, Storage & Postal Services	1405204	1232546	124145	48514
住宿和餐饮业	Hotel & Catering Trade	149961	142350	2558	5053
信息传输、计算机服务和软件业	Information Transmission, Computer Service & Software Industries	374185	349823	15794	8568
金融业	Finance	1403775	1218593	24442	160741
房地产业	Real Estate	436744	402932	16864	16949
租赁和商务服务业	Leasing & Business Service	540222	450204	68334	21685
科学研究、技术服务和地质勘查业	Scientific Research, Technology Service & Geological Prospecting	655987	621511	9845	24632
水利、环境和公共设施管理业	Water Conservancy, Environ- ment & Public Facility Management	353372	303359	15185	34827
居民服务和其他服务业	Resident & Other Services	34245	28599	2462	3184
教育	Education	4186153	4081784	12577	91792
卫生、社会保障和社会福利业	Public Health, Social Security & Social Welfare	2590866	2519328	8854	62684
文化、体育和娱乐业	Culture, Sports & Entertainment	229471	221210	2457	5804
公共管理和社会组织	Public Administration & Social Organizations	3773108	3581867	83335	107906
国际组织	International Organizations				

4—7 城镇单位从业人员平均工资（2017年）
Average Earning of Staff & Workers in Urban Units（2017）

单位：元 （yuan）

指　标	Item	单位从业人员平均工资 Average Remuneration of Staff & Workers	国有单位 State-owned Units	城镇集体单位 Urban Collective owned Units	其他类型单位 Others
总　计	**Total**	**63821**	**70407**	**46457**	**57603**
按企业、事业、机关分	**By Enterprise, Institution & Agency**				
企业	Enterprise	59115	70153	45517	57755
事业	Institution	69982	70019	52771	71586
机关	Agency	71865	71880	79876	65100
按国民经济行业分	**By Sector**				
农、林、牧、渔业	Farming, Forestry, Animal Husbandry & Fishery	36875	36205	39265	43521
采矿业	Mining	56445	28927	50247	57618
制造业	Manufacturing	54653	81725	42993	53644
电力、煤气及水的生产和供应业	Electricity,Gas & Water Production & Supply	78609	71413	49543	80059
建筑业	Construction	50900	46506	38203	53147
批发和零售业	Wholesale & Retail Trade	54245	80921	33083	49675
交通运输、仓储和邮政业	Transportation, Storage & Postal Services	74059	87952	47021	60728
住宿和餐饮业	Hotel & Catering Trade	34155	44483	31292	31986
信息传输、计算机服务和软件业	Information Transmission, Computer Service & Software Industries	93936	76270	17000	95104
金融业	Finance	96818	104855	102159	91240
房地产业	Real Estate	55688	51225	38761	56418
租赁和商务服务业	Leasing & Business Service	51375	51917	37502	52720
科学研究、技术服务和地质勘	Scientific Research, Technology Service & Geological Prospecting	79025	79085	46178	80336
水利、环境和公共设施管理业	Water Conservancy, Environment & Public Facility Management	44261	44142	34576	47516
居民服务和其他服务业	Resident & Other Services	48314	64456	41654	40381
教育	Education	67993	69055	52571	40398
卫生、社会保障和社会福利业	Public Health, Social Security & Social Welfare	79005	79316	44925	70643
文化、体育和娱乐业	Culture, Sports & Entertainment	70016	72116		64739
公共管理和社会组织	Public Administration & Social Organizations	70371	70391	74683	58844
国际组织	International Organizations				

4－8 城镇单位在岗职工平均工资（2017年）
Average Earning of Staff & Workers in Urban Units（2017）

单位：元 (yuan)

项 目	Item	在岗职工 Staff & Workers at Post	国有单位 State-owned Units	城镇集体单位 Urban Collective owned Units	其他类型单位 Others
总 计	**Total**	**66456**	**74150**	**48709**	**58992**
按企业、事业、机关分	**By Enterprise, Institution & Agency**				
企业	Enterprise	61151	75799	47556	59121
事业	Institution	73132	73138	59521	77074
机关	Agency	75712	75727	79876	69217
按国民经济行业分	**By Sector**				
农、林、牧、渔业	Farming, Forestry, Animal Husbandry & Fishery	41654	40827	39819	50654
采矿业	Mining	57054	28983	50464	58293
制造业	Manufacturing	55195	86461	43496	54077
电力、煤气及水的生产和供应业	Electricity,Gas & Water Production & Supply	80614	75815	51129	81592
建筑业	Construction	52551	47535	37546	54573
批发和零售业	Wholesale & Retail Trade	55481	82970	33283	50689
交通运输、仓储和邮政业	Transportation, Storage & Postal Services	75633	89998	51784	61116
住宿和餐饮业	Hotel & Catering Trade	34242	46383	31336	31922
信息传输、计算机服务和软件业	Information Transmission, Computer Service & Software Industries	95161	76986	17000	96390
金融业	Finance	117723	114035	104170	124421
房地产业	Real Estate	57287	56181	39967	57672
租赁和商务服务业	Leasing & Business Service	52741	54575	37855	53730
科学研究、技术服务和地质勘查业	Scientific Research, Technology Service & Geological Prospecting	82770	82838	46928	84291
水利、环境和公共设施管理业	Water Conservancy, Environment & Public Facility Management	47990	47921	48206	48803
居民服务和其他服务业	Resident & Other Services	51137	68504	41985	42555
教育	Education	71145	72305	53515	41348
卫生、社会保障和社会福利业	Public Health, Social Security & Social Welfare	80537	80838	47279	72005
文化、体育和娱乐业	Culture, Sports & Entertainment	73483	75449		68433
公共管理和社会组织	Public Administration & Social Organizations	74350	74370	75281	63035
国际组织	International Organizations				

4—9 分市城镇单位在岗职工人数（2017年）
Number of Employed Persons in Urban Units by City (2017)

单位：人 (person)

市 别	Region	在岗职工人数 Staff & Workers at Post	国有单位 State-owned Units	城镇集体单位 Urban Collective-owned Units	其他类型单位 Others
总 计	**Total**	**3167341**	**1752789**	**87795**	**1326757**
南宁市	Nanning	724807	326268	7407	391132
柳州市	Liuzhou	373053	161725	7125	204203
桂林市	Guilin	328328	180962	8986	138380
梧州市	Wuzhou	189124	87485	7440	94199
北海市	Beihai	119699	63438	3436	52825
防城港市	Fangchenggang	63390	39919	615	22856
钦州市	Qinzhou	193607	103456	11406	78745
贵港市	Guigang	163064	107580	4447	51037
玉林市	Yulin	262884	149279	17837	95768
百色市	Baise	214592	142336	8854	63402
贺州市	Hezhou	92090	68313	695	23082
河池市	Hechi	159734	114986	2801	41947
来宾市	Laibin	102856	67558	3903	31395
崇左市	Chongzuo	121538	81609	2143	37786

注：总计包括广西电网、广西中烟、南宁铁路局等单位。
Note: The total data includes Nanning Railway Bureau, Guangxi Building Engineering Group Corporation and Central Logistics Department.

4—10　分市城镇单位在岗职工平均工资（2017年）
Average Wages of Staff & Workers at Post in Urban Units by City（2017）

单位：元　(yuan)

市　别	Region	在岗职工 Staff & Workers at Post	国有单位 State-owned Units	城镇集体单位 Urban Collective-owned Units	其他类型单位 Others
总　计	**Total**	**66456**	**74150**	**48709**	**58992**
南宁市	Nanning	75481	87999	59207	68026
柳州市	Liuzhou	64958	73493	57846	60075
桂林市	Guilin	65694	73981	49852	57401
梧州市	Wuzhou	57618	70521	43845	46374
北海市	Beihai	60622	72242	48009	47826
防城港市	Fangchenggang	63484	65274	30811	61662
钦州市	Qinzhou	56863	64030	45029	49426
贵港市	Guigang	61245	68617	51406	46844
玉林市	Yulin	60901	68592	49210	51212
百色市	Baise	62528	66092	42145	57480
贺州市	Hezhou	65799	68594	61343	57692
河池市	Hechi	66085	73425	47677	48194
来宾市	Laibin	64152	70643	46752	51676
崇左市	Chongzuo	59250	64187	33929	50116

注：总计包括广西电网、广西中烟、南宁铁路局等单位。

Note: The total data includes Nanning Railway Bureau, Guangxi Building Engineering Group Corporation and Central Logistics Department.

4－11　分市城镇单位从业人员工资总额（2017年）
Earning of Employed Persons in Urban Units by City（2017）

单位：万元　　　　(10 000 yuan)

市　别	Region	单位从业人员工资总额 Wages of Employed Persons in Urban Units at the Year-end	国有单位 State-owned Units	城镇集体单位 Urban Collective-owned Units	其他类型单位 Others
总　计	**Total**	**24874547**	**14053504**	**551413**	**10269630**
南宁市	Nanning	7012975	3048643	52546	3911786
柳州市	Liuzhou	3712101	1537030	51506	2123566
桂林市	Guilin	2550998	1458556	59374	1033068
梧州市	Wuzhou	1143104	648562	35985	458557
北海市	Beihai	807308	499654	36798	270855
防城港市	Fangchenggang	476001	300576	2642	172783
钦州市	Qinzhou	1125981	670064	55950	399966
贵港市	Guigang	1061391	763074	34612	263704
玉林市	Yulin	1704618	1075219	122350	507050
百色市	Baise	1350115	939539	37670	372906
贺州市	Hezhou	648220	494758	4528	148934
河池市	Hechi	1143259	894798	21494	226967
来宾市	Laibin	736719	538036	21314	177369
崇左市	Chongzuo	760958	551619	7219	202120

注：总计包括广西电网、广西中烟、南宁铁路局等单位。
Note: The total data includes Nanning Railway Bureau, Guangxi Building Engineering Group Corporation and Central Logistics Department.

4－12　分市城镇单位从业人员平均工资（2017年）

Number of Employed Persons in Urban Units by City & Sector（2017）

单位：元　　(yuan)

市　别	Region	单位从业人员平均工资 Average Wages of Employed Persons	国有单位 State-owned Units	城镇集体单位 Urban Collective-owned Units	其他类型单位 Others
总　计	**Total**	**63821**	**70407**	**46457**	**57603**
南宁市	Nanning	72841	83540	59780	66408
柳州市	Liuzhou	63413	70732	54446	59215
桂林市	Guilin	62127	70689	47967	53835
梧州市	Wuzhou	54925	65344	42476	45676
北海市	Beihai	56929	65284	43969	47598
防城港市	Fangchenggang	57926	56402	31122	61635
钦州市	Qinzhou	55769	62145	44976	48991
贵港市	Guigang	58015	65506	40468	45539
玉林市	Yulin	58596	64989	47703	50799
百色市	Baise	62077	65641	42061	57017
贺州市	Hezhou	61903	64358	59497	55002
河池市	Hechi	61870	68081	40410	47251
来宾市	Laibin	60384	66547	41662	49216
崇左市	Chongzuo	56586	61074	33830	48097

注：总计包括广西电网、广西中烟、南宁铁路局等单位。
Note: The total data includes Nanning Railway Bureau, Guangxi Building Engineering Group Corporation and Central Logistics Department.

4—13 城镇单位分市分行业从业人员（2017年）
Number of Employed Persons in Urban Units by City & Sector（2017）

单位：人 (person)

市别 Region	合计 Total	农、林、牧、渔业 Farming, Forestry, Animal Husbandry & Fishery	采矿业 Mining	制造业 Manufac-turing	电力、煤气及水的生产和供应业 Electricity, Gas & Water Production & Supply	建筑业 Construc-tion	批发和零售业 Wholesale & Retail Trade	交通运输、仓储和邮政业 Transpor- tation, Storage & Postal Services	住宿和餐饮业 Hotel & Catering Trade	信息传输、计算机服务和软件业 Information Transmi- ssion, Computer Service & Software Industries
总　计 Total	**3980260**	**72575**	**34253**	**668708**	**117905**	**651386**	**127344**	**190175**	**44410**	**40165**
南宁市 Nanning	987743	9411	201	116298	49921	233071	45282	50257	20070	14146
柳州市 Liuzhou	600093	4187	76	147362	6117	187578	17662	15731	3963	2739
桂林市 Guilin	419575	4403	4278	72502	9690	68488	14893	9869	6947	3710
梧州市 Wuzhou	213193	736	1978	76516	6311	7096	4692	5618	1090	1530
北海市 Beihai	143904	4894	1118	37234	1960	10816	3991	4044	2292	1490
防城港市 Fangcheng-gang	83188	9750	40	6612	2560	9964	1283	6762	855	1072
钦州市 Qinzhou	207263	2896	950	28066	2554	53561	4625	4864	1106	1447
贵港市 Guigang	186051	1040		33111	7224	9481	5312	6230	763	1566
玉林市 Yulin	294750	6751	21	57081	6063	35037	8405	5063	1614	3173
百色市 Baise	222144	2427	13627	25573	7426	11318	7319	8361	1480	2537
贺州市 Hezhou	106717	1574	742	11598	4348	1281	2113	2187	466	1310
河池市 Hechi	186160	3287	5778	17863	6277	8676	5376	7454	1517	2474
来宾市 Laibin	125157	9038	1079	16408	3496	10219	2640	2858	364	1502
崇左市 Chongzuo	137221	12181	4365	19238	3958	3549	3410	2641	1084	1369

注：总计包括广西电网、广西中烟、南宁铁路局等单位。
Note: The total data includes Nanning Railway Bureau, Guangxi Building Engineering Group Corporation and Central Logistics Department.

4－13 续表 continued

单位：人 (person)

市 别 Region	金融业 Finance	房地产业 Real Estate	租赁和商务服务业 Leasing & Business Service	科学研究、技术服务和地质勘查业 Scientific Research, Technology Service & Geological Prospecting	水利、环境和公共设施管理业 Water Conservancy, Environment & Public Facility Management	居民服务和其他服务业 Resident & Other Services	教育 Education	卫生、社会保障和社会福利业 Public Health, Social Security & Social Welfare	文化、体育和娱乐业 Culture, Sports & Entertainment	公共管理和社会组织 Public Administration & Social Organizations
总 计 Total	**146658**	**78815**	**107708**	**83177**	**79014**	**7067**	**624407**	**333140**	**33127**	**540226**
南宁市 Nanning	52564	29580	32526	34061	19136	1533	114904	61493	13815	89474
柳州市 Liuzhou	10336	14481	22681	10982	13513	1306	54245	36034	3347	47753
桂林市 Guilin	18071	8382	17647	8062	10122	1004	63684	34001	4523	59299
梧州市 Wuzhou	6843	3442	1992	3110	3255	156	37487	20968	1507	28866
北海市 Beihai	7078	2895	3016	2966	4420	248	22174	12598	1344	19326
防城港市 Fangcheng-gang	1784	1550	1703	1196	2330	136	11350	6548	369	17324
钦州市 Qinzhou	4447	2385	2359	2748	3044	107	42373	21108	674	27949
贵港市 Guigang	8008	1870	1989	2023	2145	796	47964	23823	507	32199
玉林市 Yulin	8826	4684	5523	5694	6506	334	70044	31099	1902	36930
百色市 Baise	4378	2634	5430	2317	5395	224	42951	24571	1041	53135
贺州市 Hezhou	7058	1309	2740	1925	1797	68	26297	10727	1015	28162
河池市 Hechi	5127	2044	2947	1415	4055	206	41911	23680	1253	44820
来宾市 Laibin	5616	1624	1861	2319	1620	51	24250	13090	872	26250
崇左市 Chongzuo	6475	1683	4335	3670	1676	77	24773	13141	857	28739

4－14 城镇单位分市分行业女性从业人数（2017年）

Number of Female Employed Persons in Urban Units by City & Sector（2017）

单位：人 (person)

市别 Region	合计 Total	农、林、牧、渔业 Farming, Forestry, Animal Husbandry & Fishery	采矿业 Mining	制造业 Manufac-turing	电力、煤气及水的生产和供应业 Electricity, Gas & Water Production & Supply	建筑业 Construc-tion	批发和零售业 Wholesale & Retail Trade	交通运输、仓储和邮政业 Transpor-tation, Storage & Postal Services	住宿和餐饮业 Hotel & Catering Trade	信息传输、计算机服务和软件业 Information Transmi-ssion, Computer Service & Software Industries
总计 Total	**1559238**	**25909**	**7453**	**263048**	**33491**	**60466**	**63250**	**49526**	**27146**	**17397**
南宁市 Nanning	363283	3227	36	48021	13283	19682	22542	13610	12148	5308
柳州市 Liuzhou	177683	1381	18	37772	1715	10580	10339	5009	2272	1280
桂林市 Guilin	170263	1924	1414	31042	3179	6877	8025	3147	4377	1715
梧州市 Wuzhou	93789	155	242	30927	2050	1107	2045	1539	680	666
北海市 Beihai	65576	1656	152	17645	626	1411	2049	1206	1381	746
防城港市 Fangcheng-gang	33639	3724	10	2619	558	2490	538	1653	415	453
钦州市 Qinzhou	82786	1068	102	13725	730	5961	2022	1595	665	638
贵港市 Guigang	87838	293		14970	2081	2266	2452	2019	559	683
玉林市 Yulin	135775	1843	5	30851	1587	3879	3490	1716	1055	1406
百色市 Baise	88363	726	1897	8759	2468	1392	3292	2863	902	1097
贺州市 Hezhou	50443	631	206	5007	1223	304	1054	744	313	587
河池市 Hechi	83564	956	1735	8715	1850	1235	2391	3099	1066	1394
来宾市 Laibin	55051	3386	160	5670	952	2682	1277	1012	209	804
崇左市 Chongzuo	58789	4939	1476	6629	1189	344	1581	899	660	593

注：总计包括广西电网、广西中烟、南宁铁路局等单位。

Note: The total data includes Nanning Railway Bureau, Guangxi Building Engineering Group Corporation and Central Logistics Department.

4－14　续表　continued

单位：人　(person)

市　别　Region	金融业 Finance	房地产业 Real Estate	租赁和商务服务业 Leasing & Business Service	科学研究、技术服务和地质勘查业 Scientific Research, Technology Service & Geological Prospecting	水利、环境和公共设施管理业 Water Conservancy, Environment & Public Facility Management	居民服务和其他服务业 Resident & Other Services	教育 Educa-tion	卫生、社会保障和社会福利业 Public Health, Social Security & Social Welfare	文化、体育和娱乐业 Culture, Sports & Entertain-ment	公共管理和社会组织 Public Administration & Social Organizations
总　计 Total	**80946**	**31945**	**36080**	**28417**	**41026**	**3213**	**362100**	**229341**	**15500**	**182984**
南宁市 Nanning	30343	12615	12178	12568	10699	692	65401	41913	6427	32590
柳州市 Liuzhou	5753	5382	8434	3643	6903	473	33167	24688	1735	17139
桂林市 Guilin	10434	3065	3804	2525	4627	514	37350	24374	2130	19740
梧州市 Wuzhou	3708	1147	619	1001	1672	61	21896	14284	689	9301
北海市 Beihai	4230	1406	1434	978	2213	114	12616	8258	651	6804
防城港市 Fangcheng-gang	847	640	600	340	1376	21	6811	4391	178	5975
钦州市 Qinzhou	2277	997	911	903	1531	69	25815	14606	313	8858
贵港市 Guigang	4250	700	520	512	909	282	29199	14979	227	10937
玉林市 Yulin	4201	2063	1638	1754	3184	146	43753	20981	840	11383
百色市 Baise	2036	1112	1476	729	3043	175	21426	17646	482	16842
贺州市 Hezhou	3888	504	774	557	919	14	15476	7568	476	10198
河池市 Hechi	2245	863	943	431	2426	90	22464	17064	485	14112
来宾市 Laibin	3046	665	812	757	697	16	13661	9502	399	9344
崇左市 Chongzuo	3660	680	1466	1614	827	25	13065	8960	421	9761

4—15 城镇单位分市分行业从业人员平均工资（2017年）

Average Earning of Staff & Workers at Work in Urban Units by City & Sector (2017)

单位：元 (yuan)

市别 Region	合计 Total	农、林、牧、渔业 Farming, Forestry, Animal Husbandry & Fishery	采矿业 Mining	制造业 Manufacturing	电力、煤气及水的生产和供应业 Electricity, Gas & Water Production & Supply	建筑业 Times New Roman	批发和零售业 Wholesale & Retail Trade	交通运输、仓储和邮政业 Transportation, Storage & Postal Services	住宿和餐饮业 Hotel & Catering Trade	信息传输、计算机服务和软件业 Information Transmi- ssion, Computer Service & Software Industries
总　计 Total	**63821**	**36875**	**56445**	**54653**	**78609**	**50900**	**54245**	**74059**	**34155**	**93936**
南宁市 Nanning	72841	52279	53361	53903	91640	61291	59729	75300	32957	109300
柳州市 Liuzhou	63413	54501	62667	76575	64534	48191	51283	54759	37184	95361
桂林市 Guilin	62127	30976	48680	48714	69534	54035	51349	58644	34188	74247
梧州市 Wuzhou	54925	56263	37566	43706	63822	36585	45360	51417	28084	96362
北海市 Beihai	56929	37125	33383	40343	78144	41410	47220	70563	37941	96969
防城港市 Fangcheng-gang	57926	20365	44152	50307	119182	42677	77850	71924	40536	85234
钦州市 Qinzhou	55769	37035	97239	60302	90332	36713	54527	61520	27987	87321
贵港市 Guigang	58015	46456		36513	74550	37047	50120	51807	27508	85115
玉林市 Yulin	58596	28216	14524	48088	60222	40704	51812	58304	33710	83573
百色市 Baise	62077	43616	66695	58563	61483	35985	45709	54202	31196	85075
贺州市 Hezhou	61903	52476	48373	46571	71234	38712	72692	53706	34569	82360
河池市 Hechi	61870	46075	51877	38634	62585	31905	49166	51635	29467	79158
来宾市 Laibin	60384	37166	33597	49445	73534	29778	50522	51138	26480	85961
崇左市 Chongzuo	56586	29320	55003	43900	54185	39038	48688	65193	36140	86027

注：总计包括广西电网、广西中烟、南宁铁路局等单位。
Note: The total data includes Nanning Railway Bureau, Guangxi Building Engineering Group Corporation and Central Logistics Department.

4—15　续表　continued

单位：元　(yuan)

市　别	Region	金融业 Finance	房地产业 Real Estate	租赁和商务服务业 Leasing & Business Service	科学研究、技术服务和地质勘查业 Scientific Research, Technology Service & Geological Prospecting	水利、环境和公共设施管理业 Water Conservancy, Environment & Public Facility Management	居民服务和其他服务业 Resident & Other Services	教育 Education	卫生、社会保障和社会福利业 Public Health, Social Security & Social Welfare	文化、体育和娱乐业 Culture, Sports & Entertainment	公共管理和社会组织 Public Administration & Social Organizations
总　计	**Total**	**96818**	**55688**	**51375**	**79025**	**44261**	**48314**	**67993**	**79005**	**70016**	**70371**
南宁市	Nanning	114521	65102	58988	98882	50378	65334	79505	95811	86023	77868
柳州市	Liuzhou	118793	48098	44091	60622	43901	44596	67305	87451	62753	76311
桂林市	Guilin	94263	48960	45578	66219	46052	38411	70882	81516	58817	74058
梧州市	Wuzhou	79813	43331	41354	64728	34801	22147	64508	70625	50360	62554
北海市	Beihai	73948	61865	91874	65639	42552	59915	68436	65841	55250	69839
防城港市	Fangchenggang	97624	57592	45526	61783	36570	38328	61877	62038	68455	67256
钦州市	Qinzhou	82358	56603	49615	58031	39490	72486	61598	69252	48181	61464
贵港市	Guigang	67109	49768	37123	63689	52238	40082	59475	76891	66334	67954
玉林市	Yulin	98475	51095	43040	71994	43023	49131	62619	76527	56544	68738
百色市	Baise	92450	53122	55259	64232	38235	26955	68524	68162	57240	65553
贺州市	Hezhou	73811	47659	54030	70371	39816	52091	60148	76277	61340	63373
河池市	Hechi	85052	41712	47659	72574	36009	45660	68796	71537	60225	72269
来宾市	Laibin	77916	45643	41674	66996	47451	55902	69450	79143	60718	67564
崇左市	Chongzuo	65229	51152	44616	56858	44941	55506	64122	65761	56805	68327

4—16 主要年份离休、退休、退职人员和保险福利费用情况

Statistics of VCSR, Retired & Resigned, Insurance & Welfare Funds in Main Years

项目	Item	2005	2010	2013	2014	2015	2016	2017
一、截止年末离休、退休、退职人员数总计（人）	**Total Number of VCSR, Retired & Resigned at Year End (person)**	**1199346**	**1869510**	**2243670**	**1535235**	**2416388**	**2406732**	**2518653**
企业	Enterprise	755568	920376	980095	1006166	1026462	1019703	1033764
（一）内资企业	Domestic Capital	752135		973339	999030	1019222	1012575	1027904
国有企业	State Owned Units	585777		673947	665913	666089	667394	629546
集体企业	Collective Owned Units	105402		100030	89890	90804	88180	79842
其他企业	Others	60956		199362	243227	262329	257001	318516
（二）港澳台投资企业	Enterprise Funded by Hong Kong, Macao & Taiwan&Foreign Investment	3433		6756	7136	7240	7128	5860
其他人员*	Other Stuffs*	10814	460905	745870	796621	842226	902015	929388
事业	Institution	315286	372802	391202	399955	412900	224787	181506
机关	Agency	117678	115427	126503	129114	134800	259498	371892
其他单位*	Other Units*						729	2103
二、保险福利费用总计（万元）	**Total Insurance & Welfare Funds (10 000 yuan)**	**1272196**	**3244030**	**5441025**	**6133443**	**7104382**	**5995598**	**8296286**
企业	Enterprise	615790	1362997	2155958	2425804	2662397	2951393	3334975
离休金	Pensions for VCSR	14918	15229	20361	18415	17403	18533	17283
退休金（含退职人员生活费）	Pensions for Retired (including the cost-of-living for the retired)	559821	1342027	2113772	2395348	2624693	2932533	3317069
医疗卫生费	Medical Care	18829						
其他	Others	22222	5741	21825	12041	20301		
其他人员*	Other Stuffs*	6749	492671	1320829	1554116	1830426	2027933	2228591
离休金	Pensions for VCSR					4		
退休金（含退职人员生活费）	Pensions for Retired (including the cost-of-living for the retired)	6604	491805	1319431	1542068	1830407	2027933	2228591
医疗卫生费	Medical Care	44						
其他	Others	101	866	1398	12048	15		
事业	Institution	455450	965149	1438915	1581838	1926304	624559	1705651
离休金	Pensions for VCSR	10757	16285	15747	14616	20941		
退休金（含退职人员生活费）	Pensions for Retired (including the cost-of-living for the retired)	397501	948864	1423168	1567223	1905363	624559	1705651
医疗卫生费	Medical Care	13997				1926304		
其他	Others	33195						
机关	Agency	194206	423213	525323	571685	685255	388691	1018244
离休金	Pensions for VCSR	11769	28912	9345	25217	32338		
退休金（含退职人员生活费）	Pensions for Retired (including the cost-of-living for the retired)	162706	394301	507767	5464680	651117	388691	1018244
医疗卫生费	Medical Care	4904						
其他	Others	14828						
其他单位*	Other Units*						3022	8825
离休金	Pensions for VCSR							
退休金（含退职人员生活费）	Pensions for Retired (including the cost-of-living for the retired)						3022	8825
医疗卫生费	Medical Care							
其他	Others							

注：1. 此表数据由自治区人社厅提供。
2. 其他人员*是指参加城镇企业职工基本养老保险的个体经济组织以及灵活就业人员中的参保退休人员及其保险福利费用，该项指标从2005年起建立。
3. 其他单位*是指参加执行机关事业单位养老保险制度的除机关、事业单位之外的单位。
4. 机关、事业单位离休、退休退职人员是指参加城镇机关事业单位职工基本养老保险中的参保离休、退休退职人员，该项指标从2016年起建立。
5. 因2016年社保制度改革，机关事业单位退休金数据和往年数据口径不一致，无可比性。

Note: 1. The data in this table is provided by Department of Human Resources and Social Security of Guangxi.
2. The item of "Other Stuffs" starts at 2005, refers to individual operators and liberal professions who participate in the Enterprise Basic Pension Insurance System.
3. The item of "Other Units" refers to units which participate in the Institution & Agency Basic Pension Insurance System, but neither institutions nor agencies.
4. The item of "Statistics of VCSR, Retired & Resigned" start at 2016, refers to the number of retired and resigned person who participate in the Institution & Agency Basic Pension Insurance System.
5. Due to the reform of social security system in 2016, the pension data of institution and agency are inconsistent with the previous years.

4—17　参加社会保险人员
Number of Persons Joined Social Security in Main Years

单位：人　　　　(person)

项　目	Item	2016	2017
一、截止年末参加城镇基本养老保险人员总数	**Total Number of Persons Joined Urban Basic Pension Insurance at Year End**	**7519122**	**7777915**
#离休退休退职人数	Total Retired, VCSR & RRSW	2406732	2518653
（一）执行企业养老保险制度	The Enterprise Basic Pension Insurance System	5993248	6136654
1.企业	Enterprise	3916603	3982133
国有企业	State-enterprise	1983279	1895141
集体企业	Collective Enterprise	209607	187094
其他企业	Other Enterprise	1640339	1821902
港、澳、台及外资企业	Foreign Investment & Enterprise Funded by Hong Kong, Macau & Taiwan	83378	77996
2.其他人员	Other Stuffs	2076645	2154521
（二）执行机关事业单位养老保险制度	The Institution & Agency Basic Pension Insurance System	1525874	1641261
1.机关	Institution	802505	557110
2.事业	Agency	721124	1080890
3.其他单位	Others	2245	3261
二、截止年末参加失业保险人员总数	**Total Number of Persons Joined Unemployment Insurance at Year End**	**2837069**	**3021320**
（一）企业	Enterprise	1770989	1934096
1.内资企业	Domestic Capital	1659273	1814430
2.港、澳、台及外资企业	Foreign Investment & Enterprise Funded by Hong Kong, Macau & Taiwan	111716	119666
（二）事业单位	Agency	977245	1006020
（三）其他单位	Other Units	88835	81204
三、截止年末参加城镇基本医疗保险人员总数	**Total Number of Persons Joined the Urban Basic Health Care Program at Year End**	**10964222**	**51732858**
（一）城镇职工基本医疗保险参保人数	Urban Staff & Workers	5307125	5567460
#退休人数	Total Number of VCSR	1549806	1601656
1.企业	Enterprise	2900687	2994696
2.事业	Institution	1416769	1468665
3.机关	Agency	519570	509646
4.其他人员	Other Stuffs	470099	594453
（二）城镇居民基本医疗保险参保人数	Urban Residents	5657097	46165398
四、截止年末参加工伤保险人员总数	**Total Number of Persons Joined the Industrial Injury Insurance at Year End**	**3740685**	**3887915**
五、截止年末参加生育保险人员总数	**Total Number of Persons Joined the Bearing Insurance at Year End**	**3195872**	**3385751**
六、截止年末参加城乡居民基本养老保险人数	**Total Number of Residents joined The Urban & Rural Basic Pension Insurance at Year End**	**17720258**	**18059399**

注：1. 此表数据由自治区人社厅提供。
2. 因社会保险制度改革，执行机关事业单位基本养老保险制度的统计指标从2016年起建立。
3.因社会保险制度改革，城镇居民基本医疗保险与新农合从2017年起整合为城乡居民基本医疗保险。

Note: 1. The data in this table s provided by Department of Human Resources and Social Security of Guangxi.
2.The items about “The Institution & Agency Basic Pension Insurance System” start at 2016, because of the reform of social security system.

4—18 分市社会保险参保人数（2017年）
Number of Persons Joined Social Security by City（2017）

单位：人 (person)

地 区	City	城镇基本养老保险人数 Number of Persons Participating in The Basic Pension Insurance in Urban	执行企业职工基本养老保险制度 The Enterprise Basic Pension Insurance System	执行机关事业单位职工基本养老保险制度 The Institution & Agency Basic Pension Insurance System	失业保险人数 Number of Persons Participating in the Unemployment Insurance Program	基本医疗保险人数 Number of Person Participating in the Basic Health Care Program	工伤保险人数 Number of Person Participating in the Industrial Injury Insurance	生育保险人数 Number of Person Participating in the Bearing Insurance	城乡居民基本养老保险参保人数 Number of Residents Participating in The Urban & Rural Basic Pension Insurance
总 计	**Total**	**7777915**	**6136654**	**1641261**	**3021320**	**51732858**	**3887915**	**3385751**	**18059399**
南 宁 市	Nanning	1333182	1148633	184549	547046	6945605	617925	587572	2156472
柳 州 市	Liuzhou	1082854	957058	125796	422905	3834668	514291	419789	1094288
桂 林 市	Guilin	912542	748216	164326	365326	5026080	461821	393963	1998927
梧 州 市	Wuzhou	429831	339412	90419	142940	3245154	186763	177947	1205993
北 海 市	Beihai	259525	205463	54062	112599	1632072	133810	106947	390930
防城港市	Fangchenggang	158834	127922	30912	70778	915349	98713	67228	269548
钦 州 市	Qinzhou	258278	173270	85008	94754	3533982	129554	113179	1163909
贵 港 市	Guigang	311430	207423	104007	103440	5000862	167100	120736	1738942
玉 林 市	Yulin	544109	391045	153064	168267	6078436	213990	199489	2049365
百 色 市	Baise	360620	241761	118859	129610	4034196	206817	192814	1719558
贺 州 市	Hezhou	191371	130793	60578	81941	2264758	100052	90490	825239
河 池 市	Hechi	362488	241907	120581	124590	3977982	155739	163507	1602352
来 宾 市	Laibin	228681	157862	70819	86932	2345394	99087	104752	897881
崇 左 市	Chongzuo	239996	165403	74593	81765	2428741	122748	104844	945995

注：1. 此表数据由自治区人社厅提供。
2. 总计包括自治区本级。
3. 基本医疗保险人数包括城镇职工基本医疗保险与城镇居民基本医疗保险能参保人数之和。
4. 执行机关事业单位基本养老保险制度的统计指标从2016年起建立。

Note: 1. The data in this table s provided by Department of Human Resources and Social Security of Guangxi.
2. The total item include the Autonomous Region itself.
3. The number of persons participating in the Basic Health Care Program include the number of persons in the urban stuff and workers' Basic Health Care Program and the urban residents' Basic Health Care Program.
4. The items about "The Institution & Agency Basic Pension Insurance System" start at 2016.

4—19　城镇私营单位从业人员平均工资（2017年）
Average Wages of Employed Persons in Urban Private Units（2017）

单位：元　　(yuan)

行　业	Sector	2017
总　计	**Total**	**38227**
农、林、牧、渔业	Farming, Forestry, Animal Husbandry & Fishery	30417
采矿业	Mining	37331
制造业	Manufacturing	39910
电力、热力、燃气及水生产和供应业	Electricity, Gas & Water Production & Supply	40027
建筑业	Construction	38653
批发和零售业	Wholesale & Retail Trade	36784
交通运输、仓储和邮政业	Transportation, Storage & Postal Services	39545
住宿和餐饮业	Hotel & Catering Trade	30347
信息传输、软件和信息技术服务业	Information Transmission, Com- puter Service & Software Industries	41230
金融业	Finance	46606
房地产业	Real Estate	43210
租赁和商务服务业	Leasing & Business Service	38374
科学研究和技术服务业	Scientific Research, Technology Service & Geological Prospecting	46859
水利、环境和公共设施管理业	Water Conservancy, Environment & Public Facility Management	33241
居民服务、修理和其他服务业	Residents & Other Services	33624
教育	Education	33612
卫生和社会工作	Public Health,Social Security & Social Welfare	39066
文化、体育和娱乐业	Culture, Sports & Entertainment	31994

注：城镇私营单位工资统计采取抽样调查方式，样本代表性仅为省（自治区）级，无市、县（区）数据。
Note: The data of "Average Wages of Employed Persons in Urban Private Units" comes from sample survey, with the population of that in Autonomous Region, doesn't involve cities and counties.

主要统计指标解释

劳动力资源总数 指在劳动年龄内人口（16周岁及以上）总数中，具有劳动能力，在正常情况下，可能或实际参加社会劳动的人口数。

从业人员 指从事一定社会劳动并取得劳动报酬或经营收入的人员。从业人员按从业身份分组包括：（1）职工；（2）再就业的离退休人员；（3）私营业主；（4）个体户主；（5）私营企业和个体从业人员；（6）乡镇企业从业人员；（7）农村从业人员；（8）其他从业人员（包括现役军人）。

职工 指在国有、城镇集体、联营、股份制、外商和港、澳、台投资、其他单位及其附属机构中工作，并由其支付工资的各类人员。不包括下列人员：（1）乡镇企业从业人员；（2）私营企业从业人员；（3）城镇个体劳动者；（4）离休、退休、退职人员；（5）再就业的离、退休人员；（6）民办教师；（7）其他按有关规定不列入职工统计范围的人员。

城镇登记失业人员 指有非农业户口，在一定的劳动年龄内（16岁及以上男50岁以下，女45岁以下），有劳动能力，无业而要求就业，并在当地就业服务机构进行求职登记的人员。

城镇登记失业率 城镇登记失业人员与城镇单位从业人员（扣除使用的农村劳动力、聘用的离退休人员、港澳台及外方人员）、城镇单位中的不在岗职工、城镇私营业主、个体户主、城镇私营企业和个体从业人员、城镇登记失业人员之和的比。计算公式为：

$$\text{城镇登记失业率}=\frac{\text{城镇登记失业人数}}{\begin{array}{l}\text{（城镇登记单位从业人员－使用的农村劳动和－聘用的离退休人员－聘用}\\\text{的港澳台及外方人员）＋不在岗职工＋城镇私营业主＋城镇个体户主＋城}\\\text{镇私营企业及个体从业人员＋城镇登记失业人数}\end{array}}\times100\%$$

工资总额 指各单位在一定时期内直接支付给本单位全部职工的劳动报酬总额。工资总额的计算应以直接支付给职工的全部劳动报酬为根据。各单位支付给职工的劳动报酬以及其他根据有关规定支付的工资，不论是计入成本的还是不计入成本的，不论是以货币形式支付的还是以实物形式支付的，均应列入工资总额的计算范围。工资总额包括计时工资、计件工资、奖金、津贴和补贴、加班加点工资、特殊情况下支付的工资。

平均工资 指企业、事业、机关等单位的职工在一定时期内平均每人所得的货币工资额。其计算公式为：

$$\text{平均工资}=\frac{\text{报告期实际支付的全部职工工资总额}}{\text{报告期全部职工平均人数（人）}}$$

平均实际工资 是指扣除物价变动因素后的职工平均工资。其计算公式为：

$$\text{平均实际工资}=\frac{\text{报告期职工平均工资}}{\text{报告期城市居民消费价格指数}}$$

参加城镇基本养老保险人员总数 指截止报告期末参加城镇基本养老保险并在社会保险机构已建立缴费记录档案的人数，包括不能正常缴费、已中断缴费但未终止养老保险关系的人数，包括已参加基本养老保险、后进入再就业服务中心、并继续缴费的下岗职工人数。不包括只登记而未建立缴费记录档案的人数。

参加城镇基本养老保险的离退职人数 指报告期末参加城镇基本养老保险并由养老保险基金支付养老金的离休人员、退休人员、退职人员人数。

参加失业保险人员总数 指截止报告期末按照国家法律、法规和有关政策规定，参加了失业保险的城镇企业事业单位职工和地方政府规定的参加失业保险的其他人员的总数。

参加城镇基本医疗保险人员总数 指截止报告期末参加城镇基本医疗保险（实施统帐结合和单建统筹基金）的职工人数和退休人数的总数。

Explanatory Notes on Main Statistical Indicators

Total Resource of Labor Force refers to the population aged 16 and over who are capable to work , are willing to participate in or participating in social labor.

Employees refers to the persons who are engaged in social labor and receive remuneration payment or earn business income, including: (1) staff and workers at work; (2) re-employed retirees; (3) employers of private enterprises; (4) self-employed workers; (5) employers in private and individual economy; (6) employees in township; (7) employed persons in the rural areas; (8) other employed persons (including the servicemen).

Staff and Workers refer to the persons who work in (and receive payment there from) enterprise and institutions of state ownership, collective ownership, joint ownership, share holding, foreign ownership, and ownership by entrepreneurs from Hong Kong, Macao, and Taiwan, and other types of ownership and their affiliated units, excluding: (1) employed persons in rural enterprises; (2) employed persons in private enterprises; (3) urban individual laborers;(4) retired persons, VCSR and RRSW; (5) re-employed retirees and VCSR; (6) teachers in the schools run by the local people; (7) other persons aren’ t included in the statistic range of staff and workers according to related rules.

Registered Urban Unemployed Persons refer to the persons who are registered as permanent residents in the urban areas engaged in non-agricultural activities, aged within the range of working age (16 age and over, while male below 50 and female below 45), capable to labor, unemployed but desirous to be employed and have been registered at the local employment service agencies to apply for a job.

Registered Urban Unemployment Rate refers to the ratio of the number of the registered unemployed persons to the sum of the number of persons employed in various units and in private enterprises in urban areas, urban self-employed individuals and the registered urban unemployed persons. The formula is as follows:

$$\text{Registered urban unemployment rate} = \frac{\text{Number of registered urban unemployed persons}}{\begin{array}{l}\text{(number of persons employed in urban units+number of persons}\\ \text{employed in urban private enterprises+self-employed individuals in urban}\\ \text{areas+number of registered urban unemployed persons) +number of staff}\\ \text{and workers out of post+number of urban privately owners+number of}\\ \text{urban self-employed ivdividuals+number of personneel in urban privately}\\ \text{enterprises and self-employed laborers+number of the registered urban}\\ \text{unemployed persons}\end{array}} \times 100\%$$

Total Wages of Staff and Workers refer to the total remuneration payment to staff and workers in various units during a certain period of time. The calculation of total wages is based on the total remuneration payment to the staff and workers. Therefore, all the wages and salaries and other payments to staff and workers are included in the total wages regardless of their sources, category, and forms (in kind or cash). Total wages of staff and workers includes the wage calculated by time, wage calculated by volume, bonus, subsidies and allowances, wage paid in special.

Average Wage of Staff and Workers refers to the average wage in money terms per person during a certain period of time for staff and workers in enterprises, institutions and government agencies. The formula for calculating Average Wage of Staff and Workers is as follows:

$$\text{Average Wage of Staff and Workers} = \frac{\text{Total Wages of Ataff and Workers in Reference Period}}{\text{Average Number of Staff and Workers in Reference Period}}$$

Average Real Wage of Staff and Workers refers to the average wage, which has removed the factor of price change. The formula is as follows:

$$\text{Average Real Wage of Staff and Workers} = \frac{\text{Average Wago of Staff and Workers in Reference Period}}{\text{Urban Consumer Prices Indes in Reference Period}}$$

Total Number of Persons Participating in Urban Basic Pension Programs refers to the persons participating in the urban basic pension programs and registering in the social insurance institutions with payment registration, including the persons who cannot pay regularly, have stopped paid but maintained the pension insurance relation; including laid-off workers who have participated basic pension insurance, entered re-employment service center and go on paying; excluding the persons registered but without payment registration.

Total Number of Retired, VCSR & RRSW Participating in Urban Basic Pension Programs refers to number of the retired, VCSR & RRSW participating in urban basic pension programs in the report period and are paid pensions from the pension insurance funds.

Total Number of Persons Participating in Unemployment Insurance Programs refers to the number of staff and workers in urban enterprises and institutions or other persons by local government in participating in unemployment insurance programs according to national laws, rules and relative policies in the report period.

Total Number of Persons Participating Urban Basic Health Insurance Programs refers to the total number of staff, workers and retired participating urban basic health insurance programs in the report period.

第五篇

物价

PRICES

（校对编辑：蒋志华 陈 钧）

5－1 居民消费及商品零售价格总指数（1978－2017年）
Consumer & Retail General Price Indices (1978－2017)

（以上年价格为100） (preceding year=100)

年 份 Year	居民消费价格总指数 Consumer General Price Index			商品零售价格总指数 Retail General Price Index		
	全 区 Total	城 市 Urban Areas	农 村 Rural Areas	全 区 Total	城 市 Urban Areas	农 村 Rural Areas
1978	100.0	99.8	100.0	100.0	99.8	100.1
1979	102.6	102.8	101.1	102.3	102.9	101.7
1980	110.0	112.6	106.0	109.2	113.1	106.1
1981	101.6	102.7	100.1	101.7	103.0	100.5
1982	103.3	104.1	102.4	103.1	104.4	102.4
1983	102.7	103.0	102.7	102.8	103.0	102.7
1984	103.3	104.6	102.4	104.2	104.5	104.1
1985	113.0	114.7	111.8	111.2	114.5	109.3
1986	106.2	106.2	106.2	105.1	106.0	104.4
1987	108.2	110.2	105.8	108.0	110.5	105.5
1988	120.8	123.3	118.4	121.0	123.2	119.4
1989	121.1	119.7	123.3	121.3	119.1	123.5
1990	101.1	98.3	104.4	100.1	97.4	102.4
1991	102.8	102.7	103.0	102.5	102.5	102.5
1992	105.9	107.0	105.4	104.6	106.2	103.9
1993	122.0	123.3	119.1	118.9	121.9	114.8
1994	126.0	125.4	126.5	124.4	122.7	125.6
1995	118.4	118.0	118.6	116.4	115.0	117.7
1996	106.5	105.5	107.4	104.5	104.1	104.9
1997	100.8	100.7	100.8	99.6	99.9	99.4
1998	97.0	97.1	96.8	96.3	96.7	95.9
1999	97.7	97.2	98.2	97.2	96.8	97.6
2000	99.7	100.0	99.5	98.6	98.4	98.8
2001	100.6	101.3	99.6	97.8	97.3	99.0
2002	99.1	98.9	99.3	98.1	98.2	98.0
2003	101.1	100.9	101.3	100.2	99.6	100.8
2004	104.4	104.1	104.9	103.9	103.4	104.4
2005	102.4	103.0	101.6	101.1	101.3	101.0
2006	101.3	101.6	100.9	100.3	100.8	99.8
2007	106.1	105.6	106.8	104.8	104.2	105.3
2008	107.8	107.6	108.5	107.6	107.6	108.3
2009	97.9	97.9	97.5	98.0	98.1	96.9
2010	103.0	102.9	103.4	103.0	103.0	103.2
2011	105.9	105.7	106.4	106.0	105.7	106.6
2012	103.2	103.2	103.3	102.3	102.2	102.4
2013	102.2	102.1	102.4	101.2	101.1	101.3
2014	102.1	102.2	101.9	101.4	101.5	101.1
2015	101.5	101.5	101.5	100.1	100.1	100.1
2016	101.6	101.6	101.7	100.4	100.4	100.3
2017	101.6	101.9	101.1	101.2	101.2	100.8

注：1994年起商品零售价格总指数不包括农资。
Note: Retail General Price Index since 1994 has excluded agricultural means of production.

5－2 各地区商品零售和农业生产资料价格指数（2017年）

（以上年价格为100）

地 区	Region	总指数 General Index	一、食品类 Food	粮食 Grain	食用油 Edible Oil and Fats	菜 Vegetables	畜肉 Livestock Meat	禽肉 Poultry Meat	水产品 Aquatic Products
全区平均	**Average of the Whole Autonomous Region**	**101.2**	**99.4**	**101.3**	**98.7**	**96.7**	**94.2**	**97.3**	**105.0**
南宁市	Nanning	100.9	99.4	100.1	100.1	96.6	95.2	96.5	104.9
柳州市	Liuzhou	100.5	100.4	103.7	100.0	98.4	97.2	97.0	103.3
桂林市	Guilin	101.1	99.6	101.3	97.6	97.4	93.6	99.2	106.6
梧州市	Wuzhou	102.6	99.6	100.5	97.2	91.9	95.0	101.2	105.5
北海市	Beihai	101.2	102.4	104.0	100.3	95.5	97.2	94.4	105.7
防城港市	Fangchenggang	102.1	100.0	100.9	97.7	96.8	93.3	97.8	107.9
钦州市	Qinzhou	102.4	100.1	101.3	96.0	98.8	94.2	95.6	109.0
贵港市	Guigang	101.7	98.1	100.4	102.4	97.0	92.7	97.7	102.8
玉林市	Yulin	101.8	99.8	101.2	99.7	98.3	93.7	96.0	107.3
百色市	Baise	100.7	99.7	100.5	100.0	96.6	95.7	96.9	106.1
贺州市	Hezhou	100.2	98.6	100.1	99.3	95.4	92.8	96.0	105.5
河池市	Hechi	101.0	98.3	102.3	97.2	91.2	93.6	99.7	103.5
来宾市	Laibin	101.4	98.8	101.3	100.0	97.9	91.5	98.3	103.7
崇左市	Chongzuo	101.0	97.9	100.1	97.9	96.1	90.7	98.0	102.8
城市平均	**Average of Urban Areas**	**101.2**	**99.6**	**101.3**	**99.1**	**96.8**	**94.6**	**97.2**	**105.3**
农村平均	**Average of Rural Areas**	**100.8**	**97.9**	**101.2**	**95.9**	**95.7**	**91.8**	**97.8**	**102.1**

Retail & Agricultural Means of Production Price Indices by Region (2017)

(preceding year=100)

干鲜瓜果 Dry and Fresh Melons & Fruits	其他食品 Other Foods	二、饮料、烟酒类 Beverages, Tobacco & Liquor	三、服装、鞋帽类 Clothes, Shoes & Hats	服装 Garments	鞋袜帽 Shoes, Socks & Hats	四、纺织品类 Textiles
104.2	**99.5**	**100.8**	**102.0**	**102.2**	**101.4**	**102.5**
103.5	98.7	101.2	103.5	104.0	102.2	108.7
110.1	101.4	101.3	100.8	99.9	103.7	95.0
102.2	101.3	101.6	98.4	99.4	95.4	100.4
107.1	100.4	99.5	103.1	103.2	102.6	100.9
102.2	99.2	99.9	100.2	100.8	98.9	97.8
106.4	100.1	102.0	102.2	102.4	101.8	98.8
101.8	102.0	99.6	102.9	103.5	101.2	101.9
101.5	96.5	100.7	104.9	106.4	101.7	100.1
105.6	100.2	99.5	103.1	103.4	103.1	97.3
105.9	98.7	100.8	99.0	99.1	98.6	100.0
103.5	100.7	100.2	100.5	101.3	98.3	100.9
100.5	101.1	100.7	100.8	100.4	102.0	100.3
98.4	100.4	100.6	105.0	106.2	101.8	102.1
103.2	99.4	100.9	100.8	100.6	101.7	100.5
104.3	**99.9**	**100.8**	**102.0**	**102.3**	**101.4**	**102.4**
103.7	**97.5**	**100.7**	**101.7**	**101.7**	**101.9**	**103.4**

5—2 续表 1

（以上年价格为100）

地 区	Region	五、家用电器及音像器材 Household Appliances, Music & Video Equipments	家庭设备 Household Appliances	文娱用耐用消费品 Durable Consumer Goods for Recreational Use	专业音像器材类 Professional Music & Video Equip-ments	六、文化办公用品 Cultural and Office Appliances	七、日用品 Articles for Daily Use	八、体育娱乐用品 Sports & Recreation Goods
全区平均	**Average of the Whole Autonomous Region**	**100.8**	**100.8**	**101.0**	**99.5**	**99.9**	**99.8**	**100.6**
南宁市	Nanning	100.6	100.5	101.0	98.7	100.2	98.1	100.4
柳州市	Liuzhou	99.3	100.1	98.2	98.2	98.6	99.6	102.1
桂林市	Guilin	100.3	100.4	99.9	100.6	100.1	99.3	100.1
梧州市	Wuzhou	101.8	102.2	101.6	99.8	100.5	101.9	102.3
北海市	Beihai	97.1	96.6	97.9	99.5	99.5	98.7	97.5
防城港市	Fangchenggang	105.8	107.8	103.6	99.6	102.2	102.3	102.3
钦州市	Qinzhou	104.4	104.6	104.6	101.7	102.9	101.3	100.5
贵港市	Guigang	103.0	100.3	106.6	98.6	102.2	100.1	100.8
玉林市	Yulin	102.7	101.1	105.2	100.1	96.8	100.0	101.0
百色市	Baise	99.5	100.3	98.5	99.5	100.7	97.4	99.7
贺州市	Hezhou	99.6	100.8	98.1	99.8	99.5	100.9	99.6
河池市	Hechi	104.3	107.6	100.8	99.9	99.8	100.5	100.0
来宾市	Laibin	100.4	100.1	101.2	98.9	100.2	101.4	100.8
崇左市	Chongzuo	100.9	99.6	102.7	100.0	100.3	100.9	100.4
城市平均	**Average of Urban Areas**	**101.0**	**101.0**	**101.2**	**99.6**	**99.9**	**99.5**	**100.6**
农村平均	**Average of Rural Areas**	**99.5**	**99.3**	**99.9**	**98.2**	**100.0**	**101.3**	**99.6**

continued

(preceding year=100)

体育户外用品 Sports Articles	娱乐用品 Recreation Goods	九、交通、通信用品 Transporta-tion & Communi-cation Appliances	交通运输机械 Transpor-tation Appliances	通讯器材类 Communi-cation Appliances	十、家具 Furnitures	十一、化妆品类 Cosmetics	十二、金银饰品 Gold, Silver and Jewelry
100.3	**100.7**	**99.4**	**100.1**	**98.1**	**101.2**	**100.2**	**100.6**
99.6	100.9	97.0	98.8	92.6	104.8	98.6	100.4
102.5	101.9	98.0	100.2	93.7	96.5	98.7	102.4
100.0	100.1	101.0	98.1	108.5	101.9	100.8	102.4
104.5	100.6	105.0	105.0	105.1	104.6	105.2	100.8
95.5	99.1	96.4	98.2	91.8	102.2	100.8	100.1
103.0	101.9	99.8	99.1	105.8	103.9	105.5	97.2
100.4	100.5	104.7	104.9	104.5	101.6	100.6	101.9
98.2	103.1	102.2	102.7	100.6	102.1	102.6	99.0
101.7	100.6	102.6	103.7	100.5	94.7	101.0	97.5
100.6	99.1	99.0	98.5	100.2	99.9	102.3	100.6
100.0	99.4	97.3	98.0	95.9	100.1	101.8	100.0
100.1	100.0	100.1	101.7	97.8	101.5	100.1	99.6
101.1	100.7	100.4	100.4	100.3	104.5	102.9	100.1
99.2	101.2	102.3	101.0	104.7	101.0	100.9	92.6
100.4	**100.8**	**99.6**	**100.1**	**98.4**	**101.2**	**100.3**	**100.7**
99.2	**99.9**	**98.3**	**100.0**	**95.9**	**101.4**	**99.9**	**99.7**

5－2 续表2 continued

（以上年价格为100） （preceding year=100）

地 区	Region	十三、中西药品及医疗保健用品类 Traditianal Chinese &Western Medicines & Health Care Articles	医疗卫生器具 Medical Appliance and Articles	中药 Traditional Chinese Medicines	西药 Western Medicines	保健器具及用品 Health Care Appliances & Articles	十四、书报杂志及电子出版物类 Books, Newspapers, Magazines & Electronic Publications	十五、燃料 Fuels	十六、建筑材料及五金电料 Building Materials and Hardware
全区平均	**Average of the Whole Autonomous Region**	**103.9**	**100.6**	**104.3**	**104.5**	**102.4**	**100.9**	**108.1**	**102.4**
南宁市	Nanning	102.4	101.6	103.3	102.0	102.8	99.3	107.6	101.7
柳州市	Liuzhou	102.2	101.4	105.2	100.7	102.2	101.2	108.1	100.9
桂林市	Guilin	101.3	100.0	99.6	102.7	100.6	102.5	109.3	104.0
梧州市	Wuzhou	109.8	96.9	112.7	111.1	103.4	101.2	104.5	101.6
北海市	Beihai	107.2	100.6	112.4	106.2	103.8	100.5	108.5	105.1
防城港市	Fangchenggang	104.5	102.0	105.1	105.6	100.9	104.7	107.2	103.3
钦州市	Qinzhou	102.6	100.0	107.3	101.0	102.1	102.6	106.1	103.8
贵港市	Guigang	105.9	104.4	108.2	107.1	101.5	99.4	107.2	101.5
玉林市	Yulin	106.2	97.6	99.6	110.8	108.8	100.1	111.0	102.5
百色市	Baise	104.7	100.0	103.7	106.6	99.1	100.0	107.5	103.1
贺州市	Hezhou	104.0	100.0	107.3	102.6	104.7	102.1	105.6	102.6
河池市	Hechi	102.7	101.1	103.5	102.8	100.0	102.0	107.9	103.2
来宾市	Laibin	100.1	100.0	100.6	99.9	100.0	100.1	107.1	103.9
崇左市	Chongzuo	104.5	100.0	103.1	106.8	100.0	100.9	107.3	103.0
城市平均	**Average of Urban Areas**	**103.7**	**100.6**	**104.2**	**104.2**	**102.5**	**100.8**	**108.2**	**102.3**
农村平均	**Average of Rural Areas**	**105.3**	**100.6**	**104.9**	**106.6**	**101.1**	**101.7**	**107.0**	**103.2**

5－2 续表3 continued

（以上年价格为100） (preceding year=100)

地 区	Region	农业生产资料价格指数 Price Index of Agricultural Means of Production	农用手工工具 Farm Handtools	饲料 Forage	仔畜幼禽及产品畜 Newborn and Commodity Animals	半机械化农具 Semimechanized Farm Tools
全区平均	**Average of the Whole Autonomous Region**	**101.4**	**102.3**	**101.3**	**90.4**	**101.5**
贵港市	Guigang	100.2	104.6	98.7	86.5	100.0
百色市	Baise	101.6	102.5	100.2	80.0	100.0
贺州市	Hezhou	102.1	102.8	103.5	98.3	100.0

5－2 续表4 continued

（以上年价格为100） (preceding year=100)

地 区	Region	机械化农具 Mechanized Farm Machinery	化学肥料 Chemical Fertilizer	农药及农药械 Pesticide & Its Appliances	农用机油 Oil for Farm Machinery	其他农业生产资料 Others
全区平均	**Average of the Whole Autonomous Region**	**102.6**	**103.0**	**100.7**	**111.5**	**100.6**
贵港市	Guigang	102.2	102.5	98.6	109.5	103.3
百色市	Baise	100.0	103.4	101.7	111.8	100.6
贺州市	Hezhou	100.0	102.0	102.0	115.6	100.8

5—3 各地区居民消费价格指数（2017年）

（以上年价格为100）

地 区	Region	总指数 General Index	一、食品烟酒 Food, Tobacco and Liquor	1.食品 Food	（1）粮食 Grain	（2）薯类 Tubers	（3）豆类 Beans	（4）食用油 Oil or Fat	（5）蔬菜 Vegetables	（6）畜肉类 Livestock Meat
全区平均	**Average of the Whole Autonomous Region**	**101.6**	**99.7**	**98.5**	**101.2**	**98.0**	**100.7**	**97.9**	**96.6**	**93.4**
南宁市	Nanning	102.3	100.0	98.7	100.1	93.0	99.7	100.1	96.6	95.3
柳州市	Liuzhou	101.3	100.6	100.7	103.7	98.7	102.1	100.0	98.4	97.2
桂林市	Guilin	101.6	100.0	98.9	101.3	107.8	99.6	97.6	97.4	93.6
梧州市	Wuzhou	102.3	100.2	98.9	100.5	93.7	101.4	97.2	91.9	95.0
北海市	Beihai	102.9	103.3	99.8	103.9	91.8	98.1	100.3	95.4	97.2
防城港市	Fangchenggang	102.7	100.2	99.7	100.9	93.8	97.7	97.7	96.8	93.3
钦州市	Qinzhou	102.1	100.5	99.9	101.2	101.7	100.3	96.0	98.8	94.2
贵港市	Guigang	101.6	99.3	97.9	100.4	88.9	99.9	102.4	97.0	92.8
玉林市	Yulin	102.2	101.0	99.2	101.6	98.9	98.8	99.7	98.3	93.7
百色市	Baise	101.4	99.9	99.3	100.5	95.6	100.5	100.0	96.6	95.4
贺州市	Hezhou	101.4	99.3	98.6	100.3	109.9	99.5	99.3	95.4	92.8
河池市	Hechi	101.3	99.5	97.7	102.3	81.9	102.0	97.2	91.2	93.6
来宾市	Laibin	101.4	99.1	98.1	101.2	103.0	99.3	100.0	97.9	91.7
崇左市	Chongzuo	101.6	98.6	97.5	100.1	100.3	103.1	97.9	96.1	90.7
城市平均	**Average of Urban Areas**	**101.9**	**100.1**	**98.9**	**101.1**	**96.7**	**100.0**	**99.5**	**96.7**	**94.4**
农村平均	**Average of Rural Areas**	**101.1**	**99.0**	**97.9**	**101.2**	**99.5**	**101.7**	**96.0**	**96.4**	**91.8**

Consumer Price Indices by Region（2017）

（preceding year=100）

（7）禽肉类 Poultry Meat	（8）水产品 Aquatic Products	（9）蛋类 Eggs	（10）奶类 Milk	（11）干鲜瓜果类 Dry and Fresh Melons & Fruits	（12）糖果糕点类 Candy and Cake	（13）调味品 Flavoring	（14）其他食品类 Other Foods	2.茶及饮料 Tea and Beverages
97.5	**104.2**	**97.0**	**101.6**	**104.3**	**101.6**	**102.7**	**99.4**	**101.4**
96.5	104.9	94.9	100.4	103.5	98.0	101.8	98.7	103.4
97.0	103.7	99.5	102.6	110.1	101.7	101.8	101.4	101.3
99.2	106.6	97.9	100.1	102.2	101.0	104.1	101.3	100.5
101.2	105.1	101.4	100.7	107.1	101.5	100.0	100.4	100.9
94.4	105.2	97.4	103.7	102.2	103.5	103.5	99.2	100.0
97.8	107.9	96.8	100.3	106.4	101.5	107.4	100.1	101.5
95.6	109.0	98.0	103.2	101.8	103.4	104.6	102.0	99.2
97.7	102.8	98.7	97.1	101.5	99.5	105.3	96.5	102.0
96.0	105.2	94.7	100.0	105.6	105.7	105.4	100.2	99.8
96.9	106.1	97.0	99.6	105.9	103.1	103.9	98.7	101.0
96.0	105.5	99.5	106.4	103.5	104.3	103.3	100.7	100.7
99.7	103.5	102.8	100.2	100.5	102.6	104.8	101.1	101.0
98.3	104.3	98.9	102.4	98.4	101.9	103.9	100.4	100.7
98.0	102.8	95.7	102.5	103.2	102.1	103.2	99.4	101.9
97.2	**105.1**	**97.5**	**101.1**	**103.7**	**101.3**	**103.2**	**99.8**	**101.5**
98.2	**102.5**	**96.1**	**102.6**	**105.4**	**102.1**	**102.2**	**98.8**	**101.1**

5－3 续表1

（以上年价格为100）

地 区	Region	3.烟酒 Tobacco & Liquor	（1）烟草 Tobacco	（2）酒类 Liquor	4.在外餐饮 Dining Out	二、衣着 Clothing	1.服装 Garments
全区平均	**Average of the Whole Autonomous Region**	**100.4**	**99.8**	**101.4**	**103.0**	**101.9**	**102.1**
南宁市	Nanning	100.3	100.0	100.7	103.3	104.2	104.0
柳州市	Liuzhou	100.8	100.2	102.4	100.1	100.5	99.7
桂林市	Guilin	101.8	100.0	104.6	102.6	98.0	99.4
梧州市	Wuzhou	99.1	99.5	98.1	104.3	103.2	103.2
北海市	Beihai	100.0	98.9	101.1	115.3	100.5	100.8
防城港市	Fangchenggang	101.7	100.0	104.5	100.6	102.1	102.4
钦州市	Qinzhou	99.8	99.8	99.8	102.4	103.2	103.6
贵港市	Guigang	100.1	100.0	100.2	102.9	105.0	106.3
玉林市	Yulin	99.5	100.0	98.5	106.7	103.6	103.4
百色市	Baise	100.9	99.6	102.1	100.9	99.1	99.1
贺州市	Hezhou	100.0	100.0	99.9	100.8	101.1	101.3
河池市	Hechi	100.5	100.0	101.3	104.6	100.9	100.4
来宾市	Laibin	100.6	99.6	102.0	101.5	105.0	106.2
崇左市	Chongzuo	100.4	99.6	101.7	100.5	100.9	100.6
城市平均	**Average of Urban Areas**	**100.4**	**99.9**	**101.2**	**103.1**	**102.4**	**102.6**
农村平均	**Average of Rural Areas**	**100.5**	**99.7**	**101.6**	**102.8**	**100.7**	**100.6**

continued

(preceding year=100)

2.服装材料 Clothing Material	3.其他衣着及配件 Other Clothing and Accessories	4.衣着加工服务 Clothing Manufacturing Services	5.鞋类 Shoes	三、居住 Residence	1.租赁房房租 Rental	2.住房保养维修及管理 Housing Maintenance & Management	3.水电燃料 Water, Electricity and Fuels	4.自有住房 Private Housing
105.3	**100.1**	**106.6**	**101.1**	**102.4**	**102.8**	**103.3**	**101.4**	**102.5**
119.8	100.8	118.2	102.6	103.8	103.2	108.2	102.5	102.6
99.2	101.3	100.0	103.5	102.8	104.3	101.0	101.5	104.0
102.9	98.6	102.2	92.8	102.4	101.8	104.8	102.5	101.7
95.5	103.4	100.1	103.6	100.8	105.2	102.9	99.4	100.0
97.5	97.0	102.2	100.2	103.7	112.6	101.4	101.7	103.9
100.0	102.3	100.0	101.6	99.9	98.4	101.5	100.4	99.0
100.3	99.8	116.5	101.4	101.3	103.0	102.4	100.4	100.9
100.0	99.2	100.0	102.5	101.5	101.5	100.7	100.8	102.1
102.2	100.4	103.4	104.8	101.5	100.0	100.9	104.8	100.1
100.2	100.0	100.0	98.8	101.5	104.7	102.3	99.3	101.8
102.6	100.2	108.1	99.6	101.7	101.3	102.5	98.8	103.2
100.0	100.3	105.3	102.3	101.6	100.5	105.8	100.9	100.4
100.0	100.8	104.8	101.8	101.3	100.0	104.0	101.8	100.0
100.0	100.3	102.3	101.9	102.6	98.3	102.6	100.9	104.5
105.2	**100.2**	**107.7**	**101.3**	**102.3**	**102.8**	**103.9**	**101.4**	**102.0**
106.1	**100.0**	**104.5**	**100.4**	**102.6**	**102.9**	**102.2**	**101.4**	**103.5**

5−3 续表2

(以上年价格为100)

地 区	Region	四、生活用品及服务 Daily Necessities & Services	1.家具及室内装饰品 Furniture & Interior Decorations	2.家用器具 Household Appliances	3.家用纺织品 Household Textiles	4.家庭日用杂品 Goods for Daily Use	5.个人护理用品 Personal Care Applies	6.家庭服务 Household Services	五、交通和通信 Transportation & Communication	1.交通 Transportation	2.通信 Communication
全区平均	**Average of the Whole Autonomous Region**	**100.9**	**101.6**	**100.4**	**100.8**	**100.3**	**100.4**	**103.9**	**102.0**	**103.2**	**100.0**
南宁市	Nanning	100.1	103.7	99.7	102.6	97.2	97.9	103.5	101.2	102.0	99.7
柳州市	Liuzhou	99.4	96.8	100.3	95.3	100.9	98.9	101.2	100.7	101.7	99.0
桂林市	Guilin	101.2	101.8	100.6	100.0	100.1	101.1	104.4	102.4	102.3	102.7
梧州市	Wuzhou	102.5	104.3	102.1	102.6	100.6	104.0	102.7	104.4	106.0	101.6
北海市	Beihai	99.3	102.2	96.7	98.4	99.8	99.6	100.8	101.0	102.0	99.5
防城港市	Fangchenggang	103.5	103.8	107.4	99.3	101.5	105.0	100.3	102.5	103.1	101.4
钦州市	Qinzhou	102.8	101.6	104.5	103.0	100.8	100.5	110.5	103.0	104.0	101.0
贵港市	Guigang	100.9	101.9	100.7	100.8	99.5	102.0	103.0	104.4	105.8	101.3
玉林市	Yulin	100.3	95.7	101.2	97.0	99.9	100.9	107.8	103.1	104.9	100.1
百色市	Baise	100.1	99.8	100.3	99.5	97.7	100.6	107.9	101.0	101.8	99.5
贺州市	Hezhou	100.9	100.0	100.8	100.0	100.5	101.5	103.2	101.5	102.8	99.4
河池市	Hechi	101.9	101.4	107.2	100.5	100.5	100.1	95.2	102.3	103.9	99.5
来宾市	Laibin	101.3	104.0	100.1	102.0	100.3	102.1	100.2	102.1	103.2	100.0
崇左市	Chongzuo	100.8	101.0	99.7	101.3	100.3	100.9	104.4	102.5	103.6	100.6
城市平均	**Average of Urban Areas**	**100.8**	**101.6**	**100.9**	**100.5**	**99.4**	**100.2**	**103.7**	**102.0**	**103.1**	**100.3**
农村平均	**Average of Rural Areas**	**101.1**	**101.6**	**99.5**	**101.5**	**101.8**	**100.8**	**104.4**	**101.9**	**103.4**	**99.5**

continued

(preceding year=100)

六、教育文化和娱乐 Education, Culture & Recreation	1.教育 Education	2.文化娱乐 Culture & Recreation	七、医疗保健 Health Care	1.药品及医疗器具 Medical Instrument and Articles	2.医疗服务 Medical Services	八、其他用品和服务 Others	1.其他用品类 Other Supplies	2.其他服务类 Other Services
102.1	**102.3**	**101.7**	**106.1**	**103.6**	**107.5**	**101.6**	**100.0**	**102.9**
100.9	102.2	99.2	110.6	102.6	116.4	101.5	100.4	102.5
102.6	100.3	105.8	100.8	102.1	100.0	101.6	101.2	101.9
103.2	101.1	106.2	106.9	101.2	115.6	101.6	100.6	102.6
101.0	102.3	99.3	112.1	108.4	114.7	103.1	101.0	104.8
100.6	101.0	100.6	112.9	106.7	118.4	102.4	97.5	107.0
101.9	100.5	103.6	122.5	104.4	134.9	103.4	101.7	104.8
103.1	102.0	104.3	105.7	102.5	107.9	101.6	101.1	102.0
102.7	103.1	102.1	104.1	105.3	103.3	100.4	100.0	100.8
103.2	103.6	102.7	104.1	106.6	102.7	104.5	99.6	108.5
101.8	101.5	102.3	111.4	103.5	116.7	101.8	100.3	103.0
102.0	103.9	99.4	109.6	103.8	113.6	102.6	99.2	105.2
100.7	99.9	101.7	108.4	102.2	112.1	101.8	100.7	102.8
101.0	98.9	104.0	106.9	100.1	111.7	100.5	100.6	100.5
102.5	103.7	100.6	111.6	103.9	116.6	99.1	98.3	99.7
101.9	**101.9**	**102.0**	**108.5**	**103.3**	**112.0**	**101.8**	**100.3**	**103.0**
102.4	**103.1**	**100.9**	**102.5**	**104.3**	**101.6**	**101.2**	**99.2**	**102.7**

5—4 主要年份工业品出厂价格（工业生产者出厂价格）分类指数

Ex-Factory Price Indices of Industrial Products in Main Years

（以上年价格为100） (preceding year=100)

指 标	Item	1995	2000	2005	2010	2011	2012	2013	2014	2015	2016	2017
总指数	**General Index**	**117.2**	**105.5**	**104.9**	**112.0**	**108.5**	**97.8**	**98.2**	**98.4**	**97.0**	**99.1**	**107.6**
按轻重工业分	**Grouped by Light & Heavy Industry**											
轻工业	Light Industry	123.8	109.0	105.8	115.0	114.7	98.6	97.7	97.4	100.6	101.8	104.8
以农产品为原料	Using Farm Products as Raw Materials	126.6	109.9	107.5	118.9	116.1	98.0	97.1	97.0	100.8	102.2	105.1
以非农产品为原料	Using Non-farm Products as Raw Materials	113.1	100.4	101.8	105.6	106.2	102.6	100.9	99.8	99.7	100.0	103.3
重工业	Heavy Industry	111.2	103.1	104.2	110.3	106.3	97.5	98.4	98.7	95.7	98.2	108.6
采掘	Mining & Quarrying	126.6	106.1	126.5	129.1	121.2	101.7	96.3	96.6	97.9	100.8	115.9
原材料	Raw Materials Industry	105.3	106.1	105.2	113.0	106.3	98.5	98.9	99.6	96.2	96.7	108.4
加工	Manufacturing Industry	115.8	96.0	101.5	106.3	105.2	96.6	98.2	98.3	95.3	98.7	108.1
按两大部类分	**Grouped by Production & Living Materials**											
生产资料	Production Materials	114.2	103.2	104.0	110.3	107.2	97.4	98.4	98.7	95.5	98.1	109.1
生活资料	Living Materials	121.4	110.4	106.8	118.2	112.0	99.0	97.5	97.5	101.3	102.4	103.1
按工业部门分	**Grouped by Department of Industry**											
冶金工业	Metallurgical Industry	111.0	108.5	106.4	118.1	110.1	90.9	94.3	94.4	89.2	99.0	123.0
电力工业	Power Industry	107.9	112.6	100.9	102.0	99.3	106.3	100.5	100.4	99.4	98.0	99.4
煤炭及炼焦工业	Coal & Coking Industry	100.9	104.1	133.1	111.0	130.5	113.6	99.0	94.2	93.1	94.6	120.3
化学工业	Chemical Industry	129.2	95.6	108.0	114.7	113.4	95.8	99.9	100.3	97.7	98.4	105.3
机械工业	Machine Building Industry	106.2	95.7	100.6	102.3	101.4	100.0	99.7	100.1	99.8	99.0	100.3
建筑材料工业	Building Materials Industry	95.2	100.6	98.3	106.6		98.1	100.4	103.3	97.4	94.5	107.0
森林工业	Timber Industry	99.8	101.4	100.5	106.4	105.7	105.4	102.8	100.6	99.4	101.6	101.5
食品工业	Food Industry	124.4	111.1	109.4	120.3	118.2	97.5	96.0	95.7	101.0	102.9	104.6
纺织工业	Textile Industry	126.1	115.5	99.9	126.8	118.0	95.2	103.1	98.9	95.3	101.7	115.4
造纸工业	Paper Making Industry	146.6	111.2	102.0	113.5	102.7	96.1	96.2	101.1	101.2	100.3	109.2
其他工业	Others	126.1	98.4	103.8	117.0	108.9	102.4	103.6	102.1	98.3	97.6	103.4

5—4 续表 continued

(以上年价格为100) (preceding year=100)

指 标	Item	2016	2017
按工业行业分	**Grouped by Industrial Sector**		
煤炭开采和洗选业	Coal Mining & Dressing	94.6	120.3
石油和天然气开采业	Oil and Gas Mining	84.9	136.8
黑色金属矿采选业	Ferrous Metals Mining & Dressing	97.2	101.7
有色金属矿采选业	Nonferrous Metals Mining & Dressing	103.2	130.5
非金属矿采选业	Nonmetal Ores Mining & Dressing	103.5	102.2
农副食品加工业	Farm & Sideline Products Processing	103.8	105.7
食品制造业	Food Manufacturing	100.3	102.3
酒、饮料和精制茶制造业	Wine, Drink & Refined Tea Manufacturing	99.8	101.1
烟草制品业	Tobacco Products	100.0	100.0
纺织业	Textile Industry	101.7	115.4
纺织服装、服饰业	Textiles, Clothing & Dresses Manufacturing	100.3	100.4
皮革、毛皮、羽毛及其制品和制鞋业	Leather, Fur, Feather & Related Products & Shoes Manufacturing	97.4	103.1
木材加工和木、竹、藤、棕、草制品业	Timber Processing, Wood, Bamboo, Cane, Palm Fiber & Straw Products	101.5	101.4
家具制造业	Furniture Manufacturing	102.3	102.0
造纸及纸制品业	Papermaking & Paper Products	100.3	109.2
印刷和记录媒介复制业	Printing & Record Duplicating	98.5	101.3
文教、工美、体育和娱乐用品制造业	Cultural, Educational, Art, Sports & Entertainment Goods	100.1	99.2
石油加工、炼焦和核燃料加工业	Oil Processing, Coking & Nuclear Fuel Processing	94.0	116.4
化学原料和化学制品制造业	Raw Chemical Materials & Chemical Products	97.1	106.7
医药制造业	Medical & Pharmaceutical Products	103.4	103.4
橡胶和塑料制品业	Rubber & Plastic Products	96.7	104.4
非金属矿物制品业	Manufacturing of Non-metallic Minerals Mining Products	93.8	107.8
黑色金属冶炼和压延加工业	Smelting & Pressing of Ferrous Metals	100.1	125.8
有色金属冶炼和压延加工业	Smelting & Pressing of Nonferrous Metals	95.6	122.0
金属制品业	Metal Products	103.0	102.8
通用设备制造业	General Equipment Manufacturing	95.2	105.8
专用设备制造业	For Special Purposes Equipment Manufacturing	99.4	100.3
汽车制造业	Automobile Manufacturing	99.1	99.8
铁路、船舶、航空航天和其他运输设备制造业	Railway, Ship, Aerospace & Other Transportation Equipment Manufacturing	104.7	99.9
电气机械和器材制造业	Electric Equipment & Machinery	98.3	101.7
计算机、通信和其他电子设备制造业	Computer, Communication & Other Electronic Equipment Manufacturing	100.3	98.9
仪器仪表制造业	Instruments & Meters Producing	101.6	100.8
其他制造业	Other Manufacturing	94.2	100.3
废弃资源综合利用业	Utilization of Waste Resources	92.1	99.6
电力、热力的生产和供应业	Electricity & Heating Power Production & Supply	98.0	99.4
燃气生产和供应业	Gas Production & Supply	90.9	100.4
水的生产和供应业	Water Production & Supply	101.0	100.4

说明：2011年基期轮换后，工业生产者出厂价格行业数据计算有新行业和旧行业之分，但数据对外公布均使用新行业数据，2016年基期轮换后，行业数据计算均为新行业。

Note: The data calculation of ex-Factory price indices of industrial products is classificated by new industry and old indsutry, and published in new industry after the base period rotation in 2011. The data is calculated completely in new industry after the base period rotation in 2016.

5—5 主要年份工业生产者购进价格指数
Purchasing Price Indices for Industrial Producers in Main Years

(以上年价格为100) (preceding year=100)

指 标	Item	1995	2000	2005	2010	2012	2013	2014	2015	2016	2017
总 指 数	**General Index**	**112.9**	**100.9**	**108.2**	**111.2**	**99.2**	**98.9**	**98.2**	**95.7**	**98.3**	**106.5**
燃料、动力类	Fuel & Power	107.8	98.9	112.1	109.3	104.0	97.8	98.4	95.1	94.8	108.2
黑色金属材料类	Ferrous Metals	94.7	103.0	111.3	103.7	95.2	97.6	96.0	90.9	96.4	109.4
其中：钢材	Steel	94.4	105.0	105.9	105.7	96.4	97.4	96.3	93.1	96.1	108.1
有色金属材料及电线类	Non-ferrous Metals & Wire	137.6	123.8	114.5	128.6	95.2	95.5	96.7	95.4	99.8	112.5
化工原料类	Raw Chemical Materials	125.2	104.5	110.0	112.3	98.3	98.1	99.6	98.0	97.6	105.8
木材及纸浆类	Timber & Paper Pulp	108.9	99.8	94.4	111.2	97.5	100.2	100.3	99.6	100.6	103.8
建筑材料及非金属类	Building Materials & Nonmetal Mineral	88.1	92.5	103.6	114.6	98.3	98.6	100.2	95.7	98.0	107.2
其他工业原材料及半成品类	Other Industrial Raw Materials	91.7	104.7	103.7	110.3	98.5	98.6	98.2	97.9	99.5	103.5
农副产品类	Agricultural Products	148.2	90.3	116.8	116.6	101.3	103.4	98.1	93.8	102.9	105.6
纺织原料类	Textile Materials	150.5	106.3	90.6	121.4	92.1	98.5	99.8	99.7	98.2	101.4

5—6 主要年份固定资产投资价格指数
Price Indices of Investment in Fixed Assets in Main Years

(以上年价格为100) (preceding year=100)

指 标	Item	1995	2000	2005	2010	2013	2013	2014	2015	2016	2017
总 指 数	**General Index**	**103.4**	**101.4**	**101.4**	**103.1**	**100.6**	**100.1**	**101.6**	**98.8**	**99.5**	**104.4**
建筑安装、装饰工程	Construction, Installation & Decoration	101.8	102.4	101.3	103.8	100.8	99.9	102.2	98.0	99.4	106.2
设备、工器具购置	Purchase of Equipment, Tools & Instruments	106.2	95.7	100.8	101.2	99.3	99.6	100.4	99.8	99.4	100.8
其他费用	Others	105.5	104.5	102.0	102.6	101.5	101.3	100.7	100.4	100.0	100.0

主要统计指标解释

居民消费价格指数　是反映一定时期内居民所消费商品及服务项目的价格水平变动趋势和变动程度的相对数。居民消费价格水平的变动率在一定程度上反映了通货膨胀（或紧缩）的程度。编制居民消费价格指数的目的，在于分析消费品价格和服务价格变动对社会经济和居民生活的影响，满足各级政府制定政策和计划、进行宏观调控的需要，以及为国民经济核算提供参考依据。

商品零售价格指数　是反映市场商品零售价格的变动趋势和变动程度的相对数。编制商品零售价格指数，其目的在于掌握商品价格的变动趋势，为国家宏观调控和国民经济核算提供参考依据。

工业生产者出厂价格指数　反映工业企业产品第一次出售时的出厂价格的变化趋势和变动幅度。

工业生产者购进价格指数　反映工业企业产品作为中间投入产品的购进价格的变化趋势和变动幅度。

固定资产投资价格指数　是反映固定资产投资额价格变动趋势和程度的相对数。固定资产投资额是由建筑安装工程投资完成额和设备、工器具购置投资完成额和其他费用投资完成额三部分组成的。编制固定资产投资价格指数，先分别编制上述三部分投资的价格指数，然后采用加权算术平均法，计算出固定资产投资价格总指数。

Explanatory Notes on Main Statistical Indicators

Consumer Price Indices reflect the trend and degree of changes in prices of consumer goods and services purchased by households during a given period. The rate of change of CPI reflects the degree of currency inflation(or deflation) to a certain extent. The purpose of working out CPI is analyzing the effect of the price changes of consumer goods and services on the social economy and household livelihood, meeting the needs of all levels of governments' policy and plants making, carrying out macroeconomic control, and providing reference for national accounting.

Retail Price Indices reflect the trend and degree of changes in prices of retail goods in market. The purpose of working out RPI is obtaining the trend of the price changes of goods, and providing reference for macroeconomic control and national accounting.

Producer Price Indices for Industrial Products reflects the trend and degree of the ex-factory prices of industrial products in the first sale.

Purchasing Price Indices for Industrial Producers reflects the trend and degree of the purchasing prices of industrial products as intermediate inputs.

Price Indices of Investment in Fixed Assets reflect the change trend and degree of change in prices of investment goods and projects in fixed assets during a given period. The investment in fixed assets consists of three components, namely the investment in construction and installation, the investment in purchases of equipment and instrument, and the investment in other items. Price indices of investment in fixed assets are calculated as the weighted arithmetic mean of the price indices of the three components of investment in fixed assets.

第六篇

人民生活

PEOPLE'S LIVING CONDITIONS

（校对编辑：李兰澜　陆　海）

6－1　城乡居民家庭人均收入及恩格尔系数（1978－2017年）

Per Capita Income & Engle Coefficient of Urban & Rural Households（1978－2017）

年 份 Year	城镇居民人均可支配收入 Per Capita Disposable Income of Urban Households		农民人均纯收入 Per Capita Net Income of Rural Households		城镇居民家庭恩格尔系数 (%) Engle Coefficient of Urban Households (%)	农村居民家庭恩格尔系数 (%) Engle Coefficient of Rural Households (%)
	绝对数（元） Value (yuan)	比上年±% Growth Rate Over Precding Year (%)	绝对数（元） Value (yuan)	比上年±% Growth Rate Over Precding Year (%)		
1980	455		173		57.3	63.5
1981	429	-5.7	204	17.9	58.7	67.6
1982	427	-0.6	235	15.2	61.5	66.2
1983	444	4.1	262	11.5	59.2	66.2
1984	563	26.8	267	1.9	57.2	64.6
1985	683	21.4	303	13.5	56.6	62.2
1986	784	14.7	316	4.3	58.0	61.9
1987	899	14.7	354	12.0	59.1	62.1
1988	1159	28.9	424	19.8	54.6	59.6
1989	1304	12.5	483	13.9	59.3	58.3
1990	1448	11.0	639	3.5	58.6	64.4
1991	1614	11.4	658	3.0	55.3	62.0
1992	2104	30.4	732	11.2	55.9	61.8
1993	2895	37.6	885	20.9	53.7	63.6
1994	3981	37.5	1107	25.1	50.4	59.0
1995	4792	20.4	1446	30.6	51.0	61.3
1996	5033	5.0	1703	17.8	50.4	58.2
1997	5110	1.5	1875	10.1	47.4	58.2
1998	5412	5.9	1972	5.2	46.3	57.2
1999	5620	3.8	2048	3.9	44.3	58.3
2000	5834	3.8	1865	-9.0	39.9	55.4
2001	6666	14.3	1944	4.3	37.7	52.3
2002	7315	9.8	2013	3.5	40.7	51.9
2003	7785	6.4	2095	4.1	40.0	51.3
2004	8177	5.0	2305	10.0	44.0	54.3
2005	8917	9.0	2495	8.2	42.5	50.5
2006	9899	11.0	2771	11.1	42.1	49.5
2007	12200	23.2	3224	16.3	41.7	50.2
2008	14146	16.0	3690	14.5	42.4	53.4
2009	15451	9.2	3980	7.9	39.9	48.7
2010	17064	10.4	4543	14.1	38.1	48.5
2011	18854	10.5	5231	15.1	39.5	43.8
2012	21243	12.7	6008	14.8	39.0	42.8
2013	23305	9.7	6791	13.0	37.9	40.0
2014	24669	8.7	8683	11.4	35.2	36.9
2015	26416	7.1	9467	9.0	34.4	35.4
2016	28324	7.2	10359	9.4	34.4	34.5
2017	30502	7.7	11325	9.3	33.2	32.2

注：自2014年起为一体化城乡住户收支调查后新口径数据，与2013年及以前数据不可比。下同。

Note: Since 2014，the data is based on the new statistical range of the intergation survey of urban and rural residents' income and expenses, and it is not comparable with the data in and before 2013. The same as the following tables.

6－2 主要年份城镇居民家庭基本情况
Basic Conditions of Urban Households in Main Years

单位：人 (person)

项 目	Item	2013	2014	2015	2016	2017
期内住户常住成员数	**Number of Permanent Residents**	**8770**	**8794**	**9218**	**9531**	**9494**
调查样本住户数（户）	**Number of Households Surveyed (household)**	**2575**	**2611**	**2701**	**2746**	**2733**
期内人均自有现住房面积（平方米）	**Per Capita Living Floor Space of Period (sq.m)**	**36.07**	**37.72**	**38.63**	**39.24**	**39.54**
常住成员从业人数	**Number of Employees of Permanent Residents**	**4843**	**4983**	**5036**	**5129**	**5049**
户主文化程度	**Education of Household**					
1.未上过学	Not on school	35	32	31	23	22
2.小学	Primary School	371	339	319	320	315
3.初中	Junior Secondary School	924	932	1001	1014	1007
4.高中	Senior Secondary School	663	682	696	736	743
5.大学专科	College & Higher Level	341	367	386	388	384
6.大学本科	Undergraduate	219	237	241	244	238
7.研究生	Postgraduate	23	23	27	22	24
本年度就业类型	**Type of Employment in the Current Year**					
1.雇主	Employer	98	86	86	64	61
2.公职人员	Public Officials	246	259	256	273	273
3.事业单位人员	Institutions Personnel	554	529	501	479	480
4.国有企业雇员	Employees of Nationalized Business	289	260	244	235	213
5.其他雇员	Other Employees	1558	1801	2182	2348	2399
6.农业自营	Farming Self-employed	1142	1055	903	814	741
7.非农自营	Not Farming Self-employed	956	993	864	915	882
本年度从事主要行业	**Engagine Major Industries in the Current Year**					
1.第一产业	Primary Industry	1229	1138	969	870	796
2.第二产业	Secondary Industry	832	862	954	948	938
3.第三产业	Tertiary Industry	2782	2983	3114	3312	3315

注：国家统计局对城乡住户调查实施了一体化改革，统一了城乡居民收入指标名称、分类和统计标准，建立了城乡统一的一体化住户调查。广西从2014年开始，正式发布此项改革后的一体化城乡住户收支与生活状况调查数据。表11-2至11-22内的数据均来源于一体化城乡住户收支调查。与2013年及以前公布的年鉴数据不可比。

Note: National Bureau of Statistics has carried out the integrate reforming on the survey of urban & rural residents, unified the names, classification and statistical standards of the indicators on urban & rural residents' income, and built up the concordant survey for urban & rural residents. Since 2014, Guangxi has formally released the data on the integration survey of urban and rural residents' income, expenses and livelihood after this reforming. The data in tables from 11-2 to 11-22 is based on the integration survey of urban and rural residents' income and expenses, and it is not comparable with the data released before 2013.

6—3 主要年份城镇居民人均可支配收入及构成
Per Capita Disposable Income of Urban Households & Its Composition in Main Years

单位：元 (yuan)

项 目	Item	2013	2014	2015	2016	2017
可支配收入	**Disposable Income**	**22689**	**24669**	**26416**	**28324**	**30502**
一、工资性收入	Income of Wage & Subsidy	13346	13893	15163	16493	17943
（一）工资	Wage & Subsidy	12090	12730	14051	15357	16625
（二）实物福利	Physical Benefits	60	54	63	56	74
（三）其他	Other Income	1196	1109	1050	1079	1244
二、经营净收入	Net Income from Management	2504	3431	3665	4805	4904
（一）第一产业经营净收入	Net Income from Management of Primary Industry	502	551	563	856	908
1.农业	Farming	386	377	397	498	540
2.林业	Forestry	24	6	19	47	42
3.牧业	Animal Husbandry	55	91	82	137	140
4.渔业	Fishery	37	78	64	174	187
（二）第二产业经营净收入	Net Income from Management of Secondary Industry	329	461	371	422	425
（三）第三产业经营净收入	Net Income from Management of Tertiary Industry	1674	2419	2731	3527	3572
三、财产净收入	Property Net Income	1973	2235	2308	2229	2390
四、转移净收入	Transfer Net Income	4866	5110	5280	4798	5265
（一）转移性收入	Transfer Income	5759	6132	6630	6432	6980
#养老金或离退休金	Pensions for Old People & Retirement	5017	5185	5490	5282	5716
（二）转移性支出	Transfer Expenditures	893	1022	1351	1635	1715
#社会保障支出	Social Relief Expenditures	627	732	1006	1245	1324

6—4 主要年份城镇居民人均现金可支配收入及构成
Per Capita Cash disposable Income of Urban Households & Its Composition in Main Years

单位：元 (yuan)

项 目	Item	2013	2014	2015	2016	2017
现金可支配收入	**Cash Disposable income**	**21641**	**23435**	**25146**	**27120**	**29200**
一、现金工资性收入	Cash Income of Wage & Subsidy	13286	13839	15100	16437	17869
（一）工资	Wage & Subsidy	12090	12730	14051	15357	16625
（二）其他工资性收入	Other Income	1196	1109	1050	1079	1244
二、现金经营净收入	Cash Net Income from Management	2773	3595	3895	5115	5250
（一）第一产业现金经营净收入	Cash Net Income from Management of Primary Industry	452	444	469	764	847
1.农业	Farming	340	281	263	391	462
2.林业	Forestry	9	-10	1	43	40
3.牧业	Animal Husbandry	44	75	74	118	119
4.渔业	Fishery	50	98	132	212	225
（二）第二产业现金经营净收入	Cash Net Income from Management of Secondary Industry	445	554	451	496	490
（三）第三产业现金经营净收入	Cash Net Income from Management of Tertiary Industry	1876	2597	2974	3854	3914
三、现金财产净收入	Cash Property Net Income	875	1065	1098	1005	1158
四、现金转移净收入	Cash Transfer Net Income	4707	4935	5053	4564	4923
（一）现金转移性收入	Cash Transfer Income	5599	5958	6417	6198	6638
#养老金或离退休金	Pensions for Old People & Retirement	5017	5185	5490	5282	5716
（二）现金转移性支出	Cash Transfer Expenditures	893	1022	1364	1635	1715
#个人缴纳的社会保障支出	Social Relief Expenditures paid by individuals	628	732	1006	1245	1324

6—5 主要年份城镇居民人均消费支出
Per Capita Consumption Expenditure of Urban Households in Main Years

单位：元 (yuan)

项 目	Item	2013	2014	2015	2016	2017
消费支出	**Consumption Expenditures**	**14470**	**15046**	**16321**	**17268**	**18349**
一、食品烟酒	Food,Alcohol & Tobacco	4934	5293	5610	5937	6099
二、衣着	Clothing	765	794	846	886	908
三、居住	Residence	3263	3390	3629	3784	3885
四、生活用品及服务	Daily Necessities & Services	856	906	952	1033	1093
五、交通通信	Transportation & Communication	1911	1846	2249	2260	2607
六、教育文化娱乐	Education, Cultural & Recreation Services	1666	1689	1845	2003	2152
七、医疗保健	Medical Appliances & Articles	803	846	866	1066	1254
八、其他用品和服务	Other Supplies & Services	272	282	323	299	351

6—6 主要年份城镇居民人均现金消费支出
Per Capita Cash Consumption Expenditure of Urban Households in Main Years

单位：元 (yuan)

项 目	Item	2013	2014	2015	2016	2017
现金消费支出	**Cash Consumption Expenditures**	**12277**	**12698**	**13808**	**14654**	**15560**
一、食品烟酒	Food,Alcohol & Tobacco	4823	5143	5461	5785	5914
二、衣着	Clothing	764	794	846	886	908
三、居住	Residence	1339	1367	1485	1555	1615
四、生活用品及服务	Daily necessities and services	852	901	942	1023	1076
五、交通通信	Transportation & Communication	1909	1844	2243	2250	2599
六、教育文化娱乐	Education, Cultural & Recreation Services	1662	1689	1843	2002	2151
七、医疗保健	Medical Appliances & Articles	667	683	668	860	956
八、其他用品和服务	Other Supplies & Services	261	276	319	292	341

6—7 主要年份城镇居民人均消费支出细项

Breakdown of Per Capita Consumption Expenditure of Urban Households in Main Years

单位：元 (yuan)

项目	Item	2013	2014	2015	2016	2017
消费支出	**Consumption Expenditures**	**14470**	**15046**	**16321**	**17268**	**18349**
一、食品烟酒	Food,Alcohol & Tobacco	4934	5293	5610	5937	6099
（一）食品	Food	4043	4231	4470	4739	4784
（二）烟酒	Tobacco & Alcohol	258	273	272	280	302
（三）饮料	Beverages		84	84	80	92
（四）饮食服务	Catering Services	633	705	784	838	921
二、衣着	Clothing	765	794	846	886	908
（一）衣类	Garments	609	630	666	700	725
（二）鞋类	Shoes	156	164	179	186	184
三、居住	Residence	3263	3390	3629	3784	3885
（一）租赁房房租	Tenancy	170	149	139	125	142
（二）住房维修及管理	Housing Maintenance & Management	346	338	489	560	576
（三）水电燃料及其他	Water,Electricity,Fuels Fee & ect	844	909	884	877	901
（四）自有住房折算租金	Conversion Rent of Owner-occupied housing	1903	1995	2118	2223	2265
四、生活用品及服务	Daily Necessities & Services	856	906	952	1033	1093
（一）家具及室内装饰品	Furniture & Interior Decoration	138	145	162	169	185
（二）家用器具	Household Appliances	252	254	279	277	292
（三）家用纺织品	Home Textiles	68	72	72	88	83
（四）家庭日用杂品	Goods for Daily Use	257	255	263	273	282
（五）个人用品	Personal Items	91	125	131	165	184
（六）家庭服务	Household Services	50	55	45	61	67
五、交通通信	Transportation & Communication	1911	1846	2249	2260	2607
（一）交通	Transportation	1283	1143	1513	1498	1840
（二）通信	Communication	628	703	737	761	767
六、教育文化娱乐	Education, Cultural & Recreation Services	1666	1689	1845	2003	2152
（一）教育	Education	999	955	1009	1202	1346
（二）文化娱乐	Consumption Goods for Recreational Use	668	734	836	801	806
七、医疗保健	Medical Appliances & Articles	803	846	866	1066	1254
（一）医疗器具及药品	Medical Apparatus & Medicine	271	282	308	377	405
（二）医疗服务	Medical Service	532	564	558	689	849
八、其他用品和服务	Other Supplies & Services	272	282	323	299	351
（一）其他用品	Other Supplies	149	150	172	152	144
（二）其他服务	Other Services	123	132	151	147	207

6−8　主要年份城镇居民人均现金消费支出细项

Breakdown of Per Capita Cash Consumption Expenditure of Urban Households in Main Years

单位：元　(yuan)

项　目	Item	2013	2014	2015	2016	2017
现金消费支出	**Cash Consumption Expenditures**	**12277**	**12698**	**13808**	**14654**	**15560**
一、食品烟酒	Food,Alcohol & Tobacco	4823	5143	5461	5785	5914
（一）食品	Food	3944	4102	4345	4612	4631
（二）烟酒	Tobacco & Alcohol	258	273	272	280	302
（三）饮料	Beverages		84	84	80	92
（四）饮食服务	Catering Services	621	684	760	814	890
二、衣着	Clothing	764	794	846	886	908
（一）衣类	Garments	594	630	666	699	724
（二）鞋类	Shoes	156	164	179	186	184
三、居住	Residence	1339	1367	1485	1555	1615
（一）租赁房房租	Tenancy	170	149	139	125	142
（二）住房维修及管理	Housing Maintenance & Management	346	338	489	560	576
（三）水电燃料及其他	Water,Electricity,Fuels Fee & ect	805	881	857	870	896
四、生活用品及服务	Daily Necessities & Services	852	901	942	1023	1076
（一）家具及室内装饰品	Furniture & Interior Decoration	125	145	162	169	184
（二）家用器具	Household Appliances	252	254	279	277	292
（三）家用纺织品	Home Textiles	68	72	72	88	83
（四）家庭日用杂品	Goods for Daily Use	257	251	253	263	265
（五）个人用品	Personal Items	91	125	131	165	184
（六）家庭服务	Household Services	50	55	45	61	67
五、交通通信	Transportation & Communication	1909	1844	2243	2250	2599
（一）交通	Transportation	1282	1141	1507	1489	1832
（二）通信	Communication	627	703	737	761	767
六、教育文化娱乐	Education, Cultural & Recreation Services	1662	1689	1843	2002	2151
（一）教育	Education	999	955	1009	1202	1346
（二）文化娱乐	Consumption Goods for Recreational Use	663	734	834	800	805
七、医疗保健	Medical Appliances & Articles	667	683	668	860	956
（一）医疗器具及药品	Medical Apparatus & Medicine	271	282	308	376	405
（二）医疗服务	Medical Service	532	401	360	484	551
八、其他用品和服务	Other Supplies & Services	261	276	319	292	341
（一）其他用品	Other Supplies	142	150	171	151	140
（二）其他服务	Other Services	119	127	147	141	202

6—9 主要年份城镇居民人均消费主要食品数量
Per Capita Consumption of Major Foods of Urban Households in Main Years

单位：公斤 (kg)

项　目	Item	2013	2014	2015	2016	2017
食品消费情况（含自产自用）	**Conditions of Foods Consumption (including production for self consumption)**					
一、粮食消费量	Grain Consumption	112.42	110.31	106.25	102.18	97.69
（一）谷物消费量	Cereal Consumption	103.90	101.74	97.84	93.34	89.13
（二）薯类消费量	Tuber Consumption	0.93	1.07	1.20	1.25	1.36
（三）豆类消费量	Beans Consumption	7.60	7.50	7.22	7.59	7.20
1.大豆	Soybean	0.62	0.57	0.64	0.57	0.54
二、油脂类消费量	Oil & Fat	9.19	9.22	9.25	8.46	8.81
（一）植物油	Oil-bearing Crops	8.67	8.73	8.71	7.91	8.12
三、蔬菜及菜制品消费量	Vegetables & Its Products Consumption	99.03	101.82	100.06	100.07	99.08
（一）鲜菜	Fresh Vegetables	94.21	96.91	95.31	94.84	94.33
四、肉类	Meat	32.87	36.66	36.65	36.34	36.63
（一）猪肉	Pork	29.82	30.38	30.26	29.00	29.25
（二）牛肉	Beef	2.45	2.27	2.55	2.95	3.16
（三）羊肉	Mutton	0.60	0.64	0.77	1.17	1.24
五、禽类	Poultry	16.41	19.74	19.96	20.76	20.06
六、水产品	Aquatic Products	14.73	14.30	14.23	14.10	14.28
七、蛋类及蛋制品	Eggs & Its Products	6.05	6.22	6.45	6.42	6.45
八、奶和奶制品	Milk & Its Products	14.73	10.62	10.38	9.83	9.58
九、干鲜瓜果类	Dried (Fresh) Melons & Fruits	42.74	47.44	49.35	50.73	51.55
（一）鲜瓜果	Fresh Meions & Fruits	21.24	44.25	45.84	47.03	47.84
（二）坚果类	Nuts & Processed Products	2.38	2.50	2.69	2.86	2.83
十、糖果糕点类	Sweets & cakes	5.89	5.60	5.87	5.45	5.46
#食糖	Sugar	1.74	1.77	1.75	1.66	1.56

6－10　主要年份城镇居民每百户主要耐用消费品拥有量
Ownership of Major Durable Consumer Goods Per 100 Urban Households in Main Years

项　目	Item	2013	2014	2015	2016	2017
耐用消费品拥有情况	**Ownership of Major Durable Consumer Goods**					
1.家用汽车（辆）	Automobile (unit)	19.91	24.03	30.90	36.06	38.48
2.摩托车（辆）	Motorcycle (unit)	54.69	58.32	46.34	43.81	41.80
3.助力车（辆）	Helping Hand Car (unit)	57.45	63.55	70.47	81.04	87.17
4.洗衣机（台）	Washing Machine (unit)	83.92	87.59	92.59	96.51	98.79
5.电冰箱（台）	Refrigerator (unit)	87.38	90.06	94.66	97.97	99.78
6.微波炉（台）	Oven (unit)	51.02	52.87	64.92	65.39	66.43
7.彩色电视机（台）	Color Television Set (unit)	116.20	120.39	115.87	112.90	113.89
8.空调器（台）	Air Conditioner (unit)	85.17	94.81	121.13	128.57	133.84
9.淋浴热水器（台）	Shower (unit)	85.00	90.93	95.54	100.43	103.31
10.排油烟机（台）	Range Hood (unit)	49.09	51.29	61.19	62.29	64.41
11.固定电话（部）	Telephone (unit)	37.07	44.10	38.91	31.93	24.23
12.移动电话（部）	Mobile Telephone (unit)	240.42	250.45	249.87	260.09	267.69
13.家用电脑（台）	Computer (unit)	68.67	75.88	88.10	88.69	88.28
14.照相机（架）	Camera (unit)	24.67	26.25	33.36	24.98	23.46

6—11 主要年份城镇居民人均第二、三产业生产经营收支情况
Production & Management Expenditure Conditions of per Capita Secondary & Tertiary Industry of Urban Households in Main Years

单位：元 (yuan)

项 目	Item	2013	2014	2015	2016	2017
第二产业经营收入	**Operating Income of Secondary Industry**	**583**	**675**	**717**	**971**	**805**
第二产业经营现金收入	Operating Cash Income from Management of Secondary Industry	583	675	717	971	805
第二产业经营费用支出	Operating Expenditures of Secondary Industry	138	121	266	474	315
第二产业经营现金费用支出	Operating Cash Expenditures of Secondary Industry	138	121	266	474	315
第三产业经营收入	**Operating Income of Tertiary Industry**	**2128**	**2879**	**3767**	**4832**	**4764**
第三产业经营现金收入	Operating Cash Income of Tertiary industries	2150	2879	3767	4832	4764
第三产业经营费用支出	Operating Expenditures of Tertiary Industry	240	283	793	978	850
第三产业经营现金费用支出	Operating Cash Expenditures of Tertiary Industry	240	283	793	978	850

6—12 主要年份城镇居民人均可支配收入分五等份收入组
Per Capita Disposable Income of Urban Households by Income Quintile in Main Years

单位：元 (yuan)

年 份	Year	低收入户 (20%) Low Income Households	中等偏下户 (20%) Lower Middle Income Households	中等收入户 (20%) Middle Income Households	中等偏上户 (20%) Upper Middle Income Households	高收入户 (20%) High Income Households
城镇居民人均可支配收入（元）	**Per Capita Disposable Income of Urban Households (yuan)**					
2013		9314	15704	20897	28387	49602
2014		10339	16958	23205	30723	51950
2015		10400	18489	25792	33950	54483
2016		11283	19331	27006	35973	60881
2017		11759	20852	29414	39352	66417

6－13　主要年份农村居民家庭基本情况
Basic Conditions of Rural Households in Main Years

单位：人　　(person)

项　目	Item	2013	2014	2015	2016	2017
期内住户常住成员数	**Number of Permanent Residents**	**8382**	**8202**	**8361**	**8685**	**8616**
调查样本住户数（户）	**Number of Households Surveyed (household)**	**2298**	**2307**	**2345**	**2365**	**2365**
期内人均自有现住房面积（m^2）	**Per Capita Living Floor Space of Period (sq.m)**	**40.49**	**43.25**	**45.22**	**46.28**	**47.23**
常住成员从业人数	**Number of Employees of Permanent Residents**	**4957**	**4810**	**4907**	**4965**	**4819**
户主文化程度	**Education of Household**					
1.未上过学	Not on school	46	46	29	25	25
2.小学	Primary School	740	716	712	749	755
3.初中	Junior Secondary School	1155	1174	1246	1288	1281
4.高中	Senior Secondary School	335	350	343	281	280
5.大学专科	College & Higher Level	22	22	15	21	23
6.大学本科	Undergraduate				1	1
7.研究生	Postgraduate					
本年度就业类型	**Type of Employment in the Current Year**					
一、雇主	Employer	38	31	32	20	15
二、公职人员	Public Officials	27	15	8	12	9
三、事业单位人员	Institutions Personnel	46	35	31	42	45
四、国有企业雇员	Employees of Nationalized Business	10	3	5	9	7
五、其他雇员	Other Employees	664	723	910	1179	1216
六、农业自营	Farming Self-employed	3796	3600	3566	3320	3133
七、非农自营	Not Farming Self-employed	376	403	355	383	394
本季度从事主要行业	**Engagine Major industries in the Current Year**					
一、第一产业	Primary Industry	3817	3648	3578	3391	3198
二、第二产业	Secondary Industry	519	476	604	763	745
三、第三产业	Tertiary Industry	621	686	725	811	876

6—14 主要年份农村居民人均可支配收入及构成
Per Capita Disposable Income of Rural Households & Its Composition in Main Years

单位：元 (yuan)

项　目	Item	2013	2014	2015	2016	2017
可支配收入	**Disposable Income**	**7793**	**8683**	**9467**	**10359**	**11325**
一、工资性收入	Income of Wage & Subsidy	2135	2335	2549	2848	3242
（一）工资	Wage & Subsidy	1551	1934	2057	2482	2853
（二）实物福利	Physical Benefits	3	5	10	14	23
（三）其他	Other Income	581	397	481	352	366
二、经营净收入	Net Income from Management	3794	4048	4359	4759	5103
（一）第一产业经营净收入	Net Income from Management of Primary Industry	3116	3260	3509	3788	4010
1. 农业	Farming	2065	2171	2299	2417	2433
2. 林业	Forestry	296	325	326	367	435
3.牧业	Animal Husbandry	691	695	754	851	930
4. 渔业	Fishery	65	69	130	154	212
（二）第二产业经营净收入	Net Income from Management of Secondary Industry	112	129	135	118	130
（三）第三产业经营净收入	Net Income from Management of Tertiary Industry	566	659	715	852	963
三、财产净收入	Property Net Income	51	75	116	149	185
四、转移净收入	Transfer Net Income	1813	2225	2442	2603	2795
（一）转移性收入	Transfer Income	1937	2343	2594	2805	3057
#养老金或离退休金	Pensions for Old People & Retirement	301	387	424	517	569
（二）转移性支出	Transfer Expenditures	124	118	152	202	262
#社会保障支出	Social Relief Expenditures	106	90	125	161	214

6—15 主要年份农村居民人均现金可支配收入及构成

Per Capita Cash disposable Income of Rural Households & Its Composition in Main Years

单位：元 (yuan)

项 目	Item	2013	2014	2015	2016	2017
现金可支配收入	**Cash Disposable income**	**6959**	**7365**	**8330**	**9378**	**10320**
一、现金工资性收入	Cash Income of Wage & Subsidy	2132	2331	2539	2834	3219
（一）工资	Wage & Subsidy	1551	1934	2057	2482	2853
（二）其他工资性收入	Other Income	581	397	481	352	366
二、现金经营净收入	Cash Net Income from Management	3108	2930	3439	4015	4397
（一）第一产业现金经营净收入	Cash Net Income from Management of Primary Industry	2439	2046	2498	2946	3203
1. 农业	Farming	1418	1206	1447	1692	1740
2. 林业	Forestry	167	153	250	333	387
3. 牧业	Animal Husbandry	691	620	678	775	875
4. 渔业	Fishery	61	67	124	147	201
（二）第二产业现金经营净收入	Cash Net Income from Management of Secondary Industry	123	141	149	131	144
（三）第三产业现金经营净收入	Cash Net Income from Management of Tertiary Industry	546	743	791	939	1050
三、现金财产净收入	Cash Property Net Income	52	76	116	149	185
四、现金转移净收入	Cash Transfer Net Income	1668	2027	2236	2380	2519
（一）现金转移性收入	Cash Transfer Income	1792	2145	2388	2581	2781
#养老金或离退休金	Pensions for Old People & Retirement	301	387	424	517	569
（二）现金转移性支出	Cash Transfer Expenditures	124	118	152	202	262
#个人缴纳的社会保障支出	Social Relief Expenditures paid by individuals	106	90	125	161	214

6－16 主要年份农村居民人均消费支出

Per Capita Consumption Expenditure of Rural Households in Main Years

单位：元 (yuan)

项 目	Item	2013	2014	2015	2016	2017
消费支出	**Consumption Expenditures**	**6035**	**6675**	**7582**	**8351**	**9437**
一、食品烟酒	Food,Alcohol & Tobacco	2215	2463	2681	2880	3043
二、衣着	Clothing	195	209	237	252	287
三、居住	Residence	1369	1551	1730	1904	2120
四、生活用品及服务	Household Facilities, Articles & Services	367	395	456	456	495
五、交通通信	Transport, Post & Telecommunication Services	641	710	822	972	1288
六、教育文化娱乐	Cultural, Educational & Recreational Articles & Services	624	682	842	1001	1128
七、医疗保健	Medicines & Medical Services	526	554	710	782	931
八、其他用品和服务	Other Commodities & Services	99	112	106	105	145

6－17 主要年份农村居民人均现金消费支出

Per Capita Cash Consumption Expenditure of Rural Households in Main Years

单位：元 (yuan)

项 目	Item	2013	2014	2015	2016	2017
现金消费支出	**Cash Consumption Expenditures**	**4448**	**4715**	**5577**	**6277**	**7119**
一、食品烟酒	Food,Alcohol & Tobacco	1571	1646	1931	2151	2248
二、衣着	Clothing	195	208	237	252	285
三、居住	Residence	546	566	634	738	834
四、生活用品及服务	Household Facilities, Articles & Services	358	385	446	449	463
五、交通通信	Transport, Post & Telecommunication Services	641	710	819	965	1284
六、教育文化娱乐	Cultural, Educational & Recreational Articles & Services	624	682	842	1000	1127
七、医疗保健	Medicines & Medical Services	420	408	563	623	748
八、其他用品和服务	Other Commodities & Services	92	110	104	101	130

6－18　主要年份农村居民人均消费支出明细
Breakdown of Per Capita Consumption Expenditure of Rural Households in Main Years

单位：元　　　　(yuan)

项　目	Item	2013	2014	2015	2016	2017
消费支出	**Consumption Expenditures**	**6035**	**6675**	**7582**	**8351**	**9437**
一、食品烟酒	Food,Alcohol & Tobacco	2215	2463	2681	2880	3043
（一）食品	Food	1969	2154	2327	2502	2640
（二）烟酒	Tobacco & Alcohol	178	187	211	212	233
（三）饮料	Beverages		40	44	45	53
（四）饮食服务	Catering Services	68	83	100	120	117
二、衣着	Clothing	195	209	237	252	287
（一）衣类	Garments	150	157	180	193	220
（二）鞋类	Shoes	45	52	57	59	67
三、居住	Residence	1369	1551	1730	1904	2120
（一）租赁房房租	Tenancy	6	7	12	17	18
（二）住房维修及管理	Housing Maintenance & Management	320	306	321	398	451
（三）水电燃料及其他	Water, Electricity, Fuels Fee & ect	349	409	375	362	415
（四）自有住房折算租金	Conversion Rent of Owner-occupied Housing	695	829	1021	1127	1236
四、生活用品及服务	Daily Necessities & Services	367	395	456	456	495
（一）家具及室内装饰品	Furniture & Interior Decoration	77	74	84	72	79
（二）家用器具	Household Appliances	112	111	131	130	129
（三）家用纺织品	Home Textiles	30	27	36	31	26
（四）家庭日用杂品	Goods for Daily Use	123	134	140	143	171
（五）个人用品	Personal Items	18	41	56	70	82
（六）家庭服务	Household Services	7	8	9	10	8
五、交通通信	Transportation & Communication	641	710	822	972	1288
（一）交通	Transportation	457	496	560	667	943
（二）通信	Communication	185	214	262	305	345
六、教育文化娱乐	Education, Cultural & Recreation Services	624	682	842	1001	1128
（一）教育	Education	522	563	693	844	963
（二）文化娱乐	Consumption Goods for Recreational Use	102	119	149	157	165
七、医疗保健	Medical Appliances & Articles	526	554	710	782	931
（一）医疗器具及药品	Medical Apparatus & Medicine	116	129	134	150	200
（二）医疗服务	Medical Service	410	425	576	632	731
八、其他用品和服务	Other Supplies & Services	99	112	106	105	145
（一）其他用品	Other Supplies	75	72	72	67	83
（二）其他服务	Other Services	23	41	33	38	62

6—19 主要年份农村居民人均现金消费支出明细

Breakdown of Per Capita Cash Consumption Expenditure of Rural Households in Main Years

单位：元 (yuan)

项 目	Item	2013	2014	2015	2016	2017
现金消费支出	**Cash Consumption Expenditures**	**4448**	**4715**	**5577**	**6277**	**7119**
一、食品烟酒	Food,Alcohol & Tobacco	1571	1646	1931	2151	2248
（一）食品	Food	1327	1341	1586	1784	1859
（二）烟酒	Tobacco & Alcohol	178	186	210	212	233
（三）饮料	Beverages		39	44	45	53
（四）饮食服务	Catering Services	67	80	92	110	103
二、衣着	Clothing	195	208	237	252	285
（一）衣类	Garments	150	157	180	193	219
（二）鞋类	Shoes	45	52	57	59	66
三、居住	Residence	546	566	634	738	834
（一）租赁房房租	Tenancy	6	7	12	17	18
（二）住房维修及管理	Housing Maintenance & Management	320	306	321	398	451
（三）水电燃料及其他	Water, Electricity, Fuels Fee & ect	221	253	301	323	365
四、生活用品及服务	Daily Necessities & Services	358	385	446	449	463
（一）家具及室内装饰品	Furniture & Interior Decoration	69	70	82	69	68
（二）家用器具	Household Appliances	112	111	131	130	129
（三）家用纺织品	Home Textiles	30	27	36	31	26
（四）家庭日用杂品	Goods for Daily Use	123	129	132	138	150
（五）个人用品	Personal Items	18	41	56	70	82
（六）家庭服务	Household Services	7	8	9	10	8
五、交通通信	Transportation & Communication	641	710	819	965	1284
（一）交通	Transportation	457	496	557	660	939
（二）通信	Communication	185	214	262	305	345
六、教育文化娱乐	Education, Cultural & Recreation Services	624	682	842	1000	1127
（一）教育	Education	522	563	693	844	962
（二）文化娱乐	Consumption Goods for Recreational Use	102	119	149	157	165
七、医疗保健	Medical Appliances & Articles	420	408	563	623	748
（一）医疗器具及药品	Medical Apparatus & Medicine	116	129	134	150	200
（二）医疗服务	Medical Service	410	279	429	472	548
八、其他用品和服务	Other Supplies & Services	92	110	104	101	130
（一）其他用品	Other Supplies	69	69	71	65	74
（二）其他服务	Other Services	23	40	33	36	56

6－20 主要年份农村居民人均消费主要食品数量

Per Capita Consumption of Major Foods by Rural Households in Main Years

单位：公斤 (kg)

项 目	Item	2013	2014	2015	2016	2017
食品消费情况（含自产自用）	**Conditions of Foods consumption (including production for self consumption)**					
一、粮食消费量	Grain Consumption	182.68	183.62	172.21	168.27	163.27
（一）谷物消费量	Cereal Consumption	178.22	178.52	167.04	162.56	157.48
（二）薯类消费量	Tuber Consumption	0.62	0.74	0.65	0.77	136.37
（三）豆类消费量	Beans Consumption	3.85	4.36	4.52	4.94	5.05
1.大豆	Soybean	0.89	0.92	0.74	0.90	0.77
二、油脂类消费量	Oil & Fat	9.96	10.19	7.39	6.80	7.99
（一）植物油	Oil-bearing Crops	7.36	8.13	5.30	4.92	5.90
三、蔬菜及菜制品消费量	Vegetables & Its Products Consumption	87.09	95.42	87.44	79.98	78.15
（一）鲜菜	Fresh Vegetables	86.19	94.28	86.41	78.88	76.96
四、肉类	Meat	25.72	27.41	27.69	27.44	28.35
（一）猪肉	Pork	25.28	25.74	26.10	25.49	26.26
（二）牛肉	Beef	0.33	0.31	0.38	0.53	0.62
（三）羊肉	Mutton	0.12	0.12	0.18	0.36	0.39
五、禽类	Poultry	14.64	16.79	17.58	18.44	19.21
六、水产品	Aquatic Products	5.72	6.62	7.01	7.59	7.66
七、蛋类及蛋制品	Eggs & Its Products	3.88	4.41	5.19	4.49	4.92
八、奶和奶制品	Milk & Its Products	5.72	2.20	1.99	2.23	2.44
九、干鲜瓜果类	Dried (Fresh) Melons & Fruits	20.66	25.14	27.86	30.99	31.08
（一）鲜瓜果	Fresh Meions & Fruits	9.54	24.25	26.83	29.43	29.39
（二）坚果类	Nuts & Processed Products	0.76	0.76	0.87	1.35	1.40
十、糖果糕点类	Sweets & Cakes	3.41	3.45	3.45	3.47	3.48
#食糖	Sugar	1.02	1.16	1.20	1.12	1.08

6－21 主要年份农村居民每百户主要耐用消费品拥有量
Ownership of Major Durable Consumer Goods Per 100 Rural Households in Main Years

项　目	Item	2013	2014	2015	2016	2017
耐用消费品拥有情况	**Ownership of Major Durable Consumer Goods**					
一、家用汽车（辆）	Automobile (unit)	6.92	7.15	6.77	9.98	12.23
二、摩托车（辆）	Motorcycle (unit)	92.71	100.87	100.51	101.77	100.50
三、助力车（辆）	Helping Hand Car (unit)	24.10	29.70	31.26	39.88	46.17
四、洗衣机（台）	Washing Machine (unit)	45.22	51.90	54.48	65.40	68.12
五、电冰箱（台）	Refrigerator (unit)	70.17	75.87	79.56	86.23	88.82
六、微波炉（台）	Oven (unit)	14.76	16.29	14.89	16.63	18.84
七、彩色电视机（台）	Color Television Set (unit)	111.13	114.49	110.74	112.33	113.28
八、空调（台）	Air Conditioner (unit)	12.52	15.34	16.86	24.40	28.86
九、热水器（台）	Shower (unit)	40.81	47.48	50.32	62.33	68.33
十、排油烟机（台）	Range Hood (unit)	5.75	6.67	6.29	8.62	10.38
十一、固定电话（部）	Telephone (unit)	20.19	25.53	18.56	15.16	9.13
十二、移动电话（部）	Mobile Telephone (unit)	237.77	252.26	261.97	274.12	284.27
十三、计算机（台）	Computer (unit)	13.96	17.42	17.15	20.24	21.79
十四、照相机（架）	Camera (unit)	2.70	2.95	1.78	1.21	1.23

6－22　主要年份农村居民人均第一产业生产经营收支情况
Production and Management Expenditure Conditions of Per Capita Primary Industry of Rural Households in Main Years

单位：元 (yuan)

项　目	Item	2013	2014	2015	2016	2017
第一产业经营收入	**Operating Income of Primary industry**	**5505**	**6072**	**6078**	**6706**	**7289**
一、农业	Farming	3244	3543	3551	3706	3798
二、林业	Forestry	376	435	450	594	599
三、牧业	Animal Husbandry	1747	1927	1828	2152	2562
四、渔业	Fishery	117	167	249	254	330
第一产业现金经营收入	**Operating Cash Income of Primary industry**	**4413**	**4482**	**4721**	**5498**	**6091**
一、农业	Farming	2455	2389	2503	2795	2919
二、林业	Forestry	246	261	374	554	551
三、牧业	Animal Husbandry	1590	1675	1605	1908	2307
四、渔业	Fishery	111	157	239	241	314
第一产业经营费用支出	**Operating Expenditures of Primary industry**	**2226**	**2606**	**2413**	**2745**	**3124**
一、农业	Farming	1059	1241	1139	1178	1262
二、林业	Forestry	79	108	123	220	163
三、牧业	Animal Husbandry	1006	1167	1035	1253	1586
四、渔业	Fishery	50	90	116	94	113
第一产业经营现金费用支出	**Operating Cash Expenditures of Primary industry**	**2087**	**2435**	**2223**	**2552**	**3124**
一、农业	Farming	1041	1182	1056	1103	1262
二、林业	Forestry	79	108	123	220	163
三、牧业	Animal Husbandry	906	1055	927	1134	1586
四、渔业	Fishery	50	90	116	94	113

6－23　主要年份农村居民人均可支配收入五等份收入分组
Per Capita Disposable Income of Rural Households by Income Quintile in Main Years

年　份	Year	低收入户 (20%) Low Income Households	中等偏下户 (20%) Lower Middle Income Households	中等收入户 (20%) Middle Income Households	中等偏上户 (20%) Upper Middle Income Households	高收入户 (20%) High Income Households
农村居民人均可支配收入（元）	**Per Capita Disposable Income of Rural Households (yuan)**					
	2013	3245	5477	7392	9857	15121
	2014	3252	5835	7911	10647	18307
	2015	4016	6566	8922	12183	21396
	2016	5001	6990	9547	13420	24606
	2017	5670	7546	10504	14699	25972

6—24 各市城镇居民人均可支配收入和农村居民可支配收入

Per Capita Disposable Income of Urban & Rural Households by City

单位：元 (yuan)

地 区	Region	城镇居民人均可支配收入 Per Capita Disposable Income of Urban Households				农民人均可支配收入 Per Capita Disposable Income of Rural Households			
		2014年	2015年	2016年	2017年	2014年	2015年	2016年	2017年
南宁市	Nanning City	26540	28531	30728	33217	9489	10409	11398	12515
柳州市	Liuzhou City	26193	28184	30270	32661	9221	10125	11107	12151
桂林市	Guilin City	26189	28101	30124	32534	10090	11089	12176	13345
梧州市	Wuzhou City	23944	25548	27260	29359	8592	9322	10142	11085
北海市	Beihai City	25618	27514	29412	31912	9719	10623	11622	12749
防城港市	Fangchenggang City	25727	27579	29758	32079	10038	10992	12113	13373
钦州市	Qinzhou City	25501	27363	29360	31415	9172	10016	10947	11801
贵港市	Guigang City	23252	24880	26771	28806	9624	10558	11572	12544
玉林市	Yulin City	25984	28089	30083	32159	10320	11404	12590	13597
百色市	Baise City	23359	25041	26919	29126	7677	8452	9348	10171
贺州市	Hezhou City	23613	25219	26883	28899	8033	8820	9552	10498
河池市	Hechi City	20880	22237	23660	25647	6432	6927	7509	8260
来宾市	Laibin City	25391	27067	28962	31047	8319	8993	9820	10674
崇左市	Chongzuo City	23152	24634	26605	28813	8273	8918	9801	10860

主要统计指标解释

从2012年四季度起，国家统计局对分别进行的城乡住户调查实施了一体化改革，统一了城乡居民收入指标名称、分类和统计标准，建立了城乡统一的一体化住户调查。广西从2014年开始，正式发布此项改革后的一体化城乡住户收支与生活状况调查数据。

住户　指居住在一个住宅内，共同分享生活开支或收入的一群人。居住在同一房间内、不共同分享生活开支的人群，每个人都视为一个住户。住家保姆、住家家庭帮工视为单独的住户。

常住居民　指住户成员中，经常在家居住、或者调查期内居住时间超过一半的人员，以及本住户供养的学生。常住居民是住户收支的调查对象。

居民人均可支配收入　指居民可用于最终消费支出和储蓄的总和，即居民可用于自由支配的收入，既包括现金收入，也包括实物收入。按照收入的来源，可支配收入包含四项，分别为：工资性收入、经营净收入、财产净收入、转移净收入。

工资性收入　指就业人员通过各种途径得到的全部劳动报酬和各种福利，包括受雇于单位或个人、从事各种自由职业、兼职和零星劳动得到的全部劳动报酬和福利。

经营净收入　指住户或住户成员从事生产经营活动所获得的净收入，是全部经营收入中扣除经营费用、生产性固定资产折旧和生产税净额（生产税减去生产补贴）之后得到的净收入。计算公式具体为：

经营净收入＝经营收入－经营费用－生产性固定资产折旧－生产税净额（生产税－生产补贴）

财产净收入　指住户或住户成员将其所拥有的金融资产和自然资源交由其他机构单位、住户或个人支配而获得的回报并扣除相关的费用之后得到的净收入。计算公式为：财产净收入＝财产性收入－财产性支出

转移净收入　指国家、单位、社会团体对住户的各种经常性转移支付和住户之间的经常性收入转移。包括政府、非行政事业单位、社会团体对居民转移的养老金或退休金、社会救济和补助、政策性生活补贴、救灾款、经常性捐赠和赔偿以及报销医疗费等；住户之间的赡养收入、经常性捐赠和赔偿以及农村地区（村委会）在外（含国外）工作的本住户非常住成员寄回带回的收入等。计算公式为：转移净收入=转移性收入－转移性支出

居民收入五等份分组　指将所有调查户按人均收入水平从低到高顺序排列，平均分为五个等份，处于最高20%的收入群体为高收入组，依此类推依次为中高收入组、中等收入组、中低收入组、低收入组。

居民人均生活消费支出　指居民用于满足家庭日常生活消费需要的全部支出，既包括现金消费支出，也包括实物消费支出。根据用途不同，消费支出可划分为食品烟酒、衣着、居住、生活用品及服务、交通通信、教育文化娱乐、医疗保健、其他用品及服务八大类。

Explanatory Notes on Main Statistical Indicators

Since the 4th quarter of 2012, National Bureau of Statistics has carried out the integrate reforming on the survey of urban & rural residents which were once carried out separately, unified the names, classification and statistical standards of the indicators on urban & rural residents' income, and built up the concordant survey for urban & rural residents. Since 2014, Guangxi has formally released the data on the integration survey of urban and rural residents' income, expenses and livelihood after this reforming.

Household refers to a group of people living in the same residence, sharing the living expenses or incomes together. If the group of people living in the same residence, but not sharing the living expenses or incomes together, then each people in this group is count as one household. The live-in caregiver or live-in journeyman is count as one simply household.

Permanent Resident refers to the personnel living at home permanently or more than a half survey period in a household, and the students provided by this household. The permanent residents are the objects of the household income and expenses survey.

Disposable Income of Household refers to the summary of final consumption and expenses available for household, namely the income can be arranged freely by household, which includes the incomes in cash and in kind. According to the resource, the disposable income includes 4 parts: income of wage and subsidy, net income from management, property net income and transfer net income.

Income of Wage & Subsidy refers to the total labor reward and various welfares earned by employment in various ways, including the total labor reward and welfares earned by being employed by institutions or individuals, working freelance, working part-time jobs and odd jobs.

Net Income from Management refers to the net income earned by household or member of household with working management, and it is the net income gained after deducting the operating costs, productive depreciation of fixed assets and net amount of productive taxes(deducting productive subsidy from productive taxes)from the total operating income. Its calculating formulation is:

Net Income from Management= Total Operating Income

－Operating Costs

－Productive Depreciation of Fixed Assets

－Net Amount of Productive Taxes(Productive Taxes－Productive Subsidy)

Property Net Income refers to the net income after deducting the relevant costs from the return, which is gained through organizing the financial assets and natural assets owned by the household or member of household by other institutions, households or individuals. Its calculating formulation is:

Property Net Income = Property Income－Property Expenses

Transfer Net Income refers to the various usually transferring of incomes from nation, units, and social groups to household and between households. It includes the pension or retirement pay from governments, non-administrative institutions and social groups to household, social relieves and subsidy, policy subsidy for livelihood, relief money, regularly donations, compensations and applies for medical fee, etc. It also includes the supporting income, regularly donations and compensations between households, and the income sent back or brought back by the non-permanent member of the household working out of the rural area(village committee)or overseas. Its calculating formulation is:

Transfer Net Income = Transfer Income－Transfer Expenses

Five Equal Divides of Residents' Income refers to equally divide the total survey households into 5 groups according to the capita income degrees, and rank them from low to high. The group whose income in the highest 20% is called high income households, and by analogy are the upper middle income households, middle income households, lower middle income households,

and low income households.

Per Capita Consumption Expenditure for Livelihood of Household refers to the total expenses meeting the households' needs of daily livelihood consumption, including the consumption expenses in cash and in kind. According to the use, consumption expenses can be divided into 8 broad categories: food, alcohol & tobacco, clothing, residence, daily necessities & services, transportation & communication, education, cultural & recreation services, medical appliances & articles and other supplies & services.

2018广西统计年鉴

第七篇

财政、金融和保险

FINANCE, BANKING & INSURANCE

（校对编辑：黄靖贵）

7—1 公共财政预算收支总额及指数（1978—2017年）

Total Volume & Index of Public Budget Income & Expenditure（1978—2017）

单位：万元 (10 000 yuan)

年份 Year	公共财政预算收入 Public Budget Income	公共财政预算支出 Public Budget Expenditure	收支差额 Income & Expenditure Balance	指数（以上年为100） Index (preceding year =100)	
				公共财政预算收入 Public Budget Income	公共财政预算支出 Public Budget Expenditure
1978	149029	207838	-58809	123.4	143.2
1979	123898	205987	-82089	83.1	99.1
1980	125791	174440	-48649	101.5	84.7
1981	130329	160412	-30083	103.6	92.0
1982	133183	174422	-41239	102.2	108.7
1983	138862	188416	-49554	104.3	108.0
1984	137567	230558	-92991	99.1	122.4
1985	201773	297485	-95712	146.7	129.0
1986	252306	422199	-169893	125.0	141.9
1987	305368	476958	-171590	121.0	113.0
1988	338871	532723	-193852	111.0	111.7
1989	414130	577433	-163303	122.2	108.4
1990	468305	650005	-181700	113.1	112.6
1991	559225	716089	-156864	119.4	110.2
1992	611953	784754	-172801	109.4	109.6
1993	959269	1074853	-115584	156.8	137.0
1994	622617	1249283	-626666	64.9	116.2
1995	794422	1405892	-611470	127.6	112.5
1996	905102	1570121	-665019	113.9	111.7
1997	991568	1708345	-716777	109.6	108.8
1998	1196720	1983609	-786889	120.7	116.1
1999	1335647	2249775	-914128	111.6	113.4
2000	1470539	2584866	-1114327	110.1	114.9
2001	1786706	3516498	-1729792	121.5	136.0
2002	1867320	4198575	-2331255	104.5	119.4
2003	2036578	4436023	-2399445	109.1	105.7
2004	2377721	5074721	-2697000	116.8	114.4
2005	2830359	6114806	-3284447	119.0	120.5
2006	3425788	7295172	-3869384	121.0	119.3
2007	4188265	9859433	-5671168	122.3	135.2
2008	5184245	12971100	-7786855	123.8	131.6
2009	6209888	16218218	-10008330	119.8	125.0
2010	7719918	20075907	-12355989	124.3	123.8
2011	9477209	25452778	-15975569	122.8	126.8
2012	11660614	29852261	-18191647	123.0	117.3
2013	13176035	32086656	-18910621	113.0	107.5
2014	14222803	34797922	-20575119	107.9	108.4
2015	15151562	40655144	-25503582	106.5	116.8
2016	15562677	44417035	-28854358	102.7	109.3
2017	16151273	49085507	-32934234	103.8	110.5

说明：本表中公共财政预算收入和公共财政预算支出2010年以前为地方财政收入和地方财政支出。

Note: The indicator of “Public Income” and “Public Budget Expanditure” refer to Local Financial Income and Local Financial Expenditure Before 2010.

7—2 主要年份财政分项目收入

单位：万元

指 标	Item	2007	2008	2009
财政总收入	**Total Financial Revenue**	**7038810**	**8433036**	**9668808**
#上划中央收入	Turn Over Revenue to the Central Government	2850545	3248791	3458920
公共财政预算收入	**Public Budget Income**	**4188265**	**5184245**	**6209888**
税收收入	**Total Tax Revenue**	**2826809**	**3464935**	**4176820**
增值税	Taxes on Value Added	588429	658507	650089
营业税	Business Tax	1031216	1219700	1548621
企业所得税	Enterprises Income Taxes	300304	372285	360607
企业所得税退税	Return for Enterprises Income Taxes		-117	
个人所得税	Individual Income Tax	192112	194782	200448
资源税	Resource Tax	31740	41411	53448
固定资产投资方向调节税	Fixed Assets Investment Orientation Regulation Tax	534	-5	-2
城市维护建设税	City Maintenance & Construction Tax	185412	217927	240827
房产税	House Property Tax	86254	102785	113070
印花税	Stamp Tax	26670	43831	53965
城镇土地使用税	Urban Land Use Tax	39211	85333	94409
土地增值税	Land Appreciation Tax	105211	157758	151990
车船税	Tax on Vehicles and Boat Operation	8734	19452	32987
耕地占用税	Farm Land Occupation Tax	39951	131219	336245
契税	Deed Tax	184189	212325	330283
烟叶税	Tobacco Leaf Tax	6703	7574	9798
其他税收收入	Other Tax Revenue	139	168	35
非税收入	**Total Non-tax Revenue**	**1361456**	**1719310**	**2033068**
专项收入	Special Income	163642	220854	180871
行政事业性收费收入	Charge of Administrative and Institutional Units	404737	615911	593492
罚没收入	Penalty Receipts	229299	251511	243914
国有资本经营收入	Government Capital Operating Income	372212	404895	593341
国有资源（资产）有偿使用收入	Paid use of Stated-owned Resources Income	141731	133138	265671
其他收入	Other Non-tax Receipts	49835	93001	155779

Local Government Revenue by Items in Main Years

(10 000 yuan)

2010	2011	2012	2013	2014	2015	2016	2017
12286122	**15422300**	**18101386**	**20012643**	**21625355**	**23330330**	**24540771**	**26043209**
4566204	5945091	6440772	6836608	7402552	8178768	8978094	9891936
7719918	**9477209**	**11660614**	**13176035**	**14222803**	**15151562**	**15562677**	**16151273**
5338656	**6448003**	**7624567**	**8757432**	**9780659**	**10316473**	**10362194**	**10576905**
774782	861253	848105	987547	1264512	1399850	2854605	4289926
2074387	2407465	2623212	3041956	3212611	3219044	1560017	
589533	856453	859532	940375	1093533	1097392	1170262	1277460
-334							
258422	294069	241900	277433	302214	347596	401563	501884
69713	85553	101929	119681	171015	180612	172170	167753
-2	-10						
296697	405098	420483	495948	531407	635556	611496	682807
116542	142581	173472	211833	235635	275218	307071	326690
70265	81757	100136	116984	139617	142669	142017	191137
95713	118644	128883	159986	234488	260456	261403	311135
222740	339912	593007	651611	683037	570897	625848	727915
43253	54222	74962	90121	105881	124882	146200	172217
309510	339006	906846	917856	1041784	1282505	1220729	904305
411765	453475	540723	731220	752373	771470	880330	1013488
5670	8525	11377	14881	12552	8326	8483	10188
2381262	**3029206**	**4036047**	**4418603**	**4442144**	**4835089**	**5200483**	**5574368**
226704	303745	314887	407379	429901	1273125	1201637	1347960
650728	956031	1214518	1202154	1140393	978068	1051235	971369
312924	297410	381689	381520	352951	400054	409964	450768
661566	756247	991353	966988	1038912	882447	857632	690621
358740	531203	833992	1163824	1067260	965871	1150319	1616865
170600	184570	299608	296738	412727	335524	529696	496785

7—3　主要年份财政分项目支出

单位：万元

指　标	Item	2007	2008	2009
公共财政预算支出	**Public Budget Expenditure**	**9859433**	**12971100**	**16218218**
一般公共服务	General Public Service	1933693	2245366	2370751
外交	Diplomacy	82		
国防	National Defense	34323	31057	51815
公共安全	Public Security	824496	956563	1077044
教育	Education	1893837	2512210	2965980
#普通教育	Regular Education	1543495	2074491	2390167
职业教育	Vocational Education	157548	225549	334877
科学技术	Science & Technology	131873	162149	180741
#应用研究	Application Research	22223	23349	30712
技术研究与开发	Technological Research & Development	44628	66849	70661
科学技术普及	Popularization of Science & Technology	10766	14592	11115
文化体育与传媒	Culture，Sport & Media	214101	292467	292731
社会保障和就业	Social Security & Employment	1106700	1289769	2036887
#财政对社会保险基金的补助	Subsidy of Finance to the Fund of Social Security	198138	142628	432047
行政事业单位离退休	Retire of Administrative Department	399340	458704	512987
城市居民最低生活保障	Lowest Cost-of-Living of Citizens in Urban Area	59818	97871	116540
农村最低生活保障	Lowest Cost-of-Living of Peasants in Rural Area	12753	84622	144463
医疗卫生与计划生育	Public Health & Family Planning	507547	787683	1161466
#医疗服务	Public Health Service	91227	110341	216395
医疗保障	Medical Security	257360	437517	583090
节能环保支出	Energy Conservation & Environment Protection	135469	279740	499221
#污染防治	Pollution Prevention & Treatment	39033	106564	161690
退耕还林	Returning Land for Farming to Forestry	71327	79393	118652
城乡社区事务	Community Affair in Urban & Rural Area	586447	723033	1040811
农林水事务	Affairs of Agriculture, Forestry & Water Resources	898179	1393970	2107419
#农业	Agriculture	404699	640248	1135962
扶贫	Poverty Alleviation	130868	174651	171991
交通运输	Transportation	412666	584781	815499
工业商业金融等事务	Affairs of Industry, Commerce & Finance	717962	1066574	1064948
其他支出	Other Expenditures	462058	645738	552905

注：1. 按《2017年政府收支分类科目》，指标“财政对社会保险基金的补助”进行了修改调整，无法在表中体现。
2. “医疗保障”包含行政事业单位医疗、财政对基本医疗保险基金的补助、医疗救助、优抚对象医疗。

Local Government Expenditure by Accounting Items in Main Years

(10 000 yuan)

2010	2011	2012	2013	2014	2015	2016	2017
20075907	**25452778**	**29852261**	**32086656**	**34797922**	**40655144**	**44417035**	**49085507**
2687583	3221799	3863708	4131959	4059911	3952989	4507770	4553497
					4569	1103	107
72561	82131	76619	79199	99268	98706	90216	87757
1251395	1394382	1523891	1788149	1922172	2205544	2632819	2831720
3668362	4568882	5892383	6099303	6605347	7896904	8545468	9202033
2982905	3719736	4887114	5022462	5578061	6498328	7012212	7558151
349163	355561	406955	424441	473987	789090	784253	862985
216554	282470	428120	543579	599250	496321	451977	600392
31212	32775	39412	55164	50772	65724	59836	57799
89541	126866	263396	354225	414686	266765	231450	338843
12345	13656	16724	18462	19347	27401	23707	24509
327718	374814	455212	498502	685192	790041	710815	643565
2170733	2506400	2823276	3481154	3871792	4606296	5389523	6786517
446204	687335	988788	1265318	1417965	1882014	2094332	
577000	530725	483010	588726	709171	876652	1218638	2081257
129143	158387	137102	146328	139813	133889	148491	83568
254607	353717	309049	408039	408318	417310	472009	452122
1654911	2328800	2531744	2856114	3553263	4138687	4681866	5123130
836314	1248112	1405004	1668682	1911111	2264488	2596483	2843864
639887	538979	600090	642258	839981	986801	906993	851119
181610	113020	146243	145133	155892	179542	241227	272591
123239	98495	94228	91273	78883	86536	66376	55834
1038717	1187324	1620715	2123282	2693394	3175179	3649854	5296946
2602616	3148555	3690650	3718964	3912868	4975252	5734793	6468687
1233650	1099138	1347723	1356624	1397472	1642166	1669941	1564502
182179	200648	270335	302349	367640	590863	1570837	2403265
937145	2489779	2427442	2389886	2049153	2378280	2171215	2440922
2167009	2932896	3466946	3216638	3512985			
640716	395567	451465	517669	393346	267313	265715	84927

7－4 金融机构存贷款情况（期末余额，2005－2017年）
Deposits & Loans of Financial Institutions（Year-end，2005－2017）

单位：亿元 (100 million yuan)

年 份 Year	本外币存款 Balance of Deposits in RMB & Foreign Currencies	本外币贷款 Balance of Loans in RMB & Foreign currencies
2005	4262.30	3104.60
2006	5029.47	3636.90
2007	5801.04	4331.03
2008	7075.02	5110.06
2009	9638.89	7360.43
2010	11813.90	8979.87
2011	13527.97	10646.43
2012	15966.65	12355.52
2013	18400.48	14081.01
2014	20298.54	16070.95
2015	22793.54	18119.30
2016	25477.80	20640.54
2017	27899.64	23226.14

7—5 2017年全社会金融机构本外币信贷收支平衡表（期末余额）

Balance Sheet of Credit Funds in RMB & Foreign Currencies of Total Financial Institutions in Main Years（2017，Year-end）

单位：亿元 (100 million yuan)

资金来源项目	Sources of Finance	余额 Balance	比年初增加 Increasing Volume than Preceding Year
一、各项存款	Total Deposits	27899.64	2420.84
（一）境内存款	Domestic Deposits	27857.77	2415.87
1. 住户存款	Household Deposits	13814.30	1206.94
（1）活期存款	Current Deposits	7326.32	637.06
（2）定期及其他存款	Fixed deposits & Others	6487.98	569.88
2. 非金融企业存款	Non-financial Enterprises Deposits	8433.28	951.22
（1）活期存款	Current Deposits	5540.21	977.11
（2）定期及其他存款	Fixed deposits & Others	2893.07	-25.89
3. 广义政府存款	Broad Government Deposits	5048.28	579.29
（1）财政性存款	financial Deposits	547.56	154.86
（2）机关团体存款	Organization Financial Deposits	4500.72	424.43
4. 非银行业金融机构存款	Non-banking Financial Institution Financial Deposits	561.91	-321.57
（二）境外存款	Offshore deposits	41.87	4.97
二、金融债券	Financial Bonds	36.93	-55.04
其中：境外发行	Overseas		
三、卖出回购资产	Financial Assets Sold for Repurchase		-34.29
四、借款及非银行业金融机构拆入	Borrowing & Loans from Non-banking Financial Institutions	27.30	11.89
五、联行往来（净）	Interbank Transactions (net)		
六、应付及暂收款	Accounts Payable & Receivable	445.98	38.82
七、各项准备	Other Reserve Funds	664.81	52.77
八、所有者权益	Creditor's Equity	1253.33	179.33
#实收资本	Called-up Capital	349.07	25.83
九、其他	Others	-1956.37	-12.10
资金来源总计	**Total Capital Sources**	**28371.64**	**2602.22**

说明：本表中部分指标已根据中国人民银行南宁中心支行2015年报表进行了调整，下同。

Note: Several indicators in this table are adjusted by the report of Nanning Central Sub Branch of the People's Bank of China in 2015, and the same as the following tables.

7－5 续表 continued

单位：亿元 (100 million yuan)

资金运用项目	Applications of Funds	余额 Balance	比年初增加 Increasing Volume than Preceding Year
一、各项贷款	Total Deposits	23226.14	2585.60
（一）境内贷款	Domestic Loans	22954.56	2578.90
1. 住户贷款	Household Loans	8456.08	1529.46
（1）短期贷款	Short-term Loans	1199.38	206.06
消费贷款	Consumer Loans	555.13	271.50
经营贷款	Operating Loans	644.26	-65.44
（2）中长期贷款	Medium & Long-term Loans	7256.70	1323.41
消费贷款	Consumer Loans	5531.79	1123.73
经营贷款	Operating Loans	1724.90	199.68
2. 非金融企业及机关团体贷款	Non-financial Enterprises & Organizations Loans	14498.49	1049.44
（1）短期贷款	Short-term Loans	3667.18	70.59
（2）中长期贷款	Medium & Long-term Loans	10294.18	1503.99
（3）票据融资	Bill Financing	473.62	-508.17
（4）融资租赁	Finance Lease	32.90	11.50
（5）各项垫款	Advance Money	30.60	-28.46
3. 非银行业金融机构贷款	Non-banking Financial Institution Financial Loans		
（二）境外贷款	Overseas Loans	271.58	6.69
二、债券投资	Investment in Bonds	1211.07	220.50
其中：境外债券	Overseas Bonds		
三、股权及其他投资	Stock Rights & Other Investments	1624.85	289.41
四、买入返售资产	Buying Back Assets	99.40	27.69
五、存放非银行业金融机构款项	Deposits of Non-banking Financial Institutions	6.66	-0.70
六、联行往来（净）	Interbank Transactions (net)	1706.20	-553.52
其中：境内存放二级准备金	Domestic Deposits of Secondary Reserves	583.77	53.78
七、金银占款	Funds Outstanding for Gold & Silver		
八、中央银行外汇占款	Funds Outstanding for Foreign Exchange		
九、应收及预付款	Accounts Payable & Suspense Credit	251.69	24.39
十、投资性房地产	Investment Real Estate	2.71	2.23
十一、固定资产	Fixed Assets	242.91	6.63
资金运用总计	**Total Assets**	**28371.64**	**2602.22**

7－6　2017年全社会金融机构人民币信贷收支平衡表（期末余额）
Balance Sheet of Credit Funds in Renminbi of Total Financial Institutions in Main Years（2017,Year-end）

单位：亿元　　　　(100 million yuan)

资金来源项目	Sources of Finance	余额 Balance	比年初增加 Increasing Volume than Preceding Year
一、各项存款	Total Deposits	27714.24	2455.68
（一）境内存款	Domestic Deposits	27679.65	2454.72
1. 住户存款	Deposits of Households	13761.04	1211.60
（1）活期存款	Current Deposits	7293.67	639.98
（2）定期及其他存款	Fixed deposits & Others	6467.37	571.62
2. 非金融企业存款	Non-financial Enterprises Deposits	8315.34	984.28
（1）活期存款	Current Deposits	5453.84	978.28
（2）定期及其他存款	Fixed deposits & Others	2861.50	6.00
3. 广义政府存款	Broad Government Deposits	5041.97	580.26
（1）财政性存款	Financial Deposits	547.56	154.86
（2）机关团体存款	Organization Financial Deposits	4494.40	425.41
4. 非银行业金融机构存款	Non-banking Financial Institution Financial Deposits	561.29	-321.42
（二）境外存款	Offshore deposits	34.59	0.96
二、金融债券	Financial Bonds	36.93	-55.04
其中：境外发行	Overseas		
三、卖出回购资产	Financial Assets Sold for Repurchase		-34.29
四、借款及非银行业金融机构拆入	Borrowing & Loans from Non-banking Financial Institutions	2.11	-1.34
五、联行往来（净）	Interbank Transactions (net)		
六、应付及暂收款	Accounts Payable & Receivable	431.90	30.39
八、各项准备	Other Reserve Funds	648.43	56.36
九、所有者权益	Creditor' s Equity	1244.73	178.47
#实收资本	Called-up Capital	349.07	25.83
十、其他	Others	-1981.22	-12.06
资金来源总计	**Total Capital Sources**	**28097.13**	**2618.17**

7—6 续表 continued

单位：亿元 (100 million yuan)

资金运用项目	Applications of Funds	余额 Balance	比年初增加 Increasing Volume than Preceding Year
一、各项贷款	Total Deposits	22781.81	2606.04
（一）境内贷款	Domestic Loans	22767.66	2596.49
1. 住户贷款	Household Loans	8455.85	1529.48
（1）短期贷款	Short-term Loans	1199.16	206.06
消费贷款	Consumer Loans	554.91	271.50
经营贷款	Operating Loans	644.26	-65.44
（2）中长期贷款	Medium & Long-term Loans	7256.69	1323.41
消费贷款	Consumer Loans	5531.79	1123.74
经营贷款	Operating Loans	1724.90	199.68
2. 非金融企业及机关团体贷款	Non-financial Enterprises & Organizations Loans	14311.81	1067.01
（1）短期贷款	Short-term Loans	3524.41	92.41
（2）中长期贷款	Medium & Long-term Loans	10250.70	1499.71
（3）票据融资	Bill Financing	473.62	-508.17
（4）融资租赁	Finance Lease	32.90	11.50
（5）各项垫款	Advance Money	30.16	-28.44
3. 非银行业金融机构贷款	Non-banking Financial Institution Financial Loans		
（二）境外贷款	Overseas Loans	14.15	9.55
二、债券投资	Investment in Bonds	1211.07	220.50
其中：境外债券	Overseas Bonds		
三、股权及其他投资	Stock Rights & Other Investments	1624.85	289.41
四、买入返售资产	Buying Back Assets	99.40	27.69
五、存放非银行业金融机构款项	Deposits of Non-banking Financial Institutions	6.01	-0.13
六、联行往来（净）	Interbank Transactions (net)	1892.28	-550.26
其中：境内存放二级准备金	Domestic Deposits of Secondary Reserves	582.13	53.70
七、金银占款	Funds Outstanding for Gold & Silver		
八、中央银行外汇占款	Funds Outstanding for Foreign Exchange		
九、应收及预付款	Accounts Payable & Suspense Credit	236.10	16.06
十、投资性房地产	Investment Real Estate	2.71	2.23
十一、固定资产	Fixed Assets	242.90	6.63
资金运用总计	**Total Capital Applications**	**28097.13**	**2618.17**

7—7 主要年份保险业务

Major Indictors of Insurance Business in Main Years

单位：万元 (10 000 yuan)

项 目	Item	2001	2005	2010	2013	2014	2015	2016	2017
全部业务	**All Insurance Business**								
保费收入	**Premium Income**	**350616**	**731142**	**1790516**	**2754733**	**3132331**	**3857457**	**4691738**	**5650988**
保险密度（元）	Insurance Density (yuan)	73.69	149.39	389.02	583.75	661.32	804.31	969.76	1157
保险深度（%）	Insurance Depth (%)	1.6	1.8	1.9	1.9	2.0	2.3	2.6	2.8
财产保险公司业务	**Property Insurance Business**								
保费收入	Premium Income	133096	238790	691943	1188778	1406703	1606792	1798638	2132131
企业财产保险	Enterprise Property Insurance	30655	31204	44305	57998	59952	56043	53926	54973
机动车辆保险	Automobile Insurance	75637	160592	529660	902254	1037357	1172478	1329670	1517534
货物运输保险	Cargo Transportation Insurance	7653	9228	13727	18845	19107	19597	17223	17925
其他财产保险	Other Property Insurance	8425	9084	16228	47380	50906	55889	59886	69013
责任保险	Liability Insurance	8898	8060	23152	35362	43507	52424	58643	68476
信用保证保险	Credit & Guarantee Insurance	726	7878	12005	32096	45208	51578	48964	106576
农业保险	Agriculture Insurance	1102	347	7454	27640	49748	63413	88822	125307
短期健康保险	Short-term Health Insurance		308	10517	25187	50234	76974	76096	94539
意外伤害险	Accident Injury Insurance		12089	24078	42017	50685	58395	65409	77788
储金	Deposits From Insured	8446	5611	4901	4346	4352	133093	283871	192791
赔案件数（万件）	Number of Claims (10 000 cases)	11.82	28.24	79.93	147.54	176.77	294.21	265.23	295
赔款支出	Benefit Paid	62992	117165	270387	566449	710738	791312	841977	960917
企业财产保险	Enterprise Property Insurance	14836	13173	10984	26789	55184	42648	28701	29901
机动车辆保险	Automobile Insurance	36795	72637	217688	447984	514911	549783	598909	678761
货物运输保险	Cargo Transportation Insurance	3118	18904	4831	9978	13070	10080	10948	10794
其他财产保险	Other Property Insurance	2366	3322	5270	24810	28199	28066	26367	36465
责任保险	Liability Insurance	4143	2571	9114	15724	20004	20546	23291	27124
信用保证保险	Credit & Guarantee Insurance	33	1921	765	8274	3510	19682	18688	13915
农业保险	Agriculture Insurance	476	116	7148	12878	39536	52591	52916	52816
短期健康保险	Short-term Health Insurance		61	5523	11554	23131	49320	62158	86365
意外伤害险	Personal Accident Insurance		4459	6860	8457	13193	18596	20000	24776
未决赔款	Outstanding Insurance	21255	55668	158487	279890	333106	349303	378654	405587

注：2001－2007年保险密度使用平均总人口计算，2008年保险密度使用平均常住人口计算，请使用时注意口径区别。

Note: The data on "Insurance Density" from 2001 to 2007 was calculated by average total population, while the data in 2008 was calculated by average permanent population, please pay attention to the difference of coverage while using.

7—7 续表 continued

单位：万元 (10 000 yuan)

项 目	Item	2001	2005	2010	2013	2014	2015	2016	2017
人身保险公司业务	**Life Insurance Business**								
保费收入	Premium Income	217520	492352	1098573	1566045	1725628	2250665	2893100	3518857
个人业务	Personal Insurance								
人寿保险	Life Insurance Business	161293	383881	970539	1350117	1435262	1848424	2380223	2831182
分红产品	Participating	36710	250131	837623	1176250	920041	882007	1000947	1272621
投资连接产品	Unit-link	8837		603	674	773	969	1177	1425
其他产品	Others	115546	133750	132314	173193	514448	965448	1378099	1557136
意外伤害险	Personal Accident Insurance	6302	6847	21642	28861	45510	59499	61707	80228
健康险	Health Insurance	3180	21642	57851	106493	138495	193886	287417	424683
团体业务	Group Insurance								
人寿保险	Life Insurance Business	27140	43950	15804	6063	5573	5773	5724	4310
分红产品	Participating	2300	33443	0	87	6	18	32	43
投资连接产品	Unit-link								
其他产品	Others	2440	10507	15804	5975	5567	5755	5691	4267
意外伤害险	Accident Injury Insurance	16496	17875	14765	33544	31340	34242	34852	36785
健康险	Health Insurance	3109	18157	17972	40968	69449	108841	115587	141669
#新单保费	Initial Premium	104475	244075	615763	740331	822591	1257626	1663922	1821750
有效保单件数（万件）	Policies In Force (10 000 cases)	785	590	1063	1283	1191	1594	1958	2361
赔款和给付支出	Benefit Paid	83988	52123	173078	342055	380048	536356	747528	857383
个人业务	Personal Insurance								
年金给付	Annuity Paid	36306	11836	24995	37852	48230	81108	108692	137041
满期给付	Maturity Benefit	17754	6972	90873	213088	225969	313774	417729	465295
死伤医疗给付	Benefit of Deaths, Injury & Medical Treatment	7573	7936	14436	31448	36008	43817	54187	66134
团体业务	Group Insurance								
年金给付	Annuity Paid	6136	2952	6904	7984	8521	8346	9025	9952
满期给付	Maturity Benefit	4791	313	3182	4394	3650	3615	6852	7242
死伤医疗给付	Benefit of Deaths, Injury & Medical Treatment	11428	934	1085	6769	9927	12720	11696	11668
退保	Surrender	27014	83367	82797	210284	350146	417756	413876	797509

注：1. 本表由中国保险监督管理委员会广西监管局提供。
2. 2005年人身保险公司业务中人寿保险的个人业务和团体业务“投资连接保险”并入其他产品中统计。
3. 2005年赔款和给付支出中“赔款支出”从“死伤医疗给付”中剔除，但包含在赔款和给付支出总额中。

Note: 1. The data in this table is provided by Guangxi management & supervision bureau of Chinese insurance management & supervision committee.
2. The “Unit-link”, which belonging to personal insurance and group insurance of life insurance business in life insurance company business, was merged into the other business in 2005.
3. The “Benefit” was eliminated from “Benefit of Deaths, Injury & Medical Treatment” in “Benefit Paid” in 2005, but it is still belong to the “Benefit Paid”.

主要统计指标解释

财政收入 是指国家财政参与社会产品分配所取得的收入，是实现国家职能的财力保证。财政收入所包括的内容几经变化，目前主要包括：（1）各项税收，包括增值税、营业税、消费税、土地增值税、城市维护建设税、资源税、城市土地使用税、印花税、房产税、车船使用税、屠宰税、个人所得税、企业所得税、关税、契税、农牧业税和耕地占用税等。（2）专项收入：包括征收排污费收入、城市水资源费收入、教育费附加收入、矿产资源补偿费收入。（3）其他收入，包括国有资产经营收益、国有企业计划亏损补贴、基本建设贷款归还收入、基本建设收入、罚没收入、行政性收费收入、其他收入等。

地方财政收入 指按财政体制划分的地方本级收入。1994年分税制财政体制改革以后，属于中央财政的收入包括关税、海关代征消费税和增值税，消费税，中央企业所得税，地方银行和外资银行及非银行金融企业所得税，铁道、银行总行、保险总公司等集中缴纳的营业税、所得税、利润和城市维护建设税，增值税的75%部分，证券交易税（印花税）50%部分和海洋石油资源税。属于地方财政的收入包括营业税，地方企业所得税，个人所得税，城镇土地使用税，固定资产投资方向调节税，城镇维护建设税，房产税，车船使用税，印花税，屠宰税、农牧业税，农业特产税，耕地占用税，契税、增值税的25%部分，证券交易税（印花税）50%部分和除海洋石油资源税以外的其他资源税。

财政支出 是指国家为行使其职能，对筹集的财政资金进行有计划的分配使用的总称。国家财政支出，体现政府的活动范围和方向，反映财政资金的分配关系。财政支出主要包括：（1）基本建设支出；（2）企业挖潜改造资金；（3）地质勘探费；（4）科技三项费用；（5）流动资金；（6）支援农村生产支出；（7）农林水利气象等部门的事业费；（8）工业交通等部门事业费；（9）商业部门事业费；（10）城市维护费；（11）文教卫生事业费；（12）科学事业费；（13）其他部门事业费；（14）抚恤和社会福利救济费；（15）国防支出类；（16）行政管理费；（17）公检法支出；（18）价格补贴支出；（19）支援不发达地区支出；（20）专项支出；（21）农业综合开发支出；（22）行政事业单位离退休经费（23）其他支出等。

地方财政支出 指根据政府在经济和社会活动中的不同职责，划分中央和地方政府的责权，按照政府的责权划分确定的支出。中央财政支出包括国防支出，武装警察部队支出，中央行政管理费和各项事业费，重点建设支出以及中央政府调整国民经济结构、协调地区发展、实施宏观调控的支出。地方财政支出主要包括地方行政管理和各项事业费，地方统筹的基本建设、技术改造支出，支援农村生产支出，城市维护和建设费，价格补贴支出等。

地方财政用于农业的支出 指国家财政预算内资金用于农业的各项投资支出。包括：（1）对农垦、农业、畜牧、林业、农机管理、水利、水产、气象等部门的各项事业经费和基本建设、流动资金、挖潜改造资金、科技三项费用等专项拨款；（2）支援农业的各项生产支出，如小型农田水利和水土保持补助费、扶持农业经济困难的乡镇企业，农业生产队（组、户）改善生产基本条件的资金和农村开荒补助、农村草场和畜禽保护补助费、农村造林和林木保护补助费、农村水产补助费、农业发展和发展粮食生产专项资金支出、支援不发达地区资金中用于农业的支出等；（3）农业综合开发支出。

地方财政用于教育的支出 指国家财政预算内资金安排用于教育的各项支出。包括：（1）教育部门的事业费和基本建设拨款；（2）各部门事业费中用于教育的支出。如中等专业学校、技工学校经费、干部培训费等；（3）专项经费中的教育费附加支出，支援不发达地区资金中用于教育的支出。

信贷资金 指金融机构以信用方式积聚和分配的货币资金。金融机构信贷资金的来源有各项存款，对省外（国际）金融机构负债、流通中货币、银行自有资金及当年结益等；信贷资金的运用有各项贷款、黄金占款、外汇占款、财政借款及在省外（国际）金融机构中的资产等。

存款 指企业、机关、团体或居民根据资金必须收回的原则，把货币资金存入银行或其他信用机构保管并取得一定利息的一种信用活动形式。根据存款对象的不同可划分为企业存款、财政存款、机关团体存款、基本建设存款、城镇储蓄存款、农村存款等科目。它是银行信贷资金的主要来源。

贷款 指银行或其他信用机构根据资金必须归还的原则，按一定利率，为企业、个人等提供资金的一种信用活动形

式。我国银行贷款分为流动资金贷款、固定资产贷款、城乡个体工商户贷款以及农业贷款等科目。

保险公司 在中国境内的、经过保险监督部门批准设立，并依法登记注册的各类商业保险公司。

保险金额 又叫承保额，是指保险人对被保险人负提损失补偿或约定给付的金额。它是保险合同上的最高责任额，也是计算保费的依据。

保费 又叫保险费，是指投保人为取得保险人在约定范围内所承担赔偿责任而支付给保险人的费用。

赔款 指保险人根据保险合同的规定，向被保险人支付的赔偿保险责任损失的金额。

给付 包括死伤医疗给付和满期给付。死伤医疗给付是指保险人根据人寿保险及长期健康保险合同的规定，因被保险人在保险期内发生保险责任范围内的保险事故支付给被保险人（或受益人）的金额。满期给付是指被保险人生存期满，保险人按人寿保险合同规定支付给被保险人的满期保险金额。

Explanatory Notes on Main Statistical Indicators

Government Revenue refers to the revenue of the government finance by means of participating in the distribution of the social products, which are the financial resources for ensuring the government to function. The contents of government revenue have been changed several times. Now it includes the following main items: (1) Various tax revenues, including value added taxes, business tax, consumption tax, land value added tax, tax on city maintenance and construction, resources tax, tax on use of urban land, stamp tax, tax on real estate, tax on the use of vehicles and ships, slaughter tax, personal income tax, enterprise income tax, tariff, contract tax, tax on agriculture and animal husbandry and tax on occupancy of cultivated land, etc. (2) Special income: including revenue collected from imposing fee on sewage treatment, revenue collected from imposing fee on urban water resources, extra-charges for education, and revenue collected from imposing fee on mine resources. (3) Other revenues, including profits from management of state-owned assets, subsidies to loss-making state-owned enterprise, revenue from the repayment of capital construction loan, revenue from capital construction, penalty, administration income and other incomes.

Revenue of the Local Government In according with the classification of the structure of the government finance in 1994 on the basis of the classification of channels for collection of tax revenues, the revenue of the local governments have different coverage. The revenue of the central government includes tariff, consumption tax and value added tax levied by the customs, consumption tax, income tax of the enterprises subordinate to the central government, income taxes of the local banks, foreign-funded banks and non-band financial institutions, business tax, income tax and profits of railways, head office of insurance company, which are handed over to the government in a centralized way, tax on city maintenance and construction, 75% of the value added tax, tax on ocean petroleum resources, 50% of the tax on stock dealing (stamp tax). The revenue of the local government includes business tax, income tax of the enterprises subordinated to the local government, personal income tax, tax on the use of urban land, tax on the adjustment of the investment in fixed assets. Tax on town maintenance and construction, tax on real estate, tax on the use of vehicles and ships, stamp tax, slaughter tax, tax on agriculture and animal husbandry, tax on special agricultural products, tax on the occupancy of cultivated land, contract tax, 25% of the value added tax, 50% of the tax on stock dealing (stamp tax) and tax on resources other than the ocean petroleum resources.

Government Expenditure refers to the (1) Expenditure for capital construction; (2) Innovation funds of the enterprises; (3) Geological prospecting expenses; (4) Expenditures for science and technology promotion; (5) Circulating funds; (6) Expenditure for supporting rural production; (7) Operating expenses of the departments of farming, forestry, water conservancy and meteorology etc; (8) Operating expenses of the departments of industry, transport; (9) Operating expenses of the department of commerce; (10) Expenditure for city maintenance; (11) Operating expenses of the departments of culture, education and public health; (12) Operating expenses of the department of science; (13) Operating expenses of the other departments; (14) Pension for the disabled or for the families of the bereaved and relief funds for social welfare; (15) Expenditures for national defense; (16) Administrative expenses (17) Expenditure for public security agency, procurator agency and court of justice; (18) Expenditure for price subsidies; (19) Expenditure for supporting under-developed areas; (20) Special expenditure; (21) Expenditure for comprehensive development of agriculture; (22) Expenditure for retired persons in administrative department; (23) Other expenditures.

Expenditure of the Local Governments According to the different functions of the central government and local governments in the economic and social activities, the rights of affairs administration are classified between the central government and local governments are made on the basis of the classification of the rights of affairs administration between them. The expenditure of the central government includes the expenditure for national defense, expenditure for armed police forces, the administrative expenses and various operating expenses at the level of central government, expenditure for key projects and the expenditure of the central government for adjusting the national economic structure, coordinating the development among different regions and exercising the macro-economic regulation and control. The expenditure of the local governments includes mainly the administrative expenses and various operating expenses at the level of local government, expenditure for supporting rural production, expenditure for city maintenance and construction and expenditure for price subsidies, etc.

Local Government Expenditure for Agriculture refers to the investment and expenditure of national financial budgetary fund for agriculture, including: (1) Operating expenses for agricultural exclamation, agriculture, animal husbandry, forestry, agricultural machinery management, water conservancy, aquatic products and meteorology, and special appropriation for capital construction, floating funds, innovation funds and expenditures for science and technology promotion; (2) Expenditures for supporting agricultural production, such as subsidies to the small water conservancy and rural water and soil conserving, expenditure for supporting township enterprises, funds for improving capital productive conditions of agricultural production teams and subsidies on the rural waste land exclamation, subsidies to the expenditure for the protection of grasslands and cattle and fowls, subsidies on forestation and forest protection in rural areas, subsidies on the rural aquatic products industry, special fund for developing agriculture and grain production, expenditure in funds supporting under-developed areas for agriculture; (3) Expenditure for agriculture comprehensive development.

Local Government Expenditure for Education refers to expenses of national financial budgetary fund for education, including: (1) Operating expenses and capital construction appropriation of education departments; (2) Expenditure for education in operating expenses of various departments, such as expenses for specialized secondary schools and skilled workers' schools and expenditure for cadres training, etc. (3) Education expenditure added in special expenditure and expenditure in funds supporting under-developed areas for education.

Credit Funds refer to the funds issued as loans by banking institution. The sources of credit funds of the banking institutions included deposits, liabilities to international financial institutions, currency in circulation, self-owned funds and current retained profits, etc. The credit funds can be used in forms of loans, gold, foreign exchange, government debt and assets in the other provinces, autonomous regions and municipalities (international) financial institutions.

Deposit is a form of credit by which enterprises, institutions, organizations or residents can put money into banks and other credit institutions for safekeeping and interest earning under the principle of free withdrawal. According to different depositors, deposits are divided into enterprise deposits, treasury deposits, deposits of government agencies and organizations, capital construction deposits, urban savings deposits, rural deposits and other deposits. Deposits are major sources of the credit funds of banks.

Loan is a form of credit by which banks and other credit institutions provide funds at certain interest rate to enterprises and individuals in the light of the principle of unconditional repayment. Loans from Chinese banks include circulating capital loans, fixed assets loans, loans to urban and rural individuals engaged in industrial and commercial business and agricultural loans.

Insurance Companies refer to commercial insurance companies of various forms registered by law and established in China with the approval of insurance regulatory agencies.

Amount Insured refers to the maximum that the insurant will get for the claim of the case insured.

Premium is the fee paid by the insurant based on a proportion of the benefit he or she may get from the insurance plus the insurance value. It includes the income from the deposit of property insurance and personal insurance.

Settle Claim is the compensation paid by the insurer to the insurant in accordance with the insurance contact.

Payment includes payment for death, injury or medical treatment and mature payment. Payment for death, injury or medical treatment refers to the money paid to the insurant (of the beneficiary) in accordance with the life of health insurance contract when the insurant encounters accidents within the insured period covered in the contract. Mature payment refers to the mature payment to the insurant in according with the life insurance contract at the end of the insured period for the loss which has been checked and found to be in the range liability of the insurance after an accident has happened to the insured property or to a person who has insured his life. It is further divided into settled and unsettled claim.

第八篇

资源与环境

NATURAL RESOURCES & ENVIRONMENT

（校对编辑：黄浩洲　朱旭芳）

8－1 自然资源（2017年）
Natural Resources (2017)

指 标	Item	2015	2016	2017
一、土地（2014年数据）	**Land (Data in 2014)**			
土地面积（万平方公里）	Land Area (10 000 sq.km)	23.76	23.76	23.76
按土地特征分：（万公顷）	By Land Use (10 000 hectares)			
林地面积	Area of Afforested Land	1331.53	1330.64	1329.94
牧草地面积	Grass Area	0.52	0.52	0.52
水域及水利设施用地面积	Water Area & Water Conservancy Facilities Area	86.20	86.00	85.85
二、海洋	**Sea**			
海岸线长度（公里）	Length of Mainland Shore (km)	1629	1769	1707
浅海面积（平方公里）（2011年数）	Shallow Sea Area (sq.km) (Data in 2011)	6488	3593	3480
滩涂面积（平方公里）（2011年数）	Sea-beach Area (sq.km) (Data in 2011)	1005	833	1005
三、气候	**Climate**			
年平均气温（℃）	Annual Average Temperature (℃)	21.5	21.4	21.1
年平均日照时数（小时）	Annual Average Sunshine Time (hour)	1354	1604	1433
年平均降水量（毫米）	Annual Average Precipitation (mm)	1937	1660	1810
四、森林	**Forest**			
森林面积（万公顷）	Forest Area (10 000 hectares)	1478	1479	1480
人均森林面积（亩，按常住人口平均）	Per Capita Forest Area (mu，Average by Permanent Population)	4.64	4.61	4.54
活立木蓄积量（万立方米）	Stock Volume of Living Stumpage (10 000 cu.m)	70308	76194	77500

注:本表资料由自治区国土厅、海洋和渔业厅、林业厅、气象局气候中心气候变化评价室提供。

Note: Autonomous Region Territorial Resources Bureau, Department of Ocean and Fisheries,Forestry Bureau and Evaluation Office for Climatic Variation in Weather Center of Meteorological Bureau provide the data in this table.The date of the land is in 2012.

8－1 续表 1 countinued

指 标	Item	2016	2017
森林覆盖率（%）	Forest-coverage Rate (%)	62.3	62.3
按市分	Grouped by City		
南宁市	Nanning	47.7	48.3
柳州市	Liuzhou	65.0	66.4
桂林市	Guilin	70.9	71.2
梧州市	Wuzhou	75.9	75.0
北海市	Beihai	36.3	31.8
防城港市	Fangchenggang	58.7	60.2
钦州市	Qinzhou	54.2	57.1
贵港市	Guigang	46.3	46.4
玉林市	Yulin	61.0	61.9
百色市	Baise	67.4	68.5
贺州市	Hezhou	72.9	72.5
河池市	Hechi	68.7	69.7
来宾市	Laibin	51.8	52.2
崇左市	Chongzuo	54.7	54.9
五、矿产资源（保有资源储量，万吨）	**Mineral Ensured Reserves (10 000 tons)**		
锰矿（矿石）	Manganese (ore)	47449	47634
锡（Sn）	Tin	70	70
砷（As）	Arsenic	41	41
钨（Wo_3）	Wolfram	36	41
锑（Sb）	Antimony	50	50
铝土矿（矿石）	Bauxite (ore)	88625	102606
滑石（矿石）	Talcum (ore)	1620	1817
重晶石（矿石）	Barite (ore)	5249	5349
镁（白云岩，矿石）	Magnesium (dolomite,ore)	161	161
硫铁矿（矿石）	Troilite (ore)	25980	26094
煤矿（矿石）	Coal (ore)	208861	207305

8－2 主要河流基本情况（2017年）
Major Rivers（2017）

河流名称	River	流域面积（万平方公里）Drainage Area (10 000 sq.km)	年径流量（亿立方米）Annual Flow (100 million sq.m)	水力资源蕴藏量（万千瓦）Hydropower Resource (10 000 kw)	流域面积占全区总面积的比重（%）As Percentage of Total Drainage Area of Guangxi (%)
全自治区	**Total**	**23.67**	**2386.05**	**2173.90**	**100**
#红水河	Hongshuihe River	3.86	392.38	969.00	16.3
郁　江	Yujiang River	6.81	478.90	365.70	28.8
西江下游区	Lower Reaches of Xijiang River	2.14	211.10		9.0
桂　江	Guijiang River	1.82	228.88	171.90	7.7
南流江	Nanliujiang River	0.92	117.57	23.76	3.9
柳　江	Liujiang River	4.20	551.96	408.20	17.7
贺　江	Hejiang River	0.84	62.19	79.70	3.5

注：本表数据由自治区水利厅提供，下表同。
Note: The data in this table and the above one is provided by Autonomous Region Water Conservancy Bureau.

8—3 水资源基本情况
Water Resources of Guangxi

年份与市别	Year & Cities	地表水资源量（亿立方米）Volume of Surface Water Resources (100 million cu.m)	地下水资源量（亿立方米）Volume of Underground Water Resources (100 million cu.m)	人均水资源量（立方米/人）Per Capita Water Resources (cu.m/person)
2000		1592.10	385.01	3375
2001		2415.10	438.78	5031
2002		2372.60	514.50	4942
2003		1807.10	575.30	3740
2004		1604.52	321.53	3282
2005		1720.82	365.69	3494
2006		1881.00	453.20	3792
2007		1377.83	341.30	2891
2008		2282.45	504.77	4739
2009		1484.31	256.84	3069
2010		1823.60	355.80	3962
2011		1350.02	271.21	2909
2012		2086.36	587.34	4476
2013		2057.33	478.12	4360
2014		1978.06	402.97	4163
2015		2432.20	467.28	5074
2016		2177.00	529.15	4503
2017		2386.05	426.57	4889
南 宁 市	Nanning	153.28	39.98	2142.83
柳 州 市	Liuzhou	234.49	27.15	5862.25
桂 林 市	Guilin	388.14	68.21	7674.56
梧 州 市	Wuzhou	121.47	20.84	3999.14
北 海 市	Beihai	33.68	9.92	2144.53
防城港市	Fangchenggang	88.36	17.20	9398.00
钦 州 市	Qinzhou	117.46	24.90	3581.10
贵 港 市	Guigang	96.79	24.97	2212.19
玉 林 市	Yulin	133.59	34.68	2298.96
百 色 市	Baise	268.68	45.28	7368.16
贺 州 市	Hezhou	106.90	19.32	5197.50
河 池 市	Hechi	407.15	40.49	11555.24
来 宾 市	Laibin	124.77	29.83	5623.82
崇 左 市	Chongzuo	111.29	23.80	5333.05

8—4 供水用水情况（2017年）
Statistics of Water Supply & Consumption（2017）

单位：亿立方米 （100 million cu.m）

地 区	Region	供水总量 Total Volume of Water Supply	#地表水 Surface Water	用水总量 Total Volume of Water Consumption	#农田灌溉用水 Water for Irrigation of Agricultural Land	工业用水 Water Consumption for Industry	居民生活用水 Water Consumption for Household
全自治区	**Total**	**284.94**	**273.09**	**284.94**	**175.04**	**45.96**	**28.13**
南宁市	Nanning	40.93	38.89	40.93	22.37	8.69	4.43
柳州市	Liuzhou	22.30	20.57	22.30	12.36	5.31	2.44
桂林市	Guilin	39.18	38.56	39.18	27.46	3.75	3.10
梧州市	Wuzhou	13.58	13.56	13.58	7.34	2.75	1.92
北海市	Beihai	10.75	9.28	10.75	5.30	2.01	1.05
防城港市	Fangchenggang	6.47	6.37	6.47	2.91	1.69	0.51
钦州市	Qinzhou	15.68	15.32	15.68	10.86	1.89	1.60
贵港市	Guigang	27.48	26.07	27.48	18.05	3.92	2.55
玉林市	Yulin	25.07	24.11	25.07	15.00	2.99	3.26
百色市	Baise	19.86	19.01	19.86	12.34	3.14	1.99
贺州市	Hezhou	14.93	14.61	14.93	11.45	0.78	1.00
河池市	Hechi	15.14	14.31	15.14	10.40	0.88	1.98
来宾市	Laibin	21.06	20.52	21.06	10.85	6.81	1.13
崇左市	Chongzuo	12.51	11.92	12.51	8.34	1.36	1.18

注：本表由自治区水利厅提供。
Note: The data in this table is provided by Autonomous Region Water Conservancy Bureau.

8－5　主要城市气象站点平均气温（2017年）

单位：℃

城 市	City	1月 Jan.	2月 Feb.	3月 Mar.	4月 Apr.	5月 May.	6月 Jun.
南 宁	Nanning	15.6	15.1	17.1	22.3	25.4	27.6
柳 州	Liuzhou	14.1	13.8	15.3	22.3	25.4	27.5
桂 林	Guilin	11.8	11.4	13.4	20.5	24.3	25.5
梧 州	Wuzhou	14.8	14.6	16.8	21.9	25.1	27.8
北 海	Beihai	17.3	16.7	20.3	23.5	26.9	29.0
防城港	Fangchenggang	17.3	16.6	19.0	23.2	26.6	28.5
钦 州	Qinzhou	16.4	15.8	18.1	22.7	26.0	27.9
贵 港	Guigang	15.7	15.6	17.2	22.9	26.2	28.2
玉 林	Yulin	16.4	15.6	18.1	22.6	25.5	28.1
百 色	Baise	16.2	16.5	19.0	23.7	26.0	27.8
贺 州	Hezhou	12.4	12.5	14.3	20.9	24.4	26.8
河 池	Hechi	13.8	13.8	14.8	21.8	24.5	26.3
来 宾	Laibin	14.0	13.9	15.7	21.9	24.9	27.3
崇 左	Chongzuo	16.4	16.2	18.2	23.1	26.1	27.9

注：本表资料由自治区气象局气象台气候变化评价室提供。
Note: The data on this table is provided by Evaluation Office for Climatic Variation in Weather Center of Meteorological Bureau.

Monthly Average Temperature at Meteorological Stations of Major Cities（2017）

(℃)

7月 Jul.	8月 Aug.	9月 Sep.	10月 Oct.	11月 Nov.	12月 Dec.	年平均 Annual Average
27.6	27.9	28.2	23.3	18.4	14.1	21.9
29.2	29.2	29.2	24.2	17.8	13.2	21.8
28.5	28.7	28.6	22.3	16.3	11.8	20.3
27.6	27.9	28.2	23.9	18.2	14.0	21.7
28.6	29.1	28.9	24.8	20.1	16.4	23.5
28.3	28.7	28.9	24.9	20.2	16.1	23.2
27.4	27.6	28.1	23.7	19.3	15.0	22.3
28.6	29.1	29.3	24.7	18.9	14.6	22.6
27.6	28.3	28.4	23.9	19.1	14.8	22.4
27.8	27.9	27.6	23.4	19.0	14.1	22.4
28.1	28.5	28.1	22.4	16.7	12.2	20.6
27.8	27.9	27.3	22.2	16.9	12.7	20.8
27.9	28.0	28.0	23.4	17.5	13.1	21.3
27.3	27.4	27.9	23.1	18.9	14.2	22.2

8－6 主要城市气象站点降水量（2017年）

单位：毫米

城 市	City	1月 Jan.	2月 Feb.	3月 Mar.	4月 Apr.	5月 May.	6月 Jun.
南 宁	Nanning	72.5	7.5	164.9	8.2	300.8	101.3
柳 州	Liuzhou	82.6	20.2	176.0	131.6	255.8	265.4
桂 林	Guilin	49.9	57.4	218.8	134.3	244.9	667.9
梧 州	Wuzhou	33.1	35.5	189.9	80.1	213.3	175.2
北 海	Beihai	27.1	40.6	53.2	48.9	88.8	352.8
防城港	Fangchenggang	36.7	22.7	56.1	50.4	218.1	569.8
钦 州	Qinzhou	58.9	30.0	124.8	27.5	156.1	258.9
贵 港	Guigang	49.4	5.1	219.8	62.4	420.0	258.5
玉 林	Yulin	55.2	28.0	88.7	47.9	359.8	98.2
百 色	Baise	72.4	6.4	64.6	59.4	120.4	348.0
贺 州	Hezhou	60.2	19.4	250.1	96.0	180.3	285.8
河 池	Hechi	61.6	15.1	131.4	70.1	257.4	470.7
来 宾	Laibin	61.2	16.3	139.3	94.3	157.9	375.0
崇 左	Chongzuo	82.4	21.4	73.4	24.5	104.5	143.4

Monthly Average Precipitation at Meteorological Stations of Major Cities (2017)

(mm)

7月 Jul.	8月 Aug.	9月 Sep.	10月 Oct.	11月 Nov.	12月 Dec.	年平均 Annual Average
290.0	256.1	81.5	149.6	63.3	53.0	1548.7
170.5	264.2	125.4	9.8	89.3	42.6	1633.4
369.8	335.8	15.9	6.0	49.0	33.3	2183.0
243.1	247.7	130.9	8.0	104.4	13.1	1474.3
600.9	553.4	264.5	133.3	31.0	19.1	2213.6
1055.6	622.5	318.9	147.4	73.1	34.2	3205.6
526.3	638.7	197.6	301.9	85.0	56.1	2461.8
291.9	259.8	76.0	37.4	71.4	39.8	1791.5
442.3	247.5	73.1	94.6	56.0	10.5	1601.8
287.5	214.0	85.2	109.1	38.7	9.6	1415.3
226.5	137.7	78.8	13.1	1007.0	33.1	1481.7
329.5	167.9	114.1	105.9	37.9	25.3	1789.9
174.7	234.6	153.9	10.6	89.0	37.0	1543.8
258.0	204.9	54.0	185.7	23.7	43.0	1218.9

8—7 主要年份城市公用事业基本情况
Basic Statistics on Urban Public Utilities in Main Years

指 标	Item	2010	2011	2012	2013	2014	2015	2016	2017
全年供水总量（万吨）	Total Volume of Tap Water Supply (10 000 tons)	147291	154483	155501	161657	162236	173266	176719	183563
#生活用水量	Households	72823	74324	63118	78101	79239	93869	99385	103344
人均日生活用水量（升）	Per Capita Daily Water Consumption (liter)	250	242	247	240	235	256	256	257
用水普及率（%）	Percentage of Population with Access Tap Water (%)	94.7	93.9	95.3	95.9	94.4	97.5	97.7	97.6
人均城市道路面积（平方米）	Area of Roads Owned per 10 000 Persons (sq.m)	14.31	14.34	14.74	15.53	15.75	16.28	17.06	17.56
建成区路网密度（公里/平方公里）	Road Network Density of Developed Area (km/sq.km)							6	6
建成区道路面积率（%）	Road Area Ratio of Developed Area (%)							13.9	13.9
排水管道总长度（公里）	Length of Drainpipes (km)	6417	7264	7726	8309	8771	10588	11480	12305
污水处理厂座数（座）	Number of Effluent Treatment Plants (unit)	32	33	33	32	34	41	47	46
污水处理厂能力（万立方米/日）	Treatment Capacity of Polluted Water (10 000 cu.m/day)	221	257	254	262	287	303	326	323
污水处理厂集中处理率（%）	Rate of Centralized Treatment of Polluted Water (%)	46.8	53.0	60.0	59.3	60.5	67.8	70.6	72.8
液化石油气供气总量（吨）	Total Liquefied Petroleum Gas Supply (ton)	303804	297416	326110	309475	267632	262313	255863	264066
#家庭用量	Used by Residential Households	263720	246834	262661	242840	223605	212108	217047	237457
人工煤气供气总量（万立方米）	Total Manufactured Gas Supply (10 000 cu.m)	4517	4503	4423	4533	4739	4439	4428	3495
#家庭用量	Used by Residential Households	3993	3927	3788	3970	3952	3671	3517	2468
天然气供气总量（万立方米）	Total Natural Gas Supply (10 000 cu.m)	10320	13606	16904	22234	28510	38789	48713	69676
#家庭用量	Used by Residential Households	4403	5983	7591	9496	12547	15726	20792	24436
用气普及率（%）	Rate of Households with Access to Natural Gas (%)	92.4	91.1	93.3	93.6	93.0	94.5	95.9	98.0
园林绿地面积（公顷）	Area of Gardens & Green Space (hectare)	60225	64461	67149	69870	72414	82382	84484	88789
公园绿地面积（公顷）	Area of Green Space of Parks (hectare)	8331	10012	10753	10812	11086	12111	12799	14025
人均公园绿地面积（平方米）	Per Capita Public Green Space of Parks (sq.m)	9.83	11.02	11.60	11.48	11.19	11.60	11.77	12.42
建成区绿化覆盖率（%）	Coverage Area of Forestation of Developed Area (%)	35.0	37.4	37.7	37.7	39.4	37.6	37.6	39.1
公园个数（个）	Number of Parks (unit)	146	168	178	183	196	216	239	254
公园面积（公顷）	Area of Parks (hectare)	5842	7205	7603	7626	7767	8579	8928	10296
道路清扫保洁面积（万平方米）	Area Under Cleaning Program (10 000 sq.m)	11005	11133	11601	12927	14065	18189	19713	21686
生活垃圾及粪便清运量（万吨）	Volume of Garbage, Excrement & Urine Disposal (10 000 tons)	268	256	267	312	349	394	419	438.32
公共厕所数（座）	Number of Public Lavatories (unit)	1487	2104	2159	2156	2129	1496	1503	1557
生活垃圾无害化处理率（%）	Rate of Garbage No Harmful Disposal (%)	91.1	95.5	98.1	96.4	95.4	98.7	99.0	99.9

注：1.本表为21个设市城市平均水平，下表同。
2.城市建设资料由自治区住房和城乡建设厅提供。
3.有关公共交通的三个指标由自治区交通厅提供。

Note: 1.The data in this table refers to the average level of the 22 cities of Guangxi (the administrative level of Jingxi changed from county to city in 2015), and the same as the continued tables.
2.The data on city construction is provided by the Guangxi Housing & Urban & Rural Construction Department.
3.The data on public tromsportation is provided by the Guangxi Transportation Department.

8-8 城市市政公用设施水平（2017年）
Level of Urban Public Utilities in Cities（2017）

地 区 Region	人口密度（人/平方公里）Population Density (person/sq.km)	人均日生活用水量（升）Per Capita Daily Consumption of Tap Water for Residential Use (litre)	用水普及率（%）Rate of Population with Access to Water (%)	用气普及率（%）Rate of Population with Access to Gas (%)	建成区排水管道密度（公里/平方公里）Density of Drainpipes of Developed Area (km/sq.km)	人均城市道路面积（平方米）Area of Roads Owned per 10 000 Persons (sq.m)	建成区路网密度（公里/平方公里）Road Network Density of Developed Area (km/sq.km)
全区城市 All Cities	**1950**	**257**	**97.6**	**97.8**	**8.69**	**17.56**	**6.37**
南宁市 Nanning	3853	317	97.4	99.9	5.46	14.33	5.55
柳州市 Liuzhou	3565	235	97.8	94.7	7.22	13.57	5.40
桂林市 Guilin	1531	325	95.8	100.0	8.32	16.00	6.99
梧州市 Wuzhou	1264	227	92.3	94.5	8.01	17.96	9.12
北海市 Beihai	486	305	97.8	99.5	11.81	20.52	5.66
防城港市 Fangchenggang	898	290	100.0	98.0	13.59	31.11	7.98
钦州市 Qinzhou	1066	302	96.0	98.0	10.69	36.28	5.98
贵港市 Guigang	1483	171	99.5	97.7	6.00	22.70	4.94
玉林市 Yulin	2470	144	100.0	98.9	10.84	15.75	8.67
百色市 Baise	725	298	100.0	97.8	7.86	20.29	4.36
贺州市 Hezhou	3136	216	98.1	92.0	8.53	18.62	2.80
河池市 Hechi	2828	246	99.5	98.0	19.39	23.46	11.05
来宾市 Laibin	3521	162	99.9	99.0	11.63	20.19	4.06
崇左市 Chongzuo	3590	205	98.1	98.6	9.64	17.92	6.95

注：本表为21个设市城市（2017年河池宜州市撤市改区并入河池市）平均水平，下表同。
Note: The data in this table refers to the average level of the 21 cities of Guangxi, and the same as the continued tables.

8－8　续表　continued

地　区	Region	建成区道路面积率(%) Road Area Ratio of Developed Area (%)	人均公园绿地面积(平方米) Public Green Space of Parks per Population (sq.m)	建成区绿地率(%) Rate of Green Land of Developed Area (%)	建成区绿化覆盖率(%) Coverage Area of Forestation of Developed Area (%)	污水处理率(%) Treatment Rate of Polluted Water (%)	#污水处理厂集中处理率(%) Concentrated Treatment Rate by Factory (%)	生活垃圾无害化处理率(%) Rate of Garbage No Harmful Disposal (%)
全区城市	**All Cities**	**13.9**	**12.42**	**34.2**	**39.1**	**94.3**	**72.8**	**99.9**
南宁市	Nanning	15.2	11.91	36.5	42.3	96.9	82.3	100.0
柳州市	Liuzhou	10.8	13.59	36.5	43.8	95.1	49.9	100.0
桂林市	Guilin	14.4	12.20	36.1	40.2	92.9	92.7	100.0
梧州市	Wuzhou	17.2	10.83	40.3	41.2	95.5	69.4	100.0
北海市	Beihai	12.4	10.61	34.5	40.7	98.6	98.6	100.0
防城港市	Fangchenggang	16.1	24.34	32.2	36.3	91.0	33.6	100.0
钦州市	Qinzhou	15.2	12.45	33.8	38.7	96.0	87.2	100.0
贵港市	Guigang	12.8	13.54	29.0	33.7	76.3	59.6	100.0
玉林市	Yulin	15.8	14.28	35.3	39.8	99.2	99.2	100.0
百色市	Baise	10.4	12.16	34.2	38.5	69.4	69.4	100.0
贺州市	Hezhou	10.9	16.14	38.4	42.3	90.3	88.0	100.0
河池市	Hechi	19.6	10.69	28.4	32.2	95.3	79.9	100.0
来宾市	Laibin	13.3	9.68	30.2	33.5	88.1	88.1	100.0
崇左市	Chongzuo	10.1	13.18	33.6	39.6	94.1	35.5	100.0

8−9 城市人口和建设用地（2017年）
Population & Developed Areas in Cities（2017）

地 区	Region	市区人口（万人）Urban Population (10 000 persons)	市区面积（平方公里）Area of Urban (sq.km)	城区人口（万人）Population of Cities (10 000 persons)	城区（县城）暂住人口（万人）Transient Population of Cities (counties) (10 000 persons)	城区面积（平方公里）Area of Cities (sq.km)	建成区面积（平方公里）Developed Area (sq.km)	城市建设用地面积（平方公里）Land for Construction in Cities (sq.km)	#居住用地 Land for Residence	公共管理与公共服务用地 Land for Public Utilities	工业用地 Land for Industry
全区城市	**All Cities**	**2392.78**	**68539.76**	**896.60**	**232.33**	**5789.43**	**1413.65**	**1372.12**	**410.79**	**145.13**	**220.45**
南宁市	Nanning	446.95	9947.00	229.90	103.43	865.08	315.22	307.88	90.65	43.31	33.95
柳州市	Liuzhou	179.62	3555.16	125.16	53.70	501.78	225.09	225.09	62.40	21.00	53.19
桂林市	Guilin	130.45	2767.00	86.95	6.86	612.63	104.40	104.39	30.63	12.02	18.32
梧州市	Wuzhou	79.46	1850.20	48.08	13.22	485.01	58.26	56.78	19.35	5.86	8.72
北海市	Beihai	67.04	957.00	37.83	8.69	957.00	77.26	77.26	27.00	9.80	6.86
防城港市	Fangchenggang	62.12	2816.40	17.80	3.61	238.33	41.38	40.52	7.55	2.77	8.83
钦州市	Qinzhou	150.81	4767.20	33.02	4.76	354.38	90.50	89.98	22.79	7.45	21.68
贵港市	Guigang	201.50	3533.00	43.04	1.66	301.50	79.21	76.30	23.91	6.89	17.31
玉林市	Yulin	111.81	1251.30	56.51	18.08	302.04	74.24	70.61	26.60	9.62	2.21
百色市	Baise	36.15	3702.00	20.64	5.65	362.60	51.23	47.23	15.62	4.37	7.19
贺州市	Hezhou	120.12	5676.60	22.92	1.54	78.00	38.04	38.04	12.67	5.62	6.81
河池市	Hechi	100.87	6209.00	34.10	0.97	124.00	41.92	41.75	12.14	3.80	9.18
来宾市	Laibin	113.36	4363.00	30.32	2.07	92.00	49.33	49.33	11.73	2.46	6.74
崇左市	Chongzuo	37.52	2951.00	17.52	0.43	50.00	32.00	20.03	6.42	2.03	2.43

注：1. 全区城市数为21个设市合计数，14个地级市数为市本级数据，不含所辖（市）县。9-13表同。

2. 市区、城区人口及面积统计范围以国家建设部城市（县城）建设统计报表制度为准。即市区面积指的是城市行政区域内的全部土地面积（包括水域面积），城区面积指的是设市城市的城建统计的范围面积，市区、城区人口统计范围同。

Note：1.The data on all the cities of Guangxi refers to the summary of data on 21 cities, and the data on 14 prefecture-level cities excludes the under counties(county-level cities). And the same as the tables below.

2. The statistical ranges of population and area of urban area and cities subject to the statistical report system of city(county seat) construction from the Ministry of Construction. The area of city district refers to the total land area(including the area of water) in the administrative areas of a city, and the urban area refers to the statistical range of city construction in a city. And so as the statistical range of the population of city district and urban area.

8−10 城市供水情况（2017年）
Statistics of Water Supply in Cities（2017）

地 区	Region	供水综合生产能力（万立方米/日）Comprehensive Productive Capacity of Water Supply (10 000 cu.m/day)	供水管道长度（公里）Length of Water Supply Pipelines (km)	供水总量（万立方米）Total Volume of Water Supply (10 000 cu.m)	#家庭用量 Households	用水人口（万人）Number of Residents with Access to Tap Water (10 000 persons)
全区城市	**All Cities**	**701.37**	**18527.67**	**183562.61**	**81938.76**	**1102.17**
南宁市	Nanning	172.00	3779.82	56208.48	29375.49	324.80
柳州市	Liuzhou	151.10	2633.63	48246.49	11285.79	174.85
桂林市	Guilin	46.56	2026.06	15012.54	7663.57	89.84
梧州市	Wuzhou	45.30	506.23	7070.10	3367.51	56.56
北海市	Beihai	37.73	1418.30	7276.01	3670.52	45.50
防城港市	Fangchenggang	17.60	468.46	5216.82	1710.84	21.41
钦州市	Qinzhou	31.38	1047.29	6081.28	3242.56	36.27
贵港市	Guigang	24.44	1167.65	6954.42	2656.10	44.48
玉林市	Yulin	37.50	891.03	6756.59	3889.28	74.59
百色市	Baise	15.00	623.85	3521.34	2095.56	26.29
贺州市	Hezhou	10.00	917.87	2629.70	1541.30	24.00
河池市	Hechi	32.50	562.65	4300.70	2778.00	34.91
来宾市	Laibin	12.00	947.35	2359.90	1832.80	32.36
崇左市	Chongzuo	7.00	261.00	1895.00	846.00	17.60

8－11 城市园林绿化情况（2017年）

Basic Statistics on Parks, Gardens & Green Areas in Cities（2017）

地 区	Region	绿化覆盖面积（公顷）Coverage Area of Forestation (hectare)	#建成区 Developed Area	园林绿地面积（公顷）Area of Gardens & Green Area (hectare)	#建成区 Developed Area	公园绿地面积 Area of Public Green Area (hectare)	公园面积（公顷）Area of Parks (hectare)
全区城市	**All Cities**	**97094.63**	**55297.51**	**88788.88**	**48306.25**	**14024.59**	**10295.84**
#南宁市	Nanning	41766.16	13327.03	39958.89	11519.68	3968.80	2931.00
柳州市	Liuzhou	10743.06	9867.06	9293.55	8222.55	2430.00	1644.81
桂林市	Guilin	4426.15	4200.49	3974.64	3770.39	1144.63	619.44
梧州市	Wuzhou	3319.89	2402.88	3266.23	2346.14	664.00	620.59
北海市	Beihai	3144.12	3144.12	2667.87	2667.87	493.70	458.67
防城港市	Fangchenggang	1506.64	1500.14	1338.68	1332.18	521.17	565.52
钦州市	Qinzhou	12800.76	3498.19	11135.65	3056.29	470.23	433.43
贵港市	Guigang	2717.82	2668.07	2342.65	2300.35	605.28	279.06
玉林市	Yulin	3241.00	2956.00	3063.00	2620.00	1065.00	1014.00
百色市	Baise	2176.27	1974.27	1983.41	1753.41	319.70	161.00
贺州市	Hezhou	1765.86	1608.16	1618.04	1461.73	394.89	394.89
河池市	Hechi	1449.15	1350.32	1202.79	1190.79	375.07	250.62
来宾市	Laibin	1721.55	1651.51	1559.68	1489.64	313.42	60.41
崇左市	Chongzuo	1319.93	1267.93	1100.18	1076.18	236.51	158.67

8－12 城市市政设施情况（2017年）
Basic Statistics on Municipal Utilities in Cities（2017）

地 区	Region	城市道路长度（公里）Length of Roads (km)	城市道路面积（万平方米）Area of Roads (10 000 sq.m)	路灯盏数（盏）Number of Street Lights (unit)	排水管道长度（公里）Length of Drainpipes (km)	污水年排放量（万吨）Discharged Volume of Polluted Water (10 000 tons)	污水处理厂集中处理能力（万吨/日）Concentrated Treatment Capacity of Polluted Water by Factory (10 000 tons/day)	污水处理总量（万吨）Treated Total Volume of Polluted Water (10 000 tons)
全区城市	**All Cities**	**9063.73**	**19820.59**	**695594**	**12304.71**	**135948**	**323.0**	**128219**
#南宁市	Nanning	1748.74	4775.65	90631	1720.20	39573	85.0	38339
柳州市	Liuzhou	1216.19	2426.40	77743	1624.30	35196	54.0	33474
桂林市	Guilin	729.30	1501.07	69736	868.37	11220	42.0	10427
梧州市	Wuzhou	581.18	1100.67	87308	473.38	5656	18.0	5404
北海市	Beihai	437.76	954.78	31806	912.99	6403	20.0	6311
防城港市	Fangchenggang	330.13	666.09	22398	562.45	4173	4.0	3797
钦州市	Qinzhou	541.16	1370.69	23732	967.51	4257	23.0	4087
贵港市	Guigang	391.05	1014.49	20485	475.46	5414	11.0	4128
玉林市	Yulin	643.51	1174.55	33269	804.69	5278	20.0	5233
百色市	Baise	223.41	533.54	14784	402.52	2641	6.0	1832
贺州市	Hezhou	109.10	455.50	18067	326.69	1850	5.0	1670
河池市	Hechi	463.21	822.58	31624	812.63	3689	10.0	3515
来宾市	Laibin	200.47	653.84	93901	573.88	1652	5.0	1455
崇左市	Chongzuo	222.55	321.58	12713	308.46	1327	3.0	1248

8－13 城市公共交通、清洁卫生和供气情况（2017年）
Basic Statistics on Public Traffic, Urban Sanitation & Gas Supply in Cities (2017)

地 区	Region	年末实有公共汽车营运车辆（辆）Year-end Operating Public Buses (vehicle)	年末实有公共汽车标台营运车辆（标台）Year-end Operating Public Buses (standard vehicle)	运营线路网长度（公里）Length of Public Transportation Routes (km)	公共汽车客运总量（万人次）Total Passenger Traffic (10 000 person-times)	出租汽车运营车数（辆）Taxis (vehicle)	道路清扫保洁面积（万平方米）Area Under Cleaning Program (10 000 sq.m)	生活垃圾清运量（万吨）Volume of Garbage Disposal (10 000 tons)
全区城市	**All Cities**	**14599**	**15627**	**30271**	**131837**	**21678**	**21686**	**438.32**
#南宁市	Nanning	4314	5280	6144	41314	7443	6601	127.41
柳州市	Liuzhou	1385	1660	2102	21691	2056	3477	61.78
桂林市	Guilin	763	1048	971	18092	2189	2130	45.81
梧州市	Wuzhou	419	428	791	5073	806	878	20.76
北海市	Beihai	521	571	440	2162	555	1722	26.87
防城港市	Fangchenggang	300	270	864	1433	335	665	9.07
钦州市	Qinzhou	244	249	563	1529	300	1101	14.99
贵港市	Guigang	249	295	462	1604	282	656	19.12
玉林市	Yulin	185	192	247	3356	699	789	25.38
百色市	Baise	215	242	339	2325	509	582	9.14
贺州市	Hezhou	301	327	241	1017	300	386	14.97
河池市	Hechi	248	248	387	3702	475	305	9.42
来宾市	Laibin	399	407	323	2372	530	650	13.10
崇左市	Chongzuo	84	79	228	408	71	265	3.68

8－13　续表　continued

地　区	Region	垃圾无害化处理量(万吨) Volume of Garbage & Urine No Harmful Disposal (10 000 tons)	公共厕所座数(座) Number of Public Lavatories (unit)	市容环卫专用车辆设备总数(辆) Environmental Sanitation Equipment (unit)	液化石油气供气总量(吨) Total Volume of Liquid Petrol Gas Supply (ton)	人工煤气供气总量(万立方米) Total Volume of Manufactured Gas Supply (10 000 cu.m)	天然气供气总量(万立方米) Total Volume of Natural Gas Supply (10 000 cu.m)
全区城市	**All Cities**	**437.99**	**1557**	**7987**	**264066**	**3494.67**	**69676.38**
#南宁市	Nanning	127.41	226	4874	62941	0	31488.80
柳州市	Liuzhou	61.78	213	486	39071	3314.67	9742.85
桂林市	Guilin	45.81	320	558	19522	0	6783.18
梧州市	Wuzhou	20.76	98	145	7846	0	3999.46
北海市	Beihai	26.87	167	174	20002	0	4200.00
防城港市	Fangchenggang	9.07	22	224	10381	0	1223.89
钦州市	Qinzhou	14.99	91	157	11420	0	2326.27
贵港市	Guigang	19.12	53	126	14540	0	1362.08
玉林市	Yulin	25.38	78	186	22800	0	3618.00
百色市	Baise	9.14	43	388	6462	0	952.67
贺州市	Hezhou	14.97	38	81	10800	0	1020.80
河池市	Hechi	9.42	48	85	9264	180.00	122.92
来宾市	Laibin	13.10	34	51	4036	0	965.00
崇左市	Chongzuo	3.68	12	130	3411	0	116.64

8－14 主要年份工业污染治理项目建设情况

Construction of Industrial Pollution Treatment Projects in Main Years

指 标	Item	1995	2000	2005	2010	2011	2012	2013	2014	2015	2016	2017
汇总工业企业数（个）	Total Number of Industrial Enterprises (unit)			255	126	191	194	159	135	108	139	128
施工项目本年投资来源合计（万元）	Total Funds of Projects under Construction in This Year (10 000 yuan)			103730	92845	129745	127329	183218	178909	247151	130433	75847
排污费补助	Pollution Charges Subsidies			9533	770	1524	494	0	325	168	801	155
政府其他补助	Other Government Subsidies			284	388	3574	4721	9617	4331	2367	832	1040
企业自筹	Self-raising Funds			93914	91687	123639	80429	173601	174253	244616	128800	74652
#银行贷款	Loans			32665	30	19258	8193	12281	12076	1260	35	10096
施工项目本年完成投资额（万元）	Completed Investment in Construction Projects in This Year (10 000 yuan)	33191	73659	103730	92845	129745	127329	183218	178909	247151	130442	86468
治理废水	Treatment of Waste Water	17867	40020	33678	47388	58814	47863	66235	32927	15939	10906	9247
治理废气	Treatment of Waste Gas	10184	26895	56863	27250	64494	63105	110217	106049	187490	104600	46342
治理固体废物	Treatment of Solid Wastes	3771	2716	1849	17024	3249	8782	540	17201	26722	14096	237
治理噪声	Treatment of Noise Pollution	389	102	505	80	156	2	276	0	50	0	0
治理污染搬迁	Treatment of Moving away for Pollution			10	0	0	0	0	0	0	0	0
治理其他	Treatment of Other Pollution	980	3927	10824	1104	2801	7577	7051	22731	16950	840	30642
施工和竣工项目（个）	Projects under Construction & Projects Completed (unit)										0	180
当年施工项目（个）	Projects under Construction (unit)	1002	1270	389	175	315	207	143	109	137	119	102
#治理废水	Treatment of Waste Water			166	109	146	95	52	48	36	36	25
治理废气	Treatment of Waste Gas			174	36	84	40	55	40	65	60	61
治理固体废物	Treatment of Solid Wastes			34	22	37	16	6	6	7	9	3
治理噪声	Treatment of Noise Pollution			7	1	6	1	3	0	2	0	0
治理污染搬迁	Treatment of Moving away for Pollution			1	0	0	0	0	0	0	0	0
治理其他	Treatment of Other Pollution			7	7	36	55	27	15	27	14	13
当年竣工项目（个）	Projects Completed (unit)	844	1060	307	166	223	203	157	119	99	79	78
#治理废水	Treatment of Waste Water	292	443	124	104	105	92	53	49	29	24	17
治理废气	Treatment of Waste Gas	355	553	138	34	62	42	71	48	45	41	53
治理固体废物	Treatment of Solid Wastes	100	32	30	20	25	13	5	5	5	7	0
治理噪声	Treatment of Noise Pollution	62	4	7	1	6	1	3	0	1	0	0
治理污染搬迁	Treatment of Moving away for Pollution			1	0	0	0	0	0	0	0	0
治理其他	Treatment of Other Pollution		28	7	7	22	55	25	17	19	7	8

注：环保类数据为自治区环保厅提供的快报数（提供时间为2018年8月30日）。

Note: The environmental protection data were quick statistics data privided by Guangxi Zhuang Autonomous Region Department of Environmental Protection in Aug 30th, 2018.

8－15　主要年份工业污染排放及处理利用情况
Discharge, Treatment & Utilization of Industrial Pollution in Main Years

指　标	Item	1995	2000	2005	2010	2011	2012	2013	2014	2015	2016	2017
汇总工业企业数（个）	Total Number of Industrial Enterprises (unit)			1738	4443	3565	3517	3532	3464	3543	3298	2630
工业废水排放量（万吨）	Volume of Industrial Waste Water Discharged (10 000 tons)	96563	81571	145609	165211	101234	110671	89508	72936	63253	32554	35950
#经过处理达标	Treated Waste Water up to Discharge Standard	42227	30303	121873	160139							
工业废气排放总量（亿标立方米）	Volume of Industrial Waste Gas Discharged (100 million cu.m)	2797	4607	8339	14520	29853	27611	29051	18631	16773	13485	14158
#燃料燃烧过程中废气排放量	Volume of Waste Gas in the Process of Fuel Burning	1699	1787	4370	8584							
生产工艺过程中废气排放量	Volume of Waste Gas in the Process of Production	1098	2820	3969	5936							
二氧化硫排放总量（万吨）	Volume of Sulfur Dioxide Discharged (10 000 tons)	76	83	97	85	49	47	44	43	39	13	12
烟（粉）尘排放量（万吨）	Volume of Smoke (dust) Discharged (10 000 tons)					26	27	26	38	33	21	18
烟尘排放总量（万吨）	Volume of Soot Discharged (10 000 tons)	50	59	54	26							
工业粉尘排放量（万吨）	Volume of Dust Discharged (10 000 tons)	28	57	56	32							
工业固体废物产生量（万吨）	Volume of Industrial Solid Waste Product (10 000 tons)	1588	2108	3489	6232	7438	7964	7676	8038	7023	6476	6503
工业固体废物处置量（万吨）	Volume of Industrial Solid Waste Treated (10 000 tons)	238	227	109	1563	2050	2218	1609	1454	546	259	1009
工业固体废物综合利用量（万吨）	Volume of Comprehensive Utilization of Industrial Solid Waste (10 000 tons)	727	1058	2165	4231	4292	5369	5425	5058	4433	4152	3693
工业固体废物排放量（万吨）	Volume of Industrial Solid Wastes Discharged (10 000 tons)	99	127	110	9	3	0	0	0	0	0	0
“三废”综合利用产品产值（万元）	Output Value of Products Made from Utilization of Waste Gas, Waste Water & Waste Residues (10 000 yuan)	110322	84856	238923	510233							

8－16 环境污染治理投资情况

Investment in Environment Pollution Treatment

指 标	Item	2014	2015	2016	2017
环境污染源治理投资总额（万元）	**Total Investment in Treatment of Environmental Pollution (10 000 yuan)**	**2045292**	**2329068**	**1908757**	**1997742**
一、工业污染源治理项目本年完成投资	Completed Investment in Treatment of Industrial Pollution Sources Projects in This Year	178909	247151	130433	75847
二、当年完成环保验收项目环保投资	Enviornment Protection Investment in the Environmental Protection Acceptance Projects in the Year	387683	596962	176712	419467
三、城市环境基础设施建设本年完成投资额	Investment in Urban Environment Basic Facilities Construction Completed in the Year	1478700	1484955	1601612	1502428
燃气工程建设	Engineering Construction of Gas	147347	115689	117135	124129
排水工程建设	Engineering Construction of Drainage	395776	546952	517550	463399
园林绿化工程建设	Engineering Construction of Landscaping	825240	754666	831305	793495
市容环境卫生	Sanitation of Cities	110337	67648	135622	121405

8－17 重点调查工业废水排放及治理情况（2017年）
Discharge & Treatment of Waste Water by Branch of Industry（2017）

指标名称	Item	汇总工业企业数（个）Number of Industrial Enterprises (unit)	工业废水排放总量（万吨）Total Discharged Volume of Industrial Waste Water (10 000 tons)	废水治理设施数（套）Number of Facilities for Treatment of Waste Water (set)
总　计	**Total**	**2630**	**31286.6**	**1424**
煤炭采选业	Coal Mining & Processing	11	172.0	9
石油和天然气开采业	Petroleum & Natural Gas Extraction	1	6.5	1
黑色金属矿采选业	Ferrous Metals Mining & Processing	3	0	3
有色金属矿采选业	Nonferrous Metals Mining & Processing	52	2583.1	44
非金属矿采选业	Nonmetal Mining & Processing	14	411.2	11
其他采矿业	Other Mining Industries	6	557.1	7
农副食品加工业	Major Grain & Sideline Product Processing	373	3828.4	305
食品制造业	Food Production	77	980.1	57
饮料制造业	Beverage Production	53	1163.2	49
烟草制造业	Tobacco Processing	3	36.3	2
纺织业	Textile Industry	88	872.2	90
纺织服装、鞋、帽制造业	Garments, Shoes & Accessories Manufacturing	25	1026.6	25
皮革、毛皮、羽绒及其制造业	Leather, Furs, Down & Related Products	16	127.4	16
木材加工及竹、藤、棕、草制品业	Timber, Bamboo, Cane, Palm Fiber, Straw Products	151	22.4	29
家具制造业	Manufacture of Furniture	21	0	4
造纸及纸制品业	Papermaking & Paper Products	134	10397.0	146
印刷业和记录媒介的复制	Printing & Record Medium Reproduction	32	10.0	8
文教、工美、体育和娱乐用品制造业	Culture, Education, Handcraft Art, Sport & Enter tainment Goods Manufacturing	2	5.1	1
石油加工、炼焦及核燃料加工业	Petroleum Refining & Coking	9	440.4	6
化学原料及化学制品制造业	Raw Chemical Materials & Chemical Products	208	3860.4	120
医药制造业	Medical & Pharmaceutical Products	76	594.5	66

8－17 续表 continued

指标名称	Item	汇总工业企业数（个）Number of Industrial Enterprises (unit)	工业废水排放总量（万吨）Total Discharged Volume of Industrial Waste Water (10 000 tons)	废水治理设施数（套）Number of Facilities for Treatment of Waste Water (set)
橡胶和塑料制品业	Rubber & Plastic Products	29	48.9	6
非金属矿物制品业	Nonmetal Mineral Products	794	132.8	127
黑色金属冶炼及压延加工业	Smelting & Pressing of Ferrous Metals	106	1522.5	56
有色金属冶炼及压延加工业	Smelting & Pressing of Nonferrous Metals	68	535.7	39
金属制品业	Metal Products	74	142.9	38
通用设备制造业	Ordinary Machinery	13	64.3	9
专用设备制造业	Special Purpose Equipment	18	183.4	9
汽车制造业	Automobile Manufacturing	47	515.6	34
铁路、船舶、航空航天和其他运输设备制造业	Railway, Ship, Aerospace & Other Transportation Equipment Manufacturing	4	10.2	2
电气机械和器材制造业	Electric Equipment & Machinery	16	23.5	7
计算机、通信和其他电子设备制造业	Computer, Communication & Other Electronic Equipment Manufacturing	17	704.7	9
仪器仪表制造业	Instruments Manufacturing	4	1.1	3
其他制造业	Other Manufacturing	17	30.3	11
废弃资源综合利用业	Waste Resources Comprehensive Utilization	22	3.4	18
金属制品、机械和设备修理业	Metal Product, Machinery & Equipment Repair Services	4	156.5	3
电力、热力生产和供应业	Production & Supply of Electric Power & Steam	34	116.6	52
燃气生产和供应业	Production & Supply of Gas	4	0.2	2

8—18 重点调查工业废气排放及治理情况（2017年）

指标名称	Item	汇总工业企业数（个）Number of Industrial Enterprises (unit)	废气治理设施数（套）Number of Facilities for Treatment of Waste Gas (set)	工业废气排放量（亿立方米）Total Volume of Industrial Waste Gas Emission (100 million cu.m)
总　计	**Total**	**2630**	**6156**	**14158.1**
煤炭采选业	Coal Mining & Processing	11	0	0
石油和天然气开采业	Petroleum & Natural Gas Extraction	1		17.5
黑色金属矿采选业	Ferrous Metals Mining & Processing	3	36	7.2
有色金属矿采选业	Nonferrous Metals Mining & Processing	52	10	7.5
非金属矿采选业	Nonmetal Mining & Processing	14	34	7.3
其他采矿业	Other Mining Industries	6	1	…
农副食品加工业	Major Grain & Sideline Product Processing	373	430	468.0
食品制造业	Food Production	77	80	77.4
饮料制造业	Beverage Production	53	55	33.7
烟草制造业	Tobacco Processing	3	8	1.8
纺织业	Textile Industry	88	82	27.2
纺织服装、鞋、帽制造业	Garments, Shoes & Accessories Manufacturing	25	50	4.9
皮革、毛皮、羽绒及其制造业	Leather, Furs, Down & Related Products	16	21	2.6
木材加工及竹、藤、棕、草制品业	Timber, Bamboo, Cane, Palm Fiber, Straw Products	151	268	213.7
家具制造业	Manufacture of Furniture	21	51	4.3
造纸及纸制品业	Papermaking & Paper Products	134	165	336.6
印刷业和记录媒介的复制	Printing & Record Medium Reproduction	32	66	1.0
文教、工美、体育和娱乐用品制造业	Culture, Education, Handcraft, Art, Sport & Entertainment Goods Manufacturing	2	2	0.1
石油加工、炼焦及核燃料加工业	Petroleum Refining & Coking	9	8	252.5
化学原料及化学制品制造业	Raw Chemical Materials & Chemical Products	208	420	301.9
医药制造业	Medical & Pharmaceutical Products	76	79	31.1

Discharge & Treatment of Waste Gas by Branch of Industry (2017)

二氧化硫去除率 (%) Removed rate of Sulfur Dioxide (%)	二氧化硫排放量 (吨) Volume of Sulfur Dioxide Discharged (ton)	氮氧化物去除率 (%) Removed rate of Nitrogen Oxides (%)	氮氧化物排放量 (吨) Volume of Nitrogen Oxides Discharged (ton)	烟（粉）尘排放量 (吨) Volume of Smoke & Dust Discharged (ton)
95.5	**101495.3**	**64.5**	**151090.5**	**151414.4**
0	2.9	0	68.2	3.7
0	649.2	79.0	24.7	169.2
89.5	9.3	26.1	52.0	150.9
93.9	1.9	2.7	9.9	62.6
70	0.4	0	…	…
61.7	3286.4	26.3	8337.7	11262.2
56.6	325.7	64.9	360.6	545.7
76.8	935.1	33.4	818.0	537.9
47.7	9.5	0.0	10.5	4.7
67.9	78.0	2.3	196.4	930.2
21	344.1	0	137.6	254.4
83.7	48.1	44.3	28.2	37.3
49.1	451.0	47.8	1040.2	5003.2
9	6.1	0	4.0	61.4
89.6	4591.1	40.8	4781.1	3698.3
45.5	8.1	0	10.2	40.8
		0	0.3	0.1
92.0	918.6	14.3	1948.1	439.5
93.3	6033.0	38.1	2504.5	3343.0
35.9	512.0	1.1	282.6	298.2

8－18 续表

指标名称	Item	汇总工业企业数（个）Number of Industrial Enterprises (unit)	废气治理设施数（套）Number of Facilities for Treatment of Waste Gas (set)	工业废气排放量（亿立方米）Total Volume of Industrial Waste Gas Emission (100 million cu.m)
橡胶和塑料制品业	Rubber & Plastic Products	29	36	63.3
非金属矿物制品业	Nonmetal Mineral Products	794	2782	3519.6
黑色金属冶炼及压延加工业	Smelting & Pressing of Ferrous Metals	106	359	5106.0
有色金属冶炼及压延加工业	Smelting & Pressing of Nonferrous Metals	68	336	1180.7
金属制品业	Metal Products	74	86	54.5
通用设备制造业	Ordinary Machinery	13	14	3.4
专用设备制造业	Special Purpose Equipment	18	247	72.7
汽车制造业	Automobile Manufacturing	47	143	438.6
铁路、船舶、航空航天和其他运输设备制造业	Railway, Ship, Aerospace & Other Transportation Equipment Manufacturing	4	7	0.9
电气机械和器材制造业	Electric Equipment & Machinery	16	54	26.9
计算机、通信和其他电子设备制造业	Computer, Communication & Other Electronic Equipment Manufacturing	17	16	3.5
仪器仪表制造业	Instruments Manufacturing	4	1	0.1
其他制造业	Other Manufacturing	17	40	35.0
废弃资源综合利用业	Waste Resources Comprehensive Utilization	22	39	30.0
金属制品、机械和设备修理业	Metal Product, Machinery & Equipment Repair Services	4	20	48.0
电力、热力生产和供应业	Production & Supply of Electric Power & Steam	34	102	1776.7
燃气生产和供应业	Production & Supply of Gas	4	2	1.4

continued

二氧化硫去除率 (%) Removed rate of Sulfur Dioxide (%)	二氧化硫排放量 (吨) Volume of Sulfur Dioxide Discharged (ton)	氮氧化物去除率 (%) Removed rate of Nitrogen Oxides (%)	氮氧化物排放量 (吨) Volume of Nitrogen Oxides Discharged (ton)	烟（粉）尘排放量 (吨) Volume of Smoke & Dust Discharged (ton)
9.0	292.6	0	54.6	64.3
76.2	19869.2	56.1	70327.6	46480.7
68.8	19586.5	6.7	37204.4	69117.8
96.2	25577.1	66.5	9532.3	4610.4
99.9	567.9	27.8	168.6	277.0
0	0.3	72.4	3.2	5.4
0	1.1	69.8	13.2	91.7
27.8	9.7	3.8	79.1	406.3
				0.1
		0	2.7	1.0
67.8	6.2	0	16.5	9.1
0	…	0	0.1	…
73.1	75.9	56.7	386.2	244.5
71	57.6	0	64.6	104.4
91.4	0.0	3.4	2.1	482.8
95.3	17237.5	92.3	12600.8	2647.0
92.4	2.1	0	16.9	22.0

8－19 重点调查工业固体废物排放及治理情况（2017年）

指标名称	Item	汇总工业企业数（个）Number of Industrial Enterprises (unit)	工业固体废物产生量（万吨）Volume of Industrial Solid Waste Produced (10 000 tons)	#危险废物（吨）Dangerous Wastes (ton)
总　计	**Total**	**2630**	**5777.2**	**214.0**
煤炭采选业	Coal Mining & Processing	11	32.8	0
石油和天然气开采业	Petroleum & Natural Gas Extraction	1	…	
黑色金属矿采选业	Ferrous Metals Mining & Processing	3	97.0	0
有色金属矿采选业	Nonferrous Metals Mining & Processing	52	437.7	0.3
非金属矿采选业	Nonmetal Mining & Processing	14	18.8	…
其他采矿业	Other Mining Industries	6	0.8	
农副食品加工业	Major Grain & Sideline Product Processing	373	302.8	…
食品制造业	Food Production	77	8.2	0.8
饮料制造业	Beverage Production	53	37.5	…
烟草制造业	Tobacco Processing	3	…	…
纺织业	Textile Industry	88	1.5	…
纺织服装、鞋、帽制造业	Garments, Shoes & Accessories Manufacturing	25	1.2	
皮革、毛皮、羽绒及其制造业	Leather, Furs, Down & Related Products	16	0.6	…
木材加工及竹、藤、棕、草制品业	Timber, Bamboo, Cane, Palm Fiber, Straw Products	151	10.2	…
家具制造业	Manufacture of Furniture	21	0.3	…
造纸及纸制品业	Papermaking & Paper Products	134	119.2	0.2
印刷业和记录媒介的复制	Printing & Record Medium Reproduction	32	0.3	…
文教、工美、体育和娱乐用品制造业	Culture, Education, Handcraft, Art, Sport & Entertainment Goods Manufacturing	2	…	…
石油加工、炼焦及核燃料加工业	Petroleum Refining & Coking	9	0.1	2.5
化学原料及化学制品制造业	Raw Chemical Materials & Chemical Products	208	189.4	100.6
医药制造业	Medical & Pharmaceutical Products	76	6.1	0.1

Discharge & Treatment of Industrial Solid Wastes (2017)

工业固体废物综合利用量（万吨）Volume of Industrial Solid Wastes Utilized (10 000 tons)	工业固体废物贮存量（万吨）Volume of Industrial Solid Wastes Accumulated (10 000 tons)	工业固体废物处置量（万吨）Volume of Industrial Solid Wastes Treated (10 000 tons)	工业固体废物排放量（万吨）Volume of Industrial Solid Wastes Discharged (10 000 tons)
3250.8	**1774.5**	**905.7**	**0.4**
27.9	1.0	8.3	0
0	0	…	0
2.8	94.5	2.8	0
101.1	325.2	22.7	0.1
17.4	3.1	6.6	0
		0.8	…
274.3	1.5	30.4	…
6.9	…	1.3	…
36.3	…	1.3	…
…	…	0	0
1.3	0.1	0.2	…
1.2			
0.4	…	0.1	0
10.1	…	0.2	…
0.3	0	0	0
92.0	1.5	25.9	0
0.3	…	…	…
…	0	0	0
…	0	0.1	0
133.4	33.3	23.7	…
5.2	…	0.9	…

8－19　续表

指标名称	Item	汇总工业企业数（个）Number of Industrial Enterprises (unit)	工业固体废物产生量（万吨）Volume of Industrial Solid Waste Produced (10 000 tons)	#危险废物（吨）Dangerous Wastes (ton)
橡胶和塑料制品业	Rubber & Plastic Products	29	0.5	…
非金属矿物制品业	Nonmetal Mineral Products	794	336.5	1.5
黑色金属冶炼及压延加工业	Smelting & Pressing of Ferrous Metals	106	1440.1	8.3
有色金属冶炼及压延加工业	Smelting & Pressing of Nonferrous Metals	68	2133.7	81.6
金属制品业	Metal Products	74	0.8	1.8
通用设备制造业	Ordinary Machinery	13	0.3	…
专用设备制造业	Special Purpose Equipment	18	2.6	0.4
汽车制造业	Automobile Manufacturing	47	5.1	1.2
铁路、船舶、航空航天和其他运输设备制造业	Railway, Ship, Aerospace & Other Transportation Equipment Manufacturing	4	0.1	…
电气机械和器材制造业	Electric Equipment & Machinery	16	4.8	0.2
计算机、通信和其他电子设备制造业	Computer, Communication & Other Electronic Equipment Manufacturing	17	4.2	10.5
仪器仪表制造业	Instruments Manufacturing	4	…	…
其他制造业	Other Manufacturing	17	1.7	…
废弃资源综合利用业	Waste Resources Comprehensive Utilization	22	2.4	0.3
金属制品、机械和设备修理业	Metal Product, Machinery & Equipment Repair Services	4	0.4	…
电力、热力生产和供应业	Production & Supply of Electric Power & Steam	34	579.8	3.6
燃气生产和供应业	Production & Supply of Gas	4	…	…

continued

工业固体废物综合利用量（万吨）Volume of Industrial Solid Wastes Utilized (10 000 tons)	工业固体废物贮存量（万吨）Volume of Industrial Solid Wastes Accumulated (10 000 tons)	工业固体废物处置量（万吨）Volume of Industrial Solid Wastes Treated (10 000 tons)	工业固体废物排放量（万吨）Volume of Industrial Solid Wastes Discharged (10 000 tons)
0.4	…	…	…
248.6	3.4	95.3	0.2
1392.0	51.8	19.3	0
340.7	1258.9	621.6	0.1
0.7	…	0.1	0.0
0.2	…	0.1	…
1.3	0.0	1.3	…
4.5	…	0.6	0
0	…	…	0
4.8	0	…	0
4.1	…	0.1	0
…	0	…	0
1.7	…	…	0
2.3	0.1	0.1	0
0.1	0	0.3	0
538.3	0	41.6	0
…	0	0	0

主要统计指标解释

自然资源　指人类可以直接从自然界获得，并用于生产和生活的物质资源。自然资源一般可以分成可再生资源和非再生资源两大类。可再生资源指在较短时间内可以再生、可以循环利用的资源，包括土地资源、水资源、气候资源、生物资源和海洋资源等。非再生资源指在使用后不能再生的资源，包括矿产资源和地热能源。

土地资源　土地是指陆地的表层部分，它主要由岩石、岩石的风化物和土壤构成。土地资源按利用类型可以分为农用地、建筑用地和未利用地。农用地包括耕地、园地、林地、牧草地和水面。建筑用地包括居民点及工矿用地、交通用地和水利设施用地。未利用地指家用地和建筑用地以外的土地，包括滩涂、荒漠、戈壁、冰川和石山等。

林业用地面积　指生长乔木、竹类、灌木、沿海红树林等林木的土地面积，包括有林地、灌木林、疏林地、未成林造林地、迹地、苗圃等。

草地面积　指牧区和农区用于放牧牲畜或割草，植被盖度在5%以上的草原、草坡、草山等面积。包括天然的和人工种植或改良的草地面积。

海洋　是海和洋的统称。洋为地球表面上相连接的广大咸水水体的主体部分。海为地球表面相连接的广大咸水水体被陆地、岛礁、半岛包围或分隔的边缘部分。

海岸线　指平均大潮高潮时水路分界线的痕迹线。

浅海　未有国标定义，在海洋管理部门中一般指0m—10m等深线的海域。

滩涂　未有国标定义，在海洋管理部门中一般指大潮高潮位与低潮位之间的潮侵地带。

森林面积　指由乔木树种构成，郁闭度0.2以上（含0.2）的林地或冠幅宽度10米以上的林带的面积，即有林地面积。森林面积包括天然起源和人工起源的针叶林面积、阔叶林面积、针阔混交林面积和竹林面积，不包括灌木林地面积的疏林地面积。

活立木蓄积量　指一定范围内土地上全部树木蓄积的总量，包括森林蓄积、疏林蓄积、散生木蓄积和四旁树蓄积。

森林覆盖率　指一个国家或地区森林面积占土地总面积的百分比。森林覆盖率是反映森林资源的丰富程度和生态平衡善的重要指标。在计算森林覆盖率时，森林面积包括郁闭度0.2以上的乔木林地面积和竹林地面积，国家特别规定的灌木林地面积、农田林网以及四旁（村旁、路旁、水旁、宅旁）林木的覆盖面积。计算公式为：

$$森林覆盖率（\%）=\frac{森林面积}{土地总面积}\times 100\%$$

矿产资源保有储量　指探明的矿产储量（包括工业储量和远景储量）扣除已开采部分和地下损失量后的年底实有储量。它反映国家矿产资源的现状。

径流量　指在一定时段内通过河流某一过水断面的水量，用以反映一个国家或地区水资源的丰歉程度。计算公式为：

径流量=降水量－蒸发量

气温　指空气的温度，我国一般以摄氏度（℃）为单位表示。气候观测的温度表是放在离地面约1.5米处通风良好的百叶箱里测量的，因此，通常的气温指的是离地面1.5米处百叶箱中的温度。其统计计算方法为：

月平均气温是将全月各日的平均气温相加，除以该月的天数而得。

年平均气温是将12个月的平均气温累加后除以12而得。

降水量　指从天空降落到地面的液态或固态（经融化后）水，未经蒸发、渗透、流失而在地面上积聚的深度。其统计计算方法为：

月降水量是将全月各日的降水量累加而得。

年降水量是将12个月的月降水量累加而得。

日照时数　指太阳实际照射地面的时间。其统计方法与降水量相同。

工业废水排放量　指经过企业厂区所有排放口排到企业外部的工业废水量。包括生产废水、外排的直接冷却水、超标排放的矿井地下水和与工业废水混排的厂区生活污水，不包括外排的间接冷却水（清污不分流的间接冷却水应计算在内）。

工业废气排放量 指企业厂内燃料燃烧和生产工艺过程中产生的各种排入空气的含有污染物的气体总量，按标准状态（273K，101325Pa）计算。

二氧化硫排放量 指企业在燃料燃烧和生产工艺过程中排入大气的二氧化硫数量。

烟尘排放量 指企业厂内燃料燃烧产生的烟气中夹带的颗粒物数量。

工业粉尘排放量 指企业在生产工艺过程中排放的颗粒物重量，如钢铁企业的耐火材料粉尘、焦化企业的筛焦系统粉尘、烧结机的粉尘、石灰窑的粉尘、建材企业的水泥粉尘等。不包括电厂排入大气的烟尘。

工业固体废物产生量 指企业在生产过程中产生的固体状、半固体状和高浓度液体废弃物的总量，包括危险废物、冶炼废渣、粉煤灰、炉渣、煤矸石、尾矿、放射性废物和其他废物等；不包括矿山开采的剥离废石和掘进废石（煤矸石和呈酸性或碱性的废石除外）。酸性或碱性废石指采掘的废石其流经水、雨淋水的pH值小于4或pH值大于10.5者。

工业固体废物综合利用量 指通过回收、加工、循环、交换等方式，从固体废物中提取或者使其转化为可以利用的资源、能源和其他原材料的固体废物量（包括当年利用往年的工业固体废物累计贮存量），如用作农业肥料、生产建筑材料、筑路等。综合利用量由原产生固体废物的单位统计。

工业固体废物处置量 指将固体废物焚烧或者最终置于符合环境保护规定要求的场所，并不再回取的工业固体废物量（包括当年处置往年的工业固体废物累计贮存量）。处置方法有填埋（其中危险废物应安全填埋）、焚烧、专业贮存场（库）封场处理、深层灌注、回填矿井等。

工业固体废物排放量 指将所产生的固体废物排到固体废物污染防治设施、场所以外的数量，不包括矿山开采的剥离废石和掘进废石（煤矸石和呈酸性或碱性的废石除外）。

“三废”综合利用产品产值 指利用“三废”（废液、废气、废渣）作为主要原料生产的产品价值（现行价）；已经销售或准备销售的应计算产品价值，留作生产自用的不应计算产品价值。

城市统计范围 根据建设部的新规定，设市城市按城区范围统计，县的统计范围为县城。

设市城市的城区 包括：

（一）街道办事处所辖地域；

（二）城市公共设施、居住设施和市政公用设施等连接到的其他镇（乡）地域；

（三）常住人口在3000人以上独立的工矿区、开发区、科研单位、大专院校等特殊区域。

县城 包括：

（一）县政府驻地的镇（城关镇）或街道办事处地域；

（二）县城公共设施、居住设施和市政公用设施等连接到的其他镇（乡）地域；

（三）常住人口在3000人以上独立的工矿区、开发区、科研单位、大专院校等特殊区域。

市区面积 指城市行政区域内的全部土地面积（包括水域面积）。地级城市行政区不包括市辖县（市），以国务院批准的行政区划面积为准。

城区面积 指设市城市的城建统计的范围面积。

市区（县）人口 指城市（县）行政区域内有常住户口和未落常住户口的人，以及被注销户口的在押犯、劳改、劳教人员。未落常住户口是指持出生、迁移、复员转业、劳改释放、解除劳教等证件未落常住户口的、无户口的人员以及户口情况不明且定居一年以上的流入人口。

城区（县城）人口 指划定的城区（县城）范围的人口数。

Explanatory Notes on Main Statistical Indicators

Natural Resources refer to the material resources that can be get from nature directly and used for production and life. Natural resources usually can be divided into 2 kinds; renewable resources and non-renewable resources. Renewable resources refer to the resources that can reproduce or recycle in a comparatively short time, including land resource, water resource, climate resource, biology resource, ocean and sea resource and so on. Non-renewable resources refer to the resources that cannot reproduce after using, including mineral resources and geothermal resource.

Land Resource Land refers to the surface of the earth, consisting of mainly rocks and its weathering and earth. Land resource can be classified, by its utilization, as land for agriculture, land for construction and unused land. Land for agriculture includes cultivated land, plantation land, forestland, grassland and waters. Land for construction includes land for residential purpose, for manufacturing and mining, for transportation and for water conservancy projects. Unused land refers to land other than land for agriculture and construction, including beaches, deserts, Gobi, glaciers and rock mountains.

Area of Afforested Land refers to land for trees, bamboo, bushes and mangrove, including forest-covered land, bush-covered land, sparse forest land, land planned for forestation and nurseries of young trees.

Area of Grassland refers to areas of grassland, grass-slopes and grass-covered hills with vegetation covering rate of over 5% that are used for animal husbandry or harvesting of grass. It includes natural, cultivated and improved grassland area.

Oceans and Seas Oceans refer to the principal part of the large bodies of saltwater connecting on the surface of the earth. Seas refer to the edges that the large bodies of saltwater connecting on the surface of the earth encircled or isolated by land, islands, reefs and peninsulas.

Forest Area refers to the area of forest where trees and bamboo grow with canopy density above 0.2 including land of natural woods and planted woods, but excluding bush land and thin forestland. It reflects the total areas of forestation.

Stock Volume of Forest refers to total stock volume of wood growing in forest area, which shows the total size and level of forest resources of a country or a region. It is also an important indicator illustrating the richness of forest resource and the status of forest ecological environment.

Forest Coverage Rate refers to the ratio of area of forestation land to total land area. It is a very important indicator that reflects the status of abundance of forest resource and ecosystem balance. Forest area includes the area of trees and bamboo grow with canopy density above 0.2, the area of shrubby tree according to regulations of the government, the area of forest land inside farm land and the area of trees planted by the side of villages, farm houses and along roads and rivers. The formula for calculating forest coverage rate is as follows:

Forest Coverage Rate (%) = (Area of Forested Land / Area of Total Land) ×100%

Ensured Reserves of Mineral Resources refer to the proven reserves of mineral resources (including industrial reserves and future reserves), which equal to the basic reserves and volume of resources minus the part mined and underground losses. They reflect status quo of mineral resources of countries.

Volume of Runoff refers to the volume of water that run through a certain cross section of a river during a given period, and it reflects the abundance of water resource in a country or region. The formula for calculating the volume of runoff is as follows:

Volume of Runoff = Amount of Precipitation – Amount of Evaporation

Atmospheric Temperature refers to the temperature of air, and is usually measured in degree centigrade (℃) in China. The thermometer for climate observation is placed in a drafty thermometer screen in distance of 1.5 meters from ground, thus the atmospheric temperature usually called refers to the temperature in the thermometer in distance of 1.5 meters from ground. The statistical calculating method is:

Average monthly atmospheric temperature equals to add up the average atmospheric temperatures of all days over a month and then multiplies the number of days over the month.

Average annual atmospheric temperature equals to add up the average monthly atmospheric temperatures and then multiplies 12.

Amount of Precipitation refers to the depth of liquid or solid (melted) water, which falls from sky to land, collected on ground without evaporation, infiltration and loss. The statistical calculating method is:

Monthly amount of precipitation equals to add up the amount of precipitation in all days over a month.

Annual amount of precipitation equals to add up the monthly amount of precipitation in 12 months of 1 year.

Sunshine Time refers to the actual hours that the sun shining ground. The statistical calculating method is the same as amount of precipitation.

Volume of Industrial Waste Water Discharged refers to the volume of industrial waste water discharged, through all outlets, to the outside of industrial enterprises, including waste water produced, direct-cooling water, underground water from mines from mines that does not meet the standard of discharge, and the domestic sewage mixed up with industrial waste water when discharged, but excluding discharged indirect-cooling water.

Volume of Industrial Waste Gas Emission refers to waste gas emitted from burning of fuels and from production process in the area of factory, and is measured by 10 000 standard cubic meters each year under normal condition (273K, 101325Pa).

Volume of Industrial Sulphur Dioxide Discharged refers to the volume of sulphur dioxide to the air in the process of fuel burning or in the production process.

Volume of Industrial Soot Discharged refers to the volume solid soot in the smoke discharged in the process of fuel burning in the area of the factory.

Industrial Dust Discharged refers to the total weight of solid dust discharged by industrial enterprises in the production process, such as dust of refractory materials form iron plants, dust from coke-screening systems or from sintering machines of coking plants, dust form lime kilns, cements dust from building material enterprises, etc., but excluding smoke and dust discharged by power plants.

Volume of Industrial Solid Wastes Produced refers to the total volume of solid, semi-solid or high-concentration liquid residue produced by industrial enterprises in their production process, including dangerous wastes, residues from melting, fly ash, slag, gangue, tailings, radioactive residues and other residues, but excluding stripped or dug stones in mining (except gangue and acid or alkali stones which are stones washed or soaked by water with a PH value smaller than 4 or larger than 10.5).

Volume of Industrial Solid Wastes Utilized in a Comprehensive Way refers to the volume of solid wastes form which useful materials can be extracted or which can be changed to be utilizable resources, energy or other materials, including the volume of industrial solid wastes stored up in the previous years and utilized in the current year, such as the solid wastes utilized as fertilizers, building materials, for making roads or for other purpose. Solid wastes producing units collect statistical data on utilization of industrial solid wastes.

Volume of Industrial Solid Wastes Treated refers to solid wastes disposed of in a non-recoverable place that meet the requirement of environmental protection, such as burying (The dangerous wastes should be buried safely), burning, piling in designated sites, pouring water into the deep strata, filing of old mines, etc. (Including treatment of solid wastes piled up in the previous years).

Volume of Industrial Solid Wastes Discharged refers to the volume of industrial solid wastes produced and discharged at the places outside the special facilities or special sites for preventing against pollution, excluding stripped or dug stones in mining (except gangue and acid or alkali waste stones).

Output Value of Products Made from Utilization of Waste Gas, Waste Water and Industrial Solid Wastes refers to the value of products (calculated at current prices) made by industrial enterprises using recovered waste water, waste gas or solid wastes as main raw materials. Only the value of the products, which have been sold or are ready, to be sold should be included. The value of the products, which will be used in the production of the enterprises, should not be included.

Statistical Range of City According to the new regulation of Ministry of Construction, the statistical range of administratively designated city refers to the urban area, and the statistical range of county refers to the county seat.

Urban Area of Administratively Designated City includes:

1. The area ruled by sub-district offices;

2. The area of other towns (villages) joint by city public facilities, living facilities and municipal facilities;

3. The special area of independent industrial and mining areas, development zones, institutions of scientific research and universities and colleges, with the permanent population above 3000 persons.

County Seat includes:

1. The area of the seat towns of county governments or sub-district offices;

2. The area of other towns (villages) joint by public facilities of county seats, living facilities and municipal facilities;

3. The special area of independent industrial and mining areas, development zones, institutions of scientific research and universities and colleges, with the permanent population above 3000 persons.

Area of City District refers to the total land area (including water area) in the administrative areas of the city. The administrative areas of the prefecture-level city excludes the under counties (county-level cities), and subject to the area of administrative divisions authorized by the State Department.

Urban Area refers to the area of the statistical range of the administratively designated cities' construction.

Population of City District (county) refers to the population with permanent residences and not yet with permanent residences, and the residence-canceled population of criminals in custody, reform- through-labor personnel and reeducation-through-labor personnel. The population not yet with permanent residences refers to the personnel that without residences or have not registered their identifications (such as for birth, transferring, demobilization and returning to civilian work, reform- through-labor personnel released and reeducation- through-labor personnel released) as permanent residences yet, and also includes the influx of population that have uncertain residences and settle for more than 1 year.

Population of Urban Area(county seat) refers to the population in the range of the circumscribed urban area (county seat).

第九篇

能源生产与消费

ENERGY PRODUCTION & CONSUMPTION

（校对编辑：甘艳华）

9－1 能源生产、消费总量（1978－2017年）
Production & Consumption of Energy（1978－2017）

单位：万吨标准煤 （10 000 tons of SCE）

年 份 Year	能源生产总量 Total Production of Energy	原煤 Coal	原油 Crude Oil	水电及其他能源 Hydroelectricity & Other Resources of Energy	能源消费总量 Total Consumption of Energy	煤炭 Coal	石油 Oil	水电及其他能源 Hydroelectricity & Other Resources of Energy
1978	508.59	382.26		126.33	781.00	479.53	175.14	126.33
1979	475.57	341.44		134.13	765.00	437.58	193.29	134.13
1980	415.21	287.79		127.42	730.00	413.91	188.69	127.40
1981	440.82	288.59		152.23	717.00	391.55	173.22	152.23
1982	481.92	306.91		175.01	769.00	439.95	154.04	175.01
1983	524.21	333.76	3.07	187.38	810.00	461.21	161.41	187.38
1984	526.19	324.50	4.50	197.19	854.00	487.63	169.18	197.19
1985	638.52	330.16	5.13	303.23	1008.21	530.60	125.70	351.91
1986	571.19	264.64		306.55	1022.77	542.36	125.89	354.52
1987	628.55	315.04	5.39	308.12	1135.66	648.80	133.47	353.39
1988	684.25	417.56	5.20	261.49	1160.21	728.76	121.75	309.70
1989	706.28	465.87	4.67	235.74	1200.28	776.59	127.22	296.47
1990	704.63	416.27	17.14	271.22	1308.21	820.62	151.81	335.78
1991	693.59	426.95	4.49	262.15	1386.88	903.22	155.70	327.96
1992	783.88	492.88	4.59	286.41	1549.30	1034.80	157.16	357.34
1993	958.47	502.35	4.40	451.72	1809.21	1068.67	179.18	561.36
1994	1064.73	575.91	4.61	484.21	2047.95	1232.19	193.60	622.16
1995	1103.39	561.90	14.53	526.96	2256.52	1261.41	227.49	767.62
1996	1035.50	531.33	5.14	499.03	2301.11	1303.05	244.90	753.16
1997	1065.84	472.81	5.60	587.43	2327.74	1190.25	245.92	891.57
1998	975.93	430.71	4.50	540.72	2417.68	1218.87	318.95	879.86
1999	855.47	346.25	5.00	504.22	2472.73	1299.03	327.89	845.81
2000	833.28	300.26	4.70	528.32	2487.40	1226.29	378.09	883.02
2001	838.35	260.31	4.64	573.21	2700.97	1372.09	461.87	867.01
2002	770.23	185.31	5.00	579.93	2778.58	1322.61	536.27	919.71
2003	729.67	188.12	4.69	651.15	3187.66	1632.08	678.97	876.61
2004	908.43	267.06	5.13	636.24	4014.56	1971.15	863.13	1180.28
2005	1220.99	358.78	4.90	857.31	4536.74	2540.57	798.47	1197.70
2006	1359.27	288.54	4.84	1065.88	5022.95	2697.33	863.95	1461.67
2007	1467.60	305.91	4.11	1157.58	5588.61	3297.28	927.71	1363.62
2008	1926.42	191.30	4.09	1730.91	6054.22	3396.42	974.73	1683.07
2009	1820.23	259.86	4.13	1556.24	6592.74	3876.53	1068.02	1648.19
2010	1951.85	428.48	3.84	1519.53	7379.23	3977.40	1224.95	2176.88
2011	1777.24	445.37	3.24	1328.63	8005.79	4315.12	1377.00	2313.67
2012	2129.80	440.96	3.27	1685.57	8530.55	4555.32	1408.13	2567.11
2013	2517.35	369.26	62.50	2084.26	9100.37	5229.98	1443.41	2426.98
2014	2869.84	341.29	83.86	2444.69	9515.34	5025.22	1593.11	2897.01
2015	3274.39	224.60	79.30	2970.49	9760.65	4492.78	1760.29	3507.58
2016	3147.49	227.45	67.72	2852.32	10092.36	4738.59	1860.64	3493.13
2017	3255.17	206.45	62.96	2985.76	10458.46	4746.18	1922.91	3789.37

注：1. 本表指标均为常规能源折合标准煤。
2. 从1988年起电力折标系数调整，2000年－2013年因第三次经济普查数据作调整。

Note：1.The items in this table are converted into SCE.
2.Since 1988, the ratio of Hydro-Power converted into SCE has been adjusted. The data from 2000 to 2013 has been adjusted by the 3rd Economic Census.

9－2 能源生产、消费构成（1978－2017年）

Composition of Energy Production & Consumption（1978－2017）

单位：%　　(%)

年 份 Year	能源生产总量 Total Production of Energy	原煤 Coal	原油 Crude Oil	水电及其他能源 Hydroelectricity & Electricity Produced by Other Powers	能源消费总量 Total Consumption of Energy	煤炭 Coal	石油 Oil	水电及其他能源 Hydroelectricity & Electricity Produced by Other Powers
1978	100	75.2		24.8	100	61.4	22.4	16.2
1979	100	71.8		28.2	100	57.2	25.3	17.5
1980	100	69.3		30.7	100	56.7	25.9	17.4
1981	100	65.5		34.5	100	54.6	24.2	21.2
1982	100	63.7		36.3	100	57.2	20.0	22.8
1983	100	63.7	0.5	35.8	100	56.9	19.9	23.2
1984	100	61.7	0.8	37.5	100	57.1	19.8	23.1
1985	100	51.7	0.8	47.5	100	52.6	12.4	35.0
1986	100	46.3	0.9	53.7	100	53.0	12.3	34.7
1987	100	50.1	0.9	49.0	100	57.1	11.8	31.1
1988	100	61.0	0.8	38.2	100	62.8	10.5	26.7
1989	100	66.0	0.7	33.4	100	64.7	10.6	24.7
1990	100	59.1	2.4	38.5	100	62.7	11.6	25.7
1991	100	61.6	0.6	37.8	100	65.1	11.2	23.7
1992	100	62.9	0.6	36.5	100	66.8	10.1	23.1
1993	100	52.4	0.5	47.1	100	59.1	9.9	31.0
1994	100	54.1	0.4	45.5	100	60.2	9.5	30.3
1995	100	50.9	1.3	47.8	100	55.9	10.1	34.0
1996	100	51.3	0.5	48.2	100	56.6	10.6	32.8
1997	100	44.4	0.5	55.1	100	51.1	10.6	38.3
1998	100	44.1	0.5	55.4	100	50.4	13.2	36.4
1999	100	40.5	0.6	58.9	100	52.5	13.6	33.9
2000	100	36.0	0.6	63.4	100	49.3	15.2	35.5
2001	100	31.1	0.6	68.3	100	50.8	17.1	32.1
2002	100	24.1	0.7	75.2	100	47.6	19.3	33.1
2003	100	25.8	0.6	73.6	100	51.2	21.3	27.5
2004	100	32.3	0.8	66.9	100	49.1	21.5	29.4
2005	100	29.4	0.4	70.2	100	56.0	17.6	26.4
2006	100	21.2	0.4	78.4	100	53.7	17.2	29.1
2007	100	20.8	0.3	78.9	100	59.0	16.6	24.4
2008	100	9.9	0.2	89.9	100	56.1	16.1	27.8
2009	100	14.3	0.2	85.5	100	58.8	16.2	25.0
2010	100	22.0	0.2	77.9	100	53.9	16.6	29.5
2011	100	25.1	0.2	74.8	100	53.9	17.2	28.9
2012	100	20.7	0.2	79.1	100	53.4	16.5	30.1
2013	100	18.7	3.2	78.3	100	57.5	15.9	26.6
2014	100	15.6	3.5	82.1	100	52.8	16.7	30.5
2015	100	6.9	2.4	90.7	100	46.0	18.0	36.0
2016	100	7.2	2.2	90.6	100	47.0	18.4	34.6
2017	100	6.3	1.9	91.8	100	45.4	18.4	36.2

9-3 能源利用效益主要指标
Economic Results Indicators for the Utilization of Energy

年 份 Year	每万元地区生产总值消费能源（吨标准煤） Per 10 000 Yuan GDP Energy Consumption (ton of SCE)	每万元工业总产值消费能源（吨标准煤） Per10 000 Yuan Gross Output Value of Industry Energy Consumption (ton of SCE)	每吨能源消费实现的地区生产总值（元） Per Ton Energy Consumption Format Gross Domestic Product (yuan)	每吨能源消费实现的工业总产值（元） Per Ton Energy Consumption Format Gross Industrial Output Value (yuan)
1985	5.57	5.25	1795	1905
1990	2.91	2.84	3431	3526
1991	2.67	2.57	3739	3891
1992	2.40	2.16	4173	4640
1993	2.08	1.59	4818	6276
1994	1.71	1.26	5851	7912
1995	1.51	1.26	6637	7917
1996	1.36	1.16	7379	8597
1997	1.28	1.12	7807	8928
1998	1.27	1.09	7906	9161
1999	1.27	1.16	7973	8649
2000	1.20	1.13	8362	8859
2001	1.18	1.22	8439	8213
2002	1.10	1.17	9083	8575
2003	1.13	1.11	8850	8982
2004	1.17	0.95	8553	10523
2005	1.14	0.97	8182	10273
2006	1.06	0.83	9449	12081
2007	0.96	0.72	10420	13843
2008	0.86	0.63	11597	15983
2009	0.85	0.60	11769	16678
2010	0.77	0.47	12969	21277
2011	0.68	0.41	14640	24235
2012	0.65	0.38	15280	26144
2013	0.63	0.35	15799	26489
2014	0.61	0.32	16156	31467
2015	0.58	0.29	17215	34062
2016	0.55	0.30	18078	33439
2017	0.51	0.26	19502	38540

注：1. 价值指标按当年价格计算。因1998年后价值指标作调整，故本表资料相应变化。
2. 2000年－2013年数据根据第三次经济普查调整。

Note: 1.The data in value terms in this table are calculated at current prices. Due to the indicators of value have been readjusted since 1998, the data in this table have been relatively changed.
2.The data from 2000 to 2013 has been adjusted by the 3rd Economic Census.

9—4 能源消费弹性系数
Elasticity Ratio of Energy Consumption

年 份 Year	能源消费 比上年增长（%） Growth Rate of Energy Consump-tion over Preceding Year (%)	电力消费 比上年增长（%） Growth Rate of Electricity Consump-tion over Preceding Year (%)	地区生产总值 比上年增长（%） Growth Rate of GDP over Preceding Year (%)	能源消费 弹性系数 Elasticity Ratio of Energy Consumption	电力消费 弹性系数 Elasticity Ratio of Electricity Consumption
1985	6.4	15.1	11.0	0.58	1.37
1990	8.2	11.8	7.0	1.17	1.69
1991	6.0	7.8	12.7	0.47	0.61
1992	11.7	13.1	18.3	0.64	0.72
1993	16.8	10.1	18.3	0.92	0.55
1994	13.2	13.0	15.2	0.87	0.85
1995	10.2	19.8	11.4	0.90	1.74
1996	2.0	7.5	8.3	0.24	0.90
1997	1.2	3.3	8.0	0.15	0.41
1998	3.9	7.9	10.0	0.39	0.79
1999	2.3	5.7	8.0	0.29	0.71
2000	8.0	11.4	7.9	1.01	1.44
2001	8.6	3.1	8.3	1.03	0.37
2002	2.8	7.5	10.6	0.26	0.73
2003	14.7	16.5	10.2	1.44	1.58
2004	25.9	9.9	11.8	2.19	0.84
2005	15.6	11.7	13.2	1.18	0.89
2006	10.7	13.6	13.6	0.79	1.00
2007	11.3	17.6	15.1	0.75	1.17
2008	8.3	11.7	12.8	0.65	0.91
2009	8.9	11.7	13.9	0.64	0.84
2010	11.9	16.0	14.2	0.84	1.13
2011	8.5	12.0	12.3	0.69	0.98
2012	6.6	3.7	11.3	0.58	0.33
2013	6.7	7.3	10.2	0.66	0.72
2014	4.6	5.6	8.5	0.54	0.66
2015	2.6	2.0	8.1	0.32	0.25
2016	3.4	1.9	7.3	0.47	0.26
2017	3.6	6.1	7.3	0.49	0.84

9—5 主要年份分行业能源消费量和构成

行业名称	Sector	1995		2000		2005	
		消费总量（万吨标准煤）Total Consumption (10 000 tce)	构 成（%）Composition (%)	消费总量（万吨标准煤）Total Consumption (10 000 tce)	构 成（%）Composition (%)	消费总量（万吨标准煤）Total Consumption (10 000 tce)	构 成（%）Composition (%)
消 费 总 计	**Total Consumption**	**2256.52**	**100.0**	**2487.40**	**100.0**	**4536.74**	**100.0**
一、农、林、牧、渔业、水利业	**Farming,Forestry,Animal Husbandry, Fishery & Conservancy**	**45.37**	**2.0**	**52.73**	**2.1**	**96.18**	**2.1**
二、工业	**Industry**	**1848.24**	**81.9**	**1893.66**	**76.1**	**3341.76**	**73.7**
轻工业	**Light Industry**	**480.48**	**21.3**	**450.47**	**18.1**	**563.46**	**12.4**
重工业	**Heavy Industry**	**1367.76**	**60.6**	**1443.19**	**58.0**	**2778.30**	**61.2**
（一）采矿业	**Mining & Quarrying**	**92.03**	**4.1**	**83.58**	**3.4**	**92.10**	**2.0**
煤炭开采和洗选业	Mining & Washing of Coal	34.62	1.5	25.87	1.0	14.06	0.3
石油和天然气开采业	Extraction of Petroleum & Natural Gas			0.50	…	0.45	…
黑色金属矿采选业	Mining & Processing of Ferrous Metal Ores	10.55	0.5	7.96	0.3	21.78	0.5
有色金属矿采选业	Mining & Processing of Non-Ferrous Metal Ores	32.46	1.4	40.30	1.6	39.02	0.9
非金属矿采选业	Mining & processing of Nonmetal Ores	9.74	0.4	6.47	0.3	13.16	0.3
开采辅助活动	Mining Assist Activities						
其他采矿业	Mining of Other Ores	4.66	0.2	2.49	0.1	3.18	0.1
（二）制造业	**Manufacturing**	**1568.96**	**69.5**	**1679.99**	**67.5**	**3104.04**	**68.4**
农副食品加工业	Processing of Food from Agricultural Products	187.26	8.3	239.29	9.6	286.72	6.3
食品制造业	Manufacture of Foods	36.78	1.6	20.65	0.8	12.70	0.3
酒、饮料和精制茶制造业	Wine, Drink & Refined Tea Manufacturing	29.40	1.3	12.93	0.5	24.04	0.5
烟草制品业	Manufacture of Tobacco	4.18	0.2	3.73	0.2	6.35	0.1
纺织业	Manufacture of Textile	34.56	1.5	16.17	0.7	20.87	0.5
纺织服装、服饰业	Manufacture of Textile Wearing Apparel,Footwear & Caps	2.80	0.1	0.99	…	1.36	…
皮革、毛皮、羽毛及其制品业和制鞋业	Manufacture of Leather,Fur,Feather & Related Products	2.33	0.1	2.24	0.1	4.54	0.1
木材加工及木、竹、藤、棕、草制品业	Processing of Timber,Manufacture of Wood,Bamboo,Rattan, Palm & Sreaw Products	14.27	0.6	16.91	0.7	25.41	0.6
家具制造业	Manufacture of Furniture	4.56	0.2	1.49	0.1	3.18	0.1
造纸及纸制品业	Manufacture of Paper and Paper Products	66.99	3.0	61.94	2.5	120.22	2.7
印刷业和记录媒介的复制	Printing,Reproduction of Recording Media	1.92	0.1	1.74	0.1	6.35	0.1
文教、工美、体育和娱乐用品制造业	Manufacture of Articles For Culture,Education & Sport Activity	0.29	…	0.25	…	0.45	…
石油加工、炼焦和核燃料加工业	Processing of Petroleum,Coking, Processing of Nuclear Fuel	8.64	0.4	9.45	0.4	33.12	0.7
化学原料及化学制品制造业	Manufacture of Raw Chemical Materials & Chemical Products	225.44	10.0	221.63	8.9	355.23	7.8

Consumption & Composition of Energy by Sector in Main Years

2011		2012		2013		2014		2015		2016		2017	
消费总量(万吨标准煤) Total Consumption (10 000 tce)	构成(%) Composition (%)	消费总量(万吨标准煤) Total Consumption (10 000 tce)	构成(%) Composition (%)	消费总量(万吨标准煤) Total Consumption (10 000 tce)	构成(%) Composition (%)	消费总量(万吨标准煤) Total Consumption (10 000 tce)	构成(%) Composition (%)	消费总量(万吨标准煤) Total Consumption (10 000 tce)	构成(%) Composition (%)	消费总量(万吨标准煤) Total Consumption (10 000 tce)	构成(%) Composition (%)	消费总量(万吨标准煤) Total Consumption (10 000 tce)	构成(%) Composition (%)
8005.79	**100.0**	**8530.56**	**100.0**	**9100.37**	**100.0**	**9515.35**	**100.0**	**9760.65**	**100.0**	**10092.36**	**100.0**	**10458.46**	**100.0**
129.69	**1.6**	**134.78**	**1.6**	**191.27**	**2.1**	**218.38**	**2.3**	**235.13**	**2.4**	**255.13**	**2.5**	**234.47**	**2.2**
5802.60	**72.5**	**6131.77**	**71.9**	**6759.21**	**74.3**	**6848.42**	**72.0**	**6862.57**	**70.3**	**6983.35**	**69.2**	**7237.33**	**69.2**
887.84	**11.1**	**880.35**	**10.3**	**858.98**	**9.4**	**946.51**	**9.9**	**878.09**	**9.0**	**766.85**	**7.6**	**733.63**	**7.0**
4914.75	**61.4**	**5252.27**	**61.6**	**5900.23**	**64.8**	**5901.90**	**62.0**	**5984.49**	**61.3**	**6216.50**	**61.6**	**6503.70**	**62.2**
86.46	**1.1**	**80.19**	**0.9**	**86.10**	**0.9**	**85.55**	**0.9**	**87.10**	**0.9**	**94.52**	**0.9**	**116.57**	**1.1**
9.61	0.1	17.06	0.2	13.13	0.1	12.92	0.1	5.37	0.1	24.83	0.2	23.40	0.2
				1.68	0.02	1.67	…	1.41	…	1.51	…	0.53	…
32.82	0.4	15.36	0.2	12.22	0.1	12.20	0.1	12.47	0.1	13.69	0.1	15.25	0.1
30.42	0.4	23.89	0.3	30.48	0.3	29.96	0.3	34.47	0.4	26.06	0.3	25.11	0.2
13.61	0.2	23.03	0.3	28.60	0.3	28.81	0.3	33.30	0.3	28.32	0.3	39.15	0.4
												13.03	0.1
								0.09	…	0.10	…	0.10	…
5343.06	**66.7**	**5623.35**	**65.9**	**6120.14**	**67.3**	**6229.81**	**65.5**	**6270.37**	**64.2**	**6410.29**	**63.5**	**6655.98**	**63.6**
502.76	6.3	477.71	5.6	467.89	5.1	514.21	5.4	423.29	4.3	225.98	2.2	257.49	2.5
32.02	0.4	40.95	0.5	46.97	0.5	52.69	0.6	64.68	0.7	58.51	0.6	57.24	0.5
52.04	0.7	68.24	0.8	77.33	0.8	74.49	0.8	61.26	0.6	59.40	0.6	55.50	0.5
3.20	…	3.41	…	4.10	…	6.50	0.1	3.83	…	3.60	…	3.66	…
32.82	0.4	26.44	0.3	26.87	0.3	26.72	0.3	34.06	0.3	19.59	0.2	20.32	0.2
3.20	…	6.82	0.1	7.53	0.1	7.40	0.1	8.92	0.1	8.84	0.1	5.02	…
4.80	0.1	5.97	0.1	7.14	0.1	7.09	0.1	7.32	0.1	5.99	0.1	4.83	…
100.07	1.3	98.10	1.2	114.24	1.3	123.87	1.3	132.04	1.4	105.49	1.0	112.05	1.1
4.00	0.1	4.27	0.1	5.47	0.1	5.39	0.1	6.65	0.1	6.87	0.1	6.17	0.1
220.96	2.8	203.03	2.4	182.94	2.0	219.17	2.3	223.98	2.3	263.17	2.6	284.06	2.7
3.20	…	5.12	0.1	2.74	…	2.70	…	4.90	0.1	3.75	…	3.45	…
0.80	…	1.71	…	0.30	…	0.30	…	3.00	…	2.34	…	0.70	…
154.51	1.9	218.38	2.6	279.73	3.1	266.85	2.8	222.59	2.3	236.68	2.3	356.33	3.4
448.32	5.6	489.65	5.7	483.98	5.3	474.05	5.0	549.97	5.6	434.71	4.3	347.11	3.3

9—5　续表

行业名称	Sector	1995		2000		2005	
		消费总量（万吨标准煤）Total Consumption (10 000 tce)	构　成（%）Composition (%)	消费总量（万吨标准煤）Total Consumption (10 000 tce)	构　成（%）Composition (%)	消费总量（万吨标准煤）Total Consumption (10 000 tce)	构　成（%）Composition (%)
医药制造业	Manufacture of Medicines	19.76	0.9	9.95	0.4	19.51	0.4
化学纤维制造业	Manufacture of Chemical Fibers	18.37	0.8	11.94	0.5	5.44	0.1
橡胶和塑料制品业	Rubber & Plastic Products	22.83	0.7	12.19	0.5	9.53	0.2
非金属矿物制品业	Manufacture of Non-metallic Mineral Products	448.60	19.9	493.00	19.8	587.05	12.9
黑色金属冶炼及压延加工业	Smelting and Pressing of Ferrous Metals	216.38	9.6	242.52	9.8	1043.45	23.0
有色金属冶炼及压延加工业	Smelting and Pressing of Nonferrous Metals	86.10	3.8	211.18	8.5	370.65	8.2
金属制品业	Manufacture of Metal Products	20.91	0.9	13.18	0.5	21.78	0.5
通用设备制造业	Manufacture of General Purpose Machinery	24.95	1.1	13.93	0.6	19.96	0.4
专用设备制造业	Manufacture of Special Purpose Machinery	9.15	0.4	4.48	0.2	7.26	0.2
汽车制造业	Manufacture of Transport Equipment	13.76	0.6	9.20	0.4	40.38	0.9
铁路、船舶、航空航天和其他运输设备制造业	Railway, Ship, Aerospace & Other Transportation Equipment Manufacturing						
电气机械及器材制造业	Manufacture of Electrical Machinery & Equipment	6.60	0.3	7.71	0.3	9.53	0.2
通信设备、计算机及其他电子设备制造业	Manufacture of Communication Equipment,Computers & Other Electronic Equipment	1.63	0.1	1.49	0.1	3.18	0.1
仪器仪表制造业	Manufacture of Measuring Instruments & Machinery for Cultural Activity & Office Work	0.85	…	0.50	…	0.91	…
其他制造业	Other Manufacturing					51.72	1.1
废弃资源综合利用业	Recycling and Disposal of Waste					5.44	0.1
金属制品业、机械和设备修理业	Metal Product, Machinery & Equipment Repair Services						
（三）电力、燃气及水的生产和供应业	**Electric Power,Gas & Water Production & Supply**	**187.26**	**8.3**	**130.09**	**5.2**	**145.63**	**3.2**
电力、热力的生产和供应业	Production and Distribution of Electric Power & Heat Power	173.48	7.7	118.90	4.8	119.77	2.6
燃气生产和供应业	Production & Distribution of Gas	1.77	0.1	0.25	…	8.17	0.2
水的生产和供应业	Production & Distribution of Water	12.00	0.5	10.70	0.4	17.69	0.4
三、建筑业	**Construction**	**12.34**	**0.6**	**7.46**	**0.3**	**33.12**	**0.7**
四、交通运输储运业和邮政业	**Transportation,Storage & Post**	**106.17**	**4.7**	**213.67**	**8.6**	**382.90**	**8.4**
五、批发、零售业和住宿、餐饮业	**Wholesale & Retail Trade,Hotel & Catering**	**23.76**	**1.1**	**35.32**	**1.4**	**109.34**	**2.4**
六、其他行业	**Others**	**46.06**	**2.0**	**46.76**	**1.9**	**117.96**	**2.6**
七、城乡居民生活	**Residential Consumption**	**174.69**	**7.7**	**237.80**	**9.6**	**455.49**	**10.0**

continued

2011		2012		2013		2014		2015		2016		2017	
消费总量(万吨标准煤) Total Consumption (10 000 tce)	构成(%) Composition (%)	消费总量(万吨标准煤) Total Consumption (10 000 tce)	构成(%) Composition (%)	消费总量(万吨标准煤) Total Consumption (10 000 tce)	构成(%) Composition (%)	消费总量(万吨标准煤) Total Consumption (10 000 tce)	构成(%) Composition (%)	消费总量(万吨标准煤) Total Consumption (10 000 tce)	构成(%) Composition (%)	消费总量(万吨标准煤) Total Consumption (10 000 tce)	构成(%) Composition (%)	消费总量(万吨标准煤) Total Consumption (10 000 tce)	构成(%) Composition (%)
25.62	0.3	29.86	0.4	24.93	0.3	25.18	0.3	32.29	0.3	102.18	1.0	30.18	0.3
		5.12	0.1	2.45	…	2.40	…	0.03	…	2.64	…	2.03	…
7.21	0.1	23.89	0.3	28.01	0.3	28.33	0.3	49.30	0.5	35.15	0.3	115.72	1.1
1185.66	14.8	1273.61	14.9	1433.43	15.8	1346.85	14.2	1374.95	14.1	1422.38	14.1	1394.23	13.3
1488.28	18.6	1519.29	17.8	1967.96	21.6	2106.75	22.1	2030.19	20.8	2151.72	21.3	2307.03	22.1
875.03	10.9	942.63	11.1	755.37	8.3	741.29	7.8	776.67	8.0	984.01	9.8	1001.54	9.6
22.42	0.3	29.86	0.4	39.41	0.4	42.25	0.4	50.95	0.5	94.83	0.9	92.93	0.9
41.63	0.5	14.50	0.2	17.92	0.2	17.10	0.2	28.67	0.3	34.30	0.3	33.98	0.3
14.41	0.2	17.06	0.2	16.65	0.2	16.34	0.2	19.25	0.2	23.64	0.2	32.84	0.3
63.25	0.8	63.98	0.8	66.49	0.7	62.71	0.7	89.72	0.9	78.53	0.8	80.27	0.8
		8.53	0.1	9.20	0.1	9.04	0.1	5.53	0.1	5.51	0.1	7.69	0.1
28.82	0.4	29.86	0.4	32.92	0.4	32.31	0.3	43.34	0.4	20.38	0.2	20.45	0.2
8.81	0.1	11.09	0.1	12.59	0.1	12.35	0.1	15.61	0.2	12.10	0.1	12.15	0.1
0.80	…	0.85	…	1.37	…	1.35	…	1.89	…	2.03	…	3.91	…
4.00	0.1	1.71	…	2.30	…	2.28	…	3.88	…	3.98	…	2.99	…
0.80	…	0.85	…	1.74	…	1.71	…	1.44	…	1.85	…	4.11	…
				0.16	…	0.15	…	0.16	…	0.16	…	…	…
373.07	**4.7**	**429.09**	**5.0**	**552.97**	**6.1**	**533.05**	**5.6**	**505.11**	**5.2**	**478.54**	**4.7**	**464.79**	**4.4**
361.86	4.5	407.76	4.8	528.57	5.8	509.14	5.4	487.54	5.0	439.61	4.4	424.34	4.1
		0.85	…	0.86	…	0.85	…	1.34	…	11.33	0.1	10.79	0.1
11.21	0.1	21.33	0.3	23.53	0.3	23.07	0.2	16.23	0.2	27.60	0.3	29.65	0.3
40.83	**0.5**	**42.65**	**0.5**	**46.47**	**0.5**	**50.54**	**0.5**	**59.90**	**0.6**	**62.06**	**0.6**	**69.00**	**0.7**
759.75	**9.5**	**823.20**	**9.7**	**667.69**	**7.3**	**876.77**	**9.2**	**932.88**	**9.6**	**979.94**	**9.7**	**1078.80**	**10.3**
200.14	**2.5**	**215.82**	**2.5**	**178.11**	**2.0**	**215.60**	**2.3**	**233.90**	**2.4**	**244.26**	**2.4**	**257.26**	**2.5**
252.98	**3.2**	**278.95**	**3.3**	**254.59**	**2.8**	**276.74**	**2.9**	**310.49**	**3.2**	**340.10**	**3.4**	**354.32**	**3.4**
819.79	**10.2**	**903.39**	**10.6**	**1003.03**	**11.0**	**1028.90**	**10.8**	**1125.77**	**11.5**	**1227.52**	**12.2**	**1227.29**	**11.7**

9－5－1　主要年份规模以上工业分行业综合能源消费量

单位：万吨标准煤

指　标	Item
规模以上工业企业合计	**Industry above Designated Size**
#轻工业	Light Industry
#重工业	Heavy Industry
一、采矿业	**Mining & Quarrying**
煤炭开采和洗选业	Mining & Washing of Coal
石油和天然气开采业	Extraction of Petroleum & Natural Gas
黑色金属矿采选业	Mining & Processing of Ferrous Metal Ores
有色金属矿采选业	Mining & Processing of Non-Ferrous Metal Ores
非金属矿采选业	Mining & Processing of Nonmetal Ores
开采辅助活动	Mining Assist Activities
其他采矿业	Mining of Other Ores
二、制造业	**Manufacturing**
农副食品加工业	Processing of Food from Agricultural Products
食品制造业	Manufacture of Foods
酒、饮料和精制茶制造业	Wine, Drink & Refined Tea Manufacturing
烟草制品业	Manufacture of Tobacco
纺织业	Manufacture of Textile
纺织服装、服饰业	Manufacture of Textile Wearing Apparel,Footwear & Caps
皮革、毛皮、羽毛及其制品和制鞋业	Manufacture of Leather,Fur,Feather & Related Products
木材加工和木、竹、藤、棕、草制品业	Processing of Timber,Manufacture of Wood,Bamboo,Rattan,Palm & Sreaw Products
家具制造业	Manufacture of Furniture
造纸和纸制品业	Manufacture of Paper & Paper Products
印刷和记录媒介复制业	Printing ,Reproduction of Recording Media
文教、工美、体育和娱乐用品制造业	Manufacture of Articles For Culture,Education & Sport Activity
石油加工、炼焦和核燃料加工业	Processing of Petroleum,Coking,Processing of Nuclear Fuel
化学原料和化学制品制造业	Manufacture of Raw Chemical Materials & Chemical Products
医药制造业	Manufacture of Mcdicines
化学纤维制造业	Manufacture of Chemical Fibers
橡胶和塑料制品业	Rubber & Plastic Products
非金属矿物制品业	Manufacture of Non-metallic Mineral Products
黑色金属冶炼和压延加工业	Smelting and Pressing of Ferrous Metals
有色金属冶炼和压延加工业	Smelting and Pressing of Nonferrous Metals
金属制品业	Manufacture of Metal Products
通用设备制造业	Manufacture of General Purpose Machinery
专用设备制造业	Manufacture of Special Purpose Machinery
汽车制造业	Manufacture of Transport Equipment
铁路、船舶、航空航天和其他运输设备制造业	Railway, Ship, Aerospace & Other Transportation Equipment Manufacturing
电气机械和器材制造业	Manufacture of Electrical Machinery & Equipment
计算机、通信和其他电子设备制造业	Manufacture of Communication Equipment,Computers & Other Electronic Equipment
仪器仪表制造业	Manufacture of Measuring Instruments & Machinery for Cultural Activity & Office Work
其他制造业	Other Manufacturing
废弃资源综合利用业	Recycling & Disposal of Waste
金属制品、机械和设备修理业	Metal Product, Machinery & Equipment Repair Services
三、电力、燃气及水的生产和供应业	**Electric Power,Gas & Water Production & Supply**
电力、热力生产和供应业	Production & Distribution of Electric Power & Heat Power
燃气生产和供应业	Production & Distribution of Gas
水的生产和供应业	Production & Distribution of Water

注：本表中数据采用电热当量计算法。
Note: The data of this table was calculated using the Electro-thermal Equivalent Calculation Methond.

Consumption of Comprehensive Energy by Sector above Designated Size in Main Years

(10 000 tons of SCE)

2010	2011	2012	2013	2014	2015	2016	2017
4549.11	**5138.94**	**5545.10**	**6084.62**	**6116.29**	**5802.01**	**5929.64**	**6148.87**
686.42	757.34	826.50	896.44	904.75	840.30	816.69	835.10
3862.70	4381.60	4718.60	5188.18	5211.54	4961.71	5112.95	5313.77
35.91	**45.89**	**48.91**	**51.76**	**55.01**	**60.39**	**58.80**	**58.27**
3.85	4.08	4.18	3.47	2.39	2.83	1.68	2.44
			1.33	2.12	2.17	2.66	2.76
11.08	17.76	20.51	18.95	20.36	23.26	25.10	21.43
12.99	14.98	13.83	14.51	14.71	15.48	11.36	12.32
7.91	9.08	10.39	13.49	15.43	16.55	17.84	19.16
			0.01	0.01	0.01	0.02	0.01
0.09					0.10	0.15	0.13
3583.14	**4026.94**	**4357.38**	**4762.61**	**4966.20**	**4904.69**	**4972.24**	**5148.87**
350.12	368.43	399.33	429.13	433.79	386.23	366.50	363.11
19.59	23.72	31.24	33.38	38.62	37.64	38.02	35.31
44.71	47.01	54.06	53.57	45.21	44.96	43.24	43.63
2.76	2.31	2.16	2.31	2.15	2.11	1.85	1.88
20.19	19.76	21.44	20.23	21.56	25.15	22.59	21.69
0.94	1.50	2.93	3.14	3.53	3.63	3.60	3.88
4.08	3.47	3.52	3.59	3.09	3.26	2.87	2.87
43.69	51.65	57.90	67.91	75.37	79.74	83.34	82.93
1.17	1.86	2.01	2.08	2.40	2.62	2.66	2.76
123.52	160.22	175.39	197.88	198.64	176.69	172.85	196.36
1.25	1.15	2.02	2.28	1.66	1.90	2.10	2.38
0.25	0.24	0.74	0.95	1.18	1.38	1.27	1.50
84.78	144.49	213.60	213.60	264.13	247.17	253.73	275.83
302.90	352.02	345.87	376.84	381.40	342.58	286.50	269.53
18.89	19.29	20.21	22.57	20.84	20.46	22.01	20.85
0.01				0.00	0.01	0.01	0.02
13.43	13.22	15.88	18.68	19.66	22.78	21.12	18.50
896.25	1040.47	1134.40	1180.43	1163.39	1146.94	1261.36	1337.57
1077.81	1159.04	1269.53	1518.67	1635.54	1621.92	1649.38	1678.14
500.08	525.00	519.41	521.56	553.60	628.51	626.29	673.56
11.54	12.46	20.27	19.37	20.71	24.85	24.57	24.87
16.80	20.96	4.78	11.80	11.32	10.24	12.19	12.24
6.72	6.92	7.31	7.46	7.88	7.78	8.46	9.54
27.44	31.73	30.94	32.06	32.73	35.80	36.24	38.20
		2.11	2.15	2.29	2.19	2.03	1.41
7.64	12.99	13.39	14.25	17.44	18.24	16.14	16.79
2.77	3.55	4.54	4.47	5.37	6.10	7.06	8.78
0.47	0.46	0.32	0.29	0.43	0.68	0.66	1.16
1.99	2.35	1.25	1.21	1.54	2.39	2.43	1.99
1.35	0.65	0.80	0.74	0.71	0.71	1.15	0.95
		0.01	0.01	0.00	0.01	0.01	0.64
930.06	**1066.11**	**1138.82**	**1270.25**	**1095.08**	**836.92**	**898.59**	**941.74**
924.48	1061.45	1133.27	1264.50	1088.66	829.85	888.21	933.84
0.14	0.12	0.38	0.42	0.64	0.76	3.70	0.87
5.45	4.54	5.17	5.33	5.78	6.31	6.69	7.03

9－5－2　主要年份各市规模以上工业综合能源消费量

单位：万吨标准煤

地　区	City	2010	2011
全　区	**All Cities**	**4549.11**	**5138.94**
南宁市	Nanning	353.12	385.09
柳州市	Liuzhou	1009.27	1034.77
桂林市	Guilin	321.90	340.24
梧州市	Wuzhou	120.31	128.31
北海市	Beihai	103.13	136.81
防城港市	Fangchenggang	249.40	324.59
钦州市	Qinzhou	281.98	407.97
贵港市	Guigang	468.81	493.12
玉林市	Yulin	201.42	215.43
百色市	Baise	611.58	683.14
贺州市	Hezhou	48.37	79.16
河池市	Hechi	166.01	174.49
来宾市	Laibin	400.06	450.23
崇左市	Chongzuo	213.76	244.73

注：本表中数据采用电热当量计算法。
Note: The data of this table was calculated using the Electro-thermal Equivalent Calculation Methond.

Industrial Comprehensive Enevgy Consumption above Designated Size by City in Main Years

(10 000 tons of SCE)

2012	2013	2014	2015	2016	2017
5545.10	**6084.62**	**6116.29**	**5802.01**	**5929.64**	**6148.87**
527.65	586.96	524.25	471.69	470.61	469.23
1056.35	1142.94	1154.03	1064.63	1062.94	1091.72
366.84	380.67	350.84	328.85	299.17	268.98
138.59	161.68	162.68	166.63	168.04	170.22
210.76	237.15	261.12	274.11	295.97	341.15
360.04	434.71	516.40	517.72	558.48	624.77
397.47	424.05	458.05	417.77	416.01	481.38
481.55	517.71	506.95	486.12	518.31	520.65
247.80	251.54	254.57	253.47	253.97	255.54
721.39	736.78	751.35	750.52	834.45	1001.78
133.18	273.19	229.17	194.37	209.29	156.12
131.86	151.71	153.06	151.66	134.56	139.20
477.96	457.07	439.98	372.29	338.53	278.83
266.74	301.51	326.22	322.04	343.32	354.89

9－6 主要年份电力消费量

单位：亿千瓦时

指 标	Item
消费总计	**Total Consumption**
一、农、林、牧、渔业、水利业	**Farming,Forestry,Animal Husbandry,Fishery & Conservancy**
二、工业	**Industry**
轻工业	**Light Industry**
重工业	**Heavy Industry**
（一）采矿业	**Mining & Quarrying**
煤炭开采和洗选业	Mining & Washing of Coal
石油和天然气开采业	Extraction of Petroleum & Natural Gas
黑色金属矿采选业	Mining & Processing of Ferrous Metal Ores
有色金属矿采选业	Mining & Processing of Non-Ferrous Metal Ores
非金属矿采选业	Mining & Processing of Nonmetal Ores
开采辅助活动	Mining Assist Activities
其他采矿业	Mining of Other Ores
（二）制造业	**Manufacturing**
农副食品加工业	Processing of Food from Agricultural Products
食品制造业	Manufacture of Foods
酒、饮料和精制茶制造业	Wine, Drink & Refined Tea Manufacturing
烟草制品业	Manufacture of Tobacco
纺织业	Manufacture of Textile
纺织服装、服饰业	Manufacture of Textile Wearing Apparel,Footwear & Caps
皮革、毛皮、羽毛及其制品业和制鞋业	Manufacture of Leather,Fur,Feather & Related Products
木材加工及木、竹、藤、棕、草制品业	Processing of Timber,Manufacture of Wood,Bamboo,Rattan,Palm & Sreaw Products
家具制造业	Manufacture of Furniture
造纸及纸制品业	Manufacture of Paper & Paper Products
印刷和记录媒介的复制	Printing ,Reproduction of Recording Media
文教、工美、体育和娱乐用品制造业	Manufacture of Articles For Culture,Education & Sport Activity
石油加工、炼焦及核燃料加工业	Processing of Petroleum,Coking,Processing of Nuclear Fuel
化学原料及化学制品制造业	Manufacture of Raw Chemical Materials & Chemical Products
医药制造业	Manufacture of Medicines
化学纤维制造业	Manufacture of Chemical Fibers
橡胶和塑料制品业	Rubber & Plastic Products
非金属矿物制品业	Manufacture of Non-metallic Mineral Products
黑色金属冶炼及压延加工业	Smelting and Pressing of Ferrous Metals
有色金属冶炼及压延加工业	Smelting and Pressing of Nonferrous Metals
金属制品业	Manufacture of Metal Products
通用设备制造业	Manufacture of General Purpose Machinery
专用设备制造业	Manufacture of Special Purpose Machinery
汽车制造业	Manufacture of Transport Equipment
铁路、船舶、航空航天和其他运输设备制造业	Railway, Ship, Aerospace & Other Transportation Equipment Manufacturing
电气机械及器材制造业	Manufacture of Electrical Machinery & Equipment
通信设备、计算机和其他电子设备制造业	Manufacture of Communication Equipment,Computers & Other Electronic Equipment
仪器仪表制造业	Manufacture of Measuring Instruments & Machinery for Cultural Activity & Office Work
其他制造业	Other Manufacturing
废弃资源综合利用业	Recycling & Disposal of Waste
金属制品、机械和设备修理业	Metal Product, Machinery & Equipment Repair Services
（三）电力、燃气及水的生产和供应业	**Electric Power,Gas & Water Production & Supply**
电力、热力的生产和供应业	Production & Distribution of Electric Power & Heat Power
燃气生产和供应业	Production & Distribution of Gas
水的生产和供应业	Production & Distribution of Water
三、建筑业	**Construction**
四、交通运输储运业和邮政业	**Transportation,Storage & Post**
五、批发、零售业和住宿、餐饮业	**Wholesale & Retail Trade,Hotel & Catering**
六、其他行业	**Others**
七、城乡居民生活	**Residential Consumption**

注：行业分类按2011年《国民经济行业分类》（GB/T4754－2011）标准。

Note: The industry classification is based on the standard of National Economic Industry Classification (GB/T4754－2011) in 2011.

Consumption of Electricity in Main Years

(100 million kwh)

1995	2000	2005	2010	2011	2012	2013	2014	2015	2016	2017
228.08	**322.02**	**510.15**	**993.24**	**1112.21**	**1153.85**	**1237.75**	**1307.51**	**1334.32**	**1359.64**	**1422.34**
8.68	**13.17**	**14.01**	**20.09**	**22.74**	**22.49**	**23.97**	**25.02**	**26.61**	**28.63**	**30.38**
155.51	**211.41**	**384.44**	**737.55**	**815.76**	**832.73**	**869.33**	**895.49**	**892.63**	**880.88**	**917.88**
40.88	**49.10**	**53.51**	**98.74**	**89.69**	**80.87**	**84.90**	**104.71**	**103.60**	**92.86**	**114.34**
114.63	**162.31**	**330.93**	**638.81**	**726.07**	**751.86**	**784.43**	**790.78**	**789.03**	**788.02**	**803.53**
14.97	**14.80**	**16.56**	**18.91**	**23.00**	**19.18**	**20.15**	**20.15**	**20.58**	**14.31**	**22.23**
5.86	4.30	2.53	2.94	2.72	3.46	3.36	3.36	1.52	1.28	1.37
	0.16	0.13	0.50		0.11	0.11	0.11	0.32	0.35	0.53
1.26	0.87	2.96	1.80	8.87	2.75	1.55	1.55	1.32	0.78	6.45
5.99	9.00	8.11	8.54	8.74	6.76	8.49	8.49	9.97	7.19	7.62
1.47	0.22	1.80	3.87	2.67	6.10	6.64	6.64	7.45	4.71	6.26
0.39	0.25	0.83	1.26							0.35
118.75	**179.80**	**306.51**	**618.13**	**682.70**	**699.85**	**706.20**	**733.32**	**732.21**	**736.57**	**777.12**
13.68	15.03	18.13	34.14	40.14	37.02	38.66	51.55	35.50	32.51	32.93
2.61	1.26	1.56	4.32	4.28	5.79	6.79	8.19	8.19	9.43	9.23
1.71	0.89	1.40	6.59	5.17	6.71	6.86	6.86	6.86	6.86	6.71
0.31	0.33	0.89	1.14	0.46	0.51	0.63	0.63	0.75	0.75	0.73
3.96	3.58	4.01	3.55	5.29	3.27	3.44	3.44	5.82	3.43	3.68
0.43	0.21	0.35	0.58	0.91	2.14	2.31	2.31	2.73	2.69	1.69
0.30	0.45	0.65	1.15	1.00	1.26	1.53	1.53	1.53	1.40	0.88
1.76	3.35	4.73	10.71	19.51	15.64	18.83	22.35	19.55	22.68	22.85
1.04	0.38	0.76	0.27	1.01	1.18	1.36	1.36	1.72	1.77	1.78
5.29	7.67	9.95	15.86	26.02	14.78	18.93	24.45	31.92	27.62	32.34
0.38	0.54	0.96	0.57	0.94	1.52	0.80	0.80	1.51	1.10	1.01
0.04	0.05	0.05	0.04	0.15	0.52	0.07	0.07	0.92	0.70	0.14
0.50	0.83	0.92	4.03	7.63	11.52	9.52	9.52	14.73	14.38	15.98
18.46	26.18	36.01	50.77	54.62	54.08	59.23	59.23	61.00	48.42	43.77
0.93	0.65	1.86	1.99	3.33	4.25	2.29	2.29	5.40	3.02	3.60
2.43	3.73	1.21	2.14	1.66	0.78	0.78	0.78	0.01	0.83	0.02
2.11	1.99	3.12	5.96	5.34	6.67	6.67	6.67	12.07	8.15	8.16
20.01	24.27	40.98	89.03	99.35	102.31	106.00	106.00	111.26	111.73	107.52
14.86	30.56	94.12	192.27	210.95	240.84	240.56	244.35	225.49	223.42	211.24
13.06	41.74	52.62	148.67	145.02	137.51	126.55	126.55	117.64	161.18	215.54
2.27	2.50	5.06	9.08	6.07	8.55	10.29	10.29	13.12	11.28	10.09
3.01	3.11	3.77	4.52	11.12	3.48	3.48	3.48	6.64	7.69	5.81
1.34	1.00	1.16	2.37	3.89	4.51	4.51	4.51	5.66	5.96	4.50
2.09	2.18	6.45	8.45	16.91	17.76	18.09	18.09	20.79	16.63	20.68
					2.31	2.56	2.56	1.41	1.39	1.73
0.87	1.63	2.06	4.63	9.14	9.53	10.14	10.14	13.39	5.92	7.36
0.33	0.49	0.68	1.29	2.85	3.68	3.96	3.96	4.89	3.74	4.65
0.14	0.12	0.22	0.25	0.31	0.27	0.35	0.35	0.51	0.55	0.68
0.13	5.07	11.73	13.38	0.99	0.26	0.45	0.45	0.74	0.75	0.93
		1.10	0.38	0.30	0.28	0.51	0.51	0.41	0.54	0.82
					0.04	0.05	0.05	0.05	0.05	0.06
21.79	**16.81**	**61.37**	**100.51**	**110.06**	**113.70**	**142.98**	**142.02**	**139.84**	**130.00**	**118.54**
18.61	13.45	56.73	94.65	106.42	106.49	135.29	134.33	134.54	120.46	108.46
0.11	0.02	0.94	0.19	0.05	0.27	0.27	0.27	0.21	0.93	1.09
3.07	3.34	3.70	5.68	3.59	6.94	7.42	7.42	5.09	8.61	8.99
2.04	**1.00**	**5.02**	**9.84**	**11.83**	**11.89**	**14.06**	**15.51**	**16.79**	**18.43**	**20.43**
2.09	**4.39**	**6.87**	**11.52**	**13.31**	**14.35**	**15.74**	**18.85**	**23.29**	**27.12**	**34.35**
3.49	**5.97**	**13.11**	**23.92**	**27.41**	**31.13**	**36.50**	**39.92**	**43.13**	**45.94**	**50.07**
6.06	**9.67**	**17.26**	**46.20**	**51.27**	**57.83**	**66.59**	**74.22**	**80.86**	**88.43**	**101.63**
31.19	**49.58**	**69.44**	**144.12**	**169.89**	**183.43**	**211.56**	**238.50**	**251.01**	**270.21**	**287.61**

9−7 主要年份万元工业总产值电力消费量

单位：千瓦小时/万元

指 标	Item
总 计	**Total**
采矿业	**Mining & Quarrying**
煤炭开采和洗选业	Mining & Washing of Coal
石油和天然气开采业	Extraction of Petroleum & Natural Gas
黑色金属矿采选业	Mining & Processing of Ferrous Metal Ores
有色金属矿采选业	Mining & Processing of Non-Ferrous Metal Ores
非金属矿采选业	Mining & Processing of Nonmetal Ores
开采辅助活动	Mining Assist Activities
其他采矿业	Mining of Other Ores
制造业	**Manufacturing**
农副食品加工业	Processing of Food from Agricultural Products
食品制造业	Manufacture of Foods
酒、饮料和精制茶制造业	Wine, Drink & Refined Tea Manufacturing
烟草制品业	Manufacture of Tobacco
纺织业	Manufacture of Textile
纺织服装、服饰业	Manufacture of Textile Wearing Apparel,Footware & Caps
皮革、毛皮、羽毛（绒）及其制品业和制鞋业	Manufacture of Leather,Fur,Feather & Related Products
木材加工及木、竹、藤、棕、草制品业	Processing of Timber,Manufacture of Wood,Bamboo,Rattan,Palm & Sreaw Products
家具制造业	Manufacture of Furniture
造纸及纸制品业	Manufacture of Paper & Paper Products
印刷业和记录媒介的复制	Printing ,Reproduction of Recording Media
文教、工美、体育和娱乐用品制造业	Manufacture of Articles For Culture,Education & Sport Activity
石油加工、炼焦及核燃料加工业	Processing of Petroleum,Coking,Processing of Nuclear Fuel
化学原料及化学制品制造业	Manufacture of Raw Chemical Materials and Chemical Products
医药制造业	Manufacture of Medicines
化学纤维制造业	Manufacture of Chemical Fibers
橡胶和塑料制品业	Rubber & Plastic Products
非金属矿物制品业	Manufacture of Non-metallic Mineral Products
黑色金属冶炼及压延加工业	Smelting & Pressing of Ferrous Metals
有色金属冶炼及压延加工业	Smelting & Pressing of Nonferrous Metals
金属制品业	Manufacture of Metal Products
通用设备制造业	Manufacture of General Purpose Machinery
专用设备制造业	Manufacture of Special Purpose Machinery
汽车制造业	Manufacture of Transport Equipment
铁路、船舶、航空航天和其他运输设备制造业	Railway, Ship, Aerospace & Other Transportation Equipment Manufacturing
电气机械及器材制造业	Manufacture of Electrical Machinery & Equipment
通信设备、计算机及其他电子设备制造业	Manufacture of Communication Equipment,Computers and Other Electronic Equipment
仪器仪表制造业	Manufacture of Measuring Instruments & Machinery for Cultural Activity & Office Work
其他制造业	Other Manufacturing
废弃资源综合利用业	Recycling & Disposal of Waste
金属制品、机械和设备修理业	Metal Product, Machinery & Equipment Repair Services
电力、燃气及水的生产和供应业	**Electric Power,Gas and Water Production & Supply**
电力、热力的生产和供应业	Production & Distribution of Electric Power & Heat Power
燃气生产和供应业	Production & Distribution of Gas
水的生产和供应业	Production & Distribution of Water

注：2010年起工业总产值统计范围为年主营业务收入2000万元及以上工业法人企业，2012年起按当年价格，行业分类按2011年《国民经济行业分类》（GB/T4754−2011）标准。

Note: The statistical range of gross output value of industry is the industrial corporations whose annual major business income above 20,000,000 Yuan since 2010.and the gross output value is calculated bu current prices since 2012,industrial classification is based on the standard of National Economic Industry Classification （GB/T4754−2011）.

Electricity Consumption of Gross Output Value of Industry per 10,000 Yuan in Main Years

(kwh/10 000 yuan)

1995	2000	2005	2010	2011	2012	2013	2014	2015	2016	2017
1613	**1753**	**1330**	**952**	**946**	**567**	**473**	**434**	**395**	**596**	**542**
6003	**5987**	**5642**	**827**	**925**	**401**	**270**	**247**	**244**	**457**	**253**
4056	3404	3174	1732	1735	927	871	749	295	292	217
						55	46	319	548	500
2576	1311	2324	161	152	626	82	67	66	918	281
2350	1023	1090	1152	702	310	265	292	303	380	302
1056	275	498	860	816	250	372	301	304	241	201
									45	62
1085									900	999
1436	**1298**	**1222**	**862**	**865**	**544**	**432**	**397**	**350**	**560**	**322**
1000	750	827	347	404	245	189	231	151	273	123
623	450	357	420	412	254	241	242	211	282	193
754	464	354	359	332	195	162	151	127	171	128
154	139	87	101	98	30	33	29	34	51	35
1025	1555	843	279	254	263	157	138	210	266	121
391	1229	158	176	181	182	224	187	198	222	86
388	682	175	141	152	112	124	124	115	147	64
1464	2658	1416	407	411	427	281	265	187	370	157
4464	5061	418	122	131	125	118	133	145	202	162
1734	2393	1674	1039	1009	911	488	641	833	1161	796
489	833	198	98	97	171	77	74	124	187	79
272	3307	377	33	31	84	80	5	72	79	9
641	339	256	204	203	115	109	111	218	291	179
2538	2704	1972	1103	1104	659	631	578	505	547	346
434	182	343	113	105	160	68	60	123	177	78
3178	8715							114	128	97
823	1074	2835	327	317	348	262	223	346	458	214
2129	3460	2826	1757	1762	1089	832	711	654	985	533
4113	4173	2806	2551	2456	1378	1077	998	921	1539	837
2710	4088	2033	3064	3041	1536	1245	1058	930	1653	1093
1103	1988	729	1219	1185	437	363	306	309	417	185
554	488	398	317	306	130	111	108	196	339	129
521	495	212	86	83	103	98	86	108	151	79
319	252	145	67	65	107	95	84	85	118	73
					121	195	164	80	100	89
340	629	307	180	162	177	157	133	148	164	82
290	222	100	44	42	70	54	41	38	52	25
370	384	240	79	76	88	99	82	100	120	127
385	412	396	276	266	128	202	173	247	381	334
					44	42	28	14	25	21
					30	206	220	173	47	30
1358	**1436**	**1246**	**1353**	**1269**	**1046**	**1125**	**1061**	**1060**	**1332**	**971**
4818	1439	1187	1311	1261	988	1105	1053	1078	1356	974
2895	796	104	715	696	58	119	75	49	67	154
7962	4487	3317	2855	2404	1991	3083	2860	1792	2351	2430

9-8 能源消费水平
Annual Average per Capita Energy Consumption

年 份 Year	每人每年平均用能 (千克标准煤) Annual Average per Capita Energy Consumption (kilo of SCE)	每人每年平均用电 (千瓦小时) Annual Average per Capita Electricity Consumption(kwh)	每人每年平均生活用能 (千克标准煤) Annual Average per Capita Household Energy Consumption (kilo of SCE)	每人每年生活用电 (千瓦小时) Annual Average per Capita Household Electricity Consumption(kwh)
1985	251	197	25	27
1990	299	275	25	41
1991	313	293	31	48
1992	345	327	31	51
1993	408	379	38	59
1994	456	424	36	64
1995	497	502	38	69
1996	501	535	42	73
1997	502	547	48	78
1998	517	585	49	84
1999	525	613	51	92
2000	526	678	52	104
2001	566	696	56	101
2002	578	743	60	115
2003	659	857	63	127
2004	824	938	69	123
2005	974	1095	98	149
2006	1071	1228	102	171
2007	1178	1429	112	195
2008	1263	1580	120	226
2009	1363	1771	140	267
2010	1559	2099	152	305
2011	1730	2405	177	367
2012	1829	2474	194	393
2013	1936	2633	213	450
2014	2009	2760	217	503
2015	2044	2794	236	526
2016	2095	2823	255	561
2017	2151	2797	252	292

注：从2005年起按常住人口调整，2000年—2013年因第三经济普查数据作相应调整。

Note: The data in this table is adjusted by permanent population since 2005.The data from 2000 to 2013 has been adjusted by the 3rd Economic Census.

9—9 能源主要产品生活消费量
Household Energy Consumption of Main Energy Products

年 份 Year	生活用能合计 (万吨标准煤) Total Household Energy Consumption (10 000 tons of SCE)	原 煤 (万吨) Coal (10 000 tons)	液化石油气 (万吨) Liquefied Gas (10 000 tons)	煤 气 (亿立方米) Gas (100 million cu.m)	电 力 (亿千瓦时) Electricity (100 million kwh)
1985	76.12	66.71	0.07	0.00	10.56
1990	106.83	60.31	0.09	0.09	17.45
1991	133.21	59.07	6.03	0.12	20.59
1992	135.10	55.18	6.06	0.15	22.14
1993	169.27	57.57	7.89	0.21	25.97
1994	161.79	28.40	8.46	0.53	28.66
1995	174.69	27.65	15.66	0.60	31.19
1996	193.14	29.52	22.42	0.22	33.31
1997	221.23	26.16	24.40	0.37	36.30
1998	228.79	12.89	27.81	0.34	39.50
1999	238.00	10.64	32.26	0.30	43.27
2000	255.07	13.09	32.24	0.37	49.58
2001	273.02	12.96	38.94	0.25	48.44
2002	296.32	11.17	43.11	0.27	55.31
2003	316.72	13.38	45.76	0.36	61.48
2004	372.42	17.75	50.26	0.39	60.07
2005	493.28	18.56	54.26	0.41	69.44
2006	552.73	23.53	65.70	0.49	80.53
2007	582.82	29.45	70.04	0.58	93.01
2008	635.55	22.35	74.57	0.94	109.09
2009	682.64	22.56	75.80	1.10	129.00
2010	772.44	32.52	79.52	1.70	144.12
2011	878.67	32.45	84.56	0.40	169.89
2012	969.77	36.78	96.58	0.83	183.43
2013	1003.04	14.78	50.46	0.45	211.56
2014	1028.90	16.98	51.61	0.68	238.50
2015	1125.77	14.14	62.45	0.37	251.01
2016	1227.52	8.01	64.66	1.89	270.21
2017	1227.29	8.29	51.04	0.35	287.61

注：2000年—2013年数据因第三次经济普查调整。

Note: The data from 2000 to 2013 has been adjusted by the 3rd Economic Census.

9—10 主要年份石油及燃料消费量
Consumption of Petroleum & Fuel in Main Years

品 名	Type	1995	2000	2005	2010	2011	2012	2013	2014	2015	2016	2017
原 油（万吨）	Crude Oil (10 000 tons)	42.44	61.41	97.71	396.02	1018.84	1471.92	1296.13	1390.47	1428.77	1339.94	1562.5
汽 油（万吨）	Gasoline (10 000 tons)	41.32	65.87	127.75	182.68	197.56	214.53	224.21	224.30	290.89	379.03	392.29
煤 油（万吨）	Kerosene (10 000 tons)	5.60	3.79	7.00	2.73	0.28	0.08	23.83	90.32	56.36	62.51	50.95
柴 油（万吨）	Diesel Oil (10 000 tons)	72.43	136.82	234.06	332.37	376.91	400.50	430.89	506.17	573.34	537.65	561.83
燃料油（万吨）	Fuel Oil (10 000 tons)	13.57	7.67	20.96	24.64	32.45	38.42	44.83	31.22	24.10	10.21	10.36
液化石油气（万吨）	Liquefied Gas (10 000 tons)	15.89	35.27	50.70	84.85	98.94	115.36	125.88	103.02	116.32	80.94	64.07
煤 气（亿立方米）	Gas (100 million cu.m)	1.16	5.83	12.31	228.97	190.04	225.88	310.60	361.34	360.72	337.59	393.92

注：2000年－2013年部分数据根据第三次经济普查调整。
Note: The data from 2000 to 2013 has been adjusted by the 3rd Economic Census.

9—11 能源可供量（2017年）
Energy Available for Consumption (2017)

品 名	Type	综合能源可供量 Total Energy Available	生产量 Output	调入量 Transfer From Other Regions	进口量 Imports	调出量 Transfer to Other Province Regions	年初年末库存差额 Stock Balance in This Year
综合能源（万吨标准煤）	Total Energy (10 000 tons of SCE)	10458.46	3255.17	7584.5	905.90	1243.722	37.82
煤 炭（万吨）	Coal(10 000 tons)	6613.32	442.67	5222.51	1009.39		55.67
原 油（万吨）	Crude Oil (10 000 tons)	1563.03	44.07	1405.77	116.05		
电力（亿千瓦时）	Electricity(100 million kwh)	1442.35	1401.11	144.14		102.90	

注：电力可供生产量为水电、火电可供生产量，未包括回收能。
Note: Data on electricity available output refers to the total available output of hydro-power & thermal power, excluding the recycled energy.

主要统计指标解释

能源生产总量 指一定时期内一个国家或地区一次能源生产量的总和，是观察全国能源生产水平、规模、构成和发展速度的总量指标。一次能源生产量包括原煤、原油、天然气、水电、核能及其他动力能（如风能、地热能等）发电量，不包括低热值燃料生产量、生物质能、太阳能等的利用和由一次能源加工转换而成的二次能源产量。

能源消费总量 指一定时期内一个国家或地区物质生产部门、非物质生产部门和生活消费的各种能源的总和，是观察能源消费水平、构成和增长速度的总量指标。能源消费总量包括原煤和原油及其制品、天然气、电力，不包括低热值燃料、生物质能和太阳能等的利用。能源消费总量分为终端能源消费量、能源加工转换损失量和损失量三部分。

终端能源消费量 指一定时期内一个国家或地区生产和生活消费的各种能源在扣除了用于加工转换二次能源消费量和损失量以后的数量。

能源加工转换损失量 指一定时期内一个国家或地区投入加工转换的各种能源数量之和与产出各种能源产品之和的差额，是观察能源在加工转换过程中损失量变化的指标。

能源损失量 指一定时期内一个国家或地区能源在输送、分配、储存过程中发生的损失和由客观原因造成的各种损失量，不包括各种气体能源放空、放散量。

能源消费弹性系数 是反映能源消费增长速度与国民经济增长速度之间比例关系的指标。

计算公式为:

$$\text{能源消费弹性系数}=\frac{\text{能源消费量年平均增长速度}}{\text{国民经济年平均增长速度}}$$

电力消费弹性系数 反映电力消费增长速度与国民经济增长速度之间比例关系的指标。

计算公式为:

$$\text{电力消费弹性系数}=\frac{\text{电力消费量年平均增长速度}}{\text{国民经济年平均增长速度}}$$

发电煤耗计算方法 指电力按当年平均火力发电煤耗换算成标准煤。

电热当量计算法 指电力按自身热功当量换算成标准煤。采用的折标系数为1万千瓦时=1.229吨标准煤。

Explanatory Notes on Main Statistical Indicators

Total Energy Production refers to the total production of primary energy by all energy production enterprises in a country or region in a given period of time. It is a comprehensive indicator to show the capacity, scale, composition and development of energy production of the country. The production of primary energy includes that of coal, crude oil, natural gas, hydro-power and electricity generated by nuclear energy and other means such as wind power and geothermal power. However, it excludes the production of fuels of low calorific value bio-energy, solar energy and the secondary energy converted from the primary energy.

Total Domestic Energy Consumption refers to the total consumption of energy of various kinds by material production sectors, non-material production sectors and households in a country or region in a given period of time. It is a comprehensive indicator to show the scale, composition and development of energy consumption. The total energy consumption includes that of coal, crude oil and their products, natural gas and electricity. However, it excludes the consumption of fuel of low calorific value, bio-energy and solar energy. Total domestic energy consumption can be divided into three parts: final energy consumption, loss during the process of energy conversion and loss.

Volume of Terminal Energy Consumption refers to volume of various of energy consumption for production and living in a country or region during a giving period after deducting the volume consummated in processing secondhand energy and the volume losing.

Volume of Energy Lost by Processing and Conversion refers to balance between volume of various of energy put into processing and conversion and output volume of energy in one country or area in certain period, and it is an indicator to carrying out observations at changes of volume of energy lost in processing and conversion.

Volume of Energy Los refers to various of volume of energy lost in transporting, distributing and storing and for objective causes in one country or area in certain period, excludes discharged volume of various of gas energy.

Elasticity Ratio of Energy Consumption is an indicator to show the relationship between the growth rate of energy consumption and the growth rate of the national economy. The formula is:

$$\textbf{Elasticity Ratio of Energy Consumption} = \frac{\text{Average Annual Growth Rate of Energy Consumption}}{\text{Average Annual Growth Rate of National Economy}}$$

Elasticity Ratio of Energy Consumption is an indicator to show the relationship between the growth rate of energy consumption and the growth rate of the national economy. The formula is:

$$\textbf{Elasticity Ratio of Energy Consumption} = \frac{\text{Average Annual Growth Rate of Electricity Consumption}}{\text{Average Annual Growth Rate of National Economy}}$$

Calculation Method of Generation Coal Consumption Electricity is converted into SCE according to the average coal-fired power consumption of the year.

Electro-thermal Equivalent Calculation Method Electricity is converted into SCE according to its own thermal equivalent. Using the ratio of: 10 000 kWh = 1.229 tons of SCE.

第十篇

固定资产投资

INVESTMENT IN FIXED ASSETS

（校对编辑：兰佳信）

10－1 全社会固定资产投资及增长速度（1978－2017年）
Investment in Fixed Assets & Its Growth Rate（1978－2017）

年 份 Year	全社会投资总额 Total Investment	按管理渠道分 By Channel of Management						全社会投资总额中住宅 Residential Buildings
		城镇投资 Urban Investment	基本建设投资 Basic Investment	更新改造投资 Innovation	其他固定资产投资 Others	房地产开发投资 Real Estate Development	农村投资 Rural Investment	
投资额（万元） Investment（10 000 yuan）								
1978	96055	96055	96055					6745
1980	121815	121815	103067	18748				23185
1985	422191	422191	167327	71218	17599			142092
1990	685666	471432	212880	169619	35800	21933	214234	221077
1991	896479	622695	288923	220662	42900	23310	273784	285398
1992	1410395	1050784	522135	341696	76855	45413	359611	378228
1993	2780754	2288445	1099415	527724	210325	316451	492309	680317
1994	3825871	2800623	1407722	658346	146333	328408	1025248	1102233
1995	4233742	3206590	1570988	685572	162654	515050	1027152	1208881
1996	4764200	3405965	1744608	713293	105148	432305	1358235	1537400
1997	4798023	3435948	1829651	591029	145175	335374	1362075	1664245
1998	5717025	4231848	2405296	697162	156963	326838	1485177	1851688
1999	6202035	4658915	2630000	700972	394008	329735	1543120	1918970
2000	6600146	5241049	2815412	801593	592572	386747	1359097	1644650
2001	7312523	5953938	3243086	865975	646851	555826	1358585	1734899
2002	8349852	6931808	3725200	1055354	606548	882807	1418044	2008016
2003	9873063	8476445	4488309	1427401	622937	1403112	1396618	2549373
2004	12636500	11217558	6267732	1985739	847299	2116787	1418942	2863485
2005	17690715	15223560	9008716	2747259	599670	2867915	2467155	3416021
2006	22465743	19956664	11706485	3722813	827563	3699803	2509079	3978916
2007	29700845	26271518	14385378	5270504	1252801	5362835	3429327	5562505
2008	37831385	33526716	18057743	7689521	1512659	6273423	4304669	6663557
2009	57066957	51593360	26145334	15525521	1785694	8136811	5473597	9200203
2010	78590660	71618399	34794814	22158979	2602395	12062211	6972261	12279939
2011	101604527	92803004	41853857	30548054	5226437	15174656	8801523	15554926
2012	126352181	114823208	49754367	42570996	6948457	15549388	11528973	16020340
2013	119076669	107546757	45012370	43190601	3197464	16146322	11529912	16212711
2014	138432123	126067961	54182316	50389319	3111384	18384942	12364162	17861116
2015	162277817	148475604	66801531	58978498	3604642	19090933	13802213	19135552
2016	182367786	176529486	81418711	65232594	5898319	23979862	5838300	22390853
2017	204991115	199082715	114382612	53222750	4642523	26834830	5908400	20835198

10－1 续表 continued

年 份 Year	全社会投资总额 Total Investment	城镇投资 Urban Investment	按管理渠道分 By Channel of Management 基本建设投资 Basic Investment	更新改投资 Innovation	其他固定资产投资 Others	房地产开发投资 Real Estate Development	农村投资 Rural Investment	全社会投资总额中住宅 Residential Buildings
增长速度（上年=100） Growth Rate (preceding year=100)								
1978	22.1		22.1					17.2
1980	24.2		7.4	809.7				84.2
1985	49.9		54.9	55.9	129.4			72.7
1990	-4.6		2.5	-13.1	-33.5			16.4
1991	30.7	32.1	35.7	30.1	19.8	6.3	27.8	29.1
1992	57.3	68.7	80.7	54.9	79.1	94.8	31.3	32.5
1993	97.2	117.8	110.6	54.4	173.7	596.8	36.9	79.9
1994	37.6	22.4	28.0	24.8	-30.4	3.8	108.3	62.0
1995	10.7	14.5	11.6	4.1	11.2	56.8	0.2	9.7
1996	12.5	6.2	11.1	4.0	-35.4	-16.1	32.2	27.2
1997	0.7	0.9	4.9	-17.1	38.1	-22.4	0.3	8.3
1998	19.2	23.2	31.5	18.0	8.1	-2.5	9.0	11.3
1999	8.5	10.1	9.3	0.5	151.0	0.9	3.9	3.6
2000	6.4	12.5	7.0	14.4	50.4	17.3	-11.9	-14.3
2001	10.8	13.6	15.2	8.0	9.2	43.7	0.0	5.5
2002	14.2	16.4	14.9	21.9	-6.2	58.8	4.4	15.7
2003	18.2	22.3	20.5	35.3	2.7	58.9	-1.5	27.0
2004	28.0	32.3	39.6	39.1	36.0	50.9	1.6	12.3
2005	40.0	35.7	43.7	38.3	-29.2	35.5	73.9	19.3
2006	27.0	31.1	29.9	35.5	38.0	29.0	1.7	16.5
2007	32.2	31.6	22.9	41.6	51.4	44.9	36.7	39.8
2008	27.2	27.6	25.5	45.9	20.7	15.9	25.5	19.8
2009	50.8	53.9	44.8	101.9	18.1	29.7	27.2	38.1
2010	37.7	38.8	33.1	42.7	45.7	48.2	27.4	33.5
2011	29.3	29.6	20.3	37.9	100.8	25.8	26.2	26.7
2012	24.4	23.7	18.9	39.4	32.9	2.5	31.0	3.0
2013	21.4	19.8	17.8	30.0	14.6	3.8	38.5	7.3
2014	16.3	17.2	20.4	16.7	-2.7	13.9	7.2	10.2
2015	17.2	17.8	23.3	17.0	15.9	3.8	11.6	7.1
2016	12.4	12.8	21.9	10.6	63.6	25.6	1.9	17.0
2017	12.4	12.8	40.5	-18.4	-21.3	11.9	1.2	-6.9

注：1. 1978年至1981年为全民投资总额，1982年以后为全社会投资总额。2008年的数据根据经济普查数予以调整。

2. 根据相关制度要求，2013年我区固定资产投资统计起点由项目计划总投资50万元提高到500万元；2013年各增长数据根据2012年度国家口径作为基数计算；2013年度全区固定资产投资与国家公布的各省数据口径完全一致（不包含跨省项目投资），各市投资包含跨省项目投资，因此各市投资合计与全区固定资产投资不一致。

3. 根据制度设计，2016年制度取消城乡分组，故农村投资仅包含农村居民家庭固定资产，增速为同口径增速。

Note:1. Investment in fixed assets during the years 1978 to 1981 refer to total people investment, and since 1982 are total social investment in fixed assets. The data in 2008 has been adjusted by the 2nd Economic Census.

2. According to the National Statistical System, the statistical floor level of total planned projects investment in fixed assets of Guangxi has been raised from 500 000 Yuan to 5 000 000 Yuan. The data on growth rates in 2013 is calculated on the data of national statistical range in 2012. The statistical range of data on investment in fixed assets of Guangxi is completely the same as the data of other provinces published by National Bureau of Statistic (excluding investment in inter-provincial projects). Due to the investment in inter-provincial projects is included in the investment of cities separately, there are differences between the summary of investment of cities and investment of Guangxi.

3. According to the National Statistical System, the data on "Others" in this table includes 2 parts: other investment in fixed assets and private building in urban and factory & mine areas.

10－2 国有单位固定资产投资及增长速度（1978－2017年）
Investment in Fixed Assets of State-owned Units & Its Growth Rate（1978－2017）

年 份 Year	投资总额 Total Investment	中央项目 Central	地方项目 Local	地方投资占总额比重（%） Proportion of Local Investment in Total Investment (%)	新 增 固定资产 Newly Increased Fixed Assets
投资额（万元） Investment (10 000 yuan)					
1978	96055	15710	80345	83.6	54677
1980	121815	28129	93686	76.9	89031
1985	247349	88319	159030	64.3	163230
1990	411663	88657	323006	78.5	374779
1991	542295	128015	414280	76.4	419072
1992	926799	229885	696914	75.2	609629
1993	1693664	393855	1299809	76.7	960428
1994	1939743	518424	1421319	73.3	1089639
1995	2162880	623052	1539828	71.2	1917553
1996	2361406	550378	1811028	76.7	1753595
1997	2228299	467362	1760937	79.0	1946615
1998	2765781	581435	2184346	79.0	2141607
1999	3034692	689587	2345105	77.3	2112000
2000	3287710	994743	2292967	69.7	3140709
2001	3575582	922303	2653279	74.2	2332310
2002	4023603	990379	3033224	75.4	2270341
2003	4492504	1052907	3439597	76.6	3142566
2004	5394295	932227	4462068	82.7	3296786
2005	7078102	1135701	5942401	84.0	4248682
2006	8225875	1190370	7035505	85.5	4107952
2007	10056627	1167349	8889278	88.4	5110058
2008	12698400	1445195	11253205	88.6	5492696
2009	23510063	3850208	19659855	83.6	10552524
2010	30665485	5562613	25102872	81.9	11285161
2011	34849787	5196362	29653425	85.1	15927158
2012	38361748	5416951	32944797	85.9	18639488
2013	34182726	2288299	31894427	93.3	19534313
2014	38854457	2461364	36393093	93.7	22040292
2015	46135787	2251879	43883908	95.1	25625920
2016	50970596	2504243	48466353	95.1	28860824
2017	61249163	1430074	59819089	97.7	35558035

注：2006年以后国有单位固定资产投资包含了农村非农户投资，2006年数据做相应调整。根据经普对2008年数据进行调整。

Note: Investment in fixed assets of state-owned units has included investment from rural non-agriculture households in fixed assets since 2006,and the data of 2006 is adjusted relevantly.The data in 2008 has been adjusted by the 2nd Economic Census.

10－2 续表 continued

年 份 Year	投资总额 Total Investment	中央项目 Central	地方项目 Local	地方投资占总额比重（%） Proportion of Local Investment in Total Investment (%)	新 增 固定资产 Newly Increased Fixed Assets
增长速度（上年=100） Growth Rate (preceding year=100)					
1978	20.9	32.3	18.8		-8.5
1980	24.2	-4.3	36.5		13.0
1985	50.6	57.4	47.0		19.6
1990	-0.6	-8.0	1.6		2.5
1991	31.7	44.4	28.3		11.8
1992	70.9	79.6	68.2		45.5
1993	82.7	71.3	86.5		57.5
1994	14.5	31.6	9.3		13.5
1995	11.5	20.2	8.3		76.0
1996	9.2	-11.7	17.6		-8.6
1997	-5.6	-15.1	-2.8		11.0
1998	24.1	24.4	24.0		10.0
1999	9.7	18.6	7.4		-1.4
2000	8.3	44.3	-2.2		48.7
2001	8.8	-7.3	15.7		-25.7
2002	12.5	7.4	14.3		-2.7
2003	11.7	6.3	13.4		38.4
2004	20.1	-11.5	29.7		4.9
2005	31.2	21.8	33.2		28.9
2006	16.2	4.8	18.4		-3.3
2007	22.3	-1.9	26.3		24.4
2008	26.3	23.8	26.6		7.5
2009	85.1	166.4	74.7		92.1
2010	30.4	44.5	27.7		6.9
2011	13.6	-6.6	18.1		41.1
2012	10.1	4.2	11.1		17.0
2013	9.1	-48.3	18.5		28.3
2014	13.7	7.6	14.1		12.8
2015	18.7	-8.5	20.6		16.3
2016	10.5	11.2	10.4		12.6
2017	20.2	-42.9	23.4		23.2

10—3 主要年份全社会固定资产投资总额

单位：亿元

指 标	Item	1995	2000
总 计	**Total**	**423.37**	**660.01**
基本建设投资	**Basic Construction**	**157.10**	**281.54**
按经济类型分	By Economic Type		
国有经济	State-owned Units	137.15	249.95
联营经济	Joint-owned	0.86	0.45
其他经济	Others	19.09	31.14
按隶属关系分	By Administrative Relationship		
中 央	Central	43.58	71.48
地 方	Local	113.52	210.06
更新改造投资	**Innovation**	**68.56**	**80.16**
按经济类型分	By Economic Type		
国有经济	State-owned Units	55.24	64.41
联营经济	Joint-owned	0.07	0.08
其他经济	Others	13.25	15.67
按隶属关系分	By Administrative Relationship		
中 央	Central	18.81	38.51
地 方	Local	49.75	41.65
其他投资	**Others**	**16.27**	**59.26**
按经济类型分	By Economic Type		
国有经济	State-owned Units	5.41	2.96
联营经济	Joint-owned	8.10	6.92
其他经济	Others	2.76	49.38
按隶属关系分	By Administrative Relationship		
中 央	Central	0.17	0.15
地 方	Local	16.10	59.11
房地产开发投资	**Real Estate Development**	**51.51**	**38.67**
按经济类型分	By Economic Type		
国有经济	State-owned Units	18.28	11.45
联营经济	Joint-owned	9.23	3.25
其他经济	Others	23.80	23.97
农村非农户固定资产投资	**Investment from Rural Non-agriculture in Fixed Assets**	**39.67**	**50.32**
私人固定资产投资	**Individual**	**90.28**	**150.06**
城镇和工矿区私人建房	Housing Construction by Urban & Industrial & Mining Areas Individuals	27.23	64.47
农村农户投资	Rural Individuals	63.05	85.59

注：2016年国家制度修订，不设城乡分组及城镇和工矿区私人建房指标，农村农户投资数据由国家统计局广西调查总队提供。

Note: Before 2005,the data on the investment from non-agriculture households was provided by the Survey Office in Guangxi, and the housing construction by urban & industrial & mining areas refered to the total investment for individual housing construction. Since 2005, the housing construction by urban & industrial & mining areas individuals and the investment from rural non-agriculture households were calculated unitedly by sector according to the reformation of the state statistic system.

Total Investment in Fixed Assets in Main Years

(100 million yuan)

2005	2010	2011	2012	2013	2014	2015	2016	2017
1769.07	**7859.07**	**10160.45**	**12635.22**	**11907.67**	**13843.21**	**16227.78**	**18236.78**	**20499.11**
900.87	**3479.48**	**4185.39**	**4975.44**	**4501.24**	**5418.23**	**6680.15**	**8141.87**	**11438.26**
553.93	2245.94	2506.27	2868.61	2332.70	2709.51	3291.01	3482.44	4204.95
4.23	1.86	4.85	10.65	24.86	19.74	7.01	30.08	11.57
342.71	1231.67	1674.26	2096.18	2143.67	2688.98	3382.14	4629.35	897.55
118.63	490.81	446.27	471.34	170.29	188.52	184.97	250.22	183.84
782.24	2988.67	3739.12	4504.10	4330.94	5229.71	6495.19	7891.65	11254.42
274.73	**2215.90**	**3054.81**	**4257.10**	**4319.06**	**5038.93**	**5897.85**	**6523.26**	**5322.28**
106.81	538.18	616.13	684.74	633.87	771.68	936.00	1660.89	929.66
0.27	6.19	5.26	11.00	17.03	11.10	10.84	13.83	3.49
167.65	1671.52	2433.41	3561.36	3668.16	4256.15	4951.01	4848.54	4389.12
39.34	98.73	108.51	86.64	77.68	86.23	78.23	282.49	199.53
235.39	2117.17	2946.29	4170.46	4241.38	4952.70	5819.61	6240.77	5122.75
59.97	**237.25**	**441.77**	**569.99**	**313.50**	**304.48**	**349.77**	**589.83**	**464.25**
17.04	72.49	94.17	102.97	96.24	65.12	70.63	122.41	104.15
4.32	0.86	3.30	1.10	1.04	1.47	2.77	1.22	0.00
38.61	163.89	344.30	465.92	216.22	237.88	276.38	466.20	360.10
1.43	2.10	9.51	4.31	2.86	1.05	3.73	5.69	2.05
58.54	235.14	432.27	565.68	310.64	303.42	346.05	584.14	462.20
286.79	**1206.22**	**1517.47**	**1554.94**	**1614.63**	**1838.49**	**1909.09**	**2397.99**	**2683.48**
30.03	100.49	145.01	189.27	137.52	94.58	94.23	140.61	15.43
6.35	0.84	0.24	5.74	1.83	0.00	0.00	1.22	0.00
250.41	1104.90	1372.22	1359.93	1475.27	1743.92		2256.15	2668.05
99.74	**358.97**	**470.40**	**689.46**	**629.25**	**680.81**	**807.39**		
146.97	**361.25**	**490.63**	**588.29**	**529.99**	**562.27**	**583.52**		
	22.99	80.87	124.86	6.25	6.66	10.69		
146.97	338.26	409.76	463.43	523.74	555.61	572.83	583.83	590.84

10—4　主要年份固定资产投资资金来源

单位：万元

指　标	Item	1995	2000
资金来源总计	**Total Fund**	**2939513**	**4198133**
#地　方	Local	2331578	3066097
#国家预算内	State Budgetary Appropriation	78769	378744
#地　方	Local	57511	280640
国内贷款	Domestic Loans	854107	1029012
#地　方	Local	611133	617914
利用外资	Foreign Investment	220117	154224
#地　方	Local	177239	154224
自筹投资	Fundraising	1264132	1901390
#地　方	Local	1012207	1330788
在资金来源总计中:	In Total Fund		
基本建设资金来源	**Basic Construction**	**1540377**	**2714050**
#地　方	Local	1117568	1966652
#国家预算内	State Budgetary Appropriation	69741	369687
#地　方	Local	48550	272429
国内贷款	Domestic Loans	435347	738631
#地　方	Local	216517	357399
利用外资	Foreign Investment	139004	126656
#地　方	Local	103334	126656
自筹投资	Fundraising	653431	1084562
#地　方	Local	547660	863847
更新改造资金来源	**Innovation**	**669422**	**790952**
#地　方	Local	490525	410096
#国家预算内	State Budgetary Appropriation	3511	3881
#地　方	Local	3444	3035
国内贷款	Domestic Loans	204597	172464
#地　方	Local	180841	143345
利用外资	Foreign Investment	16959	7076
#地　方	Local	9751	7076
自筹投资	Fundraising	401512	579146
#地　方	Local	257846	231174

注：资金来源为城镇基建、更改、其它和房地产四部分当年资金到位数。

Note: Sources of funds refer to the funds reaching the designated positions in the current year, including basic construction, innovation, other investment & real estate by urban areas.

Investment in Fixed Assets by Source of Funds in Main Years

(10 000 yuan)

2005	2010	2011	2012	2013	2014	2015	2016	2017
16044415	**75978774**	**95911551**	**121833076**	**115286106**	**136737288**	**157003534**	**178963738**	**212853035**
14357240	70082471	72249974	116621621	112559191	133046079	153990334	145120748	192955869
1400300	3819964	4335425	6213347	5993435	8115523	10631186	16692984	19545436
889757	3108320	3814097	5657903	5762880	7854940	10474167	13339131	19348626
3026562	11669666	12032171	14654095	15569087	18439270	22163086	21807643	26575176
2495061	9637499	7499023	13073702	14654564	17271360	21009748	19617101	24832749
629035	718151	769380	420027	140943	132717	348586	205466	175372
628585	711543	699256	387026	140943	132717	348586	205466	173372
7702416	47479010	65682301	82805057	78113682	91881533	104586961	114080015	119189502
7089364	45136176	55798279	80731248	76741722	90241623	102969491	111959050	117722550
9129466	**34765422**	**41499968**	**70853235**	**67357690**	**56702552**	**69258070**	**79886111**	**110840371**
7853019	29978628	36662231	66622236	65480825	54564006	67385027	77495028	105151431
1312284	3105247	3450090	4617904	4562547	6437761	8128695	10408371	14728862
820560	2481063	2938630	4115766	4375960	6206685	8039456	8225017	14564732
2136352	6815018	6566367	10282592	10090530	8160430	11261550	10113597	14769091
1620027	4948199	4652505	8920765	9313312	7150775	10408513	9386536	14162253
349733	291442	317719	211504	90812	62250	153005	154326	138148
349283	285942	317719	178503	90812	62250	153005	154326	136148
4088562	21118834	27928690	40433080	38884501	37985530	44793887	49432818	68575491
3844733	19572221	26192105	39060701	38174715	37168991	43887098	48394995	67725701
2897512	**23214855**	**31259988**	**43925090**	**44657932**	**52670321**	**60664143**	**65953802**	**51545419**
2508256	22166358	30147586	42987692	43836557	51743433	59828842	63401344	48755070
41947	578956	722581	1362091	1151840	1471295	2234128	5815645	4498017
23128	491496	712713	1308785	1110372	1443588	2213453	4734656	4477409
303837	2301995	2771150	4238135	5398272	6795931	7420362	6578415	6179193
288661	2136647	2628207	4019569	5260967	6696676	7208388	5398234	5124604
194299	321268	367446	205748	49031	68411	168167	49628	32474
194299	320160	367446	205748	49031	68411	168167	49628	32474
2193981	19020094	26585829	36729030	36608276	42114222	48561186	48618390	36648344
1840264	18244885	25632832	36070580	35972169	41325992	47963049	47729283	36068534

10－5 按登记注册类型分的固定资产投资（2017年）

单位：万元

指 标	Item	投资合计 Total Investment
合 计	**Total**	**199082715**
内资	**Domestic Fund**	**192192935**
国有	State-owned	42203858
集体	Collective-owned	1249990
股份合作	Cooperative Share Holding	187230
国有联营	State Joint-owned	59537
集体联营	Collective Joint-owned	39467
国有与集体联营	State & Collective Joint-owned	4494
其他联营	Other Joint-owned	12250
国有独资公司	State Sole Investment	20221801
其他有限责任公司	Other Limited Companies	44186091
股份有限公司	Share Holding Limited	2988271
私营	Individual	72064472
其他	Others	8975474
港澳台商投资	**Funds from Hong Kong, Macao & Taiwan**	**2553636**
合资经营	Joint Venture	922571
合作经营	Cooperative Operation	8453
独资	Sole Investment	1515130
股份有限	Share Holding Limited	43839
其他	Others	63643
外商投资	**Foreign-funded**	**2334602**
合资经营	Joint Venture	1273664
合作经营	Cooperative Operation	9801
独资	Sole Investment	804445
股份有限	Share Holding Limited	148598
其他	Others	98094
个体经营	**Individual**	**2001542**
个体户	Private	1728882
个人合伙	Individual Partnership	272660

注：本表数据合计含城镇基建、更改、其他和房地产四部分。
Note: Total investment in this table includes basic construction, innovation, other investment & real tate development over designated size.

Investment in Fixed Assets Grouped by Registration Status（2017）

(10 000 yuan)

基本建设 Basic Construction	更新改造 Innovation	其他 Others	房地产 Real Estate Development
114382612	**53222750**	**4642523**	**26834830**
112103615	**50774963**	**4534761**	**24779596**
31711402	9296635	1041482	154339
791975	420217	35333	2465
108267	70179	8784	0
51779	7758	0	0
21244	18223	0	0
814	3680	0	0
6963	5287	0	0
15945154	3055877	139076	1081694
22335002	8597535	852514	12401040
1461023	993668	65333	468247
33285105	25946239	2161317	10671811
6384887	2359665	230922	0
580242	**810216**	**28743**	**1134435**
172045	284404	7603	458519
1353	5900	0	1200
376026	443693	20695	674716
26749	16645	445	0
4069	59574	0	0
802656	**584018**	**27129**	**920799**
432568	382877	20739	437480
4906	4895	0	0
221183	166209	5100	411953
115075	13215	0	20308
28924	16822	1290	51058
896099	**1053553**	**51890**	**0**
745395	934887	48600	0
150704	118666	3290	0

10－6　按登记注册类型分的投资资金来源（2017年）

单位：万元

指　标	Item	资金来源合　计 Total Sources of Fund	上年末结余资　金 Surplus from Fund of the End of Last Year
合　计	**Total**	**212853035**	**15609494**
内资	**Domestic Fund**	**204428313**	**14981313**
国有	State-owned	41759519	1471535
集体	Collective-owned	1294946	16778
股份合作	Cooperative Share Holding	190661	0
国有联营	State Joint-owned	53797	3838
集体联营	Collective Joint-owned	39699	0
国有与集体联营	State & Collective Joint-owned	4326	0
其他联营	Other Joint-owned	12250	0
国有独资公司	State Sole Investment	19192904	2748356
其他有限责任公司	Other Limited Companies	52278663	5822691
股份有限公司	Share Holding Limited	3211588	284222
私营	Individual	77369122	4542073
其他	Others	9020838	91820
港澳台商投资	**Funds from Hongkong, Macao & Taiwan**	**3526247**	**478305**
合资经营	Joint Venture	1320025	133836
合作经营	Cooperative Operation	8630	127
独资	Sole Investment	2089882	344342
股份有限	Share Holding Limited	44067	0
其他	Others	107710	0
外商投资	**Foreign-funded**	**2855960**	**140740**
合资经营	Joint Venture	1472058	33072
合作经营	Cooperative Operation	9801	0
独资	Sole Investment	1017814	61127
股份有限	Share Holding Limited	149655	2426
其他	Others	206632	44115
个体经营	**Individual**	**2042515**	**9136**
个体户	Private	1768857	8446
个人合伙	Individual Partnership	273658	690

注：本表含城镇基建、更改、其他和房地产四部分。
Note: Total investment in this table includes basic construction, innovation, other investment & real estate development overdesignated size.

Sources of Funds for Investment in Fixed Assets Grouped by Registration Status (2017)

(10 000 yuan)

本年资金来源小计 Surplus of Fund in This Year	预算内资金 Budgetary Appropriation	国内贷款 Domestic Loans	利用外资 Foreign Investment	自筹资金 Fundraising	其他资金 Others
197243541	**19545436**	**26575176**	**175372**	**119189502**	**31199745**
189447000	**19520883**	**25697715**	**156733**	**114955813**	**28557546**
40287984	15759065	4539290	14090	15212022	4403870
1278168	19457	41980	0	1116860	99871
190661	3200	2090	0	159054	26317
49959	7693	0	0	42266	0
39699	0	0	0	38699	1000
4326	0	0	0	4326	0
12250	0	1500	0	10750	0
16444548	2014823	5849968	1591	6444319	2074797
46455972	1107661	8141334	55175	25939259	11097874
2927366	36699	254809	2900	1926701	701026
72827049	225119	6381339	81782	57037939	9085797
8929018	347166	485405	1195	7023618	1066994
3047942	**17830**	**203400**	**1880**	**1120318**	**1704514**
1186189	7821	74439	0	363479	740450
8503	0	0	0	7883	620
1745540	4325	101880	1880	674897	962558
44067	5684	2000	0	35497	886
107710	5684	27081	0	74059	886
2715220	**3235**	**506912**	**16759**	**1312560**	**875754**
1438986	0	87887	8660	868465	473974
9801	0	5329	0	4472	0
956687	0	406009	8099	250885	291694
147229	2685	3390	0	131137	10017
162517	550	4297	0	57601	100069
2033379	**3488**	**167149**	**0**	**1800811**	**61931**
1760411	58	152649	0	1566366	41338
272968	3430	14500	0	234445	20593

10—7 按登记注册类型分的新增固定资产（2017年）

单位：万元

指 标	Item	新增固定资产合计 Newly Increased Fixed Assets
合 计	**Total**	**112975204**
内资	**Domestic Fund**	**109149187**
国有	State-owned	29654270
集体	Collective-owned	918707
股份合作	Cooperative Share Holding	111148
国有联营	State Joint-owned	50717
集体联营	Collective Joint-owned	25902
国有与集体联营	State & Collective Joint-owned	4494
其他联营	Other Joint-owned	10087
国有独资公司	State Sole Investment	5853048
其他有限责任公司	Other Limited Companies	17281810
股份有限公司	Share Holding Limited	1445503
私营	Individual	46287562
其他	Others	7505939
港澳台商投资	**Funds from Hong Kong, Macao & Taiwan**	**1307389**
合资经营	Joint Venture	718578
合作经营	Cooperative Operation	5900
独资	Sole Investment	497533
股份有限	Share Holding Limited	23041
其他	Others	62337
外商投资	**Foreign-funded**	**720767**
合资经营	Joint Venture	340684
合作经营	Cooperative Operation	10201
独资	Sole Investment	265664
股份有限	Share Holding Limited	57552
其他	Others	46666
个体经营	**Individual**	**1797861**
个体户	Private	1550200
个人合伙	Individual Partnership	247661

注：本表仅含城镇基建、更改、其他和房地产四部分。
Note: The investment in fixed assets in this table just contains 3 parts by urban areas: investment in basic construction, innovation & others.

Newly Increased Fixed Assets Grouped by Registration Status (2017)

(10 000 yuan)

基本建设 Basic Construction	更新改造 Innovation	其他 Others	房地产 Real Estate Development
67750643	**41293056**	**3931505**	**6638749**
66417597	**38894153**	**3837437**	**6404137**
22221647	6734956	697667	22912
486108	391462	41137	2400
35194	67170	8784	0
46879	3838	0	0
13247	12655	0	0
814	3680	0	0
4800	5287	0	0
4826399	962069	64580	403115
10314953	6109755	857102	3207574
699957	685859	59687	78904
22712148	21682174	1893240	2689232
5055451	2235248	215240	0
271395	**1007939**	**28055**	**227002**
91135	606443	21000	73042
0	5900	0	0
169675	320803	7055	153960
6516	16525	0	0
4069	58268	0	0
297516	**406048**	**17203**	**7610**
89904	239967	10813	4194
5306	4895	0	0
129027	131537	5100	3416
44725	12827	0	0
28554	16822	1290	0
764135	**984916**	**48810**	**0**
639755	866135	44310	0
124380	118781	4500	0

10－8 分行业固定资产投资（2017年）
Investment in Fixed Assets by Sector（2017）

单位：万元 （10 000 yuan）

指 标	Item	投资总额 Total Investment	按隶属关系分 By Administrative Relationship 中央 Central	地方 Local	新增固定资产 Newly Increased Fixed Assets
总 计	**Total**	**172247885**	**3854140**	**168393745**	**112975204**
按三次产业分	**Grouped by Three Strata of Industry**				
第一产业	Primary Industry	12035973		12035973	9571689
第二产业	Secondary Industry	70046285	2530207	67516078	51382932
第三产业	Tertiary Industry	90165627	1323933	88841694	52020583
按国民经济行业分	**By Sector**				
农、林、牧、渔业	Agriculture, Forestry, Animal Husbandry & Fishery	12035973		12035973	9571689
#农业	Farming	4508141		4508141	3460762
林业	Forestry	1626959		1626959	1204652
工业	Industry	68313828	2530207	65783621	50051519
采矿业	Mining	2700957	57421	2643536	2209741
制造业	Manufacturing	55856802	418551	55438251	42062775
电力燃气及水的生产供应业	Power, Gas & Water Production & Supply	9756069	2054235	7701834	5779003
建筑业	Construction	1732457		1732457	1331413
交通运输、仓储及邮政业	Transportation,Storage & Postal	20263158	629535	19633623	10251582
交通运输业	Transportation	19153235	615404	18537831	9568658
仓储业	Storage	1009176	14131	995045	615757
邮政业	Postal	100747		100747	67167
信息传输、计算机服务和软件业	Information Transmission, Computer Service & Software Industries	2457962	88621	2369341	1830254

注：本表仅含城镇基建、更改、其他三部分，不含房地产开发投资。
Note: The investment in fixed assets in this table just contains 3 parts by urban areas: investment in basic construction, innovation & others.

10－8 续表 continued

单位：万元 (10 000 yuan)

指 标	Item	投资总额 Total Investment	按隶属关系分 By Administrative Relationship 中 央 Central	地 方 Local	新增固定资产 Newly Increased Fixed Assets
批发和零售业	Wholesale & Retail Trades	6401552	15344	6386208	4681312
批发业	Wholesale Trades	3236822	4880	3231942	2459759
零售业	Retail Trades	3164730	10464	3154266	2221553
住宿和餐饮业	Hotel & Catering Services	2522260		2522260	1781780
#餐饮业	Catering Services	706867		706867	620248
金融业	Financial Intermeciation	533267	32371	500896	295648
房地产业	Real Estate	7860686	61548	7799138	3300742
租赁和商务服务业	Leasing & Business Services	8042535	19984	8022551	4466045
科学研究、技术服务地质勘查业	Scientific Research, Technical Services & Geological Prospecting	1534872	10333	1524539	1221982
水利、环境和公共设施管理业	Management of Water Conservancy, Environment & Public Facilities	25399088	416367	24982721	14175925
水利管理业	Water Conservancy	3192119	122816	3069303	2291355
公共设施管理业	Public Facility Management	21646251	278591	21367660	11555848
居民服务和其他服务业	Services to Households & Others	887112	4643	882469	593208
教育事业	Education	5209294	12728	5196566	3262062
卫生、社会保障和社会福利业	Public Health, Social Security & Social Welfare	2409248	9318	2399930	1588655
#卫生事业	Public Health	2068533	9318	2059215	1381334
文化、体育和娱乐业	Culture, Sports & Entertainment	3109929	1426	3108503	1798814
公共管理和社会组织	Public Management & Social Organizations	3534664	21715	3512949	2772574
国际组织	International Organizations				

10－9 工业分行业固定资产投资（2017年）
Investment in Urban Fixed Assets by Industrial Sector（2017）

单位：万元 （10 000 yuan）

指 标	Item	投资总额 Total Investment	按隶属关系分 By Administrative Relationship		新增固定资产 Newly Increased Fixed Assets
			中 央 Central	地 方 Local	
合 计	**Total**	**68313828**	**2530207**	**65783621**	**50051519**
煤炭采选业	Coal Mining & Processing	38678		38678	4182
石油和天然气开采	Extraction of Petroleum and Natural Gas	27273		27273	28538
黑色金属矿采选业	Mining and Processing of Ferrousmetal Ores	173392		173392	147054
有色金属矿采选业	Nonferrous Metals Mining & Processing	515209	48006	467203	359852
非金属矿采选业	Mining and Processing of Non-metal Ores	1772982	4115	1768867	1550824
开采辅助活动	Support Activitives for mining	69818	5300	64518	65561
其他采矿业	Mining of Other Ores	103605		103605	53730
农副食品加工	Major Grain & Sideline Food Processing	4307827	11636	4296191	3271527
#制糖业	Sugar Production	384655	11636	373019	251901
食品制造业	Food Production	2548694		2548694	2009309
饮料制造业	Beverage Production	1324548	4870	1319678	1183321
烟草加工业	Tobacco Processing	39217	24293	14924	12717
纺织业	Textile Industry	751353		751353	635778
纺织服装、鞋帽制造业	Textile Clothes, Shoes & Caps Producing	908425		908425	758247
皮革、毛皮、羽毛（绒）及其制品业	Leathers, Furs, Down & Related Products	447991		447991	352445
木材加工及竹、藤、棕、草制品业	Timber, Bamboo, Cane, Palm Fiber, Straw Products	5213908	3680	5210228	4448509
家具制造业	Furniture Manufacturing	1042739		1042739	897680
造纸及纸制品业	Papermaking & Paper Products	1185654		1185654	872410
印刷业、记录、媒介的复制	Printing & Record Medium Reproduction	646311		646311	489781
文教体育用品制造业	Culture, Education & Sports Facilities Producing	14766		14766	6801
石油加工、炼焦及核燃料加工业	Petroleum Processing, Coking Products & Nuclear Fuel Processing	577008	55758	521250	377893
化学原料及化学制品制造业	Raw Chemical Materials & Chemical Products	2852814	8169	2844645	2170043

注：1. 本表仅含基建、更改、其他三部分。
2. 2014年起，由于新国民经济行业代码调整，原办公用机械制造业已归至通用机械制造业。“仪器仪表及文化、办公用机械制造业”数据与往年不可比。

Note: 1. The investment in fixed assets in this table just contains 3 parts: investment in basic construction, innovation & others.
2. According to the code adjustment of the new national economic industry, the old indicator “Clerical Machinery Manufacturing” has been brought into the “General Machinery Manufacturing” since 2014. The data on “Instruments, Meters, Cultural & Clerical Machinery Manufacturing” in 2014 is not comparable with the former years.

10—9 续表 continued

单位：万元 (10 000 yuan)

指 标	Item	投资总额 Total Investment	按隶属关系分 By Administrative Relationship 中 央 Central	地 方 Local	新增固定资产 Newly Increased Fixed Assets
医药制造业	Medical & Pharmaceutical Products	1387682		1387682	904460
化学纤维制造业	Chemical Fiber	104004		104004	38798
橡胶和塑料制品业	Rubber & Plastic Products	1553632	6268	1547364	1250323
非金属矿物制品业	Nonmetal Mineral Products	8785147	70205	8714942	6963587
#水泥制造业	Cements Products	688063	41801	646262	716551
黑色金属冶练及压延加工业	Smelting & Pressing of Ferrous Metals	1213704	15390	1198314	972681
有色金属冶练及压延加工业	Smelting & Pressing of Nonferrous Metals	2512326	3799	2508527	1785170
金属制品业	Metal Products	1889625		1889625	1419536
通用机械制造业	General Machinery Manufacturing	1844870		1844870	1430896
专用设备制造业	Special Purpose Equipment	2188852	5130	2183722	1573604
交通运输设备制造业	Transport Equipment	5180943	145485	5035458	3265970
电气、机械及器材制造业	Electric Equipment & Machinery Manufacturing	2176301	22206	2154095	1466675
通信设备、计算机及其他电子设备制造业	Communications Equipment, Computer & Other Electric Equipment Manufacturing	2905213	41662	2863551	1737310
仪器仪表及文化、办公用机械制造业	Instruments, Meters, Cultural & Clerical Machinery	216881		216881	180427
工艺品及其他制造业	Artworks & Other Products Manufacturing	821261		821261	724631
废弃资源和废旧材料回收加工业	Abandoned Resources & Junk Materials Recycling & Processing	803731		803731	520177
金属制品、机械和设备修理业	Metal Product, Machinery & Equipment Repair Services	144660		144660	131232
电力、蒸气、热水的生成和供应业	Electricity, Steam, Hot Water Production & Supply	6970046	1992861	4977185	3834314
#水电	Hydropower	1345152	50623	1294529	647079
火电	Thermal Power	425740	122097	303643	602095
煤气生成和供应业	Gas Production & Supply	494134	50865	443269	360437
自来水的生成和供应业	Tap Water Production & Supply	2291889	10509	2281380	1584252

10－10　基本建设分行业固定资产投资（2017年）
Investment in Fixed Assets in Basic Construction by Sector（2017）

单位：万元　(10 000 yuan)

指　标	Item	投资总额 Total Investment	按隶属关系分 By Administrative Relationship		新增固定资产 Newly Increased Fixed Assets
			中　央 Central	地　方 Local	
总　计	**Total**	**114382612**	**1838369**	**112544243**	**67750643**
按三次产业分	**Grouped by Three Strata of Industry**				
第一产业	Primary Industry	10219585		10219585	7999440
第二产业	Secondary Industry	33136459	858176	32278283	20607949
第三产业	Tertiary Industry	71026568	980193	70046375	39143254
按国民经济行业分	**By Sector**				
农、林、牧、渔业	Agriculture,Forestry,Animal Husbandry & Fishery	10219585		10219585	7999440
#农业	Farming	3908571		3908571	2964144
林业	Forestry	1387044		1387044	993454
工业	Industry	31790989	858176	30932813	19627667
采矿业	Mining	1048693	10173	1038520	792766
制造业	Manufacturing	24758546	272920	24485626	15558767
电力燃气及水的生产供应业	Power, Gas & Water Production & Supply	5983750	575083	5408667	3276134
建筑业	Construction	1345470		1345470	980282
交通运输、仓储及邮政业	Transportation,Storage & Postal	13811234	369504	13441730	7387359
交通运输业	Transportation	12857828	355373	12502455	6816656
仓储业	Storage	862750	14131	848619	509767
邮政业	Postal	90656		90656	60936
信息传输、计算机服务和软件业	Information Transmission, Computer Service & Software Industries	1751646	52363	1699283	1256431

10－10 续表 continued

单位：万元 (10 000 yuan)

指 标	Item	投资总额 Total Investment	按隶属关系分 By Administrative Relationship 中 央 Central	地 方 Local	新增固定资产 Newly Increased Fixed Assets
批发和零售业	Wholesale & Retail Trades	4898819	8129	4890690	3374696
批发业	Wholesale Trades	2506577		2506577	1825249
零售业	Retail Trades	2392242	8129	2384113	1549447
住宿和餐饮业	Hotel & Catering Services	1941686		1941686	1327095
#餐饮业	Catering Services	486450		486450	442887
金融业	Financial Intermeciation	420412	32371	388041	219852
房地产业	Real Estate	6648084	47041	6601043	2538785
租赁和商务服务业	Leasing & Business Services	6712628	16360	6696268	3556505
科学研究、技术服务地质勘查业	Scientific Research, Technical Services & Geological Prospecting	1129958	7012	1122946	777533
水利、环境和公共设施管理业	Management of Water Conservancy, Environment & Public Facilities	21451982	410666	21041316	10882967
水利管理业	Water Conservancy	2641453	117976	2523477	1743204
公共设施管理业	Public Facility Management	18373847	277730	18096117	8908702
居民服务和其他服务业	Services to Households & Others	713365	4643	708722	466042
教育事业	Education	4140863	8513	4132350	2413941
卫生、社会保障和社会福利业	Public Health, Social Security & Social Welfare	1692520	9318	1683202	1043548
#卫生事业	Public Health	1453685	9318	1444367	915378
文化、体育和娱乐业	Culture, Sports & Entertainment	2717702	1426	2716276	1522002
公共管理和社会组织	Public Management & Social Organizations	2995669	12847	2982822	2376498
国际组织	International Organizations				

10—11 工业行业基本建设投资（2017年）
Investment in Basic Construction by Industrial Sector（2017）

单位：万元 (10 000 yuan)

指 标	Item	投资总额 Total Investment	按隶属关系分 By Administrative Relationship		新增固定资产 Newly Increased Fixed Assets
			中 央 Central	地 方 Local	
合 计	**Total**	**31790989**	**858176**	**30932813**	**19627667**
煤炭采选业	Coal Mining & Processing	8381		8381	4181
石油和天然气开采	Extraction of Petroleum and Natural Gas	16702		16702	16475
黑色金属矿采选业	Mining and Processing of Ferrousmetal Ores	56028		56028	39955
有色金属矿采选业	Nonferrous Metals Mining & Processing	171654	9748	161906	113848
非金属矿采选业	Mining and Processing of Non-metal Ores	718472	425	718047	571222
开采辅助活动	Support Activitives for mining	34488		34488	30231
其他采矿业	Mining of Other Ores	42968		42968	16854
农副食品加工	Major Grain & Sideline Food Processing	2158197	11636	2146561	1437344
#制糖业	Sugar Production	166612	11636	154976	64224
食品制造业	Food Production	1060707		1060707	758000
饮料制造业	Beverage Production	541429	4870	536559	444113
烟草加工业	Tobacco Processing	14924		14924	12717
纺织业	Textile Industry	316350		316350	225618
纺织服装、鞋帽制造业	Textile Clothes, Shoes & Caps Producing	385780		385780	263993
皮革、毛皮、羽毛（绒）及其制品业	Leathers, Furs, Down & Related Products	227042		227042	149350
木材加工及竹、藤、棕、草制品业	Timber, Bamboo, Cane, Palm Fiber, Straw Products	1630629		1630629	1301374
家具制造业	Furniture Manufacturing	413334		413334	344513
造纸及纸制品业	Papermaking & Paper Products	503209		503209	277807
印刷业、记录、媒介的复制	Printing & Record Medium Reproduction	206072		206072	116139
文教体育用品制造业	Culture, Education & Sports Facilities Producing	8168		8168	3216
石油加工、炼焦及核燃料加工业	Petroleum Processing, Coking Products & Nuclear Fuel Processing	247593	23310	224283	58368
化学原料及化学制品制造业	Raw Chemical Materials & Chemical Products	1390744		1390744	774956

10－11 续表 continued

单位：万元 (10 000 yuan)

指 标	Item	投资总额 Total Investment	按隶属关系分 By Administrative Relationship 中 央 Central	地 方 Local	新增固定资产 Newly Increased Fixed Assets
医药制造业	Medical & Pharmaceutical Products	659190		659190	280919
化学纤维制造业	Chemical Fiber	81604		81604	12962
橡胶和塑料制品业	Rubber & Plastic Products	676630		676630	452822
非金属矿物制品业	Nonmetal Mineral Products	3744116	38107	3706009	2611502
#水泥制造业	Cements Products	207576	9703	197873	185058
黑色金属冶练及压延加工业	Smelting & Pressing of Ferrous Metals	210019	5940	204079	212951
有色金属冶练及压延加工业	Smelting & Pressing of Nonferrous Metals	1601414		1601414	1025937
金属制品业	Metal Products	844589		844589	552998
通用机械制造业	General Machinery Manufacturing	630963		630963	404168
专用设备制造业	Special Purpose Equipment	1080698		1080698	677137
交通运输设备制造业	Transport Equipment	2173343	129481	2043862	1040789
电气、机械及器材制造业	Electric Equipment & Machinery Manufacturing	931795	21205	910590	520280
通信设备、计算机及其他电子设备制造业	Communications Equipment, Computer & Other Electric Equipment Manufacturing	1885019	38371	1846648	884800
仪器仪表及文化、办公用机械制造业	Instruments, Meters, Cultural & Clerical Machinery	58215		58215	50673
工艺品及其他制造业	Artworks & Other Products Manufacturing	311755		311755	202658
废弃资源和废旧材料回收加工业	Abandoned Resources & Junk Materials Recycling & Processing	564547		564547	295116
金属制品、机械和设备修理业	Metal Products, Machinery & Equipment Repair Services	68645		68645	71576
电力、蒸气、热水的生成和供应业	Electricity, Steam, Hot Water Production & Supply	3879746	554783	3324963	1883766
#水电	Hydropower	761458	49303	712155	206016
火电	Thermal Power	285189	81420	203769	71966
煤气生成和供应业	Gas Production & Supply	313960	9983	303977	230916
自来水的生成和供应业	Tap Water Production & Supply	1790044	10317	1779727	1161452

10－12 基本建设分行业投资项目和新增固定资产（2017年）
Basic Construction Projects & Newly Increased Fixed Assets by Sector (2017)

项 目	Item	施工项目（个）Project under Construc-tion (unit)	全部建成投产项目（个）Projects Fully Completed Put into Operation (unit)	项目建成投产率（%）Rate of Investment of Projects Completed (%)	投资总额（万元）Total Investment (10 000 yuan)	新增固定资产（万元）Newly Increased Fixed Assets (10 000 yuan)	固定资产交付使用率（%）Rate of Fixed Assets Put into Use (%)
总 计	**Total**	**31367**	**22686**	**72.3**	**114382612**	**67750643**	**59.2**
按三次产业分	**Grouped by Three Strata of Industry**						
第一产业	Primary Industry	4073	3212	78.9	10219585	7999440	78.3
第二产业	Secondary Industry	8380	6122	73.1	33136459	20607949	62.2
第三产业	Tertiary Industry	18914	13352	70.6	71026568	39143254	55.1
按国民经济行业分	**By Sector**						
农、林、牧、渔业	Agriculture,Forestry,Animal Husbandry & Fishery	4073	3212	78.9	10219585	7999440	78.3
#农业	Farming	1507	1151	76.4	3908571	2964144	75.8
林业	Forestry	514	389	75.7	1387044	993454	71.6
工业	Industry	7795	5665	72.7	31790989	19627667	61.7
采矿业	Mining	340	268	78.8	1048693	792766	75.6
制造业	Manufacturing	6250	4590	73.4	24758546	15558767	62.8
电力燃气及水的生产供应业	Power, Gas & Water Production & Supply	1205	807	67.0	5983750	3276134	54.8
建筑业	Construction	585	457	78.1	1345470	980282	72.9
交通运输、仓储及邮政业	Transportation,Storage & Postal	3036	2211	72.8	13811234	7387359	53.5
交通运输业	Transportation	2807	2064	73.5	12857828	6816656	53.0
仓储业	Storage	204	127	62.3	862750	509767	59.1
邮政业	Postal	25	20	80.0	90656	60936	67.2
信息传输、计算机服务和软件业	Information Transmission, Computer Service & Software Industries	579	492	85.0	1751646	1256431	71.7

10－12 续表 continued

项 目	Item	施工项目（个）Project under Construc-tion (unit)	全部建成投产项目（个）Projects Fully Completed Put into Operation (unit)	项目建成投产率（%）Rate of Investment of Projects Completed (%)	投资总额（万元）Total Investment (10 000 yuan)	新增固定资产（万元）Newly Increased Fixed Assets (10 000 yuan)	固定资产交付使用率（%）Rate of Fixed Assets Put into Use (%)
批发和零售业	Wholesale & Retail Trades	1692	1375	81.3	4898819	3374696	68.9
批发业	Wholesale Trades	871	721	82.8	2506577	1825249	72.8
零售业	Retail Trades	821	654	79.7	2392242	1549447	64.8
住宿和餐饮业	Hotel & Catering Services	562	442	78.6	1941686	1327095	68.3
#餐饮业	Catering Services	223	194	87.0	486450	442887	91.0
金融业	Financial Intermeciation	125	106	84.8	420412	219852	52.3
房地产业	Real Estate	1097	548	50.0	6648084	2538785	38.2
租赁和商务服务业	Leasing & Business Services	1569	1168	74.4	6712628	3556505	53.0
科学研究、技术服务地质勘查业	Scientific Research, Technical Services & Geological Prospecting	467	347	74.3	1129958	777533	68.8
水利、环境和公共设施管理业	Management of Water Conservancy, Environment & Public Facilities	5304	3488	65.8	21451982	10882967	50.7
水利管理业	Water Conservancy	1034	758	73.3	2641453	1743204	66.0
公共设施管理业	Public Facility Management	4075	2610	64.0	18373847	8908702	48.5
居民服务和其他服务业	Services to Households & Others	244	186	76.2	713365	466042	65.3
教育事业	Education	1537	1106	72.0	4140863	2413941	58.3
卫生、社会保障和社会福利业	Public Health, Social Security & Social Welfare	621	397	63.9	1692520	1043548	61.7
卫生事业	Public Health	501	330	65.9	1453685	915378	63.0
文化、体育和娱乐业	Culture, Sports & Entertainment	742	541	72.9	2717702	1522002	56.0
公共管理和社会组织	Public Management & Social Organizations	1339	945	70.6	2995669	2376498	79.3
国际组织	International Organizations						

10－13　分行业更新改造投资（2017年）
Investment in Innovation by Sector（2017）

单位：万元　　　　(10 000 yuan)

指　标	Item	投资总额 Total Investment	按隶属关系分 By Administrative Relationship 中 央 Central	地 方 Local	新增固定资产 Newly Increased Fixed Assets
总　计	**Total**	**17503604**	**1706167**	**15797437**	**12678728**
按三次产业分	**Grouped by Three Strata of Industry**				
第一产业	Primary Industry	1003485		1003485	865834
第二产业	Secondary Industry	8221790	1436754	6785036	6625929
第三产业	Tertiary Industry	8278329	269413	8008916	5186965
按国民经济行业分	**By Sector**				
农、林、牧、渔业	Agriculture,Forestry,Animal Husbandry & Fishery	1003485		1003485	865834
#农业	Farming	347695		347695	299772
林业	Forestry	124008		124008	107173
工业	Industry	8192971	1436754	6756217	6592307
采矿业	Mining	375940	27442	348498	296410
制造业	Manufacturing	5921221	12399	5908822	5479478
电力燃气及水的生产供应业	Power, Gas & Water Production & Supply	1895810	1396913	498897	816419
建筑业	Construction	28819		28819	33622
交通运输、仓储及邮政业	Transportation,Storage & Postal	3076600	253297	2823303	1182506
交通运输业	Transportation	2996753	253297	2743456	1128149
仓储业	Storage	79847		79847	54357
邮政业	Postal				
信息传输、计算机服务和软件业	Information Transmission, Computer Service & Software Industries	68425	12432	55993	62566

10－13 续表 continued

单位：万元 (10 000 yuan)

指标	Item	投资总额 Total Investment	按隶属关系分 By Administrative Relationship		新增固定资产 Newly Increased Fixed Assets
			中央 Central	地方 Local	
批发和零售业	Wholesale & Retail Trades	480375	2335	478040	417518
批发业	Wholesale Trades	171588		171588	145753
零售业	Retail Trades	308787	2335	306452	271765
住宿和餐饮业	Hotel & Catering Services	289822		289822	229635
#餐饮业	Catering Services	91274		91274	72015
金融业	Financial Intermeciation	41912		41912	14109
房地产业	Real Estate	423654		423654	337964
租赁和商务服务业	Leasing & Business Services	431953	1349	430604	228043
科学研究、技术服务地质勘查业	Scientific Research, Technical Services & Geological Prospecting	95418		95418	121547
水利、环境和公共设施管理业	Management of Water Conservancy, Environment & Public Facilities	2106427		2106427	1640684
水利管理业	Water Conservancy	282327		282327	258571
公共设施管理业	Public Facility Management	1772295		1772295	1342673
居民服务和其他服务业	Services to Households & Others	38250		38250	23450
教育事业	Education	553557		553557	473255
卫生、社会保障和社会福利业	Public Health, Social Security & Social Welfare	229541		229541	141081
卫生事业	Public Health	198452		198452	116444
文化、体育和娱乐业	Culture, Sports & Entertainment	220439		220439	140946
公共管理和社会组织	Public Management & Social Organizations	221956		221956	173661
国际组织	International Organizations				

10－14　工业分行业更新改造投资（2017年）
Investment in Innovation by Industrial Sector（2017）

单位：万元　　　　　　　　　　　　　　　　　　　　　　　　　　　　（10 000 yuan）

指　标	Item	投资总额 Total Investment	按隶属关系分 By Administrative Relationship		新增固定资产 Newly Increased Fixed Assets
			中　央 Central	地　方 Local	
合　计	**Total**	**8192971**	**1436754**	**6756217**	**6592307**
煤炭采选业	Coal Mining & Processing				
石油和天然气开采	Extraction of Petroleum and Natural Gas	6563		6563	6563
黑色金属矿采选业	Mining and Processing of Ferrousmetal Ores	36234		36234	35131
有色金属矿采选业	Nonferrous Metals Mining & Processing	81759	27442	54317	34882
非金属矿采选业	Mining and Processing of Non-metal Ores	244701		244701	216082
开采辅助活动	Support Activitives for mining	700		700	700
其他采矿业	Mining of Other Ores	5983		5983	3052
农副食品加工	Major Grain & Sideline Food Processing	477908		477908	428942
#制糖业	Sugar Production	29238		29238	33595
食品制造业	Food Production	482161		482161	401782
饮料制造业	Beverage Production	177280		177280	208981
烟草加工业	Tobacco Processing				
纺织业	Textile Industry	90710		90710	84987
纺织服装、鞋帽制造业	Textile Clothes, Shoes & Caps Producing	132358		132358	128688
皮革、毛皮、羽毛（绒）及其制品业	Leathers, Furs, Down & Related Products	54633		54633	54633
木材加工及竹、藤、棕、草制品业	Timber, Bamboo, Cane, Palm Fiber, Straw Products	673570	3680	669890	568253
家具制造业	Furniture Manufacturing	176507		176507	158722
造纸及纸制品业	Papermaking & Paper Products	182276		182276	156531
印刷业、记录、媒介的复制	Printing & Record Medium Reproduction	94368		94368	83188
文教体育用品制造业	Culture, Education & Sports Facilities Producing	2980		2980	0
石油加工、炼焦及核燃料加工业	Petroleum Processing, Coking Products & Nuclear Fuel Processing	4000		4000	4000
化学原料及化学制品制造业	Raw Chemical Materials & Chemical Products	243286	6259	237027	238576

10—14 续表 continued

单位：万元 (10 000 yuan)

指 标	Item	投资总额 Total Investment	按隶属关系分 By Administrative Relationship		新增固定资产 Newly Increased Fixed Assets
			中 央 Central	地 方 Local	
医药制造业	Medical & Pharmaceutical Products	178760		178760	135039
化学纤维制造业	Chemical Fiber	8915		8915	8915
橡胶和塑料制品业	Rubber Products	286166		286166	259203
非金属矿物制品业	Nonmetal Mineral Products	1115330		1115330	1010974
#水泥制造业	Cements Products	75457		75457	125249
黑色金属冶练及压延加工业	Smelting & Pressing of Ferrous Metals	47709		47709	33728
有色金属冶练及压延加工业	Smelting & Pressing of Nonferrous Metals	85231		85231	324921
金属制品业	Metal Products	231734		231734	197984
通用机械制造业	General Machinery Manufacturing	265969		265969	222465
专用设备制造业	Special Purpose Equipment	140849		140849	114316
交通运输设备制造业	Transport Equipment	152831		152831	136142
电气、机械及器材制造业	Electric Equipment & Machinery Manufacturing	224570		224570	188321
通信设备、计算机及其他电子设备制造业	Communications Equipment, Computer & Other Electric Equipment Manufacturing	191844	2460	189384	153423
仪器仪表及文化、办公用机械制造业	Instruments, Meters, Cultural & Clerical Machinery	23771		23771	23771
工艺品及其他制造业	Artworks & Other Products Manufacturing	97115		97115	85071
废弃资源和废旧材料回收加工业	Abandoned Resources & Junk Materials Recycling & Processing	29175		29175	22671
金属制品、机械和设备修理业	Metal Products, Machinery & Equipment Repair Services	26070		26070	23610
电力、蒸气、热水的生成和供应业	Electricity, Steam, Hot Water Production & Supply	1641506	1356031	285475	705610
#水电	Hydropower	69722		69722	47897
火电	Thermal Power	67442		67442	482920
煤气生成和供应业	Gas Production & Supply	65314	40882	24432	14504
自来水的生成和供应业	Tap Water Production & Supply	188990		188990	96305

10－15 分行业更新改造投资项目和新增固定资产（2017年）

Investment in Innovation Projects & Newly Increased Fixed Assets by Sector（2017）

指 标	Item	施工项目（个）Project under Construc-tion (unit)	全部建成投产项目（个）Projects Fully Completed Put into Operation (unit)	项目建成投产率（%）Rate of Investment of Projects Completed (%)	投资总额（万元）Total Investment (10 000 yuan)	新增固定资产（万元）Newly Increased Fixed Assets (10 000 yuan)	固定资产交付使用率（%）Rate of Fixed Assets Put into Use (%)
总 计	**Total**	**4975**	**3937**	**79.1**	**17503604**	**12678728**	**72.4**
按三次产业分	**Grouped by Three Strata of Industry**						
第一产业	Primary Industry	456	388	85.1	1003485	865834	86.3
第二产业	Secondary Industry	2127	1801	84.7	8221790	6625929	80.6
第三产业	Tertiary Industry	2392	1748	73.1	8278329	5186965	62.7
按国民经济行业分	**By Sector**						
农、林、牧、渔业	Agriculture,Forestry,Animal Husbandry & Fishery	456	388	85.1	1003485	865834	86.3
#农业	Farming	137	116	84.7	347695	299772	86.2
林业	Forestry	62	49	79	124008	107173	86.4
工业	Industry	2109	1783	84.5	8192971	6592307	80.5
采矿业	Mining	102	88	86.3	375940	296410	78.8
制造业	Manufacturing	1867	1597	85.5	5921221	5479478	92.5
电力燃气及水的生产供应业	Power, Gas & Water Produc-tion & Supply	140	98	70	1895810	816419	43.1
建筑业	Construction	18	18	100	28819	33622	116.7
交通运输、仓储及邮电通讯业	Transportation, Storage, Postal & Telecommunication Services	548	381	69.5	3076600	1182506	38.4
交通运输业	Transportation	521	360	69.1	2996753	1128149	37.6
仓储业	Storage	27	21	77.8	79847	54357	68.1
邮政业	Postal						
信息传输、计算机服务和软件业	Information Transmission, Computer Service & Software Industries	29	26	89.7	68425	62566	91.4

10－15 续表 continued

指 标	Item	施工项目（个）Project under Construc-tion (unit)	全部建成投产项目（个）Projects Fully Completed Put into Operation (unit)	项目建成投产率（%）Rate of Investment of Projects Completed (%)	投资总额（万元）Total Investment (10 000 yuan)	新增固定资产（万元）Newly Increased Fixed Assets (10 000 yuan)	固定资产交付使用率（%）Rate of Fixed Assets Put into Use (%)
批发和零售业	Wholesale & Retail Trades	215	188	87.4	480375	417518	86.9
批发业	Wholesale Trades	68	60	88.2	171588	145753	84.9
零售业	Retail Trades	147	128	87.1	308787	271765	88
住宿和餐饮业	Hotel & Catering Services	105	86	81.9	289822	229635	79.2
#餐饮业	Catering Services	42	33	78.6	91274	72015	78.9
金融业	Financial Intermeciation	11	9	81.8	41912	14109	33.7
房地产业	Real Estate	135	96	71.1	423654	337964	79.8
租赁和商务服务业	Leasing & Business Services	111	73	65.8	431953	228043	52.8
科学研究、技术服务地质勘查业	Scientific Research, Technical Services & Geological Prospecting	35	30	85.7	95418	121547	127.4
水利、环境和公共设施管理业	Management of Water Conservancy, Environment & Public Facilities	588	416	70.7	2106427	1640684	77.9
水利管理业	Water Conservancy	152	113	74.3	282327	258571	91.6
公共设施管理业	Public Facility Management	411	285	69.3	1772295	1342673	75.8
居民服务和其他服务业	Services to Households & Others	22	13	59.1	38250	23450	61.3
教育事业	Education	316	228	72.2	553557	473255	85.5
卫生、社会保障和社会福利业	Public Health, Social Security & Social Welfare	84	54	64.3	229541	141081	61.5
#卫生事业	Public Health	68	42	61.8	198452	116444	58.7
文化、体育和娱乐业	Culture, Sports & Entertainment	81	67	82.7	220439	140946	63.9
公共管理和社会组织	Public Management & Social Organizations	112	81	72.3	221956	173661	78.2
国际组织	International Organizations						

10－16 国有单位分行业投资项目和新增固定资产（2017年）
Investment Projects & Newly Increased Fixed Assets of States-owned Units (2017)

项 目	Item	施工项目（个）Project under Construc-tion (unit)	全部建成投产项目（个）Projects Fully Completed Put into Operation (unit)	项目建成投产率（%）Rate of Investment of Projects Completed (%)	投资总额（万元）Total Investment (10 000 yuan)	新增固定资产（万元）Newly Increased Fixed Assets (10 000 yuan)	固定资产交付使用率（%）Rate of Fixed Assets Put into Use (%)
总 计	**Total**	**17046**	**11955**	**70.1**	**61249163**	**35558035**	**58.1**
按三次产业分	**Grouped by Three Strata of Industry**						
第一产业	Primary Industry	944	757	80.2	2313209	2065911	89.3
第二产业	Secondary Industry	1778	1311	73.7	6388104	4294548	67.2
第三产业	Tertiary Industry	14324	9887	69.0	52547850	29197576	55.6
按国民经济行业分	**By Sector**						
农、林、牧、渔业	Agriculture,Forestry,Animal Husbandry & Fishery	944	757	80.2	2313209	2065911	89.3
#农业	Farming	300	244	81.3	794773	728413	91.7
林业	Forestry	295	232	78.6	702239	536895	76.5
工业	Industry	1396	1009	72.3	5600990	3622406	64.7
采矿业	Mining	23	20	87.0	105616	94264	89.3
制造业	Manufacturing	406	283	69.7	2219967	1187808	53.5
电力燃气及水的生产供应业	Power, Gas & Water Production & Supply	967	706	73.0	3275407	2340334	71.5
建筑业	Construction	382	302	79.1	787114	672142	85.4
交通运输、仓储及邮政业	Transportation,Storage & Postal	3140	2247	71.6	15100624	7475423	49.5
交通运输业	Transportation	3073	2205	71.8	14920282	7335615	49.2
仓储业	Storage	55	33	60.0	151631	122681	80.9
邮政业	Postal	12	9	75.0	28711	17127	59.7
信息传输、计算机服务和软件业	Information Transmission, Computer Service & Software Industries	151	134	88.7	501919	548823	109.3

注：本表仅含基建、更改、其他三部分。

Note: The investment in fixed assets in this table just contains 3 parts: investment in basic construction, innovation & others.

10－16 续表 continued

项 目	Item	施工项目(个) Project under Construc-tion (unit)	全部建成投产项目(个) Projects Fully Completed Put into Operation (unit)	项目建成投产率(%) Rate of Investment of Projects Completed (%)	投资总额(万元) Total Investment (10 000 yuan)	新增固定资产(万元) Newly Increased Fixed Assets (10 000 yuan)	固定资产交付使用率(%) Rate of Fixed Assets Put into Use (%)
批发和零售业	Wholesale & Retail Trades	112	69	61.6	449965	240666	53.5
批发业	Wholesale Trades	54	28	51.9	303822	142029	46.7
零售业	Retail Trades	58	41	70.7	146143	98637	67.5
住宿和餐饮业	Hotel & Catering Services	39	26	66.7	324011	121970	37.6
#餐饮业	Catering Services	12	10	83.3	25407	80194	315.6
金融业	Financial Intermeciation	18	10	55.6	65575	17335	26.4
房地产业	Real Estate	728	354	48.6	4195424	1549254	36.9
租赁和商务服务业	Leasing & Business Services	403	258	64.0	2180402	972127	44.6
科学研究、技术服务地质勘查业	Scientific Research, Technical Services & Geological Prospecting	147	98	66.7	466365	277873	59.6
水利、环境和公共设施管理业	Management of Water Conservancy, Environment & Public Facilities	5184	3601	69.5	18434877	10911585	59.2
水利管理业	Water Conservancy	1175	867	73.8	2588463	1964752	75.9
公共设施管理业	Public Facility Management	3801	2598	68.4	15449561	8692160	56.3
居民服务和其他服务业	Services to Households & Others	64	41	64.1	275518	107034	38.8
教育事业	Education	1694	1218	71.9	3980785	2528143	63.5
卫生、社会保障和社会福利业	Public Health, Social Security & Social Welfare	802	536	66.8	1935406	1308156	67.6
#卫生事业	Public Health	673	457	67.9	1674938	1146129	68.4
文化、体育和娱乐业	Culture, Sports & Entertainment	456	314	68.9	1477081	710683	48.1
公共管理和社会组织	Public Management & Social Organizations	1386	981	70.8	3159898	2428504	76.9
国际组织	International Organizations						

10－17 集体分行业投资项目和新增固定资产（2017年）

Investment Projects by Sector & Newly Increased Fixed Assets of Urban Collective Owned Units (2017)

指 标	Item	施工项目（个） Project under Construc-tion (unit)	全部建成投产项目（个） Projects Fully Completed Put into Operation (unit)	项目建成投产率（%） Rate of Investment of Projects Completed (%)	投资总额（万元） Total Investment (10 000 yuan)	新增固定资产（万元） Newly Increased Fixed Assets (10 000 yuan)	固定资产交付使用率（%） Rate of Fixed Assets Put into Use (%)
总 计	**Total**	**1125**	**826**	**73.4**	**3807016**	**2390112**	**62.8**
按三次产业分	**Grouped by Three Strata of Industry**						
第一产业	Primary Industry	116	104	89.7	341590	209418	61.3
第二产业	Secondary Industry	509	392	77.0	1794178	1313770	73.2
第三产业	Tertiary Industry	500	330	66.0	1671248	866924	51.9
按国民经济行业分	**By Sector**						
农、林、牧、渔业	Agriculture,Forestry,Animal Husbandry & Fishery	116	104	89.7	341590	209418	61.3
#农业	Farming	36	28	77.8	89891	70988	79.0
林业	Forestry	8	7	87.5	13384	8915	66.6
工业	Industry	502	386	76.9	1779135	1300017	73.1
采矿业	Mining	19	12	63.2	100882	44684	44.3
制造业	Manufacturing	393	313	79.6	1420366	1050560	74.0
电力燃气及水的生产供应业	Power, Gas & Water Production & Supply	90	61	67.8	257887	204773	79.4
建筑业	Construction	7	6	85.7	15043	13753	91.4
交通运输、仓储及邮政业	Transportation,Storage & Postal	59	45	76.3	109780	91010	82.9
交通运输业	Transportation	53	42	79.2	87622	77960	89.0
仓储业	Storage	6	3	50.0	22158	13050	58.9
邮政业	Postal						
信息传输、计算机服务和软件业	Information Transmission, Computer Service & Software Industries	57	37	64.9	317306	150709	47.5

注：本表仅含基建、更改、其他三部分。

Note: The investment in fixed assets in this table just contains 3 parts: investment in basic construction, innovation & others.

10－17 续表 continued

指 标	Item	施工项目（个）Project under Construc-tion (unit)	全部建成投产项目（个）Projects Fully Completed Put into Operation (unit)	项目建成投产率（%）Rate of Investment of Projects Completed (%)	投资总额（万元）Total Investment (10 000 yuan)	新增固定资产（万元）Newly Increased Fixed Assets (10 000 yuan)	固定资产交付使用率（%）Rate of Fixed Assets Put into Use (%)
批发和零售业	Wholesale & Retail Trades	60	51	85.0	136369	103072	75.6
批发业	Wholesale Trades	11	9	81.8	20530	22818	111.1
零售业	Retail Trades	49	42	85.7	115839	80254	69.3
住宿和餐饮业	Hotel & Catering Services	20	15	75.0	78679	52289	66.5
#餐饮业	Catering Services	2	1	50.0	5293	1165	22.0
金融业	Financial Intermeciation	17	13	76.5	68878	32679	47.4
房地产业	Real Estate	118	54	45.8	431261	184505	42.8
租赁和商务服务业	Leasing & Business Services	25	19	76.0	64006	37705	58.9
科学研究、技术服务地质勘查业	Scientific Research, Technical Services & Geological Prospecting	10	9	90.0	29073	25418	87.4
水利、环境和公共设施管理业	Management of Water Conservancy, Environment & Public Facilities	72	40	55.6	276623	91071	32.9
水利管理业	Water Conservancy	8	5	62.5	54194	12470	23.0
公共设施管理业	Public Facility Management	63	34	54.0	220571	74443	33.8
居民服务和其他服务业	Services to Households & Others	6	4	66.7	23823	15164	63.7
教育事业	Education	17	11	64.7	36288	32385	89.2
卫生、社会保障和社会福利业	Public Health, Social Security & Social Welfare	8	7	87.5	17125	17725	103.5
#卫生事业	Public Health	6	6	100.0	16155	17155	106.2
文化、体育和娱乐业	Culture, Sports & Entertainment	9	6	66.7	58708	8676	14.8
公共管理和社会组织	Public Management & Social Organizations	22	19	86.4	23329	24516	105.1
国际组织	International Organizations						

10—18 私营个体固定资产投资和新增固定资产（2017年）
Investment in Fixed Assets & Newly Increased Fixed Assets of Urban Private & Individual Units（2017）

指 标	Item	施工项目（个）Project under Construction (unit)	全部建成投产项目（个）Projects Fully Completed Put into Operation (unit)	项目建成投产率（%）Rate of Investment of Projects Completed (%)	投资总额（万元）Total Investment (10 000 yuan)	新增固定资产（万元）Newly Increased Fixed Assets (10 000 yuan)	固定资产交付使用率（%）Rate of Fixed Assets Put into Use (%)
总 计	**Total**	**892**	**746**	**83.6**	**2001542**	**1797861**	**89.8**
按三次产业分	**Grouped by Three Strata of Industry**						
第一产业	Primary Industry	193	163	84.5	306662	279724	91.2
第二产业	Secondary Industry	517	440	85.1	1362715	1250318	91.8
第三产业	Tertiary Industry	182	143	78.6	332165	267819	80.6
按国民经济行业分	**By Sector**						
农、林、牧、渔业	Agriculture,Forestry,Animal Husbandry & Fishery	193	163	84.5	306662	279724	91.2
#农业	Farming	46	37	80.4	58114	50823	87.5
林业	Forestry	12	12	100.0	30114	29084	96.6
工业	Industry	516	439	85.1	1362308	1247731	91.6
采矿业	Mining	39	36	92.3	104624	99543	95.1
制造业	Manufacturing	467	394	84.4	1227407	1121135	91.3
电力燃气及水的生产供应业	Power, Gas & Water Production & Supply	10	9	90.0	30277	27053	89.4
建筑业	Construction	1	1	100.0	407	2587	635.6
交通运输、仓储及邮政业	Transportation,Storage & Postal	4	4	100.0	7547	7903	104.7
交通运输业	Transportation	2	2	100.0	2517	3000	119.2
仓储业	Storage	2	2	100.0	5030	4903	97.5
邮政业	Postal						
信息传输、计算机服务和软件业	Information Transmission, Computer Service & Software Industries	1	1	100.0	662	662	100.0

注：本表仅含基建、更改、其他三部分。
Note: The investment in fixed assets in this table just contains 3 parts: investment in basic construction, innovation & others.

10—18 续表 continued

指 标	Item	施工项目（个）Project under Construction (unit)	全部建成投产项目（个）Projects Fully Completed Put into Operation (unit)	项目建成投产率（%）Rate of Investment of Projects Completed (%)	投资总额（万元）Total Investment (10 000 yuan)	新增固定资产（万元）Newly Increased Fixed Assets (10 000 yuan)	固定资产交付使用率（%）Rate of Fixed Assets Put into Use (%)
批发和零售业	Wholesale & Retail Trades	38	25	65.8	57875	44212	76.4
批发业	Wholesale Trades	8	2	25.0	13017	5400	41.5
零售业	Retail Trades	30	23	76.7	44858	38812	86.5
住宿和餐饮业	Hotel & Catering Services	67	56	83.6	121746	97912	80.4
#餐饮业	Catering Services	41	33	80.5	71192	56597	79.5
金融业	Financial Intermeciation	2	2	100.0	5990	5990	100.0
房地产业	Real Estate	3	3	100.0	9318	13090	140.5
租赁和商务服务业	Leasing & Business Services	4	3	75.0	13250	8250	62.3
科学研究、技术服务地质勘查业	Scientific Research, Technical Services & Geological Prospecting	1	1	100.0	3000	3000	100.0
水利、环境和公共设施管理业	Management of Water Conservancy, Environment & Public Facilities	5	4	80.0	5824	5520	94.8
水利管理业	Water Conservancy						
公共设施管理业	Public Facility Management	5	4	80.0	5824	5520	94.8
居民服务和其他服务业	Services to Households & Others	25	19	76.0	36255	28252	77.9
教育事业	Education	3	1	33.3	5830	4950	84.9
卫生、社会保障和社会福利业	Public Health, Social Security & Social Welfare	8	7	87.5	16265	11562	71.1
#卫生事业	Public Health	6	6	100.0	11471	9779	85.2
文化、体育和娱乐业	Culture, Sports & Entertainment	20	16	80.0	48086	35999	74.9
公共管理和社会组织	Public Management & Social Organizations	1	1	100.0	517	517	100.0
国际组织	International Organizations						

10－19　主要年份房地产开发主要指标

指　标	Item	1995	2000
一、企业（单位）个数（个）	**Number of Enterprises (unit)**	**626**	**528**
内资企业	Domestic Funds	473	407
#国有	State-owned	251	164
集体	Collective-owned	152	78
港澳台商投资企业	Funded by Enterprises form Hongkong, Macao & Taiwan	64	92
外商投资企业	Foreign Funded	86	29
二、土地开发及购置（万平方米）	**Land Development & Purchase (10 000 sq.m)**		
完成开发土地面积	Land Space Developed	1274.35	176.47
购置土地面积	Land Space Purchased	682.18	195.30
三、完成投资（万元）	**Investment Completed (10 000 yuan)**	**515050**	**386747**
#住宅	Residential Building	260541	207861
#经济适用房	Economical Houses	65078	32545
四、资金来源小计（万元）	**Sources of Funds (10 000 yuan)**	**566735**	**502039**
#国内贷款	Domestic Loans	168318	92998
利用外资	Foreign Investment	53886	12916
自筹资金	Fundraising	137817	131654
五、房屋建筑面积及价值	**Floor Space & Value of Buildings**		
施工面积（万平方米）	Floor Space under Construction (10 000 sq.m)	867.27	766.19
#住宅	Residential Building	625.77	595.25
#经济适用房	Economical Houses	133.40	112.59
竣工面积（万平方米）	Floor Space Completed (10 000 sq.m)	276.09	226.74
#住宅	Residential Building	231.99	191.17
#经济适用房	Economical Houses	59.90	50.39
竣工价值（万元）	Value of Floor Space Completed (10 000 yuan)	188746	164650
#住宅	Residential Building	148492	131042
#经济适用房	Economical Houses	37461	31137
六、商品房屋销售	**Sales of Commercial Buildings**		
销售面积（万平方米）	Floor Space of Sales (10 000 sq.m)	156.84	191.36
#住宅	Residential Building	133.98	177.80
#经济适用房	Economical Houses	38.58	43.32
销售额（万元）	Total Sales of Commercial Buildings (10 000 yuan)	158387	277384
#住宅	Residential Building	133779	245721
#经济适用房	Economical Houses	27149	39800
七、商品房待售面积（万平方米）	**Space of Commercial Buildings for sale (10 000 sq.m)**	**109.98**	**119.29**
#住宅	Residential Building	85.83	74.15
#经济适用房	Economical Houses	17.60	6.09
八、新增固定资产（万元）	**Newly Increased Fixed Assets (10 000 yuan)**	**226874**	**183837**
九、实收资本合计（万元）	**Total Capital Hold (10 000 yuan)**	**502690**	**543513**
十、经营收入总计（万元）	**Total Revenue (10 000 yuan)**	**205908**	**338043**
#土地转让收入	Land Transferred	38567	44056

Major Indicators of Real Estate Development in Main Years

2005	2010	2011	2012	2013	2014	2015	2016	2017
1730	**3212**	**3154**	**2934**	**2685**	**2491**	**2423**	**2470**	**2451**
1542	3035	2993	2793	2558	2379	2329	2377	2368
205	159	141	141	104	94	52	35	32
74	42	32	26	22	126	11	10	7
112	99	93	85	75	66	57	58	48
76	78	68	56	52	46	37	35	35
674.48	363.01							
1218.06	1193.71	978.86	541.71	4319584	610.01	415.94	639.10	675.19
2867915	**12062211**	**15174656**	**15549388**	**16146322**	**18384942**	**19090933**	**23979862**	**26834830**
1907662	8788924	10789954	10696420	11666137	12926348	14077508	17252858	19835172
74493	218072							
3395656	**15383429**	**17835008**	**20073616**	**21552380**	**24107471**	**23392870**	**31597167**	**35180380**
555493	2473098	2557343	2638371	3243473	3400275	3320395	4683828	4866248
59114	85861	70124	3294	6150	2056	15667		3400
1128707	5417241	7117514	7884479	8156908	9016015	8237208	11150353	10650091
4082.76	12048.73	14264.02	15018.46	16040.17	17472.15	18608.36	21134.65	22689.62
3164.96	9767.64	11407.86	11846.86	12419.68	13065.65	13750.52	15339.29	16453.90
94.73	402.64							
1330.74	1564.31	2303.35	2333.58	1712.68	1865.98	1675.18	1735.05	1856.24
1090.30	1342.87	1936.94	1956.57	1385.37	1441.84	1310.52	1373.27	1478.96
14.58	46.30							
1167764	2306901	3931192	4903501	3908901	4560135	4704296	4337348	5181252
913452	1922323	3262656	4077306	3101989	3388647	3589766	3350444	3958877
9191	73396							
1438.40	2793.92	2964.15	2759.26	2995.58	3156.55	3523.41	4215.39	5170.99
1314.37	2607.15	2749.33	2546.96	2765.15	2869.32	3181.51	3864.01	4687.41
42.48	92.36							
2896410	9951860	11182159	11598322	13757948	15320544	17477650	22074664	3016.64
2398083	8817021	9771009	9958158	11667241	12745691	14594268	19482272	2635.74
61184	166859							
269.86	**192.49**	**540.60**	**926.02**	**1225.46**	**1507.45**	**1677.60**	**1772.74**	**1598.85**
145.09	181.02	377.18	643.07	857.94	1024.32	1124.51	1187.21	989.74
	0.40							
1635726	**3164161**	**5410764**	**6923890**	**5584193**	**5888753**	**5858064**	**507952**	
2099130	**4812635**	**5554412**	**7352140**	**6662477**		**10763586**	**10421965**	
192426	**643311**	**711708**	**7919996**	**9067538**		**11496584**	**13950467**	
79030	45917	52231	163012	142461		80760	221189	

主要统计指标解释

全社会固定资产投资　是以货币形式表现的在一定时期内全社会建造和购置固定资产活动的工作量以及与此有关的费用的总称，它是反映固定资产投资规模、结构和发展速度的综合性指标，又是观察工程进度和考核投资效果的重要依据。全社会固定资产投资按登记注册类型可分为国有、集体、个体、联营、股份制、外商、港澳台商、其他等。按照管理渠道可分为：基本建设、更新改造、房地产开发和其他固定资产投资四个部分。

基本建设投资　基本建设指企业、事业、行政单位以扩大生产能力或工程效益为主要目的的新建、扩建工程及有关工作。其范围为总投资500万元以上（含500万元）的基本建设项目。

更新改造投资　更新改造指企业、事业单位对原有设施进行技术改造（包括固定资产更新）以及相应配套的辅助性生产、生活福利设施等工程和有关工作。其范围为总投资500万元以上的更新改造单位（或项目）。

其他固定资产投资　指全社会固定资产投资中未列入基本建设、更新改造和房地产开发投资的建造和购置固定资产的活动。

固定资产投资的资金来源　根据固定资产投资的资金来源不同，分为国家预算内资金、国内贷款、利用外资、自筹资金和其他资金来源。

（1）国家预算内资金：指中央财政和地方财政中由国家统筹安排的基本建设拨款和更新改造拨款，以及中央财政安排的专项拨款中用于基本建设的资金和基本建设拨款改贷款的资金等。

（2）国内贷款：指报告期内企、事业单位向银行及非银行金融机构借入的用于固定资产投资的各种国内借款。

（3）利用外资：指报告期内收到的用于固定资产投资的国外资金，包括统借统还、自借自还的国外贷款，中外合资项目中的外资，以及对外发行债券和股票等。国家统借统还的外资指由我国政府出面同外国政府、团体或金融组织签订贷款协议、并负责偿还本息的国外贷款。

（4）自筹资金：指建设单位报告期内收到的，用于进行固定资产投资的上级主管部门、地方和企、事业单位自筹资金。

（5）其他资金来源：指报告期内收到的除以上各种拨款、借款、自筹资金以外其他用于固定资产投资的资金。

固定资产投资按国民经济行业分　建设项目归哪个行业，按其建成投产后的主要产品或主要用途及社会经济活动性质来确定。基本建设按建设项目划分国民经济行业，更新改造、国有单位其他固定资产投资根据整个企业、事业单位所属的行业来划分。一般情况下，一个建设项目或一个企业、事业单位只能属于一种国民经济行业。为了更准确地反映国民经济各行业之间的比例关系，联合企业（总厂）所属分厂属于不同行业的，原则上按分厂划分行业。

固定资产投资按建设性质分　建设项目的性质一般分为新建、扩建、改建、迁建、恢复。基本建设按建设项目划分建设性质，更新改造、国有单位其他固定资产投资等按整个企业、事业单位的建设情况确定建设性质，房地产开发单位、农村投资等投资不划分建设性质。

（1）新建：一般是指从无到有、“平地起家”新开始建设的单位。有的单位原有的基础很小，经过建设后其新增加的固定资产价值超过原有固定资产价值（原值）三倍以上的也算新建。

（2）扩建：一般是指为扩大原有产品的生产能力，在厂内或其他地点增建主要生产车间（或主要工程）、独立的生产线或分厂的企业，事业单位和行政单位在原单位增建业务用房（如学校增建教学用房、医院增建门诊部或病床用房、行政机关增建办公楼等）也作为扩建。

（3）改建：一般是指现有企业、事业单位为了技术进步，提高产品质量，增加花色品种，促进产品升级换代，降低消耗和成本，加强资源综合利用和三废治理、劳保安全等，采用新技术、新工艺、新设备、新材料等对现有设施、工艺条件进行技术改造或更新（包括相应配套的辅助性生产、生活福利设施）。有的企业为充分发挥现有生产能力，进行填平补齐而增建不增加本单位主要产品生产能力的车间等，也属于改建。

大中小型基本建设项目划分　是根据基本建设项目的建设总规模（设计生产能力或工程效益）或计划总投资，按照

《基本建设项目大中小型划分标准》划分的建设项目类型。建设项目总规模或计划总投资划分标准原则上应按照上级批准的设计任务书或初步设计所确定的总规模或总投资为准；没有正式批准设计任务书或初步设计的，按国家或省、自治区、直辖市基本建设投资计划中所列的总规模或总投资划分；上述两条均不具备的，按本年计划施工工程的建设总规模或总投资划分。

施工项目 指报告期内曾进行建筑或安装工程施工活动的建设项目，凡是报告期内施过工的建设项目，不论施工时间长短，均作为施工项目统计。施工项目个数可以反映一定时期固定资产投资的实际规模，与同期建成投产的建设项目个数相比，可以从建设速度的角度反映固定资产投资的效果。根据建设项目施工活动的不同性质，施工项目又分为本年正式施工项目，本年收尾项目和以前年度全部停缓建项目。

全部建成投产项目 工业项目是指设计文件规定形成生产能力的主体工程及其相应配套的辅助设施全部建成，经负荷试运转，证明具备生产设计规定合格产品的条件，并经过验收鉴定合格或达到竣工验收标准，与生产性工程配套的生活福利设施可以满足近期正常生产的需要，正式移交生产的建设项目。非工业项目是指设计文件规定的主体工程和相应的配套工程全部建成，能够发挥设计规定的全部效益，经验收鉴定合格或达到竣工验收标准，正式移交使用的建设项目。

新增生产能力 指通过固定资产投资活动而增加的设计能力或工程效益，它是用实物形态表示的固定资产投资的成果的指标，也是考核投资经济效果的重要依据之一。

房屋建筑面积 指从房屋外墙线算起的各层平面面积的总和，包括可供使用的有效面积和房屋结构（如柱、墙）占用的面积。多层建筑按各层（包括地下室）面积总和计算。

住宅建筑面积 指施工和竣工房屋建筑面积中供居住用的施工和竣工房屋建筑面积。

施工面积 指报告期内施工的全部房屋建筑面积。包括本期新开工的面积、上期跨入本期继续施工的房屋面积、上期停建在本期恢复施工的房屋面积、本期竣工及本期施工后又停缓建的房屋面积。

竣工面积 指在报告期内房屋建筑按照设计要求已全部完工，达到住人和使用条件，经验收鉴定合格（或达到竣工验收标准），正式移交使用单位的各栋房屋建筑面积的总和。

房屋建筑面积竣工率 指一定时期内房屋竣工面积占同期房屋施工面积的比率。它是从房屋建筑施工速度的角度反映投资效果和建筑业经济效益的指标。

新增固定资产 指报告期内已经完成建造和购置过程，并已交付生产或使用单位的固定资产价值。该指标是表示固定资产投资成果的价值指标，也是反映建设进度，计算固定资产投资效果的指标。

建设项目投产率 指一定时期内全部建成投入生产项目个数与同期正式施工项目个数的比率。它是从项目建设速度的角度反映投资效果的指标。

固定资产交付使用率 指一定时期新增固定资产与同期完成投资额的比率。它是反映各个时期固定资产动用速度，衡量建设过程中投资效果的一个综合性指标。

房地产开发投资 指各种登记注册类型的房地产开发公司、商品房建设公司及其他房地产开发法人单位和附属于其他法人单位实际从事房地产开发或经营的活动单位统一开发的包括统代建、拆迁还建的住宅、厂房、仓库、饭店、宾馆、度假村、写字楼、办公楼等房屋建筑物和配套的服务设施，土地开发工程（如道路、给水、供电、供热、通讯、平整场地等基础设施工程）的投资，不包括单纯的土地交易活动。

商品房建设投资额 是指房地产开发企业（单位）开发建设的供出售、出租用的商品住宅、厂房、仓库、饭店、度假村、写字楼、办公楼、拆迁、回迁还建用房等房屋工程及其配套的服务设施所完成的投资额。

住宅 是指专供居住的房屋，包括别墅、公寓、职工家属宿舍和集体宿舍、职工单身宿舍和学生宿舍等。但不包括住宅楼中作为人防用、不住人的地下室等。

商业营业用房 是指商业、粮食、供销、饮食服务业等部门对外营业的用房，如度假村、饭店、商店、门市部、粮店、书店、供销店、饮食店、菜店、加油站、日杂等房屋。

完成开发土地面积 是指报告期内对土地进行开发并已完成七通一平等前期开发工程，具备进行房屋建筑物施工或出让条件的土地面积。

购置土地面积　是指报告期内通过各种方式获得土地使用权的土地面积。

商品房销售面积　指报告期内出售商品房屋合同总面积（即双方签署的正式买卖合同中所确定的建筑面积），由现房销售建筑面积和期房销售建筑面积两部分组成。

商品房销售额　指报告期内出售商品房屋的合同总价款（即双方签署的正式买卖合同中所确定的合同总价）。该指标与商品房销售面积同口径，由现房销售额和期房销售额两部分组成。

商品房待售面积　指报告期末已竣工的可供销售或出租的商品房屋建筑面积中，尚未销售或出租的商品房屋面积，包括以前年度竣工和本期竣工的房屋面积，但不包括报告期已竣工的拆迁还建、统建代建、公共配套建筑、房地产公司自用及周转房等不可销售或出租的房屋面积。

实收资本　是指企业实际收到的所有投资人投入的资本，包括以实物形式、货币形式、发明创造或技术成果等无形资产投入企业的资本。

Explanatory Notes on Main Statistical Indicators

Total Investment in Fixed Assets refers to the volume of activities in construction and purchases of fixed assets in monetary terms. It is a comprehensive indicator, which shows the size, composition and pace of the investment in fixed assets, providing basis for observing the progress of construction projects and evaluating results of investment. Total investment in fixed assets includes, by registration type of ownership, the investment by the state-owned units, collective units, individuals, joint ownership units, shareholding units, as well as investment by businessmen from foreign countries and from Hong Kong, Macao and Taiwan, and by other units. According to Chinese current management systems, the investment in fixed assets is classified into the following four parts: investment in capital construction, investment in innovation, investment in real estates development and other investment in fixed assets.

Investment in Capital Construction refers to the new construction projects or extension projects and the related work of the enterprises, institutions or administrative units mainly for the purpose of expanding production capacity or improving project efficiency covering only projects each with a total investment of 5,000,000 RMB and over.

Investment in Innovation Innovation refers to technological innovation (including the renewal of fixed assets) of the original facilities by the enterprises and institutions as well as the corresponding accessory facilities projects for production or for living and welfare purpose and the related work covering only projects each with a total investment of 5,000,000 RMB and over.

Other Investment in Fixed Assets refers to the construction and purchases of fixed assets not listed in the investment capital construction, investment in innovation and investment in real estate development.

Sources of Funds for Investment in Fixed Assets According to various sources of funds of investment in fixed assets, it is divided into state budgetary appropriation, domestic loans, foreign investment, self-raised funds, and other sources of funds.

(1) State budgetary appropriation refers to appropriation in the budget of the central and local governments earmarked for capital construction and for innovation projects, and the special appropriation from the budget of the central government for capital construction and for the transfer fund to banks to be issued as loans for capital construction projects.

(2) Domestic loans refer to various funds borrowed by enterprises and institutions from banks and non-bank financial institutions during the reference period for the purpose of investment in fixed assets.

(3) Foreign investment refers to foreign funds received during the reference period for the purpose of investment in fixed assets, including foreign funds borrowed and managed by the government, by individual units, foreign fund in joint venture program, and issue of bonds and stocks at the international financial markets. The foreign funds borrowed and managed by the government refer to foreign loans borrowed by the government from foreign governments, organizations, or financial institutions under official agreements signed by both parties, under which government is responsible for the repayment of both the principal and interests of the foreign loans.

(4) Self-raised funds refer to funds received by construction enterprises from their higher responsible authorities, local governments, or raised by enterprises or institutions themselves for the purpose of investment in fixed assets during the reference period.

(5) Other srefer to funds received during the reference period, which are not included in the above-mentioned sources.

Investment in Fixed Assets by Sector The classification of construction projects by sector is determined by the major products or the purpose of the projects when they are put into production or use, and by the nature of their social economic activities. The investment in capital construction is classified by construction projects, while investment in innovation, other investment by state-owned units are classified according to the sector which the whole enterprises or institution belongs to. In general, one project or one enterprise or institution can only belong to one sector. In order to reflect more accurately the proportions among various sectors,

the branch factories of integrated complex are classified into different sectors according to their economic activities.

Investment in Fixed Assets by Type of Construction The construction projects in general can be classified by the type of construction into new construction, expansion, reconstruction and moving away. In capital construction, the type of construction is determined by the condition of the project. In investment, in innovation, in other investment by state-owned units and investment by collective-owned units, the type of construction is determined by the condition of the whole enterprise or institution. Investment by type of construction is not applied to investment by real-estate development units, investment in rural areas.

(1) New construction in general refers to newly constructed units. In the case in which the value of the original fixed assets is quite small, and the value of newly added fixed assets exceeds the original ones by three times, the expansion construction is considered as new construction.

(2) Expansion refers to construction of new major production workshop or independent production line within a factory or in other locations, or construction of a branch factory so as to increase the production capacity of the original products. Newly constructed business houses in institutions and administrative organizations (such as the newly constructed teaching buildings in schools, clinics or bed building in hospitals, and office buildings in administrative agencies, etc.) are also classified as expansion.

(3) Reconstruction refers to technical conditions undertaken by enterprises and institutions for the purposes of technological advancement, improvement in product quality, enlarging variety of products, promoting new generation of products, reducing production consumption and cost, promoting comprehensive utilization of resources, strengthening treatment of waste gas, waste water and solid wastes, and safety in production, etc. through application of new technologies and techniques, use of new equipment and new materials(including accessory facilities for production or for living and welfare purposes). Construction of new workshops for improving existing production capacity rather than increasing production capacity is also considered as reconstruction.

Capital Construction Projects by Size is the types of construction projects based on the total scale (designed producing capacity or project efficiency) or total investment set, according to Standards for the Classification of Construction Projects into Large, Medium-sized and Small Ones. The classification of size of construction projects or total plan investment should be determined according to the total scale or total investment set in the approved construction plan by higher responsible authorities or in the tentative design, otherwise according to the total scale or total investment set in the current capital construction plan of the state, provinces, autonomous regions, and municipalities directly under central government.

Projects Under Construction refer to projects having construction and installation activities undertaken in the reference period, irrespective of the length of construction. The number of projects under construction can reflect the actual size of investment in fixed assets during a certain period, and when compared with the number of projects completed and put into use, it can reflect the efficiency of investment in fixed assets from the perspective of the speed of construction. Depending on the nature of construction activities, projects under construction can also be classified into projects under construction in current year, winding-up projects in current year and stopped or suspended projects in previous years.

Projects Completed and Put into Use Industrial projects refer to the major projects and accessory facilities completed which result in forming production capacity and have been checked and accepted while the living and welfare facilities have been completed and can ensure normal production and formally put into production. Non-industrial projects refer to the major projects and accessory facilities completed which posses the designed capacity and have been checked, accepted and formally put into production.

Newly Increased Production Capacity refers to the increase of designed capacity and project efficiency through investment in fixed assets, which reflects the accomplishment of investment in fixed assets in kind and is one of the important indicators of observing efficiency the economic efficiency of investment.

Floor Space of Buildings Under Construction and Completed refers to total floor space in each story of buildings calculated from the outside line of building walls, including both usable space and the space occupied by constructions like pillars or walls. The floor space of multi-story buildings includes the total floor space of each story (including basement).

Floor Space of Residential Buildings refers to the floor space of the residential buildings under construction and completed among the total space of buildings under construction and completed.

Floor Space under Construction refers to total floor space of all buildings under construction during the reference period, including floor space of newly started buildings during the reference period, floor space of construction extended from the previous period to the current period, floor space of construction suspended during the previous period and resumed in the current period, floor space of construction completed in the current period, and floor space of construction started and the suspended in the current period.

Floor Space of Buildings Completed refers to the total floor space of buildings completed in the reference period, which have come up to the designed standards and have been put into use.

Completed Rate of Floor Space of Buildings refers to the ratio of the floor space of buildings completed in certain period of time to the floor space of buildings under construction in the same period that reflects the investment result and economic efficiency of the construction industry from the angle of the speed of project construction.

Newly Increased Fixed Assets refers to the value of investment in fixed assets which completed the construction and purchases and put into production or use. It is a value indicator of achievements of investment in fixed assets, reflecting the progress of construction and calculating the efficiency of investment in fixed assets.

Rate of Construction Projects Completed and Put into Use refers to the ratio of the number of construction projects completed and put into use in certain period of time to the number of projects under construction in the same period. This reflects the investment efficiency from the angle of the speed of projects construction.

Rate of Projects of Fixed Assets Completed and Put into Operation refers to the ratio of the newly increase fixed assets to the total investment made in the same period. This is a comprehensive indicator, reflecting the speed of the employment of fixed assets and the investment efficiency.

Real Estate Development and Investment It includes the investment by the real estate development companies of various registration types, commercial buildings construction companies and other real estate development units of various types of ownership in the construction of house buildings, such as residential buildings, factory buildings, warehouses, hotels, guesthouses, holiday villages, office buildings, and the complementary service facilities and land development projects, such as roads, water supply, power supply, heating, telecommunications, land leveling and other projects of infrastructure. It excludes the activities in simple land transactions.

Investment in Commercial Buildings refers to the investment in residential buildings, workshops, warehouses, hotels, official buildings, houses completed pulled down and returned, unified construction buildings and related service establishment for sale or rent by real estate development enterprises.

Residential Buildings refers to houses simply for resident, including villas, apartments, dormitory for staff and workers and students. It excludes the basements without people living in residential buildings.

Commercial Buildings refer to buildings for external business belongs to commercial, grain, supply-sales and catering departments and so on. Such as buildings of holiday villages, hotels, shops, grain shops, bookstores, supply-sales stores, catering restaurants, vegetable stores, gas stations and daily facilities stores.

Developed Land Area Completed refers to the land area of land development and prophase development projects completed, which can carry out construction or remise.

Purchased Land Area in Current Year refers to the land area accessible by various means in reporting period.

Area of Commercialized Housing Sold refers to total contracted area of commercialized housing (i.e. area of floor space as designated in the formal contracts signed by both sides)during the reference time. It constitutes floor space of completed housing and floor space of future housing.

Value of Commercialized Housing Sold refers to the total contracted value (i.e. value of sales/purchase for selling/purchase of commercialized housing as designated in the contract signed by both sides) during the reference time. This indicator has the same coverage as the area of commercialized housing sold, which constitutes as the area of commercialize housing sold, which constitutes floor space of completed housing and floor space of future housing.

Space of Commercial Houses for Sale refers to the space of commercial houses which are completed, for sale or rent but not yet in report period. It includes space of houses completed in former years and this period, but excludes space of houses completed during report period but unable to be sell or rent, such as houses completed pulled down and returned, unified construction buildings, public complementary buildings, houses for real estate companies owner-occupied and houses for turnover.

Actually Got Capital refers to capital that enterprises actually got from all the investors, including capital in kind, in form of money, as intangible assets participating enterprises such as inventions or technological achievements.

第十一篇

城市概况

GENERAL SURVEY OF CITIES

（校对编辑：张　芸）

11－1 广西各市市辖区社会经济主要指标（2017年）

指 标	Item	南宁市 Nanning	柳州市 Liuzhou	桂林市 Guilin
一、人口规模	Population Size			
常住人口（万人）	Permanent Population (10 000 persons)	433.49	224.55	157.23
其中：城镇人口（万人）	Urban population (10 000 persons)	335.62	189.14	122.56
年末户籍人口（万人）	Total Household Population at the Year-end (10 000 persons)	375.38	179.68	130.4
其中：女	Famale	183.52	88.82	65.25
年平均人口（万人）	Annual Average Population (10 000 persons)	372.73	179.07	130.13
年出生人口（人）	Annual Birth Population (person)	44020	31179	23459
年死亡人口（人）	Annual Mortality Population (person)	9883	29061	23206
年末总户数（万户）	Total Households at the Year-end (10 000 households)	117.66	55.31	40.62
二、资源环境	Natural Resources & Environment			
（一）土地	Land			
行政区域土地面积（平方公里）	Gross Area (sq.km)	9947	1017	2805
建成区面积（平方公里）	Developed Area	315	225	104
现状建设用地面积（平方公里）	Area of Construction (sq.km)	307.88	225.09	104.39
其中：居住用地	Area of Living Space	90.65	62.4	30.63
公共管理与公共服务设施用地	Area of Public administration & public service facilities	43.31	21	12.02
工业用地	Area of Industry	33.95	53.19	18.32
绿化覆盖面积（公顷）	Area of Forestation (hectare)	41766	10743	4426
其中：建成区面积	Area of Forestation of Developed Area	13327	9867	4200
绿地面积（公顷）	Area of Green Space (hectare)	39958	9293	3975
公园绿地面积（公顷）	Park Green Area	3968	2430	1145
公园面积（公顷）	Water Resources	2931	1645	619
（二）水资源	Volume of Water Supply (10 000 cu.m)			
供水总量（万立方米）	Volume of Water Use (10 000 cu.m)	203785.08	105030	79020
用水总量（万立方米）	Economic Development	203785.08	105030	79020
三、经济发展	Gross Domestic Product			
（一）地区生产总值（当年价，万元）	Gross Domestic Product (current prices, 10 000 yuan)	34107409	22256613	8119388
其中：第一产业增加值	Primary Industry	2108799	560906	507699
第二产业增加值	Secondary Industry	13695677	12798304	2767121
#工业增加值	Industrial Added Value	10364965	11913002	2063127
第三产业增加值	Tertiary Industry	18302933	8897403	4844568
人均地区生产总值（元）	Per Capita Gross Domestic Product (yuan)	79292	99703	51963
地区生产总值（2015年价格，万元）	Gross Domestic Product (Prices in the year of 2015, 10 000 yuan)	32578283	21619050	8148363

注：本篇为快报数，出版前尚未经国家统计局审核反馈（数据搜集时间为2018年8月25日）。
Note: The data in this chapter are from quick statistics data, has not yet to be verified by the date of publication (August 25th, 2018).

Main Social & Economic Indicators of Municipal Districts of Cities （2017）

梧州市 Wuzhou	北海市 Beihai	防城港市 Fangcheng-gang	钦州市 Qinzhou	贵港市 Guigang	玉林市 Yulin	百色市 Baise	贺州市 Hezhou	河池市 Hechi	来宾市 Laibin	崇左市 Chongzuo
81.77	72.76	56.65	128.58	160.01	113.35	40.01	106.18	93.24	96.97	34.3
60.65	57.48	35.9	65.95	91.04	72.87	25.16	51.3	46.45	47.2	16.86
79.46	67.04	57.97	150.82	201.49	111.81	36.31	120.12	100.88	113.36	37.34
38.68	33.2	26.83	67.94	96.14	52.76	17.99	57.59	48.72	53.57	17.33
79.42	66.58	57.81	150.28	201.14	111.11	36.28	119.8	100.96	112.98	37.29
14386	11651	11570	31383	36145	21769	7016	23405	17157	25854	7488
12557	8045	8034	21209	27117	10629	7032	15571	17513	16094	6133
24.64	18.93	14.59	33.88	60.4	30.82	9.88	32.06	31.34	31.15	10.99
1793	1227	2836	4839	3533	1265	3718	5517	6203	4363	2918
58	77	41	95	79	74	51	38	42	49	32
56.78	89.13	40.52	89.98	76.3	70.61	47.23	38.04	41.75	49.33	20.03
19.35	27	7.55	22.79	23.91	26.6	15.62	12.67	12.14	11.73	6.42
5.86	9.8	2.77	7.45	6.89	9.62	4.37	5.62	3.8	2.46	2.03
8.72	18.73	8.83	21.68	17.31	2.21	7.19	6.81	9.18	6.74	2.43
3320	3144	1507	12801	2718	3241	2176	1766	1449	1722	1320
2402	3144	1500	3498	2668	2956	1974	1608	1350	1652	1268
3265	2668	1339	11136	2343	3063	1983	1618	1203	1560	1100
664	494	521	470	605	1065	320	395	375	313	237
621	459	566	433	279	1014	161	395	251	60	94
	44600	33521	11600	123300	48671	27500	70400	47087	82448	22800
	44600	33521	11600	100600	48671	27500	70400	47087	82448	22800
6247607	9651455	5657685	5918520	4597731	4928736	2872060	3141921	2565998	2936789	1936177
177614	972969	489063	1226801	704042	406476	292363	516118	580631	655902	285620
3540849	5995692	3406177	2148881	1774988	1881609	1444657	1281713	587867	1020617	924954
3373070	5596236	3010822	1382534	1252058	1311238	1201296	826879	363283	661438	806855
2529144	2682794	1762445	2542838	2118701	2640651	1135040	1344090	1397500	1260270	725603
76837	133523	100438	46302	28910	43786	72054	29728	27606	30398	56747
5939311	8208389	5546519	5438652	4254932	4707256	2499321	3088744	2571595	2746160	1674627

11－1 续表 1

指 标	Item	南宁市 Nanning	柳州市 Liuzhou	桂林市 Guilin
地区生产总值增长率	Growth Rate of Gross Domestic Product (%)	8.2	6.7	-1.3
(二) 财政	Convernment Finance			
地方一般公共预算收入（万元）	Local Government Revenue (10 000 yuan)	2989632	1584716	884497
其中：税收收入	Various Taxes	2251514	1141365	459586
#企业所得税	Enterprise Income Taxes	333023	116379	81538
个人所得税	Individual Income Taxes	120067	38275	26807
地方一般公共预算支出（万元）	General Public Budget Expenditure of Local Government	4534875	2372183	1678846
其中：一般公共服务支出	Expenditure for General Public Services	417073	188921	201564
科学技术支出	Expenditure for Science & Technology	59859	33924	17086
教育支出	Expenditure for Education	784299	455413	305611
文化体育与传媒支出	Expenditure for Culture, Sport & Media	70835	35789	30136
医疗卫生与计划生育支出	Expenditure for Health Care & birth control	354318	239789	154197
节能环保支出	Expenditure for Energy Conservation & Environment Protection	140880	38595	21050
城乡社区支出	Expenditure for Community Affair in Urban & Rural Area	817765	430352	353948
交通运输支出	Expenditure for Transpotation	180943	39534	20889
社会保障和就业支出	Expenditure for Social Security & Employment	437954	249774	203741
住房保障支出	Housing security expenditure	129953	79411	43922
(三) 金融	Finance			
年末金融机构人民币各项存款余额（万元）	Year-end Deposit Balance of Financial Institutions in RMB (10 000 yuan)	86155312	31309204	20379557
其中：住户存款余额	Household Savings Deposits	29245457	10626048	8692538
年末金融机构人民币各项贷款余额（万元）	Year-end Loans Balance of Financial Institutions in RMB (10 000 yuan)	100521464	20808351	12433176
(四) 固定资产投资	Investment in Fixed Assets			
固定资产投资（不含农户）（万元）	Total Investment in Fixed Assets (excluding rural indivduals, 10 000 yuan)	36150747	20194576	7525625
房地产开发投资（万元）	Investment in Real Estate Development	9009338	3511868	2418874
其中：住宅	Residential Buildings	6438951	2648151	1943185
全年新增固定资产（万元）	Newly Increased Fixed Assets (10 000 yuan)	19553381	10941654	2761336
(五) 房地产	Real Estate			
商品房销售面积（万平方米）	Floor Space of Selling Commercial Houses (10 000 sq.m)	1390.18	416.37	353.15
其中：住宅	Residential Building	1159.44	373.63	335.64
#别墅、高档公寓	Villa, High-grade Apartment	17.45	1.81	0.5

continued

梧州市 Wuzhou	北海市 Beihai	防城港市 Fangcheng-gang	钦州市 Qinzhou	贵港市 Guigang	玉林市 Yulin	百色市 Baise	贺州市 Hezhou	河池市 Hechi	来宾市 Laibin	崇左市 Chongzuo
2.5	10.45	7.3	9.62	9.44	8.69	11.1	5.41	9.19	6.6	10.4
534085	574747	307668	411123	285022	471376	188214	214958	147310	149500	85984
257572	409460	213269	253840	201246	289620	109174	118518	82661	77356	48970
30825	50851	16253	19693	23100	28765	12130	9673	7838	6848	9489
7481	8164	5346	6705	8517	10488	6385	4286	5543	2858	2108
1176667	1092611	733977	1145177	1082118	1046041	680412	993567	799948	748570	644573
74338	149946	95737	79735	105964	124844	65775	97184	103175	64396	56855
5572	33622	2291	6615	2319	11390	12241	3332	3630	1228	1760
160051	170981	89660	269886	200644	187526	127919	175803	141107	132908	76635
11305	14998	8637	15678	8626	13592	8830	14582	11009	6016	6337
100577	85955	54852	108405	137862	109352	64655	102289	97070	78056	43049
5297	12987	10995	11417	8237	33984	28129	14801	59474	9620	9056
420862	243347	245740	220909	190856	146907	73432	115727	42030	62836	151883
40329	20717	8054	49808	28368	37018	12353	45867	21910	15059	13243
115027	46253	67751	114671	85136	119804	60998	94678	60617	83177	49586
41337	37156	12320	46118	43651	45849	24928	62998	32737	27619	29725
5002934	6950590	4110051	5861026	6158122	7196620	3564375	4393499	4128114	3471299	2097436
2534932	3727060	1996071	3231677	3880188	4116230	1634441	2216222	2592016	1576681	818011
3499511	5244187	4960052	4662327	4422993	5090855	2632327	2837509	2572631	2716445	1312169
6385630	8439480	4872829	6408267	5104307	5555116	1800065	4332624	1227135	1961678	1651870
357424	1628057	616622	501351	733519	1014697	455757	274214	297581	300642	219231
253903	1314565	475629	394051	578998	833216	325004	235953	244654	226031	153946
3630643	4926217	2675600	3722765	1710510	3641582	703741	2165918	490495	696904	807081
81.23	315.26	217.41	120.26	143.61	263.12	84.6	83.13	78.46	94.28	46.3
75.85	302.25	196.41	116.54	127.79	244.48	77.39	78.87	72.35	88.63	41.5
0.34	3.98	1.73	2.01	6.22	2.28	1.24	2.69	0	0	5.02

11−1 续表 2

指 标	Item	南宁市 Nanning	柳州市 Liuzhou	桂林市 Guilin
商品房销售额（万元）	Total Sales of Commercial Buildings (10 000 yuan)	11466146	3529993	2201808
其中：住宅	Residential Building	9552701	3063171	2058456
#别墅、高档公寓	Villa, High-grade Apartment	266051	27884	6290
待售面积（万平方米）	Space of Commercial Buildings for Sale (10 000 sq.m)	233.94	52.49	53.22
（六）对外贸易	Foreign Trade			
外商直接投资合同项目（个）	Number of Projects for Contracted Foreign Direct Investment (unit)	70	46	18
当年实际使用外资金额（万美元）	Amount of Foreign Capital Actually Utilized (USD 10 000)	22487	65959	4179
（七）规模以上工业	Industrial Enterprises above Designated Size			
工业企业数（个）	Number Industrial Enterprises (unit)	729	642	193
其中：内资企业	Domestic Investment	664	610	175
#国有企业	State-owned Enterprises	16	7	6
私营企业	Private Enterprises	406	415	70
港、澳、台商投资企业	Enterprises with Funds from Hong Kong, Macao & Taiwan	34	13	5
外商投资企业	Foreign Funded Enterprises	31	19	13
工业总产值（当年价，万元）	Industrial Gross Output Value (current prices, 10 000 yuan)	31823134	46293927	6227093
其中：内资企业	Domestic Investment	25135686	32523338	5795965
#国有企业	State-owned Enterprises	1225074	1185154	590554
私营企业	Private Enterprises	14332794	11877191	894262
港、澳、台商投资企业	Enterprises with Funds from Hong Kong, Macao & Taiwan	5556361	1840626	87928
外商投资企业	Foreign Funded Enterprises	1131087	11929963	343200
平均用工人数（万人）	Average Number of Employees (10 000 persons)	18.8	22.29	6.34
固定资产合计（万元）	Annual Average Balance of Net Value of Fixed Assets (10 000 yuan)	6276390	7987133	2235830
流动资产合计（万元）	Annual Average Balance of Value of Circulating Funds (10 000 yuan)	10742994	17492994	3650747
主营业务收入（万元）	Income of Major Business (10 000 yuan)	29730117	42469231	5346156
主营业务成本（万元）	Cost of Major Business (10 000 yuan)	23670359	36819083	4157384
主营业务税金及附加（万元）	Tax & Extra Charges on Income of Major Business	643952	1122004	63218
利润总额（万元）	Total After-tax Profits (10 000 yuan)	1727236	1794382	467111
本年应交增值税（万元）	Value Added Taxes Receivable in This Year (10 000 yuan)	606887	938204	164698
（八）贸易	Trade			
社会消费品零售总额（万元）	Total Retail Sales of Consumer Goods (10 000 yuan)	19157836	9902509	5720836

continued

梧州市 Wuzhou	北海市 Beihai	防城港市 Fangcheng-gang	钦州市 Qinzhou	贵港市 Guigang	玉林市 Yulin	百色市 Baise	贺州市 Hezhou	河池市 Hechi	来宾市 Laibin	崇左市 Chongzuo
390885	1923192	939853	467123	809822	1252977	419597	331263	319483	268028	204259
356425	1803102	810154	439220	705362	1115525	359970	302037	267530	235750	169307
4563	47305	6945	9574	43489	17197	12357	7868	0	0	34560
106.92	170.28	55.75	113.71	7.41	40.38	30.58	31.51	23.79	49.86	5.87
8	9	2	5	4	7	1	0	4	1	1
1085	8445	74	23188	2465	1938	40	0	224	2053	87
187	137	97	147	277	114	47	129	67	82	38
151	109	81	130	260	105	43	120	64	76	30
3	2	1	2	1	4	2	1	1	1	2
77	60	50	82	183	72	15	89	24	41	18
26	20	7	12	11	5	3	8	2	4	1
10	8	9	5	6	4	1	1	1	2	7
14196134	23223078	14875399	11858470	4301833	4321936	3208355	2492970	1132389	2778143	2414617
12311185	17944566	8909438	10105615	3778942	2205979	3074636	2419912	1062545	2682884	1452499
271933	308743	187866	37792	331202	294401	429530	107952	2462	283960	248863
5601800	3660238	5711856	3378013	2066918	852703	435585	1404134	241440	672584	513637
1289485	4536184	255125	742188	240960	74884	133719	50334	50242	18246	106981
595464	742328	5710836	1010667	281931	2041073	0	22724	19602	77013	855137
6.56	6.11	2.33	3.97	4.33	3.53	2.2	2.21	2.26	1.96	1.41
2424055	2907477	5953253	2925686	1433852	1041210	1439349	677822	838227	1916691	796562
2455718	4727719	4692468	3281991	2769308	2183961	1196508	1222088	1134932	1237624	911203
12903760	22511969	11925181	11174957	4164031	4115690	2656407	2234531	1264530	2203693	1876496
10383112	18755590	10628959	9149106	3788880	3487867	2456066	1851895	983025	2063441	1271253
74294	991516	39788	678588	20235	26193	12526	13736	4644	8390	14445
1511211	2426603	822310	657407	175395	228430	51571	154746	158764	-68112	500011
591432	783138	293794	413846	113123	100495	56946	67298	42628	51957	44502
2279922	1609208	741937	2010052	2791944	3383775	864761	961660	1306908	798595	304764

11－1 续表 3

指 标	Item	南宁市 Nanning	柳州市 Liuzhou	桂林市 Guilin
限额以上批发零售业法人企业数（个）	Number of Enterprises above Designated Size in Wholesale & Retail Trades (unit)	915	398	170
其中：零售业	Retail Trade	498	196	115
限额以上批发零售业商品销售额（万元）	Total Sales of Enterprises above Designated Size in Wholesale & Retail Trades (10 000 yuan)	33929460	12146113	3619493
四、人民生活	People's Living Conditions			
（一）就业	Employment			
从业人员期末人数（城镇，人）	Total Employment at the Year-end (Urban, person)	874426	519916	266389
第一产业（农、林、牧、渔业）	Primary Industry (Farming, Forestry, Animal Husbandry & Fishery)	5843	2328	1061
第二产业	Secondary Industry	373806	322886	108991
其中：采矿业	Mining	101	76	545
制造业	Manufacturing	96759	133890	47397
电力、热力、燃气及水生产和供应业	Electricity, Gas & Water Production & Supply	48476	3902	2765
建筑业	Construction	228470	185018	58284
第三产业	Tertiary Industry	494777	194702	156337
其中：批发和零售业	Wholesale & Retail Trade	44055	16902	10597
交通运输、仓储及邮政业	Transportation, Storage & Postal	48685	14786	7662
住宿和餐饮业	Hotel & Catering Trade	19926	3531	6416
信息传输、软件和信息技术服务业	Information Transmission, Software Industries & Information Technology Services	13936	2686	3506
金融业	Finance	48005	8787	14353
房地产业	Real Estate	28347	13515	6235
租赁和商业服务业	Leasing & Commercial Services	30051	20989	15203
科学研究和技术服务业	Scientific Research & Technology Services	33352	9242	6591
水利、环境和公共设施管理业	Water Conservancy, Environment & Public Facility Management	16941	11324	5363
居民服务、修理和其他服务业	Resident & Other Services	1386	1243	863
教育	Education	83346	35125	31640
卫生和社会工作	Public Health & Social Work	46306	25436	17432
文化、体育和娱乐业	Culture, Sports & Entertainment	13342	2691	3961
公共管理、社会保障和社会组织	Public Administration & Social Organizations	67099	28445	26515
国际组织	International Organization	0	0	0
城镇私营和个体从业人员（人）	Private & Self-employed Individuals (person)	744838	534120	53970
城镇登记失业人数（人）	Registered Unemployment in Urban Areas (person)	23325	16230	3662

continued

梧州市 Wuzhou	北海市 Beihai	防城港市 Fangcheng-gang	钦州市 Qinzhou	贵港市 Guigang	玉林市 Yulin	百色市 Baise	贺州市 Hezhou	河池市 Hechi	来宾市 Laibin	崇左市 Chongzuo
154	128	50	94	101	141	70	57	72	47	27
105	93	35	60	64	82	58	39	53	30	20
1422716	1854063	1335578	1539429	1747998	2567153	1636440	845727	1083785	798522	538319
112757	107507	57808	133278	90109	101521	68560	59466	74573	63616	40515
204	4107	5365	1328	384	806	193	736	430	6550	409
51088	43416	14406	68113	24297	27412	23441	9910	19027	17054	10668
222	876	40	950	0	21	10449	28	4407	0	4026
45222	35340	5362	18645	14097	16477	5625	7113	8742	11527	4608
2717	1829	1742	2303	6559	2978	1754	2525	2368	1899	699
2927	5371	7262	46215	3641	7936	5613	244	3510	3628	1335
61465	59984	38037	63837	65428	73303	44926	48820	55116	40012	29438
3390	3637	849	3540	4346	4575	3518	1618	2938	1402	1494
3928	3608	6416	3679	3720	3052	6255	1704	4619	1580	1083
834	2239	761	743	476	976	397	122	673	212	413
1251	1393	1067	1427	1313	3167	2537	1097	2434	1089	1352
4482	6051	1784	1842	5666	5635	2119	4993	3392	2914	5620
2242	2572	986	1838	990	3371	1138	901	1439	1093	732
1332	2149	1265	1648	674	2944	779	2302	1253	1162	1940
2228	2107	699	1197	1257	2378	1021	1183	1033	1124	471
2318	3020	1735	2084	272	2851	1828	1205	1213	374	160
0	219	91	60	434	196	203	68	138	46	27
12327	11579	6338	17780	15682	17687	8098	13583	11439	11486	5911
11171	6315	4292	10409	12450	12458	6523	6126	10182	5937	2634
1122	1012	282	482	345	1042	496	577	632	415	305
14840	14083	11472	17108	17803	12971	10014	13341	13731	11178	7296
0	0	0	0	0	0		0		0	0
109875	325992	74747	43427	243290	263654	15767	117559	99613	176282	30736
4732	3265	1880	1559	1457	1066	646	4639	3006	1026	1590

11－1　续表 4

指　标	Item	南宁市 Nanning	柳州市 Liuzhou	桂林市 Guilin
（二）收入	Income			
在岗职工平均人数（万人）	Average Number of Working Staff & Workers (10 000 persons)	79.33	48.56	21.63
在岗职工工资总额（万元）	Total Wages of Working Staff & Workers (10 000 yuan)	6072517.5	3121175.3	1503753.2
五、公共服务	Public Service			
（一）教育	Education			
中等职业教育学校数（所）	Number of Secondary Schools for Vocational Education (unit)	65	20	13
普通中学数（所）	Number of Regular Secondary Schools (unit)	219	85	60
普通小学数（所）	Number of Primary Schools (unit)	525	195	160
中等职业教育专任教师数（人）	Number of Full-time Teachers of Secondary Schools for Vocational Education (person)	9594	2600	800
普通中学专任教师数（人）	Number of Full-time Teachers of Regular Secondary Schools (person)	16034	7943	5357
普通小学专任教师数（人）	Number of Full-time Teachers of Primary Schools (person)	21695	9177	6812
中等职业教育在校学生数（人）	Student Enrollment of Secondary Schools for Vocational Education	289661	65118	19004
普通中学在校学生数（万人）	Student Enrollment of Regular Secondary Schools (10 000 persons)	23.9	11.57	7.48
普通小学在校学生数（万人）	Student Enrollment of Primary Schools (10 000 persons)	39.16	16.54	11.44
（二）文体	Culture & Sports			
剧场、影剧院数（个）	Cinemas & Theatres (unit)	23	17	18
公共图书馆数（个）	Number of Public Libraries (unit)	14	6	3
公共图书馆图书藏量（万册）	Total Collection of Public Libraries (10 000 copies)	627.87	189.64	317.8
体育场馆数（个）	Gymnasiums (unit)	42	6	18
（三）医疗	Medical			
医疗卫生机构数（个）	Number of Hospitals & health institutions (unit)	2747	1057	1088
其中：医院数（个）	Number of Hospitals	82	47	29
医疗卫生机构床位数（张）	Total Number of Beds in Hospitals & health institutions (bed)	34611	15812	9181
其中：医院床位数（张）	Number of Beds in Hospitals	28786	13566	7090
卫生技术人员数（人）	Number of health technical personnel (person)	50709	22542	15425
其中：执业（助理）医师数（人）	Number of Doctors (Certified physicians & certified assistant physicians)	18474	7598	5443
注册护士（人）	Registered Nurses (person)	22959	10448	7217
（四）社会保障	Social Security			
城镇职工基本养老保险参保人数（人）	Number of Urban Staff & Workers Joined Basic Pension Insurance (person)	1066256	855243	544228
城乡居民基本养老保险参保人数（人）	Number of Persons Joined the Urban Basic Health Care Program (person)	798960	290644	274442

continued

梧州市 Wuzhou	北海市 Beihai	防城港市 Fangcheng-gang	钦州市 Qinzhou	贵港市 Guigang	玉林市 Yulin	百色市 Baise	贺州市 Hezhou	河池市 Hechi	来宾市 Laibin	崇左市 Chongzuo
9.99	9.47	4.87	12.45	7.9	9.85	6.76	5.33	6.77	5.37	3.64
607694.1	570290.4	330214.8	739870.7	517502.3	687322	436673.6	360986.8	457314.5	351031.7	241820.1
12	5	1	6	8	12	8	4	5	6	5
35	54	28	50	83	56	18	45	45	41	14
137	101	197	371	353	240	51	158	185	114	23
496	676	117	590	458	724	376	423	575	417	183
2909	4260	2033	4800	9071	4944	1748	3941	3356	1642	1351
3865	3412	2835	6680	8722	4862	1973	5549	4127	4998	1522
15200	18554	3740	13718	13146	23406	16400	18917	16298	13560	2968
4.6	5.34	3.4	10.58	14.7	8.22	3.39	6	5.7	6.54	2
7.09	8.3	5.57	14.95	17.29	11.87	3.53	10.99	8.12	9.03	2.96
11	11	6	8	4	10	4	2	4	3	2
1	2	3	2	4	2	1	2	2	2	1
60.27	47.2	30.7	296.5	67.35	76.54	34.96	28.84	37.16	44	16.81
2	2	1	11	3	5	2	4	4	7	8
480	574	382	501	1703	804	132	588	569	475	235
23	14	7	13	25	16	7	16	14	9	8
6369	3474	2539	7501	7071	8796	4002	4733	7985	4910	1748
5702	2747	1740	4311	5190	7267	3311	3429	6380	2985	1059
12862	5989	3722	9596	8789	10585	5281	5996	8938	5362	2483
3131	2118	1308	1653	2861	3576	1662	2076	2854	1763	717
4890	2672	1537	4269	3893	4920	2624	2553	4075	2238	1070
261083	96220	91982	70468	105271	28228	270238	108270	64259	88875	60160
176027	107073	125348	432400	598984	270816	1719558	362608	348870	305793	124323

11－1 续表 5

指 标	Item	南宁市 Nanning	柳州市 Liuzhou	桂林市 Guilin
城镇职工基本医疗保险参保人数（人）	Number of Workers Joined the Urban Basic Health Care Program (person)	827626	719533	443323
城镇居民基本医疗保险参保人数（人）	Number of Persons Joined the Urban Basic Health Care Program (person)	2501416	1143343	897124
失业保险参保人数（人）	Number of Persons Joined Unemployment Insurance (person)	468008	356190	254895
工伤保险参保人数（人）	Number of Persons Joined Industrial Injury Insurance (person)	530370	430317	279277
生育保险参保人数（人）	Number of Persons Joined Bearing Insurance (person)	504201	353656	269166
城镇居民最低生活保障人数（人）	Number of Urban Residents under Lowest Cost-of-living Level (person)	5029	8990	11668
（五）公共安全	Public Safety			
交通事故死亡人数（人）	Death of Traffic Accidents (person)	194	95	46
交通事故损失额（万元）	Losses of Traffic Accidents (10 000 yuan)	305	31	80
火灾事故死亡人数（人）	Death of Fire Accidents (person)	1	4	0
火灾事故损失额（万元）	Losses of Fire Accidents (10 000 yuan)	2091	570	387
刑事案件立案数（起）	Number of Criminal Cases Registered (case)	57811	13482	12262
刑事罪犯人数（人）	Number of Criminals (person)	4872	3331	2008
其中：青少年人数（年龄14-25周岁）（人）	Youth (14- 25 years old)	952	495	179
六、基础设施	Infrastructure			
（一）交通运输	Transportation			
年末实有公共汽（电）车营运车辆数（辆）	Year-end Total Operating Public Buses & Trolleys (unit)	3575	1385	774
公共汽（电）车客运总量（万人次）	Passenger Traffic Volume of Public Buses & Trolleys (10 000 person-times)	38141.61	21691.3	19672.72
年末实有出租汽车运营车数（辆）	Year-end Total Number of Taxi (unit)	6853	2056	2249
（二）邮电	Postal & Telecommunication			
年末邮政局（所）数（处）	Number of Post Offices in the Year-end (unit)	113	49	53
（三）生活设施	Living Facilities			
年末排水管道长度（公里）	Length of Sewer Pipelines at the Year-end (km)	1720	1620	868
年末供水综合生产能力（万立方米/日）	Comprehensive Productive Capacity of Water Supply at the Year-end (10 000 cu.m/day)	172	150.6	44
售水量（万吨）	Volume of Sold Water (10 000 tons)	45651.34	45245.15	12290.53
其中：居民家庭用水量（万吨）	For Residential Household Use	29375.49	11270.79	7591.31
供气总量（人工煤气、天然气）（万立方米）	Total Volume of Gas Supply Including Manufactured & Natural Gas (10 000 cu.m)	31488.8	13057.52	6783.18
其中：居民家庭用气量（万立方米）	Residential Use	9406.72	5958.85	2475.18
液化石油气供气总量（吨）	Total Volume of Liquid Petrol Gas Supply (ton)	62941	39071	19522
其中：居民家庭用量（吨）	Residential Use	62886	20232	18710

continued

梧州市 Wuzhou	北海市 Beihai	防城港市 Fangcheng-gang	钦州市 Qinzhou	贵港市 Guigang	玉林市 Yulin	百色市 Baise	贺州市 Hezhou	河池市 Hechi	来宾市 Laibin	崇左市 Chongzuo
194785	152411	76279	500601	112315	136429	3173593	100406	56150	65933	45053
573240	504251	103863	1164100	1722480	107393	3690502	1044545	817268	828229	46743
81882	85335	50461	17625	49115	65586	92186	47773	27490	27344	22366
98015	94932	61860	29800	86515	104238	152080	58958	35966	25024	35182
96080	88737	42753	33300	65550	93867	142899	54878	35479	53119	33325
3089	2547	2029	9816	1673	2536	12400	7161	1458	3171	953
30	18	21	27	78	48	27	61	113	33	26
7	7	31	20	41	36	24	45	40	19	21
0	0	0	2	0	0	0	0	0	0	0
1070	0	135	110	145	212	217	180	96	228	27
2881	0	1808	3026	926	22	1826	2296	551	2047	555
527	1951	1053	1036	1273	1467	821	1253	738	838	274
34	432	68	287	238	261	297	310	95	108	46
419	521	300	127	289	185	215	352	248	509	92
6835.87	2162	1433		1627	3356	2423.96	1016	3701.8	3157.7	366.74
806	555	335	192	330	699	509	300	475	758	71
15	16	20	36	32	17	16	28	43	30	11
473	913	562	968	475	805	406	327	813	574	308
40.5	37.73	17.6	31.38	24.44	37.5	15	10	32.5	12	5
6006.97	6838.77	4352.37	5340.09	3910.76	5998.02	3177.21	2326.6	3888	2620	1446
3367.51	3670.52	1710.84	3242.56	2464	3889.28	2095.56	1541.3	2778	2235	846
3999.46	4200	1223.89	2326.27	1362.08	3618	952.67	1020.8	302.92	965	116.64
860.08	2540	397.71	941.73	787.8	1680	259.51	11.98	205.4	439.43	116.64
7846	20002	10381	11420	14540	22800	6462	10800	9264	3995	3411
7831	20000	9862	11059	14535	21500	6439	7490	8621	3995	3410

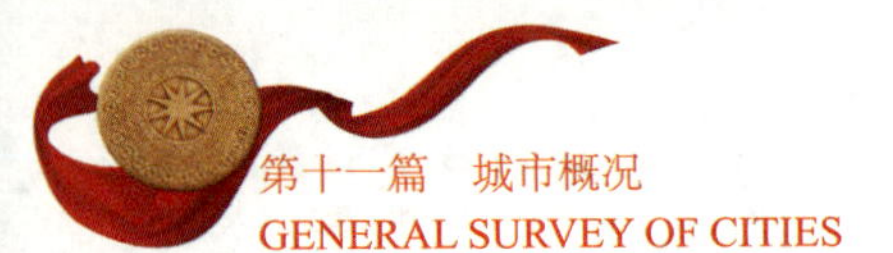

主要统计指标解释

建成区面积　指城市行政区内实际已成片开发建设、市政公用设施和公共设施基本具备的区域。对核心城市，它包括集中连片的部分以及分散的若干个已经成片建设起来，市政公用设施和公共设施基本具备的地区；对一城多镇来说，它包括由几个连片开发建设起来的，市政公用设施和公共设施基本具备的地区组成。因此建成区范围，一般是指建成区外轮廓线所能包括的地区，也就是这个城市实际建设用地所达到的范围。

居住用地　指住宅和相应服务设施的用地。

公共管理与公共服务设施用地　指行政、文化、教育、体育、卫生等机构和设施的用地，不包括居住用地中的服务设施用地。

工业用地　指工矿企业的生产车间、库房及其附属设施用地，包括专用铁路、码头和附属道路、停车场等用地，不包括露天矿用地。

绿化覆盖面积　指城市中的乔木、灌木、草坪等所有植被的垂直投影面积。包括公园绿地、防护绿地、生产绿地、附属绿地、其他绿地的绿化种植覆盖面积、屋顶绿化覆盖面积以及零散树木的覆盖面积，不含各类绿地中的水域面积以及没有被植被覆盖的面积（硬化道路、无屋顶绿化的建筑物等）。乔木树冠下重迭的灌木和草本植物不能重复计算。

绿地面积　指报告期末用作园林和绿化的各种绿地面积。包括公园绿地、生产绿地、防护绿地、附属绿地和其他绿地的面积。

公园绿地面积　指城市中向公众开放的、以游憩为主要功能，有一定的游憩设施和服务设施，同时有健全生态、美化景观、防灾减灾等综合作用的绿化用地。

城市居民最低生活保障人数　指在报告期末，家庭平均收入在当地规定的最低生活保障线以下的城市居民，并已领取补助经费的人数。包括“三无对象”，失业人员和在职、下岗、退休人员等。

道路面积只包括路面面积和与道路相通的广场、桥梁、停车场面积。不包括街心花坛、侧石、人行道和路肩的面积。

年末排水管道长度　指年末所有排水总管、干管、支管、检查井及连接井进出口等长度之和。计算时应按单管计算，即在同一条街道上如有两条或两条以上并排的排水管道时，应按每条排水管道的长度相加计算。

年末供水综合生产能力　指年末按供水设施取水、净化、送水、出厂输水干管等环节设计能力计算的综合生产能力。包括在原设计能力的基础上，经挖、革、改增加的生产能力。计算时，以四个环节中最薄弱的环节为主确定能力。原则上按设计能力填报，对于经过更新改造后，实际生产能力与设计能力相差很大的，按实际能力填报。

供水总量　指报告期内供水企业（单位）供出的全部水量，包括有效供水量和漏损水量。有效供水量指水厂将水供出厂外后，各类用户实际使用到的水量，包括售水量和免费供水量。

年末实有公共汽（电）车营运车辆数　指年末实际运营的公共汽车、公共电车的数量。

公共汽（电）车客运总量　指一年内公共汽车、公共电车总共搭载的人次。

年末实有出租汽车运营车数　指已经领取出租汽车专用牌照的运营车辆，包括技术完好的、在修的、长期行驶的以及拟报废尚未经上级机关批准的车辆。

Explanatory Notes on Main Statistical Indicators

Developed Area refers to lands expropriated in urban administrative areas and sectors actually constructed and developed for non-agricultural production and living, it includes continuous parts in downtown area and lands for city construction that spread around outskirts and have close relation with city and have general perfect public administrative facilities(such as aerodrome, waste water treatment works and communication stations).

Area of Land for Residence refers to lands for construction in cities, including residential buildings and buildings up to residential quarters and accessorial public service facilities, roads, green land and so on.

Land for Public Facilities refers to lands for construction of institutions or facilities of administration, economy, culture, education, health care, sports, scientific research, designing services and so on serving the society in cities.

Land for Industry refers to lands for construction of productive workshops, storages, yards and buildings of industry and mining enterprises in cities.

Coverage Area of Plantation in Developed Areas refers to the area of vertical projections of trees, shrubs and perennial herb for plantation managed by various units in developed areas. It includes plantation covered area of roads outside gardens and green areas(separation zones beside roads, central green islands and coverage area of boulevards and sideway trees)and coverage area of single trees.

Area of Green Areas refers to the area of all kinds of green land used as gardens and green areas by the end of reporting period, including the area of park green land, production green land, protection green land, accessorial green land and other kinds of green land.

Park Green Area refers to green areas open to the public for amusement and rest with the facilities of amusement, rest and services. Its function includes perfecting ecology, beautifying landscape, and preventing and reducing disaster. Park green areas include comprehensive park, community park, theme park, linear park and roadside green space. Total areas of comprehensive park, topic park and belt-shaped is the area of park

Number of Residents with Lowest Cost-of-living Protected refers to number of residents draw the lowest security cost in cities developing the system of lowest cost-of-living of residents, including persons without fixed habitation and work and effective identity, unemployed persons, in-service and lay-off staff, retired persons and so on.

Total Length of Sewer Pipelines Sewer pipelines refer to system made up by pipelines and their appurtenant works for collecting and discharging polluted water, waste water and rain water, including artery pipelines, branch pipelines and lines leading to treatment works. All of the pipelines operating for drainage should be counted as sewer pipeline system, wherever they are built. According to nature of drainage, pipelines can be divided into sewer pipe, rain pipe and combined pipe.

Comprehensive Productive Capacity of Water Supply refers to the comprehensive productive capacity of catching water, cleaning, transportation and supply of water sources owned by various units and tap water works belong to tap water companies of city construction department system, and it gives priority to the weakest link of these four links. The increased capacity from overwork should not be figured in.

Volume of Water Supply refers to the total volume of water supply by the tap water works, including the effective water supply and loss.

Year-end Total Operating Public Buses & Trolleys refers to total number of vehicles of city public traffic enterprises able to operate. It includes vehicles in good condition, in mending, waiting for mending, stopping operating and planning to reject but not yet approved by superior departments. It excludes the non-operating vehicles such as tank trucks, trucks and other special vehicles belonging to public traffic enterprises, and also excludes passenger vehicles borrowed or rented in.

Year-end Total Operating Public Buses & Trolleys refers to total number of passengers. It includes person-times of passengers with common tickets, person-times of passengers with commutation tickets and person-times of passengers chartering buses or trolleys.

Year-end Total Number of Taxi refers to the total number of operating vehicles approved by relevant departments exclusively for renting business. It includes number of cars, vans and buses.

⑫

2018广西统计年鉴

第十二篇

对外经济贸易

FOREIGN ECONOMY & TRADES

（校对编辑：张　茵）

12—1 外贸进出口总额（1978—2017年）
Total Import & Export Value of Foreign Trade（1978—2017）

年 份 Year	按人民币计算（万元） Calculated by RMB (10 000 yuan)				按美元计算（万美元） Calculated by USD (USD 10 000)			
	进出口总额 Total Import & Export Value	出口总额 Total Export Value	进口总额 Total Import Value	差额顺差+、逆差- Balance +,-	进出口总额 Total Import & Export Value	出口总额 Total Export Value	进口总额 Total Import Value	差额顺差+、逆差- Balance +,-
1978	45783	42305	3478	38827	26931	24885	2046	22839
1980	57112	55234	1878	53356	37823	36579	1244	35335
1985	153619	109260	44359	64901	52310	37205	15105	22100
1990	429517	348906	80611	268295	89797	72944	16853	56091
1991	544732	443062	101670	341392	102351	83248	19103	64145
1992	903567	611189	292378	318811	163850	110831	53019	57812
1993	1197113	763413	433700	329713	207760	132491	75269	57222
1994	2119857	1380777	739080	641697	245983	160222	85761	74461
1995	2689369	1880944	808425	1072519	321111	224585	96526	128059
1996	2349656	1590216	759440	830776	283132	191620	91512	100108
1997	2543484	1975177	568307	1406870	306821	238266	68555	169711
1998	2469994	2001785	468209	1533576	298377	241817	56560	185257
1999	1451332	1032287	419045	613242	175322	124701	50621	74080
2000	1686986	1236078	450908	785170	203789	149319	54470	94849
2001	1487461	1022629	464832	557797	179715	123554	56161	67393
2002	2011854	1248137	763717	484420	243032	150775	92257	58518
2003	2642161	1630853	1011308	619545	319173	197007	122166	74841
2004	3550058	1983071	1566987	416084	428847	239554	189293	50261
2005	4182696	2322127	1860569	461558	518289	287741	230548	57193
2006	5257761	2835001	2422761	412240	667398	359863	307535	52328
2007	6915250	3811510	3103740	707770	927686	511317	416369	94948
2008	9041850	5019577	4022274	997303	1324179	735117	589062	146055
2009	9699570	5715622	3983955	1731667	1420599	837110	583490	253620
2010	11808365	6408922	5399443	1009480	1770609	960988	809621	151367
2011	14818350	7912949	6905395	1007554	2333084	1245859	1087224	158635
2012	18525688	9722669	8803012	919657	2947369	1546841	1400527	146314
2013	20020330	11398148	8622181	2775967	3283690	1869499	1414191	455308
2014	24911476	14947146	9964330	4982816	4055305	2433004	1622301	810703
2015	31903077	17398601	14504476	2894125	5126215	2802570	2323645	478925
2016	31704215	15238340	16465875	-1227535	4789694	2302934	2486760	-183826
2017	38663414	18552015	20111398	-1559383	5721023	2745579	2975444	-229865

注：1. 外贸进出口数据自1999年起（含1999年）采用海关统计数据，外贸进出口数据自2015年起（含2015年）包含边民互市贸易数据。
2. 按当年12月汇率计算。

Note: 1. The imports & exports figure of the foreign trade have adopted customs statistics data since 1999 (including 1999).The total import and export value has included the border trade since 2015(including 2015).
2. The change rate of RMB yuan to US dollar is calculated as the change rate of December of current year.

12—2 主要年份外贸进出口总额（按贸易方式分）

Total Import & Export Value of Foreign Trade in Main Years (by Type of Trade)

单位：万美元 (USD 10 000)

项 目	Item	1995	2000	2005	2010	2013	2014	2015	2016 (万元)	2017 (万元)
合 计	**Total**	**321111**	**203789**	**518289**	**1770609**	**3283690**	**4055305**	**5126215**	**31704215**	**38663414**
一般贸易	Original Trade	261645	149839	358142	1068883	1491083	1466222	1426519	8284297	14235946
国家间、国际组织无偿援助和赠送的物资	Donation between Countries & from International Organizations		2	2	24	31	27		83	
华侨、港澳台同胞、外籍华人捐赠物资	Donation from Overseas Chinese Compatriots in Hong Kong, Macao & Foreign Chinese		3		11		18			
补偿贸易	Compensation Trade	3706								
来料加工装配贸易	Processing & Assembly Trade with Customers Materials	25112	16317	31841	23579	123424	325780	327683	1889135	1766039
进料加工贸易	Processing Trade with Imported Materials		21221	44497	151060	389449	512598	729633	4640842	6276506
寄售、代销贸易	Consign & Commission Trade		8	20						
边境小额贸易	Frontier Small Value Trade	24652	15013	70140	424094	1150876	1472781	1700124	7868045	8363041
来料加工装配进口的设备	Import Equipments for Processing & Assembly Trade with Customers Materials		7	311		37		22		
对外承包工程出口货物	Export Commodities for Contracted Projects with Foreign Countries & Regions		18	40	4675	2465	3688	7392	41508	30116
租赁贸易	Leasing Trade			2					1	33866
外商投资企业作为投资进口的设备物资	Import Equipments & Materials as Investment of Foreign Investment Enterprises		1134	9842	8697	2401	2539	433	3556	26227
易货贸易	Barter Trade	5996	5							
免税外汇商品	Tax Free Foreign Exchange Commodities		6							
保税监管场所进出境货物	Import & Export Commodities in Bonded Supervision Areas		156	3349	55857	68479	57449	127079	591498	680892
海关特殊监管区域物流货物	Logistics Goods in Customs Special Supervision Areas						213313	241867	1686912	880359
海关特殊监管区域进口设备	Imported Equipment in Customs Special Supervision Areas						410	263	2269	16779
其它	Others		60	103	33729	55445	480	565200	6696069	6353643

注：2016年起，外贸进出口数据以人民币计价。

Note: The data of import and export value of foreign trade was calculated by RMB since 2016.

12—3 主要年份外贸出口总额（按贸易方式分）
Total Export Value of Foreign Trade in Main Years (by Type of Trade)

单位：万美元 (USD 10 000)

项 目	Item	1995	2000	2005	2010	2013	2014	2015	2016 (万元)	2017 (万元)
合 计	**Total**	**224585**	**149319**	**287741**	**960988**	**1869499**	**2433004**	**2802570**	**15238340**	**18552015**
一般贸易	Original Trade	188402	118392	205852	462011	500380	498178	504131	3079074	5393717
国家间、国际组织无偿援助和赠送的物资	Donation Between Countries & from International Organizations			2	20	31	27		83	
华侨、港澳台同胞、外籍华人捐赠物资	Donation from Overseas Chinese Compatriots in Hong Kong, Macao & Foreign Chinese						18			
补偿贸易	Compensation Trade	3429								
来料加工装配贸易	Processing & Assembly Trade with Customers Materials	16037	7976	16583	11645	50131	148259	156800	847703	828798
进料加工贸易	Processing Trade with Imported Materials		14509	27498	109523	241636	299980	412947	2556821	3451510
寄售、代销贸易	Consign & Commission Trade		8	20						
边境小额贸易	Frontier Small Value Trade	11369	8351	37729	331945	1047220	1400883	1628344	7525758	7990166
对外承包工程出口货物	Export Commodities for Contracted Projects with Foreign Countries & Regions		18	40	4675	2465	3688	7392	41508	30116
租赁贸易	Leasing Trade			2					1	0
易货贸易	Barter Trade	5348	2							
保税监管场所进出境货物	Import & Export Commodities in Bonded Supervision Areas		59		12220	22903	13714	38436	84085	90633
海关特殊监管区域物流货物	Logistics Goods in Customs Special Supervision Areas						68203	39853	348169	283448
其它	Others		4	28949	26046	4733	54	14667	755138	483628

注：2016年起，外贸进出口数据以人民币计价。
Note: The data of import and export value of foreign trade was calculated by RMB since 2016.

12—4 主要年份外贸进口总额（按贸易方式分）
Total Import Value of Foreign Trade in Main Years（by Type of Trade）

单位：万美元 (USD 10 000)

项　目	Item	1995	2000	2005	2010	2013	2014	2015	2016（万元）	2017（万元）
合　计	**Total**	**96526**	**54470**	**230548**	**809621**	**1414191**	**1622301**	**2323645**	**16465875**	**20111398**
一般贸易	Original Trade	73243	31447	152290	606872	990703	968043	922387	5205224	8842230
国家间、国际组织无偿援助和赠送的物资	Donation between Countries & from Interna-tional Organizations		2		3					
华侨、港澳台同胞、外籍华人捐赠物资	Donation from Overseas Chinese Compatriots in Hong Kong, Macao & Foreign Chinese		3		11					
补偿贸易	Compensation Trade	277								
来料加工装配贸易	Processing & Assembly Trade with Customers Materials	9075	8341	15258	11934	73293	177521	170884	1041432	937241
进料加工贸易	Processing Trade with Imported Materials		6712	16999	41537	147813	212618	316686	2084021	2824996
寄售、代销贸易	Consign & Commission Trade									
边境小额贸易	Frontier Small Value Trade	13283	6662	32411	92149	103656	71898	71780	342287	372875
来料加工装配进口的设备	Import Equipments for Processing & Assembly Trade with Customers Materials		7	311	471	37		22		
租赁贸易	Leasing Trade									33866
外商投资企业作为投资进口的设备物资	Import Equipments & Materials as Invest-ment of Foreign Investment Enterprises		1134	9842	8697	2401	2539	433	3556	26227
易货贸易	Barter Trade	648	3							
保税监管场所进出境货物	Import & Export Commodities in Bonded Supervision Areas		97	3349	43638	45577	43735	88643	507413	590259
海关特殊监管区域物流货物	Logistics Goods in Customs Special Supervision Areas						145110	202014	1338743	596911
海关特殊监管区域进口设备	Imported Equipment in Customs Special Supervision Areas						410	263	2269	16779
其它	Others		62	88	4309	50711	427	550533	5940931	5870015

注：2016年起，外贸进出口数据以人民币计价。
Note: The data of import and export value of foreign trade was calculated by RMB since 2016.

12－5 主要年份外贸进出口总额（按企业性质分）

单位：万美元

项 目	Item	2009		2010		2011	
		出口 Export	进口 Import	出口 Export	进口 Import	出口 Export	进口 Import
总 计	**Total**	**837110**	**583490**	**960988**	**809621**	**1245859**	**1087224**
国有企业	State-owned Enterprises	101583	155850	126064	271035	195818	296411
外商投资企业	Foreign Funded Enterprises	127766	239424	203246	288202	264702	429415
#合作企业	Sino-foreign Cooperation	2678	88	2910	72	3193	220
合资企业	Sino-foreign Joint Venture	41970	51889	65776	86702	89585	156520
独资企业	Wholly Foreign-owned	83118	187447	134560	201429	171923	272676
民营企业	Civilian-owned Enterprises	607760	188037	631677	250187	785340	361012
#集体企业	Collective-owned Enterprises	15810	5175	17171	4812	17685	6588
私营企业	Private Enterprises	591803	182857	614196	245375	767196	354425
个体工商户	Individual-owned Business	146	5	311	0	460	0

注：2016年起，外贸进出口数据以人民币计价。
Note: The data of import and export value of foreign trade was calculated by RMB since 2016.

Total Import & Export Value in Main Years（by Nature of Enterprises）

(USD 10 000)

2012		2013		2014		2015		2016（万元）		2017（万元）	
出口 Export	进口 Import	出口 Export	进口 Import	出口 Export	进口 Import	出口 Export	进口 Import	出口 Export	进口 Import	出口 Export	进口 Import
1546841	**1400527**	**1869499**	**1414191**	**2433004**	**1622301**	**2802570**	**2323645**	**15238340**	**16465875**	**18552015**	**20111398**
239671	410500	238576	464816	309461	540816	297882	562402	1645782	3486276	1258119	4985329
354236	608451	366759	580622	437073	623157	442944	591354	2836282	3587751	3772075	5797114
2036	344	2559	1222	2533	544	1864	822	12434	4272	8599	2789
156513	282467	173573	301040	217059	364417	240394	343146	1518568	2272419	2187572	4079646
195687	325640	190628	278359	217481	258196	200686	247386	1305281	1311059	1575904	1714679
952935	381569	1264164	368753	1686470	458286	2047115	619658	10001358	3464390	13055750	3458460
13316	11643	10759	6944	12437	1260	12761	803	60764	1054	52656	1515
939203	369927	1253101	361788	1673675	457021	2033879	618846	9937953	3463142	13000579	3456870
415	0	304	21	358	4	475	10	2640	194	2515	76

12－6 广西同主要国家（地区）进出口商品总值（2017年）
Total Import & Export Value by Country & Region (2017)

单位：万元 (RMB 10 000)

进口原产国（地）Imported from Countries (Regions) of Origin	出口最终目的（地）Exported to Final Destination	进出口 Import & Export	出口 Export	进口 Import	2017年比2016年增减% 2017 as % of 2016 进出口 Import & Export	出口 Export	进口 Import
总　值	**Total**	**38663414**	**18552015**	**20111398**	**22.6**	**22.3**	**22.9**
亚洲	**Asia**	**26193376**	**14288082**	**11905294**	**10.4**	**13.5**	**6.9**
中国香港	Hong Kong, China	2613109	2507672	105437	43.1	38.4	661.9
印度	India	205741	162692	43048	58.0	46.8	121.8
印度尼西亚	Indonesia	673120	258962	414158	121.6	137.5	112.6
日本	Japan	492263	233303	258960	7.6	1.4	14.0
马来西亚	Malaysia	485996	178652	307343	55.9	51.9	58.4
菲律宾	the Philippines	434507	203482	231025	101.8	101.2	102.3
新加坡	Singapore	510569	403736	106833	58.1	64.2	38.5
韩国	Republic of Korea	411783	182271	229512	60.0	46.0	73.1
泰国	Thailand	465258	214784	250474	-57.3	46.7	-73.4
越南	Viet Nam	16262586	9300861	6961725	2.1	1.2	3.4
台湾省	Taiwan Province	1214296	130269	1084027	32.0	26.9	32.6
非洲	**Africa**	**1259960**	**404699**	**855261**	**124.6**	**88.0**	**147.4**
加蓬	Gabon	70368	3843	66525	544.0	312.7	565.5
南非	South Africa	613597	32280	581317	114.6	109.3	114.9
欧洲	**Europe**	**1704741**	**1146723**	**558018**	**39.7**	**72.7**	**0.3**
比利时	Belgium	63125	58053	5073	29.6	54.3	-54.1
英国	United Kingdom	203747	182348	21399	90.6	107.7	12.0
德国	Germany	308489	179100	129389	52.5	54.3	50.2
法国	France	104916	57457	47459	91.0	40.1	240.9
意大利	Italy	90454	63639	26815	44.0	51.4	29.0
荷兰	Netherlands	217257	212975	4282	44.0	68.1	-82.3
西班牙	Spain	198007	93637	104370	34.3	118.3	-0.1
芬兰	Finland	14603	4189	10415	-51.9	44.4	-62.0
瑞典	Sweden	31064	23405	7659	16.6	43.6	-25.9
俄罗斯	Russia	119162	61054	58108	-17.2	98.0	-48.6
拉丁美洲	**Latin America**	**4299991**	**442593**	**3857398**	**67.6**	**46.0**	**70.5**
北美洲	**North America**	**3690427**	**1901612**	**1788814**	**53.6**	**64.6**	**43.4**
加拿大	Canada	831819	96555	735264	50.3	91.1	46.2
美国	United States	2858608	1805058	1053550	54.5	63.4	41.4
大洋洲	**Oceanic**	**1514794**	**368307**	**1146487**	**42.8**	**52.9**	**39.8**
澳大利亚	Australia	1433025	340387	1092638	41.3	50.9	38.5
东南亚国家联盟	**Association of Southeast Asia**	**18938485**	**10624553**	**8313932**	**3.7**	**6.7**	**0.0**
欧洲联盟	**European Union**	**1435802**	**1038834**	**396968**	**49.0**	**71.4**	**11.1**
亚太经济合作组织	**Asia Pacific Economic Cooperation**	**31531319**	**16115769**	**15415550**	**17.2**	**17.5**	**16.9**

注：东南亚国家联盟包括：文莱、印度尼西亚、马来西亚、菲律宾、新加坡、泰国、越南、缅甸、柬埔寨、老挝。
欧洲联盟包括：比利时、丹麦、英国、德国、法国、爱尔兰、意大利、卢森堡、荷兰、希腊、葡萄牙、西班牙、奥地利、芬兰、瑞典、塞浦路斯、匈牙利、马耳他、波兰、爱沙尼亚、拉托维亚、立陶宛、斯洛文尼亚、捷克、斯洛伐克、罗马尼亚、保加利亚、克罗地亚。
亚太经济合作组织包括：文莱、香港、印度尼西亚、日本、马来西亚、菲律宾、新加坡、韩国、泰国、中华人民共和国、台湾省、智利、墨西哥、加拿大、美国、澳大利亚、新西兰、巴布亚新几内亚、越南、俄罗斯、秘鲁。

Note: Association of Southeast Asia includes: Brunei, Indonesia, Malaysia, the Philippines, Singapore, Thailand, Viet Nam, Myanmar, Cambodia, Laos.
European Union includes: Belgium, Denmark, United Kingdom, Germany, France, Ireland, Italy, Luxembourg, Holland, Greece, Portugal, Spain, Portugal, Spain, Austria, Finland, Sweden, Cyprus, Hungary, Malta, Poland, Estonia, Lithuania, Latvia, Slovenia, Czech, Slovakia, Romania, Bulgaria, Croatia.
Asia Pacific Economic Cooperation includes: Brunei, Hong Kong, Indonesia, Japan, Malaysia, the Philippines, Singapore, Republic of Korea, Thailand, People's Republic of China, Taiwan Province, Chile, Mexico, Canada, United States, Australia, New Zealand, Papua New Guinea, Viet Nam, Russia, Peru.

12－7　广西与东盟进出口商品总值（2017年）
Total Import & Export Value from Guangxi to ASEAN（2017）

单位：亿元　　(RMB 100 million)

主要贸易方式	Main Form of Trade	2015（亿美元）			2016			2017		
		进出口 Import & Export	出口 Export	进口 Import	进出口 Import & Export	出口 Export	进口 Import	进出口 Import & Export	出口 Export	进口 Import
合计	**Total (100 million USD)**	**290.13**	**194.55**	**95.58**	**1835.44**	**991.93**	**843.50**	**1893.85**	**1062.46**	**831.39**
边境小额贸易	Frontier Small Value Trade	170.01	162.83	7.18	786.80	752.57	34.23	836.26	798.98	37.29
一般贸易	Original Trade	28.37	15.82	12.55	152.13	89.99	62.14	250.67	142.45	108.22
其他贸易	Other Trade				667.00	75.50	591.51	633.56	46.71	586.85
海关特殊监管区域物流货物	Logistics Goods in Customs Special Supervision Areas	17.02	1.75	15.27	144.30	19.29	125.02	67.22	18.72	48.50
主要贸易国别	**Main Countries of Trade**									
#合计	Total	290.13	194.55	95.58	1835.44	991.93	843.50	1893.85	1062.46	831.39
越南	Vietnam	246.40	179.20	67.20	1589.24	916.16	673.08	1626.26	930.09	696.17
印尼	Indonesia	15.93	2.53	13.40	121.29	14.59	106.71	67.31	25.90	41.42
新加坡	Singapore	8.23	7.09	1.14	32.21	24.50	7.71	51.06	40.37	10.68
马来西亚	Malaysia	6.72	1.39	5.33	31.28	11.52	19.75	48.60	17.87	30.73
泰国	Thailand	5.15	1.48	3.68	30.25	10.84	19.42	46.53	21.48	25.05
菲律宾	the Philippines	5.79	2.15	3.65	21.06	9.64	11.42	43.45	20.35	23.10
柬埔寨	Cambodia	0.44	0.22	0.22	5.20	1.52	3.68	4.35	2.32	2.03
老挝	Laos	0.14	0.13	0.01	2.63	0.97	1.66	3.26	1.35	1.91
缅甸	Myanmar	1.32	0.35	0.96	2.22	2.14	0.08	2.73	2.44	0.30
文莱	Brunei	0.01	0.01	0	0.06	0.06	0	0.30	0.30	0.00

注：2016年起，外贸进出口数据以人民币计价。
Note: The data of import and export value of foreign trade was calculated by RMB since 2016.

12—8　各市进出口商品总值
Total Import & Export Value by City

单位：万美元　　(USD 10 000)

地　区	Region	2015 进出口 Import & Export	2015 出口 Export	2015 进口 Import	2016（万元）进出口 Import & Export	2016（万元）出口 Export	2016（万元）进口 Import	2017（万元）进出口 Import & Export	2017（万元）出口 Export	2017（万元）进口 Import
全　区	**Guangxi**	**5126215**	**2802570**	**2323645**	**31704215**	**15238340**	**16465875**	**38663414**	**18552015**	**20111398**
南宁市	Nanning City	586917	326149	260769	4162345	2111346	2051000	6070866	2756897	3313969
柳州市	Liuzhou City	222657	77924	144733	1353756	459085	894671	1722399	542460	1179939
桂林市	Guilin City	92341	81002	11338	590191	519219	70973	700117	589491	110627
梧州市	Wuzhou City	91442	46063	45379	405743	260004	145739	602406	294636	307770
北海市	Beihai City	379048	189211	189837	2047464	1102726	944738	2308381	1162528	1145853
防城港市	Fangchenggang City	860140	231166	628974	5789124	1117924	4671200	7685445	1150625	6534820
钦州市	Qinzhou City	582738	247574	335164	2921011	1061736	1859275	3404673	1162896	2241777
贵港市	Guigang City	32258	18977	13281	187879	104073	83806	238816	110306	128510
玉林市	Yulin City	45092	32872	12219	266793	221461	45332	336580	247051	89529
百色市	Baise City	164091	113945	50145	1380719	985118	395601	1884397	1506642	377754
贺州市	Hezhou City	10325	7290	3035	51915	38479	13436	48443	39065	9377
河池市	Hechi City	39168	3185	35984	181096	24373	156723	195498	22330	173168
来宾市	Laibin City	6722	4003	2719	58873	40601	18272	77312	42456	34856
崇左市	Chongzuo City	2013277	1423209	590068	12307305	7192195	5115111	13388082	8924632	4463450

注：2016年起，外贸进出口数据以人民币计价。
Note: The data of import and export value of foreign trade was calculated by RMB since 2016.

12—9 主要出口商品数量及金额（2017年）
Volume & Value of Major Export Commodities（2017）

单位：万元 （RMB 10 000）

商品名称	Item	2016		2017	
		数量 Volume	金额 Value	数量 Volume	金额 Value
活猪（种猪除外）（万头）	Live Hogs (except for the boar) (10 000 heads)	283	5393	243	4545
活家禽（万只）	Live Poultry (10 000 heads)	57	984	6	102
猪肉（吨）	Pork (ton)	37	148	15	44
水海产品（吨）	Seawater Products (ton)	68678	252073	48844	186114
粮食（吨）	Grain(ton)	98254	96764	124652	121376
谷物及谷物粉（吨）	Cereals & Cereals Flour (ton)	884	1870	939	2092
蔬菜（吨）	Vegetables (ton)	413475	363836	500312	470961
鲜、干水果及坚果（吨）	Fresh, Dried Fruits & Nuts (ton)	351125	245203	276000	247337
食用油籽（吨）	Edible Oil Seeds (ton)	521	602	10407	11185
茶叶（吨）	Tea (ton)	1404	8603	1329	10107
蘑菇罐头（吨）	Canned Mushroom (ton)				
肥料（吨）	Fertilizer(ton)	135021	25488	99531	16868
中药材及中式成药（吨）	Medicinal Materials (ton)	5004	22847	9574	71685
生丝（吨）	Raw Silk (ton)	1090	33398	831	29964
黏土及其他耐火矿物（吨）	Clay & Other Refractory Minerals (ton)	194441	1327	99804	1399
天然硫酸钡（重晶石）（吨）	Nature barium sulfate (Barite) (ton)	279738	16519	279365	16284
滑石（吨）	Talcum (ton)	279038	55173	146271	32144
氧化锌及过氧化锌（吨）	Zinc Oxide & Zinc Peroxide (ton)	398	220	405	319
锌钡白（立德粉）（吨）	Lithopone (ton)	1186	294	2866	4552
医药品（吨）	Medicinal & Pharmaceutical Products (ton)	2703	69361	2643	78676
烟花、爆竹（吨）	Fireworks & Firecrackers (ton)	20816	32357	18411	30979
松香及树脂酸（吨）	Resin & Resin Acids (ton)	3909	4668	2254	2764
家用或装饰用木制品（吨）	Wooden Products for household Use or Decoration (ton)	4139	7165	5848	9913
纸及纸板（未切成形的）（吨）	Paper & Paperboard in Rolls (ton)	118498	82882	196775	162413
纺织纱线、织物及制品	Spin Yarn, Fabric & the Products	—	1909151	—	1687818
水泥及水泥熟料（吨）	Cement (ton)	2098	128	62100	1986
平板玻璃（万平方米）	Plain Glass (10 000 sq.m)	0	1	61	418
家用陶瓷器皿（吨）	Porcelain & Pottery Wares for Family Use (ton)	122270	336949	133364	356995
珍珠、钻石、宝石及半宝石	Pearls , Precious or Semi-Stones	—	4981	—	157
钢材（吨）	Rolled Steel (ton)	482702	156246	181134	126122
未锻轧的铜及铜材（吨）	Unwrought Copper & Related Products (ton)	5104	20729	8302	39754

12—9　续表　continued

单位：万元　　(RMB 10 000)

商品名称	Item	2016		2017	
		数量 Volume	金额 Value	数量 Volume	金额 Value
未锻轧的铝及铝材（吨）	Unwrought Aluminum & Related Products (ton)	58075	99623	106874	190220
液化石油气及其他烃类气（吨）	Liquified Petroleum Gas & Other Hydrocarbon Gases				
磷酸及多磷酸（吨）	Phosphoric Acid & Polyphosphoric Acid				
未锻轧的锰（吨）	Unwrought Manganese (ton)	25571	27742	42390	53721
手用或机用工具（吨）	Hand Tools & Tools for Machines (ton)	17264	110990	18856	119047
电扇（万台）	Fans (10 000 units)	3993	54060	438485	63340
金属加工机床（台）	Machine Tools (unit)	34619	41634	39312	43732
自动数据处理设备及其部件（万台）	Automatic Data Processing Machines & Compo-nents (10 000 sets)	2785	552119	3345	890853
轴承（万套）	Bearings (10 000 units)	1745	16708	2400	19279
原电池（万个）	Primary Cells & Batteries (10 000 units)	33179	30698	11349	6844
蓄电池（万个）	Electric Accumulators (10 000 units)	2410	67684	2628	95081
扬声器（万个）	Loudspeakers (10 000 units)	3046	77916	4391	121347
电容器（吨）	Electrical Capacitors (ton)	342	14577	986	10831
电线和电缆（吨）	Electric Wires & Cables (ton)	29893	113107	38460	179446
汽车（包括整套散件）（辆）	Motor Vehicles & Chassis (unit)	25124	244728	22200	211710
汽车零件	Parts of Motor Vehicles				
摩托车（辆）	Motorcycle (unit)	232754	48798	211586	38501
船舶（艘）	Ships (unit)	8	305	12	228
家具及其零件	Furniture & Accessory	—	64074	—	96685
灯具、照明装置及类似品	Lights, Lighting Apparatus & Similar Articles	—	227848	—	381785
箱包及类似容器	Boxes, Bags & Similar Container	—	87978	—	257337
服装及衣着附件	Garments & Clothing Accessories	—	1218396	—	1849823
鞋类（吨）	Footwear(ton)	—	433075	—	612425
塑料制品（吨）	Plastic Articles (ton)	39215	181195	64685	278292
贵金属或包贵金属的首饰	Precious Metal or Jewelry of Rolled Precious Metal	—	489	—	1502
圣诞用品（吨）	Articles for Christmas (ton)	3580	26035	12066	149467
竹编结品（吨）	Bamboo Products (ton)	1462	5440	1284	5068
藤编结品（吨）	Rattan Products (ton)	3354	6987	3254	6370
草编结品（吨）	Straw Mats & Straw Products (ton)	2115	6575	1945	6158
手表（万只）	Wrist Watches (10 000 units)	625	51813	2497	59876
机电产品（包括本目录已具体列名的机电产品）	Mechanical & Electrical Products (including those have been show in this content)	—	6126798	—	7939271
高新技术产品（包括本目录已具体列名的机电产品）	High & New-tech Products (including those have been show in this content)	—	2374451	—	3153290

12－10 主要进口商品数量及金额（2017年）

Volume & Value of Major Import Commodities（2017）

单位：万元 （RMB 10 000）

商品名称	Item	2016		2017	
		数量 Volume	金额 Value	数量 Volume	金额 Value
鲜、干水果及坚果（吨）	Fresh & Dry Fruit, Nuts (ton)	763474	275114	770898	304794
大豆（万吨）	Soybean (10 000 tons)	624	1683970	9836515	2753318
食用植物油（万吨）	Edible Vegetable Oil (10 000 tons)	2	9564	252222	111246
天然橡胶（包括胶乳,吨）	Natural Rubber (including Latex, ton)	10093	7747	10990	11752
合成橡胶（包括胶乳,吨）	Synthetic Rubber (including Latex, ton)	13246	12568	3358	4986
原木（吨）	Logs (ton)	84820	8413	131992	18076
锯材（吨）	Wood Sawn (ton)	35079	11488	29137	11120
纸浆（吨）	Paper Pulp (ton)	381165	129564	435026	175123
纺织用合成纤维（吨）	Synthetic Fibers Suitable for Spinning (ton)	561	996	337	584
铁矿砂及其精矿（万吨）	Iron Ore (10 000 tons)	1622	627751	2002	1039096
锰矿砂及其精矿（万吨）	Manganese Ores (10 000 tons)	226	175137	2335171	274978
煤及褐煤（万吨）	Coal (10 000 tons)	1007	564588	11583275	813587
成品油（万吨）	Petroleum Products Refined (10 000 tons)	4	13799	36315	20114
医药品（吨）	Pharmaceutical Products (ton)	18	2499	11	1997
初级形状的塑料（吨）	Primary Plastic (ton)	28129	31544	38076	41325
牛皮革及马皮革（吨）	Cattle Hide & Horsehide (ton)	49458	54778	54619	60554
棉纱线（吨）	Cotton Yarn (ton)	2998	4719	5585	6291
合成纤维纱线（吨）	Synthetic Fibers, Continuous Filament & Yarn (ton)	101	520	73	351
合成纤维长丝机织物（万米）	Synthetic Fibers, Continuous Filament Woven Fabrics (10 000 m)	401	4380	89	1813
针织或钩编织物	Garments，knitted or Crocheted	—	7918		3618
原油（吨）	Crude Oil(ton)	4645421	912956	2860527	762984
钢材（吨）	Rolled Steel (ton)	12549	8225	8507	9142
未锻轧的铜及铜材（吨）	Unwrought Copper & Related Products (ton)	75	469	14837	61605
未锻轧的铝及铝材（吨）	Unwrought Aluminum & Related Products (ton)	148	487	52	266
液泵及液体提升机（台）	Liquid Pump & Machine with Liquid Exaltation (unit)	20013	2802	7088	2925
活塞式内燃机的零件（吨）	Accessories of Gas Engine with Liquid Exaltation (ton)	52	620	221	1906
空气调节器（台）	Air Conditioners (set)	1	1	—	—
机械提升搬运装卸设备及零件	Portage ,Load & Unload Equipments & Accessories with Machine Exaltation	—	5469	—	13336
建筑及采矿用机械及零件	Building , Mining Machinery & Accessory	—	5565	—	11496
食品、饮料工业用加工机械及零件	Food & Drink Processing Machinery & Accessory	—	783	—	416
制造纸及纸制品用机械及零件	Papermaking & Paper Products Machinery & accessory	—	6341	—	3074
印刷、装订机械及零件	Printing & Binding Machinery & Accessory	—	81893	—	51968
纺织机械及零件	Spinning Machinery & Accessory	—	3656	—	13807
金属加工机床（台）	Machine Tools (unit)	117	36580	178	43031
橡胶或塑料加工机械及零件	Rubber or Plastic Processing Machinery & Accessory	—	8153	—	8348
阀门（万套）	Valves (10 000 sets)	8	6312	10	8262
自动数据处理设备及其部件（万台）	Automatic Data Processing Machines & Components (10 000 sets)	2990	990461	596	212206
电话机（万台）	Telephone sets (10 000 set)	131	12527	3	1085
通断及保护电路装置及零件	Electrical Apparatus for Switching or Protecting Electrical Circuit	—	75474	—	112618
电线和电缆（吨）	Electric Wires & Cables (ton)	3070	91991	3978	126720
汽车（包括整套散件）（辆）	Motor Vehicles (including Complete set of spare parts)(unit)	865	21987	114	2762
汽车零配件	Parts of Motor Vehicles				
机电产品（包括本目录具体列名的机电产品）	Mechanical & Electrical Products (including those have been show in this content)	—	3349290	—	3536320
高新技术产品（包括本目录已具体列名的机电产品）	High & New-tech Products (including those have been show in this content)	—	2494820	—	2245587

12－11　外商直接投资额（1979－2017年）
Foreign Direct Investment（1979－2017）

单位：万美元　　　　(USD 10 000)

年　份 Year	外商直接投资 Foreign Direct Investments	年　份 Year	外商直接投资 Foreign Direct Investments
1979-1983	1226	2006	44740
1985	1251	2007	68396
1990	3025	2008	97119
		2009	103533
1991	3871	2010	91200
1992	18026		
1993	87203	2011	101381
1994	81506	2012	74853
1995	66952	2013	70008
1996	66618	2014	100119
1997	87986	2015	172208
1998	88613	2016	88845
1999	63730	2017	82272
2000	52466		
2001	38415		
2002	41726		
2003	45619		
2004	29579		
2005	37866		

12－12　主要年份实际利用外资及对外承包工程情况
Basic Statistics of Foreign Capital Actually Utilized Overseas Contracted Projects in Main Years

单位：万美元　　　　(USD 10 000)

项　目	Item	1995	2000	2006	2010	2013	2014	2015	2016	2017
外商直接投资	**Foreign Direct Investment**	**66952**	**52466**	**44740**	**91200**	**70008**	**100119**	**172208**	**88845**	**82272**
按投资方式分	By Investment Manner									
独资经营	Sole Investment	15163	18476	25150	65377	34258	65088	107135	39594	27971
合资经营	Joint-venture	41367	16413	18120	25770	33469	35031	64573	49251	48426
合作经营	Cooperative	10422	15477	1470	53	0	0	500	0	5864
股份制	Share Holding					2281	0	0	0	0
按国民经济行业分	By National Economic Sector									
1. 农林牧渔业	Farming, Forestry, Animal Husbandry & Fishery	2917	2092	2594	10090	625	310	10020	9139	227
2. 工业	Industry	33316	22697	34408	46989	51533	46778	63835	44065	69354
3. 建筑业	Construction	3517	6157	221	2	0	0	20	0	0
4. 交通运输、仓储和邮政业	Transport, Storage & Post	4587	2147	995	3003	5830	2263	45137	10586	664
5. 批发和零售贸易、住宿和餐饮业	Wholesale, Retail Trade, Hotel & Catering Services	1369	492	1458	14268	4016	2701	4717	5537	178
6. 房地产业	Real Estate	19997	11607	3806	11925	3794	40673	36219	11791	693
7. 其他行业	Other Sectors	1249	7274	1258	4923	4210	7394	12260	7727	11156
按国别、地区分	By Countries, Region									
# 中国香港	Hong Kong, China	37226	20204	15559	52114	37047	54020	54414	36358	29935
中国澳门	Macao, China	2420	1321	402	2579	669	972	385	194	500
日本	Japan	3175	524	1019	1347	13	21	320	88	53
新加坡	Singapore	4039	1407	1817	6010	0	1105	44931	18251	174
中国台湾	Taiwan, China	4295	4750	880	990	186	791	834	210	121
泰国	Thailand	4464	609	12	590	790	663	1056	0	2
美国	United States	2004	1282	935	135	18	719	412	56	3
英属维尔京群岛	British Virgin Islands		6815	11704	11708	9659	8589	7416	3545	1947
对外承包工程										
合同项目（个）	Contracted Projects (unit)	19	14	12	39	28	81	59	61	47
合同金额（万美元）	Contracted Value (USD 10 000)	7634	2994	1233	61019	32008	86373	65563	79521	93726
当年完成营业额（万美元）	Volume of Business Fulfilled in the Year (USD 10 000)	8292	5042	2421	56429	83002	87736	93986	84764	68825

注：1995年“房地产业”数据包含“租赁和商务服务业”

Note: The data on “Real Estate” in 1995 includes “Leasing & Business Service”.

12—13 主要年份分市新签外商直接投资项目和金额
Items & Value of Utilization of Foreign Direct Investment Through Newly Signed Agreement by City in Main Years

城 市	City	1995	2000	2005	2010	2012	2013	2014	2015	2016	2017
新签项目个数（个）	**Number of Items Newly Signed (unit)**	**571**	**246**	**351**	**190**	**109**	**109**	**138**	**142**	**139**	**183**
南宁市	Nanning	88	31	89	73	37	49	59	69	49	72
柳州市	Liuzhou	36	8	20	10	5	11	6	4	16	9
桂林市	Guilin	116	45	49	18	11	9	18	15	11	21
梧州市	Wuzhou	85	41	53	19	5	5	6	6	10	10
北海市	Beihai	56	17	32	21	6	6	9	11	8	11
防城港市	Fangchenggang	24	23	11	8	4	1	2	4	2	4
钦州市	Qinzhou	20	8	24	11	13	11	10	12	9	15
贵港市	Guigang		9	7	6	5	3	6	1	8	5
玉林市	Yulin	62	43	23	14	5	6	7	4	8	11
百色市	Baise	2	3	8	1	3	1	1	1	8	2
贺州市	Hezhou	30	7	19	3	6	2	5	4	2	6
河池市	Hechi	9	5	4	1	0	1	2	1	2	9
来宾市	Laibin	18	5	4	1	5	3	2	4	1	2
崇左市	Chongzuo	4	1	8	4	4	1	5	6	5	6
新签项目合同外资额（万美元）	**Foreign Capital to Be Utilized through the Newly Signed Agreements & Contracts (USD 10 000)**	**104177**	**71549**	**110182**	**209523**	**91192**	**215771**	**191691**	**335668**	**231861**	**519301**
南宁市	Nanning	23557	10637	31704	70743	23916	23053	77629	97978	24838	148996
柳州市	Liuzhou	8275	3380	3909	6124	3659	3388	10357	31925	34688	134341
桂林市	Guilin	10772	6550	15437	1543	3244	17335	38399	89319	61401	37227
梧州市	Wuzhou	5837	3151	12609	9325	6541	1240	599	1300	16859	13829
北海市	Beihai	10155	821	9596	30177	3217	93666	2502	3715	36100	22299
防城港市	Fangchenggang	3746	34536	14158	5296	2794	6953	1239	22916	2325	792
钦州市	Qinzhou	12048	3057	7127	20188	24278	28415	34886	55127	10367	27642
贵港市	Guigang		521	255	6246	2320	14020	10917	676	15376	24356
玉林市	Yulin	16465	2210	2834	11445	2238	2457	5542	1940	4017	11035
百色市	Baise	429	412	1502	354	4560	45	-1881	1593	7330	15
贺州市	Hezhou	2303	559	1331	26348	6976	4368	3878	11623	725	3597
河池市	Hechi	2605	4345	1826	265	-471	12807	2487	8434	13338	90156
来宾市	Laibin	947	530	637	3435	2890	3687	2414	4033	1147	1327
崇左市	Chongzuo	903	840	7257	18034	5030	4337	2723	5089	3350	3689

主要统计指标解释

进出口总额 海关进出口总额指实际进出我国国境的货物总金额，它可用以观察一个国家在对外贸易方面的总规模。进出口总额统计范围包括：对外贸易实际进出口货物，来料加工装配进出口货物，国家间、联合国及国际组织无偿援助物资和赠送品，华侨、港澳台同胞和外籍华人捐赠品，租赁期满归承租人所有的租赁货物，进料加工进出口货物，边境地方贸易及边境地区小额贸易进出口货物，中外合资、合作、外商独资企业进出口货物和公用物品，到、离岸价格在规定限额以上的进出口货样和广告品（无商业价值、无使用价值和免费提供出口的除外），从保税仓库提取在中国境内销售的进口货物，以及其他进出口货物。我国规定出口货物按离岸价格统计，进口货物按到岸价格统计。

外商直接投资 指外方投资者在我国境内通过设立外商投资企业、合作企业、与中方投资者共同进行石油、天然气和煤层气等资源的合作勘探开发以及设立外国公司分支机构等方式进行投资。外方投资者可以用现金、实物、无形资产、股权等投资。

对外承包工程 根据《对外承包工程管理条例》，对外承包工程是指中国的企业或者其他单位承包境外建设工程项目的活动。

对外承包项目分为十一大类：房屋建筑项目、工业建设项目、制造加工设施建设项目、水利建设项目、废水（物）处理项目、交通运输建设项目、危险品处理项目、电力工程建设项目、石油化工项目、通讯工程项目、其他。

Explanatory Notes on Main Statistical Indicators

Total Import & Export Value refers to the value of commodities imported into and exported from the boundary of China, it can be used to observe the total scale in foreign trade of a country. It includes: the actual imports and exports through foreign trade, imported and exported goods under the processing and assembling trades and materials, supplies and gifts as aid given gratis between governments and by the United Nations and other international organizations, the donated products of overseas Chinese, compatriot from Hong Kong, Macao and Taiwan and Chinese of foreign nationality, lease goods belonging to lessee after expiring leasing period, the imports and exports of processing with imported materials, the local trade in the border and cargoes imported and exported of small trade of border area, the imported and exported commodities and articles for public use of the Sino-foreign joint ventures, cooperative enterprises and ventures exclusively with foreign own investment, imported and exported sample of regulation and advertising product that are in the stipulated above-norm of the CIF and FOB (excluding which have no commercial value, using value and which export for free), the imports that are picked up from the bonded warehouse and sale in china, and other imports and exports. In our country, exports are calculated according to FOB, and imports are calculated according to CIF.

Foreign Direct Investment refers to the investment made in Chinese area by foreign investors in establishing foreign-funded enterprises, cooperative enterprises, cooperating with Chinese investors on the exploration and development of oil, natural gas and coalbed methane resources, and investment in the form of branches of foreign companies, etc. Foreign investors can invest in cash, real assets, intangible assets and equities.

Overseas Contracted Projects according to *The Regulations on the Administration of oversea Contracted Projects*, overseas contracted projects refers to the activities of Chinese enterprises or other entities contracting overseas construction projects.

The foreign contracting project is divided into eleven categories: Housing construction projects, industrial construction projects, manufacturing and processing facilities construction projects, water conservancy projects, waste water (material) treatment projects, transportation construction projects, dangerous goods treatment projects, electrical engineering construction projects, petrochemical projects, communication engineering projects, etc.

第十三篇
农业
AGRICULTURE

（校对编辑：磨正中　杨海玲）

13－1 主要年份农村基本情况

指 标	Item	1995	2000
乡镇个数（个）	Number of Township & Town Governments (unit)	1362	1360
#镇个数	Number of Town Governments	618	745
村委会个数（个）	Number of Villagers' Committees (unit)	14803	14849
通汽车村数	Villages with Bus Services	12072	14182
通电话村数	Villages with Telephone Communication	4842	11812
自来水受益村数	Villages with Tap Water	5617	7832
乡（镇）村户数、人口	Number of Rural (Town Governments) Households & Population		
乡（镇）村户数（万户）	Number of Rural (Town Governments) Households (10 000 households)	827.88	913.95
乡（镇）村人口（万人）	Rural Population (10 000 persons)	3881.89	4026.44
乡（镇）村从业人员（万人）	Number of Rural (Town Governments) Laborers (10 000 persons)	1964.60	2145.35
按性别分	By sex		
男	Male	1030.85	1129.86
女	Female	933.75	1015.49
按产业分	By industry		
第一产业	Primary Industry	1562.88	1556.84
第二产业	Secondary Industry	125.97	148.57
第三产业	Tertiary Industry	275.75	439.94
农业机械总动力（亿瓦特）	Total Agricultural Machinery Power (100 million watts)	107.54	146.79
农用排灌动力机械（亿瓦特）	Motor Machinery for Agricultural Drainage & Irrigation (100 million watts)	10.12	16.05
农用水泵（台）	Pumps (unit)	130684	228198
农用载重汽车（台）	Trucks for Agricultural use (unit)	24423	27501
渔业机动船（艘）	Motorized Fishing Boats (unit)	11123	13294
（亿瓦特）	(100 million watts)	3.48	4.46

注：1995年乡（镇）村从业人员为“乡（镇）村实有劳动力”。
Note: “Number of rural (town governments) laborers” in 1995 refers to “Number of Rural (Town Governments) Actual Laborers”.

Basic Statistics of Rural Area in Main Years

2005	2010	2011	2012	2013	2014	2015	2016	2017
1130	1126	1126	1126	1126	1127	1129	1128	1131
698	702	702	715	720	752	773	789	802
14453	14354	14355	14355	14337	14046	14278	14278	14256
14017	14197	14207	14246	14233				
13669	14178	14213	14250	14244				
8440	9527	9827	10113	10140	10935	10993	11354	11540
986.10	1029.14	1039.24	1060.83	1065.00	1092.10	1112.03	1109.88	1124.03
4146.19	4203.98	4221.18	4243.35	4254.00	4351.47	4403.58	4428.34	4455.61
2275.39	2387.20	2406.67	2427.11	2436.00	2469.46	2489.85	2488.47	2495.60
1202.11	1262.17	1276.01	1288.22	1293.00	1311.94	1323.32	1321.18	1330.18
1073.28	1125.03	1130.66	1138.89	1143.00	1157.52	1166.53	1167.29	1165.42
1503.06	1556.90	1546.23	1564.20	1465.00	1619.00	1651.00	1644.00	1634.58
182.84	469.46							
589.49	360.84							
190.97	276.77	299.09	319.16	338.43	352.92	376.75	375.50	360.43
23.94	31.64	37.66						
550225	834025	837376	845219	833951	867084	890894	913233	918931
33141	30137	30208						
13971	18713	19564	23332	26919	23415		24519	26482
4.87	6.99	7.09						

13－2 农林牧渔业总产值（1978－2017年）
Gross Output Value of Farming, Forestry, Animal Husbandry & Fishery（1978－2017）

（当年价格）（At current prices） 单位：亿元（100 million yuan）

年 份 Year	农林牧渔业总产值 Total	农业产值 Farming	林业产值 Forestry	牧业产值 Animal Husbandry	渔业产值 Fishery	农林牧渔专业及辅助性活动 Output Value of Service Industry for Farming, Forestry, Animal Husbandry & Fishery
一、总产值 Gross Output Value						
1978	46.17	36.99	2.28	6.37	0.53	
1980	63.31	44.41	4.39	13.64	0.87	
1985	108.02	66.34	8.09	30.43	3.16	
1990	252.22	149.69	18.05	75.50	8.98	
1991	278.15	164.73	20.87	81.99	10.56	
1992	333.12	188.65	26.77	100.71	16.99	
1993	378.62	214.24	27.47	114.15	22.76	
1994	516.46	283.71	31.78	164.02	36.95	
1995	698.28	384.17	32.56	225.57	55.98	
1996	821.55	450.52	38.14	263.80	69.09	
1997	882.60	482.48	38.64	280.67	80.81	
1998	865.90	476.24	37.75	263.96	87.95	
1999	844.78	454.85	37.48	261.87	90.58	
2000	828.97	418.83	38.76	275.33	96.05	
2001	872.90	439.93	39.44	292.34	101.19	
2002	916.50	465.47	39.81	306.50	104.72	
2003	1030.89	500.82	53.80	342.83	115.53	17.91
2004	1294.53	623.09	58.07	460.68	133.78	18.91
2005	1448.37	711.89	61.68	511.60	143.61	19.59
2006	1622.22	807.90	79.75	540.17	135.40	59.00
2007	2026.22	970.55	99.78	710.17	178.32	67.40
2008	2389.79	1106.74	124.26	871.66	206.98	80.15
2009	2380.51	1134.98	132.27	812.46	216.95	83.85
2010	2720.99	1339.58	173.47	870.73	247.16	90.05
2011	3323.37	1602.48	217.41	1096.58	303.11	103.79
2012	3490.72	1724.00	245.26	1072.77	331.74	116.95
2013	3755.19	1868.30	287.64	1101.23	366.65	131.37
2014	3947.73	1993.98	303.17	1087.25	413.12	150.21
2015	4197.12	2146.37	313.90	1140.30	429.82	166.73
2016	4591.37	2347.90	323.53	1266.37	464.25	189.31
2017	4742.76	2545.48	346.54	1136.33	500.55	213.86

13－2 续表 continued

（当年价格） (At current prices) 单位：亿元 (100 million yuan)

年份 Year	农林牧渔业总产值 Total	农业产值 Farming	林业产值 Forestry	牧业产值 Animal Husbandry	渔业产值 Fishery	农林牧渔专业及辅助性活动 Output Value of Service Industry for Farming, Forestry, Animal Husbandry & Fishery
二、构成（以总产值合计为100） Composition(Gross Output Value=100)						
1978	100.0	80.1	4.9	13.8	1.2	
1980	100.0	70.1	6.9	21.6	1.4	
1985	100.0	61.4	7.5	28.2	2.9	
1990	100.0	59.3	7.2	29.9	3.6	
1991	100.0	59.2	7.5	29.5	3.8	
1992	100.0	56.6	8.1	30.2	5.1	
1993	100.0	56.6	7.3	30.1	6.0	
1994	100.0	54.9	6.1	31.8	7.2	
1995	100.0	55.0	4.7	32.3	8.0	
1996	100.0	54.8	4.7	32.1	8.4	
1997	100.0	54.7	4.4	31.8	9.1	
1998	100.0	55.0	4.4	30.5	10.1	
1999	100.0	53.9	4.4	31.0	10.7	
2000	100.0	50.6	4.6	33.2	11.6	
2001	100.0	50.4	4.5	33.5	11.6	
2002	100.0	50.8	4.4	33.4	11.4	
2003	100.0	48.6	5.2	33.3	11.2	1.7
2004	100.0	48.1	4.5	35.6	10.3	1.5
2005	100.0	49.1	4.3	35.3	9.9	1.4
2006	100.0	49.8	4.9	33.3	8.4	3.6
2007	100.0	47.9	4.9	35.1	8.8	3.3
2008	100.0	46.3	5.2	36.5	8.7	3.3
2009	100.0	47.7	5.6	34.1	9.1	3.5
2010	100.0	49.2	6.4	32.0	9.1	3.3
2011	100.0	48.2	6.6	33.0	9.1	3.1
2012	100.0	49.4	7.0	30.7	9.5	3.4
2013	100.0	49.7	7.7	29.3	9.8	3.5
2014	100.0	50.5	7.7	27.5	10.5	3.8
2015	100.0	51.1	7.5	27.2	10.2	4.0
2016	100.0	51.1	7.1	27.6	10.1	4.1
2017	100.0	53.7	7.3	24.0	10.5	4.5

注：1. 按照国家统计口径，2003年起农林牧渔业总产值包括农业、林业、牧业、渔业以及农林牧渔专业及辅助性活动值。
2. 本表2006和2007年数据为第二次全国农业普查衔接数。

Note: 1. according to the statistic standard of our country, the gross output value of farming, forestry, animal husbandry & fishery has included the output value of the service industry of farming, forestry, animal husbandry & fishery since 2003.
2. Data of 2006 and 2007 in this table is in accordance with the second national agriculture census.

13－3 农林牧渔业总产值指数（1978－2017年）

Indices of Gross Output Value of Farming, Forestry, Animal Husbandry & Fishery（1978－2017）

（按可比价格计算，以上年为100） (at comparable prices , preceding year =100)　　单位：%（%）

年 份 Year	农林牧渔业总产值 Total	农业产值 Farming	林业产值 Forestry	牧业产值 Animal Husbandry	渔业产值 Fishery	农林牧渔专业及辅助性活动 Output Value of Service Industry for Farming, Forestry, Animal Husbandry & Fishery
1978	101.8	101.9	100.8	105.0	72.8	
1979	104.8	106.1	109.7	96.9	85.2	
1980	104.2	105.2	98.9	99.0	112.8	
1981	106.0	104.1	122.7	111.7	106.4	
1982	116.2	115.4	104.6	123.5	126.3	
1983	100.7	100.6	92.5	102.7	112.0	
1984	99.7	97.0	113.7	105.6	104.2	
1985	102.1	99.6	110.5	107.2	112.5	
1986	103.4	103.1	104.2	103.3	114.5	
1987	104.9	106.6	93.1	102.7	112.5	
1988	98.1	96.7	102.7	100.4	107.0	
1989	110.3	111.4	94.5	111.8	109.4	
1990	108.0	105.4	125.1	111.3	113.9	
1991	108.1	105.3	113.0	112.9	112.2	
1992	114.9	115.3	106.7	116.1	122.9	
1993	104.7	101.3	104.2	108.9	126.6	
1994	107.3	102.4	108.0	111.5	136.0	
1995	114.9	114.0	96.2	117.2	135.9	
1996	105.0	99.6	100.3	112.5	120.4	
1997	109.9	110.7	97.4	107.7	120.4	
1998	105.2	106.5	95.5	102.9	110.1	
1999	107.9	111.4	99.8	103.6	106.2	
2000	100.2	94.7	101.9	109.4	105.3	
2001	104.9	104.9	103.5	106.0	103.4	
2002	107.8	111.2	100.7	105.2	102.7	
2003	104.3	100.0	114.8	109.2	106.9	104.0
2004	106.3	105.8	103.4	109.0	104.8	101.6
2005	107.4	105.8	107.0	110.6	105.0	101.1
2006	107.2	105.9	121.4	107.7	105.5	104.9
2007	105.8	108.1	110.3	102.0	105.2	104.7
2008	105.4	103.6	121.4	105.9	102.4	109.7
2009	105.4	105.3	102.1	105.6	106.2	106.3
2010	104.7	103.0	115.8	105.1	105.8	104.3
2011	104.8	105.8	110.9	101.4	105.9	108.7
2012	105.7	106.0	109.2	104.5	105.4	109.2
2013	104.4	104.7	108.2	102.3	105.4	108.9
2014	103.7	105.2	102.8	100.4	104.3	110.8
2015	103.7	105.1	106.3	99.7	104.0	107.8
2016	103.3	104.7	105.9	98.3	104.3	111.3
2017	104.4	105.3	105.1	101.4	104.2	110.2

13－4 主要年份主要农作物播种面积
Sown Area of Major Farm Crops in Main Years

单位：千公顷 (1 000 hectares)

指 标	Item	1995	2000	2005	2010	2012	2013	2014	2015	2016	2017
农作物总播种面积	Total Sown Area	5745.7	6258.6	6343.9	5896.9	6089.5	6137.3	6186.1	6134.7	6145.3	6143.1
#粮食作物	Grain Crops	3662.7	3653.8	3350.9	3061.1	3069.1	3076.0	3067.7	3059.3	3023.6	2976.2
占总播种面积比重(%)	Percentage to Total Area (%)	63.7	58.4	52.8	51.9	50.4	50.1	49.6	49.9	49.2	48.4
#稻 谷	Rice	2433.0	2301.6	2099.6	2094.4	2057.6	2046.6	2026.2	1983.9	1959.8	1922.5
#早 稻	Early Rice	1150.8	1078.0	970.1	964.8	929.8	927.9	917.6	888.2	883.7	865.1
晚 稻	Late Rice	1137.7	1068.7	982.3	979.7	979.2	967.4	959.7	947.9	930.2	906.9
玉 米	Corn	550.1	608.7	607.6	538.6	580.5	587.6	584.0	622.6	609.3	597.2
大 豆	Soybean	252.5	281.4	250.4	108.8	94.4	97.0	99.6	96.0	97.3	100.4
薯 类	Tubers	312.6	341.1	294.2	244.5	255.9	265.1	273.8	274.1	274.6	272.0
#经济作物面积	Industrial Crops										
花 生	Peanuts	208.4	240.6	243.7	170.3	188.1	194.9	204.3	214.3	221.3	228.2
油菜籽	Rape Seeds	61.5	89.2	60.6	15.6	17.1	18.8	24.2	24.8	26.7	26.8
芝 麻	Sesame	9.4	7.3	4.9	5.2	5.0	5.1	5.2	5.3	5.4	5.4
黄红麻	Jute & Ambary Hemp	6.7	5.8	4.8	4.6	4.1	4.0	3.7	3.3	3.4	3.1
苎 麻	Ramie	1.2	0.9	0.4	0.5	0.5	0.5	0.5	0.6	0.6	0.5
甘 蔗	Sugarcane	454.3	508.7	747.6	1069.3	1128.0	1125.1	1081.5	973.7	951.0	935.0
烤 烟	Flue-Cured Tobacco	10.1	11.4	13.9	12.0	14.8	18.1	17.7	12.9	12.4	10.6
木 薯	Cassava	272.9	264.3	269.5	233.0	231.2	228.0	224.1	213.3	206.9	201.0
#其他农作物面积	Others										
蔬 菜（含菜瓜）	Vegetables (including vegetable melons)	555.8	899.5	1094.4	1007.6	1075.4	1104.6	1162.5	1221.0	1269.7	1314.7

注：“农作物播种面积”、“经济和其他农作物”、“蔬菜”中均不包含食用菌面积。
Note: The indicators of "Planting Area of Farm Crops", "Economic Crops" and "Vegetables" do not include the area of eatable mushrooms.
本表从属关系与农业报表制度A302表一致。

13－5 主要年份主要农作物产品产量

单位：万吨

指 标	Item	1995	2000
粮食作物	Grain Crops	1553.31	1667.24
#稻 谷	Rice	1307.66	1360.77
#早 稻	Early Rice	699.25	706.82
晚 稻	Late Rice	536.72	570.25
玉 米	Corn	155.47	188.44
大 豆	Soybean	28.97	36.43
薯 类	Tubers	49.68	67.61
油 料	Oil-bearing Crops	45.35	58.61
#花 生	Peanuts	39.17	49.55
油菜籽	Rapeseeds	5.34	8.16
芝 麻	Sesame	0.52	0.57
黄红麻	Jute & Ambary Hemp	1.29	1.15
苎 麻	Ramie	0.18	0.17
甘 蔗	Sugarcane	2555.73	2937.89
烤 烟	Flue-Cured Tobacco	1.24	1.69
蔬 菜（含菌类）	Vegetables (including ungus)		1620.75
木 薯	Cassava	124.51	132.56
茶 叶	Tea	1.94	1.79
水 果（含园林和瓜果类）	Fruits (including grove & melon fruits)	266.60	526.69
#园林水果	Grove Fruits	266.60	360.14
#蕉 类	Banana	96.35	127.32
沙田柚	Shatian Pomeloe	8.77	18.36
柑桔橙	Citrus & Orange	72.58	87.99
菠 萝	Pineapple	12.22	8.00
龙 眼	Longyan	11.86	15.67
荔 枝	Litchi	14.85	14.55
芒 果	Mango	4.38	10.96

注：1. 2000年以后的水果产量包括园林水果和果用瓜。
2. 2009年起薯类包括马铃薯。

Note: 1. The output of fruits since 2000 has included grove fruits & fruited melon.
2. The "Tubers" includes potatoes since 2009.

Output of Major Farm Crops in Main Years

(10 000 tons)

2005	2010	2011	2012	2013	2014	2015	2016	2017
1516.29	1412.32	1429.93	1484.90	1521.80	1534.41	1524.75	1521.30	1467.70
1188.09	1121.25	1084.10	1141.00	1156.20	1166.12	1137.83	1137.25	1087.90
573.03	531.50	530.41	544.90	555.20	543.30	528.80	529.69	501.60
533.55	509.40	471.93	509.70	508.04	525.31	513.10	511.04	483.00
207.26	208.70	244.72	250.60	265.95	266.40	280.70	278.60	274.40
36.87	16.69	20.11	15.30	13.51	13.65	14.20	14.94	16.30
70.63	56.18	67.84	64.80	73.00	74.15	78.40	76.05	75.20
63.18	45.81	50.14	53.94	57.21	61.30	64.68	68.95	71.62
55.13	43.50	47.46	51.09	54.10	57.57	60.70	64.86	67.50
6.33	1.47	1.61	1.71	1.90	2.50	2.62	2.79	2.80
0.46	0.59	0.61	0.64	0.67	0.72	0.74	0.76	0.78
0.96	1.08	1.08	0.95	0.58	0.98	0.87	0.91	0.88
0.11	0.14	0.15	0.15	0.17	0.18	0.20	0.21	0.21
5154.69	7119.62	7269.96	7829.71	8104.26	7952.57	7504.92	7461.32	7611.69
1.97	2.03	2.20	2.70	3.11	2.74	2.14	2.09	2.26
2130.60	2129.44	2246.40	2356.72	2435.62	2610.08	2786.37	2928.81	3086.85
173.61	173.21	180.33	181.31	182.75	182.82	175.94	172.12	172.05
2.62	3.92	4.44	4.94	5.39	5.88	6.36	6.81	7.33
766.84	1094.41	1222.98	1325.03	1433.42	1560.60	1720.02	1882.50	2066.97
571.58	841.77	943.81	1030.95	1122.63	1233.30	1369.76	1525.20	1701.30
136.44	207.95	229.08	256.60	275.21	300.33	307.23	342.57	350.16
29.38	41.33	43.57	47.28	50.25	58.80	60.18	61.91	64.98
155.08	268.29	307.70	332.72	368.39	412.80	459.07	515.46	620.41
6.54	2.76	2.93	3.05	3.27	3.43	3.43	3.42	3.55
38.17	40.55	47.36	50.41	51.57	55.81	57.36	59.67	59.30
33.48	46.58	53.19	53.06	54.63	61.85	63.77	66.75	68.13
18.59	15.62	18.34	21.76	34.04	40.84	48.98	58.44	68.41

13－6　主要年份主要农作物单位面积产量
Output of Major Farm Crops Per Hectare in Main Years

单位：公斤/公顷　　(kg/hectare)

指　标	Item	2005	2009	2010	2011	2012	2013	2014	2015	2016	2017
粮食作物	Grain Crops	4525	4770	4614	4653	4838	4947	5002	4984	5031	4931
#稻　谷	Rice	5659	5392	5354	5216	5545	5649	5755	5735	5803	5659
#早　稻	Early Rice	5907	5596	5509	5636	5860	5983	5921	5954	5994	5798
晚　稻	Late Rice	5432	5125	5200	4785	5205	5251	5473	5413	5494	5326
玉　米	Corn	3411	4212	3875	4325	4317	4526	4562	4509	4572	4595
大　豆	Soybean	1472	1652	1534	1799	1621	1393	1371	1479	1531	1624
薯　类	Tubers	2401	2723	2298	2847	2532	2754	2709	2860	2771	2765
花　生	Peanuts	2262	2477	2554	2644	2716	2776	2818	2832	2931	2958
甘　蔗	Sugarcane	68950	70836	66583	66599	69411	72032	73530	77073	78455	81409
烤　烟	Flue-Cured Tobacco	1414	1914	1694	1734	1825	1720	1548	1658	1683	2122

13－7　主要年份农业生产条件基本情况
Basic Statistics on Agricultural Production Conditions in Main Years

指　标	Item	2005	2009	2010	2011	2012	2013	2014	2015	2016	2017
机耕面积（千公顷）	Tractor Ploughed Area (1 000 hectares)	1032.8	2593.4	3163.7	3662.9	3868.8	3865.5	4305.5	4628.5	4683.3	4899.0
农村用电量（亿千瓦小时）	Electricity Consumed in Rural Areas (100 million kwh)	34.31	48.48	50.22	56.18	63.31	68.38	76.21	83.91	95.37	103.53
化肥施用量（折纯量）（万吨）	Consumption of Chemical Fertilizers (10 000 tons)	201.25	229.32	237.16	242.71	249.04	255.70	258.67	259.86	262.14	263.83
氮　肥	Nitrogenous Fertilizer	63.27	68.38	69.94	70.82	72.45	74.17	74.65	74.23	74.89	76.03
磷　肥	Phosphate Fertilizer	25.23	27.98	28.85	29.57	30.46	30.91	31.25	31.06	31.13	31.02
钾　肥	Potash Fertilizer	47.95	51.49	53.23	54.82	56.04	57.28	57.39	58.34	58.96	58.45
复合肥	Compound Fertilizer	64.81	81.47	85.15	87.50	90.09	93.34	95.38	96.23	97.16	98.33
农田有效灌溉面积（千公顷）	Irrigated Area (1 000 hectares)	1519.8	1522.3	1523.0	1529.2	1541.3	1553.6	1600.0	1618.8	1646.1	1669.9
水　库（座）	Number of Reservoirs (set)	4380	4369	4366	4348	4347	4544	4545	4545	4540	4537
#大型水库	Large Reservoirs	33	37	37	37	37	57	57	57	57	58
中型水库	Medium-sizes Reservoirs	183	185	186	186	186	228	228	229	230	230
水库库容量（亿立方米）	Capacity of Reservoirs (100 million cu.m)	252.14	328.68	321.85	321.79	321.81	679.00	679.00	658.00	679.52	708.27
#大型水库	Large Reservoirs	154.30	230.44	223.38	223.37	223.37	563.00	563.00	547.00	563.99	592.79
中型水库	Medium-sizes Reservoirs	53.02	53.66	53.94	53.93	53.93	67.00	67.00	64.00	67.08	67.08
节水灌溉面积（千公顷）	Water-saving Irrigated Area (1 000 hectares)	622.1	685.9	702.2	727.2	780.8	800.5	879.6	951.4	1030.8	1067.93
#喷滴灌面积	Sprinkling & Drip Irrigation	4.8	5.2	5.5	6.9	26.0	38.5	56.0	67.0	101.5	110.96
除涝面积（千公顷）	Flooded or Waterlogged Area (1 000 hectares)	204.2	208.8	209.6	211.4	214.0	230.9	231.4	241.3	237.4	234.92
水土流失治理面积（千公顷）	Area of Soil Erosion under Control (1 000 hectares)	1487.6	1843.7	1870.3	1952.1	2019.5	1735.7	1791.8	2017.3	2284.9	2463.76
堤防总长度（公里）	Total Length of Dikes (km)	2759	2805	2867	2948	3108	4492	4649	4885	5043	5180.94
堤防保护耕地面积（千公顷）	Area of Land Protected by Dikes (1 000 hectares)	311.3	269.5	266.8	273.8	297.3	148.2	248.8	283.8	276.9	280.43

13－8 主要年份农作物播种面积构成
Sowing Areas Structure of Farm Crops in Main Years

（以总播种面积为100） (Total Planting Structure=100) 单位：%（%）

指 标	Item	1995	2000	2005	2010	2011	2012	2013	2014	2015	2016	2017
农作物播种面积	Planting Structure of Farm Crops	100.0	100.0	100.0	100.0	100.0	100.0	100.0	100.0	100.0	100.0	100.0
一、粮食作物	Grain Crops	63.8	58.4	52.8	51.8	51.2	50.4	50.1	49.6	49.9	49.2	48.4
#稻 谷	Rice	42.3	36.8	33.1	35.3	34.7	33.8	33.3	32.8	32.3	31.9	31.3
#早 稻	Early Rice	20.0	17.2	15.3	16.2	15.7	15.3	15.1	14.8	14.5	14.4	14.1
晚 稻	Late Rice	19.8	17.1	15.5	16.5	16.4	16.1	15.8	15.5	15.5	15.1	14.8
小 麦	Wheat	0.4	0.3	0.2	0.1	0.0	0.0	0.0	0.0	0.1	0.1	0.1
玉 米	Corn	9.6	9.7	9.6	9.0	9.4	9.5	9.6	9.4	10.1	9.9	9.7
大 豆	Soybean	4.4	4.5	3.9	1.9	1.9	2.5	1.6	1.6	1.6	1.6	1.6
薯 类	Tubers	5.4	5.5	4.6	4.4	4.0	4.5	4.3	4.4	4.5	4.5	4.4
二、经济作物及其他	Economic Crops	36.2	41.6	47.2	48.2	48.8	49.6	49.9	50.4	50.1	50.8	51.6
#油料合计	Total of Oil-bearing Crops	4.9	5.5	5.0	3.3	3.4	3.5	3.6	3.8	4.0	4.2	4.3
#花 生	Peanuts	3.6	3.8	3.8	2.9	3.0	3.1	3.2	3.3	3.5	3.6	3.7
油菜籽	Rapeseeds	1.1	1.4	1.0	0.3	0.3	0.3	0.3	0.4	0.4	0.4	0.4
芝 麻	Sesame	0.2	0.1	0.1	0.0	0.1	0.1	0.1	0.1	0.1	0.1	0.1
麻 类	Fiber Crops	0.1	0.1	0.1	0.1	0.1	0.1	0.1	0.1	0.1	0.1	0.1
#黄红麻	Jute & Ambary Hemp	0.1	0.1	0.1	0.1	0.1	0.1	0.1	0.1	0.1	0.1	0.1
甘 蔗	Sugarcane & Fruit Canes	7.9	8.1	11.8	18.2	18.2	18.5	18.3	17.5	15.9	15.5	15.2
#糖 蔗	Sugarcane	7.7	7.8	11.4	17.8	17.8	18.1	17.9	17.0	15.4	15.0	14.7
烟 叶	Tobacco	0.2	0.4	0.3	0.3	0.3	0.3	0.4	0.3	0.3	0.3	0.2
#烤 烟	Flue-Cured Tobacco	0.2	0.2	0.2	0.2	0.2	0.2	0.3	0.3	0.2	0.2	0.2
木 薯	Cassava	4.8	4.2	4.2	4.0	4.0	3.8	3.7	3.6	3.5	3.4	3.3
蔬 菜（含菜用瓜）	Vegetables (including vegetable melons)	9.7	14.4	17.3	17.1	17.4	17.7	17.8	18.8	19.9	20.7	21.4
绿 肥	Green Manure	3.7	2.5	1.5	0.9	0.9	0.9	0.9	1.0	1.1	1.1	1.2

注：“农作物播种面积”、“经济和其他农作物”、“蔬菜”中均不包含食用菌面积。
Note: The indicators of “Planting Area of Farm Crops”, “Economic Crops” and “Vegetables” do not include the area of eatable mushrooms.

13－9 主要年份林业生产情况

指 标	Item	1995	2000
造林面积（年末成活率达85（%）以上，千公顷）	Afforested Area (Survival Rate above 85 (%) at Year-end, 1 000 hectares)	130.2	57.0
#飞机播种	Sown by Airplane		
用材林	Timber Forest	63.8	30.5
经济林	Economic Forest	64.2	19.5
防护林	Shelter-forest	1.7	6.0
当年迹地更新面积（千公顷）	Slash Reforestation Areas of the Current Year (1 000 hectares)	69.6	100.7
育苗面积（千公顷）	Grow Seedlings Area (1 000 hectares)	2.1	1.4
当年四旁零星植树（按实际成活计，万株）	Oddly (all around) Tree Planting of the Current Year (by actual survival rate, 10 000 roots)	3519.00	3355.00
当年幼林抚育作业面积（千公顷次）	Operative Areas of Young Growth Fostering of the Current Year (1 000 hectares times)	623.3	390.5
成林抚育实际面积（千公顷）	Actual Areas of Mature Timber Fostering (1 000 hectares)	310.2	280.3
现有封山育林面积（千公顷）	Close Hillsides to Facilitate Afforesation Areas (1 000 hectares)	4339.2	4251.2
林木种籽采集量（吨）	Forestry Seed Collection (ton)	100	154
林产品产量（吨）	Output of Forestry Products (ton)		
油茶籽	Tea-oil Seeds	86098	118620
油桐籽	Tung-oil Seeds	50854	63002
松 脂	Pine Resin	247202	216015
八 角	Anise	18382	30966
桂 皮	Cassia Bark	16716	16605
板 栗	Chestnuts	11162	22008
核 桃	Walnuts	478	262
白 果	Ginkgo	2217	3629
茴 油	Fennel Oil	1186	1601
桂 油	Laurel Oil	642	779
竹笋干	Bamboo Shoots	7453	16208
橡 胶	Rubber	2672	1403
木材采伐量（万立方米）	Felling Amount of Timber (10 000 cu.m)	372.90	270.27
毛竹采伐量（万根）	Mao Bamboo (10 000 pieces)	2679.71	4655.48

注：2000年以前的木材和毛竹采伐量为村及村以下数量，2005年以后为全社会数量。

Note: Felling amount of timber & mao bamboo before 2000 only contains the amount of village & below. The amount after 2005 contains all amounts in every aspect.

Basic Statistics on Forestry in Main Years

2005	2010	2011	2012	2013	2014	2015	2016	2017
124.0	143.3	147.8	148.9	161.4	163.6	159.4	120.1	129.8
89.4	108	113.2	99.75	93.05	91.25	76.58	50.98	40.45
8.2	9.3	12.2	20.79	35.51	31.33	29.90	32.70	20.93
26.3	25.6	22.2	27.0	24.3	30.27	23.30	17.70	15.48
53.6	119.9	135.3	151.78	153.33	130.71	141.9	125.6	159.03
1.9	1.8	1.8	3.9	17.7	8.29	16.3	22.3	19.80
3092.00	5052.00	5408.00	5671.40	5989.42	6158.37	7099.37	8187.00	7248.43
513.2	657.9	625.9	603.6	581.1	667.0	746.0	491.2	407.57
211.3	503.9	590.3	865.1	879.2	1156.1	1488.8	1180.1	1172.72
3179.0	2151.0	2010.7	1858.1	1926.3	1931.8	1887.4	1704.4	1636.87
101	154	91	69	355	316	142	354	206
117363	143749	151002	163924	167688	177650	192762	200383	225785
60372	72536	75525	77524	79935	82611	83546	83272	85374
301943	495750	532903	557141	590021	616586	651234	669185	695549
76462	99626	104821	114118	119632	129101	135105	140264	143919
20305	28655	29940	31830	34896	34323	36707	37278	40556
45951	73059	73100	82276	91897	92278	100744	105853	109563
339	929	982	1140	1219	1210	1455	2239	2426
5409	7878	8140	8471	8615	8796	9001	9196	8760
2236	2973	3297	3397	3729	3961	4152	4474	4553
701	1036	1133	1192	1292	1216	1330	1371	1396
18770	24477	26003	28014	29980	32961	34046	32893	35344
678	378	213	225	999	172	117	160	121
762.55	1743.02	2065.25	2239.06	2288.03	2409.17	2980.00	3410.00	3810
5743.21	8712.93	9521.68	10207.25	10694.52	12373.63	17030.02	13949.89	14797.57

13－10 主要年份畜牧水产主要产品生产情况

指 标	Item	1995	2000
一、畜禽产品产量	**Output of Animal Products**		
肉猪出栏头数 (万头)	Number of Slaughtered Fattened Hogs (10 000 heads)	1905.84	2756.91
肉类总产量（万吨）	Output of Meat (10 000 tons)	195.61	287.26
#猪 肉	Pork	153.63	217.87
牛 肉	Beef	6.54	9.79
羊 肉	Mutton	0.77	2.47
禽 肉	Poultry	34.52	55.85
牛 奶（吨）	Milk (ton)	9006	16816
蜂 蜜（吨）	Honey (ton)	4016	5563
蚕 茧（吨）	Silkworm Cocoons (ton)	21248	29542
禽 蛋（吨）	Eggs (ton)		144514
二、水产品产量（吨）	**Aquatic Products (ton)**	**1032871**	**2398592**
#海水产品产量	Seawater Aquatic Products	645706	1594505
按生产性质分	By Production Character		
天然生产	Naturally Grow	498192	888417
人工养殖	Artificially Cultured	147514	706088
淡水产品产量	Freshwater Aquiculture	387165	804087
按生产性质分	By Production Character		
天然生产	Naturally Grow	45818	91538
人工养殖	Artificially Cultured	341347	712549

注：1996年以前水产品产量按旧标准统计，即贝类5斤折1斤计量。1997年起按新标准统计，即海蜇按三矾后的成品、海藻按干品计量，其余所有的水产品均按捕捞起水时的鲜活实际重量计量。2016年和2017年牛肉产量，根据第三次全国农业普查数据作了调整衔接。

Note: Output of aquatic products before 1996 was calculated according to old standard, namely 5kg of shellfish were equivalent to 1 kg to count. According to new standard statistics from 1997, the jellyfish was measured according to finished product after three vitriol, marine alga was measured according to the dry product, and other aquatic products are all measured according to thelifelike actual weight while being caught from water.

Basic Statistics on Main Products of Animal Husbandry & Fishery in Main Years

2005	2010	2011	2012	2013	2014	2015	2016	2017
3852.82	3230.00	3195.12	3342.09	3456.72	3518.01	3416.79	3280.12	3355.06
418.60	387.77	391.09	410.99	420.02	420.03	417.27	407.94	412.35
300.02	241.50	239.79	252.50	261.34	266.29	258.81	249.75	254.97
16.95	13.70	14.27	13.86	14.33	14.38	14.38	11.48	11.71
3.70	3.30	3.21	3.20	3.24	3.24	3.24	3.26	3.32
95.11	124.93	128.84	136.00	135.32	128.24	132.52	134.99	133.81
53540	82000	88831	93600	95600	96500	100600	96600	100400
7775	9286	9752	11639	12417	13093	13585	14951	15248
148460	264716	296263	315703	323448	339622	360657	378000	395900
146271	200000	210000	218200	227100	221600	228800	230900	227200
2841935	**2750934**	**2888198**	**3034656**	**3190604**	**3321169**	**3456249**	**3613687**	**3787855**
1739581	1540362	1589085	1643851	1707060	1741574	1794194	1869545	1950288
845786	662954	665281	668274	651434	650599	652028	664471	623245
893795	877408	923804	975577	1055626	1090975	1142166	1205074	1327043
1102354	1210572	1299113	1390805	1483544	1579595	1662055	1744142	1837532
113148	116871	123259	129259	132687	134602	140014	150114	155125
989206	1093701	1175854	1261546	1350857	1444993	1522041	1594028	1682407

13－11 各市农林牧渔业总产值及构成（2017年）
Gross Output Value & Its Composition of Farming, Forestry, Animal Husbandry & Fishery by City（2017）

（按当年价格计算） (at current prices)

各市名称	City	农林牧渔业总产值 Total	农业 Farming	林业 Forestry	牧业 Animal Husbandry	渔业 Fishery	农林牧渔专业及辅助性活动 Output Value of Service Industry for Farming, Forestry, Animal Husbandry & Fishery
一、总产值（亿元）	**Gross Output Value (100millon yuan)**						
南宁市	Nanning	689.15	381.84	31.04	212.60	27.44	36.24
柳州市	Liuzhou	325.22	192.91	29.21	82.09	10.03	10.99
桂林市	Guilin	609.64	409.11	34.84	132.29	14.36	19.03
梧州市	Wuzhou	231.98	124.05	38.39	48.27	11.18	10.08
北海市	Beihai	302.50	59.70	4.34	31.25	201.84	5.36
防城港市	Fangchenggang	150.85	42.70	17.23	12.26	76.28	2.38
钦州市	Qinzhou	377.16	181.39	25.15	79.16	83.16	8.30
贵港市	Guigang	334.75	149.57	21.73	101.97	44.05	17.44
玉林市	Yulin	475.93	209.19	27.65	180.32	24.64	34.12
百色市	Baise	307.56	176.58	33.15	73.77	17.74	6.33
贺州市	Hezhou	181.28	101.47	18.06	48.25	7.95	5.55
河池市	Hechi	271.75	114.96	29.21	112.83	8.56	6.20
来宾市	Laibin	263.57	155.96	20.62	72.98	7.60	6.41
崇左市	Chongzuo	275.53	193.95	27.16	36.45	10.87	7.09
二、构成（%）	**Composition (%)**						
南宁市	Nanning	100.0	55.4	4.5	30.8	4.0	5.3
柳州市	Liuzhou	100.0	59.3	9.0	25.2	3.1	3.4
桂林市	Guilin	100.0	67.1	5.7	21.7	2.4	3.1
梧州市	Wuzhou	100.0	53.5	16.6	20.8	4.8	4.3
北海市	Beihai	100.0	19.7	1.4	10.3	66.7	1.8
防城港市	Fangchenggang	100.0	28.3	11.4	8.1	50.6	1.6
钦州市	Qinzhou	100.0	48.1	6.7	21.0	22.0	2.2
贵港市	Guigang	100.0	44.7	6.5	30.5	13.2	5.2
玉林市	Yulin	100.0	44.0	5.8	37.9	5.2	7.2
百色市	Baise	100.0	57.4	10.8	24.0	5.8	2.1
贺州市	Hezhou	100.0	56.0	10.0	26.6	4.4	3.1
河池市	Hechi	100.0	42.3	10.7	41.5	3.1	2.3
来宾市	Laibin	100.0	59.2	7.8	27.7	2.9	2.4
崇左市	Chongzuo	100.0	70.4	9.9	13.2	3.9	2.6

13－12 各市农作物播种面积构成（2017年）
Sowing Areas Structure of Farm Crops by City (2017)

（以总播种面积为100） (Total Planting Area=100)　　单位：%（%）

各市名称	City	农作物播种面积 Planting Area of Farm Crops	一、粮食作物 Grain Crops	#稻谷 Rice	玉米 Corn	二、经济和其他农作物 Economic Crops	#油料 Oil-bearing Crops	甘蔗 Sugarcane	木薯 Cassava	蔬菜（含菜用瓜） Vegetables (including vegetable melons)
南宁市	Nanning	100.0	44.0	28.9	10.8	56.0	5.5	14.5	2.9	24.7
柳州市	Liuzhou	100.0	41.1	32.6	4.3	58.9	3.9	21.1	0.5	26.7
桂林市	Guilin	100.0	51.9	35.8	5.8	48.1	3.6	0.7	1.0	27.2
梧州市	Wuzhou	100.0	52.4	39.6	3.7	47.6	5.1	0.7	7.6	28.2
北海市	Beihai	100.0	42.2	26.0	5.6	57.8	9.4	16.7	7.6	21.4
防城港市	Fangchenggang	100.0	39.3	24.5	7.0	60.7	2.8	35.7	1.8	18.8
钦州市	Qinzhou	100.0	54.1	40.9	4.7	45.9	2.7	13.8	6.9	17.5
贵港市	Guigang	100.0	60.4	47.1	6.3	39.6	7.4	6.2	6.4	15.3
玉林市	Yulin	100.0	62.3	50.5	4.3	37.7	3.6	3.3	4.5	23.1
百色市	Baise	100.0	56.9	19.6	26.8	43.1	2.7	10.2	0.6	22.8
贺州市	Hezhou	100.0	53.0	39.6	5.8	47.0	6.1	1.1	3.0	27.0
河池市	Hechi	100.0	56.7	20.5	23.6	43.3	3.1	12.1	3.1	18.6
来宾市	Laibin	100.0	40.3	27.0	6.7	59.7	4.1	32.5	1.6	14.7
崇左市	Chongzuo	100.0	23.4	12.8	7.0	76.6	2.4	54.7	2.7	9.8

注：“农作物播种面积”、“经济和其他农作物”、“蔬菜”中均不包含食用菌面积。12－14表为全面调查数据。

Note: The indicators of “Planting Area of Farm Crops”, “Economic Crops” and “Vegetables” do not include the area of eatable mushrooms. Data of this table is overall statistical survey.

13－13 各市主要农作物播种面积（2017年）
Sown Area of Major Farm Crops by City（2017）

单位：千公顷 （1 000 hectares）

各市名称	City	农作物播种面积 Planting Area of Farm Crops	一、粮食作物 Grain Crops	#稻谷 Rice	玉米 Corn	二、经济和其他农作物 Economic Crops	#油料 Oil-bearing Crops	甘蔗 Sugarcane	木薯 Cassava	蔬菜（含菜用瓜） Vegetables (including vegetable melons)
广西全区	Total	6164.70	2997.78	1955.58	577.00	3166.92	263.96	935.00	200.98	1314.74
南宁市	Nanning	977.04	430.38	282.00	105.33	546.66	53.34	141.31	28.81	241.25
柳州市	Liuzhou	397.98	163.41	129.94	16.92	234.57	15.37	83.90	1.90	106.08
桂林市	Guilin	711.09	369.29	254.84	41.48	341.80	25.66	4.74	7.25	193.52
梧州市	Wuzhou	297.50	155.87	117.77	10.91	141.63	15.10	2.16	22.55	83.80
北海市	Beihai	183.22	77.23	47.56	10.26	105.99	17.18	30.54	13.89	39.14
防城港市	Fangchenggang	125.75	49.45	30.82	8.82	76.30	3.47	44.94	2.30	23.67
钦州市	Qinzhou	396.96	214.90	162.29	18.51	182.06	10.85	54.79	27.37	69.46
贵港市	Guigang	449.03	271.01	211.32	28.40	178.02	33.03	27.90	28.79	68.69
玉林市	Yulin	497.63	310.16	251.27	21.41	187.47	17.96	16.47	22.54	114.83
百色市	Baise	465.77	265.09	91.24	124.73	200.68	12.36	47.36	2.77	106.10
贺州市	Hezhou	250.33	132.76	99.11	14.49	117.57	15.38	2.73	7.61	67.55
河池市	Hechi	470.35	266.49	96.66	111.07	203.86	14.70	56.72	14.41	87.68
来宾市	Laibin	422.13	170.06	113.98	28.46	252.07	17.18	137.22	6.93	62.18
崇左市	Chongzuo	519.94	121.69	66.79	36.22	398.25	12.36	284.22	13.87	50.80

注：“农作物播种面积”、“经济和其他农作物”、“蔬菜”中均不包含食用菌面积。本表为全面调查数据。

Note: The indicators of “Planting Area of Farm Crops”, “Economic Crops” and “Vegetables” do not include the area of eatable mushrooms. Data of this table is overall statistical survey.

13－14 各市主要农作物产量（2017年）
Output of Major Farm Crops by City (2017)

单位：万吨 (1 000 tons)

各市名称 City	一、粮食作物 Grain Crops	#稻谷 Rice	玉米 Corn	大豆 Soybean	薯类 Tubers	#油料 Oil-bearing	#花生 Peanuts	麻类 Fiber	甘蔗 Sugarcan	烤烟 Tobacco	木薯 Cassava	蔬菜（含食用菌） Vegetables (including mushrooms)	茶叶 tea	园林水果 Grove Fruits
广西全区 Total	1485.51	1110.38	266.85	21.15	372.83	71.62	67.50	1.09	7611.69	2.26	172.05	3086.85	7.33	1701.30
南宁市 Nanning	216.81	153.24	53.95	3.32	27.99	16.02	15.95	0.03	1161.58	0.00	35.20	568.44	0.42	248.32
柳州市 Liuzhou	82.40	71.07	7.56	0.61	14.12	3.64	3.14	0.04	658.89	0.00	1.29	237.68	1.42	96.17
桂林市 Guilin	195.79	154.84	20.61	4.75	61.95	7.78	7.07	0.22	40.09	0.00	4.77	446.57	0.54	539.74
梧州市 Wuzhou	80.85	69.62	4.73	1.22	22.11	4.41	4.31	0.00	14.29	0.00	14.10	225.97	0.34	67.12
北海市 Beihai	37.83	26.05	5.31	0.16	30.75	5.07	5.04	0.18	246.23	0.00	12.45	88.86	0.00	12.18
防城港市 Fangchenggang	19.70	13.65	4.00	0.17	8.60	0.71	0.71	0.00	311.28	0.00	2.20	30.80	0.07	8.66
钦州市 Qinzhou	108.00	89.41	8.93	0.49	41.49	3.01	2.84	0.00	398.08	0.00	24.65	151.33	1.15	204.19
贵港市 Guigang	149.63	124.09	15.53	0.49	43.17	11.54	11.44	0.14	246.32	0.00	26.33	173.92	0.48	31.05
玉林市 Yulin	176.69	153.86	11.55	0.74	48.29	5.92	5.86	0.05	180.19	0.00	16.06	335.10	0.25	108.46
百色市 Baise	114.23	51.15	55.58	3.11	13.61	1.66	0.94	0.00	255.30	1.63	1.89	247.32	1.31	115.21
贺州市 Hezhou	70.74	58.80	6.94	0.60	19.07	3.47	3.31	0.00	17.14	0.40	5.92	183.25	0.94	87.45
河池市 Hechi	102.18	50.73	44.16	3.26	15.59	1.67	0.62	0.01	345.49	0.23	8.91	155.48	0.03	41.65
来宾市 Laibin	79.51	60.77	13.16	0.92	18.94	4.17	3.73	0.05	1229.11	0.00	5.68	133.43	0.11	74.69
崇左市 Chongzuo	51.16	33.09	14.84	1.30	7.15	2.56	2.55	0.37	2507.71	0.00	12.61	108.69	0.28	66.40

注：本表为全面调查数据。

Note: Data of this table is overall statistical survey.

13－15 各市主要农产品人均占有量（2017年）
Ownership of Per Capital Major Agricultural Products by City（2017）

单位：公斤 (kg)

各市名称	City	粮食产量 Grain	油料产量 Oil-bearing Crops	甘蔗产量 Sugarcane	蔬菜产量（含菌类）Vegetable	园林水果产量 Fruits	肉类产量 Meat	水产品产量 Aquatic Products
全　区	Total	305.57	14.73	1565.71	634.96	349.95	86.82	77.92
南宁市	Nanning	305.03	22.54	1634.24	799.75	349.37	92.58	38.62
柳州市	Liuzhou	207.07	9.14	1655.77	597.29	241.67	57.23	21.21
桂林市	Guilin	388.97	15.46	79.64	887.20	1072.32	107.96	25.90
梧州市	Wuzhou	267.03	14.56	47.18	746.29	221.67	67.19	34.27
北海市	Beihai	228.77	30.67	1489.17	537.39	73.64	77.14	693.56
防城港市	Fangchenggang	210.83	7.62	3330.58	329.60	92.64	51.32	569.84
钦州市	Qinzhou	331.12	9.24	1220.54	464.00	626.07	95.03	185.37
贵港市	Guigang	343.68	26.50	565.77	399.48	71.31	87.45	57.41
玉林市	Yulin	305.52	10.23	311.56	579.41	187.55	133.92	30.02
百色市	Baise	314.39	4.57	702.66	680.70	317.09	73.42	46.56
贺州市	Hezhou	345.47	16.93	83.72	894.92	427.07	82.48	40.35
河池市	Hechi	291.01	4.75	983.96	442.81	118.62	65.59	23.83
来宾市	Laibin	359.87	18.87	5562.73	603.87	338.03	70.45	33.22
崇左市	Chongzuo	246.18	12.34	12067.90	523.03	319.56	60.43	37.74

注：本表按两年常住人口平均计算。
Note: Data in the table are calculated by average of permanent population.

主要统计指标解释

农林牧渔业总产值 农林牧渔业总产值是以货币表现的农林牧渔业的全部产品总量和农林牧渔服务业产值（即对农林牧渔业生产活动进行的各种支持性服务活动的价值）之和。它反映一定时期内农林牧渔业生产总规模和总成果，是观察农林牧渔业生产水平和发展速度，研究农林牧渔业内部比例关系、农林牧渔业与工业、农林牧渔业与国家建设、人民生活比例关系的重要指标，同时也是计算农林牧渔业劳动生产率和农林牧渔业增加值的基础资料。

农林牧渔业增加值 指农、林、牧、渔及农林牧渔服务业生产货物或提供服务活动而增加的价值，为农林牧渔业现价总产值扣除农林牧渔业现价中间投入后的余额。

农业机械总动力 指全部农业机械动力的额定功率之和。农业机械是指用于农业生产及其产品初加工等相关农事活动的机械和设备。总动力按法定计算单位千瓦计算。（注：1马力=735.5瓦特=0.735千瓦）

有效灌溉面积 指具有一定的水源，地块比较平整，灌溉工程或设备已经配套，在一般年景下能够进行正常灌溉的耕地面积。在一般的情况下，有效灌溉面积应等于灌溉工程或设备已经配套，能够进行正常灌溉的水田和水浇地面积之和。

农用化肥施用量 指在本年度内实际用于农业生产的化肥数量。包括：氮肥、磷肥、钾肥和复合肥。施用量分为按实物量及折纯量两种方法计算。按折纯量计算化肥数量，即把氮肥、磷肥、钾肥分别按含氮、含五氧化二磷、含氧化钾百分之一百折算。复合肥：是指多营养成分或元素组成的肥料，如磷铵等。其折纯量按所含的主要成分来折算。

农作物总播种面积 是指应该在本日历年度内收获农产品的各种农作物播种面积之和。其计算公式为：

农作物播种面积=上年秋冬播作物面积+本年春播作物面积+本年夏播作物面积

=本年春收作物播种面积+本年夏收作物播种面积+本年秋收作物播种面积

粮食产量 指全社会产量。包括国有经济经营、集体统一经营和农民家庭经营的粮食产量，还包括工矿企业家庭办的农场和其他生产单位的产量。

粮食：按三大类进行统计，一是谷物，包括稻谷、小麦、玉米、高粱、谷子及其他杂粮，谷物产量一律按脱粒后的原粮（晒干）计算（玉米按脱粒后的干粒计算）；二是豆类，包括大豆、绿豆、红小豆等，按去荚后的干豆计算；三是薯类（包括红薯、马铃薯，不包括芋头、木薯），1963年以前按4公斤鲜薯折1公斤粮食计算，从1964年以后改为按5公斤鲜薯折1公斤粮食计算；按国家制度，2015年开始，薯类按鲜薯重量计算，但在粮食合计中仍按5公斤鲜薯折1公斤粮食计算。2009年以前广西的马铃薯统计在蔬菜中，2009年以后统计在粮食的薯类中；2014年以前的甜玉米按粮食统计，自2014年年报始，甜玉米不在粮食统计中，纳入蔬菜统计。

林产品产量 指从人工栽培的竹木上，不经砍伐竹木的根本而取得的各种林产品产量。包括生漆、棕片、五倍子、松脂、笋干、油茶籽、油桐籽、乌桕子、核桃、板栗等各种林木籽实以及修剪竹木所获得的枝叶（包括荆条、柳条、蒲葵叶5等。不包括桑叶、茶叶和水果。也不包括野生的林产品）。如果某些林产品人工栽培的和野生的混在一起，不易划分，应根据它的主要来源决定其应计入林产品产量还是其他农业的采集野生植物产量，不要两方面都算，以免重复。

水果产量 指农业生产经营者日历年度内生产的乔木类和藤本类水果、多年草本水果及果用瓜。包括园林水果和非园林水果（瓜果类），不包括采集的野生水果。按鲜果产量计算。经脱水、晾干等处理的干果，如干枣、葡萄干、柿饼、桔饼等一律折合成鲜果计算。

园林水果：指农业生产经营者日历年度内在专业性果园、林地及零星种植果树（藤）上生产的水果。包括苹果、梨、柑桔类、热带及亚热带水果和其它园林水果如桃、葡萄、红枣等，不包括采集的野生水果。按实收的鲜果计算产量。经脱水、晾干等处理的干果，如干枣、葡萄干、柿饼、桔饼等一律折合成鲜果计算。

肉类总产量 指调查期内各种牲畜及家禽、兔等动物肉产量总计。猪、牛、羊、马、驴、骡、骆驼肉产量按去掉头蹄下水后带骨肉的胴体重量计算，兔禽肉产量按屠宰后去毛和内脏后的重量计算。猪牛羊禽四个品种肉产量由主要畜禽监测抽样调查获得，马、驴、骡、骆驼、兔肉产量由全面统计获得，其它特种养殖肉产量可用住户调查资料推算获得。

水产品产量 指渔业（捕捞和养殖）生产活动的最终有效成果，包括全部海水和淡水鱼类、甲壳类（虾、蟹）、贝类、头足类、藻类和其它类渔业产品的最终产量。不包括渔业生产过程中的中间成果，如鱼苗、鱼种、亲鱼、转塘鱼、存塘鱼和自用作饵料的产品等。水产品在上岸前已经腐烂变质，不能供人食用或加工成其它制品的，不统计在水产品产量中。

Explanatory Notes on Main Statistical Indicators

Gross Output Value of Farming, Forestry, Animal Husbandry and Fishery refers to the total amount of farming, forestry, animal husbandry, fishery products and the output value of services (refer to the supporting activities for farming, forestry, animal husbandry and fishery) that behave with the currency. It reflects the total achievement or total scale of agricultural production in form of magnitude of value during a certain period. It is an important synthesis index to observe the agricultural production level and development speed, and study proportionate relationship inside agriculture, proportionate relationship between agriculture and industry, agriculture and national construction, and proportionate relationship of people's livelihood. And it is also the basic data for calculating the agricultural productivity of labour and agricultural added value.

The Added Value of Farming, Forestry, Animal Husbandry and Fishery refers to the added value of products of farming, forestry, animal husbandry, fishery and relative services, or the added value of providing services. It is calculated by subtracting the intermediate inputs from the gross output value of farming, forestry, animal husbandry and fishery which calculated by the current prices.

Total Power of Farm Machinery refers to the summary of power rating of total power of agricultural machinery. Agricultural machinery refers to the machines and equipment for relative agricultural activities, which including agricultural producing and primary processing for relative products. The total power of farm machinery is calculated by the statutory unit of measurement: KW (note: 1 horsepower=735.5W=0.735KW).

Effective Irrigated Area refers to the cultivated areas whose irrigated project or equipments is in suit, have water source, have been ploughed, and could normally irrigated in usual years. Under normal circumstances, the effective irrigated area should include the total area of paddy fields and irrigated lands which are fitted irrigating projects or equipments and can be irrigated normally.

Consumption of Chemical Fertilizers refers to the chemical fertilizers actually used in agricultural production during the year, including nitrogenous fertilizer, phosphate fertilizer, potash fertilizer and compound fertilizer. Consumption of chemical fertilizers is calculated by 2 methods: practical amount and pure amount. Calculating by pure amount is separately converting the nitrogenous fertilizer, phosphate fertilizer and potash fertilizer into 100% according to their content of nitrogen, phosphorus pent oxide, potassium oxide. Compound fertilizer refers to fertilizer composed by various of nutritional components or elements, such as ammonium phosphate etc. Pure quantity is calculated by the percentage of its content of major component.

Total Sown Area of Farm Crops refers to the total sown area of farm crops which supposed to be harvested as products in the calendar year. Its calculation formula is:

Total Sown Area of Farm Crops = Autumn & Winter Sown Area of Last Year + Spring Sown Area of Current Year + Summer Sown Area of Current Year = Spring Harvesting Area of Current Year + Summer Harvesting Area of Current Year + Autumn Harvesting Area of Current Year

The Output of Grain refers to the output of the whole society. It includes the grain output from state-owned economy, collective-owned economy and farmer family management, and also includes the output from farms run by industrial & mining enterprises and families and other production units.

The statistics of grains is divided into 3 broad categories. 1. Cereals, including rice, wheat, corn, sorghum, millet and other coarse cereals, the output of cereals is calculated by the threshed and dried grains. 2. Beans, including soybeans, mung beans and red beans etc. Its output is calculated by the dried one without pods. 3. Tubers, including sweet potatoes and potatoes, excluding taros and cassavas, is converted into that of grain at the ratio 4:1, i.e. 4kg of fresh tubers was equivalent to 1 kg of grain up to 1963, since 1964, the ratio for conversion has been 5:1. According to national system, the tubers are calculated by the fresh weight since 2015, and 5 kg of fresh tubers is still calculated as 1 kg of grain. Potatoes and taros in Guangxi are calculated as vegetable before 2009, and since

2009 they are calculated as tubers of grains. The sweet corn was calculated as grain before 2014, and it's calculated as vegetables instead of grain since 2014.

The Output of Forestry refers to the output of various forestry products which are gained from artificial planted bamboos and trees without felling them down. It includes raw lacquer, palm sheets, Chinese gallnuts, pine resin, bamboo shoots, tea-oil seeds, bancoul nuts, Chinese tallow tree seeds, walnuts, chestnuts and various seeds of trees and branches and leaves trimmed from bamboos and trees (including twigs of the chaste trees, twigs of the willow trees, leaves of palms etc. It excludes leaves of mulberry, leaves of tea trees and fruits; it also excludes the products from wild forests). If it is difficult to discriminate certain kinds of mixed forestry products from artificial ones to wild ones, it should be accounted into the output of forestry or the output of wild plants of other agriculture according to its major resource, and it shouldn't be calculated in both sides so as to avoiding repetition.

Output of Fruits refers to the output of fruits of trees, vines, perennial herbs and fruited melons produced by agricultural operators in the calendar year. It includes grove fruits and non-grove fruits (melons), but excludes collected wild fruits. The output of fruits is calculated with fresh weight. The dried fruits which have been dehydrated or dried out, such as dried dates, raisins, dried persimmon, tangerine cake, etc. should be converted into the fresh fruit and calculated in unison.

The grove fruits: refers to the fruits produced in professional groves, forestlands and sporadically planted trees (vines) by agricultural operators in the calendar year. It includes apples, pears, oranges, tropical and subtropical fruits and other grove fruit such as peaches, grapes and dates, excludes collected wild fruits. The output of fruits is calculated with fresh weight of fruits actually harvested. The dried fruits which have been dehydrated or dried out, such as dried dates, raisins, dried persimmon, tangerine cake, etc. should be converted into the fresh fruit and calculated in unison.

Total Output of Meat refers to total output of animal meat of various livestock, poultry and rabbits. The output of meat of pigs, cattle, sheep, horses, donkeys, mules and camels is calculated with the weight of carcasses gotten rid of heads, hooves and entrails, and the output of meat of rabbits and poultry is calculated with the weight of carcasses slaughtered and gotten rid of feather and entrails. The output of meat of pigs, cattle, sheep and poultry is gained from the sample monitor investigation of major livestock and poultry, the output of meat of horses, donkeys, mules, camels and rabbits is gained from the full investigation, and the output of meat of other culture of special species could be calculated by the data of household investigation.

Output of Aquatic Products refers to the final effective products of fishery (fishing and cultivating) producing activities, including the final volume of products of all the marine fishes, freshwater fishes, crustaceans(shrimps, crabs), shellfishes, cephalopods, algae and other fishery products, excluding the intermediate products in the fishery producing activities, such as fries, fingerlings, parent fishes, pond fishes, storage pond fishes and products for self-use of fodder. The aquatic products, which have rotten before shoring and cannot be eaten or processing to other products, should not be calculated as the output, too.

第十四篇 工业

INDUSTRY

（校对编辑：白　平　黄青林）

14－1 全部工业总产值及指数
All Included Gross Industrial Output Value & Its Related Index

年 份	Year	全部工业总产值 Total	按登记注册类型分类 Grouped by Status of Registration			按轻、重工业 Grouped by Light & Heavy Industry	
			国有 State-owned	集体 Collective-owned	其他 Others	轻工业 Light Industry	重工业 Heavy Industry
总产值（当年价，万元）	**Gross Output Value (At Current Prices, 10 000 yuan)**						
1978		699727	551690	116121	31916	382292	317435
1980		786344	612702	136125	37517	468411	317933
1985		1393949	1084159	228070	81720	753461	640488
1990		3534331	2550882	586910	396539	1953243	1581088
1991		4214681	3000710	696019	517952	2270524	1944157
1992		5828107	3824655	955270	1048182	3041305	2786803
1993		9029300	5013602	1548821	2466877	4223400	4805900
1994		13216300	5921631	2246881	5047788	6492200	6724100
1995		14631700	5825904	2569475	6236321	6955900	7675800
1996		15984500	5798228	3014812	7171460	7951900	8032600
1997		16710300	5693497	3347962	7668841	8464900	8245400
1998		17276800	4980222	3601904	8694674	9103500	8173300
1999		16673250	4368813	3342196	8962241	8130100	8543200
2000		18002396	4105570	2769606	11127220	8620042	9382354
2001		19031372	3574148	2331629	13125595	9123525	9907847
2002		20365560	3489093	1942627	14933840	9760647	10604913
2003		23542453	3854711	1451699	18236043	10815312	12727141
2004		31530448	4426117	984325	26120006	13073722	18456726
2005		36840688	5534547	960144	30345997	14610518	22230170
2006		46864680	6201561	1080907	39582212	18008453	28856227
2007		61028644	7610728	1260445	52157471	22075424	38953220
2008		78019656	9005999	1319937	67693720	27725212	50294444
2009		86999513	9441093	1488212	76070208	30711524	56287989
2010		116717894	12812025	1594193	102311676	38578284	78139610
2011		150918805	18963165	1664560	130291080	49645017	101273788
2012		172046215	20500188	1859502	149686525	53959108	118087107
2013		194345536	11110367	2009015	181226155	58375567	135969969
2014		217303080	10714696	2231910	204356474	63437841	153865239
2015		233755728	9295881	2411963	222047883	67113433	166642295
2016		253714401	9994747	2491435	241228218	72733380	180981020
2017		278929062	4193125	2672834	272063103	78172286	200756776

注：1. 本表从1995年起工业总产值按新规定计算,国有指纯国有企业。
2. 工业总产值指数按可比价格计算。
3. 本篇2004年数据为第一次经济普查数据；2005－2009年数据根据第二次经济普查数据进行了相应调整衔接；2013年数据为三经普汇总数据及保密单位数据，与国家工业司汇总数一致。

Note: 1. Gross Industrial Output Value have been calculated in accordance with the new standards since 1995, State-owned refers to pure State-owned Enterprises.
2. Related Index of Gross Industrial Output Value are calculated in accordance with Constant Prices.
3. The data of 2004 in this chapter are the figures of economic census. The data from 2005 to 2009 has been adjusted for linking up with the 2nd Economic Census. The data in 2013 is the summary of the 3rd Economic Census and data of security units, and its statistical range is the same as Industrial Division of National Bureau of Statistic.

14—1 续表 continued

年 份	Year	全部工业总产值 Total	按登记注册类型分类 Grouped by Status of Registration			按轻、重工业 Grouped by Light & Heavy Industry	
			国有 State-owned	集体 Collective-owned	其他 Others	轻工业 Light Industry	重工业 Heavy Industry
指 数（上年=100）	**Index(preceding year=100)**						
1978		109.7	109.7	109.2	117.1	107.6	112.3
1980		107.1	106.5	111.7	101.8	114.5	97.9
1985		120.8	121.1	112.2	148.3	116.7	128.0
1990		108.3	106.7	106.9	120.6	110.0	105.8
1991		115.3	111.9	119.1	190.8	117.1	113.2
1992		135.4	125.5	132.7	195.8	135.7	134.9
1993		135.2	109.1	146.7	220.3	125.7	146.3
1994		130.8	104.3	140.2	193.6	131.0	131.5
1995		115.1	105.2	113.5	110.7	103.2	121.9
1996		110.8	100.7	116.3	128.8	115.2	106.6
1997		107.2	100.5	113.7	99.8	109.7	98.2
1998		106.5	97.7	106.2	107.0	110.7	108.6
1999		106.5	97.8	85.4	118.0	100.2	102.6
2000		107.4	88.8	83.0	125.8	89.2	116.3
2001		108.0	89.5	85.6	120.0	104.5	110.6
2002		111.0	97.6	89.3	118.0	113.2	108.9
2003		115.4	100.4	75.3	127.4	117.2	116.2
2004		123.1	104.6	67.1	131.5	109.3	134.8
2005		113.2	119.2	93.5	112.9	108.1	116.8
2006		118.6	102.2	110.7	121.8	111.8	123.1
2007		125.2	117.4	112.4	126.8	126.0	124.7
2008		117.8	108.6	96.9	120.0	121.1	115.9
2009		118.1	112.2	119.5	118.2	109.5	122.8
2010		120.3	121.2	96.5	120.3	109.7	126.1
2011		118.4	136.5	96.2	116.6	111.7	121.8
2012		116.1	110.5	113.8	117.0	109.5	119.4
2013		116.5	54.1	114.6	125.3	121.5	114.4
2014		112.9	98.6	111.8	113.0	109.2	114.5
2015		109.4	86.8	111.8	110.6	109.5	109.4
2016		108.7	110.1	103.6	108.6	107.4	109.2
2017		113.6	115.4	110.3	113.6	111.3	114.5

14－2 主要年份工业企业主要指标

指 标	Item	企业单位数（个）Number of Enterprises (unit)			
		2005	2010	2015	2017
总 计	**Total**	**3687**	**6583**	**5518**	**5723**
内资企业	**Civil Funded Enterprises**	**3297**	**6039**	**5057**	**5304**
国有经济	State-owned	791	384	151	71
中央企业	Central Enterprises	49	45	19	8
地方企业	Local Enterprises	742	339	132	63
集体经济	Collective-owned	256	256	98	83
股份合作企业	Cooperative Enterprises	71	50	16	11
联营企业	Joint Ownership Enterprises	11	9	3	1
有限责任公司	Limited Liability Corporations	707	1128	1544	1459
股份有限公司	Share Holding Enterprises	167	212	210	185
私营企业	Private Enterprises	1277	3931	2995	3493
其他企业	Other Enterprises			40	1
港澳台商投资企业	**Enterprises with Funds from Hong Kong, Macao & Taiwan**	**207**	**293**	**272**	**256**
外商投资企业	**Foreign Funded Enterprises**	**183**	**251**	**189**	**163**
在总计中:	Of the Total:				
国有控股企业	State Holding Enterprises	1005	632	570	538
在总计中:	Of the Total:				
轻工业	Light Industry	1487	2442	2061	1998
重工业	Heavy Industry	2200	4141	3457	3725
在总计中:	Of the Total:				
大型企业	Large-scale Industrial Enterprises	25	48	195	202
中型企业	Medium-scale Industrial Enterprises	419	798	1270	1222
小型企业	Small-scale Industrial Enterprises	3243	5737	3820	4112
微型企业	Micro-enterprises			233	187

注：本表的统计范围1995年为全部乡及乡以上独立核算工业企业，2000年为全部国有和年产品销售收入500万元及以上非国有工业法人企业，2005－2010年为年主营业务收入500万元及以上工业法人企业，2011－2017年为年主营业务收入2000万元及以上工业法人企业。

Note: The statistic in the table of 1995 covered all of the township industrial enterprises and above, and data of 2000 refer to all state-owned industrial enterprises and the non-state-owned industrial enterprises with an annual sales income of over 5 million yuan, anddata of from 2005 to 2010 refer to industrial enterprises with annual business income of the main products over 5 million yuan, since 2011-2017, the data refer to industrial enterprises with annual income of the major business over 20 million yuan.

Major Indicators of Industrial Enterprises in Main Years

工业总产值（当年价，万元）Gross Industrial Output Value (At Current Prices, 10 000 yuan)				全部从业人员年平均人数（人）Average Employed Persons (person)				流动资产合计（万元）Annual Average Balance of Circulating Funds (10 000 yuan)			
2005	2010	2015	2017	2005	2010	2015	2017	2005	2010	2015	2017
25473188	**96441278**	**225824149**	**262512136**	**912102**	**1505050**	**1677994**	**1646215**	**11249972**	**37005538**	**69815219**	**81939863**
19731000	**76682817**	**185675146**	**215757014**	**773606**	**1263500**	**1398837**	**1394091**	**8772365**	**27707681**	**55272118**	**64719485**
5534547	12812025	9295881	1615325	216272	150499	75162	23111	2708710	5079458	3796361	1013765
1700251	3791390	1220521	471261	29004	28358	14730	8210	750011	1738270	777201	668060
3834296	9020635	8075359	1138487	187268	122141	60432	14901	1958700	3341188	3019160	345705
670825	1176462	2248560	2500421	43455	37757	22233	19419	252430	372093	339404	331720
263114	1086610	459641	158251	12029	15680	3020	1724	108695	314936	66341	20728
52265	140088	41547	4006	2260	2031	466	64	15396	50299	15742	260
6321223	24121675	72932443	91562690	216067	359050	498153	483441	2925655	9029878	24256669	30727460
2779448	6887043	18968399	20008814	94413	118552	117878	95925	1445803	4319642	8145931	8838428
4069061	29503296	80503596	99897819	186661		670339	770316	1298079	8280640	18440760	23785989
		1225081	9688			11586	91			210910	1135
1357798	**5699403**	**15483948**	**18670841**	**62082**	**116632**	**157183**	**149636**	**682671**	**2206277**	**4101874**	**5704131**
4384390	**14059058**	**24665055**	**28084280**	**76414**	**124918**	**121974**	**102488**	**1794936**	**7091581**	**10441228**	**11516247**
12268731	36284650	62421736	74611222	372398	389784	363822	331416	5958746	15727556	25559237	29470397
7903693	26615080	62433801	68739619	377389	575986	649037	577122	3349354	10784576	21275188	23054157
17569495	69826198	163390348	193772517	534713	929064	1028957	1069093	7900617	26220962	48540031	58885706
7730400	26248738	76696050	92488616	127227	265881	507829	503295	3239585	10757623	26536901	30512905
8537754	33917379	74550198	82624229	303237	535571	697617	677532	4488641	16173669	23140180	26906357
9205034	36275161	73059378	85138593	481638	703598	465241	461960	3521746	10074246	19071854	23268756
		1518522	2260698			7307	3428			1066285	1251845

14－2 续表 1

单位：万元

指 标	Item	固定资产原价 Value of Fixed Assets 2005	2010	2015	2017
总 计	**Total**	**19080017**	**51408004**	**85756838**	**99224059**
内资企业	**Civil Funded Enterprises**	**16242526**	**43959624**	**71315154**	**83129490**
国有经济	State-owned	5773509	14181424	6445139	1110132
中央企业	Central Enterprises	2078259	7681474	1020072	279835
地方企业	Local Enterprises	3695250	6499950	5425067	830297
集体经济	Collective-owned	301532	273513	331460	347460
股份合作企业	Cooperative Enterprises	110521	1208176	119242	21219
联营企业	Joint Ownership Enterprises	30597	72634	8324	1494
有限责任公司	Limited Liability Corporations	6780493	16763603	36711024	50891825
股份有限公司	Share Holding Enterprises	2132785	3817158	11459115	11305113
私营企业	Private Enterprises	1100109	7507511	16015653	19451898
其他企业	Other Enterprises			225197	350
港澳台商投资企业	**Enterprises with Funds from Hong Kong, Macao & Taiwan**	**856712**	**2900474**	**4973724**	**5328720**
外商投资企业	**Foreign Funded Enterprises**	**1980780**	**4547905**	**9467960**	**10765849**
在总计中：	Of the Total:				
国有控股企业	State Holding Enterprises	13036444	30226479	44688748	53145720
在总计中：	Of the Total:				
轻工业	Light Industry	4986527	10690677	18795295	20084446
重工业	Heavy Industry	14093490	40717327	66961543	79139613
在总计中：	Of the Total:				
大型企业	Large-scale Industrial Enterprises	5845482	15607285	32644929	40622994
中型企业	Medium-scale Industrial Enterprises	7607598	18652915	30747711	32590666
小型企业	Small-scale Industrial Enterprises	5626937	17147803	21138789	25573946
微型企业	Micro-enterprises			1225409	436453

continued

(10 000 yuan)

固定资产净值 Value of Fixed Assets				实收资本 Total Capital Hold			
2005	2010	2015	2017	2005	2010	2015	2017
13126063	**36664670**	**53624955**	**61239540**	**6803910**	**15851949**	**29152575**	**28644278**
11232879	**31496168**	**44549710**	**52494467**	**5360150**	**12713358**	**23720785**	**22725934**
3783996	10582569	3939303	791026	1685247	3401392	1112934	412797
1304105	5929332	632408	140821	639194	2145031	271691	284719
2479891	4653237	3306895	650205	1046053	1256361	841243	128078
179329	154987	206397	185848	97648	98432	75438	71701
83803	949377	77899	15019	42653	299630	24758	7959
22562	53412	5983	1266	11962	17779	1264	646
4930027	11473828	22397979	31582327	2276024	4683364	14746006	11989635
1387345	2539310	7379805	7167951	653284		3205533	3448183
834968	5643092	10376653	12750705	584074	2763000	4514786	6794863
		165691	325			40065	150
614773	**2195275**	**3195725**	**2834971**	**561962**	**1274570**	**1943446**	**2206075**
1278412	**2973228**	**5879520**	**5910102**	**881799**	**1864021**	**3488344**	**3712270**
8879648	20912831	27364877	32525108	4049793	7906893	10541734	12309575
3389276	7190196	11598046	11403232	2061449	4653204	7509785	8642011
9736788	29474474	42026909	49836308	4742461	11198744	21642790	20002267
4023210	10340445	19449107	24554849	1446009	3008126	7463418	7483267
5025459	13339348	19828994	19545298	2846052	7270892	13732971	10309299
4077394	12984876	13647355	16793393	2511849	5572931	7606503	10399557
		699498	346000			349683	452155

14—2 续表 2

单位：万元

指 标	Item	负债合计 Total Liabilities 2005	2010	2015	2017
总 计	**Total**	**18534169**	**54132948**	**94028112**	**108186759**
内资企业	**Civil Funded Enterprises**	**15496001**	**44287260**	**76601490**	**89097830**
国有经济	State-owned	4829643	12182305	6219571	1007972
中央企业	Central Enterprises	1552760	6050848	950589	463897
地方企业	Local Enterprises	3276884	6131457	5268982	544076
集体经济	Collective-owned	439258	398331	230894	205811
股份合作企业	Cooperative Enterprises	148790	784013	90743	25348
联营企业	Joint Ownership Enterprises	26166	64081	9004	822
有限责任公司	Limited Liability Corporations	6285633	16144204	38223442	51000873
股份有限公司	Share Holding Enterprises	2070123	5084569	11114025	11494047
私营企业	Private Enterprises	1673542	9452050	20474977	25362614
其他企业	Other Enterprises			238833	343
港澳台商投资企业	**Enterprises with Funds from Hong Kong, Macao & Taiwan**	**927998**	**2774814**	**4899449**	**6134522**
外商投资企业	**Foreign Funded Enterprises**	**2110169**	**7070873**	**12527174**	**12954408**
在总计中：	Of the Total:				
国有控股企业	State Holding Enterprises	11301229	29019882	43679344	51409839
在总计中：	Of the Total:				
轻工业	Light Industry	4832793	11830719	22920311	23845599
重工业	Heavy Industry	13701377	42302229	71107801	84341160
在总计中：	Of the Total:				
大型企业	Large-scale Industrial Enterprises	5106233	17013726	36771160	43601925
中型企业	Medium-scale Industrial Enterprises	7264774	20990158	31265998	33862510
小型企业	Small-scale Industrial Enterprises	6163162	16129064	23963631	28910125
微型企业	Micro-enterprises			2027324	1812199

注：主营业务收入（产品销售收入）栏2000年为产品销售收入，2005—2017年为主营业务收入。

Note: In the table, data of Business Income of the Main Products (Sales Revenue) of 2000 is figure of Sales Revenue, and that from 2005 to 2017 are Business Income of the Main Products.

continued

(10 000 yuan)

主营业务收入（产品销售收入） Business Income of the Main Products (Sales Revenue)				利润总额 Total Profits			
2005	2010	2015	2017	2005	2010	2015	2017
24667860	**92358467**	**204425005**	**238050543**	**1349867**	**7715895**	**12790565**	**16109525**
19225332	**73048098**	**166875608**	**194281624**	**1018503**	**5753715**	**9854346**	**12881055**
5543125	12307051	8647019	1480252	357318	482639	-49094	87686
1688826	3407872	1118161	442233	230049	227554	12800	18702
3854299	8899179	7528858	1038019	127269	255086	-61894	68984
661895	1178772	2172943	2434053	10762	58512	176504	194005
251807	983230	441146	122816	7400	139148	57940	3227
49302	119806	42129	4006	8113	22429	5484	1
6239953	23025787	64524536	81308133	302542		3923457	5339217
2734124	7091970	16610899	18216067	232651	802764	933516	1715248
3704471	27384971	73246126	90706610	99990	2247046	4719419	5540468
		1190809	9688			87120	1203
1288361	**5349221**	**14020883**	**18086491**	**79737**	**616372**	**1229916**	**1367524**
4154166	**13961148**	**23528515**	**25682428**	**251627**	**1345808**	**1706303**	**1860946**
12429732	36027399	56807658	67859744	677038	2275089	2324215	3846278
7485388	24893120	55354189	61329431	504939	2683730	4052161	4128219
17182472	67465346	149070816	176721112	844928	5032165	8738405	11981306
7593827	26390575	71744161	85970557	476527	1816122	4161190	6528513
8565199	32014676	66019977	73952021	604357	2957365	4760550	5389993
8508834	33953216	65035250	76134778	268983	2942408	3927666	4121040
		1625616	1993187			-58841	69979

14—3　工业企业分行业主要指标（2017年）

单位：万元

行　业	Sector	企业单位数（个）Number of Enterprises (unit)	工业总产值（当年价格）Gross Industrial Output Value (At Current Prices)
工业企业	**Industrial Enterprises**	**5723**	**262512136**
煤炭的开采和洗选业	Coal Mining & Dressing	15	631431
石油和天然气开采业	Oil & Gas Mining	1	105937
黑色金属矿采选业	Ferrous Metals Mining & Dressing	38	2295006
有色金属矿采选业	Nonferrous Metals Mining & Dressing	68	2527216
非金属矿采选业	Nonmetal Minerals Mining & Dressing	157	3113495
开采辅助活动	Mining Assist Activities	1	61916
其他采矿业	Other Minerals Mining	2	35033
农副食品加工业	Farm & Sideline Products Processing	539	26866064
#制糖业	Carbohydrate Processing	87	7704840
食品制造业	Food Production	140	4778442
#罐头制造业	Canned Food Manufacturing	14.0	396590
酒、饮料和精制茶制造业	Wine, Drink & Refined Tea Manufacturing	150	5261737
#酒的制造	Beverage Manufacturing	34.0	2117300
烟草制品业	Tobacco Processing	2	2073380
#卷烟制造	Cigarettes Manufacturing	1	2065426
纺织业	Textile Industry	141	3030566
纺织服装、服饰业	Textiles, Clothing & Dresses Manufacturing	58	1957034
皮革、毛皮、羽毛及其制品和制鞋业	Leather, Fur, Feather & Related Products & Shoes Manufacturing	63	1377303
木材加工及木、竹、藤、棕、草制品业	Timber Processing, Bamboo, Cane, Palm Fiber & Straw Products	718	14599058
家具制造业	Furniture Manufacturing	50	1098316
造纸及纸制品业	Papermaking & Paper Products	165	4061256
#造纸	Papermaking	87	2344460
印刷和记录媒介复制业	Printing & Record Duplicating	68	1280073

注：工业企业分行业主要指标统计范围为年主营业务收入2000万元及以上工业法人企业。
Note: The statistic coverage of major indicators of industrial enterprises by industrial sectors is enterprises with business income ofthe main products of over 20 million yuan. the main products of over 5 million yuan.

Major Indicators of Industrial Enterprises by Industrial Sector (2017)

(10 000 yuan)

全部从业人员年平均人数（人）Average Employed Persons (person)	固定资产原价 Original Value of Fixed Assets	固定资产净值 Net Value of Fixed Assets	资产总计 Total Capital	流动资产合计 Annual Average Balance of Circulating Funds	所有者权益合计 Owner's Equity	利润总额 Total Profits	主营业务收入 Business Income of the Main Products
1646215	**99224059**	**61239540**	**175319945**	**81939863**	**67371077**	**16109525**	**238050543**
14347	292711	252980	976434	394309	298473	22447	567527
123	211779		360629	40040	311888	53602	237831
10810	411895	301117	946033	567966	420124	162327	2216286
20711	964758	551037	2650309	1352041	981803	226142	2291643
27157	595181	443054	1333257	674107	632661	219064	2817320
97	1135	948	2857	1821	2505	18092	61297
177	4201	2577	9794	7076	9379	1884	36063
128902	6532051	3476906	16148594	10303522	5978515	1787443	23399669
52285	3629053	1676261	6999803	4400980	2552168	933133	5895202
33702	1141893	858139	2730228	1275542	1437835	259399	4362677
6059	95464	68214	212752	95767	125190	54105	366530
44748	1612820	1050199	2929011	1391065	1493285	293204	4414820
13143	934758	565368	1516859	738556	733026	86670	1622987
3451	716682	294414	2021078	1351872	1442398	116208	2073516
3008	700855	294414	1968546	1307756	1394081	116135	2065249
42415	664316	462109	1566209	925160	505974	162428	2784796
21472	216110	121868	566879	393034	343066	143408	1902486
30208	237344	165214	528601	307674	270741	54426	1277548
150627	2151046	1336774	4872481	2688560	2191705	656227	13399155
8642	98018	60921	339116	197700	149803	56579	1028445
32864	3999808	1924580	6552667	2423610	1865962	168005	3665604
17629	3247132	1360458	5005364	1770821	1468385	100847	2175863
10989	520795	268274	622861	227666	383863	96552	1223252

14—3 续表

单位：万元

行 业	Sector	企业单位数（个）Number of Enterprises (unit)	工业总产值（当年价格）Gross Industrial Output Value (At Current Prices)
文教、工美、体育和娱乐用品制造业	Culture, Education, Handcraft, Art, Sport & Entertainment Goods Manufacturing	86	1620770
石油加工、炼焦及核燃料加工业	Oil Processing, Coking & Nuclear Fuel Processing	25	8935740
化学原料及化学制品制造业	Raw Chemical Materials & Chemical Products	422	12647184
医药制造业	Medical & Pharmaceutical Products	150	4597709
化学纤维制造业	Chemical Fibre Products	2	20581
橡胶和塑料制品业	Rubber & Plastic Products	149	3813339
非金属矿物制品业	Nonmetal Mineral Products	820	20165820
#水泥制造	Cement Products	100	4274525
黑色金属冶炼及压延加工业	Smelting & Pressing of Ferrous Metals	160	25228508
有色金属冶炼及压延加工业	Smelting & Pressing of Nonferrous Metals	101	19728932
金属制品业	Metal Products	161	5455912
通用设备制造业	General Equipment Manufacturing	115	4515108
专用设备制造业	For Special Purposes Equipment Manufacturing	147	5659843
汽车制造业	Automobile Manufacturing	349	28297560
#汽车整车制造	Vehicle manufacturing	8	14191960.6
铁路、船舶、航空航天和其他运输设备制造业	Railway, Ship, Aerospace & Other Transportation Equipment Manufacturing	47	1942043
电气机械及器材制造业	Electric Equipment & Machinery	140	8945650
计算机、通信和其他电子设备制造业	Computer, Communication & Other Electronic Equipment Manufacturing	133	18719074
仪器仪表制造业	Instruments Manufacturing	28	536985
其他制造业	Other Manufacturing	11	279484
废弃资源综合利用业	Waste Resources Comprehensive Utilization	35	3834118
金属制品、机械和设备修理业	Metal Product, Machinery & Equipment Repair Services	7	204255
电力、热力的生产和供应业	Production & Supply of Electric Power, Steam & Hot Water	190	11134014
#电力生产	Electric Power Production	136	3763311.4
#火力发电	Thermal Power	15	1422327.6
水力发电	Hydropower	89	1506921.7
燃气生产和供应业	Production & Supply of Gas	21	706272
水的生产和供应业	Production & Supply of Water	48	369975

continued

(10 000 yuan)

全部从业人员年平均人数（人）Average Employed Persons (person)	固定资产原价 Original Value of Fixed Assets	固定资产净值 Net Value of Fixed Assets	资产总计 Total Capital	流动资产合计 Annual Average Balance of Circulating Funds	所有者权益合计 Owner's Equity	利润总额 Total Profits	主营业务收入 Business Income of the Main Products
40977	250875	156359	471868	240071	263174	68193	1494845
5496	3371221	1967792	4426031	2127815	2683645	614178	8416842
81329	4597644	2943479	7831717	3547324	3649248	694328	11337348
40625	1894785	1018313	3353087	1755148	1858141	480626	3938986
253	3102	2054	3782	1572	1795	1810	20118
29338	664878	460899	1536595	828635	651472	142653	3342227
208848	7573881	4514136	12088129	5653843	6409685	1599536	18214749
29607	3485400	2091530	4434783	1667096	2709627	572967	3602227
68950	6785999	4052826	12103071	5999717	4224162	1822082	23904554
49849	7873166	5338117	12957114	5392613	2925827	612839	15318689
32979	817671	470300	1841703	1026016	807921	293179	4836198
30970	1335763	723691	3619679	2536163	1602635	216401	3966213
39762	1118662	691976	5208218	2939458	2364154	253881	5144485
146740	6556347	4246616	17469057	11104728	4797922	1236522	25867205
33973	2964719	2240482	7785567	5106845	1652816	749274	13424600
25108	567499	395809	1333386	826721	736420	176098	1857166
40412	1560619	1241138	3792835	2052685	1674365	588069	8286282
96937	1499715	1113685	5987767	4302684	2720193	1896519	18342149
5776	216087	140058	491116	229019	250355	35890	488003
3060	102538	57679	103116	39262	60351	32405	273467
6538	239684	218848	814935	526098	121010	194472	3581908
5380	182342	106273	661714	281024	194972	-10846	173956
92420	29826182	18544185	31447470	5307289	9485041	497443	10512190
27405	17696983	12228190	20160465	3161358	5670659	358845	3425605
6440	5118344	2891882	4369433	609461	851566	-237607	1221999
17064	7783256	5149657	9491502	1799024	3606402	506087	1402001
3099	384423	312206	720966	278662	297240	90232	615648
9927	1428432	951991	1899553	420554	871370	75580	357383

14－4 国有控股工业企业主要指标（2017年）

单位：万元

行 业	Sector	企业单位数（个）Number of Enterprises (unit)	工业总产值（当年价格）Gross Industrial Output Value (At Current Prices)
国有控股工业企业	**State-holding Industrial Enterprises**	**538**	**74605645**
在总计中:	**Of the Total:**		
轻工业	Light Industry	113	9431884
重工业	Heavy Industry	425	65173760
在总计中:	**Of the Total:**		
大型企业	Large-scale Industrial Enterprises	41	44681090
中型企业	Medium-scale Industrial Enterprises	185	22253273
小型企业	Small-scale Industrial Enterprises	288	6948754
微型企业	Micro-enterprises	24	722528
煤炭的开采和洗选业	Coal Mining & Dressing	6	485818
石油和天然气开采业	Oil & Gas Mining	1	105937
黑色金属矿采选业	Ferrous Metals Mining & Dressing	2	65612
有色金属矿采选业	Nonferrous Metals Mining & Dressing	17	671555
非金属矿采选业	Nonmetal Minerals Mining & Dressing	6	197526
农副食品加工业	Farm & Sideline Products Processing	47	5054691
#制糖业	Carbohydrate Processing	26	2119665
食品制造业	Food Production	7	169281
酒、饮料和精制茶制造业	Wine, Drink & Refined Tea Manufacturing	8	494568
#酒的制造	Beverage Manufacturing	2	452793
烟草制品业	Tobacco Processing	2	2073380
#卷烟制造	Cigarettes Manufacturing	1	2065426
纺织业	Textile Industry	9	130048
纺织服装、服饰业	Textiles, Clothing & Dresses Manufacturing	5	24061
木材加工及木、竹、藤、棕、草制品业	Timber Processing, Bamboo, Cane, Palm Fiber & Straw Products	16	747785
造纸及纸制品业	Papermaking & Paper Products	7	159101
#造纸	Papermaking	3	93282

Major Indicators of State-owned & State-holding Industrial Enterprises（2017）

(10 000 yuan)

全部从业人员年平均人数（人）Average Employed Persons (person)	固定资产原价 Original Value of Fixed Assets	固定资产净值 Net Value of Fixed Assets	资产总计 Total Capital	流动资产合计 Annual Average Balance of Circulating Funds	所有者权益合计 Owner's Equity	利润总额 Total Profits	主营业务收入 Business Income of the Main Products
331416	**53145720**	**32525108**	**78070387**	**29470397**	**27040496**	**3846278**	**67859744**
47841	3429611	1753432	8033591	4522660	3746287	462104	8258523
283575	49716109	30771676	70036796	24947737	23294209	3384174	59601222
176631	27182377	16513272	41038641	16931376	12362486	2128429	41455076
113046	14708133	8763560	23568702	8957708	9891574	1093047	19084659
40792	10944795	7006921	12216137	3157563	4410901	603611	6633493
947	310416	241355	1246908	423749	375536	21191	686516
12368	207390	194629	662480	276769	243762	15613	432552
123	211779		360629	40040	311888	53602	237831
667	9813	6618	55468	15194	20301	1968	66245
10789	536406	331559	1675674	838830	625170	112794	738869
2395	77656	42215	156914	65737	89462	33562	172285
25698	1752751	871389	4082146	2259573	1332982	190110	4269945
19314	1236919	545093	2290419	1135924	957873	152073	1563178
1763	130963	102467	163731	52499	74231	17436	146764
1304	109893	53713	93234	29084	55336	-603	474656
937	102584	49974	69532	17356	47874	-371	434535
3451	716682	294414	2021078	1351872	1442398	116208	2073516
3008	700855	294414	1968546	1307756	1394081	116135	2065249
2675	122202	79481	210185	120018	46656	7621	130958
542	15650	7704	33157	25085	23605	4821	24413
5032	270008	151842	421884	192519	75433	12473	501627
2652	152400	39685	184951	74802	20431	1438	175104
1047	105923	24007	122558	41141	-11710	-383	111673

14—4 续表

单位：万元

行 业	Sector	企业单位数（个）Number of Enterprises (unit)	工业总产值（当年价格）Gross Industrial Output Value (At Current Prices)
印刷和记录媒介复制业	Printing & Record Duplicating	14	281962
文教、工美、体育和娱乐用品制造业	Culture, Education, Handcraft, Art, Sport & Entertainment Goods Manufacturing	2	9631
石油加工、炼焦及核燃料加工业	Oil Processing, Coking & Nuclear Fuel Processing	6	7979254
化学原料及化学制品制造业	Raw Chemical Materials & Chemical Products	27	1169429
医药制造业	Medical & Pharmaceutical Products	9	585944
橡胶和塑料制品业	Rubber & Plastic Products	5	141603
非金属矿物制品业	Nonmetal Mineral Products	46	1999736
#水泥制造	Cement Products	16	1335925
黑色金属冶炼及压延加工业	Smelting & Pressing of Ferrous Metals	14	12648152
有色金属冶炼及压延加工业	Smelting & Pressing of Nonferrous Metals	25	8310116
金属制品业	Metal Products	8	351224
通用设备制造业	General Equipment Manufacturing	15	410291
专用设备制造业	For Special Purposes Equipment Manufacturing	14	1877754
汽车制造业	Automobile Manufacturing	20	16466319
铁路、船舶、航空航天和其他运输设备制造业	Railway, Ship, Aerospace & Other Transportation Equipment Manufacturing	7	250528
电气机械及器材制造业	Electric Equipment & Machinery	4	422624
计算机、通信和其他电子设备制造业	Computer, Communication & Other Electronic Equipment Manufacturing	7	349159
金属制品、机械和设备修理业	Metal Product, Machinery & Equipment Repair Services	4	193030
电力、热力的生产和供应业	Production & Supply of Electric Power ,Steam & Hot Water	132	10363828
#电力生产	Electric Power Production	84	3061638
#火力发电	Thermal Power	12	1044639
水力发电	Hydropower	53	1308183
燃气生产和供应业	Production & Supply of Gas	2	46076
水的生产和供应业	Production & Supply of Water	41	343938

continued

(10 000 yuan)

全部从业人员年平均人数（人）Average Employed Persons (person)	固定资产原价 Original Value of Fixed Assets	固定资产净值 Net Value of Fixed Assets	资产总计 Total Capital	流动资产合计 Annual Average Balance of Circulating Funds	所有者权益合计 Owner's Equity	利润总额 Total Profits	主营业务收入 Business Income of the Main Products
2672	168073	91422	208564	80140	119041	35763	292785
133	4604	1193	9569	6329	4174	195	6550
2988	3117581	1812703	3837018	1827515	2494917	543302	7611180
11706	1636072	832095	1724214	637829	606200	53386	1122813
3206	135089	123630	505298	253189	371155	90917	201472
3196	102398	90075	206012	87526	101263	-6108	142383
13837	1351685	825115	1857507	765601	1053914	227834	1676419
7043	1150861	729448	1309917	444371	810479	216157	1083271
22013	4308655	2307783	6750490	3320554	1946701	643919	11705950
21151	4233645	3094863	7132312	2516675	1634693	300746	6043217
2002	65420	42840	200938	121160	28397	-1838	347951
4356	189118	122127	570052	404577	188876	9120	391833
14478	440743	245137	3121349	1722525	1360439	68571	1648260
49785	3444643	2360269	9383789	6072105	2094195	755471	15820369
2634	187947	116277	593632	426777	320720	12678	248216
1884	79109	67477	242045	113946	64405	65	399166
3152	90542	44613	442447	315552	625102	15692	351491
4909	160062	85046	630530	272597	183783	-11274	161960
87675	27666740	17100645	28551517	4724431	8596548	459545	9846714
22957	15659772	10816442	17325238	2598777	4815585	331487	2826260
5597	3794653	2157325	3005249	420820	342923	-221559	889465
14323	7403851	4765885	8635203	1525604	3426675	493716	1240153
675	101459	79231	101104	10994	66573	11326	46196
9244	1346784	905653	1793832	396522	821003	68788	333036

14—5 国有工业企业主要指标（2017年）

单位：万元

行 业	Sector	企业单位数（个）Number of Enterprises (unit)	工业总产值（当年价格）Gross Industrial Output Value (At Current Prices)
国有工业企业	**State-holding Industrial Enterprises**	**71**	**1609748**
在总计中:	**Of the Total:**		
轻工业	Light Industry	21	518447
重工业	Heavy Industry	50	1091300
在总计中:	**Of the Total:**		
大型企业	Large-scale Industrial Enterprises	4	400733
中型企业	Medium-scale Industrial Enterprises	18	552502
小型企业	Small-scale Industrial Enterprises	49	656513
微型企业	Micro-enterprises		
煤炭的开采和洗选业	Coal Mining & Dressing		
黑色金属矿采选业	Ferrous Metals Mining & Dressing		
有色金属矿采选业	Nonferrous Metals Mining & Dressing	2	18189
非金属矿采选业	Nonmetal Minerals Mining & Dressing	1	28999
农副食品加工业	Farm & Sideline Products Processing	8	389831
#制糖业	Carbohydrate Processing	1	6087
食品制造业	Food Production	2	67074
酒、饮料和精制茶制造业	Wine, Drink & Refined Tea Manufacturing		
烟草制品业	Tobacco Processing		
纺织业	Textile Industry		
纺织服装、服饰业	Textile,Clothing & Dress Maniufacturing		
皮革、毛皮、羽毛及其制品和制鞋业	Leather, Fur, Feather & Related Products & Shoes Manufacturing		
木材加工及木、竹、藤、棕、草制品业	Timber Processing, Bamboo, Cane, Palm Fiber & Straw Products	2	126669

Major Indicators of State-owned Industrial Enterprises（2017）

（10 000 yuan）

全部从业人员年平均人数（人）Average Employed Persons (person)	固定资产原价 Original Value of Fixed Assets	固定资产净值 Net Value of Fixed Assets	资产总计 Total Capital	流动资产合计 Annual Average Balance of Circulating Funds	所有者权益合计 Owner's Equity	利润总额 Total Profits	主营业务收入 Business Income of the Main Products
23111	**1110132**	**791026**	**1978674**	**1013765**	**1420055**	**87686**	**1480252**
4565	73831	44013	145874	82513	69641	23329	494404
18546	1036301	747013	1832800	931253	1350414	64357	985848
6398	128903	56783	430978	329512	593637	10968	371249
10003	669996	551369	1088855	462390	599293	58656	542189
6710	311233	182874	458840	221863	227124	18062	566814
380	6956	3266	12045	7600	9437	1178	17507
26	147		103	66	-473	-19	7524
2663	11450	7174	43683	18858	19482	13196	369950
178	92	46	9196	9115	-1534	331	6134
508	21431	13266	24537	11271	20657	6842	67074
1068	33261	16544	39286	13348	26347	10396	108781

14—5　续表

单位：万元

行　业	Sector	企业单位数（个）Number of Enterprises (unit)	工业总产值（当年价格）Gross Industrial Output Value (At Current Prices)
印刷和记录媒介复制业	Printing & Record Duplicating	7	44912
文教、工美、体育和娱乐用品制造业	Culture, Education, Handcraft, Art, Sport & Entertainment Goods Manufacturing	1	5223
石油加工、炼焦及核燃料加工业	Oil Processing, Coking & Nuclear Fuel Processing		
化学原料及化学制品制造业	Raw Chemical Materials & Chemical Products	3	134246
医药制造业	Medical & Pharmaceutical Products	3	11408
橡胶和塑料制品业	Rubber & Plastic Products	1	12443
非金属矿物制品业	Nonmetal Mineral Products	3	29326
#水泥制造	Cement Products	1	10350
黑色金属冶炼及压延加工业	Smelting & Pressing of Ferrous Metals		
有色金属冶炼及压延加工业	Smelting & Pressing of Nonferrous Metals		
金属制品业	Metal Products	1	5578
通用设备制造业	General Equipment Manufacturing	2	31442
专用设备制造业	For Special Purposes Equipment Manufacturing	2	92081
汽车制造业	Automobile Manufacturing	1	105347
铁路、船舶、航空航天和其他运输设备制造业	Railway, Ship, Aerospace & Other Transportation Equipment Manufacturing	2	65684
电气机械及器材制造业	Electric Equipment & Machinery		
计算机、通信和其他电子设备制造业	Computer, Communication & Other Electronic Equipment Manufacturing	1	66352
金属制品、机械和设备修理业	Metal Product, Machinery & Equipment Repair Services	1	178525
电力、热力的生产和供应业	Production & Supply of Electric Power, Steam & Hot Water	9	114593
#电力生产	Electric Power Production	6	64745
#火力发电	Thermal Power		
水力发电	Hydropower	5	12870
水的生产和供应业	Production & Supply of Water	19	87405

continued

(10 000 yuan)

全部从业人员年平均人数（人）Average Employed Persons (person)	固定资产原价 Original Value of Fixed Assets	固定资产净值 Net Value of Fixed Assets	资产总计 Total Capital	流动资产合计 Annual Average Balance of Circulating Funds	所有者权益合计 Owner's Equity	利润总额 Total Profits	主营业务收入 Business Income of the Main Products
854	26067	15486	34371	17800	19816	3180	44449
42	1551	1193	2440	1056	1603	-219	2783
615	17240	23168	59853	36684	26696	877	109644
498	13333	6894	40843	33527	8084	330	10148
507	11895	11895	48229	28769	19566	1866	11114
1480	15733	11544	33292	10052	11425	226	28394
108	3916	2481	6504	497	2401	64	10348
160			2309	2174	13	13	4676
308	1869	628	11476	10768	8358	-55	25181
1254	46385	17311	102172	71946	44022	6383	92840
1244	50416	29618	102014	67370	39029	4214	105762
1668	108948	65199	323195	240612	228065	5330	66122
1247	28403	9334	111791	93539	499666	2268	68203
2589	48613	16367	215201	168095	54617	4218	146774
2546	327415	244245	282436	30196	151698	14916	109829
1808	260070	198585	221473	18238	99590	13246	64580
866	87782	57573	77652	15428	46578	831	12823
3454	339021	297893	489399	150034	231948	12546	83497

14－6 非公经济工业企业主要指标（2017年）

单位：万元

行 业	Sector	企业单位数（个）Number of Enterprises (unit)	工业总产值（当年价格）Gross Industrial Output Value (At Current Prices)
非公经济工业企业	**Non-public Industrial Enterprises**	**5045**	**181742857**
在总计中:	**Of the Total:**		
轻工业	Light Industry	1841	57667611
重工业	Heavy Industry	3204	124075246
在总计中:	**Of the Total:**		
大型企业	Large-scale Industrial Enterprises	152	44546309
中型企业	Medium-scale Industrial Enterprises	1006	59073229
小型企业	Small-scale Industrial Enterprises	3730	76706716
微型企业	Micro-enterprises	157	1416603
煤炭的开采和洗选业	Coal Mining & Dressing	9	145613
黑色金属矿采选业	Ferrous Metals Mining & Dressing	34	2154386
有色金属矿采选业	Nonferrous Metals Mining & Dressing	51	1855661
非金属矿采选业	Nonmetal Minerals Mining & Dressing	145	2752505
开采辅助活动	Mining Assist Activities	1	61916
其他采矿业	Other Minerals Mining	2	35033
农副食品加工业	Farm & Sideline Products Processing	478	21156008
#制糖业	Carbohydrate Processing	58	5428924
食品制造业	Food Production	128	4560707
#罐头制造业	Canned Food Manufacturing	14	396590
酒、饮料和精制茶制造业	Wine, Drink & Refined Tea Manufacturing	138	4282107
#酒的制造	Beverage Manufacturing	30	1195960
纺织业	Textile Industry	130	2876024
纺织服装、服饰业	Textiles, Clothing & Dresses Manufacturing	53	1932973
皮革、毛皮、羽毛及其制品和制鞋业	Leather, Fur, Feather & Related Products & Shoes Manufacturing	63	1377303
木材加工及木、竹、藤、棕、草制品业	Timber Processing, Bamboo, Cane, Palm Fiber & Straw Products	700	13840254
家具制造业	Furniture Manufacturing	50	1098316
造纸及纸制品业	Papermaking & Paper Products	153	3851976
#造纸	Papermaking	80	2206545

Major Indicators of Non-public Industrial Enterprises (2017)

(10 000 yuan)

全部从业人员年平均人数（人）Average Employed Persons (person)	固定资产原价 Original Value of Fixed Assets	固定资产净值 Net Value of Fixed Assets	资产总计 Total Capital	流动资产合计 Annual Average Balance of Circulating Funds	所有者权益合计 Owner's Equity	利润总额 Total Profits	主营业务收入 Business Income of the Main Products
1269994	**44382900**	**27723740**	**94272800**	**50881120**	**38874638**	**11875125**	**164724155**
513299	16017552	9329825	33202119	17910352	14128741	3554957	51756698
756695	28365349	18393914	61070680	32970768	24745897	8320169	112967457
310020	12441341	7421532	23766437	12953474	9914089	4146005	41632817
548065	17518844	10563832	33433083	17460912	13720231	4229715	53746888
409496	14297055	9634035	35796326	19648991	15072052	3451284	68148070
2413	125661	104341	1276954	817743	168266	48123	1196380
1979	85322	58351	313955	117540	54712	6834	134975
9910	400167	293908	866016	528814	391501	152683	2076778
9922	428351	219478	974635	513212	356633	113348	1552775
23337	494085	380663	1123487	581973	510916	181169	2481765
97	1135	948	2857	1821	2505	18092	61297
177	4201	2577	9794	7076	9379	1884	36063
99114	4636789	2564251	11679186	7770892	4488454	1565069	18617437
30758	2284750	1109675	4603608	3196422	1530939	775798	4217325
31250	1003731	751678	2542788	1205836	1352250	236770	4176187
6059	95464	68214	212752	95767	125190	54105	366530
38873	1123079	792347	2493088	1264082	1252658	250659	3570099
7778	454330	312995	1117230	634154	507533	45969	828229
39159	537922	379678	1334200	789155	457057	154603	2632981
20930	200460	114165	533722	367949	319462	138586	1878073
30208	237344	165214	528601	307674	270741	54426	1277548
145257	1879195	1182840	4441709	2492823	2112256	642767	12888155
8642	98018	60921	339116	197700	149803	56579	1028445
29219	3798703	1848492	6309257	2329053	1841664	160030	3442678
15644	3096372	1301361	4831631	1715867	1475520	94472	2018417

14—6 续表

单位：万元

行 业	Sector	企业单位数（个）Number of Enterprises (unit)	工业总产值（当年价格）Gross Industrial Output Value (At Current Prices)
印刷和记录媒介复制业	Printing & Record Duplicating	52	991183
文教、工美、体育和娱乐用品制造业	Culture, Education, Handcraft, Art, Sport & Entertainment Goods Manufacturing	84	1611139
石油加工、炼焦及核燃料加工业	Oil Processing, Coking & Nuclear Fuel Processing	19	956486
化学原料及化学制品制造业	Raw Chemical Materials & Chemical Products	355	10563228
医药制造业	Medical & Pharmaceutical Products	140	3960044
化学纤维制造业	Chemical Fibre Products	2	20581
橡胶和塑料制品业	Rubber & Plastic Products	138	3539440
非金属矿物制品业	Nonmetal Mineral Products	762	16877685
#水泥制造	Cement Products	82	2878681
黑色金属冶炼及压延加工业	Smelting & Pressing of Ferrous Metals	144	12558649
有色金属冶炼及压延加工业	Smelting & Pressing of Nonferrous Metals	76	11418816
金属制品业	Metal Products	150	5055895
通用设备制造业	General Equipment Manufacturing	96	4057620
专用设备制造业	For Special Purposes Equipment Manufacturing	132	3665374
汽车制造业	Automobile Manufacturing	318	11394595
铁路、船舶、航空航天和其他运输设备制造业	Railway, Ship, Aerospace & Other Transportation Equipment Manufacturing	36	1636956
电气机械及器材制造业	Electric Equipment & Machinery	130	7049754
计算机、通信和其他电子设备制造业	Computer, Communication & Other Electronic Equipment Manufacturing	125	18367408
仪器仪表制造业	Instruments Manufacturing	27	533875
其他制造业	Other Manufacturing	11	279484
废弃资源综合利用业	Waste Resources Comprehensive Utilization	32	3808432
金属制品、机械和设备修理业	Metal Product, Machinery & Equipment Repair Services	3	11225
电力、热力的生产和供应业	Production & Supply of Electric Power, Steam & Hot Water	53	720186
#电力生产	Electric Power Production	49	690372
#火力发电	Thermal Power	3	377689
水力发电	Hydropower	33	187437
燃气生产和供应业	Production & Supply of Gas	19	660196
水的生产和供应业	Production & Supply of Water	6	23827

continued

(10 000 yuan)

全部从业人员年平均人数（人）Average Employed Persons (person)	固定资产原价 Original Value of Fixed Assets	固定资产净值 Net Value of Fixed Assets	资产总计 Total Capital	流动资产合计 Annual Average Balance of Circulating Funds	所有者权益合计 Owner's Equity	利润总额 Total Profits	主营业务收入 Business Income of the Main Products
8189	349685	174429	405324	140975	257714	60315	924528
40844	246272	155167	462299	233742	259000	67998	1488295
2508	253639	155089	589013	300300	188728	70876	805662
61684	2905380	2078693	5963605	2830427	2994664	618405	9402202
36471	1750410	894684	2755538	1434099	1426545	376837	3679965
253	3102	2054	3782	1572	1795	1810	20118
24571	542453	350904	1265996	699821	507502	141673	3087238
188521	5891370	3491133	9769735	4753073	5030644	1220479	15279023
22165	2257727	1290561	2996227	1193716	1856226	353173	2459596
46752	2472722	1740516	5322686	2657014	2254303	1175087	12187236
28698	3639521	2243254	5824802	2875937	1291134	312093	9275472
30554	747089	424224	1619816	888301	764962	292892	4453110
25924	1133469	595486	3011125	2101035	1398502	202613	3531682
23644	663044	440633	2012210	1149902	963388	184200	3404848
93156	3017052	1834313	7826651	4837204	2627198	476041	9623674
20926	372137	276032	720123	384183	407105	162011	1556589
33308	1121640	876709	2803466	1536757	1261617	515146	6615246
93315	1408580	1068647	5544547	3986862	2095154	1880793	17988162
5312	209831	138684	480111	219411	241072	35881	484944
3060	102538	57679	103116	39262	60351	32405	273467
6277	237924	217648	728295	474268	124265	193334	3564888
471	22281	21227	31183	8427	11189	428	11996
4412	2000523	1392147	2812049	561486	857440	34662	618854
4233	1970551	1372013	2765921	543691	830078	26037	589413
843	1323691	734557	1364185	188641	508643	-16048	332534
2526	312745	344037	786994	254531	154730	11050	151916
2424	282965	232975	619862	267668	230667	78907	569452
646	80771	45908	105055	23795	49714	6742	22247

14－7 私营工业企业主要指标（2017年）

单位：万元

行 业	Sector	企业单位数（个）Number of Enterprises (unit)	工业总产值（当年价格）Gross Industrial Output Value (At Current Prices)
私营工业企业	**Collective-owned Industrial Enterprises**	**3493**	**99897819**
在总计中:	**Of the Total:**		
轻工业	Light Industry	1219	31072671
重工业	Heavy Industry	2274	68825148
在总计中:	**Of the Total:**		
大型企业	Large-scale Industrial Enterprises	82	14974659
中型企业	Medium-scale Industrial Enterprises	615	32068514
小型企业	Small-scale Industrial Enterprises	2675	51772390
微型企业	Micro-enterprises	121	1082256
煤炭开采和洗选业	Coal Mining & Dressing	6	69965
黑色金属矿采选业	Ferrous Metals Mining & Dressing	27	1217285
有色金属矿采选业	Nonferrous Metals Mining & Dressing	37	1277427
非金属矿采选业	Nonmetal Minerals Mining & Dressing	113	1622161
开采辅助活动	Mining Assist Activities	1	61916
其他采矿业	Other Minerals Mining	2	35033
农副食品加工业	Farm & Sideline Products Processing	308	9265110
#制糖业	Carbohydrate Processing	18	778370
食品制造业	Food Production	82	2139802
#罐头制造业	Canned Food Manufacturing	10	282966
酒、饮料和精制茶制造业	Wine, Drink & Refined Tea Manufacturing	89	2853742
#酒的制造业	Beverage Manufacturing	17	863892
纺织业	Textile Industry	86	1749873
纺织服装、服饰业	Textiles, Clothing & Dresses Manufacturing	37	1330519
皮革、毛皮、羽毛及其制品和制鞋业	Leather, Fur, Feather & Related Products & Shoes Manufacturing	33	526895
木材加工及木、竹、藤、棕、草制品业	Timber Processing, Bamboo, Cane, Palm Fiber & Straw Products	574	10833594
家具制造业	Furniture Manufacturing	38	680325
造纸及纸制品业	Papermaking & Paper Products	111	2182207
#造纸业	Papermaking	57	863449

Major Indicators of Private Owned Industrial Enterprises（2017）

(10 000 yuan)

全部从业人员年平均人数（人）Average Employed Persons (person)	固定资产原价 Original Value of Fixed Assets	固定资产净值 Net Value of Fixed Assets	资产总计 Total Capital	流动资产合计 Annual Average Balance of Circulating Funds	所有者权益合计 Owner's Equity	利润总额 Total Profits	主营业务收入 Business Income of the Main Products
770316	**19451898**	**12750705**	**43211506**	**23785989**	**17752197**	**5540468**	**90706610**
298185	5791806	3512632	13414934	7491439	5884342	1480477	27786338
472131	13660093	9238073	29796571	16294551	11867855	4059991	62920272
150525	4197860	3131272	7600244	3541382	3024557	1389976	14455509
331564	7425406	4591516	14716581	8002668	6265288	2075246	29281769
286262	7786002	4993944	20070914	11738456	8360838	2039520	46075111
1965	42630	33973	823767	503483	101514	35727	894221
919	35581	26410	76055	43849	23241	985	61371
3682	95371	57658	262074	163152	99303	65024	1122737
6409	278290	189547	705234	388527	311550	59500	999686
18599	378030	297592	742068	359528	332807	88214	1474004
97	1135	948	2857	1821	2505	18092	61297
177	4201	2577	9794	7076	9379	1884	36063
49597	1509868	925514	3957726	2446749	1515331	352123	8041342
7808	385833	190478	1036567	785152	226563	74896	648587
16541	405230	236296	1198880	504355	649040	146312	1993025
4950	79424	57848	137702	65138	95278	34952	271724
25349	409004	321247	1503308	886365	718034	147763	2327728
4780	141282	121670	760626	522503	298850	26551	558739
22554	392892	213928	757924	472769	226888	80285	1572094
12362	130117	88417	382192	278045	227333	99043	1279481
8214	85114	68596	242777	132989	137716	20295	492292
113077	1357755	905822	3183619	1839247	1356518	457797	10131100
5436	54491	36331	252530	152376	105553	32452	641816
18981	621168	405786	1391457	708036	450877	97805	1963093
8720	373148	248218	542464	257668	183146	32311	838656

14－7 续表

单位：万元

行 业	Sector	企业单位数（个） Number of Enterprises (unit)	工业总产值（当年价格） Gross Industrial Output Value (At Current Prices)
印刷业和记录媒介的复制	Printing & Record Medium Reproduction	41	751200
文教、工美、体育和娱乐用品制造业	Culture, Education, Handcraft, Art, Sport & Entertainment Goods Manufacturing	54	1103100
石油加工、炼焦及核燃料加工业	Oil Processing, Coking & Nuclear Fuel Processing	9	227361
化学原料及化学制品制造业	Raw Chemical Materials & Chemical Products	226	6327957
医药制造业	Medical & Pharmaceutical Products	72	1807126
化学纤维制造业	Chemical Fibre Products	2	20581
橡胶和塑料制品业	Rubber & Plastic Products	104	2431426
非金属矿物制品业	Nonmetal Mineral Products	552	11101766
#水泥制造	Cement Products	41	995479
黑色金属冶炼及压延加工业	Smelting & Pressing of Ferrous Metals	88	6884264
有色金属冶炼和压延加工业	Smelting & Pressing of Nonferrous Metals	50	3947862
金属制品业	Metal Products	113	4375526
通用设备制造业	Production & Supply of Electric Power & Heating Power	67	1801181
专用设备制造业	For Special Purposes Equipment Manufacturing	97	2235428
汽车制造	Automobile Manufacturing	233	7258866
铁路、船舶、航空航天和其他运输设备制造业	Railway, Ship, Aerospace & Other Transportation Equipment Manufacturing	29	1494326
电气机械及器材制造业	Electric Equipment & Machinery	92	4025968
计算机、通信和其他电子设备制造业	Computer, Communication & Other Electronic Equipment Manufacturing	57	5167128
仪器仪表制造业	Instruments Manufacturing	16	299097
其他制造业	Other Manufacturing	3	126495
废弃资源综合利用业	Waste Resources Comprehensive Utilization	20	2477637
金属制品、机械和设备修理业	Repair Service of Metal Products, Machinery & Equipment	3	11225
电力、热力的生产和供应业	Production & Supply of Electric Power & Heating Power	16	113338
#电力生产	Electric Power Production	16	113338
#火力发电	Thermal Power	1	21803
水力发电	Hydropower	15	91534
燃气生产和供应业	Production & Supply of Gas	3	57237
水的生产和供应业	Production & Supply of Water	2	5874

continued

(10 000 yuan)

全部从业人员年平均人数（人）Average Employed Persons (person)	固定资产原价 Original Value of Fixed Assets	固定资产净值 Net Value of Fixed Assets	资产总计 Total Capital	流动资产合计 Annual Average Balance of Circulating Funds	所有者权益合计 Owner's Equity	利润总额 Total Profits	主营业务收入 Business Income of the Main Products
6645	303316	139755	327093	107470	214136	49840	709770
26076	177213	107822	314135	153446	177803	47840	1004570
1027	52066	29428	119350	79234	33910	3972	109451
39987	1291417	789436	2621324	1309965	1388796	393948	5840699
17204	730877	332065	932807	483084	427303	129213	1765139
253	3102	2054	3782	1572	1795	1810	20118
16178	249183	154419	757511	469237	320332	104155	2168760
139652	3169839	2028178	5367387	2673609	2313169	641410	10244121
8149	581576	372980	736614	313506	205925	56588	896511
23435	1642387	1316387	3602250	1764475	1655304	615407	6738682
13577	1141347	458479	1966577	1138915	400458	103594	3439053
24641	562352	303438	1250652	700536	570326	266605	3820481
12590	183388	130557	578544	349547	254712	63123	1480940
15439	421149	272223	1043198	617264	472438	113159	2080210
59744	1756488	1175826	4470527	2700035	1220575	225322	6073797
20045	356255	270466	529034	237507	321048	150112	1426602
20148	814814	693214	1956496	953987	804548	164884	3709080
23003	363162	390968	1646555	1110811	709582	616484	5018967
2281	71850	39533	90624	46747	55770	19543	269341
728	55031	36465	47115	10600	31131	15583	126152
3720	150027	147705	451090	278943	89021	136127	2344893
471	22281	21227	31183	8427	11189	428	11996
1171	142059	107737	342037	151793	62985	1062	65334
1171	142059	107737	342037	151793	62985	1062	65334
95	23396	23396	40499	3053	19857	2169	10846
1076	118663	84340	301538	148741	43128	-1108	54488
223	15852	13786	62346	39880	26463	5892	35444
84	18200	12871	31394	14024	23327	3384	5879

14－8 大中型工业企业分行业主要指标（2017年）

单位：万元

行 业	Sector	企业单位数（个）Number of Enterprises (unit)	工业总产值（当年价格）Gross Industrial Output Value (At Current Prices)
大中型工业企业	**Large-scale & Medium-scale Industrial Enterprises**	**1424**	**175112845**
在总计中:	**Of the Total:**		
轻工业	Light Industry	600	40387035
重工业	Heavy Industry	824	134725810
在总计中:	**Of the Total:**		
大型企业	Large-scale Industrial Enterprises	202	92488616
中型企业	Medium-scale Industrial Enterprises	1222	82624229
煤炭的开采和洗选业	Coal Mining & Dressing	8	493641
黑色金属矿采选业	Ferrous Metals Mining & Dressing	9	1224824
有色金属矿采选业	Nonferrous Metals Mining & Dressing	19	1318819
非金属矿采选业	Nonmetal Minerals Mining & Dressing	18	904345
农副食品加工业	Farm & Sideline Products Processing	151	15891883
#制糖业	Carbohydrate Processing	78	7564809
食品制造业	Food Production	26	2806407
#罐头制造业	Canned Food Manufacturing	6	226395
酒、饮料和精制茶制造业	Wine, Drink & Refined Tea Manufacturing	36	2723197
#酒的制造	Beverage Manufacturing	7	1410013
烟草制品业	Tobacco Processing	2	2073380
#卷烟制造	Cigarettes Manufacturing	1	2065426
纺织业	Textile Industry	48	1722441
纺织服装、服饰业	Textiles, Clothing & Dresses Manufacturing	36	1694688
皮革、毛皮、羽毛及其制品和制鞋业	Leather, Fur, Feather & Related Products & Shoes Manufacturing	28	1029448
木材加工及木、竹、藤、棕、草制品业	Timber Processing, Bamboo, Cane, Palm Fiber & Straw Products	122	6008348
家具制造业	Furniture Manufacturing	11	582527
造纸及纸制品业	Papermaking & Paper Products	28	1930203
#造纸	Papermaking	14	1378717
印刷和记录媒介复制业	Printing & Record Duplicating	8	332001

注：工业企业分行业主要指标统计范围为年主营业务收入2000万元及以上工业法人企业。

Note: The statistic coverage of major indicators of industrial enterprises by industrial sectors is enterprises with business income of the main products of over 20 million yuan.

Major Indicators of Large-scale & Medium-scale Industrial Enterprises by Industrial Sector (2017)

(10 000 yuan)

全部从业人员年平均人数（人） Average Employed Persons (person)	固定资产原价 Original Value of Fixed Assets	固定资产净值 Net Value of Fixed Assets	资产总计 Total Capital	流动资产合计 Annual Average Balance of Circulating Funds	所有者权益合计 Owner's Equity	利润总额 Total Profits	主营业务收入 Business Income of the Main Products
1180827	**73213660**	**44100147**	**124088935**	**57419262**	**47062665**	**11918506**	**159922578**
417926	14067121	7443510	28652903	15823708	12485790	2741974	36043911
762901	59146539	36656637	95436032	41595554	34576874	9176532	123878667
503295	40622994	24554849	66241760	30512905	23089834	6528513	85970557
677532	32590666	19545298	57847175	26906358	23972830	5389993	73952021
13510	240832	209131	857231	335012	277822	22549	440281
8403	327762	254106	684533	396143	328571	120569	1251204
15636	654663	339061	1794949	874306	663763	156258	1291335
15547	257408	199525	356196	127531	218417	111353	895543
92612	5233810	2576944	11781662	7564914	4303586	1228018	13658705
50774	3564398	1646632	6712584	4205093	2600386	939520	5809691
19674	709598	600191	1743477	751317	908221	165251	2594078
4760	76544	53936	162972	81158	88764	23974	212298
32613	911944	564929	1498474	778394	764929	162105	2288647
9176	648458	359416	997141	529576	512127	62770	1032019
3451	716682	294414	2021078	1351872	1442398	116208	2073516
3008	700855	294414	1968546	1307756	1394081	116135	2065249
28839	340836	311099	945168	543194	292157	86817	1568345
17931	180840	101685	467296	320355	283107	129395	1661620
27464	198090	139679	415099	222802	231023	51731	954262
81898	1074397	655242	1933051	996087	920954	377627	5627032
5052	50294	26729	123837	80631	61703	32744	542205
17499	3147525	1283756	4548237	1578301	1344776	82764	1703778
9509	2788133	1046222	4030699	1360352	1209929	60937	1221560
3396	120914	49128	185051	83087	118045	33715	324440

14－8 续表

单位：万元

行 业	Sector	企业单位数（个）Number of Enterprises (unit)	工业总产值（当年价格）Gross Industrial Output Value (At Current Prices)
文教、工美、体育和娱乐用品制造业	Culture, Education, Handcraft, Art, Sport & Entertainment Goods Manufacturing	47	1087682
石油加工、炼焦及核燃料加工业	Oil Processing, Coking & Nuclear Fuel Processing	5	8100139
化学原料及化学制品制造业	Raw Chemical Materials & Chemical Products	85	4624190
医药制造业	Medical & Pharmaceutical Products	41	2496120
橡胶和塑料制品业	Rubber & Plastic Products	28	1094290
非金属矿物制品业	Nonmetal Mineral Products	195	11990059
#水泥制造	Cement Products	34	3182274
黑色金属冶炼及压延加工业	Smelting & Pressing of Ferrous Metals	36	21835155
有色金属冶炼及压延加工业	Smelting & Pressing of Nonferrous Metals	41	16750333
金属制品业	Metal Products	30	2494802
通用设备制造业	General Equipment Manufacturing	18	2588915
专用设备制造业	For Special Purposes Equipment Manufacturing	35	3124783
汽车制造	Automobile Manufacturing	103	24394016
铁路、船舶、航空航天和其他运输设备制造业	Railway, Ship, Aerospace & Other Transportation Equipment Manufacturing	24	1623337
电气机械及器材制造业	Electric Equipment & Machinery	37	5987650
计算机、通信和其他电子设备制造业	Computer, Communication & Other Electronic Equipment Manufacturing	64	15053733
仪器仪表制造	Instruments Manufacturing	7	166654
其他制造业	Other Manufacturing	4	165213
废弃资源综合利用业	Waste Resources Comprehensive Utilization	8	1477742
电力、热力的生产和供应业	Production & Supply of Electric Power, Steam & Hot Water	49	8786183
#电力生产	Electric Power Production	19	1905903
#火力发电	Thermal Power	11	1178289
水力发电	Hydropower	6	272361
燃气生产和供应业	Production & Supply of Gas	3	124057
水的生产和供应业	Production & Supply of Water	9	216604

continued

(10 000 yuan)

全部从业人员年平均人数（人）Average Employed Persons (person)	固定资产原价 Original Value of Fixed Assets	固定资产净值 Net Value of Fixed Assets	资产总计 Total Capital	流动资产合计 Annual Average Balance of Circulating Funds	所有者权益合计 Owner's Equity	利润总额 Total Profits	主营业务收入 Business Income of the Main Products
35020	95651	67020	226894	129777	120892	50012	1053938
3187	3059884	1799424	3713833	1733985	2487129	602201	7686703
51242	2439132	1374140	3248322	1445720	1485580	373250	4440858
26220	1231857	720798	2206705	1074324	1376193	347261	1967077
15779	443491	320846	776011	346622	322763	58211	947101
150206	5318025	3095122	7101066	2921658	4304054	1221700	11107913
22657	2851277	1623709	3497188	1332852	2349446	511377	2603082
57379	6254409	3682825	10553904	5044102	3633752	1760603	20831682
42985	7689571	5220737	11478682	4661304	2417592	556059	12502427
18364	394962	185130	754625	409139	358627	218476	2415486
19493	938961	482357	2549797	1856511	1165306	146376	2338013
26608	721668	415976	3988919	2185674	1765794	150275	2785607
115266	5866760	3797207	15277983	9638502	4080904	1154135	22423216
23045	457568	311231	978948	634250	587235	148034	1582889
26802	967982	953657	2686567	1387145	1147570	465673	5546107
86920	1039831	850822	4083431	2949393	2044353	1538228	14814156
3601	113681	88432	361112	163914	176559	12517	165265
1997	56443	26634	53214	22736	27643	20038	160765
3302	127155	115362	282053	166691	40590	112625	1397434
78247	20440050	11948237	22093704	3976621	6434104	-90	8388671
16169	8847025	5973110	11396146	1963224	2939252	-125104	1760015
5590	4604803	2479204	3777519	517670	702260	-196244	1070826
8578	1095565	546887	3447005	976560	1598934	54555	234053
1719	237217	203516	406603	149865	175796	60345	116206
4675	993658	750007	1280278	244370	566608	56707	212111

14—9 工业企业主要经济效益指标（2017年）
Major Economic Efficiency Indicators of Industrial Enterprises（2017）

行 业	Sector	企业亏损面（%）Composition of Loss-making Enterprises (%)	百元主营业务收入实现利润（元）Per-tax Profits Per 100 yuan of Core Business Sales (yuan)	成本费用利润率（%）Ratio of Profits to Industrial (%)
总 计	**Total**	**14.1**	**6.77**	**7.3**
在总计中:	**Of the Total:**			
国有企业	State-owned	14.1	5.92	6.3
中央企业	Central Enterprises	4.23		4.1
地方企业	Local Enterprises	15.9	6.65	7.3
集体企业	Collective-owned	9.6	7.97	8.9
其他经济	Others	14.2	6.62	7.2
#外商及港澳台商投资企业	Foreign Funded Enterprises & Enterprises with Funds from Hong Kong , Macao & Taiwan	14.1	7.38	7.9
在总计中:	**Of the Total:**			
轻工业	Light Industry	12.2	6.73	7.4
重工业	Heavy Industry	15.1	6.78	7.3
在总计中:	**Of the Total:**			
大型企业	Large-scale Industrial Enterprises	5.0	7.60	8.2
中型企业	Medium-scale Industrial Enterprises	11.4	7.29	8.0
小型企业	Small-scale Industrial Enterprises	15.1	5.36	5.7
微型企业	Micro-enterprises	21.4	3.44	3.6
煤炭的开采和洗选业	Coal Mining & Dressing	40.0	3.96	4.0
石油和天然气开采业	Oil & Gas Mining		22.54	30.2
黑色金属矿采选业	Ferrous Metals Mining & Dressing	18.4	7.32	8.0
有色金属矿采选业	Nonferrous Metals Mining & Dressing	17.6	9.87	11.0
非金属矿采选业	Nonmetal Minerals Mining & Dressing	11.5	7.78	8.6
开采辅助活动	Mining Assist Activities		29.51	44.0
其他采矿业	Other Minerals Mining		5.22	5.6
农副食品加工业	Farm & Sideline Products Processing	14.3	7.64	8.2
#制糖	Carbohydrate Processing	27.6	15.83	18.3
食品制造业	Food Production	13.6	5.95	6.4
#罐头食品制造	Canned Food Manufacturing	7.1	14.76	17.3
酒、饮料和精制茶制造业	Wine, Drink & Refined Tea Manufacturing	8.7	6.64	7.2
#酒的制造	Liquor & Beverage Manufacturing	14.7	5.34	5.6
烟草制品业	Tobacco Processing		5.60	13.3
#卷烟制造	Cigarettes Manufacturing		5.62	13.4
纺织业	Textile Industry	16.3	5.83	6.1

14—9 续表 continued

行业	Sector	企业亏损面(%) Composition of Loss-making Enterprises (%)	百元主营业务收入实现利润（元） Per-tax Profits Per 100 yuan of Core Business Sales (yuan)	成本费用利润率(%) Ratio of Profits to Industrial (%)
纺织服装、服饰业	Manufacture of Textile, Wearing Apparel & Accessories	5.2	7.54	8.2
皮革、毛皮、羽毛及其制品和制鞋业	Leather, Fur, Feather & Related Products & Shoes Manufacturing	19.0	4.26	4.5
木材加工及木、竹、藤、棕、草制品业	Timber Processing, Bamboo, Cane, Palm Fiber & Straw Products	12.0	4.90	5.3
家具制造业	Furniture Manufacturing	4.0	5.50	5.9
造纸及纸制品业	Papermaking & Paper Products	21.8	4.58	4.9
#造纸	Papermaking	21.8	4.63	4.7
印刷业和记录媒介的复制	Printing & Record Duplicating	4.4	7.89	8.7
文教、工美、体育和娱乐用品制造业	Culture, Education, Handcraft, Art, Sport & Entertainment Goods Manufacturing	3.5	4.56	4.8
石油加工、炼焦及核燃料加工业	Oil Processing, Coking & Nuclear Fuel Processing	28.0	7.30	9.7
化学原料及化学制品制造业	Raw Chemical Materials & Chemical Products	14.5	6.12	6.6
医药制造业	Medicine Products	11.3	12.20	14.2
化学纤维制造业	Chemical Fiber Products	0.0	9.00	10.0
橡胶和塑料制品业	Rubber & Plastic Products	10.7	4.27	4.8
非金属矿物制品业	Nonmetal Mineral Products	12.7	8.78	9.7
#水泥制造	Cement Products	18.0	15.91	18.9
黑色金属冶炼及压延加工业	Smelting & Pressing of Ferrous Metals	23.8	7.62	8.1
有色金属冶炼及压延加工业	Smelting & Pressing of Nonferrous Metals	26.7	4.00	4.1
金属制品业	Metal Products	17.4	6.06	6.5
通用设备制造业	General Equipment Manufacturing	18.3	5.46	5.5
专用设备制造业	For Special Purposes Equipment Manufacturing	10.2	4.94	5.2
汽车制造业	Automobile Manufacturing	20.1	4.78	5.0
#汽车整车制造	Vehicle manufacturing		5.58	5.9
铁路、船舶、航空航天和其他运输设备制造业	Railway, Ship, Aerospace & Other Transportation Equipment Manufacturing	4.3	9.48	10.3
电气机械及器材制造业	Electric Equipment & Machinery	10.0	7.10	8.0
计算机、通信和其他电子设备制造业	Computer, Communication & Other Electronic Equipment Manufacturing	6.8	10.34	11.5
仪器仪表制造业	Instruments Manufacturing	14.3	7.35	8.1
其他制造业	Other Manufacturing	9.1	11.85	13.6
废弃资源综合利用业	Waste Resources Comprehensive Utilization	14.3	5.43	5.8
金属制品、机械和设备修理业	Metal Product, Machinery & Equipment Repair Services	28.6	-6.23	-5.4
电力、热力的生产和供应业	Production & Supply of Electric Power & Heating Power	19.5	4.73	4.9
#电力生产	Electric Power Production	23.5	10.48	11.5
#火力发电	Thermal Power	86.7	-19.44	-15.8
水力发电	Hydropower	19.1	36.10	55.5
燃气生产和供应业	Production & Supply of Gas	19.0	14.66	15.0
水的生产和供应业	Production & Supply of Water	12.5	21.15	24.7

14－10 国有控股工业企业主要经济效益指标（2017年）

Major Economic Efficiency Indicators of State-owned & State Holding Industrial Enterprises (2017)

行 业	Sector	企业亏损面 (%) Composition of Loss-making Enterprises (%)	百元主营业务收入实现利润（元） Per-tax Profits Per 100 yuan of Core Business Sales (yuan)	成本费用利润率 (%) Ratio of Profits to Industrial (%)
总 计	**Total**	**23.0**	**5.67**	**6.2**
在总计中:	**Of the Total:**			
轻工业	Light Industry	22.1	5.60	6.8
重工业	Heavy Industry	23.3	5.68	6.1
在总计中:	**Of the Total:**			
大型企业	Large-scale Industrial Enterprises	17.1	5.13	5.5
中型企业	Medium-scale Industrial Enterprises	24.9	5.73	6.5
小型企业	Small-scale Industrial Enterprises	22.9	9.10	10.0
微型企业	Micro-enterprises	20.8	3.09	3.2
煤炭的开采和洗选业	Coal Mining & Dressing	26.9	9.73	10.2
石油和天然气开采业	Oil & Gas Mining		22.54	30.2
黑色金属矿采选业	Ferrous Metals Mining & Dressing	50.0	2.97	3.1
有色金属矿采选业	Nonferrous Metals Mining & Dressing	11.8	15.27	18.0
非金属矿采选业	Nonmetal Minerals Mining & Dressing	33.3	19.48	24.5
农副食品加工业	Farm & Sideline Products Processing	23.4	4.45	4.6
#制糖	Carbohydrate Processing	26.9	9.73	10.2
食品制造业	Food Production	14.3	11.88	13.6
酒、饮料和精制茶制造业	Wine, Drink & Refined Tea Manufacturing	37.5	-0.13	-0.1
#酒的制造	Liquor & Beverage Manufacturing	50.0	-0.09	-0.1
烟草制品业	Tobacco Processing		5.60	13.3
#卷烟制造	Cigarettes Manufacturing		5.62	13.4
纺织业	Textile Industry	11.1	5.82	5.9
纺织服装、服饰业	Textiles, Clothing & Dresses Manufacturing		19.75	23.7
木材加工及木、竹、藤、棕、草制品业	Timber Processing, Bamboo, Cane, Palm Fiber & Straw Products	68.8	2.49	2.5
造纸及纸制品业	Papermaking & Paper Products	28.6	0.82	0.8
#造纸	Papermaking	33.3	-0.34	-0.3

14—10 续表 continued

行 业	Sector	企业亏损面(%) Composition of Loss-making Enterprises (%)	百元主营业务收入实现利润（元） Per-tax Profits Per 100 yuan of Core Business Sales (yuan)	成本费用利润率(%) Ratio of Profits to Industrial (%)
印刷和记录媒介复制业	Printing & Record Duplicating	14.3	12.21	14.0
文教、工美、体育和娱乐用品制造业	Culture, Education, Handcraft, Art, Sport & Entertainment Goods Manufacturing	50.0	2.97	2.9
石油加工、炼焦及核燃料加工业	Oil Processing, Coking & Nuclear Fuel	16.7	7.14	9.7
化学原料及化学制品制造业	Raw Chemical Materials & Chemical Products	25.9	4.75	4.6
医药制造业	Medical & Pharmaceutical Products	22.2	45.13	83.9
橡胶和塑料制品业	Rubber & Plastic Products	40.0	-4.29	-4.4
非金属矿物制品业	Nonmetal Mineral Products	17.4	13.59	15.6
#水泥制造	Cement Products		19.95	24.3
黑色金属冶炼及压延加工业	Smelting & Pressing of Ferrous Metals	21.4	5.50	5.6
有色金属冶炼及压延加工业	Smelting & Pressing of Nonferrous Metals	44.0	4.98	5.1
金属制品业	Metal Products	25.0	-0.53	-0.5
通用设备制造业	General Equipment Manufacturing	26.7	2.33	2.3
专用设备制造业	For Special Purposes Equipment Manufacturing	14.3	4.16	4.2
汽车制造业	Automobile Manufacturing	15.0	4.78	5.0
铁路、船舶、航空航天和其他运输设备制造业	Railway, Ship, Aerospace & Other Transportation Equipment Manufacturing		5.11	5.2
电气机械及器材制造业	Electric Equipment & Machinery	25.0	0.02	
计算机、通信和其他电子设备制造业	Computer, Communication & Other Electronic Equipment Manufacturing	14.3	4.46	4.6
金属制品、机械和设备修理业	Metal Product, Machinery & Equipment Repair Services	50.0	-6.96	-6.0
电力、热力的生产和供应业	Production & Supply of Electric Power, Steam & Hot Water	21.2	4.67	4.9
#电力生产	Electric Power Production	27.4	11.73	13.1
#火力发电	Thermal Power	91.7	-24.91	-19.6
水力发电	Hydropower	20.8	39.81	64.6
燃气生产和供应业	Production & Supply of Gas		24.52	30.0
水的生产和供应业	Production & Supply of Water	14.6	20.65	23.9

14－11 大中型工业企业主要经济效益指标（2017年）
Major Economic Efficiency Indicators of Large & Medium Industrial Enterprises（2017）

行 业	Sector	企业亏损面 (%) Composition of Loss-making Enterprises (%)	百元主营业务收入实现利润（元） Per-tax Profits Per 100 yuan of Core Business Sales (yuan)	成本费用利润率 (%) Ratio of Profits to Industrial (%)
大中型工业企业	**Large & Medium Industrial Enterprises**	**10.5**	**7.45**	**8.1**
在总计中:	**Of the Total:**			
轻工业	Light Industry	10.2	7.61	8.5
重工业	Heavy Industry	10.7	7.41	8.0
在总计中:	**Of the Total:**			
大型企业	Large-scale Industrial Enterprises	5.0	7.59	8.2
中型企业	Medium-scale Industrial Enterprises	11.4	7.29	8.0
煤炭的开采和洗选业	Coal Mining & Dressing	50.0	5.12	5.2
黑色金属矿采选业	Ferrous Metals Mining & Dressing	11.1	9.64	10.7
有色金属矿采选业	Nonferrous Metals Mining & Dressing	10.5	12.10	13.7
非金属矿采选业	Nonmetal Minerals Mining & Dressing		12.43	14.3
农副食品加工业	Farm & Sideline Products Processing	15.9	8.99	9.8
#制糖业	Carbohydrate Processing	23.1	16.17	18.8
食品制造业	Food Production	11.5	6.37	6.8
#罐头制造业	Canned Food Manufacturing	16.7	11.29	12.7
酒、饮料和精制茶制造业	Wine, Drink & Refined Tea Manufacturing	2.8	7.08	7.6
#酒的制造	Beverage Manufacturing		6.08	6.3
烟草制品业	Tobacco Processing		5.60	13.3
#卷烟制造	Cigarettes Manufacturing		5.62	13.4
纺织业	Textile Industry	10.4	5.54	5.7
纺织服装、服饰业	Textiles, Clothing & Dresses Manufacturing	5.6	7.79	8.6
皮革、毛皮、羽毛及其制品和制鞋业	Leather, Fur, Feather & Related Products & Shoes Manufacturing	3.6	5.42	5.9
木材加工及木、竹、藤、棕、草制品业	Timber Processing, Bamboo, Cane, Palm Fiber & Straw Products	4.9	6.71	7.3
家具制造业	Furniture Manufacturing	9.1	6.04	6.5
造纸及纸制品业	Papermaking & Paper Products	28.6	4.86	4.9
#造纸	Papermaking	35.7	4.99	5.0
印刷和记录媒介复制业	Printing & Record Duplicating		10.39	11.4

14－11 续表 continued

行 业	Sector	企业亏损面 (%) Composition of Loss-making Enterprises (%)	百元主营业务收入实现利润（元） Per-tax Profits Per 100 yuan of Core Business Sales (yuan)	成本费用利润率 (%) Ratio of Profits to Industrial (%)
文教、工美、体育和娱乐用品制造业	Culture, Education, Handcraft, Art, Sport & Entertainment Goods Manufacturing	2.1	4.75	5.0
石油加工、炼焦及核燃料加工业	Oil Processing, Coking & Nuclear Fuel Processing	0.0	7.83	10.7
化学原料及化学制品制造业	Raw Chemical Materials & Chemical Products	7.1	8.40	9.2
医药制造业	Medical & Pharmaceutical Products	7.3	17.65	21.3
橡胶和塑料制品业	Rubber & Plastic Products	14.3	6.15	7.0
非金属矿物制品业	Nonmetal Mineral Products	7.7	11.00	12.4
#水泥制造	Cement Products	5.9	19.65	24.2
黑色金属冶炼及压延加工业	Smelting & Pressing of Ferrous Metals	16.7	8.45	9.0
有色金属冶炼及压延加工业	Smelting & Pressing of Nonferrous Metals	26.8	4.45	4.6
金属制品业	Metal Products	10.0	9.04	10.0
通用设备制造业	General Equipment Manufacturing	5.6	6.26	6.1
专用设备制造业	For Special Purposes Equipment Manufacturing	8.6	5.39	5.6
汽车制造业	Automobile Manufacturing	14.6	5.15	5.4
铁路、船舶、航空航天和其他运输设备制造业	Railway, Ship, Aerospace & Other Transportation Equipment Manufacturing	4.2	9.35	10.4
电气机械及器材制造业	Electric Equipment & Machinery	8.1	8.40	9.4
计算机、通信和其他电子设备制造业	Computer, Communication & Other Electronic Equipment Manufacturing	3.1	10.38	11.5
仪器仪表制造业	Instruments Manufacturing		7.57	8.1
其他制造业	Other Manufacturing	25.0	12.46	14.5
废弃资源综合利用业	Waste Resources Comprehensive Utilization		8.06	8.8
电力、热力的生产和供应业	Production & Supply of Electric Power, Steam & Hot Water	26.5		
#电力生产	Electric Power Production	68.4	-7.11	-6.5
#火力发电	Thermal Power	90.9	-18.33	-14.9
水力发电	Hydropower	50.0	23.31	29.5
燃气生产和供应业	Production & Supply of Gas		51.93	54.5
水的生产和供应业	Production & Supply of Water	11.1	26.73	33.6

14—12 主要年份主要工业产品产量

产品名称	Item	1995	2000
锰矿石（万吨）	Manganese Ore (10 000 tons)	265.40	118.65
铁矿石（万吨）	Iron Ore (10 000 tons)	272.32	68.61
粗钢（万吨）	Steel (10 000 tons)	88.78	104.73
生铁（万吨）	Pig Iron (10 000 tons)	96.76	125.32
钢材（万吨）	Rolled Steel (10 000 tons)	80.50	102.63
铁合金（万吨）	Ferroalloys (10 000 tons)	31.14	41.58
十种有色金属（吨）	10 Nonferrous Metal (ton)	272700	605902
#铝	Aluminum	64960	185867
锌	Zinc	129076	235535
锡	Tin	23457	45874
氧化铝（万吨）	Oxide of Aluminum (10 000 tons)		40.81
发电量（亿千瓦小时）	Electricity (100 million kwh)	217.29	289.09
#水电	Hydropower	136.54	168.87
原煤（万吨）	Coal (10 000 tons)	1391.42	706.67
硫酸（万吨）	Sulfuric Acid (10 000 tons)	57.43	86.04
烧碱（吨）	Caustic Soda (ton)	101700	140719
农用化肥（折100%，万吨）	Chemical Fertilizers (10 000 tons)	43.12	53.30
水泥（万吨）	Cement (10 000 tons)	1980.47	2198.35

Output of Major Industrial Products in Main Years

2005	2010	2011	2012	2013	2014	2015	2016	2017
75.18	564.39	353.41	494.77	605.79	741.45	821.99	977.48	1127.52
62.16	353.06	423.25	484.03	908.40	871.15	799.28	495.82	283.32
496.29	1204.57	1212.11	1341.65	2223.65	2085.62	2146.05	2109.57	2265.26
485.39	1113.46	959.98	1302.70	1571.63	1235.20	1222.00	1216.59	1310.75
519.88	1560.34	1766.40	2149.54	2791.68	3263.68	3545.75	3645.08	3271.11
126.28	269.44	315.87	388.57	668.84	488.39	542.39	521.08	521.15
666284	1405548	1339961	1112295	1238592	1375375	1576687	1804491	2302130
246263	667180	631218	656208	658842	515272	575629	783554	1205529
170110	500762	471706	318971	410139	524798	501797	462049	461717
35338	29306	27393	15903	12846	14103	11664	11028	15033
92.46	528.84	529.21	672.24	727.99	796.80	846.01	906.00	1045.80
446.04	1032.15	1039.01	1186.12	1249.53	1310.03	1299.90	1346.50	1401.11
195.82	475.26	415.48	536.46	479.39	629.36	749.30	654.40	555.67
700.34	757.57	784.52	753.61	640.34	615.43	425.50	432.50	442.68
171.77	264.27	269.49	284.29	281.75	330.60	368.32	367.37	385.32
240172	430064	488177	449042	434025	416681	437556	462022	957397
84.02	86.90	95.67	124.41	105.71	111.49	116.91	95.56	84.90
3306.13	7516.51	8746.48	6986.88	11202.83	10744.58	11144.43	12056.42	12218.75

14－12 续表

产品名称	Item	1995	2000
汽车（辆）	Motor Vehicles (set)	73824	131238
#客车	Buses		59137
小型拖拉机（台）	Mini-tractors (set)	100900	90966
纱（万吨）	Yarn (10 000 tons)	7.70	9.22
布（万米）	Cloth (10 000 m)	16800	8714
机制纸及纸板（万吨）	Machine-made Paper & Paperboard (10 000 tons)	95.02	82.55
成品糖（万吨）	Machine-made Sugar (10 000 tons)	178.12	325.76
发酵酒精（万吨）	Liquor (10 000 tons)	13.93	21.46
化学原料药（吨）	Chemical Medicine (ton)	2804	2482
中成药（吨）	Traditional Chinese Medicine (ton)	57071	49719
表（万只）	Watches (10 000 units)	86.90	1016.88
原盐（万吨）	Salt (10 000 tons)	9.69	15.62
卷烟（万箱）	Cigarettes (10 000 cases)	98.35	72.33
罐头（吨）	Canned Food (ton)	234700	135747
饮料酒（千升）	Alcoholic Beverages (kilo-liter)	314889	546848
原油加工量（万吨）	Volume of Crude Oil Processing		
发动机（万千瓦）	(10 000 tons)		

注：本表统计范围为全部工业产品产量。

Note: The statistical range of this table is the total output of industrial enterprises.

continued

2005	2010	2011	2012	2013	2014	2015	2016	2017
377184	1366096	1423467	1673293	1869086	2092254	2294032	2454531	2486056
288683	1076891	1116201	1245007	828835	617016	5340	6286	4616
117804	282254	386795	442446	457024	431257	163181	150438	138258
11.87	11.01	12.45	11.78	11.77	10.81	9.76	10.08	10.44
5472	4633	5970	5550	5067	4480	4506	4478	21077
125.37	225.11	276.52	336.37	413.90	338.67	284.05	289.03	301.21
504.34	705.46	742.28	861.47	1010.89	1077.16	925.74	914.69	936.20
22.45	55.76	56.18	55.95	65.59	86.17	69.56	59.74	79.25
5449	5920	7334	6034	6915	7090	7197	7237	9260
74712	213336	189188	232036	324318	293524	344856	437518	502580
95.34	102.15	98.41	97.06	99.02	88.68	76.34	32.21	52.93
10.72	8.80	6.54	7.14	11.08	8.94	7.90	7.08	3.84
106.90	143.30	148.30	150.70	153.70	156.80	156.84	147.73	144.26
171994	478805	487164	516198	559740	483416	565830	541756	589115
832112	1878833	2104674	2322123	2437584	2426751	2391867	2186628	1933313
	418.93	1108.01	1550.66	1296.13	1390.47	1428.80	1339.94	1562.50
	15377.04	15505.84	14045.63	16730.11	16973.37	18551.83	19657.61	20585.59

14—13 广西分市规模以上工业企业主要经济指标（2017年）

单位：万元

分市名称	Sector	企业单位数（个） Number of Enterprises (unit)	工业总产值（当年价格） Gross Industrial Output Value (At Current Prices)	全部从业人员年平均人数（人） Average Employed Persons (person)	固定资产原价 Original Value of Fixed Assets	固定资产净值 Net Value of Fixed Assets
广西	Guangxi	5723	262512136	1646215	99224059	61239540
南宁市	Nanning	960	37130696	231101	15005942	8430985
柳州市	Liuzhou	835	50313265	262966	15319093	9365413
桂林市	Guilin	646	17290627	169226	7322142	4896767
梧州市	Wuzhou	399	25143723	189651	5985476	4499164
北海市	Beihai	212	25008663	68282	5187350	3125367
防城港市	Fangchenggang	151	17724363	30867	7435578	5939846
钦州市	Qinzhou	326	18111483	101584	6726741	3353844
贵港市	Guigang	500	10705960	142610	3865285	2292857
玉林市	Yulin	549	18924180	186494	4142221	2724384
百色市	Baise	354	17872575	82967	9864008	6145257
贺州市	Hezhou	204	4163170	33601	2342671	1263905
河池市	Hechi	173	4066081	45644	6579031	3642357
来宾市	Laibin	227	6059036	39689	4333668	2474410
崇左市	Chongzuo	201	9405821	41702	3534750	1780610

Major Indicators Economic of Industrial Enterprises above Designated Size by City（2017）

(10 000 yuan)

资产总计 Total Capital	流动资产合计 Annual Average Balance of Circulating Funds	所有者权益合计 Owner's Equity	利润总额 Total Profits	主营业务收入 Business Income of the Main Products
175319945	81939863	67371077	16109525	238050543
26289270	12633414	10475843	2085922	34775110
32790529	18539075	10694530	1862519	45924080
13026349	5916450	6184116	961661	15794393
9616110	3841186	5025795	2867623	23520956
10213712	5266062	4062392	2533399	23964899
13300362	5188413	3932613	828244	13687407
9715661	4092175	4494467	939465	16827395
9284039	4254669	4338672	707488	10394178
8849809	4889268	3889647	904186	17400524
15450629	6136307	4722527	620088	13486784
5006901	2012351	1885736	253633	3854569
7803806	2971336	2147112	620612	3782056
5932520	2093115	1041497	-4377	5182394
6025314	3289069	2645836	1402942	8097958

主要统计指标解释

工业 指从事自然物质资源采掘和对工业品原料及农产品原料进行加工和再加工的物质生产部门。具体包括：（1）对自然资源的开采，如采矿、晒盐等，但不包括禽兽捕猎和水产捕捞；（2）对农副产品的加工、再加工，如粮油加工、食品加工、缫丝、纺织、制革等；（3）对采掘品的加工、再加工，如炼铁、炼钢、化工生产、石油加工、机器制造、木材加工等，以及电力、自来水、煤气的生产和供应等；（4）对工业品的修理、翻新，如机器设备的修理、交通运输工具（如汽车）的修理等。

独立核算法人工业企业 指从事工业生产经营活动的单位。独立核算法人工业企业应同时具备以下条件：①依法成立，有自己的名称、组织机构和场所，能够承担民事责任；②独立拥有和使用资产，承担负债，有权与其他单位签订合同；③独立核算盈亏，并能够编制资产负债表。

集体企业 指企业资产归集体所有，并按《中华人民共和国企业法人登记管理条例》规定登记注册的经济组织。是社会主义公有制经济的组成部分。包括城乡所有使用集体投资举办的企业，以及部分个人通过集资自愿放弃所有权并依据工商行政管理机关认定为集体所有制的企业。

国有控股：包括：（1）在企业的全部实收资本中，国有经济成分的出资人拥有的实收资本（股本）所占企业全部实收资本（股本）的比例大于50%的国有绝对控股。（2）在企业的全部实收资本中，国有经济成分的出资人拥有的实收资本（股本）所占比例虽未大于50%，但相对大于其他任何一方经济成分的出资人所占比例的国有相对控股；或者虽不大于其他经济成分，但根据协议规定拥有企业实际控制权的国有协议控股。（3）投资双方各占50%，且未明确由谁绝对控股的企业，若其中一方为国有经济成分的，一律按国有控股处理。

股份制经济 是指以合作制为基础，由企业职工共同出资入股，吸收一定比例的社会资产投资组建，实行自主经营，自负盈亏，按劳分配与按股分红相结合的一种集体经济组织。

联营企业 是指两个及两个以上相同或不同所有制性质的企业法人或事业单位法人，按自愿、平等、互利的原则，共同投资组成的经济组织。包括国有联营、集体联营、国有与集体联营、其他联营等。

有限责任公司 是指根据《中华人民共和国公司登记管理条例》规定登记注册，由两个以上，五十个以下的股东共同出资，每个股东以其所认缴的出资额对公司承担有限责任，公司以其全部资产对其债务承担责任的经济组织。包括国有独资公司以及其他有限责任公司。

股份有限公司 是指根据《中华人民共和国公司登记管理条例》规定登记注册，其全部注册资本由等额股份构成并通过发行股票筹集资本，股东以其认购的股份对公司承担有限责任，公司以其全部资产对其债务承担责任的经济组织。

私营企业 是指由自然人投资设立或由自然人控股，以雇佣劳动为基础的营利性经济组织。包括按照《公司法》、《合伙企业法》、《私营企业暂行条例》以及《个人独资企业法》规定登记注册的私营独资企业、私营合伙企业、私营有限责任公司、私营股份有限公司和个人独资企业。

轻工业 指主要提供生活消费品和制作手工工具的工业。按其所使用的原料不同，可分为两大类：（1）以农产品为原料的轻工业，是指直接或间接以农产品为基本原料的轻工业。主要包括食品制造、饮料制造、烟草加工、纺织、缝纫、皮革和毛皮制作、造纸以及印刷等工业；（2）以非农产品为原料的轻工业，是指以工业品为原料的轻工业。主要包括文教体育用品、化学药品制造、合成纤维制造、日用化学制品、日用玻璃制品、日用金属制品、手工工具制造、医疗器械制造、文化和办公用机械制造等工业。

重工业 指为国民经济各部门提供物质技术基础的主要生产资料的工业。按其生产性质和产品用途，可以分为下列三类：（1）采掘（伐）工业，是指对自然资源的开采，包括石油开采、煤炭开采、金属矿开采、非金属矿开采和木材采伐等工业；（2）原材料工业，指向国民经济各部门提供基本材料、动力和燃料的工业。包括金属冶炼及加工、炼焦及焦炭化学、化工原料、水泥、人造板以及电力、石油和煤炭加工等工业；（3）加工工业，是指对工业原材料进行再加工制造的工业。包括装备国民经济各部门的机械设备制造工业、金属结构、水泥制品等工业，以及为农业提供的生产资料如化肥、农药等工业。

根据上述划分原则，修理业中以重工业产品为修理作业对象的划为重工业，反之划为轻工业。

工业总产值 是以货币表现的工业企业在一定时期内生产的已出售或可供出售工业产品总量，它反映一定时期内工业生产的总规模和总水平。包括在本企业内不再进行加工，经检验、包装入库（规定不需包装的产品除外）的成品价值，对外加工费收入，自制半成品、在产品期末期初差额价值。工业总产值采用“工厂法”计算，即以工业企业作为一个整体，按企业工业生产活动的最终成果来计算，企业内部不允许重复计算，不能把企业内部各个车间（分厂）生产的成果相加。但在企业之间、行业之间、地区之间存在着重复计算。

轻重工业总产值的划分也是按“工厂法”计算的，即一个工业企业在正常情况下生产的主要产品的性质属于轻工业，则该企业的全部总产值作为轻工业总产值；一个工业企业生产的主要产品的性质属于重工业，则该企业的全部总产值作为重工业总产值。

固定资产原价 指企业在建造、购置、安装、改建、扩建、技术改造某项固定资产时所支出的全部货币总额。它一般包括买价、包装费、运杂费和安装费等。

固定资产净值 指固定资产原价减去历年已提折旧额后的净额。

主营业务收入 指企业在报告期内生产的成品、自制半成品和工业性劳务取得的收入。

Explanatory Notes on Main Statistical Indicators

Industry refers to the material production sector which is engaged in excavation of natural material resources, processing and reprocessing of industrial and agricultural raw materidls, including: (1) exploitation of natural resources, such as mining, solar salt, but not including hunting and fishing ; (2) processing and reprocessing of farm and sideline products, such as rice husking, wine making, oil pressing, cotton ginning, silk reeling, spinning and weaving, and leather making; (3) manufacture of industrial products, such as steel making, iron smelting, chemicals manufacturing, petroleum processing, machine building, timber processing; water and gas production and electricity generation and supply; (4) repairing of industrial products such as the repairing of machinery and means of transport (such as cars) .

Corporate Industrial Enterprises with Independent Accounting System refer to enterprises engaging in industrial production activities, which meet the following requirements: 1. They are established legally, having their own names, organizations, location, able to take civil liability; 2. They possess and use their assets independently, assume liabilities, and are entitled to sign contracts with other units; 3.They are financially independent, and compile their own balance sheets.

Collective-owned Enterprises refer to industrial enterprises where the means of production are owned collectively, including urban and rural enterprises invested by collectives and some enterprises which were formerly owned privately but have been registered in industrial and commercial administration agency as collective units through raising fund from the public.

State-holding Enterprises includes: (1) absolutely state-holding enterprises whose state paid-up capital(stock) shares are more than 50%. (2) relatively state-holding enterprises that state shares are less than 50%,but relatively more than other economic units, or no more than other economic units, but according to agreement, the state have actuary controlling ability to the enterprises. (3) enterprises that one of the two 50-50 investors is state-owned, without conforming which investor is absolute holding.

Share-holding Enterprises refer to economic units set up on cooperative basis, with funding party from members of the enterprises and partly from outside investment, where the operation and management is decided by the members who also participate in the production, and the distribution of income is based both on work (labor input) and on shares (capital input).

Joint-operation Enterprises refer to economic units that are established by joint investment by two or more corporate enterprise or institution of the same or different types of ownership on voluntary, equal and mutual-beneficial basis. They include state-owned joint-operation enterprises, collective joint-operation enterprises, state-collective joint-operation enterprises, other joint-operation etc.

Share-holding Liability Corporations refers to economic units registered in accordance with the Regulation of the People's Republic of China on the registration of corporation enterprises, assets are collected by above 2 investors, bellow 50 investors, each investor bears limited liability to the corporation depending on the holding of shares, and the corporation bears liability to its debt to the maximum of its total assets. They include state-owned enterprises and other share-holding liability corporations.

Share-holding Corporations Lid. refer to economic units registered in accordance with the Regulation of the People's Republic of China on the Management of Registration of Corporation Enterprises, with total registered capital divided into equal shares and raised through issuing stocks. Each investor bears limited liability to the corporation depending on the holding of shares, and the corporation bears to its debt to the maximum of its total assets.

Private Enterprises refer to economic units invested or controlled (by holding the majority of the shares) by natural persons who hire labors for profit-making activities. Included in this category are private limited liability corporations, private share-holding corporations ltd., private partnership and private sole investment enterprises registered in accordance with the Corporation law, Partnership law, Tentative Regulation on Private Enterprises and Individual Proprietorship Enterprise Law.

Light Industry refers to the industry that produces consumer goods and hand tools. It consists of two categories, depending on the materials used: (1) Industries using farm products as raw materials. These are branches of light industry which directly or indirectly use farm products as basic raw materials, including the manufacture of food and beverages, tobacco processing, textile, clothing, fur and leather manufacturing, paper making, printing, etc. (2) Industries using non farm products as raw materials. These are branches of light industry which use manufactured goods as raw materials, including the manufacture of cultural, educational articles and sports goods, chemicals, synthetic fiber, chemical products for daily use, glass products for daily use, metal products for daily use, hand tools, medical apparatus and instruments, and the manufacture of cultural and clerical machinery.

Heavy Industry refers to the industry whose produces capital goods, and provides various sectors of the national economy with necessary material and technical basis. It consists of the following three branches according to the purpose of production or the use of products: (1) Mining, quarrying and logging industry refers to the industry that extracts natural resources, including extraction of petroleum, coal, metal and non metal ores and logging. (2) Raw materials industry refers to the industry that provides various sectors of the national economy with raw materials, fuels and power. It includes smelting and processing of metals, coking and coke chemistry, chemical materials and building materials such as cement, plywood, and power, petroleum refining and coal dressing. (3) Manufacturing industry refers to the industry that processes raw materials. It includes machine manufacturing industry which equips sectors of the national economy, industries of metal structure and cement products, industries producing means of agricultural production, such as chemical fertilizers and pesticides.

According to the above principle of classification, the repairing trades that are engaged primarily in repairing products of heavy industry are classified into heavy industry while these engaged in repairing products of light industry are classified into light industry.

Gross Industrial Output Value is the total volume of industrial products sold or available for sale in value terms that reflects the total achievements and overall scale of industrial production during a given period. It includes the value of the finished products, which are not to be further processed in the enterprises and have been inspected, packed and put in storage, the value of industrial services rendered to other units, and the changes in the value of the semi- finished products and products in process between the beginning and closing of the period. The gross industrial output value is calculated with "factory method". No double calculations are to be made within the same enterprise. However, double counting does occur among different enterprises.

Output value of light and heavy industries is also classified with the "factory" method. Under normal conditions, if the major products of an industrial enterprise belong to light industry products, the gross output value of that enterprise is classified wholly into light industry; the same principle applies to heavy industry.

Original Value of Fixed Assets refers to the original value of all fixed assets owned by industrial enterprises, calculated at the cost paid at the time of purchase, installation, reconstruction, expansion, and technical innovation and transformation of the said assets, which includes expenses on purchase, package, transportation, and installation, etc. Net value of fixed assets is obtained by deducting depreciation over years from the original value of fixed assets.

Net Value of Fixed Assets is obtained by deducting depreciation over years from the original value of fixed assets.

Business Income of Main Products refers to the revenue form the sales of finished and semi-finished products and from rendering of industrial services by industrial services by industrial enterprises during the reference period.

第十五篇

建筑业

CONSTRUCTION

（校对编辑：陈李全）

15－1 主要年份三级及三级以上建筑业企业主要指标
Major Indicators of the Third & Higher Grade Construction Enterprises in Main Years

指 标	Item	2000	2005	2010	2013	2014	2015	2016	2017
企业个数（个）	**Number (unit)**	**1078**	**1047**	**1160**	**1245**	**1163**	**1152**	**1203**	**1326**
#国有及国有控股企业	State-owned & State-holding Enterprises	260	216	169	152	142	137	135	134
城镇集体企业	Urban Collective-owned Enterprises	623	314	229	197	182	167	157	172
1. 内资企业	1.Domestic Enterprises	1067	1042	1153	1241	1161	1149	1201	1324
2. 港澳台商投资企业	2.Funded from Hong Kong, Macao & Taiwan	4	4	5	4	2	3	2	2
3. 外商投资企业	3.Foreign Funded Enterprises	7	1	2	0	0	0	0	0
总产值（亿元）	**Gross Output Value (10 000 yuan)**	**150.92**	**425.21**	**1222.31**	**2289.88**	**2608.91**	**2953.42**	**3434.33**	**4209.72**
#国有及国有控股企业	State-owned & State-holding Enterprises	88.82	248.35	645.72	1109.61	1216.28	1335.06	1516.96	1709.64
城镇集体企业	Urban Collective-owned Enterprises	46.62	63.89	117.02	152.69	171.74	192.34	203.91	235.77
1. 内资企业	1.Domestic Enterprises	150.27	422.85	1200.77	2289.30	2608.65	2952.50	3434.06	4206.05
2. 港澳台商投资企业	2.Funded from Hong Kong , Macao & Taiwan	0.067	0.17	0.88	0.58	0.26	0.92	0.27	3.67
3. 外商投资企业	3.Foreign Funded Enterprises	0.581	2.19	20.65	0	0	0	0	0
年末从业人员（万人）	**Number of Employed Persons (10 000 persons)**	**33.3**	**43.0**	**59.06**	**76.50**	**77.92**	**85.67**	**113.29**	**139.29**
#国有及国有控股企业	State-owned & State-holding Enterprises	16.1	20.4	26.4	30.73	31.90	35.02	43.02	46.43
城镇集体企业	Urban Collective-owned Enterprises	13.5	10.5	7.39	6.88	6.87	6.83	7.75	7.99
1. 内资企业	1.Domestic Enterprises	15.5	42.8	58.01	76.46	77.91	85.65	113.27	139.09
2. 港澳台商投资企业	2.Enterprises Funded by Enterprises from Hong Kong, Macao & Taiwan	…	0.03	0.01	0.04	0.01	0.02	0.02	0.17
3. 外商投资企业	3.Foreign Funded Enterprises	0.1	0.1	1.03	0	0	0	0	0
房屋建筑施工面积（万平方米）	**Floor Space of Buildings under Construction (10 000 sq.m)**	**2327.5**	**5518.1**	**10742.3**	**18316.08**	**21168.07**	**23431.97**	**26463.48**	**25305.93**
房屋建筑竣工面积（万平方米）	**Floor Space of Buildings Completed (10 000 sq.m)**	**1188.7**	**2209.7**	**4093.82**	**5787.59**	**6733.02**	**7720.70**	**7933.69**	**8438.74**

15－2 主要年份国有及国有控股建筑企业主要指标
Major Indicators of State-owned & State-holding Construction Enterprises in Main Years

指 标	Item	2000	2005	2010	2013	2014	2015	2016	2017
企业个数（个）	Number of Enterprises (unit)	260	216	169	152	142	137	135	134
计算建筑业劳动生产率的平均人数（万人）	Average Number of Staff & Workers to Calculate Labor Productivity (10 000 persons)	15.6	19.7	25.1	28.8	35.4	38.7	40.6	46.4
建筑业总产值（万元）	Gross Output Value of Construction (10 000 yuan)	888224	2483506	6457240	11096091	12162752	13350594	15169598	17096397
竣工产值（万元）	Output Value of Construction Completed (10 000 yuan)	824396	1600790	3109693	5952729	4528612	6927922	6657249	8239957
房屋建筑施工面积（万平方米）	Floor Space of Buildings under Construction (10 000 sq.m)	1050.1	2380.9	4640.4	8708.35	10645.75	11767.78	12794.31	13194.08
#本年新开工	Newly Started Buildings in the Year	416.6	1069	1658.8	2467.15	3268.01	2388.66	2531.94	3161.98
房屋建筑竣工面积（万平方米）	Floor Space of Buildings Completed (10 000 sq.m)	464.9	808.1	1260.6	1605.30	1752.24	2157.42	2426.74	2485.23
#住 宅	Residential Building	281.6	529.6	844.2	1117.35	1132.70	1284.77	1543.74	1777.04
年末自有机械设备总台数（台）	Number of Machinery & Equipment Owned at Year-end (set)	42514	46905	36782	37728		37146	31656	33944
年末自有机械设备净值（万元）	Net Value of Machinery & Equipment Owned at Year-end (10 000 yuan)	125314	174423	183742	162130		185266	160287	139898
年末自有机械设备总功率（万千瓦）	Total Power of Machinery & Equipment Owned at Year-end (10 000 kw)	98.2	104.6	107.4	110.1		114.3	88.9	82.1
年末固定资产原值（万元）	Original Value of Fixed Assets (10 000 yuan)	751637	758096	782614	847846	989844	1033633	1362935	1095886
年末固定资产净值（万元）	Net Value of Fixed Assets (10 000 yuan)	597232	505996	477123	438954	558453	577324	852362	576104
本年固定资产折旧（万元）	Depreciation of Fixed Assets (10 000 yuan)	20662	32117	53040	49627	68112	64642	62764	65729
利润总额（万元）	Total Profits (10 000 yuan)	440	15102	51373	77453	104659	127681	200782	218349
利税总额（万元）	Total Pre-tax Profits (10 000 yuan)	30485	95195	251929	393578	446876	511979	366429	366528
按建筑业总产值计算的劳动生产率（元/人）	Overall Labor Productivity in Terms of Gross Output Value (yuan/person)	56937	125917	257132	385924	343180	344720	373289	368255
按竣工面积计算的劳动生产率（平方米/人）	Overall Labor Productivity in Terms of Floor Space of Buildings Completed (sq.m/person)	29.8	41	50.2	55.8	49.4	55.7	59.72	53.5
产值利润率（%）	Ratio of Profit to Gross Output Value (%)	0.1	0.6	0.8	0.7	0.9	1.0	1.3	1.3
产值利税率（%）	Ratio of Pre-tax Profit to Gross Output Value (%)	3.4	3.8	3.9	3.5	3.7	3.8	2.4	2.1
房屋建筑面积竣工率（%）	Rate of Floor Space of Buildings Completed (%)	44.3	33.9	27.2	18.4	16.5	18.3	19.0	18.8
技术装备率（元/人）	Value of Machines per Laborer (yuan/person)	7784	8843	6960	5280		5292	3726	3139
动力装备率（千瓦/人）	Power of Machines per Laborer (kw/person)	6	5	4	4		3	2	2

15－3 主要年份地方国有建筑企业主要指标

Major Indicators of Local State-owned Construction Enterprises in Main Years

指 标	Item	2000	2005	2010	2013	2014	2015	2016	2017
企业个数（个）	Number of Enterprises (unit)	238	200	156	118	103	96	128	83
计算建筑业劳动生产率的平均人数（万人）	Average Number of Staff & Workers to Calculate Labor Productivity (10 000 persons)	13.3	16.7	20.3	24.6	29.7	28.1	28.8	26.37
建筑业总产值（万元）	Gross Output Value of Construction (10 000 yuan)	691699	1949218	4878699	8778188	8368281	9059867	9941288	9001850
竣工产值（万元）	Output Value of Construction Completed (10 000 yuan)	601947	1213806	2560959	4065692	3683812	5425079	4602114	4388651
房屋建筑施工面积（万平方米）	Floor Space of Buildings under Construction (10 000 sq.m)	1004.7	2203.8	4415.9	8391.64	8351.79	9265.25	10034.17	7800.23
#本年新开工	Newly Started Buildings in the Year	400.3	961.1	1490.9	2326.70	2701.83	2015.00	1785.32	1812.48
房屋建筑竣工面积（万平方米）	Floor Space of Buildings Completed (10 000 sq.m)	444.3	702.3	1238.1	1543.35	1372.58	1669.52	1935.13	1496.42
#住 宅	Residential Building	273.2	446.7	838.5	1076.52	928.01	965.83	1262.45	1113.34
年末自有机械设备总台数（台）	Number of Machinery & Equipment Owned at Year-end (set)	34428	34397	23962	20031		19042	16406	15748
年末自有机械设备净值（万元）	Net Value of Machinery & Equipment Owned at Year-end (10 000 yuan)	93670	107045	86709	89364		114434	107069	66828
年末自有机械设备总功率（万千瓦）	Total Power of Machinery & Equipment Owned at Year-end (10 000 kw)	74.9	63.2	57.6	42.3		59.5	56.55	38.45
年末固定资产原值（万元）	Original Value of Fixed Assets (10 000 yuan)	647397	427785	423670	492979	488579	488910	781761	392748
年末固定资产净值（万元）	Net Value of Fixed Assets (10 000 yuan)	532899	299639	298090	308085	328598	321051	551868	205292
本年固定资产折旧（万元）	Depreciation of Fixed Assets (10 000 yuan)	14028	3118	15029	22496	21244	25981	23454	23583
利润总额（万元）	Total Profits (10 000 yuan)	3789	7854	33002	79950	74325	85246	184145	119066
利税总额（万元）	Total Pre-tax Profits (10 000 yuan)	25426	61464	186674	330131	320206	344675	320443	226393
按建筑业总产值计算的劳动生产率（元/人）	Overall Labor Productivity in Terms of Gross Output Value (yuan/person)	52007	116991	239954	356200	343180	322102	345646	341323
按竣工面积计算的劳动生产率（平方米/人）	Overall Labor Productivity in Terms of Floor Space of Buildings Completed (sq.m /person)	33	42.2	60.9	62.6	49.4	59.4	67.3	56.7
产值利润率（%）	Ratio of Profit to Gross Output Value (%)	0.5	0.4	0.7	0.9	0.9	0.9	1.9	1.3
产值利税率（%）	Ratio of Pre-tax Profit to Gross Output Value (%)	3.7	3.2	3.8	3.8	3.7	3.8	3.2	2.5
房屋建筑面积竣工率（%）	Rate of Floor Space of Buildings Completed (%)	44.2	31.9	28	18	16.4	18.0	19.3	19.2
技术装备率（元/人）	Value of Machines per Laborer (yuan/person)	6788	6425	3900	3386		4472	3646	2827
动力装备率（千瓦/人）	Power of Machines per Laborer (kw/person)	5	4	3	2		2	2	1

15—4 建筑企业生产情况（2017年）
Major Production Indicators of Construction Enterprises (2017)

指标	Item	总计 Total	#国有经济 State-owned Economic	中央企业 Central	地方企业 Local	#城镇集体经济 Urban Collective-owned Economic
企业个数（个）	Number of Enterprises (unit)	1326	100	17	83	172
#亏损企业个数	Number of Loss-making Enterprises	210	14	1	13	40
建筑业总产值(万元)	Gross Output Value of Construction (10 000 yuan)	42097228	12306459	3304609	9001850	2357657
建筑工程	Construction Projects	35940152	10194659	2750288	7444371	2180994
安装工程	Installation Projects	3645432	1460221	510671	949550	84593
其他	Others	2511643	651579	43650	607929	92075
竣工产值（万元）	Output Value of Construction Completed (10 000 yuan)	22690094	5540714	1152063	4388651	1525105
房屋建筑施工面积（万平方米）	Floor Space of Buildings under Construction (10 000 sq.m)	25305.93	8194.01	393.78	7800.23	1845.73
#本年新开工	Newly Started Buildings in the Year	9001.03	1981.17	168.69	1812.48	930.22
#投标承包	Number of Bidding Projects	0	0	0	0	0
房屋建筑竣工面积（万平方米）	Floor Space of Buildings Completed (10 000 sq.m)	8438.74	1508.68	12.26	1496.42	921.49
#住宅面积	Residential Buildings	5219.51	1114.02	0.68	1113.34	483.09
年末自有机械设备总台数（台）	Number of Machinery & Equipment Owned at Year-end (set)	155543	29662	13914	15748	16455
年末自有机械设备总功率（万千瓦）	Total Power of Machinery & Equipment Owned at Year-end (10 000 kw)	306.01	76.14	37.69	38.45	40.87
年末自有机械设备净值（万元）	Net Value of Machinery & Equipment Owned at Year-end (10 000 yuan)	634527	119607	52779	66828	62491
计算建筑业劳动生产率的平均人数(万人)	Average Number of Staff & Workers to Calculate Labor Productivity (10 000 persons)	139.29	32.61	6.23	26.37	7.99

15—5 按主要行业分组的建筑企业生产情况（2017年）
Major Production Indicators of Construction Enterprises by Sector (2017)

指　标	Item	总　计 Total	房屋 建筑业 Housing Industry	土木工程 建筑业 Civil Engineering	建筑 安装业 Construction & Installation	建筑装饰 和其他 建筑业 Architectual Ornament & Others
企业个数（个）	Number of Enterprises (unit)	1326	828	249	121	128
#亏损企业个数	Number of Loss-making Enterprises	210	128	27	29	26
建筑业总产值(万元)	Gross Output Value of Construction (10 000 yuan)	42097228	32310496	8433238	925077	428417
建筑工程	Construction Projects	35940152	28547789	6702756	345004	344604
安装工程	Installation Projects	3645432	1982891	1109298	529935	23308
其他	Others	2511643	1779816	621184	50138	60505
竣工产值（万元）	Output Value of Construction Completed (10 000 yuan)	22690094	17245928	4775930	429661	238575
房屋建筑施工面积（万平方米）	Floor Space of Buildings under Construction (10 000 sq.m)	25305.93	24133.64	1027.43	137.98	6.87
#本年新开工	Newly Started Buildings in the Year	9001.03	8630.93	298.74	69.38	1.98
#投标承包	Number of Bidding Projects	0	0	0	0	0
房屋建筑竣工面积（万平方米）	Floor Space of Buildings Completed (10 000 sq.m)	8438.74	8176.69	241.32	17.85	2.88
#住宅面积	Residential Buildings	5219.51	5018.66	181.86	16.90	2.10
年末自有机械设备总台数（台）	Number of Machinery & Equipment Owned at Year-end (set)	155543	120325	24235	4956	6027
年末自有机械设备总功率（万千瓦）	Total Power of Machinery & Equipment Owned at Year-end (10 000 kw)	306.01	217.96	76.27	6.34	5.43
年末自有机械设备净值（万元）	Net Value of Machinery & Equipment Owned at Year-end (10 000 yuan)	634527	432093	160279	15721	26435
计算建筑业劳动生产率的平均人数(万人)	Average Number of Staff & Workers to Calculate Labor Productivity (10 000 persons)	139.29	114.50	21.01	2.57	1.22

15－6 建筑企业主要财务状况（2017年）
Major Financial Indicators of Construction Enterprises（2017）

单位：万元 （10 000 yuan）

指 标	Item	总 计 Total	# 国有经济 State-owned Economic			# 城镇集体经济 Urban Collective-owned Economic
				中央企业 Central	地方企业 Local	
实收资本合计	Total Capital Hold	4712778	1056379	260111	796268	193779
流动资产合计	Total Circulating Funds	18435971	6461196	2314546	4146650	540822
固定资产合计	Total Fixed Assets	2028874	647833	223169	424664	130189
固定资产原价	Original Value of Fixed Assets	2489859	838076	445328	392748	128427
累计折旧	Add Up Depreciation	1050611	424006	236550	187456	35540
#本年折旧	Depreciation of the Year	160890	49908	26325	23583	3592
资产总计	Total Assets	22859494	7512692	2662302	4850390	819430
流动负债合计	Total Liquid Liabilities	12448485	4990151	2177573	2812578	339937
非流动负债合计	Total Non-liquid Liabilities	1542828	823586	143246	680340	31574
所有者权益合计	Total Creditors Equity	8134743	1668677	341483	1327194	345864
主营业务收入	Income from Major Business	31338827	9446170	2750913	6695257	1702860
主营业务成本	Cost of Major Business	28692723	8919369	2606830	6312540	1505827
主营业务税金及附加	Taxes & Extra Charges of Major Business	403391	50237	11486	38750	51530
其他业务利润	Other Profits	28174	8156	3621	4535	3396
管理费用	Management Expenses	943336	247343	72463	174880	47921
财务费用	Property Expenses	225385	90545	25671	64875	3174
利润总额	Total Profits	755796	158124	39058	119066	50202
利税总额	Total Pre-tax Profits	1040596	273648	47256	226393	97308

15—7 按主要行业分组的建筑企业财务状况（2017年）
Major Financial Indicators of Construction Enterprises by Sector（2017）

单位：万元 (10 000 yuan)

指 标	Item	总 计 Total	房屋建筑业 Housing Industry	土木工程建筑业 Civil Engineering	建筑安装业 Construction & Installation	建筑装饰和其他建筑业 Architectual Ornament & Others
实收资本合计	Total Capital Hold	4712778	3063454	1330521	220332	98471
流动资产合计	Total Circulating Funds	18435971	11405427	5868140	818672	343733
固定资产合计	Total Fixed Assets	2028874	1134188	769494	66624	58569
固定资产原价	Original Value of Fixed Assets	2489859	1262610	1085712	92462	49075
累计折旧	Add Up Depreciation	1050611	441947	533533	46886	28246
#本年折旧	Depreciation of the Year	160890	78837	71316	7735	3003
资产总计	Total Assets	22859494	14179060	7290303	971215	418916
流动负债合计	Total Liquid Liabilities	12448485	7444677	4154069	632970	216769
非流动负债合计	Total Non-liquid Liabilities	1542828	777585	709493	12442	43309
所有者权益合计	Total Creditors Equity	8134743	5354562	2310872	320359	148950
主营业务收入	Income from Major Business	31338827	23089881	7055909	878273	314764
主营业务成本	Cost of Major Business	28692723	21361054	6277168	787143	267358
主营业务税金及附加	Taxes & Extra Charges of Major Business	403391	326028	67548	7113	2702
其他业务利润	Other Profits	28174	12816	12726	2537	96
管理费用	Management Expenses	943336	572086	293595	54763	22893
财务费用	Property Expenses	225385	153877	62559	7894	1055
利润总额	Total Profits	755796	495930	229080	12927	17859
利税总额	Total Pre-tax Profits	1040596	800096	196995	28756	14750

15－8 各种分组的建筑企业主要经济效益指标（2017年）
Major Economic Efficiency Indicators of Construction Enterprises by Various Groups（2017）

指 标	Item	劳动生产率 Labor Productivity			房屋建筑面积竣工率（%） Rate of Floor Space of Buildings Completed (%)
		按总产值计算（元/人） Calculated by Gross Output Value (yuan/person)	按竣工产值计算（元/人） Calculated by Completed Output Value (yuan/person)	按房屋竣工面积计算（平方米/人） Calculated by Floor Space of Building Completed (sq.m/person)	
总 计	**Total**	**302614**	**162968**	**60.56**	**33.3**
按经济类型分	By Economic units				
#国有经济	State-owned Economic	377414	169922	46.27	18.4
中央企业	Central Enterprises	530103	184806	1.97	3.1
地方企业	Local Enterprises	341323	166404	56.74	19.2
集体经济	Collective-owned Economic	295279	191008	115.41	49.9
按企业资质等级分	By the Classes of Enterprises				
O、一级	Zero, One Classes	319825	159499	54.15	26.8
二、三级	Two, Three Classes	268504	169844	73.26	51.6
按行业分	By Sector				
房屋建筑业	Building Construction	282621	150681	71.41	33.8
土木工程建筑业	Civil Engineering	401415	227330	11.49	23.5
建筑安装业	Construction	360204	167300	6.95	12.9
建筑装饰和其他建筑业	Installation	352403	196245	2.37	41.9

15—8 续表 continued

指 标	Item	资产利润率(%) Ratio of Profit to Funds (%)	资产利税率(%) Ratio of Per-tax Profit to Funds (%)	产值利润率(%) Ratio of Profit to Gross Output Value (%)	产值利税率(%) Ratio of Pre-tax Profit to Gross Output Value (%)
总 计	**Total**	**3.3**	**4.6**	**1.8**	**2.5**
按经济类型分	By Economic units				
#国有经济	State-owned Economic	2.1	3.6	1.3	2.2
中央企业	Central Enterprises	1.5	1.8	1.2	1.4
地方企业	Local Enterprises	2.5	4.7	1.3	2.5
集体经济	Collective-owned Economic	6.1	11.9	2.1	4.1
按企业资质等级分	By the Classes of Enterprises				
O、一级	Zero, One Classes	3.1	4.7	1.4	2.1
二、三级	Two, Three Classes	3.6	4.4	2.7	3.3
按行业分	By Sector				
房屋建筑业	Building Construction	3.5	5.6	1.5	2.5
土木工程建筑业	Civil Engineering	3.1	2.7	2.7	2.3
建筑安装业	Construction	1.3	3.0	1.4	3.1
建筑装饰和其他建筑业	Installation	4.3	3.5	4.2	3.4

主要统计指标解释

建筑业统计单位 指从事房屋、构筑物建造和设备安装活动的法人企业。

建筑业总产值 建筑业总产值是以货币表现的建筑业企业在一定时期内生产的建筑业产品和提供的服务的总和。建筑业总产值包括:

(1) 建筑工程产值:指列入建筑工程预算内的各种工程价值。

(2) 安装工程产值:指设备安装工程价值,不包括被安装设备本身价值。

(3) 其他产值:建筑业总产值中除建筑工程、安装工程以外的产值。包括房屋构筑物修理产值、非标准设备制造产值、总包企业向分包企业收取的管理费以及不能明确划分的施工活动所完成的产值。

竣工产值 指以货币表现的建筑业生产所形成的成品的价值。竣工产值一般是以单位工程为对象,当该工程按照设计所规定工程内容全部完成,达到了设计规定的交工条件,经有关部门检查验收鉴定合格的单位工程价值。竣工产值包括报告期内竣工单位工程从开工到竣工的全部自行完成的价值。如果一个单位工程跨两个年度施工,其竣工价值应当包括上年度完成的价值。竣工产值不包括附属辅助企业或内部核算的其他单位为外单位生产和服务的价值。

房屋建筑施工面积 是指报告期内施工的全部房屋建筑面积,它包括本期新开工的面积、上期跨入本期继续施工的房屋面积、上期停缓建在本期恢复施工的房屋面积、本期竣工的房屋面积以及本期施工后又停缓建的房屋面积。

房屋竣工面积 是指在报告期内房屋建筑按照设计要求已全部完工,达到了使用条件,经检查验收鉴定合格的房屋建筑面积。计算房屋竣工面积,必须严格执行房屋竣工验收标准。

自有机械设备年末总功率 是指本企业(或单位)自有施工机械、生产设备、运输设备以及其他设备等列为固定资产的生产性机械设备年末总功率,按设定能力或查定能力计算。包括机械本身的动力和为该机械服务的单独动力设备,如电动机等。计量单位用千瓦,动力换算可按1马力=0.735千瓦折合成千瓦数。电焊机、变压器、锅炉不计算动力。

自有机械设备净值 是指本企业(或单位)自有机械设备经过使用、磨损后实际存在的价值,即原值减去折旧后的净额。

房屋建筑面积竣工率 是指报告期内房屋建筑竣工面积占同期房屋建筑施工面积的比重。

技术装备率 指在报告期末自有机械设备净值与期末从业人数的比重。

动力装备率 指在报告期末自有机械设备总功率与期末从业人数的比重。

产值利润率 指在报告期内每百元产值所实现的利润。它的计算方法是:利润总额除以建筑业总产值。

产值利税率 指在报告期内每百元产值所实现的利税。它的计算方法是:利税总额除以建筑业总产值。

Explanatory Notes on Main Statistical Indicators

Statistical Unit in Construction refers to corporate enterprise engaged in the construction of buildings and structures and in the installation of equipment

Gross Output Value of Construction (Output Value of Projects Under Construction) refers to total of construction products, expressed, in money terms, completed by construction and installation enterprises during a given period of time. It includes:

(1)Output value of construction projects, that is the value of projects covered by the project budgets;

(2)Output value of installation projects, that is the value of the installation equipment,(excluding the value of the equipment to be installed);

(3)Output value of others, that is the output value of construction industry excluding of construction projects and installation projects. It includes: output value of repairs of buildings or structures; output value of non-standard equipment manufacturing; overhead expenses received by contracted enterprises the sub-contracted enterprises and the completed output value of construction activities that have no clear definition.

Output Value Completed refers to the value of the finished products make from construction producing that displays with the currency. It is the value of unit projects completed, which has come up to the designed standards and has been checked and accepted as qualified project by related departments. Output value completed includes the value of unit project completed that is all finished by itself from going into operation to completing during the report period. If the project of a unit is stepped for two years, its completed value should include the value that is finished in prior year. Output value completed does not include the value of attaching auxiliary enterprises or other checked-inside units that produce and serve for the other unit.

Floor Space of Buildings Under Construction refers to floor space of buildings under construction during the reference period including newly started buildings buildings started earlier and continued during the reference period and buildings suspended earlier restarted during the reference period, buildings completed during the reference period, and building under construction and then suspended during the reference period.

Floor Space of Buildings Completed refers to the floor space of buildings that are completed in reference period in accordance with the requirements of the design, up to the standard for putting into use, and have been checked and accepted by concerned departments as qualified ones.

Total Power of Machinery and Equipment Owned by the End of Year refers to the total power of machinery and equipment owned by the enterprises, and listed as the fixed assets of the enterprises by the end of the yea r'including machinery and equipment for construction, production and transportation. The power of the machinery is calculated on basis of the designed or verified capacity covering the power of the machinery / equipment and the separate power equipment serving the machinery / equipment (such as electric motors) but excluding welders, transformers and boilers. The unit used for the calculation of power is kilowatt, with horsepower converted to kilowatt by 1 horsepower = 0.735 kilowatt. Arc welding generator, voltage transformer and boiler don't calculate power.

Net Value of Machinery and Equipment Owned refers to the actual value of machinery and equipment owned by the enterprises after being used and broken, is obtained by deducting net value after depreciation from original value.

Rate of Floor Space of Buildings Completed refers to the ration of the floor space of buildings completed in certain period of time to the floor space of buildings under Construction in the same period.

Value of Machines per Laborer refers to the proportion of net value of machinery and equipment owned with persons employed of construction at year-end during the reference period.

Power of Machines per Laborer refers to the proportion of total power of machinery and equipment owned with persons employed of construction at year-end during the reference period.

Ratio of Profit to Gross Output Value refers to the profits that per 100 yuan make. It can be calculated as: total profits /gross output value of construction.

Ratio of Pre-tax Profit to Gross Output Value that is ratio of pre-tax profit to gross output value. Refers to the profits that per 100 yuan make. It can be calculated as: total Pre-tax profits /gross output value of construction.

第十六篇

批发和零售业

WHOLESALE & RETAIL TRADES

（校对编辑：闫室丞）

16－1 限额以上批发和零售业企业基本情况（2017年）

Basic Conditions of Enterprises above Designated Size in Wholesale & Retail（2017）

项 目	Item	2016		2017	
		法人企业（个）Corporation Enterprises (unit)	年末从业人员（人）Year-end Persons Employed (person)	法人企业（个）Corporation Enterprises (unit)	年末从业人员（人）Year-end Persons Employed (person)
总 计	**Total**	**3178**	**188602**	**3624**	**205096**
一、批发业	**Ⅰ.Wholesale**	**1212**	**68435**	**1331**	**74139**
1.按登记注册类型分组	**1.Grouped by Status of Registration**				
内资企业	Domestic Funded Enterprises	1203	68101	1321	73914
国有企业	State-owned Industry	53	9827	50	9060
集体企业	Collective-owned Industry	21	1104	20	1454
股份合作企业	Cooperative Enterprises	2	43	1	29
联营企业	Joint Ownership Enterprises				
国有联营企业	State Joint Ownership Enterprises				
集体联营企业	Collective Joint Ownership Enterprises				
国有与集体联营企业	Joint State-Collective Ownership Enterprises				
其他联营企业	Other Joint Ownership Enterprises				
有限责任公司	Limited Liability Corporations	349	24255	357	26199
国有独资企业	Sole State-funded Corporations	45	7268	64	7500
其他有限责任公司	Other Limited Liability Corporations	304	16987	293	18699
股份有限公司	Share Holding Enterprises	43	8749	39	7188
私营企业	Private Enterprises	727	23402	844	29218
私营独资企业	Private-funded Enterprises	6	215	6	179
私营合伙企业	Private Partnership Enterprises	1	23	2	10
私营有限责任公司	Private Limited Liability Corporations	698	22428	814	26482
私营股份有限公司	Private Share Holding Enterprises	22	736	22	2547
其他企业	Others	8	721	10	766
港、澳、台商投资企业	Enterprises with Funds from Hong Kong, Macao & Taiwan	5	202	4	72
合资经营企业	Joint Venture Enterprises	2	68		
合作经营企业	Cooperative Enterprises				
独资经营企业	Enterprises with Sole Investment	3	134	4	72
投资股份有限公司	Share-holding Corporations Ltd. with Investment				
其他港澳台投资企业	Others				
外商投资企业	Foreign-investment Enterprise	4	132	6	153
中外合资经营企业	Joint Venture Enterprises	2	98	2	99
中外合作经营企业	Cooperative Enterprises				
外资企业	Enterprises with Sole Foreign Investment	2	34	4	54
外商投资股份有限公司	Share-holding Corporations Ltd. with Foreign Investment				
其他外商投资企业	Others				
2.按国民经济行业分组	**2.Grouped by National Economic Sector**				
农、林、牧、渔产品批发业	Wholesale of the Agricultural & Animal Products	75	2667	86	2696
食品、饮料及烟草制品批发业	Wholesale of Food , Beverage & Tobacco Products	161	18279	205	19416
#米、面制品及食用油批发业	Wholesale of Rice, Flour Products & Edible Oil	32	3154	36	3663

16-1 续表1 continued

项 目	Item	2016 法人企业(个) Corporation Enterprises (unit)	2016 年末从业人员(人) Year-end Persons Employed (person)	2017 法人企业(个) Corporation Enterprises (unit)	2017 年末从业人员(人) Year-end Persons Employed (person)
烟草制品批发业	Wholesale of Tobacco Products	14	7240	14	7114
纺织、服装及家庭用品批发业	Wholesale of Textile, Garments & Daily Necessities	107	6350	99	5958
#服装批发业	Wholesale of Garments	16	775	11	560
文化、体育用品及器材批发业	Wholesale of Culture, Sports Goods & Apparatus	23	786	24	744
医药及医疗器材批发业	Wholesale of Medicine & Medical Apparatus	115	9406	147	11658
矿产品、建材及化工产品批发业	Wholesale of Mineral Products, Building Materials & Chemical Products	509	22277	555	24926
#煤炭及制品批发业	Wholesale of Coal & Related Products	60	1071	65	1264
石油及制品批发业	Wholesale of Petroleum & Related Products	72	12436	80	12779
金属及金属矿批发业	Wholesale of Metal & Metallic Ore	177	2765	166	3783
建材批发业	Wholesale of Building Materials	71	1338	101	2043
化肥批发业	Wholesale of Chemical Fertilizer	61	2556	64	2518
机械设备、五金产品及电子产品批发业	Wholesale of Mechanical Equipment, Hardware & Electrical Equipment & Electronic Product	189	8088	183	8269
#汽车及零配件批发业	Wholesale of Motor Vehicles	33	1050	43	1840
计算机、软件及辅助设备批发业	Wholesale of Computer, Software & Auxiliary Equipment	21	724	30	913
贸易经纪与代理	Trade Manager & Acting as Agent	5	48	5	47
其他批发业	Others	28	534	27	425
二、零售业	**Ⅱ.Retail**	**1966**	**120167**	**2293**	**130957**
1.按登记注册类型分组	**1. Grouped by Status of Registration**				
内资企业	Domestic Funded Enterprises	1915	109673	2241	120367
国有企业	State-owned Industry	31	2005	33	1946
集体企业	Collective-owned Industry	32	1394	33	1426
股份合作企业	Cooperative Enterprises	1	30	1	30
联营企业	Joint Ownership Enterprises				
国有联营企业	State Joint Ownership Enterprises				
集体联营企业	Collective Joint Ownership Enterprises				
国有与集体联营企业	Joint State-Collective Ownership Enterprises				
其他联营企业	Other Joint Ownership Enterprises				
有限责任公司	Limited Liability Corporations	615	44958	621	45613
国有独资企业	Sole State-funded Corporations	63	2833	78	3618
其他有限责任公司	Other Limited Liability Corporations	552	42125	543	41995
股份有限公司	Share Holding Enterprises	60	10865	45	8705
私营企业	Private Enterprises	1171	50340	1506	62585
私营独资企业	Private-funded Enterprises	70	1441	90	1618
私营合伙企业	Private Partnership Enterprises	12	415	13	446
私营有限责任公司	Private Limited Liability Corporations	1047	46705	1361	58403
私营股份有限公司	Private Share Holding Enterprises	42	1779	42	2118
其他企业	Others	5	81	2	62

16－1 续表2 continued

项 目	Item	2016 法人企业（个） Corporation Enterprises (unit)	2016 年末从业人员（人） Year-end Persons Employed (person)	2017 法人企业（个） Corporation Enterprises (unit)	2017 年末从业人员（人） Year-end Persons Employed (person)
港、澳、台商投资企业	Enterprises with Funds from Hong Kong, Macao & Taiwan	42	8680	42	8727
合资经营企业	Joint Venture Enterprises	12	3377	12	3630
合作经营企业	Cooperative Enterprises	1	179	1	167
独资经营企业	Enterprises with Sole Investment	25	4479	23	3594
投资股份有限公司	Share-holding Corporations Ltd. with Investment	2	141	1	45
其他港澳台投资企业	Others	2	504	5	1291
外商投资企业	Foreign-investment Enterprise	9	1814	10	1863
中外合资经营企业	Joint Venture Enterprises	1	222	1	205
中外合作经营企业	Cooperative Enterprises	1	10	1	10
外资企业	Enterprises with Sole Foreign Investment	5	1349	5	1368
外商投资股份有限公司	Share-holding Corporations Ltd. with Foreign Investment	1	214	2	211
其他外商投资企业	Others	1	19	1	69
2.国民经济行业分组	**2. Grouped by National Economic Sector**				
综合零售业	Comprehensive Retail	315	44081	339	44879
#百货零售业	Retail of Consumer Goods	124	17392	136	18580
超级市场零售业	Retail of Supermarket	171	25666	178	25162
食品、饮料及烟草制品专门零售业	Special Retail of Food, Beverage & Tobacco Products	98	3238	163	4727
纺织、服装及日用品专门零售业	Special Retail of Textile, Garments & Daily Necessities	47	1876	67	2488
#服装零售业	Retail of Garments	15	517	18	745
文化、体育用品及器材专门零售业	Special Retail of Culture, Sports Goods & Apparatus	114	4651	129	5073
#体育用品及器材零售业	Retail of Sports Goods	3	885	3	896
图书、报刊零售业	Retail of Books	74	2768	83	2975
医药及医疗器材专门零售业	Special Retail of Medicine & Medical Apparatus	113	15932	123	17975
#西药零售业				95	15116
中药零售业	Retail of Medicines	104	15676	19	2667
汽车、摩托车、零配件和燃料及其他动力零售业	Special Retail of Motor Vehicles, Motorcycles & Parts	819	34089	927	37210
#汽车新车零售业	Retail of Motor Vehicles	638	30055	728	32944
机动车燃油零售业	Fuel Retail of Motor Vehicle	90	2273	93	2366
家用电器及电子产品专门零售业	Special Retail of Household Appliances & Electronic Products	326	11434	363	12324
#日用家电零售业	Retail of Home Electronic & Electrical Appliances	128	5530	130	5835
#计算机、软件及辅助设备零售业	Retail of Computer, Software & Auxiliary Equipment	97	1904	118	2510
通讯设备零售业	Retail of Communication Apparatus	33	1871	43	2157
五金、家具及室内装饰材料专门零售业	Special Retail of Hardware, Furniture & Indoor Renovation Material	54	1087	81	1459
货摊、无店铺及其他零售业	Retail without Shop & Others	80	3779	97	4598

16－2 主要年份限额以上批发和零售业企业商品购进、销售和库存总额
Total Purchases, Sales & Stock of Enterprises above Designated in Wholesale & Retail Sale Trade in Main Years

单位：万元 (10 000 yuan)

项 目	Item	2000	2005	2010	2012	2013	2014	2015	2016	2017
一、法人企业数（个）	**Number of Corporation Enterprises (unit)**	**681**	**902**	**1465**	**2176**	**2375**	**2705**	**2920**	**3178**	**3624**
二、年末从业人员（人）	**Number of Persons Employed (person)**	**100057**	**119358**	**122788**	**159978**	**170027**	**175267**	**180103**	**188602**	**205096**
三、商品购进总额	**Ⅰ.Total Purchases**	**3890602**	**11143383**	**24393191**	**41578059**	**45048592**	**46415288**	**48709342**	**56399803**	**66307177**
#进 口	Imports	66953	136366	399495	789367	714536	1018980	949068	993713	1910310
四、商品销售总额	**Ⅱ.Total Sales**	**4181138**	**11682006**	**25892641**	**42275981**	**48675175**	**51919397**	**57516783**	**64032093**	**74307630**
1.批 发	1.Wholesale	3071302	8699573	18000452	30424752	34300190	35702255	39614680	44244014	52724015
#出 口	Exports	371065	331529	465449	582354	470110	1076534	1802295	2340145	3225646
2.零 售	2.Retail	1109836	2982433	7892189	11851228	14374985	16217142	17902103	19788078	21583615
五、年末库存总额	**Ⅲ.Total Inventory at Year-end**	**394164**	**694048**	**1887898**	**3770048**	**3794962**	**4148921**	**3792495**	**4708162**	**4518135**

16−3 限额以上批发和零售业企业商品购进、销售、库存总额（2017年）

Total Purchases, Sales & Stock of Enterprises above Designated in Wholesale & Retail Sale Trade by Sector (2017)

单位：万元 (10 000 yuan)

项 目	Item	购进总额 Total Purchases	#进口 Imports	销售总额 Total Sales 合计 Total	批发 Wholesale	#出口 Exports	零售 Retail Sale	年末库存总额 Total Inventory at Year-end
总 计	**Total**	**66307176.7**	**1910310.3**	**74307630.2**	**52724014.8**	**3225646.1**	**21583615.4**	**4518134.8**
一、批发业	**Ⅰ.Wholesale**	**49463847.9**	**1645628.1**	**55011285.7**	**50352630.2**	**3208673.0**	**4658655.5**	**2836379.3**
1.按登记注册类型分组	**1.Grouped by Status of Registration**							
内资企业	Domestic Funded Enterprises	49175701.1	1600659.7	54700855.5	50048280.7	3171814.2	4652574.8	2823915.1
国有企业	State-owned Industry	3270938.4	1310.8	4755670.5	4718089.7	571.8	37580.8	336313.0
集体企业	Collective-owned Industry	676937.2	220.0	736220.3	695293.4		40926.9	16371.1
股份合作企业	Cooperative Enterprises	3748.0		3750.0	2064.4		1685.6	108.0
联营企业	Joint Ownership Enterprises							
国有联营企业	State Joint Ownership Enterprises							
集体联营企业	Collective Joint Ownership Enterprises							
国有与集体联营企业	Joint State-Collective Ownership Enterprises							
其他联营企业	Other Joint Ownership Enterprises							
有限责任公司	Limited Liability Corporations	29987041.6	854482.8	32028010.6	29135718.4	489123.7	2892292.2	1378950.2
国有独资企业	Sole State-funded Corporations	10401946.2	39690.2	10028504.3	8096513.3	3220.9	1931991.0	359215.0
其他有限责任公司	Other Limited Liability Corporations	19585095.4	814792.6	21999506.3	21039205.1	485902.8	960301.2	1019735.2
股份有限公司	Share Holding Enterprises	2138606.2	1723.3	2758546.9	1583078.7	31572.1	1175468.2	106504.5
私营企业	Private Enterprises	13059846.3	742068.3	14377118.4	13874330.3	2650546.6	502788.1	985353.9
私营独资企业	Private-funded Enterprises	44121.2		65726.9	62859.5		2867.4	5276.7

16－3 续表1 continue

单位：万元 (10 000 yuan)

项 目	Item	购进总额 Total Purchases	#进口 Imports	销售总额 Total Sales 合计 Total	批发 Wholesale	#出口 Exports	零售 Retail Sale	年末库存总额 Total Inventory at Year-end
私营合伙企业	Private Partnership Enterprises	29497.5		33073.3	31952.2		1121.1	270.1
私营有限责任公司	Private Limited Liability Corporations	12741552.8	741933.6	14002943.2	13520473.8	2650545.8	482469.4	957292.5
私营股份有限公司	Private Share Holding Enterprises	244674.8	134.7	275375.0	259044.8	0.8	16330.2	22514.6
其他企业	Others	38583.4	854.5	41538.8	39705.8		1833.0	314.4
港、澳、台商投资企业	Enterprises with Funds from Hong Kong, Macao & Taiwan	161060.8	36350.2	168704.0	168161.6	32834.8	542.4	1770.3
合资经营企业	Joint Venture Enterprises							
合作经营企业	Cooperative Enterprises							
独资经营企业	Enterprises with Sole Investment	161060.8	36350.2	168704.0	168161.6	32834.8	542.4	1770.3
投资股份有限公司	Share-holding Corporations Ltd. with Investment							
其他港澳台投资企业	Others							
外商投资企业	Foreign-investment Enterprise	127086.0	8618.2	141726.2	136187.9	4024.0	5538.3	10693.9
中外合资经营企业	Joint Venture Enterprises	89609.9		99597.8	94059.5		5538.3	4585.8
中外合作经营企业	Cooperative Enterprises							
外资企业	Enterprises with Sole Foreign Investment	37476.1	8618.2	42128.4	42128.4	4024.0		6108.1
外商投资股份有限公司	Share-holding Corporations Ltd. with Foreign Investment							
其他外商投资企业	Others							
2.按国民经济行业分组	**2.Grouped by National Economic Sector**							
农、林、牧、渔产品批发业	Wholesale of the Agricultural & Animal Products	1271435.6	59137.2	1364908.4	1272013.2	45110.6	92895.2	203928.9

16－3　续表2　continued

单位：万元　　　　(10 000 yuan)

项　目	Item	购进总额 Total Purchases	#进口 Imports	销售总额 Total Sales 合计 Total	批发 Wholesale	#出口 Exports	零售 Retail Sale	年末库存总额 Total Inventory at Year-end
食品、饮料及烟草制品批发业	Wholesale of Food , Beverage & Tobacco Products	10056838.1	325899.6	12347440.6	12185374.2	347890.0	162066.4	675996.3
#米、面制品及食用油批发业	Wholesale of Rice, Flour Products & Edible Oil	545836.3	27970.2	902679.2	868140.8	2651.9	34538.4	93945.6
烟草制品批发业	Wholesale of Tobacco Products	2898707.5	136.8	4338489.3	4336289.9		2199.4	204684.0
纺织、服装及家庭用品批发业	Wholesale of Textile, Garments & Daily Necessities	2022150.7	142108.4	2118982.1	2043232.5	979627.3	75749.6	206928.9
#服装批发业	Wholesale of Garments	159619.6	52.0	167748.4	152512.9	103166.1	15235.5	13510.1
文化、体育用品及器材批发业	Wholesale of Culture , Sports Goods & Apparatus	446400.9		499339.5	462343.2	11986.7	36996.3	36970.1
医药及医疗器材批发业	Wholesale of Medicine & Medical Apparatus	2126257.5	29647.3	2628229.7	2388768.8	10491.7	239460.9	314805.3
矿产品、建材及化工产品批发业	Wholesale of Mineral Products , Building Materials & Chemical Products	29754259.0	1069058.8	31965140.9	28110632.8	304100.5	3854508.1	1144309.2
#煤炭及制品批发业	Wholesale of Coal & Related Products	2695692.6	140883.3	2958855.1	2928351.0	525.5	30504.1	96955.2
石油及制品批发业	Wholesale of Petroleum & Related Products	8486673.7	78191.1	9555766.7	5821080.2	1741.4	3734686.5	289341.8
金属及金属矿批发业	Wholesale of Metal & Metallic Ore	14244932.1	826514.3	14880166.1	14858693.8	80679.0	21472.3	485545.0
建材批发业	Wholesale of Building Materials	2902019.6	18060.4	3002737.0	2976971.4	162251.7	25765.6	158837.5
化肥批发业	Wholesale of Chemical Fertilizer	534157.2		628819.7	592545.5	11949.2	36274.2	60199.7
机械设备、五金产品及电子产品批发业	Wholesale of Mechanical Equipment, Hardware & Electrical Equipment & Electronic Product	3005446.3	6125.1	3252640.7	3056680.3	1132141.3	195960.4	234159.6

16—3 续表3 continued

单位：万元 (10 000 yuan)

项 目	Item	购进总额 Total Purchases	#进口 Imports	销售总额 Total Sales 合计 Total	批发 Wholesale	#出口 Exports	零售 Retail Sale	年末库存总额 Total Inventory at Year-end
#汽车及零配件批发业	Wholesale of Motor Vehicles	774130.6		896066.2	807925.6	75677.8	88140.6	57696.9
计算机、软件及辅助设备批发业	Wholesale of Computer, Soft-ware & Auxiliary Equipment	218908.1		231286.8	156440.9	16683.7	74845.9	30989.4
贸易经纪与代理	Trade Manager & Acting as Agent	15689.2	37.6	18208.3	18178.3	15164.3	30.0	2189.5
其他批发业	Others	765370.6	13614.1	816395.5	815406.9	362160.6	988.6	17091.5
二、零售业	**Ⅱ. Retail**	**16843328.8**	**264682.2**	**19296344.5**	**2371384.6**	**16973.1**	**16924959.9**	**1681755.5**
1.按登记注册类型分组	**1. Grouped by Status of Registration**							
内资企业	Domestic Funded Enterprises	15460602.1	173001.9	17749458.2	2256178.4	10146.5	15493279.8	1580052.4
国有企业	State-owned Industry	142262.6		166054.0	19801.5		146252.5	11024.7
集体企业	Collective-owned Industry	290676.8		324375.7	126555.9		197819.8	13843.6
股份合作企业	Cooperative Enterprises	1184.9		1588.3			1588.3	4.6
联营企业	Joint Ownership Enterprises							
国有联营企业	State Joint Ownership Enterprises							
集体联营企业	Collective Joint Ownership Enterprises							
国有与集体联营企业	Joint State-Collective Ownership Enterprises							
其他联营企业	Other Joint Ownership Enterprises							
有限责任公司	Limited Liability Corporations	7065734.4	41130.8	8186148.3	800973.8	2900.0	7385174.5	667772.5
国有独资企业	Sole State-funded Corporations	399951.3		455741.0	71925.6		383815.4	43832.2

16－3　续表4　continued

单位：万元　　　　(10 000 yuan)

项　目	Item	购进总额 Total Purchases	#进口 Imports	销售总额 Total Sales 合计 Total	批发 Wholesale	#出口 Exports	零售 Retail Sale	年末库存总额 Total Inventory at Year-end
其他有限责任公司	Other Limited Liability Corporations	6665783.1	41130.8	7730407.3	729048.2	2900.0	7001359.1	623940.3
股份有限公司	Share Holding Enterprises	1789983.9	70.0	1978409.5	588557.3		1389852.2	146076.4
私营企业	Private Enterprises	6169403.3	131801.1	7090690.6	720289.9	7246.5	6370400.7	740372.2
私营独资企业	Private-funded Enterprises	104904.6		119155.4	9400.9		109754.5	9977.6
私营合伙企业	Private Partnership Enterprises	30594.8		35094.7	856.5		34238.2	1132.8
私营有限责任公司	Private Limited Liability Corporations	5857077.9	131801.1	6726101.5	673037.3	7246.5	6053064.2	706253.4
私营股份有限公司	Private Share Holding Enterprises	176826.0		210339.0	36995.2		173343.8	23008.4
其他企业	Others	1356.2		2191.8			2191.8	958.4
港、澳、台商投资企业	Enterprises with Funds from Hong Kong, Macao & Taiwan	1220336.2	60708.9	1365498.8	96253.1	5851.0	1269245.7	79951.5
合资经营企业	Joint Venture Enterprises	352358.5	19630.8	376315.6	7842.0		368473.6	27417.6
合作经营企业	Cooperative Enterprises	9022.6		8619.0			8619.0	2247.0
独资经营企业	Enterprises with Sole Investment	596680.1	4004.2	665994.2	81796.9		584197.3	39481.5
投资股份有限公司	Share-holding Corporations Ltd. with Investment	4175.4		5061.4			5061.4	886.0
其他港澳台投资企业	Others	258099.6	37073.9	309508.6	6614.2	5851.0	302894.4	9919.4
外商投资企业	Foreign-investment Enterprise	162390.5	30971.4	181387.5	18953.1	975.6	162434.4	21751.6
中外合资经营企业	Joint Venture Enterprises	22100.7		24470.9			24470.9	1919.1
中外合作经营企业	Cooperative Enterprises	3847.4		4428.2			4428.2	294.0
外资企业	Enterprises with Sole Foreign Investment	113765.4	24540.5	129325.6	18953.1	975.6	110372.5	14473.4
外商投资股份有限公司	Share-holding Corporations Ltd. with Foreign Investment	12491.1		17272.3			17272.3	769.7
其他外商投资企业	Others	10185.9	6430.9	5890.5			5890.5	4295.4
2.按国民经济行业分组	**2.Grouped by National Economic Sector**							
综合零售业	Comprehensive Retail	2726237.9	5730.6	3605942.6	158417.8	4537.3	3447524.8	302831.0

16－3 续表5 continued

单位：万元 (10 000 yuan)

项 目	Item	购进总额 Total Purchases	#进口 Imports	销售总额 Total Sales 合计 Total	批发 Wholesale	#出口 Exports	零售 Retail Sale	年末库存总额 Total Inventory at Year-end
#百货零售业	Retail of Consumer Goods	1598539.3	4607.4	2047434.0	93907.3	4537.3	1953526.7	116307.7
超级市场零售业	Retail of Supermarket	996361.5	105.4	1400842.0	6978.5		1393863.5	176134.3
食品、饮料及烟草制品专门零售业	Special Retail of Food, Beverage & Tobacco Products	292779.4	1527.1	344694.8	96815.8	40.0	247879.0	49606.9
纺织、服装及日用品专门零售业	Special Retail of Textile, Garments & Daily Necessities	205590.5	1718.7	237300.8	37821.9		199478.9	35581.4
#服装零售业	Retail of Garments	85570.9		90378.1	15210.4		75167.7	16410.2
文化、体育用品及器材专门零售业	Special Retail of Culture, Sports Goods & Apparatus	315862.5		403156.0	56097.7		347058.3	49659.0
#体育用品及器材零售业	Retail of Sports Goods	4193.0		49380.3	7219.5		42160.8	1163.6
图书、报刊零售业	Retail of Books	253062.1		279457.0	36893.4		242563.6	28697.4
医药及医疗器材专门零售业	Special Retail of Medicine & Medical Apparatus	2912759.8	928.6	3248771.8	1055975.7		2192796.1	262967.5
#西药零售业		2539902.1		2774954.3	923997.2		1850957.1	236335.5
中药零售业	Retail of Medicines	348567.9		441712.2	129795.8		311916.4	25033.8
汽车、摩托车、零配件和燃料及其他动力零售业	Special Retail of Motor Vehicles, Motorcycles & Parts	8449848.5	238354.3	9171854.1	334199.2	773.8	8837654.9	746996.7
#汽车新车零售业	Retail of Motor Vehicles	7723556.4	238122.1	8331597.9	248004.3		8083593.6	692522.1
机动车燃油零售业	Fuel Retail of Motor Vehicle	457536.1		548028.4	74050.4		473978.0	16911.7
家用电器及电子产品专门零售业	Special Retail of Household Appliances & Electronic Products	1431738.1	12677.1	1687735.1	457873.2	6826.6	1229861.9	197781.4
#日用家电零售业	Retail of Home Electronic & Electrical Appliances	913239.1		1046733.1	291248.3		755484.8	120939.0
计算机、软件及辅助设备零售业	Retail of Computer , Software & Auxiliary Equipment	168562.6		218568.3	61692.3		156876.0	18606.3
通讯设备零售业	Retail of Communication Apparatus	176162.6	11329.4	222851.1	70505.8	975.6	152345.3	38022.9
五金、家具及室内装饰材料专门零售业	Special Retail of Hardware, Furniture & Indoor Renovation Material	278138.4	2840.5	296734.2	102000.3	4795.4	194733.9	24587.3
货摊、无店铺及其他零售业	Retail without Shop & Others	194478.2	881.9	253990.1	44418.9		209571.2	9735.0

16－4 限额以上批发和零售业企业主要财务指标（2017年）

单位：万元

项目	Item	流动资产小计 Circulating Funds	#存货 Deposit Products	固定资产原价 Original Value of Fixed Assets	累计折旧 Add Up Depreciation	#本年折旧 Depreciation of the Year	资产合计 Total Assets	负债合计 Total Liabilities
总　计	**Total**	**27578416.3**	**4319730.6**	**3350462.2**	**1304108.7**	**205874.6**	**35805864.7**	**25384510.7**
一、批发业	**Ⅰ.Wholesale**	**19886269.7**	**2784780.9**	**1940210.9**	**764556.5**	**107427.1**	**26026383.5**	**18543961.8**
1.按登记注册类型分组	**1.Grouped by Status of Registration**							
内资企业	Domestic Funded Enterprises	19687312.3	2772306.1	1932938.0	761307.2	106870.9	25718940.5	18328297.2
国有企业	State-owned Industry	1091451.4	343782.4	419809.6	197307.6	21404.8	1458516.2	489078.1
集体企业	Collective-owned Industry	122472.5	14154.3	14098.0	6728.8	471.9	141758.7	119729.5
股份合作企业	Cooperative Enterprises	80.3		126.0	65.3	6.0	436.1	432.9
联营企业	Joint Ownership Enterprises							
国有联营企业	State Joint Ownership Enterprises							
集体联营企业	Collective Joint Ownership Enterprises							
国有与集体联营企业	Joint State-Collective Ownership Enterprises							
其他联营企业	Other Joint Ownership Enterprises							
有限责任公司	Limited Liability Corporations	11648578.2	1372082.1	921165.2	328094.0	36693.3	15477974.8	11330592.3
国有独资企业	Sole State-funded Corporations	3260429.0	473408.6	528395.4	190829.2	21429.1	4478816.3	3317478.5
其他有限责任公司	Other Limited Liability Corporations	8388149.2	898673.5	392769.8	137264.8	15264.2	10999158.5	8013113.8
股份有限公司	Share Holding Enterprises	649999.3	121133.6	264287.2	121168.6	26276.6	1610548.3	539484.3
私营企业	Private Enterprises	6171859.5	920318.9	310112.1	106748.5	21739.3	7022023.6	5845415.6
私营独资企业	Private-funded Enterprises	34721.1	9655.7	3373.2	1733.5	204.8	36915.1	31239.3
私营合伙企业	Private Partnership Enterprises	6182.0	1097.4	235.5	147.1	4.2	6270.4	2753.3
私营有限责任公司	Private Limited Liability Corporations	6018337.2	886283.8	287307.4	99279.3	20309.8	6838437.9	5720239.8
私营股份有限公司	Private Share Holding Enterprises	112619.2	23282.0	19196.0	5588.6	1220.5	140400.2	91183.2
其他企业	Others	2871.1	834.8	3339.9	1194.4	279.0	7682.8	3564.5
港、澳、台商投资企业	Enterprises with Funds from Hong Kong, Macao & Taiwan	49735.6	2257.4	3479.6	1293.7	337.1	51925.4	37139.7
合资经营企业	Joint Venture Enterprises							
合作经营企业	Cooperative Enterprises							
独资经营企业	Enterprises with Sole Investment	49735.6	2257.4	3479.6	1293.7	337.1	51925.4	37139.7
投资股份有限公司	Share-holding Corporations Ltd. with Investment							
其他港澳台投资企业	Others							

Main Financial Indicators of Enterprises above Designated in Wholesale & Retail Sale Trade（2017）

（10 000 yuan）

所有者权益合计 Total Creditors Equity	#实收资本 Capital Hold	#国家资本 State Capital	主营业务收入 Business Income of the Main Products	主营业务成本 Core Business Cost	主营业务税金及附加 Core Business Tax & Extra Charges	销售费用 Operating Cost	管理费用 Manage-ment Expenses	财务费用 Financial Expenses	#利息支出 Interest Expenditure	营业利润 Business Profits	利润总额 Gross Profits
10421354.0	**7755017.5**	**4309265.9**	**64952384.9**	**60315714.2**	**627877.4**	**1931989.0**	**1091423.0**	**315711.3**	**323894.7**	**920355.6**	**1063730.0**
7482421.7	**5030417.5**	**3044615.5**	**48150918.4**	**45204740.1**	**571277.4**	**987849.0**	**640571.4**	**247973.9**	**281325.6**	**591737.6**	**635383.4**
7390643.3	4977999.4	3044615.5	47879723.7	44941546.4	570966.7	985414.3	637425.2	244627.4	278259.1	592861.9	637205.6
969438.1	64645.5	63001.8	4140495.1	3045188.9	504687.0	106361.9	183022.0	-13449.0	5294.1	325337.4	341614.9
22029.2	11389.1		630988.8	608993.4	1080.0	15038.2	7749.7	660.2	79.5	1892.5	3161.3
3.2	135.4	78.0	3636.7	3453.9	5.2	177.6	104.6	5.0	5.0	-1.5	-1.5
4147382.5	3043812.1	2185780.9	27657661.6	26657550.0	42528.7	440447.9	241653.8	164446.5	202252.1	193152.2	209486.9
1161337.8	1300461.4	1018317.4	8557509.2	8245658.4	12577.4	146304.0	70761.6	32104.7	78402.6	67301.8	68753.4
2986044.7	1743350.7	1167463.5	19100152.4	18411891.6	29951.3	294143.9	170892.2	132341.8	123849.5	125850.4	140733.5
1071064.0	901031.2	793054.8	2339707.1	2155295.1	4898.9	110677.5	25297.5	9552.2	5324.9	21192.0	23858.8
1176608.0	954611.5	2700.0	13066502.4	12434521.9	17687.5	311427.4	178733.3	83409.2	65302.7	49331.3	57568.2
5675.8	1250.0		59333.1	55954.9	704.4	562.5	2088.3	4.1		-735.2	-739.7
3517.1	3490.0	2392.0	29790.7	29270.9	49.4	132.9	87.4	15.9		427.1	351.9
1118198.1	912230.1	308.0	12667978.2	12060659.2	16519.6	300577.0	169559.9	81479.3	63910.1	47684.2	55576.7
49217.0	37641.4		309400.4	288636.9	414.1	10155.0	6997.7	1909.9	1392.6	1955.2	2379.3
4118.3	2374.6		40732.0	36543.2	79.4	1283.8	864.3	3.3	0.8	1958.0	1517.0
14785.7	17271.6		147779.5	146413.6	127.6	1284.6	711.1	646.3	578.3	-1399.4	-2092.3
14785.7	17271.6		147779.5	146413.6	127.6	1284.6	711.1	646.3	578.3	-1399.4	-2092.3

16—4 续表 1

单位：万元

项 目	Item	流动资产小计 Circulating Funds	#存货 Deposit Products	固定资产原价 Original Value of Fixed Assets	累计折旧 Add Up Depreciation	#本年折旧 Depreciation of the Year	资产合计 Total Assets	负债合计 Total Liabilities
外商投资企业	Foreign-investment Enterprise	149221.8	10217.4	3793.3	1955.6	219.1	255517.6	178524.9
中外合资经营企业	Joint Venture Enterprises	108680.9	4181.3	3472.9	1761.6	203.8	209115.4	133025.0
中外合作经营企业	Cooperative Enterprises							
外资企业	Enterprises with Sole Foreign Investment	40540.9	6036.1	320.4	194.0	15.3	46402.2	45499.9
外商投资股份有限公司	Share-holding Corporations Ltd. with Foreign Investment							
其他外商投资企业	Others							
2.按国民经济行业分组	**2.Grouped by National Economic Sector**							
农、林、牧、渔产品批发业	Wholesale of the Agricultural & Animal Products	777002.7	220633.5	78939.8	27206.5	2541.6	1025498.0	830324.9
食品、饮料及烟草制品批发业	Wholesale of Food, Beverage & Tobacco Products	4785697.7	602523.3	448331.4	209742.8	24504.9	5947305.5	4301714.3
#米、面制品及食用油批发业	Wholesale of Rice, Flour Products & Edible Oil	492525.3	91649.4	18872.6	7628.2	685.5	716378.6	519550.2
烟草制品批发业	Wholesale of Tobacco Products	780865.7	210789.5	320390.8	152211.7	18853.1	1036159.8	233575.3
纺织、服装及家庭用品批发业	Wholesale of Textile, Garments & Daily Necessities	815980.3	200875.8	42932.4	13161.4	2596.9	1047395.3	812524.1
#服装批发业	Wholesale of Garments	35351.9	12561.6	2081.5	1713.7	311.0	35932.2	31256.1
文化、体育用品及器材批发业	Wholesale of Culture, Sports Goods & Apparatus	368790.0	44790.9	25094.7	9478.6	1263.2	625580.7	381263.9
医药及医疗器材批发业	Wholesale of Medicine & Medical Apparatus	1259279.1	200320.4	105924.1	33293.2	8564.5	1424529.5	1130606.1
矿产品、建材及化工产品批发业	Wholesale of Mineral Products, Building Materials & Chemical Products	10487419.5	1255488.9	1167146.2	438088.4	63158.2	14398662.1	9895814.8
#煤炭及制品批发业	Wholesale of Coal & Related Products	1921060.9	84925.3	31773.4	9781.0	2350.5	2739543.5	1799969.5
石油及制品批发业	Wholesale of Petroleum & Related Products	2165456.7	437386.4	891389.7	341734.7	52771.1	3660962.8	2249773.9
金属及金属矿批发业	Wholesale of Metal & Metallic Ore	4115503.0	474641.6	91229.8	34299.2	3848.8	5320577.4	3782409.1
建材批发业	Wholesale of Building Materials	1095198.6	148003.3	15896.5	5625.7	949.1	1311279.9	904218.0
化肥批发业	Wholesale of Chemical Fertilizer	237784.3	69887.6	21151.0	5340.5	723.8	285004.3	200196.3
机械设备、五金产品及电子产品批发业	Wholesale of Mechanical Equipment, Hardware & Electrical Equipment & Electronic Product	1299455.0	241819.7	65772.8	31820.2	4489.6	1445694.5	1111466.9
#汽车及零配件批发业	Wholesale of Motor Vehicles	333930.3	57182.6	12074.6	5822.0	660.2	365458.5	315617.5
计算机、软件及辅助设备批发业	Wholesale of Computer, Software & Auxiliary Equipment	41364.7	15634.0	1417.4	895.5	131.5	50124.0	30042.1
贸易经纪与代理	Trade Manager & Acting as Agent	4462.7	1867.3	29.4	20.4	2.9	4533.0	3720.2
其他批发业	Others	88182.7	16461.1	6040.1	1745.0	305.3	107184.9	76526.6

continued

（10 000 yuan）

所有者权益合计 Total Creditors Equity	#实收资本 Capital Hold	#国家资本 State Capital	主营业务收入 Business Income of the Main Products	主营业务成本 Core Business Cost	主营业务税金及附加 Core Business Tax&Extra Charges	销售费用 Operating cost	管理费用 Manage-ment Expenses	财务费用 Financial Expenses	#利息支出 Interest Expen-diture	营业利润 Business Profits	利润总额 Gross Profits
76992.7	35146.5		123415.2	116780.1	183.1	1150.1	2435.1	2700.2	2488.2	275.1	270.1
76090.4	26646.5		85414.4	81746.0	97.9	926.9	1427.5	2721.8	2442.9	-1468.4	-1484.7
902.3	8500.0		38000.8	35034.1	85.2	223.2	1007.6	-21.6	45.3	1743.5	1754.8
195173.1	119204.8	68421.6	1258552.1	1183688.2	3799.4	23390.3	16209.4	21491.9	19176.3	14262.9	24238.3
1645591.2	488029.4	194848.8	10735587.3	9457716.9	514292.3	183122.4	223000.6	53010.8	60831.8	329655.7	347839.7
196828.4	114888.5	17824.0	800257.5	766383.3	801.4	29963.2	9765.5	5164.2	6995.1	-3516.5	-429.9
802584.5	25470.7	24891.5	3733779.8	2660833.4	503982.9	87159.5	171229.5	-16611.7		331661.8	335388.3
234871.2	102635.7	2700.0	1966001.1	1865956.6	2788.0	61030.0	32500.3	9808.3	4460.8	-8327.5	-7652.5
4676.1	11189.0		158703.9	152735.3	286.5	5351.4	1096.6	-48.3	116.9	-723.1	-1196.6
244316.8	153775.2	126444.3	431539.8	396246.7	855.5	19647.9	10130.7	1901.3	3549.3	1890.8	1631.0
293923.4	208130.9	1139.8	2337096.6	2034257.4	7346.0	157752.3	76026.7	11949.7	6355.2	50277.7	43468.8
4502847.3	3832039.6	2637023.3	27589839.1	26621370.3	36779.4	457317.4	239689.7	143845.5	181867.3	148505.2	165781.8
939574.0	471656.8	193956.6	2565644.3	2464696.3	3626.2	36112.0	65467.3	20812.9	22335.6	-21351.8	-11751.5
1411188.9	1515230.8	1397171.2	7988799.1	7512712.6	11103.2	255788.4	79795.4	13893.9	11241.3	121634.2	120634.6
1538168.3	1276097.7	771367.4	12983519.4	12771829.4	14454.2	74656.4	47913.3	58687.3	105731.8	26793.7	26660.3
407061.9	372343.7	184350.1	2604825.2	2517142.1	5382.1	32257.3	16122.7	14277.1	7257.2	37634.4	38552.3
84808.0	59770.6	14547.4	584042.7	544511.5	545.7	27448.0	6690.5	1954.1	1730.7	5873.4	5724.3
334227.6	109189.8	13008.5	3054056.0	2886441.2	4367.1	79218.8	37822.5	5365.0	4954.6	49130.4	53012.9
49841.0	36744.5	10670.9	790698.5	764466.6	1024.9	16668.0	6809.9	1278.9	866.9	5915.5	9249.0
20081.9	16730.1		198275.1	187694.5	284.7	5030.8	4571.1	366.0	162.9	677.7	387.8
812.8	1700.0	1000.0	16940.8	15837.6	12.7	460.7	204.4	118.9		306.5	318.7
30658.3	15712.1	29.2	761305.6	743225.2	1037.0	5909.2	4987.1	482.5	130.3	6035.9	6744.7

16－4 续表2

单位：万元

项 目	Item	流动资产小计 Circulating Funds	#存货 Deposit Products	固定资产原价 Original Value of Fixed Assets	累计折旧 Add Up Depreci-ation	#本年折旧 Depreciat-ion of the Year	资产合计 Total Assets	负债合计 Total Liabilities
二、零售业	**Ⅱ.Retail**	**7692146.6**	**1534949.7**	**1410251.3**	**539552.2**	**98447.5**	**9779481.2**	**6840548.9**
1.按登记注册类型分组	**1.Grouped by Status of Registra-tion**							
内资企业	Domestic Funded Enterprises	7265681.9	1446020.6	1163106.9	456804.9	78786.0	9059977.5	6419945.7
国有企业	State-owned Industry	82226.2	12640.2	24677.7	13027.5	708.1	114642.6	86527.3
集体企业	Collective-owned Industry	28714.5	7824.5	11821.3	3136.1	499.0	47967.6	34486.3
股份合作企业	Cooperative Enterprises	434.7	3.9	37.3	31.4		440.6	188.0
联营企业	Joint Ownership Enterprises							
国有联营企业	State Joint Ownership Enterprises							
集体联营企业	Collective Joint Ownership Enterprises							
国有与集体联营企业	Joint State-Collective Ownership Enterprises							
其他联营企业	Other Joint Ownership Enterprises							
有限责任公司	Limited Liability Corporations	3597413.1	582753.2	430833.2	200914.0	35221.7	4341110.8	3090904.1
国有独资企业	Sole State-funded Corporations	190091.1	36544.4	56006.8	27659.9	2915.3	282813.2	113155.6
其他有限责任公司	Other Limited Liability Corporations	3407322.0	546208.8	374826.4	173254.1	32306.4	4058297.6	2977748.5
股份有限公司	Share Holding Enterprises	870228.9	139630.7	294869.0	103886.1	10075.0	1291336.8	714189.0
私营企业	Private Enterprises	2685475.5	702209.7	400070.4	135443.5	32210.1	3262381.3	2493250.4
私营独资企业	Private-funded Enterprises	34369.4	10816.4	9459.3	2420.9	572.9	46654.9	27145.7
私营合伙企业	Private Partnership Enterprises	11722.7	1184.1	1971.3	1004.9	170.1	14633.0	10041.7
私营有限责任公司	Private Limited Liability Corporations	2553340.6	665637.7	357882.8	120754.5	29156.5	3071888.9	2394095.6
私营股份有限公司	Private Share Holding Enterprises	86042.8	24571.5	30757.0	11263.2	2310.6	129204.5	61967.4
其他企业	Others	1189.0	958.4	798.0	366.3	72.1	2097.8	400.6
港、澳、台商投资企业	Enterprises with Funds from Hong Kong, Macao & Taiwan	321453.0	67613.4	225444.9	74804.5	18067.2	580400.2	345786.5
合资经营企业	Joint Venture Enterprises	108886.9	24449.0	110674.1	25300.3	3586.6	213407.6	144634.3
合作经营企业	Cooperative Enterprises	13953.4	2247.0	224.1	206.4	11.3	13971.1	12507.6
独资经营企业	Enterprises with Sole Investment	150986.6	31207.0	80331.6	29137.5	6191.3	218294.3	125456.3
投资股份有限公司	Share-holding Corporations Ltd. with Investment	494.2	65.4	1253.0	367.9	367.9	1396.5	1205.9
其他港澳台投资企业	Others	47131.9	9645.0	32962.1	19792.4	7910.1	133330.7	61982.4

continued

(10 000 yuan)

所有者权益合计 Total Creditors Equity	#实收资本 Capital Hold	#国家资本 State Capital	主营业务收入 Business Income of the Main Products	主营业务成本 Core Business Cost	主营业务税金及附加 Core Business Tax&Extra Charges	销售费用 Operating Cost	管理费用 Manage-ment Expenses	财务费用 Financial Expenses	#利息支出 Interest Expen-diture	营业利润 Business Profits	利润总额 Gross Profits
2938932.3	**2724600.0**	**1264650.4**	**16801466.5**	**15110974.1**	**56600.0**	**944140.0**	**450851.6**	**67737.4**	**42569.1**	**328618.0**	**428346.6**
2640031.8	2602411.8	1264059.1	15464962.7	13972900.5	52012.3	813609.8	413459.1	65050.6	39093.9	273228.2	271286.6
28115.3	13504.5	11486.0	134729.0	111760.6	1268.8	15017.1	4754.0	468.7	779.4	4052.8	5665.1
13481.3	6300.1		276024.2	246833.7	1877.0	8131.0	7171.1	1868.9	862.6	9502.9	9621.2
252.6	50.0		1358.0	1006.4	6.1	99.8	115.4	0.2		130.1	130.1
1250206.7	1803726.3	1233881.7	7059407.8	6359126.0	22195.2	412594.1	150947.8	22366.0	13704.4	153493.9	147853.1
169657.6	129327.3	122801.1	414857.0	351453.0	1597.2	32973.7	17947.4	856.8	947.2	14987.4	16773.8
1080549.1	1674399.0	1111080.6	6644550.8	6007673.0	20598.0	379620.4	133000.4	21509.2	12757.2	138506.5	131079.3
577147.8	141320.8	18150.4	1683578.2	1532893.7	7236.4	48568.2	56841.8	4000.0	2115.9	49199.1	47677.3
769130.9	636009.7	541.0	6308219.2	5719679.4	19428.8	329199.2	193557.2	36346.6	21631.6	56832.5	60364.6
19509.2	9446.2		107849.6	94668.6	735.5	5495.2	3491.1	582.3	384.2	2748.2	2609.3
4591.3	3729.5		30164.9	26024.5	79.9	1682.6	1314.6	59.0	0.1	1035.7	989.3
677793.3	584681.3	541.0	5983522.4	5435764.4	18189.7	313055.5	179686.0	34528.3	20635.2	48277.5	50074.8
67237.1	38152.7		186682.3	163221.9	423.7	8965.9	9065.5	1177.0	612.1	4771.1	6691.2
1697.2	1500.4		1646.3	1600.7		0.4	71.8	0.2		16.9	-24.8
234613.7	103809.4	591.3	1177797.9	1006487.2	4129.9	110372.9	33969.4	2741.6	3405.7	48333.4	151014.0
68773.3	49286.8	591.3	311949.8	262232.4	853.2	30681.7	11235.6	1583.2	1218.7	14854.2	66109.4
1463.5	409.9		8619.0	7510.1	12.6	552.1	166.3	9.6		368.3	368.3
92838.0	46474.7		598277.9	523170.8	2055.2	48409.9	13530.1	1910.5	1950.9	18238.4	24224.2
190.6	1000.0		4288.9	3882.8	28.1	296.6	273.1	47.0		-238.7	-220.4
71348.3	6638.0		254662.3	209691.1	1180.8	30432.6	8764.3	-808.7	236.1	15111.2	60532.5

16—4 续表3

单位：万元

项 目	Item	流动资产小计 Circulating Funds	#存货 Deposit Products	固定资产原价 Original Value of Fixed Assets	累计折旧 Add Up Depreciation	#本年折旧 Depreciation of the Year	资产合计 Total Assets	负债合计 Total Liabilities
外商投资企业	Enterprises With Foreign Investment	105011.7	21315.7	21699.5	7942.8	1594.3	139103.5	74816.7
中外合资经营企业	Joint Venture Enterprises	1941.4	1683.4	1770.1	1298.2	109.0	12530.2	5096.5
中外合作经营企业	Cooperative Enterprises	10729.0	294.0	218.2	205.0	2.1	10929.1	9895.3
外资企业	Enterprises with Sole Foreign Investment	81716.5	14159.7	15163.2	5507.6	1279.8	100428.7	47383.4
外商投资股份有限公司	Share-holding Corporations Ltd. with Foreign Investment	4748.7	860.9	985.2	801.0	72.4	5013.7	2801.6
其他外商投资企业	Others	5876.1	4317.7	3562.8	131.0	131.0	10201.8	9639.9
2.按国民经济行业分组	**2.Grouped by National Economic Sector**							
综合零售业	Comprehensive Retail	1011634.3	239345.3	603492.0	251923.5	39501.1	1806553.8	1267777.0
#百货零售业	Retail of Consumer Goods	547610.2	110213.2	442393.9	163543.3	22475.5	1147783.5	795115.7
超级市场零售业	Retail of Supermarket	441289.8	122766.9	152049.3	85879.7	16756.1	623593.1	445674.0
食品、饮料及烟草制品专门零售业	Special Retail of Food, Beverage & Tobacco Products	216082.7	50229.3	31132.4	10332.6	1944.0	301771.8	193824.4
纺织、服装及日用品专门零售业	Special Retail of Textile, Garments & Daily Necessities	408799.8	33648.2	7252.5	3400.3	988.8	542015.0	345870.2
#服装零售业	Retail of Garments	32170.8	14918.0	1213.0	744.7	115.5	34650.3	37014.8
文化、体育用品及器材专门零售业	Special Retail of Culture, Sports Goods & Apparatus	208112.0	37768.1	69882.0	32963.3	3178.7	312406.2	135385.1
#体育用品及器材零售业	Retail of Sports Goods	2850.3	815.3	2843.5	1542.2	685.8	4173.1	1904.6
图书、报刊零售业	Retail of Books	151285.4	22086.2	62031.0	28853.2	2291.0	246990.2	86373.6
医药及医疗器材专门零售业	Special Retail of Medicine & Medical Apparatus	1527644.1	249937.3	144787.6	29920.5	6135.7	1745782.9	1194941.7
#西药零售业		1364236.3	223573.0	115226.8	22761.4	5010.7	1551449.8	1053320.8
中药零售业	Retail of Medicines	150470.6	25087.1	28353.6	6267.3	705.3	180872.3	133181.7
汽车、摩托车、零配件和燃料及其他动力零售业	Special Retail of Motor Vehicles, Motorcycles & Parts	2853183.2	680935.2	426608.2	167062.3	38886.3	3425563.5	2425385.3
#汽车新车零售业	Retail of Motor Vehicles	2579334.2	624781.1	378906.2	149195.4	35693.8	3072346.2	2231550.5
机动车燃油零售业	Fuel Retail of Motor Vehicle	181480.5	19201.1	37668.2	13716.4	2409.8	237802.7	113010.3
家用电器及电子产品专门零售业	Special Retail of Household Appliances & Electronic Products	1236088.1	204062.7	46023.1	16342.2	2815.8	1318410.5	1087036.0
#日用家电零售业	Retail of Home Electronic & Electrical Appliances	914685.5	132789.8	26372.4	8960.2	1529.1	963721.3	881719.7
计算机、软件及辅助设备零售业	Retail of Computer, Software & Auxiliary Equipment	96797.6	18260.4	7527.8	3086.1	596.3	107748.5	62181.6
通讯设备零售业	Retail of Communication Apparatus	126425.9	24736.5	3016.3	1451.9	139.8	138076.4	64451.7
五金、家具及室内装修材料专门零售业	Special Retail of Hardware, Furniture & Indoor Renovation Material	97195.1	24803.6	10229.8	3047.9	805.9	111374.8	75120.4
货摊、无店铺及其他零售业	Retail without Shop & Others	112388.1	12216.0	68048.3	23569.9	3464.5	191684.3	102829.2

continued

（10 000 yuan）

所有者权益合计 Total Creditors Equity	#实收资本 Capital Hold	#国家资本 State Capital	主营业务收入 Business Income of the Main Products	主营业务成本 Core Business Cost	主营业务税金及附加 Core Business Tax&Extra Charges	销售费用 Operating Cost	管理费用 Management Expenses	财务费用 Financial Expenses	#利息支出 Interest Expenditure	营业利润 Business Profits	利润总额 Gross Profits
64286.8	18378.8		158705.9	131586.4	457.8	20157.3	3423.1	-54.8	69.5	7056.4	6046.0
7433.7			21465.7	17083.1	79.1	2001.4	243.4	53.2	5.4	2439.5	2438.1
1033.8	796.0		4428.2	3712.6	10.7	421.1	97.5	19.3		167.0	167.0
53045.3	15558.8		114754.6	93908.2	323.2	14968.1	2663.1	-130.6	64.1	4444.1	3397.3
2212.1	1024.0		12324.0	11076.0	43.4	2493.6	216.9	1.2		451.8	481.7
561.9	1000.0		5733.4	5806.5	1.4	273.1	202.2	2.1		-446.0	-438.1
538776.8	268306.2	16723.6	2985298.9	2511731.7	17106.8	349344.3	127020.3	16825.9	10754.5	52668.4	101726.7
352667.8	173681.1	14964.5	1601188.2	1333520.6	11706.9	175920.0	84559.4	10680.6	7558.2	26418.2	73738.0
177919.1	87999.2	1723.1	1262126.3	1070562.5	4486.6	167149.1	38705.0	5476.3	2541.3	24107.4	25755.9
107947.4	80999.8	16615.7	301116.8	259533.7	1201.9	17583.8	19182.3	2640.9	1841.5	2242.6	5492.0
196144.8	201512.0	896.1	212696.0	167946.1	958.1	28218.1	7629.2	3622.0	266.7	1049.4	4598.3
-2364.5	3196.2		80856.4	62819.8	424.3	16136.1	2490.7	45.6	35.5	-1037.2	-830.5
177021.1	134786.5	101961.0	374539.4	291863.6	2612.8	38606.3	25017.8	221.9	468.3	21520.2	22025.5
2268.5	1686.5		43385.8	32311.0	187.8	7950.3	2116.3	10.1	2.5	907.3	912.1
160616.6	118077.2	101961.0	265422.1	202830.2	1634.0	27587.6	18898.1	-154.5	159.2	20125.2	20790.5
550841.2	171816.7	50630.0	2784115.9	2516418.0	6968.6	123243.6	61972.9	8519.9	7480.6	76319.3	125915.3
498129.0	147142.6	50630.0	2369509.7	2154142.1	5755.4	95473.4	47590.5	6226.0	5564.3	68810.9	118410.6
47690.6	21414.1		388225.9	341275.1	1016.3	25064.8	12554.6	2119.2	1771.9	7033.7	7040.9
1000178.2	634019.7	72490.3	8146571.1	7606578.3	19903.2	257823.1	142578.2	28921.9	16875.5	132896.7	128618.7
840795.7	542576.9	25751.4	7412126.6	6940366.5	17861.8	227856.5	129138.2	26445.4	15648.2	110097.7	105232.8
124792.4	72893.8	41602.7	469469.6	419040.5	1402.0	22325.1	8344.4	903.4	781.3	20073.5	20053.7
231374.5	137769.4	841.6	1450606.5	1293439.2	5213.9	90371.5	44883.4	5303.3	3537.1	19303.7	17409.1
82001.6	49233.2	335.6	873896.0	784044.5	3069.1	58459.5	18922.1	3445.1	2277.7	8873.7	6881.8
45566.9	35047.4	506.0	197970.0	168573.7	1223.9	8872.8	13213.8	442.1	208.5	6141.1	6515.9
73624.7	31646.7		198330.7	181547.3	350.4	12752.8	6178.4	166.2	659.5	1529.7	861.5
36254.4	25472.8	55.2	258320.7	243839.7	1172.9	4708.6	5138.1	977.5	717.6	6167.2	5410.8
88855.1	1059059.2	1004436.9	246736.1	190201.6	1273.2	25510.7	14809.5	600.4	511.3	16049.8	16989.5

16-5 按登记注册类型分连锁批发和零售企业基本情况（2017年）

Basic Condictions of Chain-retail Enterprises by Categories of Registration (2017)

项 目	Item	总店数（个）Number of Head Offices	门店总数（个）Number of Stores (unit)	年末从业人数（人）Engaged Persons (10 000 persons)	年末零售营业面积（平方米）Operating Area (10 000 sq.m)	商品销售总额（万元）Total Sales of Commodities (10 000 yuan)	商品购进总额（万元）Total Purchases Value (10 000 yuan)	统一配送商品购进额（万元）Centralized Purchases & Delivery (10 000 yuan)
总 计	**Total**	**82**	**5904**	**42801**	**4607576**	**8473194**	**7542818**	**7470866**
内资企业	Domestic Funded Enterprises	80	5521	40967	4549020	8398969	7492383	7420432
国有企业	State-owned Industry							
集体企业	Collective-owned Industry							
股份合作企业	Cooperative Enterprises							
联营企业	Joint Ownership Enterprises							
国有联营企业	State Joint Ownership Enterprises							
集体联营企业	Collective Joint Ownership Enterprises							
国有与集体联营企业	Joint State-Collective Ownership Enterprises							
其他联营企业	Other Joint Ownership Enterprises							
有限责任公司	Limited Liability Corporations	37	3279	20126	2417877	6252023	5835568	5819865
国有独资公司	Sole State-funded Corporations	14	1142	7418	1950239	5346981	5143131	5143131
其他有限责任公司	Other Limited Liability Corporations	23	2137	12708	467638	905042	692437	676734
股份有限公司	Share Holding Enterprises	17	724	12532	1923976	1850576	1469810	1413561
私营企业	Private Enterprises	26	1518	8309	207167	296370	187006	187006
私营独资企业	Private-funded Enterprises							
私营合伙企业	Private Partnership Enter-prises							
私营有限责任公司	Private Limited Liability Corporations	24	1493	7934	199165	219035	154707	154707
私营股份有限公司	Private Share Holding Enterprises	2	25	375	8002	77335	32299	32299
其他企业	Others							
港、澳、台商投资企业	Enterprises with Funds from Hong Kong, Macao & Taiwan	2	383	1834	58556	74226	50435	50435
合资经营企业（港或澳、台资）	Joint Venture Enterprises	1	200	1200	43506	53929	34122	34122
合作经营企业（港或澳、台资）	Cooperative Enterprises							
港、澳、台商独资经营企业	Enterprises with Sole Investment	1	183	634	15050	20297	16313	16313
港、澳、台商投资股份有限公司	Share-holding Corporations Ltd. with Investment							
其他港澳台商投资	Others							
外商投资企业	Enterprises With Foreign Investment							
中外合资经营企业	Joint Venture Enterprises							
中外合作经营企业	Cooperative Enterprises							
外资企业	Enterprises with Sole Foreign Investment							
外商投资股份有限公司	Share-holding Corporations Ltd. with Foreign Investment							
其他外商投资	Others							

16－6 亿元以上商品交易市场基本情况（2017年）

Basic Conditions of Commodity Exchange Markets of Transaction Value over 100 Million Yuan (2017)

项 目	Item	市场数量（个）Number of Markets (unit)	摊位数（个）Number of Booths (unit)	营业面积（平方米）Operating Area (sq.m)	成交额（万元）Turnover (10 000 yuan)
总 计	**Total**	**86**	**85158**	**3995467**	**10526937**
1.综合市场	**Integrated Markets**	**24**	**40523**	**1017859**	**1957709**
工业消费品综合市场	Industrial Consumable Comprehensive Markets	2	6626	207800	175203
农产品综合市场	Farm Produce Comprehensive Markets	14	23278	594543	1354389
其他综合市场	Other Comprehensive Markets	8	10619	215516	428117
2.专业市场	**Special Markets**	**62**	**44635**	**2977608**	**8569228**
生产资料市场	Production Markets	17	6066	917054	2731605
#农用生产资料市场	Agricultural Production Markets	3	933	71043	271105
木材市场	Wood Markets	2	280	135000	41870
建材市场	Building Material Markets	7	1974	245380	289662
金属材料市场	Metal Material Markets	3	1529	325631	1850600
机械设备市场	Mechanical Equipment Markets	1	500	30000	78400
其他生产资料市场	Others	1	850	110000	199968
农产品市场	Farm Produce Markets	18	16448	825785	3347992
#粮油市场		1	94	10000	10123
肉禽蛋市场	Meat, Poultry & Eggs Markets	7	8876	104624	547823
水产品市场	Aquatic Products Markets	1	371	13000	48610
蔬菜市场	Vegetables Markets	4	2343	351620	799502
干鲜果品市场	Dried & Fresh Melons & Fruits Markets	3	1450	122165	878785
其他农产品市场	Others	2	3314	224376	1063149
食品、饮料及烟酒市场	Food, Beverages, Tobacco & Liquor Markets	6	1852	41883	189076
#食品饮料市场	Food & Beverages Markets				
茶叶市场	Tea Markets	2	240	12500	96906
其他食品饮料及烟酒市场	Others	4	1612	29383	92170
纺织、服装、鞋帽市场	Textiles, Clothing, Shoes & Hats Markets	10	12176	430128	562232
#服装市场	Clothing Markets	6	8866	346068	429317
其他纺织服装鞋帽市场	Others	4	3310	84060	132915
电器、通讯器材、电子设备市场	Electrical Appliances, Communication Appliances & Electronical Appliances Markets	1	700	20678	79000
#计算机及辅助设备市场	Computer & Accessory Equipment Markets	1	700	20678	79000
医药、医疗用品及器材市场	Medicine, Medical Materials & Medical Instruments Markets	1	1116	23000	946000
#中药材市场	Traditional Chinese Medicinal Materials Markets	1	1116	23000	946000
家具、五金及装饰材料市场	Furniture, Hardware & Decoration Materials Markets	6	4936	630080	603545
#家具市场	Furniture Markets	1	976	59640	196448
装饰材料市场	Decoration Materials Markets	2	899	205500	59722
厨具、盥洗设备市场		1	2111	164940	49875
五金材料市场	Hardware Materials Markets	1	400	50000	60000
其他装修市场	Others	1	550	150000	237500
汽车、摩托车及零配件市场	Cars, Motorcycles & Spare Parts Markets	3	1341	89000	109778
#汽车市场	Cars Markets	2	1006	79200	94028
摩托车市场	Motorcycles Markets	1	335	9800	15750

16－7　社会消费品零售总额及指数

Total Retail Sales of Consumer Goods & Relate Indices

年　份 Year	绝对数（万元） Absolute Number (10 000 yuan)	指数（上年=100） Relate Indices (Preceding year=100)
1978	335918	
1980	457228	117.9
1985	886005	129.1
1990	1754369	103.2
1991	2002276	114.1
1992	2436189	121.7
1993	3149992	129.3
1994	3991040	126.7
1995	4981172	124.8
1996	5718385	114.8
1997	6301661	110.2
1998	6868810	109.0
1999	7404577	107.8
2000	8041371	108.6
2001	8757053	108.9
2002	9597730	109.6
2003	10768653	112.2
2004	12222421	113.5
2005	14055459	115.0
2006	16203133	115.3
2007	19327097	119.3
2008	23957870	124.0
2009	27907047	116.5
2010	33120000	118.7
2011	39082000	118.0
2012	45166000	115.6
2013	51331000	113.6
2014	57728317	112.5
2015	63480633	110.0
2016	70273061	110.7
2017	78130335	111.2

注：本表数据1993－2008年已按经济普查资料口径调整。
Note: The data in this table from 1993 to 2008 was adjusted by the economic census.

16—8 各市社会消费品零售总额
Total Retail Sales of Consumer Goods by City

单位：亿元 (100 million yuan)

地 区	Region	2008	2009	2010	2011	2012	2013	2014	2015	2016	2017
全 区	**Total**	**2395.79**	**2790.70**	**3312.00**	**3908.20**	**4516.60**	**5133.10**	**5772.83**	**6348.06**	**7027.31**	**7813.03**
南宁市	Nanning	647.46	757.01	905.93	1073.15	1255.59	1442.84	1616.90	1786.68	1980.36	2204.16
柳州市	Liuzhou	344.33	400.98	480.00	568.80	661.84	758.42	858.20	944.11	1045.13	1155.64
桂林市	Guilin	284.77	330.92	391.53	462.36	536.35	604.03	682.87	751.96	836.45	928.12
梧州市	Wuzhou	146.54	171.09	191.77	224.08	257.21	292.34	328.30	364.93	395.95	445.87
北海市	Beihai	82.08	95.40	108.00	127.29	146.51	167.03	185.81	202.99	225.34	250.13
防城港市	Fangchenggang	39.09	45.33	51.84	61.16	71.30	81.43	91.67	101.03	111.89	124.02
钦州市	Qinzhou	124.01	145.09	172.19	204.27	237.56	268.82	303.25	333.50	373.63	411.75
贵港市	Guigang	155.86	181.08	209.54	245.97	284.05	321.72	359.56	389.06	431.89	480.70
玉林市	Yulin	224.88	262.92	307.24	362.81	422.83	482.91	545.71	600.34	660.43	728.86
百色市	Baise	83.56	97.10	113.85	134.34	156.67	178.60	201.06	221.18	246.84	277.35
贺州市	Hezhou	59.81	68.94	78.68	92.36	106.39	119.00	133.63	146.94	160.98	178.85
河池市	Hechi	99.98	115.07	131.73	154.79	176.98	198.97	223.79	243.38	267.96	301.20
来宾市	Laibin	57.57	66.84	79.46	94.42	109.53	120.87	134.17	145.11	159.11	180.29
崇左市	Chongzuo	45.99	53.45	61.08	72.40	84.37	96.38	108.44	119.39	131.34	146.09

注：本表数据2008年为第二次经济普查后修订数据。
Note: The data in this table in 2008 is adjusted by the 2nd Economic Census.

16—9 主要年份个体工商业发展情况

指 标	Item	1995	2000	2005
一、户数（户）	**Number of Households (household)**	**923679**	**967512**	**1015941**
按城乡分	by Urban & Rural			
城 镇	Urban	362450	451020	558987
农 村	Rural	561229	516492	456954
按行业分	by Sector			
农林牧渔业	Farming, Forestry, Animal Husbandry & Fishery	2432	12888	15414
制造业	Manufacturing	76662	85900	71105
建筑业	Construction	762	1164	1234
批发和零售业	Wholesale & Retail Trade	546260	529569	619773
交通运输、仓储和邮政业	Transport, Storage & Postal Service	82886	85435	112534
住宿和餐饮业	Hotels & Catering Services			85031
租赁和商务服务业	Leasing & Business Services			8658
居民服务、修理和其他服务业	Residents Services, Repairing & Other Services			78261
文化、体育和娱乐业	Culture, Sports & Entertainment			6847
二、从业人员（人）	**Number of Employed Persons (person)**	**1307050**	**1394187**	**1635767**
按城乡分	by Urban & Rural			
城 镇	Urban	529941	678565	897945
农 村	Rural	777109	715622	
按行业分	by Sector			
农林牧渔业	Farming, Forestry, Animal Husbandry & Fishery	3515	23066	30040
制造业	Manufacturing	139534	146868	152766
建筑业	Construction	1759	3627	2710
批发和零售业	Wholesale & Retail Trade	732757	726665	945430
交通运输、仓储和邮政业	Transport, Storage & Postal Service	104559	117835	138763
住宿和餐饮业	Hotels & Catering Services			174077
租赁和商务服务业	Leasing & Business Services			13662
居民服务、修理和其他服务业	Residents Services, Repairing & Other Services			126714
文化、体育和娱乐业	Culture, Sports & Entertainment			13456

注：1.本表数据来自自治区工商行政管理局。
2.1995、2000年无住宿和餐饮业、租赁和商务服务业、居民服务修理和其他服务业、文化体育和娱乐业数据。

Note:1. The data in the table comes from Guangxi Administration for industry and commerce.
2. There is no data on"Hotels & Catering Services", "Leasing & Business Services", "Residents Services, Repairing & Other Services" and "Culture, Sports & Entertainment" in 1995 and 2000.

Development of Individual Industrial &Commercial Enterprises in Main Years

2010	2011	2012	2013	2014	2015	2016	2017
1158725	**1141622**	**1173252**	**1243444**	**1375799**	**1493192**	**1543576**	**1688950**
772103	837283	768197	929419	1038234	1129739	1179604	1271626
386622	304339	405055	314025	337565	363453	363972	417324
15600	16671	17132	18108	17994	20449	27443	37416
71804	64128	60681	60415	62311	64192	65529	71956
2183	2213	2246	2683	3382	4102	4736	5691
750112	757149	716542	833537	933560	1013120	1035289	1083444
110416	95636	149214	93631	96772	79091	57931	80282
86229	85323	90840	102371	114636	144685	165933	200861
11765	12555	12954	13982	15662	17234	19811	23905
88774	87770	89294	96424	109136	124889	138180	158527
6887	6522	6653	6496	6795	6607	6797	7249
2231412	**2172283**	**2296637**	**2492428**	**2811454**	**3079374**	**3432599**	**3833882**
1410110	1566973	1391497	1677987	1906493	2124167	2524130	2703029
821302	605310	905140	814441	904961	955207	908469	1130853
33017	36215	41514	48835	54852	62497	86658	112544
227193	223490	204294	215910	227211	228584	241250	270414
5702	5484	5781	6940	8599	10873	13232	16279
1325885	1280985	1196093	1444283	1659230	1810012	2024016	2151853
154101	139274	339393	153356	157604	118939	87815	130960
226910	222327	224595	304023	346542	434021	497267	600864
20667	23383	25721	28659	32645	36985	45350	55459
166122	169895	174652	223546	255618	298550	353378	408757
23133	23900	25128	25543	27723	28320	31135	36412

主要统计指标解释

商品购进额 指从本企业以外的单位和个人购进（包括从国外直接进口）作为转卖或加工后转卖的商品金额（含增值税）。本指标反映批发和零售业从国内外市场上购进商品的总价。商品购进包括：（1）从工农业生产者、批发和零售业企业、住宿和餐饮业企业、出版社或报社的出版发行部门和其他服务业企业购进的商品；（2）从机关团体、事业单位购进的商品；（3）从海关、市场管理部门购进的缉私和没收的商品；（4）从居民收购的废旧商品等。不包括：（1）企业为本单位自身经营用，不是作为转卖而购进的商品，如材料物资、包装物、低值易耗品、办公用品等；（2）未通过买卖行为而收入的商品，如接受其他部门移交的商品、借入的商品、收入代其他单位保管的商品、其他单位赠送的样品、加工回收的成品等；（3）经本单位介绍，由买卖双方直接结算，本单位只收取手续费的业务；（4）销售退回和买方拒付货款的商品；（5）商品溢余。

商品销售额 指对本单位以外的单位和个人出售的商品金额（包括售给本单位消费用的商品，含增值税），本指标反映批发和零售业在国内市场上销售商品以及出口商品的总价。商品销售包括：（1）售给城乡居民和社会集团消费用的商品；（2）售给农业、工业、建筑业、服务业等国民经济各行业用于生产、经营用的商品，包括售予批发和零售业作为转卖或加工后转卖的商品；（3）对国（境）外直接出口的商品。不包括：（1）未通过买卖行为付出的商品，如随机构变动移交给其他企业单位的商品、借出的商品、归还受其他单位委托代保管的商品、付出的加工原料和赠送给其他单位的样品等；（2）经本单位介绍，由买卖双方直接结算，本单位只收取手续费的业务；（3）购货退回的商品；（4）商品损耗和损失；（5）出售本单位自用的废旧物资。

批发额 指售给国民经济各行业用于生产、经营用的商品金额。

零售额 指售给城乡居民用于生活消费和社会集团用于公共消费的商品金额。

商品库存额 对于批发和零售业法人单位和个体经营户，是指报告期末取得所有权的全部商品金额（含增值税）；对于批发和零售业产业活动单位，是指报告期末实际在库且归属法人具有所有权的全部商品金额（含增值税）。这个指标反映批发和零售业的商品库存情况，以及对市场商品供应的保证程度。库存商品包括：（1）存放在本单位（如门市部、批发站、采购站、经营处）的仓库、货场、货柜和货架中的商品；（2）挑选、整理、包装中的商品；（3）已记入购进而尚未运到本单位的商品，即发货单或银行承兑凭证已到而货未到的商品；（4）寄放他处的商品，如因购货方拒绝付款而暂时存在购货方的商品；（5）委托其他单位代销（未作销售或调出）尚未售出的商品；（6）代其他单位购进尚未交付的商品。不包括：（1）所有权不属于本单位的商品，如商品已作销售但买方尚未取走的商品，代替他人保管、运输、加工的商品，代其他单位销售（未做购进或调入）而未售出的商品；（2）委托外单位加工的商品（包括本单位所属加工厂和其他生产单位加工生产尚未收回成品的商品）；（3）外贸企业代理其他单位从国外进口，尚未付给订货单位的商品；（4）代国家储备部门保管的商品。

亿元以上商品交易市场 指年成交额在亿元及以上的商品交易市场。商品交易市场是指经有关部门和组织批准设立，有固定场所、设施，有经营管理部门和监管人员，若干市场经营者入内，常年或实际开业三个月以上，集中、公开、独立地进行生活消费品、生产资料等现货商品交易以及提供相关服务的交易场所，包括各类消费品市场、生产资料市场等。

连锁总店（总部） 负责连锁企业资源（商号、商誉、经营模式、服务标准、管理模式等等）的开发、配置、控制或使用等功能的企业核心管理机构。连锁经营是指经营同类商品或服务，使用统一商号的若干店铺，在同一总店（总部）的管理下，采取统一采购或特许经营等方式，实现规模效益的组织形式，包括直营连锁、特许连锁和自愿连锁三种形式。

直营连锁是指连锁店铺由连锁公司全资或控股开设，在总部的直接控制下，开展统一经营的连锁经营形式；特许连锁是指拥有注册商标、企业标志、专利、专有技术等经营资源的企业（特许人），以合同形式将其拥有的经营资源许可其他经营者（被特许人）使用，被特许人按合同约定在统一的经营模式下开展经营，并向特许人支付特许经营费用的连锁经营形式；自愿连锁是指若干个店铺或企业自愿组合起来，在不改变各自资产所有权关系的情况下，以同一个品牌形象面对消费者，以共同进货为纽带开展的连锁经营形式。

社会消费品零售总额 指企业（单位、个体户）通过交易直接售给个人、社会集团非生产、非经营用的实物商品金额，以及提供餐饮服务所取得的收入金额。个人包括城乡居民和入境人员，社会集团包括机关、社会团体、部队、学校、企事业单位、居委会或村委会等。

Explanatory Notes on Main Statistical Indicators

Total Purchases of Commodities refer to the total value of purchases of commodities by enterprises (establishments) from other establishments or individuals (including direct import from abroad) for the purpose of re-selling, either with or without further processing of the commodities purchased. This indicator is used to show the total value of purchases of commodities by wholesale and retail establishments from domestic and overseas markets. The purchases include: (1) agricultural and industrial products purchased from producers; (2) books, magazines and newspapers purchased from distribution departments of the publishers; (3) commodities purchased from wholesale and retail establishments of different status of registration; (4) commodities purchased from other units, such as surplus materials purchased from government agencies, enterprises or institutions, commodities purchased from hotels and catering services establishments, confiscated goods purchased from customs authorities or market management agencies, second-hand goods and wastes purchased from residents; and (5) commodities directly imported from abroad. Excluded are commodities purchased by enterprises (establishments) for use in their own business operation, commodities obtained without buying or selling procedures, rejected commodities, etc.

Total Sales of Commodities refer to value of commodities sold by the establishments to other establishments and individuals (including direct export to abroad and value-added taxes). This indicator is used to show the total value of sales of commodities at domestic markets and export. The sales include: (1) commodities sold to urban and rural residents and social institutions for their consumption; (2) commodities sold to establishments in industry, agriculture, construction, post and telecommunications, wholesale and retail trades, hotels and catering services for their production and operation; (3) commodities for direct export to abroad. Excluded are: (1) commodities transferred without buying or selling procedures, such as hand-over commodities to other enterprises with institution changing, lent commodities, returned commodities that had been administered by other enterprises, processing raw materials sent out and samples present to other enterprises etc. (2) commission income from brokerage in transactions for which settlement is directly handled by buyers and sellers, (3) rejected commodities in the purchase, (4) loss in commodities, (5) self-using junk materials sold by enterprises etc.

Sales of Wholesale Trades refers to the amount of money of commodities sold to various national economic industries for producing and operating.

Sales of Retail Trades refers to the amount of money of commodities sold to urban and rural residents for household consumption and to social institutions for public consumption.

Total Stock of Commodities refers to wholesale and retail units and individual enterprises, it refers to total commodities possessed at the end of report periods (including value-added taxes); to wholesale and retail corporation units, it refers to total commodities actually in stock and possessed at the end of report periods (including value-added taxes). This indicator reflects the commodity stock level of various wholesale and retail enterprises and the potential for market supply. It includes: (1) commodities located in storage, garages, counters, and shelves of operating units (such as sale stores, wholesale centers, and operating offices) of wholesale and retail enterprises; (2) commodities in the process of being selected, sorted, and packed; (3) commodities not arrived but recorded as purchase in the account, i.e. commodities not arrived but payment receipts for the commodities from the sellers or the banks arrived; (4) commodities deposited in other places rather than places mentioned above, for instance: commodities in the hold of purchasers temporarily due to the refusal of payment and commodities not taken back after going through the formalities; (5) commodities entrusted to other units to sell but not sold yet; (6) commodities purchased for other units but not delivered yet. Commodities not included as: (1) stock are those not owned by the enterprises (units), (2) commodities on commission for processing but not yet delivered, (3) imported commodities of agency of foreign trade enterprise but not yet delivered to ordering units, (4) finally those put in stock on behalf of the state material reserves units.

Volume of Transaction at Large Commodity Markets with Transaction Value over 100 Million Yuan refers to the markets with an annual transaction of over 100 million yuan markets approved by the industrial and commercial administration departments, which specialize in wholesale and retail trades of commodities with an annual transaction of over 100 million yuan. The sum of sales of all sellers in the market makes up the transaction value of the market.

Head Chain Store (Head Office) refers to the core managing institution in charge of development, allocation, controlling or using chain enterprise' s resources (such as firms, business credits, operating modes, servicing standards and managing modes etc.).Chain operation refers to the type of organization of several stores selling the same commodities or providing the same services use a uniform firm, and they under the management of the same head store(head office), realizing scaled efficient by modes of uniform purchases or licensed operating. The modes of chain operation include Regular Chain, Licensed Chain and Voluntary Chain.

Regular Chain refers to chain that are invested or controlled by the headquarters. They operate under direct and unified management from the headquarters. Licensed chain refers to chain that enterprises(licensing units)owning operating resources like registered trade marks, enterprise' s symbols, patents and special techniques license their resources to other operators(licensed units) in type of contracts. Licensed units operate in uniform operation mode according to contracts, and pay the licensed fees to licensing units. Voluntary Chain refers to chain that various stores or enterprises combine together voluntarily, and face the consumers with the same brand image while the own ship of assets did not changed.

Total Retail Sales of Consumer Goods refer to the summary of retail sales of commodities sold directly by wholesale and retail trades, catering services and other service industries to urban and rural households for household consumption and to social institutions for public consumption. The Retail Sales of Consumer Goods to households refer to sales of commodities sold to urban and rural households for household consumption. The Retail Sales of Consumer Goods to social institutions refer to sales of commodities sold to departments, social institutions, armies, schools, enterprises and public institutions, neighborhood committees or village committees for non-production, non-operation and public consumption purposes, paid with government expenses. Total Retail Sales of Consumer Goods includes: sales of commodities and building materials sold to urban and rural households for household and building houses, sales of Consumer Goods sold to foreigners, overseas Chinese and Chinese compatriots from Hong Kong, Macao and Taiwan visiting China, and sales of commodities sold to social institutions for non-production, non-operation and public consumption purposes. It excludes: sales of commodities between urban households, sales of commodities sold by urban households through trust shops and sales of commodities sold to agriculture, industry, and construction and so on for production.

第十七篇

住宿餐饮业和旅游

HOTELS,CATERING SERVICES & TOURISM

（校对编辑：钟业宁　闫室丞）

17—1 限额以上住宿和餐饮业企业基本情况（2017年）

Basic Conditions of Accommodation above Star-rated & Catering Service above Designated Size (2017)

项 目	Item	2016		2017	
		法人企业（个）Corporation Enterprises (unit)	年末从业人员（人）Year-end Persons Employed (person)	法人企业（个）Corporation Enterprises (unit)	年末从业人员（人）Year-end Persons Employed (person)
总 计	**Total**	**841**	**74288**	**912**	**77637**
一、住宿业	**Ⅰ.Accommodation**	**521**	**45965**	**566**	**46720**
1.按登记注册类型分组	**1.Grouped by Status of Registration**				
内资企业	Domestic Funded Enterprises	502	41179	548	42180
国有企业	State-owned Industry	49	5352	43	5024
集体企业	Collective-owned Industry	5	315	5	255
股份合作企业	Cooperative Enterprises	2	182	1	28
联营企业	Joint Ownership Enterprises				
国有联营企业	State Joint Ownership Enterprises				
集体联营企业	Collective Joint Ownership Enterprises				
国有与集体联营企业	Joint State-Collective Ownership Enterprises				
其他联营企业	Other Joint Ownership Enterprises				
有限责任公司	Limited Liability Corporations	147	13798	146	13886
国有独资企业	Sole State-funded Corporations	4	423	5	674
其他有限责任公司	Other Limited Liability Corporations	143	13375	141	13212
股份有限公司	Share Holding Enterprises	26	3248	21	2686
私营企业	Private Enterprises	259	17456	331	20204
私营独资企业	Private-funded Enterprises	33	1509	33	1531
私营合伙企业	Private Partnership Enterprises	15	643	19	829
私营有限责任公司	Private Limited Liability Corporations	195	14205	262	16670
私营股份有限公司	Private Share Holding Enterprises	16	1099	17	1174
其他企业	Others	14	828	1	97
港、澳、台商投资企业	Enterprises with Funds from Hong Kong, Macao & Taiwan	17	4719	17	4473
合资经营企业	Joint Venture Enterprises	3	690	3	627
合作经营企业	Cooperative Enterprises	1	484	1	485
独资经营企业	Enterprises with Sole Investment	13	3545	13	3361
投资股份有限公司	Share-holding Corporations Ltd. with Investment				
其他港澳台投资企业	Others				
外商投资企业	Foreign-investment Enterprise	2	67	1	67
中外合资经营企业	Joint Venture Enterprises	1	67	1	67
中外合作经营企业	Cooperative Enterprises				
外资企业	Enterprises with Sole Foreign Investment	1	0		
外商投资股份有限公司	Share-holding Corporations Ltd. with Foreign Investment				
其他外商投资企业	Others				
2.按国民经济行业分组	**2.Grouped By Sector**				
旅游饭店	Tourist Hotel	355	36182	364	35316
一般旅馆	General Hotel	154	9021	190	10777
民宿服务	Homestay			1	25
露营地服务	Camp				
其他住宿业	Other Accommodation Service	12	762	11	602

17－1 续表 continued

项 目	Item	2016 法人企业(个) Corporation Enterprises (unit)	2016 年末从业人员(人) Year-end Persons Employed (person)	2017 法人企业(个) Corporation Enterprises (unit)	2017 年末从业人员(人) Year-end Persons Employed (person)
二、餐饮业	**Ⅱ.Catering Trades**	**320**	**28323**	**346**	**30917**
1.按登记注册类型分组	**1. Grouped by Status of Registration**				
内资企业	Domestic Funded Enterprises	314	23590	338	25221
国有企业	State-owned Industry	9	513	10	557
集体企业	Collective-owned Industry	3	137	4	226
股份合作企业	Cooperative Enterprises	1	38	2	145
联营企业	Joint Ownership Enterprises				
国有联营企业	State Joint Ownership Enterprises				
集体联营企业	Collective Joint Ownership Enterprises				
国有与集体联营企业	Joint State-Collective Ownership Enterprises				
其他联营企业	Other Joint Ownership Enterprises				
有限责任公司	Limited Liability Corporations	81	8291	81	9290
国有独资企业	Sole State-funded Corporations			1	292
其他有限责任公司	Other Limited Liability Corporations	81	8291	80	8998
股份有限公司	Share Holding Enterprises	14	1025	8	625
私营企业	Private Enterprises	193	12895	233	14378
私营独资企业	Private-funded Enterprises	44	1860	47	2090
私营合伙企业	Private Partnership Enterprises	8	346	6	226
私营有限责任公司	Private Limited Liability Corporations	132	10092	173	11679
私营股份有限公司	Private Share Holding Enterprises	9	597	7	383
其他企业	Others	13	691		
港、澳、台商投资企业	Enterprises with Funds from Hong Kong, Macao & Taiwan	5	407	6	514
合资经营企业	Joint Venture Enterprises	2	241	2	252
合作经营企业	Cooperative Enterprises				
独资经营企业	Enterprises with Sole Investment	3	166	4	262
投资股份有限公司	Share-holding Corporations Ltd. with Investment				
其他港澳台投资企业	Others				
外商投资企业	Foreign-investment Enterprise	1	4326	2	5182
中外合资经营企业	Joint Venture Enterprises			1	165
中外合作经营企业	Cooperative Enterprises				
外资企业	Enterprises with Sole Foreign Investment	1	4326	1	5017
外商投资股份有限公司	Share-holding Corporations Ltd. with Foreign Investment				
其他外商投资企业	Others				
2.按国民经济行业分组	**2.Grouped By Sector**				
正餐服务业	Dinner	296	19793	321	20824
快餐服务业	Snack	17	8229	16	9682
饮料及冷饮服务业	Beverage & Cold Drink	5	240	6	253
餐饮配送及外卖送餐服务	Catering Distribution & Delivery				
其他餐饮业	Others	2	61	2	95

17－2　限额以上住宿和餐饮业企业经营情况（2017年）

Business of Enterprises above Designated Size of Hotels & Catering Services（2017）

单位：万元　　(10 000 yuan)

项　目	Item	营业额 Business Revenue	客房收入 From Hotels	餐费收入 From Catering
总　计	**Total**	**1243130.6**	**491285.0**	**648433.4**
一、住宿业	**Ⅰ.Accommodation**	**782076.9**	**459719.6**	**244531.6**
1.按登记注册类型分组	**1. Grouped by Status of Registration**			
内资企业	Domestic Funded Enterprises	683795.7	409098.7	202873.5
国有企业	State-owned Industry	73168.8	23536.4	26300.1
集体企业	Collective-owned Industry	4729.0	2451.9	1115.4
股份合作企业	Cooperative Enterprises	230.9	199.9	1.2
联营企业	Joint Ownership Enterprises			
国有联营企业	State Joint Ownership Enterprises			
集体联营企业	Collective Joint Ownership Enterprises			
国有与集体联营企业	Joint State-Collective Ownership Enterprises			
其他联营企业	Other Joint Ownership Enterprises			
有限责任公司	Limited Liability Corporations	239390.1	149362.3	65689.8
国有独资企业	Sole State-funded Corporations	6943.8	2996.6	3582.2
其他有限责任公司	Other Limited Liability Corporations	232446.3	146365.7	62107.6
股份有限公司	Share Holding Enterprises	42521.3	20355.1	16767.9
私营企业	Private Enterprises	322994.1	212662.1	92768.6
私营独资企业	Private-funded Enterprises	22341.9	13077.3	8522.4
私营合伙企业	Private Partnership Enterprises	11777.1	7770.1	3881.9
私营有限责任公司	Private Limited Liability Corporations	268660.7	180268.0	73313.8
私营股份有限公司	Private Share Holding Enterprises	20214.4	11546.7	7050.5
其他企业	Others	761.5	531.0	230.5
港、澳、台商投资企业	Enterprises with Funds from Hong Kong, Macao & Taiwan	94907.5	47279.8	41658.1
合资经营企业	Joint Venture Enterprises	8222.2	5330.1	2558.0
合作经营企业	Cooperative Enterprises	3130.0	1472.3	1412.0
独资经营企业	Enterprises with Sole Investment	83555.3	40477.4	37688.1
投资股份有限公司	Share-holding Corporations Ltd. with Investment			
其他港澳台投资企业	Others			
外商投资企业	Foreign-investment Enterprise	3373.7	3341.1	
中外合资经营企业	Joint Venture Enterprises	3373.7	3341.1	
中外合作经营企业	Cooperative Enterprises			
外资企业	Enterprises with Sole Foreign Investment			
外商投资股份有限公司	Share-holding Corporations Ltd. with Foreign Investment			
其他外商投资企业	Others			
2.按国民经济行业分组	**2.Grouped By Sector**			
旅游饭店	Tourist Hotel	586988.1	317625.0	205509.0
一般旅馆	General Hotel	180966.2	135147.2	37532.9
民宿服务	Homestay	270.0	221.0	49.0
露营地服务	Camp			
其他住宿业	Other Accommodation Service	13852.6	6726.4	1440.7

17—2 续表 continued

单位：万元 (10 000 yuan)

项 目	Item	营业额 Business Revenue	客房收入 From Hotels	餐费收入 From Catering
二、餐饮业	**Ⅱ.Catering Trades**	**461053.7**	**31565.4**	**403901.8**
1.按登记注册类型分组	**1. Grouped by Status of Registration**			
内资企业	Domestic Funded Enterprises	380120.3	31099.8	323565.2
国有企业	State-owned Industry	5848.2	1780.5	3632.6
集体企业	Collective-owned Industry	2609.7		2609.7
股份合作企业	Cooperative Enterprises	1718.5	18.0	1619.2
联营企业	Joint Ownership Enterprises			
国有联营企业	State Joint Ownership Enterprises			
集体联营企业	Collective Joint Ownership Enterprises			
国有与集体联营企业	Joint State-Collective Ownership Enterprises			
其他联营企业	Other Joint Ownership Enterprises			
有限责任公司	Limited Liability Corporations	145789.3	9342.9	118249.6
国有独资企业	Sole State-funded Corporations	3529.6	1354.4	2136.5
其他有限责任公司	Other Limited Liability Corporations	142259.7	7988.5	116113.1
股份有限公司	Share Holding Enterprises	7546.9	2502.7	4755.8
私营企业	Private Enterprises	216607.7	17455.7	192698.3
私营独资企业	Private-funded Enterprises	25155.6	3924.0	20899.2
私营合伙企业	Private Partnership Enterprises	2015.0	471.9	1520.4
私营有限责任公司	Private Limited Liability Corporations	185652.6	12356.3	167265.4
私营股份有限公司	Private Share Holding Enterprises	3784.5	703.5	3013.3
其他企业	Others			
港、澳、台商投资企业	Enterprises with Funds from Hong Kong, Macao & Taiwan	11794.5		11663.3
合资经营企业	Joint Venture Enterprises	3174.7		3174.7
合作经营企业	Cooperative Enterprises			
独资经营企业	Enterprises with Sole Investment	8619.8		8488.6
投资股份有限公司	Share-holding Corporations Ltd. with Investment			
其他港澳台投资企业	Others			
外商投资企业	Foreign-investment Enterprise	69138.9	465.6	68673.3
中外合资经营企业	Joint Venture Enterprises	1295.8	465.6	830.2
中外合作经营企业	Cooperative Enterprises			
外资企业	Enterprises with Sole Foreign Investment	67843.1		67843.1
外商投资股份有限公司	Share-holding Corporations Ltd. with Foreign Investment			
其他外商投资企业	Others			
2.按国民经济行业分组	**2.Grouped By Sector**			
正餐服务业	Dinner	310782.6	30697.1	263460.1
快餐服务业	Snack	145853.0		137613.1
饮料及冷饮服务业	Beverage & Cold Drink	2313.5		1770.2
餐饮配送及外卖送餐服务	Catering Distribution & Delivery			
其他餐饮业	Others	714.4		714.4

17－3 限额以上住宿和餐饮业企业主要财务指标（2017年）

单位：万元

项 目	Item	流动资产小计 Circulating Funds	#存货 Deposit Products	固定资产原价 Original Value of Fixed Assets	累计折旧 Add Up Depreciation	#本年折旧 Depreciation of the Year	资产合计 Total Assets	负债合计 Total Liabilities
总 计	**Total**	**1104287.4**	**73538.6**	**1773219.9**	**766761.4**	**80437.3**	**2790623.8**	**2189820.8**
一、住宿业	**Ⅰ.Accommodation**	**914182.6**	**58445.1**	**1580781.7**	**696168.0**	**69380.2**	**2388155.6**	**1873995.6**
1.按登记注册类型分组	**1. Grouped by Status of Registration**							
内资企业	Domestic Funded Enterprises	762138.4	24276.7	1133140.8	467019.6	51769.3	1905647.2	1430502.9
国有企业	State-owned Industry	47650.9	1575.9	181090.9	103908.5	8349.5	200144.8	129368.8
集体企业	Collective-owned Industry	3223.2	43.3	6530.5	4265.4	261.3	6667.0	2586.0
股份合作企业	Cooperative Enterprises	411.6	46.3	1886.1	1434.5	50.2	917.1	864.4
联营企业	Joint Ownership Enterprises							
国有联营企业	State Joint Ownership Enterprises							
集体联营企业	Collective Joint Ownership Enterprises							
国有与集体联营企业	Joint State-Collective Ownership Enterprises							
其他联营企业	Other Joint Ownership Enterprises							
有限责任公司	Limited Liability Corporations	234571.7	11177.4	487443.0	165060.8	17981.2	746812.5	530392.2
国有独资企业	Sole State-funded Corporations	8550.4	632.5	38656.4	12088.9	3524.8	46231.1	40280.5
其他有限责任公司	Other Limited Liability Corporations	226021.3	10544.9	448786.6	152971.9	14456.4	700581.4	490111.7
股份有限公司	Share Holding Enterprises	27569.4	1135.2	92459.6	38140.8	3194.1	122878.7	74104.8
私营企业	Private Enterprises	448697.2	10295.0	363729.6	154209.1	21932.7	828026.5	693079.2
私营独资企业	Private-funded Enterprises	18119.1	1013.7	42890.1	24223.2	1764.0	50781.6	21328.5
私营合伙企业	Private Partnership Enterprises	6032.2	263.9	16875.3	7172.6	913.0	22308.5	11097.4
私营有限责任公司	Private Limited Liability Corporations	395381.9	8829.4	286361.8	114859.9	18518.0	708037.4	612150.2
私营股份有限公司	Private Share Holding Enterprises	29164.0	188.0	17602.4	7953.4	737.7	46899.0	48503.1
其他企业	Others	14.4	3.6	1.1	0.5	0.3	200.6	107.5
港、澳、台商投资企业	Enterprises with Funds from Hong Kong, Macao & Taiwan	151710.4	34138.9	447406.7	228993.4	17551.9	481546.1	442707.7
合资经营企业	Joint Venture Enterprises	14223.2	151.3	44830.4	30212.9	370.6	79197.0	91740.7
合作经营企业	Cooperative Enterprises	3713.6	95.3	20128.1	14939.3	964.0	9125.9	8287.2
独资经营企业	Enterprises with Sole Investment	133773.6	33892.3	382448.2	183841.2	16217.3	393223.2	342679.8
投资股份有限公司	Share-holding Corporations Ltd. with Investment							
其他港澳台投资企业	Others							
外商投资企业	Foreign-investment Enterprise	333.8	29.5	234.2	155.0	59.0	962.3	785.0
中外合资经营企业	Joint Venture Enterprises	333.8	29.5	234.2	155.0	59.0	962.3	785.0
中外合作经营企业	Cooperative Enterprises							
外资企业	Enterprises with Sole Foreign Investment							
外商投资股份有限公司	Share-holding Corporations Ltd. with Foreign Investment							
其他外商投资企业	Others							
2.按国民经济行业分组	**2.Grouped By Sector**							
旅游饭店	Tourist Hotel	616670.1	51404.8	1418800.0	633045.7	57377.1	1894020.6	1477813.4
一般旅馆	General Hotel	288265.8	6929.4	148389.6	61619.8	11363.6	462047.5	376566.5
民宿服务	Homestay	148.3	27.6				2274.7	530.1
露营地服务	Camp							
其他住宿业	Other Accommodation Service	9098.4	83.3	13592.1	1502.5	639.5	29812.8	19085.6

Main Financial Indicators of Enterprises above Designated in Wholesale & Retail Sale Trade（2017）

(10 000 yuan)

所有者权益合计 Total Creditors Equity	#实收资本 Capital Hold	#国家资本 State Capital	主营业务收入 Business Income of the Main Products	主营业务成本 Core Business Cost	主营业务税金及附加 Core Business Tax&Extra Charges	销售费用 Operating Cost	管理费用 Manage-ment Expenses	财务费用 Financial Expenses	#利息支出 Interest Expen-diture	营业利润 Business Profits	利润总额 Gross Profits
600802.9	**983089.3**	**121363.4**	**1163658.7**	**489501.0**	**19364.0**	**375666.3**	**258952.4**	**43204.2**	**33700.0**	**-10266.2**	**-7863.7**
514160.0	**872640.6**	**114868.0**	**728949.7**	**260956.5**	**14358.9**	**246461.8**	**207143.9**	**35812.8**	**29704.7**	**-26253.2**	**-23852.3**
475144.3	637920.2	111579.7	638683.2	242221.5	10300.1	218056.6	163145.7	31796.6	23385.0	-18125.8	-16080.3
70776.0	54074.0	41693.1	66012.3	23655.9	1655.4	28002.3	19099.1	2363.2	2213.9	-5205.5	-4678.0
4081.0	1182.2		4363.2	1676.8	113.4	1741.5	814.8	-4.5	1.1	80.1	84.3
52.7	81.0		207.6	3.6	10.9	115.5	149.5	1.1		-49.6	-49.6
216420.3	221971.0	68535.2	224404.0	81433.4	3754.1	71950.0	62396.4	13876.8	10403.6	-5058.6	-5827.1
5950.6	13338.5	12629.4	6919.3	3046.5	103.4	4094.8	2959.9	819.1	116.7	-4042.8	-4049.9
210469.7	208632.5	55905.8	217484.7	78386.9	3650.7	67855.2	59436.5	13057.7	10286.9	-1015.8	-1777.2
48773.9	52919.7	550.4	38921.2	15865.2	419.9	11284.6	11111.0	2153.5	2083.2	-372.7	-811.6
134947.3	307692.3	801.0	304013.4	119380.3	4341.4	104523.9	69498.5	13403.3	8680.0	-7572.0	-4851.8
29453.1	149991.7		21634.4	11967.1	570.4	3409.1	3558.7	676.5	533.5	1173.1	1027.1
11211.1	6938.3		11398.1	5287.2	356.6	2758.7	1889.8	504.6	389.9	608.5	458.6
95887.2	142440.3	800.0	251979.1	94856.7	3206.8	92666.1	60621.9	10867.9	6883.6	-9820.4	-6385.3
-1604.1	8322.0	1.0	19001.8	7269.3	207.6	5690.0	3428.1	1354.3	873.0	466.8	47.8
93.1			761.5	206.3	5.0	438.8	76.4	3.2	3.2	52.5	53.5
38838.4	234687.4	3288.3	87393.0	18271.0	3895.8	26984.3	43558.2	3996.2	6319.7	-8493.0	-8134.0
-12543.7	40983.7	3288.3	7744.7	946.7	165.0	3965.9	3146.5	916.9	1059.0	-1219.2	-890.1
838.7	13908.7		3682.1	955.9	30.1	1401.9	1713.2	256.4	250.6	-674.1	-669.5
50543.4	179795.0		75966.2	16368.4	3700.7	21616.5	38698.5	2822.9	5010.1	-6599.7	-6574.4
177.3	33.0		2873.5	464.0	163.0	1420.9	440.0	20.0		365.6	362.0
177.3	33.0		2873.5	464.0	163.0	1420.9	440.0	20.0		365.6	362.0
416207.2	780642.7	110595.1	542301.7	192412.3	11794.7	183596.8	166960.4	28557.1	26664.9	-32702.7	-32722.8
85481.0	87282.6	4272.9	173579.2	66298.8	2411.3	60016.2	37628.1	6985.8	2761.2	1098.4	3431.9
1744.6	1000.0		270.0	87.6	1.4		72.9	15.6	15.6	92.5	92.5
10727.2	3715.3		12798.8	2157.8	151.5	2848.8	2482.5	254.3	263.0	5258.6	5346.1

17−3 续表

单位：万元

项　目	Item	流动资产小计 Circulating Funds	#存货 Deposit Products	固定资产原价 Original Value of Fixed Assets	累计折旧 Add Up Depreciation	#本年折旧 Depreciation of the Year	资产合计 Total Assets	负债合计 Total Liabilities
二、餐饮业	**Ⅱ.Catering Trades**	**190104.8**	**15093.5**	**192438.2**	**70593.4**	**11057.1**	**402468.2**	**315825.2**
1.按登记注册类型分组	**1.Grouped by Status of Registration**							
内资企业	Domestic Funded Enterprises	180738.3	14378.6	179626.7	64579.2	10578.2	373257.0	303783.9
国有企业	State-owned Industry	2277.5	133.2	9679.3	5372.3	146.4	7013.0	6289.8
集体企业	Collective-owned Industry	483.6	25.6	165.5	51.2	18.6	687.7	428.0
股份合作企业	Cooperative Enterprises	4018.4	42.9	1635.3	969.3	60.9	5126.7	3181.0
联营企业	Joint Ownership Enterprises							
国有联营企业	State Joint Ownership Enterprises							
集体联营企业	Collective Joint Ownership Enterprises							
国有与集体联营企业	Joint State-Collective Ownership Enterprises							
其他联营企业	Other Joint Ownership Enterprises							
有限责任公司	Limited Liability Corporations	62804.2	4716.4	60102.4	14687.3	3471.5	146005.5	144787.1
国有独资企业	Sole State-funded Corporations	1684.8	463.7	772.5	341.5	169.0	2726.3	2624.5
其他有限责任公司	Other Limited Liability Corporations	61119.4	4252.7	59329.9	14345.8	3302.5	143279.2	142162.6
股份有限公司	Share Holding Enterprises	3399.9	348.6	17670.1	7661.9	827.5	14240.3	13538.9
私营企业	Private Enterprises	107754.7	9111.9	90374.1	35837.2	6053.3	200183.8	135559.1
私营独资企业	Private-funded Enterprises	11622.1	1831.3	16970.4	5205.6	720.2	30115.8	12620.6
私营合伙企业	Private Partnership Enterprises	1699.1	113.9	1595.6	386.8	56.0	3059.9	2372.8
私营有限责任公司	Private Limited Liability Corporations	83920.5	7079.0	66533.0	29073.1	5221.2	148801.4	109610.1
私营股份有限公司	Private Share Holding Enterprises	10513.0	87.7	5275.1	1171.7	55.9	18206.7	10955.6
其他企业	Others							
港、澳、台商投资企业	Enterprises with Funds from Hong Kong, Macao & Taiwan	6839.9	79.8	2612.4	2030.7	171.5	7622.7	3528.6
合资经营企业	Joint Venture Enterprises	829.2		333.5	245.2	4.4	918.0	918.5
合作经营企业	Cooperative Enterprises							
独资经营企业	Enterprises with Sole Investment	6010.7	79.8	2278.9	1785.5	167.1	6704.7	2610.1
投资股份有限公司	Share-holding Corporations Ltd. with Investment							
其他港澳台投资企业	Others							
外商投资企业	Foreign-investment Enterprise	2526.6	635.1	10199.1	3983.5	307.4	21588.5	8512.7
中外合资经营企业	Joint Venture Enterprises	964.1	31.2				964.1	909.1
中外合作经营企业	Cooperative Enterprises							
外资企业	Enterprises with Sole Foreign Investment	1562.5	603.9	10199.1	3983.5	307.4	20624.4	7603.6
外商投资股份有限公司	Share-holding Corporations Ltd. with Foreign Investment							
其他外商投资企业	Others							
2.按国民经济行业分组	**2.Grouped By Sector**							
正餐服务业	Dinner	160294.0	13070.8	157871.2	57178.3	9164.4	327417.2	277019.8
快餐服务业	Snack	16224.1	1840.2	21153.8	7479.9	1064.3	52189.3	26453.3
饮料及冷饮服务业	Beverage & Cold Drink	10883.7	107.3	6713.1	3295.1	375.2	15012.9	10485.3
餐饮配送及外卖送餐服务	Catering Distribution & Delivery							
其他餐饮业	Others	147.5	39.8	220.4	132.5	132.3	235.8	25.8

continued

(10 000 yuan)

所有者权益合计 Total Creditors Equity	#实收资本 Capital Hold	#国家资本 State Capital	主营业务收入 Business Income of the Main Products	主营业务成本 Core Business Cost	主营业务税金及附加 Core Business Tax&Extra Charges	销售费用 Operating Cost	管理费用 Manage-ment Expenses	财务费用 Financial Expenses	#利息支出 Interest Expen-diture	营业利润 Business Profits	利润总额 Gross Profits
86642.9	**110448.7**	**6495.4**	**434709.0**	**228544.5**	**5005.1**	**129204.5**	**51808.5**	**7391.4**	**3995.3**	**15987.0**	**15988.6**
69473.0	105054.9	6495.4	358597.0	194324.1	4880.9	107035.8	44613.2	7408.4	3991.2	2815.4	2525.7
723.2	4217.8	2766.9	5644.5	2682.9	73.9	1843.8	1372.4	38.2	28.9	-361.0	-360.7
259.7	227.1		2557.8	1292.8	49.1	753.0	247.7	4.3	1.7	239.0	156.0
1945.7	523.9		1697.0	1382.0	5.0	89.2	199.8	3.9	3.7	-2.0	-5.9
1218.3	26328.5	3540.0	134070.0	64098.7	1088.4	49795.5	15598.1	3257.7	912.8	1013.3	920.3
101.8	3500.0	3500.0	3329.8	689.0	7.5	2141.5	1593.4	50.2	-19.2	-1151.7	-1145.9
1116.5	22828.5	40.0	130740.2	63409.7	1080.9	47654.0	14004.7	3207.5	932.0	2165.0	2066.2
701.4	2315.6	160.0	7872.8	4573.9	189.7	2055.1	1190.3	167.9	138.7	-280.4	-265.3
64624.7	71442.0	28.5	206754.9	120293.8	3474.8	52499.2	26004.9	3936.4	2905.4	2206.5	2081.3
17495.2	11620.3	6.5	24597.8	14461.9	708.4	4398.9	2809.6	284.4	83.3	1872.3	1567.5
687.1	1345.0		1886.1	1249.4	72.1	242.0	190.3	46.6	36.9	155.7	155.7
39191.3	46458.5	22.0	176621.3	102854.0	2649.0	46336.2	22447.0	3506.1	2718.5	452.4	622.4
7251.1	12018.2		3649.7	1728.5	45.3	1522.1	558.0	99.3	66.7	-273.9	-264.3
4094.1	3059.0		11137.4	4348.7	55.4	5315.0	1259.4	22.2	4.1	629.6	834.5
-0.5	130.0		3064.1	1645.3	13.3	1282.3	50.2	6.4		66.6	67.9
4094.6	2929.0		8073.3	2703.4	42.1	4032.7	1209.2	15.8	4.1	563.0	766.6
13075.8	2334.8		64974.6	29871.7	68.8	16853.7	5935.9	-39.2		12542.0	12628.4
55.0	100.0		1295.8	368.7	8.8	232.2	718.0	3.1		65.0	68.7
13020.8	2234.8		63678.8	29503.0	60.0	16621.5	5217.9	-42.3		12477.0	12559.7
50397.3	90321.9	6495.4	294444.4	165035.0	4641.7	80677.6	40302.6	6451.9	3446.9	-1953.1	-1785.1
25736.0	9747.0		136009.5	61617.0	279.8	46690.5	10474.0	465.1	81.5	17592.9	17705.1
4527.6	2176.7		2345.2	1070.5	81.1	1144.8	335.7	470.8	466.9	415.0	134.8
210.0	203.1		714.4	574.4	0.4	60.0	45.0	0.4		34.0	34.9

17—4 主要年份限额以上住宿和餐饮业企业经营情况

Business Circumstance of Enterprises above Designated Size in Hotel & Catering in Major Years

单位：万元 (10 000 yuan)

项 目	Item	2000	2005	2010	2011	2012	2013	2014	2015	2016	2017
一、法人企业数（个）	Number of Corporation Enterprises (unit)	85	393	581	662	734	802	818	828	841	912
二、年末从业人员（人）	Number of Persons Employed (person)	21621	59652	70818	52483	83526	81461	77844	75538	74288	77637
三、营业额（万元）	Business Revenue (10 000 yuan)	70028	352590	675506	848208	965256	926203	932172	1003531	1083573	1243131
四、客房间数（间）	Number of Guest Rooms (room)			63915	69897	96443	81777	87037	115733	204719	262564
五、床位数（个）	Number of Beds (bed)		80315	112690	121624	161065	139771	147920	189627	323589	437085
六、餐位数（位）	Number of Catering Seatings (seat)		213534	292875	315285	367388	365375	389320	399120	416588	947127
七、年末餐饮营业面积（平方米）	Area of Catering Business (sq.m)		680358	812365	1421726	1783501	1736158	1863541	1916088	1976210	2300859

注：1. 2005年住宿业为星级以上住宿企业，未设置“客房间数”指标。
2. 2000年统计范围为限额以上餐饮业，未包括住宿业；未设置四至七项指标。

Note: 1. The data on hotel in 2005 refers to the hotels above star-rate, and the indicator of “Number of Guest Rooms” has not been set.
2. The statistical range in 2000 is the catering enterprises above designated size, excluding hotel enterprises, and the relative indicators have not been set.

17—5 旅游机构数（2017年）

Number of Tourism Institutions (2017)

单位：家 (unit)

城 市	City	旅游管理部门 Tourist Management Department	旅行社 Travel Agencies	星级饭店 Star-rated Hotels	五星 5 Star	四星 4 Star	三星 3 Star	二星 2 Star
总 计	**Total**	**195**	**830**	**457**	**12**	**96**	**264**	**85**
南宁市	Nanning	19	131	49	2	14	27	6
柳州市	Liuzhou	15	58	41	2	10	20	9
桂林市	Guilin	22	282	58	5	13	30	10
梧州市	Wuzhou	8	32	34		2	17	15
北海市	Beihai	6	60	35	1	5	23	6
防城港市	Fangchenggang	12	30	25		6	19	
钦州市	Qinzhou	7	63	17	1		16	
贵港市	Guigang	6	19	13		5	5	3
玉林市	Yulin	17	29	25		8	10	7
百色市	Baise	13	19	31		6	24	1
贺州市	Hezhou	6	20	18		3	13	2
河池市	Hechi	28	41	50		9	30	11
来宾市	Laibin	10	11	16	1	3	10	2
崇左市	Chongzuo	26	35	45		12	20	13

17—6 主要年份旅游人数及消费

Number of Oversea Visitor Arrivals & Tourism Consumption in Main Years

指 标	Item	1995	2000	2005	2010	2012	2013	2014	2015	2016	2017
接待入境旅游者人数(人次)	**Number of Oversea Visitor Arrivals (person-time)**	**418499**	**1240265**	**1461605**	**2502363**	**3502732**	**3915435**	**4211845**	**4500562**	**4825160**	**5124381**
港澳和台湾同胞	Compatriots from Hong Kong, Macao & Taiwan	107672	730706	585557	1088493	1575725	1792289	1995074	2108234	2305390	2570577
外国人	Foreigners	307428	506288	873103	1413870	1927007	2123146	2216771	2392328	2519770	2553804
#越南	Vietnam	1110	66327	140396	292332	486694	450799	427548	453556	482492	484933
韩国	South Korea		86769	57304	94461	190446	221023	278608	369949	403583	308493
马来西亚	Malaysia	15546	11672	145537	190128	242491	281445	279697	281679	287182	277124
新加坡	Singapore	7164	6174	15545	53995	100808	129784	131404	151725	154324	149314
美国	United States	34878	58517	78709	101540	111172	109754	119674	125262	134230	135248
印度尼西亚	Indonesia	15057	14351	19065	67624	96765	134099	117725	121311	129923	134718
泰国	Thailand	5166	8256	48322	30552	81646	106747	86644	105457	96006	100714
法国	France	23241	40519	43425	85921	79163	77597	67293	63252	67551	75047
英国	United Kingdom	12374	15795	24757	53996	49105	52467	56935	62462	69710	80695
加拿大	Canada	5497	6376	15969	38181	71526	71338	63390	57282	63026	74386
德国	Germany	22987	27802	32045	51535	55234	55984	50064	51057	53482	57084
日本	Japan	72706	86469	91117	84576	59235	31241	38638	48944	59578	65388
澳大利亚	Australia	5587	7782	20036	45321	45516	42880	46792	42282	51748	48771
菲律宾	The Philippines				6778	8063	13367	18158	37297	39395	50447
印度	India				4428	8670	19667	20539	28069	32371	37007
意大利	Italy	10075	8732	15079	17164	19940	20117	23507	23387	28810	31212
新西兰	New Zealand	1178	1440	3168	8626	8403	11515	14214	13519	15114	16775
国内游客人数(万人次)	**Number of Domestic Visitors (10 000 person-times)**	**1450**	**3951**	**6493**	**14074**	**20778**	**24264**	**28565**	**33661**	**40419**	**51812**
国际旅游外汇消费(亿美元)	**Foreign Exchange from International Tourism (100 million dollars)**	**1.21**	**3.07**	**3.59**	**8.07**	**12.79**	**15.47**	**17.28**	**19.17**	**21.64**	**23.96**
国内旅游消费(亿元)	**Domestic Tourist Consumption (100 million yuan)**	**17.4**	**146.8**	**277.8**	**898.1**	**1578.9**	**1961.3**	**2495.0**	**3136.4**	**4047.7**	**5418.6**
旅游总消费(亿元)	**Total Tourist Expenditure (100 million yuan)**	**28.3**	**168.6**	**303.7**	**952.9**	**1659.7**	**2057.1**	**2601.2**	**3254.2**	**4191.4**	**5580.4**
星级饭店数(个)	**Number of Star-rated Hotels (unit)**	**41**	**162**	**350**	**423**	**456**	**477**	**466**	**466**	**472**	**457**

注：2000年及以前的星级饭店总数为涉外饭店数。

Note: The number of star-rated hotels before 2000 refers to the number of hotels for foreign tourists.

17—7 主要年份各市接待入境旅游者人数

单位：人次

城 市	City	2000		2005		2010		2011	
		合计 Total	外国人 Foreigners	合计 Total	外国人 Foreigners	合计 Total	外国人 Foreigners	合计 Total	外国人 Foreigners
南宁市	Nanning	45586	23746	83317	65338	167527	123267	236144	161735
柳州市	Liuzhou	20268	4148	33778	24072	81100	59153	105958	73209
桂林市	Guilin	950172	403872	1000912	585391	1486202	897491	1643935	1037220
梧州市	Wuzhou	49858	3110	37612	17959	90017	8736	130119	14588
北海市	Beihai	38087	4523	30228	18657	73008	37249	83073	41703
防城港市	Fangchenggang					70122	66388	103275	99002
钦州市	Qinzhou					24367	2950	35630	5220
贵港市	Guigang					40485	9992	55847	12724
玉林市	Yulin					33128	10209	43006	9855
百色市	Baise					26741	7466	40106	14483
贺州市	Hezhou					164018	41557	227152	57336
河池市	Hechi					30155	9935	41385	13179
来宾市	Laibin					8163	3703	12030	4904
崇左市	Chongzuo					207330	135774	270263	169670

Number of Oversea Visitor Arrivals & International Tourism Receipts by City in Main Years

(person-time)

2012		2013		2014		2015		2016		2017	
合计 Total	外国人 Foreigners	合计 Total	外国人 Foreigners	合计 Total	外国人 Foreigners	合计 Total	外国人 Foreigners	合计 Total	外国人 Foreigners	合计 Total	外国人 Foreigners
300674	209892	351068	233107	432967	309542	510850	396336	555424	422601	591288	407692
137760	87005	167394	100150	174132	114121	181221	126170	188769	134079	200355	149927
1824141	1092967	1936542	1170849	2047792	1171655	2163406	1216381	2333247	1287124	2489026	1329359
152816	12087	182851	14655	190255	15263	196278	16172	202724	17985	209257	15387
98759	53205	115820	61427	120938	63113	129053	65264	135536	66498	145410	76008
127497	122183	146715	140034	153803	144795	160987	150294	168593	156605	176622	163625
41631	6220	46112	6829	50312	7227	53573	7300	61916	8350	68793	9438
68086	12025	79323	12734	82853	11847	86921	11897	90678	11216	96278	9950
57942	15832	81054	20745	95939	17969	105432	19511	122301	26173	136733	28058
51516	26950	63698	34334	70106	35489	73928	37585	78164	39002	83155	41160
267251	69630	309624	66541	330696	63829	351569	64722	376544	52380	389077	29412
53546	15543	70037	21146	91705	32793	100570	35080	106764	34262	112560	33122
14500	6002	16848	7364	18561	6545	19629	6437	21586	6373	22733	5752
306613	197466	348349	233234	351771	222583	367145	239179	382914	257122	403094	254914

17－8 主要年份各市国际旅游消费

International Tourism Expenditure by City in Main Years

单位：万元 (10 000 yuan)

城 市	City	2000	2005	2010	2011	2012	2013	2014	2015	2016	2017
南宁市	Nanning	5736	20320	37858	53449	67629	85067	100629	125962	154268	175520
柳州市	Liuzhou	1031	9560	18241	23476	30073	36428	40488	44579	52866	63892
桂林市	Guilin	188712	191951	341244	401305	463936	538503	582964	638154	784966	888722
梧州市	Wuzhou	3004	3195	15589	22907	26725	34971	40236	43284	50068	54143
北海市	Beihai	8367	5326	14768	16728	21662	26677	29164	31259	36992	41032
防城港市	Fangchenggang			11731	17546	22595	27139	30148	32476	38570	42681
钦州市	Qinzhou			5589	7334	8418	9332	10822	11929	16221	18719
贵港市	Guigang			8129	11376	13766	16389	18813	20157	23744	26870
玉林市	Yulin			9947	11327	14555	20280	25936	28799	38049	41312
百色市	Baise			7298	9920	12221	14552	16522	18031	21978	24202
贺州市	Hezhou			28408	41088	48201	58482	66281	73613	89936	97727
河池市	Hechi			7744	10122	12644	15913	21843	25541	30666	34009
来宾市	Laibin			2368	3134	3800	4342	4998	5545	6653	7361
崇左市	Chongzuo			39591	53743	61664	70118	72879	78582	92097	101294

17—9 主要年份各市接待入境旅游者平均每人消费额
Per Capita Expenditure of Oversea Visitor Arrivals by City in Main Years

单位：元 (yuan)

城 市	City	2000	2005	2010	2011	2012	2013	2014	2015	2016	2017
南宁市	Nanning	1258	2439	2260	2263	2249	2423	2324	2466	2777	2968
柳州市	Liuzhou	509	2830	2249	2216	2183	2176	2326	2460	2801	3189
桂林市	Guilin	1986	1918	2296	2441	2543	2781	2847	2950	3364	3571
梧州市	Wuzhou	603	849	1732	1760	1749	1913	2115	2205	2470	2587
北海市	Beihai	2197	1762	2023	2014	2193	2303	2411	2422	2729	2822
防城港市	Fangchenggang			1673	1699	1772	1850	1960	2017	2288	2417
钦州市	Qinzhou			2294	2058	2022	2024	2151	2227	2620	2721
贵港市	Guigang			2008	2037	2022	2066	2271	2319	2618	2791
玉林市	Yulin			3003	2634	2512	2502	2703	2732	3111	3021
百色市	Baise			2729	2473	2372	2285	2357	2439	2812	2911
贺州市	Hezhou			1732	1809	1804	1889	2004	2094	2388	2512
河池市	Hechi			2568	2446	2361	2272	2382	2540	2872	3021
来宾市	Laibin			2901	2605	2621	2577	2693	2825	3082	3238
崇左市	Chongzuo			1910	1989	2011	2013	2072	2140	2405	2513

17－10 各市接待国内游客人数
Number of Domestic Visitors by City

单位：万人次 (10 000 persons-times)

城 市	City	2010	2011	2012	2013	2014	2015	2016	2017
南宁市	Nanning	3542.70	4374.74	5122.07	5840.26	6905.19	8159.14	9499.62	11001.08
柳州市	Liuzhou	1300.25	1519.63	1904.10	2266.32	2605.43	2901.14	3297.26	4018.78
桂林市	Guilin	2097.71	2623.78	3110.25	3390.52	3737.84	4253.61	5152.55	7983.89
梧州市	Wuzhou	655.91	840.33	975.98	1131.39	1279.13	1527.79	1727.66	2205.06
北海市	Beihai	938.43	1100.79	1311.20	1521.16	1770.67	2143.69	2473.24	3069.82
防城港市	Fangchenggang	550.08	675.59	806.53	965.11	1168.40	1345.77	1568.79	2016.35
钦州市	Qinzhou	469.33	570.42	692.74	774.25	868.31	1077.07	1801.21	2564.30
贵港市	Guigang	623.02	744.62	918.75	1095.16	1266.25	1435.85	1666.60	2090.70
玉林市	Yulin	712.55	837.47	1023.28	1355.97	1653.75	2027.02	2787.85	3989.88
百色市	Baise	952.24	1119.78	1356.29	1680.45	1997.80	2321.92	2716.69	3265.21
贺州市	Hezhou	487.43	640.12	785.12	999.13	1257.17	1526.53	1775.52	2171.47
河池市	Hechi	728.01	849.13	1063.11	1281.76	1530.09	1841.95	2154.20	2635.58
来宾市	Laibin	353.36	581.56	753.35	855.99	1197.65	1539.39	1806.63	2260.28
崇左市	Chongzuo	662.48	779.44	954.81	1106.45	1327.35	1560.50	1991.54	2539.48

17－11 各市国内旅游消费
Tourist Consumption of Domestic Visitors by City

单位：亿元 （100 million yuan）

城 市	City	2010	2011	2012	2013	2014	2015	2016	2017
南宁市	Nanning	234.78	307.05	397.13	469.64	598.73	729.93	903.24	1109.80
柳州市	Liuzhou	88.59	117.38	150.66	182.27	229.09	281.02	351.48	443.49
桂林市	Guilin	134.17	178.21	230.48	294.63	373.77	453.51	558.81	882.89
梧州市	Wuzhou	50.02	64.53	81.26	100.11	123.22	153.78	192.68	240.33
北海市	Beihai	67.17	86.07	110.17	137.28	173.11	219.74	284.34	364.52
防城港市	Fangchenggang	27.89	38.73	50.36	61.79	76.73	97.40	125.37	164.83
钦州市	Qinzhou	27.04	40.03	51.02	60.99	75.67	101.12	172.02	252.68
贵港市	Guigang	34.53	48.59	65.66	85.88	107.53	135.62	176.79	235.16
玉林市	Yulin	49.55	66.95	88.21	115.83	147.53	196.44	277.74	415.49
百色市	Baise	56.64	73.23	95.08	121.84	156.01	200.02	259.59	334.46
贺州市	Hezhou	34.87	50.62	67.77	96.05	124.96	162.44	208.38	262.84
河池市	Hechi	43.32	58.41	88.97	111.81	144.39	179.60	230.51	297.22
来宾市	Laibin	15.86	32.88	41.52	50.15	70.59	101.18	133.12	180.23
崇左市	Chongzuo	33.66	46.79	60.64	73.05	93.66	124.59	173.58	234.67

17－12 各市旅游总消费
Total Tourist Consumption by City

单位：亿元 (100 million yuan)

城　市	City	2010	2011	2012	2013	2014	2015	2016	2017
南宁市	Nanning	238.57	312.40	403.89	478.15	608.79	742.53	918.67	1127.35
柳州市	Liuzhou	90.42	119.73	153.67	185.92	233.14	285.48	356.77	449.88
桂林市	Guilin	168.30	218.34	276.87	348.48	432.07	517.33	637.30	971.76
梧州市	Wuzhou	51.58	66.82	83.93	103.61	127.24	158.11	197.69	245.75
北海市	Beihai	68.64	87.74	112.34	139.94	176.03	222.86	288.04	368.62
防城港市	Fangchenggang	29.07	40.48	52.62	64.51	79.75	100.64	129.23	169.10
钦州市	Qinzhou	27.60	40.76	51.86	61.92	76.75	102.31	173.64	254.55
贵港市	Guigang	35.34	49.73	67.03	87.52	109.41	137.64	179.16	237.85
玉林市	Yulin	50.54	68.08	89.67	117.86	150.12	199.32	281.55	419.62
百色市	Baise	57.37	74.23	96.31	123.30	157.66	201.82	261.79	336.88
贺州市	Hezhou	37.71	54.73	72.59	101.89	131.59	169.80	217.37	272.62
河池市	Hechi	44.10	59.42	90.23	113.40	146.57	182.16	233.58	300.62
来宾市	Laibin	16.10	33.19	41.90	50.59	71.09	101.74	133.79	180.97
崇左市	Chongzuo	37.62	52.16	66.81	80.06	100.95	132.45	182.79	244.79

17－13　广西国家A级旅游景区一览表（2017年）
Schedule of National A-Grade Scenic Spots in Guangxi（2017）

类　别 Classification	风景名胜区名称	Name	所在地	Location
AAAAA	桂林漓江景区	Lijiang River Scenic Spot	桂林市	Guilin
	桂林乐满地休闲世界	Lemandi World for Leisure of Guilin		
	桂林独秀峰—王城景区	Guilin Duxiu Peak & Imperial City Scenic Zone		
	桂林两江四湖·象山景区	Two Rivers & Four Lakes Scenic Spot of Guilin , Xiangshan Scenic Spot		
	南宁青秀山风景旅游区	Qingxiu Mountain Scenic Spot of Nanning	南宁市	Nanning
AAAA	南宁嘉和城景区	Jiahe Town Scenic Spot of Nanning	南宁市	Nanning
	南宁九曲湾温泉景区	Jiuquwan Hotspring Scenic Spot of Nanning		
	广西八桂田园	Bagui Fields and Gardens of Guangxi		
	南宁市动物园	Nanning Zoo		
	广西药用植物园	Guangxi Medicinal Botanical Garden		
	南宁大明山风景旅游区	Damingshan Mountain Scenic Spot of Nanning		
	广西科技馆	Guangxi Science & Technology Museum		
	广西民族博物馆	Guangxi Ethnographical Museum		
	南宁市乡村大世界景区	World of Countryside of Nanning		
	南宁市武鸣县伊岭岩景区	Yilingyan Rock Scenic Spot of Wuming in Nanning		
	南宁市良凤江森林景区	Liangfengjiang Forest Tourist Area of Nanning		
	广西规划馆景区	Guangxi Capital Exhibition		
	南宁市民歌湖景区	Minge Lake of Nanning		
	隆安县龙虎山旅游景区	Longhu Hill Scenic Spot of Long’an County		
	南宁市凤岭儿童公园	Fengling Children’s Park of Nanning		
	南宁马山金伦洞景区	Jinlun Cave Scenic Spot of Mashan County in Nanning		
	上林县金莲湖景区	Jinlian Lake Scenic Spot of Shanglin County		
	南宁市人民公园	People's Park in Nanning City		
	南宁花花大世界景区	Huahua Flower World in Nanning City		
	南宁昆仑关旅游风景区	Kunlun Pass Scenic Spot of Nanning		
	南宁上林县大龙湖景区	Dalong Cave Scenic Spot of Shanglin County in Nanning		
	九龙瀑布景区	Jiulong Waterfall Scenic Spot		
	水锦·顺庄	Shuijin Shunzhuang Scenic Spot		
	龙门水都景区	Longmen water translation scenic spot		
	柳州龙潭景区	Longtan Scenic Spot of Liuzhou	柳州市	Liuzhou
	柳侯公园	Liuhou Park		
	柳州市鱼峰风景区	Liyu Hill Scenic Spot of Liuzhou		
	三江程阳侗族八寨景区	Dong Bazhai Scenic Spot of Sanjiang Chengyang		
	柳州博物馆	Liuzhou Museum		
	广西鹿寨香桥岩风景区	Xiangqiao Rock Scenic Spot of Luzhai County in Guangxi		
	柳州市三江县丹洲景区	Danzhou Scenic Spot of Sanjiang County in Liuzhou		
	柳州文庙景区	Confucian Temple Scenic Spot of Liuzhou		
	柳州城市规划展览馆	Liuzhou Urban Planning Exhibition Hall		

17－13 续表1 continued

类 别 Classification	风景名胜区名称	Name	所在地	Location
AAAA	柳州市马鹿山奇石博览园景区	Malu Hill Stones Exposition Garden of Liuzhou	柳州市	Liuzhou
	柳州市三江县大侗寨景区	Dadongzhai Scenic Spot in Sanjiang County of Liuzhou		
	柳州市工业博物馆景区	Industrial Museum Scenic Spot of Liuzhou		
	柳州市百里柳江旅游景区	Liujiang River Scenic Spot of Liuzhou		
	柳州园博园景区	Liuzhou Garden Expro Scenic Spot		
	柳州市融安石门仙湖旅游景区	Liuzhou Rongan Xianhu Shimen Tourist Attractions		
	柳州柳城县知青城景区	Zhiqing Town Scenic Spot of Liucheng County in Liuzhou		
	柳州市都乐岩景区	Dule Cave Scenic Spot in Liuzhou		
	柳州市融水元宝山龙女沟景区	Longnv Ravine Scenic Spot of Yuanbao Mountain of Rongshui County in Liuzhou		
	柳江县凤凰河生态旅游度假区	Fenghuang River Original Scenic Spot of Liujiang County		
	柳州市动物园	The Liuzhou City Zoo		
	柳州融水·民族体育公园	Folk Sports Park of Rongshui County in Liuzhou		
	柳州市雀儿山公园景区	Que'er Moutain Residential District		
	柳州市融水县老君洞景区	Rongshui Laojun Hole		
	七星景区	Qixing Scenic Spot	桂林市	Guilin
	芦笛景区	Ludi Scenic Spot		
	桂林世外桃源旅游区	Shiwaitaoyuan Scenic Spot of Guilin		
	桂林冠岩景区	Guanyan Rock Scenic Spot of Guilin		
	桂林愚自乐园艺术园	Art Garden in Yuzi Fairyland of Guilin		
	桂林银子岩旅游度假区	Yinzi Rock Scenic Spot of Guilin		
	桂林古东瀑布景区	Gudong Waterfall Scenic Spot of Guilin		
	兴安灵渠景区	Lingqu Scenic Spot of Xing'an County		
	桂林丰鱼岩旅游度假区	Fengyu Rock Scenic Spot of Guilin		
	桂林龙胜温泉旅游度假区	Longsheng Hotspring Scenic Spot of Guilin		
	桂林穿山景区	Chuanshan Scenic Spot of Guilin		
	桂林尧山景区	Yaoshan Hill Scenic Spot of Guilin		
	荔浦荔江湾景区	Lijiang Bay Scenic Spot of Lipu		
	桂林义江缘景区	Yijiangyuan Scenic Spot of Guilin		
	阳朔图腾古道—聚龙潭景区	Totem Ancient Road & Julong Lake Scenic Spot of Yangshuo County		
	永福金钟山旅游度假区	Jinzhongshan Hill Scenic Spot of Yongfu County		
	龙胜龙脊梯田景区	Longji Rice Terrace Scenic Spot of Longsheng County		
	桂林市南溪山景区	Nanxishan Hill Scenic Spot of Guilin		
	桂林经典刘三姐大观园景区	Scenery Park of Liusanjie in Guilin		
	桂林阳朔县蝴蝶泉旅游景区	Butterfly Spring Scenic Spot in Yangshuo County of Guilin		
	桂林西山景区	Guilin Xishan Scenic Spot		
	桂林市逍遥湖景区	Xiaoyao Lake Scenic Spot in Guilin		
	桂林罗山湖玛雅水上乐园景区	Maya Water World of Luoshan Lake in Liuzhou		
	桂林市猫儿山景区	Mao'er Moutain Scenic Spot of Guilin City		
	阳朔西街	Yang Shuo West Street		

17－13 续表2 continued

类 别 Classification	风景名胜区名称	Name	所在地	Location
AAAA	梧州骑楼城一龙母庙景区	City of Arcade-Longmu Temple Scenic Spot of Wuzhou	梧州市	Wuzhou
	藤县石表山休闲旅游景区	Shibiao Hill Scenic Spot of Tengxian		
	蒙山县永安王城景区	Yongan Ancient City Scenic Spot of Mengshan County		
	梧州苍海旅游区	Canghai Scenic Spot of Wuzhou		
	长坪水韵瑶寨景区			
	梁羽生公园	Liang Yusheng		
	梧州市军事体育文化园景区			
	梧州李济深故里文化旅游区			
	梧州天龙顶山地公园景区	Wuzhou Tianlong Peak National Moutain Area		
	北海银滩旅游区	Yintan Coast Scenic Spot of Beihai	北海市	Beihai
	北海海底世界	Submarine World of Beihai		
	北海海洋之窗	Oceanorama of Beihai		
	北海涠洲岛国家地质公园鳄鱼山景区	E'yushan Hill Scenic Spot of Weizhoudao Island National Geopark		
	北海市嘉和一冠山海景区	Jiahe-Guanshanhai Scenic Spot in Beihai		
	北海老城历史文化旅游区	Oldtown Historical & Cultural Tourism Area in Beihai		
	北海金海湾红树林生态旅游区	Jinhaiwan Mangrove Forest Scenic Spot in Beihai		
	北海园博园景区	Beihai Garden Expo Scenic Spot		
	北海汉闾文化园	Hanlv Cultural World in Beihai		
	涠洲岛圣堂景区	Shengtang Scenic Spot of Beihai		
	上思十万大山国家森林公园景区	Shiwandashan Mountain National Forest Park of Shangsi County	防城港市	Fangcheng-gang
	防城港东兴市京岛风景名胜区	Jingdao Island Scenic Spot of Dongxing City in Fangchenggang		
	东兴市屏峰雨林景区	Pingfeng Rainforest Scenic Spot of Dongxing City		
	防城港市江山半岛白浪滩旅游景区	Bailangtan Beach in Jiangshan Peninsula of Fangchenggang		
	防城港市西湾旅游区	Western Bay Tourism Area in Fangchenggang		
	上思县十万大山百鸟乐园景区	Shiwandashan Mountain Paradise of Birds of Shangsi County		
	钦州三娘湾景区	Sanniang Bay Scenic Spot of Qinzhou	钦州市	Qinzhou
	钦州刘冯故居景区	Former Residence of Liuyongfu & Fengzicai Scenic Spot of Qinzhou		
	钦州八寨沟旅游景区	Bazhai Ravine Scenic Spot of Qinzhou		
	钦州市浦北县五皇山景区	Wuhuang Hill Scenic Spot of Pubei County in Qinzhou		
	钦州园博园景区	Qinzhou Garden Expo Park		
	钦州市灵山县六峰山风景名胜区	Liufeng Hill Scenic Spot of Lingshan in Qinzhou City		
	钦州市浦北县越州天湖景区			
	钦州市林湖森林公园	Linhu Forest Park of Qinzhou City		
	钦州市大芦古村文化生态旅游区	Dalu Ancient Village Culture Original Scenic Spot of Qinzhou City		
	桂平西山风景名胜区	Xishan Hill Scenic Spot of Guiping	贵港市	Guigang
	贵港市龙潭国家森林公园景区	Longtan National Forest Park of Guiping		
	桂平市太平天国金田起义地址景区	The Site of the Jintian Uprising of the Taiping Heavenly Kingdom of Guiping City		

17－13 续表3 continued

类别 Classification	风景名胜区名称	Name	所在地	Location
AAAA	兴业鹿峰山风景区	Lufeng Mountain Scenic Spot of Xingye	玉林市	Yulin
	陆川谢鲁温泉休闲景区	Xielu Hotspring Scenic Spot of Luchuan		
	广西五彩田园现代特色农业示范区	Wucaitianyuan Modern Featured Agricultrue Demonstration Distrct		
	广西玉林市大容山国家森林公园	DaRong Mountain National Forest Park in Yulin City		
	玉林云天文化城	Yuntian Folk Cultural World in Yulin City		
	玉林容州古城	Rongzhou Ancient City Scenic Spot of Yulin City		
	玉林容县都峤山风景区	Duqiao Mountain Scenic Spot of Rong County		
	铜石岭国际旅游度假区	Tongshiling Mountain International Scenic Spot		
	北流市会仙河公园			
	六万大山森林公园	Liuwandashan Moutain Forest Park		
	玉林容州·民国小镇			
	靖西通灵大峡谷景区	Tongling Canyon Scenic Spot of Jingxi	百色市	Baise
	百色乐业大石围天坑群景区	Leye Dashiwei Sky Hole Cluster Scenic Spot of Baise		
	百色起义纪念馆	Memorial of Baise Uprising		
	靖西古龙山峡谷群生态旅游景区	Gulong Mountain Canyon Cluster Natural Scenic Spot of Jingxi		
	百色大王岭景区	Dawang Hill Scenic Spot of Baise		
	凌云茶山金字塔景区	Pyramid of Tea Hill Scenic Spot of Lingyun County		
	百色市德保县吉星岩景区	Jixing Rock Scenic Spot in Debao County of Baise		
	百色市德保县红叶森林旅游景区	Red Leaves Forest Scenic Spot in Debao County of Baise		
	百色市平果黎明通天河旅游景区	Baise Pingguo Liming Tongtian River Scenic Area		
	百色市田阳聚之乐休闲农业景区	Baise Tianyang Poly Music Leisure Agriculture Area		
	百色田州古城	Tianzhou Ancient Town of Baise		
	百色西林县宫保府景区			
	百色靖西市鹅泉旅游景区	Baise Jingxi E'quan Spring Scenic Spot		
	贺州姑婆山旅游区	Gupo Mountain Scenic Spot in Hezhou City	贺州市	Hezhou
	昭平黄姚古镇风景名胜区	Huangyao Town Scenic Spot of Zhaoping		
	贺州市十八水原生态园景区	Shibashui Original Scenic Spot in Hezhou City		
	贺州市玉石林景区	Jade Stone Forest Scenic Spot of Hezhou City		
	昭平县南山茶海景区	Tea Garden of Nanshan of Zhaoping		
	昭平县黄姚花海景区	Flower Garden of Huangyao Town of Zhaoping		
	巴马盘阳河景区	Panyang River Scenic Spot of Bama County	河池市	Hechi
	巴马水晶宫景区	Crystal Palace Scenic Spot of Bama County		
	广西凤山国家地质公园景区	Fengshan National Geopark in Guangxi		
	河池市东兰红色旅游区	Red Tourism Area in Donglan County of Hechi		
	河池市宜州刘三姐故里旅游区	Liusanjie's Homeland Scenic Spot in Yizhou City of Hechi		
	河池天峨县龙滩大峡谷景区	Longtan Grand Canyon Scenic Spot of Tian'e County in Hechi		
	宜州市会仙山景区	Huixian Mountain Scenic Spot of Yizhou City		
	南丹县歌娅思谷·中国白裤瑶生态民俗风情园景区	Geyasigu Baiku Yao Original Folkcustom Scenic Spot of Nandan County		
	广西大化七百弄国家地质公园景区	Qibainong National Geopark in Dahua County		

17－13　续表4　continued

类　别 Classification	风景名胜区名称	Name	所在地	Location
AAAA	广西丹泉洞天酒文化旅游景区	Danquan Dongtian Liquor Cultrue Scenic Spot of Guangxi	河池市	Hechi
	河池宜州拉浪生态休闲区	Lalang Woodland Scenic Spot of Yizhou City		
	河池宜州怀远古镇景区	Huaiyuan Town Scenic Spot of Yizhou City		
	金秀莲花山旅游景区	Lianhua Mountain Scenic Spot of Jinxiu County	来宾市	Laibin
	来宾市象州古象旅游区	Guxiang Scenic Spot of Xiangzhou County in Laibin		
	来宾市金秀圣堂湖景区	Shengtang Lake Scenic Spot of Jinxiu County in Laibin		
	金秀县圣堂山景区	Shengtang Moutain Scenic Spot of Jinxiu County		
	金秀县山水瑶城景区	Shanshuiyaocheng Scenic Spot of Jinxiu County		
	忻城县薰衣草庄园景区	Lavender Villa Scenic Spot of Xincheng County		
	来宾金秀银杉森林公园	Silver Fir Park Scenic Spot of Jinxiu County in Laibin		
	大新德天跨国瀑布景区	Detian International Waterfall Scenic Spot of Daxin	崇左市	Chongzuo
	凭祥市友谊关景区	Youyiguan Scenic Spot of Pingxiang City		
	凭祥红木文博城景区	Rosewood Exposition of Pingxiang City		
	龙州县龙州起义纪念园景区	Memorial of Longzhou Uprising of Longzhou County		
	大新县明仕景区	Mingshi Scenic Spot of Daxin County		
	崇左市宁明县花山景区	Huashan Scenic Spot of Ningming County		
	崇左石景林・园博园	Shijinglin Garden Expo Park in Chongzuo		
	崇左大新德天・老木棉景区	Detian Laomumian Garden of Daxin County		
	大新龙宫仙境景区	Longgongxianjing Scenic Spot of Daxin County		
	龙州县小连城景区	Xiaoliancheng Scenic Spot of Longzhou County		
	龙州县左江景区	Zuojiang River Scenic Spot of Longzhou County		
	大新县安平仙河景区	Anping Xianhe scenic spot		
	广西派阳山森林公园	Paiyang Mountain Forest Park of Guangxi		
	扶绥县龙谷湾景区			
	左江斜塔景区			
AAA	南宁金花茶公园	Golden Camellia Park of Nanning	南宁市	Nanning
	横县西津湖景区	Xijin Lake Scenic Spot in Hengxian		
	宾阳蔡氏书香古宅群景区	Caishi Oldhouse Scenic Spot of Binyang		
	南宁市大王滩风景区	Dawang Beach Scenic Spot of Nanning		
	南宁市凤凰谷景区	Fenghuang Valley Scenic Spot of Nanning		
	南宁海底世界景区	Sea World Scenic Spot of Nanning		
	南宁金湖地王云顶观光旅游景区	Top Tour of Diwang Building of Nanning		
	宾阳县白鹤观旅游度假区	Baihe Taoist Temple Scenic Spot in Binyang County		
	南宁市华南城景区	Huanancheng Scenic Spot of Nanning		
	上林县鼓鸣寨养生旅游度假区	Guming Village Healthy Tourism Resort of Shanglin County		
	上林县禾田农耕文化园	Hetian Farming Culture Garden of Shanglin County		
	上林县霞客桃园壮乡旅游度假区	Xiaketaoyuan Zhuang Minority Village for Tourism of Shanglin County		
	南宁市江南区扬美古镇景区	Yangmei Ancient Town of Jiangnan District in Nanning City		
	横县中华茉莉园景区	Chinese Jasmine Garden of Hengxian County		
	青秀区花雨湖生态休闲旅游区	Huayu Lake Natural Scenic Spot of Qingxiu District		

17—13　续表5　continued

类　别 Classification	风景名胜区名称	Name	所在地	Location
AAA	上林县云里湖景区	Yunli Lake Scenic Spot of Shanglin County	南宁市	Nanning
	上林县万古茶园景区	Wangu Tea Garden Scenic Spot of Shanglin County		
	横县莲塘圣茶谷景区	Shengcha Tea Garden of Liantang in Hengxian County		
	兴宁区狮山公园	Shishan Park of Xingning District		
	向阳红农业庄园	Sunny Farm		
	那贵樱花园	Nagui Sakura Garden		
	海王科普馆	Neptunus Group's Science Museum		
	柳州花果山生态景区	Huaguo Mountain Natural Scenic Spot of Liuzhou	柳州市	Liuzhou
	三江石门冲景区	Shimenchong Scenic Spot of Sanjiang County		
	柳州市君武森林公园景区	Junwu Forest Park of Liuzhou City		
	鹿寨月岛湖景区	Yuedao Lake Scenic Spot of Luzhai County		
	融水雨卜苗寨景区	Yubu Miaotse Scenic Spot of Rongshui County		
	融水老子山景区	Laozi Hill Scenic Spot of Rongshui County		
	融水县田头苗寨景区	Tiantou Miaotse Scenic Spot of Rongshui County		
	柳城县红马山景区	Hongma Hill Scenic Spot in Liucheng County		
	柳州市万聚休闲农庄	Leisure Farm Wanju of Liuzhou City		
	三江县冠洞景区	Guandong Cave Scenic Spot in Sanjiang County		
	柳城古砦仫佬族乡民俗风情旅游区	Guzhai Mulam Folklore Scenic Spot of Liucheng County		
	柳州三江甜水寨旅游度假景区	Tianshuizhai Scenic Spot of Sanjiang County		
	融水县龙宝大峡谷景区	Longbao Canyon Scenic Spot of Rongshui County		
	融水县石上人家景区	Village-on-rock Scenic Spot of Rongshui County		
	三江县产口景区	Chankou Scenic Spot of Sanjiang County		
	三江县侗族博物馆	Museum of Dong Minority of Sanjiang County		
	鹿寨县中渡古镇景区	Zhongdu Ancient Town of Luzhai County		
	融安县沙子石岩生态旅游景区	Shazishi Cave Original Scenic Spot of Rong'an County		
	柳江县百朋镇下伦荷花景区	Xialun Lotus Garden of Baipeng Town of Liujiang County		
	融水田塘瑶寨景区	Tiantang Yao Minority Scenic Spot of Rongshui County		
	鹿寨拉沟乡五家景区	Wujia Scenic Spot of Lagou in Luzhai County		
	鹿寨县鹿鸣谷景区			
	桂林阳朔文化古迹山水园	Park of Cultural & Historic Site & Landscape of Yangshuo in Guilin	桂林市	Guilin
	桂林资江景区	Zijiang River Scenic Spot of Guilin		
	临桂十二滩漂流景区	Twelve Beach Drift Scenic Spot of lingui		
	阳朔鉴山寺景区	Jianshan Temple Scenic Spot of Yangshuo		
	阳朔九马画山景区	Nine horses Paint Mountain Scenic Spot of Yangshuo		
	荔浦天河瀑布景区	Tianhe Waterfall Scenic Spot of Lipu County		
	灵川龙门瀑布景区	Longmen Waterfall County Scenic Spot of Lingchuan County		
	平乐仙家温泉景区	Xianjia Hotspring Scenic Spot of Pingle County		
	资源县八角寨景区	Bajiaozhai Scenic Spot in Ziyuan County		
	恭城县红岩景区	Hongyan Scenic Spot in Gongcheng County		
	恭城县三庙一馆景区	Three Temples & Guild Hall Scenic Spot in Gongcheng County		

17—13 续表6 continued

类 别 Classification	风景名胜区名称	Name	所在地	Location
AAA	桂林多耶古寨-蛇王李景区	Guilin ? Village-Snake King Li Scenic Spot	桂林市	Guilin
	灵川县江头景区	Jiang Tou Lingchuan County Area		
	桂林兴安县红军长征突破湘江战役纪念公园	Memorial Park for the Battle of the Red Army Breaking Through the Xiangjiang River of Xing'an County		
	桂林旅苑景区	Lvyuan Scenic Spot of Guilin		
	桂林芦笛岩鸡血玉文化艺术中心景区	Jixue Jade Culture & Art Centro of Ludi Cavc in Guilin		
	桂林全州县湘山寺景区	Xiangshan Temple Scenic Spot of Quanzhou County		
	龙胜县白面瑶寨景区	Baimian Yao Minority Scenic Spot of Longsheng County		
	龙胜艺江南中国红玉文化园景区	Yijiangnan Chinese Red Jade Cultural Garde of Longsheng County		
	龙胜县龙脊特色旅游小镇景区	Longji Featured Tourism Town of Longsheng County		
	龙胜县金车生态民族村景区	Jinche Original Minority Village of Longsheng County		
	桂林崇华中医街	Chonghua Chinese Medicine Street in Guilin		
	全州县炎井温泉	Yanjing Hotspring Scenic Spot of Quanzhou County		
	桂林市神龙水世界景区	ShenLong Water Paradise Resort		
	万福广场·休闲旅游城			
	荔浦县马岭鼓寨民族风情园			
	荔浦县柘村景区 (橘子红了乡村旅游区)	Ripe Tangerines Rural Tourism Area		
	荔浦县鹅翎寺景区	Goose Quill Temple		
	资源县宝鼎景区			
	资江灯谷景区			
	塘洞景区			
	藤县黎寨蝴蝶谷景区	Lizhai Butterfly Valley of Tengxian County	梧州市	Wuzhou
	梧州市珠山景区	Zhushan Hill Scenic Spot of Wuzhou		
	梧州市中山公园	Zhongshan Park of Wuzhou		
	白云山公园	Baiyun Hill Park of Wuzhou		
	夏宜醉美瑶乡	Zzuimei Yao Minority Village of Xiayi in Wuzhou		
	西炮台公园	Xipaotai Park of Wuzhou City		
	石燕山			
	古皮橙柿亲情谷			
	东乡积翠景区			
	羽生谷休闲养生基地			
	天书侠谷			
	蒙山县丝绸工业旅游景区			
	六堡茶生态旅游景区			
	岑溪市博物馆·东山公园			
	北海大江埠民俗风情村	Dajiangbu Folk Custom Village in BeiHai	北海市	Beihai
	北海贝雕博物馆	Museum of Shell Carving in Beihai City		
	北海南珠博物馆	Museum of Nanzhu Pearl in Beihai City		
	槐园景区	Huaiyuan Garden Scenic Spot in Beihai City		
	合浦县东坡亭景区	Dongpo Pavilion Scenic Spot of Hepu County		

17—13 续表7 continued

类 别 Classification	风景名胜区名称	Name	所在地	Location
AAA	合浦县古海角景区	Guhaijiao Scenic Spot of Hepu County	北海市	Beihai
	合浦县观音山生态旅游区	Guanyin Mountain Eco-tourism Area of Hepu County		
	合浦县曲樟客家土围城	Quzhang Hakkas Clay Castle		
	合浦县永安大士阁景区	Yongan Dashi Pavilion Scenic Spot		
	合浦县梦唤滨海体育文化园	Dreamlike Coastal Sports Culture Park		
	合浦县东园家酒产业园	Dongyuanjia Wine Industry Park		
	合浦县四方岭考古遗址景区	Sifangling Archaeological Site		
	涠洲岛石螺口景区	Shiluokou Scenic Spot		
	涠洲岛城仔景区	Chengzai Scenic Spot		
	涠洲岛滴水丹屏景区	Dishui Danping Scenic Spot		
	涠洲岛湿地公园景区	Wetland Park		
	东兴陈公馆景区	Chen Mansion Scenic Spot of Dongxing	防城港市	Fangcheng-gang
	防城港市北仑河源头景区	The Headstream of Beilun River Scenic Spot in Fangchenggang		
	东兴市意景园旅游景区	Yijingyuan Garden Scenic Spot in Dongxing City		
	东兴市百业东兴.红木社区旅游购物景区	Baiyedongxing Rosewood Tourism & Shopping Area of Dongxing City		
	东兴市北仑河口景区	Beilun River Scenic Spot in Dongxing City		
	钦州龙门群岛海上生态公园	Longmen Archipelago Natural Ocean Park of Qinzhou	钦州市	Qinzhou
	钦州市浦北县文昌景区	Wenchang Scenic Spot of Pubei County in Qinzhou		
	钦州市浦北县大朗书院景区	Dalang Ancient College of Pubei County in Qinzhou		
	钦州坭兴陶艺术馆	Nixing Pottery Art Gallery Scenic Spot of Qinzhou		
	钦州市火龙果农业文化休闲园	Huolongguo Farming Culture Scenic Spot in Qinzhou City		
	钦州市登峰陶艺馆	Dengfeng Pottery Art Gallery in Qinzhou City		
	广西钦州保税港区国际商品直销中心旅游景区	International Merchandise Outlet of Bonded Port Area in Qinzhou City		
	钦州市白石湖景区	Baishi Lake Scenic Spot in Qinzhou City		
	钦州市钦北区碗窑梨花谷景区	Wanyao Pear Valley Scenic Spot of Qinbei District in Qinzhou City		
	广西钦州市浦北县公猪脊景区	Gongzhuji Scenic Spot of Pubei County in Qinzhou City		
	钦州长融水世界旅游景区	Changrong Water Park of Qinzhou City		
	钦州市欢乐农庄旅游景区	Paradise Country Scenic Spot of Qinzhou City		
	钦州学院滨海校区景区	Binhai Campus Scenic Spot of Qinzhou University		
	钦州市灵山桂味生态园			
	钦州市那雾山森林公园			
	中国广西东盟商贸城	China Guangxi Asean Trade City		
	钦州市千年古陶城景区	Qinzhou Millennium Ancient City		
	贵港市平天山国家森林公园	Pingtian Moutain National Forest Park in Guigang City	贵港市	Gugang
	平南县龚州公园	Gongzhou Park of Pingnan County		
	桂平市大藤峡景区	Dateng Canyon Scenic Spot of Guiping City		
	桂平市北回归线标志公园	Park of the Sign of the Tropic of Cancer of Guiping City		
	桂平市中山公园	Zhongshan Park of Guiping City		
	桂平市革命烈士纪念碑公园	Guiping Revolutionary Martyrs Monument Park		

17－13 续表8 continued

类 别 Classification	风景名胜区名称	Name	所在地	Location
AAA	桂平市滨江文化公园	Guiping Riverside Cultural park	贵港市	Gugang
	桂平市东塔景区	Guiping East Tower Spot		
	桂平市罗丛岩景区	Guiping Luocong Rock Spot		
	九凌湖旅游风景区	Jiuling Lake Tourism Resort		
	北流勾漏洞景区	Goulou Hole Scenic Spot of Beiliu	玉林市	Yulin
	陆川龙珠湖风景名胜区	Longzhu Lake Scenic Spot of Luchuan County		
	玉林市龟山公园景区	Guishan Hill Scenic Spot of Yulin		
	玉林市容县天堂湖温泉度假山庄景区	Tiantanghu Hotspring Holiday Village of Rongxian County in Yulin		
	玉林市狮子山公园景区	Shizi Hill Park of Yulin		
	容县抗日烈士纪念馆	Memorial Hall for Anti-Japanese Martyrs of Rongxian County		
	北流市扶新佰仁生态旅游风景区	Fuxinbairen Original Scenic Spot of Beiliu City		
	容县兰花生态园	Orchid Eco-park of Rongxian County		
	黄绍竑故居	Huang Shaohong's Former Residence		
	南方黑芝麻博物馆	Museum of Nanfang Black Sesame		
	容县沙田柚王国	Plantation of Shatian Pomelo in Rongxian County		
	都峤山森林公园	Duqiao Moutain Forest Park		
	绿碧山风景区	Lvbi Moutain Scenic Spot		
	北流市城西公园			
	北流市梧村狮峰生态旅游区			
	北流市陶瓷名城			
	北流市陶瓷小镇			
	北流市九龙湾生态旅游度假区			
	北流市容心谷生态旅游度假区			
	北流市金斗岭生态旅游度假区			
	博白县宴石山风景区			
	田东十里莲塘景区	Shili Lotus Scenic Spot of Tiandong	百色市	Baise
	凌云县泗城文庙景区	Sicheng Literature Temple of Lingyun County		
	田东县右江工农民主政府旧址景区	The Site of Youjiang Former Workers & Peasants Democratic Government of Tiandong County		
	凌云县纳灵河谷景区	Naling Valley of Lingyun County		
	百色乐业罗妹莲花洞景区	Luomei Lotus Cave Scenic Spot in Leye County of Baise		
	靖西市龙潭湿地公园景区	Longtan Lake Wetland Park of Jingxi City		
	田阳县敢壮山布洛陀遗址景区	The Site of Buluotuo on Ganzhuang Mountain of Tianyang County		
	靖西市渠洋湖景区	Quyang River Scenic Spot of Jingxi City		
	百色乐业布柳河仙人桥景区	Xianren Bridge over the Buliu River of Leye County in Baise		
	靖西市岜蒙福峒山生态旅游景区			
	乐业县红七红八军纪念馆景区			
	乐业县龙云山故事小镇景区			

17—13 续表9 continued

类 别 Classification	风景名胜区名称	Name	所在地	Location
AAA	贺州紫云景区	Ziyun Scenic Spot of Hezhou	贺州市	Hezhou
	贺州市贺州博学园景区	Boxue Park Scenic Spot of Hezhou		
	昭平县桂江生态旅游景区	Guijiang River Original Scenic Spot of Zhaoping County		
	贺州八步区西溪森林温泉度假村	Xixi Stream Forest & Hotspring Holiday Village of Babu District		
	昭平县故乡茶博园景区	Homeland Tea Expo Garden of Zhaoping County		
	昭平县黄姚世外田园景区	Paradise Garden of Huangyao Town of Zhaoping County		
	贺州市博物馆	Museum of Hezhou City		
	客家围屋	Scenic Spot of Hakka Buildings		
	广西省工委历史博物馆景区			
	走马观画无边际景区	Zouma View Painting No Boundary Tourist Center		
	南丹温泉公园	Hotspring Park of Nandan	河池市	Hechi
	河池市天峨县龙滩水电站景区	Longtan Hydroelectric Station of Tian'e County		
	南丹白裤瑶生态博物馆	Eco-museum of Baiku Yao in Nandan County		
	金城江小三峡旅游景区	Xiaosanxia Scenic Spot of Jinchengjiang		
	南丹县铜江公园景区	Tongjiang River Scenic Spot in Nandan County		
	河池市金城江公园	Jinchengjiang Park in Hechi City		
	河池市环江县牛角寨瀑布群景区	Niujiaozhai Waterfalls Scenic Spot of Huanjiang County		
	河池市巴马长寿岛景区	Changshou Island Scenic Spot of Bama County		
	河池市巴马仁寿源景区	Renshouyuan Scenic Spot of Bama County		
	河池宜州市古龙河漂流景区	Gulong River Rafting Scenic Spot of Yizhou district		
	罗城县成龙湖公园景区	Chenglong Lake Park of Luocheng County		
	天峨县大山原始森林景区	Dashan Primeval Forest Scenic Spot of Tian'e County		
	巴马县西山红色旅游区	Western Hill Red Tourism Scenic Spot of Bama Coutny		
	宜州嘉联丝绸工业园	Jialian Silk Industry Park of Yizhou district		
	巴马活泉水文化景区	Huoquan Spring Cultural Scenic Spot of Bama Coutny		
	都安密洛陀文化公园			
	武宣百崖大峡谷景区	Baiya Canyon Scenic Spot of Wuxuan	来宾市	Laibin
	忻城莫土司衙署景区	Ancient Government Office of Mo Tusi of Xincheng County		
	忻城县盘鹤岭森林公园	Panhe Mountain Forest Park of Xincheng County		
	金秀县青山瀑布景区	Qingshan Waterfall Scenic Spot of Jinxiu County		
	金秀县古沙沟景区	Gusha Gully Scenic Spot of Jinxiu County		
	来宾市桂中水城盘古公园	Pangu Park of Waters in Mid-Guangxi in Laibin City		
	忻城县神秘湖景区	Mysterious Lake Scenic Spot of Xincheng County		
	合山市国家矿山公园	National Mine Park of Heshan City		
	合山28号铁轨·十里花廊景区	The No.28 Railroad Scenic Spot of Heshan City		
	兴宾区红河红景区			
	象州县象郡文化公园			

17—13 续表10 continued

类 别 Classification	风景名胜区名称	Name	所在地	Location
AAA	武宣县下莲塘景区		来宾市	Laibin
	忻城县蓝莓生态园			
	合山市红河公园景区			
	合山市奇石文化公园	Strange Stones Gallery of Heshan City		
	扶绥县逐羊景区	Zhuyang Scenic Spot in Fusui County	崇左市	Chongzuo
	凭祥市金鸡山景区	Jinji Hill Scenic Spot of Pingxiang City		
	凭祥市大连城景区	Daliancheng Defense Scenic Spot of Pingxiang City		
	凭祥市兰花谷景区	Park of Orchids Valley of Pingxiang City		
	凭祥市浦寨文化旅游不夜城景区	The Never-Sleep-City Cultural Scenic Spot of Puzhai Town of Pingxiang City		
	凭祥市平岗岭地下长城景区	Pinggangling Greatwall Underground Scenic Spot of Pingxiang City		
	凭祥市世界珍稀林木生态园景区	The World's Rare Trees Original Scenic Spot of Pingxiang City		
	江洲区雨花石景区	Yuhuashi Scenic Spot of Jiangzhou District in Chongzuo		
	大新县小灵珑景区	Xiaolinglong Scenic Spot of Daxin County		
	大新县凤凰岭景区	Fenghuang Valley Scenic Spot of Daxin County		
	江州区如意岛景区	Ruyi Island Scenic Spot of Jiangzhou District in Chongzuo		
	扶绥甜蜜之光旅游景区	Tianmizhiguang Agricultural Park of Fusui County		
	扶绥县炎鑫景区	Yanxin Scenic Spot of Fusui County		
	龙州县胡志明展馆景区	Ho Chi Minh Memorial Site of Longzhou County		
	狮子头森林公园	Shizitou Forest Park		
	崇左市壮族博物馆	Chongzuo Museum of Zhuang Ethnic Group		
	龙州县业秀园景区			
	龙州（水陇－甫茶）红军路景区			
	龙州县独山景区			
AA	防城港火山岛景区	Volcano Island Scenic Spot of Fangchenggang	防城港市	Fangcheng-gang
	钦州市北部湾坭兴玉陶景区	The Nixing Potery Scenic Spot of Beibu Gulf in Qinzhou	钦州市	Qinzhou
	钦州市灵山县锦泉生态旅游度假村	Jinquan Original Holiday Village of Lingshan County in Qinzhou City		
	玉林市欢天喜地园艺乐园	Huantianxidi Gardening Paradise in Yulin	玉林市	Yulin
	罗城青明山庄园景区	Qingming Villa Scenic Spot of Luocheng County	河池市	Hechi
	罗城县武阳江景区	WuYang River Scenic Spot of Luocheng County		
	大化莲花山景区	Lianhua Mountain Scenic Spot of Dahua County		
	河池市都安县石头开花景区	Jianjiang River Scenic Spot of Luocheng County		
	河池市罗城县剑江景区	Jianjiang River Scenic Spot of Luocheng County		
	都安县八仙乐园景区	Baxian Fairyland Scenic Spot of Du'an County		
	象州县凉泉景区	Liangquan Scenic Spot of Xiangzhou County	来宾市	Laibin
	来宾市金海公园	Jinhai Park in Laibin		
	桂中第一支部	The 1st Party Branch of Mid Guangxi		
	广西武宣县文庙景区	The Confucian Temple of Wuxuan County in Guangxi		

主要统计指标解释（旅游）

游客 指任何为休闲、娱乐、观光、度假、探亲访友、就医疗养、购物、参加会议或从事经济、文化、体育、宗教活动，离开常住国（或常住地）到其他国家（或地区），其连续停留时间不超过12个月，并且在其他国家（或其他地区）的主要目的不是通过所从事的活动获取报酬的人。游客不包括因工作或学习在两地有规律往返的人，按出游地分国际游客（即海外游客）和国内游客，按出游时间分为过夜游客和一日游游客。

入境游客 指报告期内来中国（大陆）观光、度假、探亲访友、就医疗养、购物、参加会议或从事经济、文化、体育、宗教活动的外国人、港澳台同胞等游客（即入境旅游人数）。统计时，入境游客按每入境一次统计1人次。入境游客包括入境过夜游客和入境一日游游客。

国内游客 指报告期内在中国（大陆）观光游览、度假、探亲访友、就医疗养、购物、参加会议或从事经济、文化、体育、宗教活动的中国（大陆）居民，其出游的目的不是通过所从事的活动谋取报酬。统计时，国内游客按每出游一次统计1人次。国内游客包括国内过夜旅游者和国内一日游游客。

旅游消费 游客（入境游客和国内游客）在旅游过程中（由游客或游客的代表为游客）支付的一切支出就是国内（省、市、区）的旅游消费。旅游支出应包括过夜游客和一日游游客在整个游程中行、游、住、食、购、娱，以及为亲友、家人购买纪念品、礼品等方面的旅游支出，不包括为商业的购物、购买房、地、车船等资本性或交易性的投资、馈赠亲友的现金及给公共机构的捐赠。旅游消费包括国际旅游（外汇）消费和国内旅游消费。

国际旅游（外汇）消费 入境游客在中国（大陆）境内旅行、游览过程中用于交通、参观游览、住宿、餐饮、购物、娱乐等全部花费。

国内旅游消费 指国内游客在国内旅行、游览过程中用于交通、参观游览、住宿、餐饮、购物、娱乐等全部花费。

Explanatory Notes on Main Statistical Indicators

Tourists refers to the persons leaving their resident countries (or resident districts) for other countries (or districts) for the purposes of leisure, entertainment, sight-seeing, vacation, visiting relatives or friends, medical treatment, shopping, attending conference, or to engage in economic, cultural, sports and religious activities, continuously staying for less than 12 months, and not having the main purpose of being paid by their activities. Tourists excludes the persons regularly traveling round for studying or working, and is divided into overnight tourists and one-day tourists by the length of their visiting periods.

Number of Visitor Arrivals refers to the number of tourists of foreigners, Chinese compatriots from Hong Kong, Macao and Taiwan who come to China (mainland) within the reference period for sight-seeing, vacation, visiting relatives, medical treatment, shopping, attending conference, or to engage in economic, cultural, sports and religious activities. In compiling statistics, each time of visitor arrival is counted as one person-time. The number of visitor arrivals includes the number of overnight visitor arrivals and one-day visitor arrivals.

Number of Domestic Tourists refers to the number of Chinese (mainland) residents who travel within China (mainland) for sight-seeing, vacation, visiting relatives, medical treatment, shopping, attending conference, or to engage in economic, cultural, sports and religious activities. In compiling statistics, each time of traveling is counted as one person-time.

Number of Chinese Residents Going Abroad refers to the number of Chinese (mainland) residents going to other countries, Hong Kong Special Administrative region, Macao Special Administrative region and Taiwan for on official or private purposes, for sight-seeing, vacation, visiting relatives, medical treatment, shopping, attending conference, or to engage in economic, cultural, sports and religious activities. In compiling statistics, each time of leaving is counted as one person-time.

Tourist Consumption refers to the total expenditure paid by tourists or delegates of tourists (visitor arrivals or domestic tourists) during their journeys. It should include the tourist (overnight or one-day) expenditure for transportation, visiting, accommodation, catering, shopping, entertainment, purchasing gifts and souvenirs for families and friends during the whole journey, and exclude shopping for business purposes, capital or trading investment for buying real estates, lands, motor vehicles and ships, cash given to relatives and friends, and donations for public institutions. Tourist income includes foreign exchange earnings from international tourism and income from domestic tourism.

International Tourist Expenditure refers to the total expenditure of foreigners, overseas Chinese, Chinese compatriots from Hong Kong, Macao and Taiwan during their stay in the mainland of China on transportation, sighting, accommodation, food, shopping and entertainment.

Domestic Tourist Expenditure refers to expenditure of domestic tourists on transportation, sighting, accommodation, food, shopping and entertainment while they travel.

第十八篇

交通、运输和邮电通信业

TRANSPORTATION,POSTAL & TELECOMMUNICATION SERVICES

（校对编辑：邓海梅）

18－1　主要年份民用车辆保有量
Possession of Civil Vehicles in Main Years

指　标	Item	1995	2000	2005	2010	2012	2013	2014	2015	2016	2017
一、汽车（万辆）	Civil Motor Vehicles (10 000 units)	24.90	29.13	63.54	155.73	231.03	279.81	322.36	366.52	427.34	504.33
#私人	Private	6.51	13.27	33.49	111.71	180.76	226.29	269.83	316.66	378.12	452.65
1. 载客汽车（万辆）	Number of Buses and Cars (100 000 units)	10.72	15.23	38.00	113.13	175.77	217.94	258.96	302.56	360.24	431.16
#私人	Private	1.89	6.03	21.07	88.01	146.94	187.31	229.08	274.28	332.77	402.74
载客量（万客位）	Passenger Vehicles Seats (10 000 sets)	111.16	192.57		793.31	1163.91	1404.28	1623.22	1861.34	2186.99	2583.88
大型（万辆）	Large (10 000 units)	1.30	1.70	2.45	3.22	3.53	3.53	3.37	3.33	3.44	3.62
#私人	Private	0.31	0.53	0.19	0.12	0.13	0.10	0.04	0.02	0.02	0.03
载客量（万客位）	Passenger Vehicles Seats (10 000sets)	48.02	68.60		125.95	143.47	147.12	145.45	144.86	152.07	161.81
轿车（万辆）				16.03	62.81	101.01	126.90	152.41	176.65	208.76	251.03
#私人				9.48	52.68	89.03	113.88	139.39	164.28	196.69	238.29
2. 载货汽车（万辆）	Ordinary Trucks (10 000 units)	13.07	13.16	19.48	36.82	49.20	55.74	57.73	58.71	62.13	68.45
#私人	Private	4.59	7.15	8.45	20.00	29.91	34.93	37.05	38.99	42.11	46.83
载重量（万吨位）	General Trucks (10 000 tons)	48.76	58.20		127.93	166.10	188.46	185.37	182.40	191.20	215.02
大（重）型（万辆）	Large (10 000 units)	8.93	7.38	9.36	8.97	11.79	13.45	13.55	13.51	14.43	16.75
#私人	Private	3.24	3.98	3.55	3.14	4.73	5.43	5.12	5.10	5.51	6.49
载重量（万吨位）	General Trucks (10 000 tons)	44.33	39.70		83.01	112.32	130.57	129.84	128.93	136.14	156.13
3. 其他汽车（万辆）	Other Special Motor Vehicles (10 000 units)	1.11	0.75	6.05	5.78	6.06	6.13	5.67	5.24	4.98	4.72
#私人	Private	0.04	0.09	3.97	3.69	3.91	4.05	3.70	3.40	3.24	3.08
二、拖拉机（万辆）	Wheel Tractor (10 000 units)	23.52	29.17	49.07	37.95	41.45	42.67	48.72	47.82	47.85	45.73
#私人	Private	22.61	28.37	49.79	37.95	41.45	42.67	48.72	47.82	47.85	45.73
手扶拖拉车（万辆）	Walking Tractor (10 000 units)	19.16	21.21		21.68	23.60					
#私人	Private	18.60	20.90		21.68	23.60					
三、摩托车（万辆）	Motorcycles (10 000 units)	45.69	160.15	433.80	638.52	693.17	700.64	692.80	671.96	561.20	654.33
#私人	Private	37.55	145.57	425.97	633.02	689.78	697.54	689.69	668.75	558.40	651.19
普通（万辆）	Motor Bikes (10 000 units)	37.45	145.50	414.12	633.40	688.42	695.64	688.33	667.73	558.73	650.63
#私人	Private	33.34	137.09	407.31	627.93	685.05	692.55	685.22	664.53	555.94	647.49
四、挂车（万辆）	Trailers (10 000 units)	0.91	0.45	0.89	1.46	2.03	2.39	2.73	2.92	3.36	4.19
#私人	Private	0.39	0.22	0.28	0.38	0.61	0.74	0.86	0.96	1.16	1.47
五、其他类型车（万辆）	Other Motor Vehicles (10 000 units)	1.09	3.40		0.02	0.01	0.01	0.01	0.01	0.01	—
#私人	Private	0.86	1.93		—	—	—	—	—	—	—

说明：根据2006年口径，2005年民用汽车拥有量及其中私人民用汽车拥有量数据已做调整，不再包含农机部门的三轮汽车和低速汽车。
Note: The number of Civil Motor Vehicles and Private Civil Motor Vehicles in 2005 have been adjusted according to the new standard in 2006, and exclude the motor pedicabs and low-speed motor vehicles belong to the Agricultual Machinery Department.

18－2　主要年份民用运输船舶拥有量
Possession of Civil Transport Vessels in Main Years

指　标	Item	1995	2000	2005	2010	2012	2013	2014	2015	2016	2017
一、机动船（艘）	**Ⅰ.Motor Vessels (unit)**	**12360**	**8472**	**8307**	**8800**	**8873**	**8658**	**9074**	**9000**	**8756**	**7964**
#私人	Private	6457	3978	3450	3493	3023	2590	3033	2877	2706	2536
载客量（客位）	Passenger Vehicles Seats (set)	93152	83676	89716	112138	111394	103685	114367	119982	117832	103656
净载重量（吨位）	Net Haulage Capacity (ton)	917539	849281	2036048	5140009	6811525	7426921	7727187	8197392	8902086	8832801
总功率（千瓦）	Total Power (kw)	491044	411586	674658	1485400	1831268	1970310	2013192	2084065	2138175	203181
1. 客船（艘）	1.Passenger Vessels (unit)	1379	1872	2269	2725	2611	2357	2525	2462	2297	2031
#私人	Private	998	1456	1684	2168	2010	1658	1966	1934	1814	1644
载客量（客位）	Passenger Vehicles Seats (set)	59758	74087	88283	110731	109987	101826	112508	118307	116157	101281
2. 客货船（艘）	2.Passenger and Cargo Vessels (unit)	1150	166	5	5	5	6	6	4	4	5
#私人	Private	1084	143	1							
载客量（客位）	Passenger Vehicles Seats (set)	33394	9589	1433	1407	1407	1859	1859	1675	1675	2375
净载重量（吨位）	Net Haulage Capacity (ton)	11912	2420		2555	2555	5099	5101	4041	4041	4526
3. 货船（艘）	3.Cargo Boat (unit)	9638	6403	6030	6060	6254	6293	6541	6532	6453	5928
#私人	Private	4367	2379	1765	1325	1013	932	1067	943	892	892
净载重量（吨位）	Net Haulage Capacity (ton)	905627	846861	2034599	5131300	6808970	7421822	7722086	8193351	8898045	8811052
4. 拖船（艘）	4.Drawing (unit)	193	31	3	3	3	2	2	2	2	
二、驳船（艘）	**Ⅱ.Barges (unit)**	**597**	**110**	**10**	**7**	**7**	**4**	**4**	**4**	**4**	**2**
净载重量（吨位）	Net Haulage Capacity (ton)	106289	32725	6740	6138	6138	3250	3250	3250	3250	1250

18－3　主要年份内河、沿海规模以上港口基本情况
Basic Statistics of Major Ports of Inland & Coast in Main Years

指　标	Item	码头长度（米） Length of Quay Lines (m)										
		1995	2000	2005	2010	2011	2012	2013	2014	2015	2016	2017
内　河	**Navigable Inland Waterways**				**17386**	**17616**	**20649**	**21358**	**23126**	**23451**	**24490**	**24338**
南宁港	Nanning Port	1115	2197	1643	3417	3319	4155	5044	5796	5796	5796	5796
柳州港	Liuzhou Port	350	1150	1056	751	981	1556	1556	1556	1556	1724	1892
梧州港	Wuzhou Port	1559	6376	4234	3970	4068	4586	4406	5120	5250	5250	4930
贵港港	Guigang Port	890	5150	5951	7083	7083	7311	7311	7613	7745	8529	8529
来宾港	Laibin Port				2165	2165	3041	3041	3041	3104	3191	3191
广西北部湾港	**Ports of Beibu Gulf in Guangxi**				**24868**	**27703**	**31191**	**31496**	**34097**	**35937**	**37197**	**37953**
其中：北海港域	Beihai Port	1210	1900	2504	5142	5142	6040	6040	6040	6739	7672	7672
防城港域	Fangchenggang Port	2371	3211	4080	12194	12194	13945	14223	14897	15260	15587	16343
钦州港域	Qinzhou Port	360	1730	3696	7532	10367	11206	11233	13160	13938	13938	13938

18－4 主要年份运输线路里程

Length of Transportation Routes in Main Years

单位：公里 (km)

指 标	Item	1995	2000	2005	2010	2012	2013	2014	2015	2016	2017
一、铁路营业里程	Extension Length of Central Railways	2473	3109	3097	3174	3164	3982	4711	5086	5141	5140
高铁里程	Extension Length of High-speed Rail	—	—	—	—	—	785	1482	1703	1751	1751
复线里程	Length of Double track Lines	179	408	482	455	456	1377	2163	2400	2434	2644
电气化里程	Length of Electric Lines				779	779	1622	2377	3066	3289	3374
二、铁路正线延展里程	Extensive Length of Railway Lines	2621	3349	3462	3675	3647	5367	5884	7501	7596	7809
三、公路里程	Length of Highways	40904	52910	62003	101782	107906	111384	114900	117993	120547	123259
#高速公路里程	Length of Expressway		812	1411	2574	2883	3305	3722	4288	4603	5259
四、内河航道通航里程	Length of Navigable Inland Waterways			5591	5591	5638	5634	5866	5873	5873	5873

注：1. 2006年度国家交通部将村道纳入公路里程统计范围。

2. 根据2016年口径调整了历年高铁里程。2010年起，铁路里程为广西境内路段。

Note: 1. The village road has been brought into the statistical range of Length of Highways by National Department of Transportation since 2006.

2. We recalculate the length of expressway according to the new standard in 2016.

18－5 主要年份规模以上港口货物吞吐量

Cargo Handled at Major Ports in Main Years

单位：万吨 (10 000 tons)

港口名称	Name of Ports	1995	2000	2005	2010	2011	2012	2013	2014	2015	2016	2017
规模以上港口货物吞吐量合计	**Total Volume of Cargo Handled in Ports above Designated Size**	**1717**	**2879**	**6877**	**18575**	**23335**	**26873**	**29276**	**31025**	**31421**	**32041**	**34449**
#内河港口	**Ports of Navigable Inland Waterways**	**998**	**1112**	**3208**	**6652**	**8004**	**9435**	**10603**	**10836**	**10939**	**11649**	**12586**
南宁港	Nanning Port	82	58	73	485	777	1070	1292	1150	1004	1312	1380
柳州港	Liuzhou Port	74	36	56	189	124	197	239	252	234	129	98
梧州港	Wuzhou Port	160	85	403	1601	2071	2608	3015	3142	3202	3385	3634
贵港港	Guigang Port	362	468	1507	3807	4108	4512	4900	5242	5334	5763	6322
来宾港	Laibin Port				569	924	1048	1157	1050	1166	1061	1152
广西北部湾港	**Ports of Beibu Gulf in Guangxi**	**719**	**1768**	**3669**	**11923**	**15331**	**17438**	**18673**	**20189**	**20482**	**20392**	**21862**
北海港域	Beihai Port	201	265	437	1251	1591	1757	2078	2276	2468	2750	3169
防城港域	Fangchenggang Port	464	919	2006	7650	9024	10058	10501	11501	11504	10688	10355
钦州港域	Qinzhou Port	9	140	511	3022	4716	5622	6035	6412	6510	6954	8338

18－6　全社会客运量及旅客周转量（1978－2017年）
Total Passenger Traffic & Turnover of Passenger Traffic（1978－2017）

年　份 Year	客运量（万人）Passenger Traffic (10 000 persons)	铁路 Railways	公路 Highways	水运 Waterways	民航 Civil Aviation
1978	6398	1368	4628	383	10
1980	9369	1869	7054	429	17
1985	20018	2456	16993	526	43
1990	26272	2391	22826	984	69
1991	24685	2346	21175	1089	75
1992	27262	2703	23189	1273	95
1993	39398	2980	33968	2344	106
1994	34274	3030	29954	1177	113
1995	34317	2819	30024	1192	283
1996	36066	2385	32582	805	294
1997	38343	2495	34752	802	294
1998	39670	2576	36006	786	302
1999	41009	2496	37412	779	322
2000	42952	2508	39321	766	357
2001	44451	2270	41020	755	373
2002	45868	2148	42459	850	410
2003	43595	1936	40524	785	350
2004	48870	1938	45578	861	439
2005	52197	2037	48740	883	536
2006	56635	2347	52609	1023	656
2007	61716	2578	57213	1119	806
2008	64745	2937	60645	340	823
2009	69740	2956	65045	302	1077
2010	76967	3163	72208	395	1201
2011	84431	3383	79300	417	1331
2012	91656	3310	86449	470	1427
2013	50846	3275	45606	394	1571
2014	49926	4770	42841	512	1803
2015	50986	7046	41522	533	1885
2016	50765	8388	39750	561	2066
2017	51056	9838	38083	657	2478

注：1. 2013年公路水路数为交通运输部《公路运输量统计试行方案（2014）》和《水路运输量统计试行方案（2014）》确认数。
2. 2015年公路水路数为交通运输部开展的小样本调查推算数，2014年数已按2015年1－12月累计增速作了相应调整。
3. 铁路数据口径调整：客运量2015年起由售票人数改为乘车人数，上年同期数相应调整。
4. 2013年按旧口径快报数为：总计97780，铁路3275，公路92378，水运556，民航1571。

Note: 1. The data on highways and waterways in 2013 is confirmed by Pilot Scheme of Highways Ttaffic Statistic (2014) and Pilot Scheme of Highways Ttaffic Statistic (2014) from Ministry of Transport.
2. The data of highways and waterways in 2015 comes from a small sample survey conducted by the Ministry of Transport, the data in 2014 has already adjusted by the cumulative growth in 2015.
3. The adjustment of statistical range about railways 2015 are: The data of "Passenger Traffic" refers to the number of passengers instead of tickets, data in the same period of last year as well.
4. The corresponding data in old statistical range 2013 is: Total 97780, Raiways 3275, Highways 92378, Waterways 556, Civil Aviation 1571.

18－6 续表 continued

年 份 Year	旅客周转量（亿人公里） Turnover of Passenger Traffic (100 million passenger-km)	铁路 Railways	公路 Highways	水运 Waterways	民航 Civil Aviation
1978	41.20	21.64	16.89	2.67	
1980	60.25	31.11	25.05	4.09	
1985	127.77	55.72	66.50	5.55	
1990	174.79	66.79	101.21	6.76	
1991	183.70	71.33	105.18	7.19	
1992	223.94	83.19	133.39	7.31	
1993	283.77	112.00	164.04	7.72	
1994	289.39	118.59	165.32	5.48	
1995	298.41	112.14	180.78	5.49	
1996	323.69	93.79	225.97	3.93	
1997	378.18	94.40	280.32	3.46	
1998	386.97	91.77	292.63	2.57	
1999	440.19	105.36	332.30	2.52	
2000	464.96	114.48	347.94	2.54	
2001	490.92	116.23	372.07	2.63	
2002	502.42	117.02	382.70	2.70	
2003	475.09	105.46	367.35	2.27	
2004	529.43	116.18	410.64	2.61	
2005	573.08	131.73	438.77	2.58	
2006	625.34	150.90	471.43	3.01	
2007	714.27	174.05	536.93	3.29	
2008	753.27	188.10	563.52	1.65	
2009	787.42	167.44	618.28	1.70	
2010	879.23	182.13	695.32	1.78	
2011	973.01	194.48	776.51	2.01	
2012	1047.98	187.72	857.98	2.28	
2013	611.32	193.67	415.73	1.92	
2014	670.05	236.96	430.60	2.48	
2015	731.75	318.22	410.82	2.71	
2016	743.83	351.08	390.05	2.70	
2017	777.57	403.87	370.38	3.32	

注：2013年按旧口径快报数为：总计1126.83，铁路193.67，公路930.63，水运2.53。

Note: The corresponding data in old statistical range 2013 is: Total 1126.83, Raiways 193.67, Highways 930.63, Waterways 2.53.

18－7　全社会货运量及货物周转量（1978－2017年）
Total Freight Traffic & Turnover of Freight Traffic（1978－2017）

年　份 Year	货运量（万吨） Freight Traffic (10 000 tons)	铁路 Railways	公路 Highways	水运 Waterways	民航 Civil Aviation
1978	5885	2118	2697	1070	
1980	4496	1833	1772	891	0.10
1985	12909	2224	9898	787	0.58
1990	19888	3798	14711	1338	0.50
1991	22469	3920	17146	1403	0.70
1992	23457	4167	17567	1666	0.90
1993	35509	4434	27723	3352	1.00
1994	28132	4920	20391	2820	1.00
1995	28622	5072	20686	2862	1.60
1996	29441	5166	22386	1887	1.70
1997	31473	5315	24349	1808	1.00
1998	32671	5364	25482	1823	1.80
1999	30862	5293	23720	1846	3.20
2000	31270	5843	23514	1910	3.38
2001	33267	6316	23747	2024	3.76
2002	33392	6636	24325	2423	7.64
2003	33457	6516	24164	2774	3.80
2004	37118	7860	25822	3432	4.20
2005	41025	8517	27861	4642	4.80
2006	45454	9374	30525	5549	5.60
2007	50152	10503	32920	6722	6.90
2008	84950	9861	64884	10198	6.80
2009	95076	9564	75766	9738	8.03
2010	113445	7052	93552	12832	9.49
2011	136143	6770	113549	15813	11.00
2012	161368	6846	135112	19398	12.24
2013	151155	6916	124677	19549	12.94
2014	137794	6687	108270	22824	13.30
2015	149727	5779	119194	24741	13.36
2016	160774	5898	128247	26615	14.11
2017	174656	6634	139602	28405	14.61

注：1. 2013年公路水路数为交通运输部《公路运输量统计试行方案（2014）》和《水路运输量统计试行方案（2014）》确认数。
2. 2015年公路水路数为交通运输部开展的小样本调查推算数，2014年数已按2015年1－12月累计增速作了相应调整。
3. 铁路数据口径调整：货运量2012年起增加了行包运量，但2012年度数据仍为原口径数据。
4. 2013年按旧口径的快报数为：总计179795，铁路6916，公路151841，水运21025，民航12.9。

Note: 1.The data on highways and wateways in 2013 is confirmed by Pilot Scheme of Highways Ttaffic Statistic (2014) and Pilot Scheme of Highways Traffic Statistic (2014) from Ministry of Transport.
2.The data of highways and waterways in 2015 comes from a small sample survey conducted by the Ministry of Transport, the data in 2014 has already adjusted by the cumulative growth in 2015.
3.The adjustment of statistical range about railways 2015 are: The data of "Freight Traffic" include the data of baggage and parcel volume since 2012, but annual data in 2012 remains the same.
4.The corresponding data in old statistical range 2013 is: Total 179795, Raiways 6916, Highways 151841, Waterways 21025, Civil Aviation 12.9.

18－7 续表 continued

年 份 Year	货物周转量（亿吨公里） Turnover of Freight Traffic (100 million ton-km)	铁路 Railways	公路 Highways	水运 Waterways	民航 Civil Aviation
1978	183.78	153.93	7.54	22.31	
1980	160.46	132.52	5.77	22.17	
1985	276.26	200.52	47.30	28.44	
1990	428.02	268.17	116.95	42.82	
1991	429.61	286.31	91.62	51.68	
1992	487.27	310.98	102.72	64.42	
1993	511.96	335.21	103.23	73.51	
1994	588.98	348.14	140.36	100.48	
1995	592.93	351.61	143.39	97.93	
1996	606.12	346.30	170.58	89.23	
1997	642.30	366.73	183.48	92.08	
1998	695.35	413.46	190.48	91.41	
1999	698.20	414.60	202.10	81.50	
2000	770.61	485.14	209.44	76.03	
2001	799.42	504.15	212.10	83.16	
2002	860.74	540.92	218.51	101.31	
2003	942.55	606.39	217.10	119.06	
2004	1095.66	713.35	235.62	146.69	
2005	1208.91	777.73	258.43	172.75	
2006	1338.95	846.02	286.85	206.08	
2007	1516.55	928.94	302.23	285.34	
2008	2210.23	912.86	799.96	497.41	
2009	2365.62	825.25	934.70	605.67	
2010	2926.77	891.33	1173.45	861.99	
2011	3478.23	895.38	1494.04	1088.81	
2012	4110.64	860.01	1878.29	1372.34	
2013	3856.37	809.43	1857.18	1189.76	
2014	3869.91	770.85	1902.70	1196.36	
2015	4061.82	674.53	2122.60	1264.69	
2016	4260.41	679.03	2248.46	1332.92	
2017	4613.32	709.68	2456.69	1446.95	

注：1. 2015年公路水路数为交通运输部开展的小样本调查推算数，2014年数已按2015年1－12月累计增速作了相应调整。

2. 2013年按旧口径的快报数为：总计4320.13，铁路809.43，公路2140.30，水运1370.36。

Note: 1. The data of highways and waterways in 2015 comes from a small sample survey conducted by the Ministry of Transport, the data in 2014 has already adjusted by the cumulative growth in 2015.

2. The corresponding data in old statistical range 2013 is: Total 4320.13, Raiways 809.43, Highways 2140.30, Waterways 1370.36.

18－8　公路线路长度（按等级分类，1978－2017年）
Total Length of Highways（Grouped by Class,1978－2017）

单位：公里　(km)

年份 Year	公路里程总计 Total Length of Highways	等级公路合计 Expressway & Class I to IV Highway	高速 Expressway	一级 Class Ⅰ	二级 Class Ⅱ	三级 Class Ⅲ	四级 Class Ⅳ	等外 Below Class Ⅳ	公路等级里程占总里程（%） Proportion of Expressway & Class I to IV Highway in Total Length of Highways(%)
1978	29773							14996	
1979	30692	13771			83	1341	12347	16921	44.87
1980	31624	14703			83	1348	13272	16921	46.49
1981	31823	14902			83	1373	13446	16921	46.83
1982	32156	15264			83	1465	13716	16892	47.47
1983	32529	15740			84	1531	14125	16789	48.39
1984	32757	16061			84	1531	14446	16696	49.03
1985	32972	16329			104	1633	14592	16643	49.52
1986	33222	16703			105	1670	14928	16519	50.28
1987	33928	17604			139	1763	15702	16324	51.89
1988	35400	19193			202	1803	17188	16207	54.22
1989	35945	19829			214	1875	17740	16116	55.16
1990	36214	20098		8	358	2031	17701	16116	55.50
1991	36660	20711		11	428	1919	18353	15949	56.49
1992	37291	21488		11	682	1917	18878	15803	57.62
1993	38495	22754		11	1035	1910	19798	15741	59.11
1994	39550	23890		48	1074	2017	20751	15660	60.40
1995	40904	25509		66	1330	2163	21950	15395	62.36
1996	42696	27375		66	1448	2222	23639	15321	64.12
1997	45378	30283	193	189	1670	2208	26023	15095	66.73
1998	51073	43319	439	389	2107	16741	23643	7754	84.82
1999	51378	43671	575	389	2319	16721	23667	7707	85.00
2000	52910	45430	812	442	2628	16620	24928	7480	85.86
2001	54752	40192	822	449	4316	5213	29392	14560	73.40
2002	56297	42155	822	449	4773	5348	30763	14142	74.86
2003	58451	45284	1011	482	5351	5611	32829	13167	77.47
2004	59704	47304	1157	514	5783	5337	34314	12400	79.23
2005	62003	51046	1411	546	6299	5813	36977	10957	82.33
2006	90318	52101	1545	705	6847	5589	37415	38216	57.69
2007	94202	62861	1879	733	7325	5625	47296	31340	66.73
2008	99273	73051	2181	818	8114	6311	55624	26221	73.58
2009	100491	77154	2395	827	8559	6889	58484	23337	76.78
2010	101782	81239	2574	876	8646	7942	61200	20543	79.82
2011	104889	87296	2754	944	9132	8261	66205	17592	83.23
2012	107906	91583	2883	984	9720	8320	69676	16322	84.87
2013	111384	96343	3305	1008	10392	8258	73380	15041	86.50
2014	114900	100647	3722	1026	10618	8334	76947	14252	87.60
2015	117993	105019	4288	1079	11147	8269	80236	12974	89.00
2016	120547	108947	4603	1372	11934	8016	83021	11600	90.38
2017	123259	112619	5259	1443	12714	8296	84907	10640	91.37

注：1. 从2001年起以第二次全国公路普查数据为调整基数。
2. 2006年度国家交通部将村道纳入公路里程统计范围，与往年数据不可比。

Note: 1. The data in the table have been readjusted basing on the data of the Second National Highway Census since 2001.
2. Since 2006, the Ministry of Transportation has broght the country roads under the statistical range of highway length, thus the data in 2006 is incomparable with the former years.

18－9 主要年份邮电通信水平

Level of Postal & Telecommunications Services in Main Years

指 标	Item	1995	2000	2005	2010	2011	2012	2013	2014	2015	2016	2017
平均每人每年发函件数（件）	Per Capita Annul Average Number of Letters (piece)	4.6	3.6	2.4	1.4	1.4	1.3	1.1	1.1	0.8	0.6	0.6
平均每人订有报刊数（件）	Annul Average Number of Newspapers & Magazines Per Capita Subscribed (piece)	13.1	9.5	4.0	6.2	7.4	7.8	8.0	8.1	8.2	7.9	7.7
平均每万人拥有电话机数（部）	Average Number of Telephone Subscribers per 10 000 Persons Owned (set)	234	1102	3853	6177	6880	7469	8152	8558	8572	8522	9607
设有邮电局、所乡（镇）比重（%）	Proportion of townships with Post & Telecommunication Office (%)	85.4	90.3	91.3	95.5	95.7	96.0	100.0	100.0	100.0	100.0	100.0
通电话的乡（镇）比重（%）	Proportion of townships with Telephone Communication (%)	96.8	100.0	100.0	100.0	100.0	100.0	100.0	100.0	100.0	100.0	100.0
按固定班期投递邮件的乡（镇）比重（%）	Proportion of townships with Delivery by Regularly Time (%)	98.2	99.9	98.7	100.0	100.0	100.0	100.0	100.0	100.0	100.0	100.0
通电话的行政村比重（%）	Proportion of Administrative Village with Telephone (%)		91.5	99.1	100.0	100.0	100.0	100.0	100.0	100.0	100.0	100.0
互联网宽带接入通达的行政村比重（%）	Proportion of Administrative V:Uage with Broadband internet (%)										98.1	99.4

注：1. 1995年以来的"平均每万人拥有电话机数"含移动电话用户。

2. 平均每人每年发函件数、平均每人每年订报刊数、平均每万人拥有电话机数等指标根据2004年和2005年实际情况做相应修改。

Note: 1. "Number of Telephone Subscribers per 10 000 persons owned" have included mobile telephones subscribers since 1995.

2. The data on "Per Capita Annul Average Number of Letters", "Annul Average Number of Newspapers & Magazines per Capita Subscribed" & "Average Number of Telephone Subscribers per 10 000 persons owned" was adjusted by practical situation in 2004 & 2005.

18－10 主要年份邮政和电信主要指标
Major Indicators of Postal & Telecommunications Services in Main Years

指 标	Item	2000	2005	2010	2014	2015	2016	2017
邮政行业各类营业网点	Number of Post & Telecommunication Offices (unit)	1674	1613	1518	3419	4849	6166	7631
#快递服务网点（处）				263	1453	2739	4461	6067
邮路及快递网路总长度（单程，万公里）	Total Length of Postal Route & Express Network (one way, 10 000 km)	17.70	17.86	19.44	63.31	54.55	64.24	78.70
邮政行业汽车（辆）	Postal Vehicles (unit)	1084	1318	1554	3908	4315	5436	6074
长途业务电路总数（万路）	Total Lines of Long Distance Business (line)	8.40	57.90	64.20	231.17	309.16	510.27	913.53
光缆线路长度（万公里）				17.16	55.52	65.30	88.94	109.35
邮电业务总量（亿元）	Business Volume of Post & Telecommunication Services (100 million yuan)	96.36	322.87	807.81	503.24	651.74	452.66	799.92
#电信业务总量	Telecommunication Services	92.05	311.15	779.23	467.01	608.10	388.96	711.88
邮政业务总量	Post	4.31	11.72	28.58	36.23	43.64	63.70	88.04
快递业务量（万件）	Express (10 000 pcs)			2278	9055	12541	22835	31750
函件（亿件）	Number of Letters (100 million pcs)	1.67	1.20	0.72	0.50	0.36	0.28	0.30
报刊期发数（万份）	Newspapers & Magazines Circulation (10 000 copies)	667.40	340.10	360.22	407.00	396.70	331.96	324.93
订销报纸累计数（万份）	Total Number of Newspaper Subscribed & Sold (10 000 copies)	40934.00	22387.00	27900.00	34913.00	36059.93	35236.58	34794.74
订销杂志累计数（万份）	Total Number of Magazines Subscribed & Sold (10 000 copies)	3324.00	2490.00	3825.00	3663.00	3295.02	2781.21	2647.64
固定电话年末户数（万户）	Number of Subscribers of Fixed-line Telephone (10 000 subscribers)	319.10	869.40	708.90	499.85	439.67	348.94	307.71
#公用电话（万户）	Public Telephone (10 000 subscribers)	9.92	61.80	57.40	42.06	18.77	9.65	7.15
#城市电话	Urban	233.48	557.70	430.30	336.91	312.01	244.36	221.31
农村电话	Rural	85.64	311.70	278.60	162.94	127.65	104.58	86.40
移动电话用户合计（万户）	Number of Mobile Telephone Subscribers (10 000 subscribers)	166.86	1021.00	2214.50	3553.78	3594.96	3774.15	4385.08
#3G移动电话用户数（万户）	3G Mobile Telephone Subscribers			98	1359.02	666.72	442.90	368.09
#4G移动电话用户数（万户）	4G Mobile Telephone Subscribers					1297.60	2325.27	3131.72
互联网用户数（万户）	Number of Subscribers of Internet (10 000 subscribers)	23.80	186.00	1579.60	3186.51	3521.63	3961.35	4771.64
#互联网宽带接入用户数	Broadband Internet Access	23.20	80.00	330.10	592.43	715.78	789.95	1050.97
移动互联网用户数	Mobile Internet			1240.30	2586.52	2798.31	3163.95	3713.35
#手机上网用户数（万户）					2565.9	2788.3	3116.58	3628.5
移动互联网接入流量（万GB）	Accessflow of Mobile Internet (10 000 GB)					10157	21703	63283

注：1. 邮电业务总量2000年及以前按1990年不变价格计算，以后按2000年不变价格计算。订销杂志累计数根据2005年实际情况做相应修改。
2. 2014年起，邮政快递网点、邮路总长度、邮政汽车三个指标包含快递服务企业数据，之前仅含邮政公司数。
3. 2016年起电信业务总量按2015年不变价格计算，其余年份不改变。
4. 2016年原口径（2010年变价）：电信业务总量936.87亿元、邮电业务总量1000.57亿元。

Note: 1.The business volume of post & telecommunication services of 2000 and before were calculated at 1990's constant prices; and these since 2000 were calculated at 2000's constant prices. The Total Number of Magazines Subscribed & Sold was adjusted by the practical situation in 2005.
2.Data of "Number of Post & Telecommunication Offices", "Total Length of Postal Route & Express Network" and "Postal Vehicles" include data of express services since 2014, before then was data of China Post only.
3.Data of "Business Volume of Post & Telecommunication Services" were calculated at 2015's constant prices since 2016, data before then remains the same.
4.Data using old statistical range for 2016 at 2010's constant prices are:Telecommunication Services 936.87 (100 million yuan), Business Volume of Post & Telecommunication Services 1000.57 (100 million yuan).

主要统计指标解释

铁路营业里程 又称营业长度（包括正式营业和临时营业里程），指办理客货运输业务的铁路正线总长度。凡是全线或部分建成双线及以上的线路，以第一线的实际长度计算；复线、站线、段管线、岔线和特殊用途线以及不计算运费的联络线都不计算营业里程。

公路里程 指在一定时期内实际达到《公路工程技术标准JTG B01-2003》规定的技术等级的公路，并经公路主管部门正式验收交付使用的公路里程数。包括大、中城市的郊区公路，以及公路通过小城镇（指县城、集镇）街道的公路里程和公路桥梁长度、隧道长度、渡口的宽度以及分期修建的公路已验收交付使用的里程，不包括大中城市的街道、厂矿、林区生产用道和农业生产用道的里程。两条或多条公路共同经由同一路段，只计算一次，不得重复计算里程长度。按公路技术等级分为等级公路和等外公路，其中等级公路分为高速公路、一级公路、二级公路、三级公路和四级公路。

内河航道通航里程 指在一定时期内，能通航运输船舶及排筏的天然河流、湖泊水库、运河及通航渠道的长度。包括全年季节性通航累计三个月以上的航道，不包括仅供零散流放竹、木排的河道。两省以河为界的航道里程，双方均按一半计算，以免重复。该指标可以反映内河水运网的规模、水平和发展情况。

铁路旅客运量 指一定时期内使用铁路客车运送的旅客人数。铁路旅客运量的计算方法：不论票价多少或行程长短，均按单程计算为一人次；不足购票年龄免购客票的儿童，不计算运量；月、季票按每月往返各21人次计算。

铁路旅客周转量 指一定时期内使用铁路客车运送的旅客人数与运输距离的乘积之和。计算公式为：

旅客周转量（人公里）=∑（实际运送的每一乘客×该旅客出发站与到达站间距离）

=实际运送的旅客人数×旅客平均运程

铁路货物运量 指使用铁路货车实际运送的货物重量。

铁路货物周转量 指一定时期内使用铁路货车完成的货物运量与运送距离的乘积之和。计算公式为：

货物周转量（吨公里）=∑（每批货物重量×该批货物的运送距离）

=实际运送货物吨数×货物平均运程

公路客运量 指公路运输企业及由其组织的其它单位在一定时期内实际运送的旅客人数。公路客运量的计算方法：不论乘车路程远近和票价的多少，以客票为依据，“人”为计量单位；不足购票年龄的免票儿童不计算客运量。

公路旅客周转量 指一定时期内由各种公路运输工具实际运送的旅客人数与相应的运送距离的乘积之和。计算公式为：

旅客周转量（人公里）=∑（实际运送的每一旅客×该旅客出发站与到达站间距离）

公路货运量 指一定时期内由各种公路运输工具实际运送到目的地并卸完的货物数量。反映公路货运量的指标有发送货物吨数、到达货物吨数和运送货物吨数。

公路货物周转量 指一定时期内由各种公路运输工具实际完成的货物运量与相应的运送距离的乘积之和。计算公式为：

货物周转量（吨公里）=∑（每批货物重量×该批货物的运送距离）

水路客运量 指水运企业及由其组织的其他单位在一定时期内实际运送的旅客人数。

水路旅客周转量 指水运企业和由其组织的其他单位在一定时期内实际运送的旅客人数与相应的运送距离的乘积之和。

水路货运量 指在一定时期内由各种水运工具实际运送的货物数量，包括内河、江海、远洋货运量。

水路货物周转量 指一定时期内由各种水路运输工具实际完成的货物运量与相应的运送距离的乘积之和。

港口货物吞吐量 指经由水路进、出港区范围，并经过装卸的货物数量。按货物流向分为进港吞吐量和出港吞吐量，按货物的贸易性质分为内贸和外贸吞吐量。按货物的类别分，可根据现行的交通行业标准《运输货物分类和代码》分类。

民用航空客运量 指公共航空运输飞行所载运的旅客人数。成人和儿童各按一人计算，婴儿不计人数。每一特定航班

的每一旅客只计算一次。唯一例外的是，乘坐定期航班既经过国内航段又经过国际航段的旅客，同时计算一个国内旅客和一个国际旅客。不定期航班运送的旅客每一特定航班（同一航班）只计算一次。

民用航空货邮运量 指公共航空运输飞行所载运的货物、邮件重量，货物包括外交信袋和快件。原始数据以吨位计算单位，保留一位小数。每一特定航班（同一航班）的货邮只计算一次，不能按航段重复计算。但对于既经过国内航段、又经过国际航段运输的货邮，则同时统计为国内货邮和国际货邮。不定期航班运输的货物每一特定航班（同一航班）只计算一次。

电信业务总量 指以货币形式表现的电信企业为社会提供各类电信服务的总数量。计算方法为各类电信业务的实物量分别乘以相应的不变单价，求出各类电信业务的货币量后加总求得。该指标反映了一定时期电信通信业务发展的总成果，是观察电信通信业务发展变化总趋势的综合性指标。

邮政行业业务总量 指以货币形式表现的邮政企业为社会提供各类邮政通信服务或其他服务的总数量。计算方法为各类邮政通信服务业务的实物量分别乘以相应的不变单价，求出各类业务的货币量后加总求得。该指标反映了一定时期邮政通信业务发展的总成果，是观察邮政通信业务发展变化总趋势的综合性指标。

Explanatory Notes on Main Statistical Indicators

Length of Railways in Operation refers to the total length of the trunk line for passenger and freight transportation (including both full operation and temporary operation). The calculation is based on the actual length of the first line if this line has a full or partial double (or more). Not included are double tracks, station sidings, tracks under the charge of stations, branch lines, special-purpose lines and non-payable connecting lines. The length of railways in operation is an important indicator to show the development of the infrastructure of railway transport. It is also essential data to calculate volume of passenger freight transport, traffic density and utilization efficiency of locomotives and carriages.

Length of Highways refers to the length of highways which are built in conformity with the grades specified by the highway engineering standard [Highways WTBZ-Technical Standard JTG B01-2003] formulated by the Ministry of Transport, and have been formally checked and accepted by the departments of highways and put into use. The length of highways includes that of the suburb highways at large and medium-sized cities, highways passing through streets at small cities and towns, and also the length of bridges, tunnels, ferry piers, and the checked and accepted length of the installment highways being put to use. It does not include the length of streets in big and medium-sized cities and highways built for the production purpose at factories, mines, forest areas and agricultural areas. If two or more highways go the same section of the way, the length of the section is only calculated for once and no duplication is allowed. According to the technical grade, they are divided into grade highways and off-grade highways, and grade highways include express highways, Class I, Class II, Class III and Class IV. The length of highways is an indicator to show the development of the scale of highway construction and to provide essential information to calculate the transport network density.

Length of Navigable Inland Waterways is an indicator reflecting the size and development of inland water network. It refers to the length of the natural rivers, lakes, reservoirs, canals, and ditches open to navigation during a given period, which enables transportation by ships and rafts. It includes the channels open to navigation for over an accumulated period of 3 months in a year, yet this does not include the river courses which are only used to float odd logs and bamboo rafts. For fear of repeating calculation, the length of waterways of boundary rivers between two provinces is reckon in a half for each province. This indicator can reflect the scale, level and development situation of the inland waterway network.

Railway Passenger Traffic refers to the volume of passenger transported with railway within a specific period of time. It is calculated by the principle that one person can be counted only once in one trip and takes no account of the ticket price and traveling distance. The free tickets for under-aged children are not calculated in. Monthly tickets and season tickets are calculated as 21 person-times per 1 month.

Turnover of Railway Passenger Traffic refers to the summary of products of the number of passengers transported with railway trains and the distance of transportation within a specific period of time. It is calculated as:

Turnover of Passenger Traffic (person-km)

= ∑ (each passenger actually transported × distance between this passenger' s starting and arriving station)

= number of passengers actually transported × average distance of passengers transported

Railway Freight Traffic refers to the weight of goods actually transported with railway goods trains.

Turnover of Railway Freight Traffic refers to the summary of products of the volume of goods transported with railway goods trains and the distance of transportation within a specific period of time. The calculating formula is:

Turnover of Freight Traffic (ton-km)

= ∑ (weight of each batch of goods × distance of this batch of goods transported)

= tonnage of goods actually transported × average distance of goods transported

Highway Passenger Traffic refers to volume of passenger transported with highway transportation enterprises and other units being organized by highway transportation enterprises within a specific period of time. It is calculated by the principle that one person can be counted as "1 person" and takes no account of the traveling distance and ticket price, according to the ticket. The free tickets for under-aged children are not calculated in.

Turnover of Highway Passenger Traffic refers to the summary of products of the number of passengers actually transported with kinds of highway conveyances and the distance of transportation within a specific period of time. It is calculated as:

Turnover of Passenger Traffic (person-km)

= ∑ (each passenger actually transported × distance between this passenger' s starting and arriving station)

Highway Freight Traffic refers to the volume of goods actually transported to destinations and completely discharged with kinds of highway conveyances within a specific period of time. To reflecting Highway Freight Traffic, there are indicators such as the tonnage of goods sending off, the tonnage of goods receiving and the tonnage of goods transporting.

Turnover of Highway Freight Traffic refers to the summary of products of the volume of goods actually transported with kinds of highway conveyances and the distance of transportation within a specific period of time. The calculating formula is:

Turnover of Freight Traffic (ton-km)

= ∑ (weight of each batch of goods × distance of this batch of goods transported)

Waterway Passenger Traffic refers to the volume of passenger transported with waterway transportation enterprises and other units being organized by highway transportation enterprises within a specific period of time.

Turnover of Waterway Passenger Traffic refers to the summary of products of the number of passengers actually transported with waterway transportation enterprises and other units being organized by waterway transportation enterprises the distance of transportation within a specific period of time.

Waterway Freight Traffic refers to the volume of goods actually transported with kinds of waterway conveyances within a specific period of time. It includes the freight traffic of inland rivers, seas and oceans.

Turnover of Waterway Freight Traffic refers to the summary of products of the volume of goods actually

Volume of Freight Handled in Coastal Ports refers to the volume of cargo passing in and out of the harbor area of the major coastal ports and having been loaded and unloaded. The volume of freight handled may be classified by direction of flow as freight for import and freight for export, or by nature of cargo as freight for domestic trade and freight for foreign trade. The volume of freight handled maybe classified by the classification of cargo, or the current transport standard of The Classification and Code of Cargo Type.

Civil Aviation Passenger Traffic refers to the volume of passenger transported with public air transportation. An adult or child is counted as 1 person, and babies are not calculated in. One passenger in a certain flight is just counted once. The exception is that one passenger taking a fix-date flight both including domestic part and international part is calculated as 1 domestic passenger and 1 international passenger contemporarily.

Civil Aviation Freight Traffic of Goods and Posts refers to the weight of goods and posts transported with public air transportation. The data well be calculated by the unit of tons. The goods and posts of one certain flight can be just counted once. The exception is that the goods and posts taking a fix-date flight both including domestic part and international part arc calculated as 1 domestic goods and posts and 1 international goods and posts contemporarily.

Business Volume of Telecommunications refers to the total amount of telecommunication services, expressed in value terms, provided by the telecommunications departments for society. It can be classified as: long distance telephones, rent circuitries, mobile phones, packet switching digital communication and lease and maintenance etc. This indicator reflects the overall results of development of telecommunication services in a certain period, and it is an important indicator for researching construction and development of business volume of telecommunications. The calculating formula is:

Business Volume of Telecommunications

= ∑ (various Business Volume of Telecommunications × fixed unit prices) + lease and maintenance and other business incomes

Business Volume of Post refers to the total amount of postal services, expressed in value terms, provided by the departments for society. It can be classified as: letters, parcels, drafts, circulating presses, postal expresses, EMS, postal savings, stamp collecting etc. This indicator reflects the overall results of development of postal services in a certain period, and it is an important indicator for researching construction and development of business volume of post. The calculating formula is:

Business Volume of Post

= ∑ (various Business Volume of Post × fixed unit prices) + lease and maintenance and other business incomes

第十九篇
教育、科技和文化
EDUCATION,SCIENCE, TECHNOLOGY & CULTURE

（校对编辑：卢启函　付晓霞）

19－1 主要年份各类学校基本情况
Basic Statistics of Schools by Type in Main Years

项 目	Item	1995	2000	2005	2010	2013	2014	2015	2016	2017
培养研究生单位（所）	Institutions of Postgraduate Education(unit)	9	9	9	11	12	13	13	13	13
毕业生人数（人）	Graduates (person)	228	444	1652	5396	7518	8007	8444	8840	9000
招生人数（人）	New Student Enrollment (person)	318	912	4561	7720	9417	9238	9619	10025	11000
在校学生数（人）	Student Enrollment (person)	747	2057	10711	20823	24905	25888	26731	27713	29400
普通高等学校（所）	Regular Institutions of Higher Education (unit)	27	30	51	70	70	70	70	73	74
毕业生人数（万人）	Graduates (10 000 persons)	1.78	2.02	6.49	13.81	16.50	17.41	18.27	18.94	21.07
招生人数（万人）	New Student Enrollment (10 000 persons)	2.04	4.72	11.67	18.38	20.07	22.77	24.14	25.95	27.99
在校学生数（万人）	Student Enrollment (10 000 persons)	6.00	11.79	33.83	56.75	64.42	70.19	75.12	81.03	86.67
专任教师（人）	Number of Full-time Teachers (person)	7542	9326	19610	31650	37437	37680	38625	41502	43246
普通中等专业学校（所）	Regular Specialized Secondary Schools (unit)	123	127	93	357	309	295	280	276	271
毕业生人数（万人）	Graduates (10 000 persons)	3.83	4.17	4.96	16.36	26.75	23.05	23.19	22.44	19.97
招生人数（万人）	New Student Enrollment (10 000 persons)	4.07	4.10	5.96	38.09	30.36	27.12	25.69	25.63	25.28
在校学生数（万人）	Student Enrollment (10 000 persons)	11.67	15.87	17.04	80.95	82.22	78.27	73.64	69.86	68.68
专任教师（人）	Number of Full-time Teachers (person)	7797	8800	7040	20469	20459	20417	20151	20733	20942
技工学校（所）	Skilled Workers' Schools (unit)	120	82	55	54	48	47	48	43	44
毕业生人数（万人）	Graduates (10 000 persons)	2.05	1.60	1.80	3.41	3.21	3.01	2.56	2.51	2.85
招生人数（万人）	New Student Enrollment (10 000 persons)	3.07	1.80	3.13	5.14	4.32	5.20	5.56	5.55	5.18
在校学生数（万人）	Student Enrollment (10 000 persons)	6.39	4.14	7.97	10.82	10.39	11.40	10.97	11.16	12.15
专任教师（人）	Number of Full-time Teachers (person)	3780	3405	3879	3622	6305	4662	4694	4623	4537
普通中学（所）	Regular Secondary Schools (unit)	3077	3019	2887	2437	2289	2288	2284	2262	2217
毕业生人数（万人）	Graduates (10 000 persons)	48.73	74.07	93.89	86.56	88.21	87.19	88.48	91.81	91.92
招生人数（万人）	New Student Enrollment (10 000 persons)	76.73	109.84	107.06	97.22	98.63	96.89	97.95	103.58	106.29
在校学生数（万人）	Student Enrollment (10 000 persons)	194.05	285.63	303.87	275.79	276.96	278.90	282.88	290.64	300.94
专任教师（人）	Number of Full-time Teachers (person)	97749	126660	152381	160840	169750	166162	169741	176797	185744
普通高中（所）	Senior Secondary Schools (unit)	437	464	529	463	453	445	445	450	460
毕业生人数（万人）	Graduates (10 000 persons)	6.60	8.20	19.35	23.90	24.19	25.33	25.73	26.85	28.18
招生人数（万人）	New Student Enrollment (10 000 persons)	7.84	15.34	25.69	27.07	29.77	30.46	31.04	33.85	35.07
在校学生数（万人）	Student Enrollment (10 000 persons)	20.93	36.93	69.96	75.40	81.89	83.82	86.57	91.89	97.48
专任教师（人）	Number of Full-time Teachers (person)	14344	18913	35249	42120	58412	48357	50733	53370	55988
普通初中（所）	Junior Secondary Schools (unit)	2640	2555	2358	1974	1836	1843	1839	1812	1757
毕业生人数（万人）	Graduates (10 000 persons)	42.13	65.87	74.54	62.66	64.02	61.86	62.75	64.96	63.74
招生人数（万人）	New Student Enrollment (10 000 persons)	68.89	94.50	81.37	70.15	68.86	66.43	66.91	69.73	71.22
在校学生数（万人）	Student Enrollment (10 000 persons)	173.12	248.70	233.91	200.39	195.08	195.08	196.31	198.75	203.46
专任教师（人）	Number of Full-time Teachers (person)	83405	107747	117132	118720	111338	117805	119008	123427	129756
普通小学（所）	Regular Primary Schools (unit)	16005	16109	15500	13942	13499	12946	11849	10173	8454
毕业生人数（万人）	Graduates (10 000 persons)	81.05	103.70	84.42	71.82	70.06	67.54	67.36	69.85	71.36
招生人数（万人）	New Student Enrollment (10 000 persons)	107.48	76.76	73.46	74.11	75.29	74.97	77.08	81.29	83.7
在校学生数（万人）	Student Enrollment (10 000 persons)	639.92	536.79	452.79	430.06	426.26	431.81	440.10	451.37	463.75
专任教师（人）	Number of Full-time Teachers (person)	194780	198977	204788	220183	209529	210666	221962	224260	237848
幼儿园（所）	Kindergartens (unit)	2555	3846	3152	5349	8886	9734	10397	11013	11787
在园儿童（万人）	Student Enrollment (10 000 persons)	100.07	72.84	88.78	118.53	181.71	197.33	206.90	209.64	213.99
专任教师（人）	Number of Full-time Teachers (person)	22956	22942	22395	31109	52110	61256	68407	74163	82306

注：2005年以后的普通中等专业学校统计范围为中等职业教育（学校）。

Note: The statistical range of "Regular Specialized Secondary Schools" refers to vocational schools for secondary education.

19－2　普通高等学校本科学生数（2017年）

Student Statistics in Institutions of Higher Education by Field of Study（2017）

单位：人　　　　(person)

项　目	Item	毕业生数 Graduates	招生数 New Student Enrollment	在校学生数 Student Enrollment	预计毕业生数 Number of Expecting Graduates
总　计	**Total**	**79001**	**109683**	**398173**	**90395**
哲　学	Philosophy	76	96	394	94
经济学	Economics	4875	6017	22845	5509
法　学	Law	2506	3432	12730	2591
教育学	Education	4566	6877	23193	4740
文　学	Literature	9866	14209	48638	10384
历史学	History	341	369	1427	335
理　学	Science	5753	7579	26961	6178
工　学	Engineering	23645	35009	126851	29334
农　学	Agriculture	812	952	2990	728
医　学	Medicine	8205	10507	44800	9556
管理学	Administration	18356	24636	87344	20946

19－3　普通高等学校专科学生数（2017年）

Student Statistics in Institutions of Higher Education by Field of Study（2017）

单位：人　　　　(person)

项　目	Item	毕业生数 Graduates	招生数 New Student Enrollment	在校学生数 Student Enrollment	预计毕业生数 Number of Expecting Graduates
总　计	**Total**				
农林牧渔大类	Farming, Forestry, Animal Husbandry & Fishery	1710	2448	6475	1947
交通运输大类	Transportation	5817	9195	23016	6155
生化与药品大类	Biochemistry & Medicine				
资源开发与测绘大类	Resource Developing, Survey & Draw				
材料与能源大类	Material & Energy	1860	2400	6356	1920
土建大类	Construction	18746	17423	51440	17896
水利大类	Water Conservancy	373	534	1500	453
制造大类	Manufacture	12723	15855	42620	13350
电子信息大类	Electronic Information	8772	15882	37796	9967
环保、气象与安全大类	Environmental Protection, Meteorology & Weather Safty				
轻纺食品大类	Textile & Food Industry				
财经大类	Finance & Economy	30886	32906	95043	31327
医药卫生大类	Medical & Health Care	11147	13610	36458	10956
旅游大类	Tourism	3838	5627	14753	4415
公共事业大类	Public Affairs				
文化教育大类	Culture & Education				
艺术设计传媒大类	Art Design & Media				
公安大类	Public Security	3309	2349	5671	1566
法律大类	Law				

19－4　中等职业专业学校分科学生数（2017年）

Number of Students by Field of Study in Secondary Vocational Schools（2017）

单位：人　(person)

项　目	Item	毕业生数 Graduates	招生数 New Student Enrollment	初中毕业 Graduates from Junior Secondary Schools	在校学生数 Student Enrollment	预计毕业生数 Number of Expecting Graduates
合　计	**Total**	**199722**	**252803**	**190321**	**686797**	**211948**
农林牧渔类	Farming, Forestry, Animal Husbandry & Fishery	14249	14441	8615	37411	13540
资源环境类	Resouwes & Environment	25	70	62	181	37
能源与新能源类	Energy & New Energy	260	261	201	725	242
土木水利类	Construction & Water Conservancy	8066	6408	4963	17836	5618
加工制造类	Processing & Manufacturing	34535	35118	24376	107572	37645
石油化工类	Petrochemical Engineering	32	701	698	941	72
轻纺食品类	Textile & Food	816	924	501	2663	1107
交通运输类	Transportation	32374	40197	30142	113749	36268
信息技术类	Information Technique	32875	41283	28429	110292	33825
医药卫生类	Medical & Health Care	17937	19392	17132	55706	17111
休闲保健类	Leisure & Health Keeping	731	1818	1074	4822	1420
财经商贸类	Finance & Business	23451	33617	25164	90028	27012
旅游服务类	Tourism Services	10329	19686	16194	48196	12539
文化艺术类	Culture & Art	8242	11217	7682	27732	7953
体育与健身	Sports & Body Building	388	1032	944	2482	695
教育类	Education	13153	21887	20999	55292	13130
司法服务类	Jurisdiction Services	563	840	586	1761	518
公共管理与服务类	Public Administration & Services	1463	1835	1168	5875	2148
其他	Others	233	2076	1391	3533	1068

19—5 主要年份教师负担学生数

Student-teacher Ratio of School by Field in Main Years

单位：人 (person)

指 标	Item	1995	2000	2005	2010	2013	2014	2015	2016	2017
普通高等学校	Regular Institutions of Higher Education									
教师人数	Number of Teachers	7542	9326	19610	32616	37437	37680	38625	41502	44325
平均每个教师负担学生数	Student-teacher Ratio	8.0	12.6	17.2	17.9	18.1	18.6	18.1	19.5	20.0
中等学校	Secondary Schools									
教师人数	Number of Teachers	116084	145397	171287	184931	196514	186579	194586	237213	211223
平均每个教师负担学生数	Student-teacher Ratio	19.2	20.6	20.2	19.9	18.8	19.1	18.9	15.2	18.1
小学	Primary Schools									
教师人数	Number of Teachers	194780	198977	204788	220183	209529	210666	221962	224260	237848
平均每个教师负担学生数	Student-teacher Ratio	32.9	27.0	22.1	19.5	19.7	20.5	19.8	20.1	19.5

注：中等学校包括初中、普通高中、普通中专、职业高中、技工学校。

Note: Secondary school includes junior secondary schools, senior secondary schools, specialized secondary schools, vocational secondary schools and skilled workers' schools.

19—6 主要年份各级各类教育平均每万人在校学生数

Number of Students Enrollment by Level & Type per 10 000 Persons in Main Years

单位：人 (person)

指 标	Item	1995	2000	2005	2010	2013	2014	2015	2016	2017
1. 高等学校	Institutions of Higher Education	25.0	46.0	99.3	156.9	192.4	198.2	215.9	225.9	260.26
普通高校	Regular Institutions of Higher Education	13.0	25.0	69.2	123.3	136.5	147.6	156.6	173.2	235.13
成人高校	Adult Education Schools	12.0	21.0	27.9	33.6	48.1	50.6	53.7	52.7	51.48
2. 高中阶段	Step of Senior Schools	135.0	158.0	232.0	363.0	370.0	364.9	358.2	357.3	340.1
#中职学校	Vocational Secondary Schools			75.7	199.4	196.3	188.6	177.7	167.4	140.6
普通高中	Regular Senior Secondary Schools	47.0	78.0	143.1	163.8	173.5	176.3	180.5	189.9	199.5
3. 初中阶段	Step of Junior Schools	387.0	535.0	479.3	435.3	413.4	410.4	409.3	410.8	416.5
#普通初中	Regular Junior Secondary Schools	385.0	528.0	478.5	435.3	413.4	410.4	409.3	410.8	416.5
4. 小学	Primary Schools	1424.0	1139.0	926.1	934.3	903.3	908.3	917.6	933.0	949.3
5. 幼儿园	Kindergartens	189.0	155.0	181.6	257.5	385.1	415.1	431.4	433.3	438.1

19－7　主要年份各级成人教育在校学生数

Student Enrollment in Various Adult Education in Main Years

单位：人　　　　(person)

项　目	Item	1995	2000	2005	2010	2013	2014	2015	2016	2017
成人高等学校	**Adult Education Schools**	**52200**	**100992**	**136579**	**166095**	**227016**	**253141**	**270202**	**268958**	**251528**
广播电视大学	Ratio & TV Universities	12142	13784		673	982	1052	1141	1092	931
职工（农民）高等学校	Schools of Higher Education for Staff, Workers (Peasants)	5518	3180		543	546	452	262	153	114
管理干部学院	Colleges for Management Cadres	4142	10502		11540	2086	10738	11001	11311	1809
教育学院	Pedagogical Colleges	10995	6421		6883	3109	8101	7956	10053	6926
普通高等学校举办	Run by Institutions of Higher Schools	19403	67105	115699	146456	220293	232798	249842	246349	241748

19－8　主要年份义务教育普及程度

Level of Compulsory Education Popularization in Main Years

单位：%　　　　(%)

指　标	Item	1995	2000	2005	2010	2013	2014	2015	2016	2017
小学学龄儿童入学率	Percentage of School-age Children Enrolled	98.2	98.7	99.1	99.4	99.6	99.6	99.4	99.6	99.8
男童	Male Students	98.8	98.7	99.1	99.4	99.6	99.6	99.4	99.6	99.8
女童	Female Students	97.5	98.6	99.0	99.3	99.6	99.6	99.4	99.6	99.8
初中毛入学率	Crude Percentage of Children Enrolled in Junior Schools	66.3	91.7	101.9	106.7	108.8	108.9	109.2	110.0	112.5
男生	Male Students	69.3	92.4	102.2	106.8	108.9	109.1	109.5	110.4	112.8
女生	Female Students	62.8	90.9	101.6	106.5	108.7	108.7	108.9	109.6	112.2
小学生辍学率	Drop-out Rate of Primary Students	3.0	0.8	1.5	2.1	1.3	0.5	0.4	0.1	0.03
男生	Male Students	2.9	0.9	1.6	2.3	1.5	0.5	0.4	0.1	0.1
女生	Female Students	3.2	0.8	1.3	1.9	1.1	0.4	0.3	0.03	-0.1
普通初中辍学率	Drop-out Rate of Regular Junior Students	7.4	5.0	5.6	6.6	3.3	2.5	1.9	1.4	1.5
男生	Male Students	8.4	5.5	6.7	8.0	4.1	3.0	2.5	1.7	1.9
女生	Female Students	6.2	4.3	4.3	5.0	2.5	2.0	1.2	1.1	1.0
小学毕业生升学率	Percentage of Graduates of Primary Schools Entering Junior Secondary Schools	85.9	92.6	96.5	97.7	98.3	98.4	99.3	99.8	99.8
男生	Male Students	89.1	93.9	96.9	96.9	97.3	97.6	98.7	99.4	99.5
女生	Female Students	81.9	91.1	96.0	98.6	99.4	99.2	100.0	100.3	100.1
初中毕业生升学率	Percentage of Graduates of Junior Secondary Schools Entering Senior Secondary Schools		39.8	58.4	79.6	80.1	85.7	83.6	90.3	92.4
小学生五年保留率	Percentage of 5-year Primary Schools Maintained	73.5	91.6	96.7	88.4	89.0	91.1	91.0	96.8	99.2
男生	Male Students	73.3	91.9	96.6	87.7	88.1	90.6	90.4	96.6	99.2
女生	Female Students	73.7	91.1	96.7	89.0	89.7	91.8	91.6	97.0	99.2
普通初中生三年保留率	Percentage of 3-year Junior Secondary Schools Maintained	83.5	82.0	83.6	82.0	90.9	94.2	94.7	96.3	95.8
男生	Male Students	79.4	79.8	80.5	78.0	88.6	93.1	93.6	95.1	94.6
女生	Female Students	89.5	84.8	87.2	86.4	92.9	95.5	95.9	97.8	97.0

19—9 主要年份科技活动基本情况
Basic Statistics for Scientific & Technical Activities in Main Years

指　标	Item	2000	2005	2010	2013	2014	2015	2016	2017
科技机构数（个）	**Number of Scientific & Technological Research Institutions (unit)**	**732**	**639**	**714**	**825**	**847**	**842**	**825**	**860**
#科技部门属科研机构	Institutions of Research & Technological Development	234	209	138	120	121	124	118	119
大中型工业企业属技术开发机构	Technological Development Institutions in Large & Medium Industrial Enterprises	181	122	211	284	267	234	189	193
全日制高等院校属科研机构	Institutions of Research in Full-time Universities & Colleges	131	74	159	186	233	285	314	363
科技活动人员数（万人）	**Number of Persons Engaged in Scientific & Techno-logical Activities (10 000 persons)**	**4.86**	**5.67**	**8.91**	**10.87**	**10.72**	**11.37**	**12.08**	
#R&D活动人员折合全时人员（人年）	Number of Full-time Personnel Converted from the Persons Engaged in Scientific & Techno-logical Activities (person-year)	13015	17996	33982	40664	41208	38535	39903	36857.3
研究与发展经费内部支出（万元）	**Inner Expenditure of Funds for Research & Develop-ment (10 000 yuan)**	**83597**	**146745**	**628695**	**1076790**	**1119033**	**1059124**	**1177487**	**1421787**
（一）按活动类型分	By Type of Activities								
#基础研究支出	Expenditure for Basic Research	5443	9488	36005	54832	78630	108296	120475	173376
应用研究支出	Expenditure for Application Research	14786	39076	95585	122770	129914	131781	148577	193218
试验发展支出	Expenditure for Experimental Development	63367	93048	497105	899187	910488	819047	908435	1055194
（二）按支出用途分	By Use of Expenditure								
#日常性支出	# Ordinary Expenditure	53976	141611	526983	864559	946395	912865	1030691	1269675
#人员劳务费	# Fees for Personel Labor Service	39621	39202	150318	283417	313399	326517	345391	388145
（三）按资金来源分	By Resource of Funds								
#政府资金	Funds from Government	19198	32549	152128	210060	234760	249685	272643	384486
企业资金	Funds from Enterprises	56972	105062	451914	804800	826558	759182	851352	971908
境外资金	Funds from Foreign Countries	149	270	866	237	615	335	743	746

19—10　大中型工业企业科技活动基本情况（2017年）

单位：万元

指　标	Item	R&D人员折合全时当量（人年）Number of Full-time Personnel Converted from the Persons Engaged in R&D Activities (person-year)	其中：研究人员 Researchers	基础研究 Basic Research	应用研究 Application Research	试验发展 Testing Development	R&D经费内部支出 Inner Expenditure of R&D Funds	1.日常性支出 Recurrent Expenditure
总　计	**Total**	**13360**	**5202**		**190**	**13171**	**812910.9**	**752872.8**
一、按登记注册类型分组	**I. Grouped by Type of Registration**							
内资企业	**Domestically-funded Enterprises**	**6934**	**2696**		**187**	**6747**	**426855.1**	**388748.5**
国有企业	State-owned Enterprises	250	66			250	8188.2	7485.6
集体企业	Collective-owned Enterprises	3	0			3	52.6	30.4
股份合作企业	Cooperative Stock Enterprises							
有限责任公司	Limited Liability Corporations	3110	1292		105	3005	188826.3	173022.6
股份有限公司	Share Holding Enterprises	2276	881		48	2228	96428.8	92032.1
私营企业	Private Enterprises	1295	456		34	1261	133359.2	116177.8
港、澳、台商投资企业	**Enterprises with Funds from Hong Kong, Macao or Taiwan**	**941**	**333**		**3**	**938**	**43868.9**	**37421.1**
合资经营企业（港或澳、台资）	Joint Equity (Funds from Hong Kong, Macao or Taiwan)	715	267		3	713	38266.7	32622.2
港、澳、台商独资经营企业	Enterprises Wholly Owned by Hong Kong, Macao or Taiwan	221	64			221	5516.4	4713.1
外商投资企业	**Foreign Funded Enterprises**	**5486**	**2173**			**5486**	**342186.9**	**326703.2**
中外合资经营企业	Sino-foreign Joint Equity	4608	1743			4608	287139.4	276067.6
外资企业	Wholly Foreign-owned Enterprises	120	49			120	3766.8	2205.0
外商投资股份有限公司	Foreign-funded Share Holding Enterprises	758	381			758	51280.7	48430.6
二、按工业行业大类分组	**II. Grouped by Major Defect of Industrial Branch**							
采矿业	**Mining**	**150**	**65**			**150**	**10345.7**	**5298.0**
煤炭开采和洗选业	Coal Mining & Dressing	3	1			3	4510.2	1942.0
有色金属矿采选业	Nonferrous Metals Mining & Processing	29	15			29	651.8	323.4
制造业	**Manufacturing**	**13189**	**5129**		**190**	**12999**	**802492.2**	**747550.3**
农副食品加工业	Farm & Sideline Products Processing	426	145		8	418	15940.9	14190.3

Basic Statistics for Scientific & Technical Activities Organized by Large &Medium Industrial Enterprises（2017）

(10 000 yuan)

人员劳务费 Remunera-tion	内部经费支出中: In Recurrent Expenditure			2. 资产性支出 Capital Expenditure	#1. 土建工程 Projects of Construc-tion	2. 仪器设备 Instruments & Equipment	内部经费支出中: In Inner Expenditure				R&D经费外部支出 Exterior Expend-iture
	基础研究 Basic Research	应用研究 Application Research	试验发展 Testing Develop-ment				政府资金 Government Funds	企业资金 Funds from Enterprises	国外资金 Foreign Funds	其他资金 Others	
241065.2		**13848.1**	**799062.8**	**60038.1**	**1480.2**	**58557.9**	**30245.1**	**781585.4**	**419.4**	**661.0**	**61166.3**
105363.0		**13417.2**	**413437.9**	**38106.6**	**884.7**	**37221.9**	**24240.5**	**402460.0**	**23.0**	**131.6**	**37045.2**
1634.6			8188.2	702.6	1.3	701.3	1386.7	6801.5			41.1
10.4			52.6	22.2		22.2		52.6			
53900.2		10264.8	178561.5	15803.7	675.7	15128.0	9104.4	179669.2	21.2	31.5	30885.8
29061.7		966.3	95462.5	4396.7	122.1	4274.6	10040.6	86304.3	1.8	82.1	4431.1
20756.1		2186.1	131173.1	17181.4	85.6	17095.8	3708.8	129632.4		18.0	1687.2
10623.0		**430.9**	**43438.0**	**6447.8**	**4.3**	**6443.5**	**650.9**	**42798.9**	**396.4**	**22.7**	**214.8**
7948.5		430.9	37835.8	5644.5	4.2	5640.3	647.9	37199.7	396.4	22.7	210.8
2670.4			5516.4	803.3	0.1	803.2	3.0	5513.4			4.0
125079.2			**342186.9**	**15483.7**	**591.2**	**14892.5**	**5353.7**	**336326.5**		**506.7**	**23906.3**
107516.5			287139.4	11071.8	154.5	10917.3	2958.6	283674.1		506.7	11908.5
396.7			3766.8	1561.8	8.8	1553.0	427.9	3338.9			579.0
17166.0			51280.7	2850.1	427.9	2422.2	1967.2	49313.5			11418.8
886.2			**10345.7**	**5047.7**	**234.7**	**4813.0**	**490.7**	**9348.3**		**506.7**	**1603.2**
537.6			4510.2	2568.2	224.5	2343.7		4510.2			1075.7
24.7			651.8	328.4		328.4	413.7	238.1			361.1
240174.0		**13848.1**	**788644.1**	**54941.9**	**1245.5**	**53696.4**	**29746.4**	**772172.1**	**419.4**	**154.3**	**59361.6**
2103.4		399.0	15541.9	1750.6	6.6	1744.0	1606.8	14334.1			853.6

19—10 续表

单位：万元

指 标	Item	R&D人员折合全时当量（人年）Number of Full-time Personnel Converted from the Persons Engaged in R&D Activities (person-year)	其中：研究人员 Researchers	基础研究 Basic Research	应用研究 Application Research	试验发展 Testing Develop-ment	R&D经费内部支出 Inner Expenditure of R&D Funds	1. 日常性支出 Recurrent Expenditure
食品制造业	Food Production	52	20		0	52	5659.6	5624.7
酒、饮料和精制茶制造业	Beverage Production	70	15		18	52	10043.9	9942.8
烟草制品业	Tobacco Processing	205	99			205	14972.7	14734.9
纺织业	Textile Industry	176	33			176	4248.5	3703.1
木材加工和木、竹、藤、棕、草制品业	Processing of Timbers, Manufacture of Wood, Bamboo, Rattan, Palm, and Straw Products	15	5			15	1203.2	1175.6
造纸和纸制品业	Papermaking & Paper Products	31	4			31	2274.9	1182.6
印刷业和记录媒介复制业	Printing & Record Duplicating	43	6			43	1913.9	1913.9
化学原料和化学制品制造业	Raw Chemical Materials & Chemical Products	441	176		4	437	16034.3	13071.5
医药制造业	Medical & Pharmaceutical Products	420	187		2	418	20696.5	19223.5
橡胶和塑料制品业	Rubber Products	139	33			139	3222.4	2825.5
非金属矿物制品业	Nonmetal Mineral Products	247	75			247	15417.6	14205.3
黑色金属冶炼和压延加工业	Smelting & Pressing of Ferrous Metals	361	185			361	87260.0	74901.6
有色金属冶炼和压延加工业	Smelting & Pressing of Nonferrous Metals	545	161		8	537	42984.6	41352.4
通用设备制造业	General Equipment Manufacturing	875	435			875	52080.2	48793.0
专用设备制造业	For Special Purposes Equipment Manufacturing	1548	602		26	1522	58618.1	55718.9
汽车制造业	Automobile Manufacturing	6300	2496		4	6296	381745.4	361113.1
铁路、船舶、航空航天和其他交通运输设备制造业	Railway, Ships, Aerospace & other Transport Equipment Manufacturing							
电气机械和器材制造业	Electric Equipment & Machinery	575	198			575	26028.5	22951.3
计算机、通信和其他电子设备制造业	Communicaition Equipment, Computer & other Electronic Equipment Manufacturing	490	177		116	373	27705.7	27232.1
仪器仪表制造业	Instruments, Meters Cultural & Office Machinery	44	9			44	1581.9	1525.6
电力、热力、燃气及水生产和供应业	Production & Supply of Electric Power, Gas & Water	21	8			21	73.0	24.5
电力、热力生产和供应业	Production & Supply of Electric Power & Steam	21	8			21	73.0	24.5

continued

(10 000 yuan)

	内部经费支出中: In Recurrent Expenditure						内部经费支出中：In Inner Expenditure				
人员劳务费 Remunera-tion	基础研究 Basic Research	应用研究 Application Research	试验发展 Testing Develop-ment	2. 资产性支出 Capital Expenditure	1. 土建工程 Projects of Construc-tion	2. 仪器设备 Instruments & Equipment	政府资金 Government Funds	企业资金 Funds from Enterprises	国外资金 Foreign Funds	其他资金 Others	R&D经费外部支出 Exterior Expend-iture
921.3		62.8	5596.8	34.9	23.2	11.7	78.0	5581.6			
2299.4		516.3	9527.6	101.1		101.1	160.2	9883.7			106.3
2326.9			14972.7	237.8		237.8		14972.7			2503.0
976.1			4248.5	545.4		545.4	138.0	4101.2		9.3	65.2
221.2			1203.2	27.6		27.6	15.0	1188.2			
254.3			2274.9	1092.3	0.1	1092.2	19.5	2255.4			
553.7			1913.9					1913.9			
4146.7		211.7	15822.6	2962.8	74.3	2888.5	1029.9	14995.7		8.7	158.1
3878.0		544.6	20151.9	1473.0	84.9	1388.1	2499.0	18164.2	1.8	31.5	4914.3
1024.7			3222.4	396.9		396.9	398.9	2823.5			
4033.7			15417.6	1212.3	2.8	1209.5	1608.8	13808.8			20.0
11060.3			87260.0	12358.4	4.5	12353.9	1410.1	85849.9			478.2
7755.4		675.6	42309.0	1632.2	83.4	1548.8	673.1	42311.5			638.7
17963.7			52080.2	3287.2	429.1	2858.1	2095.7	49984.5			11271.4
20568.1		168.8	58449.3	2899.2	47.7	2851.5	7493.7	51120.6		3.8	781.0
144409.9		710.9	381034.5	20632.3	473.6	20158.7	6521.9	374804.4	396.4	22.7	37288.0
5233.9			26028.5	3077.2	4.6	3072.6	1652.3	24376.2			235.4
8351.8		10322.0	17383.7	473.6	1.6	472.0	442.2	27185.2		78.3	45.0
571.1			1581.9	56.3	8.2	48.1	31.6	1550.3			
5.0			73.0	48.5		48.5	8.0	65.0			201.5
5.0			73.0	48.5		48.5	8.0	65.0			201.5

19－11 主要年份工业企业科技活动情况

Statistics for Technical Activities of Large & Medium Industrial Enterprises in Main Years

指 标	Item	2000	2007	2010	2013	2014	2015	2016	2017
大中型工业企业(个)	**Number of Enterprises (unit)**								
#有研发机构的单位数	Units Engaged in Scientific & Technological Activities	293	191	232	186	173	139	121	117
#有R&D活动的单位数	Units Engaged in New Products Developing Activities		138	167	225	233	214	219	235
科技活动人员（万人）	**Personnel Engaged in Scientific & Technological Activities (10 000 persons)**	**2.15**	**2.68**	**3.78**	**5.37**	**5.48**	**4.83**	**4.98**	
研究与发展经费内部支出（万元）	**Inner Expenditure of Funds for Research & Development (10 000 yuan)**			**438669**	**817063**	**848808**	**769190**	**827248**	**935996**
(一) 按活动类型分	By Type of Activities								
#基础研究支出	Expenditure for Basic Research	171	3748	167	602	370	386	276	
应用研究支出	Expenditure for Application Research	5601	26154	9083	6525	23160	22162	17978	14680
试验发展支出	Expenditure for Experimental Development	50462	117480	429420	809937	825278	746643	808994	921316
(二) 按支出用途分	By Use of Expenditure								
#日常性支出	Ordinary Expenditure	42987	147382	378741	660528	740385	684371	750524	862915
#人员劳务费	Fees for Personel Labor Service	16912	31817	91657	202106	230884	242333	236884	263583
(三) 按资金来源分	By Resource of Funds								
#政府资金	Funds from Government	2930	5704	22168	36970	38907	32000	33126	36617
企业资金	Funds from Enterprises	48390	140294	413173	777281	796270	732074	788248	896603
境外资金	Funds from Foreign Countries	132	68	161	66	369	75	204	459
新产品开发经费支出（万元）	**Expenditure for New Product Development (10 000 yuan)**	**50304**	**174798**	**460413**	**849395**	**850464**	**903957**	**905498**	**1120030**
科技活动产出情况	**Output from Scientific & Technological Activities**								
专利申请数（项）	Patent Applications Examined (item)	162	627	1591	4468	4840	4613	5555	5428
#发明专利	Patent for Invention	20	190	488	2234	2423	2005	2660	2502
拥有有效发明专利数（项）	Number of Patent for Invention Owned (item)	78	233	950	1889	2670	3731	6010	6557
技术改造和技术获取情况	**Technological Transformation & Technical Acquisition**								
技术改造经费支出（万元）	Expenditure for Technological Transformation (10 000 yuan)	126898	713690	1374075	1223981	850900	915924	795169	789278.7
引进境外技术经费支出（万元）	Expenditure for Technological Recommendation from Foreign Countries (10 000 yuan)	27910	8180	8137	3599	12392	5697	4210	8059.9
引进技术的消化吸收经费支出（万元）	Expenditure for Technological Digesting & Absorbing (10 000 yuan)	754	3411	5988	3605	6329	2621	1952	3183.2
购买境内技术经费支出（万元）	Expenditure for Buying Domestic Technological (10 000 yuan)	6657	3779	12092	12881	16032	11610	6951	32622.8

19－12 主要年份县及县以上政府部门所属研究与开发机构基本情况

Basic Statistics on Governmental Department Research & Development Institutions at & above County Level in Main Years

项 目	Item	1995	2000	2005	2010	2012	2013	2014	2015	2016	2017
机构数（个）	Number of Institutions (unit)	230	224	210	207	202	200	199	195	166	165
从事科技活动人员（人）	Number of Persons Engaged in Scientific & Technological Activities (person)	9227	7954	7574	8757	9152	9586	10025	10034	7418	7516
#科学家、工程师	Scientists & Engineers	5048	4787	4461							
#大学本科及以上学历	University Degree or above				5400	6138	6719	7068	7449	5505	5692
经费筹集总额（万元）	Funds for Scientific & Technological Activities (10 000 yuan)	44526	54820	72749	187190	254351	286173	284221	278240	456973	511634
#政府拨款	Funds from Government	16910	31272	60359	136474	196158	230582	232426	224073	240075	280262
经费使用总额（万元）	Expenditure of Funds for Scientific & Technological Activities (10 000 yuan)	39087	53090	73823	170741	248668	271088	293345	274085	242160	280336
#固定资产购建支出	Purchases of Fixed Assets	8910	7818	12445	28939	51612	58966	80274	52689	51678	53570

注：1. 2009年，指标“科学家工程师”取消，改为“大学本科及以上学历”（县属机构使用“大专以上学历”）。2011年，均使用“大学本科及以上学历”。

2. 2016年度数据口径已剔除转制院所数据（因科技厅报表改版，转制院所报表已为企业报表，不属于政府部门属机构，科技部不作汇总）。

Note: 1.The indicator of “Scientists & Engineers” has been canceled since 2009, and it was replaced by “University Degree or above”(it is changed as “Junior College Degree or above” in county level institutions) Both in dicators were replaced by “University Degree of above” since 2011.

2.The statistical range of 2016 excluding data from reformed institutions (due to the revision of reports inside the Science & Techuology Department, reports of reformed institutions become part of enterprises’ report instead of government’ s report, the science & Technology Department has no response for the summary).

19－13 县及县以上政府部门所属研究与开发机构情况（2017年）

Basic Statistics on Governmental Department Research & Development Institutions at & above County Level (2017)

项　目	Item	机构数（个）Number of Institutions (unit)	从事科技活动人员合计（人）Personnel in Scientific & Technological Activities (person)	#大学本科及以上学历 University Degree or above	经费筹集总额（万元）Funds for Scientific & Technological Activities (10 000 yuan)	#政府拨款 Funds from Government	经费使用总额（万元）Total Expenditure (10 000 yuan)
总　计	**Total**						
一、按单位类型分	**By Unit Type**	**165**	**7516**	**5692**	**511633.6**	**280261.6**	**280335.9**
科学研究与技术开发机构	Institutions of Research & Technological Development	146	7070	5307	499833.1	271516.7	271493.5
科技情报与文献机构	Scientific & Technological Information & Literature Institutions	19	446	385	11800.5	8744.9	8842.4
二、按隶属关系分	**By Relationship**						
中央属	Central	1	225	210	36017.1	29279	32695
自治区属	Autonomous	50	5152	4167	415853	213543.6	209343.3
地（市）属	Prefectural	67	1810	1235	54337.4	32649.6	34337.6
县属	County	47	329	80	5426.1	4789.4	3960
三、按学科领域分	**By Programmes**						
自然科学	Natural Sciences	5	749	549	56224.9	46186	51764.3
农业科学	Agricultural Sciences	50	2942	2104	139257.3	114852.5	100490.5
医药科学	Medical Sciences	11	1737	1427	238827.4	64536.9	73120.6
工程与技术科学	Engineering & Technology	23	1002	861	48466.2	29965.7	32020.7
人文与社会科学	Humanities & Social Sciences	29	757	671	23431.7	19931.1	18979.8

注：科技部汇总表上没有将县属机构按科学领域分组，所以这里的“按科学领域分”只包含了市级以上政府部门属机构数据。

Note: Since the summary table given by the science & Technology Department didn't have data of county's institutions by programmes, so the related data of this table only include the institutions in cities.

19－14 县及县以上政府部门所属研究与开发机构课题情况（2017年）

Projects of Governmental Department Research & Development Institutions at & above County Level (2017)

项 目	Item	课题数（项）Projects (unit)	投入人员（人年）Personnel Engaged in Projects (person-year)	#研究人员 Researchers	投入经费（万元）Funds of Projects (10 000 yuan)
总 计	**Total**	**2805**	**4438**		**82204.9**
按单位类型分	**By Unit Type**				
科学研究与技术开发机构	Institutions of Research & Technological Development	2724	4236		79646.4
科技情报与文献机构	Scientific & Technological Information & Literature Institutions	81	202		2558.5
按活动类型分	**By Activity Type**				
基础研究	Basic Research	589	832		10546.1
应用研究	Application Research	649	1207		28411.8
实验发展	Testing Development	849	1292		28842.4
研究与实验发展成果应用	Application of R&D Achievement	398	629		8827.2
科技服务	Technological Services	297	480		5577.3

注：1.投入的人员和经费为直接投入数据，不包括间接投入数据。
2.课题数的汇总缺县属机构按活动类型分的数据。
3.“研究人员”缺所有汇总数据。

Note: 1. The data on Personnel engaged and Funds of Projects is direct input, excluding indirect input.
2. The summary data of projects by activity type in the county agency are missing.
3. All the summary data of “Reseachers” are missing.

19－15　县及县以上政府部门所属研究与开发机构成果情况（1990－2017年）
Achievement of Governmental Department Research & Development Institutions at & above County Level (1990－2017)

年　份 Year	科学著作（种） Scientific & Technological Works (10 000 words)	科学论文（篇） Scientific & Technological Works (unit)
1990	887	579
1991	1520	675
1992	881	945
1993	1027	1072
1994	841	1135
1995	583	1274
1996	35	1403
1997	23	1691
1998	50	1505
1999	79	1525
2000	84	1839
2001	62	1456
2002	58	1400
2003	51	1673
2004	34	1756
2005	50	1918
2006	62	2274
2007	58	2331
2008	62	2550
2009	63	2736
2010	72	3104
2011	39	3178
2012	48	3342
2013	87	3328
2014	102	3868
2015	96	3731
2016	108	3024
2017	85	2897

注：1999年以后科学著作计量单位为：种；1990年科学著作、科学论文不包含科技情报与文献机构数。

Note: Since 1999, the term of scientific & technological works is *Kind*; In the year of 1990, scientific & technological works & papers exclude ones from scientific & technological information & literature institutions.

19－16 文化及相关产业机构和从业人员（2017年）
Institutions, Staff & Workers of Cultural & Relevant Industries（2017）

项 目	Item	总计 Total		文化部门 Cultural Department		其他部门 Other Departments	
				合计 Total			
		机构数（个） Number of Institutions (unit)	从业人员数（人） Number of Staff & Workers (person)	机构数（个） Number of Institutions (unit)	从业人员数（人） Number of Staff & Workers (person)	机构数（个） Number of Institutions (unit)	从业人员数（人） Number of Staff & Workers (person)
总 计	**Total**	**7877**	**56826**	**1955**	**17455**	**5922**	**39371**
艺术业	Art	151	5450	40	1470	111	3980
图书馆业	Library	115	1660	115	1660		
群众文化服务业	Service for Mass Culture	1298	5236	1298	5236		
艺术教育业	Art Education	2	190	2	190		
文化市场经营机构（不含非公有制艺术表演团体）	Units in Operation in Culture Market (excluding non-public-owned art peformance groups)	5774	35159			5774	35159
文艺科研	Culture & Art Researching	9	174	9	174		
文物业	Cultural Relics	216	2830	180	2629	36	201
其他文化产业	Other Industries						

注：统计范围为文化系统,以下各表相同。

Note: The statistical range is the cultural system, and the same as the continued tables.

19—17 文化及相关产业增加值（2017年）
Added Value of Culture & Relevant Industries（2017）

单位：万元 (10 000 yuan)

项 目	Item	总产出 Total Output	中间消耗 Consum-ption Therein	增加值 Added Value	劳动者报酬 Remuneration for Labors	生产税净额 Net Value of Production Tax	固定资产折旧 Depreciation of Fixed Assets	营业盈余 Surplus of Operation
总 计	**Total**	**734430**	**252152**	**482279**	**307019**	**27757**	**28671**	**118832**
艺术业	Art	104859	57276	47584	21739	18000	6823	1022
#艺术表演团体	Art Performance Groups	103043	56606	46436	21244	17929	6517	746
艺术表演场馆	Art Performance Places	5348	2759	2589	1420	145	307	718
图书馆	Library	53674	14534	39140	32383	70	6683	4
群众文化	Mass Culture	57772	7275	50497	44914	23	5553	8
艺术教育	Art Education	3894	1103	2790	2445	4	342	0
文化市场经营机构	Operating Units of Culture Marlcet	321995	120800	201195	125920	7690	0	67585
动漫企业	Comic & Animation	3473	1090	2383	1302	151	228	702
文艺科研	Culture & Art Research	1930	429	1501	1490	0	10	1
文物业	Relic Industry	41073	17717	23356	17194	129	5024	1009
其他文化及相关产业	Other Culture & Relative Industries	145760	31927	113833	59633	1689	4009	48502

19—18 文化部门主要文化产业单位基本情况
Basic Situation of Major Units of Culture Industries in Culture Department

项 目	Item	1995	2000	2005	2010	2012	2013	2014	2015	2016	2017
艺术表演团体	**Art Performance Groups**										
机构数（个）	Number of Institutions (unit)	117	118	118	141	68	59	67	92	100	108
从业人员（人）	Employees (person)	4408	4518	4352	4946	2744	3777	3042	4613	4716	4747
国内演出场次（千场次）	Times of Domestic Performance (1 000 performances)	10.87	13.40	12.34	14.93	11.07	15.41	9.20	13.17	11.98	14.43
国内演出观众人次（千人次）	Person-times of Audiences of Domestic Performance (1 000 person-times)	9867	16184	13182	15076	7579	8818	6639		8484	9732
本年收入合计（万元）	Total Income in This Year (10 000 yuan)	3806	6503	12018	23855	17507	35747	32238	65365	15470	15945
#财政补助收入	Income from Financial Allowance	2589	4913	9022	17951	12709	22824	21449	24937	12726	13124
演出收入	Income from Performance	507	717	1550	3679	4631	9109	5497	34801	30885	72554
本年支出合计（万元）	Total Expenditure in This Year (10 000 yuan)	3670	6492	11761	23871	15820	35657	29397	54129	14710	17588

注：本表中艺术表演团体基本情况数据自2010年开始，将在广西文化市场管理机构登记办证的艺术表演单位纳入统计范畴。

Note: The data on the basic situation of art performance groups has brought the art performance units of culture market in Guangxi into the statistical rarge since 2010.

19－18 续表 1 continued

项 目	Item	1995	2000	2005	2010	2012	2013	2014	2015	2016	2017
公共图书馆	**Public Library**										
机构数（个）	Number of Institutions (unit)	99	94	95	108	112	112	112	112	114	115
从业人员（人）	Employees (person)	1335	1540	1459	1509	1467	1519	1508	1509	1589	1660
总藏量（千册/件）	Total Collection of Books (1 000 copies/ collects)	12430	13122	14908	18809	21267	21098	24815	26063	27195	27860
总流通人次（千人次）	Total Circulation Person-times (1 000 person-times)	8090	9268	12257	13428	13664	14705	19980	20652	20670	23443
书刊外借册次（千册次）	Copy-time of Lending Books (1 000 copy-times)	5281	6878	7614	7328	8058	8539	7542	11550	11418	11829
本年收入合计（万元）	Total Income in This Year (10 000 yuan)	1821	3361	6305	13320	25084	29032	25969	35997	33215	477477
#财政补助收入	Income from Financial Allowance	1563	2851	5469	12191	22675	23491	23347	32734	29939	459831
本年支出合计（万元）	Total Expenditure in This Year (10 000 yuan)	1769	3077	6288	13369	18759	25286	26425	35915	32947	459915
#图书购置费	Expenditure for Book Purchasing	291	520	674	1676	2484	2845	2281		3757	4434
本年新购图书（千册）	New Books Purchased in This Year (1 000 copies)	157	201	260	563	913	968	1426	1492	1316	1282
群众文化	**Mass Culture**										
群艺馆机构数（个）	Number of Institutions of Mass Culture (unit)	14	15	15	15	15	15	15	15	15	15
从业人员（人）	Employees (person)	319	337	335	345	487	557	512	519	543	547
举办展览个数（个）	Number of Exhibitions Held (unit)	57	53	84	70	80	128	113	151	114	113
组织文艺活动次数（次）	Times of Culture & Art Actions Organized (time)	119	276	289	1264	1186	1142	1126	1288	1075	2330
本年收入合计（万元）	Total Income in This Year (10 000 yuan)	611	849	1454	4055	8269	11144	1123640	129517	136940	55713
#财政补助收入	Income from Financial Allowance	332	567	1249	3372	6394	10075	10025	11299	12216	50554
本年支出合计（万元）	Total Expenditure in This Year (10 000 yuan)	652	877	1515	4006	7366	11484	11323	11817	12303	55119

19－18 续表 2 continued

项 目	Item	1995	2000	2005	2010	2012	2013	2014	2015	2016	2017
文化馆机构数（个）	Number of Insitutions of Cultural Centers (unit)	98	99	100	107	108	108	108	108	109	109
从业人员（人）	Employees (person)	1280	1273	1195	1145	1605	1629	1630	1595	1596	1613
举办展览个数（个）	Number of Exhibitions Held (unit)	316	730	340	354	564	623	629	608	618	601
组织文艺活动次数（次）	Times of Culture & Art Actions Organizated (time)	1288	2166	2249	4740	6215	5950	6364	6600	7351	8594
本年收入合计（万元）	Total Income in This Year (10 000 yuan)	1248	1509	2607	6743	13130	16063	16460	18663	20238	20994
#财政补助收入	Income from Financial Allowance	897	1234	2258	6443	12091	13869	15090	16706	18268	19522
本年支出合计（万元）	Total Expenditure in This Year (10 000 yuan)	1218	1485	2537	6672	12557	15284	16195	17639	19492	20388
文化站机构数（个）	Number of Insitutions of Cultural Stations (unit)	1412	1294	1139	1162	1167	1167	1167	1168	1168	1174
从业人员（人）	Employees (person)	1835	1777	2273	2585	2735	2832	2967	3168	3399	3076
博物馆	**Museum**										
机构数（个）	Number of Institutions (unit)	37	39	49	64	79	104	106	124	125	132
从业人员（人）	Employees (person)	566	667	753	1096	1529	1696	1703	1996	2013	2212
文物藏品（件、套）	Collection of Relics (unit, set)	180956	170336	239327	279452	362854	397058	411224	422677	342356	254298
#一级品	1st Class	296	293	279	312	316	316	316	360	320	298
举办展览（个）	Number of Exhibitions Held (unit)	102	102	126	194	250	171	207	445	277	570
参观人次（千人次）	Number of Visitors (1 000 person-times)	1443	1802	1442	7441	11250	12532	15078	16555	19516	18279
#未成年人参加人次	Juveniles				2067	2762	3382	3843	5115	5638	5211
#外宾人次	Foreign Visitors	41	34	37		156					
本年收入合计（万元）	Total Income in This Year (10 000 yuan)	906	1792	4905	17239	32873	39463	40183	40712	44058	44880
#财政补助收入	Income from Financial Allowance	611	976	2430	14244	27635	23213	29615	29745	40251	43011
门票收入	Income from Ticket	51	122	229	39	165	75				
本年支出合计（万元）	Total Expenditure in This Year (10 000 yuan)	899	1852	4326	14344	30701	27714	32573	38965	36106	41629

注：1.公共图书馆中自2013年起“图书购置费”为“新增藏量购置费”，“本年新购图书”为“本年新增藏量”。
2.博物馆中自2013年起“举办展览”为“临时展览”。

Note: 1. The indicator of “Expenditure for Book Burchasing” of Public Library since 2013 is changed to “Expenditure for New Added Collection” “New Books Purchased in This Year” is changed to “New Added Collection in This Year”.
2. The indicator of “Number of Exhibitions Held” of Museum since 2013 is changed to “Temporary Exhibitions Held”.

19－19 主要年份广播事业发展情况
Basic Statistics on Broadcasting in Main Years

项 目	Item	1995	2000	2005	2010	2013	2014	2015	2016	2017
基本情况	**Basic Statistics**									
中短波转播发射台（座）	Medium-and-short-wave Broadcasting Transmision Stations & Relaying Stations (set)	24	25	21	20	20	20	20	20	20
调频转播发射台（座）	Frequency Modulation Broadcasting Transmision Stations & Relaying Stations (set)	32	100	89	150	261	392	604	712	769
节目（套）	Programmes (unit)	31	34	60	63	65	70	72	74	75
全年公共广播节目播出时间（小时）	Daily Broadcasting Hours (hour)	117560	158714	257463	276733	324793	358518	376961	401239	421299
广播综合人口覆盖率（%）	Listener Rating (%)	66.3	85.2	88.7	95.0	96.2	96.6	96.7	96.9	97.2
制作广播节目（小时）	Broadcasting Programmes Producing (hour)	47053	90269	165012	176577	188549	221858	220838	232673	237853
新闻资讯节目	News & Information Programmes	6801	11186	23447	36670	36504	42427	41919	44128	44272
专题服务节目	Subject Service Programmes	11999	23109	46634	43832	35929	39176	34445	39469	43931
综艺益智	Comprehensive Entertainment Programmes	17362	27912	60556	62601	67584	74870	61424	68564	82162
广播剧节目	Radio Play Programmes			769	409	484	1131	1035	939	1438
广告节目	Advertisement Programmes		2323	15326	13071	15800	18140	17851	18923	14941
其他节目	Other Programmes	10891	25739	18280	19994	32246	46111	64163	60651	51108

19－20 各市公共图书馆基本情况（2017年）

地 区	Region	机构数（个）Number of Institutions (unit)	从业人员（人）Employed Persons (person)	总藏量（千册）Library Holdings (1 000 copies)	当年购买的报刊种类（种）Newspapers & Periodicals Purchased in the Year (kind)	总流通人次（千人次）Total Circulation of Persons(1 000 person-times)
广西壮族自治区	**Guangxi**	**115**	**1660**	**27859.83**	**37896**	**23442.98**
自治区本级	**Autonomous Region Level**	**3**	**323**	**7145.35**	**8274**	**5131.86**
南宁市	Nanning	14	219	3071.52	4915	3668.29
柳州市	Liuzhou	11	150	1926.46	2604	2892.43
桂林市	Guilin	13	100	1561.95	2146	651.65
梧州市	Wuzhou	5	104	1113.68	1816	4672.26
北海市	Beihai	3	82	673.62	696	548.23
防城港市	Fangchenggang	5	49	447.99	797	377.84
钦州市	Qinzhou	5	62	3177.05	1384	482.22
贵港市	Guigang	6	45	1210.66	1399	552.18
玉林市	Yulin	8	107	1794.44	1877	1495.05
百色市	Baise	13	153	1988.44	3168	1211.39
贺州市	Hezhou	4	59	752.13	1416	363.48
河池市	Hechi	11	83	1260.91	3736	462.52
来宾市	Laibin	7	65	917.11	1989	560.81
崇左市	Chongzuo	7	59	818.56	1679	372.77

Basic Situation of Public Libraries by City（2017）

为读者举办各种活动 Activities Held for Readers				本年支出合计（万元）Total Cost of the Year (10 000 yuan)	资产合计（万元）Total Capitals (10 000 yuan)	实际使用公用房屋建筑面积（千平方米）Area of Public Building Actual Used (sq.m)
组织各类讲座次数（次）Number of Lectures Held (time)	参加人次（千人次）Number of Persons Attending (1 000 person-times)	举办展览（次）Number of Exhibitions Held (time)	参观人次（千人次）Number of Persons Visiting(1 000 person-times)			
1777	**328.11**	**942**	**3931.19**	**45992**	**115851**	**422.49**
197	**31.00**	**63**	**1465.02**	**17451**	**55515**	**109.96**
343	90.82	148	220.41	3691	11980	37.52
123	11.91	104	1395.22	3767	7249	31.17
210	56.57	89	78.19	1297	2104	17.99
123	28.25	28	13.30	1320	2172	19.09
112	8.95	85	56.30	1465	2843	23.16
97	22.73	9	37.36	1476	2346	16.54
61	6.85	25	41.42	6000	7585	16.31
74	13.77	35	35.94	1046	2462	18.88
110	9.60	43	50.58	2029	6429	30.26
105	11.89	77	215.47	2452	6190	29.84
38	5.39	30	56.21	730	1887	7.62
71	9.88	53	167.69	1416	2918	30.82
60	4.79	47	57.06	1001	2172	20.68
53	15.68	106	41.02	849	1997	12.68

19—21 主要年份电视事业发展情况
Basic Statistics on Television Stations in Main Years

项 目	Item	1995	2000	2005	2010	2013	2014	2015	2016	2017
基本情况	**Basic Statistics**									
电视转播台（座）	Television Relaying Stations (set)	1009	237	65	128	128	128	128	128	
节目（套）	Programmes (unit)	20	23	39	41	41	41	42	41	41
全年公共电视节目播出时间（小时）	Television Broadcasting Hours of Whole Year (hour)	42572	74166	276597	481171	543051	548710	576257	595786	596046
电视综合人口覆盖率（%）	Viewer Rating (%)	79.5	90.0	93.5	97.0	98.0	98.2	98.3	98.4	98.6
制作电视节目	Programmes Producing	5732	15200	60033	80594	106334	104166	97532	82568	93848
新闻资讯节目（小时）	News & Information Programmes (hour)	1591	2793	17833	25367	34943	34540	33830	32398	32698
专题服务节目（小时）	Subject Service Programmes (hour)	1387	3357	12123	15071	24981	27125	25481	21663	16227
综艺益智节目（小时）	Comprehensive Entertainment	768	2999	7793	9101	12014	12855	9041	5826	8592
影视剧节目（小时）	Programmes (hour)			692	416	117	91	104	509	481
广告节目（小时）	TV Play Programmes (hour)		4011	15168	21730	22156	20584	20665	15557	18860
其他节目（小时）	Advertisement Programmes (hour)	1986	2040	6424	8909	12120	8968	8411	6615	6989
电视剧（部/集）	Other Programmes (hour)	3/21	11/80	9/448	10/341	2/52	4/108	2/60	4/156	5/240
动画电视（小时）	TV Plays (collection/episode)				3	71	4	45	277	28

19—22 主要年份图书、报纸及杂志出版情况
Basic Statistics of Books, Newspaper & Magazines in Main Years

项 目	Item	1995	2000	2005	2010	2013	2014	2015	2016	2017
图 书	**Books**									
种 数（种）	Number of Publications (kind)	2694	2739	3500	7344	8795	13146	7537	7419	7319
印 数（万册）	Printed Copies (10 000 copies)	25397	23691	18818	24810	34376	39773	29978	29193	29022
印 张（千印张）	Printed Sheets (1 000 sheets)	1031173	1153943	1331175	1545018	2400209	2854019	2165681	2075167	2107198
报 纸	**Newspapers**									
种 数（种）	Number of Publications (kind)	66	60	50	55	54	54	54	53	53
印 数（万份）	Printed Copies (10 000 copies)	47475	56008	58222	69560	71812	72972	68974	64275	57997
印 张（千印张）	Printed Sheets (1 000 sheets)	451524	834192	1668812	2855711	2516898	2326772	2082133	1738851	1395607
期 刊	**Magazines**									
种 数（种）	Number of Publications (kind)	159	191	180	183	179	182	180	181	181
印 数（万册）	Printed Copies (10 000 copies)	4630	5242	5571	4268	4870	4808	4754	4236	4090
印 张（千印张）	Printed Sheets (1 000 sheets)	129001	149238	277555	176235	201151	196245	193264	180387	177766

主要统计指标解释

普通高等学校 指按国家规定的设置标准和审批程序批准建立的，通过全国普通高等教育统一招生考试，招收高中毕业生为主要培养对象，实施高等学历教育的全日制大学、独立设置的学院和高等专科学校、高等职业学校和其他机构。

大学、独立设置的学院主要实施本科及本科层次以上教育。高等专科学校、高等职业学校实施专科层次教育。其他机构是承担国家普通招生计划任务不计校数的机构。包括普通高等学校分校和批准筹建的普通高等学校等（注：高等学校在校学生数均不包括在校研究生）。

成人高等学校 指按国家规定的设置标准和审批程序批准举办的，通过全国成人高等教育统一招生考试，招收具有高中毕业或同等学历的人员为主要培养对象，利用函授、业余、脱产的多种形式对其实施高等学历教育的学校。包括职工高等学校、农民高等学校、管理干部学院、教育学院、独立函授学院、广播电视大学、其他机构。

中等职业教育 调整后的中等职业学校是指将普通中等专业学校（中等技术学校、中等师范学校）、成人中等专业学校、职业高中学校、其他机构等各种实施中等职业教育的办学类型，通过合并、共建、联办、划转等形式调整为统一的办学类型。

艺术表演团体 指由文化部门主办或实行行业管理（经文化市场行政部门审批或已申报登记并领取相关许可证），专门从事表演艺术等活动的各类专业艺术表演团体，含民间职业剧团。不包括群众业余文艺表演团体。

艺术表演场馆 指由文化部门主办或实行行业管理（经文化市场行政部门审批或已申报登记并领取相关许可证），有观众席、舞台、灯光设备，公共售票、专供文艺团体演出的文化活动场所。

广播节目综合人口覆盖率 是指根据国家广电总局制定的《广播电视人口覆盖率统计技术标准和方法》，在对象区内采用无线、有线、卫星等技术手段能够收听到包括中央、省、地市、县广播节目其中任意一套的人口数与全国总人口的比。

电视节目综合人口覆盖率 是指根据国家广电总局制定的《广播电视人口覆盖率统计技术标准和方法》，在对象区内采用无线、有线、卫星等技术手段能够收看到包括中央、省、地市、县级电视节目中任意一套的人口数与全国总人口的比。

科技活动 指在自然科学、农业科学、医药科学、工程与技术科学、人文与社会科学领域（简称科学技术领域）中，与科技知识的产生、发展、传播和应用密切相关的有组织的活动。可分为科学研究与试验发展（R&D）、科学研究与试验发展成果应用及相关的科技服务三类活动。

科学研究与试验发展（R&D） 指在科学技术领域，为增加知识总量、以及运用这些知识去创造新的应用而进行的系统的创造性的活动，包括基础研究、应用研究、试验发展三类活动。

基础研究 指为获得关于现象和可观察事实的基本原理的新知识（揭示客观事物的本质、运动规律，获得新发现、新学说）而进行的实验性或理论性研究，它不以任何专门或特定的应用或使用为目的。其成果以科学论文和科学著作为主要形式。

应用研究 指为获得新知识而进行的创造性研究，主要针对某一特定的目的或目标。应用研究是为了确定基础研究成果可能的用途，或是为达到预定的目标探索应采取的新方法（原理性）或新途径。其成果形式以科学论文、专著、原理理性模型或发明专利为主。

试验发展 指利用从基础研究、应用研究和实际经验所获得的现有知识，为产生新的产品、材料和装置，建立新的工艺、系统和服务，以及对已产生和建立的上述各项作实质性的改进而进行的系统性工作。其成果形式主要是专利、专有技术，具有新产品基本特征的产品原型或具有新装置基本特征的原始样机等。在社会科学领域，试验发展是指把通过基础研究、应用研究获得的知识转变成可以实施的计划（包括为进行检验和评估实施示范项目）的过程。人文科学领域没有对应的试验发展活动。

R&D人员 指单位内部从事基础研究，应用研究和试验发展三类活动的人员。包括直接参加上述三类项目活动的人员

以及这三类项目的管理人员和直接服务人员。为研发活动提供直接服务的人员包括直接为研发活动提供资料文献、材料供应、设备维护等服务的人员。

政府资金　指从各级政府部门获得的计划用于科技活动的经费，包括科学事业费、科技三项费、科研基建费、科学基金、教育等部门事业费中计划用于科技活动的经费以及政府部门预算外资金中计划用于科技活动的经费等。

Explanatory Notes on Main Statistical Indicators

Regular Institutions of Higher Learning refer to educational establishments set up according to the govern-ment evaluation and approval procedures, enrolling graduates from senior secondary schools and providing higher education courses and training for senior professionals. They include full-time universities, colleges, high professional schools and short-term profes-sional universities.

Institutions of Higher Learning for Adults refer to educational establishments, set up in line with relevant rules approved by the government, enrolling staff and workers with senior secondary school or equivalent education, and providing higher education courses in many forms of full-time, part-time, spare-time, or correspondence for adults. Professionals thus trained receive a qualification equivalent to graduates studying regular courses at regular universities, colleges and professional colleges. Institutions of higher learning for adults include Radio and TV universities, schools of high education for staff and workers and peasants, college for management cadres, pedagogical colleges, independent correspondence colleges.

Art Troupe refers to the troupe which is engaged in drama, opera, music, dance, acrobatics or other art performance, opens independent accounts with banks and has self-supporting accounting system; excluding the troupes which are engaged partly in industrial or agricultural activities, partly in art performance and the professional troupes organized by the people.

Scientific and Technological Activities (S&T Activities) refer to organized activities which are closely related with the creation, development, dissemination, and application of the scientific and technical knowledge in the fields of natu-ral sciences, agricultural science, medical science, engineering and technological science, humanities and social sciences (referred to as scientific and technological fields). S&T activities can be classified into 3 categories: research and development (R&D) activities, application of R&D results, and related S&T services.

Research and Development (R&D) refers to systematic and creative activities in the field of science and tech-nology aiming at increasing the knowledge and using the knowledge for new application. R&D includes 3 categories of activities: basic research, applied research and experiments and development.

Basic Research refers to empirical or theoretical research aiming at obtaining new knowledge on the fundamental principles of phenomena of observable facts to reveal the nature and law of movement of objects and to acquire new discoveries or new theories. Basic research takes no specific or designated application as the aim of the research are mainly released or disseminated in the form of scientific papers or monographs.

Applied Research refers to creative research aiming at obtaining new knowledge on a specific objective or target. Pur-pose of the applied research is to identity the possible use of results from basic research, or to explore new (fundamental) methods of new approaches. Results of applied research are expressed in the form of scientific papers, monographs, fundamental models or in-vention patents.

Experiments and Development refer to systematic activities aiming at using the knowledge form basic and applied researches or form practical experience to develop new products, materials and equipment, to establish new production process, systems and services, or to make substantial improvement on the existing products, process or services. Results of experiment and development activities are embodied in patents, exclusive technology, and monotype of new products or equipment. In social sci-ences, experiment and development activities refer to the process of converting the knowledge from basic or applied researches into feasible programs (including conduct of demonstration projects for assessment and evaluation). There is on experiment and devel-opment activities in the science of humanities.

R&D Personnel refer to persons engaged in research, management and supporting activities of R&D, including persons in the project teams, persons engaged in the management of S&T activities of enterprises and supporting staff providing direct ser-vice to the research projects.

Government Funds refer to funds obtained from government agencies at all levels to be used for S&T activities, including fund for scientific undertakings, 3 kinds of fund for S&T activities, fund for capital construction for scientific researches, science fund, funds from education expenditures by education departments for S&T activities, and extra-budget fund from government agencies for S&T activities.

第二十篇

体育、卫生与社会福利

SPORT, PUBLIC HEALTH & SOCIAL WELFARE

（校对编辑：卢启函）

20－1　主要年份体育事业发展情况
Statistics on Sports in Main Years

项　目	Item	2000	2005	2010	2011	2012	2013	2014	2015	2016	2017
体育系统从业人员（人）	Number of Staff & Workers in Sports System (person)	3335	3917	5183	5231	5319	3670	3971	4457	4440	3981
#优秀运动队	Splendid Sports Team		1110	1535	1761	1776	119	881	956	1056	963
体育运动学校	Physical Education & Sports Schools	180		199	168	176	523	499	512	535	476
业余体校	Spare Time Sports Schools	1028	1119	1886	1626	1786	716	743	793	790	732
训练基地	Training Bases	184	129	127	62	97	856	295	300	285	280
体育场馆	Sports Places	272	213	248	126	209	308	271	272	256	277
举办综合运动会次数（次）	Number of Comprehensive Athletic Meetings Held (time)		0	4	1	0	0	0	1	12	1
举办单项比赛次数（次）	Number of Single Game Items Held (time)		23	34	14	26	25	27	30	131	305
举办全民健身活动次数（次）	Number of Exercises Held for All the People (time)		2675	3265	3726	2851			511	2685	2819
#1 000人以上的活动	Above 1 000 Persons		448	973	748	568			511	664	85
举办全民健身活动人数（万人）	Number of Persons Taking Part in Exercises Held for All the People (10 000 persons)		331	454	856	1731			130	218	229
等级运动员发展人数（人）	Number of Athletes in Grades (person)	2552	707	1711	690	927	635	743	607	882	644
#国际级健将	International Masters of Sports		4	7	3	0	0	0	0	0	0
运动健将	Masters of Sports	27	36	45	29	21	24	1	7	1	0
一级运动员	First Grade Sportsmen	41	75	184	165	177	133	223	31	336	170
二级运动员	Second Grade Sportsmen	354	592	1475	493	729	478	523	370	545	494
等级裁判员发展人数（人）	Number of Referees in Grades (person)	2154	865	1894	2685	5411	2652	2755	2170	1357	
#国家级裁判	National Referees	10	11	1	7	12	5	0	10	0	10
一级裁判员	First Grade Referees		78	113	161	290	185	271	233	33	
二级裁判员	Second Grade Referees		776	1780	2190	1944	2458	2484	1934	1324	

20－2　运动队体育比赛成绩（2017年）
Scores of Sports Groups in Sport Matches　(2017)

单位：个　　(unit)

项　目	Item	名次 Position								破记录情况 Situation of Record Breaking
		1	2	3	4	5	6	7	8	
世界三大赛	The Three Worldwide Big Matches	6	5	1		2	1	2	1	
一般国际比赛	Common Worldwide Matches	7	5	5		4		1	2	
亚洲大赛	Big Matches of Asia	10	4	5		2	2			
全国大赛	National Big Matches	62	58	84	67	84	54	30	30	
全国青少年比赛	National Matches of Youth	94	91	88	84	74	39	29	17	
一般国内大赛	Common National Matches	8	8	6	8	8	13	6	10	
合　计	**Total**	**187**	**171**	**189**	**159**	**174**	**109**	**68**	**60**	

20—3 主要年份卫生事业基本情况
Basic Situation of Public Health in Main Years

项 目	Item	1995	2000	2005	2010	2013	2014	2015	2016	2017
一、各类卫生机构、卫生技术人员	Health Care Institutions & Medical Technical Personnel by Type									
卫生机构数（个）	Number of Health Care Institutions (unit)	5571	13707	9432	10341	11195	11469	11770	11991	12288
#医院、卫生院	Hospitals	1709	1868	1753	1728	1755	1756	1794	1810	1853
社区卫生服务中心（站）	Community Sanitation Service Center			156	285	261	269	277	279	300
疗养院	Sanatoriums	11	8	8	5	5	5	5	5	5
门诊部、诊所、医务室	Clinics	3333	11361	7050	7891	8725	9041	9255	9403	9700
疾病预防控制中心(防疫站)	Sanitation & Antiepidemic Agencies	132	136	106	105	109	113	115	115	117
卫生监督所（局）	Sanitation Supervision Agencies			63	109	110	112	112	111	114
专科疾病防治院（所、站）	Specialized Prevention Hospitals (Stations)	66	66	62	43	40	41	41	37	34
妇幼保健院（所、站）	Maternity & Child Care Hospitals (Stations)	81	103	103	103	104	104	104	103	104
医学学科研究机构	Research Institutions of Medical Science	26	22	15	14	13	14	13	14	13
其他卫生机构	Others	126	147	41	28	39	14	15	15	14
病床总数（张）	Total Number of Beds (bed)	83963	85422	93767	143695	187216	201600	214485	224710	240713
#医院、卫生院病床数	Hospitals	78788	82975	87061	133887	174001	187702	199712	209021	224114
每千人中医院、卫生院病床数（张）	Number of Hospital Beds per 1 000 Persons (bed)	1.73	1.74	1.77	2.60	3.69	4.16	4.06	4.32	5.00
卫生技术人员（人）	Medical Technical Personnel (person)	116547	127036	129210	185715	233777	258618	274663	289865	305316
#执业医师、执业助理医师	Practitioner Doctors & Practitioner Assistant Doctors	41305	45981	54652	67314	77825	86525	91580	96678	101141
注册护士	Registered Nurses	35636	40331	44604	69906	93887	103955	113202	122595	131711
每千人中有卫生技术人员数（人）	Number of Medical Technical Personnel per 1 000 Persons (person)	2.56	2.67	2.63	3.60	4.87	5.44	5.73	5.99	6.00
疾病预防控制中心（防疫站）（个）	Center for Disease Control and Prevention (Epidemic Prevention Stations) (unit)	132	136	106	105	109	113	115	115	117
卫生技术人员（人）	Medical Technical Personnel (person)	5152	5340	4839	4852	5354	5435	5735	6004	6003
妇幼保健院（所、站）（个）	Women and Children Care Agencies (unit)	81	103	103	103	104	104	104	103	104
卫生技术人员（人）	Medical Technical Personnel (person)	2190	5879	7193	12763	16997	18357	19380	20790	23082
乡镇卫生院（个）	Rural Hospitals (unit)	1273	1134	1295	1278	1279	1270	1267	1267	1264
床位数（张）	Number of Beds (bed)	18470	12720	20963	44974	55526	58319	59406	60541	63035
卫生技术人员（人）	Medical Technical Personnel (person)	23829	20134	28258	43687	53395	56298	58007	59957	62357
乡村医生和卫生员人数（人）	Doctors or Health Workers in Rural Areas (person)	44617	47099	36236	36386	33353	36725	36101	34981	34151
二、医院病床使用情况	Utilization of Hospital Beds									
病床周转次数（次）	Turnover of Beds (time)	19	19	25	42	38	38	37	36	36
病床工作日数（日）	Days Per Bed in Use (day)	264	219	256	300	357	347	328	321	321
病床使用率（%）	Utilization Rate of Beds (%)	73	60	70	82	98	95	90	88	88
出院者平均住院日数（日）	Average Hospitalization Period (day)	14	11	10	7	9	9	9	9	9
参合率（%）	Participation Rate of NCMS(%)				93.1	98.9	99.0	99.2	99.3	

注：1. 本表的卫生机构数不含村卫生室和计生机构。

2. 1995年、2000年的执业医师、执业助理医师为中医师、西医师、中西医结合医师，注册护士为护师、护士。

Note: 1. The indicator “Number of Health Care Institutions” in this table excludes village clinics and institutions of family planning.

2. The practitioner doctors and practitioner assistant doctors in 1995, 2000 refer to doctors of Chinese medicine, doctors of Western medicine, senior doctors who integrate traditional Chinese therapeutics with Western therapeutics in practice, registered nurses refer to primary nurses and nurses.

20—4 医疗机构诊疗人次和入院人数（2017年）
Number of Hospital Patients & Admissions (2017)

医院类别	Hospital Type	诊疗人次数（万人次）Total Number of Patients Treated (10 000 person-times)	#门、急诊 Out-patients & Emergency Patients	入院人数（万人）Hospital Admissions (10 000 persons)	每百名门急诊的入院人数（人）Hospital Admissions Per 100 Patient-times (person)
总　计	**Total**	**26050.3**	**25370.3**	**901.0**	**5.2**
医院	Hospital	9846.2	9572.7	571.7	6.0
疗养院	Sanatoriums	5.4	4.9	0.9	19.0
社区卫生服务中心	Community Sanitation Service Center	783.5	739.6	3.3	0.5
卫生院	Rural Hospitals	5005.8	4898.6	247.0	5.0
门诊部	Out-patients Department	157.1	152.4	0.1	
妇幼保健院（所、站）	Hospitals for Maternity & Child Care	2058.0	2013.4	77.3	3.8
专科疾病防治院（所、站）	Specialized Stations	96.6	91.2	0.7	0.7

20—5 收养性社会福利单位基本情况（2017年）
Basic Statistics of Adopting Social Welfare Units (2017)

项　目	Item	机构（个）Number of Institutions (unit)	职工人数（人）Number of Staff & Workers (person)	床位（张）Number of Beds (bed)	年在院总人天数（人天）Number of Persons in Social Welfare Home (person-day)
总　计	**Total**	**555**	**11172**	**55478**	**7733374**
荣誉军人康复医院	Recuperative Hospital for Soldiers with Honour	1	48	241	78533
光荣院	Homes for Disabled Veterans	57	234	2046	181961
复退军人精神病院	Mental Hospitals for Demobilized Soldiers & Veterans	4	890	1750	571943
社会福利院	Social Welfare Homes	91	2108	10390	1696555
儿童福利机构	Social Welfare Homes for Children	41	901	3442	321593
社会福利医院	Social Welfare Homes for Mental				
城镇收养性老年福利机构	Adopting Welfare Units for the Elderly in Urban Areas	193	4499	27222	3646003
农村收养性老年福利机构	Adopting Welfare Units for the Elderly in Rural Areas	44	313	3259	443969
其他收养性福利单位	Others	124	2179	7128	792817

注：收养性社会福利单位不包括五保村。
Note: The adopting social welfare units excludes the five guarantees villages.

20－6 主要年份优抚和社会福利单位机构和人员
Institutions & Persons Engaged for Martyrs & Social Welfare in Main Years

项　目	Item	1995	2000	2005	2010	2012	2013	2014	2015	2016	2017
机 构（个）	**Institutions (unit)**										
一、收养性社会福利单位	Adopting Social Welfare Units	423	634	5992	1446	1471	1496	492			555
# 优抚类收养性单位	Adopting Units for Martyrs	20	22	44	70	77					93
福利类收养性单位	Adopting Units for Welfare	403	612	5948	1376	1394					462
二、优抚安置单位	Administration Units for Martyrs			62	80	68			72	68	64
#军休所	Homes for Retired & Resigned Soldiers	10	18	32	37	36	36	36	35	35	34
军供站	Institutions for Army Facilities Supply	11	12	12	12	12	13	13	13	13	14
烈士纪念建筑物管理单位	Administrative Agencies of Martyr Memorial Buildings			18	31	20	21	23	24	20	16
三、社会福利企业单位	Number of Total Social Welfare Enterprises	482	325	276	199	137	143	124	112		
#国有社会福利企业	Run by Government			42							
集体社会福利企业	Run by Communities			174							
民办社会福利企业	Run by the Local People			60							
四、救助类单位	Units for Relief	17	17	20	37	46	55	81	93	68	92
#救助管理站	Stations for Relief Management	15	15	17	30	39	48	58	66	68	67
流浪儿童救助保护中心	Helping & Protecting Centers for Waifs			3	7	7	7	23	27	26	25
五、殡仪服务单位	Funeral Institutions	24	44	56	71	71	56	107	108	97	89
六、福利彩票发行单位	Welfare Lottery-ticked Issuance Units			91	53	36	33	32	30	28	19
七、慈善团体	Charities			15							
八、社区服务中心	Community Service Centers		70	93	104	91	86	80	88	178	321
#提供住宿	Providing with Lodging			2							
不提供住宿	Providing without Lodging			91							
职工人数（人）	**Number of Staff & Workers (person)**										
一、收养性社会福利单位	Adopting Social Welfare Units	2135	3134	9136	7846	7864	8724	5900			11172
# 优抚类收养性单位	Adopting Units for Martyrs	409	446	673	792	923					545
福利类收养性单位	Adopting Units for Welfare	1704	2688	8463	7054	6941					10627
二、优抚安置单位	Administration Units for Martyrs			770							
#军休所	Homes for Retired & Resigned Soldiers	93	141	224	242	246	246	36	35	225	244
军供站	Institutions for Army Facilities Supply	388	395	391	381	293	301	13	13	232	229
烈士纪念建筑物管理单位	Administrative Agencies of Martyr Memorial Buildings			155	185	218	243	307		247	199
三、社会福利企业单位	Number of Total Staff & Workers Engaged in Social Welfare Enterprises	12398	9981	9389	11292	9095	8815	8139	7619		
#国有社会福利企业	Run by Government			1546							
集体社会福利企业	Run by Communities			6184							
民办社会福利企业	Run by the Local People			2105							
四、救助类单位	Units for Relief	715	645	297	348	441	474	556	553	486	684
#救助管理站	Stations for Relief Management	245	255	276	306	369	406	433	439	486	502
流浪儿童救助保护中心	Helping & Protecting Centers for Waifs			21	42	72	68	123	114	158	182
五、殡仪服务单位	Funeral Institutions	613	784	1261	1581	1513	1435	1942	2075	2032	1886
六、福利彩票发行单位	Welfare Lottery-ticked Issuance Units			482	323	494	589	669	740	747	744
七、慈善团体	Charities			50							
八、社区服务中心	Community Service Centers		413	901	1576	728	654	304		863	1199
#提供住宿	Providing with Lodging			5							
不提供住宿	Providing without Lodging			896							

注：收养性社会福利单位数、收养人数不包括五保村机构数、床位数和收养人数。优抚、福利类收养性单位和优抚安置单位的调查口径自2013年起已取消。

Note: The number of adopting social welfare units and the number of adopting persons excludes the number of five guarantees villages,beds and adopting persons. The adjusted statistical range of adopting units for martyrs and welfare and administration units for martyrs has been canceled since 2013.

20—7 主要年份社会救济对象享受救济情况

Basic Statistics of Persons Receiving Subsidies or Relief Funds in Main Years

项 目	Item	2000	2005	2010	2013	2014	2015	2016	2017
一、城镇居民最低生活保障人数（人）	Population Receiving Lowest Cost-of-living in Urban Area (person)	108173	568957	601935	494366	448016	385308	226134	190843
城镇居民最低生活保障家庭数（户）	Number of Families Receiving Lowest Cost-of-living in Urban Area (household)		273349	306368	252800	228360	198698	121741	102814
城镇临时救济人次数（人次）	Population Receiving Temporary Almsgiving in Urban Area (person-time)	31226	67043	4732	7164	5088	7402		
二、农村居民最低生活保障人数（人）	Population Receiving Lowest Cost-of-living in Rural Area (person)	204293	42745	3156789	3458922	3289710	2921414	2905689	2539255
农村居民最低生活保障家庭数（户）	Number of Families Receiving Lowest Cost-of-living in Rural Area(household)		26019	1296975	1334863	1294495	1179258	1019010	890723
三、农村传统定期定量救济人数（人）	Population Receiving Traditional Relief in Rural Area (person)	50292	470169	6308	111153	117691	118118	112853	111903
农村临时救济人次数（人次）	Population Receiving Temporary Almsgiving (person-time)	1298570	2058208	6308	251163	76608			
四、农村五保户供养人数（人）	Population Enjoying the Five Guarantees (person)			327349	294670	289490	280486	269643	250418
农村五保户供养户数（户）	Households Enjoying the Five Guarantees (household)			320567					
五、医疗救助（人）	Medical Assistance (person)								
民政部门资助参保人数	Number of Persons Aided by Civil Affairs Departments				250598	211705	148784		
民政部门资助参合人数	Number of Persons Joined CMS and being Aided by Civil Affairs Departments				2439585	2326681	1860604		
民政部门直接救助人次数	Number of Person-times Directly Aided by Civil Affairs Departments				413584	373903	931603	595218	282881
#住院救助人次数	Number of Person-times of Hospital Assistance				295485	337638	908789	258213	260198
门诊救助人次数	Number of Person-times of Outpatients Assistance				118099	36265	22814	337005	22683

注：医疗救助情况，民政部从2013年开始使用新口径，数据与2012年以前不可比。

Note: The new statistical range of Medical Assitatnce is used by Ministry of Civil Affairs since 2013, and it is not comparable with the data before 2012.

20—8 主要年份殡葬管理情况

Condition of Burial Administration in Main Years

项 目	Item	2008	2009	2012	2013	2014	2015	2016	2017
一、单位数（个）	Number of Units(unit)	69	68	71	75	107	108	97	89
二、年末职工人数（人）	Number of Staff & Workers in Year-end (person)	1568	1501	1513	1435	1942	2075	2032	1886
三、业务活动	Operation								
（一）火化炉数（台）	Number of Cremators(unit)	71	76	88	88	91	99	104	110
（二）全年处理遗体数（具）	Annual Number of Remains Dealed(body)	58627	59506	70044	71536	77139	78448	82200	85653
（三）穴位数（个）	Number of Graves(unit)	155059	169135	138549	121945	255235	348434	378223	349263
#本年销售穴位数	# Annual Number of Sold Graves	21798	19182	8884	9948	9372	14058	15469	13231
（四）安葬数（具）	Number of Remains Buried(body)	107176	127623	88555	94365	122806	212613	229221	180216
#本年安葬数	# Annual Number of Buried Remains	8809	11746	5935	6291	7482	13649	15876	14260

20−9 广西残疾人工作主要情况
The Major Situation of the Disabled Work in Guangxi Autonomous Region

指 标	Item	2017
一、康复	**Rehabilitation**	
康复机构数（个）	**Number of rehabilitation institutions (a)**	**220**
其中：残联办	Disabled Persons' Office	110
卫生办	Health office	56
民政办	Civil Affairs Office	8
教育办	Education Office	8
民 办	Civilian	27
其他	Others	11
康复机构在岗人员（人）	**On duty personnel of rehabilitation institutions (person)**	**6868**
其中：业务人员	business personnel	4620
管理人员	Management	713
其他人员	Other personnel	1535
二、教育	**Education**	
专项资助残疾人接受学前教育（人）	Special funding for disabled people to receive preschool education (person)	2135
特殊教育普通高中在校生（人）	Students Enrollment Receiving Special Cripple Education in Ordinary Senior Schools (person)	44
残疾人中等职业学校在校生（人）	Disabled Students Enrollment in Vacational Secondary Schools (person)	219
普通高等教育院校录取残疾考生（人）	Enrolled at Schools of Higher Education (person)	315
三、就业	**Employment**	
就业残疾人数	**Employment disability**	**322419**
其中：按比例就业	Proportional employment	9034
个体就业	engaged persons	14600
公益性岗位就业	Public welfare post employment	2018
从事农业种养加工	Engaged in agricultural cultivation and processing	226523
灵活就业	Flexible employment	24792
四、社会保障	**Social Security**	
符合参加城乡社会养老保险的残疾居民（人）	Disabled residents who are eligible to participate in urban and rural social retirement insurance(person)	1412722
实际参加城乡社会养老保险的残疾居民（人）	Disabled residents who actually participate in urban and rural social retirement insurance (person)	1122555
其中：（一）领取待遇	Receiving treatment	591910
（二）60岁以下参加城乡社会养老保险的残疾居民（人）	Disabled residents under 60 years old who participate in urban and rural social retirement insurance(person)	530645
五、培训	**Training**	
本年度实用技术培训（人次）	**Practical technical training this year(person)**	**29944**
其中：扫盲教育（人）	Literacy Education (person)	1186
六、文化	**Culture**	
公共图书馆盲文及盲人有声读物图书室	Braille in Public Library & Sound book library for the blind	
其中：省级	Provincial level	1
地市级	City level	9
县（市、区）级	County (city, district) level	9

主要统计指标解释

等级运动员人数 指经考核正式批准授予等级运动员称号的人数。运动员等级分为国际级运动健将、运动健将、一级运动员、二级运动员、三级运动员、少年级运动员。

等级裁判员人数 指经考核正式批准授予等级裁判员称号的人数。裁判员等级分为国际裁判、国家级裁判、一级裁判、二级裁判、三级裁判。

卫生机构 是指从卫生行政部门取得《医疗机构执业许可证》，或从民政、工商行政、机构编制管理部门取得法人单位登记证书，为社会提供医疗保健、疾病控制、卫生监督服务或从事医学科研和教育等工作的单位。

卫生技术人员 包括执业助理医师、注册护士、药剂人员、检验和影像人员等卫生专业人员。不包括从事管理工作的卫生技术人员。

执业医师 指具有《医师执业证》及其“级别”为“执业医师”且实际从事医疗、预防保健工作的人员，不包括实际从事管理工作的执业医师。执业医师类别分为临床、中医、口腔和公共卫生。

执业助理医师 指具有《医师执业证》及其“级别”为“执业助理医师”且实际从事医疗、预防保健工作的人员，不包括实际从事管理工作的执业助理医师。执业助理医师类别分为临床、中医、口腔和公共卫生。

注册护士 指具有注册护士证书且实际从事护理工作的人员，不包括从事管理工作的护士。

收养性社会福利单位数 是指提供食宿的、不以盈利为目的的革命伤残军人休养院、复退军人慢性病疗养院、复退军人精神病院、光荣院、社会福利院、儿童福利院、老年收养性机构(敬老院、养老院、老年公寓)等收养性的社会福利事业单位的总称。这些单位，分事业单位、企业和民办非企业3类。

收养性社会福利单位床位数 指提供食宿的、不以盈利为目的的革命伤残军人休养院、复退军人慢性病疗养院、复退军人精神病院、光荣院、社会福利院、儿童福利院、精神病福利院、老年收养性机构等收养性单位报告期末床位的实际收养能力。

农村定期定量救济 指由民政部门发给农村收入水平很低、生活确有困难的五保户、贫困户的生活救济。

残疾人灵活就业 指截止到本年度12月31日，以非全日制、临时性和弹性工作等灵活形式就业的就业年龄段城乡持证残疾人数。

领取待遇 指在“实际参保的残疾居民”中，已年满60周岁、未享受城镇职工基本养老保险待遇、直接按月领取城乡居民社会养老保险基础养老金的残疾居民。

60周岁以下参保残疾居民 指在“实际参保的残疾居民”中，60周岁以下，实际缴费参加城乡居民社会养老保险并已建立缴费记录档案的残疾居民。

Explanatory Notes on Main Statistical Indicators

Number of Athletes in Grades refers to the number of athletes who have been given titles through examination. The titles of athletes include international masters of sports, masters of sports, first grade, second grade and third grade sportsmen and young athletes.

Number of Referees in Grades refers to the number of referees who have been given titles after examination. They are classified as international masters of referees, masters of referees and referees of the first, second and third grades.

Stadiums refer to stadiums for track and field events with six lane 400-meter tracks around soccer fields, permanent track marks and permanent bleachers. Stadiums are classified according to seating capacity. They include: Class A stadiums seating 25000 people each, Class B stadiums seating 15000 to 25000 people each, Class C stadium seating 5000 to 15000 people each, and Class D stadiums seating fewer than 5000 people.

Gymnasiums refer to indoor sports grounds with permanent seats in which basketball, volleyball, badminton, table tennis and gymnastics can be held. Gymnasiums are classified according to seating capacity. They include Class A gymnasiums seating over 6000 people, Class B gymnasiums seating 4000 to 6000 people, Class C gymnasiums seating 2000 to 4000 people, and Class D gymnasiums seating fewer than 2000 people.

Hospitals refer to medical institutions with permanent hospital beds, which are able to take in patients and provide them with medical and nursing services. Hospitals are classified into three categories: hospitals at or above the country level, hospitals of rural townships, and other hospitals. According to their ownership, hospitals can be classified into three categories: hospitals under the public health departments, hospitals under industrial and other departments and collective-owned hospitals. Hospitals at or above county level are divided into comprehensive and specialized hospitals.

Medical Technical Personnel refers to all medical staff and workers employed by medical institutions, including doctors of Chinese and Western medicine, senior doctors who integrate traditional Chinese therapeutics with Western therapeutics in practice, senior nurse, pharmacists of Chinese and Western medicine, laboratory specialists, other specialists, paramedics of Chinese and Western medicine, nurses, midwives, druggists in Chinese and Western medicine, laboratory technicians, other technicians, other practitioners of Chinese medicine, nursing attendants, pharmacological workers of Chinese and Western medicine, laboratory workers, and other primary medical personnel.

Actual Expenditure of Funds refers to the total actual expenditure of administrative units in this year, including wages, allow-ance wages, other wages, welfare funds for staff and workers, social security funds, grants, funds for official duties, expenditure for equipment purchasing, expenditure for repairing, funds for business and expenditure for other use (the 11 kinds of expenditure above are of the same to items of expenditure detail account).

Off-budget Expenditure refers to actual expenditure of accounting administrative units for off-budget expenditure. This indicator is filled by list according to total number of “off-budget expenditure” of accounting items.

Specific Fund Expenditure refers to total actual expenditure of administrative units for specific funds. Specific funds refer to specially own and owner-occupied funds, which are reserved or set by administrative units according to governmental rules, such as fund for rewards, fund of institutions and fund for appraised fixed assets.

Special Fund Expenditure refers to actual expenditure of specific fund appropriated. Specific fund refers to fund appointed use, for specific purposes and independently accounted, such as expenditure for equipment purchasing, expenditure for large scale repairing and expenditure for special survey.

Expenditure for Business refers to actual total expenditure for business and other items of units in this year, including wages, allowance wages, other wages, welfare funds for staff and workers, social security funds, funds for official duties, expenditure for equipment purchasing, expenditure for repairing, funds for business and expenditure for other use (the 10 kinds of expenditure above are of the same to items of detail account of expenditure for business).

第二十一篇

区域经济

ECONOMIC ZONES

（校对编辑：黄浩洲）

21－1 各个经济区域主要经济指标

指 标	Item	2015			
		北部湾经济区（4市）The Beibu Gulf Economic Zone (4 cities)	北部湾经济区（6市）The Beibu Gulf Economic Zone (6 cities)	桂西资源富集区 The Resource-rich Area of Western Guangxi	珠江—西江经济带广西七市 The Zhujiang River-Xijiang River Economic Belt (7 cities)
土地面积（平方公里）	Local Land Area（sq.km)	43221	73377	87009	130785
年末常住人口（万人）	Population at the Year-end (10 000 persons)	1273.95	2050.12	912.80	2603.51
城镇化率（%）	Urbanization Rate（%）	52.89	49.45	34.97	49.66
地区生产总值（亿元）	Gross Domestic Product（100 million yuan）	5867.15	7995.88	2281.27	9873.72
第一产业	Primary Industry	810.31	1224.51	465.25	1295.86
第二产业	Secondary Industry	2530.03	3440.47	986.30	4622.06
# 工业	Industry	1990.31	2726.33	807.13	3852.38
第三产业	Tertiary Industry	2526.83	3330.92	829.72	3955.80
地区生产总值指数（上年=100）	Indices of Gross Domestic Product（preceding year = 100）	109.1	109.0	107.0	107.7
第一产业	Primary Industry	103.9	103.2	103.4	103.7
第二产业	Secondary Industry	110.8	110.7	106.6	107.4
# 工业	Industry	111.2	110.7	106.3	107.2
第三产业	Tertiary Industry	108.7	109.0	110.0	109.4
固定资产投资（亿元）	Investment in Fixed Assets（100 million yuan）	5623.51	7647.19	2109.31	9315.31
公共财政预算收入（亿元）	Public Budget Income（100 million yuan）	447.06	594.33	154.55	732.05
公共财政预算支出（亿元）	Public Budget Expenditure（100 million yuan）	990.42	1461.28	755.21	1873.95
社会消费品零售总额(亿元)	Total Retail Sales of Consumer Goods（100 million yuan）	2424.19	3143.92	583.95	3970.46
进出口（亿美元）	Total Exports & Imports（100 million USD ）	240.88	446.72	221.65	311.74
#出口	Exports	99.41	245.02	154.03	201.03

说明：1. 北部湾经济区（4市）指南宁、北海、防城港、钦州4市合计，北部湾经济区（6市）指南宁、北海、防城港、钦州、玉林、崇左6市合计，桂西资源富集区指百色、河池、崇左3市合计，珠江—西江经济带广西七市指南宁、柳州、梧州、贵港、百色、来宾、崇左7市合计。
2. 2016年起，外贸进出口数据以人民币计价。

Main Economic Indicators of Each Economic Zone

2016				2017			
北部湾经济区(4市) The Beibu Gulf Economic Zone (4 cities)	北部湾经济区(6市) The Beibu Gulf Economic Zone (6 cities)	桂西资源富集区 The Resource-rich Area of Western Guangxi	珠江—西江经济带广西七市 The Zhujiang River-Xijiang River Economic Belt (7 cities)	北部湾经济区(4市) The Beibu Gulf Economic Zone (4 cities)	北部湾经济区(6市) The Beibu Gulf Economic Zone (6 cities)	桂西资源富集区 The Resource-rich Area of Western Guangxi	珠江—西江经济带广西七市 The Zhujiang River-Xijiang River Economic Belt (7 cities)
43221	73377	87009	130785	43223	73379	87009	130785
1287.79	2070.31	918.84	2626.12	1303.68	2093.44	925.68	2651.80
53.80	50.32	35.98	50.74	54.96	51.42	37.04	51.87
6488.07	8808.10	2537.69	10784.30	7400.11	10007.27	3003.98	12227.83
873.39	1319.21	500.91	1395.22	918.95	1377.11	529.45	1454.18
2810.80	3786.52	1105.25	4986.48	3314.39	4446.74	1419.02	5775.76
2231.66	3009.90	912.96	4168.83	2658.52	3557.90	1193.17	4851.69
2803.88	3702.36	931.54	4402.60	3166.77	4183.42	1055.51	4997.89
107.8	107.8	107.5	107.3	108.3	108.3	108.7	107.9
103.5	103.2	103.5	103.4	104.0	103.9	104.3	104.2
108.1	108.3	107.4	106.8	109.0	109.0	109.8	107.2
108.1	108.0	107.2	106.8	109.7	109.3	109.7	107.4
108.8	109.0	110.0	109.1	109.0	109.2	109.7	109.7
6386.86	8685.37	2296.83	10437.26	7169.25	9829.08	2650.11	11948.18
468.02	613.58	153.60	765.75	496.90	636.52	152.79	791.11
1058.70	1579.12	833.79	2070.61	1131.96	1705.21	927.06	2274.50
2691.21	3482.99	646.15	4390.62	2990.05	3865.01	724.65	4890.11
1491.99	1518.67	1386.91	1985.66	1946.94	3319.40	1546.80	2398.43
539.37	561.52	820.17	1115.24	623.29	1540.46	1045.36	1417.80

Note: 1. The Beibu Gulf Economic Zone (4 cities) includes 4 cities of Nanning, Beihai, Fangchenggang and Qinzhou, the Beibu Gulf Economic Zone (6 cities) includes 6 cities of Nanning, Beihai, Fangchenggang, Qinzhou, Yulin and Chongzuo, the Resource-rich Area of Western Guangxi includes 3 citise of Baise, Hechi and Chongzuo, and the Zhujiang River-Xijiang River Economic Belt (7 cities) includes 7 cities of Nanning, Liuzhou, Wuzhou, Guigang, Baise, Laibin and Chongzuo.

2. The data of import and export value of foreign trade was calculated by RMB since 2016.

21－2　各个经济区域主要经济指标占全区比重

单位：%

指　标	Item	2015			
		北部湾经济区（4市）The Beibu Gulf Economic Zone (4 cities)	北部湾经济区（6市）The Beibu Gulf Economic Zone (6 cities)	桂西资源富集区 The Resource-rich Area of Western Guangxi	珠江—西江经济带广西七市 The Zhujiang River-Xijiang River Economic Belt (7 cities)
土地面积	Local Land Area	18.2	30.9	36.6	55.0
年末常住人口	Population at the Year-end	26.6	42.7	19.0	54.3
地区生产总值	Gross Domestic Product	34.8	47.4	13.5	58.5
第一产业	Primary Industry	31.6	47.7	18.1	50.5
第二产业	Secondary Industry	32.6	44.3	12.7	59.5
#工业	Industry	31.1	42.5	12.6	60.1
第三产业	Tertiary Industry	38.6	50.9	12.7	60.5
固定资产投资	Investment in Fixed Assets	35.9	48.8	13.5	59.5
公共财政预算收入	Public Budget Income	29.5	39.2	10.2	48.3
公共财政预算支出	Public Budget Expenditure	24.4	35.9	18.6	46.1
社会消费品零售总额	Total Retail Sales of Consumer Goods	38.2	49.5	9.2	62.5
进出口	Total Exports & Imports	47.0	87.1	43.2	60.8
#出口	Exports	35.5	87.4	55.0	71.7

Percentage of Main Regional Economic Indicators to Guangxi

(%)

2016				2017			
北部湾经济区（4市）The Beibu Gulf Economic Zone (4 cities)	北部湾经济区（6市）The Beibu Gulf Economic Zone (6 cities)	桂西资源富集区 The Resource-rich Area of Western Guangxi	珠江—西江经济带广西七市 The Zhujiang River-Xijiang River Economic Belt (7 cities)	北部湾经济区（4市）The Beibu Gulf Economic Zone (4 cities)	北部湾经济区（6市）The Beibu Gulf Economic Zone (6 cities)	桂西资源富集区 The Resource-rich Area of Western Guangxi	珠江—西江经济带广西七市 The Zhujiang River-Xijiang River Economic Belt (7 cities)
18.2	30.9	36.6	55.0	18.2	30.9	36.6	55.0
26.6	42.8	19.0	54.3	26.7	42.9	18.9	54.3
35.4	48.0	13.8	58.8	36.0	48.7	14.6	59.5
31.5	47.6	18.1	50.3	31.7	47.4	18.2	50.1
33.6	45.3	13.2	59.6	35.0	47.0	15.0	61.1
32.3	43.6	13.2	60.4	34.1	45.6	15.3	62.2
38.9	51.3	12.9	61.0	38.7	51.2	12.9	61.1
36.2	49.2	13.0	59.1	36.0	49.4	13.3	60.0
30.1	39.4	9.9	49.2	30.8	39.4	9.5	49.0
23.8	35.6	18.8	46.6	23.0	34.7	18.9	46.3
38.3	49.6	9.2	62.5	38.3	49.5	9.3	62.6
47.1	86.7	43.7	62.6	50.4	85.9	40.0	62.0
35.4	84.0	53.8	73.2	33.6	83.0	56.3	76.4

21－3 北部湾经济区主要经济指标（4市，2006—2017年）
Main Economic Indicators of the Beibu Gulf Economic Zone (4 cities, 2006—2017)

年 份 Year	地区生产总值（亿元） Gross Domestic Product (100 million yuan)	第一产业 Primary Industry	第二产业 Secondary Industry	第三产业 Tertiary Industry	#工业 Industry
2006	1418.09	314.25	484.67	619.16	381.40
2007	1764.60	371.74	615.46	777.40	496.05
2008	2156.01	417.90	778.79	959.32	630.11
2009	2492.99	443.36	912.17	1137.46	724.33
2010	3042.75	511.24	1198.05	1333.45	954.80
2011	3770.17	635.08	1545.18	1589.92	1228.75
2012	4268.59	678.30	1787.21	1803.08	1408.75
2013	4817.43	742.96	2097.47	1977.00	1660.52
2014	5448.72	768.70	2385.35	2294.67	1880.28
2015	5867.15	810.31	2530.03	2526.83	1990.31
2016	6488.07	873.39	2810.80	2803.88	2231.66
2017	7400.11	918.95	3314.39	3166.77	2658.52

21－3 续表 1 continued

年 份 Year	地区生产总值指数（上年＝100） Index of Gross Domestic Product (preceding year=100)	第一产业 Primary Industry	第二产业 Secondary Industry	第三产业 Tertiary Industry	#工业 Industry
2006	116.0	106.7	126.0	113.9	129.9
2007	117.7	106.7	123.2	118.8	126.3
2008	115.6	104.5	117.8	118.8	119.1
2009	116.0	105.5	120.3	116.7	117.8
2010	115.6	105.1	122.1	114.0	121.3
2011	115.4	105.2	123.6	112.0	124.6
2012	113.5	105.4	120.3	109.5	120.8
2013	110.5	104.7	115.0	107.7	114.8
2014	109.5	103.5	112.8	107.6	113.2
2015	109.1	103.9	110.8	108.7	111.2
2016	107.8	103.5	108.1	108.8	108.1
2017	108.3	104.0	109.0	109.0	109.7

21－3 续表 2 continued

年 份 Year	全社会固定资产投资（亿元） Investment in Fixed Assets (100 million yuan)	公共财政预算收入（亿元） Public Budget Income (100 million yuan)	公共财政预算支出（亿元） Public Budget Expenditure (100 million yuan)	社会消费品零售总额（亿元） Total Retail Sales of Consumer Goods (100 million yuan)	进出口（亿美元） Total Exports & Imports (100 million USD)	#出口 Exports
2006	722.25	86.34	156.96	595.69		
2007	965.03	109.96	203.54	706.14	40.84	18.29
2008	1292.30	137.20	272.35	871.01	60.55	28.45
2009	1994.51	177.16	361.15	1042.84	66.39	34.76
2010	2796.72	228.65	454.88	1237.96	76.94	35.38
2011	3671.74	277.22	544.25	1465.88	113.11	46.13
2012	4513.52	339.98	672.64	1710.96	148.90	55.31
2013	4246.04	384.02	738.99	1968.12	149.50	58.50
2014	4810.12	415.19	813.54	2197.63	191.17	78.85
2015	5623.51	447.06	990.42	2424.19	240.88	99.41
2016	6386.86	468.02	1058.70	2691.21	1491.99	539.37
2017	7169.25	496.90	1131.96	2990.05	1946.94	623.29

说明：1. 北部湾经济区（4市）指南宁、北海、防城港、钦州4市合计。
2. 全社会固定资产投资包含固定资产投资和农户投资两部分，本表数据自2014年起为固定资产投资数据。
3. 2016年起，外贸进出口数据以人民币计价。

Note: 1. The Beibu Gulf Economic Zone (4 cities) includes 4 cities of Nanning, Beihai, Fangchenggang and Qinzhou.
2. The "Total Investment in Fixed Assets" includes 2 parts: investment in fixed assets and investment from rural households, and the data in this table refers to the investment in fixed assets since 2014.
3. The data of import and export value of foreign trade was calculated by RMB since 2016.

21—4　北部湾经济区主要经济指标（6市，2006—2017年）
Main Economic Indicators of the Beibu Gulf Economic Zone (6 cities, 2006—2017)

年　份 Year	地区生产总值（亿元） Gross Domestic Product (100 million yuan)	第一产业 Primary Industry	第二产业 Secondary Industry	第三产业 Tertiary Industry	#工业 Industry
2006	2025.71	488.59	702.43	834.68	571.96
2007	2500.52	574.88	885.16	1040.48	733.14
2008	3031.82	648.84	1110.78	1272.20	920.92
2009	3480.84	682.36	1296.72	1501.76	1056.28
2010	4275.37	797.82	1720.55	1756.99	1406.46
2011	5281.97	993.87	2201.18	2086.92	1793.96
2012	5901.17	1050.45	2486.50	2364.23	1997.19
2013	6600.52	1136.22	2872.33	2591.97	2305.20
2014	7439.95	1164.76	3254.45	3020.74	2592.44
2015	7995.88	1224.51	3440.47	3330.92	2726.33
2016	8808.10	1319.21	3786.52	3702.36	3009.90
2017	10007.27	1377.11	4446.74	4183.42	3557.90

21—4　续表 1　continued

年　份 Year	地区生产总值指数（上年＝100） Index of Gross Domestic Product (preceding year=100)	第一产业 Primary Industry	第二产业 Secondary Industry	第三产业 Tertiary Industry	#工业 Industry
2006	115.6	107.2	124.6	113.9	127.5
2007	117.1	106.4	122.8	118.5	125.1
2008	114.7	104.9	117.2	117.5	118.2
2009	115.4	105.6	119.5	116.4	117.2
2010	115.4	105.5	122.0	113.8	121.0
2011	114.1	105.4	120.8	111.5	121.1
2012	112.8	105.6	118.9	109.4	118.9
2013	110.4	104.5	114.8	107.7	114.5
2014	109.2	103.5	112.3	107.5	112.3
2015	109.0	103.2	110.7	109.0	110.7
2016	107.8	103.2	108.3	109.0	108.0
2017	108.3	103.9	109.0	109.2	109.3

21－4 续表 2 continued

年 份 Year	全社会固定资产投资（亿元） Investment in Fixed Assets (100 million yuan)	公共财政预算收入（亿元） Public Budget Income (100 million yuan)	公共财政预算支出（亿元） Public Budget Expenditure (100 million yuan)	社会消费品零售总额（亿元） Total Retail Sales of Consumer Goods (100 million yuan)	进出口（亿美元） Total Exports & Imports (100 million USD)	#出口 Exports
2006	948.46	112.60	225.08	781.15	35.91	18.66
2007	1262.91	143.14	297.74	927.57	53.86	29.07
2008	1708.15	179.55	396.80	1163.51	81.03	45.07
2009	2651.40	228.40	527.42	1359.20	98.60	62.69
2010	3721.12	291.79	658.80	1606.28	118.73	72.62
2011	4879.07	356.33	804.52	1901.09	170.21	96.37
2012	6049.93	445.04	981.52	2218.15	226.12	126.95
2013	5692.24	506.98	1081.28	2547.67	256.44	158.98
2014	6482.47	552.45	1192.49	2851.78	342.98	213.87
2015	7647.19	594.33	1461.28	3143.92	446.72	245.02
2016	8685.37	613.58	1579.12	3482.99	1518.67	561.52
2017	9829.08	636.52	1705.21	3865.01	3319.40	1540.46

说明：1. 北部湾经济区（6市）指南宁、北海、防城港、钦州、玉林、崇左6市合计。
2. 全社会固定资产投资包含固定资产投资和农户投资两部分，本表数据自2014年起为固定资产投资数据。
3. 2016年起，外贸进出口数据以人民币计价。

Note: 1. The Beibu Gulf Economic Zone (6 cities) includes 6 cities of Nanning, Beihai, Fangchenggang, Qinzhou, Yulin and Chongzuo .
2. The "Total Investment in Fixed Assets" includes 2 parts: investment in fixed assets and investment from rural households, and the data in this table refers to the investment in fixed assets since 2014.
3. The data of import and export value of foreign trade was calculated by RMB since 2016.

21－5　桂西资源富集区主要经济指标（2006—2017年）
Main Economic Indicators of the Resource-rich Area of Western Guangxi (2006—2017)

年　份 Year	地区生产总值（亿元）Gross Domestic Product (100 million yuan)	第一产业 Primary Industry	第二产业 Secondary Industry	第三产业 Tertiary Industry	#工业 Industry
2006	734.79	200.91	305.00	228.89	252.69
2007	902.79	227.97	397.20	277.63	339.30
2008	1054.10	249.30	481.09	323.70	416.40
2009	1139.99	259.91	499.04	381.04	418.82
2010	1435.10	317.93	679.37	437.79	581.10
2011	1667.90	390.45	772.83	504.62	661.29
2012	1778.46	406.43	805.51	566.51	678.94
2013	1917.12	432.27	870.62	614.23	727.51
2014	2168.84	443.22	972.73	752.89	802.61
2015	2281.27	465.25	986.30	829.72	807.13
2016	2537.69	505.91	1105.25	931.54	912.96
2017	3003.98	529.45	1419.02	1055.51	1193.17

21－5　续表 1　continued

年　份 Year	地区生产总值指数（上年＝100）Index of Gross Domestic Product (preceding year=100)	第一产业 Primary Industry	第二产业 Secondary Industry	第三产业 Tertiary Industry	#工业 Industry
2006	115.1	106.7	123.6	113.1	124.1
2007	115.6	103.6	122.7	116.8	125.5
2008	112.8	106.0	118.6	110.5	122.7
2009	112.0	104.5	113.3	115.8	110.5
2010	113.7	105.9	118.8	111.8	118.0
2011	107.0	104.8	107.4	107.9	107.9
2012	106.8	105.9	106.6	107.8	105.6
2013	108.3	104.6	111.1	106.6	110.7
2014	108.3	103.9	111.0	107.1	110.4
2015	107.0	103.4	106.6	110.0	106.3
2016	107.5	103.5	107.4	110.0	107.2
2017	108.7	104.3	109.8	109.7	109.7

21－5 续表 2 continued

年 份 Year	全社会固定资产投资(亿元) Investment in Fixed Assets (100 million yuan)	公共财政预算收入(亿元) Public Budget Income (100 million yuan)	公共财政预算支出(亿元) Public Budget Expenditure (100 million yuan)	社会消费品零售总额(亿元) Total Retail Sales of Consumer Goods (100 million yuan)	进出口(亿美元) Total Exports & Imports (100 million USD)	#出口 Exports
2006	509.25	41.88	123.74	156.07	11.61	7.40
2007	627.55	53.54	173.66	183.48	16.33	11.06
2008	665.11	64.14	232.01	229.53	24.09	18.10
2009	1020.23	70.38	274.92	265.62	37.26	30.06
2010	1310.50	83.01	342.11	306.66	47.77	37.45
2011	1616.39	93.25	409.29	361.53	62.91	50.46
2012	1810.06	118.24	520.32	418.03	81.68	71.80
2013	1676.96	140.16	564.31	473.95	113.56	101.83
2014	1787.09	149.24	638.88	533.28	159.02	137.33
2015	2109.31	154.55	755.21	583.95	221.65	154.03
2016	2296.83	153.60	833.79	646.15	1386.91	820.17
2017	2650.11	152.79	927.06	724.65	1546.80	1045.36

说明：1. 桂西资源富集区指百色、河池、崇左3市合计。
2. 全社会固定资产投资包含固定资产投资和农户投资两部分，本表数据自2014年起为固定资产投资数据。
3. 2016年起，外贸进出口数据以人民币计价。

Note: 1. The Resource-rich Area of Western Guangxi includes 3 citise of Baise, Hechi and Chongzuo.
2. The "Total Investment in Fixed Assets" includes 2 parts: investment in fixed assets and investment from rural households, and the data in this table refers to the investment in fixed assets since 2014.
3. The data of import and export value of foreign trade was calculated by RMB since 2016.

21－6 珠江—西江经济带广西七市主要经济指标（2006—2017年）

Main Economic Indicators of the Zhujiang River-Xijiang River Economic Belt (7 cities, 2006—2017)

年 份 Year	地区生产总值（亿元） Gross Domestic Product (100 million yuan)	第一产业 Primary Industry	第二产业 Secondary Industry	第三产业 Tertiary Industry	#工业 Industry
2006	2720.33	535.40	1138.77	1046.16	968.32
2007	3315.59	622.86	1449.82	1242.91	1252.45
2008	3960.79	696.91	1781.41	1482.47	1538.98
2009	4522.50	727.35	2055.33	1739.83	1750.10
2010	5611.10	859.82	2736.76	2014.52	2353.01
2011	6806.61	1067.24	3356.56	2382.82	2870.66
2012	7635.59	1130.95	3773.94	2730.70	3205.87
2013	8451.39	1218.24	4244.34	2988.81	3599.10
2014	9343.02	1233.24	4531.33	3578.44	3804.76
2015	9873.72	1295.86	4622.06	3955.08	3852.38
2016	10784.30	1395.22	4986.48	4402.60	4168.83
2017	12227.83	1454.18	5775.76	4997.89	4851.69

21－6 续表 1 continued

年 份 Year	地区生产总值指数（上年＝100） Index of Gross Domestic Product (preceding year=100)	第一产业 Primary Industry	第二产业 Secondary Industry	第三产业 Tertiary Industry	#工业 Industry
2006	115.5	107.1	122.5	113.0	124.5
2007	116.3	105.6	122.5	115.1	124.3
2008	113.1	104.7	116.3	113.4	117.4
2009	115.3	105.2	119.0	115.2	117.2
2010	115.2	105.4	120.5	112.5	120.1
2011	111.3	105.5	114.0	110.2	113.5
2012	111.7	106.0	114.4	110.2	114.1
2013	109.6	104.9	112.2	107.7	112.0
2014	107.7	103.4	108.6	108.1	108.6
2015	107.7	103.7	107.4	109.4	107.2
2016	107.3	103.4	106.8	109.1	106.8
2017	107.9	104.2	107.2	109.7	107.4

21－6 续表2 continued

年 份 Year	全社会固定资产投资(亿元) Investment in Fixed Assets (100 million yuan)	公共财政预算收入(亿元) Public Budget Income (100 million yuan)	公共财政预算支出(亿元) Public Budget Expenditure (100 million yuan)	社会消费品零售总额(亿元) Total Retail Sales of Consumer Goods (100 million yuan)	进出口(亿美元) Total Exports & Imports (100 million USD)	#出口 Exports
2006	1315.03	153.48	322.85	997.25	35.05	21.09
2007	1672.24	187.56	420.75	1181.37	48.59	31.90
2008	2121.82	239.94	558.21	1481.31	71.81	48.60
2009	3293.76	294.72	709.68	1727.55	86.77	62.54
2010	4597.06	369.56	911.03	2041.63	101.42	65.03
2011	5983.92	437.36	1076.92	2413.16	119.98	82.26
2012	7772.67	571.95	1348.79	2809.26	164.87	111.36
2013	7169.31	647.89	1463.46	3219.13	202.86	140.40
2014	7950.42	692.17	1600.72	3606.63	241.67	178.71
2015	9315.31	732.05	1873.95	3970.46	311.74	201.03
2016	10437.26	765.75	2070.61	4390.62	1985.66	1115.24
2017	10088.91	622.99	1997.97	4890.11	2398.43	1417.80

说明：1. 珠江—西江经济带广西七市指南宁、柳州、梧州、贵港、百色、来宾、崇左7市合计。
2. 全社会固定资产投资包含固定资产投资和农户投资两部分，本表数据自2014年起为固定资产投资数据。
3. 2016年起，外贸进出口数据以人民币计价。

Note: 1. The Zhujiang River-Xijiang River Economic Belt (7 cities) includes 7 cities of Nanning, Liuzhou, Wuzhou, Guigang, Baise, Laibin and Chongzuo.
2. The "Total Investment in Fixed Assets" includes 2 parts: investment in fixed assets and investment from rural households, and the data in this table refers to the investment in fixed assets since 2014.
3. The data of import and export value of foreign trade was calculated by RMB since 2016.

第二十二篇

各市基本情况

BASIC STATISTICS OF CITIES

（校对编辑：黄浩洲）

22—1 各市社会经济主要指标（2017年）

指 标	Item	南宁市 Nanning	柳州市 Liuzhou	桂林市 Guilin
行政区域土地面积（平方公里）	Administrative Region Land Area(sq.km)	22099	18597	27667
地区生产总值（当年价，亿元）	Gross Domestic Product (At current prices, 100 million yuan)	4118.83	2755.64	2045.18
第一产业	Primary Industry	404.18	189.49	381.83
第二产业	Secondary Industry	1599.50	1487.08	791.94
# 工业	Industry	1189.89	1345.13	609.71
第三产业	Tertiary Industry	2115.15	1079.07	871.41
人均地区生产总值（元）	Per Capita GDP (yuan)	57948	69249	40632
地区生产总值指数（%，上年=100）	Indices of Gross Domestic Product (%, preceding year=100)	108.0	107.1	103.9
第一产业	Primary Industry	104.1	103.7	104.3
第二产业	Secondary Industry	108.6	104.4	99.5
#工业	Industry	109.5	104.5	98.7
第三产业	Tertiary Industry	108.4	111.6	108.5
人均地区生产总值指数（%，上年=100）	Indices of Per Capita GDP (%, preceding year=100)	106.7	106.1	102.9
户籍年末总人口（万人）	Total Population at Year-end (10 000 persons)	756.87	386.60	534.08
男性	Male	394.48	199.70	276.55
女性	Female	362.38	186.90	257.53
出生人口（万人）	Birth (10 000 person)	15.33	6.46	9.11
死亡人口（万人）	Death (10 000 person)	14.36	6.14	9.16
年末总户数（万户）	Total Households at Year-end (10 000 households)	225.78	113.65	163.26
就业人员（万人）	Employed Persons (10 000 persons)			
城镇登记失业率（%）	Urban Registered Unemployment Rate (%)	2.63	2.51	2.40
城镇非私营就业人员（万人）	Number of Employed Persons in Urban Units (10 000 persons)	98.77	76.35	41.96
#国有单位	State-owned Units	36.79	22.10	20.75
城镇集体单位	Urban Collective-owned Units	0.97	0.92	1.24
城镇私营单位就业人数（万人）	Number of Employed Persons in Urban Private Enterprises (10 000 persons)			
城镇单位就业人员（含劳务派遣）平均工资（元）	Average Wages of Employed Persons in Urban Units (yuan)	72841	64958	62127
国有单位	State-owned Units	83540	70732	70689
城镇集体单位	Urban Collective-owned Units	59780	54446	47967
固定资产投资（亿元，不含农户）	Investment in Fixed Assets (excluding rural registents)	4307.75	2697.20	2234.24
#房地产开发	Investment in Real Estate Development	958.09	395.08	300.40
商品房销售额（亿元）	Sales of Commercial Houses (100 million yuan)	1200.77	392.98	293.07
#住宅	Residential Buildings	1006.96	343.22	267.74

注：本表统计范围为全市数。
Note: The statistic indicators in this table refer to the whole city(including the counties belonging to the city).

Main Social & Economic Indicators by City (2017)

梧州市 Wuzhou	北海市 Beihai	防城港市 Fangcheng-gang	钦州市 Qinzhou	贵港市 Guigang	玉林市 Yulin	百色市 Baise	贺州市 Hezhou	河池市 Hechi	来宾市 Laibin	崇左市 Chongzuo
12572	3989	6239	10897	10602	12824	36201	11753	33476	13382	17332
1338.10	1229.84	741.62	1309.82	1082.18	1699.54	1361.76	548.83	734.60	663.69	907.62
136.41	190.54	89.27	234.95	193.65	276.91	189.24	115.76	158.96	159.96	181.25
785.71	668.66	421.23	625.01	465.86	734.14	789.33	210.91	231.49	250.08	398.20
729.57	612.00	369.45	487.18	378.53	564.86	690.07	132.15	168.58	183.98	334.52
415.98	370.64	231.12	449.86	422.68	688.49	383.20	222.16	344.15	253.65	328.17
44193	74378	79351	40160	24857	29387	37479	26802	20921	30037	43678
106.7	110.2	106.7	108.8	109.0	107.6	108.8	105.3	107.8	107.4	109.3
104.4	103.7	103.9	103.9	104.2	103.2	104.5	104.3	103.8	104.6	104.4
105.2	110.5	106.4	111.2	111.3	108.1	109.5	101.6	109.4	105.3	110.8
105.5	111.3	106.3	111.9	111.3	107.4	109.6	97.1	108.4	105.4	110.5
110.4	113.3	108.3	108.9	108.8	109.1	109.8	109.9	108.7	111.5	110.6
106.0	108.9	105.5	107.6	108.0	106.6	108.1	104.5	107.1	106.5	108.5
349.06	175.42	97.79	410.92	555.71	724.19	417.57	243.53	429.87	268.11	249.94
185.57	91.95	52.84	224.02	294.97	388.20	217.28	128.39	223.83	140.82	131.90
163.49	83.47	44.95	186.91	260.74	335.99	200.28	115.14	206.04	127.29	118.04
7.32	2.98	1.98	8.00	1.01	14.80	7.54	4.54	8.39	5.06	4.03
4.55	2.24	1.35	5.66	7.79	6.02	6.78	3.13	6.11	3.90	4.30
99.48	44.54	25.34	98.48	156.75	207.71	111.58	64.69	125.22	78.26	70.78
				317.24					176.37	155.29
2.39	1.88	1.20	2.28	1.07	1.50	2.80	2.35	2.57	2.60	2.14
21.32	14.39	8.32	20.73	18.61	29.48	22.21	10.67	16.44	12.52	13.72
10.02	7.69	5.42	10.94	11.74	16.74	14.46	7.80	11.71	8.20	9.10
0.90	0.94	0.08	1.27	0.99	2.71	0.91	0.08	0.28	0.52	0.22
10.48		4.19	16.05	19.23			6.43	4.78	6.09	7.45
54925	60622	50175	56863	58015	60901	62528	65799	66085	64152	59250
65344	72242	31465	64030	65506	68592	66092	68594	73425	70643	64187
42476	48009	25391	45029	40468	49210	42145	61343	47677	46752	33929
1330.15	1099.68	672.77	1088.85	983.81	1689.33	1226.41	722.02	453.20	432.16	970.50
66.40	168.28	73.90	80.00	136.59	184.35	107.92	42.20	60.06	49.95	60.24
71.75	212.92	102.23	69.00	173.63	203.22	94.09	48.69	49.50	44.76	60.02
67.41	198.90	88.13	62.88	160.62	182.44	82.03	42.81	41.22	39.95	51.44

22－1　续表1

指　标	Item	南宁市 Nanning	柳州市 Liuzhou	桂林市 Guilin
商品房屋销售面积（万平方米）	Selling Space of Commercial Houses (10 000 sq.m)	1544.13	528.76	528.60
#住宅	Residential Buildings	1307.68	481.71	494.92
公共财政预算收入（亿元）	Public Budget Income (100 million yuan)	332.15	179.79	144.16
#税收收入	Tax Revenue	248.10	128.22	72.29
#国内增值税	Value-added Tax	68.88	46.60	21.58
营业税	Sales Tax	0.14	0.09	0.07
企业所得税	Enterprises Income Tax	34.66	12.54	10.19
个人所得税	Individual Income Tax	12.57	4.20	3.52
公共财政预算支出（亿元）	Public Budget Expenditure (100 million yuan)	646.31	374.56	434.71
#教育支出	Expenditure for Education	117.14	70.77	77.44
社会保障和就业支出	Expenditure for Social Security & Employment	68.14	40.85	55.84
医疗卫生（与计划生育）支出	Expenditure for Medical & Health Care	61.22	41.58	53.27
农林水利事务支出	Expenditure for Affairs of Agriculture, Forestry & Water Resources	69.60	49.50	52.76
农村居民人均可支配收入（元）	Per Capita Disposable Income of Rural Households (yuan)	12515	12151	13345
农村居民人均生活费支出（元）	Per Capita Living Expenditure of Rural Households (yuan)	9839	8804	8620
#食品烟酒支出	Expenditure for Food & liquid	3362	3761	3413
城镇居民人均可支配收入（元）	Per Capital Disposable Income of Urban Households (yuan)	33217	32661	32534
城镇居民人均生活消费性支出(元)	Per Capita Living Expenditure of Urban Households (yuan)	17279	20909	19005
#食品烟酒支出	Expenditure for Food & liquid	6102	8414	6916
农村人均住房面积（平方米）	Per Capita Living Floor Space of Rural Households (sq.m)		41.3	48.80
城镇人均住房建筑面积（平方米）	Per Capita Living Building Space of Urban Households (sq.m)		37.90	40.50
乡村户数（万户）	Rural Households(10 000 households)	138.80	63.88	107.11
常用耕地面积（千公顷）	Daily Cultivated Area (1000 hectares)	681.18	348.46	328.98

注：2014年起农民人均纯收入调整口径为农村居民人均可支配收入，各表同。
Note: The indicator of "per capital annual net income of rural households" was replaced by "Per Capita Annual Net Income of Rural Households" since 2014, same as other tables.

Continued

梧州市 Wuzhou	北海市 Beihai	防城港市 Fangcheng-gang	钦州市 Qinzhou	贵港市 Guigang	玉林市 Yulin	百色市 Baise	贺州市 Hezhou	河池市 Hechi	来宾市 Laibin	崇左市 Chongzuo
175.93	376.61	239.64	187.20	310.22	459.84	245.81	123.34	125.96	159.15	166
168.53	360.63	218.08	177.41	291.22	430.54	228.07	114.42	113.06	150.20	151
84.55	64.34	47.60	52.81	50.41	105.55	82.50	30.89	36.22	27.64	34
45.26	45.12	32.24	32.64	33.63	65.05	50.43	18.05	21.88	16.00	41
9.26	19.36	5.35	8.57	10.73	14.19	16.36	4.10	9.42	5.84	5
0.06	0.19	0.13	0.07	0	0.13	0.06	0.03	0.03	0.06	0
3.98	5.35	2.04	2.41	3.48	5.39	3.82	1.49	2.35	1.53	2.46
1.09	0.94	0.70	0.90	1.32	1.61	1.53	0.60	1.11	0.59	0.67
242.30	157.54	120.47	205.94	233.93	351.62	376.52	179.99	328.92	178.18	221.62
49.71	28.52	16.61	49.92	52.88	85.41	69.94	32.09	61.20	31.47	34.51
29.02	10.85	11.65	25.81	27.79	46.78	44.92	20.16	36.36	21.53	25.49
29.51	15.45	9.96	25.98	34.15	47.79	46.24	20.79	38.27	21.38	23.36
24.04	17.13	9.64	18.47	25.49	34.87	78.16	31.51	70.75	37.86	43.72
11085	12749	13373	11801	12544	13597	10171	10498	8260	10674	10860
7430	8930	10873	7427	8186	9512	8026	7664	6844	8953	7037
2825	3145	3664	2898	3431	2885	2946	3027	2323	3124	2533
29359	31912	32079	31415	28806	32159	29126	28899	25647	31047	28813
19017	20238	20538	18392	17791	18306	17985	16335	16784	18619	17453
7755	8703	6884	6493	7010	7194	6155	6267	5446	6674	7084
	41.00	43.61	42.00	50.91	39.40	40.10	49.50	46.77		45.11
	46.00	53.00	49.00	47.30	56.70	43.80	54.40	45.31		43.75
77.57	26.92	16.72	87.28	123.08	141.58	85.54	51.39	95.94	54.44	53.78
126.50	123.03	91.19	208.10	299.19	238.89	447.75	143.65	364.33	406.46	519.55

22－1 续表2

指 标	Item	南宁市 Nanning	柳州市 Liuzhou	桂林市 Guilin
农业机械总动力（万千瓦）	Total Agricultural Machinery Power (10 000 kw)	481.15	222.01	503.47
化肥使用量(折纯量，万吨)	Consumption of Chemical Fertilizers (Pure quantity, 10 000 tons)	53.83	18.97	24.42
农村用电量（亿千瓦时）	Electricity Consumed in Rural Areas (100 million kwh)	11.83	8.55	7.83
有效灌溉面积（千公顷）	Irrigated Area (1 000 hectares)	231.56	112.47	219.79
农作物总播种面积（不含食用菌）（千公顷）	Total Sown Area of Farm Crops (exclude mushrooms) (1 000 hectares)	977.04	397.98	711.09
#粮食作物	Grain Crops	430.38	163.41	369.29
粮食产量（万吨）	Grain Output (10 000 tons)	216.81	82.40	195.79
甘蔗产量（万吨）	Output of Sugarcane (10 000 tons)	1161.58	658.89	40.09
油料产量（万吨）	Output of Oil Plants (10 000 tons)	16.02	3.64	7.78
蔬菜产量（含食用菌）（万吨）	Output of Vegetables (10 000 tons)	568.44	237.68	446.57
园林水果产量（万吨）	Output of Fruits (10 000 tons)	248.32	96.17	539.74
肉类总产量（万吨）	Total Output of Meat (10 000 tons)	65.81	22.77	54.34
奶类产量（万吨）	Output of Milk (10 000 tons)	4.86	0.66	0.12
禽蛋产量（万吨）	Output of Eggs (10 000 tons)	4.11	1.81	6.59
水产品产量（万吨）	Output of Aquatic Products (10 000 tons)	27.45	8.44	13.04
工业企业单位数（个）	Number of Industrial Enterprises (unit)	946	835	646
工业总产值（规模以上，当年价，亿元）	Gross Industrial Output Value (Above designated size, at current prices, 100 million yuan)	3713.07	5031.33	1729.06
#轻工业	Light Industry	1495.62	492.67	699.93
重工业	Heavy Industry	2217.45	4538.66	1029.13
#大型企业	Large Enterprises	782.10	2724.16	397.78
中型企业	Medium Enterprises	1193.58	1018.19	529.22
小微型企业	Small Enterprises	1737.39	1288.98	802.06
#内资企业	Domestic Funds Enterprises	2996.76	3650.59	1654.32
港澳台商投资企业	Enterprises with Funds from Hong Kong, Macao & Taiwan	572.81	184.28	19.21
外商投资企业	Foreign Funded Enterprises	143.50	1196.45	55.53
工业企业资产总计（亿元）	Total Assets of Industrial Enterprises (100 million yuan)	2628.93	3279.05	1302.63
工业企业负债合计（亿元）	Total Liabilities of Industrial Enterprises (100 million yuan)	1578.69	2208.73	718.85
工业企业所有者权益（亿元）	Owner's Equity of Industrial Enterprises (100 million yuan)	1047.58	1069.45	618.41
工业企业主营业务收入（亿元）	Business Income of the Major Products of Industrial Enterprises (100 million yuan)	3477.51	4592.41	1579.44
工业企业利润总额（亿元）	Total Profits of Industrial Enterprises (100 million yuan)	208.59	186.25	96.17
工业企业本年应交增值税（亿元）	Value Added Tax Payable of Industrial Enterprises (100 million yuan)	67.41	103.06	48.93
工业企业从业人员年平均人数（万人）	Annual Average Number of Employed Persons of Industrial Enterprises (10 000 persons)	23.11	26.30	16.92
建筑企业单位数（个）	Number of Construction Enterprises (unit)	422	92	128
建筑业企业从业人员（万人）	Number of Persons Employed in Construction Enterprises (10 000 persons)	45.75	18.40	9.41
建筑业总产值（亿元）	Gross Output Value of Construction (100 million yuan)	1469.11	717.30	349.85

Continued

梧州市 Wuzhou	北海市 Beihai	防城港市 Fangcheng-gang	钦州市 Qinzhou	贵港市 Guigang	玉林市 Yulin	百色市 Baise	贺州市 Hezhou	河池市 Hechi	来宾市 Laibin	崇左市 Chongzuo
137.51	148.02	77.65	184.70	365.85	305.74	299.64	124.06	314.31	197.34	258.80
7.07	6.08	5.56	24.30	19.52	16.32	12.48	5.52	13.99	26.28	30.11
4.85	2.24	2.45	6.80	5.90	9.99	9.42	4.44	10.30	10.62	3.63
61.03	45.69	29.87	79.40	151.46	143.09	109.27	81.02	82.37	105.58	74.53
297.50	183.22	125.75	396.96	449.03	497.63	465.76	250.33	470.35	471.94	519.94
155.87	77.23	49.45	214.90	271.01	310.16	265.09	132.76	266.49	170.06	121.69
80.85	37.83	19.70	108.00	149.63	176.69	114.23	70.74	102.18	79.51	51.16
14.29	246.23	311.28	398.10	246.32	180.19	255.30	17.14	345.49	1229.11	2507.71
4.41	5.07	0.71	3.00	11.54	5.92	1.66	3.47	1.67	4.16	2.56
225.97	88.84	30.80	151.33	173.92	335.10	247.32	183.25	155.48	133.43	108.69
67.12	12.18	8.66	204.20	31.05	108.46	115.21	87.45	41.65	74.69	66.40
20.35	12.75	4.80	31.00	38.07	77.45	26.68	16.89	23.03	15.57	12.56
0.10	0.17	0.49	3.80	0.54	0.56	0.00	1.77	0.00	0.57	0.00
0.90	2.04	0.68	2.80	2.73	7.87	0.86	0.87	0.83	0.48	0.31
10.38	114.68	53.26	60.50	25.00	17.36	16.92	8.26	8.37	7.34	7.84
399	212	151	327	499	549	335	204	173	227	195
2514.37	2500.87	1772.44	1846.31	1182.25	1892.42	1787.26	416.32	406.61	605.90	938.86
382.60	243.27	666.63	624.70	470.95	916.21	136.88	78.03	104.21	200.11	502.74
2131.77	2257.59	1105.80	1221.61	711.30	976.20	1650.38	338.29	302.39	405.79	436.12
1106.42	984.55	680.93	86.89	223.34	622.74	668.55	0	124.01	93.49	219.96
831.70	1099.52	420.86	1133.80	473.30	603.63	504.88	157.21	151.42	184.22	325.96
576.25	416.80	670.64	625.62	485.62	666.05	613.83	259.11	131.17	328.19	392.94
2248.47	1937.37	1149.75	1635.85	1017.33	1541.24	1724.86	371.38	397.76	585.18	707.50
176.86	470.50	51.60	52.77	105.33	101.28	60.90	37.62	6.89	11.87	17.20
89.04	92.99	571.08	157.69	59.59	249.90	1.50	7.32	1.96	8.85	214.20
961.61	1021.37	1356.31	1019.29	908.42	884.98	1545.06	500.69	780.38	593.25	591.32
457.32	614.73	961.57	567.33	472.51	496.02	1071.15	312.22	565.77	489.10	331.65
502.58	406.24	393.26	449.45	435.91	388.96	472.25	188.57	214.61	104.15	213.74
2352.10	2396.49	1386.82	1720.25	1099.56	1740.05	1348.68	385.46	378.21	518.24	803.56
286.76	253.34	94.21	91.16	76.64	90.42	60.01	25.36	62.04	-0.44	124.34
107.13	35.17	32.39	50.08	23.78	43.97	29.12	11.49	23.99	10.77	20.81
18.97	6.83	3.22	10.44	17.00	18.65	8.30	3.36	4.56	3.97	4.70
42	45	75	81	48	97	99	46	56	47	39
1.41	2.29	2.34	20.73	2.14	9.12	1.13	0.78	2.02	2.64	1.22
35.90	94.81	143.43	595.70	141.82	376.79	69.82	25.73	72.69	75.34	41.27

22－1　续表3

指　标	Item	南宁市 Nanning	柳州市 Liuzhou	桂林市 Guilin
房屋建筑施工面积（万平方米）	Floor Space of Buildings under Construction (10 000 sq.m)	8246.58	6763.41	3238.61
房屋建筑竣工面积（万平方米）	Floor Space of Buildings Completed (10 000 sq.m)	1842.88	1365.68	764.03
公路里程（公里）	Length of Highways (km)	12795	8714	13596
#等级公路	Length of Expressway & Class I to IV Highway	12212		11711
民用汽车拥有量（辆）	Number of Civil Motor Vehicles Owned (vehicle)	1315448	611327	580863
#私人汽车	Private Motor Vehicles	1131833	54486	527079
邮政业务总量（亿元）	Business Volume of Post Service(100 million yuan)	5.64	5.91	6.85
电信业务总量（亿元）	Business Volume of Telecommunications Service(100 million yuan)	185.79	32.62	78.12
固定电话用户（万户）	Local Telephone Subscribers (10 000 subscribers)	71.90	24.36	31.38
移动电话用户（万户）	Number of Mobile Telephone Subscribers (10 000 subscribers)	937.80	438.16	465.80
互联网用户数（万户）	Number of Internet Subscribers (10 000 subscribers)	713.85	104.10	104.75
社会消费品零售总额（亿元）	Total Retail Sales of Consumer Goods (100 million yuan)	2204.16	1155.64	928.12
限额以上批发和零售业法人企业数（个）	Number of Corporation Enterprises above Designated Size in Wholesale & Retail (unit)	1007	451	316
限额以上批发和零售业年末从业人数（人）	Number of Year-end Employed Persons above Designated Size in Wholesale & Retail (person)	75226	26103	21291
限额以上批发和零售业商品销售额（亿元）	Sales of Goods above Designated Size of Wholesale & Retail (100 million yuan)	3525.11	1237.01	453.16
限额以上住宿和餐饮业法人企业数（个）	Number of Corporation Enterprises above Designated Size in Hotel & Catering (unit)	245	71	165
限额以上住宿和餐饮业年末从业人数（人）	Number of Year-end Employed Persons above Designated Size in Hotel & Catering (person)	38949	7016	12979
限额以上住宿和餐饮业营业额（亿元）	Turnover above Designated Size of Hotel & Catering (100 million yuan)	65.90	10.95	24.35
进出口总额（人民币，万元）	Total Import & Export (RMB, 10 000 yuan)	6070866	1722399	700117
进口额	Import	3313969	1179939	110627
出口额	Export	2756897	542460	589491
实际外商直接投资（万美元）	Foreign Actual Direct Investment(USD 10 000)	95753	67893	4179
入境国际旅游者人数（万人次）	Number of International Tourists Through Guangxi (10 000 person-times)	59.13	20.04	248.90
#外国人	Foreigners	40.77	14.99	132.94
国际旅游外汇收入（万美元）	Foreign Exchange Earnings From International Tourism (USD 10 000)	25996.00	9462.99	131627.23
国内旅游人数（万人次）	Number of Domestic Tourists (10 000 person-times)	11001.08	4018.78	7983.89
国内旅游总收入（亿元）	Total Domestic Tourism Receipts (100 million yuan)	1109.80	443.49	882.89
星级饭店数（个）	Total Number of Tourist Hotel (unit)	49	40	58
金融机构本外币存款（亿元）	Saving Deposit in RMB & Foreign Currencies of Financial Institutions (100 million yuan)	9492.18	3714.64	3284.51
金融机构人民币存款（亿元）	Saving Deposit in RMB of Financial Institutions (100 million yuan)	9367.53	3700.55	3265.31
#住户存款	Deposit of Households	3176.69	1447.92	1809.30

说明：根据海关报表调整，2015年起进出口总额使用人民币口径。
Note: According to the adjustment of the reports from the customhouse, the data of indicator "Total Import & Export" is calculated in RMB since 2015.

Continued

梧州市 Wuzhou	北海市 Beihai	防城港市 Fangcheng-gang	钦州市 Qinzhou	贵港市 Guigang	玉林市 Yulin	百色市 Baise	贺州市 Hezhou	河池市 Hechi	来宾市 Laibin	崇左市 Chongzuo
902.40	520.38	440.80	1536.05	947.30	2418.72	272.60	106.69	191.65	596.82	111.00
56.80	212.54	296.88	1112.32	596.50	1418.24	153.66	73.14	149.28	285.55	89.69
6727	2393	3116	7092	7665	10363	17293	5093	13348	7173	7299
6485		2472		6629	8915	16592	5076	12949	5917	6851
198550	207422	115564	236571	280575	492469	292626	161148	248654	169840	163020
182183	189623	105543	207611	261856	460856	268184	149195	229590	158477	132201
4.17	2.81	2.34	39.85	5.36	9.82	3.44	1.81	2.93	1.61	3.88
33.62	32.93	16.69	36.90	43.19	61.85	46.33	22.79	42.15	24.89	28.83
13.36	17.13	9.94	24.24	37.27	35.39	14.27	7.25	14.15	7.49	9.85
224.96	200.38	104.47	259.72	426.74	430.43	311.31	151.59	293.99	195.60	198.67
49.26	46.42	22.31	49.85	87.40	117.17	53.80	30.75	54.80	33.11	32.98
445.87	250.13	124.02	411.75	480.70	728.86	277.35	178.85	301.20	180.29	146.09
250	156	85	189	155	270	277	76.00	150	83	159
9104	7143	3681	8210	7183	18197	11498	5290.00	7617	3567	4454
157.62	195.47	190.43	281.59	191.17	344.81	255.50	86.43	136.84	89.32	392.63
50	45	25	30	30	57	94	14.00	36	18	31
2333	3246	1687	2505	1973	4496	4133	1510.00	2228	1560	2166
3.72	5.36	2.86	2.66	2.20	6.57	5.25	2.48	2.25	1.65	3.82
602406	2308381	7685445	3404673	238816	336580	1884397	48443	195498	77312	13388082
307770	1145853	6534820	2241777	128510	89529	377754	9377	173168	34856	4463450
294636	1162528	1150625	1162896	110306	247051	1506642	39065	22330	42456	8924632
1084.88	8445.00	57159	23187.00	3405.00	3179.00	7331.00	667.35	10.17	1147.00	370.23
20.93	14.54	17.66	6.88	9.63	13.67	8.32	38.91	11.26	2.36	40.31
1.54	7.60	16.36	0.94	1.00	2.81	4.12	2.94	3.31	0.66	25.49
8018.97	6077.00	6321.41	2772.40	3980.00	6118.64	3854.58	14474.21	5037.07	1090.00	15002.44
2205.06	3069.82	2016.35	2564.30	2090.71	3989.88	3265.21	2171.47	2635.58	2260.28	2539.48
240.33	364.51	164.83	254.55	235.16	415.49	334.46	262.84	297.22	180.20	234.67
34	35	25	16	14	25	32	18	50	14	45
1136.18	947.09	624.97	979.97	1263.37	1878.56	1236.80	725.31	1127.79	702.83	785.44
1133.48	938.84	618.88	976.54	1262.28	1876.23	1235.81	724.80	1126.69	702.47	784.81
729.86	578.55	341.84	652.17	912.82	1379.83	729.01	424.11	694.33	389.49	495.12

22—1　续表4

指　标	Item	南宁市 Nanning	柳州市 Liuzhou	桂林市 Guilin
金融机构本外币贷款（亿元）	Loans in RMB & Foreign Currencies of Financial Institutions (100 million yuan)	10880.58	2462.39	2149.77
金融机构人民币贷款（亿元）	Loans in RMB of Financial Institutions (100 million yuan)	10470.44	2459.49	2145.76
境内贷款	Domestic Loans	10457.38	2459.32	2145.64
短期贷款	Short-term Loans	1700.53	98.86	499.63
中长期贷款	Medium & Long-term Loans	8445.02	813.62	1602.96
境外贷款	Overseas Loans	13.06	0.17	0.12
幼儿园数（所）	Number of Kindergartens (unit)	1693	802	944
在园儿童数（万人）	Student Enrollment (10 000 persons)	32.01	13.73	17.17
普通小学学校数（所）	Number of Regular Primary Schools (unit)	1168	339	559
普通小学专任教师数（人）	Full-time Teachers in Regular Primary Schools (person)	35362	16830	21624
普通小学招生数（万人）	New Student Enrollment in Regular Primary Schools (10 000 persons)	12.07	5.13	6.64
普通小学在校学生数（万人）	Regular Primary Student Enrollment (10 000 persons)	64.68	30.37	37.92
普通小学毕业生数（万人）	Graduates of Regular Primary Schools (10 000 persons)	9.60	4.94	5.56
普通中学学校数（所）	Number of Regular Secondary Schools (unit)	358	153	214
普通中学专任教师数（人）	Full-time Teachers in Regular Secondary Schools (person)	26941	13402	19472
普通中学招生数（万人）	New Student Enrollment in Secondary Schools (10 000 persons)	14.39	7.35	8.30
普通中学在校学生数（万人）	Student Enrollment in Regular Secondary Schools (10 000 persons)	40.87	20.34	23.12
普通中学毕业生数（万人）	Graduates in Regular Secondary Schools (10 000 persons)	12.69	5.85	7.08
普通高等学校数（所）	Regular Institutions of Higher Education (unit)	33	6	13
普通高等学校专任教师数（人）	Full-time Teachers in Regular Institutions of Higher Education (person)	20651	4235	9135
普通高等学校招生数（万人）	New Student Enrollment in Regular Institutions of Higher Education (10 000 persons)	13.99	1.12	5.82
普通高等学校在校学生数（万人）	Student Enrollment in Regular Institutions of Higher Education(10 000 persons)	42.67	8.22	19.22
普通高等学校毕业生数（万人）	Graduates in Regular Institutions of Higher Education (10 000 persons)	10.86	0.71	4.67
公共图书馆（个）	Public Libraries (unit)	16	11	14
卫生机构数（个）	Number of Health Institutions (unit)	4532	2355	5042
#医院、卫生院	Hospitals, Village Clinics	236	65	210
卫生机构床位数（张）	Number of Beds in Health Institutions (bed)	47082	23695	22159
#医院、卫生院	Hospitals, Village Clinics	43811	17890	20295
卫生机构人员数（人）	Number of Employed Personnel in Health Institutions (person)	80884	39243	44279
#卫生技术人员	Medical & Technical Personnel	65642	31844	32864
#执业医师、执业助理医师	Certified Physicians , Certified Assistant Physicians	23469	10330	11434
注册护士	Senior Nurses	29163	14105	14096

Continued

梧州市 Wuzhou	北海市 Beihai	防城港市 Fangcheng-gang	钦州市 Qinzhou	贵港市 Guigang	玉林市 Yulin	百色市 Baise	贺州市 Hezhou	河池市 Hechi	来宾市 Laibin	崇左市 Chongzuo
788.51	672.43	632.93	664.82	814.54	1205.07	0.36	454.68	661.06	467.37	449.34
787.52	654.52	629.76	661.13	814.51	1205.05	922.29	454.68	660.19	467.14	449.33
787.36	654.46	629.68	660.96	814.39	1204.96	922.28	454.66	660.19	467.13	449.26
203.24	49.78	33.69	55.24	70.03	100.26	68.26	111.34	154.62	29.11	114.12
575.84	384.49	186.53	261.89	385.53	850.79	328.09	342.04	504.60	157.55	334.46
0.16	0.06	0.08	0.17	0.12	0.09	0.01	0.02	0.00	0.01	0.07
679	327	261	309	968	1619	1358	482	953	939	515
13.42	7.91	4.20	6.86	20.31	30.75	17.14	9.20	15.89	8.91	8.08
672	326	521	1004	855	1339	1427	316	709	223	267
15973	7640	5317	19264	22678	31034	18429	11368	19541	10574	9759
5.11	2.92	1.80	6.87	8.65	12.80	5.35	4.04	6.19	3.32	2.79
28.96	16.13	9.71	36.73	46.29	64.85	34.16	21.30	36.48	19.05	17.14
4.66	2.63	1.41	5.55	7.23	9.73	5.82	2.96	5.84	3.02	2.77
135	92	43	123	215	223	165	103	189	79	86
12060	7656	3469	22519	21358	17363	13311	7679	12577	8171	7042
6.66	5.46	1.94	7.75	11.96	9.73	5.81	4.19	8.46	4.29	3.97
19.09	11.04	5.58	21.95	34.72	28.42	23.23	11.53	23.71	12.59	10.92
5.97	3.26	1.66	6.89	11.41	9.03	5.01	3.55	7.10	3.83	3.00
2	4	1	2	0	1	5	1	2	2	6
1261	2089	155	1094	0	929	2267	743.00	657	618	2218
1.10	0.55	0.19	0.58	0.00	0.44	1.38	0.44	0.65	0.52	2.43
3.36	3.40	0.55	1.90	0.00	1.75	4.24	1.59	1.94	1.36	4.18
0.69	0.53	0	0.41	0.00	0.47	1.11	0.25	0.52	0.24	1.24
5	3	5	5	6	8	13	4	11	7	7
1618	1061	670	2255	4278	3113	2672	1164	2356	1504	1392
101	25	42	86	124	180	209	85	184	95	120
13986	8685	3907	15571	16314	25614	17871	8434	17828	11020	8549
13214	5793	3636	13021	15676	24130	16496	7946	16843	10253	7721
25662	17952	7795	25607	28692	36488	29427	14984	27534	19911	15806
18748	10055	5772	18055	20017	26640	21633	10853	20568	11552	11171
5945	3514	2042	5316	6589	9116	6382	3449	6286	3772	5893
8416	4383	2406	7907	8003	11087	9269	4581	8916	4587	4833

22—2 南宁市主要经济指标情况（1978—2017年）
Main Economic Indicators of Nanning (1978—2017)

年 份 Year	生产总值(按当年价格，亿元) Gross Domestic Product (current prices,100 million yuan)	第一产业 Primary Industry	第二产业 Secondary Industry	#工业 Industry	第三产业 Tertiary Industry	生产总值指数(上年=100) Indices of Gross Domestic Product (Preceding year=100)	第一产业 Primary Industry	第二产业 Secondary Industry	#工业 Industry	第三产业 Tertiary Industry
1978	14.74	6.19	5.22	4.75	3.33	111.5	110.3	112.1	108.1	112.6
1979	10.68	2.90	5.17	4.73	2.61	119.7	111.1	134.1	133.9	106.2
1980	18.01	7.01	7.00	6.45	4.00	105.5	105.3	108.0	112.6	101.7
1981	12.44	3.32	5.62	5.02	3.50	109.0	109.2	102.2	102.6	121.9
1982	13.72	4.11	5.99	5.26	3.62	108.8	120.2	107.2	105.6	102.0
1983	14.95	4.11	6.58	5.82	4.26	108.8	98.1	110.7	111.5	115.8
1984	15.38	4.12	6.51	5.65	4.75	100.0	98.3	96.4	95.6	107.4
1985	30.93	11.83	10.84	9.59	8.27	112.7	103.4	122.1	117.7	113.1
1986	35.15	12.64	12.72	11.10	9.79	107.9	101.4	111.7	110.1	114.1
1987	42.05	14.64	15.67	13.75	11.75	112.6	105.2	117.6	118.3	114.2
1988	53.78	17.88	19.13	16.67	16.76	109.7	92.8	109.0	108.3	129.6
1989	62.04	19.16	21.92	20.06	20.96	107.4	107.7	102.8	108.0	114.9
1990	70.88	23.10	24.84	22.83	22.94	109.6	111.1	111.6	112.1	107.8
1991	79.32	23.91	27.46	25.20	27.95	106.3	100.6	106.9	106.7	111.6
1992	91.81	27.77	30.47	27.59	33.56	112.7	115.1	109.3	107.9	114.3
1993	134.62	34.44	49.93	43.65	50.25	123.5	106.9	134.4	129.7	128.3
1994	187.23	49.10	67.51	57.80	70.61	116.5	107.7	119.6	117.1	120.7
1995	235.81	61.52	80.79	65.22	93.49	114.5	112.6	114.9	108.3	115.7
1996	267.20	69.05	84.59	66.64	113.56	111.4	105.9	110.4	107.7	116.5
1997	304.49	78.59	92.22	70.98	133.69	112.5	113.9	108.8	106.3	115.2
1998	339.55	83.44	99.73	76.71	156.38	111.5	108.4	110.3	110.3	114.8
1999	356.99	85.26	101.99	77.23	169.73	109.4	107.4	108.1	106.4	111.7
2000	377.94	87.66	105.37	79.09	184.91	107.7	100.7	104.6	105.4	113.9
2001	418.17	90.74	113.16	85.25	214.26	108.8	102.2	106.4	106.7	113.2
2002	463.18	94.35	125.56	93.39	243.27	110.9	107.7	112.0	112.2	111.6
2003	521.78	99.70	152.35	109.62	269.73	110.9	103.7	119.3	113.4	109.4
2004	619.12	107.68	193.38	137.83	318.06	113.2	105.9	118.2	116.8	113.1
2005	727.90	124.25	231.21	165.18	372.44	113.4	108.2	115.6	115.0	114.0
2006	880.11	144.34	297.31	221.29	438.46	116.8	108.4	125.3	129.9	114.4
2007	1089.07	178.00	372.27	284.09	538.80	117.4	107.3	121.2	124.2	117.9
2008	1320.43	203.11	457.94	352.27	659.39	114.7	105.3	114.8	116.9	117.4
2009	1524.71	212.38	527.46	395.80	784.88	115.1	105.8	117.0	113.5	116.3
2010	1800.26	244.43	651.88	483.78	903.94	114.2	105.7	117.8	115.9	113.7
2011	2211.44	305.55	829.61	612.59	1076.28	113.5	105.7	118.3	118.1	112.2
2012	2503.18	322.96	960.75	706.11	1219.48	112.3	105.2	118.1	118.7	109.6
2013	2803.54	349.93	1110.89	820.60	1342.73	110.3	104.8	114.6	114.8	108.1
2014	3148.32	354.69	1251.54	923.49	1542.09	108.5	104.2	109.9	110.3	108.2
2015	3410.08	371.10	1345.15	1000.37	1693.83	108.6	104.1	110.4	111.4	107.9
2016	3703.33	395.93	1426.50	1063.14	1880.90	107.0	103.2	105.8	105.6	108.8
2017	4118.83	404.18	1599.50	1189.89	2115.15	108.0	104.1	108.6	109.5	108.4

22—2 续表 continued

年 份 Year	固定资产投资（不含农户）（亿元） Investment in Fixed Assets (excluding rural registents) (100 million yuan)	社会消费品零售总额（亿元） Total Retail Sales of Consumer Goods (100 million yuan)	进出口（万美元） Total Import & Export (USD 10 000)	#出口 Exports	财政收入（亿元） Finance Revenue (100 million yuan)	#公共财政预算收入 Public Budget Income	公共财政预算支出（亿元） Public Budget Expenditure (100 million yuan)	城镇居民人均可支配收入（元） Per Capital Disposable Income of Urban Households (yuan)	农村居民人均纯收入（元） Per Capita Net Income of Rural Households (yuan)
1978	1.77	3.47			2.01	2.01	0.71		88
1979	2.47	4.02			1.98	1.98	0.60		105
1980	1.67	4.94			2.37	2.37	0.74	386	107
1981	1.34	5.50			2.45	2.45	0.74	445	135
1982	1.65	6.24			2.60	2.60	0.81	478	158
1983	1.96	6.93			2.63	2.63	0.77	513	239
1984	2.39	8.42			2.74	2.74	0.95	624	316
1985	4.46	11.72			3.54	3.54	1.80	716	367
1986	5.93	12.50			3.89	3.89	2.67	851	404
1987	6.80	15.16			4.41	4.41	2.90	949	461
1988	9.15	20.59			5.11	5.11	4.05	1166	521
1989	7.39	23.79			5.74	5.74	3.94	1274	574
1990	7.59	25.16	13732	9983	6.39	6.39	4.77	1454	624
1991	8.44	30.63	15884	11153	7.01	7.01	4.84	1659	683
1992	11.36	36.76	15903	10121	7.35	7.35	4.84	2106	778
1993	23.65	52.09	23324	9463	10.65	10.65	6.69	3081	912
1994	33.90	66.79	25234	9424	15.02	7.35	8.58	4543	1093
1995	56.35	83.99	17594	6988	17.11	9.12	9.46	5544	1326
1996	64.39	100.66	13703	6210	19.05	10.36	10.58	5973	1553
1997	74.78	115.36	36368	29434	21.58	11.68	11.95	5931	1788
1998	82.36	128.64	39753	33228	24.52	13.16	13.99	6570	1942
1999	88.08	137.14	57100	40094	27.01	14.97	17.29	6847	2079
2000	113.17	212.43	66164	51238	36.46	21.65	29.07	7448	1791
2001	121.41	231.35	53733	43053	45.29	29.19	34.86	7906	1954
2002	145.56	256.78	49668	40746	52.53	31.28	45.26	8796	2111
2003	190.36	288.45	65792	51143	61.06	36.24	52.50	9162	2231
2004	262.76	332.05	63625	52421	74.63	43.25	62.12	8059	2467
2005	362.90	380.34	71916	57716	100.22	45.20	73.55	9203	2680
2006	447.22	438.20	92853	71681	120.36	56.62	93.08	10193	3033
2007	560.22	518.81	128596	101316	150.84	70.15	118.00	11877	3462
2008	693.44	647.46	186666	158604	191.17	92.88	166.08	14446	4001
2009	1043.91	757.01	278735	238172	231.37	120.46	203.55	16254	4385
2010	1483.02	905.93	220407	158638	300.88	156.10	261.28	18032	5005
2011	2018.95	1073.15	251042	166236	363.52	186.29	301.85	20005	5848
2012	2585.18	1255.59	414678	251734	422.00	229.72	376.51	22561	6777
2013	2475.01	1450.84	442117	235270	473.66	256.25	418.40	24817	7685
2014	2933.87	1616.90	481410	261702	526.59	274.85	465.77	27075	8576
2015	3366.89	1786.68	585153	325095	572.48	297.05	527.69	29106	9408
2016	3824.73	1980.36	628556	319017	613.87	312.79	586.98	30728	11398
2017	4307.95	2204.16	607.09	275.69	687.98	332.15	646.31	33217	12515

注：1. 城镇居民人均可支配收入2004年（含2004年）以前为城市居民人均可支配收入。
2. 2000年以后农民人均纯收入统计口径调整。2014年后口径调整为农村居民人均可支配收入。
3. 2017年起，外贸进出口数据以人民币计价，单位为亿元。

Note:1. The statistical range of indicator "Per Capita Disposable Income of Urban Households" is the household in cities in and before 2004.
2. After 2000,2014 the statistical range of Per Capita Net Income of Farmers has been adjusted.
3. The data of import and export value of foreign trade was calculated by RMB（100 million yuan） since 2017.

22－3 柳州市主要经济指标情况（1978—2017年）
Main Economic Indicators of Liuzhou (1978—2017)

年 份 Year	生产总值（按当年价格，亿元）Gross Domestic Product (current prices,100 million yuan)	第一产业 Primary Industry	第二产业 Secondary Industry	#工业 Industry	第三产业 Tertiary Industry	生产总值指数（上年=100）Indices of Gross Domestic Product (Preceding year=100)	第一产业 Primary Industry	第二产业 Secondary Industry	#工业 Industry	第三产业 Tertiary Industry
1978	9.89	2.70	4.86	4.53	2.33	106.6	104.7	106.4	107.2	109.5
1979	10.87	2.76	5.31	4.94	2.80	104.5	98.8	106.8	108.1	106.6
1980	12.26	3.16	6.11	5.67	2.99	112.9	104.8	116.7	116.5	114.2
1981	13.47	3.73	6.56	6.09	3.18	106.4	110.7	104.9	106.2	105.0
1982	14.10	3.99	6.68	6.23	3.43	105.2	103.4	105.0	105.6	107.3
1983	16.29	4.31	7.76	7.27	4.23	109.9	105.5	108.9	109.0	116.1
1984	18.74	4.57	9.14	8.40	5.04	114.0	101.8	121.1	120.4	112.5
1985	23.16	5.18	11.53	10.77	6.45	120.1	102.2	127.9	128.2	119.6
1986	26.87	5.94	13.57	12.50	7.36	113.2	105.7	118.5	119.4	107.3
1987	35.51	6.93	18.87	17.27	9.72	117.0	108.9	115.4	114.2	126.4
1988	42.78	8.12	21.53	19.79	13.13	107.6	96.5	105.4	105.9	118.9
1989	49.01	9.61	24.06	22.43	15.34	102.7	111.2	100.8	101.8	102.3
1990	52.80	11.98	24.23	22.88	16.59	102.8	106.4	100.6	101.0	104.9
1991	61.67	11.97	28.85	26.41	20.85	111.5	98.1	113.9	113.5	117.0
1992	76.34	13.73	36.49	33.42	26.12	119.2	115.1	120.2	120.5	120.2
1993	105.48	16.23	56.71	52.77	32.54	110.3	105.0	123.0	123.8	101.7
1994	141.56	21.04	78.94	72.80	41.57	115.1	100.7	130.7	130.4	105.6
1995	177.64	29.25	93.46	85.68	54.93	116.5	114.7	117.8	116.8	115.8
1996	178.75	31.93	82.52	73.56	64.30	102.2	108.3	98.7	97.4	104.0
1997	201.07	33.54	91.26	82.07	76.27	115.0	110.8	110.4	110.8	122.8
1998	216.86	34.74	96.04	87.48	86.08	107.9	101.8	105.6	106.7	113.0
1999	228.37	35.60	99.09	91.10	93.68	107.3	106.8	105.9	106.3	109.1
2000	251.56	37.36	107.26	99.70	106.93	109.0	105.3	108.7	109.6	110.7
2001	283.68	39.40	119.84	111.59	124.45	111.1	106.8	112.2	112.8	111.4
2002	314.63	42.86	135.51	124.07	136.27	113.7	106.9	117.8	115.8	111.7
2003	361.57	44.61	168.73	150.61	148.23	111.9	104.6	117.2	112.4	108.7
2004	440.83	54.56	226.06	203.54	160.21	114.2	107.9	120.4	120.5	109.0
2005	512.00	58.95	266.11	241.78	186.95	114.0	107.3	117.5	118.6	111.6
2006	622.34	65.75	345.79	319.71	210.79	115.2	108.0	121.0	122.5	109.3
2007	755.12	77.20	437.93	407.55	239.99	115.6	106.8	119.4	119.9	112.2
2008	905.26	85.52	543.66	505.78	276.08	114.1	105.1	118.6	119.2	109.0
2009	1046.05	90.45	636.43	588.07	319.18	116.3	105.4	120.1	119.1	112.4
2010	1315.31	109.48	839.96	776.84	365.87	115.8	105.4	120.4	119.9	109.8
2011	1579.72	135.86	1003.68	923.21	440.17	110.8	105.7	111.7	111.3	110.3
2012	1820.61	147.38	1147.36	1055.69	525.87	111.5	106.1	111.7	111.6	112.6
2013	2010.05	159.29	1274.93	1166.65	575.84	110.0	105.0	111.6	111.0	107.6
2014	2208.51	160.01	1312.54	1191.11	735.90	108.5	103.3	108.5	108.6	109.7
2015	2298.62	167.10	1300.11	1174.93	831.41	107.2	103.3	105.2	105.2	112.4
2016	2476.94	179.46	1361.81	1232.52	935.67	107.3	103.1	105.7	105.9	110.5
2017	2755.64	189.49	1487.08	1345.13	1079.07	107.1	103.7	104.4	104.5	111.6

22－3 续表 continued

年 份 Year	固定资产投资(不含农户)(亿元) Investment in Fixed Assets (excluding rural registents) (100 million yuan)	社会消费品零售总额(亿元) Total Retail Sales of Consumer Goods (100 million yuan)	进出口(万美元) Total Import & Export (USD 10 000)	#出口 Exports	财政收入(亿元) Finance Revenue (100 million yuan)	#公共财政预算收入 Public Budget Income	公共财政预算支出（亿元） Public Budget Expenditure (100 million yuan)	城镇居民人均可支配收入（元） Per Capital Disposable Income of Urban Households (yuan)	农村居民人均纯收入（元） Per Capita Net Income of Rural Households (yuan)
1978	1.23	3.63			2.79	2.79	1.15		82
1979	0.96	3.93			2.99	2.99	0.73		91
1980	1.73	4.75			2.96	2.96	0.79	384	81
1981	1.33	5.45			3.24	3.24	0.80	431	103
1982	1.68	6.04			3.41	3.41	0.96	467	159
1983	1.81	6.61			2.92	2.92	0.97	489	254
1984	2.99	7.30			3.34	3.34	1.17	586	270
1985	4.88	9.43			4.37	4.37	1.95	668	316
1986	5.37	10.96			4.91	4.91	3.32	841	352
1987	8.67	12.54			5.76	5.76	3.95	966	392
1988	9.76	16.97			6.43	6.43	4.10	1119	453
1989	7.63	18.25			7.23	7.23	4.88	1260	518
1990	6.59	18.84			7.55	7.55	5.26	1515	586
1991	10.71	21.66			7.81	7.69	5.35	1794	694
1992	15.64	26.54			8.40	8.40	5.72	2105	783
1993	35.34	39.75			13.10	13.10	9.22	3267	890
1994	45.78	48.38			17.07	6.92	8.35	3912	1120
1995	38.68	60.48			18.78	8.26	9.71	4508	1440
1996	40.54	63.06			18.34	7.78	11.68	4805	1701
1997	41.36	72.65			20.90	9.32	12.06	5457	2035
1998	46.17	74.45			25.74	13.05	13.95	5552	2155
1999	45.46	77.43			27.93	13.93	16.60	5328	2183
2000	44.83	81.15			33.09	16.86	19.48	5740	1658
2001	50.77	94.57	21317	14022	42.20	21.76	27.43	7547	1797
2002	75.78	102.86	26813	14632	49.00	23.24	30.77	7928	1954
2003	109.37	90.90	28454	13922	58.19	27.13	38.37	8370	2082
2004	141.32	175.50	59342	19236	67.74	29.81	43.73	9155	2250
2005	171.76	200.25	69599	21250	80.19	28.18	49.48	9556	2534
2006	200.69	230.50	101256	39472	95.20	34.85	62.61	11002	2914
2007	302.04	274.08	133110	68613	116.38	40.37	74.93	12866	3497
2008	430.30	344.33	202586	93049	140.13	52.44	96.36	14474	3956
2009	681.86	400.98	167882	36484	157.64	61.41	127.48	16017	4330
2010	1004.88	480.00	281894	62952	201.18	74.64	155.03	17766	4935
2011	1304.57	568.80	278372	92446	229.60	89.45	184.29	19615	5721
2012	1683.13	661.84	311234	90678	260.18	113.55	221.17	22181	6746
2013	1566.71	758.42	288429	87472	285.06	125.12	240.58	24355	7663
2014	1810.94	858.20	226825	80197	316.55	133.16	261.61	26693	8606
2015	2082.89	944.11	222657	77924	343.81	146.68	309.72	28722	9449
2016	2338.61	1045.13	1353756	459085	370.16	159.16	339.56	30270	11107
2017	2697.20	1155.64	172.24	54.25	403.82	179.79	374.28	32661	12151

注：1. 城镇居民人均可支配收入2004年（含2004年）以前为城市居民人均可支配收入。

2. 2000年以后农民人均纯收入统计口径调整。2014年后口径调整为农村居民人均可支配收入。

3. 2017年起，外贸进出口数据以人民币计价，单位为亿元。

Note:1. The statistical range of indicator "Per Capita Disposable Income of Urban Households" is the household in cities in and before 2004.

2. After 2000,2014 the statistical range of Per Capita Net Income of Farmers has been adjusted.

3. The data of import and export value of foreign trade was calculated by RMB（100 million yuan） since 2017.

22—4 桂林市主要经济指标情况（1978—2017年）
Main Economic Indicators of Guilin (1978—2017)

年 份 Year	生产总值（按当年价格，亿元） Gross Domestic Product (current prices,100 million yuan)	第一产业 Primary Industry	第二产业 Secondary Industry	#工业 Industry	第三产业 Tertiary Industry	生产总值指数（上年=100） Indices of Gross Domestic Product (Preceding year=100)	第一产业 Primary Industry	第二产业 Secondary Industry	#工业 Industry	第三产业 Tertiary Industry
1978	11.22	4.87	3.96	3.66	2.39	111.2	105.1	109.9	109.7	123.8
1979	12.57	5.70	4.32	3.94	2.55	108.3	111.1	107.8	106.1	103.3
1980	13.76	6.11	4.73	4.26	2.92	103.7	97.9	109.2	108.3	107.6
1981	14.54	6.44	4.85	4.28	3.25	103.3	102.9	99.9	98.4	109.8
1982	15.96	7.36	4.95	4.36	3.65	107.4	109.0	103.6	103.6	110.0
1983	17.71	8.26	5.35	4.77	4.10	107.4	107.4	106.1	107.6	109.2
1984	19.69	8.54	6.02	5.26	5.13	109.9	100.5	114.4	114.5	120.9
1985	24.42	10.47	7.54	6.55	6.40	114.9	107.4	121.1	118.1	118.4
1986	28.54	11.30	9.31	7.89	7.93	109.5	102.3	113.0	113.5	114.9
1987	34.47	12.92	11.37	9.16	10.19	110.4	100.7	111.8	108.1	120.6
1988	41.82	16.08	13.21	11.00	12.53	105.3	101.7	105.6	107.3	108.7
1989	45.06	16.96	14.23	12.22	13.87	100.8	104.9	100.4	102.7	97.1
1990	49.88	20.45	14.44	12.36	15.00	103.0	102.4	101.7	102.0	105.3
1991	57.13	22.20	17.01	15.06	17.93	113.5	109.3	116.8	120.9	116.1
1992	70.87	25.95	23.27	20.42	21.64	117.8	110.3	131.4	132.2	114.2
1993	96.93	32.33	35.29	30.65	29.31	119.8	107.9	137.2	138.5	118.2
1994	134.28	50.33	43.41	37.88	40.54	112.4	111.2	113.1	113.7	113.0
1995	178.03	65.00	57.62	49.75	55.41	118.5	119.4	117.4	114.9	118.9
1996	223.11	80.71	69.17	59.33	73.22	121.0	116.8	120.3	119.9	126.7
1997	247.31	90.03	74.85	64.18	82.42	111.9	118.2	106.9	106.5	110.7
1998	259.64	90.67	82.92	70.89	86.05	107.8	102.7	113.7	113.8	107.4
1999	278.32	96.27	85.33	72.39	96.72	109.5	106.2	109.2	108.5	113.3
2000	302.49	99.50	93.57	79.49	109.42	110.1	105.2	111.3	111.7	113.6
2001	332.53	104.96	101.41	86.81	126.16	109.8	107.3	109.1	110.5	112.7
2002	360.78	107.50	112.47	95.60	140.81	109.2	102.5	111.6	110.9	112.8
2003	391.54	105.63	139.89	117.51	146.02	109.8	106.0	112.1	110.2	110.5
2004	459.16	118.05	170.73	143.52	170.38	113.1	109.2	115.9	115.8	113.4
2005	512.03	119.89	186.99	155.67	205.15	113.6	107.9	118.8	119.9	112.7
2006	595.52	133.42	234.83	200.34	227.27	112.2	106.5	116.3	117.8	111.8
2007	724.05	157.72	290.76	250.60	275.56	114.8	105.8	121.2	122.7	113.7
2008	851.59	171.42	357.46	308.71	322.71	112.9	106.0	118.2	119.7	111.1
2009	948.23	177.90	412.00	354.05	358.33	113.8	105.3	117.6	116.7	113.9
2010	1103.56	203.31	492.35	417.93	407.89	113.8	104.8	120.7	120.2	110.3
2011	1327.57	247.11	615.08	519.85	465.37	111.8	105.2	118.7	118.9	106.7
2012	1485.02	271.84	697.46	585.55	515.71	113.1	106.7	119.3	119.8	108.0
2013	1657.90	299.44	792.87	662.66	565.59	111.0	105.2	115.5	115.3	107.3
2014	1826.27	320.63	865.05	717.27	640.59	108.0	104.9	109.9	110.0	106.6
2015	1942.90	339.59	900.98	745.22	702.33	108.0	104.4	108.2	108.1	109.2
2016	2054.82	361.27	916.74	750.07	776.81	107.0	104.5	106.6	106.3	108.7
2017	2045.18	381.83	791.94	609.71	871.41	103.9	104.3	99.5	98.7	108.5

22－4 续表 continued

年 份 Year	固定资产投资（不含农户）（亿元） Investment in Fixed Assets (excluding rural registents) (100 million yuan)	社会消费品零售总额（亿元） Total Retail Sales of Consumer Goods (100 million yuan)	进出口（万美元） Total Import & Export (USD 10 000)	#出口 Exports	财政收入（亿元） Finance Revenue (100 million yuan)	#公共财政预算收入 Public Budget Income	公共财政预算支出（亿元） Public Budget Expenditure (100 million yuan)	城镇居民人均可支配收入（元） Per Capital Disposable Income of Urban Households (yuan)	农村居民人均纯收入（元） Per Capita Net Income of Rural Households (yuan)
1978	0.91	4.17			0.92				
1979	0.98	4.74			0.94				
1980	1.48	5.60			0.96				
1981	1.38	6.00			1.09				
1982	1.73	6.34			1.24				
1983	1.73	6.70			1.40				
1984	1.76	8.03			1.56				
1985	3.27	11.02			1.74				
1986	5.75	12.17			2.07				
1987	8.77	15.17			2.74				
1988	9.58	19.88	435	435	3.72				
1989	7.60	20.71	1841	1653	4.65				
1990	7.34	22.22	2696	1791	5.07				513
1991	7.50	24.86	4143	2737	8.03				689
1992	12.71	28.84	5185	4278	8.87				735
1993	25.36	37.57	8404	5736	9.48				872
1994	33.09	50.75	9204	8454	12.86				1137
1995	42.58	67.28	19114	16360	15.32				1575
1996	53.02	82.49	23661	14763	17.97				2075
1997	58.62	90.30	24253	16044	20.68				2347
1998	63.20	95.92	23945	13300	22.73	14.76	19.92		2570
1999	69.83	104.17	20887	11267	23.16	15.21	21.77		2673
2000	79.23	113.52	26167	12909	24.22	15.89	24.15		2878
2001	88.51	124.12	21277	11940	29.52	20.52	30.92		2063
2002	97.41	136.04	23813	14158	32.90	20.19	36.57		2195
2003	111.05	103.95	26227	16488	37.04	22.13	40.95		2354
2004	146.90	142.88	35468	23861	42.74	25.52	45.09	8149	2638
2005	198.73	164.78	44155	30843	51.61	24.78	54.62	9268	3003
2006	260.87	191.17	58426	42871	59.33	29.70	64.80	10713	3391
2007	403.05	228.79	79243	53074	72.50	36.32	84.67	12908	3908
2008	485.96	284.77	101058	69541	85.55	45.18	117.15	14636	4465
2009	659.35	330.92	73600	51547	97.64	55.15	141.71	16221	4833
2010	908.56	391.53	90743	62220	121.08	67.08	183.59	17949	5487
2011	1140.53	462.36	95655	71700	141.94	80.75	232.67	19882	6325
2012	1462.40	536.35	97487	78858	163.56	106.01	261.33	22300	7328
2013	1390.32	604.03	92370	75889	180.37	111.00	286.56	24552	8361
2014	1627.30	682.87	94327	77225	195.18	123.89	304.43	26811	9431
2015	1970.83	751.96	88271	77420	209.19	134.53	356.04	28768	10365
2016	2131.62	836.45	89500	78700	223.76	145.33	399.03	30124	12176
2017	2234.24	928.12	70.01	58.95	239.54	144.16	434.71	32534	13345

注：1. 城镇居民人均可支配收入2004年（含2004年）以前为城市居民人均可支配收入。
2. 2000年以后农民人均纯收入统计口径调整。2014年后口径调整为农村居民人均可支配收入。
3. 2017年起，外贸进出口数据以人民币计价，单位为亿元。

Note:1. The statistical range of indicator "Per Capita Disposable Income of Urban Households" is the household in cities in and before 2004.
2. After 2000,2014 the statistical range of Per Capita Net Income of Farmers has been adjusted.
3. The data of import and export value of foreign trade was calculated by RMB (100 million yuan) since 2017.

22－5　梧州市主要经济指标情况（1978—2017年）
Main Economic Indicators of Wuzhou (1978—2017)

年　份 Year	生产总值（按当年价格，亿元） Gross Domestic Product (current prices,100 million yuan)	第一产业 Primary Industry	第二产业 Secondary Industry	#工业 Industry	第三产业 Tertiary Industry	生产总值指数（上年=100） Indices of Gross Domestic Product (Preceding year=100)	第一产业 Primary Industry	第二产业 Secondary Industry	#工业 Industry	第三产业 Tertiary Industry
1978	6.07	3.07	1.77	1.64	1.22	125.2	109.8	172.9	175.3	117.0
1979	6.32	3.17	1.87	1.68	1.28	113.8	123.4	107.7	105.7	101.3
1980	6.99	3.42	2.11	1.91	1.46	105.6	107.3	103.4	103.0	104.5
1981	7.88	3.46	2.46	2.22	1.96	109.2	93.4	116.0	116.8	130.5
1982	9.07	4.23	2.73	2.43	2.11	106.2	111.7	106.3	160.1	104.6
1983	9.85	4.50	2.81	2.52	2.49	105.2	104.0	100.8	99.7	113.5
1984	10.62	5.03	2.89	2.59	2.70	105.7	107.4	102.5	103.2	106.0
1985	12.68	5.75	3.54	3.14	3.40	97.4	110.5	116.1	114.0	115.4
1986	14.41	6.20	4.02	3.58	4.18	127.8	107.3	107.7	109.1	117.1
1987	17.91	7.68	5.17	4.65	5.06	113.2	111.8	114.3	115.9	114.4
1988	21.96	9.16	6.43	5.71	6.36	109.2	103.9	112.5	110.9	114.1
1989	25.35	10.61	7.25	6.48	7.49	106.1	108.1	105.0	107.5	104.6
1990	30.69	13.08	7.09	6.36	10.52	119.7	114.5	104.6	102.0	142.9
1991	35.02	14.31	7.86	7.04	12.85	117.3	114.5	113.9	118.7	125.1
1992	45.24	17.51	11.03	9.75	16.70	116.6	111.1	109.4	106.4	129.5
1993	59.36	21.16	17.51	15.67	20.69	120.5	109.0	155.1	162.0	112.7
1994	73.24	27.81	21.77	19.29	23.66	104.4	102.6	114.6	114.1	98.0
1995	86.27	32.72	25.00	21.75	28.56	105.9	106.9	105.5	103.3	105.0
1996	96.55	35.96	28.98	25.69	31.60	108.5	106.1	115.8	118.0	104.4
1997	107.21	37.57	33.95	29.91	35.69	112.4	105.2	119.3	119.0	113.9
1998	112.00	38.85	34.19	29.63	38.96	105.5	99.7	105.0	104.2	112.9
1999	115.78	39.95	34.67	30.51	41.16	108.2	107.5	107.3	108.9	109.7
2000	127.08	41.77	38.51	33.27	46.79	108.1	101.9	110.2	108.9	112.1
2001	139.05	43.13	41.64	35.86	54.28	108.4	105.2	107.8	108.1	111.8
2002	153.16	46.10	47.06	39.86	60.00	110.2	106.8	111.5	109.7	111.9
2003	162.00	40.22	56.02	46.32	65.76	109.5	100.8	120.2	116.5	107.6
2004	196.61	47.74	75.93	60.42	72.95	114.2	109.7	124.8	119.9	108.1
2005	228.40	49.83	97.61	81.07	80.96	114.6	105.8	121.0	119.4	114.1
2006	270.42	52.96	126.23	109.40	91.22	114.6	105.2	123.0	127.6	110.2
2007	319.57	59.67	165.00	145.61	94.91	115.6	102.8	126.6	129.0	108.4
2008	400.12	66.45	215.50	190.96	118.17	114.9	104.1	123.6	124.9	107.0
2009	453.65	69.53	246.60	215.91	137.52	117.6	106.6	123.7	122.9	113.0
2010	579.28	79.96	341.23	304.60	158.10	117.8	104.8	125.3	126.8	110.2
2011	742.49	96.02	465.84	422.43	180.62	114.3	105.6	119.6	120.9	107.4
2012	832.58	104.84	525.22	479.88	202.52	113.6	105.1	117.5	119.0	108.5
2013	991.71	115.32	654.83	605.03	221.55	113.2	104.8	116.8	117.5	107.9
2014	1062.00	117.18	646.06	595.31	298.76	106.0	102.1	107.0	107.8	105.0
2015	1078.65	122.44	623.96	572.62	332.25	108.3	103.9	108.1	108.4	110.6
2016	1175.65	131.31	679.35	627.01	364.99	107.6	103.3	108.6	109.2	107.2
2017	1338.10	136.41	785.71	729.57	415.98	106.7	104.4	105.2	105.5	110.4

22－5 续表 continued

年 份 Year	固定资产投资（不含农户）（亿元） Investment in Fixed Assets (excluding rural registents) (100 million yuan)	社会消费品零售总额（亿元） Total Retail Sales of Consumer Goods (100 million yuan)	进出口（万美元） Total Import & Export (USD 10 000)	#出口 Exports	财政收入（亿元） Finance Revenue (100 million yuan)	#公共财政预算收入 Public Budget Income	公共财政预算支出（亿元） Public Budget Expenditure (100 million yuan)	城镇居民人均可支配收入（元） Per Capital Disposable Income of Urban Households (yuan)	农村居民人均纯收入（元） Per Capita Net Income of Rural Households (yuan)
1978	0.33	2.53			0.90	0.90	0.60	442	85
1979	0.40	2.78			0.82	0.82	0.56	449	88
1980	0.50	3.30			0.95	0.95	0.61	458	94
1981	0.58	3.61		16735	1.04	1.04	0.71	459	93
1982	0.84	3.79		16577	1.06	1.06	0.75	486	133
1983	0.90	4.01		16374	1.05	1.05	0.81	472	230
1984	0.88	4.40		14713	1.14	1.14	1.02	589	264
1985	1.31	6.15		15454	1.42	1.42	1.21	776	327
1986	2.00	7.17		19573	1.54	1.54	1.77	942	385
1987	2.41	8.57	29089	20611	1.89	1.89	1.95	1093	453
1988	3.32	10.82	28502	19393	2.34	2.34	2.43	1571	516
1989	3.94	11.74	23785	18333	2.62	2.62	2.86	1724	555
1990	4.10	12.10	22940	19171	2.71	2.71	3.26	1890	598
1991	5.00	13.89	24707	19556	3.44	3.44	3.49	2314	662
1992	9.72	17.53	37416	23636	3.75	3.75	4.02	2315	803
1993	16.51	23.10	44064	24692	5.16	5.16	4.92	3246	1054
1994	19.55	31.61	47494	26422	4.07	3.29	5.32	4309	1247
1995	24.86	37.76	42880	23103	6.61	4.13	5.85	4909	1565
1996	21.48	42.49	24490	16105	7.58	4.65	6.36	4945	2015
1997	23.10	46.21	21211	13956	8.18	5.31	6.87	4934	2212
1998	23.95	48.27	18951	9781	8.84	5.92	8.25	4838	2302
1999	13.42	52.17	17340	9818	9.08	6.16	8.96	5415	2394
2000	20.73	57.55	19569	12400	9.88	6.87	10.27	5221	2442
2001	26.32	63.32	10621	14300	11.32	8.12	13.76	5838	1784
2002	30.14	69.54	15406	18293	12.59	8.20	16.46	6282	1897
2003	41.70	76.40	21223	21975	14.26	9.17	19.25	6785	2007
2004	73.04	71.31	37304	25724	17.64	11.94	22.02	7062	2292
2005	99.89	85.55	45805	29260	20.25	11.99	27.21	8118	2575
2006	121.94	98.04	44051	29073	23.08	13.71	33.84	9449	2879
2007	151.37	115.59	51494	32191	27.03	15.27	43.66	11362	3252
2008	198.31	146.54	50845	36114	32.42	18.13	50.91	13268	3854
2009	330.37	171.09	55835	38763	40.06	23.49	71.71	14747	4218
2010	468.42	191.77	64221	44548	56.13	32.42	90.96	16427	4879
2011	631.65	224.08	79616	52508	76.14	44.91	118.55	18239	5651
2012	858.09	257.21	121038	44127	101.02	73.83	159.21	20563	6592
2013	850.30	292.30	176506	49932	118.23	85.74	175.95	22537	7475
2014	926.36	328.30	124948	50777	122.42	90.45	184.05	24272	8342
2015	1061.33	364.93	567181	285673	123.74	92.37	214.73	25898	9051
2016	1168.51	395.95	61037	39424	127.59	95.61	227.99	27260	10142
2017	1330.15	445.87	60.24	29.46	121.09	84.55	242.30	29359	11085

注：1. 城镇居民人均可支配收入2004年（含2004年）以前为城市居民人均可支配收入。

2. 2000年以后农民人均纯收入统计口径调整。2014年后口径调整为农村居民人均可支配收入。

3. 2017年起，外贸进出口数据以人民币计价，单位为亿元。

Note:1. The statistical range of indicator "Per Capita Disposable Income of Urban Households" is the household in cities in and before 2004.

2. After 2000,2014 the statistical range of Per Capita Net Income of Farmers has been adjusted.

3. The data of import and export value of foreign trade was calculated by RMB（100 million yuan） since 2017.

22—6 北海市主要经济指标情况（1978—2017年）
Main Economic Indicators of Beihai (1978—2017)

年 份 Year	生产总值（按当年价格，亿元） Gross Domestic Product (current prices,100 million yuan)	第一产业 Primary Industry	第二产业 Secondary Industry	#工业 Industry	第三产业 Tertiary Industry	生产总值指数（上年=100） Indices of Gross Domestic Product (Preceding year=100)	第一产业 Primary Industry	第二产业 Secondary Industry	#工业 Industry	第三产业 Tertiary Industry
1978	2.86	1.72	0.78	0.73	0.35	100.8	98.8	101.9	101.2	109.6
1979	3.21	1.82	1.92	0.86	0.47	103.7	101.1	102.7	102.3	118.4
1980	3.67	1.86	1.19	0.99	0.61	110.4	104.5	123.4	110.9	116.7
1981	3.77	1.94	1.16	1.04	0.67	105.4	104.8	99.6	107.5	116.4
1982	4.44	2.48	1.14	1.01	0.83	108.4	115.8	99.5	97.0	95.1
1983	4.79	2.51	1.28	1.12	1.00	107.7	104.4	116.1	111.8	109.8
1984	5.16	2.33	1.45	1.24	1.38	110.2	98.0	100.4	108.4	171.4
1985	6.83	3.04	2.27	1.65	1.52	107.8	93.8	140.1	128.2	111.8
1986	8.01	3.28	2.77	2.10	1.96	117.7	105.7	128.3	126.1	128.8
1987	9.47	3.98	3.02	2.24	2.47	103.3	110.4	105.0	106.8	105.1
1988	12.08	5.01	3.75	3.16	3.32	110.0	105.6	120.5	124.1	106.1
1989	13.81	6.30	3.94	3.43	3.57	104.6	109.2	101.2	103.2	101.4
1990	17.61	8.05	4.78	4.19	4.78	125.6	138.9	108.4	107.2	123.0
1991	21.21	9.52	5.92	5.08	5.77	107.9	98.1	116.7	114.0	117.8
1992	31.55	11.94	9.82	7.37	9.79	142.1	115.5	164.3	150.0	162.3
1993	54.31	15.03	20.51	12.78	18.77	146.3	104.3	179.2	162.0	160.4
1994	75.45	19.72	28.24	20.94	27.49	118.1	111.6	123.7	140.0	116.6
1995	88.26	26.16	27.61	21.04	34.49	102.6	117.9	89.2	89.6	108.1
1996	91.62	29.23	24.04	18.63	40.03	102.6	105.7	94.3	97.9	108.7
1997	95.33	29.99	26.03	21.85	39.31	101.6	101.1	101.0	105.6	102.4
1998	102.63	32.58	30.02	24.19	40.03	109.4	108.7	115.0	111.8	105.2
1999	107.63	34.96	29.75	24.63	42.97	106.9	107.4	103.7	105.9	109.6
2000	113.67	35.46	31.81	26.98	46.40	107.7	103.8	110.0	112.7	108.6
2001	123.44	37.39	33.87	29.26	52.18	109.3	103.4	115.6	119.8	109.4
2002	134.39	39.43	36.77	31.05	58.19	110.4	104.6	113.5	112.3	112.3
2003	140.14	39.08	42.82	33.29	58.24	111.8	102.9	123.6	116.4	110.7
2004	155.53	42.76	51.92	44.57	60.85	111.3	103.1	120.2	123.7	110.7
2005	164.61	51.76	49.81	41.64	63.04	121.9	107.9	137.8	139.9	123.9
2006	179.25	56.08	59.32	50.36	63.85	110.9	104.2	118.9	120.9	110.2
2007	225.95	63.53	71.79	61.32	90.62	117.9	104.8	128.0	130.6	119.5
2008	276.50	70.60	96.60	82.50	109.30	116.8	103.7	125.8	126.0	117.8
2009	321.06	77.07	118.40	100.70	125.60	116.2	104.7	123.0	122.0	116.5
2010	401.41	87.17	167.88	144.92	146.36	117.6	103.7	132.3	133.5	110.0
2011	496.60	115.50	207.40	176.10	173.80	118.2	103.1	131.9	132.9	111.4
2012	630.09	127.37	303.75	267.77	198.97	121.7	104.3	138.3	141.9	108.7
2013	735.00	142.81	373.65	332.78	218.53	113.3	104.1	119.1	119.8	108.1
2014	856.54	149.49	454.51	407.81	252.54	112.4	101.9	118.7	119.7	105.7
2015	891.94	159.35	450.13	401.25	282.46	111.4	103.2	113.2	113.9	111.4
2016	1006.98	175.09	516.14	464.42	315.75	108.6	104.1	109.6	109.9	109.7
2017	1229.84	190.54	668.66	612.00	370.64	110.2	103.7	110.5	111.3	113.3

22－6 续表 continued

年 份 Year	固定资产投资（不含农户）（亿元）Investment in Fixed Assets (excluding rural registents) (100 million yuan)	社会消费品零售总额（亿元）Total Retail Sales of Consumer Goods (100 million yuan)	进出口（万美元）Total Import & Export (USD 10 000)	#出口 Exports	财政收入（亿元）Finance Revenue (100 million yuan)	#公共财政预算收入 Public Budget Income	公共财政预算支出（亿元）Public Budget Expenditure (100 million yuan)	城镇居民人均可支配收入（元）Per Capital Disposable Income of Urban Households (yuan)	农村居民人均纯收入（元）Per Capita Net Income of Rural Households (yuan)
1978	0.27	1.15	3005	3005	0.32	0.32	0.21		
1979	0.29	1.31	3040	3040	0.33	0.33	0.23		
1980	1.01	1.67	3893	3893	0.37	0.37	0.30		
1981	0.61	1.94	3676	3676	0.40	0.40	0.33		
1982	0.64	2.24	3948	3948	0.45	0.45	0.34		
1983	0.55	2.46	4192	4191	0.46	0.46	0.31	539	239
1984	1.06	2.75	3731	3731	0.52	0.52	0.54	754	316
1985	2.03	3.84	10236	9218	0.78	0.78	0.73	828	400
1986	2.77	4.69	8409	7389	0.86	0.86	1.21	998	417
1987	2.65	5.00	10634	9218	0.93	0.93	1.14	1122	458
1988	3.01	6.77	8353	6929	1.10	1.10	1.10	1296	546
1989	2.35	6.74	16828	8794	1.32	1.32	1.65	1376	586
1990	3.11	7.07	14510	8998	1.59	1.59	1.82	1591	738
1991	3.85	7.86	17182	8462	1.95	1.95	2.25	1910	786
1992	10.05	9.72	24409	9430	2.85	2.85	2.70	2727	869
1993	36.58	15.42	13865	9318	5.68	5.68	5.27	4516	1281
1994	34.75	18.61	16592	8373	6.77	5.33	6.88	5649	1635
1995	25.81	21.57	39655	8260	8.30	5.87	7.96	6365	2224
1996	17.48	24.01	26976	7768	7.69	4.95	6.08	6396	2348
1997	17.58	26.30	32096	10406	8.41	5.46	5.95	6558	2394
1998	24.11	28.68	19381	15178	9.70	6.63	8.26	6301	2366
1999	25.65	31.16	16812	13250	10.69	7.56	8.79	6483	2427
2000	21.83	34.01	7403	4876	10.20	6.54	8.98	6167	2155
2001	19.94	37.34	7327	5040	10.68	6.85	10.72	7013	2265
2002	26.60	40.75	10782	6738	11.63	7.19	13.33	7692	2454
2003	43.06	34.24	14429	8668	13.06	8.27	13.21	8015	2587
2004	51.40	40.71	15073	10656	15.32	9.72	14.63	8773	2790
2005	51.40	46.24	20079	13770	19.27	10.86	17.77	9520	3180
2006	67.24	53.41	29172	19574	23.10	14.04	24.98	10380	3414
2007	87.40	64.36	49838	30671	30.03	19.02	33.57	12334	3846
2008	200.30	82.08	71075	43863	27.03	14.34	31.26	13989	4309
2009	321.85	95.40	79643	47351	35.75	17.22	50.99	15134	4697
2010	485.26	108.00	137122	83948	47.10	27.51	63.04	16798	5426
2011	603.19	127.29	171242	113143	57.50	37.06	84.64	18656	6249
2012	725.36	146.51	207820	118382	100.10	41.13	98.73	21202	7227
2013	674.90	167.30	269833	136611	113.60	42.11	99.47	23407	8239
2014	797.71	185.81	350016	175176	127.39	47.25	104.97	25818	9079
2015	932.54	202.99	379048	189211	142.99	47.61	131.76	27729	9923
2016	1011.10	225.34	310157	167007	166.31	50.07	150.06	29412	11622
2017	1099.68	250.13	230.84	116.25	200.67	64.34	157.54	31912	12749

注：1. 城镇居民人均可支配收入2004年（含2004年）以前为城市居民人均可支配收入。

2. 2000年以后农民人均纯收入统计口径调整。2014年后口径调整为农村居民人均可支配收入。

3. 2017年起，外贸进出口数据以人民币计价，单位为亿元。

Note:1. The statistical range of indicator “Per Capita Disposable Income of Urban Households” is the household in cities in and before 2004.

2. After 2000,2014 the statistical range of Per Capita Net Income of Farmers has been adjusted.

3. The data of import and export value of foreign trade was calculated by RMB（100 million yuan） since 2017.

22—7　防城港市主要经济指标情况（1978—2017年）
Main Economic Indicators of Fangchenggang (1978—2017)

年　份 Year	生产总值（按当年价格，亿元）Gross Domestic Product (current prices,100 million yuan)	第一产业 Primary Industry	第二产业 Secondary Industry	#工业 Industry	第三产业 Tertiary Industry	生产总值指数（上年=100）Indices of Gross Domestic Product (Preceding year=100)	第一产业 Primary Industry	第二产业 Secondary Industry	#工业 Industry	第三产业 Tertiary Industry
1978	1.08	0.56	0.29	0.22	0.23	-	-	-	-	-
1980	1.26	0.68	0.30	0.21	0.28	102.5	105.4	90.3	102.1	108.7
1985	2.56	1.56	0.42	0.30	0.58	103.3	101.7	103.9	99.3	107.2
1986	3.09	1.73	0.62	0.51	0.75	124.4	118.0	143.7	164.1	127.8
1987	3.71	1.89	0.70	0.58	1.12	114.0	107.2	106.9	107.5	136.1
1988	4.68	2.34	0.86	0.65	1.48	102.6	90.5	110.8	103.3	120.6
1989	5.82	3.30	0.90	0.73	1.62	117.4	140.0	104.3	110.3	92.3
1990	6.98	4.02	1.04	0.84	1.92	110.1	104.2	121.2	119.4	115.9
1991	8.24	4.33	1.59	1.20	2.32	116.7	100.8	124.9	118.8	142.3
1992	12.38	6.08	2.02	1.37	4.29	127.9	105.1	143.0	143.2	150.8
1993	17.49	6.12	4.33	3.00	7.04	124.8	100.2	150.6	148.6	134.2
1994	24.66	8.95	7.51	5.71	8.20	122.3	120.9	151.6	160.3	104.9
1995	29.26	11.73	7.01	5.60	10.52	112.2	115.2	106.4	113.3	115.1
1996	36.66	13.96	10.27	8.17	12.43	116.8	121.0	126.4	122.3	105.3
1997	44.64	18.11	12.08	9.72	14.45	115.1	116.5	118.1	118.4	110.7
1998	49.04	19.27	13.12	10.30	16.65	112.0	109.3	111.8	109.5	114.8
1999	52.05	19.46	14.06	11.35	18.54	108.2	104.5	107.3	108.2	112.6
2000	55.03	19.99	14.28	11.57	20.77	107.4	100.6	111.0	113.2	110.0
2001	60.03	20.18	16.12	13.12	23.72	108.8	103.3	114.2	114.9	110.5
2002	66.53	20.40	20.05	17.41	26.09	113.1	102.7	129.6	138.6	110.6
2003	72.53	20.70	21.41	18.09	30.42	110.7	106.2	116.1	114.9	109.8
2004	83.32	21.67	27.38	22.34	34.28	111.7	104.8	118.9	114.3	110.8
2005	99.14	26.04	35.22	29.72	37.87	116.0	105.3	130.9	135.6	111.0
2006	122.78	29.54	48.55	41.23	44.70	119.8	107.6	132.9	133.2	116.0
2007	162.91	32.87	72.71	64.34	57.33	120.8	105.7	127.3	130.3	123.5
2008	213.34	36.45	99.38	87.94	77.50	120.2	104.9	120.7	120.3	127.9
2009	251.04	39.88	124.93	109.73	86.23	122.6	104.7	136.2	136.0	116.5
2010	320.42	47.43	159.77	138.19	113.21	117.8	105.7	120.1	117.4	119.9
2011	413.77	57.79	217.63	187.32	138.35	115.3	105.8	119.0	117.4	114.0
2012	443.99	61.16	233.56	197.64	149.28	112.2	105.7	117.8	117.8	106.5
2013	530.40	67.30	295.36	255.59	167.74	112.4	105.5	117.9	119.5	105.9
2014	588.89	70.57	340.36	298.41	177.96	110.4	101.6	115.2	117.1	105.2
2015	620.71	75.49	353.00	310.52	192.23	110.2	103.7	112.6	113.8	107.8
2016	676.04	82.60	386.26	340.88	207.18	109.1	104.0	111.5	112.1	106.5
2017	741.62	89.27	421.23	369.45	231.12	106.7	103.9	106.4	106.3	108.3

注：2013年更新为全国第三次经济普查数据。
Note: The data in 2013 has been adjusted according to the 3rd National Economic Census.

22—7 续表 continued

年 份 Year	固定资产投资(不含农户)(亿元) Investment in Fixed Assets (excluding rural registents) (100 million yuan)	社会消费品零售总额(亿元) Total Retail Sales of Consumer Goods (100 million yuan)	进出口(万美元) Total Import & Export (USD 10 000)	#出口 Exports	财政收入(亿元) Finance Revenue (100 million yuan)	#公共财政预算收入 Public Budget Income	公共财政预算支出(亿元) Public Budget Expenditure (100 million yuan)	城镇居民人均可支配收入(元) Per Capital Disposable Income of Urban Households (yuan)	农村居民人均纯收入(元) Per Capita Net Income of Rural Households (yuan)
1978	0.32	0.57			0.08	0.08	0.18		72
1980	0.35	0.77			0.91	0.91	0.22		78
1985	0.58	1.12			0.17	0.17	0.41		246
1986	0.76	1.92			0.21	0.21	0.60		286
1987	0.90	2.11			0.25	0.25	0.72		296
1988	1.41	2.84			0.33	0.33	0.75		338
1989	0.68	3.34			0.50	0.50	0.89		387
1990	0.92	3.52	1348	1043	0.58	0.51	1.17		443
1991	1.90	3.68	1642	1399	0.93	0.56	1.33		535
1992	2.45	5.11	1348	1063	1.57	0.94	1.93		862
1993	8.56	6.70	1738	1049	2.92	2.92	2.71		877
1994	10.41	9.83	3730	2417	3.64	2.30	4.08		1020
1995	13.13	12.79	17715	10863	3.84	2.47	4.72		1443
1996	11.39	14.86	19800	10146	4.04	2.62	3.97	4508	1855
1997	11.88	16.56	30353	23214	4.51	3.04	4.38	5122	2269
1998	14.42	17.93	41202	28015	5.21	3.69	5.43	5456	2503
1999	14.69	19.38	33083	21789	5.42	3.86	5.47	5591	2626
2000	15.23	20.94	24073	12593	4.13	3.26	4.74	6200	1844
2001	17.53	22.66	10459	1855	4.53	3.61	6.61	6661	2026
2002	16.03	24.29	34444	5742	5.03	3.57	7.54	7664	2163
2003	19.70	17.60	48685	7358	5.61	3.84	8.37	7869	2334
2004	30.40	20.28	73486	8358	6.78	4.72	9.14	6324	2517
2005	42.96	22.89	84953	9924	8.04	4.51	10.22	7254	2704
2006	68.96	26.37	102900	11610	10.59	5.21	13.92	9113	3172
2007	103.53	31.41	145857	19495	15.76	7.74	19.08	12159	3791
2008	146.32	39.09	220775	30660	21.92	11.70	26.22	14364	4474
2009	254.10	45.33	216891	39202	27.39	18.47	40.10	16067	4930
2010	376.84	51.84	279774	77906	35.12	22.69	52.57	17831	5628
2011	491.27	61.16	410586	94431	44.35	28.30	60.77	19722	6502
2012	550.39	71.30	489826	82804	52.38	35.55	74.73	22203	7539
2013	475.45	81.43	430030	107839	59.26	40.71	88.48	24423	8557
2014	499.91	91.67	546866	150522	65.33	45.45	97.52	26523	9524
2015	549.74	101.03	860140	231166	70.64	52.05	131.72	28433	10429
2016	600.14	111.89	875753	169314	75.61	55.65	127.60	29758	12113
2017	672.77	124.02	768.54	115.06	74.51	47.60	120.47	32079	13373

注：1. 城镇居民人均可支配收入2004年（含2004年）以前为城市居民人均可支配收入。
2. 2000年以后农民人均纯收入统计口径调整。2014年后口径调整为农村居民人均可支配收入。
3. 2017年起，外贸进出口数据以人民币计价，单位为亿元。

Note:1. The statistical range of indicator "Per Capita Disposable Income of Urban Households" is the household in cities in and before 2004.
2. After 2000,2014 the statistical range of Per Capita Net Income of Farmers has been adjusted.
3. The data of import and export value of foreign trade was calculated by RMB (100 million yuan) since 2017.

22—8 钦州市主要经济指标情况（1978—2017年）
Main Economic Indicators of Qinzhou (1978—2017)

年 份 Year	生产总值（按当年价格，亿元）Gross Domestic Product (current prices,100 million yuan)	第一产业 Primary Industry	第二产业 Secondary Industry	#工业 Industry	第三产业 Tertiary Industry	生产总值指数（上年=100）Indices of Gross Domestic Product (Preceding year=100)	第一产业 Primary Industry	第二产业 Secondary Industry	#工业 Industry	第三产业 Tertiary Industry
1978	4.46	2.80	0.85	0.70	0.80	107.0	97.1	137.7	116.7	121.3
1979	4.80	2.93	0.99	0.80	0.88	108.3	106.1	114.0	114.8	109.9
1980	6.15	4.01	1.15	0.93	0.99	122.0	127.6	115.5	114.3	110.6
1981	6.50	4.15	1.26	1.00	1.06	106.9	107.3	111.0	112.6	101.0
1982	7.79	5.38	1.22	0.95	1.19	113.6	120.7	93.0	90.2	110.2
1983	8.20	5.39	1.34	1.02	1.46	104.2	100.0	107.7	109.0	118.9
1984	8.40	5.26	1.42	1.07	1.72	95.6	88.3	105.0	104.4	114.0
1985	9.72	5.93	1.76	1.39	2.03	105.8	99.7	116.6	120.9	114.1
1986	11.79	7.20	2.25	1.82	2.34	111.8	108.2	125.4	126.8	108.9
1987	14.48	8.66	2.78	2.33	3.03	112.6	111.5	116.1	118.5	111.8
1988	16.70	9.12	3.36	2.81	4.22	101.4	90.1	106.3	107.3	124.7
1989	18.85	10.03	3.60	3.03	5.21	111.9	119.3	95.8	94.8	113.2
1990	23.92	13.33	4.07	3.46	6.52	119.8	108.7	136.8	143.1	128.0
1991	28.50	14.91	4.97	4.30	8.62	118.4	113.5	117.8	119.4	129.0
1992	38.79	21.28	7.19	5.82	10.33	132.1	139.5	140.7	135.1	113.7
1993	52.65	26.73	12.30	9.83	13.61	113.4	102.1	154.4	157.9	109.7
1994	70.12	37.74	15.03	12.36	17.35	110.0	113.5	108.4	109.9	104.3
1995	86.89	47.03	16.41	13.73	23.45	107.0	105.9	98.4	98.3	118.5
1996	97.82	51.81	17.54	14.00	28.47	108.9	102.7	115.0	112.4	116.1
1997	109.58	57.86	20.46	16.33	31.26	113.8	116.9	111.1	109.6	110.5
1998	118.23	62.98	22.29	17.58	32.96	111.9	112.0	116.4	116.7	108.0
1999	122.86	66.01	22.06	17.46	34.78	110.5	115.6	102.5	102.1	108.0
2000	131.25	68.69	23.49	19.49	39.07	104.7	101.9	103.4	106.9	111.5
2001	142.55	72.79	26.28	21.22	43.48	108.7	107.4	112.7	109.8	108.6
2002	148.12	71.02	29.02	22.98	48.08	110.9	109.8	112.1	109.9	111.9
2003	152.89	70.02	34.98	28.62	47.89	106.4	101.3	113.2	111.5	111.0
2004	171.25	72.67	43.99	35.91	54.60	113.3	113.3	116.2	114.8	111.3
2005	188.02	76.45	51.50	41.65	60.08	114.9	107.2	138.7	143.4	111.0
2006	235.95	84.29	79.50	68.52	72.15	115.1	105.3	131.4	136.4	113.6
2007	286.67	97.34	98.69	86.30	90.65	116.9	107.4	124.6	127.6	120.6
2008	345.75	107.77	124.85	107.37	113.13	115.4	103.4	121.3	120.3	122.0
2009	396.18	114.04	141.38	118.10	140.76	115.2	105.8	119.6	116.4	119.2
2010	520.67	132.21	218.51	187.91	169.90	118.0	104.9	130.6	131.4	115.5
2011	646.65	156.00	290.70	252.90	199.91	120.1	105.1	136.6	140.3	110.7
2012	691.32	166.81	289.15	237.24	235.35	111.8	106.5	114.4	111.5	111.6
2013	753.74	181.77	316.85	250.12	255.13	107.9	104.6	110.3	107.3	106.3
2014	854.96	193.95	338.94	250.57	322.07	109.8	104.0	113.6	110.8	107.5
2015	944.42	204.37	381.75	278.17	358.31	108.4	103.9	108.4	105.7	111.4
2016	1102.05	220.10	481.90	363.22	400.05	109.0	103.5	111.3	109.9	109.7
2017	1309.82	234.95	625.01	487.18	449.86	108.8	103.9	111.2	111.9	108.9

22—8 续表 continued

年 份 Year	固定资产投资(不含农户)(亿元) Investment in Fixed Assets (excluding rural registents) (100 million yuan)	社会消费品零售总额(亿元) Total Retail Sales of Consumer Goods (100 million yuan)	进出口(万美元) Total Import & Export (USD 10 000)	#出口 Exports	财政收入(亿元) Finance Revenue (100 million yuan)	#公共财政预算收入 Public Budget Income	公共财政预算支出(亿元) Public Budget Expenditure (100 million yuan)	城镇居民人均可支配收入(元) Per Capital Disposable Income of Urban Households (yuan)	农村居民人均纯收入(元) Per Capita Net Income of Rural Households (yuan)
1978	0.51	1.66			0.40	0.40	0.46		117
1979	0.57	1.93			0.42	0.42	0.44		136
1980	0.66	2.37			0.47	0.47	0.5		182
1981	0.61	2.59			0.67	0.67	0.54		206
1982	0.89	2.95			0.74	0.74	0.55		244
1983	1.01	3.29			0.61	0.61	0.51		259
1984	0.92	3.67			0.60	0.60	0.65		250
1985	0.78	4.49			0.65	0.65	0.82	620	278
1986	1.30	5.11			0.81	0.81	1.26	745	302
1987	1.27	6.14			0.93	0.93	1.4	865	455
1988	1.96	7.70			1.12	1.12	1.63	1242	506
1989	1.82	9.31			1.35	1.35	3.01	1507	494
1990	1.69	9.77			1.62	1.62	2.32	1640	655
1991	2.45	13.07			2.04	2.04	2.58	1852	663
1992	5.59	15.56			2.28	2.28	2.68	2095	800
1993	12.61	21.65			3.41	3.41	3.49	3091	985
1994	13.28	20.50			3.91	2.22	3.61	4030	1231
1995	14.16	25.18			4.39	2.68	3.97	4635	1670
1996	15.50	28.39			4.93	3.20	4.69	5098	1930
1997	15.47	32.29			5.70	3.84	5.51	5027	2174
1998	20.76	35.42			6.64	4.67	6.29	5433	2362
1999	20.80	39.06			7.44	5.79	7.68	5672	2475
2000	23.02	42.81	3357	1146	8.26	6.72	9.27	5692	2092
2001	28.93	47.37	1772	1208	8.35	5.52	11.68	6328	2278
2002	35.30	51.23	3202	2059	9.24	6.23	13.25	6734	2442
2003	44.50	55.87	4320	3598	10.19	6.99	15.59	7437	2610
2004	63.00	62.47	9056	5191	11.75	7.84	16.78	7922	2783
2005	89.85	70.76	19846	11415	14.11	9.08	20.87	8942	3091
2006	117.88	80.72	44040	13458	17.17	10.47	24.91	10041	3405
2007	165.93	95.32	84089	31384	23.56	13.04	32.37	12057	3934
2008	248.91	124.01	127008	51370	32.00	18.28	48.80	14106	4444
2009	374.65	145.09	88572	22566	38.02	21.01	66.51	15768	4843
2010	451.60	172.19	131101	32558	58.37	22.36	78.00	17356	5340
2011	558.34	204.27	298225	87518	123.10	25.57	96.98	19248	6167
2012	652.59	237.56	376656	100190	139.20	33.58	122.67	21600	7140
2013	609.72	268.82	353042	105243	136.12	44.95	134.26	23695	8054
2014	726.95	303.05	533447	201112	138.31	47.64	141.27	25425	8892
2015	866.23	333.5	582738	247574	162.23	50.34	192.54	27281	9710
2016	950.89	373.63	442813	161508	154.08	49.50	200.08	29360	10947
2017	1088.85	411.75	340.47	116.29	145.08	52.81	205.94	31415	11801

注：1. 城镇居民人均可支配收入2004年（含2004年）以前为城市居民人均可支配收入。
2. 2000年以后农民人均纯收入统计口径调整。2014年后口径调整为农村居民人均可支配收入。
3. 2017年起，外贸进出口数据以人民币计价，单位为亿元。

Note:1. The statistical range of indicator "Per Capita Disposable Income of Urban Households" is the household in cities in and before 2004.
2. After 2000,2014 the statistical range of Per Capita Net Income of Farmers has been adjusted.
3. The data of import and export value of foreign trade was calculated by RMB (100 million yuan) since 2017.

22－9　贵港市主要经济指标情况（1996—2017年）
Main Economic Indicators of Guigang (1996—2017)

年　份 Year	生产总值（按当年价格，亿元）Gross Domestic Product (current prices,100 million yuan)	第一产业 Primary Industry	第二产业 Secondary Industry	#工业 Industry	第三产业 Tertiary Industry	生产总值指数（上年=100）Indices of Gross Domestic Product (Preceding year=100)	第一产业 Primary Industry	第二产业 Secondary Industry	#工业 Industry	第三产业 Tertiary Industry
1996	108.26	50.95	19.70	18.17	37.60	100.5	94.7	91.9	91.6	116.1
1997	111.58	52.03	20.58	19.26	38.98	106.7	108.9	106.5	107.8	104.2
1998	113.66	51.73	21.58	20.06	40.35	107.6	108.7	106.6	106.3	106.9
1999	115.38	51.31	21.98	20.54	42.08	105.6	106.8	103.2	103.5	105.7
2000	120.81	51.17	24.87	23.16	44.77	104.3	98.3	109.8	109.5	108.1
2001	132.35	52.59	28.11	25.98	51.65	108.5	104.7	113.4	112.9	110.0
2002	139.82	52.92	29.94	27.24	56.96	110.8	109.5	111.3	110.3	111.9
2003	156.92	52.51	38.58	33.98	65.83	111.4	104.9	125.0	121.4	110.6
2004	191.18	62.21	53.52	46.24	75.45	112.8	106.9	123.9	121.0	111.5
2005	222.82	66.01	72.63	60.23	84.19	116.2	107.4	137.8	133.2	109.3
2006	260.02	70.08	88.85	75.17	101.09	112.9	105.1	120.3	122.6	112.7
2007	330.56	83.30	127.51	111.25	119.75	117.0	102.9	133.2	136.4	112.4
2008	386.82	96.34	153.46	133.62	137.02	111.3	105.2	111.8	112.0	115.0
2009	437.73	96.92	182.21	158.37	158.61	115.2	104.8	120.7	120.2	115.6
2010	544.66	108.05	248.25	218.78	188.35	114.0	104.6	120.6	120.8	112.0
2011	630.82	138.79	264.49	228.92	227.54	106.1	105.4	105.2	104.4	107.8
2012	679.18	148.68	273.38	229.15	257.13	110.2	106.1	112.0	110.4	110.1
2013	742.01	160.76	303.35	253.11	277.90	108.2	104.9	111.1	110.7	106.2
2014	805.40	162.14	325.50	270.65	317.75	105.2	103.0	105.2	105.2	106.4
2015	865.20	173.95	348.50	285.89	342.75	107.5	103.8	108.5	107.0	107.9
2016	958.76	190.01	393.20	319.38	375.55	107.9	103.8	110.0	108.4	107.9
2017	1082.18	193.65	465.86	378.53	422.68	109.0	104.2	111.3	111.3	108.8

22—9 续表 continued

年 份 Year	固定资产投资（不含农户）（亿元） Investment in Fixed Assets (excluding rural registents) (100 million yuan)	社会消费品售总额（亿元） Total Retail Sales of Consumer Goods (100 million yuan)	进出口（万美元） Total Import & Export (USD 10 000)	#出口 Exports	财政收入（亿元） Finance Revenue (100 million yuan)	#公共财政预算收入 Public Budget Income	公共财政预算支出（亿元） Public Budget Expenditure (100 million yuan)	城镇居民人均可支配收入（元） Per Capital Disposable Income of Urban Households (yuan)	农村居民人均纯收入（元） Per Capita Net Income of Rural Households (yuan)
1996	7.75	45.39	6432	4560	6.42	4.19	5.22		1906
1997	9.06	43.90	7063	5359	6.46	4.21	5.35		2103
1998	12.26	46.79	3115	2502	7.24	4.98	6.58		2179
1999	13.04	49.37	1173	749	7.41	5.39	7.33		2114
2000	17.29	53.67	1892	1628	8.03	5.81	8.12		1868
2001	21.09	58.58	1553	1122	9.00	6.46	10.97		1979
2002	29.47	63.46	5046	2513	10.03	6.59	12.88		2091
2003	36.35	70.70	5666	4254	12.04	8.09	15.47		2228
2004	58.61	79.96	6306	5130	14.31	9.56	18.42	6209	2399
2005	129.43	91.42	7777	5443	17.05	9.21	22.01	7642	2693
2006	149.56	104.50	9544	6144	19.08	10.97	27.33	8938	2961
2007	155.90	123.80	11474	8515	23.02	12.29	35.31	10717	3472
2008	220.07	155.86	16388	9525	29.07	15.62	47.44	12666	4049
2009	290.18	181.08	14324	11131	34.03	19.53	64.24	13915	4504
2010	385.29	209.54	17386	12090	40.02	21.44	90.80	15531	5289
2011	430.02	245.97	27228	14033	43.33	21.69	106.07	17017	6257
2012	552.24	284.05	23144	10609	50.03	26.57	126.24	19314	7253
2013	496.26	321.72	22123	12143	57.42	31.22	140.46	21361	8189
2014	611.41	359.56	30603	18703	66.11	36.45	146.84	23262	9131
2015	778.61	389.10	32258	13281	72.75	42.57	186.38	24890	10017
2016	841.69	431.89	28527	15816	78.96	47.62	212.55	26771	11572
2017	983.81	480.70	23.88	11.03	90.03	50.41	233.82	28806	12544

注：1. 城镇居民人均可支配收入2004年（含2004年）以前为城市居民人均可支配收入。

2. 2000年以后农民人均纯收入统计口径调整。2014年后口径调整为农村居民人均可支配收入。

3. 2017年起，外贸进出口数据以人民币计价，单位为亿元。

Note:1. The statistical range of indicator "Per Capita Disposable Income of Urban Households" is the household in cities in and before 2004.

2. After 2000,2014 the statistical range of Per Capita Net Income of Farmers has been adjusted.

3. The data of import and export value of foreign trade was calculated by RMB（100 million yuan） since 2017.

22—10　玉林市主要经济指标情况（1978—2017年）
Main Economic Indicators of Yulin (1978—2017)

年份 Year	生产总值（按当年价格，亿元）Gross Domestic Product (current prices,100 million yuan)	第一产业 Primary Industry	第二产业 Secondary Industry	#工业 Industry	第三产业 Tertiary Industry	生产总值指数（上年=100）Indices of Gross Domestic Product (Preceding year=100)	第一产业 Primary Industry	第二产业 Secondary Industry	#工业 Industry	第三产业 Tertiary Industry
1978	9.12	5.79	1.66	1.43	1.67	102.0	101.2	107.6	116.1	97.2
1979	9.18	5.75	1.61	1.30	1.82	99.7	93.9	95.9	90.5	127.3
1980	10.42	6.76	1.66	1.41	2.00	110.8	109.9	94.4	112.7	113.5
1981	11.64	7.45	1.89	1.59	2.30	112.8	112.1	114.5	113.3	113.5
1982	13.86	9.01	2.17	1.84	2.69	118.5	120.7	113.2	106.1	116.7
1983	14.36	9.01	2.34	1.94	3.01	100.7	95.6	108.5	100.5	109.9
1984	15.45	9.41	2.58	2.02	3.46	106.4	101.3	109.1	94.8	117.7
1985	17.63	10.11	3.42	2.92	4.10	105.2	93.9	120.5	167.7	119.4
1986	20.74	11.55	4.32	3.64	4.87	112.4	108.7	121.9	125.5	111.9
1987	26.98	14.67	5.75	4.92	6.56	120.9	111.9	128.9	133.9	130.0
1988	33.57	18.31	7.31	6.23	7.95	106.6	101.4	114.8	113.7	107.8
1989	35.97	19.62	7.78	6.51	8.58	101.2	108.8	101.9	106.0	89.9
1990	41.13	23.99	8.24	6.79	8.90	109.1	107.8	103.3	107.3	117.0
1991	50.40	27.30	11.31	9.61	11.79	112.6	106.4	128.9	129.0	118.9
1992	65.31	30.29	18.97	16.69	16.04	126.6	109.3	156.1	156.1	135.0
1993	97.97	36.08	36.67	33.29	25.22	125.2	103.8	143.2	153.1	117.5
1994	134.92	52.92	49.25	45.40	32.75	115.6	119.0	112.5	112.1	115.4
1995	156.08	63.65	50.71	46.01	41.71	111.2	110.0	113.1	113.5	110.0
1996	168.34	72.91	51.46	46.67	43.97	104.5	106.0	101.9	101.8	103.6
1997	173.51	77.16	51.58	47.14	44.77	104.3	107.0	101.3	101.2	104.7
1998	187.40	80.87	57.77	52.88	48.76	109.2	106.5	111.2	112.4	110.6
1999	191.15	80.37	57.10	52.59	53.68	106.5	107.4	102.8	103.3	111.0
2000	199.64	78.42	60.70	55.58	60.52	106.1	98.5	109.4	109.4	112.9
2001	213.91	81.59	61.17	55.55	71.14	107.4	105.1	107.8	107.9	110.1
2002	231.70	80.61	71.50	65.34	79.59	110.4	105.8	116.7	117.6	110.1
2003	258.45	79.68	84.99	77.24	93.78	108.3	98.0	116.8	116.4	111.9
2004	312.68	99.49	101.03	87.80	112.16	115.2	112.3	122.1	117.2	110.8
2005	352.60	100.62	120.80	104.41	131.19	113.1	106.8	117.5	116.8	114.6
2006	410.96	107.62	148.64	129.90	154.70	113.5	107.0	119.2	120.1	113.4
2007	501.39	128.88	187.06	164.60	185.45	115.2	105.1	121.6	122.4	116.5
2008	602.83	149.49	230.32	201.70	223.02	112.8	105.8	114.7	114.7	115.4
2009	683.49	152.06	277.14	241.11	254.29	114.8	106.2	120.7	119.3	114.0
2010	840.25	171.73	373.39	324.14	295.13	115.7	105.7	123.7	122.5	112.8
2011	1019.94	213.81	458.59	395.50	347.55	111.0	105.4	113.7	113.0	110.9
2012	1102.08	229.20	482.33	404.39	390.55	110.9	106.1	114.6	113.3	108.7
2013	1210.44	243.57	526.26	421.03	451.61	110.0	104.2	113.8	112.9	107.8
2014	1314.52	248.78	591.66	479.53	501.08	108.4	103.4	111.3	110.3	106.7
2015	1445.91	259.14	635.83	509.64	550.94	108.9	101.4	111.1	110.2	109.4
2016	1553.83	278.16	665.03	521.11	610.64	108.0	102.1	109.6	108.2	109.0
2017	1699.54	276.91	734.14	564.86	688.49	107.6	103.2	108.1	107.4	109.1

22－10 续表 continued

年 份 Year	固定资产投资（不含农户）（亿元）Investment in Fixed Assets (excluding rural registents) (100 million yuan)	社会消费品零售总额（亿元）Total Retail Sales of Consumer Goods (100 million yuan)	进出口（万美元）Total Import & Export (USD 10 000)	#出口 Exports	财政收入（亿元）Finance Revenue (100 million yuan)	#公共财政预算收入 Public Budget Income	公共财政预算支出（亿元）Public Budget Expenditure (100 million yuan)	城镇居民人均可支配收入（元）Per Capital Disposable Income of Urban Households (yuan)	农村居民人均纯收入（元）Per Capita Net Income of Rural Households (yuan)
1978	0.39	3.11			0.89		0.68		
1979	0.46	3.50			0.79		0.69		
1980	0.46	3.93			0.87		0.77		
1981	0.35	4.36			1.06		0.92		
1982	0.82	5.03			1.22		0.93		
1983	1.20	5.83			1.15		0.93		
1984	0.62	7.15			1.06		1.07		
1985	0.99	8.85			1.41		1.61		
1986	1.40	10.25			1.46		1.94		
1987	1.98	12.49			1.95		2.28		
1988	3.89	17.56			2.69		3.04		
1989	2.46	22.02	1010		2.95		3.52		
1990	2.38	23.15	2083		3.23		4.01		
1991	7.52	25.88	2471		3.70		4.35		
1992	12.92	29.18	5542		4.21		4.89		
1993	21.46	34.53	6409		7.24		6.74		
1994	34.65	47.49	17887		9.32	5.36	8.54		
1995	42.03	61.34	19100		11.16	6.82	10.72		
1996	39.77	72.84	18482		12.54	8.19	10.82		
1997	26.11	76.48	18145		13.19	9.04	11.44		
1998	29.43	80.73	23280	21149	13.95	9.59	12.44		
1999	25.79	83.39	6690	6324	15.24	10.85	14.11		
2000	28.15	75.77	17854	17163	16.65	12.09	16.11		1736
2001	30.03	82.62	9800	8400	15.44	10.53	18.86		1839
2002	33.86	90.53	13280	9945	18.32	10.87	20.84		1959
2003	48.33	99.63	26001	17510	21.43	12.06	24.07		2035
2004	92.30	113.97	30143	21422	25.42	14.13	26.76	7136	2259
2005	131.31	130.80	36916	25866	28.64	14.86	31.97	8297	2573
2006	176.11	151.39	34807	26705	33.68	17.74	40.42	10175	3041
2007	230.68	180.96	37023	29780	40.68	20.88	54.89	12202	3536
2008	290.69	224.88	44214	31665	47.75	25.57	71.59	14156	4123
2009	444.61	262.92	35401	21663	54.67	30.61	96.21	15827	4531
2010	615.56	307.24	45148	31594	68.96	36.84	129.37	17642	5302
2011	792.18	362.81	63457	34069	85.86	48.94	159.73	19590	6269
2012	1004.26	422.83	58807	35843	100.36	65.57	192.65	22171	7269
2013	974.78	482.91	41679	28992	113.81	75.48	203.73	24366	8272
2014	1154.39	545.71	48681	32224	128.17	88.81	229.10	26681	9341
2015	1332.12	600.34	45092	32872	139.57	97.16	285.76	28842	10292
2016	1467.10	660.43	40427	33567	148.95	104.81	317.55	30083	12590
2017	1689.33	728.86	33.66	24.71	160.18	105.55	351.63	32159	13597

注：1. 城镇居民人均可支配收入2004年（含2004年）以前为城市居民人均可支配收入。
2. 2000年以后农民人均纯收入统计口径调整。2014年后口径调整为农村居民人均可支配收入。
3. 2017年起，外贸进出口数据以人民币计价，单位为亿元。

Note:1. The statistical range of indicator "Per Capita Disposable Income of Urban Households" is the household in cities in and before 2004.
2. After 2000,2014 the statistical range of Per Capita Net Income of Farmers has been adjusted.
3. The data of import and export value of foreign trade was calculated by RMB（100 million yuan） since 2017.

22－11 百色市主要经济指标情况（1978—2017年）
Main Economic Indicators of Baise (1978—2017)

年 份 Year	生产总值（按当年价格，亿元）Gross Domestic Product (current prices,100 million yuan)	第一产业 Primary Industry	第二产业 Secondary Industry	#工业 Industry	第三产业 Tertiary Industry	生产总值指数（上年=100）Indices of Gross Domestic Product (Preceding year=100)	第一产业 Primary Industry	第二产业 Secondary Industry	#工业 Industry	第三产业 Tertiary Industry
1978	6.15	3.92	1.09	0.93	1.14	112.9	111.7	115.2	106.7	114.2
1979	6.53	4.06	1.15	0.98	1.32	107.1	104.9	108.7	109.3	112.0
1980	6.74	4.10	1.23	0.99	1.41	96.4	94.8	99.0	97.3	98.6
1981	7.46	4.67	1.25	1.04	1.54	110.8	117.2	93.5	96.2	109.0
1982	8.38	5.34	1.30	1.07	1.74	106.6	106.4	102.3	100.8	110.5
1983	9.09	5.64	1.46	1.20	1.99	107.9	104.6	112.5	113.0	113.7
1984	9.40	5.47	1.56	1.30	2.37	98.7	90.9	106.7	110.2	113.3
1985	10.56	5.99	1.80	1.50	2.77	102.5	99.9	108.3	107.5	103.9
1986	12.85	7.41	2.16	1.89	3.28	110.3	110.4	108.8	114.2	111.0
1987	15.21	8.26	2.96	2.57	3.99	110.3	104.8	124.1	122.4	111.7
1988	17.87	9.52	3.42	2.87	4.93	103.7	101.7	104.2	101.5	107.0
1989	19.92	10.60	3.83	3.34	5.49	101.3	103.0	104.4	106.4	96.0
1990	23.14	11.84	4.35	3.73	6.95	103.3	101.0	103.3	102.1	107.5
1991	26.91	13.41	5.54	4.59	7.96	108.7	105.3	119.4	113.4	107.8
1992	31.04	14.12	7.04	5.39	9.88	111.3	105.2	120.9	115.0	114.8
1993	41.56	18.31	10.69	7.42	12.56	112.7	108.0	124.3	116.7	111.4
1994	58.68	26.50	13.54	10.33	18.64	115.3	112.4	112.7	122.0	121.9
1995	77.13	32.62	20.53	15.66	23.98	116.3	112.6	127.7	122.7	112.7
1996	89.18	37.10	23.20	20.43	28.88	114.4	114.5	112.6	130.7	115.7
1997	97.14	40.49	24.50	21.11	32.15	113.1	112.0	115.3	114.3	112.7
1998	106.08	44.56	27.04	23.09	34.48	110.9	112.2	112.0	111.6	108.3
1999	112.02	47.28	28.66	24.17	36.08	109.1	109.4	110.5	109.4	107.3
2000	119.50	47.85	32.43	26.81	39.22	107.2	103.1	107.8	105.6	110.7
2001	128.37	49.45	35.25	28.42	43.67	107.1	101.0	111.4	110.3	111.1
2002	143.97	48.09	47.43	37.25	48.45	113.1	104.7	130.4	129.4	108.1
2003	162.13	50.32	58.38	47.28	53.43	112.9	103.4	129.9	133.2	106.2
2004	203.76	61.04	82.83	69.22	59.89	115.9	106.0	127.4	129.9	112.2
2005	239.36	63.91	105.70	88.06	69.75	115.2	106.1	120.3	118.8	117.1
2006	297.28	67.32	149.11	126.14	80.85	115.0	103.8	122.8	121.6	112.5
2007	352.73	79.98	176.49	151.47	96.26	115.4	104.0	122.2	124.1	113.8
2008	416.24	88.07	217.61	189.29	110.56	113.4	103.2	120.2	123.7	109.7
2009	452.86	90.77	225.78	191.66	136.31	114.8	104.1	119.8	119.1	113.8
2010	573.99	105.21	313.89	273.49	154.80	115.0	104.9	121.1	121.4	110.5
2011	656.71	125.61	357.84	312.26	173.26	106.5	104.6	107.7	108.3	105.2
2012	755.24	137.14	414.21	361.92	203.89	109.2	107.4	109.7	109.1	109.6
2013	803.58	148.76	432.59	373.87	222.22	108.6	105.3	110.1	109.8	107.2
2014	917.95	158.71	490.02	417.90	269.22	108.4	104.2	109.9	108.7	107.8
2015	980.42	169.38	511.68	433.61	299.36	108.1	104.7	107.3	106.7	111.8
2016	1114.31	182.25	594.73	508.74	337.33	108.8	103.9	109.5	109.2	110.2
2017	1361.76	189.24	789.33	690.07	383.20	108.8	104.5	109.5	109.6	109.8

22－11 续表 continued

年 份 Year	固定资产投资(不含农户)(亿元) Investment in Fixed Assets (excluding rural registents) (100 million yuan)	社会消费品零售总额(亿元) Total Retail Sales of Consumer Goods (100 million yuan)	进出口(万美元) Total Import & Export (USD 10 000)	#出口 Exports	财政收入(亿元) Finance Revenue (100 million yuan)	#公共财政预算收入 Public Budget Income	公共财政预算支出(亿元) Public Budget Expenditure (100 million yuan)	城镇居民人均可支配收入(元) Per Capital Disposable Income of Urban Households (yuan)	农村居民人均纯收入(元) Per Capita Net Income of Rural Households (yuan)
1978	0.58	2.05			0.54	0.54	0.83		57
1980	0.95	2.75			0.47	0.47	0.96		64
1985	1.47	4.56			0.77	0.77	1.87		139
1986	1.33	5.56			0.87	0.87	2.29		166
1987	1.53	6.56			1.14	1.14	2.74		191
1988	2.76	8.46			1.42	1.42	3.07		218
1989	2.09	8.64			1.67	1.67	3.53		259
1990	2.74	8.91			1.95	1.95	3.84	1546	283
1991	4.67	10.36			2.23	2.23	4.03	1620	330
1992	8.77	14.57			2.36	2.36	4.85	2002	382
1993	18.47	14.14	62	62	3.74	3.74	5.42	2703	483
1994	20.63	18.76	986	986	4.53	2.71	6.34	4017	643
1995	27.92	23.55	1736	1552	5.78	3.70	8.55	5035	909
1996	13.31	24.67	1985	1805	7.13	4.56	8.07	5180	1261
1997	13.75	27.40	4259	3014	8.57	5.42	9.53	5049	1642
1998	18.80	29.83	4392	3335	10.04	6.90	12.01	5495	1848
1999	21.38	31.82	2770	1460	11.24	7.62	13.50	5607	1985
2000	29.46	34.02	2433	1393	12.78	8.18	14.68	5747	1183
2001	37.32	36.82	3210	2205	14.67	9.38	20.64	6806	1258
2002	58.08	39.99	11439	5484	16.69	9.54	23.55	7215	1331
2003	76.31	43.72	13358	7090	20.10	11.64	27.00	7378	1403
2004	102.74	37.22	17110	4775	24.80	14.15	32.82	6687	1550
2005	175.56	48.72	18560	6943	32.37	15.23	39.74	8077	1783
2006	249.92	56.23	32489	12104	40.08	20.19	52.73	9887	2110
2007	293.66	66.22	43980	17046	50.08	26.79	75.19	12197	2463
2008	325.45	83.56	48921	33994	55.10	29.46	98.48	13169	2820
2009	530.15	97.10	37238	26212	56.85	28.55	111.46	14573	3064
2010	639.71	113.85	39415	20264	72.32	33.86	137.67	15976	3461
2011	764.01	134.34	42887	25521	84.07	39.69	162.89	17384	4052
2012	1000.07	156.67	50866	29286	98.11	56.58	214.85	19561	4774
2013	845.44	178.60	59786	38667	107.69	65.70	231.69	21458	5409
2014	895.23	201.06	72850	53059	108.70	70.91	261.13	23282	6145
2015	1051.22	221.18	164091	113945	114.51	72.98	310.99	25041	6766
2016	1061.40	246.84	200104	142771	123.22	79.48	341.16	26919	9348
2017	1226.41	277.35	188.44	150.66	135.05	82.50	376.52	29126	10171

注：1. 城镇居民人均可支配收入2004年（含2004年）以前为城市居民人均可支配收入。
2. 2000年以后农民人均纯收入统计口径调整。2014年后口径调整为农村居民人均可支配收入。
3. 2017年起，外贸进出口数据以人民币计价，单位为亿元。

Note:1. The statistical range of indicator "Per Capita Disposable Income of Urban Households" is the household in cities in and before 2004.
2. After 2000,2014 the statistical range of Per Capita Net Income of Farmers has been adjusted.
3. The data of import and export value of foreign trade was calculated by RMB (100 million yuan) since 2017.

22—12　贺州市主要经济指标情况（2002—2017年）
Main Economic Indicators of Hezhou (2002—2017)

年　份 Year	生产总值（按当年价格，亿元） Gross Domestic Product (current prices,100 million yuan)	第一产业 Primary Industry	第二产业 Secondary Industry	#工业 Industry	第三产业 Tertiary Industry	生产总值指数（上年=100） Indices of Gross Domestic Product (Preceding year=100)	第一产业 Primary Industry	第二产业 Secondary Industry	#工业 Industry	第三产业 Tertiary Industry
2002	110.26	42.54	30.68	27.74	37.04	107.6	102.0	109.0	108.9	113.7
2003	114.98	40.71	38.24	31.86	36.03	110.5	104.9	116.6	112.6	112.1
2004	139.50	49.43	54.28	44.77	35.79	112.6	106.3	122.8	116.5	108.9
2005	141.07	51.25	48.52	35.38	41.30	114.6	105.2	123.9	121.7	109.8
2006	162.15	53.61	61.40	46.40	47.15	113.3	105.1	118.6	119.8	114.3
2007	205.43	48.39	100.39	83.19	56.65	115.0	105.0	120.5	122.4	116.5
2008	227.36	55.28	104.30	84.00	67.77	106.4	103.9	106.1	106.0	108.8
2009	249.22	56.31	112.07	85.21	80.84	112.6	104.3	113.8	107.8	117.2
2010	296.87	63.68	139.57	105.91	93.62	113.1	104.5	119.6	119.2	110.0
2011	356.40	78.92	165.09	124.77	112.39	110.6	105.2	113.5	114.6	109.8
2012	394.21	85.43	183.53	136.10	125.25	109.0	106.2	110.9	109.1	108.0
2013	423.85	92.58	196.30	143.55	134.97	108.7	104.4	112.0	112.2	106.1
2014	448.97	98.59	192.02	134.23	158.36	106.1	104.2	105.5	105.6	108.1
2015	468.11	103.14	188.68	126.87	176.29	107.6	104.0	106.6	105.5	111.2
2016	518.19	111.44	211.55	144.67	195.20	108.1	104.1	110.0	110.6	108.3
2017	548.83	115.76	210.91	132.15	222.16	105.3	104.3	101.6	97.1	109.9

22－12 续表 continued

年 份 Year	固定资产投资(不含农户)(亿元) Investment in Fixed Assets (excluding rural registents) (100 million yuan)	社会消费品零售总额(亿元) Total Retail Sales of Consumer Goods (100 million yuan)	进出口(万美元) Total Import & Export (USD 10 000)	#出口 Exports	财政收入(亿元) Finance Revenue (100 million yuan)	#公共财政预算收入 Public Budget Income	公共财政预算支出(亿元) Public Budget Expenditure (100 million yuan)	城镇居民人均可支配收入(元) Per Capital Disposable Income of Urban Households (yuan)	农村居民人均纯收入(元) Per Capita Net Income of Rural Households (yuan)
2002	12.51	25.72	9901	7731	6.26	3.67	10.25		1793
2003	22.49	28.29	11671	9011	7.06	4.63	12.76		1894
2004	45.98	31.06	11251	9401	8.78	5.98	13.89	6415	2090
2005	82.96	34.85	11220	9290	11.22	6.95	17.23	7516	2351
2006	106.10	39.87	10281	8760	13.56	8.50	21.84	8619	2682
2007	133.66	45.65	9853	8614	15.81	9.72	28.43	10790	3093
2008	159.19	59.81	10558	9502	16.01	8.52	35.47	12772	3458
2009	254.68	68.94	14085	12749	18.15	10.39	47.98	14151	3776
2010	363.3	78.68	10953	9140	22.08	12.13	61.23	15802	4298
2011	464.71	92.36	15499	11580	26.65	14.02	78.91	17606	4963
2012	591.58	106.39	15589	9061	32.04	19.21	97.69	19855	5823
2013	483.19	119.00	19951	7220	35.76	21.95	107.26	21682	6557
2014	566.02	133.63	17306	7351	40.60	24.41	118.32	23590	7337
2015	662.05	146.94	64051	45190	47.14	28.97	154.75	25194	8056
2016	650.83	160.98	51915	38479	50.9	32.42	161.15	26883	9552
2017	722.02	178.85	4.84	3.91	53.11	30.89	179.99	28899	10498

注：1. 城镇居民人均可支配收入2004年（含2004年）以前为城市居民人均可支配收入。
2. 2000年以后农民人均纯收入统计口径调整。2014年后口径调整为农村居民人均可支配收入。
3. 2017年起，外贸进出口数据以人民币计价，单位为亿元。

Note:1. The statistical range of indicator "Per Capita Disposable Income of Urban Households" is the household in cities in and before 2004.
2. After 2000,2014 the statistical range of Per Capita Net Income of Farmers has been adjusted.
3. The data of import and export value of foreign trade was calculated by RMB (100 million yuan) since 2017.

22－13　河池市主要经济指标情况（1978—2017年）
Main Economic Indicators of Hechi (1978—2017)

年　份 Year	生产总值（按当年价格，亿元）Gross Domestic Product (current prices,100 million yuan)	第一产业 Primary Industry	第二产业 Secondary Industry	#工业 Industry	第三产业 Tertiary Industry	生产总值指数（上年=100）Indices of Gross Domestic Product (Preceding year=100)	第一产业 Primary Industry	第二产业 Secondary Industry	#工业 Industry	第三产业 Tertiary Industry
1978	5.67	2.53	1.69	1.40	1.46	108.9	95.8	126.8	120.6	133.7
1979	6.57	3.14	2.02	1.71	1.42	103.1	102.1	112.0	108.3	95.4
1980	7.82	3.89	2.19	1.85	1.73	107.7	103.4	110.0	106.2	116.3
1981	7.58	3.84	1.90	1.67	1.84	95.9	98.2	85.2	93.8	104.1
1982	8.44	4.52	1.89	1.68	2.31	109.6	117.4	94.5	95.6	107.6
1983	8.56	4.17	2.23	1.94	2.16	100.9	94.9	113.5	112.0	104.3
1984	9.84	4.71	2.68	2.23	2.46	109.3	105.7	115.8	112.4	111.1
1985	12.72	5.49	4.33	3.72	2.90	121.7	107.5	159.8	152.8	112.8
1986	14.25	6.02	4.74	3.83	3.49	100.8	98.4	93.5	92.9	116.3
1987	17.34	7.11	5.84	4.69	4.39	115.9	109.5	121.6	102.5	120.2
1988	20.78	8.90	6.74	5.70	5.15	100.4	96.8	102.4	107.1	103.8
1989	24.43	10.08	8.24	6.86	6.11	115.9	125.7	114.0	115.8	103.7
1990	27.91	11.43	8.65	7.43	7.83	108.0	112.0	105.6	106.2	123.4
1991	31.56	12.59	9.18	7.98	9.79	109.8	108.1	103.7	104.9	119.0
1992	37.17	14.41	10.86	9.37	11.90	111.3	105.9	115.8	117.1	114.2
1993	51.33	17.86	18.12	16.04	15.35	121.0	108.6	145.7	151.1	112.1
1994	73.14	24.75	27.16	23.89	21.23	121.1	111.1	133.4	132.8	117.3
1995	98.89	30.24	37.70	32.89	30.95	118.5	110.6	122.4	120.1	121.9
1996	108.77	35.20	36.32	31.34	37.24	105.0	104.4	99.2	98.3	114.0
1997	122.84	39.04	40.90	34.00	42.91	110.3	110.8	109.3	106.8	111.1
1998	130.03	42.52	43.62	35.01	43.89	110.9	108.5	112.6	110.9	111.1
1999	137.75	43.70	46.08	37.37	47.97	109.3	106.7	110.8	111.8	109.8
2000	141.39	41.81	56.31	48.95	43.27	108.0	102.9	111.0	111.5	108.6
2001	145.31	43.05	54.58	45.53	47.68	103.8	104.3	98.1	93.1	109.2
2002	137.64	42.94	42.00	32.17	52.69	95.2	102.0	74.6	65.6	108.8
2003	148.58	44.34	46.08	34.17	58.16	106.9	104.1	108.4	103.5	108.3
2004	178.45	54.58	58.68	43.32	65.20	113.7	110.2	122.2	118.5	109.4
2005	206.96	58.55	76.08	57.36	72.34	113.5	107.9	124.7	126.2	108.3
2006	248.89	64.80	100.87	78.48	83.22	114.1	107.2	122.1	123.4	111.1
2007	319.31	73.86	144.43	120.07	101.02	116.7	105.5	122.2	127.3	119.2
2008	367.31	80.26	166.45	142.63	120.60	113.0	103.8	117.3	121.2	114.3
2009	382.77	82.20	165.86	136.33	134.72	108.2	104.2	105.3	100.1	114.5
2010	468.74	97.87	216.29	180.08	154.58	112.5	105.8	117.0	114.7	111.4
2011	511.96	119.81	211.65	173.39	180.50	104.1	103.6	100.8	101.5	109.1
2012	492.71	126.34	174.34	132.96	192.02	99.3	104.9	93.2	90.5	103.9
2013	528.62	133.78	189.78	143.02	205.06	106.0	103.9	108.1	107.0	104.9
2014	601.17	137.23	205.26	152.07	258.68	108.2	103.7	112.4	113.1	105.9
2015	618.03	140.81	200.01	147.14	277.21	104.5	102.2	103.7	104.0	106.8
2016	657.18	150.99	199.82	147.09	306.36	104.9	103.2	101.2	101.4	108.5
2017	734.60	158.96	231.49	168.58	344.15	107.8	103.8	109.4	108.4	108.7

22—13 续表 continued

年 份 Year	固定资产投资（不含农户）（亿元） Investment in Fixed Assets (excluding rural registents) (100 million yuan)	社会消费品零售总额（亿元） Total Retail Sales of Consumer Goods (100 million yuan)	进出口（万美元） Total Import & Export (USD 10 000)	#出口 Exports	财政收入（亿元） Finance Revenue (100 million yuan)	#公共财政预算收入 Public Budget Income	公共财政预算支出（亿元） Public Budget Expenditure (100 million yuan)	城镇居民人均可支配收入（元） Per Capital Disposable Income of Urban Households (yuan)	农村居民人均纯收入（元） Per Capita Net Income of Rural Households (yuan)
1978	1.43	2.26			0.47	0.47	0.78		54
1979	1.16	2.54			0.42	0.42	0.78		55
1980	1.14	2.73			0.43	0.43	0.84		55
1981	0.90	2.86			0.44	0.44	0.83		61
1982	1.04	3.03			0.45	0.45	0.92		75
1983	1.36	3.59			0.51	0.51	1.13		96
1984	1.86	4.09			0.58	0.58	1.46		133
1985	2.60	5.36			0.76	0.76	1.76		145
1986	3.54	5.80			0.81	0.81	2.33		174
1987	4.30	6.95			1.11	1.11	2.52		214
1988	4.71	10.32			1.39	1.39	3.03		254
1989	5.64	9.98			1.78	1.78	3.40		302
1990	5.61	9.93			1.96	1.96	3.86		332
1991	6.42	10.91			2.20	2.20	4.20		368
1992	9.16	13.14			2.54	2.54	4.71		413
1993	14.14	15.57		50	4.43	2.59	6.26		519
1994	20.81	20.83		846	5.70	3.21	7.17		656
1995	26.02	29.02	2625	2408	7.85	4.55	8.76		900
1996	24.29	34.41	2586	2056	9.12	5.46	9.43	3890	1170
1997	30.32	38.88	4027	3441	10.58	6.59	11.08	3976	1591
1998	36.76	42.70	4869	4861	11.84	7.70	13.34	4662	1748
1999	36.16	46.66	1730	1666	13.20	8.87	15.17	4726	1885
2000	40.55	50.95	1834	1812	14.50	9.56	16.42	4800	1386
2001	50.15	55.62	1350	1336	18.68	12.38	23.36	5292	1384
2002	53.45	59.03	1348	1143	16.63	9.43	23.98	5033	1419
2003	60.81	46.24	4115	2665	16.65	9.85	25.30	5238	1497
2004	92.05	52.01	10369	5837	20.03	12.15	28.40	6156	1727
2005	137.00	60.50	14567	8667	23.04	11.60	33.72	7170	1912
2006	188.28	68.78	28276	18241	27.40	13.18	43.24	8619	2186
2007	218.74	80.55	26083	15546	34.32	14.45	58.64	10752	2592
2008	211.17	99.98	31406	12506	40.23	17.91	80.68	12042	2944
2009	277.80	115.07	48624	16474	40.32	21.04	93.40	13369	3183
2010	361.95	131.73	64621	12634	47.34	22.95	120.97	14889	3599
2011	437.24	154.79	78614	10839	50.72	23.36	142.45	16448	4118
2012	277.84	176.99	52444	8112	44.56	22.17	175.95	17964	4620
2013	349.14	198.97	48148	3758	50.23	26.97	198.04	19653	5198
2014	399.65	223.79	47929	2291	54.67	29.93	226.19	21363	5723
2015	454.48	243.38	39168	3185	56.14	31.45	259.12	22752	6164
2016	404.02	267.96	27558	3691	62.24	33.36	289.76	23660	7509
2017	453.20	301.20	19.55	2.23	69.45	36.22	328.92	25647	8260

注：1. 城镇居民人均可支配收入2004年（含2004年）以前为城市居民人均可支配收入。

2. 2000年以后农民人均纯收入统计口径调整。2014年后口径调整为农村居民人均可支配收入。

3. 2017年起，外贸进出口数据以人民币计价，单位为亿元。

Note:1. The statistical range of indicator "Per Capita Disposable Income of Urban Households" is the household in cities in and before 2004.

2. After 2000,2014 the statistical range of Per Capita Net Income of Farmers has been adjusted.

3. The data of import and export value of foreign trade was calculated by RMB（100 million yuan） since 2017.

22－14　来宾市主要经济指标情况（1978—2017年）
Main Economic Indicators of Laibin(1978—2017)

年　份 Year	生产总值（按当年价格，亿元）Gross Domestic Product (current prices, 100 million yuan)	第一产业 Primary Industry	第二产业 Secondary Industry	#工业 Industry	第三产业 Tertiary Industry	生产总值指数（上年=100）Indices of Gross Domestic Product (Preceding year=100)	第一产业 Primary Industry	第二产业 Secondary Industry	#工业 Industry	第三产业 Tertiary Industry
1978	3.60	2.32	0.71	0.59	0.57	101.9				
1979	3.68					102.4				
1980	3.86	2.48	0.76	0.67	0.62	102.2	101.2	115.6	95.7	111.6
1981	4.28									
1982	5.02									
1983	5.71									
1984	6.36									
1985	6.97	4.04	1.46	1.18	1.48	101.9	88.7	113.8	102.9	132.5
1986	7.65									
1987	9.43									
1988	11.69									
1989	14.35									
1990	16.78	8.98	4.54	4.07	3.26	106.3	97.4	103.5	102.9	130.4
1991	20.40	10.33	5.48	4.90	4.59	115.1	111.5	108.8	108.2	133.3
1992	23.57	12.17	6.04	5.37	5.36	110.4	109.8	109.6	109.2	112.7
1993	32.77	15.38	10.03	9.06	7.36	114.6				
1994	45.47	21.33	14.11	12.64	10.03	103.3	97.8	108.8	107.1	108.5
1995	59.31	28.80	17.98	16.19	12.53	116.3	118.8	114.1	113.1	114.0
1996	72.23	34.77	21.56	19.75	15.90	115.4	110.1	116.8	118.4	125.0
1997	79.73	37.81	23.94	21.50	17.98	112.9	114.9	110.5	107.6	112.2
1998	86.89	36.86	30.37	22.38	19.67	114.9	100.9	140.6	109.7	109.0
1999	87.49	39.44	27.55	21.51	20.50	106.4	111.3	100.9	110.7	106.9
2000	98.95	42.34	33.87	30.46	22.73	104.7	102.3	101.8	115.9	114.2
2001	109.21	45.55	37.39	34.42	26.27	110.9	109.3	108.1	110.6	113.2
2002	114.71	46.13	39.05	35.01	29.54	109.7	108.4	111.0	108.6	110.1
2003	126.30	48.71	44.21	39.57	33.38	110.7	106.8	115.6	115.7	110.7
2004	154.75	58.91	57.13	51.45	38.71	113.1	108.6	119.7	119.9	110.8
2005	165.22	52.54	65.17	58.05	47.51	113.4	107.9	118.2	118.4	113.6
2006	200.06	65.88	77.41	69.50	56.77	113.9	108.6	116.4	116.7	116.3
2007	235.64	70.10	96.86	87.23	68.68	115.3	106.4	122.2	123.4	115.1
2008	273.47	76.22	113.87	100.25	83.38	112.8	105.0	114.9	113.2	117.4
2009	303.14	80.36	129.45	109.47	93.33	112.9	104.6	116.5	112.1	114.8
2010	405.22	97.83	192.35	168.00	115.04	118.0	105.0	125.0	123.1	117.8
2011	486.21	120.37	231.75	195.60	134.09	113.0	105.1	118.9	116.3	109.9
2012	514.29	127.01	236.07	189.06	151.22	111.7	107.7	114.6	112.1	109.8
2013	515.57	134.45	219.51	169.21	161.61	103.0	105.1	99.5	98.0	107.8
2014	551.12	133.17	228.21	173.67	189.75	106.1	102.1	105.9	106.3	109.4
2015	557.93	136.83	218.05	158.59	203.05	103.4	102.0	102.1	99.9	106.7
2016	589.11	148.60	220.20	160.92	220.31	103.9	103.0	101.5	102.0	107.1
2017	663.69	159.96	250.08	183.98	253.65	107.4	104.6	105.3	105.4	111.5

22－14 续表 continued

年 份 Year	固定资产投资（不含农户）（亿元） Investment in Fixed Assets (excluding rural registents) (100 million yuan)	社会消费品零售总额（亿元） Total Retail Sales of Consumer Goods (100 million yuan)	进出口（万美元） Total Import & Export (USD 10 000)	#出口 Exports	财政收入（亿元） Finance Revenue (100 million yuan)	#公共财政预算收入 Public Budget Income	公共财政预算支出（亿元） Public Budget Expenditure (100 million yuan)	城镇居民人均可支配收入（元） Per Capital Disposable Income of Urban Households (yuan)	农村居民人均纯收入（元） Per Capita Net Income of Rural Households (yuan)
1978	0.73	1.47	436	436	0.52	0.20	0.39		
1979	0.68	1.59		840	0.41	0.25	0.36		
1980	0.83	1.84	979	979	0.44	0.25	0.34		
1981	0.43	2.20		935	0.46	0.24	0.36		
1982	0.47	2.28		859	0.51	0.33	0.41		
1983	0.63	2.95		607	0.65	0.38	0.46		
1984	0.83	3.08		414	0.74	0.38	0.81		
1985	1.06	3.70	204	204	0.91	0.52	0.76		259
1986	1.81	3.99		224	1.40	0.61	1.00		
1987	2.51	4.54		455	1.88	0.86	1.38		
1988	3.75	6.12		518	2.22	1.08	1.66		
1989	2.89	7.14		542	2.67	1.50	2.03		
1990	1.58	7.07	265	265	2.19	1.65	2.43		591
1991	1.27	8.04		409	2.45	1.69	2.46		604
1992	2.03	8.85		2813	3.49	2.09	3.49		660
1993	4.05	7.99		69	3.77	2.75	3.77		794
1994	7.01	9.88		245	3.97	1.80	3.94		945
1995	10.04	11.54	2268	2268	3.89	2.41	4.12		1219
1996	11.32	12.94	5166	3630	4.90	3.01	5.24		1512
1997	13.66	13.95	5718	3952	6.04	3.45	5.17		1845
1998	30.86	14.33	2586	1014	6.99	4.39	6.20		1998
1999	27.35	16.54	10829	3537	7.63	4.91	6.85		2142
2000	18.01	18.09	6009	4554	8.39	5.49	8.20		1458
2001	16.52	20.06	7088	4763	9.16	5.53	9.42		1639
2002	24.11	22.59	7956	4969	10.23	5.35	14.15		1769
2003	34.92	25.41	9034	5646	11.31	5.86	14.25		1927
2004	45.62	28.77	17814	10013	13.74	6.26	16.11	6428	2113
2005	56.89	32.97	14329	7356	17.51	6.64	20.89	8166	2385
2006	74.65	38.71	15009	8810	21.06	8.63	25.49	10051	2829
2007	93.90	46.15	23985	13243	26.07	10.39	33.83	12089	3245
2008	125.77	57.57	52149	20200	30.29	14.64	46.09	14037	3767
2009	205.01	66.84	26929	16725	34.14	20.48	61.18	15609	4094
2010	306.90	79.46	17127	10213	43.05	24.94	89.76	17334	4659
2011	419.58	94.42	13091	3563	47.66	25.10	100.17	19233	5382
2012	561.80	109.53	14321	6565	52.55	32.20	119.82	21499	6231
2013	453.22	120.87	11965	4634	56.13	36.37	123.68	23563	7085
2014	482.83	134.17	10688	4699	58.11	37.95	129.29	25401	7751
2015	498.15	145.11	6722	4003	50.02	30.29	139.33	27077	8379
2016	370.91	159.11	8925	6145	49.60	30.32	159.52	28962	9820
2017	432.16	180.29	7.73	4.25	48.25	27.64	179.78	31047	10674

注：1. 城镇居民人均可支配收入2004年（含2004年）以前为城市居民人均可支配收入。

2. 2000年以后农民人均纯收入统计口径调整。2014年后口径调整为农村居民人均可支配收入。

3. 2017年起，外贸进出口数据以人民币计价，单位为亿元。

Note:1. The statistical range of indicator “Per Capita Disposable Income of Urban Households” is the household in cities in and before 2004.

2. After 2000,2014 the statistical range of Per Capita Net Income of Farmers has been adjusted.

3. The data of import and export value of foreign trade was calculated by RMB（100 million yuan） since 2017.

22—15 崇左市主要经济指标情况（2003—2017年）
Main Economic Indicators of Chongzuo (2003—2017)

年 份 Year	生产总值（按当年价格，亿元）Gross Domestic Product (current prices,100 million yuan)	第一产业 Primary Industry	第二产业 Secondary Industry	#工业 Industry	第三产业 Tertiary Industry	生产总值指数（上年=100）Indices of Gross Domestic Product (Preceding year=100)	第一产业 Primary Industry	第二产业 Secondary Industry	#工业 Industry	第三产业 Tertiary Industry
2003	104.22	40.96	24.97	19.31	38.28	108.3	103.8	111.5	109.9	111.9
2004	125.55	48.34	31.08	25.26	46.13	112.8	110.2	118.6	117.9	112.1
2005	151.13	55.34	43.63	36.29	52.17	113.9	108.8	129.4	130.3	107.5
2006	194.03	66.45	66.58	58.13	61.00	117.1	110.1	127.8	130.4	114.5
2007	231.87	76.24	78.12	67.97	77.51	116.6	107.1	122.9	123.9	119.7
2008	272.98	81.45	101.67	89.11	89.86	111.8	105.7	118.9	119.9	110.0
2009	304.36	86.94	107.41	90.83	110.01	112.6	105.1	111.6	108.1	120.1
2010	392.37	114.85	149.11	127.53	128.41	113.1	107.0	116.6	115.0	114.0
2011	491.85	144.98	197.42	169.71	149.45	110.5	106.2	116.0	115.6	108.1
2012	530.51	142.95	216.96	184.06	170.60	111.8	105.2	117.4	117.4	110.4
2013	584.63	149.44	248.24	210.62	186.95	110.2	104.2	115.7	115.9	107.8
2014	649.72	147.28	277.45	232.64	224.99	108.3	103.8	111.5	111.0	107.5
2015	682.82	155.06	274.61	226.38	253.15	108.0	103.2	108.1	107.6	111.5
2016	766.20	167.66	310.69	257.13	287.85	108.2	103.4	107.9	107.0	111.5
2017	907.62	181.25	398.20	334.52	328.17	109.3	104.4	110.8	110.5	110.6

22—15 续表 continued

年 份 Year	固定资产投资（不含农户）（亿元） Investment in Fixed Assets (excluding rural registents) (100 million yuan)	社会消费品零售总额（亿元） Total Retail Sales of Consumer Goods (100 million yuan)	进出口（万美元） Total Import & Export (USD 10 000)	#出口 Exports	财政收入（亿元） Finance Revenue (100 million yuan)	#公共财政预算收入 Public Budget Income	公共财政预算支出（亿元） Public Budget Expenditure (100 million yuan)	城镇居民人均可支配收入（元） Per Capital Disposable Income of Urban Households (yuan)	农村居民人均纯收入（元） Per Capita Net Income of Rural Households (yuan)
2003	32.49	20.11	26185	22009	13.01	8.86	18.38	—	1927
2004	40.73	23.90	32628	28005	14.84	8.31	20.61	6208	2122
2005	52.81	26.98	49490	41380	16.74	8.46	23.78	7102	2298
2006	71.05	31.06	55332	43609	20.50	8.51	27.77	8640	2767
2007	115.15	36.71	93233	78026	26.94	12.30	39.83	11070	3290
2008	128.49	45.99	160531	134526	32.07	16.77	52.85	12732	3754
2009	212.28	53.45	286765	257935	36.73	20.79	70.06	14032	4028
2010	308.84	61.08	373711	341557	47.54	26.16	85.53	15620	4621
2011	415.14	72.40	507571	468275	57.65	30.23	103.11	17301	5370
2012	532.15	84.37	713458	680593	66.00	39.49	130.99	19370	6263
2013	482.38	96.38	1027713	975800	73.02	47.49	140.92	21289	7077
2014	581.49	108.44	1469407	1317965	73.16	48.40	155.51	23184	7707
2015	691.57	119.39	2013277	1423209	75.15	50.12	185.10	24668	8308
2016	831.41	131.34	1857407	1086290	58.20	40.76	202.87	26605	9801
2017	970.50	146.09	1338.81	892.46	55.25	34.07	221.62	28813	10860

注：1. 城镇居民人均可支配收入2004年（含2004年）以前为城市居民人均可支配收入。
2. 2000年以后农民人均纯收入统计口径调整。2014年后口径调整为农村居民人均可支配收入。
3. 2017年起，外贸进出口数据以人民币计价，单位为亿元。

Note:1. The statistical range of indicator "Per Capita Disposable Income of Urban Households" is the household in cities in and before 2004.
2. After 2000,2014 the statistical range of Per Capita Net Income of Farmers has been adjusted.
3. The data of import and export value of foreign trade was calculated by RMB（100 million yuan） since 2017.

22－16 广西农垦管区社会经济主要指标
Main Social & Economic Indicators by Guangxi State Farms

指 标	Item	2010	2011	2012	2013	2014	2015	2016	2017
辖区土地面积(平方公里)	Administrative Region Land Area (sq.km)	1701.84	1681.88	1681.88	1681.88	1681.88	1681.88	1681.88	1607.18
地区生产总值（当年价，亿元)	Gross Domestic Product (At current prices, 100 million yuan)	236.88	296.67	341.92	382.72	417.90	449.59	494.05	544.08
第一产业	Primary Industry	33.06	39.73	41.81	45.93	47.19	49.91	57.30	61.43
第二产业	Secondary Industry	145.79	180.48	213.03	240.82	262.64	280.90	305.04	333
#工业	Industry	113.53	137.25	160.32	183.38	199.34	218.42	234.24	263.45
建筑业	Construction	32.26	43.23	52.71	57.44	63.30	62.48	70.80	69.55
第三产业	Tertiary Industry	58.03	76.46	87.08	95.97	108.07	118.78	131.71	149.65
年末总人口（万人）	Total Population at Year-end (10 000 persons)	28.51	31.82	35.28	36.93	37.98	39.61	41.46	41.70
男性	Male	16.54	18.78	20.51	21.67	22.51	23.57	24.62	24.70
女性	Female	11.97	13.04	14.77	15.26	15.47	16.04	16.84	17.00
年末总户数（万户）	Total Households at Year-end (10 000 households)	8.36	9.88	10.69	11.07	11.45	11.72	11.98	12.09
就业人员（万人）	Employed Persons (10 000 persons)	16.93	18.51	20.13	20.46	20.85	21.69	22.73	23.33
第一产业	Primary Industry	5.92	6.09	6.17	6.31	6.18	6.20	6.40	6.67
第二产业	Secondary Industry	7.03	8.25	9.31	9.31	9.55	9.96	10.42	10.46
第三产业	Tertiary Industry	3.98	4.17	4.65	4.84	5.13	5.53	5.91	6.20
国有单位就业人员(万人)	Number of Employed Persons in State-owned Units (10 000 persons)	5.76	5.89	5.90	6.07	5.94	5.99	6.13	6.07
在岗职工人数（万人）	Number of Staff & Workers (10 000 persons)	3.23	3.16	3.01	2.91	2.77	2.59	2.50	2.32
在岗职工工资总额(万元)	Total Wage of Staff & Workers (100 million yuan)	64937	71739	79755	87731	92626	91669	95368	99551
在岗职工平均工资（元）	Average Wage of Staff & Workers (yuan)	19455	22583	26585	29662	32609	34182	37819	41964
全社会固定资产投资（亿元）	Total Investment in Fixed Assets (100 million yuan)	131.31	180.21	235.41	270.79	281.00	300.60	343.94	329.72
#基本建设	Basic Construction	83.87	107.39	150.79	176.22	181.01	182.66	227.49	219.7
更新改造	Innovation	9.86	15.78	7.93	11.06	11.64	9.85	9.37	8.88
其他投资	Others	5.53	9.09	10.75	11.30	12.14	17.56	11.78	16.24
房地产开发	Real Estate Development	27.45	33.36	32.88	47.97	61.52	81.10	88.04	78.4
私人建房	Housing Construction by Individuals	4.60	14.59	33.06	24.24	14.69	9.43	7.26	6.5
城镇固定资产投资(亿元)	Urban Investment in Fixed Assets (100 million yuan)	127.67	173.67	229.33	257.25	266.95	285.57	329.84	318.11
城镇居民人均可支配收入（元）	Per Capita Disposable Income of Household (yuan)	13310	14775	17550	19654	21641	23446	25331	27114
农林牧渔业从业人口(万人)	Farming, Forestry, Animal Husbandry & Fishery Employed Persons (10 000 persons)	5.92	6.09	6.17	6.31	6.18	6.20	6.40	6.67
常用耕地面积（千公顷）	Daily Cultivated Area (1000 hectares)	32.65	32.91	32.81	33.76	33.85	33.88	33.96	33.68
农林牧渔业总产值(当年价，亿元)	Gross Output Value of Farming, Forestry, Animal Husbandry & Fishery (At current prices, 100 million yuan)	51.56	63.00	70.44	75.92	78.79	86.54	94.83	102.36

注：地区生产总值与各行业增加值增长速度按可比价计算；规模以上工业的统计口径2008-2010年为“年主营业务收入500万元及以上的工业法人企业”，2011年及以后为“年主营业务收入2000万元及以上的工业法人企业”。

Note:The growth of “Gross Domestic Product” and other sectors’ added value were calculated by comparable price; the statistical range of Industrial Enterprises above Designated Size is industrial enterprises which has the prime operating revenue of 5 million yuan and above between 2008 and 2010, and it was replaced by industrial enterprises which has the prime operating revenue of 20 million yuan and above since 2011.

22－16 续表 continued

指 标	Item	2010	2011	2012	2013	2014	2015	2016	2017
农业机械总动力(万千瓦)	Total Agricultural Machinery Power (10 000 kw)	23.62	25.30	25.43	27.30	27.7	31.83	33.19	35.13
化肥使用量（折纯量，万吨）	Consumption of Chemical Fertilizers (Pure quantity, 10 000 tons)	4.97	5.53	5.52	5.82	5.51	5.27	5.59	6.02
农场用电量(万千瓦小时)	Electricity Consumed in Rural Areas (10 000 kwh)	32097	38711	48746	49132	49518	52350	52378	52694
有效灌溉面积（千公顷）	Irrigated Area (1 000 hectares)	11.52	12.61	12.99	12.83	13.57	15.37	15.81	18.29
农作物总播种面积（千公顷）	Total Sown Area of Farm Crops (1 000 hectares)	32.39	32.63	32.76	32.76	32.97	33.51	32.95	32.56
#甘蔗	Sugarcane	22.55	22.62	22.91	22.62	21.98	22.17	21.60	21.71
甘蔗产量（万吨）	Output of Sugar cane (10 000 tons)	227.75	223.72	239.43	242.19	234.56	232.83	226.82	238.6
剑麻纤维产量（万吨）	Output of Sisal fiber (10 000 ton)	1.80	2.02	2.11	2.19	1.94	1.80	1.93	1.99
干毛茶产量（吨）	Output of Primary tea (ton)	881	849	1137	1068	968	770	664	600
水果产量（万吨）	Output of Fruits (10 000 tons)	16.14	18.02	23.50	25.28	25.68	30.67	31.87	36.84
生猪年末存栏头数(万头)	Number of Pigs in Livestock (10 000 heads)	90.15	100.29	127.40	145.71	164.43	141.44	145.07	168.51
肉猪出栏头数（万头）	Number of Slaughtered Fattened Hogs (10 000 heads)	130.66	130.94	154.46	179.99	193.3	215.86	207.01	221.76
肉类总产量（万吨）	Total Output of Meat (10 000 tons)	10.07	10.10	11.91	13.73	14.71	16.53	15.91	16.99
#猪牛羊肉	Pork, Beef & Mutton	9.17	9.19	10.85	12.63	13.59	15.18	14.56	15.6
牛奶产量（吨）	Output of Cow milk (10 000 tons)	4366	4471	4017	3989	4111	4641	5238	5334
水产品产量（万吨）	Output of Aquatic Products (10 000 ton)	1.50	1.57	1.66	1.70	1.63	1.71	1.70	1.91
工业企业单位数（规模以上，个）	Number of Industrial Enterprises (Above designated size,unit)	369	248	274	300	329	347	384	409
工业总产值（规模以上，当年价，亿元）	Gross Industrial Output Value (Above designated size, at current prices, 100 million yuan)	266.40	315.10	387.54	450.07	514.19	588.37	635.54	707.67
工业企业增加值（规模以上，当年价，亿元）	Value-added of Industrial Enterprises (Above designated size,at current prices,100 million yuan)	105.99	118.47	144.33	161.94	183.19	200.88	217.18	248.06
工业企业税金（规模以上，亿元）	Taxation expense of Industrial Enterprises (Above designated size, 100 million yuan)	10.13	10.27	10.55	11.29	12.55	13.65	14.10	17.24
工业企业利润（规模以上，亿元）	Total Profits of Industrial Enterprises (Above designated size, 100 million yuan)	20.11	24.23	26.62	27.07	29.94	31.32	32.51	38.36
成品糖产量（万吨）	Machine-made Sugar (10 000 tons)	61.30	67.55	69.82	83.16	84.77	80.52	65.60	64.39
发酵酒精产量（万吨）	Output of Alcohol (10 000 tons)	21.47	20.02	25.22	22.12	22.35	20.39	18.10	8.73
剑麻制品（万吨）	Sisal Product (10 000 tons)	4.31	4.88	5.71	4.57	4.35	4.86	4.36	4.46
淀粉产量（万吨）	Output of Starch (10 000 tons)	28.57	29.96	29.66	32.80	32.67	27.67	27.36	31.63
软饮料产量（万吨）	Output of Soft drinks	28.21	30.06	31.64	25.65	17.81	16.88	16.72	12.86
成品茶（吨）	Refined Tea (ton)	2298	2188	2761	2873	2710	2463	2292	2169
人造板产量（万立方米）	Output of Wood-based Plate (10 000 cu.m)	95.87	106.61	141.22	143.44	161.21	160.05	166.23	205.31
水泥（万吨）	Cement (10 000 tons)	46.46	53.76	44.52	48.00	49.46	45.31	20.20	9.50
饲料产量（万吨）	Output of Feed (10 000 tons)	31.36	41.16	46.37	54.67	63.78	73.82	84.24	92.83
工农业产品进出口总额（亿元）	Import & Export of Industrial & Agricultural Products (100 million yuan)	17.10	17.17	14.46	16.88	18.29	20.47	14.15	14.63
年末实有外来投资企业及项目个数（个）	Actual Number of External Investment Enterprises & Projects in Year-end (unit)	759	820	892	980	1057	1129	1208	1294

第二十三篇

县（市、区）基本情况

BASIC STATISTICS OF COUNTIES (CITIES, DISTRICTS)

（校对编辑：杨海玲）

23－1 110个县域社会经济主要指标（2017年）

指 标	Item	兴宁区 Xingning District	青秀区 Qingxiu District
行政区域面积（平方公里）	Administrative Region Land Area (sq.km)	723	865
常住户数（户）	Total Households at Year-end (household)	159064	230985
年末常住人口（万人）	Total Population at Year-end (10 000 persons)	43.54	79.17
年末户籍人口（万人）	Registered Population at Year-end (10 000 persons)	33.41	73.34
地区生产总值（万元）	Gross Domestic Product (10 000 yuan)	4135500	9139620
第一产业增加值	Primary Industry	109843	178800
第二产业增加值	Secondary Industry	701936	1047785
#工业	Industry	121246	130873
第三产业增加值	Tertiary Industry	3323721	7913035
人均生产总值（元）	Per Capital GDP (yuan)	95696	116488
地区生产总值指数（上年＝100）	Indices of Gross Domestic Product (preceding year=100)	108.0	106.1
第一产业	Primary Industry	104.7	102.0
第二产业	Secondary Industry	103.9	105.8
#工业	Industry	99.0	102.0
第三产业	Tertiary Industry	109.0	106.2
人均生产总值指数（上年=100）	Indices of Per Capital GDP (preceding year＝100)	106.3	104.4
公共财政预算收入（万元）	Government Revenue (10 000 yuan)	91542	310514
税收收入（万元）	Total Tax Revenue (10 000 yuan)	72199	282827
公共预算支出（万元）	Government Expenditure (10 000 yuan)	179925	371204
年末金融机构各项存款余额（万元）	Year-end Deposits of Financial Institutions (10 000 yuan)		
#居民储蓄存款余额	Urban & Rural Savings Deposits		
年末金融机构各项贷款余额（万元）	Year-end Loans of Financial Institutions (10 000 yuan)		
耕地面积（公顷）	Farmland (hectare)	14757	19045
设施农业占地面积（公顷）	Protected Agriculture Covered (hectare)	60	285
农业机械总动力（万千瓦特）	Total Agricultural Machinery Power (10 000 watts)	19.93	18.22
农作物总播种面积（公顷）	Total Sown Area of Major Farm Crops (hectare)	27524	38071
#粮食	Grain Crops	10694	14841
油料	Oil Crops	1506	2900
糖料	Sugar Crops	620	6329
蔬菜	Vegetables	8881	8180
粮食总产量（吨）	Yield of Grain (ton)	52746	84457
#稻谷	Rice	44882	65612

注：本表由各县（市）区2018年7月30日上报，截止出版前未经国家审核反馈。
Note: The data in this table is reported by relevant counties (cities, districts), has yet to be verified by the date of publication.

Main Social & Economic Indicators by County (2017)

江南区 Jiangnan District	西乡塘区 Xixiangtang District	良庆区 Liangqing District	邕宁区 Yongning District	武鸣县 Wuming County	隆安县 Long' an County	马山县 Mashan County	上林县 Shanglin County
1183	1076	1369	1231	3389	2306	2341	1871
188718	417552	93312	91354	232880	90373	159465	146356
64.03	123.38	37.61	28.58	57.18	31.54	41.11	36.32
52.43	79.60	28.85	36.18	71.57	42.24	57.12	49.97
6029689	8884120	1562091	908814	3531974	731841	551826	567493
300192	199421	230493	276546	811704	279486	202636	219900
4228928	4963915	863570	227126	1623616	197709	103532	107291
3910302	4144455	503596	136708	1378885	106233	33066	51916
1500569	3720784	468028	405142	1096654	254645	245658	240302
95173	72479	41862	32034	62117	23311	13487	15727
110.0	108.5	108.2	112.5	108.7	106.6	105.2	104.8
102.3	102.2	103.9	103.2	104.9	104.1	104.3	104.3
111.7	110.1	108.6	114.0	105.0	106.9	101.4	102.2
113.0	110.5	103.1	142.6	105.4	109.0	102.8	101.1
107.5	106.5	109.7	119.3	118.3	109.2	107.7	106.4
107.3	107.1	107.0	111.0	107.7	105.7	104.3	103.9
51532	80226	78862	29858	49043	27062	19496	25322
41548	67259	68322	25474	23415	18609	11145	16267
197772	288649	192164	234480	373993	259101	339297	313600
				2572166	978390	979908	944504
				1678445	780289	640502	763043
				1736775	518139	477818	551956
38422	44273	35598	44444	125973	62260	46185	47992
581	158	128	187	471	94	118	30
19.44	38.16	28.88	21	79.38	29.71	29.51	49.84
74546	41339	59095	66188	177721	67866	60705	60930
16359	11985	18300	26439	67780	38282	39053	38073
3829	3136	2618	5169	14648	2466	1394	3572
15280	2796	17056	15480	21307	6670	3301	9465
23241	15669	13863	12970	52698	14259	9420	7237
88495	61935	92540	138639	349042	172042	178620	178124
65013	39159	77160	115569	209922	76884	80001	128205

23－1 续表1

指 标	Item	兴宁区 Xingning District	青秀区 Qingxiu District
油料产量（吨）	Yield of Oil-bearing Crops (ton)	4094	9525
糖料产量（吨）	Yield of Sugar Crops (ton)	40049	545240
蔬菜产量（吨）	Yield of Vegetables (ton)	166352	179078
园林水果（不含瓜类水果）产量（吨）	Yield of Fruit (ton)	8477	21749
肉类总产量（吨）	Output of Meat (ton)	18519	33609
#猪肉（吨）	Pork (ton)	9678	20610
禽蛋产量（吨）	Output of Eggs (ton)	2578	2651
奶类产量（吨）	Output of Milk (ton)	1352	0
水产品产量（吨）	Aquatic Products (ton)	8573	8013
规模以上工业企业个数（个）	Number of Industrial Enterprises above Designated Size (unit)	25	30
规模以上工业总产值（当年价，万元）	Included Gross Industrial Output Value above Designated Size (at current price，10 000 yuan)	352559	500623
规模以上工业企业从业人员年平均人数（人）	Annual Average Number of Employed Persons (person)	2976	4014
规模以上工业企业主营业务收入（万元）	Income from Major Business (10 000 yuan)	349997	490643
公路里程（公里）	Length of Domestic Highways (km)	551	622
民用汽车拥有量（辆）	Number of Civil Motor Vehicles Owned (vehicle)		
年末实有公共汽（电）车营运数（辆）	Year-end Total Operating Public Buses (vehicle)		
年末实有出租汽车数（辆）	Year-end Total Taxis (vehicle)		
固定电话年末用户（户）	Number of Local Telephone Subscribers in Year-end (subscriber)		
年末移动电话用户数（户）	Number of Mobile Telephone Subscribers at Year-end (subscriber)		
互联网宽带接入用户（户）	Number of Internet Subscribers (subscriber)		
全社会用电量（万千瓦时）	Total Consumption of Electricity (10 000 kwh)	138700	307100
#居民生活用电量	Household Consumption of Electricity	43900	75100
社会消费品零售总额（亿元）	Total Retail Sale of Consumer Goods 100 million yuan)	464.93	448.64
固定资产投资（不含农户）（亿元）	Investment in Fixed Assets (100 million yuan)	274.62	885.21
新增固定资产（万元）	Newly Increased Fixed Assets (10 000 yuan)	1397156	955581
房地产开发投资完成额（万元）	Real Estate Development (10 000 yuan)	950088	1424731
#住宅	Residential Buildings	771275	969534
住宅竣工面积（万平方米）	Completed Floor Space of Residential Buildings (10 000 sq.m)	27.17	156.25
普通中学数（所）	Number of Regular Secondary Schools (unit)	16	15

Continued

江南区 Jiangnan District	西乡塘区 Xixiangtang District	良庆区 Liangqing District	邕宁区 Yongning District	武鸣县 Wuming County	隆安县 Long' an County	马山县 Mashan County	上林县 Shanglin County
12516	9457	6298	14161	46528	5718	2712	8094
1527620	185358	1078368	1103031	1725126	571179	205636	547790
528784	321628	368222	283876	1338498	312924	231124	142320
59766	592182	75186	59538	1004990	444397	21101	11075
30601	37129	38502	62764	146290	46356	40253	40844
13017	17750	11264	20568	92924	31406	27955	33928
4076	3817	813	673	16900	1180	840	666
4286	1528	786	0	1474	0		0
16731	13915	14036	14350	49940	16678	12850	22814
159	228	56	24	195	37	13	16
13390961	9217465	1584300	553931	4893087	506991	81599	191952
47746	65086	9525	4613	34627	5252	1694	2764
11964223	8723523	1216847	451475	4467499	521297	68370	177349
	690	1461	1091	2297		1123	1026
			29996	30655		24815	19954
			146	205	52	25	70
			0	181	23	40	35
			490			28011	14933
			121405			306012	288697
			69524			37012	65359
258100			13105	163789	68963	39225	33006
55200	126200		4125	35239	15504	21371	17922
206.76	391.36	37.14	23.21	83.73	21.22	25.34	21.97
507.68	677.81	428.39	219.01	386.49	57.81	42.19	46.25
2805821	2203518		202374	1149975			258365
1447436	916962	2860189	1117516	292416	206923	18875	102765
1012157	666143	1872007	770236	249388	194637	18875	85645
27.66	64.15	43.78	0.00	38.45	22.29	0.91	14.87
29	41	19	14	25	16	20	18

23－1 续表2

指 标	Item	兴宁区 Xingning District	青秀区 Qingxiu District
小学数（所）	Number of Primary Schools (unit)	49	82
普通中学专任教师数（人）	Full-time Teachers in Regular Secondary Schools (person)	724	1286
小学专任教师数（人）	Full-time Teachers in Primary Schools (person)	1843	3821
普通中学在校学生数（人）	Student Enrollment in Regular Secondary Schools (person)	11279	10444
小学在校学生数（人）	Primary Student Enrollment (person)	37514	64606
专业技术人员（人）	Number of Professionals (person)	1884	3684
#农业技术人员	Agricultural Professionals (person)	33	0
医疗卫生机构床位数（张）	Number of Beds in Heathcare Institutions (bed)	4698	12540
医疗卫生机构技术人员（人）	Medical & Technical Personnel of Heathcare Institutions (person)	6398	20461
#执业（助理）医师	Practitioner (assistant) Doctors	2291	19505
居民人均可支配收入（元）	Per Capita Annual Disposable Income of Households (yuan)		39614
城镇居民人均可支配收入（元）	Per Capita Annual Disposable Income of Urban Households (yuan)	36322	42138
农村居民人均可支配收入（元）	Annual Per Capita Net Income of Rural Residents (yuan)	13585	14021
各种社会福利收养性单位数（个）	Number of Adopting Units of Social Welfare (unit)	3	9
各种社会福利收养性单位床位数（张）	Number of Beds in Adopting Units of Social Welfare (bed)	120	1156
城镇基本养老保险参保人数（人）	Number of Persons Joining Basic Pension Insurance (person)	66639	63476
城镇基本医疗保险参保人数（人）	Number of Persons Joining Basic Health Care Insurance (person)		179843
失业保险参保人数（人）	Number of Persons Joining Unemployment Insurance (person)		
新型农村合作医疗参保人数（人）	Number of Persons Joining New-type Rural Cooperative Medical Service (person)	176107	
新型农村社会养老保险参保人数（人）	Number of Persons Joining New-type Rural Social Pension Insurance (person)		
城镇居民最低生活保障人数（人）	Number of Urban Residents Receiving Lowest Cost-of-living (person)	1107	469
农村居民最低生活保障人数（人）	Number of Rural Residents Receiving Lowest Cost-of-living (person)	2161	2185
森林面积（公顷）	Forest Area (10 000 hectares)	25188	43970
工业二氧化硫排放量（吨）	Volume of Sulfur Dioxide Discharged (ton)	179	
氮氧化物排放量（吨）	Volume of Nitrogen Oxides Discharged (ton)	166	
烟（粉）尘排放量（吨）	Volume of Smoke & Dust Discharged (ton)	523	
污水处理厂数（座）	Number of Effluent Treatment Plants (unit)		4
污水处理厂集中处理率（%）	Rate of Centralized Treatment of Polluted Water (%)		
垃圾处理站数（个）	Number of Garbage Station (unit)		

Continued

江南区 Jiangnan District	西乡塘区 Xixiangtang District	良庆区 Liangqing District	邕宁区 Yongning District	武鸣县 Wuming County	隆安县 Long'an County	马山县 Mashan County	上林县 Shanglin County
87	97	40	70	104	135	105	105
1535	2230	980	1063	2059	1175	1568	1395
3621	5753	1948	1497	2524	1380	2186	1912
19889	29954	14910	15246	28176	20119	23515	20455
70365	103704	36396	22575	41019	32148	37092	30804
7880	18301	2782	3339	9117	3834	5706	5189
140	66	93	71	235	76	136	141
708	8060	1987	1587	3851	1770	1726	1714
496	6011	789	1574	3352	1574	2625	2339
228	3362	139	533	1139	773	601	646
		24228	19264	22075	15173	13966	
32156	31188	28901	30609	32014	25912	25889	25225
13819	12679	13356	12559	14594	10720	9807	10199
9	17	27	7	15	16	13	28
772	701	305	448	648	421	506	485
25199	10417	1117	16706	372400	39119		18726
80048	48824		17312	667500	46652		35188
	888		17125	19200	14730	8810	9816
251813	319616	217979	284650		362824		430452
92748	102586	72829	103604		163355	199514	164265
604	29568	173	204	5140	341	5037	3995
2107	31783	4592	6470	7908	16592	47473	28756
41136	30482	56084	50535	160254	124620	147435	100185
101	4811	59	94	1780	1115		135
527	1962	171	203	2425	2188	92	139
192	4659	31	180	2118	1859	472	402
2	0	4	0	1	1	1	1
100.0				79.9	79.0	100.0	68.0
4	0	2		4	5	4	10

23－1 续表3

指　标	Item	宾阳县 Binyang County	横　县 Hengxian County
行政区域面积（平方公里）	Administrative Region Land Area (sq.km)	2298	3448
常住户数（户）	Total Households at Year-end (household)	258950	306206
年末常住人口（万人）	Total Population at Year-end (10 000 persons)	82.03	90.84
年末户籍人口（万人）	Registered Population at Year-end (10 000 persons)	105.59	126.56
地区生产总值（万元）	Gross Domestic Product (10 000 yuan)	2183924	3045838
第一产业增加值	Primary Industry	502419	728680
第二产业增加值	Secondary Industry	681795	1208939
#工业	Industry	454005	888782
第三产业增加值	Tertiary Industry	999710	1108219
人均生产总值（元）	Per Capital GDP (yuan)	26722	33654
地区生产总值指数（上年＝100）	Indices of Gross Domestic Product (preceding year=100)	109.4	107.0
第一产业	Primary Industry	103.8	103.9
第二产业	Secondary Industry	106.1	104.5
#工业	Industry	107.2	104.2
第三产业	Tertiary Industry	115.2	112.3
人均生产总值指数（上年=100）	Indices of Per Capital GDP (preceding year＝100)	108.8	106.3
公共财政预算收入（万元）	Government Revenue (10 000 yuan)	126005	134252
税收收入（万元）	Total Tax Revenue (10 000 yuan)	75734	77760
公共预算支出（万元）	Government Expenditure (10 000 yuan)	479621	537073
年末金融机构各项存款余额（万元）	Year-end Deposits of Financial Institutions (10 000 yuan)	2127211	2490014
#居民储蓄存款余额	Urban & Rural Savings Deposits	1683495	2036401
年末金融机构各项贷款余额（万元）	Year-end Loans of Financial Institutions (10 000 yuan)	1191999	1443034
耕地面积（公顷）	Farmland (hectare)	91948	110278
设施农业占地面积（公顷）	Protected Agriculture Covered (hectare)	469	465
农业机械总动力（万千瓦特）	Total Agricultural Machinery Power (10 000 watts)	75.46	68.59
农作物总播种面积（公顷）	Total Sown Area of Major Farm Crops (hectare)	141136	160690
#粮食	Grain Crops	71573	76734
油料	Oil Crops	6790	5247
糖料	Sugar Crops	19274	20839
蔬菜	Vegetables	32408	41362
粮食总产量（吨）	Yield of Grain (ton)	362401	407651
#稻谷	Rice	306442	322945

Continued

城中区 Chengzhong District	鱼峰区 Yufeng District	柳南区 Liunan District	柳北区 Liubei District	柳江县 Liujiang County	柳城县 Liucheng County	鹿寨县 Luzhai County	融安县 Rong' an County
78	474	164	301	2537	2114	2975	2898
68381	152414	198201	153895	159651	124174	116983	99429
17.39	48.94	52.27	45.05	60.90	37.11	35.20	30.01
16.28	35.09	36.07	35.12	57.12	40.97	40.97	32.76
3080601	4385826	7010443	5259334	2520409	1363600	1625024	743890
10569	22022	26237	95329	406749	465754	346633	176407
1088531	2860772	4905957	2724790	1218256	448946	771678	281285
753977	2823446	4726066	2552663	1056850	370434	580101	233985
1981502	1503033	2078249	2439215	895404	448900	506713	286198
178431	90448	134777	117396	41550	36934	46290	24917
109.5	108.1	107.6	100.2	113.2	109.3	111.0	109.5
103.0	93.0	98.4	101.2	104.2	104.4	103.5	104.5
109.7	104.2	106.3	93.7	113.2	111.0	112.2	110.0
112.8	104.3	106.7	93.6	114.0	113.1	110.5	112.2
109.4	116.7	111.0	108.7	117.8	112.5	114.5	112.4
107.9	106.4	106.5	99.2	112.2	108.4	110.4	108.6
59778	68593	87334	79138	103169	57965	59458	27036
53009	62795	78402	70751	79718	39211	41884	17883
74018	72994	113230	105445	323804	270975	265446	222507
				1936525	1049253	1560441	864175
				1294572	750648	1057374	617241
				1742249	603780	1332045	490756
409	4343	2563	8141	86338	77543	58987	26852
50		69	330	216	337	258	69
0.8	8.9	1.98	8.73	45.49	38	51.8	20.77
1028	9030	3587	11916	88592	88447	71989	43398
260	2983	1400	3150	33336	32291	31973	20732
30	245	191	741	1752	3695	3827	1972
	2876	0	2200	19578	34496	14745	4666
738	2506	1910	5030	33926	13275	21438	11329
1212	14945	6700	15200	170780	166170	163215	99188
600	12239	6085	12848	141062	148598	135235	91054

23－1　续表4

指　标	Item	宾阳县 Binyang County	横　县 Hengxian County
油料产量（吨）	Yield of Oil-bearing Crops (ton)	21315	19593
糖料产量（吨）	Yield of Sugar Crops (ton)	1705787	2000425
蔬菜产量（吨）	Yield of Vegetables (ton)	709832	845281
园林水果（不含瓜类水果）产量（吨）	Yield of Fruit (ton)	33664	97271
肉类总产量（吨）	Output of Meat (ton)	63967	81153
#猪肉（吨）	Pork (ton)	39107	47255
禽蛋产量（吨）	Output of Eggs (ton)	1789	2896
奶类产量（吨）	Output of Milk (ton)	11	6719
水产品产量（吨）	Aquatic Products (ton)	43335	49190
规模以上工业企业个数（个）	Number of Industrial Enterprises above Designated Size (unit)	64	100
规模以上工业总产值（当年价，万元）	Included Gross Industrial Output Value above Designated Size (at current price, 10 000 yuan)	1656512	2833566
规模以上工业企业从业人员年平均人数（人）	Annual Average Number of Employed Persons (person)	19717	28009
规模以上工业企业主营业务收入（万元）	Income from Major Business (10 000 yuan)	1504165	2798113
公路里程（公里）	Length of Domestic Highways (km)	956	1903
民用汽车拥有量（辆）	Number of Civil Motor Vehicles Owned (vehicle)	16000	37644
年末实有公共汽（电）车营运数（辆）	Year-end Total Operating Public Buses (vehicle)	344	23
年末实有出租汽车数（辆）	Year-end Total Taxis (vehicle)	120	134
固定电话年末用户（户）	Number of Local Telephone Subscribers in Year-end (subscriber)	25773	29075
年末移动电话用户数（户）	Number of Mobile Telephone Subscribers at Year-end (subscriber)	638746	671642
互联网宽带接入用户（户）	Number of Internet Subscribers (subscriber)	523029	518087
全社会用电量（万千瓦时）	Total Consumption of Electricity (10 000 kwh)	127737	143941
#居民生活用电量	Household Consumption of Electricity	41093	47783
社会消费品零售总额（亿元）	Total Retail Sale of Consumer Goods 100 million yuan)	115.82	104.02
固定资产投资（不含农户）（亿元）	Investment in Fixed Assets (100 million yuan)	276.10	270.52
新增固定资产（万元）	Newly Increased Fixed Assets (10 000 yuan)	2020949	2230210
房地产开发投资完成额（万元）	Real Estate Development (10 000 yuan)	118266	124700
#住宅	Residential Buildings	105549	105546
住宅竣工面积（万平方米）	Completed Floor Space of Residential Buildings (10 000 sq.m)	24.79	0.19
普通中学数（所）	Number of Regular Secondary Schools (unit)	35	40

Continued

城中区 Chengzhong District	鱼峰区 Yufeng District	柳南区 Liunan District	柳北区 Liubei District	柳江县 Liujiang County	柳城县 Liucheng County	鹿寨县 Luzhai County	融安县 Rong' an County
90	460	515	1514	4246	10638	11017	3456
	156636	15	243312	1629124	2968826	947720	272970
9506	44475	43528	172120	909812	296485	422716	189874
657	13882	2486	35670	136799	386570	149740	165679
2809	3520	4701	14264	52459	46518	32831	22088
1008	2193	2904	7135	31675	32762	21555	11521
	5	8990	2840	863	1766	1591	865
250	2151	90	2745	618	20	776	
327	737	1330	10409	18356	20760	11135	7656
8	176	119	148	113	37	66	36
1084689	7558831	6057593	11870551	3229491	907080	1782651	601135
5724	59918	35504	36662	23000	9416	19279	5175
1251226	7029712	4859275	11111629	2127564	754768	1453197	537000
71		53	163	1276	1169	1578	1029
				69883	51256	11747	25347
					232	132	39
					31	121	60
				214035	15212	25837	10532
				341613	306816	228805	232125
				52016	38690	59178	77299
		244593	774381	88365	74308	120751	35368
		48417	41673	30959	16707	18292	12576
179.21	214.67	310.31	163.36	51.00	39.56	41.35	30.55
243.05	901.39	289.61	284.11	301.29	139.01	221.27	122.17
1252050	2766600	1307000	2421406	2168793	1448273	1888715	890611
589217	1139500	557200	419740	218555	54426	121742	49689
428803	1139500	400600	273776	156899	31779	106951	32869
52.97	24.50	11.50	37.95	16.50	4.52	18.00	2.52
6	9	17	15	18	15	7	14

23－1 续表5

指 标	Item	宾阳县 Binyang County	横 县 Hengxian County
小学数（所）	Number of Primary Schools (unit)	192	207
普通中学专任教师数（人）	Full-time Teachers in Regular Secondary Schools (person)	3249	3520
小学专任教师数（人）	Full-time Teachers in Primary Schools (person)	3623	4539
普通中学在校学生数（人）	Student Enrollment in Regular Secondary Schools (person)	51289	52854
小学在校学生数（人）	Primary Student Enrollment (person)	69278	85931
专业技术人员（人）	Number of Professionals (person)	11029	10524
#农业技术人员	Agricultural Professionals (person)	272	241
医疗卫生机构床位数（张）	Number of Beds in Heathcare Institutions (bed)	3628	3632
医疗卫生机构技术人员（人）	Medical & Technical Personnel of Heathcare Institutions (person)	4431	4457
#执业（助理）医师	Practitioner (assistant) Doctors	1347	1837
居民人均可支配收入（元）	Per Capita Annual Disposable Income of Households (yuan)	20520	19955
城镇居民人均可支配收入（元）	Per Capita Annual Disposable Income of Urban Households (yuan)	31489	31762
农村居民人均可支配收入（元）	Annual Per Capita Net Income of Rural Residents (yuan)	12867	12703
各种社会福利收养性单位数（个）	Number of Adopting Units of Social Welfare (unit)	25	234
各种社会福利收养性单位床位数（张）	Number of Beds in Adopting Units of Social Welfare (bed)	1382	5396
城镇基本养老保险参保人数（人）	Number of Persons Joining Basic Pension Insurance (person)	390705	54338
城镇基本医疗保险参保人数（人）	Number of Persons Joining Basic Health Care Insurance (person)	940767	90623
失业保险参保人数（人）	Number of Persons Joining Unemployment Insurance (person)	24354	20005
新型农村合作医疗参保人数（人）	Number of Persons Joining New-type Rural Cooperative Medical Service (person)		1100288
新型农村社会养老保险参保人数（人）	Number of Persons Joining New-type Rural Social Pension Insurance (person)		432126
城镇居民最低生活保障人数（人）	Number of Urban Residents Receiving Lowest Cost-of-living (person)	822	767
农村居民最低生活保障人数（人）	Number of Rural Residents Receiving Lowest Cost-of-living (person)	14869	23289
森林面积（公顷）	Forest Area (10 000 hectares)	95092	167203
工业二氧化硫排放量（吨）	Volume of Sulfur Dioxide Discharged (ton)	1420	3424
氮氧化物排放量（吨）	Volume of Nitrogen Oxides Discharged (ton)	1714	6010
烟（粉）尘排放量（吨）	Volume of Smoke & Dust Discharged (ton)	1805	2587
污水处理厂数（座）	Number of Effluent Treatment Plants (unit)	8	1
污水处理厂集中处理率（%）	Rate of Centralized Treatment of Polluted Water (%)	97.3	99.6
垃圾处理站数（个）	Number of Garbage Station (unit)	17	4

Continued

城中区 Chengzhong District	鱼峰区 Yufeng District	柳南区 Liunan District	柳北区 Liubei District	柳江县 Liujiang County	柳城县 Liucheng County	鹿寨县 Luzhai County	融安县 Rong' an County
17	38	42	48	115	143	65	87
692	732	1241	1126	1646	838	861	949
1059	1654	2217	1637	2556	1575	1297	1210
8900	11422	18167	13705	19655	9459	15797	13806
18030	30602	43477	28649	37676	22155	25479	17884
1510		2903	7480	7488	4331	3414	3679
5		18	45	286	232	162	115
3699	5327	1876	2582	1766	1696	1598	1722
6035	5416	2776	3281	1905	1906	1820	1381
1847	993	948	1230	698	549	685	622
39567			35436		19936	22317	17292
39678	36346	37724	36360	32835	31056	33044	27097
20675	21151	19399	15569	12292	12574	12865	11674
4	6	9	5	11	46	30	29
465	928	1489	833	450	540	553	468
135440	131339		186371	64633	42472	61502	109226
220009	188072		169352	33165	27381	356682	292259
60516	44113	93912	80518	22582	14382	21738	8156
18810		39602	60962	427188	312025		
912		8660	19105	231584	139000	167381	
660	873	2370	55139	405	719	723	1103
59	4	289	11712	8960	6477	11503	19799
3123		5072	900	117682	96593	194782	226597
	1973	1210	32600	838	514	3672	73
	654	6498	28900	245	636	1975	114
	2957	3403	66000	2988	4523	2358	467
	1		1	2	6	2	3
	100.0	0.0	94.3	76.2	90.0	28.0	93.5
			0	3	1	15	3

23－1 续表6

指　标	Item	融水苗族自治县 Rongshui County	三江侗族自治县 Sanjiang County
行政区域面积（平方公里）	Administrative Region Land Area (sq.km)	4638	2417
常住户数（户）	Total Households at Year-end (household)	133004	89812
年末常住人口（万人）	Total Population at Year-end (10 000 persons)	42.01	31.12
年末户籍人口（万人）	Registered Population at Year-end (10 000 persons)	51.97	40.26
地区生产总值（万元）	Gross Domestic Product (10 000 yuan)	985737	518281
第一产业增加值	Primary Industry	160927	184249
第二产业增加值	Secondary Industry	440623	99395
#工业	Industry	290608	32627
第三产业增加值	Tertiary Industry	384186	234637
人均生产总值（元）	Per Capital GDP (yuan)	23568	16719
地区生产总值指数（上年＝100）	Indices of Gross Domestic Product (preceding year=100)	111.7	109.3
第一产业	Primary Industry	104.0	104.7
第二产业	Secondary Industry	111.9	103.5
#工业	Industry	111.2	103.2
第三产业	Tertiary Industry	115.1	116.4
人均生产总值指数（上年=100）	Indices of Per Capital GDP (preceding year＝100)	110.8	108.5
公共财政预算收入（万元）	Government Revenue (10 000 yuan)	46672	22098
税收收入（万元）	Total Tax Revenue (10 000 yuan)	25952	15880
公共预算支出（万元）	Government Expenditure (10 000 yuan)	351633	262403
年末金融机构各项存款余额（万元）	Year-end Deposits of Financial Institutions (10 000 yuan)	1372153	850283
#居民储蓄存款余额	Urban & Rural Savings Deposits	886863	541008
年末金融机构各项贷款余额（万元）	Year-end Loans of Financial Institutions (10 000 yuan)	881770	478183
耕地面积（公顷）	Farmland (hectare)	55715	20737
设施农业占地面积（公顷）	Protected Agriculture Covered (hectare)		137
农业机械总动力（万千瓦特）	Total Agricultural Machinery Power (10 000 watts)	27.31	20.75
农作物总播种面积（公顷）	Total Sown Area of Major Farm Crops (hectare)	42842	27767
#粮食	Grain Crops	23334	14106
油料	Oil Crops	1664	1273
糖料	Sugar Crops	4945	92
蔬菜	Vegetables	9516	6412
粮食总产量（吨）	Yield of Grain (ton)	116368	70320
#稻谷	Rice	102425	60664

Continued

叠彩区 Diecai District	象山区 Xiangshan District	七星区 Qixing District	雁山区 Yanshan District	临桂区 Lingui District	阳朔县 Yangshuo County	灵川县 Lingchuan County	全州县 Quanzhou County
52	90	71	302	1436	2247	2302	3979
49174	86581	90565	27660	144513	93794	118117	247037
18.82	29.44	30.72	13.83	47.91	28.82	37.23	66.57
15.06	24.24	21.69	6.93	51.34	32.86	39.09	84.15
861863	2257615	1944258	257728	1780481	1282351	1324110	1710192
14416	12076	15860	53019	405905	270734	381286	518900
173648	712088	927120	47209	789543	447817	466226	558681
83002	532972	842300	27617	516393	228227	362226	432942
673799	1533451	1001279	157499	585033	563801	476598	632611
46151	77031	63538	18923	37385	44619	35772	25789
107.0	107.2	102.6	106.2	91.3	106.7	102.0	106.2
104.0	100.7	96.2	103.9	103.3	105.5	103.2	104.4
102.0	106.4	98.0	102.0	79.6	104.4	97.5	103.2
105.4	107.7	98.3	102.0	72.5	107.9	97.9	102.2
108.4	107.7	108.2	108.5	110.7	109.2	106.8	110.8
105.3	106.3	101.8	102.6	90.3	106.0	100.9	105.3
34765	76808	107174	11632	198771	47189	107536	49384
19576	31553	58123	6786	106575	23258	53929	29282
49387	99030	143231	62964	353976	199469	312977	395923
				4823790	1079339	1921029	2047129
					828493	1368960	1569926
				2443185	639537	1563970	1165246
1005	1424	753	5951	47059	13990	27867	70908
31	20	23	138	555	174	263	225
0.8	2.82	2.26	11.6	36.41	30.2	49.23	57.82
2369	2582	2161	9834	82525	46837	63866	130371
572	1301	469	3894	46907	23229	32715	76506
45	29	34	216	604	2224	788	5222
4				676	418	139	594
1596	905	1550	4018	21191	13489	22042	25629
3737	6605	2531	18808	246814	113992	165770	405965
3364	5817	2109	13491	226358	87512	135864	348434

23－1 续表7

指 标	Item	融水苗族自治县 Rongshui County	三江侗族自治县 Sanjiang County
油料产量（吨）	Yield of Oil-bearing Crops (ton)	2555	1925
糖料产量（吨）	Yield of Sugar Crops (ton)	336490	7496
蔬菜产量（吨）	Yield of Vegetables (ton)	147154	70049
园林水果（不含瓜类水果）产量（吨）	Yield of Fruit (ton)	56505	13657
肉类总产量（吨）	Output of Meat (ton)	29108	19443
#猪肉（吨）	Pork (ton)	15949	9913
禽蛋产量（吨）	Output of Eggs (ton)	263	900
奶类产量（吨）	Output of Milk (ton)		
水产品产量（吨）	Aquatic Products (ton)	9200	4490
规模以上工业企业个数（个）	Number of Industrial Enterprises above Designated Size (unit)	37	9
规模以上工业总产值（当年价，万元）	Included Gross Industrial Output Value above Designated Size (at current price，10 000 yuan)	707632	39100
规模以上工业企业从业人员年平均人数（人）	Annual Average Number of Employed Persons (person)	5640	809
规模以上工业企业主营业务收入（万元）	Income from Major Business (10 000 yuan)	608356	40200
公路里程（公里）	Length of Domestic Highways (km)	1864	1158
民用汽车拥有量（辆）	Number of Civil Motor Vehicles Owned (vehicle)	30595	26863
年末实有公共汽（电）车营运数（辆）	Year-end Total Operating Public Buses (vehicle)	30	39
年末实有出租汽车数（辆）	Year-end Total Taxis (vehicle)	98	80
固定电话年末用户（户）	Number of Local Telephone Subscribers in Year-end (subscriber)	8861	9559
年末移动电话用户数（户）	Number of Mobile Telephone Subscribers at Year-end (subscriber)	335004	269914
互联网宽带接入用户（户）	Number of Internet Subscribers (subscriber)	50308	47251
全社会用电量（万千瓦时）	Total Consumption of Electricity (10 000 kwh)	55641	31144
#居民生活用电量	Household Consumption of Electricity	28536	13880
社会消费品零售总额（亿元）	Total Retail Sale of Consumer Goods 100 million yuan)	30.23	23.70
固定资产投资（不含农户）（亿元）	Investment in Fixed Assets (100 million yuan)	122.15	73.15
新增固定资产（万元）	Newly Increased Fixed Assets (10 000 yuan)	799384	555817
房地产开发投资完成额（万元）	Real Estate Development (10 000 yuan)	145217	67897
#住宅	Residential Buildings	117683	60053
住宅竣工面积（万平方米）	Completed Floor Space of Residential Buildings (10 000 sq.m)	5.58	8.00
普通中学数（所）	Number of Regular Secondary Schools (unit)	14	16

Continued

叠彩区 Diecai District	象山区 Xiangshan District	七星区 Qixing District	雁山区 Yanshan District	临桂区 Lingui District	阳朔县 Yangshuo County	灵川县 Lingchuan County	全州县 Quanzhou County
106	57	89	295	1351	7294	1932	14308
442				67606	37982	11733	41518
43894	17596	48644	88311	485037	301425	599121	558806
207	170	142	33284	179674	499738	412704	416017
2679	4171	4112	18095	101640	28190	54709	74864
1711	3151	3038	6264	33316	16441	31014	57234
166	431	152	2959	18215	2616	10888	9007
	240	656			66	0	
250	1968	1014	3173	18215	9540	11591	26930
10	26	66	7	80	22	75	58
411400	1519259	3159271	91971	2261916	544436	1390754	1326855
1506	16314	23221	1073	22500	12193	215	5155
233878	1067831	2443512	77057	1943009	541350	1348782	1175453
42	56	73	299	866	659	887	2276
30922	50361	40006	8124	45827	37269	44492	48481
			22	330	65	151	497
		139	1		48		100
				23100	15201	27000	19753
				369018	189466	354287	294130
				54736	35100	62567	32714
	160075	81725	18305	99904	42207	73012	140900
	29674	26708	9740	33752	19075	23758	35194
122.12	162.28	92.90	3.91	45.72	29.45	54.35	35.52
83.55	164.68	125.11	44.72	150.81	250.01	149.98	219.04
428844	626618	286342	198195	2053425	1333621	867192	935066
500413	278829	515681	39420	911578	2372	254783	59503
394370	167815	424822	39420	806321	2372	151679	49002
5.58	14.37	2.20	11.95	17.82	0.00	7.55	
1	9	3	2	22	11	20	25

23－1 续表8

指 标	Item	融水苗族自治县 Rongshui County	三江侗族自治县 Sanjiang County
小学数（所）	Number of Primary Schools (unit)	118	226
普通中学专任教师数（人）	Full-time Teachers in Regular Secondary Schools (person)	1402	1108
小学专任教师数（人）	Full-time Teachers in Primary Schools (person)	1924	1667
普通中学在校学生数（人）	Student Enrollment in Regular Secondary Schools (person)	24711	18990
小学在校学生数（人）	Primary Student Enrollment (person)	38195	34673
专业技术人员（人）	Number of Professionals (person)	5169	5254
#农业技术人员	Agricultural Professionals (person)	429	107
医疗卫生机构床位数（张）	Number of Beds in Heathcare Institutions (bed)	1761	1172
医疗卫生机构技术人员（人）	Medical & Technical Personnel of Heathcare Institutions (person)	2269	1316
#执业（助理）医师	Practitioner (assistant) Doctors	616	286
居民人均可支配收入（元）	Per Capita Annual Disposable Income of Households (yuan)	16632	15224
城镇居民人均可支配收入（元）	Per Capita Annual Disposable Income of Urban Households (yuan)	26935	27048
农村居民人均可支配收入（元）	Annual Per Capita Net Income of Rural Residents (yuan)	11413	11125
各种社会福利收养性单位数（个）	Number of Adopting Units of Social Welfare (unit)	25	135
各种社会福利收养性单位床位数（张）	Number of Beds in Adopting Units of Social Welfare (bed)	493	974
城镇基本养老保险参保人数（人）	Number of Persons Joining Basic Pension Insurance (person)	35858	15275
城镇基本医疗保险参保人数（人）	Number of Persons Joining Basic Health Care Insurance (person)	98756	31455
失业保险参保人数（人）	Number of Persons Joining Unemployment Insurance (person)	14833	6597
新型农村合作医疗参保人数（人）	Number of Persons Joining New-type Rural Cooperative Medical Service (person)	440401	339445
新型农村社会养老保险参保人数（人）	Number of Persons Joining New-type Rural Social Pension Insurance (person)	215022	152418
城镇居民最低生活保障人数（人）	Number of Urban Residents Receiving Lowest Cost-of-living (person)	3312	4216
农村居民最低生活保障人数（人）	Number of Rural Residents Receiving Lowest Cost-of-living (person)	37284	47033
森林面积（公顷）	Forest Area (10 000 hectares)	367193	193328
工业二氧化硫排放量（吨）	Volume of Sulfur Dioxide Discharged (ton)	474	490
氮氧化物排放量（吨）	Volume of Nitrogen Oxides Discharged (ton)	467	83
烟（粉）尘排放量（吨）	Volume of Smoke & Dust Discharged (ton)	916	167
污水处理厂数（座）	Number of Effluent Treatment Plants (unit)	3	1
污水处理厂集中处理率（%）	Rate of Centralized Treatment of Polluted Water (%)	94.0	88.5
垃圾处理站数（个）	Number of Garbage Station (unit)	16	16

Continued

叠彩区 Diecai District	象山区 Xiangshan District	七星区 Qixing District	雁山区 Yanshan District	临桂区 Lingui District	阳朔县 Yangshuo County	灵川县 Lingchuan County	全州县 Quanzhou County
15	23	30	12	88	88	51	270
64	563	158	190	1740	890	1221	2344
524	1242	1312	334	2252	1198	1433	3204
676	6721	1910	2019	19860	12374	15748	34150
10737	23060	22935	4388	36427	19786	26169	53625
579	1175	1470	743	5216	3523	3927	7486
4	8	4	35	269	160	255	269
1254	3305	884	100	1175	773	1343	1879
2016	4531	1901	134	2430	1325	2009	2396
607	1482	809	61	901	466	729	1015
	33293	34168	24860		22781	22582	
32993	33214	34785	30614	36003	35286	33680	30961
13704	13463	16329	12449	15907	15045	13893	13651
7	7	10	6	68	12	12	213
215	1395	1136	118	960	276	504	2503
2315	2451			26347	13954	21985	46443
	51853			59724	34629	54899	79511
				19140	10720	12500	13400
26334	23453	14711	53181	388635	281884	336001	663599
4815	5487		25444	220650	151160	184702	357303
1331	2331	18064	66	6222	401	811	5246
368	517	12792	2428	20090	8584	9276	32315
1132	2570	2320	14195	137285	78178	163297	244598
230		1600	27	733	413	3137	2272
92		400	5	472	63	1599	369
26		235		219	260	2483	563
	1	2	2	3	5	1	2
				75.0	97.1	92.0	89.2
1	1	5	4	4	5	5	7

23－1　续表9

指　标	Item	兴安县 Xing' an County	永福县 Yongfu County
行政区域面积（平方公里）	Administrative Region Land Area (sq.km)	2333	2795
常住户数（户）	Total Households at Year-end (household)	124658	74082
年末常住人口（万人）	Total Population at Year-end (10 000 persons)	34.50	24.67
年末户籍人口（万人）	Registered Population at Year-end (10 000 persons)	39.09	28.87
地区生产总值（万元）	Gross Domestic Product (10 000 yuan)	1364691	1331784
第一产业增加值	Primary Industry	358009	288743
第二产业增加值	Secondary Industry	510977	807188
#工业	Industry	400394	642631
第三产业增加值	Tertiary Industry	495706	235852
人均生产总值（元）	Per Capital GDP (yuan)	39694	54281
地区生产总值指数（上年＝100）	Indices of Gross Domestic Product (preceding year=100)	106.3	106.7
第一产业	Primary Industry	104.5	104.9
第二产业	Secondary Industry	101.5	107.4
#工业	Industry	103.0	107.4
第三产业	Tertiary Industry	114.7	106.4
人均生产总值指数（上年=100）	Indices of Per Capital GDP (preceding year＝100)	105.5	105.6
公共财政预算收入（万元）	Government Revenue (10 000 yuan)	96495	44814
税收收入（万元）	Total Tax Revenue (10 000 yuan)	33681	18370
公共预算支出（万元）	Government Expenditure (10 000 yuan)	266465	198510
年末金融机构各项存款余额（万元）	Year-end Deposits of Financial Institutions (10 000 yuan)	1484762	784477
#居民储蓄存款余额	Urban & Rural Savings Deposits	1199335	565778
年末金融机构各项贷款余额（万元）	Year-end Loans of Financial Institutions (10 000 yuan)	1375702	608712
耕地面积（公顷）	Farmland (hectare)	26556	26942
设施农业占地面积（公顷）	Protected Agriculture Covered (hectare)	141	290
农业机械总动力（万千瓦特）	Total Agricultural Machinery Power (10 000 watts)	51.2	29
农作物总播种面积（公顷）	Total Sown Area of Major Farm Crops (hectare)	65451	48357
#粮食	Grain Crops	37942	25956
油料	Oil Crops	2154	601
糖料	Sugar Crops	49	1176
蔬菜	Vegetables	16004	11368
粮食总产量（吨）	Yield of Grain (ton)	204711	123003
#稻谷	Rice	160608	104358

Continued

灌阳县 Guanyang County	龙胜各族自治县 Longsheng County	资源县 Ziyuan County	平乐县 Pingle County	荔浦县 Lipu County	恭城瑶族自治县 Gongcheng County	万秀区 Wanxiu District	长洲区 Changzhou District
1835	2451	1941	1893	1760	2139	449	373
105754	47788	56996	142373	106420	90676	103372	63850
24.32	16.11	15.50	38.71	36.15	25.94	32.31	20.80
29.57	17.25	18.03	46.19	38.24	30.36	29.90	18.43
778809	666258	601189	1147400	1669382	818974	2251855	2395180
189435	120859	114920	454932	342114	270692	39114	47191
379697	349289	293357	355989	767831	291852	1141830	1436428
329919	290562	233015	283432	655876	251355	1073063	1397262
209677	196111	192912	336479	559437	256430	1070912	911561
32162	41537	39026	29756	46326	31682	70009	116128
104.9	106.4	107.4	104.4	106.8	105.3	113.7	85.4
104.8	105.0	105.1	104.9	105.2	104.4	104.4	104.4
103.3	105.7	103.3	98.1	104.9	103.0	118.1	73.4
102.3	105.5	103.9	94.9	106.0	103.6	119.1	72.7
108.1	108.8	115.9	111.5	110.8	109.5	109.1	111.8
103.9	105.4	106.2	103.7	106.2	104.6	112.9	84.1
24553	23620	19490	39515	64258	40239	17674	26320
12747	13535	9326	21574	30504	17146	11091	15069
222741	196758	167094	236857	255703	211580	93880	100025
840421	578212	659616	932345	1230278	718266	0	239151
650277	420089	465195	807603	963503	563162	0	238376
478138	422522	464192	515109	1280822	510514	0	328111
19671	17754	16498	20751	25528	5888	4133	2791
73	9	22	58	61	32	11	9
29.95	28	24	49.24	44.25	57.27	10	5
44232	22612	23243	71722	54116	44246	7831	10108
28040	10701	9371	30239	23173	17959	4629	3280
1549	235	522	4326	1731	5381	360	554
120	0		613	828	41	8	
9358	7641	7469	23887	15949	10884	2722	5310
178263	63094	54650	158531	124402	79629	22938	15660
135803	40257	39740	113320	86371	43097	20382	14374

23－1　续表10

指　标	Item	兴安县 Xing' an County	永福县 Yongfu County
油料产量（吨）	Yield of Oil-bearing Crops (ton)	7381	2228
糖料产量（吨）	Yield of Sugar Crops (ton)	2409	93530
蔬菜产量（吨）	Yield of Vegetables (ton)	366651	268706
园林水果（不含瓜类水果）产量（吨）	Yield of Fruit (ton)	454606	323248
肉类总产量（吨）	Output of Meat (ton)	46074	49485
#猪肉（吨）	Pork (ton)	36362	26806
禽蛋产量（吨）	Output of Eggs (ton)	3484	2680
奶类产量（吨）	Output of Milk (ton)	50	113
水产品产量（吨）	Aquatic Products (ton)	12738	7782
规模以上工业企业个数（个）	Number of Industrial Enterprises above Designated Size (unit)	46	50
规模以上工业总产值（当年价，万元）	Included Gross Industrial Output Value above Designated Size (at current price，10 000 yuan)	1117669	2218188
规模以上工业企业从业人员年平均人数（人）	Annual Average Number of Employed Persons (person)	8212	8496
规模以上工业企业主营业务收入（万元）	Income from Major Business (10 000 yuan)	1092178	2126048
公路里程（公里）	Length of Domestic Highways (km)	1213	542
民用汽车拥有量（辆）	Number of Civil Motor Vehicles Owned (vehicle)	34509	22710
年末实有公共汽（电）车营运数（辆）	Year-end Total Operating Public Buses (vehicle)	111	173
年末实有出租汽车数（辆）	Year-end Total Taxis (vehicle)	110	25
固定电话年末用户（户）	Number of Local Telephone Subscribers in Year-end (subscriber)	13028	8249
年末移动电话用户数（户）	Number of Mobile Telephone Subscribers at Year-end (subscriber)	260114	253046
互联网宽带接入用户（户）	Number of Internet Subscribers (subscriber)	45998	29711
全社会用电量（万千瓦时）	Total Consumption of Electricity (10 000 kwh)	85552	57129
#居民生活用电量	Household Consumption of Electricity	14961	13034
社会消费品零售总额（亿元）	Total Retail Sale of Consumer Goods 100 million yuan)	45.37	32.11
固定资产投资（不含农户）（亿元）	Investment in Fixed Assets (100 million yuan)	218.25	143.78
新增固定资产（万元）	Newly Increased Fixed Assets (10 000 yuan)	1795002	1239711
房地产开发投资完成额（万元）	Real Estate Development (10 000 yuan)	21581	10648
#住宅	Residential Buildings	20891	10137
住宅竣工面积（万平方米）	Completed Floor Space of Residential Buildings (10 000 sq.m)	5.12	9.01
普通中学数（所）	Number of Regular Secondary Schools (unit)	13	13

Continued

灌阳县 Guanyang County	龙胜各族自治县 Longsheng County	资源县 Ziyuan County	平乐县 Pingle County	荔浦县 Lipu County	恭城瑶族自治县 Gongcheng County	万秀区 Wanxiu District	长洲区 Changzhou District
3843	443	1418	14939	6469	15685	469	1759
5384	0		61771	74278	4204	630	
175098	122393	160976	602733	297481	163007	43394	99986
421586	98363	73861	891779	454014	1138043	13946	8519
29301	11837	10495	31622	50293	24599	7347	6702
24368	6023	5994	20461	37036	13629	5137	4357
1799	766	833	5220	3091	3559	450	659
0	0			60		297	83
5924	860	1500	11339	7661	8504	6996	10228
29	24	29	39	58	23	68	20
683849	628149	614360	777298	2172675	720723	2619309	5505225
2821	6609	3471	7035	35130	5400	214	34562
608819	629349	469148	707929	1810113	669265	1780204	5524200
805	994	908	797	911	780	197	247
19126	1495	13883	27828	85712	24327	17202	5348
108	18	45	182	175	59	325	0
42	61	30	20	146	62		
15506	3500	5900	14000	30321	13288	39321	62435
165780	156215	80000	262535	282281	231789	75448	68712
20612	27263	20000	29326	51608	42759	1144820	119780
64179	32637	44772	40281	56301	45908	64365	137900
13612	7168	6101	18264	22104	14081	9226	108010
20.48	9.97	13.08	25.26	61.07	29.38	105.40	82.73
74.26	56.39	74.56	121.89	179.46	93.25	204.09	193.19
661600	393512	377068	1137147	1548265	813111	778618	1502000
	3021	30043	22488	78291	33197	54752	224338
	2446	17046	12207	72369	23084	43278	180587
38.80	0.00	7.37	6.96	15.32	4.39	0.00	22.50
12	3	9	14	14	14	2	4

23－1　续表11

指　标	Item	兴安县 Xing' an County	永福县 Yongfu County
小学数（所）	Number of Primary Schools (unit)	104	81
普通中学专任教师数（人）	Full-time Teachers in Regular Secondary Schools (person)	2302	762
小学专任教师数（人）	Full-time Teachers in Primary Schools (person)	1218	1005
普通中学在校学生数（人）	Student Enrollment in Regular Secondary Schools (person)	7294	10560
小学在校学生数（人）	Primary Student Enrollment (person)	24681	18677
专业技术人员（人）	Number of Professionals (person)	3540	3480
#农业技术人员	Agricultural Professionals (person)	64	144
医疗卫生机构床位数（张）	Number of Beds in Heathcare Institutions (bed)	1845	875
医疗卫生机构技术人员（人）	Medical & Technical Personnel of Heathcare Institutions (person)	1809	1258
#执业（助理）医师	Practitioner (assistant) Doctors	1021	814
居民人均可支配收入（元）	Per Capita Annual Disposable Income of Households (yuan)		19028
城镇居民人均可支配收入（元）	Per Capita Annual Disposable Income of Urban Households (yuan)	32879	33502
农村居民人均可支配收入（元）	Annual Per Capita Net Income of Rural Residents (yuan)	15926	12913
各种社会福利收养性单位数（个）	Number of Adopting Units of Social Welfare (unit)	17	51
各种社会福利收养性单位床位数（张）	Number of Beds in Adopting Units of Social Welfare (bed)	250	472
城镇基本养老保险参保人数（人）	Number of Persons Joining Basic Pension Insurance (person)	42273	10921
城镇基本医疗保险参保人数（人）	Number of Persons Joining Basic Health Care Insurance (person)	360939	14663
失业保险参保人数（人）	Number of Persons Joining Unemployment Insurance (person)	13950	8635
新型农村合作医疗参保人数（人）	Number of Persons Joining New-type Rural Cooperative Medical Service (person)	305412	249423
新型农村社会养老保险参保人数（人）	Number of Persons Joining New-type Rural Social Pension Insurance (person)	165207	115083
城镇居民最低生活保障人数（人）	Number of Urban Residents Receiving Lowest Cost-of-living (person)	1689	2488
农村居民最低生活保障人数（人）	Number of Rural Residents Receiving Lowest Cost-of-living (person)	13597	33214
森林面积（公顷）	Forest Area (10 000 hectares)	173475	209090
工业二氧化硫排放量（吨）	Volume of Sulfur Dioxide Discharged (ton)	1133	6400
氮氧化物排放量（吨）	Volume of Nitrogen Oxides Discharged (ton)	3096	6182
烟（粉）尘排放量（吨）	Volume of Smoke & Dust Discharged (ton)	2162	623
污水处理厂数（座）	Number of Effluent Treatment Plants (unit)	2	2
污水处理厂集中处理率（%）	Rate of Centralized Treatment of Polluted Water (%)	98.6	91.5
垃圾处理站数（个）	Number of Garbage Station (unit)	1	1

Continued

灌阳县 Guanyang County	龙胜各族自治县 Longsheng County	资源县 Ziyuan County	平乐县 Pingle County	荔浦县 Lipu County	恭城瑶族自治县 Gongcheng County	万秀区 Wanxiu District	长洲区 Changzhou District
139	62	108	34	107	22	43	42
931	521	595	1171	1178	918	89	102
1206	1169	776	1621	1646	1355	1313	1117
10526	6623	7729	18040	14994	12657	1066	2248
17903	10059	12879	31129	23655	21349	22855	20037
4042	2677	2370	5118	3712	3419	1479	1195
213	99	100	295	184	130	11	42
978	565	508	1312	1413	925	4304	816
1232	856	591	2084	2558	1420	7895	878
357	283	370	887	643	484	1837	378
	15167	15750		22028	16992	28720	29033
30454	31172	30334	31319	32792	30551	30439	31032
9796	10572	9968	12724	13803	11880	14338	13560
60	46	9	38	1	1	13	7
421	408	134	503	72	70	437	649
16995	84025	12010	27815	29000	18702	35579	20580
29867	17088	35396	21508	26100	20863	22161	143447
8015	9539	5594	8210	10002	9800	21062	9890
250165	145999	149640	379482	309808	272030	67967	
125401	75992	66132	195955	155558	141418	28593	
3042	1187	850	2130	1396	7182	2288	1505
19347	17158	13288	24611	16090	223590	2359	3013
135390	194193	153737	133937	123200	178141	31900	27802
407	1	135	547	291	568	1532	354
68	2	54	111	144	2188	533	66
308	39	70	317	328	900	599	1311
5	1	2	5	1	8	2	2
94.0	83.5	82.0	89.0	96.0	85.0	0.0	
10	1	1	11	1	17	0	1

23－1　续表12

指　标	Item	龙圩区 Longxu District	苍梧县 Cangwu County
行政区域面积（平方公里）	Administrative Region Land Area (sq.km)	971	2782
常住户数（户）	Total Households at Year-end (household)	84916	98105
年末常住人口（万人）	Total Population at Year-end (10 000 persons)	28.66	33.01
年末户籍人口（万人）	Registered Population at Year-end (10 000 persons)	31.14	40.72
地区生产总值（万元）	Gross Domestic Product (10 000 yuan)	1621324	415456
第一产业增加值	Primary Industry	91309	160740
第二产业增加值	Secondary Industry	984270	144290
#工业	Industry	924397	91032
第三产业增加值	Tertiary Industry	545744	110427
人均生产总值（元）	Per Capital GDP (yuan)	56853	12618
地区生产总值指数（上年＝100）	Indices of Gross Domestic Product (preceding year=100)	113.4	109.2
第一产业	Primary Industry	104.5	104.9
第二产业	Secondary Industry	115.8	113.0
#工业	Industry	118.2	123.1
第三产业	Tertiary Industry	111.9	111.4
人均生产总值指数（上年=100）	Indices of Per Capital GDP (preceding year＝100)	112.3	108.6
公共财政预算收入（万元）	Government Revenue (10 000 yuan)	22336	33506
税收收入（万元）	Total Tax Revenue (10 000 yuan)	17787	16682
公共预算支出（万元）	Government Expenditure (10 000 yuan)	116996	248343
年末金融机构各项存款余额（万元）	Year-end Deposits of Financial Institutions (10 000 yuan)		1770400
#居民储蓄存款余额	Urban & Rural Savings Deposits		1188100
年末金融机构各项贷款余额（万元）	Year-end Loans of Financial Institutions (10 000 yuan)		1226200
耕地面积（公顷）	Farmland (hectare)	11015	20834
设施农业占地面积（公顷）	Protected Agriculture Covered (hectare)		27
农业机械总动力（万千瓦特）	Total Agricultural Machinery Power (10 000 watts)	15.21	26.56
农作物总播种面积（公顷）	Total Sown Area of Major Farm Crops (hectare)	26288	40810
#粮食	Grain Crops	16679	24235
油料	Oil Crops	1718	2167
糖料	Sugar Crops	70	110
蔬菜	Vegetables	5811	7782
粮食总产量（吨）	Yield of Grain (ton)	82539	127780
#稻谷	Rice	77706	115674

Continued

藤 县 Tengxian County	蒙山县 Mengshan County	岑溪市 Cenxi City	海城区 Haicheng District	银海区 Yinhai District	铁山港区 Tieshangang District	合浦县 Hepu County	港口区 Gangkou District
3946	1282	2770	182	541	504	2762	410
302428	69971	267703	94506	49850	36544	248371	52138
87.70	20.23	81.03	37.39	19.94	15.43	93.57	17.49
110.40	22.39	96.09	31.39	17.18	18.47	108.37	13.97
2706193	886224	3125570	5072048	1270648	3308760	2486281	4153115
530656	129466	365664	263153	407822	301994	932476	176759
1578094	491367	2102484	2919093	331439	2745160	662309	2774110
1421450	453732	1956417	2626188	261924	2708124	495215	2516869
597443	265391	657421	1889802	531387	261606	891495	1202246
30926	43927	38647	136254	64386	215931	26715	239442
112.2	108.0	110.6	110.7	109.0	110.6	108.4	106.8
104.6	104.8	104.5	103.4	103.7	103.9	103.9	103.9
115.6	108.1	112.1	110.2	106.2	112.0	111.0	106.0
117.2	110.2	112.9	110.9	108.0	112.3	113.8	106.3
111.5	109.6	109.9	112.6	115.2	109.0	111.4	109.3
111.7	107.2	110.2	109.7	106.9	109.1	107.3	105.1
118817	20094	139014	43482	32127	23487	68614	63850
77875	12745	87698	37567	26184	20714	41773	51291
436451	163685	397820	117509	124493	91451	483175	110626
2012606	556039	1992798	9388400			2437786	4110051
1570343	404461	1600714	5785500			2058470	1996071
1294683	371531	1483249	6545200			1301056	4960052
38222	12777	37314	2238	21844	17208	81743	3186
18	15	33	249	854	604	1120	16
39.26	12.25	29.06	18.3	27.59	25.73	76.3	13.28
101476	32525	78590	4335	26166	21506	132203	7341
48376	12779	46168	1337	5550	5879	64459	4265
4473	1818	4013	484	2213	3542	10943	807
719	168	1084	109	8797	3868	17764	79
29959	15225	16991	1794	4798	4051	28500	1984
263702	66351	229560	4540	22975	27475	323275	17811
231998	52513	183534	1480	13627	16864	228555	10423

23－1 续表13

指 标	Item	龙圩区 Longxu District	苍梧县 Cangwu County
油料产量（吨）	Yield of Oil-bearing Crops (ton)	5438	6632
糖料产量（吨）	Yield of Sugar Crops (ton)	3864	6291
蔬菜产量（吨）	Yield of Vegetables (ton)	100839	171901
园林水果（不含瓜类水果）产量（吨）	Yield of Fruit (ton)	70982	136045
肉类总产量（吨）	Output of Meat (ton)	15514	23956
#猪肉（吨）	Pork (ton)	10265	16468
禽蛋产量（吨）	Output of Eggs (ton)	134	191
奶类产量（吨）	Output of Milk (ton)		
水产品产量（吨）	Aquatic Products (ton)	7542	12353
规模以上工业企业个数（个）	Number of Industrial Enterprises above Designated Size (unit)	30	13
规模以上工业总产值（当年价，万元）	Included Gross Industrial Output Value above Designated Size (at current price，10 000 yuan)	752580	300276
规模以上工业企业从业人员年平均人数（人）	Annual Average Number of Employed Persons (person)	244	1553
规模以上工业企业主营业务收入（万元）	Income from Major Business (10 000 yuan)	465493	298945
公路里程（公里）	Length of Domestic Highways (km)	288	1198
民用汽车拥有量（辆）	Number of Civil Motor Vehicles Owned (vehicle)		21571
年末实有公共汽（电）车营运数（辆）	Year-end Total Operating Public Buses (vehicle)	65	
年末实有出租汽车数（辆）	Year-end Total Taxis (vehicle)		
固定电话年末用户（户）	Number of Local Telephone Subscribers in Year-end (subscriber)		15979
年末移动电话用户数（户）	Number of Mobile Telephone Subscribers at Year-end (subscriber)		385442
互联网宽带接入用户（户）	Number of Internet Subscribers (subscriber)		58546
全社会用电量（万千瓦时）	Total Consumption of Electricity (10 000 kwh)	51474	20695
#居民生活用电量	Household Consumption of Electricity	13319	10172
社会消费品零售总额（亿元）	Total Retail Sale of Consumer Goods 100 million yuan)	39.86	23.82
固定资产投资（不含农户）（亿元）	Investment in Fixed Assets (100 million yuan)	122.07	35.54
新增固定资产（万元）	Newly Increased Fixed Assets (10 000 yuan)	419799	175279
房地产开发投资完成额（万元）	Real Estate Development (10 000 yuan)	78334	
#住宅	Residential Buildings	64088	
住宅竣工面积（万平方米）	Completed Floor Space of Residential Buildings (10 000 sq.m)		
普通中学数（所）	Number of Regular Secondary Schools (unit)	10	17

Continued

藤 县 Tengxian County	蒙山县 Mengshan County	岑溪市 Cenxi City	海城区 Haicheng District	银海区 Yinhai District	铁山港区 Tieshangang District	合浦县 Hepu County	港口区 Gangkou District
12995	6623	10157	1307	7991	10653	30769	1591
49492	12899	69676	9655	757686	236963	1458040	2803
1128037	244546	465961	46965	139583	85377	616593	21660
179090	45276	217335	13749	10876	6167	90975	1692
56291	14337	79303	5557	15142	11720	95130	2333
36063	11463	38903	4219	8176	7640	54896	786
2955	1669	2989	37	1014	150	19197	2176
6	215	411	451	540	0	690	0
31988	12233	22411	249319	241244	190600	465631	222725
81	24	90	96	12	14	75	54
4304675	940695	6303950	13142176	69777	9096159	1882940	12879897
84300	5493	44454	45939	1393	7326	12619	18598
4098150	857913	6109018	13294709	62998	8620997	1452982	10691046
1989	121	1698	75	697	394	2036	312
3089	7600	78588	175200		17000	82320	
93	8	65	521			26	
54	10	60	555			208	
28667	7539	28544	237900			59599	42356
529285	170128	589301	571890			806623	95101
85290	25946	124184	236500			129837	61679
139740	32770	99951	204752	62025	320040	128156	457147
32220	9383	34589	47618	27803	10093	49797	23568
92.64	17.74	83.67	129.66	19.85	11.42	89.21	24.72
278.54	69.01	308.50	367.14	265.65	211.16	255.73	348.80
1771505	606611	2951240	2186975	209739	1630441	2090491	1776530
140737	32109	133728	838866	764600		54713	451415
111877	23009	114185	620752	665290		52469	361056
23.79	14.63	14.53	85.30	70.72		80.85	14.67
38	9	34	14	10	7	39	5

23－1 续表14

指 标	Item	龙圩区 Longxu District	苍梧县 Cangwu County
小学数（所）	Number of Primary Schools (unit)	64	133
普通中学专任教师数（人）	Full-time Teachers in Regular Secondary Schools (person)	608	1280
小学专任教师数（人）	Full-time Teachers in Primary Schools (person)	1515	1916
普通中学在校学生数（人）	Student Enrollment in Regular Secondary Schools (person)	11477	20751
小学在校学生数（人）	Primary Student Enrollment (person)	29049	30402
专业技术人员（人）	Number of Professionals (person)	2123	4571
#农业技术人员	Agricultural Professionals (person)		54
医疗卫生机构床位数（张）	Number of Beds in Heathcare Institutions (bed)	585	390
医疗卫生机构技术人员（人）	Medical & Technical Personnel of Heathcare Institutions (person)	1116	720
#执业（助理）医师	Practitioner (assistant) Doctors	521	200
居民人均可支配收入（元）	Per Capita Annual Disposable Income of Households (yuan)		12214
城镇居民人均可支配收入（元）	Per Capita Annual Disposable Income of Urban Households (yuan)	27206	21952
农村居民人均可支配收入（元）	Annual Per Capita Net Income of Rural Residents (yuan)	10680	8115
各种社会福利收养性单位数（个）	Number of Adopting Units of Social Welfare (unit)		5
各种社会福利收养性单位床位数（张）	Number of Beds in Adopting Units of Social Welfare (bed)		105
城镇基本养老保险参保人数（人）	Number of Persons Joining Basic Pension Insurance (person)		237
城镇基本医疗保险参保人数（人）	Number of Persons Joining Basic Health Care Insurance (person)		4389
失业保险参保人数（人）	Number of Persons Joining Unemployment Insurance (person)		10243
新型农村合作医疗参保人数（人）	Number of Persons Joining New-type Rural Cooperative Medical Service (person)	236796	348822
新型农村社会养老保险参保人数（人）	Number of Persons Joining New-type Rural Social Pension Insurance (person)	125872	200151
城镇居民最低生活保障人数（人）	Number of Urban Residents Receiving Lowest Cost-of-living (person)	626	516
农村居民最低生活保障人数（人）	Number of Rural Residents Receiving Lowest Cost-of-living (person)	11954	24953
森林面积（公顷）	Forest Area (10 000 hectares)	68778	225619
工业二氧化硫排放量（吨）	Volume of Sulfur Dioxide Discharged (ton)		209
氮氧化物排放量（吨）	Volume of Nitrogen Oxides Discharged (ton)		66
烟（粉）尘排放量（吨）	Volume of Smoke & Dust Discharged (ton)		237
污水处理厂数（座）	Number of Effluent Treatment Plants (unit)		1
污水处理厂集中处理率（%）	Rate of Centralized Treatment of Polluted Water (%)		40.0
垃圾处理站数（个）	Number of Garbage Station (unit)		17

Continued

藤　县 Tengxian County	蒙山县 Mengshan County	岑溪市 Cenxi City	海城区 Haicheng District	银海区 Yinhai District	铁山港区 Tieshangang District	合浦县 Hepu County	港口区 Gangkou District
270	62	446	34	40	50	290	27
3423	772	3761	558	674	449	3861	294
5255	926	4404	2013	1043	704	4827	822
57287	10805	55987	5189	7332	5085	58548	4082
89067	16001	85404	46699	22610	13004	79211	15221
10466	3718	10754	2060	1850	1153	11070	1102
536	82	266	12	50	0	614	47
2741	766	3312	3322	761	219	5080	432
2820	712	3149	4880	361	372	4066	674
1278	245	1072	1672	117	103	1681	243
17418	15456	22320	32594				30898
26878	26438	30910	32625	31751	31252	31217	34137
10979	9481	13353	13746	14163	13307	12512	14310
26	8	18	8	19	17	121	3
763	142	413	420	717	173	1251	112
62123	22786	42826	23566	55021	25238	65872	32644
113458	14120	37938	135415	151057	23318	68457	37999
25505	6807	20910				27264	12692
882395	185601	854033	48314		138939	906645	63278
382653	81500	366712	3753		34723	290874	18018
2245	1263	3696	1331	577	356	7168	735
83104	14194	53205	238	2724	4845	30362	2450
283010	99668	202484	735	12117	7400	106254	10200
1229	378	330	5			184	15598
5215	286	724	254			584	13896
1051	414	531	4			231	4318
1	2	3	1	1	4	1	1
90.0	95.6	93.0	100.0	85.0	95.2	95.0	0.0
2	7	1	12	0	3	2	0

23－1 续表15

指 标	Item	防城区 Fangcheng District	上思县 Shangsi County
行政区域面积（平方公里）	Administrative Region Land Area (sq.km)	2426	2814
常住户数（户）	Total Households at Year-end (household)	104120	68265
年末常住人口（万人）	Total Population at Year-end (10 000 persons)	39.16	21.45
年末户籍人口（万人）	Registered Population at Year-end (10 000 persons)	44.00	24.85
地区生产总值（万元）	Gross Domestic Product (10 000 yuan)	1504570	808784
第一产业增加值	Primary Industry	312304	216054
第二产业增加值	Secondary Industry	632068	359731
#工业	Industry	493954	329665
第三产业增加值	Tertiary Industry	560199	232999
人均生产总值（元）	Per Capital GDP (yuan)	38594	37944
地区生产总值指数（上年＝100）	Indices of Gross Domestic Product (preceding year=100)	108.6	104.9
第一产业	Primary Industry	103.7	104.5
第二产业	Secondary Industry	110.1	100.9
#工业	Industry	109.8	99.4
第三产业	Tertiary Industry	109.4	112.6
人均生产总值指数（上年=100）	Indices of Per Capital GDP (preceding year＝100)	107.6	103.7
公共财政预算收入（万元）	Government Revenue (10 000 yuan)	59105	62867
税收收入（万元）	Total Tax Revenue (10 000 yuan)	41537	43766
公共预算支出（万元）	Government Expenditure (10 000 yuan)	233011	229907
年末金融机构各项存款余额（万元）	Year-end Deposits of Financial Institutions (10 000 yuan)		617553
#居民储蓄存款余额	Urban & Rural Savings Deposits		354927
年末金融机构各项贷款余额（万元）	Year-end Loans of Financial Institutions (10 000 yuan)		391831
耕地面积（公顷）	Farmland (hectare)	24763	58010
设施农业占地面积（公顷）	Protected Agriculture Covered (hectare)	63	29
农业机械总动力（万千瓦特）	Total Agricultural Machinery Power (10 000 watts)	23.84	29.63
农作物总播种面积（公顷）	Total Sown Area of Major Farm Crops (hectare)	51519	57308
#粮食	Grain Crops	27347	11889
油料	Oil Crops	1631	762
糖料	Sugar Crops	5605	38989
蔬菜	Vegetables	14643	4002
粮食总产量（吨）	Yield of Grain (ton)	109106	46686
#稻谷	Rice	75212	31827

Continued

东兴市 Dongxing City	钦南区 Qinnan District	钦北区 Qinbei District	灵山县 Lingshan County	浦北县 Pubei County	港北区 Gangbei District	港南区 Gangnan District	覃塘区 Qintang District
589	2596	2217	3558	2526	1097	1099	1352
44179	140959	186461	388462	240658	217713	169597	174513
15.92	57.26	71.32	121.96	77.46	62.04	54.52	43.45
14.96	64.58	86.23	166.17	93.93	70.88	70.00	60.61
1039648	2819385	3099135	2849333	2230291	2194608	1001553	1401570
187582	704333	522468	696240	413639	212881	227053	264108
449829	755243	1393638	1182922	1204505	677870	390045	707073
357473	453212	929322	887072	894905	352370	290495	609193
402236	1359809	1183029	970171	612147	1303857	384455	430389
65738	49576	43677	23488	28959	35575	18496	32448
107.0	109.7	109.5	108.3	109.5	109.0	107.9	111.3
103.8	104.0	104.0	103.9	104.1	103.8	104.0	104.5
110.5	107.3	108.0	112.1	108.9	108.5	109.3	114.4
110.8	106.2	106.3	113.5	110.3	108.1	111.4	115.1
104.6	114.2	113.9	107.6	114.6	110.2	108.9	111.5
105.7	108.5	108.3	107.2	108.2	107.8	106.5	109.9
105476	38788	37941	66892	50068	84774	36692	45298
65365	25702	24017	40340	32193	72656	30003	35810
244970	188932	263560	523877	384339	204663	191324	200516
1461186			2289017	1615400	4403571		
1067436			1986569	1303500			
945688			1134102	814900	3207238	76100	
5543	37890	47675	80201	41983	37046	44162	61548
61	592	302	380	361	689	191	231
10.91	33.9	38.65	63.11	49.28	43.94	57.47	50.4
9709	85156	97959	134972	78915	40218	60109	74583
5946	39159	54712	74452	46490	24821	40630	39413
273	1806	4301	1958	2788	2692	3523	6055
266	14739	14054	18311	7687	6081	2906	14148
3040	20527	17500	19861	11555	4582	5848	9820
23438	175229	272405	384206	247844	151315	229218	217105
19048	124237	226157	336797	206659	116045	190455	153068

23－1　续表16

指　标	Item	防城区 Fangcheng District	上思县 Shangsi County
油料产量（吨）	Yield of Oil-bearing Crops (ton)	3202	1760
糖料产量（吨）	Yield of Sugar Crops (ton)	464787	2630615
蔬菜产量（吨）	Yield of Vegetables (ton)	191335	50409
园林水果（不含瓜类水果）产量（吨）	Yield of Fruit (ton)	55189	18189
肉类总产量（吨）	Output of Meat (ton)	26104	11700
#猪肉（吨）	Pork (ton)	16615	4879
禽蛋产量（吨）	Output of Eggs (ton)	3379	757
奶类产量（吨）	Output of Milk (ton)		4784
水产品产量（吨）	Aquatic Products (ton)	151801	19433
规模以上工业企业个数（个）	Number of Industrial Enterprises above Designated Size (unit)	45	26
规模以上工业总产值（当年价，万元）	Included Gross Industrial Output Value above Designated Size (at current price，10 000 yuan)	1987462	1264145
规模以上工业企业从业人员年平均人数（人）	Annual Average Number of Employed Persons (person)	422	4490
规模以上工业企业主营业务收入（万元）	Income from Major Business (10 000 yuan)	1234458	557754
公路里程（公里）	Length of Domestic Highways (km)	1086	1287
民用汽车拥有量（辆）	Number of Civil Motor Vehicles Owned (vehicle)		1021
年末实有公共汽（电）车营运数（辆）	Year-end Total Operating Public Buses (vehicle)	104	20
年末实有出租汽车数（辆）	Year-end Total Taxis (vehicle)	204	25
固定电话年末用户（户）	Number of Local Telephone Subscribers in Year-end (subscriber)	26279	
年末移动电话用户数（户）	Number of Mobile Telephone Subscribers at Year-end (subscriber)	476054	
互联网宽带接入用户（户）	Number of Internet Subscribers (subscriber)	45706	
全社会用电量（万千瓦时）	Total Consumption of Electricity (10 000 kwh)	66170	26462
#居民生活用电量	Household Consumption of Electricity	22745	12369
社会消费品零售总额（亿元）	Total Retail Sale of Consumer Goods 100 million yuan)	49.47	22.28
固定资产投资（不含农户）（亿元）	Investment in Fixed Assets (100 million yuan)	138.48	55.99
新增固定资产（万元）	Newly Increased Fixed Assets (10 000 yuan)	899070	583445
房地产开发投资完成额（万元）	Real Estate Development (10 000 yuan)	165207	29817
#住宅	Residential Buildings	106793	
住宅竣工面积（万平方米）	Completed Floor Space of Residential Buildings (10 000 sq.m)	14.68	
普通中学数（所）	Number of Regular Secondary Schools (unit)	17	7

Continued

东兴市 Dongxing City	钦南区 Qinnan District	钦北区 Qinbei District	灵山县 Lingshan County	浦北县 Pubei County	港北区 Gangbei District	港南区 Gangnan District	覃塘区 Qintang District
573	4260	12857	5327	7679	8852	12711	19529
14554	869590	1065240	1471502	573083	602251	275531	1117665
43449	425985	469230	404950	209954	135368	133491	181314
11507	75800	442889	814339	708910	17659	15430	16171
7826	43610	106927	95216	63659	58449	46320	47656
4583	14476	21860	40881	41781	45359	34831	38531
469	9349	2379	11373	4693	3386	1925	6195
0	0	0	37266	707	3344	0	87
138616	455853	47689	51784	41187	17597	30477	21464
28	65	56	88	105	75	95	100
1580859	2335633	3293361	3045132	3459800	1843200	1168449	1873301
4626	11635	22223	28958	26021	18800	14287	11174
1276763	1845049	3192867	2959287	3151300	1854800	1080298	1333036
278	1149	1185	2260	1946	655	885	1200
			283500	22704	40960	24211	
100			58	28	220	39	
210			150	55	293	71	
34461			98960	100000		56210	48888
252448			716850	578488		50225	40150
36712			122580	45258		18555	15480
53397		43105	112345	65892	159968	72357	199121
29192		8159	53056	32401	37689	27496	18918
27.55	88.92	112.09	106.55	85.57	186.46	46.86	45.88
129.50	300.32	230.40	225.62	222.40	232.40	153.08	124.95
1176668	1436648	1686985	1653043	1395349	821105	786662	527736
92560	381097	120254	211501	87200	689957	18570	24992
66726	264611	103343	102840	68413	518124	11193	23367
24.81	49.36	39.20	12.48	17.23	8.03	8.24	20
8	20	20	43	26	20	20	24

23－1 续表17

指 标	Item	防城区 Fangcheng District	上思县 Shangsi County
小学数（所）	Number of Primary Schools (unit)	63	273
普通中学专任教师数（人）	Full-time Teachers in Regular Secondary Schools (person)	925	701
小学专任教师数（人）	Full-time Teachers in Primary Schools (person)	1830	1180
普通中学在校学生数（人）	Student Enrollment in Regular Secondary Schools (person)	15854	11473
小学在校学生数（人）	Primary Student Enrollment (person)	37269	19413
专业技术人员（人）	Number of Professionals (person)	3376	117
#农业技术人员	Agricultural Professionals (person)	105	
医疗卫生机构床位数（张）	Number of Beds in Heathcare Institutions (bed)	1014	911
医疗卫生机构技术人员（人）	Medical & Technical Personnel of Heathcare Institutions (person)	1613	1116
#执业（助理）医师	Practitioner (assistant) Doctors	458	353
居民人均可支配收入（元）	Per Capita Annual Disposable Income of Households (yuan)	24251	
城镇居民人均可支配收入（元）	Per Capita Annual Disposable Income of Urban Households (yuan)	33617	21971
农村居民人均可支配收入（元）	Annual Per Capita Net Income of Rural Residents (yuan)	13883	10939
各种社会福利收养性单位数（个）	Number of Adopting Units of Social Welfare (unit)	37	16
各种社会福利收养性单位床位数（张）	Number of Beds in Adopting Units of Social Welfare (bed)	838	373
城镇基本养老保险参保人数（人）	Number of Persons Joining Basic Pension Insurance (person)	35445	26821
城镇基本医疗保险参保人数（人）	Number of Persons Joining Basic Health Care Insurance (person)	92472	72709
失业保险参保人数（人）	Number of Persons Joining Unemployment Insurance (person)	17250	11162
新型农村合作医疗参保人数（人）	Number of Persons Joining New-type Rural Cooperative Medical Service (person)	298806	149452
新型农村社会养老保险参保人数（人）	Number of Persons Joining New-type Rural Social Pension Insurance (person)	115188	91048
城镇居民最低生活保障人数（人）	Number of Urban Residents Receiving Lowest Cost-of-living (person)	1280	2312
农村居民最低生活保障人数（人）	Number of Rural Residents Receiving Lowest Cost-of-living (person)	15721	11228
森林面积（公顷）	Forest Area (10 000 hectares)	161553	157157
工业二氧化硫排放量（吨）	Volume of Sulfur Dioxide Discharged (ton)		
氮氧化物排放量（吨）	Volume of Nitrogen Oxides Discharged (ton)		
烟（粉）尘排放量（吨）	Volume of Smoke & Dust Discharged (ton)		
污水处理厂数（座）	Number of Effluent Treatment Plants (unit)		4
污水处理厂集中处理率（%）	Rate of Centralized Treatment of Polluted Water (%)	90.1	91.8
垃圾处理站数（个）	Number of Garbage Station (unit)	8	16

Continued

东兴市 Dongxing City	钦南区 Qinnan District	钦北区 Qinbei District	灵山县 Lingshan County	浦北县 Pubei County	港北区 Gangbei District	港南区 Gangnan District	覃塘区 Qintang District
50	158	338	410	382	99	126	133
735	1689	1240	4238	2867	2065	2010	2396
1302	3173	4548	7380	4290	3605	2661	2306
10303	24871	31120	86441	47184	28841	28010	33633
22550	62397	88197	144332	73420	71703	51633	44792
2217	4298	6905	13538	8032	5083	5271	5465
32	222	65	886	319	73	70	65
457	889	1828	4643	3328	3689	842	1411
934	1114	2053	6645	4055	1380	856	1518
414	342	587	1604	797	1260	363	146
31275	23793	20298	16165	31069	26482	19457	20549
37652	32113	31024	31467	31069	30704	29651	29155
16471	12211	11777	11777	11573	13277	12720	13213
27	134	1	276	221	9	21	11
337	1585	271	3665	11052	96	355	240
1777	28700	28692	9497	63843	199310	39437	
28754	63547	22932	36389	82047	581914	53304	
9155	9900	6500	28700	17157			
105901	369200	683692	1315482	728458	583517	545745	540452
52747	111400	278999	496559	288325	199310	203469	179909
459	3960	1366	2707	2680	840	466	394
2746	20051	27591	74241	47225	12070	11728	26760
32026		112557	199994	149194	46865	37630	45788
249			556	820	16502	181	2747
47			247	168	10506	193	12464
80			251	658	32568	354	
3		9	14	1	1	0	1
95.3		100.0	96.0	95.1		0.0	25.0
6		17	41	6	1	0	0

23－1 续表18

指 标	Item	平南县 Pingnan County	桂平市 Guiping City
行政区域面积（平方公里）	Administrative Region Land Area (sq.km)	2984	4071
常住户数（户）	Total Households at Year-end (household)	428606	534892
年末常住人口（万人）	Total Population at Year-end (10 000 persons)	119.16	158.37
年末户籍人口（万人）	Registered Population at Year-end (10 000 persons)	152.47	201.74
地区生产总值（万元）	Gross Domestic Product (10 000 yuan)	2681731	3574288
第一产业增加值	Primary Industry	562707	669737
第二产业增加值	Secondary Industry	1116304	1772209
#工业	Industry	1014604	1523559
第三产业增加值	Tertiary Industry	1002720	1132342
人均生产总值（元）	Per Capital GDP (yuan)	22608	22663
地区生产总值指数（上年＝100）	Indices of Gross Domestic Product (preceding year=100)	108.7	108.6
第一产业	Primary Industry	104.0	104.6
第二产业	Secondary Industry	111.4	110.8
#工业	Industry	112.4	110.4
第三产业	Tertiary Industry	108.9	107.8
人均生产总值指数（上年=100）	Indices of Per Capital GDP (preceding year＝100)	107.8	107.8
公共财政预算收入（万元）	Government Revenue (10 000 yuan)	117696	101439
税收收入（万元）	Total Tax Revenue (10 000 yuan)	74294	60722
公共预算支出（万元）	Government Expenditure (10 000 yuan)	572451	685055
年末金融机构各项存款余额（万元）	Year-end Deposits of Financial Institutions (10 000 yuan)	2631837	3832830
#居民储蓄存款余额	Urban & Rural Savings Deposits	2221941	3026121
年末金融机构各项贷款余额（万元）	Year-end Loans of Financial Institutions (10 000 yuan)	1732896	1989225
耕地面积（公顷）	Farmland (hectare)	61080	116632
设施农业占地面积（公顷）	Protected Agriculture Covered (hectare)	1	88
农业机械总动力（万千瓦特）	Total Agricultural Machinery Power (10 000 watts)	86.19	127.82
农作物总播种面积（公顷）	Total Sown Area of Major Farm Crops (hectare)	106074	169264
#粮食	Grain Crops	63810	102340
油料	Oil Crops	9220	11538
糖料	Sugar Crops	1838	2835
蔬菜	Vegetables	16781	31657
粮食总产量（吨）	Yield of Grain (ton)	347291	551340
#稻谷	Rice	302132	479214

Continued

玉州区 Yuzhou District	福绵区 Fumian District	容 县 Rongxian County	陆川县 Luchuan County	博白县 Bobai County	兴业县 Xingye County	北流市 Beiliu City	右江区 Youjiang District
436	829	2255	1554	3830	1468	2452	3718
190461	117778	210108	327412	519820	215211	418790	108826
73.33	40.02	66.99	80.28	141.30	58.87	120.29	40.01
68.09	43.72	86.63	110.11	188.11	76.02	151.50	36.31
4146828	781907	2160937	2492622	2544497	1628259	3240459	2872060
171599	234877	382394	334959	805084	367859	472342	292363
1586563	295046	1138324	1162067	797820	716302	1541844	1444657
1166645	144592	1024218	999924	591750	410698	1207320	1201296
2388666	251985	640218	995595	941593	544098	1226273	1135040
57040	19614	32398	31193	18074	27762	27064	72054
108.9	107.8	108.3	105.5	107.8	108.0	108.1	111.1
103.5	102.9	103.9	103.1	103.8	102.5	102.6	103.9
109.2	111.4	109.1	103.2	107.5	109.0	109.0	110.5
107.8	104.6	108.8	103.7	106.7	107.6	109.2	109.8
109.1	108.5	109.9	109.5	112.0	110.9	109.1	113.7
107.3	107.0	107.5	104.6	107.0	107.3	107.1	110.4
154378	37341	102398	113700	125073	80494	162475	64086
94478	22921	64640	68684	77758	50318	99438	45462
286881	166229	394379	491539	693231	348930	526161	251281
		2314229	1892528	2799705	1342981	3193221	3564375
		1767487	1581898	2388282	1132879	2623840	1634441
		1277601	1050878	1739127	855876	2074967	2632327
27596		28978	33344	71543	33660	41110	30032
	9144	136	270	451	751	181	56
18.05	24.82	56.47	53.9	60.4	38.46	58.28	17.95
25959	46127	60441	60757	145271	64750	89979	47616
14959	27137	38370	43765	85248	40174	57450	17567
1030	1081	1430	2131	4711	2371	4420	796
122	2102	280	1439	10112	1120	1094	11667
9085	12301	15519	9737	33744	13568	19584	13526
88927	159624	218530	256785	467613	236456	319937	78493
84265	147730	197672	234798	356951	213900	285774	39580

23－1 续表19

指 标	Item	平南县 Pingnan County	桂平市 Guiping City
油料产量（吨）	Yield of Oil-bearing Crops (ton)	32787	42061
糖料产量（吨）	Yield of Sugar Crops (ton)	159178	261627
蔬菜产量（吨）	Yield of Vegetables (ton)	597499	668084
园林水果（不含瓜类水果）产量（吨）	Yield of Fruit (ton)	127423	133791
肉类总产量（吨）	Output of Meat (ton)	108828	119490
#猪肉（吨）	Pork (ton)	82646	82644
禽蛋产量（吨）	Output of Eggs (ton)	6940	8847
奶类产量（吨）	Output of Milk (ton)	602	1353
水产品产量（吨）	Aquatic Products (ton)	92866	88561
规模以上工业企业个数（个）	Number of Industrial Enterprises above Designated Size (unit)	127	112
规模以上工业总产值（当年价，万元）	Included Gross Industrial Output Value above Designated Size (at current price，10 000 yuan)	2980385	4005758
规模以上工业企业从业人员年平均人数（人）	Annual Average Number of Employed Persons (person)	54821	62397
规模以上工业企业主营业务收入（万元）	Income from Major Business (10 000 yuan)	2801941	3932389
公路里程（公里）	Length of Domestic Highways (km)	1524	2896
民用汽车拥有量（辆）	Number of Civil Motor Vehicles Owned (vehicle)	33925	74896
年末实有公共汽（电）车营运数（辆）	Year-end Total Operating Public Buses (vehicle)	131	81
年末实有出租汽车数（辆）	Year-end Total Taxis (vehicle)	100	281
固定电话年末用户（户）	Number of Local Telephone Subscribers in Year-end (subscriber)	110520	52265
年末移动电话用户数（户）	Number of Mobile Telephone Subscribers at Year-end (subscriber)	559015	995347
互联网宽带接入用户（户）	Number of Internet Subscribers (subscriber)	71740	156938
全社会用电量（万千瓦时）	Total Consumption of Electricity (10 000 kwh)	186971	164261
#居民生活用电量	Household Consumption of Electricity	53701	62596
社会消费品零售总额（亿元）	Total Retail Sale of Consumer Goods 100 million yuan)	72.27	129.24
固定资产投资（不含农户）（亿元）	Investment in Fixed Assets (100 million yuan)	205.80	267.59
新增固定资产（万元）	Newly Increased Fixed Assets (10 000 yuan)	1108385	1601288
房地产开发投资完成额（万元）	Real Estate Development (10 000 yuan)	361355	271053
#住宅	Residential Buildings	315258	233860
住宅竣工面积（万平方米）	Completed Floor Space of Residential Buildings (10 000 sq.m)	11.28	5.00
普通中学数（所）	Number of Regular Secondary Schools (unit)	62	74

Continued

玉州区 Yuzhou District	福绵区 Fumian District	容　县 Rongxian County	陆川县 Luchuan County	博白县 Bobai County	兴业县 Xingye County	北流市 Beiliu City	右江区 Youjiang District
3321	3807	3905	6575	15694	6659	18630	1703
12505		21098	114660	1219590	89238	100560	610950
280031	436759	391895	344578	831019	279533	718081	362907
25810	58692	198445	72443	346398	48590	329605	237094
31266	58590	86738	114964	216619	169391	90313	30624
20821	19672	42981	79129	171239	55559	57543	15239
7087	26615	17450	10086	5840	4072	6069	343
30		294	154	507		4663	0
16150	14773	14267	29044	47529	9761	35730	27920
59	24	86	83	86	41	139	49
2648800	196046	3018494	3665548	2331865	1310191	4263089	3204448
21968		34782	15339	26923	5573	77868	16049
2458226		2882270	3270635	2148156	1032307	4176626	2640086
1159		1347	1671	2733	1053	1687	1549
75630	16785	33467	41966	77063	42370	56446	127211
1319	45	374	283	527	19	476	214
653		119	85	75	53	72	620
162249	509	58108	47300	64342	26000	102997	38712
968953	222868	551389	448856	912019	407500	153524	553451
191204	13526	100114	91800	77552	84423	82018	104655
240700		74927	99240	145028	87314	159690	452578
62300		32060	34839	63808	21470	50075	40000
320.02	18.36	70.41	64.08	109.68	36.31	110.00	86.48
446.62	108.89	188.77	223.30	271.81	172.33	277.61	180.01
	127541	971667	2233000	1778437	1138327	1612254	703741
975359	39338	174675	97899	202172	23011	324578	455757
848		142690	97889	171912	19804	217424	325004
		25.59	7.29	28.42	4.75	65.10	11.86
18	12	31	34	79	27	51	21

23－1 续表20

指 标	Item	平南县 Pingnan County	桂平市 Guiping City
小学数（所）	Number of Primary Schools (unit)	280	252
普通中学专任教师数（人）	Full-time Teachers in Regular Secondary Schools (person)	3800	7042
小学专任教师数（人）	Full-time Teachers in Primary Schools (person)	7000	7885
普通中学在校学生数（人）	Student Enrollment in Regular Secondary Schools (person)	76027	112168
小学在校学生数（人）	Primary Student Enrollment (person)	120301	166905
专业技术人员（人）	Number of Professionals (person)	25622	89489
#农业技术人员	Agricultural Professionals (person)	195	184
医疗卫生机构床位数（张）	Number of Beds in Heathcare Institutions (bed)	4922	4819
医疗卫生机构技术人员（人）	Medical & Technical Personnel of Heathcare Institutions (person)	5076	6158
#执业（助理）医师	Practitioner (assistant) Doctors	1715	2013
居民人均可支配收入（元）	Per Capita Annual Disposable Income of Households (yuan)	19919	19200
城镇居民人均可支配收入（元）	Per Capita Annual Disposable Income of Urban Households (yuan)	28767	28270
农村居民人均可支配收入（元）	Annual Per Capita Net Income of Rural Residents (yuan)	12399	12644
各种社会福利收养性单位数（个）	Number of Adopting Units of Social Welfare (unit)	167	222
各种社会福利收养性单位床位数（张）	Number of Beds in Adopting Units of Social Welfare (bed)	2571	2413
城镇基本养老保险参保人数（人）	Number of Persons Joining Basic Pension Insurance (person)	42821	90072
城镇基本医疗保险参保人数（人）	Number of Persons Joining Basic Health Care Insurance (person)	130637	123951
失业保险参保人数（人）	Number of Persons Joining Unemployment Insurance (person)	26825	33500
新型农村合作医疗参保人数（人）	Number of Persons Joining New-type Rural Cooperative Medical Service (person)	1254986	1664188
新型农村社会养老保险参保人数（人）	Number of Persons Joining New-type Rural Social Pension Insurance (person)	491277	649970
城镇居民最低生活保障人数（人）	Number of Urban Residents Receiving Lowest Cost-of-living (person)	9860	4288
农村居民最低生活保障人数（人）	Number of Rural Residents Receiving Lowest Cost-of-living (person)	70898	63887
森林面积（公顷）	Forest Area (10 000 hectares)	177706	194762
工业二氧化硫排放量（吨）	Volume of Sulfur Dioxide Discharged (ton)	1850	609
氮氧化物排放量（吨）	Volume of Nitrogen Oxides Discharged (ton)	11000	1302
烟（粉）尘排放量（吨）	Volume of Smoke & Dust Discharged (ton)	18757	226
污水处理厂数（座）	Number of Effluent Treatment Plants (unit)	5	1
污水处理厂集中处理率（%）	Rate of Centralized Treatment of Polluted Water (%)	87.3	87.4
垃圾处理站数（个）	Number of Garbage Station (unit)	1	1

Continued

玉州区 Yuzhou District	福绵区 Fumian District	容　县 Rongxian County	陆川县 Luchuan County	博白县 Bobai County	兴业县 Xingye County	北流市 Beiliu City	右江区 Youjiang District
89	107	144	160	346	161	359	55
1773	958	2822	3367	5599	1887	5150	2227
2429	1369	3151	4892	8890	2906	8059	2182
25898	15817	51620	58586	101313	32482	95741	38821
63617	30933	81609	92111	158605	52955	171458	32825
	2327	7943	10564	19043	5406	14687	3767
		316	206	333	59	280	111
5896	556	2860	2727	3710	1551	3768	4123
	588	2825	2771	3052	1503	3896	5093
	212	1717	1130	1193	655	1556	1644
32071		0		18234	17994	25229	24807
36922	34360	29856	28950	27071	27663	34006	31810
15487	13231	12979	12783	12883	12228	14605	13503
19	7	77	76	68	131	46	41
708	174	982	1374	3560	1426	716	2114
59156	146695	40265	38426	91346	241003	88863	31068
139635	366396	124702	110956	165900	655335	207730	78712
16145	4285	21008	22011	24071	10594	24130	11228
441272		608241	902764	1341000	641955	1277870	224994
133592		334650	319300	588220	241003	368041	120723
3587	58	1367	6886	7537	729	7969	1033
23698	8849	33415	74668	60909	32953	82034	12696
14783		160554	91236	245240	90313	150675	238897
1320		158	1460	1102	584	3011	1929
349		93	5706	602	3241	6906	452
1726		246	4568	2255	1386	3861	3629
2		6	9	3	13	2	1
99.2		88.2	95.0	94.0	96.8	98.0	69.4
1		19	3	3	9	1	1

23－1　续表21

指　标	Item	田阳县 Tianyang County	田东县 Tiandong County
行政区域面积（平方公里）	Administrative Region Land Area (sq.km)	2373	2811
常住户数（户）	Total Households at Year-end (household)	105797	112965
年末常住人口（万人）	Total Population at Year-end (10 000 persons)	32.80	37.60
年末户籍人口（万人）	Registered Population at Year-end (10 000 persons)	35.61	43.66
地区生产总值（万元）	Gross Domestic Product (10 000 yuan)	1750447	1600133
第一产业增加值	Primary Industry	289508	292111
第二产业增加值	Secondary Industry	1111199	947263
#工业	Industry	1000267	790739
第三产业增加值	Tertiary Industry	349739	360760
人均生产总值（元）	Per Capital GDP (yuan)	53621	42699
地区生产总值指数（上年＝100)	Indices of Gross Domestic Product (preceding year=100)	110.6	104.9
第一产业	Primary Industry	105.6	104.3
第二产业	Secondary Industry	112.4	104.5
#工业	Industry	113.1	105.1
第三产业	Tertiary Industry	110.4	106.4
人均生产总值指数（上年=100)	Indices of Per Capital GDP (preceding year＝100)	109.7	104.2
公共财政预算收入（万元）	Government Revenue (10 000 yuan)	82457	73230
税收收入（万元）	Total Tax Revenue (10 000 yuan)	41892	43494
公共预算支出（万元）	Government Expenditure (10 000 yuan)	296992	297133
年末金融机构各项存款余额（万元）	Year-end Deposits of Financial Institutions (10 000 yuan)	1031826	1215394
#居民储蓄存款余额	Urban & Rural Savings Deposits	674607	827006
年末金融机构各项贷款余额（万元）	Year-end Loans of Financial Institutions (10 000 yuan)	884984	1046009
耕地面积（公顷）	Farmland (hectare)	36742	70507
设施农业占地面积（公顷）	Protected Agriculture Covered (hectare)	86	3288
农业机械总动力（万千瓦特）	Total Agricultural Machinery Power (10 000 watts)	40.64	33.91
农作物总播种面积（公顷）	Total Sown Area of Major Farm Crops (hectare)	52687	64111
#粮食	Grain Crops	22009	24326
油料	Oil Crops	697	743
糖料	Sugar Crops	3245	15771
蔬菜	Vegetables	25129	20370
粮食总产量（吨）	Yield of Grain (ton)	115346	115067
#稻谷	Rice	63198	70089

Continued

平果县 Pingguo County	德保县 Debao County	那坡县 Napo County	凌云县 Lingyun County	乐业县 Leye County	田林县 Tianlin County	西林县 Xilin County	隆林各族自治县 Longlin County
2457	2575	2223	2047	2633	5524	2997	3518
146610	97545	50428	59727	49850	60722	38423	107507
46.07	30.83	16.14	19.53	15.59	23.37	14.64	35.83
51.60	36.87	21.74	22.36	17.81	26.55	16.15	43.00
2010727	996916	267894	342789	251798	565246	252956	540189
163164	107809	72704	85351	71170	144672	101156	112715
1429617	671718	67769	142116	56026	231272	50136	207774
1317400	566309	49521	102744	19415	197004	25004	173817
417946	217389	127421	115322	124603	189302	101664	219700
43840	32394	16696	17642	16203	24275	17361	15110
110.8	109.3	105.3	106.3	107.8	112.0	106.3	105.5
104.3	104.3	103.9	104.9	104.4	105.6	106.2	104.4
112.4	111.2	102.0	105.6	113.4	120.2	115.3	103.5
112.2	112.1	103.1	108.8	108.5	121.0	113.1	104.2
109.1	107.1	107.7	108.2	107.6	110.1	102.6	108.2
109.9	108.9	104.2	105.3	107.0	111.2	105.4	104.9
164088	61375	22660	14248	12607	22512	10919	33047
99850	40565	13492	9903	8314	15623	7361	23730
374632	261088	233520	236464	181026	236740	180067	291217
1387776	678032	456185	504133	404236	652791	371317	774848
949548	458492	287141	324874	223985	386827	200893	512054
1367310	515167	231285	315871	237044	448206	228253	506553
45916	40110	27384	16986	25129	20946	22035	50821
150	40	14	2	42	0	15	
34	24.38	19	9	16	23.4	18.11	29
40200	37116	24776	20544	19488	36016	22050	32985
26277	25833	16731	13944	11725	20385	14170	22267
476	705	229	1346	2285	801	1510	1754
3698	2526	161	229	48	6300	487	525
7852	6505	4441	3501	3280	6033	3686	3875
108056	100813	62246	51229	51232	94339	55263	88917
53374	48140	23566	21134	18077	39094	21127	36264

23－1　续表22

指　标	Item	田阳县 Tianyang County	田东县 Tiandong County
油料产量（吨）	Yield of Oil-bearing Crops (ton)	1491	1644
糖料产量（吨）	Yield of Sugar Crops (ton)	180261	784740
蔬菜产量（吨）	Yield of Vegetables (ton)	707115	482290
园林水果（不含瓜类水果）产量（吨）	Yield of Fruit (ton)	238951	319073
肉类总产量（吨）	Output of Meat (ton)	28612	32026
#猪肉（吨）	Pork (ton)	19788	20969
禽蛋产量（吨）	Output of Eggs (ton)	335	2795
奶类产量（吨）	Output of Milk (ton)	0	0
水产品产量（吨）	Aquatic Products (ton)	21703	20800
规模以上工业企业个数（个）	Number of Industrial Enterprises above Designated Size (unit)	38	37
规模以上工业总产值（当年价，万元）	Included Gross Industrial Output Value above Designated Size (at current price，10 000 yuan)	2690156	2251659
规模以上工业企业从业人员年平均人数（人）	Annual Average Number of Employed Persons (person)	7636	9566
规模以上工业企业主营业务收入（万元）	Income from Major Business (10 000 yuan)	1328782	1295766
公路里程（公里）	Length of Domestic Highways (km)	183	1359
民用汽车拥有量（辆）	Number of Civil Motor Vehicles Owned (vehicle)	68573	75953
年末实有公共汽（电）车营运数（辆）	Year-end Total Operating Public Buses (vehicle)	84	127
年末实有出租汽车数（辆）	Year-end Total Taxis (vehicle)	106	245
固定电话年末用户（户）	Number of Local Telephone Subscribers in Year-end (subscriber)	13909	16270
年末移动电话用户数（户）	Number of Mobile Telephone Subscribers at Year-end (subscriber)	263272	92772
互联网宽带接入用户（户）	Number of Internet Subscribers (subscriber)	50595	37980
全社会用电量（万千瓦时）	Total Consumption of Electricity (10 000 kwh)	503724	163181
#居民生活用电量	Household Consumption of Electricity	16510	20260
社会消费品零售总额（亿元）	Total Retail Sale of Consumer Goods 100 million yuan)	28.29	24.46
固定资产投资（不含农户）（亿元）	Investment in Fixed Assets (100 million yuan)	172.23	196.91
新增固定资产（万元）	Newly Increased Fixed Assets (10 000 yuan)	157843	1039390
房地产开发投资完成额（万元）	Real Estate Development (10 000 yuan)	73173	184615
#住宅	Residential Buildings	73173	123641
住宅竣工面积（万平方米）	Completed Floor Space of Residential Buildings (10 000 sq.m)	9.06	8.10
普通中学数（所）	Number of Regular Secondary Schools (unit)	7	17

Continued

平果县 Pingguo County	德保县 Debao County	那坡县 Napo County	凌云县 Lingyun County	乐业县 Leye County	田林县 Tianlin County	西林县 Xilin County	隆林各族自治县 Longlin County
828	1130	332	1229	2171	807	1727	2091
188989	151100	9301	15846	2539	355395	32042	36304
153981	132922	75863	61865	63331	121048	62718	74750
58406	43228	9120	8611	10185	43570	127252	29340
37037	20477	12156	12789	9614	22298	11018	20202
21191	11169	7994	9104	6581	14330	6285	13194
1159	1230	211	115	133	514	380	1065
0			0		0	0	
10250	2330	920	1090	20328	4634	19360	31436
60	24	11	22	9	40	7	20
3479123	1418646	108200	273866	29068	539291	58426	362300
16894	7466	1233	2578	841	3307	1030	2242
2612104	956201	85685	229095	22810	430578	39299	354000
1257	1117	333	1379	1220	1897	849	1859
14046	16931	34600	35002	31285	50993	7485	72355
161	65	32	28	50	67	42	45
87	79	17	11	43		42	
17918	11574	5691	5746	3217	6565	4931	7512
383229	223087	134074	145796	119757	179238	127685	257106
71617	36940	21146	21904	17087	27967	17018	39148
228075	145931	25516	25913	12200	36444	12629	90486
25977	13783	7056	11934	7747	10479	6355	1065
32.92	13.52	7.04	7.71	12.14	6.93	17.16	31.53
205.96	106.80	28.53	43.26	32.74	36.17	32.08	43.57
1870201	269917	280549	249280	90320	203851	144992	181665
189445	3180	7000		16347	2358	12954	100
157413	2930				2358	10992	40
5.80	0.00				2.78	6.20	15.00
11	13	10	10	13	15	9	19

23－1　续表23

指　标	Item	田阳县 Tianyang County	田东县 Tiandong County
小学数（所）	Number of Primary Schools (unit)	71	152
普通中学专任教师数（人）	Full-time Teachers in Regular Secondary Schools (person)	932	1205
小学专任教师数（人）	Full-time Teachers in Primary Schools (person)	1165	1790
普通中学在校学生数（人）	Student Enrollment in Regular Secondary Schools (person)	15047	15381
小学在校学生数（人）	Primary Student Enrollment (person)	27488	34878
专业技术人员（人）	Number of Professionals (person)	3233	5111
#农业技术人员	Agricultural Professionals (person)	143	101
医疗卫生机构床位数（张）	Number of Beds in Heathcare Institutions (bed)	1366	2286
医疗卫生机构技术人员（人）	Medical & Technical Personnel of Heathcare Institutions (person)	1328	2133
#执业（助理）医师	Practitioner (assistant) Doctors	353	1416
居民人均可支配收入（元）	Per Capita Annual Disposable Income of Households (yuan)	19111	20359
城镇居民人均可支配收入（元）	Per Capita Annual Disposable Income of Urban Households (yuan)	30337	31425
农村居民人均可支配收入（元）	Annual Per Capita Net Income of Rural Residents (yuan)	12109	13516
各种社会福利收养性单位数（个）	Number of Adopting Units of Social Welfare (unit)	47	107
各种社会福利收养性单位床位数（张）	Number of Beds in Adopting Units of Social Welfare (bed)	653	1055
城镇基本养老保险参保人数（人）	Number of Persons Joining Basic Pension Insurance (person)	19161	31728
城镇基本医疗保险参保人数（人）	Number of Persons Joining Basic Health Care Insurance (person)	26076	49998
失业保险参保人数（人）	Number of Persons Joining Unemployment Insurance (person)	9471	11911
新型农村合作医疗参保人数（人）	Number of Persons Joining New-type Rural Cooperative Medical Service (person)	302222	384844
新型农村社会养老保险参保人数（人）	Number of Persons Joining New-type Rural Social Pension Insurance (person)	178501	166873
城镇居民最低生活保障人数（人）	Number of Urban Residents Receiving Lowest Cost-of-living (person)	829	1998
农村居民最低生活保障人数（人）	Number of Rural Residents Receiving Lowest Cost-of-living (person)	34593	47675
森林面积（公顷）	Forest Area (10 000 hectares)	164927	115121
工业二氧化硫排放量（吨）	Volume of Sulfur Dioxide Discharged (ton)	4865	1273
氮氧化物排放量（吨）	Volume of Nitrogen Oxides Discharged (ton)	2500	2677
烟（粉）尘排放量（吨）	Volume of Smoke & Dust Discharged (ton)	1527	1050
污水处理厂数（座）	Number of Effluent Treatment Plants (unit)	1	2
污水处理厂集中处理率（%）	Rate of Centralized Treatment of Polluted Water (%)	95.1	85.0
垃圾处理站数（个）	Number of Garbage Station (unit)	1	1

Continued

平果县 Pingguo County	德保县 Debao County	那坡县 Napo County	凌云县 Lingyun County	乐业县 Leye County	田林县 Tianlin County	西林县 Xilin County	隆林各族自治县 Longlin County
158	49	101	40	74	92	49	159
1779	933	470	696	656	630	560	1102
2023	1688	912	1075	1019	1240	921	1959
28750	15561	7578	20726	11420	15925	10519	26151
38986	24448	16467	17510	15552	24128	15816	45290
5131	5169	4509	2299	1985	3013	2245	3880
168	52	101	37	135	152	72	90
1884	1113	878	710	413	977	567	1297
2702	1169	475	563	512	972	737	1507
866	274	238	83	129	218	93	396
20497	15731	11688	12957	13408	14167	13760	13415
31924	30585	23318	26551	27856	27241	24122	28961
11465	9469	7628	8098	8241	10286	9275	8401
167	12	31	11	9	16	11	18
2780	890	480	267	230	269	360	681
15730	7072	109044	5196	9099	11467	69301	14588
24508	11925	201507	21385	12876	30124	17341	15476
11163	6031	5230	7983	3238	5615	3880	6991
415841	323006		192936	152344	217108	142287	362314
150047	182340		91916	74839	113970	70041	166037
1950	1465	2234	2983	1222	2121	1713	2164
43771	44930	33459	37933	19527	51746	19309	56349
142755	138969	163785	160091	195017	384723	193018	269354
2961	4517	341	73	30	17	380	188
1031	3770	175	485	20	49	140	1
632	688	208	396	15	465	30	132
1	1	1	4	1	1	1	1
99.2	92.2	98.1	80.0	95.8	96.6	90.6	98.4
30	4	1	1	1	1	5	1

23－1　续表24

指　标	Item	靖西市 Jingxi City	八步区 Babu District
行政区域面积（平方公里）	Administrative Region Land Area (sq.km)	3326	5517
常住户数（户）	Total Households at Year-end (household)	147897	199636
年末常住人口（万人）	Total Population at Year-end (10 000 persons)	52.24	64.95
年末户籍人口（万人）	Registered Population at Year-end (10 000 persons)	65.91	74.02
地区生产总值（万元）	Gross Domestic Product (10 000 yuan)	2154823	1724822
第一产业增加值	Primary Industry	159655	314636
第二产业增加值	Secondary Industry	1622588	521489
#工业	Industry	1546057	294665
第三产业增加值	Tertiary Industry	372579	888697
人均生产总值（元）	Per Capital GDP (yuan)	41363	26677
地区生产总值指数（上年＝100）	Indices of Gross Domestic Product (preceding year=100)	107.1	103.5
第一产业	Primary Industry	104.3	104.3
第二产业	Secondary Industry	106.5	91.7
#工业	Industry	106.4	84.8
第三产业	Tertiary Industry	110.0	114.2
人均生产总值指数（上年=100）	Indices of Per Capital GDP (preceding year＝100)	106.5	102.8
公共财政预算收入（万元）	Government Revenue (10 000 yuan)	139618	52027
税收收入（万元）	Total Tax Revenue (10 000 yuan)	90924	37904
公共预算支出（万元）	Government Expenditure (10 000 yuan)	495971	337969
年末金融机构各项存款余额（万元）	Year-end Deposits of Financial Institutions (10 000 yuan)	1314485	4393499
#居民储蓄存款余额	Urban & Rural Savings Deposits	831032	2216222
年末金融机构各项贷款余额（万元）	Year-end Loans of Financial Institutions (10 000 yuan)	807169	2837509
耕地面积（公顷）	Farmland (hectare)	67254	30083
设施农业占地面积（公顷）	Protected Agriculture Covered (hectare)	266	731
农业机械总动力（万千瓦特）	Total Agricultural Machinery Power (10 000 watts)	34	32.61
农作物总播种面积（公顷）	Total Sown Area of Major Farm Crops (hectare)	68776	72968
#粮食	Grain Crops	50327	33870
油料	Oil Crops	1018	3518
糖料	Sugar Crops	2703	1809
蔬菜	Vegetables	7955	22940
粮食总产量（吨）	Yield of Grain (ton)	221294	184014
#稻谷	Rice	77840	163300

Continued

平桂区 Pinggui District	昭平县 Zhaoping County	钟山县 Zhongshan County	富川瑶族自治县 Fuchuan County	金城江区 Jinchengjiang District	宜州区 Yizhou District	南丹县 Nandan County	天峨县 Tian' e County
	3224	1472	1540	2346	3857	3905	3184
121770	105985	96684		105084	196236	97425	50595
41.23	35.66	36.74	27.09	34.81	58.43	29.23	16.28
46.10	44.81	44.85	33.75	34.36	66.52	32.43	17.55
1417099	681109	989065	702930	1295798	1270200	1115634	685382
201482	212265	172290	256899	134822	445809	119878	71846
760224	186636	427528	221878	332472	255395	539529	437581
532214	64465	281025	157815	213706	149577	476061	401898
455393	282208	389247	224153	828504	568996	456227	175955
34530	19159	27061	26059	37370	21797	38312	42334
108.1	106.5	108.0	104.5	112.0	106.2	108.0	107.9
104.1	104.1	104.2	105.0	103.9	104.0	103.8	103.1
109.0	106.1	108.5	99.8	115.2	106.9	109.3	109.3
105.8	98.9	108.5	98.4	118.8	107.7	109.9	110.0
108.8	108.8	109.4	110.0	111.7	107.6	108.0	107.0
107.3	105.8	107.1	103.6	111.2	105.6	107.2	106.8
55080	23150	31887	38916	29306	39925	50579	22772
34261	14402	21652	25969	20698	26954	34947	16003
243631	288780	252898	276000	185458	308481	257747	199066
	905601	1118845	830096	2541121	1596938	859676	480466
	593075	790265	641508	1246953	1252705	606555	262011
	494133	664284	550843	1591093	990270	754800	400837
13977	13834	37405	41787	23013	99123	23564	12753
642	173	445	106	36	44	18	5
21.06	25.05	26.4	18.93	28.45	48.91	25.54	21.2
51268	39121	36965	50919	35619	95006	36167	26189
23120	25340	25350	25079	16695	47575	19828	16901
3172	915	1896	5877	777	2376	2653	973
478	2	113	162	4693	23107	1336	53
14694	8543	6177	15115	9960	14790	8910	4943
119025	137324	140029	127022	71200	217516	84313	64173
96078	115129	119937	93546	40899	117583	49940	22287

23－1 续表25

指 标	Item	靖西市 Jingxi City	八步区 Babu District
油料产量（吨）	Yield of Oil-bearing Crops (ton)	1437	8395
糖料产量（吨）	Yield of Sugar Crops (ton)	185526	108505
蔬菜产量（吨）	Yield of Vegetables (ton)	170882	612025
园林水果（不含瓜类水果）产量（吨）	Yield of Fruit (ton)	27286	104897
肉类总产量（吨）	Output of Meat (ton)	29913	48825
#猪肉（吨）	Pork (ton)	19473	34056
禽蛋产量（吨）	Output of Eggs (ton)	336	1279
奶类产量（吨）	Output of Milk (ton)	40	2
水产品产量（吨）	Aquatic Products (ton)	8401	20872
规模以上工业企业个数（个）	Number of Industrial Enterprises above Designated Size (unit)	25	47
规模以上工业总产值（当年价，万元）	Included Gross Industrial Output Value above Designated Size (at current price，10 000 yuan)	3828894	826705
规模以上工业企业从业人员年平均人数（人）	Annual Average Number of Employed Persons (person)	7590	11692
规模以上工业企业主营业务收入（万元）	Income from Major Business (10 000 yuan)	2878333	798831
公路里程（公里）	Length of Domestic Highways (km)	2111	1108
民用汽车拥有量（辆）	Number of Civil Motor Vehicles Owned (vehicle)	89393	161148
年末实有公共汽（电）车营运数（辆）	Year-end Total Operating Public Buses (vehicle)	115	200
年末实有出租汽车数（辆）	Year-end Total Taxis (vehicle)	105	300
固定电话年末用户（户）	Number of Local Telephone Subscribers in Year-end (subscriber)	11000	40700
年末移动电话用户数（户）	Number of Mobile Telephone Subscribers at Year-end (subscriber)	311000	1615700
互联网宽带接入用户（户）	Number of Internet Subscribers (subscriber)	24000	235000
全社会用电量（万千瓦时）	Total Consumption of Electricity (10 000 kwh)	515892	329163
#居民生活用电量	Household Consumption of Electricity	24569	39862
社会消费品零售总额（亿元）	Total Retail Sale of Consumer Goods 100 million yuan)	9.18	62.65
固定资产投资（不含农户）（亿元）	Investment in Fixed Assets (100 million yuan)	148.15	226.40
新增固定资产（万元）	Newly Increased Fixed Assets (10 000 yuan)	946715	1138121
房地产开发投资完成额（万元）	Real Estate Development (10 000 yuan)	124890	182111
#住宅	Residential Buildings	19000	147452
住宅竣工面积（万平方米）	Completed Floor Space of Residential Buildings (10 000 sq.m)	5.47	2.31
普通中学数（所）	Number of Regular Secondary Schools (unit)	22	28

Continued

平桂区 Pinggui District	昭平县 Zhaoping County	钟山县 Zhongshan County	富川瑶族自治县 Fuchuan County	金城江区 Jinchengjiang District	宜州区 Yizhou District	南丹县 Nandan County	天峨县 Tian' e County
6591	1857	4654	13174	1142	2938	3379	1016
13140	114	10493	5249	283267	1428300	80870	2178
396995	242663	203756	356868	247171	460192	183256	32079
52974	71136	130565	514947	42578	85973	42847	36974
27297	24717	33237	34810	13794	27562	20745	11688
19623	17065	21682	29252	9794	16857	10244	8300
899	1249	2090	3147	3029	931	301	418
12	35	17630	0	0			
13240	20614	18215	9678	9760	18681	2003	7954
79	14	43	20	28	41	11	7
1735000	215591	1037490	495864	577223	490675	1593774	471226
9000	1961	7151	2739	16050	9300	7646	883
1421500	164999	1030487	463652	576000	530400	1217978	460829
1461	1086	721	792	934	1516	1181	1311
	12034	16320		30000	49629	22094	1856
	74	31	16	147	71	68	27
	13	64	60	300	175	131	62
	28923	7293	8420	30090	17151	12753	9168
	294734	295613	224245	285875	549883	279200	148134
	69716	45844	48866	107607	115619	49500	19790
67204	37526	50438	43763	108867	103160	231093	13738
31178	15205	16290	13580	25089	32560	14601	8188
33.52	26.56	39.26	16.86	75.86	54.84	30.77	13.41
206.86	65.85	121.38	101.52	77.80	44.91	54.18	21.77
1027797	272999	827596	661393	221221	269274	360531	106829
92103	49338	59299	39124	163787	133794	72786	
48143	33798	48785	22385	123387	97471	41864	
		3.15	2.07	62.30	8.95	29.67	2.09
21	19	22	11	12	23	13	10

23－1 续表26

指 标	Item	靖西市 Jingxi City	八步区 Babu District
小学数（所）	Number of Primary Schools (unit)	233	244
普通中学专任教师数（人）	Full-time Teachers in Regular Secondary Schools (person)	1767	1779
小学专任教师数（人）	Full-time Teachers in Primary Schools (person)	2543	3386
普通中学在校学生数（人）	Student Enrollment in Regular Secondary Schools (person)	29042	29401
小学在校学生数（人）	Primary Student Enrollment (person)	46388	69278
专业技术人员（人）	Number of Professionals (person)	5929	6353
#农业技术人员	Agricultural Professionals (person)	197	212
医疗卫生机构床位数（张）	Number of Beds in Heathcare Institutions (bed)	1781	4157
医疗卫生机构技术人员（人）	Medical & Technical Personnel of Heathcare Institutions (person)	2107	5095
#执业（助理）医师	Practitioner (assistant) Doctors	519	1746
居民人均可支配收入（元）	Per Capita Annual Disposable Income of Households (yuan)	14165	20410
城镇居民人均可支配收入（元）	Per Capita Annual Disposable Income of Urban Households (yuan)	27019	30761
农村居民人均可支配收入（元）	Annual Per Capita Net Income of Rural Residents (yuan)	9344	11156
各种社会福利收养性单位数（个）	Number of Adopting Units of Social Welfare (unit)	121	110
各种社会福利收养性单位床位数（张）	Number of Beds in Adopting Units of Social Welfare (bed)	1297	1392
城镇基本养老保险参保人数（人）	Number of Persons Joining Basic Pension Insurance (person)	34448	23639
城镇基本医疗保险参保人数（人）	Number of Persons Joining Basic Health Care Insurance (person)	64735	23379
失业保险参保人数（人）	Number of Persons Joining Unemployment Insurance (person)	12745	16163
新型农村合作医疗参保人数（人）	Number of Persons Joining New-type Rural Cooperative Medical Service (person)	584788	639055
新型农村社会养老保险参保人数（人）	Number of Persons Joining New-type Rural Social Pension Insurance (person)	276433	147149
城镇居民最低生活保障人数（人）	Number of Urban Residents Receiving Lowest Cost-of-living (person)	3267	1951
农村居民最低生活保障人数（人）	Number of Rural Residents Receiving Lowest Cost-of-living (person)	92196	30435
森林面积（公顷）	Forest Area (10 000 hectares)	217954	263397
工业二氧化硫排放量（吨）	Volume of Sulfur Dioxide Discharged (ton)	8177	2950
氮氧化物排放量（吨）	Volume of Nitrogen Oxides Discharged (ton)	4857	2579
烟（粉）尘排放量（吨）	Volume of Smoke & Dust Discharged (ton)	1179	2096
污水处理厂数（座）	Number of Effluent Treatment Plants (unit)	1	1
污水处理厂集中处理率（%）	Rate of Centralized Treatment of Polluted Water (%)	96.5	100.0
垃圾处理站数（个）	Number of Garbage Station (unit)	1	7

Continued

平桂区 Pinggui District	昭平县 Zhaoping County	钟山县 Zhongshan County	富川瑶族自治县 Fuchuan County	金城江区 Jinchengjiang District	宜州区 Yizhou District	南丹县 Nandan County	天峨县 Tian' e County
138	49	80	28	72	207	164	96
1994	1330	1263	1087	872	1263	837	770
1866	3024	2073	1649	1664	2368	2079	936
25604	19838	20482	14513	13068	33981	16450	13300
39559	36363	39524	26970	30602	50603	33388	16430
	5727	4918	5737	3639	7763	5318	2627
	251	71	118	167	311	137	111
1143	1145	1461	1068	3580	4129	1088	584
1220	1824	1784	1438	4230	4588	1476	735
402	482	493	349	1370	1305	433	161
18569	18022	16879	16548	19285	18626	19301	13833
27627	27944	27597	27099	32718	32198	31240	23980
10519	10040	10098	10079	9755	10628	9867	7948
9	161	1	7	15	18	15	11
196	718	36	108	407	521	380	377
3457	188678	19017	11607	23428	55501	17368	14614
21159	399977	42726	19582	246089	70588	60064	158872
7897	12162	12706	9428	10803	16687	9410	6418
375876		366188	278267	196250	533191	245336	
133740		147662	156177	169113	242043	117016	76000
5210	1287	1393	3294	8317	814	2880	664
25352	30024	29617	23018	139113	19795	42968	14510
138428	264923	91093	88090	229000	228168	269549	250977
558	128	324	1105	0	359	6237	0
184	105	82	2293	0	567	416	0
	362	294	1008	0	1715	748	23
	28	1	2	1	2	1	3
90.3	91.2	80.0	90.0	91.1	96.3	98.0	93.2
	2	1	2	6	4	7	6

23－1　续表27

指　标	Item	凤山县 Fengshan County	东兰县 Donglan County
行政区域面积（平方公里）	Administrative Region Land Area (sq.km)	1730	2437
常住户数（户）	Total Households at Year-end (household)	53811	80752
年末常住人口（万人）	Total Population at Year-end (10 000 persons)	16.97	22.35
年末户籍人口（万人）	Registered Population at Year-end (10 000 persons)	22.05	31.19
地区生产总值（万元）	Gross Domestic Product (10 000 yuan)	228620	284016
第一产业增加值	Primary Industry	58659	73305
第二产业增加值	Secondary Industry	46052	58738
#工业	Industry	13961	13895
第三产业增加值	Tertiary Industry	123909	151973
人均生产总值（元）	Per Capital GDP (yuan)	13532	12765
地区生产总值指数（上年＝100）	Indices of Gross Domestic Product (preceding year=100)	106.3	108.3
第一产业	Primary Industry	103.8	104.0
第二产业	Secondary Industry	107.7	112.7
#工业	Industry	97.2	105.6
第三产业	Tertiary Industry	107.0	108.8
人均生产总值指数（上年=100）	Indices of Per Capital GDP (preceding year＝100)	105.3	107.5
公共财政预算收入（万元）	Government Revenue (10 000 yuan)	9193	14461
税收收入（万元）	Total Tax Revenue (10 000 yuan)	5817	9653
公共预算支出（万元）	Government Expenditure (10 000 yuan)	196234	244383
年末金融机构各项存款余额（万元）	Year-end Deposits of Financial Institutions (10 000 yuan)	450087	795893
#居民储蓄存款余额	Urban & Rural Savings Deposits	258278	405100
年末金融机构各项贷款余额（万元）	Year-end Loans of Financial Institutions (10 000 yuan)	227762	403758
耕地面积（公顷）	Farmland (hectare)	14687	14001
设施农业占地面积（公顷）	Protected Agriculture Covered (hectare)	22	0
农业机械总动力（万千瓦特）	Total Agricultural Machinery Power (10 000 watts)	25.92	28.59
农作物总播种面积（公顷）	Total Sown Area of Major Farm Crops (hectare)	20985	23710
#粮食	Grain Crops	12935	15326
油料	Oil Crops	568	1293
糖料	Sugar Crops	89	467
蔬菜	Vegetables	4869	4642
粮食总产量（吨）	Yield of Grain (ton)	40352	53179
#稻谷	Rice	15220	28019

Continued

罗城仫佬族自治县 Luocheng County	环江毛南族自治县 Huanjiang County	巴马瑶族自治县 Bama County	都安瑶族自治县 Du'an County	大化瑶族自治县 Dahua County	兴宾区 Xingbin District	忻城县 Xincheng County	象州县 Xiangzhou County
2651	4553	1976	4088	2750	4404	2522	1918
120990	106176	72864	184105	102861	311464	101795	105545
31.13	28.21	23.42	53.88	37.64	96.97	32.89	29.88
38.70	37.69	29.42	72.06	47.90	113.36	43.09	36.92
464593	515327	429573	487373	562799	2936789	638933	1145269
164809	186161	106328	134542	93559	655902	210103	325333
86828	105696	121086	86505	239286	1020616	181419	548765
42436	63617	76405	36590	191933	661438	140109	446378
212956	223470	202159	266326	229954	1260270	247412	271171
14960	18316	18437	9067	15016	30398	19524	38451
104.5	105.8	112.1	108.6	102.6	106.6	105.9	110.3
103.9	103.9	104.9	103.7	103.8	104.5	105.3	105.7
100.2	104.8	121.8	111.2	100.0	103.1	99.9	111.7
100.2	99.6	114.4	116.2	97.4	103.7	100.6	110.6
107.0	107.9	111.0	110.7	105.4	110.7	111.8	112.6
103.9	105.3	111.1	108.1	101.9	105.8	104.8	109.6
18673	23808	16858	25867	32716	49741	15609	27265
9906	11963	11013	17128	19662	30517	9423	12835
294733	283272	245291	447486	322930	410238	251962	210500
932012	1034300	597654	1113383	775444	3471299	640693	846841
596130	590100	412932	696007	524407	1576681	482862	595675
424405	464237	314075	558192	481214	2716445	336327	506356
44780	60528	18851	30822	25318	189611	60237	71300
52	27	23	1	1	1274	41	31
23.12	33.64	14.71	43.61	20.58	85.74	22.38	35.68
56902	43463	38991	58926	35976	198674	53998	65880
26051	23452	17806	44356	25568	63977	27440	33246
2847	810	1647	103	652	8682	1281	1635
9733	6811	2869	3434	4122	85255	5613	15984
12685	8481	6565	8211	4121	27711	10298	8463
112037	124639	59195	123121	72089	301734	108314	177471
76704	84793	20140	34895	16818	227781	56612	157257

23－1　续表28

指　标	Item	凤山县 Fengshan County	东兰县 Donglan County
油料产量（吨）	Yield of Oil-bearing Crops (ton)	642	975
糖料产量（吨）	Yield of Sugar Crops (ton)	6196	34903
蔬菜产量（吨）	Yield of Vegetables (ton)	36982	50598
园林水果（不含瓜类水果）产量（吨）	Yield of Fruit (ton)	14463	29605
肉类总产量（吨）	Output of Meat (ton)	10304	13661
#猪肉（吨）	Pork (ton)	7544	7989
禽蛋产量（吨）	Output of Eggs (ton)	305	373
奶类产量（吨）	Output of Milk (ton)		0
水产品产量（吨）	Aquatic Products (ton)	370	5991
规模以上工业企业个数（个）	Number of Industrial Enterprises above Designated Size (unit)	4	5
规模以上工业总产值（当年价，万元）	Included Gross Industrial Output Value above Designated Size (at current price，10 000 yuan)	19225	35351
规模以上工业企业从业人员年平均人数（人）	Annual Average Number of Employed Persons (person)	125	850
规模以上工业企业主营业务收入（万元）	Income from Major Business (10 000 yuan)	20018	30650
公路里程（公里）	Length of Domestic Highways (km)	862	1328
民用汽车拥有量（辆）	Number of Civil Motor Vehicles Owned (vehicle)	9965	7892
年末实有公共汽（电）车营运数（辆）	Year-end Total Operating Public Buses (vehicle)	33	16
年末实有出租汽车数（辆）	Year-end Total Taxis (vehicle)	0	23
固定电话年末用户（户）	Number of Local Telephone Subscribers in Year-end (subscriber)	6067	11538
年末移动电话用户数（户）	Number of Mobile Telephone Subscribers at Year-end (subscriber)	136651	136892
互联网宽带接入用户（户）	Number of Internet Subscribers (subscriber)	24797	24497
全社会用电量（万千瓦时）	Total Consumption of Electricity (10 000 kwh)	14354	23089
#居民生活用电量	Household Consumption of Electricity	8315	11138
社会消费品零售总额（亿元）	Total Retail Sale of Consumer Goods 100 million yuan)	9.23	16.03
固定资产投资（不含农户）（亿元）	Investment in Fixed Assets (100 million yuan)	26.70	45.90
新增固定资产（万元）	Newly Increased Fixed Assets (10 000 yuan)	75756	144739
房地产开发投资完成额（万元）	Real Estate Development (10 000 yuan)	33691	4310
#住宅	Residential Buildings	21537	2693
住宅竣工面积（万平方米）	Completed Floor Space of Residential Buildings (10 000 sq.m)	2.54	
普通中学数（所）	Number of Regular Secondary Schools (unit)	14	12

Continued

罗城仫佬族自治县 Luocheng County	环江毛南族自治县 Huanjiang County	巴马瑶族自治县 Bama County	都安瑶族自治县 Du'an County	大化瑶族自治县 Dahua County	兴宾区 Xingbin District	忻城县 Xincheng County	象州县 Xiangzhou County
3626	761	1518	76	583	21629	3155	3139
583980	393291	154237	233100	254247	7779208	421141	1292913
121382	136760	104989	99107	53957	555953	223306	169522
58146	24677	36977	29610	14667	198967	58061	201756
22044	21351	19748	40466	28937	67609	18654	18939
16227	13624	11928	29028	21361	45374	9833	11459
616	517	327	920	543	1866	606	1239
0		0		0	5024		0
6956	4018	5407	3262	19284	35236	6285	13413
15	22	13	16	6	81	17	57
129827	188425	195550	131702	207460	2806761	383388	1262527
2334	4876	1407	1768	1226	21262	2821	8046
108963	184508	142563	128052	205010	2188000	366563	1232922
64	1178	927	1765	1602	3221	1055	788
19149	22687	9863	25544	8231	45139	15110	29515
27	36	74	64	28	381	4	9
24	134	60	160	80	530	27	28
9867	91498	16563	42140	21466	40850	3582	20118
198335	589189	150263	299121	241109	908605	244707	289782
28480	251679	23869	50156	34679	167023	32062	73319
27821	29836	24049	56247	32678	780176	29827	42394
14082	13581	14326	32563	19999	106002	24734	14486
19.28	23.49	14.96	24.50	18.83	79.86	24.95	26.14
28.37	34.76	48.48	40.26	30.07	196.17	40.76	76.41
184150	193321	108053	238507	149312	651285	286325	325298
30494	10502	42072	30134	49547	300642	42517	23033
21358	4985	38802	24791	34169	225441	39549	17109
13.62	5223.00	8566.00	8.47	0.11	17.54	2.56	0.00
14	16	13	24	20	28	7	10

23－1　续表29

指　标	Item	凤山县 Fengshan County	东兰县 Donglan County
小学数（所）	Number of Primary Schools (unit)	114	101
普通中学专任教师数（人）	Full-time Teachers in Regular Secondary Schools (person)	911	648
小学专任教师数（人）	Full-time Teachers in Primary Schools (person)	1110	1312
普通中学在校学生数（人）	Student Enrollment in Regular Secondary Schools (person)	8038	11965
小学在校学生数（人）	Primary Student Enrollment (person)	18967	24368
专业技术人员（人）	Number of Professionals (person)	2778	3242
#农业技术人员	Agricultural Professionals (person)	236	187
医疗卫生机构床位数（张）	Number of Beds in Heathcare Institutions (bed)	646	1014
医疗卫生机构技术人员（人）	Medical & Technical Personnel of Heathcare Institutions (person)	757	816
#执业（助理）医师	Practitioner (assistant) Doctors	263	274
居民人均可支配收入（元）	Per Capita Annual Disposable Income of Households (yuan)	10825	10628
城镇居民人均可支配收入（元）	Per Capita Annual Disposable Income of Urban Households (yuan)	21772	22211
农村居民人均可支配收入（元）	Annual Per Capita Net Income of Rural Residents (yuan)	7216	7216
各种社会福利收养性单位数（个）	Number of Adopting Units of Social Welfare (unit)	35	17
各种社会福利收养性单位床位数（张）	Number of Beds in Adopting Units of Social Welfare (bed)	464	314
城镇基本养老保险参保人数（人）	Number of Persons Joining Basic Pension Insurance (person)	8017	8255
城镇基本医疗保险参保人数（人）	Number of Persons Joining Basic Health Care Insurance (person)	11141	14617
失业保险参保人数（人）	Number of Persons Joining Unemployment Insurance (person)	6710	5817
新型农村合作医疗参保人数（人）	Number of Persons Joining New-type Rural Cooperative Medical Service (person)	187988	255907
新型农村社会养老保险参保人数（人）	Number of Persons Joining New-type Rural Social Pension Insurance (person)	82343	133454
城镇居民最低生活保障人数（人）	Number of Urban Residents Receiving Lowest Cost-of-living (person)	1423	413
农村居民最低生活保障人数（人）	Number of Rural Residents Receiving Lowest Cost-of-living (person)	26995	17154
森林面积（公顷）	Forest Area (10 000 hectares)	140737	188360
工业二氧化硫排放量（吨）	Volume of Sulfur Dioxide Discharged (ton)	52	62
氮氧化物排放量（吨）	Volume of Nitrogen Oxides Discharged (ton)	3	7
烟（粉）尘排放量（吨）	Volume of Smoke & Dust Discharged (ton)	8	60
污水处理厂数（座）	Number of Effluent Treatment Plants (unit)	1	1
污水处理厂集中处理率（%）	Rate of Centralized Treatment of Polluted Water (%)	67.0	93.0
垃圾处理站数（个）	Number of Garbage Station (unit)	3	3

Continued

罗城仫佬族自治县 Luocheng County	环江毛南族自治县 Huanjiang County	巴马瑶族自治县 Bama County	都安瑶族自治县 Du'an County	大化瑶族自治县 Dahua County	兴宾区 Xingbin District	忻城县 Xincheng County	象州县 Xiangzhou County
158	133	116	447	158	114	119	101
832	1316	627	1921	1524	2727	942	953
1301	1652	1554	3389	2250	4998	1537	1276
14792	17369	12932	42849	27499	38214	14852	14811
27346	25827	30604	64176	44586	90307	26778	22270
3956	4178	3325	8110	5432	14649	4033	5115
211	334	176	276	247	1183	74	159
1185	912	711	1578	1690	2076	1862	1709
1920	1089	1113	1860	1564	2256	1291	1356
395	332	327	699	382	719	568	65
11537	13689	11613	12707	11357	20650	16655	18787
21549	25027	24281	22233	22010	31586	30951	31326
7262	8861	7376	7237	7426	11245	10097	11071
54	23	8	6	17	44	14	11
541	298	190	1966	473	1070	489	345
9325	17971	9060	8950	16000	305793	13772	151049
31400	23145	11194	29268	27294	852302	35778	331950
6803	10558	7780	10997	8200	15315	8131	9183
334473	325572	253299	654499	391321		368961	320809
166126	153721	108173	264000	164043		173962	151049
1108	882	710	10988	552	3171	432	907
48796	27439	25119	111009	39906	35128	31835	15859
179086	313797	144880	254439	182957	168933	148664	74356
1181	6	0	610	376		34	942
247	53	28	58	117		58	482
179	64	134	0	256		112	1075
3	4	3	1	1		1	1
92.0	95.0	93.8	97.0	95.0	89.7	91.0	85.3
1	18	10	29	3	18	1	20

23－1　续表30

指　标	Item	武宣县 Wuxuan County	金秀瑶族自治县 Jinxiu County
行政区域面积（平方公里）	Administrative Region Land Area (sq.km)	1704	2469
常住户数（户）	Total Households at Year-end (household)	131460	48579
年末常住人口（万人）	Total Population at Year-end (10 000 persons)	37.13	13.13
年末户籍人口（万人）	Registered Population at Year-end (10 000 persons)	45.49	15.69
地区生产总值（万元）	Gross Domestic Product (10 000 yuan)	1192132	322296
第一产业增加值	Primary Industry	274317	90067
第二产业增加值	Secondary Industry	562847	65535
#工业	Industry	491421	42125
第三产业增加值	Tertiary Industry	354968	166694
人均生产总值（元）	Per Capital GDP (yuan)	32224	24716
地区生产总值指数（上年＝100）	Indices of Gross Domestic Product (preceding year=100)	107.7	110.1
第一产业	Primary Industry	103.3	105.2
第二产业	Secondary Industry	107.7	105.1
#工业	Industry	106.9	106.5
第三产业	Tertiary Industry	111.2	115.2
人均生产总值指数（上年=100）	Indices of Per Capital GDP (preceding year＝100)	106.9	108.6
公共财政预算收入（万元）	Government Revenue (10 000 yuan)	48861	9222
税收收入（万元）	Total Tax Revenue (10 000 yuan)	37020	6507
公共预算支出（万元）	Government Expenditure (10 000 yuan)	258593	163779
年末金融机构各项存款余额（万元）	Year-end Deposits of Financial Institutions (10 000 yuan)	1238400	455896
#居民储蓄存款余额	Urban & Rural Savings Deposits	686700	273689
年末金融机构各项贷款余额（万元）	Year-end Loans of Financial Institutions (10 000 yuan)	633900	293292
耕地面积（公顷）	Farmland (hectare)	60221	12738
设施农业占地面积（公顷）	Protected Agriculture Covered (hectare)	139	23
农业机械总动力（万千瓦特）	Total Agricultural Machinery Power (10 000 watts)	34.03	11.08
农作物总播种面积（公顷）	Total Sown Area of Major Farm Crops (hectare)	70572	21144
#粮食	Grain Crops	28785	10635
油料	Oil Crops	4408	706
糖料	Sugar Crops	24117	2495
蔬菜	Vegetables	8742	4804
粮食总产量（吨）	Yield of Grain (ton)	131959	46869
#稻谷	Rice	105781	34698

Continued

合山市 Heshan City	江州区 Jiangzhou District	扶绥县 Fusui County	宁明县 Ningming County	龙州县 Longzhou County	大新县 Daxin County	天等县 Tiandeng County	凭祥市 Pingxiang City
366	2918	2841	3704	2311	2748	2165	645
47510	111407	148159	113392	73070	89437	90723	33778
11.86	34.30	40.18	35.39	22.72	30.73	33.42	11.94
13.56	37.34	46.00	44.13	27.23	38.26	45.55	11.44
330122	1936177	1836920	1380516	1216076	1287297	618939	759826
43844	285620	471446	343751	271421	247016	137644	55612
117194	924953	878267	622557	519511	615742	207147	220241
53863	806855	788408	534469	423015	540609	141206	117038
169083	725603	487207	414208	425144	424539	274148	483973
27976	56747	45906	39180	53702	42027	18581	64147
105.4	110.4	110.3	108.6	108.2	108.1	107.4	113.2
102.5	103.2	106.9	106.1	104.7	103.9	101.6	103.2
96.7	110.8	114.8	110.2	107.8	108.4	106.0	113.3
88.3	110.6	114.1	110.0	107.8	107.4	106.6	113.3
113.9	112.8	107.4	108.5	110.9	110.2	111.7	114.4
104.7	109.3	109.5	107.7	107.6	107.5	106.7	111.6
17302	26097	96119	37519	31738	23680	14048	51621
9613	18098	57856	27055	19710	16288	9447	21208
138524	210179	345188	306252	257646	246366	245208	170910
371582	2097435	1346195	957620	919863	873522	823668	829847
279278	818011	909478	697688	597139	687278	599327	642277
185057	1312169	741157	458894	600141	525969	477066	367910
12354	113586	132822	83387	64867	69367	46531	9692
20	0	255	102	34	54	0	5
8.43	44.56	42.11	35.94	26.53	60.13	43.78	5.75
12510	93018	141693	76543	68718	71854	55549	12612
5973	10467	15743	16202	12066	26900	36197	4117
472	1646	5180	1750	1634	693	1180	279
3754	72761	79193	47936	41690	33672	3806	5123
2157	3067	15278	7946	5830	5532	10761	2388
28802	43002	64201	70604	48005	118703	149536	17504
25540	30317	49374	55794	32785	80149	70818	11706

23－1　续表31

指　标	Item	武宣县 Wuxuan County	金秀瑶族自治县 Jinxiu County
油料产量（吨）	Yield of Oil-bearing Crops (ton)	11101	1625
糖料产量（吨）	Yield of Sugar Crops (ton)	2259869	226004
蔬菜产量（吨）	Yield of Vegetables (ton)	208418	99865
园林水果（不含瓜类水果）产量（吨）	Yield of Fruit (ton)	206272	65802
肉类总产量（吨）	Output of Meat (ton)	37815	8544
#猪肉（吨）	Pork (ton)	30917	6396
禽蛋产量（吨）	Output of Eggs (ton)	501	376
奶类产量（吨）	Output of Milk (ton)	725	0
水产品产量（吨）	Aquatic Products (ton)	13766	1942
规模以上工业企业个数（个）	Number of Industrial Enterprises above Designated Size (unit)	50	14
规模以上工业总产值（当年价，万元）	Included Gross Industrial Output Value above Designated Size (at current price，10 000 yuan)	1415709	107691
规模以上工业企业从业人员年平均人数（人）	Annual Average Number of Employed Persons (person)	5040	354
规模以上工业企业主营业务收入（万元）	Income from Major Business (10 000 yuan)	1045078	108562
公路里程（公里）	Length of Domestic Highways (km)	1032	948
民用汽车拥有量（辆）	Number of Civil Motor Vehicles Owned (vehicle)	25844	9485
年末实有公共汽（电）车营运数（辆）	Year-end Total Operating Public Buses (vehicle)	165	
年末实有出租汽车数（辆）	Year-end Total Taxis (vehicle)	40	150
固定电话年末用户（户）	Number of Local Telephone Subscribers in Year-end (subscriber)	11095	18832
年末移动电话用户数（户）	Number of Mobile Telephone Subscribers at Year-end (subscriber)	325606	160021
互联网宽带接入用户（户）	Number of Internet Subscribers (subscriber)	53521	15735
全社会用电量（万千瓦时）	Total Consumption of Electricity (10 000 kwh)	62290	15165
#居民生活用电量	Household Consumption of Electricity	17327	6049
社会消费品零售总额（亿元）	Total Retail Sale of Consumer Goods 100 million yuan)	27.48	9.69
固定资产投资（不含农户）（亿元）	Investment in Fixed Assets (100 million yuan)	81.26	18.74
新增固定资产（万元）	Newly Increased Fixed Assets (10 000 yuan)	435423	118360
房地产开发投资完成额（万元）	Real Estate Development (10 000 yuan)	96787	26260
#住宅	Residential Buildings	69445	18163
住宅竣工面积（万平方米）	Completed Floor Space of Residential Buildings (10 000 sq.m)		8.61
普通中学数（所）	Number of Regular Secondary Schools (unit)	12	6

Continued

合山市 Heshan City	江州区 Jiangzhou District	扶绥县 Fusui County	宁明县 Ningming County	龙州县 Longzhou County	大新县 Daxin County	天等县 Tiandeng County	凭祥市 Pingxiang City
1040	2995	11065	3910	3439	1675	1844	717
312005	6025939	6666615	4433232	3962989	3258365	335901	388225
59012	55289	452118	143046	117515	98470	178792	40783
16042	114942	212916	48807	161560	85428	28169	12220
4101	7953	15225	19687	8478	31977	36412	5841
2279	4123	9546	14473	4257	22944	30229	3938
175	236	1057	452	296	446	349	250
0		0		0		0	
2759	11658	20323	9412	17866	11757	4088	3285
8	38	69	22	15	24	12	29
153755	2220492	2279011	1637266	1217441	1368948	282760	386811
2627	10328	11871	3930	6178	9550	2381	1160
126992	1654196	1749105	1576976	1166873	1321466	251275	333209
292	1400	1234	1423	954	1000	986	430
11696	23987	20912	20161	2741	31768		37682
38	74	110	12	36	31	44	73
104	71	90	71	35	12	30	129
9368		10434	10787	11748	13722	12185	17057
122730		170508	272192	182229	267378	193721	178373
23099		7556	38833	35663	40270	26032	27834
34709	44580	133179	30900	33285	37253	31836	22751
5882	16650	19871	16000	13319	14399	14049	9539
12.19	30.48	24.76	16.99	20.91	15.29	11.89	25.77
18.81	165.19	206.57	142.36	119.44	131.22	74.34	131.38
209526		1555917	929675	649588	1100987	432732	1077241
7020	219231	95974	71147	61116	64088	61563	45259
6820	153946	58311	26648	45111	52509	56837	17364
		4.15		18.86	12.50		1.70
3	11	15	14	6	12	15	3

23－1 续表32

指 标	Item	武宣县 Wuxuan County	金秀瑶族自治县 Jinxiu County
小学数（所）	Number of Primary Schools (unit)	24	92
普通中学专任教师数（人）	Full-time Teachers in Regular Secondary Schools (person)	1112	303
小学专任教师数（人）	Full-time Teachers in Primary Schools (person)	1528	806
普通中学在校学生数（人）	Student Enrollment in Regular Secondary Schools (person)	20869	4278
小学在校学生数（人）	Primary Student Enrollment (person)	32607	9863
专业技术人员（人）	Number of Professionals (person)	4188	2681
#农业技术人员	Agricultural Professionals (person)	232	153
医疗卫生机构床位数（张）	Number of Beds in Heathcare Institutions (bed)	1683	825
医疗卫生机构技术人员（人）	Medical & Technical Personnel of Heathcare Institutions (person)	1811	712
#执业（助理）医师	Practitioner (assistant) Doctors	664	281
居民人均可支配收入（元）	Per Capita Annual Disposable Income of Households (yuan)	18940	
城镇居民人均可支配收入（元）	Per Capita Annual Disposable Income of Urban Households (yuan)	30819	31393
农村居民人均可支配收入（元）	Annual Per Capita Net Income of Rural Residents (yuan)	11167	9280
各种社会福利收养性单位数（个）	Number of Adopting Units of Social Welfare (unit)	12	10
各种社会福利收养性单位床位数（张）	Number of Beds in Adopting Units of Social Welfare (bed)	509	348
城镇基本养老保险参保人数（人）	Number of Persons Joining Basic Pension Insurance (person)	29567	56899
城镇基本医疗保险参保人数（人）	Number of Persons Joining Basic Health Care Insurance (person)	41588	15265
失业保险参保人数（人）	Number of Persons Joining Unemployment Insurance (person)	11519	5600
新型农村合作医疗参保人数（人）	Number of Persons Joining New-type Rural Cooperative Medical Service (person)	377342	127126
新型农村社会养老保险参保人数（人）	Number of Persons Joining New-type Rural Social Pension Insurance (person)	173026	50306
城镇居民最低生活保障人数（人）	Number of Urban Residents Receiving Lowest Cost-of-living (person)	507	639
农村居民最低生活保障人数（人）	Number of Rural Residents Receiving Lowest Cost-of-living (person)	18365	10514
森林面积（公顷）	Forest Area (10 000 hectares)	85029	219998
工业二氧化硫排放量（吨）	Volume of Sulfur Dioxide Discharged (ton)		3
氮氧化物排放量（吨）	Volume of Nitrogen Oxides Discharged (ton)		25
烟（粉）尘排放量（吨）	Volume of Smoke & Dust Discharged (ton)		85
污水处理厂数（座）	Number of Effluent Treatment Plants (unit)	1	2
污水处理厂集中处理率（%）	Rate of Centralized Treatment of Polluted Water (%)	88.1	84.0
垃圾处理站数（个）	Number of Garbage Station (unit)	11	5

Continued

合山市 Heshan City	江州区 Jiangzhou District	扶绥县 Fusui County	宁明县 Ningming County	龙州县 Longzhou County	大新县 Daxin County	天等县 Tiandeng County	凭祥市 Pingxiang City
6	62	97	197	51	141	82	37
337	716	1508	794	557	888	727	320
503	1584	1735	1801	988	1560	1612	652
4106	10897	21777	13733	9824	14467	14607	5327
8702	27663	32084	31515	15025	22080	30096	10593
2210	2951	4583	4854	2322	4020	3815	1468
65	125	120	151	65	56	79	20
449	1458	1387	1191	1209	1182	1219	281
630	867	1590	1784	1283	1518	1219	679
187	261	657	480	378	434	384	298
23563	21104	20071	15051	15945	16463	13738	22363
30175	30910	30193	25862	26902	30217	25169	32124
11055	12223	12487	10637	9799	11336	9551	10997
4	20	16	16	16	33	13	2
200	192	280	631	445	865	312	166
24208		145005	162745	18528	146321	13300	11849
113800		60743	36707	44762	353694		30829
5807		14716	11198	9325	9404	7672	6930
		332625	386260	223441	348881	421444	82095
35200				124105	144855	190021	49105
934	797	7404	1963	1145	27493	1404	1754
3064	11095	10788	27163	18250		28464	3798
20000	131032	124099	243233	136042	178745	140080	36292
1369		829	143		1064		1
897		7646	684		304		10
125		5473			2028		42
1		4	5	4	3	1	1
75.1		89.0	85.0	97.0	98.0	85.8	78.0
9		16	3	22	1	1	8

附录

GENERAL SURVEY

2017年广西壮族自治区国民经济和社会发展统计公报

广西壮族自治区统计局　国家统计局广西调查总队

2018年3月30日

2017年，全区上下在自治区党委、政府的坚强领导下，不断增强政治意识、大局意识、核心意识、看齐意识，深入学习宣传贯彻党的十九大精神，以习近平新时代中国特色社会主义思想为指导，全面贯彻落实习近平总书记赋予广西“三大定位”新使命和提出的“五个扎实”新要求，坚持稳中求进工作总基调，坚定不移贯彻新发展理念，坚持以提高发展质量和效益为中心，以推进供给侧结构性改革为主线，统筹推进稳增长、促改革、调结构、惠民生、防风险各项工作，全区经济运行总体平稳、稳中提质、稳中增效，经济社会保持平稳健康发展。

一、综　合

初步核算，全年全区生产总值[2]（GDP）20396.25亿元，比上年增长7.3%。其中，第一产业增加值2906.87亿元，增长4.1%；第二产业增加值9297.84亿元，增长6.6%；第三产业增加值8191.54亿元，增长9.2%。第一、二、三产业增加值占地区生产总值的比重分别为14.2%、45.6%和40.2%，对经济增长的贡献率分别为8.3%、41.9%和49.8%。按常住人口计算，全年人均地区生产总值41955元。

图1　2013—2017年广西生产总值（GDP）及其增长速度

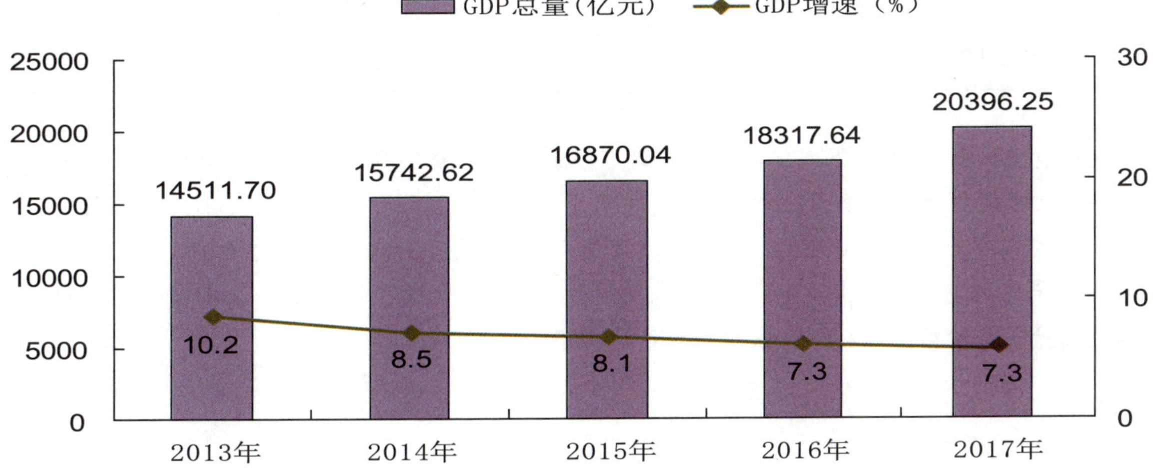

图2 2013—2017年广西人均GDP

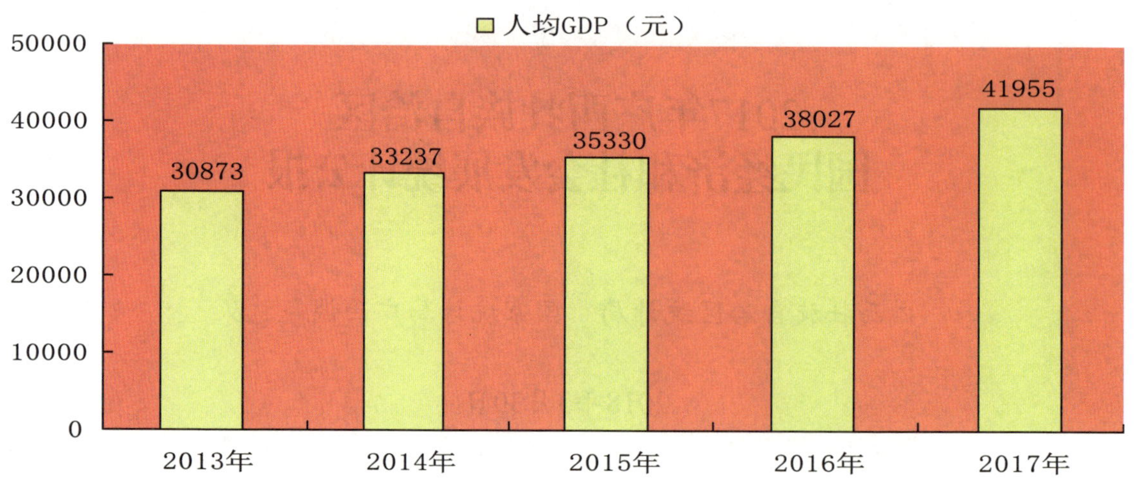

年末全区户籍总人口5600万人，比上年末增加21万人。年末全区常住人口[3]4885万人，比上年末增加47万人，其中城镇人口2404万人，占总人口比重（常住人口城镇化率）为49.21%，比上年末提高1.13个百分点。户籍人口城镇化率为31.23%，比上年末提高0.56个百分点。全年出生人口81.7万人，出生率为15.14‰；死亡人口31.6万人，死亡率为6.22‰；自然增长率为8.92‰。

表1 2017年常住人口数及其构成

指　　标	年末数（万人）	比重（%）
全区常住人口	4885	—
其中：城镇	2404	49.21
乡村	2481	50.79
其中：男性	2535.8	51.91
女性	2349.2	48.09
其中：0—14岁	1080.07	22.11
15—64岁	3318.87	67.94
65岁及以上	486.06	9.95

年末全区就业人员2841.52万人（按常住人口口径统计）。全年城镇新增就业44.61万人，比上年增加2.74万人。年末城镇登记失业率为2.21%，比上年末下降0.72个百分点。全区农民工总量1276万人，比上年增长3.6%。其中，外出农民工922万人，增长2.7%；本地农民工354万人，增长6.0%。

全年全区居民消费价格比上年上涨1.6%，工业生产者出厂价格上涨7.6%，工业生产者购进价格上涨6.5%，固定资产投资价格上涨4.4%，农产品生产者价格下降1.8%。

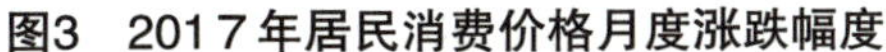

图3　2017年居民消费价格月度涨跌幅度

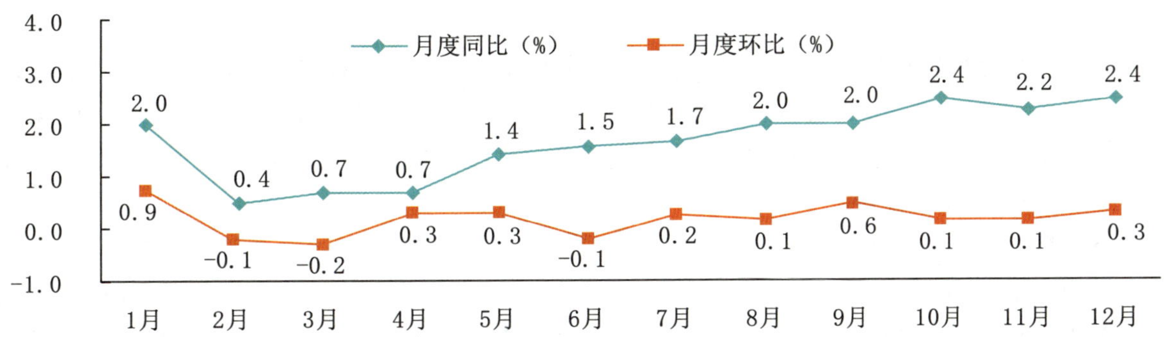

表2　2017年广西居民消费价格比上年涨跌幅度

单位：%

指　　标	广　西	城　市	农　村
居民消费价格	1.6	1.9	1.1
其中：食品烟酒	-0.3	0.1	-1.0
衣　着	1.9	2.4	0.7
居　住	2.4	2.3	2.6
生活用品及服务	0.9	0.8	1.1
交通和通信	2.0	2.0	1.9
教育文化和娱乐	2.1	1.9	2.4
医疗保健	6.1	8.5	2.5
其他用品和服务	1.6	1.8	1.2

全年全区财政收入2604.21亿元，比上年增长6.1%。一般公共预算收入1615.03亿元，增长5.2%，其中，税收收入1057.59亿元，增长6.3%。一般公共预算支出4912.89亿元，增长10.6%。

图4　2013—2017年广西财政收入

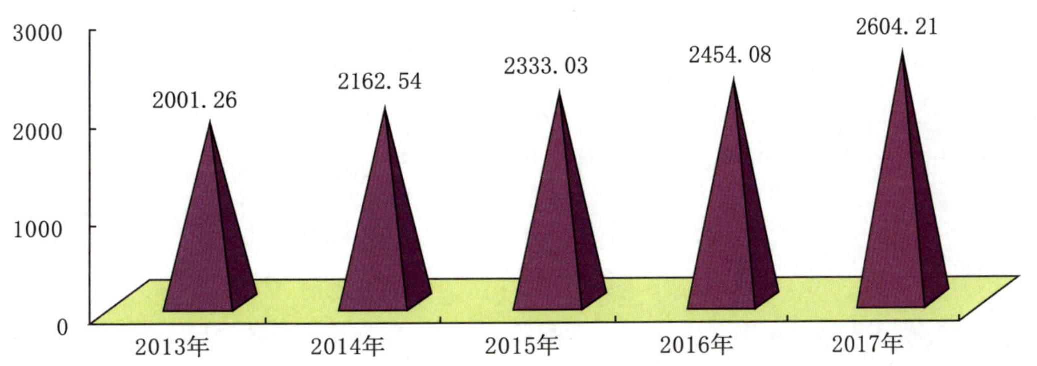

二、农 业

全年全区粮食种植面积2976.2千公顷，比上年减少47.4千公顷;甘蔗种植面积935.0千公顷，减少16.03千公顷；油料种植面积263.96千公顷，增加6.75千公顷；蔬菜种植面积1314.74千公顷，增加44.99千公顷；木薯种植面积200.98千公顷，减少5.9千公顷；果园面积1307.93千公顷，增加75.33千公顷；桑园面积207.86千公顷，增加2.08千公顷。

全年全区粮食产量1467.7万吨，比上年减少53.6万吨，减产3.5%。其中，春收粮食产量31.8万吨，减产7.3%；早稻产量501.6万吨，减产5.3%；秋粮产量934.3万吨，减产2.4%。全年谷物产量1366.2万吨，减产3.8%。其中，稻谷产量1087.9万吨，减产4.3%；玉米产量274.4万吨，减产1.8%。油料产量71.62万吨，增产3.9%；甘蔗产量7611.69万吨，增产2.0%；蔬菜产量（含食用菌）3086.85万吨，增产5.4%；园林水果产量1701.30万吨，增产11.6%。

图5 2013—2017年广西粮食产量

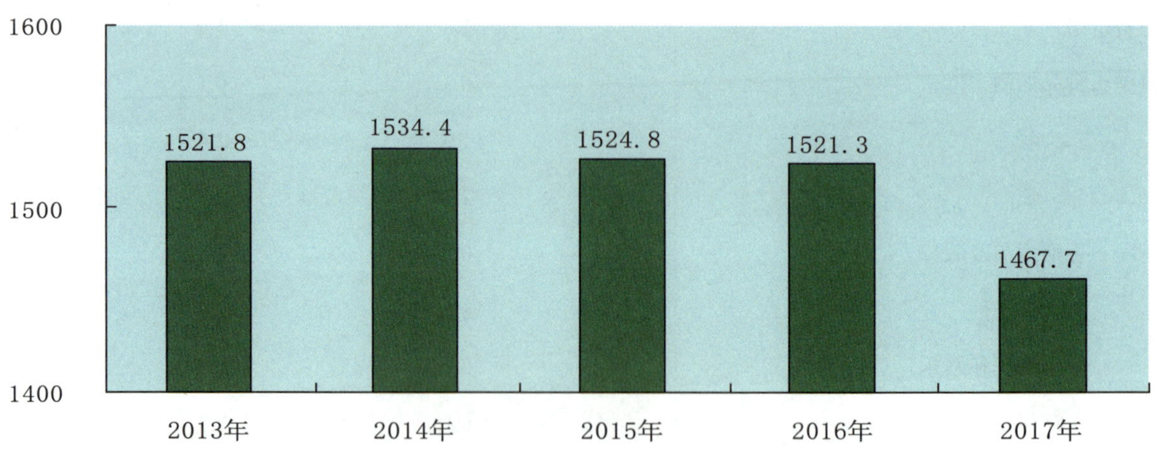

表3 2017年主要农产品产量及其增长速度

产品名称	产 量（万吨）	比上年增长（%）
粮 食	1467.7	-3.5
其中：稻 谷	1087.9	-4.3
其中：早 稻	501.6	-5.3
油 料	71.62	3.9
其中：花 生	67.50	4.1
甘 蔗	7611.69	2.0
蔬 菜（含菌类）	3086.85	5.4
烤 烟	2.26	8.3
木 薯	172.05	-0.04
园林水果	1701.30	11.6
其中：柑橘类	686.66	18.8

续表

产品名称	产　量（万吨）	比上年增长（%）
香　蕉	324.43	1.4
菠　萝	3.55	3.7
荔　枝	68.13	2.1
龙　眼	59.30	-0.6
芒　果	68.41	17.1
茶　叶	7.33	7.7
蚕　茧	39.59	4.8

全年全区猪牛羊禽肉总产量403.8万吨，比上年增长1.1%。其中，猪肉产量255.0万吨，增长2.1%；牛肉产量11.7万吨，增长2.0%；羊肉产量3.3万吨，增长1.8%；禽肉产量133.8万吨，下降0.9%。禽蛋产量22.7万吨，下降1.6%；牛奶产量10.0万吨，增长3.9%。全年生猪出栏3355.1万头，比上年增长2.3%；年末生猪存栏2293.7万头，比上年末增长3.5%。全年蚕茧产量39.59万吨，增长4.8%。水产品产量379.08万吨，增长4.9%，其中海水产品产量195.32万吨，增长4.5%。

全年全区木材采伐量3810万立方米，比上年增长11.7%。松脂产量69.55万吨，增长3.9%。

三、工业和建筑业

全年全区全部工业增加值7663.71亿元，比上年增长6.8%。全区规模以上工业增加值增长7.1%。在规模以上工业中，分经济类型看，国有控股企业增长9.4%，集体企业增长8.3%，股份合作企业下降47.2%，股份制企业增长7.6%，外商及港澳台商投资企业增长6.5%，其他经济类型企业下降0.3%。分门类看，采矿业增长2.8%，制造业增长6.9%，电力热力燃气及水生产和供应业增长11.5%。

图6　2013—2017年广西全部工业增加值

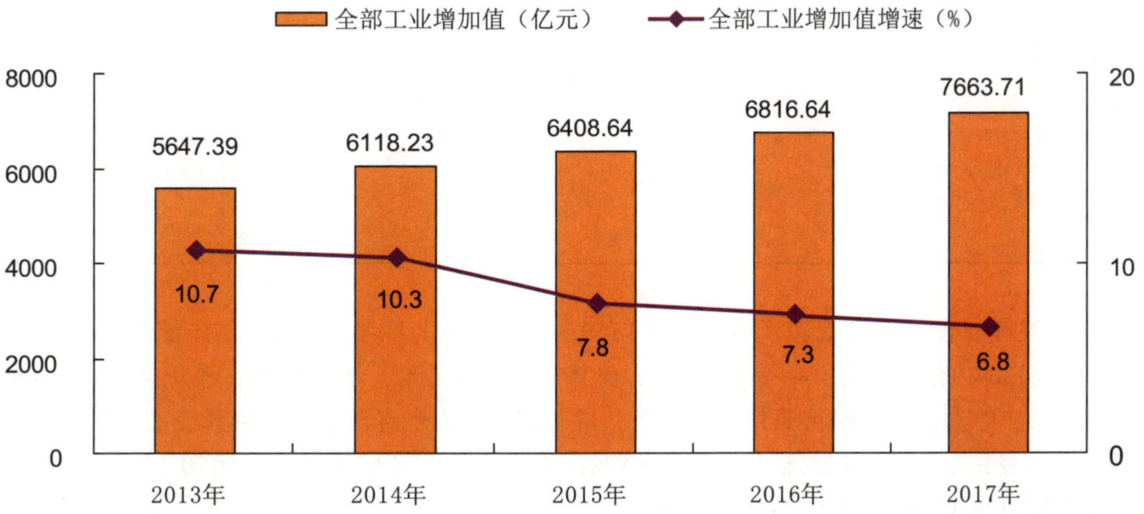

全年全区规模以上工业中，农副食品加工业增加值比上年增长6.4%，木材加工和木竹藤棕草制品业增长17.5%，通用设备制造业增长10.7%，专用设备制造业增长10.7%，计算机通信和其他电子设备制造业

增长19.7%，电气机械及器材制造业增长5.6%，汽车制造业增长5.1%，非金属矿物制品业增长6.6%，化学原料及化学制品制造业增长7.7%，有色金属冶炼及压延加工业增长14.1%，黑色金属冶炼及压延加工业下降18.6%，电力热力生产和供应业增长11.4%，石油加工炼焦及核燃料加工业增长14.8%。高技术制造业增加值增长15.4%，占规模以上工业增加值的比重为7.8%。装备制造业增加值增长9.2%，占规模以上工业增加值的比重为23.1%。六大高耗能行业增加值增长3.9%，占规模以上工业增加值的比重为39.7%。

表4　2017年规模以上工业主要产品产量及其增长速度

产品名称	单　位	产　量	比上年增长（%）
成品糖	万吨	935.96	4.4
发酵酒精	万千升	79.25	7.1
卷　烟	万箱	144.26	-2.4
机制纸及纸板	万吨	300.89	4.1
原　煤	万吨	415.37	0.3
发电量	亿千瓦小时	1321.62	5.9
其中：火电[4]	亿千瓦小时	617.32	7.4
水电	亿千瓦小时	555.67	-0.6
粗　钢	万吨	2265.26	7.5
钢　材	万吨	3270.73	-9.0
十种有色金属	万吨	230.00	27.4
其中：电解铝	万吨	120.55	53.9
氧化铝	万吨	1045.80	15.4
水　泥	万吨	12179.38	2.0
显示器	万台	1668.47	-17.5
电子元件	亿只	280.99	41.5
化　肥（折100%）	万吨	84.90	-11.6
发动机	万千瓦	20585.59	4.7
汽　车	万辆	248.61	1.3
铁合金	万吨	521.15	0.5

全年全区规模以上工业企业实现利润总额1559.3亿元，比上年增长25.2%。分经济类型看，国有控股企业实现利润364.9亿元，比上年增长39.1%；集体企业19.7亿元，增长9.4%；股份合作企业0.6亿元，上年同期亏损1.1亿元；股份制企业1135.7亿元，增长32.0%；外商及港澳台商投资企业326.1亿元，增长10.9%；其他经济类型企业62.3亿元，增长2.8%。分门类看，采矿业实现利润70.1亿元，比上年增长31.0%；制造业1426.3亿元，增长27.2%；电力、热力、燃气及水生产和供应业63.0亿元，下降11.4%。全年规模以上工业企业每百元主营业务收入中的成本为85.45元，比上年下降0.20元。年末规模以上工业企业资产负债率为61.3%，比上年末下降0.4个百分点。

表5　2017年规模以上工业企业利润总额及其增长速度

指　　标	利润总额（亿元）	比上年增长（%）
规模以上工业企业	1559.3	25.2
其中：国有控股企业	364.9	39.1
其中：大中型企业	1138.1	25.7
其中：国有企业	14.9	11.2
集体企业	19.7	9.4
股份合作企业	0.6	亏转赢
股份制企业	1135.7	32.0
外商及港澳台投资企业	326.1	10.9
其他经济类型企业	62.3	2.8
其中：轻工业	410.2	14.8
重工业	1149.1	29.4

全年全区全社会建筑业增加值1635.71亿元，比上年增长5.6%。全区具有资质等级的总承包和专业承包建筑业企业实现利润75.21亿元，比上年增长15.6%。其中，国有控股企业18.10亿元，下降4.5%。

四、固定资产投资

全年全区全社会固定资产投资20499.11亿元，比上年增长12.4%。其中，固定资产投资（不含农户）19908.27亿元，比上年增长12.8%。

图7　2013—2017年广西全社会固定资产投资

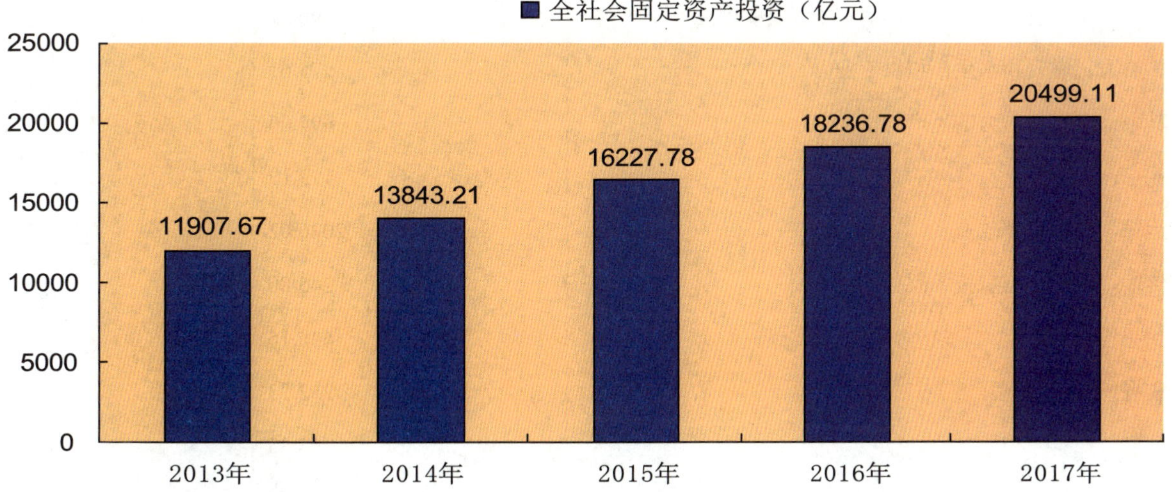

注：2013年起广西固定资产投资统计口径从计划总投资50万元项目提高至500万元。

在固定资产投资（不含农户）中，第一产业投资1202.26亿元，比上年增长26.7%；第二产业投资7004.23亿元，增长7.3%，其中工业投资6831.04亿元，增长6.7%；第三产业投资11701.78亿元，增长

15.0%。基础设施投资6722.28亿元，增长13.7%，占固定资产投资（不含农户）的比重为33.8%。民间固定资产投资11797.47亿元，增长8.5%，占固定资产投资（不含农户）的比重为59.3%。高技术产业投资981.70亿元，增长17.6%，占固定资产投资（不含农户）的比重为4.9%。六大高耗能行业投资2291.10亿元，增长10.8%，占固定资产投资（不含农户）的比重为11.5%。

表6 2017年分行业固定资产投资（不含农户）及其增长速度

行　　业	投资额（亿元）	比上年增长（%）
总　计	19908.27	12.8
农、林、牧、渔业	1202.26	26.7
采矿业	270.10	-2.5
制造业	5585.34	7.7
其中：农副食品加工业	430.78	17.3
造纸和纸制品业	118.57	-12.9
石油加工、炼焦和核燃料加工业	57.70	110.6
化学原料和化学制品制造业	285.28	11.8
非金属矿物制品业	878.51	1.8
黑色金属冶炼和压延加工业	121.37	21.6
有色金属冶炼和压延加工业	251.23	72.2
金属制品业	188.96	-6.7
通用设备制造业	187.78	6.8
专用设备制造业	218.89	-13.5
交通运输设备制造业	65.21	61.4
电气机械和器材制造业	217.63	1.8
通信设备计算机和其他电子设备制造业	290.37	58.5
电力、热力、燃气和水生产和供应业	975.61	3.8
其中：电力、热力的生产与供应业	697.00	3.0
建筑业	173.19	41.7
交通运输、仓储和邮政业	2026.02	9.9
信息传输、软件和信息技术服务业	245.80	10.1
批发和零售业	640.16	-15.3
住宿和餐饮业	252.23	24.8
金融业	53.33	-26.0
房地产业	3469.55	15.7
租赁和商务服务业	804.25	43.6
科学研究和技术服务业	153.49	持平
水利、环境和公共设施管理业	2539.91	21.7

续表

行　　业	投资额（亿元）	比上年增长（%）
居民服务、修理和其他服务业	88.54	-6.0
教育	520.93	9.1
卫生和社会工作	240.92	10.0
文化、体育和娱乐业	310.99	38.3
公共管理、社会保障和社会组织	353.47	34.7

全年全区房地产开发投资2683.48亿元，比上年增长11.9%。其中，住宅投资1983.52亿元，增长15.0%；办公楼投资102.79亿元，增长9.9%；商业营业用房投资323.67亿元，增长1.1%。商品房销售面积5170.99万平方米，增长22.7%，其中住宅4687.41万平方米，增长21.3%。年末商品房待售面积1598.85万平方米，比上年末减少173.71万平方米。年末商品住宅待售面积989.74万平方米，比上年末减少197万平方米。

表7　2017年房地产开发和销售主要指标完成情况及其增长速度

指　　标	单　位	绝对数	比上年增长%
投资额	亿元	2683.48	11.9
其中：住宅	亿元	1983.52	15.0
其中：90平方米及以下	亿元	562.29	2.2
房屋施工面积	万平方米	22689.62	7.4
其中：住宅	万平方米	16453.90	7.3
房屋新开工面积	万平方米	1912.21	-1.4
其中：住宅	万平方米	3662.39	2.4
房屋竣工面积	万平方米	1856.24	7.0
其中：住宅	万平方米	1478.96	7.7
商品房销售面积	万平方米	5170.99	22.7
其中：住宅	万平方米	4687.41	21.3
本年资金来源	亿元	3518.04	11.3
其中：国内贷款	亿元	486.62	3.9
其中：个人按揭贷款	亿元	787.87	24.5
本年购置土地面积	万平方米	675.49	5.6
土地成交价款	亿元	217.18	5.2

五、国内贸易

全年全区社会消费品零售总额7813.03亿元，比上年增长11.2%，扣除价格因素，实际增长9.9%。按经营地统计，城镇消费品零售额6874.20亿元，增长11.0%；乡村消费品零售额938.83亿元，增长12.6%。按消费类型统计，商品零售额7064.92亿元，增长11.1%；餐饮收入额748.11亿元，增长12.0%。

图8 2013—2017年广西社会消费品零售总额

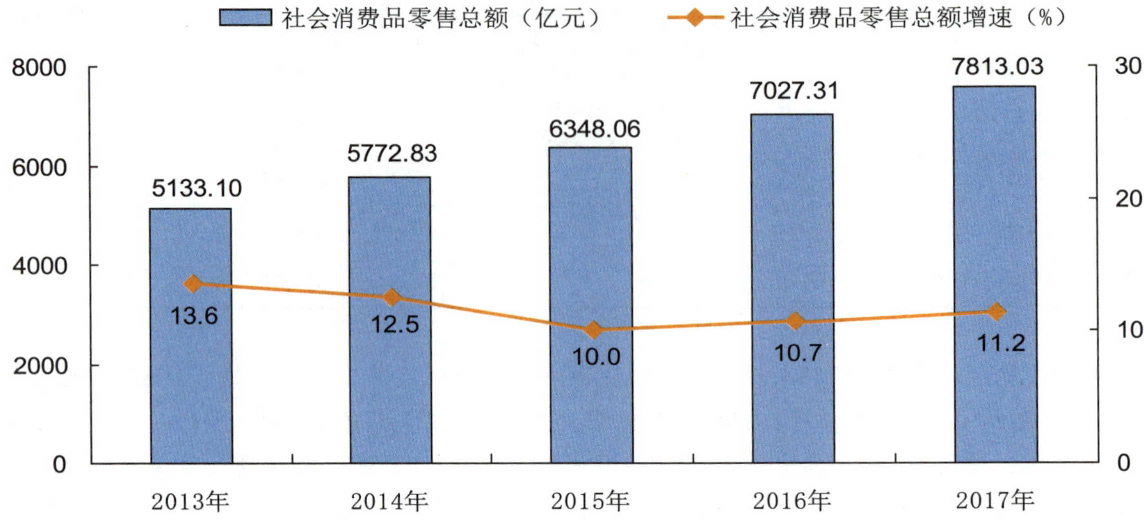

在限额以上企业商品零售额中，粮油、食品、饮料、烟酒类零售额比上年增长8.5%，服装、鞋帽、针纺织品类增长8.7%，化妆品类增长18.7%，金银珠宝类增长11.7%，日用品类增长4.4%，家用电器和音像器材类增长8.5%，中西药品类增长16.2%，文化办公用品类增长8.5%，家具类增长10.8%，通讯器材类下降1.3%，建筑及装潢材料类增长23.3%，汽车类增长10.4%，石油及制品类增长5.5%。

六、对外经济

全年全区货物进出口总额3866.34亿元，比上年增长22.6%。其中，出口1855.20亿元，增长22.3%；进口2011.14亿元，增长22.9%。贸易逆差（出口小于进口）155.94亿元，比上年增加36.19亿元。对东盟国家进出口总额1893.85亿元，比上年增长3.7%。其中，出口1062.46亿元，增长6.7%；进口831.39亿元，与上年基本持平。

表8 2017年货物进出口总额及其增长速度

指 标	绝对数（亿元）	比上年增长（%）
货物进出口总额	3866.34	22.6
其中：一般贸易	1423.59	70.4
其中：货物出口额	1855.20	22.3
其中：一般贸易	539.37	73.0
来料加工	82.88	-2.2
进料加工	345.15	41.6
边境小额贸易	799.02	5.8
货物进口额	2011.14	22.9

表9 2017年对主要国家和地区货物进出口总额及其增长速度

国家和地区	货物出口额（亿元）	比上年增长（%）	货物进口额（亿元）	比上年增长（%）
亚洲	1428.81	13.5	1190.53	6.9
其中：东盟	1062.46	6.7	831.39	0.0
其中：越南	930.09	1.2	696.17	3.4

续表

国家和地区	货物出口额（亿元）	比上年增长（%）	货物进口额（亿元）	比上年增长（%）
其中：中国香港	250.77	38.4	10.54	661.9
日本	23.33	1.4	25.90	14.0
韩国	18.23	46.0	22.95	73.1
非洲	40.47	88.0	85.53	147.4
欧洲	114.67	72.7	55.80	0.3
其中：欧盟	103.88	71.4	39.70	11.1
拉丁美洲	44.26	46.0	385.74	70.5
北美洲	190.16	64.6	178.88	43.4
其中：美国	180.51	63.4	105.36	41.4
大洋洲	36.83	52.9	114.65	39.8

全年全区批准项目合同外资额（商务部口径，下同）51.93亿美元，比上年增长124.0%；实际利用外资额8.23亿美元，下降7.4%。

全年全区对外承包工程和劳务合作完成营业额6.90亿美元，比上年下降18.9%。

七、交通、邮电和旅游

全年全区交通运输、仓储和邮政业增加值932.61亿元，比上年增长6.5%。

年末全区公路总里程12.33万公里，比上年新增0.27万公里；其中，高速公路里程5259公里，比上年新增656公里。年末铁路营业总里程5140公里，比上年减少1公里；其中，高速铁路营业里程1751公里。

表10　2017年旅客、货物运输量及其增长速度

指　　标	单　位	绝对数	比上年增长（%）
旅客运输总量	亿人次	5.11	0.6
旅客运输周转量	亿人公里	777.57	4.5
货物运输总量	亿吨	17.47	8.6
货物运输周转量	亿吨公里	4613.32	8.3

全年全区货物运输总量17.47亿吨，比上年增长8.6%。货物运输周转量4613.32亿吨公里，增长8.3%。全年规模以上港口完成货物吞吐量3.44亿吨，比上年增长7.4%，其中外贸货物吞吐量1.21亿吨，下降0.7%。规模以上港口集装箱吞吐量318.37万标准箱，增长26.6%。

全年全区旅客运输总量5.11亿人次，比上年增长0.6%。旅客运输周转量777.57亿人公里，增长4.5%。

年末全区民用汽车保有量504.33万辆，比上年末增长18.0%，其中私人汽车保有量452.65万辆，增长19.7%。民用轿车保有量251.03万辆，增长20.2%，其中私人轿车238.29万辆，增长21.2%。

全年全区完成邮电业务总量799.92亿元，比上年增长76.6%。其中，邮政业务总量88.04亿元，增长38.2%；电信业务总量711.88亿元（2015年不变单价），增长82.9%。年末全区电话用户总数4693万户，其中移动电话用户4385万户。移动电话普及率上升至89.8部/百人。固定互联网宽带接入用户1051万户，比上年增加195万户，其中固定互联网光纤宽带接入用户808万户，比上年增加240万户；移动宽带用户3500

万户，增加732万户。互联网用户4764万户，增加744万户，其中手机上网用户3629万户，增加512万户。互联网宽带接入通达的行政村比重达到99.4%。全年移动互联网接入流量6.33亿G，比上年增长191.6%。

全年全区入境过夜游客512.44万人次，比上年增长6.2%；国际旅游（外汇）消费23.96亿美元，增长10.7%。接待国内旅客5.18亿人次，增长28.2%，国内旅游消费5418.61亿元，增长33.9%。旅游总消费5580.36亿元，增长33.1%。

八、金 融

全年全区金融业增加值1273.40亿元，比上年增长8.7%。

年末全区金融机构本外币各项存款余额27899.64亿元，比年初增加2420.84亿元，其中人民币各项存款余额27714.24亿元，增加2455.68亿元。年末金融机构本外币各项贷款余额23226.14亿元，比年初增加2585.60元，其中人民币各项贷款余额22781.81亿元，增加2606.04亿元。

表11 2017年金融机构本外币存贷款余额及其增长速度

指 标	年末数（亿元）	比上年末增长（%）
各项存款余额	27899.64	9.5
其中：住户存款	13814.30	9.6
其中：人民币	13761.04	9.7
非金融企业存款	8433.28	12.5
各项贷款余额	23226.14	12.5
其中：境内短期贷款	1199.38	20.8
境内中长期贷款	7256.70	22.3

年末全区上市公司（A股）数量36家，市价总值3082.56亿元，比上年末下降13.0%。

全年全区保险公司原保险保费收入565.10亿元，比上年增长20.5%。其中，财产险业务原保险保费收入196.0亿元，增长18.3%；寿险业务原保险保费收入283.50亿元，增长18.8%；健康险和意外险业务原保险保费收入85.60亿元，增长31.9%。支付各类赔款及给付181.80亿元，增长14.4%。其中，财产险业务赔款96.10亿元，增长14.1%；寿险业务给付65.80亿元，增长13.5%；健康险和意外险业务赔款及给付31.0亿元，增长24.3%。

九、居民收入消费和社会保障

全年全区居民人均可支配收入19905元，比上年名义增长8.7%，扣除价格因素，实际增长7.0%。全区居民人均可支配收入中位数[5]16707元，名义增长9.2%。按常住地分，城镇居民人均可支配收入30502元，名义增长7.7%，扣除价格因素，实际增长5.7%；城镇居民人均可支配收入中位数为29108元，名义增长7.1%。农村居民人均可支配收入11325元，名义增长9.3%，扣除价格因素，实际增长8.1%；农村居民人均可支配收入中位数为10414元，名义增长10.2%。农民工月均收入水平3237元，增长5.4%。

全年全区居民人均消费支出13424元，比上年名义增长9.2%，扣除价格因素，实际增长7.5%。按常住地分，城镇居民人均消费支出18349元，名义增长6.3%，扣除价格因素，实际增长4.3%；农村居民人均消费支出9437元，名义增长13.0%，扣除价格因素，实际增长11.8%。恩格尔系数为32.9%，下降1.5个百分点，其中城镇为33.2%，农村为32.2%。

表12　2013—2017年城乡居民生活改善情况

指标 \ 年份	2013	2014	2015	2016	2017
城镇居民人均可支配收入（元）	22689	24669	26416	28324	30502
农村居民人均可支配收入（元）	7793	8683	9467	10359	11325
城镇居民家庭恩格尔系数（%）	37.9	35.2	34.4	34.4	33.2
农村居民家庭恩格尔系数（%）	40.0	36.9	35.4	34.5	32.2

按照每人每年2952元的农村贫困标准计算，2017年末，全区农村贫困人口246万人，比上年末减少95万人。2017年，全区贫困发生率5.7%，比上年下降2.2个百分点。贫困地区（33个国家贫困县）农村居民人均可支配收入9719元，比上年增长10.4%。

年末全区参加城镇职工（包括企业和机关事业单位）基本养老保险人数777.79万人，比上年末增加25.88万人。参加城乡居民基本养老保险人数1805.94万人，增加33.91万人。参加基本医疗保险人数5173.29万人。其中，参加城镇职工基本医疗保险人数556.75万人，增加26.04万人；参加城乡居民基本医疗保险人数4616.54万人。参加失业保险人数302.13万人，增加18.42万人。年末全区领取失业保险金人数5.38万人。参加工伤保险人数388.79万人，增加14.72万人，其中参加工伤保险的农民工46.24万人，减少5.81万人。参加生育保险人数338.58万人，增加18.99万人。

年末全区社会保障卡持卡人数3344.89万人，比上年末增加758.52万人。全区共有19.1万人享受城市居民最低生活保障，253.9万人享受农村居民最低生活保障，25.4万人享受特困人员救助供养。全年民政部门资助188.4万人参加基本医疗保险，直接救助26.5万人次。

十、教育、科学技术和文化体育

全年全区研究生教育招生1.1万人，在校研究生2.94万人，毕业生0.9万人。普通高等教育招生27.99万人，在校生86.67万人，毕业生21.07万人。各类中等职业教育（不含技工）招生25.28万人，在校生68.68万人，毕业生19.97万人。普通高中招生35.07万人，在校生97.48万人，毕业生28.18万人。普通初中招生71.22万人，在校生203.46万人，毕业生63.74万人。普通小学招生83.7万人，在校生463.75万人，毕业生71.36万人。特殊教育招生0.46万人，在校生2.2万人，毕业生0.18万人。学前教育在园幼儿213.99万人。九年义务教育巩固率为94%，高中阶段毛入学率为88.5%。

表13　2017年各类教育发展情况

指　　标	招生人数（万人）	在校生人数（万人）	毕业生人数（万人）
研究生	1.1	2.94	0.9
普通高等教育	27.99	86.67	21.07
中等职业教育（不含技工）	25.28	68.68	19.97
普通高中	35.07	97.48	28.18
普通初中	71.22	203.46	63.74
普通小学	83.7	463.75	71.36
特殊教育	0.46	2.2	0.18

全年安排科学研究与技术开发计划项目2018项，资助经费81492万元。其中，科技重大专项经费6800万元，重点研发计划经费16943万元，技术创新引导专项（基金）经费10663万元，科技基地和人才专项经费35693万元，自然科学基金11393万元。取得省部级以上登记科技成果4109项，其中，应用技术成果3384项，软科学研究成果7项，基础理论成果718项。全年全区获广西科技进步奖项目148项，其中，特别贡献奖2项，自然科学奖20项，技术发明奖23项，科学技术进步奖103项。全年全区专利申请量56957件，比上年增长8.2%，其中发明专利申请量37968件，比上年增长0.5%。全年全区授权专利15263件，比上年增长1.0%，其中授权发明专利4552件，比上年下降11.0%。每万人口发明专利拥有量为3.81件，比上年增长27.0%。全年共签订技术合同2037项，技术合同成交金额39.41亿元，比上年增长16.0%。全年全区创新驱动发展专项资金项目142项，资助经费71610万元，其中，科技重大专项经费55210万元，科技基地和人才专项经费16400万元。

年末全区共有产品检测实验室（指全区获得省级实验室资质认定的检验检测实验室）1162个，国家级检测中心8个，自治区级检测中心30个。全区累计完成产品认证企业个数（有效期内）5919个。全区共有法定计量技术机构88个，全年强制检定计量器具381万台（件）。累计制、修订地方标准数1657个，有效期内广西名牌产品数495个，地理标志保护产品68个。

年末全区共有地震台站244个，地震监测台网6个。

全年全区各级气象台共发布气象预警信号9733次，全年自治区气象台发布预警73次。全区共有海洋观测站5个。

年末全区共有县级以上公共图书馆114个，文化馆124个，博物馆131个，国有艺术表演团体100个，娱乐场所3590个，互联网上网服务营业场所（网吧）4918个。全区共有52个项目列入国家级非物质文化遗产名录，618个项目列入自治区级非物质文化遗产名录。

年末全区共有广播电台7座，电视台6座，广播电视台84座。有线广播电视用户725.16万户，数字电视用户678.73万户。年末广播节目综合人口覆盖率为97.2%；电视节目综合人口覆盖率为98.6%。全年全区出版各类报纸6.12亿份，各类期刊0.42亿册，图书2.89亿册。年末全区共有档案馆155个，已开放各类档案83.31万卷。

全年全区运动员在世界三大赛中获金银铜牌12枚，其中金牌6枚，银牌5枚，铜牌1枚。

十一、卫生和社会服务

年末全区共有医疗卫生机构34012个，其中，医院589个，乡镇卫生院1264个，社区卫生服务中心159个，诊所（卫生所、医务室）9487个，村卫生室20770个，疾病预防控制中心117个，卫生监督所（中心）114个，妇幼保健院（所、站）104个。卫生技术人员30.54万人，其中执业医师和执业助理医师10.12万人，注册护士13.17万人，乡村医生和卫生员3.42万人。医疗卫生机构床位24.13万张，其中医院16.15万张，乡镇卫生院6.32万张。

年末全区共有提供住宿的养老服务机构和设施11661个，床位16.7万张，年末收养7.4万人。为儿童提供救助收养服务的机构41个，床位0.29万张，年末收养0.14万人。各类社区服务设施2149个，其中社区服务中心184个，社区服务站1539个。

十二、资源、环境和安全生产

全年全区国有建设用地供应总量1.9万公顷，比上年增长28.5%。其中，工矿仓储用地0.3万公顷，下降1.2%；住宅用地0.3万公顷，增长14.2%；基础设施等用地1.3万公顷，增长41.6%。

全年全区水资源总量2377.3亿立方米。全年平均降水量1806毫米。年末全区监测的58座大型水库蓄水总量289.2亿立方米，比上年增长1.4%。全年总用水量283.1亿立方米，比上年下降2.6%。其中，生活用水增长0.4%，工业用水下降7.8%，农业用水下降4.0%，生态补水增长9.6%。万元地区生产总值用水量[6]138.8立方米，比上年下降13.8%。万元工业增加值用水量60立方米，下降17.8%。人均用水量579立方米，比上年下降3.4%。

全年全区完成造林面积236千公顷，其中人工造林面积76.7千公顷，占全部造林面积的32.5%。截至年底，全区建成自然保护区达78个，其中国家级自然保护区23个，获批国家级生态文明建设示范区1个。自然保护区面积135万公顷。森林覆盖率62.31%。活立木蓄积量7.8亿立方米。新增水土流失治理面积1788.7平方公里。

全年全区平均气温为21.1℃，比上年下降0.3℃，共有4个热带气旋直接影响广西。

初步核算，全年全区万元地区生产总值能耗比上年下降3.4%。电力消费量增长6.1%。规模以上万元工业增加值综合能源消耗比上年下降4.8%。重点耗能工业企业单位油气产量综合能耗下降4.6%，单位水泥综合能耗下降1.2%，吨钢综合能耗下降3.6%，单位氧化铝综合能耗下降4.2%，单位电解铝综合能耗上升0.9%，每千瓦时火力发电标准煤耗上升1.1%。

在监测的14个设区市中，城市空气质量达标的市占42.9%，未达标的市占57.1%，城市区域声环境质量较好的市占100%。

年末全区城市污水处理厂日处理能力326.2万立方米，比上年末增长0.2%；城市污水处理率为93.6%，提高1.5个百分点。城市生活垃圾无害化处理率为99.3%，提高0.4个百分点。城市建成区绿地率为33.3%，提高0.7个百分点；人均公园绿地面积12.0平方米，增加0.3平方米。

全年全区各类生产安全事故共死亡1182人，比上年下降25.2%。道路交通事故造成伤亡人数5920人，比上年上升1.02%。

注释：

［1］本公报中2017年数据均为初步统计数。部分数据因四舍五入的原因，存在与分项合计不等的情况。

［2］地区生产总值、各产业增加值绝对数按现价计算，增长速度按不变价格计算。

［3］常住人口指在广西居住半年以上的人口，以及户口在广西、外出广西不满半年或在境外工作学习的人口。

［4］火电包括燃煤发电量，燃油发电量，燃气发电量，余热、余压、余气发电量，垃圾焚烧发电量，生物质发电量。

［5］人均收入中位数是指将所有调查户按人均收入水平从低到高顺序排列，处于最中间位置的调查户的人均收入。

［6］万元地区生产总值用水量、万元工业增加值用水量、万元地区生产总值能耗按2015年价格计算。

［7］自2017年起，自治区本级财政科技计划整合为广西科技重大专项、广西重点研发计划、广西技术创新引导专项（基金）、广西科技基地和人才专项、广西自然科学基金五大类。

资料来源：

本公报中城镇新增就业、登记失业率、社会保障数据来自人力资源社会保障厅；户籍总人口数据来自公安厅；财政数据来自财政厅；物价、城乡居民收入和支出、恩格尔系数、农民工、贫困人口、部分农业数据来自国家统计局广西调查总队；进出口数据来自南宁海关；外商直接投资、对外承包工程和劳务合作等数据来自商务厅；金融数据来自中国人民银行南宁中心支行；保险数据来自中国保险监督委员会广西监管局；旅游数据来自旅游发展委；公路里程、港口数据来自交通运输厅；旅客、货物运输量和周转量数据来自交通运输厅、中国铁路南宁局集团有限公司和广西机场集团；铁路营业里程、高速铁路数据来自南宁铁路局；汽车保有量数据来自自治区交警总队；邮政业务数据来自自治区邮政管理局；电信业务数据来自自治区通信管理局；教育数据来自教育厅；安排科技计划课题、专利数据、技术合同等数据来自科技厅；质量检验、标准制定修订数据来自自治区质量技术监督局；地震数据来自自治区地震局；艺术表演团体、博物馆、公共图书馆、文化馆、娱乐场所、互联网上网服务营业场所（网吧）、非物质文化遗产数据来自文化厅；广播电视、报纸、期刊、图书数据来自自治区新闻出版广电局；档案数据来自自治区档案局；卫生数据来自卫计委；体育数据来自自治区体育局；社会服务及救助数据来自民政厅；安全生产数据来自自治区安全生产监督管理局；交通事故数据来自公安厅；气象预警、平均气温、热带气旋数据来自自治区气象局；国有建设用地供应数据来自国土资源厅；水资源、新增水土流失治理面积数据来自水利厅；林业数据来自林业厅；自然保护区、环境监测数据来自环境保护厅；城市污水处理、建成区绿地覆盖率来自住房城乡建设厅；其他数据均来自自治区统计局。